# HANDBOOK OF

# Metrics *for* Research *in* Operations Management

# HANDBOOK OF

# Metrics *for* Research *in* Operations Management

## Multi-item Measurement Scales and Objective Items

Aleda V. Roth
*Clemson University*

Roger G. Schroeder
*University of Minnesota*

Xiaowen Huang
*Miami University*

M. Murat Kristal
*York University*

SAGE Publications
Los Angeles • London • New Delhi • Singapore

*For information:*

Sage Publications, Inc.
2455 Teller Road
Thousand Oaks, California 91320
E-mail: order@sagepub.com

Sage Publications Ltd.
1 Oliver's Yard
55 City Road
London EC1Y 1SP
United Kingdom

Sage Publications India Pvt. Ltd.
B 1/I 1 Mohan Cooperative Industrial Area
Mathura Road, New Delhi 110 044
India

Sage Publications Asia-Pacific Pte. Ltd.
33 Pekin Street #02-01
Far East Square
Singapore 048763

Printed in the United States of America

*Library of Congress Cataloging-in-Publication Data*

Handbook of metrics for research in operations management: Multi-item measurement scales and objective items/Aleda Roth . . . [et al.].
p. cm.
Includes bibliographical references and index.
ISBN 978-1-4129-5451-8 (cloth)
1. Industrial management—Research—Statistical methods—Handbooks, manuals, etc. 2. Operations research—Statistical methods—Handbooks, manuals, etc. 3. Production management—Research—Statistical methods—Handbooks, manuals, etc. 4. Research, Industrial—Statistical methods—Handbooks, manuals, etc. I. Roth, Aleda V.

HD30.215.H356 2008
658.4′034—dc22 2007008885

This book is printed on acid-free paper.

07 08 09 10 11 10 9 8 7 6 5 4 3 2 1

*Acquisitions Editor:* Al Bruckner
*Editorial Assistant:* MaryAnn Vail
*Production Editor:* Diane S. Foster
*Copy Editor:* QuADS Prepress (P) Ltd.
*Typesetter:* C&M Digitals (P) Ltd.
*Proofreader:* Penelope Sippel
*Cover Designer:* Candice Harman
*Marketing Manager:* Nichole M. Angress

# CONTENTS

**Preface** **vii**

**1. Introduction** **1**
The Purpose of the Book 1
Coverage and Scope 3
Caveats and Cautions 3
Organization of the Book 4
Selected Bibliography of Methods for Scale Development 7

**2. Classification of Scales** **9**

**3. Objective Measures of Operations** **12**
Introduction 12
IndustryWeek Best Plants Program 13
Global Manufacturing Research Group Study 14
High Performance Manufacturing Study 14
Vision in Manufacturing Survey 15
Retail Banking Futures Study 15
Appendixes 3.1 to 3.5: Survey Instruments/Selected Items 19

**4. List of Scale Summaries (Alphabetically by First Author)** **42**
Authors A–B 43
Authors C–D 113
Authors E–G 198

Authors H–J 275
Authors K–M 326
Authors N–R 425
Authors S–T 515
Authors V–Z 613

**Appendixes** **665**

1: Classification of Scales 665
2: List of Scale Names 714
3: List of Papers Summarized 753

**About the Authors** **763**

# Preface

The aim of this book is to provide a comprehensive review of constructs and metrics useful in furthering empirical science in operations management. We provide a list of 1,803 multi-item perceptual scales and several hundred objective items that can be used to construct surveys or other structured approaches to data collection by researchers. These metrics are provided in one place for the convenience of scholars and others who are constructing questionnaires or other types of data collection instruments.

In constructing this book, we have gathered multi-item scales and objective measures from many different publications. We have classified these measures in a convenient format so that researchers can easily find a construct of interest. This book will aid scholars in finding published scales that can be used directly or modified to suit their needs.

A brief summary of the 1,803 scales is provided for each of the 230 original, published articles selected from primary academic journals. The format for these article summaries includes the following:

A complete citation of the original article

A listing of all scales and items from the article

The description of each construct and its origin

A summary of the measurement, survey development process, and sample

A report of construct reliability and validity

The scoring method (summation or factor loadings)

Other evidence and references, if any

Using this standard format for each of the 230 articles, researchers can easily determine if a particular scale meets their needs.

The book also lists hundreds of objective (single-item) measures in Chapter 3 and in some of the various scale summaries where objective items are used. Objective items can be very helpful in constructing surveys and instruments, especially if the measure is not primarily perceptual in nature. However, the reader should be cautioned that measurement errors and bias may exist with both objective and perceptual measures.

We hope that researchers and scholars will find this book helpful. We have started a Web site that will be updated annually with additional summaries that are published (http://www.carlsonschool.umn.edu/Schroeder/Scalebook). The Web site will use the same classification system and summary format as the book. This Web site will insure that current, recently published metrics can also be found. Please refer to Appendixes 1 and 2 for the classification systems used in this book.

We are grateful to a number of people who have worked with us in summarizing and reviewing articles. We acknowledge the support of Zeynep Camdereli, Yi-Su Chen, Jeff Correll, Kristy Cua, John Gray, Sebastian Heese, Yunsook Hong, Sung Kang, Yoousoon Kim, Chris Liu, Gensheng

(Jason) Liu, Larry Menor, Chad Mayer, Michael Naor, Sriram Narayanan, Pedro Oliveira, Enno Siemsen, Jeff Stratman, Sriram Thirumalai, Rung Ting Tu, Yimin Wang, and Muge Yayla who helped prepare the research summaries, and especially to Craig Froehle, Eve Rosenzweig, Arash Azedagan, and Kim Scales for their added assistance in coordinating aspects of the work. We are also grateful to Katie Williams, Jeff Shockley, and Robin Weng for their editorial assistance.

*Aleda V. Roth*
*Roger G. Schroeder*
*Xiaowen Huang*
*M. Murat Kristal*

# 1

# INTRODUCTION

## THE PURPOSE OF THE BOOK

Empirical science in operations management (OM) has advanced dramatically since the early 1990s. This advancement has been driven largely by scholarly inquiry into manufacturing and service operations strategy, and subsequently in areas such as quality management, just-in-time (JIT), supply chain management, service operations, and e-operations. These topics are inherently less understood, boundary spanning, and relatively unstructured in contrast to more traditional inventory theory, for example. As a consequence, the time was ripe to open the OM field to new approaches and methods of scholarly inquiry. The era of OM empiricism began. Yet studying complex OM phenomena, typically through empirically based survey and case research methods, oftentimes requires the development of new constructs and perceptual measures that define them. Moreover, the use of objective metrics that are drawn from secondary data sources necessitates a reasonable assessment of data quality.

A primary tenet of good empirical science is this: *Reliable and valid metrics are vital to the advancement of theory.* The pioneers of OM empirical research have had little guidance from their own discipline for developing appropriate metrics. Few early OM scholars had expertise in the social science and the statistical foundations of multi-item measurement scale development. Thus, to improve the theory and practice of OM, a deeper understanding of items and scale construction of perceptual measures was needed. No one study makes a measurement scale "valid." Validity first requires that metrics be reliable in that they are consistent, and second, it requires replication and refinement of existing metrics to adequately glean the meaning of the intended constructs and their posited interrelationships.

This handbook is a compilation of multi-item measurement scales and objective metrics that have been used to construct surveys and questionnaires in published, empirical OM research and/or have been derived from secondary data sources. Some of these constructs have also been deployed in case research investigations, and more recently in behavioral operations experiments. We envisioned this handbook as providing a broad-based picture of the empirical side of the field and serving as a springboard for stimulating future OM empirical research.

Historically, research in OM employs both analytical models and empirical science. The empirical science applications in OM are relatively new compared with analytical modeling, which traditionally dominated the field's research landscape. The past two decades witnessed a significant rise in prominence of the empirical side of OM scholarship, which builds on social, economic and behavioral science approaches. Much of the empirical work to date employs perceptual metrics that consist of multiple-item scales as well as objective measures. Yet the OM field lags the more mature management disciplines, such as marketing, management, strategy, and information systems, which employ rigorous social and behavioral science methods in the conduct of empirical research. It also falls short of economics, finance, and accounting in the use of objective measures that are frequently derived from publicly available secondary sources, such as COMPUSTAT, CRSP, Hoovers, and EdgarScan.

Until recently, there were few metrics available that operationalize OM concepts and constructs; and there was little experience from which to build the substantive areas of our discipline. Many of the original measures used in pioneering OM research were developed from scratch or were drawn from research in other disciplines. As the OM field matures and theories and frameworks are empirically tested, higher quality perceptual and objective metrics are required if the resulting research is to be useful for explanation, prediction, decision making, and testing of assumptions.

We conceptualized this handbook as a source in which the body of empirical studies in OM could be mapped via the constructs and multi-item measures that tap into them. As the amount of empirical research in OM expands, it has become increasingly obvious that many of the metrics employed are being redeveloped over and over again, and oftentimes different constructs use subsets of the same items. This lack of semantic clarity in our constructs and reuse of the same items in scales that are intended to capture different constructs pose serious threats to validity. Invalid measures can have a dire impact on the ability of OM to develop sound theory in the longer term.

Our reviews indicate that the accumulated experience of iterative development has not been systematically summarized and mistakes in measurement scale development are repeated in exploratory modes of investigation. Perceptual metrics in OM research are not being refined and honed for different contexts as required for good empirical research and their quality varies widely. For example, Rosenzweig and Roth (2004) report that no adequate multi-item scales were available for testing the elements of competitive progression theory. Since this handbook summarizes the existing set of perceptual metrics in the OM field, others can learn from the pioneers and, in turn, can begin the iterative multi-item, scale development that over time will have the high degrees of reliability and validity needed for theory building and testing. Similarly, many objective items, which are used as proxy variables for theoretical constructs and performance outcomes, are offered for others to build on.

The multi-item scales presented here can be used to measure constructs that have a large OM empirical base, including total quality management (TQM), JIT or lean manufacturing, operations capabilities and strategy, technology and supply chain management, performance of operations, as well as emerging areas such as new product development, service operations, environmental and sustainable operations, and cross-functional and organizational interfaces. Thus, this handbook is a broad compilation of the literature and measures that serve as reference work to provide researchers a guide for construction of surveys and other structured data collection on OM topics. It sets the stage for the second generation of OM empirical science, that is, it builds on more confirmatory, as opposed to first generational exploratory approaches to measurement.

Our book is designed to be a basic reference source for furthering scholarly research in OM. Among others, this reference book is particularly useful to four key groups: (1) OM professionals conducting survey and other empirical research or teaching empirical science to graduate students; (2) researchers wishing to conduct meta-analyses of the psychometric properties of items and measurement scales; (3) OM faculty and doctoral students who are interested in empirical research and desire to become familiar with available constructs and measurement instruments; and (4) scholars in other fields who are interested in investigating OM-related research, especially regarding the interfaces of OM with other disciplines and across business and supply chain entities. Researchers now have ready access to the body of existing multi-item scales and objective items published in the extant OM literature and their known psychometric properties as reported by the authors.

## Coverage and Scope

Since our focus is to identify and compile a body of knowledge on relevant multi-item measurement scales and objective measures, we began our search with articles starting in 1990, which is generally recognized as the year when empirical research in OM was taking off. To find them, we first reviewed every issue of production and operations management related journals: *Journal of Operations Management (JOM), Production and Operations Management (POM), Manufacturing and Service Operations Management (M&SOM), Decision Sciences (DS), Journal of Service Research (JSR), International Journal of Production Research (IJPR), Management Science (MS), and International Journal of Operations and Production Management (IJOPM).* The first four journals (*JOM, POM, M&SOM,* and *DS*) were searched manually. The last four journals (*JSR, IJPR, MS,* and *IJOPM*) were reviewed through computer databases (i.e., ABI and EBSCO). In addition, we used a keyword search of the following terms: *empirical and operations, empirical and manufacturing,* and *empirical and service.* We found at least one article in other journals, including *Academy of Management Journal (AMJ), Strategic Management Journal (SMJ), Technovation,* and *Resource Policy.* We also supplemented these with multi-item measurement scales found in selected book chapters. While we have attempted to be as thorough as possible in our coverage of important OM scales, we do not claim that this book covers every multi-item measurement scale in OM to date. Articles that do not give sufficient information on measurement, such as the lack of a scale listing, were excluded. Our search produced 230 journal articles in the literature that have published one or more OM-related scales. Additionally, we illustrate questions that employ single-item objective measures in Chapter 3. In total, 1,803 multi-item measurement scales and numerous objective measures have been found.

To the extent that the authors provided the information, each article has been summarized in a standard format consisting of the following elements:

*Citation:* The full citation for the article being summarized is provided.

*Scale listing:* A list of the questions (items) included in each of the scales or objective measures tested in the article is given.

*Construct description:* A description of the meaning of the scales, the literature used, and grounding of the constructs are provided. A further description of the items is also included if presented in the original journal article.

*Measurement description:* We summarize (1) how measurement was performed, (2) whether the scales were grouped into factors, and (3) what format was used (e.g., Likert) for the scaling of the questions.

*Development:* A description of the measurement and survey development process is summarized. This covers the process used to develop the scales, including pretesting, split-sample approaches, exploratory factor analysis, or other methods.

*Sample:* The nature of the sample employed is given. This part includes the following information as indicated by the author(s) of the manuscript: the data collected to demonstrate reliability and validity; the survey respondents (e.g., managers, nurses, students); the sample size and the response rate; the measures taken to reach nonrespondents and to test for possible response bias.

*Reliability and validity:* The psychometric properties of the tests are summarized as reported in the original manuscript. The summary covers (1) the measures reported to test for reliability of the scale (e.g., Cronbach alpha, split halves methods, or measurement model statistics derived from confirmatory factor analyses); (2) tests used for convergent and discriminant validity; and (3) the demonstration of unidimensionality.

*Scores:* The methods used to obtain a scale score are provided if given in the text. Most frequently used methods are the averaging of items comprising the scale or the use of factor loadings. Any other scoring information that the authors of the manuscript made available is also reported.

*Other evidence:* Any other evidence related to the measurement reliability and validity of the scale is given.

*References:* Citations for the references used in the summary are reported.

## Caveats and Cautions

The criteria above are given to provide the reader with some notion about the constructs, items, and scales as reported in the original source materials. They are intended to offer some insights into the psychometric properties of the scales, but the measurement quality cannot be guaranteed since we provide only a simple description of the psychometric properties as reported by the authors. The measurement quality of reported OM metrics varies widely. Many potentially interesting and insightful OM empirical articles have paid inadequate attention to and demonstrated a lack of rigor in the development of perceptual metrics used in the study design. Furthermore, efforts to rectify inadequate metrics after the full study has been implemented have been problematic in that many scales have been modified on a post hoc basis without further replication on a separate validation or holdout sample. By identifying these items and scales, OM researchers can replicate and refine them in the same and different contexts.

We also caution that it is difficult to interpret and compare the quality of the metrics because of differences in the statistical procedures, contexts, and response rates reported in the original source material. Oftentimes, the methods information is insufficient for study replication. Moreover, some authors may not have fully disclosed all the limitations of their research. We, therefore, urge researchers interested in particular scales to review the original sources for obtaining a deeper understanding of the scales and the context of the original research and to assess the theoretical rationale for constructs and items comprising their operationalization.

Also, for most of the literature-based measurement scales in OM, and especially those in the early years of OM empirical research or for emerging topics, the psychometric properties may not be consistently reported. As indicated earlier, our review discovered a lack of semantic clarity and well-defined, construct definitions. Similar items tapping into one construct in some studies will be reported in different constructs in another, which pose a threat to validity. Future research will be required to rectify these conceptual and operational issues. Consequently, the metrics here should be viewed as a *starting point* for further refinement and scale assessment.

We recognize that the literature in multi-item, measurement scale development is rich and varied. Much of the early work in scale development was based on exploratory, first-generation multivariate techniques, such as principal components analysis or common factor analyses. Some studies used a combination of exploratory procedures and confirmatory data analysis on the same samples, which is not recommended because of data fitting. There are many useful statistical approaches for developing new perceptual metrics in the extant literature that can add to the second generation of OM empirical science. Building on Churchill (1979), Menor and Roth (2007) offer a two-stage approach for developing and assessing items and measurement scales (*see* Figure 1.1). In contrast to many perceptual scale development efforts, these authors suggest that researchers focus on the "front-end" stage of survey research—*before* pilot testing and field implementation of questionnaires—for tentative item and scale assessment. They demonstrate that attention to the front end can yield an efficient and effective means of improving overall measurement quality. Figure 1.2 illustrates the Menor and Roth (2007a, 2007b) statistics that can be used for establishing tentative reliability and validity at the front-end stage. Examples of the Menor and Roth approach can be found in Stratman and Roth (2002), Menor and Roth (2007b), and Rosenzweig and Roth (forthcoming).

Froehle and Roth (2004) provide yet another rigorous approach for addressing the front end of multi-item scale development when samples are large, and Froehle and Roth (2007) offer a new methodology for developing and defining constructs. In addition, comparison of the pros and cons of various survey data collection methodologies for OM researches can be found in Rosenzweig, Roth, and Gilland (2006).

A selected bibliography listed at the end of this chapter reports on issues that need to be considered in a careful construction of new items and a rigorous analysis of perceptual data that will increase the rigor of the researcher's efforts to further develop and refine psychometrically sound multi-item scales.

## Organization of the Book

Chapter 2 offers a classification scheme for the scales. This method is unique to this book and provides a typology for scales in OM. It is based

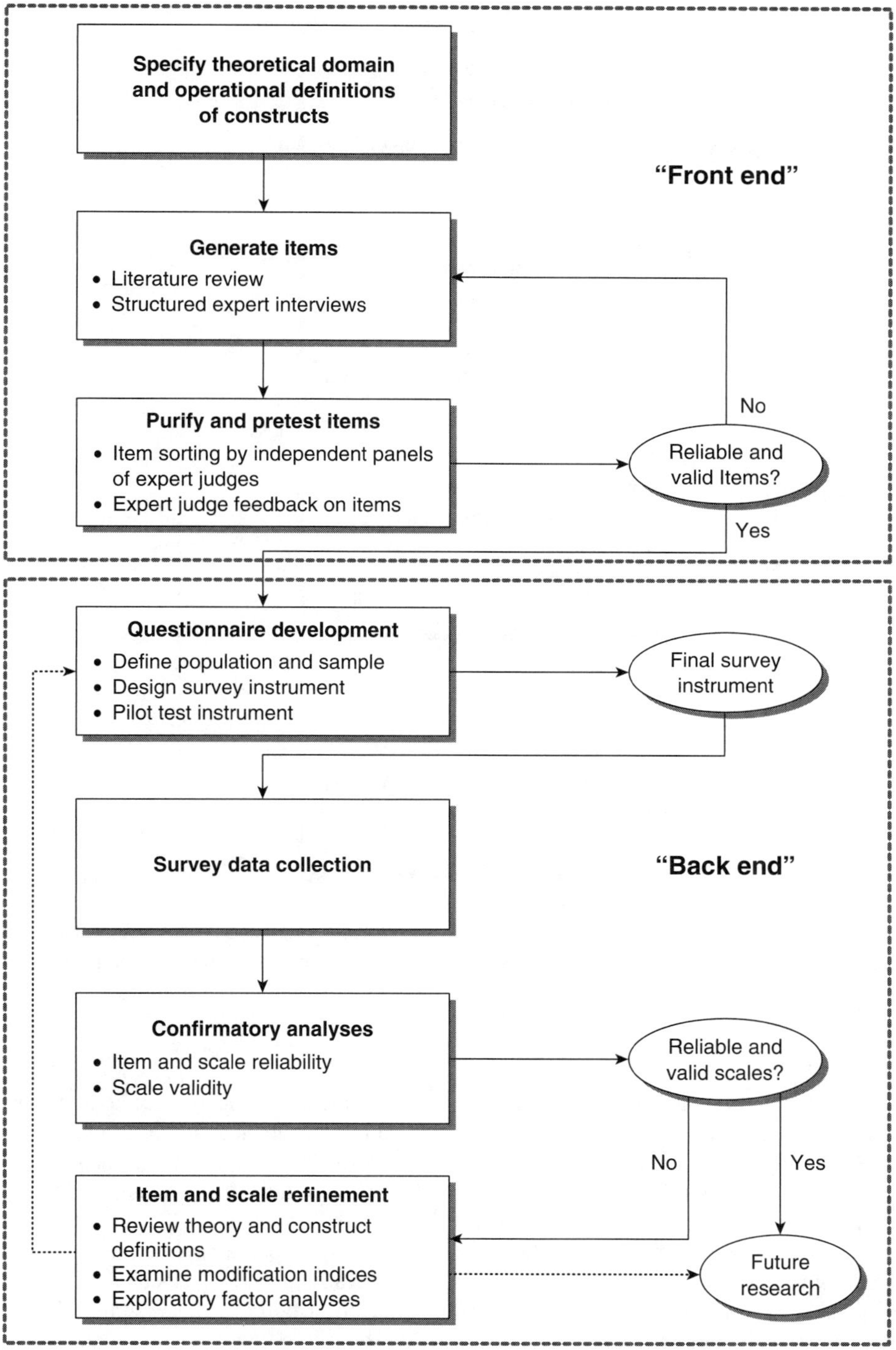


**Figure 1.1** Menor and Roth's Two-Stage Approach for New Item and Scale Development

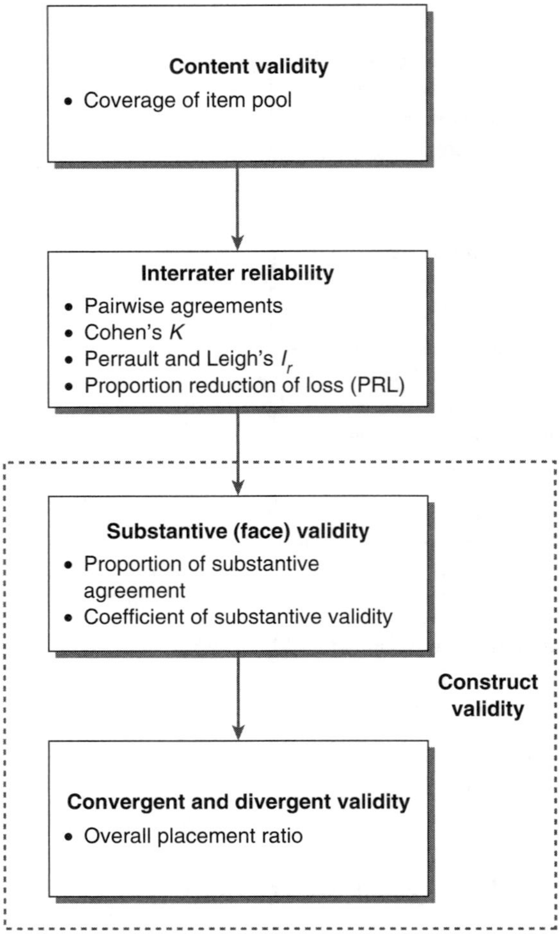


**Figure 1.2** Statistics for Establishing Tentative Reliability and Construct Validity at the Front End

SOURCE: Menor and Roth (2007a, 2007b).

on the classification systems used for research topics accepted by major journals in the OM field.

Chapter 3 discusses objective, single-item metrics that have been covered in OM research. It also includes illustrative questions from five sample surveys used in OM. The unit of analysis is theoretically and pragmatically important to OM empirical research, and it varies across studies. In Chapter 3, three of the surveys highlight questions at the "plant" level, and two represent the "operations business unit" level of analyses, one from manufacturing and the other from service. Less frequent, but also of increasing importance, to understanding the customer/buyer side of operations, is the use of "individuals" as the unit of analysis (*see,* e.g., Froehle and Roth 2004; Siemsen, Balasubramanian, and Roth, forthcoming).

Chapter 4 contains 230 summaries of journal articles arranged in alphabetical order by last name of the first author. These summaries are useful for those looking for a particular scale in the published literature.

A particular scale of interest can be found in three ways by using the appendixes to this book.

If only the general category of the scale is known (e.g., manufacturing strategy, JIT, quality management), one or more scales can be found in Appendix 1. On the other hand, if the specific scale name is known (e.g., employee involvement), it can be found in Appendix 2. If the author of the scales is known, the location of the relevant article summary can be found in the author listing in Appendix 3 and in the alphabetical table of contents for Chapter 4.

## Selected Bibliography of Methods for Scale Development


Anderson, J. C., and D. W. Gerbing. 1991. Predicting the performance of measures in a confirmatory factor analysis with a pretest assessment of their substantive validities. *Journal of Applied Psychology* 76 (5): 732–40.

Blalock, H. M. 1979. Measurement and conceptualization problems: The major obstacle to integrating theory and research. *American Journal of Sociological Review* 44:881–94.

Bollen, K. A. 1989. *Structural equations with latent variables.* New York: Wiley.

Campbell, D. T. 1960. Recommendations for APA test standards regarding construct, trait, or discriminant validity. *American Psychologist* 15:546–53.

Campbell, D. T., and D. W. Fiske. 1959. Convergent and discriminant validation by the multitrait-multimethod matrix. *Psychological Bulletin* 56: 81–105.

Churchill, G. A. 1979. A paradigm for developing better measures of marketing constructs. *Journal of Marketing Research* 6:64–73.

Cohen, J. 1960. A coefficient of agreement for nominal scales. *Educational and Psychological Measurement* 20:37–46.

Cortina, J. M. 1993. What is coefficient alpha? An examination of theory and applications. *Journal of Applied Psychology* 78 (1): 98–104.

Crittenden, K. S., and R. J Hill. 1971. Coding reliability and validity of interview data. *American Sociological Review* 36:1073–80.

Cronbach, L. J. 1951. Coefficient alpha and the internal structure of tests. *Psychometrika* 16: 297–334.

Drolet, A. L., and D. G. Morrison. 2001. Do we really need multiple-item measures in service research? *Journal of Service Research* 3 (3): 196–204.

Fleiss, J. L. 1971. Measuring nominal scale agreement among many raters. *Psychological Bulletin* 76 (5): 378–82.

Forza, C. 2002. Survey research in operations management: A process-based perspective. *International Journal of Operations & Production Management* 22 (2): 152–94.

Froehle, C., and A. V. Roth. 2004. New measurement scales for evaluating perceptions of the technology-mediated customer experience. *Journal of Operations Management* 22 (1): 1–21.

Froehle, C., and A. V. Roth. 2007. A resource-process framework of new service development. *Production and Operations Management* , 16 (2): 169–188.

Frolich, M. T. 2002. Techniques for improving response rates in OM survey research. *Journal of Operations Management* 20:53–62.

Gerbing, D. W., and J. G. Hamilton. 1996. Viability of exploratory factor analysis as a precursor to confirmatory factor analysis. *Structural Equation Modeling* 3:62–72.

Handfield, R. B., and S. A. Melnyk. 1998. The scientific theory-building process: A primer using the case of TQM. *Journal of Operations Management* 16: 321–39.

Harmon, H. H. 1976. *Modern factor analysis.* 3rd ed. Chicago, IL: University of Chicago Press.

Hensley, R. L. 1999. A review of operations management studies using scale development techniques. *Journal of Operations Management* 17:343–58.

Menor, L., & A. V. Roth, 2007a. *Improving perceptual measurement in operations management survey research.* Toronto, Ontario, Canada: Ivey Business School, University of Western Ontario.

Menor, L. and A. V. Roth. 2007b. New service development competence in retail banking: Construct development and measurement validation. *Journal of Operations Management,* 25 (4): 825–846.

Meredith, J. R., A. Raturi, K. Amoako-Gyampah, and B. Kaplan. 1989. Alternative research paradigms in operations. *Journal of Operations Management* 8 (4): 297–326.

Miller, M. B. 1995. Coefficient alpha: A basic introduction from the perspective of classical test theory and structural equation modeling. *Structural Equation Modeling* 2 (3): 255–73.

Mitchell, S. K. 1979. Interobserver agreement, reliability, and generalizability of data collected in observational studies. *Psychological Bulletin* 86 (2): 376–90.

Nunnally, J. C., and I. H. Bernstein. 1994. *Psychometric theory.* New York: McGraw-Hill.

O'Leary-Kelly, S. W., and R. J. Vokurka. 1998. The empirical assessment of construct validity. *Journal of Operations Management* 16:387–405.

Perreault, W. D., and L. E. Leigh. 1989. Reliability of nominal data based on qualitative judgments. *Journal of Marketing Research* May:135–48.

Reise, S. P., K. F. Widaman, and R. G. Pugh. 1993. Confirmatory factor analysis and item response theory: Two approaches for exploring measurement invariance. *Psychological Bulletin* 114 (3): 552–66.

Rosenzweig, E., and A. V. Roth. 2004. Towards a theory of competitive progression: Evidence in high tech manufacturing. *Production and Operations Management* 13 (4): 354–68.

Rosenzweig, E., and A. V. Roth. Forthcoming. B2B seller competence: Construct development and measurement using an operations strategy lens. *Journal of Operations Management.*

Rosenzweig, E. D., A. V. Roth, and W. Gilland. 2006. *Web-based survey best practices for the operations management researcher toolkit.* Atlanta, GA: Goizueta Business School, Emory University.

Roth, A. V. Forthcoming 2007. Special issue on applications of empirical science in operations management. *Manufacturing and Service Operations Management.*

Rungtusanatham, M. 1998. Let's not overlook content validity. *Decision Line* July:10–13.

Rust, R. T., and B. Cooil. 1994. Reliability measures for qualitative data: Theory and implications. *Journal of Marketing Research* February:1–14.

Schmitt, N., and D. Stults. 1986. Methodology review: Analysis of multitrait-multimethod matrices. *Applied Psychological Measurement* 10:1–22.

Schriesheim, C. A., K. J. Powers, T. A. Scandura, C. C. Gardiner, and M. J. Lankau. 1993. Improving construct measurement in management research: Comments and a quantitative approach for assessing the theoretical content adequacy of paper-and-pencil survey-type instruments. *Journal of Management* 19 (2): 385–417.

Schwab, D. P. 1980. Construct validity in organizational behavior. *Research in Organizational Behavior* 2:3–43.

Siemsen, E., S. Balasubramanian, and A. V. Roth. Forthcoming. Incentives that induce task-related effort, helping, and knowledge sharing in workgroups. *Management Science.*

Singleton, R. A., B. C. Straits, and M. M. Straits. 1993. *Approaches to social research.* 2nd ed. New York: Oxford University Press.

Stephenson, W. 1953. *The study of behavior: Q-Technique and its methodology.* Chicago, IL: University of Chicago Press.

Stratman, J. K., and A. V. Roth. 2002. Enterprise resource planning (ERP) competence constructs: Two-stage multi-item scale development and validation. *Decision Sciences* 33 (4): 601–28.

Swamidass, P. M. 1991. Empirical science: New frontier in operations management research. *Academy of Management Review* 16 (4): 793–814.

# 2

# Classification of Scales

Several aids are provided to help readers find perceptual scales or objective measures of interest. A classification system for measures is provided in Appendix 1 and described below. An alphabetical listing of all measures by the name used by the original authors of the article is provided in Appendix 2. This should help readers who are looking for a particular scale or measure. If the first author of the article containing the scale is known, then the article reference can be found in Appendix 3 and the scale summary found in Chapter 4.

We provide a convenient classification system in Appendix 1. Our conceptual typology is useful in classifying scales that are intended to define similar constructs or concepts but different names may appear in the source articles. Our classification system draws on similar classification systems used by journals such as *Journal of Operations Management* and *Production and Operations Management* to classify articles and broadly define the content of the operations management field.

The classification system has the following major topic headings:

- Context and environment
- Operations strategy
- Business strategy
- Core quality practices
- Planning and control
- Human resources/organization issues
- Organizational learning
- Performance/capabilities
- Information systems/e-business
- Supply chain
- Technology
- Product/service development
- Other measures

*Context and environment* includes measures such as industry, competition, and plant size. These are the variables that capture the external and internal environment. They are frequently modeled as either control variables or contextual variables in empirical studies. Specific measures for the context and environment category include the competition faced by operations, for example, competitive hostility, competitive intensity, entry barriers, marketplace environment, munificence, and rivalry. This category also contains uncertainty measures such as agility assessment, demand uncertainty, dynamism, environmental stability, market newness, supply uncertainty, and technology uncertainty. Several measures of industry type are provided along with measures of the business unit, plant, process, and product type.

The *operations strategy* category includes measures related to the formulation, the content, and the implementation of operations strategy. Note that we have reserved this category for operations as a functional strategy and use a separate category for business strategy. While business strategy is not in the usual domain of operations, but considering the interrelationship between operations strategy and business strategy, we include business strategy for completeness. Operations strategy includes measures for both manufacturing and service. Specific measures listed in Appendix 1 are competitive priorities of various types, including cost, delivery, flexibility, and quality. A number of structure, infrastructure, and integration choices are also provided, such as adoption of manufacturing practices, capability building, human resources, information systems, capacity, vertical integration, and other strategic issues. The operations strategy category also includes measures of the strategy process, for example, communication of strategy, critical success factors, customer focus, manufacturing involvement, and long-term orientation. Finally, measures for various types of operations strategies that cover topics such as lean, time-based, mass customization and service strategy are provided.

*Business strategy* includes measures on business strategy elements such as differentiation, low cost, niche strategies, and integration between strategies. Also presented are a number of measures on marketing strategy and other functional strategies.

The *core quality practices* category has measures that are specifically related to quality management and is thus narrowly defined. Human resources and organization practices such as teamwork, training, and empowerment could be considered part of quality management or total quality management (TQM) but are included in the human resources/organization category. The core quality category includes many measures on quality leadership/management support, strategic quality planning, information and analysis, process management, supplier/customer quality management, quality dimensions, customer focus, quality management philosophies, and service recovery/failure. This category also includes scales that are used to measure different dimensions of quality as used in the literature.

*Planning and control* is a category that encompasses measures frequently associated with just-in-time (JIT) or other production control and scheduling practices. This category has, for example, multiple measures on scheduling and planning, process modification and material flow, setup and lot size, production control, layout, inventory control, and overall JIT and related constructs.

*Human resources/organization issues* contain a large number of scales devoted to human resources in operations. While many of these scales have roots in the organization behavior field, they have been used in articles published in operations management journals. Scales in this category include organization culture/structure, organizational processes, hiring/selection, employee development/training, teamwork, measurement/rewards, employee satisfaction/attitude, and work design/employee empowerment.

Closely related to human resources/organization issues are scales from *organizational learning,* which is a category that highlights metrics spanning learning organization, knowledge transfer, and knowledge management.

Measures from the *performance/capabilities* are frequently used in empirical studies in operations management. They include the generic OM performance criteria of cost, quality, flexibility, and delivery plus measures related to management accounting, business performance, and customer satisfaction. Note that these measures refer to the actual performance achieved (i.e., "realized" competitive capabilities) and not to the competitive priorities that are considered performance goals or objectives under the operations strategy category. This category also includes measures of supply chain capabilities, financial/marketing measures, and individual/team performance.

There is a separate category for information systems in operations that consists of e-operations, enterprise resource management (ERP), and related measures. This category is closely related to supply chain measures such as computer networking with suppliers and customers; however, the supply chain category also contains other supply chain measures involving supplier development and strategic purchasing. The *information systems/e-business* category is divided into groups of measures on IT that incorporates metrics on IT strategy/management, ease of use, system usefulness, value and satisfaction, barriers/motivations/pressure, attitude and intentions toward information system adoption, and use of IT in operations.

*Supply chain measures* encompass a variety of issues and notions. Measures on buyer-supplier relationships, integration/collaboration, power, communications, transaction cost, and environmental purchasing are contained in this category.

The *technology* and *product/service* categories, while closely related conceptually, are distinctive enough in the extant literature to warrant separate classifications. *Technology* refers to the methods of work and it comprises internal process (or "hard") technologies such as advanced manufacturing technologies (AMT), flexible manufacturing systems (FMS), group technology (GT), as well as associated practices like enablers and drivers of technology adoption and implementation strategies. *Product/service development* has measures that are typically associated with cross-functional new product development practices, concurrent development, design for manufacturing (DFM), and project selection.

The *other measures* category contains miscellaneous metrics. These are activity-based costing, altruism, career advancement, compliance, management accounting system, and public responsibility.

The classification framework described here is detailed in Appendix 1 so that readers can find scales and objective measures that may have different names but are closely related.

Appendix 2 is a complete alphabetical list of the metrics by the name given to the measure by the authors of the original article.

Appendix 3 is a listing of the 230 articles that have been summarized in this handbook, organized alphabetically by the last name of the first author.

# 3

# OBJECTIVE MEASURES OF OPERATIONS

## INTRODUCTION

Most of this book contains perceptual measures using multi-item scales. Nevertheless, the use of single objective measures in operations management (OM) is exceedingly important. Like perceptual scales, objective measures too are also subject to measurement and sampling errors and potential bias. Oftentimes, objective measures are also used as proxy variables for constructs because they are available from secondary sources. Sometimes these proxies are a stretch in that they require many assumptions; and as a result, good multi-item perceptual scales may be more desirable. For example, research in finance has established measurement problems and bias in the well-known COMPUSTAT databases used in some OM empirical research (Rosenberg and Houglet 1974; Kinney and Swanson 1993; Guenther and Rosman 2002). In the existing OM empirical literature, these issues are too easily dismissed. Consequently, the use of objective measures can also pose significant threats to validity, if care is not taken. As a general rule, it is good practice to use a combination of objective and multi-item measurement scales or have literature showing their equivalence for the intended research purpose.

An objective measure is one that can be quantitatively determined and perhaps verified by others. Examples are things that can be counted (e.g., units produced, number of defects, number of parts, and number of employees), things that can be measured (length of time, weight, dollars), or simply yes/no questions that can be objectively answered.

As indicated above, objective questions should be subject to reliability and validity analyses just like perceptual scales. While this has rarely been done in the OM literature, interrater reliability is a good statistic to use. Interrater reliability varies from zero to one depending on the amount of agreement among two or more raters who answer the same question. For example, suppose the question is "How many suppliers does the plant have?" At first blush, this seems like a perfectly objective question, yet two individuals can give dramatically different answers depending on whether one counts all suppliers to the plant or only those that are considered as major suppliers. A study by one of the authors exemplifies this point. The answers to this question were 150 suppliers and 550 suppliers by two different respondents. This example illustrates the importance of clarifying the question as to what type of suppliers should be included, so that interrater reliability is improved. Another example is to ask two respondents what the number of employees is at the plant? The two answers could diverge depending on whether part-time workers, temporary workers, or contract employees are included, whether only those within the manufacturing function are counted, or whether some attached functions such as R&D or purchasing are counted, and so on. It is quite possible in this case that reliable responses (e.g., consistent responses) between the two respondents might be obtained; however, validity would require that in addition to being reliable, the objective data gathered properly reflected the intended definition of employee counts. Among the most important issues in using objective questions are to very clearly establish the scope of the question, operational definition, the context, and the assumptions that should be used. For this reason, it is important to pretest objective questions and also to check for interrater reliability in the context of the research study and theory. Researchers, who obtain objective measures from secondary data sources, must also be mindful of potential measurement errors and risks (Roth, Shockley, and Weng, 2007). Gray, Roth, and Tomlin (2007), for example, used a Delphi approach with a panel of experts to develop and validate an objective measure of plant quality risk. The secondary data source was the U.S. Food and Drug Administration's (FDA) audit data reports.

The five prominent OM studies that have made extensive use of objective measures are summarized as follows: *IndustryWeek,* Global Manufacturing Research Group (GMRG), High-Performance Manufacturing (HPM), Vision in Manufacturing (VIM) research, and the Retail Banking Futures (RBF) study. The first four of these studies are manufacturing oriented, and the RBF study illustrates metrics for services. The first three are conducted at the plant level. The VIM study and the RBF studies are conducted at the highest level in the organization, where manufacturing/service operations and marketing strategies are made. Typically, cross-functional strategies are set at the business unit level of analysis. None of them, however, have verified interrater reliability of the measures. Summaries and updates for these five studies are given below. Two other seminal OM studies—the International Service Study (ISS) and the Boston University Manufacturing Project—that employ objective and perceptual measures are described in Roth et al. (1997).

## *IndustryWeek* Best Plants Program

This program has been done by *IndustryWeek* magazine since 1990 in order to provide an award to outstanding manufacturing plants. The questionnaire is available to be used with permission from *IndustryWeek* and selected questions from the 2006 version of the questionnaire are included as Appendix 3.1 to this chapter. *IndustryWeek* also maintains an online interactive database of all entrants, finalists, and winners of the Best Plants Program. This database is available for sale to academics and practitioners. See the *IndustryWeek* Web site (www.industryweek.com/Benchmarking/BestPlants/) for the most recent version of the questionnaire and details on the database.

One advantage of the *IndustryWeek* study is that it is very comprehensive, containing more than 250 different questions. All questions in their survey are objective, and it does not use multi-item perceptual scales. Some of the questions, however, must be regarded with caution since different respondents' interpretations may not be the same. For example, one question is "Quality techniques extensively implemented: Total quality management: No, Yes." Since this is a yes/no question, different individuals could interpret use of the words "extensively implemented" or "total quality management" in dissimilar ways leading to low interrater reliability. Nevertheless, many of the *IndustryWeek* questions are specific and would probably produce acceptable variance among different respondents. Understanding the measurement properties of the *IndustryWeek*-like variables is an important area for future research.

The *IndustryWeek* questionnaire is organized as follows:

General questions

Quality and quality performance

Employment practices

Safety

Customer focus

Product innovation

Supply chain and logistics

Technology

Manufacturing and flexibility

Maintenance

Inventory management

Environmental

Competitiveness and market results

As one can see, the *IndustryWeek* questions cover a wide range of topics and deal with both practices being implemented and performance of the plant.

## Global Manufacturing Research Group Study

This study of plant practices is led by Professor D. Clay Whybark of the University of North Carolina at Chapel Hill and includes a large group of academics worldwide. The most recent questionnaire is available at the Web site http://gmrg.org. A sample questionnaire from round 3 is reproduced in Appendix 3.2 and contains mostly objective items, but some perceptual multi-item scales as well. Questions from round 3 are organized into the following categories:

Outsourcing and supplier relations

Manufacturing planning and control information systems

Sales forecasting

Demographics

Competitive goal measurement

Internal manufacturing practices

Purchasing

The GMRG questionnaire is much more limited than the *IndustryWeek* Best Plants Study, since it does not include quality, employment practices, technology, maintenance, innovation, safety, environmental practices, and performance. This study has been restricted to supply chain, forecasting, inventory, scheduling, goals, materials management, and purchasing topics. Nevertheless, the depth of coverage in these areas is impressive and the questionnaire has published results available from it. A bibliography of publications can be obtained from the GMRG Web site. We leave it to the reader to evaluate the quality of the metrics based on the information provided.

## High Performance Manufacturing Study

The HPM study, formerly called the World Class Manufacturing Study, is led by Roger Schroeder from the University of Minnesota and Barbara Flynn from Indiana University along with a large group of researchers from around the world. Details of this study are contained in the book *High Performance Manufacturing: Global Perspectives* (Schroeder and Flynn 2001). The book contains the results of the past studies and references to many academic articles written from rounds 1 and 2 of the data collected at different time periods. The questionnaires and data are not yet publicly available; however, many scales have been published in journals and are available with permission.

The HPM study surveyed both perceptual and objective items on various issues related to plant operations. For many constructs, both objective items and multi-item perceptual items are captured, which allows for the evaluation of criterion validity. In the current round 3 of data collection efforts, twenty-one questionnaires are given to ten managers and eleven workers/supervisors to collect a broad profile of data about the plant. All perceptual questions are answered by at least three respondents to establish interrater reliability. Appendix 3.3 to this chapter contains the selected objective questions used in the HPM study from round 3 of data collection conducted in 2004–2005. This will give the reader an idea of the scope of the entire data available in the HPM study.

The topics covered by the HPM study are as follows:

Environment of the plant

Supply chain

Human resources

Improvement

Information systems

JIT and theory of constraints

Manufacturing strategy

Quality management

Total productive maintenance

Technology

New product development

Plant performance

## Vision in Manufacturing Survey

Since the mid-1980s Aleda Roth (currently at Clemson University) and Craig Giffi, Gregory Seal, Michael Fradette, and Deloitte Research of Deloitte and Touche has been periodically following the strategic developments and trends in manufacturing through the VIM study. The VIM survey was developed from theory and grounded by a comprehensive investigation of world-class manufacturing funded by the National Center for Manufacturing Sciences (Giffi et al. 1990). The purpose of the study was to develop measures suitable for testing research hypotheses about capabilities-based manufacturing, technology, and supply chain strategies in a global context and to benchmark trends in best operations-based practices, and operations-driven business performance. The unit of analysis is the manufacturing business unit (MBU)—defined operationally as the highest level in the organization where manufacturing and marketing join together to set strategy for the primary products in the firm's primary line of business. Over the years, the survey instrument and methodology have been honed and fine-tuned to improve the measurement properties of established scales and items, and to introduce new ones, as well as to improve the sampling processes.

To ensure academic rigor, all survey instruments were designed by Aleda Roth in collaboration with Deloitte and Touche. In most recent years, Deloitte Research hired professional survey research groups to develop the sampling frame and collect the data. A typical survey may consist of over 900 items, in 50 perceptual scales. Objective measures of performance and business characteristics are also captured. Over 3,000 leading manufacturing executives and their management teams, from industrialized and emerging markets, have participated in the survey since its inception, making it the most comprehensive study of global manufacturing strategies and performance ever conducted. Follow-up studies of smaller groups have been periodically undertaken to ensure reliability and validity of the instrument. The subject areas covered in versions of the survey include the following:

Competitive environment

Business context and strategic directions

Competitive capabilities and priorities

Manufacturing strategy

World-class manufacturing practices

Manufacturing and information technology strategies

Outsourcing and supply chain strategies

New product development

Business process reengineering

Human resources

Performance

For more details of the most recent studies, see Roth (1996), and Rosenzweig and Roth (2004), and Appendix 3.4.

## Retail Banking Futures Study

The retail banking futures study is a collaborative survey initiative led by Aleda Roth and the Bank Administration Institute (headquartered in

Chicago). From the late 1980s through the mid-1990s, trends in retail banking service operations have been assessed biennially. The study takes into account the retail banking operational and service delivery system strategies that American retail banks either have adopted or had planned to implement in support of the overall business strategies. The research was conceptualized on theory and propositions given in the extant OM literature that link service operations choices to performance. Thus, the RBF study covers the strategic role that service operations plays in orchestrating resources in delivery systems for building competitive advantage. It tracks the critical success factors, including competitive capabilities and priorities, as well as market direction, performance, technology implementation, quality progress, and other best practices.

The unit of analysis of the study is the retail banking unit (RBU). A RBU is operationally defined as the strategic business unit, which may be an entire bank, a holding company, a division or group, or department, depending on how the retail side of the bank is organized. For example, in a decentralized, highly diversified bank, the RBU is most likely to be a division or group. A common thread spanning RBUs in the study is that each represents the highest level in the organization where strategic delivery system decisions are made. The sampling frame was derived from Federal Deposit Insurance Corporation (FDIC) Call Report tapes of all commercial banks in the United States and their asset sizes. A stratified sampling plan was established to ensure adequate coverage of small, medium, and large banks according to assets.

Data were obtained through mail surveys to senior retail banking executives who served as coordinators of data collection. These executives were responsible for gathering consensus from cross-functional teams of senior managers who were responsible for the RBU strategy and from individuals who were assigned to specific functional areas. Rigorous methodological initiatives, such as focused groups, pilot studies, pretests, and post-hoc analyses of prior data, were taken to ensure the psychometric properties of the instruments. Refinements were made over time to improve reliability and validity (see Huete and Roth 1987; Roth 1993; Roth and Jackson 1995; Roth and van der Velde 1991, 1992; Menor et al. 2001). The survey comprises many objective and perceptual items, starting in 1987 with over 900 items. About half of the items were fixed over time, and the other half were varied in order to hone in on some specific aspect of service operations strategy that was of general interest to researchers and practice at the time of the survey. The number of respondents varied, as well, ranging from 120 to 150 RBUs. For detailed examples see Appendix 3.5. The topics included in this study are as follows:

- Competitive environment
- Business strategic directions
- Competitive capabilities and priorities
- Management concerns
- Areas of change
- Market leader practices/activities/tools
- Investments in infrastructure
- New service development
- OM-marketing strategy interfaces
- Human resources practices
- Performance indicators

## Survey Summary

Taken together, these five studies provide a wide range of objective items for questionnaire construction. While there is some overlap among the questions in the five studies, there are also some unique ways of measuring operations constructs presented in each study. The challenge for OM in the future is to perfect the constructs and questions that have been used to ensure they are specific, well defined, and well formulated; and in turn, they can pass the test of interrater reliability along with other reliability and validity tests. These five studies also illustrate the deliberate design trade-offs in terms of scale and scope of research (see Rosenzweig and Roth 2004; Roth

2007; Roth et al. 1997). A large number of items in a survey instrument and multiple respondents can potentially allow for more in-depth coverage of a topic; however, usually smaller samples are obtained (i.e., $n < 100$), which may limit the overall assessment of the instrument, precision of estimates, and potentially the generalizability[1] of the results to a wider group than the current study. Smaller samples restrict the researcher's ability to evaluate adequately the psychometric properties, say, for example, using hold-out samples and/or using the measurement model of structural equation modeling. Moreover, modifications of multi-item scales may lead to data fitting when samples are small. On the other hand, gathering data from a large number of respondents using a well-defined sampling plan and research approach oftentimes limits the number of questions and constructs in a single survey. Advocates of Web surveys have found these trade-offs to be exacerbated.

It should be noted in closing that there are many published studies that use a few objective measures along with perceptual scales. Examples of these objective measures can be found in the summaries provided in this book.

## Note

1. Generalizability is a function of many factors, such as geographic, time, and population dimensions, and not necessarily sample size.

## Selected Illustrative References

Giffi, C., A. V. Roth, and G. Seal. 1990. *Competing in world class manufacturing: America's 21st century challenge.* Homewood, IL: Business One Irwin.

Gray, J., A. V. Roth, and B. Tomlin. 2007. Quality risk in outsourcing: Evidence from the U.S. drug industry. Fisher College of Business Working Paper. The Ohio State University, Columbus, OH. (Also in the Seventh Annual Technology Mini-Conference Papers, Wharton, University of Pennsylvania. http://mackcenter.wharton.upenn.edu)

Guenther, D. A., and A. J. Rosman. 1994. Differences between COMPUSTAT and CRSP SIC codes and related effects on research. *Journal of Accounting and Economics* 18 (1): 115–28.

Huete, L., and A. V. Roth. 1988. The industrialization and span of retail banks' delivery systems. *International Journal of Operations & Production Management* 8 (3): 46–66.

Kinney, M. R., and E. P. Swanson. 1993. The accuracy and adequacy of tax data in COMPUSTAT. *Journal of the American Taxation Association* 15 (1): 121–35.

Menor, L. J., A. V. Roth, and C. H. Mason. 2001 Agility in retail banking: A numerical taxonomy of strategic service groups. *Manufacturing & Service Operations Management* 3 (4): 273–92.

Rosenberg, B., and M. Houglet. 1974. Error rates in CRSP and COMPUSTAT data bases and their implications. *Journal of Finance* 29 (4): 1303–10.

Rosenzweig, E. D., and A. V. Roth. 2004. Towards a theory of competitive progression: Evidence in high-tech manufacturing. *Production and Operations Management Journal* 13 (4): 354–68.

Rosenzweig, E. D., A. V. Roth, and J. Dean. 2003. The influence of integration intensity on competitive capabilities and business performance: An exploratory investigation of consumer products manufacturers. *Journal of Operations Management* 21 (4): 437–56.

Roth, A. V. 1993. Assessing performance in service organizations. In *Service superiority: The design and delivery of effective service operations,* ed. R. Johnston and N. D. Slack, 367–74. Warwick, UK: Warwick Printing.

———. 1996. Neo-operations strategies: Linking capabilities-based competition to technology. In *The handbook of technology management,* ed. G. H. Gaynor, 38.1–38.44. New York: McGraw-Hill.

———. Forthcoming 2007. Applications of empirical science in manufacturing and service operations. *Manufacturing and Service Operations Management.*

Roth, A. V., A. E. Gray, J. Singhal, and K. Singhal. 1997. International technology and operations management: Resource toolkit for research and teaching. *Production and Operations Management* 6 (2): 167–87.

Roth, A. V., and W. Jackson. 1995. Strategic determinants of service quality and performance: Evidence from the banking industry. *Management Science* 41 (11): 1720–33.

Roth, A. V., J. Shockley, and H. H. Weng. 2007. The use of secondary data to measure performance in operations management research: Looking backward and forward. College of Business and Behavioral Science Working Paper, Clemson University, Clemson, SC.

Roth, A. V., and M. van der Velde. 1988. *The future of retail banking delivery systems.* Chicago, IL: Bank Administration Institute.

———. 1989. Investing in retail delivery system technology. *Journal of Retail Banking* 11 (2): 23–34.

———. 1990. *Retail banking strategies: Opportunities for the 1990s.* Chicago, IL: Bank Administration Institute.

———. 1992. *World class banking: Benchmarking the market leaders.* Chicago, IL: Bank Administration Institute.

Schroeder, Roger, and Barbara Flynn, eds. 2001. *High performance manufacturing: Global perspetives.* New York: Wiley.

# APPENDIX 3.1

## *IndustryWeek* Best Plants Program Metrics

### Selected Items from the Total Survey of 250 Items

**General Questions**

| | |
|---|---|
| Public or Private: | Private, Public |
| Years since plant startup: | 0–5, 6–10, 11–20, over 20 |
| Number of days operating per week? | Numerical |
| Number of shifts: | Numerical |
| Square footage of plant: | 0–49,999; 50,000–99,999; 100,000–249,999; 250,000–499,999; 500,000–999,999; 1,000,000+ |
| Number of employees: | Fewer than 100, 100–249, 250–499, 500–999, 1,000 or more |
| Are plant workers represented by a union? | Nonunion, union |
| Product type: | Discrete, process, both |
| In general, in which value chain does this plant primarily participate? | Aerospace, automotive, chemicals, construction, consumer packaged goods/nondurables, consumer product durables, high tech, industrial equipment and machinery, pharmaceuticals, biotechnology, medical, printing and publishing, none of the above |
| Annual savings (as a percentage of cost of goods sold) achieved due to Improvement methodologies, %: | Numerical |
| Labor cost as a percentage of costs of goods sold, %: | Numerical |
| Overhead as a percentage of costs of goods sold, %: | Numerical |
| Material costs as a percentage of costs of goods sold, %: | Numerical |
| Dedicated improvement people as a percentage of total workforce: | Numerical |
| Total documented cost savings as a result of specific improvement programs over the most recent year per employee: | Numerical |
| Number of kaizen blitz or kaizen event programs conducted In most recent 12-month period? | Numerical |

**Quality**

| | |
|---|---|
| Has the plant received ISO 9000:2000 certification? | No, Yes |
| Has the plant received TS 16969 certification? | No, Yes |
| People dedicated 100% to quality control, percentage of total plant workforce | Numerical |
| Cost of quality as a percentage of cost of goods sold: | Numerical |
| Quality techniques extensively implemented: Six Sigma | No, Yes |

*(Continued)*

(Continued)

| | |
|---|---|
| Quality techniques extensively implemented: Quality function deployment | No, Yes |
| Quality techniques extensively implemented: Poka-yoke (mistake proofing) methods | No, Yes |
| Quality techniques extensively implemented: Failure mode effect analysis (FMEA) | No, Yes |
| Quality techniques extensively implemented: Total quality management | No, Yes |
| Quality techniques extensively implemented: Employee problem-solving teams | No, Yes |
| Quality techniques extensively implemented: Plan/do/check/verify | No, Yes |
| Quality techniques extensively implemented: Advanced product quality planning (APQP) | No, Yes |
| Quality techniques extensively implemented: Manual SPC | No, Yes |
| Quality techniques extensively implemented: Computerized SPC | No, Yes |
| Quality techniques extensively implemented: Design of experiments | No, Yes |
| Quality techniques extensively implemented: Taguchi methods | No, Yes |
| Finished product current first-pass yield, %: | Numerical |
| Finished product yield improvement within the past three years, % (five years reported prior to 2002): | Numerical |
| First-pass yield for all finished products (weighted average that accounts for differences in product volumes or in value-added), %: | Numerical |
| First-pass yield for all finished products (weighted average that accounts for differences in product volumes or in value-added), %: | Less than 75, 75–89.9, 90–94.9, 95–96.9, 97–98.9, 99–100 |
| Does plant calculate rolled throughput yield? | No, Yes |
| In-plant defect rate (fallout rate) on manufactured components and finished products, ppm; | Numerical |
| Percent reduction in in-plant defect rate in the past three years, % (five years reported prior to 2002): | Numerical |
| Customer reject rate on shipped products, ppm: | Numerical |
| Percent reduction in customer reject rate in the past three years (five years reported prior to 2002), %: | Numerical |
| Scrap/rework costs as a percentage of sales, %: | Numerical |
| Scrap/rework costs as a percentage of sales, %: | Less than 1, 1–1.9, 2–4.9, 5–14.9, 15 or higher |
| Percent reduction in scrap/rework as a percentage of sales in the past three years (five years reported prior to 2002), %: | Numerical |
| Warranty costs as a percentage of sales, %: | Numerical |
| Warranty costs as a percentage of sales, %: | Less than 0.5, 0.5–0.9, 1–1.9, 2–2.9, 3–9.9, 10 or more |
| Percent reduction in warranty costs as a percentage of sales within the past three years (five years reported prior to 2002), %: | Numerical |

SOURCE: Reprinted with permission. These questions are an illustrative, partial listing of the *IndustryWeek* survey items. For the following areas, permission was not granted by *IW* to include the detailed items: employment practices, safety, customer focus, product innovation, supply chain and logistics, technology, manufacturing and flexibility, maintenance, inventory management, environmental, and competitiveness and market results. The information in this appendix is not to be used without the express written permission of *IndustryWeek*.

## APPENDIX 3.2

### Global Manufacturing Research Group (GMRG)

### Manufacturing Practices Survey: Round 3 Questionnaire

**1. Company Description and Background Information**

The information in this section of the survey will be useful to researchers in studying relationships between company characteristics and manufacturing practices. As with the answers to questions in subsequent sections of the survey, the information that you provide will not be used to identify individual companies. Feel comfortable giving **approximate responses**; in most cases, our research has shown that it is important to have approximate answers than none at all.

In this survey, we have used the word "company" to represent the unit for which you are answering questions. We ask that you be consistent throughout the survey and report the sales, employment, practices, etc. for the unit, whether it is a company, strategic business unit, or plant.

1.01 **Approximately** how many employees work for the company? ___employees

1.02 How many of these employees are production workers (direct and indirect)? ___workers

1.03 About what percentage of the production workers are contract or temporary? ___% of workers

1.04 How many hours per year does a production employee typically work? ___hours per year

1.05 How many product lines or product families does the company produce?

___ product lines or families

1.06 What percentage of company sales comes from the company's largest selling product line?

___% of sales

1.07 About what percentage of the company's products is make-to-order? ___% make-to-order

1.08 What percentage of the machines in the company is grouped as follows?

______% of machines grouped by machine type (e.g., all lathes together)

______% of machines grouped by product or product families (e.g., manufacturing cells)

1.09 On average, over the past two years, what has been the capacity utilization rate for plant machinery or equipment? ____% capacity utilization rate

1.10 What were the company's sales last year? (State currency units.) ___total sales

1.11 What were the company's sales **two years before that**? (State currency units.) ___total sales

1.12 What percentage of the company's sales last year was for export? ___% export sales

1.13 What percentage of the company's sales **two years before that** was for export?

___% export sales

1.14 What percentage of the ownership of the company is each of the following? (These should sum to 100%.) ___% domestic (within the country) ___% foreign (outside the country)

1.15 About what percentage of the company's **sales** is the total manufacturing cost? ___% of sales

*(Continued)*

(Continued)

1.16 About what percentage of the company's total manufacturing cost is for labor? ___% of cost

1.17 About what percentage of the company's total manufacturing cost is for material? ___% of cost

1.18 What is the approximate average age of the company's production equipment? ___years

1.19 On average, over the past two years, about what **percentage of annual sales** has been invested in new manufacturing equipment? ___% of annual sales

1.20 Approximately how many suggestions are offered per year per employee? ___suggestions

1.21 Approximately how many employees are absent per day? ___employees

1.22 Approximately how many employees leave the company a year? ___employees

1.23 For each of the items listed below, how does the company compare with its competitors? (Circle a number.)

| | Far Worse Than Competitors | | | | Far Better Than Competitors | | |
|---|---|---|---|---|---|---|---|
| Production costs | 1 | 2 | 3 | 4 | 5 | 6 | 7 |
| Total product costs | 1 | 2 | 3 | 4 | 5 | 6 | 7 |
| Supply chain costs | 1 | 2 | 3 | 4 | 5 | 6 | 7 |
| Product features | 1 | 2 | 3 | 4 | 5 | 6 | 7 |
| Product performance | 1 | 2 | 3 | 4 | 5 | 6 | 7 |
| Perceived overall product quality | 1 | 2 | 3 | 4 | 5 | 6 | 7 |
| Supply chain integration | 1 | 2 | 3 | 4 | 5 | 6 | 7 |
| Order fulfillment speed | 1 | 2 | 3 | 4 | 5 | 6 | 7 |
| Delivery speed | 1 | 2 | 3 | 4 | 5 | 6 | 7 |
| Delivery as promised | 1 | 2 | 3 | 4 | 5 | 6 | 7 |
| Delivery flexibility | 1 | 2 | 3 | 4 | 5 | 6 | 7 |
| Flexibility to change output volume | 1 | 2 | 3 | 4 | 5 | 6 | 7 |
| Flexibility to change product mix | 1 | 2 | 3 | 4 | 5 | 6 | 7 |
| Manufacturing throughput time | 1 | 2 | 3 | 4 | 5 | 6 | 7 |
| Product design time | 1 | 2 | 3 | 4 | 5 | 6 | 7 |
| Solid waste disposal | 1 | 2 | 3 | 4 | 5 | 6 | 7 |
| Air emissions | 1 | 2 | 3 | 4 | 5 | 6 | 7 |
| Water emissions | 1 | 2 | 3 | 4 | 5 | 6 | 7 |
| Health and safety record | 1 | 2 | 3 | 4 | 5 | 6 | 7 |
| ISO certifications | 1 | 2 | 3 | 4 | 5 | 6 | 7 |

1.24 In the past two years, to what extent has the company invested resources (money, time, and/or people) in programs in the following areas? (Circle a number for each program.)

| | Not at All | | | | To a Great Extent | | |
|---|---|---|---|---|---|---|---|
| Cellular manufacturing | 1 | 2 | 3 | 4 | 5 | 6 | 7 |
| Factory automation | 1 | 2 | 3 | 4 | 5 | 6 | 7 |
| Process redesign | 1 | 2 | 3 | 4 | 5 | 6 | 7 |
| Enterprise resource planning (e.g., SAP) | 1 | 2 | 3 | 4 | 5 | 6 | 7 |
| Just-in-time | 1 | 2 | 3 | 4 | 5 | 6 | 7 |

| | Not at All | | | | | | To a Great Extent |
|---|---|---|---|---|---|---|---|
| Material requirements planning | 1 | 2 | 3 | 4 | 5 | 6 | 7 |
| Manufacturing throughput time reduction | 1 | 2 | 3 | 4 | 5 | 6 | 7 |
| Setup time reduction | 1 | 2 | 3 | 4 | 5 | 6 | 7 |
| ISO 9000 certification | 1 | 2 | 3 | 4 | 5 | 6 | 7 |
| Supplier certification | 1 | 2 | 3 | 4 | 5 | 6 | 7 |
| Statistical process control | 1 | 2 | 3 | 4 | 5 | 6 | 7 |
| Total quality management | 1 | 2 | 3 | 4 | 5 | 6 | 7 |
| ISO 14000 certification | 1 | 2 | 3 | 4 | 5 | 6 | 7 |
| Pollution prevention | 1 | 2 | 3 | 4 | 5 | 6 | 7 |
| Recycling of materials | 1 | 2 | 3 | 4 | 5 | 6 | 7 |
| Waste reduction | 1 | 2 | 3 | 4 | 5 | 6 | 7 |
| Workplace health and safety | 1 | 2 | 3 | 4 | 5 | 6 | 7 |

**2. Sales Forecasting**

This section of the survey is about the methods that the company uses to anticipate demand for its products. We have found that manufacturing firms use a wide range of methods, and that both formal and informal approaches are effective. Thus, as with the other sections, your answers will provide us with insights about actual company practices and there are no right or wrong answers. Please note, also, that for questions which ask for numerical answers, your answers may be **approximate.**

2.01 Which of the following best describes the **position** (level) of the person who has the **primary** authority for producing the company's sales forecasts? (Mark only one.)

___president/CEO/managing director ___department/division head

___vice president/director ___ group/section manager

2.02 Which of the following best describes the **function** of the person who has the **primary** authority for producing the company's sales forecasts? (Mark only one.)

___administration ___production ___sales ___finance

___planning ___engineering ___marketing ___accounting

2.03 To what extent does the company use these techniques for sales forecasting? (Circle a number for each.)

| | Not at All | | | | | | To a Great Extent |
|---|---|---|---|---|---|---|---|
| Quantitative models (e.g., regression) | 1 | 2 | 3 | 4 | 5 | 6 | 7 |
| Qualitative models (e.g., survey) | 1 | 2 | 3 | 4 | 5 | 6 | 7 |
| Management opinion | 1 | 2 | 3 | 4 | 5 | 6 | 7 |

2.04 To what extent is each of the following considered in the company's forecast? (Circle a number for each.)

| | Not at All | | | | | | To a Great Extent |
|---|---|---|---|---|---|---|---|
| Current economic conditions | 1 | 2 | 3 | 4 | 5 | 6 | 7 |
| Customer information | 1 | 2 | 3 | 4 | 5 | 6 | 7 |
| Supplier information | 1 | 2 | 3 | 4 | 5 | 6 | 7 |
| Results of market research | 1 | 2 | 3 | 4 | 5 | 6 | 7 |

*(Continued)*

(Continued)

2.05 To what extent is the company's sales forecast used for the following purposes? (Circle a number for each.)

| | Not at All | | | | | | To a Great Extent |
|---|---|---|---|---|---|---|---|
| Budget preparation | 1 | 2 | 3 | 4 | 5 | 6 | 7 |
| Production planning | 1 | 2 | 3 | 4 | 5 | 6 | 7 |
| Subcontracting decisions | 1 | 2 | 3 | 4 | 5 | 6 | 7 |
| Material/inventory planning | 1 | 2 | 3 | 4 | 5 | 6 | 7 |
| Sales planning | 1 | 2 | 3 | 4 | 5 | 6 | 7 |
| Human resource planning | 1 | 2 | 3 | 4 | 5 | 6 | 7 |
| New product development | 1 | 2 | 3 | 4 | 5 | 6 | 7 |
| Facilities planning | 1 | 2 | 3 | 4 | 5 | 6 | 7 |
| Equipment purchase planning | 1 | 2 | 3 | 4 | 5 | 6 | 7 |

2.06 For about how many individual products or product lines does the company develop forecasts?

___products are forecast ___product lines are forecast

2.07 How many months into the future does the company forecast (e.g., the time horizon)? ___months

2.08 What is the smallest time period into which the time horizon of the company's sales forecast is divided? (Please mark only one.)

___ days ___ weeks ___ months ___ years

2.09 What has been the **approximate** average percent forecast error over the past two years?

___ % error

2.10 How many times per year is the company sales forecast modified? ___times per year

2.11 What percentage of the company's sales forecasts do production personnel change for production planning purposes? ___ % changed

### 3. Production Planning and Scheduling

This section is about your company's practices in the areas of planning and scheduling production. Planning refers to activities that express units of production and inventory in aggregated terms for the purpose of specifying overall output and capacity requirements for several months or even years into the future. Scheduling refers to more detailed activities (often known as master production scheduling) that determine the timing and output levels for specific products or components in the next few weeks or months.

*3a. Production Planning (Having to Do with Aggregated Units for the Next Several Months)*

3.01 For about how many individual products or product lines does the company develop production plans? ___ products in production plan ___ product lines in production plan

3.02 How far into the future does the company's production plan extend? ___ months

3.03 What is the smallest increment into which the company's production plan is divided? (Mark only one.) ___days ___weeks ___months ___years

3.04 About how many times per year is the company's production plan revised? ___ times per year

3.05 To what extent is each of the following factors considered in the development of the company's production plan? (Circle a number for each factor.)

| | Not at All | | | | | | To a Great Extent |
|---|---|---|---|---|---|---|---|
| Customer order backlogs | 1 | 2 | 3 | 4 | 5 | 6 | 7 |
| Previous sales | 1 | 2 | 3 | 4 | 5 | 6 | 7 |
| Machine capacity | 1 | 2 | 3 | 4 | 5 | 6 | 7 |
| Labor capacity | 1 | 2 | 3 | 4 | 5 | 6 | 7 |
| Customers' future plans | 1 | 2 | 3 | 4 | 5 | 6 | 7 |
| Inventory levels | 1 | 2 | 3 | 4 | 5 | 6 | 7 |
| The forecast | 1 | 2 | 3 | 4 | 5 | 6 | 7 |

3.06 How often are the following considered when subcontracting or outsourcing? (Circle a number for each.)

| | Never | | | | | | Very Often |
|---|---|---|---|---|---|---|---|
| Excess production load at your company | 1 | 2 | 3 | 4 | 5 | 6 | 7 |
| Production difficulty at your company | 1 | 2 | 3 | 4 | 5 | 6 | 7 |
| Top management directive | 1 | 2 | 3 | 4 | 5 | 6 | 7 |
| Subcontracting allows earlier delivery dates | 1 | 2 | 3 | 4 | 5 | 6 | 7 |
| Subcontractor's costs are lower | 1 | 2 | 3 | 4 | 5 | 6 | 7 |
| Subcontractor's quality is higher | 1 | 2 | 3 | 4 | 5 | 6 | 7 |

3.07 When **demand exceeds capacity**, how often does the company respond in each of the following ways? (Circle a number for each alternative.)

| | Never | | | | | | Very Often |
|---|---|---|---|---|---|---|---|
| Hire more workers | 1 | 2 | 3 | 4 | 5 | 6 | 7 |
| Use overtime | 1 | 2 | 3 | 4 | 5 | 6 | 7 |
| Add shifts | 1 | 2 | 3 | 4 | 5 | 6 | 7 |
| Subcontract production work | 1 | 2 | 3 | 4 | 5 | 6 | 7 |
| Backlog customer order | 1 | 2 | 3 | 4 | 5 | 6 | 7 |
| Lease temporary capacity | 1 | 2 | 3 | 4 | 5 | 6 | 7 |
| Turn away customers | 1 | 2 | 3 | 4 | 5 | 6 | 7 |

3.08 When **demand is less than capacity**, how often does the company respond in each of the following ways? (Circle a number for each alternative.)

| | Never | | | | | | Very Often |
|---|---|---|---|---|---|---|---|
| Lay off workers | 1 | 2 | 3 | 4 | 5 | 6 | 7 |
| Allow idle capacity | 1 | 2 | 3 | 4 | 5 | 6 | 7 |
| Eliminate shifts | 1 | 2 | 3 | 4 | 5 | 6 | 7 |
| Reduce work day or week | 1 | 2 | 3 | 4 | 5 | 6 | 7 |
| Build inventory | 1 | 2 | 3 | 4 | 5 | 6 | 7 |
| Lease capacity to others | 1 | 2 | 3 | 4 | 5 | 6 | 7 |

*(Continued)*

(Continued)

3.09 To what extent is the company's production plan used for the following purposes? (Circle a number for each.)

| | Not at All | | | | | | To a Great Extent |
|---|---|---|---|---|---|---|---|
| Budget preparation | 1 | 2 | 3 | 4 | 5 | 6 | 7 |
| Production planning | 1 | 2 | 3 | 4 | 5 | 6 | 7 |
| Subcontracting decisions | 1 | 2 | 3 | 4 | 5 | 6 | 7 |
| Material/inventory planning | 1 | 2 | 3 | 4 | 5 | 6 | 7 |
| Sales planning | 1 | 2 | 3 | 4 | 5 | 6 | 7 |
| Human resource planning | 1 | 2 | 3 | 4 | 5 | 6 | 7 |
| Facilities planning | 1 | 2 | 3 | 4 | 5 | 6 | 7 |
| Equipment purchase planning | 1 | 2 | 3 | 4 | 5 | 6 | 7 |
| New product development plans | 1 | 2 | 3 | 4 | 5 | 6 | 7 |

*3b. Production Scheduling (This Has to Do with Products, Product Lines, or Components over the Next Few Weeks or Months)*

3.10 How far into the future does the company's production **schedule** extend? ___weeks

3.11 What is the **smallest** time increment of the company's production schedule? (Mark only one.)

___days ___weeks ___months ___years

3.12 How far into the future does the company freeze the production schedule?

(0 = the firm does not freeze the production schedule.) ___weeks

3.13 How good are the factors that affect your ability to schedule effectively?

About how accurate are the company's inventory records (0 = do not measure)? ___%
About how accurate are the company's bills of material (0 = do not measure)? ___%
About how accurate are routings (0 = do not measure)? ___%

**4. Shop-Floor Control**

Shop-floor control refers to the set of operating-level activities associated with the implementation of detailed production schedules. This includes decisions about lot sizes, when to start a production order, sequencing at work centers, and when to make changes in the schedule. Our research has shown that a wide range of practices is used. As with the other sections, your answers to these questions will assist us in understanding actual practices.

4.01 Which of the following best describes the **position** of the person in the company who authorizes the plant to start work on an order? (Mark only one.)

___ president/CEO/managing director ___ department/division head
___ vice president/director ___ group/section manager

4.02 Which of the following best describes the **functional group** in the company who authorizes the plant to start work on an order? (Mark only one.)

___ administration ___ production ___ sales ___finance
___ planning ___engineering ___ marketing ___accounting

4.03 On approximately what percentage of orders do **customers make changes** after the start of production? ___% of orders

4.04 On approximately what percentage of orders do **engineering changes** occur after the start of production? ___after the start of % of orders

4.05 What is the approximate percent breakdown of the production time for a typical production batch?

___ % of elapsed factory time spent in set-up operations

___ % of elapsed factory time spent on other processing operations

___ % of elapsed factory time spent on nonprocessing operations (queue time, move time)

4.06 To what extent is each of the following considered in company decisions to authorize start of work on a production order? (Circle a number for each factor.)

| | Never | | | | | | Very Often |
|---|---|---|---|---|---|---|---|
| Actual customer order | 1 | 2 | 3 | 4 | 5 | 6 | 7 |
| Production plan | 1 | 2 | 3 | 4 | 5 | 6 | 7 |
| Detailed production schedule | 1 | 2 | 3 | 4 | 5 | 6 | 7 |
| Parts shortage list | 1 | 2 | 3 | 4 | 5 | 6 | 7 |
| Inventory level | 1 | 2 | 3 | 4 | 5 | 6 | 7 |
| Importance of the customer | 1 | 2 | 3 | 4 | 5 | 6 | 7 |
| Idle labor or equipment available | 1 | 2 | 3 | 4 | 5 | 6 | 7 |

4.07 How often is the processing sequence at machines or work centers in the company established by the following criteria? (Circle a number for each factor.)

| | Never | | | | | | Very Often |
|---|---|---|---|---|---|---|---|
| Order in which jobs arrive | 1 | 2 | 3 | 4 | 5 | 6 | 7 |
| Customer order due date | 1 | 2 | 3 | 4 | 5 | 6 | 7 |
| Processing time of the job | 1 | 2 | 3 | 4 | 5 | 6 | 7 |
| Work remaining at subsequent stations | 1 | 2 | 3 | 4 | 5 | 6 | 7 |
| Minimize the number of setups | 1 | 2 | 3 | 4 | 5 | 6 | 7 |
| Top management directive | 1 | 2 | 3 | 4 | 5 | 6 | 7 |
| How easy or difficult the job is | 1 | 2 | 3 | 4 | 5 | 6 | 7 |
| Past experience | 1 | 2 | 3 | 4 | 5 | 6 | 7 |

4.08 How often does each of the following factors **change** the company's production schedule priorities **after** the plant has started an order? (Circle a number for each factor.)

| | Never | | | | | | Very Often |
|---|---|---|---|---|---|---|---|
| Pressure from customer | 1 | 2 | 3 | 4 | 5 | 6 | 7 |
| Labor shortage | 1 | 2 | 3 | 4 | 5 | 6 | 7 |
| Material shortage | 1 | 2 | 3 | 4 | 5 | 6 | 7 |
| Energy shortage | 1 | 2 | 3 | 4 | 5 | 6 | 7 |
| Equipment shortage | 1 | 2 | 3 | 4 | 5 | 6 | 7 |
| Change in sales plan or demand | 1 | 2 | 3 | 4 | 5 | 6 | 7 |
| Change in delivery due date | 1 | 2 | 3 | 4 | 5 | 6 | 7 |
| Engineering design change | 1 | 2 | 3 | 4 | 5 | 6 | 7 |
| Top management directive | 1 | 2 | 3 | 4 | 5 | 6 | 7 |

*(Continued)*

(Continued)

4.09 What percentage of the original due dates that are promised to customers are determined by each of the following? (Should add to 100%)

the customer ___% the company ___% negotiation with the customer ___%

4.10 Approximately how many calendar days into the future has the company promised delivery?

| | Currently | Two Years Ago |
|---|---|---|
| **Minimum** days to delivery promise date | ___ days | ___ days |
| **Maximum** days to delivery promise date | ___ days | ___ days |
| **Usual** days to delivery promise date | ___ days | ___ days |

4.11 On average, what percentage of the company's orders is delivered to customers **after** the promised date?

| | Currently | Two Years Ago |
|---|---|---|
| Percentage of orders delivered **after** promised date | ___% | ___% |

4.12 For customer orders that are **delivered late**, what is the average number of days late?

| | Currently | Two Years Ago |
|---|---|---|
| Average number of days late | ___ days | ___days |

4.13 When finished goods are delivered late to customers, how often is each of the following the cause of lateness? (Circle a number for each factor.)

| | Never | | | | | | Very Often |
|---|---|---|---|---|---|---|---|
| Insufficient machine capacity | 1 | 2 | 3 | 4 | 5 | 6 | 7 |
| Machine breakdown | 1 | 2 | 3 | 4 | 5 | 6 | 7 |
| Material shortage | 1 | 2 | 3 | 4 | 5 | 6 | 7 |
| Energy shortage | 1 | 2 | 3 | 4 | 5 | 6 | 7 |
| Insufficient labor capacity | 1 | 2 | 3 | 4 | 5 | 6 | 7 |
| Material quality problem | 1 | 2 | 3 | 4 | 5 | 6 | 7 |
| Production quality problem | 1 | 2 | 3 | 4 | 5 | 6 | 7 |
| Scheduling error | 1 | 2 | 3 | 4 | 5 | 6 | 7 |
| Change of schedule priorities | 1 | 2 | 3 | 4 | 5 | 6 | 7 |
| Finished goods transportation problem | 1 | 2 | 3 | 4 | 5 | 6 | 7 |

4.14 What percentage of the company's orders is completed on or before the time specified by the **production schedule**?

| | Currently | Two Years Ago |
|---|---|---|
| Percentage of orders completed on time or early | ___% | ___% |

4.15 What are the company's **approximate reject or return percentages** at each of the following stages? (Please provide an answer for each one.)

| | Currently | Two Years Ago |
|---|---|---|
| Percentage of rejects of incoming material | ___% | ___% |
| Percentage of rejects during processing (scrap rate) | ___% | ___% |
| Percentage of rejects at the final inspection | ___% | ___% |

4.16 About how much time typically elapses from the start of the first operation until a batch of the company's products is finished?

| | Currently | Two Years Ago |
|---|---|---|
| **Average** time from start to completion | ___ days | ___ days |

4.17 About how much time typically elapses from the receipt of a customer order until it is shipped?

| | Currently | Two Years Ago |
|---|---|---|
| **Average** time from order to shipment | ___days | ___ days |

4.18 Using an index of 100 as the starting point two years ago, give the current index for the following (e.g., a 5 percent increase would be 105).

| | |
|---|---|
| Physical output (units, meters, etc.) . | _______index |
| Manufacturing cost (without inflation) | _______index |
| Labor productivity | _______index |
| Capital productivity | _______index |

4.19 Using 100 as the base two years ago, give the current index for the following (e.g., a 20 percent decrease would be 80).

| | |
|---|---|
| Product design time | _______index |
| Cost of manufacturing | _______index |
| Manufacturing throughput time | _______index |
| Delivery speed | _______index |

**5. Materials Management**

Materials management includes a wide range of activities associated with purchasing, managing, distributing, and controlling inventories within the plant. Inventory includes raw materials, component parts, work in process, and finished goods. As in the other sections, we are interested in the practices employed in your plant. Since many approaches to materials management have been shown to be effective, there are no right or wrong answers.

5.01 Approximately what percentage of the parts and components that comprise the company's products are fabricated within the plant? ___% fabricated in plant

5.02 What percentage of the company's purchase orders do suppliers deliver as follows? (These should sum to 100%.)

| | Currently | Two Years Ago |
|---|---|---|
| Percentage delivered **early** | ___% | ___% |
| Percentage delivered **on time** | ___% | ___% |
| Percentage delivered **late** | ___% | ___% |

5.03 What is the approximate average lateness of the purchase orders that are delivered **late**?
___days late

*(Continued)*

(Continued)

5.04 About how many suppliers does the company have, on average, per part?

___suppliers per part

5.05 What is the **approximate** total number of part numbers in each segment of the company's inventory system?

___ raw material part numbers

___ component part numbers

___ finished goods part numbers

5.06 How often does the company use each of the following policies when initiating purchase orders? (Circle a number for each factor.)

| | Never | | | | | | Very Often |
|---|---|---|---|---|---|---|---|
| Order at periodic interval (e.g., monthly) | 1 | 2 | 3 | 4 | 5 | 6 | 7 |
| Order based on inventory level | 1 | 2 | 3 | 4 | 5 | 6 | 7 |
| Order based on production plan or schedule | 1 | 2 | 3 | 4 | 5 | 6 | 7 |
| Order based on material shortage list | 1 | 2 | 3 | 4 | 5 | 6 | 7 |
| Order for actual customer order | 1 | 2 | 3 | 4 | 5 | 6 | 7 |
| Order based on past experience | 1 | 2 | 3 | 4 | 5 | 6 | 7 |
| No order, supplier delivers as needed | 1 | 2 | 3 | 4 | 5 | 6 | 7 |

5.07 What is the **approximate** value of the company's total inventory in all stages of production including finished goods? (State currency units.)

___ total inventory value

5.08 What is the approximate distribution of the company's inventory value? (These should sum to 100%.)

Percentage of value in purchased materials and parts ___%

Percentage of value in work-in-process ___%

Percentage of value in finished goods ___%

**6. Summary**

Thank you for your help with this survey. Your participation will contribute to a better worldwide understanding of manufacturing practices. Are there any important issues that you feel have been left out? If so, please comment in the space provided on this page.

Please let us know if there are other areas that we should consider for future study.

Comments and additional remarks:

## APPENDIX 3.3

### High-Performance Manufacturing (HPM) Study

### Selected Objective Measures from Round 3 Survey

**Environment: Objective Items**

*Complexity of the Environment*

| | |
|---|---|
| ERCEN01 | In a typical year, what is the ratio of monthly plant sales between the month with the highest sales and the month with the lowest sales? (For example, if the peak month has $100,000 in sales and the lowest month has $50,000 in sales, the ratio is 2.0.) |
| ERCEN02 | This plant's output requires approximately how many individual active part numbers or material items? |
| ERCEN05 | How much does the master production schedule change from month to month, in aggregate? Measure this by the average percent change in plant output dollars from one month to the next, over the course of a year. |
| ERCEN06 | How many labor grades are there in the plant? |
| ERCEN07 | How many levels of management are there in the plant, from first level supervisor on up to plant manager? (Example: supervisor, superintendent, plant manager = 3 levels). |
| ERCEN08 | How many product models are manufactured at this plant? |
| ERCEN20 | What is the number of final product configurations sold to customers (last year)? |

What percentage of production volume is manufactured in each of the following ways?

| | | | |
|---|---|---|---|
| ERCEN15 % | Manufacturing cells | ERCEN16 % | Dedicated flow line(s) |
| ERCEN17 % | Mixed model line(s) | ERCEN18 % | Other ways |

| | |
|---|---|
| ERCEN19 | What is the average life cycle of your products (years)? |
| ERCEN23 | How many levels are there in the bill of materials? |
| ERCEN24 % | What is the percentage of common parts, among all products? |

*Plant Focus*

| | |
|---|---|
| ERPFN01 | Number of product families used for production purposes |
| ERPFN02 % | Percentage of sales of largest product family |
| ERPFN04 % | Percentage of final products assembled to order |
| ERPFN05 % | Percentage of final products produced or purchased based on forecasts |

*Unions*

For each union within your plant, list the year that it was certified as the representative for its bargaining unit, along with the name of the union.

| *Union Name* | *Year Certified* |
|---|---|
| ERDSN50 | ERDSN51 |
| ERDSN52 | ERDSN53 |
| ERDSN54 | ERDSN55 |
| ERDSN56 | ERDSN57 |

*(Continued)*

(Continued)

## Supply Chain: Objective Items

### *Supply Chain Characteristics*

*Please Indicate the Extent to Which You Outsource the Following Activities*

| | | *Totally Internal* | *Predominately Internal* | *About Half and Half* | *Predominately Outsourced* | *Totally Outsourced* |
|---|---|---|---|---|---|---|
| PRSCN01 % | Warehousing | | | | | |
| PRSCN02 % | Transportation | | | | | |
| PRSCN03 % | Manufacturing | | | | | |
| PRSCN04 % | Assembly | | | | | |
| PRSCN05 % | Design | | | | | |
| PRSCN06 % | Administration (e.g., HR, IS, etc.) | | | | | |
| PRSCN07 % | Reverse logistics | | | | | |

| | |
|---|---|
| PRSCN08 % | What percentage of purchases come from your home country? |
| PRSCN09 % | What percentage of sales are made to customers in your home country? |

What percentage of your materials is purchased from each of the following sources?

| | | | |
|---|---|---|---|
| PRSCN10 % | Raw material suppliers | PRSCN11 % | Manufacturers |
| PRSCN12 % | Assemblers | PRSCN13 % | Distributors |
| PRSCN14 % | Wholesalers | | |

What percentage of your sales is to each of the following types of customers?

| | | | |
|---|---|---|---|
| PRSCN15 % | End consumers | PRSCN16 % | Retailers |
| PRSCN17 % | Wholesalers | PRSCN18 % | Distributors |
| PRSCN19 % | Assemblers | PRSCN20 % | Manufacturers |

## Human Resources: Objective Items

### *Compensation, Rewards, and Incentives*

Absenteeism

| | |
|---|---|
| HRTRN04 % | What is the annual absenteeism rate for hourly employees? |
| HRTRN05 % | What is the annual absenteeism rate for salaried employees? |

Stable Employment

| | |
|---|---|
| HRSEN01 | How many employees have been laid off during the past five years? |
| HRSEN02 | Of these, how many have been returned to their former positions? |
| HRSEN03 | In which years, over the past 20, has the plant had a layoff? |

Suggestions

| | |
|---|---|
| IRQIN03 | How many suggestions per worker are provided annually in this plant? |
| IRQIN04 | How many employee suggestions are implemented annually in this plant? |

**Improvement: Objective Items**

*Improvement Initiatives*

Please indicate the year in which each of the following was implemented at this plant. Enter "N" if a practice has not been implemented.

| | *Year Started* |
|---|---|
| Quality improvement | IRINN01 |
| Just-in-time | IRINN04 |
| Employee involvement | IRINN07 |
| Manufacturing strategy | IRINN10 |
| Use of manufacturing cells | IRINN16 |
| Reduction in suppliers | IRINN22 |
| Fewer levels of management | IRINN25 |
| Supplier partnership | IRINN31 |
| Simultaneous engineering | IRINN34 |
| Computer-aided design (CAD) | IRINN37 |
| Computer-aided engineering (CAE) | IRINN40 |
| Materials requirement planning | IRINN42 |
| Enterprise resource planning (ERP) | IRINN44 |
| Business process reengineering | IRINN46 |
| Electronic data interchange (EDI) | IRINN48 |
| Internet connection with customers | IRINN50 |
| Internet connection with suppliers | IRINN52 |
| Supply chain management | IRINN54 |
| Benchmarking | IRINN56 |

**Information Systems/Information Technology: Objective Items**

*E-Sales*

For which of the following marketing and sales activities does your plant use the Internet?

| | |
|---|---|
| CRESN01 | Presenting information about your plant |
| CRESN02 | Presenting your sales products catalog |
| CRESN03 | Providing online customized customer service, where customers can configure the product within the constraints stated by the plant |
| CRESN04 | Providing fixed pricing offers to potential buyers |
| CRESN05 | Providing dynamic pricing offers to potential buyers |
| CRESN06 | Online order entry |
| CRESN07 | Customers can check delivery status of their orders |

*Expenses*

| | |
|---|---|
| CREXN01 % | Plant information technology expenses (hardware, software, telecommunications, services, personnel) as a percentage of total plant manufacturing costs for last year |
| CREXN02 % | Percent increase or decrease in information technology expenses in the past year |

*(Continued)*

(Continued)

*Product Configurator*

Please check the activities for which you use a product configurator.

| | |
|---|---|
| CRPCN01 | Allowing salespeople to select appropriate features |
| CRPCN02 | Allowing customers to select appropriate features |
| CRPCN03 | Dynamically generating the product code for new product configurations |
| CRPCN04 | Dynamically generating the bill of materials for new product configurations |
| CRPCN05 | Dynamically generating the production cycle for new product configurations |
| CRPCN06 | Dynamically calculating the cost of new product configurations |
| CRPCN07 | Dynamically pricing new product configurations |

*Structure of Information*

| | |
|---|---|
| CRISN01 Yes No | Our information system allows B2B/B2C reception and transmission of structureless information from and to suppliers and customers |

Please check the structured information format for which your system allows transmission and reception.

| | |
|---|---|
| CRISN02 | Supply chain management for both suppliers and customers |
| CRISN03 | Supplier relationship management for suppliers only |
| CRISN04 | Customer relationship management for customers only |

**Manufacturing Strategy: Objective Items**

*Distinctive Competence*

*Please Indicate Your Opinion About How Your Plant Compares with Its Competition in Your Industry, on a Global Basis*

| | *Superior* | *Better than Average* | *Equivalent to Competition* | *Below Average* | *Poor; at Low End of Industry* |
|---|---|---|---|---|---|
| SRDCN06 | Employee relations | | | | |
| SRDCN07 | Degree of vertical integration | | | | |
| SRDCN09 | Supplier relations | | | | |
| SRDCN10 | Customer relations | | | | |
| SRDCN11 | Enterpdrise resource planning | | | | |
| SRDCN12 | Quality improvement program | | | | |
| SRDCN14 | Degree of mass customization | | | | |
| SRDCN15 | Supply chain management | | | | |
| SRDCN16 | Web-based interfaces with customers and suppliers | | | | |
| SRDCN17 | Just-in-time | | | | |
| SRDCN18 | Lean manufacturing | | | | |

| *Please Position the Products of Your Strategic Business Unit, Relative to Those of Your Leading Competitors* | | | | | |
|---|---|---|---|---|---|
| | *Significantly Lower* | *Lower* | *About the Same* | *Higher* | *Significantly Higher* |
| SRPCN01 | Product selling price | | | | |
| SRPCN02 | Percentage of sales spent on R&D | | | | |
| SRPCN03 | Percentage of sales spent on marketing expenses | | | | |
| SRPCN04 | Product quality | | | | |
| SRPCN05 | Brand image | | | | |
| SRPCN06 | Product features | | | | |

**Performance: Objective Items**

*Competitive Performance*

| *Please Indicate Your Opinion About How Your Plant Compares With Its Competition in Your Industry, on a Global Basis* | | | | | |
|---|---|---|---|---|---|
| | *Superior* | *Better than Average* | *Average* | *Equivalent to Competition* | *Poor, Low End of Industry* |
| GRCPN01 | Unit cost of manufacturing | | | | |
| GRCPN02 | Conformance to product specifications | | | | |
| GRCPN03 | On-time delivery performance | | | | |
| GRCPN04 | Fast delivery | | | | |
| GRCPN05 | Flexibility to change product mix | | | | |
| GRCPN06 | Flexibility to change volume | | | | |
| GRCPN07 | Inventory turnover | | | | |
| GRCPN08 | Cycle time (from raw materials to delivery) | | | | |
| GRCPN09 | Speed of new product Introduction into the plant (development lead time) | | | | |
| GRCPN10 | Product capability and performance | | | | |
| GRCPN11 | On-time new product launch | | | | |
| GRCPN12 | Product innovativeness | | | | |
| GRCPN13 | Customer support and service | | | | |

*Customer Satisfaction Assessment*

| | |
|---|---|
| QRATN01 | Do you regularly survey your customers for satisfaction? |

If so, what do your results show compared to industry average?

| Excellent | Superior | Comparable | Below | Very low |
|---|---|---|---|---|

*(Continued)*

(Continued)

**Quality: Objective Items**

*Dimensions of Quality*

*How Does the Quality of Your Products Compare with Your Competitors' Products?*

| | | *Significantly Worse* | *Worse* | *A Little Worse* | *About the Same* | *A Little Better* | *Better* | *Much Better* |
|---|---|---|---|---|---|---|---|---|
| QRDQN01 | Primary product performance characteristics | | | | | | | |
| QRDQN02 | Secondary options or features; characteristics that supplement the basic functioning of the product | | | | | | | |
| QRDQN03 | Reliability of the product; probability of failure in a specified time | | | | | | | |
| QRDQN04 | Conformance to established standards | | | | | | | |
| QRDQN05 | Durability; amount of use before the product deteriorates or needs to be replaced | | | | | | | |
| QRDQN06 | Serviceability; ease of repair | | | | | | | |
| QRDQN07 | Aesthetics; how the product looks, feels, sounds, tastes, or smells | | | | | | | |
| QRDQN08 | Overall product quality perceived by customers | | | | | | | |

*Problem-Solving Teams*

| | |
|---|---|
| QRTMN02 % | What percentage of the workers in the plant are involved in problem-solving teams? |
| QRTMN03 % | What percentage of the workers in the plant are capable of performing their own statistical process control? |

**Total Productive Maintenance: Objective Items**

*Maintenance*

| | |
|---|---|
| MROQN01 % | What percentage of operators have been cross-trained on maintenance tasks? |
| MROQN02 % | What is the average percent downtime of machines due to failure, during a normal shift? |
| MROQN03 % | What percentage of machines in the plant have information concerning maintenance, operation, setup, etc., posted on them or readily available? |

**Technology: Objective Items**

*Automation Level*

TRATN02 What term describes your production equipment, relative to your industry?

| | | |
|---|---|---|
| Absolutely state of the art | Better than most companies in our industry | About equal to the industry average |
| Below the industry average | | Poor, near the bottom of the industry |

*New-Product Development Speed*

TRNPN12 How many months does it take, on average, to introduce a typical new product into the plant, from initial conceptual design through prototypes, tooling, and initial production?

*Willingness to Introduce New Products*

TRNAN01 Which term best describes the plant's posture toward new products?

| | |
|---|---|
| Leader in new products | Among the first to adopt new products, but not the leader |
| Adopts new products when it becomes more or less the general rule | Usually, among the last to adopt new products |
| Never adopts new products | |

# APPENDIX 3.4

## Vision in Manufacturing (VIM) Survey

### Selected Objective Question

1. Which processes are the focus of ongoing reengineering initiatives? Which are planned over the next three years [year]? *Check all that apply.* (RESPONSES: New product development, Marketing and sales, order fulfillment, Procurement/purchasing, Logistics management, Customer service/support, Business planning, Finance/managerial accounting, Human resources, Information systems, Others—Specify.)
2. Which of the following geographic areas will receive your business focus over the next three years? (RESPONSES: North America, Western Europe, Former Soviet Union, Japan, China, Southeast Asia, Other Far East, Australia/New Zealand, Middle East, Indian Sub-Continent, North Africa, South Africa, Mexico, Central/South America, Brazil, Other—Specify.)
3. For each Region/Country (in #2), what is the primary method of operation or entry that will be used for each. (RESPONSES: Alliance, Joint venture, Merger/acquisition, Expand existing facilities, Establish new facilities, Other—Specify.)
4. What types of measurements does your business unit use to judge performance? *Check all that apply.* (RESPONSES: Manufacturing/operations performance: (a) Total manufacturing labor costs, (b) Total manufacturing indirect costs, (c) Percentage of products reworked, (d) Manufacturing cycle time, (e) Procurement cycle time, (f) Inventory reduction, (g) Speed of new product introduction, (h) Reduced engineering change orders, (i) Machine availability/utilization, (j) Materials yields, (k) Scrap rates, (l) Vendor quality, (m) Parts shortages, (n) Direct labor productivity, (o) Worker safety record, (p) Organizational learning rate; Business Unit Performance Measurement: (a) Sales growth, (b) Return to shareholders, (c) Percentage of revenue from new products, (d) Market share of primary products in target markets, (e) Meeting overall business unit goals, (f) Highly desired as an employer, (g) Workforce loyalty/retention, (h) Pretax return on assets, (i) Customer loyalty/retention, (j) Overall customer satisfaction, (k) Overall level of employee satisfaction, and (l) Reduced voluntary employee turnover.)
5. Please estimate the share of total manufacturing costs represented by the following categories—three years ago [year], Current [year], and planned in three years [year]. (Categories: __% Materials, __% Direct labor, __% Energy, __% Overhead, __% Other—Specify. *Totals should add to 100%, each for current and planned.*)
6. What is your current annual sales volume—check one category for your business unit and total company, respectively? (RESPONSES: (a) under $50 million U.S., (b) over $50 million to $100 million U.S., (c) over $100 million to $500 million U.S., (d) over $500 million to $1 billion U.S., (e) over $1 billion to $5 billion U.S., and (f) over $5 billion U.S.)
7. What is the appropriate number of full-time equivalent personnel employed in your business unit and total company, respectively? (RESPONSES: (a) less than 100, (b) over 100 to 500, (c) over 500 to 1,000, (d) over 1,000 to 5,000, (e) over 5,000 to 10,000, (f) over 10,000. Don't know.)
8. What was your business unit's and total company's pretax profit level for the most recent fiscal year? (RESPONSES (a) negative, (b) break even, (c) up to 5%, (d) over 5% to 10%, (e) over 10% to 15%, (f) over 15% to 25%, (g) over 25%. Don't know.)
9. What are your current inventory turns, per year? (RESPONSES: (a) less than 2× per year, (b) 2× to 3×, (c) over 3× to 5×, (d) over 5× to 8×, (e) over 8× to 15×, (f) over 15×. Don't know.)

SOURCE: Deloitte and Touche/Aleda Roth. These questions are not to be reproduced or used without written permission of the authors. *Note*: Items/wording may vary over time with different versions of the survey instrument. All responses are in terms of the manufacturing business unit, which is the highest level in the organization where manufacturing and marketing strategies are determined for the primary product.

## APPENDIX 3.5

### Retail Banking Futures Survey

### Selected Objective Questions

Instructions: All the questions in the survey refer to a **retail banking unit**. A retail banking unit may be a holding company, an entire bank, a division, or in some instances a department or branch, depending on your position and the way your bank is organized. In general, you should answer for the unit of analysis you know best. If your overall view is a corporate one, then answer for the overall corporation. If you are in a division, then answer for that division. If you have a corporate or divisional position, but there is too much diversity among divisions or departments to make generalizations across them, then answer for the one retail division or department that you know best. Whatever you choose as the unit of analysis, it is important that your answers consistently apply to the same retail banking unit throughout the survey.

**Retail Banking Unit Profile**

1. Check the one category that best describes the retail banking unit for which you are responding to in this questionnaire. (RESPONSES: ___ bank holding company, ___ bank, division, ___ department, ___ other—specify.)
   a. What is the name of the banking unit for which you are responding?
   b. What is the name of the highest level (or parent company) of which your retail banking unit is a part?

2. Please address the following questions: (a) for the retail banking unit and (b) for the financial institution to which your banking unit belongs, as of [year]: ___Total assets in millions of $, ___total revenues in millions of $, ___ratio of earnings to average assets (%), ___annual growth rate in total deposits___(%).
   a. Retail Banking Unit
   b. Overall Financial Institution (Parent Company)

3. Estimate the current [year] and planned in next three years [year] revenue and expense structures for your retail banking unit. Percentages in each column should add to 100%.

| | Revenue Structure | Expenses Structure |
|---|---|---|
| a. Fees | | |
| Consumer service charges | ____% | ____% |
| Correspondent service charges | ____% | ____% |
| Special service and analysis | ____% | ____% |
| b. Interest | ____% | ____% |
| c. Noninterest | ____% | ____% |
| d. Other (specify) | ____% | ____% |
| | Total 100% | Total 100% |

4. Estimate the current [year] and planned in next three years [year] breakdown of your retail banking unit's noninterest expenses. (*Column percentages should add to 100%.*)

| | Current (%) | Planned (%) |
|---|---|---|
| a. Marketing | ____% | ____% |
| b. Back-office/operations | ____% | ____% |
| c. Retail delivery systems (branches/staff) | ____% | ____% |
| d. Banking unit overhead | ____% | ____% |
| e. Corporate overhead allocation | ____% | ____% |
| f. Depreciation | ____% | ____% |
| g. All other | | |
| | Total 100% | Total 100% |

*(Continued)*

(Continued)

5. Estimate the total investments (a) made over the past five years and (b) planned over the next three years:

| | Past Five Years | Next Three Years |
|---|---|---|
| a. Brick and mortar branches | $_________,000 | $_________,000 |
| b. ATMs (proprietary) | $_________,000 | $_________,000 |
| c. Point of sale (POS) | $_________,000 | $_________,000 |
| d. Other self-service technologies* | $_________,000 | $_________,000 |

*Computer voice telephone, home banking, etc.

6. Listed below are retail banking demographic and geographic market segments:
   (a) Check the category that describes (i) your current primary *demographic market* [year] and (ii) the planned target market in three years [year]. (RESPONSES: ___ mass market, ___ middle consumer market, ___ upscale consumer market, ___ small business, ___executive/professional market, ___ not-for-profit organizations, ___ other—specify.)
   (b) Check the category that best describes (i) the current [year] and (ii) planned in three years [year] *geographical markets* served by your retail banking unit. (RESPONSES: ___local or countrywide, ___statewide, ___ regional, ___ national, ___ international.)

**Delivery Systems Profile**

1. In a typical day, approximately how many customer transactions and inquires are handled by the retail banking unit? ______ No. of Transactions

2. Please provide the approximate percentage of allocations of current [year] transactions and customer inquiries according to the manner in which they were processed by the retail banking unit. Also, provide the expected percentage of allocations of customer transactions and inquires in three years [year]. (RESPONSES: ___% tellers and platform officers, ___% customer-service phone contact, ___% incoming mail, ___% ATMS,

   ___ % other technology-based self-service*, ___% other—specify. *Total should add to 100%.*)

   *Other technology-based self-service is defined as the means of service delivery besides ATMs, where the customer does not come face-to-face with employees.

3. What is the number of persons employed in the retail banking unit front- and back-offices, respectively? *Please indicate in full-time equivalents (FTEs).*

| | FTE (Front Office) | FTE (Back Office) |
|---|---|---|
| **Customer contact personnel*** | | |
| a. Full-time (nonexempt) | _____ | _____ |
| b. Part-time in FTEs (nonexempt) | _____ | _____ |
| c. Managers/supervisors (exempt) | _____ | _____ |
| d. Other professional (exempt) | _____ | _____ |
| **Noncustomer contact personnel**** | | |
| a. Full-time (nonexempt) | _____ | _____ |
| b. Part-time in FTEs (nonexempt) | _____ | _____ |

| | | |
|---|---|---|
| c. Managers/supervisors (exempt) | _____ | _____ |
| d. Other professional (exempt) | _____ | _____ |

*Spends more than 25% of the working day dealing directly with customers — face-to-face, telephone, and online.

**Spends less than 25% of work time interacting directly with customers.

4. Approximately, what percentages of the retail banking unit employees do you anticipate will be involved in customer and noncustomer contact positions in three years [year]? (*See* definitions of customer contact personnel in Q3.)

| | Percent |
|---|---|
| **Customer contact personnel** | |
| Nonexempt | _____ |
| Exempt | _____ |
| **Noncustomer contact personnel** | |
| Nonexempt | _____ |
| Exempt | _____ |
| Total | 100% |

5. If a workforce reduction program is in effect or planned in the next three years [year], indicate the relative percentage of the overall reductions due to the following factors: *Check if **no** reductions are planned and skip to the next question [ ].* (RESPONSES: —_____% consolidation/reorganization, _____% automation to enhance or increase labor productivity, _____% automation to substitute for direct labor, _____% reduced consumer demand, outside sourcing [subcontracting, temporary agencies, etc.] _____% improved methods, other—specify.)

6. Estimate the current [year] and planned in three years [year] of branches (brick and mortar offices) of your retail banking unit (e.g., total number of branches in the retail banking unit).

7. Estimate the current [year] and planned in three years [year] number of proprietary automated teller machines (ATMs) in your retail banking unit.

8. Indicate whether or not your retail banking unit belongs currently [year] to an ATM network with other institutions. Also, indicate if the retail banking unit plans to belong to a network in the next three years [year] and specify the type (local, national, etc.). *Check all that apply.* (RESPONSES: ___belongs to a local/regional network, ___ belongs to a national network, ___ does not belong to any network, ___ other—specify.)

SOURCE: Bank Administration Institute and Aleda Roth. These questions are not to be reproduced or used without written permission of the authors.

# 4

# LIST OF SCALE SUMMARIES

*Alphabetically by First Author*

# Adam

### Article Summarized

Adam, Everett E., Jr. 1994. Alternative quality improvement practices and organization performance. *Journal of Operations Management* 12 (1): 27–44.

### Scales (Actual Questions Used)[a]

1. QUALITY IMPROVEMENT at this company is best described as . . .
   - Applying no formal approach
   - Statistical process control (SPC)
   - Involving employees; each employee's responsibility; behavioral in nature

Quality products and services depend upon the degree to which a company (1) understands an specifies customer requirements (design) and (2) produces and services there requirements (conformance). AT MY COMPANY . . .

2. Customers' opinions and views regarding their needs are actively sought through direct contact; sales calls, focus groups, and so forth
3. Customers regularly and formally receive customer satisfaction questionnaires
4. Senior executive (responsible for company profit and loss) create and sustain clear and visible quality values

Productivity can be improved by introducing behavioral, engineering, and accounting practices. At my company PRODUCTIVITY IS IMPROVED BY . . .

5. Traditional industrial engineering applications: process flow analyses, work measurement, standards, layouts, and so forth
6. Effective inventory planning and control

[a]Note: Above are a part of the measurement items for quality and productivity improvement. The author did not provide the complete questionnaire in the article.

### Construct Description

Not available.

### Measurement Description

A primary source of questions was Benson, Saraph, and Schroeder (1991). The 26 measurement items for organizational quality context were assessed by Benson, Saraph, and Schroeder. Accepting the results from Benson, Saraph, and Schroeder, this study used items relating to corporate support for quality, managerial knowledge, past quality performance, and marketplace. In this study, 7-point Likert scales were used.

### Development

Not available.

### Sample

There were two primary sources of companies for this research: (1) U.S. Department of Commerce's Standard Industrial Classification (SIC) and geographical listings and (2) membership in the Operations Management Association. The target respondents were the production/operations executives within the companies. For the first source (the primary source), "a systematic random sampling procedure was used. Responding and nonresponding companies were similar in industrial types (SIC) and had similar geographical dispersion" (p. 33). For this group, questionnaires were mailed out after telephone solicitation for participation. As a result, the author obtained 163 usable returns from 243 questionnaires mailed, which led to a high response rate of 67.1%. For the second source, direct mailing was used with no telephone contact. The author "obtained 24 usable returns from 166 questionnaires mailed. No statistically significant differences were detected in this group between respondents and nonrespondents" (p. 33). Overall, a total of 187 usable responses were received from 409 questionnaires mailed from both sources. The overall response rate was 47.5%.

### Reliability and Validity

The instrument was validated by Saraph, Benson, and Schroeder (1989).

### Scores

The scores are presented in Tables 4–6 in the article.

### Other Evidence

Not available.

### References

Benson, P. G., J. V. Saraph, and R. G. Schroeder. 1991. The effects of organizational context on quality management: An empirical investigation. *Management Science* 31 (9): 1107–24.

Saraph, J. V., P. G. Benson, and R. G. Schroeder. 1989. An instrument for measuring critical success factors of quality management. *Decision Sciences* 20 (4): 810–29.

---

## Adam, Corbett, Flores, Harrison, Lee, Rho, Ribera, Samson, and Westbrook

### Article Summarized

Adam, Everett E., Jr., Lawrence M. Corbett, Benito E. Flores, Norma J. Harrison, T. S. Lee, Boo-Ho Rho, Jaime Ribera, Danny Samson, and Roy Westbrook. 1997. An international study of quality improvement approach and firm performance. *International Journal of Operations & Production Management* 17 (9): 842–73.

### Scales (Actual Questions Used)

*Employee Involvement (INVOLV)*

1. Training in total quality concept
2. Programs address employee skill and knowledge
3. Employees contribute to objectives

4. Involving employees
5. Identify and resolve improvement projects
6. Adequate resources made available
7. Management involvement and responsibility
8. Applying a formal approach to quality improvement
9. Provide objective feedback on performance
10. Job training and development for employees
11. Improving quality

*Senior Executive Involvement*

12. Quality, a key strategic opportunity
13. Senior executive assumes responsibility for quality
14. Senior executive commitment compares with others
15. Senior executive creates quality values
16. Senior executive rewarded for performance
17. Comparisons and benchmarking
18. Strategic quality-planning process

*Employee Satisfaction*

19. Employees satisfied with the company
20. Employees satisfied with their jobs
21. Employees satisfied with pay
22. Employees satisfied with management
23. Employees satisfied with coworkers

*Compensation*

24. Employees paid for superior performance
25. Output-based individual incentive plans
26. Reward focused
27. Group incentive plans
28. Employees recognized for performance

*Customers*

29. Customers received acceptable quality
30. Customers perceive our past year's quality as good
31. Customers receive the quality expected
32. Customers demand quality

*Design and Conformance*

33. Quality practice reflects on both design and conformance
34. Quality practice reflects on design
35. Quality practice reflects on conformance
36. Design and manufacturing engineers work closely together

*Knowledge*

37. Tried to expand knowledge in quality area
38. Familiar with various quality programs
39. Knowledge of quality compares with others

*Employee Selection and Development*

40. Employee biographical data used in selection
41. Pre-employment testing used in employee selection

42. Job training and development for employees
43. Responsibility and decision making at lower levels

*Inventory Reduction*

44. Reducing inventories
45. Implementing just-in-time (JIT) production
46. Effective inventory planning and control

*Performance Quality*

47. Average percent items defective
48. Cost of quality as a percentage of sales:
    - Training and development
    - Inspection
    - Rework
    - Internal waste/scrap
    - Return and warranty or adjustment
    - Total cost of quality
49. Customer satisfaction

*Financial Performance*

50. Past year's net profit as a percentage of sales
51. Past year's return-on-assets
52. Past 3 years' return-on-assets
53. Past 3 years' average sales growth

*Other*

54. Employee annual turnover rate (percent)

**Construct Description**

The explicit definitions of each construct were not available in the article. However, most of the constructs were grounded in the literature. Among the 46 items retained in the final instrument, 39 of them were related to the quality improvement practices and 13 were related to the productivity improvement indicators. The quality improvement practices were grouped into nine factors: employee involvement, senior executive involvement, employee satisfaction, compensation, customers, design and conformance, knowledge, employee selection and development, and inventory reduction. The construct of quality examined in the study was focused on design and conformance dimensions.

**Measurement Description**

Both 7-point Likert and ordinal scales were used to measure the constructs. Several examples of measurement items for quality and productivity improvement can be found in the Appendix (p. 872).

**Development**

The initial quality improvement items were developed from the total quality literature and the productivity improvement literature. Those items were further reduced to eleven broader factors. The questionnaire was pretested in the United States. Through a factor analysis of the items, two factors with loadings less than .70 were dropped from the initial questionnaire, along with six items defining the factors. Therefore, 32 items were retained in the final questionnaire.

**Sample**

The data were collected from 977 participating firms. These firms came from three regions—Asia/South Pacific, North America, and Europe—and nine countries. Some firms were selected randomly; and the remainder was chosen based on the consideration of accessibility. Of the participating firms, 61% were from Asia, 29% from North America, and 10% from Europe. Because of the national differences, the data collection procedures varied. Three countries followed the telephone contact/mail survey approach. The five Asian/South Pacific countries adopted mail-only survey approach. Unlike other surveys conducted by researchers, the survey in Mexico was completed by having undergraduate business students make personal contacts with individual respondents. The characteristics of the sample firms and respondents are listed in Table II (p. 855).

### Reliability and Validity

The internal consistency was tested by calculating the Cronbach coefficient alpha value. Table IV in the article showed that the coefficient alpha values for each scale ranged from .74 to .89. These results demonstrated good scale reliability (p. 859).

### Scores

The means for the nine quality improvement practice factors, which were calculated based on 7-point Likert scales, are listed in Table IV (p. 859) in the article.

### Other Evidence

Not available.

### References

Adam, E. E., Jr. 1994. Alternative quality improvement practices and organization performance. *Journal of Operations Management* 12 (1): 27–44.

Benson, P. G., J. V. Saraph, and R. G. Schroeder. 1991. The effects of organizational context on quality management: An empirical investigation. *Management Science* 31 (9): 1107–24.

Dean, J. W., Jr., and D. E. Bowen. 1994. Management theory and total quality: Improving research and practice through theory development. *Academy of Management Review* 19 (3): 392–418.

Reeves, C. A., and D. A. Bednor. 1994. Defining quality: Alternatives and implications. *Academy of Management Review* 19 (3): 419–45.

Roth, A. V., and C. A. Giffi. 1994. Critical factors for achieving world class manufacturing governance. *Operations Management Review* 10 (2): 1–29.

U.S. Department of Commerce. 1991. *1991 Application guidelines of Malcolm Baldrige National Quality Award.* Washington, DC: U.S. Department of Commerce.

## Ahire, Golhar, and Waller

### Article Summarized

Ahire, Sanjay L., Damodar Y. Golhar, and Matthew A. Waller. 1996. Development and validation of TQM implementation constructs. *Decision Sciences* 27 (1): 23–56.

### Scale (Actual Questions Used)

*Top Management Commitment (TMC)*

1. Top-level managers view quality as being more important than cost.
2. Top-level managers view quality as being more important than meeting production schedules.
3. Our performance evaluation by the top-level management depends heavily on quality.
4. Top-level managers allocate adequate resources toward efforts to improve quality.

5. We have clear quality goals identified by top-level managers.
6. At company-wide meetings, top-level managers often discuss the importance of quality.

*Supplier Quality Management (SQM)*

7. Quality is a more important criterion than price in selecting suppliers of the major component.
8. Our supplier rating system considers the supplier's engineering capability.
9. Our supplier rating system considers the supplier's financial stability.
10. Our supplier rating system considers the supplier's delivery performance.
11. We provide technical assistance to our suppliers of this component.
12. We are more interested in developing a long-term relationship with these suppliers than reducing prices.

*Supplier Performance (SPERF)*

13. Suppliers send us shipments of the critical components that conform to specifications.
14. Most quality problems in the past with our suppliers have been easily resolved.
15. Our suppliers are always eager to solve quality problems.
16. The critical components are durable.
17. The critical components' performance is excellent.
18. The critical components are reliable.

*Customer Focus (CUSF)*

19. Manufacturing managers are aware of the results of customer-satisfaction surveys.
20. A summary of customer complaints is given to manufacturing managers regularly.
21. To achieve greater customer satisfaction, our company actively seeks ways to improve our primary product.
22. Our company has been customer focused for the past 2 years.

*Statistical Process Control (SPC) Usage*

23. SPC is used extensively in our plant.
24. SPC has been effective in improving the quality of our primary product.
25. We will continue to use SPC in the manufacture of our primary product.
26. Production workers are well trained in SPC.

*Benchmarking (BENCH)*

27. We are engaged in extensive benchmarking of competitors' products that are similar to our primary product.
28. Our benchmarking activities have reduced costs.
29. We have engaged in extensive benchmarking of other companies' business processes in other industries.
30. Benchmarking has helped improve our product.
31. We will definitely continue benchmarking.

*Internal Quality Information Usage (IQIU)*

32. Scrap rates of our primary product are readily available.
33. Rework rates of our primary product are readily available.
34. Cost of quality data concerning our primary product is readily available.
35. Quality information is displayed at most of the workstations.
36. Progress toward quality-related goals is displayed in our plant.
37. Information about defects is conveyed to the appropriate workstations.

*Employee Involvement*

38. There are several quality circles in our plant now.*
39. Cross-functional teams are often used.
40. All employee suggestions are evaluated.
41. Most employee suggestions are implemented.
42. Employees are encouraged to give suggestions.*
43. Financial awards are given to individuals for excellent suggestions.*
44. Groups of employees are given financial awards for excellent suggestions.*
45. We have an effective profit-sharing program.*

*Employee Training (TRAIN)*

46. Resources are available for employee quality training in our plant.
47. There is almost always some kind of employee quality training going on in our plant.
48. Plant managers are often involved in quality training.
49. Most employees in our plant are trained to use quality problem-solving techniques such as cause-and-effect diagrams.
50. Most employees in our plant do *not* view each new quality seminar or training program as "just another fad."

*Design Quality Management (DESQM)*

51. Our design engineers are required to have some shop-floor experience.*
52. Our design engineers are required to have some marketing experience.*
53. We use Taguchi methods extensively.
54. We use error-prevention techniques, such as Shingo, in designing the manufacturing processes.
55. Quality function deployment (QFD) is used in the design of the primary product.
56. There are engineers from other functional departments on a design team.

*Employee Empowerment (EMPOW)*

57. Our line workers inspect the quality of their own work; inspection is not the responsibility of an inspector.
58. Line workers are encouraged to fix the problems they find.
59. Line workers are given the resources necessary to correct the quality problems they find.
60. Line workers have the technical assistance available to them to help them solve quality problems.
61. A problem-solving network is available to line workers in solving quality-related problems.

*Product Quality (PRODQ)*

62. Functional performance
63. Reliability
64. Conformance to specifications
65. Durability

*Note: The asterisked items (*) were dropped during scale refinement.*

## Construct Description

The above 12 constructs were operationalized as multi-item measurement scales. The total quality management (TQM) implementation constructs ranged from top management's commitment to quality to planning issues, such as design quality management, to human resource management (HRM) issues, including employee training and employee empowerment to customer and supplier involvement. The TQM operational outcomes at the plant level were developed in terms of the product quality. Product quality was measured with respect to four of eight dimensions from Garvin (1987). These dimensions included performance, conformance, reliability, and durability. In addition, the process quality construct was also used in the main study. This construct was operationalized through the following two items: percentage of scrap generated and percentage of rework.

### Measurement Description

The items on constructs 1 through 11 (except the supplier quality management construct) solicited answers from the respondent (plant manager) regarding quality practices with respect to the *primary product* (by volume). Practices were measured on 7-point Likert scales with item response categories, ranging from 1 = "strongly disagree," to 7 = "strongly agree," where 4 = "neutral." The items on the supplier quality management construct (construct 2 above) solicited answers regarding supplier management practices with respect to the *most critical component* of the primary product. The items on the product quality scale (construct 12) compared the quality of the firm's *primary product* with competition along a 7-point Likert scale, where 1 = "worst-in-industry," 4 = "average," and 7 = "best-in-industry."

### Development

The instrument was developed through a comprehensive literature review of TQM-related articles over the period from 1972 to 1992. The detailed literature review was reported in Ahire, Landeros, and Golhar (1995; *see* References). The survey instrument was then pretested on a random sample of 100 auto parts firms listed in Elm International, Inc. in Detroit, Michigan. The pretest questionnaire was modified based on the feedback. Confirmatory factor analysis (CFA) was conducted to further refine the scales. To enhance reliability, the employee involvement scale was modified from the initial eight-item to a final three-item scale that included three items: the use of cross-functional teams, evaluation of employee suggestions, and implementation of suggestion.

### Sample

After the pretest, the main mail survey was conducted in two waves on a sample of 1,000 plants listed in Elm International, Inc. All plants were from the automotive parts manufacturing industry (U.S. Bureau of Commerce's Standard Industrial Classification code [SIC 3714]) and had 100 or more employees. The resulting sample size was 371, which corresponded to an overall 37.1% response rate. The plant managers were the key respondents in the study.

The sample consisted of diverse firms in terms of size (e.g., revenue and employment), production type, and unionization. The number of employees ranged from 100 to 3,600, with 364 employees on average. The reported annual sales revenue varied between $9 million and $900 million, with an average of $62 million. Sixty-two of the firms were unionized. Of the 371 firms, 61% had a make-to-order production process; 38%, a make-to-inventory process; and 1%, a combination of both.

### Reliability and Validity

CFA was conducted to examine unidimensionality, reliability, convergent validity, and discriminant validity. All the scales exhibited good unidimensionality (e.g., goodness-of-fit [GFI] indices ranging from .93 for SPERF to .99 for CUSF, SPC, and INVOLV). Cronbach's coefficient alpha ($\alpha$) ranged from .72 for CUSF to .92 for PRODQ. The Werts-Linn-Jöreskog (Werts, Linn, and Jöreskog 1974) coefficient of composite reliability ranged from .73 for CUSF to .93 for BENCH. The values of these two coefficients provided evidence of reliability. The Bentler-Bonett coefficient of convergent validity ranged from .87 for DESQM to .99 for INVOLV, which showed convergent validity.

Chi-square difference tests for pairs of constructs revealed statistically significant differences for all scales at $p < .01$ and demonstrated solid evidence of discriminant validity. Structural equation modeling was used to test for criterion-related validity. Correlations between the operationalized constructs were all positive, and ranged from .17 (SPERF-BENCH) to .78 (TMC-CUSF). All the scales had statistically significant positive correlations with product quality at $p < .01$. Therefore, criterion-related validity was supported for all the scales. Since the scales were developed based on a thorough analysis of quality-related literature, the authors also claim that reasonable evidence of content validity was established.

### Scores

| *Construct* | *Mean* | *s.d.* | *Construct* | *Mean* | *s.d.* |
|---|---|---|---|---|---|
| TMC | 5.44 | 1.10 | IQIU | 5.74 | 1.13 |
| SQM | 5.38 | 1.02 | INVOLV | 5.21 | 1.25 |
| SPERF | 5.27 | 0.99 | TRAIN | 5.03 | 1.31 |
| CUSF | 6.08 | 1.03 | DESQM | 3.77 | 1.30 |
| SPC | 5.15 | 1.51 | EMPOW | 5.45 | 1.18 |
| BENCH | 3.44 | 1.93 | PRODQ | 5.99 | 1.18 |

### Other Evidence

The above results were based on the original study in the U.S. auto parts industry (SIC 3714) by Ahire, Golhar, and Waller (1996). Later, this study was replicated in Canadian auto parts firms (N = 139). Ahire and O'Shaughnessy (1998) report the results of analysis of the composite sample. They provide similar values of reliabilities of scale correlations and reliabilities. The individual scales of the above instrument are being used in other studies pertaining to quality management.

### References

Ahire, S. L., R. Landeros, and D. Y. Golhar. 1995. Total quality management: A literature review and an agenda for future research. *Production and Operations Management* 4 (3): 277–306.

Ahire, S. L., and K. C. O'Shaughnessy. 1998. The role of top management commitment in quality management: An empirical analysis of the auto parts industry. *International Journal of Quality Science* 3 (1): 5–37.

Black, S. A., and L. J. Porter. 1996. Identification of the critical factors of TQM. *Decision Sciences* 27 (1): 1–22.

Flynn, B. B., R. G. Schroeder, and S. Sakakibara. 1994. A framework for quality management research and an associated measurement instrument. *Journal of Operations Management* 11: 339–66.

Garvin, D. A. 1987. Competing on the eight dimensions of quality. *Harvard Business Review* 65 (6): 101–109.

Saraph, J. V., P. G. Benson, and R. G. Schroeder. 1989. An instrument for measuring the critical factors of quality management. *Decision Sciences* 20 (4): 810–29.

Werts, C. E., R. L. Linn, and K. G. Jöreskog. 1974. Interclass reliability estimates: Testing structural assumptions. *Educational and Psychological Measurement* 34 (1): 25–33.

## Ahmad and Schroeder (2001)

### Article Summarized

Ahmad, Sohel, and Roger G. Schroeder. 2001. The impact of electronic data interchange on delivery performance. *Production and Operations Management* 10 (1): 16–30.

**Scales (Actual Questions Used)**

*Daily Schedule Adherence*

1. Because of production stoppages for quality problems, our schedule is designed to allow time for catching up.
2. We usually meet the production schedule each day.
3. There is no time in the schedule for machine breakdowns or production stoppages.
4. Our daily schedule is reasonable to complete on time.
5. We usually complete our daily schedule as planned.

*Equipment Layout*

6. We have laid out the shop floor so that production processes and machines are in proximity to each other.
7. We have organized our plant floor by means of manufacturing cells.
8. We do not have many long conveyors to move materials.
9. Our machines are grouped according to the product family to which they are dedicated.
10. The layout of the shop floor facilitates low inventories and fast throughput.
11. Our processes are located close together so that material handling and part storages are minimized.
12. We tend to use smaller equipment that is moveable and flexible.

*JIT Delivery by Suppliers*

13. Our suppliers deliver to us on a JIT basis.
14. We receive daily shipments from most suppliers.
15. Our suppliers are certified, or qualified, for quality.
16. We have long-term arrangements with our suppliers.
17. Our suppliers deliver to us on short notice.
18. We can depend on on-time delivery from our suppliers.
19. Our suppliers are linked with us by a pull system.

*JIT Link with Customers*

20. Our customers receive JIT deliveries from us.
21. Most of our customers receive frequent shipment from us.
22. We are expected to supply on short notice to our customers.
23. We always deliver on time to our customers.
24. We can adapt our production schedule to sudden production stoppages by our customers.
25. Our customers have a pull-type link with us.

*Kanban*

26. Suppliers fill our Kanban containers rather than filling purchase orders.
27. Our suppliers deliver to us in Kanban containers, without the use of separate packaging.
28. We use a Kanban pull system for production control.
29. We use Kanban squares, containers, or signals for production control.

*Setup Time Reduction*

30. We are aggressively working to lower setup times in our plant.
31. We have converted most of the setup time to external time while the machine is running.
32. We have low setup times of equipment in our plant.
33. Our crews practice setups to reduce the time required.
34. Our workers are trained to reduce setup time.
35. Management emphasizes the importance of setup time reduction.

*Customer Focus*

36. We are frequently in close contact with our customers.
37. Our customers seldom visit our plant.
38. Our customers give us feedback on quality and delivery performance.
39. Our customers are actively involved in the product design process.
40. We strive to be highly responsive to our customers' needs.
41. We regularly survey our customers' requirements.

*Feedback*

42. Charts showing defect rates are posted on the shop floor.
43. Charts showing schedule compliance are posted on the shop floor.
44. Charts plotting the frequency of machine breakdowns are posted on the shop floor.
45. I am never told whether I am doing a good job.
46. Information on quality performance is readily available to employees.
47. Information on productivity is readily available to employees.
48. My manager never comments about the quality of my work.

*Process Control*

49. Customer requirements are thoroughly analyzed in the new product design process.
50. Processes in our plant are designed to be foolproof.
51. A large percentage of the equipment or processes on the shop floor are currently under statistical quality control.
52. We make extensive use of statistical techniques to reduce variance in processes.
53. We use charts to determine whether our manufacturing processes are in control.
54. We monitor our processes using statistical process control.

*Supplier Quality Involvement*

55. We strive to establish long-term relationships with our suppliers.
56. Our suppliers are actively involved in our new product development (NPD) process.
57. Quality is our number 1 criterion in selecting suppliers.
58. We rely on a small number of high-quality suppliers.
59. We use mostly suppliers that we have certified.
60. We maintain close communication with suppliers about quality considerations and design changes.

## Construct Description

In this study, product instability referred to the unpredictability of demand because of uncertainty of the environment, seasonality, unreliable suppliers, machine breakdowns, implementation of new technology and/or software, production schedule changes to satisfy important customers, inefficient inventory management, poor coordination among departments, and so on. Just-in-time (JIT) management practices referred to the practices that are used by an organization to reduce setup time and lot size through multi-skilled workers and flexible equipment layout. Also, to apply JIT management practices, organizations maintain close relationships with its customers and suppliers to support a pull-based supply chain. Quality management practices referred to the efforts by the organization to "ensure a predictable production process. This reduces scrap and rework and thus minimizes the production time" (p. 19).

## Measurement Description

Objective variables were operationalized as given below:

Product diversity was computed as the log-transformed number of final product configurations sold to customers by the plant.

Product customization indicated the classification (in percentages) of the "products into the following categories: highly customized, somewhat customized, standard with custom options, somewhat standardized, and highly standardized" (p. 22). A composite measure was formed using a weighted average.

Product instability was quantified as the "average percentage change in plant output (in terms of respective currency) from one month to the next over the course of a year" (p. 22).

Size of organization was computed as the log-transformed sum of salaried and hourly personnel employed.

Electronic data interchange *(EDI)* was measured by two variables. "The first variable is EDIAVYN, an indicator variable that represents whether a plant uses EDI or not . . . The second variable, however, represents the level or extent of use of EDI for the plants that used EDI . . . This variable is measured by averaging two objective responses: (1) percentage of purchase orders sent to suppliers by means of EDI and (2) percentage of customer orders received via EDI" (p. 22).

On-time delivery indicated the percentage of orders that were shipped on time in the past 1-year period, according to company records.

### Development

Not available.

### Sample

A total of 85 plants from the electronics, machinery, and automobile industries in four different countries were included in the study.

### Reliability and Validity

Each scale was checked for reliability and unidimensionality. One or more items were dropped from a scale when they did not contribute to the psychometric properties of the scale. A scale having a value of .70 or more for Cronbach's coefficient alpha was considered reliable (Nunnally 1978). Factor analysis was performed to assure that each scale was also unidimensional. A value of one or more for the eigenvalue was the criteria used to assess unidimensionality. During the test for unidimensionality, it was sometimes necessary to modify the scale by dropping items. The reliability analysis was repeated to ensure that the modified scales remained reliable (e.g., Cronbach's a > .70). Refer to the Appendix in the article for reliability analyses (p. 23).

### Scores

The scores are given in Tables 2–4 in the article.

### Other Evidence

Not available.

### Reference

Nunnally, J. C. 1978. *Psychometric theory.* New York: McGraw-Hill.

## Ahmad and Schroeder (2003)

### Article Summarized

Ahmad, Sohel, and Roger G. Schroeder. 2003. The impact of human resource management practices on operational performance: Recognizing country and industry differences. *Journal of Operations Management* 21 (1): 19–43.

**Scales (Actual Questions Used)**

*Human-Resources Management (HRM) Practices Scales*

Employment Insecurity

1. The number of employees laid off in the past 5 years divided by the number of employees in the organization times 100.

Manufacturing and Human Resources Fit

2. The human resources department communicates closely with manufacturing when writing job descriptions.
3. Job design at this plant is closely coordinated with manufacturing.
4. The human resources department has a close and positive working relationship with manufacturing.
5. Staffing, training, and development of employees are closely coordinated with manufacturing.
6. Manufacturing works well with human resources staff when changes take place in the manufacturing process.
7. Human resources staff know what manufacturing considers important in the training of employees for new skills.

Behavior and Attitude

8. We use attitude/desire to work in a team as a criterion in employee selection.
9. We use problem-solving aptitude as a criterion in employee selection.
10. We use work values and behavioral attitudes as a criterion in employee selection.
11. We select employees who can provide ideas to improve the manufacturing process.
12. We select employees who are able to work well in small groups.

*Use of Teams and Decentralization*

Team Activities

13. During problem-solving sessions, we make an effort to get all team members' opinions and ideas before making a decision.
14. Our plant forms teams to solve problems.
15. In the past 3 years, many problems have been solved through small group sessions.
16. Problem-solving teams have helped improve manufacturing processes at this plant.
17. Employee teams are encouraged to try to solve their problems as much as possible.

*Interaction Facilitation*

18. Supervisors encourage the persons who work for them to work as a team.
19. Supervisors encourage people who work for them to exchange opinions and ideas.
20. Supervisors frequently hold group meetings where the people who work for them can really discuss things together.

*Compensation/Incentive Contingent on Performance*

Contingent Compensation

Which of the following types of pay/compensation plans are used in the plant for direct labor?

21. Group incentive plans (GRPINCEN) (Y/N)
22. Profit-sharing (PROFITSH) (Y/N)

*Incentives to Meet Objectives*

23. Our incentive system encourages us to vigorously pursue plant objectives.
24. The incentive system at this plant is fair in rewarding people who accomplish plant objectives.
25. Our reward system really recognizes the people who contribute the most to our plant.

26. Our incentive system at this plant encourages us to reach plant goals.
27. Our incentive system is at odds with our plant goals.
28. Persons (and/or teams) who achieve plant goals are rewarded the same as those who do not achieve plant goals.

*Extensive Training*

Training on Job Skills

29. Our plant has a low skill level compared with our industry.
30. At this plant, some employees lack important skills.
31. Plant employees receive training and development in workplace skills on a regular basis.
32. The management at this plant believes that continual training and upgrading of employees' skills are important.
33. Employees at this plant have skills that are above average in this industry.

Training in Multiple Functions

34. Employees receive training to perform multiple tasks.
35. Employees at this plant learn how to perform a variety of tasks/jobs.
36. The longer an employee has been at this plant, the more tasks or jobs that employee learns to perform.
37. Employees are cross-trained at this plant so that they can fill in for others if necessary.
38. At this plant, employees only learn how to do one job/task.
39. At this plant, employees are encouraged to learn skills in depth rather than develop a broad skill base.

*Status Difference*

Existing Status Differences

40. The use of assigned parking spots (Y/N)
41. The use of uniforms by workers only (Y/N)
42. Access restriction to the cafeteria for some employees (Y/N)
43. The use of separate restrooms (Y/N) for different employees in the plant

*Sharing Information*

Communication of Strategy

44. In our plant, goals, objectives, and strategies are communicated to me.
45. Strategies and goals are communicated primarily to managers.
46. I know how we are planning to be competitive at this plant.
47. I understand the long-run competitive strategy of this plant.

Feedback on Performance

48. Charts showing defect rates are posted on the shop floor.
49. Charts showing schedule compliance are posted on the shop floor.
50. Charts plotting the frequency of machine breakdowns are posted on the shop floor.
51. I am never told whether I am doing a good job or not. Information on quality performance is readily available to employees.
52. Information on productivity is readily available to employees.
53. My manager never comments about the quality of my work.

*Organizational Performance*

Organizational Commitment

54. I am willing to put in a great deal of effort beyond that normally expected to help this organization be successful.
55. I talk up this organization to my friends as a great organization to work for.

56. I would accept almost any type of job assignment to keep working for this organization.
57. I find that my values and the organization's values are very similar.
58. I am proud to tell others that I am part of this organization.
59. This organization really inspires the best in me in the way of job performance.
60. I am extremely glad that I chose this organization to work for over others I was considering at the time I joined.
61. I really care about the fate of this organization.
62. For me, this is the best of all organizations for which to work.

Operational Performance

63. Unit cost of manufacturing
64. Quality of product conformance
65. On-time delivery performance
66. Flexibility to change volume
67. Speed of new product introduction

**Construct Description**

The constructs were developed on two streams of research, HRM practices and organizational performance literature. Seven HRM practices—employment insecurity, selective hiring, use of teams and decentralization, compensation/incentive contingent on performance, extensive training, status differences, and sharing information—were proposed in the study. These practices were identified based on literature by Pfeffer (1998). The measures for operational performance were drawn from Wheelwright (1978), Schmenner (1981), Hayes and Wheelwright (1984), Hill (1989), and Vickery, Dröge, and Markland (1997). The other organizational performance construct, organizational commitment, represents an intangible performance outcome. It emphasizes on psychological links between organizational and employee goals.

**Measurement Description**

Ten scales were defined in this article to measure the HRM practices. For these questions, items were measured using a 5-point Likert scale, where 1 represented "strongly disagree" and 5 represented "strongly agree." Three other variables were measured using objective items. In the validation process, the authors dropped any item that did not contribute to the construct reliability, though they do not enumerate the specific items that were dropped. The value of each construct was then computed by averaging all the remaining items in the related scale. The authors also determined the ideal HRM practices scores and argue that the degree of misfit between the ideal HRM scores and the firm's HRM practices scores were negatively related to the organizational performance. Misfit and organizational performance were linked by a regression model. Detailed measurement description for each HRM practice was presented next.

Employment insecurity was measured by the number of employees laid off in the past 5 years divided by the number of employees in the organization times 100.

Selective hiring was created by two first-order constructs: (1) manufacturing and HR fit, defined as the degree of cooperation between manufacturing and HR in designing job descriptions and staffing activities; and (2) behavior and attitude, defined as the importance given to a prospective employee's attitudes and behavior toward teamwork and problem solving during the selection process.

Use of teams and decentralization was derived from two first-order constructs: (1) team activities that were "defined as effective use of teams on the shop floor" (p. 24); and (2) interaction facilitation, which captured the extent to which supervisors encourage workers and facilitate workers to work as a team.

Compensation/incentive contingent on performance was derived from two first-order constructs: (1) contingent compensation that checks if the organization had a practice of sharing profits or had incentive plans; and (2) "incentives to meet objectives, which measures whether the plant's reward system is consistent with manufacturing objectives and goals" (p. 24).

Extensive training was captured from two first-order constructs: (1) training on job skills, "which measures if employees' on the job skills and knowledge are being upgraded in order to maintain a work force with cutting edge skills and abilities" (p. 24); and (2) training in multiple functions, "which measures the extent to which employees receive cross-training so that they can perform multiple tasks or jobs" (p. 24).

Status differences referred to "a construct that indicates if there are perceived status differences among the various employees of the firm" (p. 24).

Sharing information was developed as a second-order construct that was composed of two first-order constructs: (1) "communication of strategy, which measures the efforts made by management to communicate the plant's competitive strategy to all employees" (p. 24); and (2) "feedback on performance which measures the extent to which management provides shop floor personnel with information regarding their performance in a timely and useful manner" (p. 24).

Operational performance was described as the performance of a plant on cost, quality, delivery, flexibility, and speed of new product development (NPD). On each dimension, respondents were asked to evaluate their plant's performance as it compared with their competitors in the same industry, where 5 = "superior or better than average;" 4 = "better than average"; 3 = "average or equal to the competition"; 2 = "below average"; and 1 = "poor or low end of the industry." A single performance index was created by summing up measures over all five dimensions. This composite index reflected a plant's overall, aggregate achievement in operations.

The other performance construct, organization commitment, was measured using a set of Likert scales. The initial set included eight items. When purifying the scales, the authors dropped several items and averaged the remaining items to obtain the score for the scale.

### Development

All the measures came from the world class manufacturing (WCM) database. The authors selected scales from the existing literature whenever possible. The questionnaire instrument was pretested using 10 industry experts and academics. As a result, some items were modified to better capture the meaning of the intended constructs. In addition, revisions on the scales were also made based on experience from the prior round of data collection and analysis of the WCM project. The U.S. instrument was finalized and translated into German, Italian, and Japanese. These foreign language versions were then translated back into English and examined for discrepancies. Finally, after the data were collected through the large-scale survey, the authors further purified the scales by dropping some items while they evaluated the construct reliability and unidimensionality.

### Sample

The data used by the authors were a part of the WCM project database, which addressed HRM issues. The WCM project collected data from manufacturing plants operating in four countries (Germany, Italy, Japan, and the United States) and three industries (electronics, machinery, and automobile). The four countries were chosen to represent the major industrial regions of the world. Three industries were selected to represent those that face significant global competition and that seek improvement by implementing various manufacturing practices. The response rate for the overall project was approximately 60%.

The data used in this study consisted of 107 manufacturing plants having 1,153 employees on average, after eliminating responses with missing data. The number of plants by country and industry are reported in Table 1. The mean age of these 107 plants was 37 years. Each plant has 32 product lines on average.

Different targeted respondents for the performance variables and the HRM variables (i.e., managers, engineers, supervisors, and/or workers) were identified through the joint effort from the research team and the plant research coordinators. The plant research coordinators appointed in each plant were "managers who had at least 3 years of experience in the plants and were knowledgeable about the major responsibilities of the employees working in the plant" (p. 23).

### Reliability and Validity

Face validity of the constructs was ensured by development of the instrument from three different researchers. Content validity was ensured through a pretesting exercise. The construct reliability and validity were formally tested in the prior round of data collection, based on data from more than 800 respondents in

43 U.S. plants. The Cronbach's coefficient alpha values were used to test the internal consistency among the items included in each construct in the study sample. A threshold level of .70 was applied for acceptable construct reliability. The authors also stated that each scale was evaluated for unidimensionality. However, no detailed info was given in the article.

### Scores

Means, standard deviations, and correlations of the variables are reported in Table 5 of the article. The results of the canonical correlation analysis are given in Table 6 of the article.

### Other Evidence

Not available.

### References

Hayes, R. H., and S. C. Wheelwright. 1984. *Restoring our competitive edge: Competing through manufacturing.* New York: Wiley.

Hill, T. 1989. *Manufacturing strategy: Text and cases.* Homewood, IL: Irwin.

Pfeffer, J. 1998. Seven practices of successful organizations. *California Management Review* 40 (2): 96–124.

Schmenner, R. W. 1981. *Production/operations management: Concepts and situations.* 1st ed. Chicago, IL: Science Research Associates.

Vickery, S. K., C. Dröge, and R. E. Markland. 1997. Dimensions of manufacturing strength in the furniture industry. *Journal of Operations Management* 15 (4): 317–30.

Wheelwright, S. C. 1978. Reflecting corporate strategy in manufacturing decisions. *Business Horizons* 21 (1): 57–66.

---

## Ahmed, Montagno, and Firenze

### Article Summarized

Ahmed, Nazim U., Ray V. Montagno, and Robert J. Firenze. 1996. Operations strategy and organizational performance: An empirical study. *International Journal of Operations and Production Management* 16 (5): 41–53.

### Scales (Actual Questions Used)

*Operations Strategy*

1. Total quality management (TQM)
2. JIT production method
3. Manufacturing cells
4. Concurrent engineering
5. Computer networking with suppliers and customers
6. Benchmarking
7. Flexible manufacturing systems (FMS)

*Performance Measures*

Market

8. Market share
9. Sales volume

Product

10. Product quality
11. New and improved product information
12. Productivity
13. Ability to improve

Economic

14. Annual earnings
15. Profitability
16. Return on investment (ROI)

Employees

17. Employee skills related to technology
18. Employee flexibility

## Construct Description

The operations strategies considered in the study were conceptualized as "efforts with the purpose of accomplishing the goals of the firm through better utilization of multiple factors in the production process" (p. 42). Specifically, "TQM is an enterprise-wide strategy with a central focus of customer satisfaction through continuous improvement. JIT strategy is based on the principle of getting the right material at the right time. Manufacturing cells attempt to organize the production process by combining machines and equipment to produce a family of parts more efficiently than the traditional job shop. FMS allow a firm to respond to the market demand by making its operations flexible" (p. 43). Benchmarking is a strategy used to compare an organization's current performance with that of its competitors. Computer networking with suppliers and customers enables responsive decision making through effective communication with an organization's outside partners. Concurrent engineering allows integration between product and process design.

The performance constructs were defined as goals that an organization establishes to measure its success. These goals were classified into four areas relating to markets, products, economic outcomes, and employees, which, taken together, capture a broad range of outcome important to an organization.

## Measurement Description

"The performance measures were self reports from participants and reflect their perceptions of changes in the performance over the last five years" (p. 47). Each performance item was measured on a 5-point Likert scale, indicating whether the firm performance had "increased" (5), "decreased" (1), or "remained the same" (3). A composite performance score based on the 11 performance dimensions listed in the questionnaire was also formed for each firm.

For each operation strategy practice, the respondents were asked "whether they are using a particular strategy currently, plan to use it in the future or are not using it currently" (p. 46). Accordingly, the firms were defined as "users" if they were deploying the strategy currently; otherwise, they were classified as "nonusers" of the strategy-based practices.

## Development

Questions on operations strategies were first developed based on an extensive literature review. Then inputs were collected from a panel of manufacturing managers. Revisions of questionnaire items were made based on suggestions from the panel members to improve clarity and readability of the instrument.

## Sample

"Companies in the sample were identified from the following sources: Indiana Labor Management Council, Harris Industrial Directory, Society of Manufacturing Engineers, and National Electrical

Manufacturing Association. Approximately 10,000 surveys were mailed and 655 were returned for a response rate of 6.55%" (p. 45). The responding companies were located in 40 states and covered a wide range of industries. However, the majority of them were located in midwestern states and were more likely to be "traditional" manufacturers that produce engineered products. The number of employees in the responding companies varied from less than 100 to more than 2,000. On average, the hourly employees in the responding companies had 37.4 years of service; and the salaried employees had 39.8 years of service. The target respondent was the senior executive of each firm. These senior executives were asked to complete the survey themselves, or if they were not the most appropriate respondent, to assign it to the most knowledgeable person to complete.

### Reliability and Validity

Not available.

### Scores

The scores are presented in Tables III–X in the article.

### Other Evidence

Not available.

### Reference

Kim, Y., and J. Lee. 1993. Manufacturing strategy and production systems: An integrated framework. *Journal of Operations Management* 11 (1): 3–15.

---

## Amoako-Gyampah and Boye

### Article Summarized

Amoako-Gyampah, Kwasi, and Samuel S. Boye. 2001. Operations strategy in an emerging economy: The case of the Ghanaian manufacturing industry. *Journal of Operations Management* 19 (1): 59–79.

### Scales (Actual Questions Used)

*Business Cost*

1. Rising labor cost
2. Rising material cost
3. Rising transport cost
4. Rising telecommunication cost
5. Rising utilities cost
6. Rising rental cost
7. Rising health care cost
8. Strong Ghanaian Cedis

*Labor Availability*

9. Shortage of managerial and administrative staff
10. Shortage of technicians

11. Shortage of clerical and related workers
12. Shortage of skilled workers
13. Shortage of production workers
14. Inability to operate third shift

*Competitive Hostility*

15. Keen competition in local markets
16. Keen competition in foreign markets
17. Low profit margins
18. Declining demand in local market
19. Declining demand in foreign market
20. Producing to the required quality standards
21. Unreliable vendor quality

*Dynamism*

22. Rate at which products and services become outdated
23. Rate of innovation of new products and services
24. Rate of innovation of new operation processes
25. Rate of change in taste and preferences of customers in your industry

*Low Cost Priority*

26. Reduce unit costs
27. Reduce material costs
28. Reduce overhead costs
29. Reduce inventory level

*Quality*

30. Reduce defective rates
31. Improve product performance and reliability
32. Improve vendor's quality
33. Implement quality control circles
34. Obtaining ISO 9000 certification

*Flexibility*

35. Reduce manufacturing lead time
36. Reduce procurement lead time
37. Reduce NPD cycle
38. Reduce setup/changeover time

*Delivery Performance*

39. Increase delivery reliability
40. Increase delivery speed
41. Improve presales service and technical support
42. Improve after sales service

**Construct Description**

Explicit definitions of each construct were not given in the article. However, most of the construct items are grounded in the extant literature. Among the 42 items retained in the final instrument, 16 of them pertained to competitive priorities; and the remaining 25 items were used to assess the business environment (Ward et al. 1995).

### Measurement Description

In this study, all constructs were measured using multi-item scales. A variety of 5-point Likert-type scales were used to assess question items.

### Development

The questionnaire was adapted from Ward et al. (1995); and as indicated above, the questionnaire employed the same indicator variables for the business environment and competitive priority constructs. However, this research did not include the firm performance questions from Ward et al. (1995).

### Sample

The surveys were mailed to 78 manufacturing companies in Ghana. A total of 61 responses were received, representing a 78% of response rate. The target respondents were production managers, who are high-level officials within manufacturing firms in Ghana. According to the authors, production managers in this study correspond to vice president of operations in an U.S.-based manufacturing company. The authors present the details of the respondent companies in Table II of the article.

### Reliability and Validity

Internal consistency was tested by calculating the coefficient alpha value. Table V (p. 69) reported that the coefficient alpha values for each scale ranged from .52 to .81.

### Scores

The mean scores for the measures were calculated based on 5-point Likert scales and are listed in Table V (p. 69) of the article. The correlation matrix for the constructs was presented in Table VI (p. 69).

### Other Evidence

The measures used in this study were derived from Ward et al. (1995).

### Reference

Ward, P. T., R. Duray, G. K. Leong, and C. H. Sum. 1995. Business performance, operations strategy, and performance: An empirical study of Singapore manufacturers. *Journal of Operations Management* 13 (2): 99–115.

---

## Anand and Ward

### Article Summarized

Anand, Gopesh, and Peter T. Ward. 2004. Fit, flexibility and performance in manufacturing: Coping with dynamic environments. *Production and Operations Management* 13 (4): 369–85.

### Scales (Actual Questions Used)

*Manufacturing Flexibility*

For your manufacturing plant, how important is the ability to (1 = no importance, 4 = very important, 7 = absolutely critical, and 9 = N/O).

Mobility

1. Make rapid design changes
2. Adjust capacity quickly
3. Make rapid volume changes

Range

4. Offer a large number of diverse product features
5. Offer a large degree of product variety
6. Adjust product mix

*Environmental Dynamism*

Unpredictability

How would you rate the predictability of the following? (Reverse coded such that higher scores indicate more unpredictability: 1 = unpredictable, 7 = highly predictable, and 9 = N/O).

7. Business unit upswings and downswings
8. Rate of product innovation in your industry
9. Rate of innovation in operating processes in your industry
10. Business unit labor relations

Volatility

Indicate the rate of change for the following: (1 = slow, 7 = rapid, and 9 = N/O).

11. Rate at which your products and services become outdated
12. Rate of innovation of new products and services
13. Rate of innovation of new operating processes
14. Tastes and preferences of customers in your industry

*Business Performance*

Compared with your competitors, indicate your position on the following dimensions: (1 = significantly lower, 3 = equal, 7 = significantly higher, and 9 = N/O).

15. Market share
16. Sales growth

## Construct Description

Among the constituent measures—munificence, dynamism, and complexity—of an environment as classified by Dess and Beard (1984), the authors selected dynamism to assess environment. Furthermore, adopting the suggestions of Miller and Friesen (1983), Bourgeois and Eisenhardt (1988), and Volberda (1996), the authors divided the dynamism scale into *unpredictability* and *volatility,* which are two dimensions of environmental dynamism that are often associated with high velocity or hypercompetitive environments. The first dimension of dynamism was characterized as the unpredictability of change in the different elements of the external environment: market, product, technology innovations, and labor. The second dynamism measure—volatility—was described as the degree of instability in the various factors that constitute the firm's environment and that indicates the rate of change. Volatility was grounded in Miller and Friesen's (1983) division of the dynamism dimension.

The measures of manufacturing flexibility were constructed to assess the strategic orientation of the plants in two dimensions: mobility and ranges. Mobility implies the ability to alter production, while range suggests the ability to manage product and/or process diversity.

### Measurement Description

This study used perceptual measures of the environment, perceived importance scales for flexibility, and business performance. The scales for assessing environment consisted of eight items. The scales for assessing plant's flexibility consisted of six items. The three mobility items captured the importance of making transitions in volumes and design. The three range items tapped into the product variety and features that a plant was geared to offer. Each item was measured using a 7-point Likert-type scale response, ranging from "no importance" (1) to "absolute critical" (7). The option of "N/O" was also provided.

Business performance was measured using two single-item perceptual measures—one for market share and the other for sales growth. The respondents were asked to evaluate the plant performance in these two areas compared with their competitors based on a 7-point scale—1 representing "significantly lower" and 7 representing "significantly higher." The respondents could also choose "N/O."

### Development

The scale items for measuring unpredictability were developed based on the definition of the construct provided by previous researchers (Bourgeois and Eisenhardt 1988). The authors did not provide any information on how the other scale items were developed.

### Sample

For sampling purposes, this study used data that were obtained from a survey of U.S. manufacturing firms conducted in 1994 (Ward, Leong, and Boyer 1994; Ward and Duray 2000). The primary product types of the businesses involved fell into one of three sectors: fabricated metal products, electrical devices, and electronic controls (U.S. Department of Commerce, Standard Industrial Classification [SIC] codes 34, 36, and 38). Both privately and publicly owned firms were covered in the sample. Only businesses with more than 150 employees at the location were included. The target respondents were plant manager, marketing manager, and manufacturing manager/engineer. For each question, two independent respondents at each plant were solicited to complete the survey. The final sample had 101 usable responses, consisting of two responses to each question. The response rate was 37%. The nonresponse bias was tested by comparing the sales volume and number of employees for nonrespondent firms, industry-wide, with those of the respondent firms. The nonsignificant *t*-tests confirmed that no nonresponse bias was indicated. The authors also made postsurvey telephone calls to investigate the reasons for nonresponse. They found that lack of time and the possibility of revealing proprietary information were the most common reasons given for nonparticipation.

### Reliability and Validity

Content validity was ensured by a thorough literature review. As this study used two perceptual measures for performance, the authors also incorporated related objective performance measures in the survey instrument. However, less than half of the respondents provided information on these objective measures. Correlations between objective and perceptual performance measures were, however, found to be significant ($p < .01$), using a method similar to that described in Vickery, Dröge, and Markland (1993).

For each of the four measurement scales covering the environment and flexibility constructs, construct validity was assessed statistically using the approach suggested by Ahire and Devaraj (2001) and Flynn, Schroeder, and Flynn (1999). Two confirmatory factor analyses (CFA) models using maximum likelihood estimation were conducted to assess convergent validity. One CFA was for the two environment constructs and the other for the two flexibility constructs. Overall, the CFA provided adequate support for the existence of convergent validity of the constructs. Various fit indices indicated reasonable fit: $\chi^2$(d.f.) = 130.96 (75) with the $\chi^2$/d.f. of 1.75, nonnormed fit index (NNFI) = .94, comparative fit index (CFI) = .89; root mean square error of approximation (RMSEA) = .09. All the items had significant factor loadings ($p < .01$) (*see* Table 3).

To test unidimensionality, principal component analyses (PCAs) were conducted for each of the scales. For each construct, the within-scale PCA showed only one eigenvalue greater than 1 and all factor loadings on a single factor were greater than .40. The authors claimed that these results provided support for unidimensionality and also additional evidence of convergent validity.

Three tests were used to examine divergent validity of the scale. First, the authors reported that the Cronbach's alpha coefficients for the scales were greater than their correlations with other scales. Second, the average item-total correlations with items not in the scales were substantially lower than the average item-total correlations with items within the related scales. Finally, the percentage variance extracted using within-scale PCAs was greater than the squared interscale correlation for each scale.

Cronbach's coefficient alpha was also used to evaluate construct reliability. Cronbach coefficient alpha values were above .70 for all the constructs, except for unpredictability with an alpha value of .59. Nonetheless, the authors decided to retain the unpredictability scale, as constructed, because the composition was supported by its earlier definitions; and coefficient alpha for the scale was close to the cutoff point. Nunnally and Bernstein (1994) recommended .60 as threshold for alpha in constructing new measurement scales.

In addition, given the existence of two independent responses for each question, the authors evaluated interrator reliability by calculating interrater correlations. The correlation coefficients for the four multi-item scales ranged from .45 to .71 and were statistically significant ($p < .01$). The interrater correlation coefficients for two single-item performance measures were also statistically significant ($p < .001$). The interrater correlation coefficients were .76 for market share and .59 for sales growth, respectively.

### Scores

The scores for each question were averaged over the two independent respondents at each plant. Summated scales were then constructed for each multi-item scale. The correlations between scale items are given in Table 1. The CFA parameter estimates and descriptive statistics for summated scales are displayed in Table 3. The correlations between scales are shown in Table 5.

### Other Evidence

Not available.

### References


Ahire, S. L., and S. Devaraj. 2001. An empirical comparison of statistical construct validation approaches. *IEEE Transactions on Engineering Management* 48 (3): 319–29.

Bourgeois, L. J., III, and K. Eisenhardt. 1988. Strategic decision processes in high velocity environments: Four cases in the microcomputer industry. *Management Science* 34 (7): 816–35.

Dess, G., and D. Beard. 1984. Dimensions of organizational task environments. *Administrative Science Quarterly* 29 (1): 52–73.

Flynn, B. B., R. G. Schroeder, and E. J. Flynn. 1999. World class manufacturing: An investigation of Hayes and Wheelwright's foundation. *Journal of Operations Management* 17 (3): 249–69.

Miller, D., and P. H. Friesen. 1983. Strategy-making and environment: The third link. *Strategic Management Journal* 4 (3): 221–35.

Nunnally, J. C., and I. H. Bernstein. 1994. *Psychometric theory.* New York: McGraw-Hill.

Vickery, S. K., C. Dröge, and R. R. Markland. 1993. Production competence and business strategy: Do they affect business performance? *Decision Sciences* 24 (2): 435–55.

Volberda, H. W. 1995. Toward the flexible form: How to remain vital in hypercompetitive environments. *Organization Science* 7 (4): 359–74.

Ward, P. T., and R. Duray. 2000. Manufacturing strategy in context: Environment, competitive strategy and manufacturing strategy. *Journal of Operations Management* 18 (2): 123–38.

Ward, P. T., G. K. Leong, and K. K. Boyer. 1994. Manufacturing proactiveness and performance. *Decision Sciences* 25 (3): 337–58.

# Anderson, Rungtusanatham, Schroeder, and Devaraj

**Article Summarized**

Anderson, John C., Manus Rungtusanatham, Roger G. Schroeder, and Sarvanan Devaraj. 1995. A path analytic model of a theory of quality management underlying the Deming Management method: Preliminary empirical findings. *Decision Sciences* 26 (5): 637–58.

**Scales (Actual Questions Used)**

*Visionary Leadership*

1. All major department heads within our plant accept responsibility for quality.
2. Plant management provides personal leadership for quality products and quality improvement.
3. Our top management strongly encourages employee involvement in the production process.
4. Financial goals are the most important at our plant (reverse coded).
5. Management outside the plant is primarily concerned with short-range financial performance (reverse coded).
6. Short-term losses affect our decision making but are less important than pursuing long-term goals.
7. In our plant, goals, objectives, and strategies are communicated to me.
8. Strategies and goals are communicated primarily to managers (reverse coded).

*Internal and External Cooperation*

9. Generally speaking, everyone in the plant works well together.
10. Departments in the plant communicate frequently with each other.
11. Departments within the plant seem to be in constant conflict (reverse coded).
12. Management works well together on all decisions.
13. Our plant is organized into permanent production teams.
14. During problem-solving sessions, we make an effort to get all team members' opinions and ideas before making a decision.
15. Problems are usually solved by supervisors (reverse coded).
16. In the past 3 years, many problems have been solved through small group sessions.

*Learning*

17. Employees receive training to perform multiple tasks.
18. Plant employees are rewarded for learning new skills.
19. Direct labor technical competence is high in this plant.

*Process Management*

20. Charts showing defect rates are posted on the shop floor.
21. Charts plotting frequency of machine breakdowns are posted on the shop floor.
22. We have standardized process instructions that are given to personnel.
23. A large percentage of the equipment or process on the shop floor are currently under statistical control.
24. We make extensive use of statistical techniques to reduce variance in processes.

*Continuous Improvement*

25. All employees believe that it is their responsibility to improve quality in the plant.
26. Continuous improvement of quality is stressed in all work processes throughout our plant.

*Employee Fulfillment*

27. I would feel unhappy if I could not take pride in my job.
28. Doing a good job should mean as much to a worker as a good paycheck.
29. If I do a sloppy job at work, I feel a little ashamed of myself.

*Customer Satisfaction*

30. How does your plant compare with its competitors in your industry in terms of customer relations?
31. How does your plant compare with its competition in your industry in terms of quality of product conformance?
32. In general, our plant's level of quality performance over the past 3 years has been low, relative to industry norms (reverse coded).
33. Our customers have been well satisfied with the quality of our products over the past 3 years.

## Construct Description

Seven basic constructs capturing the essence of Deming Management method were developed, including (1) visionary leadership, (2) internal and external cooperation, (3) learning, (4) process management, (5) continuous improvement, (6) employee fulfillment, and (7) customer satisfaction. Nominal definitions of the above constructs can be found in Table 1 of the article.

## Measurement Description

A total of 33 items that were grouped under seven scales were used for the final study. A 5-point Likert scale was used for each item, with response categories ranging from 1 = "strongly agree" to 5 = "strongly disagree." Several statements were reverse coded with 1 = "strongly disagree" to 5 = "strongly agree"; and two statements required informants to choose from 1 = "superior/better than average" to 5 = "poor/low end of the industry."

## Development

Seven experts from both industry and academia in a three-round Delphi study developed the constructs. The constructs were operationalized using measurement statements developed by the world class manufacturing (WCM) research project at the University of Minnesota and Iowa state University. Selected measurement statements were then pooled to create a multi-item perceptual scale.

## Sample

The plant was used as the unit of analysis for the study. Plants were selected from three types, including U.S. plants with Japanese ownership, U.S. plants with a reputation for being world class, and U.S. plants selected at large; and belonging to three different industries—electronics, machinery, and transportation components. A dual stratified random sampling strategy was employed. Only plants with more than 100 employees were considered. Out of a total of 72 plants, 41 chose to participate, yielding a response rate of 60%. The managers or vice presidents of the plants were then contacted to obtain approval and to assign a coordinator for the study. Questionnaires were then allocated to individuals with different job titles and responsibilities in the plant.

## Reliability and Validity

Principal component analyses (PCA) without rotation supported the unidimensionality for each construct. Each of the Cronbach alpha values exceeded the minimum ($\alpha = .60$) confirming the internal consistency reliability. The values can be found in Table 2.

## Scores

The mean values are listed in Table 4 in the article.

## Other Evidence

None.

## Reference

None.

# Athanassopoulos and Iliakopoulos

**Article Summarized**

Athanassopoulos, Andreas D., and Anastasios Iliakopoulos. 2003. Modeling customer satisfaction in telecommunications: Assessing the effects of multiple transaction points on the perceived overall performance of the provider. *Production and Operations Management* 12 (2): 224–45.

**Scales (Actual Questions Used)**

*Directory Enquiries*

1. Easy access to directory
2. Wait time prior to getting contact
   - Overall time to service
   - Staff knowledge to provide service
   - Staff courtesy
   - Correct information

*Billing*

3. Timely arrival
4. Information span
5. Understanding info
6. Trust of billing

*Branch Network*

7. Time of operation
8. Image
9. Overall time to service
10. Courtesy
11. Knowledge of personnel
12. Understanding of needs
13. Correcting mistakes

*Corporate Image (Orientation)*

14. General image
15. Continuous improvement
16. Customer orientation
17. Competitor orientation
18. Interfunctional coordination

*Fault Repair*

19. Speed of service
20. Correct operation
21. Personnel

*Service Provisioning*

22. Speed of service
23. Correct operation
24. Personnel

*Satisfaction from the Product*

25. Continuous operation of telecom line
26. Quality of voice transmission
27. Access at peak time

*Perceived Performance*

28. Overall satisfaction with telecom
29. Value for money of services
30. Recommendation to other customers
31. Relationship marketing

## Construct Description

The constructs used in the study are described below. The article stated that the constructs relate to the basic service contact points between customers and the provider.

"Directory enquiries are traditionally conceived as a basic point of reference for customers of the telecommunications sector" (p. 232). The authors used Ruyter and Wetzels (2000) research instrument to construct these items. "Billing is a traditional performance dimension upon which telecommunications operators are monitor for the satisfaction of their customers" (p. 232). This construct was developed based on Hu and Bentler (1999). "Branch network corresponds to the physical network of activity units that are visited by telecom customers for purposes that include (based on empirical evidence) payment of bills, service provision, purchases of new products, and complaint handling" (p. 232). The corporate image (orientation) indicated "the corporate image exhibited by the operator that has also been found previously (Athanassopoulos 2000)" (p. 234). Fault repair "has been operationalized for customers that had experienced faults over the last two years prior to the survey" (p. 234). The items from Spence (1975) and Collier and Wilson (1997) were used to construct the measures. Service provisioning "was measured for customers that had inquired for services over the last two years prior to the survey" (p. 234).

The construct satisfaction from the product stands for "the core product element of the telecommunication organization upon which extended product offerings are provided" (p. 234). The perceived performance "is an overall representation of the performance of the telecommunications organization by diverse measurement attributes" (p. 235). The items that are used to define this construct are used as independent constructs in Anderson and Lehman (1994).

## Measurement Description

The satisfaction constructs were measured based on a scale from 0 to 10, 0 being very dissatisfied and 10 being very satisfied. The exact phrasing of the questions relating to the satisfaction constructs is as follows: "We would like now to ask you about your overall satisfaction or dissatisfaction with the telecommunications organization. Please give me a rating from 0 to 10 (0 being very dissatisfied and 10 being very satisfied) concerning your satisfaction or dissatisfaction with XX telecommunications operator" (p. 231).

## Development

The instrument aims at capturing "customer satisfaction with different transaction points between the customers and telecommunications operator" (p. 231). The measurement instrument was first developed based on the existing literature on customer satisfaction and the results from eight qualitative customer focus groups. Then, the authors adopted half-split analysis methods to evaluate the reliability and validity of the scale development process. The subsample used in the evaluation was a random sample of 400 responses out of 2,900 original responses.

## Sample

The empirical data were drawn from a large-scale project undertaken on behalf of a major European telecommunications firm during the developmental stages of its customer satisfaction system. The target respondents were the fixed-line, residential customers, who were between 18 and 65 years old, and were covered by one of the firm's 10 different geographical divisions. The customers were contacted by telephone first and approached three more times for those that failed to respond to the initial interview. This approach led to a total of 2,900 effective interviews. Among the 2,900 responses, 400 were randomly selected for questionnaire validation and the remaining 2,500 were used for model estimation. The response rate was 65% on the first contact of the sample and the overall response rate was 87%. The sample used in the study had good representation in terms of age, gender, and occupation.

**Reliability and Validity**

The split-half method was employed to assess reliability and validity. The authors used both principal component analysis (PCA) with varimax rotation and confirmatory factor analysis (CFA). The average reliability values ranged from .81 for billing and corporate image/orientation to .98 for directory enquiries. The average variance explained ranged from .48 for corporate image/orientation to .92 for directory enquiries. Test statistics for comparative fit index (CFI), goodness-of-fit index (GFI), and root mean square error of approximation (RMSEA) criterion as well as $\chi^2$ values and the standardized factor loadings were reported in Table 1 (p. 233). Additional validity tests were conducted for "the five factors representing customer points for all customers included in the sample" (p. 235) to further support the dimensionality of customer transaction points. Discriminant validity was tested by examining the correlation coefficients among the five factors representing customer satisfaction dimensions.

**Scores**

The dimensionality of customer transaction points can be found in Table 2, and correlation coefficients are reported in Table 3.

**Other Evidence**

Not available.

**References**

Anderson, E., and D. Lehman. 1994. Customer satisfaction, market share and profitability: Findings from Sweden. *Journal of Marketing* 58: 53–66.

Athanassopoulos, A. D. 2000. Customer satisfaction cues to support market segmentation and explain switching behavior. *Journal of Business Research* 47 (3): 191–207.

Collier, D. A., and D. Wilson. 1997. The role of automation and labor in determining customer satisfaction in a telephone repair service process. *Decision Sciences* 28 (3): 689–708.

Hu, L., and P. Bentler. 1999. Cutoff criteria for fit indices in covariance structure analysis: Conventional criteria versus new approaches. *Structural equation modeling* 6 (1): 1–55.

Ruyter, K., and M. Wetzels. 2000. The impact of perceived listening behavior in voice-to-voice service encounters. *Journal of Service Research* 2 (3): 276–84.

Spence, A. M. (1975). Monopoly, quality and regulation. *Bell Journal of Economics* 6 (2): 417–29.

## Bates, Amundson, Schroeder, and Morris

**Article Summarized**

Bates, Kimberly A., Susan D. Amundson, Roger G. Schroeder, and William T. Morris. 1995. The crucial interrelationship between manufacturing strategy and organizational culture. *Management Science* 41 (10): 1565–80.

## Scales (Actual Questions Used)

*Manufacturing Strategy Scales*

Strategic Role: Stage 1

1. We use internal control systems to control manufacturing.
2. Manufacturing at our plant is kept flexible and unfocused.
3. Fire fighting is common at our plant.
4. Short-term performance is emphasized at our plant.
5. At our plant, external experts are used in making important decisions.

Strategic Role: Stage 2

6. At our plant, common industry practices are followed.
7. We rely on vendors for most of our equipment.
8. We use industry-wide wage rates.
9. Our planning horizon is one business cycle.
10. We consider capital investment to be our primary means of competing.

Strategic Role: Stage 3

11. We systematically address long-term manufacturing trends.
12. We have a manufacturing strategy that is actively pursued.
13. Our business strategy is translated into manufacturing terms.
14. Potential manufacturing investments are screened for consistency with our business strategy.
15. At our plant, manufacturing is kept in step with our business strategy.

Strategic Role: Stage 4

16. We actively develop propriety equipment.
17. At our plant, manufacturing is centrally involved in marketing and engineering decisions.
18. The functions of our firm are well integrated.
19. We pursue long-range programs to acquire manufacturing capabilities in advance of our needs.
20. We make an effort to anticipate the potential of new manufacturing practices and technologies.

Long-Range Orientation

21. At our plant, financial goals are the most important.
22. There is a lot of emphasis on quarterly manufacturing cost targets.
23. Management outside the plant is primarily concerned with short-range financial performance.
24. Our plant is long-run oriented and does not change its goals or objectives each year.
25. Short-term losses affect our decision making but are less important than pursuing long-term goals.

Manufacturing Strategy Strength

26. We have a regular system of monitoring plant performance against formal criteria.
27. We have a well developed manufacturing strategy in our plant.
28. Out plant is well focused.
29. Manufacturing provides competitive strength for our business.

Formal Strategic Planning

30. Our plant has a formal strategic planning process, which results in a written mission, long-range goals, and strategies for implementation.
31. Plant management is not included in the formal strategic planning process. It is conducted at higher levels in the corporation.

Communication of Strategy

32. In our plant, goals, objectives, and strategies are communicated to me.
33. Strategies and goals are communicated primarily to managers.
34. I know how we are planning to be competitive at this plant.
35. I understand the long-run competitive strategy of this plant.

*Organizational Culture Scales*

Coordination of Decision Making

36. Generally speaking, everyone in the plant works well together.
37. Departments in the plant communicate frequently with each other.
38. Departments within the plant seem to be in constant conflict.
39. Management works together well on all important decisions.

Supervisors as Team Leaders

40. Supervisors encourage the persons who work for them to work as a team.
41. Supervisors encourage people who work for them to exchange opinions and ideas.
42. Supervisors frequently hold group meetings where the people who work for them can really discuss things together.

Rewards for Group Performance

43. Our plant has an annual bonus system based on plant productivity.
44. Nonfinancial incentives, such as jackets, coffee cups, etc., are used to reward quality improvement.
45. Promotion implies team participation and experience with the firm.
46. Quality of team participation is signification part of managerial performance evaluation.
47. Managers are rewarded for making continuous improvements.

Small Group Problem Solving

48. Our plant is organized into permanent production teams.
49. During problem-solving sessions, we make an effort to get all team members' opinions and ideas before making a decision.
50. Our plant forms team to solve problems.
51. In the past 3 years, many problems have been solved through small group sessions.

*Power Distance Scales*

Shop-Floor Contact

52. Most of our manufacturing engineers have their offices located directly on the shop floor.
53. Managers in the plant believe in using a lot of face-to-face contact.
54. We hardly ever see managers on the shop floor.
55. Managers here are more likely to send a memo than to tell us something face-to-face.
56. Our engineers are located near the shop floor to provide quick assistance when production stops.
57. We see the plant manager on the shop floor almost every day.

Centralization of Authority

58. I can do almost everything I want without consulting my boss.
59. Even small matters have to be referred to someone higher up for a final answer.
60. This plant is a good place for a person who likes to make his own decisions.
61. Any decision I make has to have my boss's approval.
62. There can be little action taken here until a supervisor approves a decision.

Hierarchical Index

63. Are parking spots assigned on the basis of rank at this plant?
64. Do direct laborers punch a time clock at this plant?
65. Do direct laborers wear uniforms at this plant? Do management and staff wear uniforms at this plant?
66. Are hourly employees allowed to eat in the same cafeteria as the salaried employees at this plant?
67. Do salaried employees have their own restroom at this plant?

*Cultural Congruence Scales*

Loyalty

68. I am willing to put a great deal of effort, beyond that normally expected, to help this organization be successful.
69. I talk up this organization to my friends as a great organization to work for.
70. I would accept almost any type of job assignment to keep working for this organization.
71. I find that my values and the organization's values are very similar.
72. I am proud to tell others that I am part of this organization.
73. This organization really inspires the best in me in the way of job performance.
74. I am extremely glad that I chose this organization to work for over others I was considering at the time I joined.
75. I really care about the fate of this organization.
76. For me, this is the best of all organizations for which to work.

Philosophy

77. This plant doesn't have a very definite idea about how things should be done.
78. This plant produces a very special kind of employee.
79. This plant has a clear view about how to achieve goals.
80. Stories are often told within the plant about accomplishments of past employees.
81. Sayings that embody organizational wisdom are often told within the plant.

**Construct Description**

The constructs were developed to empirically test the links between organizational culture and the manufacturing strategy process within manufacturing plants. Manufacturing strategy process was defined in terms of a "well aligned and implemented manufacturing strategy" (p. 1570). A "well aligned and implemented manufacturing strategy" consisted of the following dimensions: formal strategic planning, communication of strategy, long-range orientation, manufacturing strategy strength, and strategic roles—stages 3 and 4 (from Hayes and Wheelwright 1984).

The organizational culture within manufacturing plants was characterized as hierarchically oriented cultures, which depended primarily on authority relationship for control of behavior, or clan-oriented cultures, which relied on shared values and beliefs. They were measured based on three dimensions: individualism/collectivism, power distance, and cultural congruency.

**Measurement Description**

A total of eight scales, copyrighted by Roger G. Schroeder and Barbara Flynn, to measure manufacturing strategy were used. Two of them (strategic role—stage 1 and strategic role—stage 2) were dropped because of low reliability. The formal strategic planning process consisted of aligning the manufacturing strategy with the business strategy by translating the business strategy into manufacturing terms. Communication of strategy referred to the communication of the manufacturing throughout the plant. Long-range orientation indicated whether a firm's manufacturing strategy delved into the future to anticipate its needs and to acquire manufacturing capabilities in advance of those needs. Manufacturing strategy strengths measured whether a firm's manufacturing strategy was viewed as integral to reaching performance goals and providing competitive strength for the organization. The strategic role—stage 3 and strategic role—stage 4 were based on the work of Hayes and Wheelwright. Stage 3 described manufacturing as "providing credible support to the business strategy," and stage 4 described organizations that "pursue a manufacturing-based competitive advantage."

A total of nine scales for three constructs were used: individualism/collectivism (four scales), power distance (three scales), and cultural congruency (two scales). Individualism/collectivism indicated the fundamental difference in the organization's beliefs about the role of the individual versus that of the group and was measured in this study by coordination of decision making, supervisors as team leaders, rewards for group performance, and small group problem solving. Power distance described the distribution of authority within the plant and is measured by shop-floor contact, centralization of authority, and hierarchical index. Cultural congruency indicated the extent to which values and beliefs are shared within an organization and is measured by loyalty and philosophy.

All responses were on Likert-type scales, except for the Hierarchical Index, which was based on objective information.

## Development

Several scales for manufacturing strategy were created in this article. These new scales were pretested in a pilot study and revised accordingly to improve clarity and validity. Two scales (strategic role—stage 1 and strategic role—stage 2) were dropped because of low reliability. The rest of the scales were adapted from the existing literature.

## Sample

The data were collected in 41 plants from three industries: electronics, automotive components, and machinery. The plants included both American-owned and Japanese-owned plants located in the United States. Thirteen plants were drawn from a list of Japanese-owned plants located in the United States. The list was obtained from the Japanese External Trade Organization (1988). Two samples of U.S.-owned plants were drawn; 14 plants from Dun's Industrial Guide (1988) and 15 plants from a sampling frame composed by the authors from Schonberger's (1986) honor roll of world class firms or from favorable reviews in *Target,* the periodical of the Association for Manufacturing Excellence (1985–89). Sixty percent of the plants selected participated in this study.

The questionnaires were designed so that multiple respondents could answer all perceptual questions. Nine different types of questionnaires were distributed among 21 employees in each plant, 11 managers and 10 randomly selected workers. A total of 822 usable individual questionnaires from the 41 participating plants were returned.

## Reliability and Validity

To ensure the reliability of each factor, Cronbach's coefficient alpha was used to test the internal consistency among the items included in each factor. A threshold level of .60 was applied for acceptable reliability for newly developed scales and a threshold level of .70 for the previously developed scales.

Content validity was assessed using expert opinion and informed judgment. Factor analysis was used to examine the unidimensionality of each scale. Except for rewards for group performance, factor analyses indicated the unidimensionality.

## Scores

Plant scores were constructed using the mean of the respondents' scores.

| | *Number of Respondents* | *Cronbach's Alpha* |
|---|---|---|
| Manufacturing strategy scales | | |
| Strategic role: stage 1 | 72 | .25 |
| Strategic role: stage 2 | 72 | .35 |
| Strategic role: stage 3 | 72 | .79 |
| Strategic role: stage 4 | 72 | .67 |
| Formal strategic planning | 71 | .62 |
| Communication of strategy | 698 | .77 |
| Long-range orientation | 231 | .62 |
| Manufacturing strategy strength | 113 | .74 |
| Organizational culture | | |
| *Collectivism* | | |
| Coordination of decision making | 699 | .74 |
| Supervisors as team leaders | 505 | .73 |
| Small group problem solving | 626 | .65 |
| Rewards for group performance | 426 | .63 |
| *Power distance* | | |
| Centralization of authority | 665 | .77 |
| Shop-floor contact | 505 | .71 |
| Hierarchical index | 70 | N/A |
| *Cultural congruency* | | |
| Loyalty | 665 | .88 |
| Philosophy | 617 | .71 |

**Other Evidence**

Not available.

**References**

Aiken, M., and J. Hage. 1966. Organizational alienation: A comparative analysis. *American Sociological Review* 31:497–507.

The Association for Manufacturing Excellence. 1985–1989. *Target*. Vols. 1–5. Wheeling, IL: Association for Manufacturing Excellence.

*Dun's industrial guide: The metalworking directory*. 1988. Dun & Bradstreet: Parsippany, NJ.

Georgopoulos, Basil Spyros. 1986. *Organizational structure, problem solving, and effectiveness*. San Francisco, CA: Jossey-Bass

Hayes, R. H., and S. C. Wheelwright. 1984. *Restoring our competitive edge: Competing through manufacturing*. New York: Wiley.

Japanese External Trade Organization (JETRO). 1988. Zaibei Nikei Seizogyo Keiei o Jitsutai (in Japanese), February, 1988.

Schonberger, Richard J. 1986. *World class manufacturing*. New York: Free Press.

Taylor, J. C., and D. B. Bowers. 1972. *Survey of organizations: A machine-scored standardized questionnaires instrument*. Ann Arbor, MI. University of Michigan, Institute for Social Research.

# Benson, Saraph, and Schroeder

**Article Summarized**

Benson, P. George, Jayant V. Saraph, and Roger G. Schroeder. 1991. The effects of organizational context on quality management: An empirical investigation. *Management Science* 37 (9): 1107–24.

**Scales (Actual Questions Used)**

*Managerial Knowledge*

1. Experience in quality
2. Participation in professional quality organizations
3. Familiarity with various quality programs (zero defects, total quality control [TQC])
4. Expertise in quality concepts
5. Overall knowledge of quality

*Corporate Support for Quality*

6. Level of corporate goal setting in quality
7. Rewards for corporate management for quality performance
8. Corporate leadership for quality
9. Quality viewed by corporate management as strategic variable
10. Corporate quality emphasis throughout the organization
11. Corporate management's commitment to quality
12. Progressiveness and innovativeness of corporate management
13. Corporate-sanctioned rewards for divisional management for quality performance
14. Resources made available by corporate management for quality improvement
15. Appropriateness of corporate systems (plants, equipment, systems) for quality improvement

*Market Environment*

16. Degree of competition faced by the business unit
17. Barriers to entry in the industry
18. Quality demands of customers
19. Quality demands because of legal and regulatory requirements

*Product/Process Environment*

20. Rate of change of product/process
21. Proportion of product/service purchased outside
22. Degree of manufacturing content (as opposed to service content)
23. Degree of batch-type process (as opposed to flow-type process)
24. Degree of product complexity

*Past Quality Performance*

25. Past 3 years' quality performance
26. Perceived customer satisfaction for past 3 years

**Construct Description**

The constructs were operationalized as follows: Divisional top management leadership for quality was defined as the acceptance of quality responsibility by general manager and department head, the evaluation of management on quality, the degree of participation by management in quality improvement efforts, the specificity of quality goals, the importance attached to quality in relation to cost and schedule, and comprehensive quality planning. See Table 1 in the article (p. 1111).

Role of the quality department was defined as "Visibility and autonomy of the quality department. The quality department's access to top management. Use of quality staff for consultation. Coordination between quality department and other departments. Effectiveness of quality department" (p. 1111). Training was explained as "Extent of statistical training, trade training, and quality-related training for all employees" (p. 1111). Product/service design was expressed as "an in depth understanding of customer requirements. Thorough scrub-down process, extensive involvement of all affected departments in design reviews, clarity of specifications, emphasis on quality—not roll-out schedule, and avoidance of frequent redesigns" (p. 1111). Supplier quality management was defined as "Fewer dependable suppliers, reliance on supplier process control, strong interdependence, purchasing policy emphasizing quality rather than price, supplier participation in quality control and product design" (p. 1111.)

Process management was referred to as "Clarity of process ownership, boundaries, and steps; less reliance on inspection, use of statistical process control, selective automation, 'fool-proof' process design, preventative maintenance, employee self-inspection, automated testing, and effective management of customer contact" (p. 1111). Quality data and reporting was defined as "Use of cost quality data, feedback of quality data to employees and managers for problem solving, timely quality measurement, evaluation of managers and employees based on quality. Customer perceptions of quality" (p. 1111). Employee relations represented "Implementation of employee involvement and quality circles, open employee participation in quality decisions, responsibility of employees for quality, employee recognition for superior quality performance, effectiveness of supervision in handling quality issues, and on-going quality awareness by all employees" (p. 1111).

### Measurement Description

A two-stage process was used for the data collection. In the first stage, the managers were asked to rate the ideal and actual quality management of their plants. In the second stage, the managers focused on assessing their organizational context. The "eight critical factors" of quality management were measured using 78 separate items. A complete list of these items was shown in Saraph, Benson, and Schroeder (1989). A 5-point Likert scale was used in the current study.

### Development

Please refer to Saraph, Benson, and Schroeder (1989).

### Sample

The 70 companies in this study were classified based on type—service or manufacturing—and size—large, medium, and small. A select random group of 22 firms was chosen to be contacted for participation. From this list, five companies declined to participate because of various organizational issues or "lack of interest." These were replaced by other randomly selected organizations.

### Reliability and Validity

The instrument was validated by Saraph, Benson, and Schroeder (1989).

### Scores

The scores are presented in Tables 4, 6, and 7 in the article.

### Other Evidence

Not available.

### Reference

Saraph, J. V., P. G. Benson, and R. G. Schroeder. 1989. An instrument for measuring the critical factors of quality management. *Decision Sciences* 20 (4): 810–29.

# Benton and Maloni

### Article Summarized

Benton, W. C., and Michael Maloni. 2005. The influence of power driven buyer/seller relationships on supply chain satisfaction. *Journal of Operations Management* 23 (1): 1–22.

### Scales (Actual Questions Used)

*Relationship Elements*

Cooperation

1. The relationship better described as a "cooperative."
2. Perform well together.
3. Our future goals best reached by working with XXX.[1]
4. We cannot count on XXX to give us the support others receive.
5. XXX helps us in getting job done.

Commitment

6. Do not want to replace XXX as a partner.
7. Committed to preservation of good relationships with XXX.
8. Our firm believes in XXX as a partner.

Trust

9. XXX is concerned about our welfare.
10. XXX considers how its decisions/actions affect us.
11. We cannot trust XXX.
12. XXX looks out for our best interests.

Conflict

13. We do not like things XXX does.
14. XXX prevents us from doing what we want to do.
15. XXX does not have our best interests at heart.
16. We disagree with XXX on critical issues.

Conflict Resolution

17. Discussions within areas of disagreement are productive.
18. Discussions intend to create more problems.
19. Discussions increase effectiveness/strength of relationship.

Compliance

20. Our private views are different from those we express publicly.
21. Unless rewarded, we see no reason to expend extra effort.
22. How hard we work for XXX is linked to reward.
23. Bargaining is necessary to obtain favorable terms of trade.

Satisfaction

24. Dealings with XXX benefits our company.
25. We are satisfied with dealings with XXX.

26. If we could, we would discontinue selling to XXX.
27. XXX is a good company to do business with.

*Performance Elements*

Performance-Supplier

28. The performance of our firm has improved as a result of our association with XXX.
29. The efficiency of relationship has improved our performance.
30. Without XXX, our performance was not as good.

Performance-Manufacturer

31. The performance of XXX has improved.
32. The efficiency of relationship has improved the performance of XXX.
33. Without us, the performance of XXX was not as good.

Performance-Supply Chain

34. The performance of supply chain has improved.
35. The efficiency of relationship has improved supply chain performance.
36. Without relationship, supply chain performance would not be as good.

### Construct Description

Mediated and nonmediated forms of power were used in this study to list "forms of power" per Brown, Lusch, and Nicholson (1995) and Maloni and Benton (2000). However, the 19 items used to measure power were not included in the article. According to French and Raven (1959), the "most appropriate dichotomization of the supply chain environment is based on mediated and nonmediated power sources" (p. 4). These authors listed the mediated power sources to include reward, coercive, and legal legitimate. These involve influence strategies that "the source (buyer) specifically administers to the target (seller)" (p. 4). Nonmediated power sources were more relational and positive in orientation. These included expert, referent, and traditional legitimate. "These power bases occur as a natural part of buyer-seller business transactions and do not necessitate intention from the source" (p. 4).

Supplier satisfaction was defined as "the feeling of equity with the relationship no matter what power imbalance exists" (p. 5). For this study, the three sources of power influence the measures of performance. In addition, the buyer-seller relationship affected the measures of performance for the supplier, manufacturer, and the supply chain, which in turn affect supplier satisfaction.

### Measures

Each construct in the study was measured using multi-item scales. The respondents were asked to evaluate each statement using a 7-point Likert scale, where 1 = "strongly disagree" to 7 = "strongly agree," with 4 indicating a "neutral" score.

### Development

The authors used two-stage process to design the questionnaire. First, they conducted extensive literature review to generalize the survey items. In the second stage, they refined the questionnaire by seeking advice from industry experts. The authors conducted a survey pilot testing with industry experts, which led to the final questionnaire.

## Sample

Daimler-Chrysler and Honda, considered major auto manufacturers, provided lists of their most "critical" tier-one suppliers, supplying 178 and 392 contracts, respectively. A total of 570 contact names were provided. After data cleansing, 525 contacts were considered usable. Of these, 33.7% were from Daimler-Chrysler and 66.3% from Honda.

## Reliability and Validity

The authors used a three-step validation process. Content validity, construct validity, and nomological validity based on suggestions by O'Leary-Kelly and Vokurka (1998). The authors used a literature review and in-depth interviews with business executives and researchers to establish the basis of content validity. The authors established unidimensionality of measures using "target rotation factor analysis." A .40 value is normally "considered to be the lowest significant factor loading to define the construct (Guadagnoli and Velicer, 1998; Hair et al., 1998)" (p. 11). The authors also computed Cronbach's alpha coefficients for the items of each survey construct. Once verification of unidimensionality was completed, five power constructs remained. According to the authors, each of the five constructs retained an acceptable level of alpha. The authors also noted that the Cronbach alpha levels for the five relationship constructs maintained were acceptable, with commitment at .83, cooperation at .71, trust at .89, conflict at .81, and conflict resolution at .86. In addition, the supplier performance, manufacturer performance, and supply chain performance measures also retained high threshold values of coefficient alpha at .83, .84, and .85, respectively. Last, satisfaction had a coefficient alpha value of .80. Thus, the authors asserted that the reliabilities of the research constructs were established.

## Scores

Table 4 provides descriptive statistics for each survey statement.

## Other Evidence

Not available.

## Note

1. XXX is the supplier name.

## References

Brown, J. R., R. F. Lusch, and C. Y. Nicholson. 1995. Power and relationship commitment: Their impact on marketing channel member performance. *Journal of Retailing* 71 (4): 363–92.

French, J. R., and B. Raven. 1959. The basis of social power. In *Studies in social power,* ed. C. Dorwin, 150–67. Ann Arbor, MI. University of Michigan Press.

Guadagnoli, E., and W. F. Velicer. 1998. Relation of sample size to the stability of component patterns. *Psychological Bulletin* 103 (2): 265–75.

Hair, J. F., Jr., R. E. Anderson, R. L. Tatham, and W. C. Black. 1998. *Multivariate data analysis.* 5th ed. Englewood Cliffs, NJ: Prentice Hall.

Maloni, M. J., and W. C. Benton. 2000. Power influences in the supply chain. *Journal of Business Logistics* 21 (1): 42–73.

O'Leary-Kelly, S. W., and R. J. Vokurka. 1998. The empirical assessment of construct validity. *Journal of Operations Management* 16 (4): 387–405.

# Black and Porter

### Article Summarized

Black, Simon A., and Leslie J. Porter. 1996. Identification of the critical factors of TQM. *Decision Sciences* 27 (1): 1–27.

### Scales (Actual Questions Used)

*People and Customer Management*

1. HRM in line with company quality performance plans
2. Employee recognition/measurement to support quality/performance
3. Management of customer relations

*Supplier Partnerships*

4. Assurance of supplier quality
5. Action to assist and improve the quality and responsiveness of suppliers
6. Strategic management of suppliers

*Communications of Improvement Information*

7. Determination of quality costs to support the prioritization of improvements
8. Assessment of needs for quality training and subsequent delivery and review
9. Benchmarking of processes in noncompeting organizations
10. Promotion of quality improvement with outside groups

*Customer Satisfaction Orientation*

11. Commitments to customers through strengthening of warranties/policies, etc.
12. Comparisons of customer satisfaction with competitors and internal indicators
13. Determination of improvements in customer satisfaction
14. Benchmarking of direct competitors' products and processes

*External Interface Management*

15. Recognition of responsibilities for public health and safety, and the environment
16. Determination of customers' future requirements
17. Integration of the design process with customer and operational requirements

*Strategic Quality Management*

18. Process control and improvement of core processes in accordance with design
19. Active leadership by managers in quality issues
20. Inclusion of employee well-being considerations in improvement activities
21. Senior executive commitment to quality through involvement and communication
22. Development/implementation of long-term plans/strategies focused on quality
23. Analysis of performance and cost data support improvement priorities

*Teamwork Structures for Improvement*

24. Use of specific organizational structures to support quality improvement
25. Use of techniques to identify key processes, customers, and suppliers

*Operational Quality Planning*

26. Development/implementation of short-term plans/strategies focused on quality
27. Consideration of performance requirements in developing short-term goals

*Quality Improvement Measurement Systems*

28. Assessment and improvement of processes, practices, and products/services
29. Management of data/information to support quality improvement efforts
30. Procedures to ensure the reliability and improvement of data gathering

*Corporate Quality Culture*

31. Consideration of requirements in developing long-term goals
32. Encouragement of a company-wide culture committed to quality improvement

### Construct Description

The definitions of each construct were not available in the article. However, most of the constructs are adopted from the Baldrige Award model and others are grounded in the literature. Appendix A in the article provided a description for each item used in the questionnaire. The 32 items retained in the final instrument are grouped into 10 factors: people and customer management, supplier partnerships, communications of improvement information, customer satisfaction orientation, external interface management, strategic quality management, teamwork structures for improvement, operational quality planning, quality improvement measurement systems, and corporate quality culture.

### Measurement Description

In the questionnaire, 39 items were randomly presented to respondents. The item pertaining to "assessment and improvement of quality systems and documentation" was chosen to be the reference item, with a score fixed at 100. Every other item was scored proportionally based on its importance relative to that of the reference item.

### Development

The initial questionnaire consisted of 39 items. Of these, 32 were developed from the Baldrige Award model, and the other seven "non-Baldrige" items were identified from the total quality management (TQM) literature. The authors conducted factor analysis on 38 items. The reference item—assessment and improvement of quality systems and documentation—was excluded from the analysis. Among the 38 items, 6 had structure loadings less than .58 and were dropped from the initial questionnaire. Therefore, 32 items were kept in the final questionnaire.

### Sample

A target sample was drawn from members of the European Foundation for Quality Management (EFQM), which includes both U.S.- and European-owned organizations operating in Europe. A total of 263 questionnaires were mailed to 33 different EFQM member organizations. In addition, another 199 questionnaires were mailed to 28 other organizations that had attended workshops run by the European Center for TQM at the University of Bradford. Out of the 462 questionnaires, 204 correctly completed questionnaires were returned, yielding a 44.2% response rate.

### Validity

The internal consistency was tested by calculating the Cronbach's coefficient alpha. Table 1 in the article showed that the coefficient alpha values for each scale ranged from .68 to .87. In addition, reliability was also examined using split-halves tests. The results provided evidence of repeatability of the factor structure. Besides, the factor structure was proved to be robust to different rotation methods too.

The content validity was established based on the systematic redefinition of the 1992 Baldrige criteria. The rational judgments by both the independent nonexperts and the experts in TQM further supported the content validity. In addition, the item analyses provided the empirical evidence for the content validity. Construct validity was examined using factor tests. All the 10 factors were proved to be unidimensional. The Kaiser-Meyer-Olkin (KMO) measure of sampling adequacy confirmed the suitability of the data set for each unifactorial determination. Variance explained by the single factors in unifactorial tests is reported in Table 2.

### Scores

The scores are reported in Tables 1 and 2 in the article.

### Other Evidence

Not available.

### Reference

None.

## Borgatti and Cross

### Article Summarized

Borgatti, Stephen P., and Rob Cross. 2003. A relational view of information seeking and learning in social networks. *Management Science* 49 (4): 432–45.

### Scales (Actual Questions Used)

*Knowing*

1. I understand this person's knowledge and skills. This does not necessarily mean that I have these skills or am knowledgeable in these domains but that I understand what skills this person has and domains they are knowledgeable in.

*Value*

2. This person has expertise in areas that are important in the kind of work I do.

*Access*

3. One issue in getting information or advice from others is your ability to gain access to their thinking. The extent to which you can access another person's thinking and knowledge is a continuum. At one end of the spectrum are people who do not make themselves available to you quickly enough to help solve your problem. At the other end of the spectrum are those who are willing to engage actively in problem solving with you in a timely fashion. With this continuum in mind, how would you rate your overall ability to assess this person's thinking and knowledge?

*Cost*

4. Seeking information or advice from other people can be costly. For example, with some people you may not feel comfortable revealing your lack of knowledge on a given topic. Alternatively, people you ask for information may make you feel excessively indebted to them. In light of such interpersonal risks and obligations, please indicate the extent to which you feel that seeking information or advice from this person is costly.

*Information*

5. Please indicate how often you have turned to this person for information or knowledge on work-related topics in the past 3 months.
6. Please indicate how often this person has turned to you for information or knowledge on work-related topics in the past 3 months.

## Construct Description

The constructs were described as follows: Knowing was defined as the "awareness that the individual is a possible source in light of the current problem or opportunity" (p. 434). Value was defined as how the knowledge seeker evaluates "the knowledge and skills of the person sought" (p. 434). Access was defined as one's being available at the time the information is needed, and how well the person will mindfully focus on the knowledge seeker's needs. Cost was defined as the cost to the knowledge seeker, both in term of interpersonal risk (e.g., embarrassment) or obligations incurred (e.g., implicit debt for taking the other person's time).

## Measurement Description

With the exception of information, each construct was measured using a 5-point, Likert-type, single-item scale. Respondents assessed aspects of general information and knowledge-seeking behaviors and attributes. To measure the dependent variable information, two questions were used (*see* the previous section). The authors averaged these two questions to form a two-item, measurement scale for the information construct.

## Development

Not available.

## Sample

The social network data were collected from two groups. The first group consisted of 37 information scientists (16 men and 21 women) in a pharmaceutical organization. The second group consisted of 35 researchers (16 men and 19 women). Surveys were sent to the target respondents through e-mail. All the 37 information scientists and 34 of the 35 researchers completed the study.

## Reliability and Validity

The authors comment on the single-item measures as follows: "While some have faulted the practice of asking a single sociometric question to measure each theoretical variable . . . , a review by Marsden (1990) suggest that these indices are largely reliable when appropriate procedures are followed to help individuals accurately report their network links" (p. 436).

Validity was argued logically in discussions on each construct; e.g., the authors offered justification for the content validity using logical arguments. With single-item scales, it was difficult to establish construct validity more rigorously.

### Scores

The correlations are given in Table 2 and regression results are given in Table 3 in the article.

### Other Evidence

Not available.

### Reference

Marsden, P. 1990. Network data and measurement. *Annual Review of Sociology* 16: 435–63.

## Bowen, Cousins, Lamming, and Faruk

### Article Summarized

Bowen, Frances E., Paul D. Cousins, Richard C. Lamming, and Adam C. Faruk. 2001. The role of supply management capabilities in green supply. *Production and Operations Management* 10 (2): 174–89.

### Scales (Actual Questions Used)

*Corporate Environmental Proactivity*

1. We always attempt to go beyond basic compliance with laws and regulations on environmental issues.
2. Our corporate management gives a high priority to environmental issues.
3. The top managers in our business unit give environmental issues a high priority.
4. We lead our industry on environmental issues.
5. We effectively manage the environmental risks that affect our business.

*Strategic Purchasing*

6. The purchasing function has a formally written long-range plan (e.g., 5- to 10-year plan).
7. The long-range plan for purchasing includes the kinds of materials of services to be purchased.
8. The long-range plan for purchasing includes various types of relationships to be established with suppliers.

*Supply Management Capabilities*

9. Liaison between purchasing and other functions
10. Detailed purchasing policies and procedures
11. Partnership approach with suppliers
12. Technical skills of purchasing professionals
13. Advanced understanding of environmental issues and how they affect supply

*Product-Based Green Supply*

Have you implemented any of the following?

14. Recycling initiatives that require cooperation with a supplier
15. Collaboration with a supplier to eliminate packaging
16. Efforts with suppliers to reduce waste

*Greening the Supply Process*

Have you implemented any of the following?

17. Environmental supplier questionnaire
18. Supplier environmental award
19. Scoring system to rank suppliers on their environmental performance
20. Requirement on suppliers to have an environmental management system

Have you built environmental criteria into any of the following?

21. Vendor assessment system
22. Selection of strategic suppliers

### Construct Description

The green supply constructs described the activities of manufacturers to improve the environmental performance of purchased inputs or of the suppliers that provide them. Accordingly, greening the supply process indicates the changes made to the firm's supplier management activities that incorporate environmental considerations. The product-based green supply involved changes to the product supply and attempts to manage the by-products of supplied inputs, such as packaging.

### Measurement Description

Corporate environmental proactivity, strategic purchasing, and supply management capabilities were measured using 7-point Likert scales. The product-based green supply and greening the supply process were captured using the following categories: 2 ("yes"), 1 ("planned"), and 0 ("not planned").

### Development

The model was developed in a two-phase, research process. The first phase involved interviews with senior managers in 24 business units in a broad cross-selection of industries. Looking at industries broadly helped avoid the bias by focusing only on environmentally engaged industries. In the second phase, questionnaires were sent to key respondents in operating units within the business units interviewed in phase 1. The authors reported improved validity because they collected data from respondents at the appropriate level of the firm; and also since they gathered systemic data on each of the key resources identified in theory and interviews. Reliability was enhanced by triangulating the findings by consulting with other informants in the same firm. Two questionnaires were mailed—one for the operating unit general manager and the other for the person responsible for purchasing. Both questionnaires were pretested on a sample of 19 managers at a regular progress meeting on a research project.

### Sample

A total of 24 business units within UK public-limited companies were targeted for data collection. The industry and company breakdowns are reported in Table 1. Two questionnaires were mailed to key respondents in operating units within each business unit, one questionnaire for the general manager of the operating unit and the other for the individual responsible for purchasing at the operating unit. Of the 138 sets of questionnaires sent out, 95 usable general manager questionnaires and 70 purchasing questionnaires were returned, yielding response rates of 69% and 51%, respectively. "The response rate for matched pairs of general manager and purchasing manager responses within individual business units ranged from 20% (water provision) to 100% (home and personal products, printing)" (p. 181).

### Reliability and Validity

"Scale reliabilities and intercorrelations for all study variables are presented in Table 3. The Cronbach's alpha of all the scale is well above the conventional reliability criterion of .70 (Nunnally 1978)" (p. 183).

### Scales

The scores are given in Tables 3 and 4 in the article.

### Other Evidence

Not available.

### Reference

Nunnally, J. C. 1978. *Psychometric theory.* New York: McGraw-Hill.

---

## Boyer and Hult

### Article Summarized

Boyer, Kenneth K., and G. Tomas M. Hult. 2006. Customer behavioral intentions for online purchases: An examination of fulfillment method and customer experience level. *Journal of Operations Management* 24 (2): 124–47.

### Scales (Actual Questions Used)

*Service Quality*

1. Grocer X employees are reliable in providing the service I expect.
2. Grocer X employees understand my service needs.
3. Grocer X employees are responsive to my service requests.
4. Grocer X employees are competent in providing the expected service.
5. I feel secure in service encounters with Grocer X employees.
6. Grocer X employees are courteous in providing me service.
7. Grocer X employees are available to answer my service-related questions.
8. The tangible (appearance of trucks, staff, and products) aspects of Grocer X service are excellent.
9. Grocer X has good credibility in providing the service I need.
10. I have access to communicate with Grocer X regarding my service needs.

*Product Quality*

11. Grocer X has prestigious products.
12. Grocer X has an excellent assortment of products.
13. The products of Grocer X are among the best. (Dropped)
14. Grocer X has a sufficient range of product choices (I can get what I want).
15. The products are the same quality as I can get in the store.
16. The number of substitutions or out of stock item is reasonable. (Dropped)

*Product Freshness*

17. Freshness of food
18. Quality of fresh produce
19. Quality of meats

*Time Savings*

20. Time to place the most recent order in minutes divided by the time to place the first order in minutes

*Behavioral Intentions*

21. I would classify myself as a loyal customer of Grocer X.
22. I do not expect to switch to another online grocer to get better service in the future.
23. I would continue to do business with Grocer X even if I had to pay more.
24. I would complain to other customers if I experienced a problem with Grocer X service.
25. I would complain to the employees of Grocer X if I experienced a problem with their service. (Dropped)

**Construct Description**

These authors defined service quality based on the existing literature (Zeithmal, Berry, and Parasuraman 1996). Product quality captured customers' perception of quality of the physical products and the variety of choices relative to what they can get in the physical store. Product freshness specifically referred to the quality of fresh produce and meats. Time savings was defined as the reduction in the time to place orders as customers place more orders (Ellis 2003). Behavioral intentions were based on Zeithmal, Berry, and Parasuraman (1996), who stated that "positive behavioral intentions are reflected in the service provider's ability to get its customers to (a and b) remain loyal to them, (c) pay price premiums, (d) communicate concerns to other customers, and (e) communicate concerns to the company" (p. 134).

**Measurement Description**

Not available.

**Development**

The authors adopted the existing scales where possible and developed customized scales when appropriate to reflect the nature of the online grocery shopping. The initial scale development of each process is described next.

The authors adopted the 10-item service quality scale based on the 10 original dimensions of service quality proposed by Parasuraman, Zeithmal, and Berry (1985). The original 10 items were modified to be generalizable across different grocers and countries. The product quality scale was derived from the prior research by Boyer and Hult (2005). Product freshness was constructed to specifically measure the quality of fresh produce and markets. The behavioral intentions scale was taken from Cronin, Brady, and Hult (2000).

After data were collected, the authors conducted a variety of measurement tests. During the development process, five items were dropped to improve psychometric properties of the constructs. The final set of scales consisted of 19 purified items.

**Sample**

Five online/home delivery grocers participated in the data collection. Two of them are in the United States, two in the United Kingdom, and one in Canada. Two different sampling selection approaches were used—stratified sampling for four grocers and random sampling for one grocer. Among the five grocers, Web survey was conducted for four of them and mail survey was used for the fifth grocer. Small incentives were implemented to increase the completion rates; and follow-up invitations to participate in the study were implemented during the survey. The overall response rate for the entire sample is 2,125 responses, out of 16,577 customers contacted, or 18%. To assess nonresponse bias, the authors "conducted chi-square tests on the proportion of positive responses for the number of orders placed online with the sponsoring grocer" (p. 133). The analyses indicated the existence of potential response biases for two out of the four participating grocers. The authors noted that for these two grocers, the customers that have placed more orders with a grocer were more likely to complete the survey.

### Reliability and Validity

The measurement testing process started with the evaluation of item-level robustness across segmented samples using $\chi^2$ tests. Then the authors used confirmatory factor analysis (CFA) to evaluate construct reliability and validity. Specifically, the latent factors' reliability was assessed by calculating a composite reliability for each construct (Fornell and Larcker 1981). The authors also examined the parameter estimates and their associated *t*-values as well as the average variance extracted (AVE). The measurement scale reliabilities ranged from .47 to .94 ($p < .01$); and the AVE ranged from 37% to 84%.

Following the reliability analyses, the authors "established discriminant validity by two independent methods" (p. 138). First, following Fornell and Larcker (1981) they "calculated the shared variance between each pair of constructs and verified that it was lower than the variances extracted for the involved constructs" (p. 138). Second, they examined all possible pairs of constructs, as suggested by Anderson (1987) and Bagozzi and Phillips (1982).

Finally, a series of Harmon's one-factor tests were used to assess the possibility of common method variance.

### Scores

The variable means, standard deviations, and correlations for overall sample and for each of the segmented samples are reported in Table 2. The results from CFA, including factor loadings, AVE, composite reliabilities, and fit indices are presented in Tables 4 and 5 in the article.

### Other Evidence

Not available.

### References

Anderson, J. C. 1987. An approach for confirmatory measurement and structural equation modeling of organizational properties. *Management Science* 33 (4): 525–41.

Bagozzi, R. P., and L. W. Phillips. 1982. Representing and testing organizational theories: A holistic construal. *Administrative Science Quarterly* 27 (3): 459–89.

Boyer, K. K., and G. T. M. Hult. 2005. Extending the supply chain: Integrating operations and marketing in the online grocery industry. *Journal of Operations Management* 23 (6): 642–61.

Cronin, J. J., M. K. Brady, and G. T. M. Hult. 2000. Assessing the effects of quality, value, and customer satisfaction on consumer behavioral intentions in service environments. *Journal of Retailing* 76 (2): 193–218.

Ellis, C. 2003. Lessons from online groceries. *Sloan Management Review* 44 (2): 8.

Fornell, C., and D. F. Larcker. 1981. Evaluating structural equation models with unobservable variables and measurement error. *Journal of Marketing Research* 18 (1): 39–50.

Parasuraman, A., V. A. Zeithmal, and L. L. Berry. 1985. A conceptual model of service quality and its implications for future research. *Journal of Marketing* 49 (4): 41–50.

Zeithmal, V. A., L. L. Berry, and A. Parasuraman. 1996. The behavioral consequences of service quality. *Journal of Marketing* 60 (2): 31–46.

# Boyer, Leong, Ward, and Krajewski

## Article Summarized

Boyer, Kenneth K., G. Keong Leong, Peter T. Ward, and Lee J. Krajewski. 1997. Unlocking the potential of advanced manufacturing technologies. *Journal of Operations Management* 15 (4): 331–47.

## Scales (Actual Questions Used)

*Advanced Manufacturing Technologies (TECH)*

1. Computer-aided manufacturing (CAM)
2. Computer-aided design (CAD)
3. Computer-aided engineering (CAE)
4. Computer-aided process planning (CAPP)
5. Robotics
6. Real-time process control systems
7. Group technology (GT)
8. Flexible manufacturing systems
9. Electronic mail
10. Electronic data interchange
11. Office automation
12. Computerize numerical control machines (CNC)
13. Automated material handling systems
14. Environmental control systems
15. Bar coding/automatic identification
16. Knowledge-based systems
17. Decision support systems
18. Material requirements planning (MRP)
19. Manufacturing resource planning (MRP II, including capacity requirements planning)
20. Activity-based accounting systems

*Infrastructure*

QLEAD

21. All major department heads within our plant accept responsibility for quality.
22. Plant management provides personal leadership for quality improvement.
23. The top priority in evaluating plant management is quality performance.
24. All major department heads within our plant work to encourage JIT production.
25. Our top management strongly encourages employee involvement in the production process.

SOFT

26. Direct contact (i.e., design reviews, informal contact in coffee lounges, ad hoc meetings, etc.)
27. Physical proximity (locating departments close together)
28. Electronic mail
29. Liaisons (matching employees in different departments)
30. Secondment (transferring employees between departments for 1 to 2 years)
31. Cross-functional project teams
32. Permanent project teams (with people from different functional areas)
33. Matrix organization (people working on a project report functionally within their department but report to a project manager for project work)

WEMP

34. Giving workers a broader range of tasks
35. Giving workers more planning responsibility
36. Giving workers more inspection/quality responsibility
37. Changing labor/management relationships
38. Improving direct labor motivation
39. Improving supervisor training
40. Improving direct labor training

*Performance*

Growth

41. Market share growth
42. Sales growth

Profit

43. Return on investment (ROI)
44. Growth in ROI
45. Return on sales (ROS)

Flexibility

46. Volume is the ease with which your plant can respond to changes in production volume.
47. Mix is the ability to produce a number of different products at the same point in time.
48. Changeover is the ability to add or remove new products from the product mix.
49. Modification is the ability to make design changes (revisions) in existing products.

**Construct Description**

In this article, "the term AMT was used . . . as an umbrella term to describe a variety of technologies which primarily utilize computers to control, track, or monitor manufacturing activities, either directly, or indirectly" (p. 332). "The term, manufacturing infrastructure, was described by Hayes and Wheelwright (1984) and Hill (1994) as including workforce and organizational policies, as well as procedural systems such as manufacturing planning and control, and quality assurance" (p. 332).

**Measurement Description**

The response to each item was captured on a 7-point Likert-type scale. The degree of investment in advanced manufacturing technologies (AMTs) was composed of 20 items, each of which was measured on a scale ranging from 1 = "no investment" to 7 = "heavy investment," with 4 indicating "moderate investment." The final scale TECH was constructed by taking the average of all the items. Infrastructure was measured by three scales: worker empowerment, quality leadership, and soft integration. The Likert scale for quality leadership (QLEAD) ranged from 1 = "strongly disagree" to 7 = "strongly agree." The Likert scale used for SOFT and work empowerment (WEMP) ranged from 1 = "no emphasis" to 4 = "moderate emphasis" and to 7 = "extreme emphasis."

Three performance constructs were used in the study. The first two performance constructs—growth and profit—consisted of five questions. Respondents were asked to rate each item on a scale ranging from 1 = "significantly lower" to 7 = "significantly higher" compared with their competitors over the past 2 years. Among the five questions, the first two questions related to market share growth and sales. The average of these two questions was used as the score for GROWTH. The next three questions were used to measure profit, and their average scores were labeled as PROFIT. The last performance construct—flexibility consisted of four items. Each item was evaluated on a Likert scale, ranging from 1 = "less than competitors" to 7 = "more than competitors;" and their average was labeled as FLEXIBILITY.

### Development

The multi-item scales were all developed from the existing literature. Specifically, the items for AMT were derived from the Boston University Manufacturing Futures project. The scale used to measure worker empowerment was based on Ward, Leong, and Boyer (1994). The scale for quality leadership was based on Flynn, Schroeder, and Sakakibara (1994). The soft integration scale was based on Twigg, Voss, and Winch (1992). Similarly, the growth items were adopted from Swamidass and Newell (1987). The measurement items for the other two performance constructs were based on Vickery, Dröge, and Markland (1993) and Gerwin (1987).

### Sample

Data were gathered from executives in U.S. plants with 50 or more employees "in standard industrial classification codes 33 to 37, the metal-working industries. The instrument was pretested and then delivered by mail to a sample of 491 manufacturing plants. The survey yielded 202 usable responses, 41.1% response rate" (p. 334). In the article, Table 1 (p. 335) presented a profile of the final companies that participated in the survey.

### Validity and Reliability

Cronbach's coefficient alpha was used to assess reliability of the scales (Table 2). It ranged between .79 and .93. Reliability was also tested by a subsample of 124 responding firms that were contacted to achieve a second response from another informant in the plant. "A total of 73 responses were obtained, for a second-rater response rate of 58.9%. Interrater reliability results are described in Table 2. In addition, two comparisons of respondents and nonrespondents on the basis of industry membership and plant size were conducted by chi-square tests, with neither test showing a significant difference" (p. 334).

### Scores

The scores are presented in Tables 1–7 in the article.

### Other Evidence

Not available.

### References

Flynn, B. B., R. G. Schroeder, and S. Sakakibara. 1994. A framework for quality management research and an associated measurement instrument. *Journal of Operations Management* 11 (4): 339–66.

Gerwin, D. 1987. An agenda for research on the flexibility of manufacturing processes. *International Journal of Operations and Production Management* 7 (1): 38–49.

Hayes, R. H., and S. C. Wheelwright. 1984. *Restoring our competitive edge: Competing through manufacturing.* New York: Wiley.

Hill, T. J. 1994. *Manufacturing strategy: Text and cases.* 2nd ed. Burr Ridge, IL: Irwin.

Swamidass, P. M., and W. T. Newell. 1987. Manufacturing strategy, environmental uncertainty and performance: A path analytic model. *Management Science* 33 (4): 509–24.

Twigg, D., C. A. Voss, and G. M. Winch. 1992. Implementing integrating technologies: Developing managerial integration for CAD/CAM. *International Journal of Operations and Production Management* 12 (7/8): 76–91.

Vickery, S. K., C. Dröge, and R. E. Markland. 1993. Production competence and business strategy: Do they affect business performance? *Decision Sciences* 24 (2): 435–55.

Ward, P., G. K. Leong, and K. K. Boyer. 1994. Manufacturing proactiveness and performance. *Decision Sciences* 25 (3): 337–58.

# Boyer and McDermott

## Article Summarized

Boyer, Kenneth K., and Christopher McDermott. 1999. Strategic consensus in operations strategy. *Journal of Operations Management* 17 (3): 289–305.

## Scales (Actual Questions Used)

*Competitive Priorities*

Cost

1. Reduce inventory
2. Increase capacity utilization
3. Reduce production costs
4. Increase labor productivity

Quality

5. Provide high-performance products
6. Offer consistent, reliable quality
7. Improve conformance to design specifications

Delivery

8. Provide fast deliveries
9. Meet delivery promises
10. Reduce production lead time

Flexibility

11. Make rapid design changes
12. Adjust capacity quickly
13. Make rapid volume changes
14. Offer a large number of product features
15. Offer a large degree of product variety
16. Adjust product mix

*Infrastructural Investments*

Worker Empowerment

17. Giving workers a broader range of tasks
18. Giving workers more planning responsibility
19. Giving workers more inspection/quality responsibility
20. Changing labor/management relationships
21. Improving direct labor motivation
22. Improving supervisor training
23. Improving direct labor training

Quality Leadership (QLEAD)

24. All major department heads within our plant accept responsibility for quality.
25. Plant management provides personal leadership for quality improvement.
26. The top priority in evaluating plant management is quality performance.

27. All major department heads within our plant work to encourage JIT production.
28. Our top management strongly encourages employee involvement in the production process.

Team

29. Our plant forms teams to solve problems.
30. In the past 3 years, many problems have been solved through team efforts.
31. During problem-solving sessions, all team members' opinions and ideas are considered before making a decision.

*Structural (Advanced Manufacturing Technology) Investments*

Design

32. Computer-aided design
33. Computer-aided engineering
34. Computer-aided process planning

Manufacturing

35. Computer-aided manufacturing
36. Robotics
37. Real-time process control systems
38. Group technology
39. Flexible manufacturing systems
40. Computerized numerical control machines
41. Automated material handling systems
42. Environmental control systems
43. Bar coding/automatic identification

Administrative

44. Electronic mail
45. Electronic data interchange
46. Office automation
47. Knowledge-based systems
48. Decision support systems
49. Material requirements planning
50. Manufacturing resource planning (including capacity requirements planning)
51. Activity-based accounting systems

**Construct Description**

In this research, strategic consensus was operationally defined as "the level of agreement within an organization regarding the relative importance of cost, quality, delivery and flexibility to the organization's operational goals, as well as the relationships between these competitive priorities and operational polices" (p. 290). This article investigated the strategic consensus regarding competitive priorities, structural decisions, and infrastructural decisions. Specifically, competitive priorities referred to four primary components that researchers agree on: cost, quality, flexibility, and delivery (Adam and Swamidass 1989; Leong, Snyder, and Ward 1990).

Infrastructural investments included three constructs: worker empowerment, quality leadership, and teamwork. Structural investments consisted of the investment on design-based AMTs, manufacturing-based AMTs, and administrative-based AMTs. Worker empowerment (WEMP) was defined as "giving workers more responsibility and control of the manufacturing process, as well as increased levels of training to build the skills needed to effectively exercise increased responsibility" (p. 295). This construct was directly related to the workforce element of infrastructure as described by Hayes and Wheelwright (1984). Quality leadership (QLEAD) captured "where the responsibility for quality lies in the firm" (p. 295). This construct is directly related to organizational aspects of infrastructure as described by Hayes and Wheelwright (1984). The use of small teams emphasized the cooperative atmosphere that teams help foster as well as the generation of new ideas and approaches that these teams help encourage. This aspect of infrastructural capability development had been investigated by other researchers in operations strategy, TQM, and JIT (Sakakibara, Flynn, and Schroeder 1993; Flynn, Schroeder, and Sakakibara 1994).

Design-based AMTs (DESIGN) focused on the design of products and processes. "Manufacturing-based AMTs (MANUFACTURING) focused on the actual manufacturing and physical transformation of the product. Administrative-based AMTs (ADMINISTRATIVE) were used primarily to track operations inputs and outputs" (p. 295).

### Measurement Description

All scales were based on 7-point Likert scales. Responses were averaged within each scale to form an aggregate score, ranging from a low of 1 to a high of 7.

### Development

The scales were adapted from prior research (Miller and Vollmann 1984; Ward, Leong, and Boyer 1994; Flynn, Schroeder, and Sakakibara 1994; Boyer, Ward, and Leong 1996). The survey instruments were developed to fit two contrasting groups of manager and operators as respondents with slight modifications in wording. The survey questions were also discussed and elaborated on during interviews. "Discrepancies between survey responses and interview discussion were noted and clarified" (p. 294). Standard reliability analyses were conducted along with comparisons of survey and case study results.

### Sample

"Seven manufacturing plants were studied via a combination of plant visits and the completion of a common survey instrument. The plants under study are manufacturing firms in standard industrial classification codes 33–37, the metalworking industries" (p. 293). Each plant was selected "based on prior experience of the authors in working with that plant" (p. 293). The survey instruments were "administered to two different groups of respondents in each plant: middle and upper level managers who had authority over operational decisions and operational level employees. The targeted size of each group was approximately 10 respondents" (p. 294).

More qualitative data were also collected through "semi-structured interviews performed on-site with either the plant manager, vice president of operations or president of each firm. Issues relating to the historical development of the firm, its main competition, main markets, structural (e.g. AMT) and infrastructural (e.g. worker training) investments were explored in these discussions" (p. 294).

### Reliability and Validity

Inter-item and interrater reliability were assessed, but not reported since all scales in this study had been employed and validated in prior research. The data analysis focused on comparisons between two different groups of respondents: (1) managers and (2) plant floor operators. Analyses of variance and rank ordering were used to assess strategic consensus.

### Scores

The mean scores for each measurement scale are presented on a company-by-company and group-by-group (managers or operators) basis in Tables 2–4 in the article.

### Other Evidence

The scales for AMT, worker empowerment, and quality leadership were also used in the study of Boyer et al. (1997).

**References**

Adam, E. E., and P. M. Swamidass. 1989. Assessing operations management from a strategic perspective. *Journal of Management* 15 (2): 181–203.

Boyer, K. K., P. T. Ward, and G. K. Leong. 1996. Approaches to the factory of the future: An empirical taxonomy. *Journal of Operations Management* 14 (4): 297–313.

Boyer, K. K., G. K. Leong, P. T. Ward, and M. L. Krajewski. 1997. Unlocking the potential of advanced manufacturing technologies. *Journal of Operations Management* 15 (4): 331–47.

Flynn, B. B., R. G. Schroeder, and S. Sakakibara. 1994. A framework for quality management research and an associated measurement instrument. *Journal of Operations Management* 11 (4): 339–66.

Hayes, R. H., and S. C. Wheelwright. 1984. *Restoring our competitive edge: Competing through manufacturing.* New York: Wiley.

Leong, G. K., D. Snyder, and P. Ward, 1990. Research in the process and content of manufacturing strategy. *Omega* 18: 109–122.

Miller, J. G., and T. E. Vollmann. 1984. *1984 North American manufacturers' survey: Summary of survey responses* (Boston University Manufacturing Roundtable Report Series). Boston, MA: Boston University Press.

Sakakibara, S., B. B. Flynn, and R. G. Schroeder. 1993. A framework and measurement instrument for just-in-time manufacturing. *Production and Operations Management* 2 (3): 177–95.

Ward, P., G. K. Leong, and K. K. Boyer. 1994. Manufacturing proactiveness and performance. *Decision Sciences* 25 (3): 337–58.

## Boyer, Ward, and Leong

**Article Summarized**

Boyer, Kenneth K., Peter T. Ward, and G. Keong Leong. 1996. Approaches to the factory of the future: An empirical taxonomy. *Journal of Operations Management* 14 (4): 297–313.

**Scales (Actual Questions Used)**

*Design*

1. Computer-aided design (CAD)
2. Computer-aided engineering (CAE)
3. Computer-aided process planning (CAPP)

*Manufacturing*

4. Computerized numerical control (CNC)
5. Computer-aided manufacturing (CAM)
6. Environmental control systems
7. Bar coding/automatic identification
8. Real-time process control systems
9. Flexible manufacturing systems (FMS)
10. Automated material handling systems
11. Group technology (GT)
12. Robotics

*Administrative*

13. Material requirements planning (MRP)
14. Office automation
15. Manufacturing resource planning (MRP II)
16. Activity-based accounting systems
17. Electronic mail
18. Electronic data interchange (EDI)
19. Decision support systems
20. Knowledge-based systems

*Integration*

21. Design and production process planning (i.e., CAD data directly linked to CAPP)
22. Design and production (i.e., CAD data directly controlling production equipment, such as CNC machines, robots, or FMS)
23. Design and resource planning (i.e., parts data from CAD linked to MRP software)
24. Process planning and shop-floor production
25. Production planning and shop-floor production (i.e., production schedules generated by MRP-controlling production equipment)
26. Between manufacturing equipment (i.e., various robots or computer-controlled machines linked by computerized material handling devices)

*Performance*

27. Sales growth
28. Return on sales
29. Earnings growth

**Construct Description**

Not available.

**Measurement Description**

The authors adapted "a set of items developed for use in the Boston University Manufacturing Futures Project (Miller and Vollman, 1984; Miller and Roth, 1994)" (p. 304). For each question, the participants were asked "to rate the degree of investment that their plant currently has in each particular AMT" (p. 304). They used a 7-point Likert scale ranging from 1 = "no investment" to 7 = "heavy investment." Similarly, the respondents are asked to answer the performance outcomes on 7-point Likert scales.

**Development**

All measurement scales were developed based on existing literature.

**Sample**

The "sample consists of companies in the metal working industries (SIC Codes 33–37). Data were collected during the first half of 1994. The unit of analysis is individual manufacturing plants with 50 or more employees. The instrument was pretested and sent by mail to a sample of individuals from 491 manufacturing plants. After discarding 8 incomplete survey forms, the survey yielded 202 usable responses, resulting in 41.1% response rate" (p. 303).

**Reliability and Validity**

The process of validating the proposed taxonomy required that the authors "assess it in the context of its nomological" (p. 301) network; e.g., other related constructs (Schwab, 1980). While reviewing the literature, the authors asserted that they began "to establish the nomological validity of the taxonomy by demonstrating a clear conceptual linkage between the taxonomy developed in their research and its antecedents in earlier research" (p. 301). "To check the reliability of the answers provided by the respondents, a random sample of 124 responding firms was contacted to obtain a second response from another informant in that plant. A total of 73 responses were received from this sample. The responses of the second raters are used solely as a check for interrater reliability, or the level of agreement between two informants within the same company" (p. 303).

### Scores

The scores are presented in Tables 2–6 in the article.

### Other Evidence

The scales in this study were used in the studies of Boyer et al. (1997) and Boyer and McDermott (1999).

### References

Boyer, K. K., G. K. Leong, P. T. Ward, and M. L. Krajewski. 1997. Unlocking the potential of advanced manufacturing technologies. *Journal of Operations Management* 15 (4): 331–47.

Boyer, Kenneth K., and Christopher McDermott. 1999. Strategic consensus in operations strategy. *Journal of Operations Management* 17 (3): 289–305.

Miller, J. G., and A. V. Roth. 1994. A taxonomy of manufacturing strategies. *Management Science* 40 (3): 285–304.

Miller, J. G., and T. E. Vollman. 1984. *North American manufacturers' survey: Summary of survey responses* (Boston University Manufacturing Roundtable Report Series). Boston, MA: Boston University.

Schwab, D. P. 1980. Construct validity in organizational behavior. *Research in Organizational Behavior* 2: 3–43.

---

## Bozarth and Edwards

### Article Summarized

Bozarth, Cecil, and Steve Edwards. 1997. The impact of market requirements focus and manufacturing characteristics focus on plant performance. *Journal of Operations Management* 15 (3): 161–80.

### Scales (Actual Questions Used)

*Market Requirements Focus*

Major Customer (Major)

1. Number of customers accounting for 80% of plant's dollar volume

Variability in Customer's Needs (Needva)

Variability in customer's needs with regard to

2. Conformance quality
3. Delivery reliability
4. Cost
5. Delivery speed
6. Design capability
7. Product range

Number of Product Lines (Lines)

8. Number of product lines

Variability in the Level of Product Customization (Varcust)

9. Variability in the level of product customization

*Manufacturing Characteristics Focus*

Strategy

10. Degree of focus reflected in plant's strategic orientation

*Manufacturing Similarity across the Product Set*

MFGSIM1

11. Degree of manufacturing similarity across the product set

MFGSIM2

12. Product demand patterns are similar across products (reverse scored)
13. Material handling procedures differ from one product to the next
14. Different scheduling rules for some products or customers

*Degree of Similarity across Focused Work Cells or PWPs*

PWPSEP1

Use the items listed below to complete the following statement:———was a key factor in our plant's decision to use work cells and/or "mini-plants"?

15. Volume differences
16. Differences in equipment needs
17. Labor skill differences
18. Differences in the physical product characteristics
19. Setup/tooling differences

PWPSEP2

In your plant, dedicated work cells or "mini-plants" are characterized by

20. Dedicated workforces
21. Separate training systems
22. Separate planning and control systems
23. Separate performance measurement systems
24. Separate quality control systems
25. Dedicated customer support personnel
26. Dedicated purchasing personnel
27. Separate inventory systems
28. Separate distribution systems

*Manufacturing Performance (WPERFORM)*

29. Cost
30. Conformance quality
31. Delivery speed

32. Delivery reliability
33. Product range
34. Design capability

**Construct Description**

Manufacturing characteristics addressed both physical product requirements and customers' performance criteria. Manufacturing characteristics focus was defined as "the degree of internal consistency found in the physical processes and infrastructural elements that define the manufacturing organization" (p. 162). Market requirements focus referred to a consistent and limited set of market demands faced by the plants.

**Measurement Description**

The measures of market requirements focus included two customer-based and three product-based variables. These variables were measured using objective questions. To define manufacturing characteristics focus, the authors used five variables. The first variable, *STRATEGY,* captured "the degree of focus reflected in the plant's strategic orientation" (p. 168). Two variables, *MFGSIM1* and *MFGSIM2,* measured the degree of manufacturing similarity across the product set. The last two variables, *PWPSEP1* and *PWPSEP2,* connoted the degree of similarity across focused work cells or PWPs. Three out of the five constructs were gauged using multi-item perceptual scales. *MFGSIM2* was measured using three items. Responses to each item were evaluated on 7-point Likert scales ranging from "strongly agree" to "strongly disagree." The value of MFGSIM2 was calculated by summing scores across these three items. *PWPSEP1* focused on measuring the degree of similarity in volumes, equipment, labor skills, product characteristics, and setups across focused work cells/PWPs using a set of five questions. *PWPSEP2* addressed the degree of organizational sharing across work cells/PWPs, using a set of nine questions. These 14 questions (five for *PWPSEP1* and nine for *PWPSEP2*) were all on a 7-point Likert scale. Like MFGSIM2, the values for PWPSEP1 and PWPSEP2 were computed by summing scores across corresponding items.

Manufacturing performance was calculated as the weighted average of performance on six competitive priorities: cost, conformance quality, delivery speed, delivery reliability, product range, and design capability. Performance on each priority was ranked on a scale from 1 to 5, with 1 indicating that performance was "nearly always worse" than the plant's major competitors, and 5 indicating that performance was "nearly always better." The priority weight represented the importance of each performance dimension, which was ranked on a 5-point scale with 1 indicating "totally unimportant" and 5 indicating "more important" than any other criteria.

**Development**

Not available.

**Sample**

The data collection targeted North Carolina plants serving as original equipment (OE) and aftermarket suppliers to the automotive industry. The sampling frame consisted of 52 automotive-related manufacturers selected the North Carolina Manufacturers Directory. In the study, 28 plants agreed to participate. A comparison of average plant age and size between these participating plants and a sample of 1,632 plants of the first-tier, U.S. automotive supplier plants indicated that the study plants tended to be younger and smaller.

**Reliability and Validity**

To assess internal consistency, the authors evaluated Cronbach's coefficient alpha values for all three multi-item constructs. The alpha values were .66 for MFGSIM2, .71 for PWPSEP1, and .72 for PWPSEP2, indicating acceptable levels of inter-item correlations for each scale.

### Scores

The scores are presented in Tables 2–9 of the article.

### Other Evidence

Not available.

### Reference

None.

---

## Brady and Cronin

### Article Summarized

Brady, Michael K., and J. Joseph Cronin, Jr. 2001. Customer orientation: Effects on customer service perceptions and outcome behaviors. *Journal of Service Research* 3 (3): 241–51.

### Scales (Actual Questions Used)

The list of actual questions was not provided in the article. The following was the related information collected from the article:

*Customer Orientation*

Customer orientation is quantified using 12 items from the sales orientation/customer orientation scale listed in Saxe and Weitz (1982).

*Physical Goods Quality*

"Items were similar to Oliver (1997), with the exception that the respondents were specifically directed to assess the quality of the physical products received during the transaction" (p. 246).

*Servicescape Quality*

The scale required the respondents to rate 26 aspects of the physical environment in accordance with the servicescape dimensions, as suggested by Bitner (1992).

*Performance Service Quality*

"A five item scale assessed the degree to which the service received was reliable, trustworthy, delivered in a timely manner, whether the employees were dressed properly, and whether they made an effort to understand the customers needs" (p. 246).

*Overall Service Quality*

In the three items scale, respondents were asked to describe the quality of service, with attributes ranging from inferior to superior, low quality to high quality, and low standards or high standards.

*Customer Satisfaction*

Respondents were asked using a three-item, unipolar adjective scale "to report the degree to which they were happy, pleased and delighted" (p. 247).

*Value*

"Value of the service product received, value of what was received to what was paid and whether the overall service experience delivered" (p. 247) was good.

*Behavioral Outcomes*

"Respondents were asked to assess

1. The probability that they would use the service again
2. Whether they would recommend the service to a friend
3. The likelihood that they would say good things to others
4. Their loyalty to the service firm" (p. 247)

**Construct Description**

Not available.

**Measurement Description**

All items contained in the two new measurement scales—value and physical goods and quality—were captured on a 9-point Likert-type and semantic differential scales. The measurement descriptions of other constructs were summarized in the scales section.

**Development**

Whenever possible, existing scales were used or adapted for use in this research. The exceptions were measures for value and physical goods quality constructs, which were newly developed in this study. The development process follows the guidance from Churchill (1979).

**Sample**

The data collection focused on three specific service industries, which represented a wide array of service experience. Two service providers per industry were included in the data collection process. Of the surveys within each industry, roughly half were collected at a transaction specific level, whereas the other half were based on cumulative responses. A sample of 649 consumers was recruited by trained student assistants. "Responses were collected in multiple locations in a medium sized metropolitan area" (p. 245). To be included in the sample, potential respondents needed at least one experience with the service provider in the past 6 months. The authors noted that the respondents in this study were generally better educated and younger than the average population.

**Reliability and Validity**

According to the authors, "Validity was tested using the procedure of Fornell/Lackner. Convergent validity was assessed by verifying the significance of the *t*-values associated with the parameter estimates. All *t*-values were positive and significant. Discriminant validity was tested by comparing the average variance extracted by each construct to the shared variance between the construct and all other variables. For each comparison, the explained variance exceeded all combinations of shared variances" (p. 247). In addition, the Cronbach's coefficient alpha values for each construct were estimated to assess construct reliability. All constructs demonstrated an acceptable level of internal consistency. The alpha values ranged from .76 for the value construct to .95 for customer satisfaction.

**Scores**

Not available.

**Other Evidence**

Not available.

### References

Bitner, M. J. 1992. Servicescapes: The impact of physical surroundings on customers and employees. *Journal of Marketing* 56 (2): 57–71.
Churchill, G. A. 1979. A paradigm for developing better measures of marketing constructs. *Journal of Marketing Research* 16 (February): 64–73.
Oliver, R. L. 1997. *Satisfaction: A behavioral perspective on the consumer.* New York: McGraw-Hill.
Saxe, R., and B. A. Weitz. 1982. The SOCO scale: A measure of the customer orientation of salespeople. *Journal of Marketing Research* 19 (3): 343–51.

## Brockman and Morgan

### Article Summarized

Brockman, Beverly K. and Robert M. Morgan. 2003. The role of existing knowledge in new product innovativeness and performance. *Decision Sciences* 34 (2): 385–419.

### Scales (Actual Questions Used)

*Entrepreneurship*

1. In general, the managers of my organization favor a strong emphasis on the marketing of tried and true products or services, a strong emphasis on R&D, technological leadership, and innovations.
2. In my organization over the past five years no new lines of products or services have been marketed/very many new lines of products or services have been marketed.
3. In my organization over the past five years changes in product or service lines have been mostly of a minor nature/changes in product or service lines have usually been quite dramatic.
4. In dealing with its competitors, my organization typically responds to actions which competitors initiate/typically initiates actions to which competitors then respond.
5. In dealing with its competitors, my organization is very seldom the first business to introduce new products/services, administrative techniques, operating technologies, etc./is very often the first business to introduce new products/services, administrative techniques, operating technologies, etc.
6. In general, the managers of my organization have a strong proclivity for low-risk projects (with normal and certain rates of return)/have a strong proclivity for high-risk projects (with chances of very high return).
7. In general, the managers of my organization believe that owing to the nature of the environment, it is best to explore gradually via cautious, incremental behavior/owing to the nature of the environment, bold, wide-ranging acts are necessary to achieve the firm's objectives.
8. When confronted with decision-making situations involving uncertainty, my organization typically adopts a cautious, "wait and see" posture to minimize the probability of making costly decisions/typically adopts a bold, aggressive posture to maximize the probability of exploiting potential opportunities.

*Cohesiveness*

In general, the management philosophy in my organization emphasizes

9. United employee effort in trying to reach the goals for the organization
10. That employees work together as a team
11. That all employees take responsibility for poor business performance

12. That all employees share similar aspirations for the unit's performance
13. That everyone pitches in and helps if a few members of the unit have difficulty solving a work problem

*Knowledge*

Prior to the project, compared with firms in our industry, my organization had

14. A great deal of knowledge about this product category
15. A great deal of information about this product category
16. A strong understanding of this product category
17. A great deal of insight regarding this product category

*Innovative Information*

Compared with information gathered during other product development projects, the information acquired for this project was

18. Typical/innovative,
19. "Old Hat"/original,
20. Old/new,
21. Common/fresh,
22. Dull/creative,
23. Ordinary/unique, and
24. Unimaginative/inventive.

*Information Acquisition Efficiency*

Please rate the extent to which the project members' process of acquiring information for the new product reflects the following statements.

25. "Proficient" is a good description for the process of information acquisition engaged in during the development of the product.
26. The development team for this product was efficient in acquiring useful information.
27. We displayed a high level of competence in acquiring the information needed to develop the product.
28. The process of information acquisition engaged in during the development of the product was productive.

*Shared Interpretation*

Please rate the extent to which people working on the project were in agreement regarding the meaning of the acquired information for development of the new product.

29. Everyone working on the project shared a similar understanding of the role the acquired information would play in developing the new product.
30. There was general agreement among project members regarding how acquired information would be used for the new product's development.
31. Everyone had the same intent for how the acquired information would be used in developing the new product.
32. Project members shared a high degree of consensus with regard to the importance of the acquired information for developing the new product.

*New Product Innovativeness*

Please rate the extent to which the product has achieved the following outcomes during the first 12 months of its life in the marketplace.

33. Did not challenge existing ideas for this category/challenged existing ideas for this category
34. Did not offer new ideas to the category/offered new ideas to the category
35. Not creative/creative

*New Product Performance*

Please rate the extent to which the product has achieved the following outcomes during the first 12 months of its life in the marketplace.

36. Profit margin relative to objective
37. Return on assets relative to objective
38. ROI relative to objective

*Organization Structure*

In general, the management philosophy in my organization favors

39. Highly structured channels of communication/open channels of communication
40. Highly restricted access to important financial and operating information/important financial and operating information flowing quite freely throughout the business unit
41. A strong insistence on a uniform managerial style throughout the organization/managers' operating styles allowed to range freely from the very formal to the very informal
42. A strong emphasis on giving the most say in decision making to formal line managers/a strong tendency to let the expert in a given situation have the most say in decision making even if this means temporary bypassing of formal line authority
43. A strong emphasis on holding fast to tried and true management principles despite any changes in business conditions/a strong emphasis on adapting freely to changing circumstances without too much concern for past practice
44. A strong emphasis on always getting personnel to follow formal procedures/a strong emphasis on getting things done even if it means disregarding formal procedures
45. Tight formal control of most operations by means of sophisticated control and information systems (IS)/loose, informal control; heavy dependence on informal relationships and norms of cooperation for getting work done
46. A strong emphasis on getting line and staff personnel to adhere closely to formal job descriptions/a strong tendency to let the requirements of the situation and the individual's personality define proper on-job behavior.

## Construct Description

The construct definitions were taken from the article as follows: Entrepreneurship was characterized as "the degree to which an organization favors risk taking, proactiveness, and innovativeness" (p. 393). Existing knowledge was defined as "the amount of stored information an organization has about a particular phenomenon" (p. 387). Cohesiveness was described as "the tendency for the group to stick together and remain united in the pursuit of its goals and objectives" (p. 393). Innovative information was given as "the degree to which information is fresh or original and stimulates the insight for development of a new product" (p. 389). Information acquisition efficiency was defined as "the ability to acquire useful information for product development with a minimum expenditure of time, energy, and resources" (p. 391). Shared interpretation of acquired information connoted "the degree of consensus among project members on the meaning of acquired information in terms of its implications for development of the product" (p. 391). New product performance was captured by "the products level of profitability in the first 12 months of its life in the market place" (p. 388); new product innovativeness, by "the degree to which the product is novel and has generative capacity" and generative capacity, "the potential to change thinking and practice" (p. 388). Finally, organization structure, based on Khandwalla (1977), referred to an organization as "a network of durable and formally sanctioned organizational arrangements and relationships" (p. 482).

## Measurement Description

Among the nine constructs studied in the article, three constructs—entrepreneurship, cohesiveness, and organization structure—are measured using formative indicator variables. All other constructs employ reflective indicators (*see* Bollen 1989). Responses to each indicator were captured either on 7-point semantic differential scales or on 7-point Likert scales.

### Development

For six out of the nine constructs, items were taken or adapted from the existing scales. The entrepreneurship measures came from Covin and Selvin (1986, 1988). The existing organizational knowledge measure was an adapted version of the scale from Moorman and Miner (1997). The cohesiveness measures were based on Widmeyer, Brawley, and Carron (1985). The organization structure measure was obtained from Khandwalla (1977). The new product creativity and short-term new product performance measures were adapted from Moorman and Miner (1997).

New measurement scales were developed for three constructs—innovative information, information acquisition efficiency, and shared interpretation. Each was based on conceptual definitions from existing literature on the related constructs. Scales were purified after the measurement model was evaluated. Four items were dropped because of weak performance.

### Sample

The sample for the study consisted of firms that were involved in new product development (NPD) and earned a minimum of $100 million in sales revenue. The firms were selected based on 38 product classifications. A total of 1,820 firms were initially asked to participate; and of these 323 surveys were returned, yielding a response rate of 28%.

### Reliability and Validity

The composite construct reliability scores were reported by the authors for the constructs given above. Composite reliability scores of at least .60 and average variances extracted scores of at least .50 were used as the threshold values in the study (Bagozzi and Yi 1988). The authors also conducted validity tests for discriminant convergent and nomological validity, following the two-step approach recommended by Anderson and Gerbing (1988). First, both exploratory factor analysis and confirmatory factor analysis were used to test for convergent and discriminant validity. "Convergent validity was supported in each of the constructs, with the lowest parameter estimate being $\lambda = .69$ ($t = 13.58$, $p < .001$) for items 4 of the information acquisition efficiency measure. Discriminant validity was assessed by comparing the variance-extracted estimate to the square of the phi matrix. In each case, the variance-extracted estimate was greater than .50, with the smallest being .61 for information acquisition efficiency . . . and exceeded the square of the phi matrix" (p. 399). At the second stage, the authors estimate the structural model to assess nomologic validity.

### Scores

The intercorrelations are given in Table 1 of the article. The results of the structural model are in Figure 3 and those of the measurement model are in Table 2.

### Other Evidence

Not available.

### References

Anderson, J. C., and D. W. Gerbing. 1988. Structural equation modeling in practice: A review and recommended two-step approach. *Psychological Bulletin* 103 (3): 411–23.

Bagozzi, R. P., and Y. Yi. 1988. On the evaluation of structural equation models. *Journal of the Academy of Marketing Science* 16 (1): 74–94.

Bollen, K. A. 1989. *Structural equations with latent variables.* New York: Wiley.

Covin, J. G., and D. P. Slevin. 1986. The development and testing of an organizational-level entrepreneurship scale. In *Frontiers of entrepreneurship research,* eds. R. Ronstadt, J. Hornaday, R. Peterson, and K. Vesper, 628–39. Wellesley, MA: Babson College Center for Entrepreneurship Research.

———. 1988. The influence of organization structure on the utility of an entrepreneurial top management style. *Journal of Management Studies* 25 (3): 217–34.

Khandwalla, P. N. 1977. *The design of organizations.* New York: Harcourt, Brace, Jovanovich.

Miller, D. 1983. The correlates of entrepreneurship in three types of firms. *Management Science* 29 (**7**): 770–91.

Moorman, C., and A. S. Miner. 1997. The impact of organizational memory on new product performance and creativity. *Journal of Marketing Research* 34 (1): 91–106.

Widmeyer, W. N., L. R. Brawley, and A. V. Carron. 1985. *The measurement of cohesion in sport teams: The group environment questionnaire.* London, Ontario, Canada: Sports Dynamics.

# Brown

### Article Summarized

Brown, Steve. 1998. Manufacturing seniority, strategy and innovation. *Technovation* 18 (3): 149–62.

### Scales (Actual Questions Used)

*Identifying Traditional and Enlightened Plants*

1. How often is the business plan reviewed? (months: 12 and 18)
2. Level of seniority of management (M = manager, D = director)
3. Manufacturing involvement in business strategy (N = none, R = reactive, P = passive, A = active, and L = leader)
4. Is there a manufacturing strategy? (Yes and No)
5. Time period in manufacturing strategy
6. How often is the manufacturing strategy reviewed? (Months: 6, 12, and N/A.)
7. Common links between manufacturing and business strategies

*New Product Development*

8. What is the percentage of present turnover from product development within the past 5 years?
9. In 5 years' time, what percentage of turnover is envisaged from products not yet launched?
10. What is the percentage of present turnover from new products developed within past 2 years?
11. In 2 years' time, what percentage of turnover is envisaged from products not yet launched?
12. Average speed of NPD (months)
13. Manufacturing involvement (C = concept, D = design, B = business evaluation, P = production)

### Construct Description

This study investigated three key factors that may explain in part the differences in speed and success of new product development (NPD). Antecedent factors were "(1) the seniority of manufacturing personnel within the firms, (2) the involvement of these senior managers in the business, and (3) the contribution of a manufacturing strategy which feeds into, and forms part of, the overall business plan within the plant" (p. 149). Based on diverse characteristics of the plants, the author argued that they could be divided into those that were more traditional plants and those that could be called "enlightened." And, these differences were posited to determine the business performance.

### Measurement Description

Several key enablers were associated with the identification of enlightened versus traditional plants. They are (1) the seniority and role of manufacturing personnel within the plant, (2) whether a manufacturing strategy existed within the plant, (3) the common links between business and manufacturing strategies, and (4) the time synchronization between business and manufacturing strategies. Most constructs were measured by objective data. However, the study did not provide detailed information on measurement description.

### Development

Not available.

### Sample

"The analysis for this research was gained, essentially, from case study material derived from interviews with 29 divisions/plants of firms within the automobile, telecommunications, and computing industries between 1992 and 1996. The three industries were chosen for the following reasons: (1) interest to the author, (2) dynamic exciting industries (the nature of the chosen industries), and (3) all three industries tend to share the same manufacturing process choice—largely based around line processes, with flexible manufacturing, group technology, and other hybrid systems" (p. 154).

### Reliability and Validity

Not available.

### Scores

Table 3 in the article showed the data in identifying traditional and enlightened plants. Table 4 contained descriptive statistics on NPD.

### Other Evidence

Not available.

### Reference

None.

---

## Byrd and Turner

### Article Summarized

Byrd, Terry A., and Douglas E. Turner. 2001. An exploratory analysis of the value of skills of IT personnel: Their relationship to IS infrastructure and competitive advantage. *Decision Sciences* 32 (1): 21–54.

### Scales (Actual Questions Used)

*Information Technology (IT) Personnel Skills*

Technology Management

1. Our IT personnel are knowledgeable about the key success factors that must go right if our organization is to succeed.
2. Our IT personnel are encouraged to learn new technologies.
3. Our IT personnel closely follow the trends in current technologies.
4. Investments in IT are best described as long-term and consistent.

5. Our organizations often use IT as component for an information-based innovation.
6. The strategies of the IT group and our organization's strategies are well aligned.

Business Skills

7. Our IT personnel understand our organization's policies and plans.
8. Our IT personnel are encouraged to learn about business functions.
9. Our IT personnel are able to interpret business problems and develop appropriate technical solutions.
10. Our IT personnel are knowledgeable about business functions.
11. Out IT personnel are knowledgeable about the environmental constraints within which the organization operates (e.g., government regulation, competition).
12. Our IT personnel are free to assist end users as they deem necessary.
13. Out IT personnel are knowledgeable about our organization's product delivery/logistics system methodology (e.g., KANBAN, JIT, continuous operation).
14. Problem resolution between IT and business units is identified as a specific job task in our organization.

Interpersonal Skills

15. Our IT personnel are very capable in teaching others.
16. Our IT personnel have the ability to plan, organize, and lead projects.
17. Our IT personnel have the ability to plan and execute work in a collective environment.
18. Our IT personnel have the ability to accomplish multiple assignments.
19. Our IT personnel work well in cross-functional teams addressing business problems.
20. Our IT personnel have the ability to work cooperatively in a project team environment.
21. Our IT personnel have the ability to work closely with clients and customers.
22. Our IT personnel have the ability to write clear, concise, and effective memos, reports, and documentation.
23. Our IT personnel are cross-trained to support other IT services outside their primary knowledge domain (e.g., programmers trained to support telecommunications).

Technical Skills

24. Our IT personnel are skilled in multiple programming languages.
25. Our IT personnel are skilled in multiple structured programming, CASE methods or tools.
26. Our IT personnel are skilled in multiple mainframe computer operating systems.
27. Our IT personnel are skilled in multiple microcomputer operating systems.
28. Our IT personnel are skilled in expert systems or artificial intelligence.
29. Our IT personnel are skilled in decision support systems.
30. Our IT personnel are competent in managing the development of life cycle of projects.
31. Our IT personnel are skilled in distributed processing or distributed computing.
32. Our IT personnel are skilled in network management and maintenance.
33. Our IT personnel are skilled in developing Web-based applications.
34. Out IT personnel are skilled in warehousing, mining, or marts.

*Flexible Information Systems (IS) Infrastructure*

IS Connectivity

35. Compared with rivals within our industry, our organization has the foremost in available IT systems and connections (e.g., ADSL, VDSL, ATM, SDV).
36. Our organization has formally addressed the issue of data security with access to a number of protocols (e.g., Kerberos V.5, MIME, PGP, S-HTTP).
37. All remote, branch, and mobile offices are connected to the central office.
38. Out organization uses open systems network mechanisms to boost connectivity.
39. There are very few identifiable communications bottlenecks within our organization.
40. Our organization uses a virtual network or virtual local network (VLAN) to connect to end users.

Applications Functionality

41. Reusable software modules are widely used in new systems development.
42. End users use object-oriented tools to create their own applications.
43. IT personnel use object-oriented technologies to minimize the development time for new applications.
44. Legacy systems within our organization restrict the development of new applications.

IS Compatibility

45. Remote, branch, and mobile offices do not have to perform any additional steps or procedures to access data from home or central office.
46. End users throughout the organization use a common operating system (e.g., UNIX, OS/2).
47. Software applications can be easily transported and used across multiple platforms.
48. Our organization offers a wide variety of types of information to end users (e.g., multimedia).
49. Our users' interfaces provide transparent access to all platforms and applications.
50. Our organization provides multiple interfaces or entry points (e.g., Web access) for external end users.

Data Transparency

51. Our corporate database is able to communicate through many different protocols (e.g., SQL, ODBC).
52. Mobile users have ready access to the same data used at desktops.
53. Our organization easily adapts to various vendors' database management systems protocols and standards.
54. Data captured in one part of our organization are immediately available to everyone in the organization.

*CAPIS (Competitive Advantage Provided by IS)*

Support Activity Efficiency

55. In our organization, IT applications assist in reducing the cost of recruiting, hiring, and training organizational personnel.
56. In our organization, IT reduces the cost of general management activities (e.g., planning, accounting, finance).
57. In our organization, IT reduces the cost of coordinating activities (e.g., purchasing, marketing, sales).

Primary Activity Efficiency

58. In our organization, IT reduces the cost of transforming material inputs into customer deliverable outputs (e.g., manufacturing technologies).
59. In our organization, IT reduces the cost of receiving and warehousing product inputs (e.g., material handling).
60. In our organization, IT reduces the cost of collecting, storing, and distributing products (e.g., order processing, scheduling).
61. In our organization, IT reduces the cost of providing service to maintain or enhance the value of the product.

Resource Management Functionality

62. In our organization, IT assists the activity of monitoring the use of resources (e.g., tracking, power utilization).
63. In our organization, IT assists the activity of upgrading a resource (e.g., adding an additional production).
64. In our organization, IT assists the activity of transferring or disposing of a resource.

Threat

65. IT assists our organization's ability to threaten suppliers and customers with vertical integration (e.g., assimilate external functions).
66. IT assists in our organization's ability to evaluate and select the most appropriate supplier.

67. IT assists in our organization's ability to evaluate and choose the most appropriate customers.
68. Our customers would incur significant cost increases if they were to change to alternate suppliers.

### Construct Description

IS infrastructure flexibility was described by two dimensions, integration, and modularity. Integration consists of two concepts, connectivity, and compatibility. "Connectivity is the ability of a component of the IS infrastructure to link to any other component inside or outside the organizational environment" (p. 25). The compatibility is identified as "the ability of the IS infrastructure to share any type of information across any technology component" (p. 25). Modularity was defined as "the ability of the IS infrastructure to add, modify and remove any software or data components with ease and with no major overall effect" (p. 25).

### Measurement Description

Multiple items were tapped into each construct. Each item was captured on a 5-point Likert scale.

### Development

Four dimensions were first identified. "Using these dimensions, a content analysis of the literature was employed resulting in an initial pool of items that were used in the development of the initial instrument" (p. 32). The original questionnaire was then pretested with eight IT managers, four in higher education and four in the private sector. A few items were omitted as a result of this pretest. "The resulting questionnaire was then pilot tested by IT personnel in three different types of firms: a textile manufacturer, a mass retailer, and a financial institution" (p. 32). Again, after the pilot some additional items were weeded out.

### Sample

A questionnaire was sent to a sample of 1,000 of the *Fortune* Magazine's top 2,000 companies. Addressees were the top computer executives of those companies. A total of 207 executives responded.

### Reliability and Validity

Convergent validity was assessed through a factor analysis. Items with factor loadings above .30 were retained in the study. Following Bagozzi, Yi, and Phillip (1991) and Venkatraman (1989), discriminant validity was evaluated by performing statistical comparisons between two nested models—one with no constraints on correlation between the two factors included in the model, and the other with a correlation of 1. The comparison was conducted for each of the factor pairs. The results found statistically significant differences in each comparison, which provided evidence supporting discriminant validity.

The authors also asserted that, according to Nunnally (1978), construct reliability was acceptable since they were all at or above 0.50.

### Scores

The scores are given in Tables 5 and 6 of the article.

### Other Evidence

Not available.

### References

Bagozzi, R. P., Y. Yi, and L. W. Phillips. 1991. Assessing construct validity in organizational research. *Administrative Science Quarterly* 36 (3): 421–58.

Nunnally, J. C. 1978. *Psychometric theory.* New York: McGraw-Hill.

Venkatraman, N. 1989. Strategic orientation of business enterprise: The construct, dimensionality, and measurement. *Management Science* 35 (8): 942–62.

# Calantone, Dröge, and Vickery

### Article Summarized

Calantone, Roger, Cornelia Dröge, and Shawnee Vickery. 2002. Investigating the manufacturing-marketing interface in new product development: Does context affect the strength of relationships. *Journal of Operations Management* 20 (3): 273–87.

### Scales (Actual Questions Used)

*Uncertainty*

1. The rate at which products/services are getting obsolete is very slow (e.g., base metal such as copper)/the rate of obsolescence is very high as in some fashion goods.
2. Actions of competitors are quite easy to predict (as in some primary industries)/actions of competitors are unpredictable.
3. Demand and consumer tastes are fairly easy to predict (e.g., for milk companies)/demand and consumer tastes are almost unpredictable (e.g., high fashion goods).

*New Product Introduction Rate*

4. The rate, relative to competitors, of new product/service introduction by the firm.

*Marketing Knowledge of Manufacturing*

5. Marketing understands manufacturing process.
6. Marketing knows manufacturing limits and capabilities.

*Marketing-Manufacturing Relationship Quality*

7. Marketing appreciates manufacturing managers' efforts.
8. Marketing is friendly and social with manufacturing.
9. Marketing cares about manufacturing managers.

*Manufacturing Evaluation of Marketing Communication*

10. Overall, we receive superior intelligence on competitors.
11. Overall, we receive superior marketing information on customers.
12. Overall, we receive marketing information useful to our needs.

*Marketing-Manufacturing Integration*

13. There is mutual understanding of marketing and manufacturing of the technical knowledge aspects regarding new project policies.
14. In NPD, there is (little = 1; total = 7) cooperation between marketing and manufacturing.

### Construct Description

In this study, six constructs were used. Of these, uncertainty and NPD introduction rate were employed as constructs for contingency analysis. Although there was no formal definition provided for these constructs, both of them were rooted in the literature. Environmental uncertainty construct was based on the works of Miles and Snow (1978) and Lawrence and Lorsch (1967). New product development (NPD) introduction rate construct was "designed to capture the internal environment of the firm in terms of the pressures exerted by a continual 'need for speed' manifested in attempts to accelerate the rate of new product introductions relative to the competition" (p. 279).

Marketing-manufacturing integration captured "the extent of cooperation in NPD and the degree of shared understanding of the technical knowledge domain of NPD policies enjoyed by two functions" (p. 276). Marketing-manufacturing relationship quality gauged "the strength of the relationship between marketing and manufacturing with respect to interpersonal relations" (p. 276).

Manufacturing's evaluation of marketing communication was defined as "manufacturing's evaluation of the value, usefulness or more generally, quality of information received from marketing (information about competitors and customers, for example)" (p. 277). Marketing's knowledge of manufacturing was stated as "marketing's understanding of the manufacturing process, its limitations and capabilities (as perceived by manufacturing)" (p. 277).

### Measurement Description

Most of the items were measured on 5-point Likert scales, except the contingency constructs. Both uncertainty and NPD introduction rate are measured on bipolar scales.

### Development

Not available.

### Sample

The data collection was administered by a large marketing research company and its internal lists were used to locate potential respondents. The sampling frame consisted of "500 senior manufacturing engineers and plant managers in the automotive industry (primarily associated with first and second tier suppliers) . . . Of 500 original inquiries, 226 useable responses were obtained, yielding a response rate of approximately 45%" (p. 279).

### Reliability and Validity

The validity and reliability of the scales were evaluated by Cronbach's coefficient alpha and confirmatory factor analysis (CFA). The authors reported the results of these analyses in Tables 1 and 2 of the article.

### Scores

The scores for the structural models are presented in Figure 2 (p. 282) in the article.

### Other Evidence

Not available.

### References

Lawrence, P. R., and J. W. Lorsch. 1967. *Organization and environment: Managing differentiation and integration.* Boston, MA: Harvard Business School Press.

Miles, R. E., and C. C. Snow. 1978. *Organizational strategy, structure and process.* New York: McGraw-Hill.

## Cao and Dowlatshahi

### Article Summarized

Cao, Qing, and Shad Dowlatshahi. 2005. The impact of alignment between virtual enterprise and information technology on business performance in an agile manufacturing environment. *Journal of Operations Management* 23 (5): 531–50.

**Scales (Actual Questions Used)**

*Virtual Enterprise*

Circle the number to indicate the degree to which the following are a current immediate concern to your business unit (1 = low, 5 = high).

1. Sharing of infrastructures, R&D, and financial resource
2. Linking complementary core competencies
3. Reducing concept-to-cash time through information sharing
4. Expending production capabilities
5. Gaining access to markets and sharing markets or customer loyalty
6. Focusing on solutions rather than selling products

*Information Technology*

Circle the number to indicate the degree of emphasis that your business unit places on the following activities (1 = less important, 5 = very important).

7. EDI in conducting the business unit operations
8. Groupware in conducting the business unit operations
9. Intranets in conducting the business unit operations
10. Extranets in conducting the business unit operations
11. Enterprise resource planning (ERP) in conducting the business unit operations

*Business Performance*

Circle the number to indicate your business unit achievement (perceived) on the following dimensions (1 = low, 5 = high).

Market Growth

12. Market share gain
13. Sales growth
14. Revenue growth

Financial Performance

15. Return on investment
16. Return on sales
17. Liquidity
18. Cash flow
19. Profitability

Product/Service Innovation

20. Development in business operations
21. Development in products and services

Company Reputation

22. Reputation among major customer segments

Agile Manufacturing Criteria

23. Marketplace nature (1 = least turbulent, 10 = most turbulent)
24. Competitor's circumstances (1 = least turbulent, 10 = most turbulent)
25. Technology changing situation (1 = least turbulent, 10 = most turbulent)
26. Criticality of relation with suppliers (1 = least turbulent, 10 = most turbulent)

27. Customer requirements change level and rate (1 = least turbulent, 10 = most turbulent)
28. Social/structural changes (1 = least turbulent, 10 = most turbulent)
29. Products/processes complexity (1 = least turbulent, 10 = most turbulent)

### Construct Description

Virtual enterprise (VE) was conceptualized as one of the enablers of agile manufacturing (AM) that facilitates manufacturers' ability to deliver rapidly the products (Cho et al. 1996; Sharp et al. 1999). VE was "described as a network of organizations or firms from which temporary alignments are formed. These alignments combine the specific core capabilities of its members in order to rapidly exploit manufacturing opportunities associated with a specific product or service" (p. 534).

IT was "regarded as a major enabler and facilitator of the AM (Sharp, Irani, and Desai 1999; Coronado, Sarhadi, and Millar 2002)" (p. 532). "Frayret et al. (2001) described a framework for designing and operating AM through a distributed network of interdependent and responsible manufacturing centers" (p. 534). Similarly, IT applications also maintain the needed communication between "VE environments." The article suggested that powered managerial control, team setup of workers, and empowerment enabled higher agility. The authors also noted that five of the most commonly referenced information technologies supporting VE and AM were electronic data interchange (EDI), Groupware, Intranets, Extranets, and ERP (Strader and Shaw 1997; Khalil and Wang 2002). These five technologies were posited as the dimensions of IT construct in their study.

The authors described the business performance construct as complex and multifaceted (Chan et al. 1997). They referred to the business strategy literature, where multiple measures were typically used when attempting to evaluate business performance (Venkatraman and Ramanujam 1987; Chan et al. 1997; Chan, Huff, and Copeland 1997; Sabherwal and Chan 2001). Also noted were the shortcomings in operations strategy research where only one dimensional measure—typically profitability—was used (Badri, Davis, and Davis 2000; Ward and Duray 2000).

### Measurement Description

Five-point Likert-type scales were used to measure the items.

### Development

This study used a two-part research design. In the first part, the authors analyzed and reviewed the previous and current literature, developing the framework in Section 3. They conducted interviews with key employees of several AM companies. Based on their findings, the authors constructed a questionnaire, which had items covering the key constructs. Then they conducted a pilot study with the managers of several manufacturing companies in the Midwest region of the United States. "Managers were asked to examine the degree to which the preliminary questionnaire captured the measured constructs and how easy or difficult the preliminary questionnaire was to complete" (p. 537). In the second part, after revising the questionnaire based on the results of the pilot study, the authors gathered more data from 500 manufacturing companies.

### Sample

The authors distributed a total of 500 questionnaires in one mailing, from which 114 responses were received (22.8% response rate). Out of 114 responses, 102 were usable resulting in an actual response rate of 20.4%. Accordingly, this response rate is "not unusual when the unit of analysis is the firm level and the questionnaire involves extensive organizational level questions (Griffin, 1997)" (p. 537).

### Reliability and Validity

According to the authors, each scale item in this research met the requirements of normality, scale reliability, and instrument validity tests. To evaluate scale reliability, the authors followed suggestions from Vickery and Dröge (1993) to calculate Cronbach's coefficient alpha for each construct and dimension.

The resulting Cronbach's alpha scores were above .70, which is "generally considered as adequate for assessing reliability in empirical research" (Kline 1998, 81).

The authors also calculated skewness values for all the 47 scale items. All values were below 1.50; and in turn, met the requirement for the normality test of skewness. They also determined that none of the scale items had an absolute value of kurtosis greater than 2.2, which meets normality test values for kurtosis. The authors, therefore, assumed that all the 47 scale items are normally distributed and proceeded to complete an analysis using structural equation modeling. The results of this analysis using a $\chi^2$ difference test are given in Table B.5 of the article. Pairwise comparisons were performed for each of the three sets and the $\chi^2$ difference between the unconstrained model and the constrained model was statistically significant ($p = .01$). The authors concluded that all three constructs were "related" but that they "conceptually presented distinct traits."

### Scores

The scores are presented in Tables 4–7 in the article.

### Other Evidence

Not available.

### References


Badri, M. A., D. Davis, and D. Davis. 2000. Operations strategy, environment uncertainty and performance: A path analytic model of industries in developing countries. *Omega* 28 (2): 155–73.

Chan, Y. E., S. L. Huff, D. W. Barclay, and D. G. Copeland. 1997. Business strategic orientation, information systems strategic orientation, and strategic alignment. *Information Systems Research* 8 (2): 125–50.

Chan, Y. E., S. L. Huff, and D. G. Copeland. 1997. Assessing realized information systems strategy. *Journal of Strategic Information Systems* 6 (4): 273–98.

Cho, H., M. Jung, and M. Kim. 1996. Enabling technologies of agile manufacturing and its related activities in Korea. *Computers Industrial Engineering* 30 (3): 323–34.

Coronado, A. E., M. M. Sarhadi, and C. Millar. 2002. Defining a framework for information systems requirements for agile manufacturing. *International Journal of Production Economics* 75 (1/2): 57–68.

Frayret, J.-M., S. D'Amours, B. Montreuil, and L. Cloutier. 2001. A network approach to operate agile manufacturing systems. *International Journal of Production Economics* 74 (1/3): 239–59.

Griffin, A. 1997. PDMA research on new product development practices: Updating trends and benchmarking best practices. *Journal of Product Innovation Management* 14 (6): 429–58.

Heizer, J., and B. Render. 2004. *Operations management.* Upper Saddle River, NJ: Prentice Hall.

Khalil, O., and S. Wang. 2002. Information technology enabled metamanagement for virtual organizations. *International Journal of Production Economics* 75 (1/2): 127–34.

Kline, R. B. 1998. *Principles and practices of structural equation modeling.* New York: Guilford Press.

Sabherwal, R., and Y. E. Chan. 2001. Alignment between business and IS strategies: A study of prospectors, analyzers, and defenders. *Information Systems Research* 12 (1): 11–33.

Sharp, J. M., Z. Irani, and S. Desai. 1999. Working towards agile manufacturing in the UK industry. *International Journal of Production Economics* 62 (1/2): 155–69.

Strader, T. J., and M. J. Shaw. 1997. Characteristics of electronic markets. *Decision Support Systems* 21 (3): 185–98.

Venkatraman, N., and V. Ramanujam. 1987. Measurement of business economic performance: An examination of method convergence. *Journal of Management* 13 (1): 109–22.

Vickery, S. K., and C. Dröge. 1993. Production competence and business strategy: Do they affect business performance? *Decision Sciences* 24 (2): 435–55.

Ward, P. T., and R. Duray. 2000. Manufacturing strategy in context: Environment, competitive strategy and manufacturing strategy. *Journal of Operations Management* 18 (2): 123–38.

# Carr and Pearson

## Article Summarized

Carr, Amelia S., and John N. Pearson. 1999. Strategically managed buyer-supplier relationships and performance outcomes. *Journal of Operations Management* 17 (5): 497–519.

## Scales (Actual Questions Used)

*Strategic Purchasing*

1. The purchasing function has a formally written long-range plan.
2. Purchasing's long-range plan is reviewed and adjusted to match changes in the company's strategic plans on a regular basis.
3. Purchasing's long-range plan includes the various types of relationships to be established with suppliers.

*Supplier Evaluation System*

4. We have a formal supplier certification program.
5. Our company has a formal system to track the performance of the suppliers we deal with.
6. Our firm has a formal program for evaluating and recognizing suppliers.

*Buyer-Supplier Relationships*

7. We enter into special agreements with suppliers who have improved their performance.
8. We are loyal to key suppliers.
9. We have very frequent face-to-face planning/communication with key suppliers.
10. There is high corporate-level communication on important issues with key suppliers.
11. There are direct computer-to-computer links with key suppliers.
12. Purchasing can influence first-tier supplier's responsiveness to purchasing requirements.

*Firm's Financial Performance over the Past 5 Years*

13. Return on investment
14. Profits as percentage of sales
15. The firm's net income before taxes
16. The present value of the firm

## Construct Description

Strategic purchasing was defined as "the process of planning, evaluating, implementing, and controlling" (p. 499) strategic and operating purchasing decisions. Strategic purchasing was viewed as a part of the firm's strategic planning process. No formal definition was given for the remaining constructs.

## Measurement Description

Sixteen items were grouped into four factors (i.e., strategic purchasing, supplier evaluation system, buyer-supplier relationships, and firm's financial performance over the past 5 years). Most items were operationalized using 5-point Likert scales using response formats, 1 = "strongly disagree" and 5 = "strongly agree." Other items were captured using similar 5-point Likert scales. For example, the items of the firm's financial performance over the past 5 years used a rating of 1 = "decreased significantly" to 5 = "increased significantly." More information can be found in Table 3 of the article.

## Development

This study chose 49 related questions out of a larger study as the initial survey instrument. This initial item set was tested by two groups. The first group consisted of college-level purchasing students; and the second group had 7 purchasing executives, 8 academics, and 30 purchasing professionals. After these two pretest exercises, the initial instrument was modified.

The scale was further purified by using correlation and exploratory factor analysis (EFA). Of the 49 variables included in the EFA, 16 variables were kept in the final model.

## Sample

Firms were chosen from members of the National Association of Purchasing Management (NAPM). The majority of them was small to medium in size and represented a wide cross-section of industries with no one industry accounting for more than 8.2% of the sample. The data were collected through multiple informants. The first key informant sample had 739 respondents, which consisted primarily of executives at the director and vice president levels. Of these respondents, 55% were directors of purchasing, 16% were presidents of purchasing, and 8% were vice presidents of materials management. The response rate for this sample was 34.6%. The second informant sample had 168 respondents, which consisted of 71% executives at the director and vice president level and 22% with other titles.

The 168 firms provided two responses to the survey and were retained as a holdout sample. The remaining 571 firms in the first key informant sample were used as a separate sample for a correlation analysis and EFA. The mean comparisons of the survey items between the two samples indicated no response bias.

## Reliability and Validity

Interrater reliability was checked by calculating the interclass correlation (ICC) between the two groups of respondents. The overall ICC was +.63. Of 16 items, 12 had ICC greater than .60. The Cronbach's coefficient alpha was calculated to examine the internal consistency. The alpha levels ranged from .70 to .88. Detailed information is shown in Table 3.

Structural equation modeling was used to examine the construct validity. Confirmatory factor analysis (CFA) on the holdout sample showed a close fit of the data to the measurement model (e.g., comparative fit index [CFI] = .9871). In addition, *t*-statistic for each item was greater than 2.0 and no standard errors were near zero. Therefore, convergent validity was demonstrated. Discriminant validity was also reported since the confidence interval around the correlation for each pair of factors did not include 1.0. Evidence in support of the predictive validity was provided by empirical tests of the five hypotheses given in the article.

## Scores

The factor loadings and the standard errors for each item are reported in Table 4 in the article.

## Other Evidence

Not available.

## Reference

Watts, C. A., and C. K. Hahn. 1993. Supplier development programs: An empirical analysis. *International Journal of Purchasing and Materials Management* 29 (2): 10–17.

# Carr

### Article Summarized

Carr, Christopher L. 2002. A psychometric evaluation of the expectations, perceptions, and difference-scores generated by the IS-adapted SERVQUAL instrument. *Decision Sciences* 33 (2): 281–96.

### Scales (Actual Questions Used)

*Expected IS Service Quality*

Reliability

1. When excellent information services promise to do something by a certain time, they will do so.
2. Excellent information services will perform the service right the first time.
3. Excellent information services will provide their services at the time they promise to do so.

Responsiveness

4. Employees in excellent information services will give prompt service to users.
5. Employees in excellent information services will always be willing to help users.
6. Employees in excellent information services will never be too busy to respond to users' requests.

Assurance

7. The behavior of employees in excellent information services will instill confidence in users.
8. Employees in excellent information services will be consistently courteous to users.
9. Employees in excellent information services will have the knowledge to answer users' questions.

Empathy

10. Excellent information services will give users individual attention.
11. Excellent information services will have employees who give users personal attention.
12. Excellent information services will have the user's best interests at heart.
13. The employees of excellent information services will understand the specific needs of their users.

*Perceived IS Service Quality*

Reliability

14. When our information services promises to do something by a certain time, it does so.
15. Our information services perform the service right the first time.
16. Our information services provide its services at the time it promises to do so.

Responsiveness

17. Employees in our information services give you prompt service.
18. Employees in our information services are always willing to help you.
19. Employees in our information services are never too busy to respond to your requests.

Assurance

20. The behavior of employees in our information services instills confidence in you.
21. Employees in our information services are consistently courteous with you.
22. Employees in our information services have the knowledge to answer your questions.

Empathy

23. Our information services give you individual attention.
24. Our information service has employees who give you personal attention.
25. Our information services has best interests at heart.
26. Employees of our information services understand your specific needs.

### Construct Description

The following construct definitions were provided in the source article. Reliability was defined as the "ability to perform the proposed service dependably and accurately" (p. 282). Responsiveness indicated a "willingness to help customers and provide prompt service" (p. 282). Assurance connoted the "knowledge and courtesy of employees and their ability to inspire trust and confidence" (p. 282). Empathy was characterized as the "caring, individualized attention the service provider gives its customers" (p. 282).

### Measurement Description

These following sets of data were measured: SERVEXP, SERVPERF, and SERVQUAL. The SERVQUAL data for each item were measured "as the algebraic difference between the raw perception-of-performance score and the raw expectation score" (p. 282).

### Development

The 26-item instrument was derived from Kettinger and Lee's (1997) IS-adapted SERVQUAL instrument.

### Sample

The sample consisted of "adults who had significant experience using information systems as a part of their everyday work environment and had experienced technical support service interaction via direct contact with internal organizational help desks" (p. 284). The respondents' ages ranged from 18 to 71 years. They held a wide variety of titles, covering the gamut from secretaries to professionals to top executives. Of the 1,000 surveys mailed out, 455 responses were returned leading to a complete and usable response rate of 40.1%.

### Reliability and Validity

Reliability was reported on the indicator level. $R^2$s, the portion of the variance in each indicator that is not random or specific to error variance, measures the indicator reliability. The results shown in Table 2 revealed low reliability in general. "Out of the 13 possible measures, four measures (three Reliability, and one Responsiveness measures) associated with IS-SERVPERF exhibit adequate indicator reliability. Six of the 13 IS-Adapted SEREXP measures (two Reliability, one Responsiveness, and three Empathy measures) exhibit adequate indicator reliability. Six of the 13 difference-score measures (three Reliability measures, two Responsiveness measures, and one Empathy measure) exhibit adequate indicator reliability" (p. 286).

The scales were based on existing scales, which had been tested with expert judges and were shown to be content valid according to the authors. The authors reported on the convergent and discriminant validity and reliability of the measures. "Confirmatory factor analysis is used to assess convergent and discriminant validity and reliability" (p. 285). The examination of average variance extracted (AVE) for each construct in Table 2 of the article indicated that only the construct of reliability exhibits partial convergent validity with the criterion of AVE greater than .5. Discriminant validity was tested by comparing AVE and the square of the correlations among the latent variables. Table 3 in the article contains the results of the test for discriminant validity (p. 285). Only the construct pair of reliability and responsiveness showed an AVE score that "is greater than the square of the correlation, which exhibits some level of discriminant validity. . . . No other constructs exhibits invariant discriminant validity with all other constructs in either instrument or based on difference-scores" (p. 285).

Nomological validity was assessed using the full structural equation modeling that included one overall service quality variable and four latent variables. Fit statistics in Table 4 "indicate moderately poor fit of the model" (p. 290). Also, multicollinearity suggested additional problems for the nomological validity.

### Scores

The scores are provided in Tables 1–5 in the article.

### Other Evidence

Not available.

### Reference

Kettinger, W. J., and C. C. Lee. 1997. Pragmatic perspectives on the measurement of information systems service quality. *MIS Quarterly* 21 (2): 223–40.

---

## Carter and Carter

### Article Summarized

Carter, Craig R., and Joseph R. Carter. 1998. Interorganizational determinants of environmental purchasing: Initial evidence from the consumer products industries. *Decision Sciences* 29 (3): 659–84.

### Scales (Actual Questions Used)

*Environmental Purchasing*

Currently, our department

1. purchases recycled packaging,
2. purchases packaging that is of lighter weight,
3. uses a life-cycle analysis to evaluate the environmental friendliness of products and packaging,
4. participates in the design of products for disassembly
5. asks suppliers to commit to waste reduction goals, and
6. participates in the design of products for recycling or reuse.

*Verbal Coordination*

Our department has

7. created partnerships with suppliers of recycled packaging,
8. created partnerships with suppliers of recycled raw materials,
9. consolidated purchases with suppliers to motivate the suppliers to provide a more environmentally friendly product,
10. established long-term contracts to assure supply of recycled raw materials,
11. formed closer relationships with suppliers of recycled materials (such as processors, collectors, and municipalities) to assure supply,
12. developed new suppliers to procure recycled raw materials.
13. increased communication flows and information sharing with current suppliers or recycled raw materials, and
14. worked with trade associations to assure supply of environmentally friendly raw materials.

*Supply Uncertainty*

If today we had to terminate relations with our current suppliers of environmentally friendly materials

15. Environmentally friendly materials would still be available.
16. There would exist a great number of additional suppliers of environmentally friendly materials.
17. We could easily continue to assure supply of environmentally friendly materials.

*Competitive Sector*

My department's environmental activities have been motivated by

18. competitors undertaking environmental activities and
19. actions by competitors.

*Input Sector*

My department's environmental activities have been motivated by

20. actions by suppliers,
21. new product offerings by suppliers, and
22. supplier salespeople.

*Regulatory Sector*

My department's environmental activities have been motivated by

23. current government legislation,
24. the threat of future legislation, and
25. targeted threat of future activist groups.

*Output Sector*

My department's environmental activities have been motivated by

26. requests by retailers or distributors to reduce primary packaging,
27. consumer pressures,
28. demands by retailers or distributors for maximum selling/shelf space, and
29. demands by customers to take back packaging waste.

*Quality*

30. Environmentally friendly products conform to standards at least as well as standard products.
31. Environmentally friendly products that we purchase are less durable than alternative, standard products.
32. The quality level of environmentally friendly products is lower than those of standard products.
33. The quality of environmentally friendly products is sometimes less than what we expect.

*Resource Dependence*

Our department

34. depends on environmentally friendly purchases,
35. depends on suppliers of environmentally friendly products to attain its goals, and
36. requires the support of suppliers of environmentally friendly suppliers.

**Construct Description**

Where possible, existing scales were employed to tap into the constructs in this study. "These included Duncan's (1972) operationalization of the construct of uncertainty and Van de Ven and Ferry's (1980) operationalization of resource dependence. In addition, scale items for vertical coordination were based on the continuums of Heide and John (1992) and Webster (1992), along with the case study findings of

Kopocki et al. (1993). The quality construct was operationalized based on the environmental supply chain literature, which suggested that Garvin's (1988) manufacturing and product-based definitions were the most germane (Bronstad & Evans-Correia 1992; Kopicki et al. 1993)" (p. 666).

### Measurement Description

The items were measured by 5-point Likert-type scales.

### Development

While developing the scales, the authors followed Churchill's (1979) recommended guidelines to address reliability and validity. They used interviews of purchasing managers to assess the validity of the overall model (McCracken 1989). Next they pretested an initial survey to assess the face validity (Heeler and Ray 1972). "A pilot test was then run with a group of 50 purchasing managers. After completion of the pilot instrument, an open discussion of the instrument and model with the purchasing managers led to additional modification of the survey instrument. Reliability and validity were evaluated using the data from the pilot test. Some scale items were deleted or reworded, and additional questions were added in order to increase reliability and validity" (p. 667).

### Sample

The authors administered the survey to purchasing executives at the manager level or higher within their firms. The list of the respondents was generated from the membership list of the National Association of Purchasing Management (NAPM). "The names and addresses of purchasing personnel were provided based on two digit Standard Industrial Classification (SIC) codes" (p. 668). The authors received a total of 437 usable questionnaires, resulting in a 41.7% response rate.

### Reliability and Validity

The validity of the overall model and the face validity of the instrument were explained in the Development section of the article. The authors then assessed the reliability and validity by "using the data from the pilot test. Some scale items were deleted or reworded, and additional questions were added in order to increase reliability and validity" (p. 669).

### Scores

The scores are presented in Tables 1 and 2 in the article.

### Other Evidence

Not available.

### References

Bronstad, G. H., and K. Evans-Correia. 1992. Green purchasing: The purchasing agent's role in corporate recycling. Paper presented at the 1992 Conference of the National Association of Purchasing Management, Orlando, FL.

Churchill, G. A., Jr. 1979. A paradigm for developing better measures of marketing constructs. *Journal of Marketing Research* 16 (1): 64–73.

Duncan, R. B. 1972. Characteristics of organizational environments and perceived concern as a noneconomic buying criterion. *Journal of Marketing* 58 (3): 1–19.

Garvin, D. A. 1988. *Managing quality: The strategic and competitive edge.* New York: Free Press.

Heeler, R. M., and M. L. Ray. 1972. Measure validation in marketing. *Journal of Marketing Research* 9 (4): 361–70.

Heide, J. B., and G. John. 1992. Do norms matter in marketing relationships? *Journal of Marketing* 56 (2): 32–44.
Kopicki, R. J., L. L. Legg, and K. E. Novak. 1993. Reuse and recycling: Reverse logistics opportunities. Paper presented at the Annual conference of the Council of Logistics Management, Washington, DC, October 3–6.
McCracken, G. 1989. *The long interview.* Newbury Park, CA: Sage.
Van de Ven, A. H., and D. L. Ferry. 1980. *Measuring and assessing organizations.* New York: Wiley.
Webster, F. E., Jr. 1992. The changing role of marketing in the corporation. *Journal of Marketing* 56 (4), 1–17.

---

# Chen and Paulraj

### Article Summarized

Chen, Injazz J., and Antony Paulraj. 2004. Towards a theory of supply chain management: The constructs and measurements. *Journal of Operations Management* 22 (2): 119–50.

### Scales (Actual Questions Used)

*Environmental Uncertainty*

Supply Uncertainty

1. The suppliers consistently meet our requirements.
2. The suppliers produce materials with consistent quality.
3. We have extensive inspection of incoming critical materials from suppliers.
4. We have a high rejection rate of incoming critical materials from suppliers.

Demand Uncertainty

5. Our master production schedule has a high percentage of variation in demand.
6. Our demand fluctuates drastically from week to week.
7. Our supply requirements vary drastically from week to week.
8. We keep weeks of inventory of the critical material to meet the changing demand.
9. The volume and/or composition of demand is difficult to predict.

Technology Uncertainty

10. Our industry is characterized by rapidly changing technology.
11. If we don't keep up with the changes in technology, it will be difficult for us to remain competitive.
12. The rate of process obsolescence is high in our industry.
13. The production technology changes frequently and sufficiently.

*Customer Focus*

14. We anticipate and respond to customers' evolving needs and wants.
15. We emphasize the evaluation of formal and informal customer complaints.
16. We follow-up with customers for quality/service feedback.
17. We interact with customers to set reliability, responsiveness, and other standards.
18. Satisfying customer needs is the central purpose of our business.
19. Customer focus is reflected in our business planning.
20. We produce products that satisfy and/or exceed customer expectations.

*Competitive Priorities*

21. Our strategy cannot be described as the one to offer products with the lowest price.
22. Our strategy is based on quality performance rather than price.
23. We place greater emphasis on innovation than price.
24. We place greater emphasis on customer service than price.
25. Our strategy places importance on delivering products with high performance.
26. We emphasize launching new products quickly.

*Strategic Purchasing*

27. Purchasing is included in the firm's strategic planning process.
28. The purchasing function has a good knowledge of the firm's strategic goals.
29. Purchasing performance is measured in terms of its contributions to the firm's success.
30. Purchasing professionals' development focuses on elements of the competitive strategy.
31. Purchasing department plays an integrative role in the purchasing function.
32. Purchasing's focus is on longer-term issues that involve risk and uncertainty.
33. The purchasing function has a formally written long-range plan.

*Top-Management Support*

34. Top management is supportive of our efforts to improve the purchasing department.
35. Top management considers purchasing to be a vital part of our corporate strategy.
36. Purchasing's views are important to most top managers.
37. The chief purchasing officer has high visibility within top management.
38. Top management emphasizes the purchasing function's strategic role.
39. Requests for increased resources are mostly satisfied by top management.
40. Top management supports the need for interorganizational IS.

*Information Technology*

41. There are direct computer-to-computer links with key suppliers.
42. Interorganizational coordination is achieved using electronic links.
43. We use IT-enabled transaction processing.
44. We have electronic mailing capabilities with our key suppliers.
45. We use electronic transfer of purchase orders, invoices, and/or funds.
46. We use advanced IS to track and/or expedite shipments.

*Supply Network Structure*

47. We have a permeable organizational boundary that facilitates better communication and/or relationship with our key suppliers.
48. Our relation with the suppliers is based on interdependence rather than power.
49. Our organizational structure can be characterized as a flexible value-adding network.
50. Our organizational/supply network structure does not involve power-based relationships.
51. The decision-making process in our organization is decentralized.
52. We have few management levels in our relationship with suppliers.

*Supply-Base Reduction*

53. We rely on a small number of high-quality suppliers.
54. We maintain close relationship with a limited pool of suppliers.
55. We get multiple price quotes from suppliers before ordering.
56. We drop suppliers for price reasons.
57. We use hedging contracts in selecting our suppliers.

*Long-Term Relationship*

58. We expect our relationship with key suppliers to last for a long time.
59. We work with key suppliers to improve their quality in the long run.
60. The suppliers see our relationship as a long-term alliance.
61. We view our suppliers as an extension of our company.
62. We give a fair profit share to key suppliers.
63. The relationship we have with key suppliers is essentially evergreen.

*Communication*

64. We share sensitive information (financial, production, design, research, and/or competition).
65. Suppliers are provided with any information that might help them.
66. Exchange of information takes place frequently, informally, and/or in a timely manner.
67. We keep each other informed about events or changes that may affect the other party.
68. We have frequent face-to-face planning/communication.
69. We exchange performance feedback.

*Cross-Functional Teams*

70. We collocate employees to facilitate cross-functional integration.
71. We coordinate joint planning committees with our suppliers.
72. We promote task force teams with our suppliers.
73. We share ideas and information with our supplier through cross-functional teams.
74. We use supplier-involved ad hoc teams based on our strategic objectives.
75. We encourage teamwork between our suppliers and us.

*Supplier Involvement*

76. We involve key suppliers in the product design and development stage.
77. We have key supplier membership/participation in our project teams.
78. Our key suppliers have major influence on the design of new products.
79. There is a strong consensus in our firm that supplier involvement is needed in product design/development.
80. We involve our key suppliers in business and strategy planning.
81. We have joint planning committees/task forces on key issues with key suppliers.

*Logistics Integration*

82. Interorganizational logistic activities are closely coordinated.
83. Our logistics activities are well integrated with the logistics activities of our suppliers.
84. We have a seamless integration of logistics activities with our key suppliers.
85. Our logistics integration is characterized by excellent distribution, transportation, and/or warehousing facilities.
86. The inbound and outbound distribution of goods with our suppliers is well integrated.
87. Information and materials flow smoothly between our supplier firms and us.

**Construct Description**

In this study, the authors considered supply, demand, and technology as forms of uncertainty. "Supply uncertainty includes indicators that represent quality, timeliness and the inspection requirements of the suppliers. Demand uncertainty is measured in terms of fluctuations and variations in demand. Technology uncertainty measures the extent of technological changes evident within the industry" (p. 123).

Customer focus was described as the importance given to customers in the execution of strategic planning, quality initiatives, product customization, and responsiveness. "Top management support is characterized in terms of time and resources contributed by the top management to strategic purchasing, supplier relationship development and adoption of advanced information technology" (p. 123).

Supply network structure was based on the notions of "non-power base relationships and inter-firm coordination as well as the informal social systems that are linked through a network of relations" (p. 125). Supplier-base reduction was characterized as a required element of contemporary supply chain management. "The construct of supply base reduction includes indicators measuring the domain of reduced numbers of suppliers, contractual agreements and supplier retention policies utilized by the buying firm" (p. 125).

The long-term relationships construct "is operationalized to involve the initiatives taken by the buying firm to encourage long-term relationships with their suppliers" (p. 125). Construct of communication was conceptualized in terms of the involvement of the buyers in two-way communication and interaction with suppliers. The construct of cross-functional teams was operationalized to "define the efforts taken to encourage as well as to use such supplier-involved teams" (p. 126). Supplier involvement was labeled based "on the involvement of the suppliers in crucial project and planning processes" (p. 126). Logistics integration construct was "derived to include the seamless integration of the logistics function of the various supply chain partners" (p. 126).

"In this study, the supplier performance construct is measured in terms of quality, cost, flexibility, delivery, and prompt response" (p. 127). Buyer performance was "measured using indicators of operational performance in addition to financial indicators such as return on investment, profit, present value, and net income" (p. 127).

### Measurement Description

Seven-point Likert scales were used to measure the items.

### Development

The authors employed a three-stage continuous improvement (CI) cycle for developing the measures to assess the requirements of reliability, validity, and unidimensionality (*see* Figure 3 in the article). This cycle used confirmatory factor analysis (CFA). Also, the authors established the content validity by strong grounding of the work in literature prior to data collection. In developing the measurements, the authors' second stage of the development process involved exploratory factor analysis (EFA). Varimax rotation with Kaiser normalization was used to achieve simple structure and to clarify the factor solutions (Loehlin 1998). This analysis aided in the determination of the exact number of factors to be extracted.

### Sample

Mail surveys were the primary means of data collection for this study. A four-page questionnaire was distributed to various locations in the United States. Members of the Institute for Supply Management (ISM), drawn from firms in the 34-to-39 two-digit U.S. Department of Commerce's, Standard Industrial Classification (SIC) codes were used for this purpose. The study targeted higher-level executives in purchasing, supply, and materials management. Most items were assessed using the 7-point Likert scale. The authors attempted to increase the response rate by following the suggestions of Dillman (1978). They mailed letters and other documents using first-class mail and followed up with reminder postcards 2 weeks after the original mailer. A second reminder was also sent in pursuit of the nonrespondents. This resulted in a response rate of 24.3%. A majority of the respondents included directors (62%) and presidents/vice presidents (16%). A majority of the firms (60%) had gross income rates larger than $100 million and were distributed evenly among the six SIC codes targeted. Tables 1 and 2 summarize the information noted. Nonresponse bias was further tested by splitting the samples into two based on the date of response receipt; *t*-tests indicated no difference between the groups. Last, the authors randomly selected and analyzed company information for evaluation.

**Reliability and Validity**

The authors used Cronbach's coefficient alpha for evaluating reliability to test the "strongly grounded" measures of their study. Alpha values of .60 were treated as the cutoff values for reliability. Variables with adequate psychometric properties were thus claimed by the authors. Content validity was determined subjectively (Emory 1980) by grounding the work in literature (more than 400 articles) and by pretesting the measurement instrument before the field collection of data. The authors noted that executives of the ISM and researchers were both involved in the pretesting process. As a result, some minor changes to the questionnaires were made as a result of possible ambiguities in the survey.

Unidimensionality was established by the empirical representation of each item and that it is only associated with one construct. The authors used a confirmatory factor analysis (CFA) and implemented four separate LISREL measurement models. In Appendix B in the article, unidimensionality results of these measurement models were given. Chi-square statistics, the adjusted goodness-of-fit index (AGFI), root-mean square error approximation (RMSEA) (Jöreskog and Sörbom 1997), and Bentler and Bonett's nonnormed fit index (NNFI) were used for the purpose. All measurement models reflected acceptable fit indices.

Convergent validity was assessed using both exploratory factor anaylsis (EFA) and CFA. The authors first assessed whether the items cross-loaded into different constructs with EFA, then they confirmed their results with CFA. The authors note that convergent validity was assessed by checking whether or not each individual item's regression loading was greater than twice its standard error. The proportion of variance ($r^2$) in the observed variables was used to estimate the reliability of an indicator. The authors determined that all indicators are significantly related to their underlying theoretical constructs.

Discriminant validity, which measures the extent to which each individual items of a construct is exclusive and does not measure other constructs, was established using the CFA. Models were constructed for all possible pairings of latent constructs. By allowing for correlation between constructs and by fixing the correlations at 1.0, the authors assessed distinctness of the two constructs (Bagozzi and Phillips 1982; Bagozzi, Yi, and Phillips 1991). They also conducted $\chi^2$ tests, using a $p < .001$ confidence level. One hundred and five discriminant validity checks were made for the 15 constructs, excluding the supply chain performance factors. The results are summarized in Table 3 of the article.

**Scores**

The scores are presented in Tables 3–5 and in Appendixes A and B of the article.

**Other Evidence**

Not available.

**References**

Bagozzi, R. P., and L. W. Phillips. 1982. Representing and testing organizational theories: A holistic construal. *Administrative Science Quarterly* 27 (3): 459–89.

Bagozzi, R. P., Y. Yi, and L. W. Phillips. 1991. Assessing construct validity in organizational research. *Administrative Science Quarterly* 36 (3): 421–58.

Dillman, D. A. 1978. *Mail and telephone surveys: The total design method.* New York: Wiley.

Emory, C. W. 1980. *Business research methods.* Homewood, IL: Richard D. Irwin.

Jöreskog, K. G., and D. Sörbom. 1997. *LISREL 8: User's reference guide.* Chicago, IL: Scientific Software.

Loehlin, J. C. 1998. *Latent variable models: An introduction to factor, path, and structural analysis.* Mahwah, NJ: Lawrence Erlbaum.

# Chen, Paulraj, and Lado

## Article Summarized

Chen, Injazz J., Antony Paulraj, and Augustine A. Lado. 2004. Strategic purchasing, supply management, and firm performance. *Journal of Operations Management* 22 (5): 505–23.

## Scales (Actual Questions Used)

*Strategic Purchasing*

1. Purchasing is included in the firm's strategic planning process.
2. The purchasing function has a good knowledge of the firm's strategic goals.
3. Purchasing performance is measured in terms of its contributions to the firm's success.
4. Purchasing professional's development focuses on elements of the competitive strategy.
5. Purchasing department plays an integrative role in the purchasing function.
6. The purchasing function has a formally written long-range plan.

*Limited Number of Suppliers*

7. We rely on a small number of high-quality suppliers.
8. We maintain close relationship with a limited pool of suppliers.
9. We get multiple price quotes from suppliers before ordering.
10. We drop suppliers for price reasons.
11. We use hedging contracts in selecting our suppliers.

*Long-Term Orientation*

12. We expect our relationship with key suppliers to last for a long time.
13. We work with key suppliers to improve their quality in the long run.
14. The suppliers see our relationship as a long-term alliance.
15. We view our suppliers as an extension of our company.
16. We give a fair profit share to key suppliers.
17. The relationship we have with key suppliers is essentially evergreen.

*Communication*

18. We share sensitive information (financial, production, design, research, and/or competition).
19. Suppliers are provided with any information that might help them.
20. Exchange of information takes place frequently, informally, and/or in a timely manner.
21. We keep each other informed about events or changes that may affect the other party.
22. We have frequent face-to-face planning/communication.
23. We exchange performance feedback.

*Customer Responsiveness*

24. Rapid confirmation of customer orders.
25. Rapid handling of customer complaints.

*Financial Performance*

26. Return on investment
27. Profits as a percentage of sales
28. Firm's net income before tax

### Construct Description

Not available.

### Measurement Description

The items were measured using 7-point Likert scales with anchors ranging from 1 = "strongly disagree" to 7 = "strongly agree." The dependent variables were captured by asking the respondents to indicate the changes in performance measures over the past 3 years. These indicators were measured using 7-point Likert scales with anchors ranging from 1 = "decreased significantly" to 7 = "increased significantly."

### Development

The survey instrument was pretested for content validity in two stages. In the first stage, the authors asked six experienced researchers to critique the questionnaire for ambiguity, clarity, and appropriateness of the items used. Next, the survey instrument was mailed to 42 purchasing executives affiliated to the Institute for Supply Management (ISM) to review the questionnaire for structure, readability, ambiguity, and completeness.

### Sample

The data collection was administered by mail surveys. The ISM database served as the sampling frame. The survey was sent to title 1 and 2 managers, primarily consisting of vice president or director of purchasing, supply chain management, and materials management. A total of 232 responses were returned, leading to an effective response rate of 23.2%. The final sample consisted of 35 presidents/vice presidents (16%), 138 directors (62%), 33 purchasing managers (15%), and 15 others (7%).

### Reliability and Validity

The authors assessed the reliability of the items by using Cronbach's coefficient alpha that varied from .65 to .97. Construct validity was assessed first by exploratory factor analysis (EFA) and then by confirmatory factor analysis (CFA). The CFA results indicated that the final measures had sufficient convergent and discriminant validity. Unidimensionality of the measures were addressed by evaluating the overall fit of the CFA model.

### Scores

The scores are presented in Tables 1–3 as well as in Figure 2 in the article.

### Other Evidence

Not available.

### Reference

None.

---

## Chesteen, Helgheim, Randall, and Wardell

### Article Summarized

Chesteen, Susan, Berit Helgheim, Taylor Randall, and Don Wardell. 2005. Comparing quality of care in non-profit and for-profit nursing homes: A process perspective. *Journal of Operations Management* 23 (2): 229–42.

## Scales (Actual Questions Used)[1]

*Process Quality*

Leadership

Immediate Supervisor

1. Rate the level of trust between you and your immediate supervisor.
2. Rate the level of praise that you get for your work from your immediate supervisor.
3. My supervisors set good examples.
4. My direct supervisor gives fair evaluations of my work.
5. My direct supervisor listens to my problems and concerns.

Director of Nursing

6. Rate the level of trust between you and your director (Director of nursing).
7. Rate the level of praise you get for your work from your director (Director of nursing).

Patient Focus

8. Are residents in your facility treated with the respect and/or compassion that you would want for yourself or a family member?
9. In your facility, do you feel that there is enough time available for certified nurse assistants (CNAs) to have personal interaction with their residents?
10. In your facility, do you feel there is sufficient time available to allow CNAs the opportunity to attend to the resident's personal needs as well as their clinical needs?
11. In your facility, are there enough trained CNAs per shift to handle the work load effectively?

Staff Focus

Training

12. Rate the initial training you received when you were hired.
13. Rate the amount of one-on-one training and/or staff development available to new CNAs.
14. Do you think you have enough training to do your job well?

*Teamwork*

15. Rate the level of communication between you and other care-giving staff.
16. How do you rate the ability of your facility's care givers to function as a team?

Cross-Functional

17. How often are you involved in your facility's interdisciplinary team (IDT) meetings?
18. Rate the level of input you have in your facility's decision-making processes within the context of your position.
19. Rate the level of patient information that is relayed between CNAs at each shift change.

Knowledge Dissemination

Task Expectations

20. Do you know exactly what is expected of you in your job?
21. Are you given clear explanations of what has to be done?

*Feedback*

22. How quickly do you receive feedback regarding your problem?
23. How satisfied are you with the way problems are usually handled?

Process Management

Responsiveness

24. How promptly are residents' call lights answered?
25. How do you rate the availability of the equipment you use?

Procedures

26. How familiar are you with your facilities emergency procedures?
27. How comfortable are you with the approved procedures in responding to medical emergencies?

**Construct Description**

The authors applied the Baldrige definitions and criteria as the framework for judging process quality. According to the Baldrige award framework, outcomes are a direct result of organizations improving their internal process quality. Five general categories corresponding to the Baldrige criteria considered in this study were as follows: "(1) leadership, (2) patient focus, (3) staff focus, (4) knowledge management, and (5) process management. The general categories are divided into subcategories in many cases and result in 10 different constructs, including leadership of the immediate supervisor, leadership of the Director of nursing, patient focus, staff training, staff teamwork, staff cross-functional ability, task expectations, feedback, responsiveness, and procedures" (pp. 233–34).

**Measurement Description**

Not available.

**Development**

The authors pilot tested the questionnaire with 60 certified nurse assistants (CNAs). They then sent "the survey to 80 nursing homes and skilled care facilities" (p. 233).

**Sample**

The authors used members of "the Utah Health Care Association's nursing homes and skilled care facilities for this study" (p. 233). They used a data set gathered in 1999 and accumulated from various sources. The primary source of data was from a survey of 890 CNAs. An approximate response rate of 40% was estimated by the authors. They also justified the use of CNAs as a preferred level of analysis based on a report from Eaton (2000) suggesting that more than "85% of the labor-intensive tasks of nursing homes are conducted by these individuals" (p. 233). In addition, the authors note that CNAs interface between both management and patients, providing a unique perspective from different angles. A pilot-tested survey instrument followed by survey mailer to 80 nursing homes and skilled care facilities were used by the authors. On average 21.2 questionnaires from each nursing home were deemed useable by the authors.

**Reliability and Validity**

Differences in size and organizational status (for- and nonprofit status) of the nursing homes were investigated by the authors as possible explanation for how sample data may be different from population data (p. 233). The authors note that nonrespondent nursing homes seemed to be "smaller in size (76.89 beds versus 96.60 beds), have lower patient days (19,893 patient days versus 28,625 patient days), and had lower revenue per patient day ($104.48 per day versus $115.37 per day)" (p. 233). Nonprofit nursing homes had similar nonresponse rates (12%) as compared with responding rates (14%).

Using a confirmatory factor analysis (CFA), the authors verified the validity of their model, which consisted of 10 latent variables. The model also included 27 observed indicators. The authors noted significance "in the skewness and kurtosis of the observed variables" (p. 234). As a result, the model had to be transformed using normal scores to reach normality (based on the works of Jöreskog et al. 2001). All 10 underlying variables were considered as latent variables and were measured using observable indicators. Satisfactory factor loadings between all variables were noted, all exceeding .52. The authors noted significance for 23 of the tems at the .05 level with others showing significance at .1 level.

### Scores

The scores are presented in Tables 1–5 in the article.

### Other Evidence

Not available.

### Note

1. Questions were asked of CNAs. The responses were based on a 6-point scale, where 1 was "poor or strongly disagree" and 6 was "excellent or strongly agree."

### References

Eaton, S. C. 2000. Beyond "unloving care": Linking human resource management and patient care quality in nursing homes. *International Journal of Human Resource Management* 11 (3): 591–616.

Jöreskog, K. G., D. Sörbom, S. Du Toit, and M. Du Toit. 2001. *LISREL 8: New statistical features.* 2nd ed. Lincolnwood, IL: Scientific Software.

---

## Chikan and Demeter

### Article Summarized

Chikan, Attila, and Krisztina Demeter. 1995. Manufacturing strategies in Hungarian industry: The effects of transition from planned to market economy. *International Journal of Operations and Production Management* 15 (11): 5–19.

### Scales (Actual Questions Used)

*Focuses of Managerial Control*

1. Product quality
2. Production quality
3. Reliable delivery
4. Low production cost
5. Fast delivery
6. Customer service
7. Adaptation to individual customer demand
8. Fast product innovation
9. Fast quantity adaptation
10. Wide product line

*Causes of Late Delivery*

11. Due date changes
12. Quality problems
13. Materials shortage
14. Production bottlenecks

15. Labor shortage
16. Insufficient overall capacity

*Reasons for Subcontracting*

17. Production load
18. Production difficulty
19. Company policy
20. Lower costs
21. Higher quality
22. Faster production

*Causes of Priority Changes*

23. Pressure from marketing
24. Pressure from customers
25. Orders from management
26. Changes in delivery dates
27. Sudden surges in demand
28. Manufacturing problems
29. Material shortages
30. Changes in sales plan
31. Engineering problem

*Alternative Ways to Change Capacity: Increases*

32. Hire additional workers
33. Use overtime
34. Subcontract production
35. Backorder the production
36. Lease temporary capacity

*Alternative Ways to Change Capacity: Decreases*

37. Lay off extra workers
38. Idle time
39. Reduce the work time
40. Build inventory
41. Lease capacity to others

*Degree of Computerization*

42. Sales forecast
43. Production planning
44. Capacity planning
45. Material usage planning
46. Job shop order recording
47. Production scheduling
48. Quality control
49. Production design
50. Sales order recording
51. Purchase order recording
52. Inventory recording
53. Material accounting
54. Wage recording

**Construct Description**

Not available.

### Measurement Description

Most items were measured based on 5-point Likert scales. In the survey of year 1994, delivery time was measured as the minimum, maximal, and usual delivery time the firm offered to its customers. *See* Whybark and Vastag (1993) for details.

### Development

The details of survey development were explained by Whybark and Vastag (1993).

### Sample

The data stem from the Global Manufacturing Research Group survey (*see* Whybark and Vastag 1993). The survey was administered in Hungary at three time intervals: 1986, 1991, and 1994 (p. 7). The modifications in the questionnaire were small enough to maintain comparability of the results. The sample sizes were about the same during each survey administration year (78, 77, and 75, respectively). The sample contains "one-third machine industry, one-third textile industry and one-third other industries" (p. 8). Owing to the transition process in Hungary, the samples differed substantially in structure (*see* Table I, p. 8 in the article for details).

### Reliability and Validity

Not available.

### Scores

Average weights for all items and for each of the three surveys are given in Tables 4–8 in the article.

### Other Evidence

Not available.

### Reference

Whybark, D. C., and G. Vastag. 1993. *Global manufacturing practices: A worldwide survey of practices in production planning and control.* Amsterdam, The Netherlands: Elsevier.

## Choi and Eboch

### Article Summarized

Choi, Thomas Y., and Karen Eboch. 1998. The TQM paradox: Relations among TQM practices, plant performance, and customer satisfaction. *Journal of Operations Management* 17 (1): 59–75.

### Scales (Actual Questions Used)

*Total Quality Management*

Management of Process Quality

1. Machines are maintained by the workers on the shop floor.
2. Problem-solving techniques are actively used by the workers on the shop floor.
3. We view work standards as something we need to continuously update.

4. Mechanics typically work on the machines only when they are down.
5. Quality data are generated mostly just to show to customers.
6. Problem-solving techniques are primarily used by the technical people.

Human Resources Development and Management

7. Employees are rewarded for quality.
8. We encourage individuals to acquire new skills.
9. Reward systems are mostly based on seniority (reversed scale).
10. Employees actively make production-improvement suggestions.
11. Employees are given timely feedback on their suggested ideas.
12. We have a profit-sharing program for all employees.
13. We use team-based rewards.
14. Company performance data are shared with employees.
15. Company financial data are shared with employees.

Strategic Quality Planning

16. The entire organization views quality improvement as their top priority.
17. Our top management demonstrates a commitment to quality.
18. Our annual objectives reflect the organization's long-term focus on quality.
19. The production layout is designed around the company's strategic goals.
20. The organization consistently supports the need to improve quality.
21. Everyone is aware of the mission and vision statements.
22. We set short- and long-term objectives for quality performance.
23. Three- to five-year organizational objectives are understood by everyone.

Information and Analysis

24. Workers use SPC data mostly to look for points out of bounds.
25. SPC data are used for machine maintenance.
26. Tolerance specifications typically drive the production processes.
27. Employees can easily gain access to the company's database.
28. Decisions are usually made based on the actual facts of the situation.
29. Customer input is used to help determine quality improvements.
30. Customer satisfaction is tracked and analyzed.
31. Quality is interpreted as hitting a target right on.

Plant Performance

32. In general, how would you rate the performance of your plant compared with the industry average?

Quality

33. External reject rate (reversed scale)
34. Internal reject rate (reversed scale)
35. Production down time (reversed scale)

Delivery

36. On-time delivery
37. Machine cycle time (reversed scale)
38. Flow time (reversed scale)

Cost

39. Work-in-process inventory (reversed scale)
40. Costs per unit produced (reversed scale)

41. Weeks of raw materials supply (reversed scale).
42. Inventory turnover ratio

*Customer Satisfaction*

43. What is the general level of your major customer with your plant's performance in the following areas?

Quality

44. Product reliability
45. Technical innovation
46. Rapid design changes
47. Conformance to specifications

Cost

48. Cost-reduction capacity
49. Low price for our customer

Delivery

50. Consistent delivery
51. Short delivery lead times
52. Rapid volume changes

**Construct Description**

The construct of management of process quality described the monitoring of work processes and improving operational variations. Human resource management practices referred to whether "workers on the shop floor become the center of the plant's improvement efforts" (p. 61). "Strategic quality planning can be referred to as designing internal functions to reflect the organization's mission. It is used to keep the organization focused on the chosen objectives. . . . Information and analysis practices are used to emphasize the importance of data-based, factual decision making" (p. 61). Plant performance was indicated by the quality, cost, and delivery outcomes of the plant.

**Measurement Description**

Items under total quality management (TQM) were placed into four categories that gauged each plant manager's perceptions of how these quality practices were implemented in the plant. Each item was captured using 5-point Likert scales, ranging from 1 = "strongly disagree" to 5 = "strongly agree." Items under "plant performance" were factored into three categories that used 5-point Likert scales, which had anchors from 1 = "well below" to 5 = "well above." Items under "customer satisfaction" were factored into three categories and were measured by Likert scales, ranging from 1 = "very low" to 5 = "very high."

**Development**

The authors refined the survey by the help of operations management faculty and executive MBA students. Operations management faculty assisted with the survey development by ensuring that a degree of content validity existed; and executive MBA students and plant managers at six manufacturing sites further aided in scale development. They identified "any language ambiguities and perceived omissions of other TQM practices used in manufacturing plants but not included in the survey. The discrepancies and comments were used to further refine the instrument" (p. 63).

**Sample**

The authors "compiled a list of transportation and electronics parts manufacturers located in Ohio as the target sample, based on the *1994 Ohio Manufacturer's List*" (p. 63). As respondents, the authors selected companies from U.S. Department of Commerce, Standard Industrial Classification (SIC) codes that range between "3400 to 3700 range of industries, which represents fabricated metal products, industrial machinery and equipment, electronic and other electric equipment, and transportation equipment. Based on the industry descriptions provided at the four-digit level, 55 classifications were selected that related to automotive and electrical manufacturing" (p. 63).

The authors stated that "plant managers were determined as the most appropriate respondents, since they are most familiar with their plant's operating practices and performance outcomes. Of the 1679 mailed surveys, 67 were returned as undeliverable. Within two months of mailing, 339 completed surveys were returned, which was a 21 percent response rate" (p. 64).

### Reliability and Validity

"Confirmatory factor analysis was conducted to address the convergent and discriminant validity of the constructs" (p. 64). As a result, "two items of plant performance, on-time delivery and inventory turnovers, were dropped due to lack of convergent validity. In addition, several other items with alpha value less than .6 were dropped to enhance reliability" (p. 66). Other indicators showed significant loadings on the related constructs, which indicated convergent validity. The $\chi^2$ difference tests for pairs of constructs revealed statistically significant differences for all scales ($p < .05$) and demonstrated strong discriminant validity. The scales were further purified by examining the internal consistency by ownership (i.e., U.S. ownership, non-U.S. ownership) and industry (i.e., auto, electronics, and metal stamping and coating).

### Scores

The scores are reported in Tables 1–6 in the article.

### Other Evidence

Not available.

### Reference

None.

---

## Choi and Hartley

### Article Summarized

Choi, Thomas Y., and Janet L. Hartley. 1998. An exploration of supplier selection practices across the supply chain. *Journal of Operations Management* 14 (4): 333–43.

### Scales (Actual Questions Used)

*Finances*

1. Financial conditions
2. Profitability of supplier
3. Financial records disclosure
4. Performance awards

*Consistency*

5. Conformance quality
6. Consistent delivery

7. Quality philosophy
8. Prompt response

*Relationship*

9. Long-term relationship
10. Relationship closeness
11. Communication openness
12. Reputation of integrity

*Flexibility*

13. Product volume changes
14. Short setup time
15. Short delivery lead time
16. Conflict resolution

*Technological Capability*

17. Design capability
18. Technical capability

*Service*

19. After-sales support
20. Sales rep's competence

*Reliability*

21. Incremental improvement
22. Product liability

*Price*

23. Low initial price

**Construct Description**

Not available.

**Measurement Description**

Twenty-six supplier selection items were captured on 4-point scales that were anchored from "low importance" to "high importance."

**Development**

The authors refined the survey in multiple steps. First, to determine content validity, they obtained feedback from academics who were familiar with the study. The authors then "visited several sites, which included a major auto maker and a cross-section of suppliers (e.g. stamping plants, plastic molding plants) and reviewed the instrument with purchasing managers to ensure that its questions were interpreted in the way that we intended them to be as well as in the same way by different respondents" (p. 335).

**Sample**

The authors chose the business unit as unit of analysis. They compiled a list of potential respondents from three resources: (a) the National Association of Purchasing Managers (NAPM) membership list (1994),

(b) the Ohio Manufacturers List (1994), and (c) Japanese Automotive Supplier Directory. The U.S. Department of Commerce's, Standard Industrial Classification (SIC) code 37 was employed to further develop the sampling frame. The authors "excluded heavy truck and bus manufacturers because of differences in product cycles, production volumes, and level of customization, compared to passenger cars, light trucks, and minivans" (p. 336).

"Surveys were mailed to 733 potential respondents, and 156 surveys were returned for a response rate of 21%. (Among the surveys received) 41% of the respondents came from plants, 24% from divisions, and 33% from corporate levels. Further, 60% of the responses came from business units that had more than $50 million in annual sales" (p. 336).

### Reliability and Validity

As indicated in the Development section, the authors used academicians to ensure content validity of the survey. They also "visited several sites, which included a major auto maker and a cross-section of suppliers and reviewed the instrument with purchasing mangers to ensure that its questions were interpreted in the way that we intended them to be as well as in the same way by different respondents" (p. 335).

### Scores

The scores are presented in Tables 1–6 in the article.

### Other Evidence

Not available.

### References

Dickson, G. W. 1966. An analysis of vendor selection systems and decisions. *Journal of Purchasing* 2 (1): 5–17.

Weber, C. A., J. R. Current, and W. C. Benton. 1991. Vendor selection criteria and methods. *European Journal of Operational Research* 50 (1): 2–18.

## Choi and Liker

### Article Summarized

Choi, Thomas Y., and Jeffrey K. Liker. 1995. Bringing Japanese continuous improvement approaches to U.S. manufacturing: The roles of process orientation and communications. *Decision Sciences* 26 (5): 589–620.

### Scales (Actual Questions Used)

*Value Construction*

How would each of those listed below (including yourself) respond in each of the following situations? For each person, check either A or B for all the three situations.

1. When doing a job,
   A. Get it done right at ALL costs.
   B. Get it done as efficiently as possible in MINIMUM time.

2. I just worked on a product and found out that it has what I would consider a minor quality problem. I suspect that this problem will not affect product functioning.
   A. Call the customer and ask for an extension so that I can fix the problem.
   B. Send it out since I feel the deadline is important.

3. Someone suggests my company invest in a new program.
   A. Vote for investing if it sounds like the right thing to do.
   B. Vote for investing only if the payback schedule is reasonable.

*Continuous Improvement Communication Question*

4. Your company joined the Continuous Improvement Users Group (CIUG) last October. Since then, your company has been involved in making various types of CI changes. Make one checkmark for each person. How frequently has each of the following persons talked to you about CI?

*Outcome Variables*

5. Please rate the general impact of CI on your company.

## Construct Description

Based on Imai (1986), continuous improvement (CI) was defined in terms of a concept that "optimizes Japan's process-oriented thinking, which has been proven much more effective in quality management than the results-oriented thinking characteristic of the West. Process-oriented management, which supports and stimulates the efforts for continuous improvement, is more effective in achieving lean production than results-oriented management, which controls the performance of the workers with a carrot and stick" (pp. 594–95).

## Measurement Description

Not available.

## Development

Not available.

## Sample

The authors chose seven manufacturing sites located in Detroit area. These manufacturers were "all members of the same CI training and support group known as the CI Users Group (CIUG). The sample sites were small- to medium-sized companies, ranging from 25 to 160" (p. 597). "The survey respondents were identified as the 'key organizational actors' in the implementation of the CI program. All managers were first identified as key actors because of their authority to make decisions that affect CI activities in the company. Then, a group of staff and workers who participated in CI activities were identified using a snowball sampling technique" (p. 598).

## Reliability and Validity

Not available.

## Scores

The scores are presented in Tables 5–9 in the article.

## Other Evidence

Not available.

**Reference**

Imai, M. 1986. *Kaizen (ky'zen), the key to Japan's competitive success.* New York: Random House.

## Christensen, Germain, and Birou

### Article Summarized

Christensen, William J., Richard Germain, and Laura Birou. 2005. Build-to-order and just-in-time as predictors of applied supply chain knowledge and market performance. *Journal of Operations Management* 23 (5): 470–81.

### Scales (Actual Questions Used)

*Build-to-Order (BTO) Strategy: Open-Ended Scale*

1. Percentage of customer output made to customer order (as opposed to stock)

*JIT Strategy: Open-Ended Scales*

2. JIT purchasing percentage
3. JIT production percentage
4. JIT sales percentage

*Applied Customer Supply Chain Knowledge: Seven-Point Scales (Endpoints of Low and High)*

5. Information from customers on expected product quality levels
6. Joint design of products with customers
7. Information from customers on their future production plans
8. Information from customers that improves your product quality
9. Information from customers that improves outbound delivery and inventory management

*Applied Supplier Supply Chain Knowledge: Seven-Point Scales (Endpoints of Low and High)*

10. Information from alternative suppliers on their product quality levels
11. Joint design of products with suppliers
12. Suppliers' use of your production plans
13. Information from suppliers that improves your product quality
14. Information from suppliers that improves inbound delivery and inventory management

*Market Performance: Seven-Point Scales (Endpoints Well below and Well above Industry Average)*

15. Market share growth over the past 3 years
16. Sales growth over the past 3 years

### Construct Description

Build-to-order (BTO) characterized "the production or assembly of products after orders are received from customers. When viewed along a continuum, the opposite strategy would consist of production in anticipation of demand, usually according to a forecast" (p. 471). Just-in-time (JIT) captured a "philosophy of continuous and forced problem solving that supports lean production . . . driven by the 'pull' of the customer's order (Heizer and Render, 2004)" (p. 472).

Applied customer supply chain knowledge referred to "the use of knowledge resources to downstream inter-firm trading partners for economic gain. If that knowledge is difficult to transfer (e.g., cannot be readily purchased in a market) or difficult to imitate, then a competitive advantage may ensue due to knowledge asymmetries across firms (Kuwada, 1998; Nonaka, 1991)" (p. 472). Note that the authors considered applied supplier supply chain knowledge to be analogous to applied customer supply chain knowledge, with the exception that company resources were more aimed at the suppliers. The authors also proposed that the presence of "transference and imitative difficulties" can lead to differences in understanding between organizations and that leads to competitive advantage by some firms.

Finally, market performance pertained to "sustained growth in sales and market share" (p. 471).

### Measurement Description

The items were measured by 7-point Likert scales.

### Development

Not available.

### Sample

Executive members of the Institute for Supply Management (ISM); formerly the National Association of Purchasing Management were the "target population" for the survey. The 1,264 ISM members were asked about the positions they held in their organizations; and those they targeted had reached a higher level of supply management. The target sample size was 200, which resulted in the need to contact 400 ISM managers to achieve their response objective. Next a random set of managers from the sample list were contacted via phone to further perform "key informant" checks and also to ensure that the participants did not have any reluctance in participating. Once the respondent list was verified, questionnaires were faxed and e-mailed. On receipt of the surveys, it was determined that some respondents did not meet the requirements for the study and their questionnaires were not used. In this case, another target respondent was drawn randomly and administered the survey. A total of 402 qualified individuals were contacted. The authors also used referrals to contact a second individual in 78 cases. Of these, 17 returned completed surveys. The authors indicated that the purpose of obtaining two surveys in a limited number of instances was "to assess inter-rater agreement across multiple respondents" (p. 474). In the final count, the study included 480 surveys sent to 402 firms. Of these, 227 were returned from 210 firms. "The survey response rate was 47% (227/480) and the firm rate was 52% (210/402). Two hundred and twenty-five surveys from 208 firms were kept for analysis" (p. 474). Seventy-two percent of the surveys were from managers in purchasing and supply management. Materials management (10%) and manufacturing (5%) were the next two main categories. A director title was held in most of the cases (66%), manager title in 16% of the cases, and vice president in 14% of the cases.

### Reliability and Validity

As a first step in assessing reliability and validity, the authors "collapsed the data" by reducing the data set to 208 firms by taking the mean of the 17 instances where there were two respondents per firm. The authors then developed an interrater agreement score ($r_{wg}$) for each of the five constructs in the model (James et al. 1993). They also assumed a uniform distribution, which they reported could inflate $r_{wg}$ values. An $r_{wg}$ value of .70 is considered acceptable and the ranges of $r_{wg}$ values for this study were between .77 and .92. The authors note that "data folding was thus undertaken with caution" (p. 475).

The authors then conducted a confirmatory factor analysis (CFA), using LISREL (Jöreskog and Sörbom 1997) to test the overall measurement model adequacy, construct validity, and reliability. The observed $\chi^2$ was found to be significant ($\chi^2 = 172.523$; d.f. = 97; $p < .01$) (p. 475); and the authors noted that this result "indicated that the observed and predicted covariance matrices differ" (p. 475). Accordingly, authors then evaluated the RMSEA, which specified the "tendency to reject any model given the observed covariance matrix and the utilized sample size" (p. 475). They report an RMSEA value of .062. The authors also used the comparative fit index (CFI) as another additional fit statistic. CFI values above .90 are considered acceptable and this study, the CFI was found to be .93. Based on the RMSEA and CFI indicators, the overall model fit was deemed to be acceptable.

The standardized estimates of the effect of the latent constructs on observable variables were above .40 and significant ($p < .01$). The authors evaluated the reliability of their scales with the composite reliability estimates that showed values ranging from .72 and .91. These results indicated an acceptable scale reliability. Further tests revealed discriminant validity. Each of the correlations between pairs of latent variables was set constant at unity. The authors then compared these models with a CFA that was "less constrained" with a single degree of freedom $\chi^2$-test. According to the authors, this was important especially "for the correlation between applied customer and applied supplier supply chain knowledge" (p. 475). The authors deduced from these "results that the applied customer and applied supplier supply chain knowledge are different constructs" (p. 475). Also the remaining nine single degrees of freedom differences between the latent variables were found to be significant.

### Scores

The scores are presented in Tables 2–5 in the article.

### Other Evidence

Not available.

### References

Heizer, J., and B. Render. 2004. *Operations management.* Upper Saddle River, NJ: Prentice Hall.

James, L. R., R. G. Demaree, and G. Wolf. 1993. $r_{wg}$: An assessment of within-group interrater agreement. *Journal of Applied Psychology* 78 (2): 306–309.

Jöreskog, K. G., and D. Sörbom. 1997. *LISREL 8: User's reference guide.* Chicago, IL: Scientific Software.

Kuwada, K. 1998. Strategic learning: The continuous side of discontinuous strategic change. *Organization Science* 9 (6): 719–36.

Nonaka, I. 1991. The knowledge-creating company. *Harvard Business Review* 69 (6): 96–104.

---

## Cleveland, Schroeder, and Anderson

### Article Summarized

Cleveland, Gary, Roger G. Schroeder, and John C. Anderson. 1989. A theory of production competence. *Decision Sciences* 20 (4): 655–68.

### Scales (Actual Questions Used)

*Production Competence*

1. Business Strategy
   - Cost broad
   - Cost focused

- Differentiation broad
- Differentiation focused

2. Production Process
   - Job shop (JS)
   - Batch (BT)
   - Connected line flow (LF)
   - Continuous line flow (CF)
3. Strengths and/or weaknesses in the nine key performance areas are as follows:
   - Adaptive manufacturing
   - Cost-effectiveness of labor
   - Delivery performance
   - Logistics
   - Production economies of scale
   - Process technology
   - Quality performance
   - Throughput and lead time
   - Vertical integration

*Business Performance*

4. Manufacturing performance
   - Cost (*T*)
   - Quality (*Q*)
   - Dependability (*D*)
   - Flexibility (*F*)
5. Marketing performance
   - Market share (*S*)
   - Growth rate (*G*)
6. Financial performance
   - Pretax return on assets (ROA; *R*)

## Construct Description

In the article, production competence was defined as "the preparedness, skill, or capability that enables manufacturers to prosecute a product-market specific business strategy." This concept was consistent with Skinner's argument on the missing link between production operations and corporate strategy. Note that production competence was treated as a variable rather than as reflective attributes. It was operationalized as a measure of the overall combined effects of a manufacturer's strengths and weaknesses in nine key performance areas: adaptive manufacturing, cost-effectiveness of labor, delivery performance, logistics, production economies of scale, process technology, quality performance, throughput and lead time, and vertical integration. The relative strengths and weaknesses were gauged on "the capability of the process to achieve a desired objective or meet a particular performance criterion."

Business strategy was based on Michael Porter's (1980) generic strategies: cost, differentiation, and focus. Production process connoted Hayes and Wheelwright's (1979) four process life cycle states: job shop, batch, connected line flow, and continuous flow.

Business performance was developed as a composite measure of manufacturing, marketing, and financial performance relative to competitors. Specifically, manufacturing performance consisted of cost, quality, dependability, and flexibility. Marketing performance included market share and growth rate. Financial performance referred to the pretax ROAs.

**Measurement Description**

Production competence was operationalized by a competence index that was computed as $\Sigma_{t=1}^{9}$ $w_i$ log ($k_i$), where *i* represented the nine performance areas; *i* = 1, 2, . . . , 9 (*see* Scales). *W* measured the strengths and weaknesses of each of the nine performance areas. $W_i$ = +1 (strength), 0 (neutral), or −1 (weakness). $K_i$ was the inverse rank order of performance area *i;* $K_i$ = 9 (most important to the business strategy), 8, 7, 6, 5, 4, 3, 2, 1 (least important to the business strategy).

The overall business performance was captured by a performance index, which was the summation of the relative performances in manufacturing, marketing, and finance: $P = T + Q + D + F + S + G + R$ (*see* Scale). Each of the relative performance variables—*T, Q, . . . , R*—was rated on a 5-point Likert scale, where respondents were asked to compare their firm's performance with competitors. The response categories were 5 = "best in industry," 4 = "better than average," 3 = "average," 2 = "worse than average," 1 = "worst in the industry."

**Development**

The instruments were "designed to collect the data needed to classify process and strategy, rank and evaluate the key performance area, and diagnose performance" (p. 659). Metrics were largely based on the existing literature and clarified through interviews.

**Sample**

The research sample consisted of six hard-goods manufacturers located in the upper Midwest. The companies were specifically selected to obtain a wide degree of variance in the study's scales. Within the sample, business performances varied from poor to excellent, strategies were from broad to focused, and processes ranged from job shop to continuous. Two research instruments were used to facilitate data collection: (1) a technical interview schedule for process design and process performance, and (2) a policy interview schedule for business strategy and relative performance. Both schedules contained closed- and open-ended questions.

**Reliability and Validity**

Theoretical knowledge about production competence, either as an element in a broader concept or as a concept in and of itself, is tenuous as best. The objective of the study was to generate grounded theory using a small sample, multiple-case study, which was based on the approach advocated by Glaser and Strauss in 1967. For that reason, it would be premature to formulate a priori hypotheses for rigorous empirical verification. Therefore, the study was exploratory.

**Scores**

The competence index and performance index are reported in Tables 4 and 3 in the article, respectively. The competence index ranged from -1.72 (very poor) to +2.92 (excellent), and the performance index ranged from 16.5 (very poor) to 30.0 (excellent). Linear regression was used to establish the relationship between production competence (expressed as *C*) and relative performance (expressed as *P*). A strong coefficient of determination ($r^2$ = .97) indicated that production competence explains much of the variance in a company's business performance.

No statistical confirmation was provided, as the results of the study were interpreted on a strictly exploratory basis. No attempt was made to predict or confirm the relationship observed. Nevertheless, the correlation between *C* and P (r = .986) indicates that a strong relationship does indeed exist.

**Other Evidence**

Not available.

**References**

Andrews, K. R. 1980. *The concept of corporate strategy.* Homewood, IL: Irwin.

Buffa, E. S. 1984. *Meeting the competitive challenge: Manufacturing strategy for U.S. companies.* Homewood, IL: Irwin.

Glaser, B. G., and A. L. Strauss. 1967. *The discovery of grounded theory: Strategies for qualitative research.* Chicago, IL: Aldine.

Hayes, R. H., and R. W. Schmenner. 1978. How should you organize manufacturing? *Harvard Business Review* 56 (1): 105–18.

Hayes, R. H., and S. C. Wheelwright. 1979. Link manufacturing process and product life cycles. *Harvard Business Review* 57 (1): 133–40.

———. 1984. *Restoring our competitive edge: Competing through manufacturing.* New York: Wiley.

Porter, M. E. 1980. *Competitive strategy: Techniques for analyzing industries and competitors.* New York: Free Press.

Schroeder, R. 1984. Operations strategy: Missing link in corporate planning. *Management Review* 73 (8): 20–23.

Skinner, W. 1969. Manufacturing: Missing link in corporate strategy. *Harvard Business Review* 47 (3): 136–45.

Wheelwright, S. C. 1978. Reflecting corporate strategy in manufacturing decisions. *Business Horizons* 21 (1): 57–66.

---

# Collins, Cordon, and Julien

**Article Summarized**

Collins, Robert S., Carlos Cordon, and Denyse Julien. 1998. An empirical test of the rigid flexibility model. *Journal of Operations Management* 16 (2/3): 133–46.

**Scales (Actual Questions Used)**

*Flexibility*

1. Inventory management
2. Warehousing
3. Product cycle time
4. Total cycle time
5. New product introduction
6. Customer delivery time

*Simplicity*

7. Problem solving
8. Supplier lead times
9. Supplier relations
10. Kanban

*Discipline*

11. Business process documentation
12. Manufacturing strategy
13. Training
14. Quality vision

15. Process capability
16. Defects
17. Scrap, rework
18. Performance measurement

### Construct Description

The constructs were defined in the article as follows. Flexibility was captured by "an explicit statement of customer and end-user requirements that are to be met by manufacturing, e.g., the customization of products, shorter delivery lead times, etc." (p. 134). Simplicity involved "the streamlining of the business processes concerned with the flow of material and information through the supply chain" (p. 133). Discipline was "concerned with the procedures involved in staffing, planning, scheduling and controlling of these processes" (p. 133).

### Measurement Description

Eighteen items were used to tap into constructs of flexibility, simplicity, and discipline. Two first-order factors emerged for simplicity: (1) lean management systems and (2) lean attitude. Three first-order factors were derived for discipline: (1) quality management process, (2) process capability, and (3) strategic processes.

### Development

The development of the instrument involved pilot testing and statistical validity checking. Of the 18 items that were developed to measure the flexibility, simplicity, discipline, and performance, their initial assignment to each construct was made by their fit with the interpretation of the construct definitions. After that, factor analysis was conducted to infer the factors that these items measured.

### Sample

The data were collected from 816 manufacturing plants in five European countries representing 18 industries. The sample distribution by industry type is given in Table 1 of the article and the final sample distribution by country is given in Figure 3.

### Reliability and Validity

Not available.

### Scores

The scores of the factor analyses are reported in Appendix B in the article. The regression summary and the correlation matrix for the independent variables are given in Tables 4 and 5. In Table 6, $r^2$ values for flexibility factors are provided by country (p. 139).

### Other Evidence

Not available.

### Reference

Collins, R. S., and R. Schmenner. 1993. Achieving rigid flexibility: Factor focus for the 1990s. *European Management Journal* 11 (4): 443–47.

# Conlon, Devaraj, and Matta

### Article Summarized

Conlon, Edward, Sarv Devaraj, and Khalil F. Matta. 2001. The relationship between initial quality perceptions and maintenance behavior: The case of the automotive industry. *Management Science* 47 (9): 1191–202.

### Scales (Actual Questions Used)

*Proactivity*

1. Wherever I have been, I have been a powerful force for constructive change.
2. I enjoy facing and overcoming obstacles to my ideas.
3. Nothing is more exciting than seeing my ideas turn into reality.
4. If I see something I don't like, I fix it.
5. No matter what the odds, if I believe in something, I will make it happen.
6. I love being a champion for my ideas, even against others' opposition.
7. I am always looking for better ways to do things.
8. If I believe in an idea, no obstacle will prevent me from making it happen.
9. When I have a problem, I tackle it head on.
10. I can spot a good opportunity long before others can.

*Service Satisfaction*

Based on your experience, please rate the service department on the following measures:

11. Cost
12. Convenience
13. Ease of getting an appointment
14. Knowledge of "target" car
15. Honesty and integrity
16. Ability to do the job right
17. Ability to do the job on time
18. Cleanliness and appearance of the facility
19. Friendliness of personnel

*Dealer Belief*

20. The general reputation of the dealer was a major influence on my buying decision.
21. The friendliness and the trustworthiness of the dealer's employees was a major influence on my buying decision.
22. The service department of the dealer was a major influence on my buying decision.
23. Positive prior experience with the dealer was a major influence on my buying decision.

### Construct Description

Based on Crant (1995), proactivity was defined as "the extent to which persons show initiative, take action and persevere until they bring about meaningful change" (p. 1193). Constructs for service satisfaction and dealer belief were intended to reflect the personal beliefs of the buyers regarding the quality reputation of the dealer at the time of the vehicle purchase, the perceived quality of the dealership, its service department, and satisfaction with the service department subsequent to purchase.

### Measurement Description

Both proactivity and dealer belief items were based on a 7-point Likert scale ranging from 1 = "strongly disagree" to 7 = "strongly agree." Service satisfaction consisted of nine items, and each item was captured on a 5-point Likert scale, ranging from 1 = "very poor" to 5 = "very good." Quality rating was gauged on consumer reports that used 5-point Likert scales to evaluate the quality, reliability, and performance of vehicles by model. According to the authors, "The graphical scores used by Consumer reports were translated into a 5-point numerical scale, anchored with 5 for vehicle models ranked best and 1 for ranked worst. The quality-rating variable was the average score of each model for the years 1988 to 1990" (p. 1197).

### Development

The proactivity scale was adopted from Bateman and Crant (1993).

### Sample

Maintenance data were collected on the 1991 car model year for two competing brands sold by one local dealer. The sampling time frame was 1991 to 1996. A total of 2,338 vehicles, 66.6% of which were Brand A (domestic) and 33.4% were Brand B (imported), were serviced by the local dealer. Questionnaires were mailed to each of the 2,338 vehicle owners. Owners were asked to have the survey completed by the member of the household who was primarily responsible for vehicle care. Five hundred and four usable responses were received with a response rate of 28.3%. Descriptive statistics on the sample and the attendants of the study are provided in Table 1 in the article.

### Reliability and Validity

The validity of the proactivity scale was established with previously published studies (Bateman and Crant 1993; Crant 1995). The construct validity of proactivity scale was examined by using principal component analysis (PCA) with a "scree" test, which revealed that all 10 items loaded on a single factor. PCA was also used to assess the constructs of service satisfaction and dealer belief. The results revealed nine items loaded on service satisfaction with an eigenvalue of 4.64, and four items loaded on dealer belief of the dealer with an eigenvalue of 2.81.

Cronbach's coefficient alpha values were computed to assess reliability of each multi-item measurement scale. The reported Cronbach alpha scores were .89, .88, and .86 for proactivity, service satisfaction, and dealer belief, respectively.

### Scores

The descriptive statistics for the items are provided in Table 2 of the article. The conceptual model fit statistics from structural equation modeling (SEM) are given in Table 3, whereas individual factor loadings are reported in Figures 2a and b.

### Other Evidence

Not available.

### References

Bateman, T. S., and J. M. Crant. 1993. The proactive component of organizational behavior: A measure and correlates. *Journal of Organizational Behavior* 14 (2): 103–18.

Crant, J. M. 1995. The proactive personality scale and objective job performance among real estate agents. *Journal of Applied Psychology* 80 (4): 532–37.

# Cua, McKone, and Schroeder

**Article Summarized**

Cua, Kristy O., Kathleen E. McKone, and Roger G. Schroeder. 2001. Relationships between implementation of TQM, JIT, and TPM and manufacturing performance. *Journal of Operations Management* 19 (6): 675–94.

**Scales (Actual Questions Used)**

*Committed Leadership*

1. All major department heads within our plant accept their responsibility for quality.
2. Plant management provides personal leadership for quality products and quality improvement.
3. All major department heads within our plant work toward encouraging JIT production.
4. Our top management strongly encourages employee involvement in the production process.
5. Plant management creates and communicates a vision focused on quality improvement.
6. Plant management is personally involved in quality improvement projects.

*Strategic Planning*

7. Our plant has a formal strategic planning process that results in a written mission, long-range goals, and strategies for implementation.
8. Plant management is not included in the formal strategic planning process. It is conducted at higher levels in the corporation.
9. The plant has a strategic plan that is put in writing.
10. Plant management routinely reviews and updates a long-range strategic plan.
11. The plant has an informal strategy that is not very well-defined.

*Cross-Functional Training*

12. Employees receive training to perform multiple tasks.
13. Employees at this plant learn how to perform a variety of tasks/jobs.
14. Employees are cross-trained at this plant so that they can fill in for others, if necessary.
15. At this plant, employees learn to do only one job/task.

*Employee Involvement*

16. During problem-solving sessions, we make an effort to get all team members' opinions and ideas before making a decision.
17. Our plant forms teams to solve problems.
18. In the past 3 years, many problems have been solved through small group sessions.
19. Problem-solving teams have helped improve manufacturing processes at this plant.
20. Employee teams are encouraged to try to solve their problems as much as possible.

*Information and Feedback*

21. Charts showing defect rates are posted on the shop floor.
22. Charts showing schedule compliance are posted on the shop floor.
23. Charts plotting the frequency of machine breakdowns are posted on the shop floor.
24. Information on quality performance is readily available to employees.
25. Information on productivity is readily available to employees.

*Process Management*

26. A large percentage of the equipment or processes on the shop floor are currently under statistical quality control.
27. We make extensive use of statistical techniques to reduce variance in processes.
28. We use charts to determine whether our manufacturing processes are in control.
29. We monitor our processes using SPC.

*Cross-Functional Product Design*

30. Direct labor employees are involved to a greater extent (on teams or consulted) before introducing new products or making product changes.
31. Manufacturing engineers are involved to a greater extent before the introduction of new products.
32. There is little involvement of manufacturing and quality people in the early design of products, before they reach the plant.
33. We work in teams, with members from a variety of areas (marketing, manufacturing, etc.) to introduce new products.

*Supplier Quality Management*

34. Quality is our number one criterion in selecting suppliers.
35. We use mostly suppliers whom we have certified.
36. Our suppliers are certified, or qualified for quality.

*Customer Involvement*

37. We are frequently in close contact with our customers.
38. Our customers give us feedback on quality and delivery performance.
39. We strive to be highly responsive to our customers' needs.
40. We regularly survey our customers' requirements.

*Setup Time Reduction*

41. We are aggressively working to lower setup times in our plant.
42. We have low setup times of equipment in our plant.
43. Our crews practice setups to reduce the time required.
44. Our workers are trained to reduce setup time.

*Pull System Production*

45. Suppliers fill our kanban containers rather than purchase orders.
46. Our suppliers deliver to us in kanban containers, without the use of separate packaging.
47. We use a kanban pull system for production control.
48. We use kanban squares, containers, or signals for production control.

*JIT Delivery by Suppliers*

49. Our suppliers deliver to us on a JIT basis.
50. Our suppliers deliver to us on short notice.
51. We can depend on on-time delivery from our suppliers.

*Equipment Layout*

52. We have laid out the shop floor so that processes and machines are in close proximity to each other.
53. Our machines are grouped according to the product family to which they are dedicated.

54. The layout of the shop floor facilitates low inventories and fast throughput.
55. Our processes are located close together so that material handling and part storage are minimized.

*Schedule Adherence*

56. We usually meet the production schedule each day.
57. Our daily schedule is reasonable to complete on time.
58. We usually complete our daily schedule as planned.

*Autonomous and Planned Maintenance*

59. We dedicate a portion of every day solely to maintenance.
60. We emphasize good maintenance as a strategy for achieving quality and schedule compliance.
61. We have a separate shift, or a part of a shift, reserved each day for maintenance activities.
62. Our maintenance department focuses on assisting machine operators perform their own preventive maintenance.

*Technology Emphasis*

63. Our plant stays on the leading edge of new technology in our industry.
64. We are constantly thinking of the next generation of technology.
65. We search for continuing learning and improvement after installation of the equipment.

*Proprietary Equipment Development*

66. We actively develop proprietary equipment.
67. We rely on vendors for most of our equipment.
68. We have equipment that is protected by the firm's patents.
69. Proprietary equipment helps us gain a competitive advantage.

*Process Orientation*

70. The production process in this plant is best characterized as follows (what percentage of product volume falls into each category?)

*Capacity Utilization*

71. During the past year, what was the average percentage of plant capacity utilization?

*Number of Employees*

72. Number of personnel employed (hourly personnel) in the current year
73. Number of personnel employed (salaried personnel) in the current year

*Manufacturing Performance*

74. Quality of product performance
75. Unit cost of manufacturing
76. Delivery performance
77. Flexibility to change volume

## Construct Description

Not available.

## Measurement Description

The items were measured using 5-point Likert scales with anchors ranging from 1 = "strongly disagree" to 5 = "strongly agree." Performance was assessed by asking the plant managers to evaluate plant performance relative to its competitors.

**Development**

The data used in this study were collected as part of an on-going world class manufacturing (WCM) study (Flynn, Schroeder, and Sakakibara 1994; Schroeder and Flynn 2001).

**Sample**

The database used in this study contained data from manufacturing plants located in the United States, Japan, Italy, Germany, and the United Kingdom. The authors provided the distribution of the plants in Table 2 in the article.

**Reliability and Validity**

The authors assessed the reliability of the items by using Cronbach's coefficient alpha. They used confirmatory factor analysis (CFA) to assess for unidimensionality and convergent and discriminant validity.

**Scores**

The scores are presented in Tables 5–7 in the article.

**Other Evidence**

Not available.

**References**

Flynn, B. B., R. G. Schroeder, and S. Sakakibara. 1994. A framework for quality management research and an associated measurement instrument. *Journal of Operations Management* 11 (4): 339–66.
Schroeder, R. G., and B. B. Flynn. 2001. *High performance manufacturing: Global perspectives.* New York: Wiley.

---

# Curkovic, Vickery, and Dröge

**Article Summarized**

Curkovic, Sime, Shawnee Vickery, and Cornelia Dröge. 2000. Quality-related action programs: Their impact on quality performance and firm performance. *Decision Sciences* 31 (4): 885–905.

**Scales (Actual Questions Used)**

*Quality-Related Action Programs*

1. Committed leadership
2. Employee empowerment
3. Cross-functional quality teams
4. Quality training
5. Measurement
6. Statistical process control
7. Benchmarking
8. Continuous improvement
9. Supplier development
10. Closer customer relationships

*Dimensions of Quality Performance*

11. Product reliability
12. Product durability
13. Conformance to specifications
14. Design quality
15. Company reputation
16. Presale customer service
17. Product support
18. Responsiveness to customers

**Construct Description**

Ten quality action programs that cover the people, process, and integration aspects of total quality management (TQM) were identified based on three TQM literature streams: anecdotal, empirical-based research, and formal assessment processes. These 10 programs were defined in Table 1 of the article as follows:

"Committed leadership: Top level management commitment to TQM.

Employee Empowerment: Allowing employees to decide on their own how to go about doing their work and ensuring action is taken on employee input.

Cross-functional quality teams: Cross-functional teams to support TQM initiatives.

Quality training: Formal employee training to support TQM.

Measurement: Goal-orientation and zeal for performance data, with constant performance measurement.

Statistical Process Control: The monitoring of a process by analyzing outputs using statistical techniques that provide feedback for maintaining, or improving process capability.

Benchmarking: Selecting data and information for competitive comparisons to support performance planning, evaluation, and improvement.

Continuous Improvement: A never-ending effort to expose and eliminate root causes of problems in an incremental manner.

Supplier Development: Policies, procedures, and practices for assessing and improving supplier capability and performance in multiple areas such as quality, design support, and delivery.

Closer Customer Relationship: Determining customers' requirements (both inside and outside the firm), then meeting those requirements no matter what it takes." (p. 887)

Quality performance was mainly developed based on Garvin's (1987) conceptualization of eight dimensions of quality. The definition of each dimension was presented in Table 2 of the article as follows:

"Product Reliability: The ability to maximize the time to product failure or malfunction.

Product Durability: The ability to maximize the time to product replacement.

Conformance to Specifications: The ability to manufacture a product whose operating characteristics meet established performance standards.

Design Quality: The ability to provide a product with capabilities, features, styling, and/or operating characteristics that are either superior to those of competing products or unavailable with competing products.

Company Reputation: The ability to create a positive or favorable image in the customer's mind when s/he hears the company's name.

Pre-sale Customer Service: The ability to service the customer during the purchase decision process (i.e. before the customer buys the product).

Product Support: The ability to service the customer in providing product support after the sale of the product to ensure continuing customer satisfaction.

Responsiveness to Customers: The ability to respond in a timely manner to the needs and wants of the company's customer's including potential customers." (p. 889)

### Measurement Description

A 7-point Likert scale was used to measure the extent of use for each quality-related action program with the endpoints 1 = "extremely low use of action program" and 7 = "extremely high use of action program." If an action program was not used, the respondent was asked to circle "not used." Similarly, for each dimension of quality performance, a 7-point Likert scale was used to measure quality performance relative to major competitors with 1 = "poor" and 7 = "excellent." The overall firm performance was assessed using four financially based measures (pre-tax ROA, after-tax ROA, ROI, growth in ROI), and two market share measures (market share and growth in market shares). These six indicators were measured based on the 7-point Likert scale ranging from 1 = "worst in industry" to 7 = "best in industry."

### Development

The scales were adapted from existing TQM literature. In addition, they were assessed and pretested by the industry experts from the panel of the Automotive Industry Action Group (AIAG).

### Sample

The sample consisted of independently owned first-tier suppliers to General Motors, Ford, and Chrysler that are at the top 150, in terms of annual sales. The unit of analysis was the strategic business unit (SBU). Questionnaires were mailed to chief executive officers (CEOs). The effective sample size was 57 firms with a response rate of 38%. Mean sales for the 57 firms were $501,516, and the mean number of employees was 2,810. The mean percentage of SBU sales direct to North American original equipment manufacturers (OEMs) was 83.67%.

### Reliability and Validity

The validity of the subjective assessment of performance was verified by correlation analyses with objective measures obtained from about half of the sample.

### Scores

The statistical results are presented in Tables 3–5 in the article.

### Other Evidence

Not available.

### Reference

Garvin, D. A. 1987. Competing on the eight dimensions of quality. *Harvard Business Review* 65 (6): 101–109.

# da Silveira

## Article Summarized

da Silveira, Giovani J. C. 2005. Market priorities, manufacturing configuration, and business performance: An empirical analysis of the order-winners framework. *Journal of Operations Management* 23 (6): 662–75.

## Scales (Actual Questions Used)

*Delivery Speed*

1. Degree of importance of "offer faster deliveries" as order winner

*Unique Design Capability*

2. Degree of importance of "offer newer products more frequently" as order winner

*Price*

3. Degree of importance of "have lower selling prices" as order winner

*Type of Product*

4. Frequency with which designs are subject to change orders

*Level of Capital Investment*

5. Proportion of revenues spent on process equipment over the past 3 years

*Work-in-Progress*

6. Days of production carried in work-in-progress inventories

*Process Choice*

7. Extent of activity organized in dedicated lines

*Business Performance*

8. Domestic market share
9. Return on sales
10. Return on investment

## Construct Description

Not available.

## Measurement Description

This study used single-item scales for operationalization of the constructs. The items for delivery speed, unique design capability, price, and type of product were measured using 5-point Likert scales. The remaining items were captured by percentages.

## Development

The data were collected as part of on-going International Manufacturing Strategy Survey (IMSS; Voss and Blackmon 1998).

### Sample

The database used in this study contained data from manufacturing plants that were located in various countries, such as the United States, Italy, Germany, and the United Kingdom. The authors provided a distribution of the plants and a complete list of the countries in Table I of the article.

### Reliability and Validity

Not available.

### Scores

The scores are presented in Tables 4 and 5 in the article.

### Other Evidence

Not available.

### Reference

Voss, C., and K. Blackmon. 1998. Differences in manufacturing strategy decisions between Japanese and Western manufacturing plants: The role of strategic time orientation. *Journal of Operations Management* 16 (2/3): 147–58.

---

## Das and Narasimhan

### Article Summarized

Das, Ajay, and Ram Narasimhan. 2001. Process-technology fit and its implications for manufacturing performance. *Journal of Operations Management* 19 (5): 521–40.

### Scales (Actual Questions Used)

*Manufacturing Technology*

1. The use of flexible integrated manufacturing (IM) systems
2. The use of CNC technology
3. The use of CAM
4. The use of robotics

*Manufacturing Design*

5. The use of CAD
6. The use of CAE
7. The use of computer-aided testing
8. Modularization in design

*Manufacturing Infrastructure*

9. The use of automated material handling systems
10. The use of kanban/similar manufacturing practices
11. The use of in-plant EDI systems

12. The use of real-time process controls
13. The use of bar coding
14. The use of setup time reduction techniques
15. The use of preventive maintenance
16. JIT supplier deliveries
17. Cellular manufacturing organizations
18. Group technology
19. Maintaining safety stock only for unique components

*Human Resources Management*

20. The use of cross-trained employees
21. The use of teams in manufacturing
22. The use of decentralized decision making in manufacturing

*Manufacturing Cost Reduction*

23. Relative to internal goals
24. Relative to primary competition

*Quality Performance*

25. Number of defects/product reduction relative to internal goals
26. Number of defects/product reduction relative to primary competition

*New Product Introduction*

27. New product introduction time reduction relative to internal goals
28. New product introduction time reduction relative to primary competition

*Delivery Performance*

29. Delivery speed relative to internal goals
30. Delivery speed relative to primary competition
31. Delivery dependability relative to internal goals
32. Delivery dependability relative to primary competition

*Customization Responsiveness Performance*

33. Meeting customization requests relative to internal goals
34. Meeting customization requests relative to primary competition

**Construct Description**

No formal definitions of the constructs were provided in the study.

**Measurement Description**

The items were measured on 5-point Likert scales.

**Development**

The questionnaire was developed in two phases. In the first phase, the authors made site visits to ensure that the managers would understand the content of the questionnaire. In the second phase, they conducted telephone interviews for further refinement of the questionnaire.

**Sample**

The data were collected from senior level National Association of Purchasing Managers (NAPM) members. The authors received 322 usable questionnaires leading to an effective response rate of 19%. The sampling frame consisted of manufacturing industries with U.S. Department of Commerce, Standard Industrial Classification (SIC) codes of 34, 35, 36, 37, and 38. The authors presented the sampling frame in Table 2 in the article.

**Reliability and Validity**

The validity and reliability of the scales used were evaluated by Cronbach's coefficient alpha, exploratory factor analysis (EFA), and confirmatory factor analysis (CFA). The authors report the results of these analyses in Tables 4 and 5 in the article.

**Scores**

The results of the regression analyses are reported in Tables 6–9 (pp. 533–34) in the article. In Table 10, the authors presented the correlation between "lack of fit" and the composite manufacturing performance (p. 536).

**Other Evidence**

Not available.

**Reference**

None.

---

# de Jong and de Ruyter

**Article Summarized**

de Jong, Ad, and Ko de Ruyter. 2004. Adaptive versus proactive behavior in service recovery: The role of self-managing teams. *Decision Sciences* 35 (3): 457–91.

**Scales (Actual Questions Used)**

*Empowerment*

1. In our team, we are permitted to use our own judgment in solving problems.
2. In our team, we are encouraged to take initiative.
3. Our team is allowed a high degree of initiative.
4. In our team, we are allowed complete freedom in our work.
5. In our team, we are allowed to do our work the way we think best.
6. As a team, we are able to handle all tasks assigned to us.

*Customer Complaint Management*

7. In our bank, external customer complaints are used to evaluate the quality of the delivery services.
8. Our bank informs our team about customer evaluations of service recovery delivered by our team.

9. Our bank regularly asks our team to report possible customer complaints about the service delivered by our team.
10. Following customer reactions, our bank continuously adjusts the service delivery process.
11. The management of our bank seriously considers customer reactions.

*Interteam Support*

12. Other teams act in a responsive manner when we forward customer complaints.
13. The knowledge of other teams assists us in service customers.
14. The quality of service delivered by other teams to our team is good.
15. Because of insufficient feedback from other teams our service to customers is substandard (reversed item).
16. Other teams provided good feedback on how to serve customers.
17. The cooperation between teams within the bank is good.
18. The employees of other teams are helpful in solving problems of customers.

*Intrateam Support*

19. In our team, we help each other in serving the customer.
20. The mutual support of team members is highly valued.
21. Each team member is personally responsible for the assistance of other members in serving the customer.
22. In our team, members need not formally be monitored with regard to the assistance of colleagues.

*Adaptive Recovery Behavior*

23. When we feel that one service recovery effort is not working, we can easily change to another.
24. In our team, we feel that each unhappy customer requires a unique approach.
25. Our team is very sensitive to the needs of our customers.
26. In our team, our service style may vary from one recovery situation to another.
27. In our team, we try to understand how one customer differs from another in service recovery expectations.
28. In our team, it is easy to modify our service approach if the situation calls for it.

*Proactive Recovery Behavior*

29. In our team, we actively seek out areas for continuous improvement of our service recovery.
30. In our team, we continuously revise service recovery processes.
31. In our team, we seek alternative solutions to service recovery problems.
32. In our team, we seek innovative solutions to service recovery problems.
33. In our team, we address service recovery issues before they become major problems.
34. In our team, we are constantly on the lookout for improving our service recovery effort.

*Service Recovery Satisfaction*

35. How satisfied are you with the way your complaints are processed by the employees?

*Loyalty Intentions*

36. I consider the XXX bank to be my first choice for all financial services that I need.
37. If I want to open a savings account or get a loan, I will probably do this at the XXX bank.
38. Over 5 years, I will still consider the XXX bank to be my most important bank.

*Share of Customer*

39. The average customer usage rates (%) of the different services offered are as follows:

    Nonroutine services: mortgages, loans, investment funds, stocks, and insurances

    Routine services: checking accounts, savings accounts, electronic banking/telebanking, currency exchange, credit application accounts, and travel services

**Construct Description**

The following constructs have been defined by the authors. Empowerment was defined as the amount of autonomy delegated to employees to self-manage their daily task responsibilities (Cook et al. 1981). Customer complaint management was associated with managing "the provision of information and feedback about customer complaints and evaluations to front-line employees (Lawler, 1986; Ledford, 1993; Schneider, White, & Paul, 1998)" (p. 461). Interteam support referred to the "internal service and communication between teams and other units within the organization" (p. 461), while intrateam support referred to "the mutual willingness of team members to help and to deliver service to each other to reach common group goals (Campion, Medsker, and Higgs, 1993)" (p. 461).

Adaptive recovery behavior assessed the team members' ability to adjust their behavior toward customers to deal with diverse service recovery situations effectively. The concept of proactive behavior followed Bateman and Crant's (1999, p. 63) explanation that "proaction involves creating change, not merely anticipating it" (p. 460). Proactive behavior involved "challenging the status quo of the operational aspects of the service delivery process rather than passively adapting to the present service conditions (e.g., Iacobucci, 1998; Morrison & Phelps, 1999)" (p. 460).

The authors did not provide formal definitions for service recovery satisfaction and loyalty intention. However, they distinguished these two constructs by arguing that loyalty intention was based on behavioral intention while service recovery satisfaction assessed subjective satisfaction. Share of customers was defined as the number of services purchased from a specific frontline employee.

**Measurement Description**

All indicator variables of the employee survey were captured on 7-point scales. "The assessment of adaptive recovery behavior was based on a 16-item adaptive selling scale developed by Spiro and Weitz (1990). To measure adaptive recovery behavior, we modified this scale by dropping redundant items and rewording the remaining items to emphasize team and service recovery aspects. The final 6-item scale assesses team members' ability to adapt to diverse service recovery situations by altering their approach toward customers" (p. 466).

Items from Hyatt and Rudy (1997) were used for the proactive recovery behavior construct. Seven items in the empowerment scale were "largely based upon the tolerance of freedom instrument of the LBDQ XII, which measured the amount of autonomy delegated to employees to self-manage their daily task responsibilities (Cook, Hepworth, Wall, & Warr, 1981)" (p. 467). A customer survey was designed to assess "service recovery satisfaction, loyalty intentions, and share of customer" (p. 467). Service recovery satisfaction indicators were assessed by 5-point single-item scales, ranging from 1 = "strongly dissatisfied" to 5 = "strongly satisfied." In addition to this, an extra answer category 6 = "not available" was included, to exclude those customers who did not have any recovery experiences from the analysis.

The authors drew from Zeithaml, Berry, and Parasuraman's (1996) behavioral intentions battery of scales to form their measures of loyalty intentions, which were anchored on 5-point scales, ranging from "strongly disagree" (1) to "strongly agree" (5) (p. 467).

**Development**

All measurement scales were modified from the extant literature, as described in the previous section.

### Sample

The data were collected from individual bank employees who are members of 61 self-managed teams (SMTs) and from their customers. All "members of the SMT [in the bank] were invited to participate. In total, 939 questionnaires were returned (76.4%). For the customer survey, a random sample of 150 customers per SMT was drawn. In total, 1,884 questionnaires were returned to the researchers by mail (2.6%). For the employee survey, 809 questionnaires from 61 teams were used for further analysis. Regarding the customer survey, 1,724 questionnaires of customers of the 61 service teams were employed for the analysis" (p. 467).

The employees responding to the survey had the following profiles, as reported in the article. "Fifty-four percent of the employees are younger than 31 years. A large part of respondents are high school graduates (45.5%) and/or have completed tertiary education (3.8%). Most respondents have been with the institution for a relatively longer period (55.9% > 4 years)" (p. 467). The characteristics of the customers surveyed indicated that "most respondents were male (63.8%) and older than 44 years (59.2%). The great majority of the respondents had a long-lasting relationship with the bank (93.5% > 5 years) and about half of them visited the bank at least once a month (46.5%)" (p. 467).

Nonresponse bias was examined through an abbreviated telephone survey of employees who did not participate in the mail survey. No significant differences between respondents and nonrespondents were found on selected items. A similar procedure was carried out for the customer survey data. Again, no significant differences between respondents and nonrespondents were discovered.

### Reliability and Validity

Fit indices of a two-factor model were compared against the common factor model to ensure the discriminant validity of the adaptive and proactive recovery behavior constructs. The authors applied confirmatory factor analysis (CFA) to determine the psychometric characteristics of all scales—empowerment, customer complaint management, interteam support, intrateam support, adaptive recovery behavior, proactive recovery behavior, service recovery satisfaction, loyalty intentions, share of customer. In Table 2 of the article, they reported the fit indices of the proposed factor model, construct reliabilities of the scales, and confirmatory factor loadings with *t*-values for each item. The indices of the proposed factor model yielded a good fit (goodness-of-fit index (GFI) = .91, adjusted goodness-of-fit index (AGFI) = .90, root-mean square error approximation (RMSEA) = .047, normal fit index (NFI) = .91, and comparative fit index (CFI) = .94), revealing unidimensionality of the scales. All measures have Cronbach's coefficient alphas of .71 or higher, indicating that the reliability of all constructs was acceptable.

### Scores

The factor loadings and the *t*-values are reported in Table 2 of the article.

### Other Evidence

Not available.

### References

Bateman, T. S., and J. M. Crant. 1999. Proactive behavior: Meaning, impact, recommendations. *Business Horizons* 42 (3): 63–70.

Campion, M. A., G. J. Medsker, and A. C. Higgs. 1993. Relations between work group characteristics and effectiveness: Implications for designing effective work groups. *Personnel Psychology* 46 (4): 823–50.

Cook, J. D., S. J. Hepworth, T. D. Wall, and P. B. Warr. 1981. *The experience of work: A compendium and review of 249 measures and their use*. London, Academic Press.

Lawler, E. E., III. 1986. *High-involvement management: Participative strategies for improving organizational performance*. San Francisco, CA: Jossey-Bass.

Ledford, G. E., Jr. 1993. Employee involvement: Lessons and predictions. In *Organizing for the future: The new logic for managing complex organizations,* ed. J. R. Galbraith and E. E. Lawler III, 142–71. San Francisco, CA: Jossey-Bass.

Morrison, E. W., and C. C. Phelps. 1999. Taking charge at work: Extrarole efforts to initiate workplace change. *Academy of Management Journal* 42 (4): 403–19.
Schneider, B., S. S. White, and M. C. Paul. 1998. Linking service climate and customer perceptions to service quality: Test of a causal model. *Journal of Applied Psychology* 83 (2): 150–63.
Spiro, R. L., and B. A. Weitz. 1990. Adaptive selling: Conceptualization, measurement, and nomological validity. *Journal of Marketing Research* 27 (1): 61–69.

# de Jong, de Ruyter, and Wetzels

**Article Summarized**

de Jong, Ad, Ko de Ruyter, and Martin Wetzels. 2005. Antecedents and consequences of group potency: A study of self-managing service teams. *Management Science* 51 (11): 1610–25.

**Scales (Actual Questions Used)**

*Employee Data*

Group Potency

1. Our team has confidence in performing the job requirements.
2. Our team believes it can become usually good at self-managing.
3. Our team expects to be known as a high-performing team.
4. Our team feels it can solve any problem it encounters.
5. No task is too tough for tour team.
6. Our team can get a lot done when it works hard.

Management Support

7. Our team members feel comfortable speaking with management about business issues.
8. Our team always receives timely information from management.
9. Our team is treated with respect by management.
10. Our team communicates with management as needed.
11. Our team has access to the recourses we need to perform effectively as a team.

Interteam Support

12. Other teams act in a responsive manner when we forward customer complaints.
13. Other teams support us through knowledge sharing when we are servicing customers.
14. The quality of service delivered by other teams to our team is good.
15. Because of insufficient feedback from other teams our service to customers is substandard (reversed item).
16. Other teams provide good feedback on how to serve customers.
17. The cooperation between teams within the bank is good.
18. The employees of other teams are helpful in solving problems of customers.

Social Support

19. In our team, members can always count on each other for support.
20. Each team member is involved with what is going on in our team.
21. In our team, members are always willing to help each other.

*Customer Data*

Customer-Perceived Service Quality

22. The extent to which employees make clear appointments
23. The competence of the service by employees
24. The attention employees pay to you
25. The politeness of employees
26. The extent to which the employees show empathy
27. The readiness of the employees to help you

### Construct Description

According to the article, the constructions were defined as follows: Group potency connoted "the jointly held belief that the team could effect changes and take control, resulting in more effective functioning" (p. 1611). Management support was related to "facilitate an external service orientation by providing the means and resources to function on the boundary between company and market" (p. 1612). Interteam support captured "cooperative interaction and information sharing with other teams in front-line operations" (p. 1612). Team tenure measured the length of time during which teams have been established. Functional diversity means the level of diversity in knowledge, skills, and abilities by team members within a team. Social support indicated that team members "help each other and have supportive social interactions" (p. 1612).

### Measurement Description

The survey consisted of two parts, employee data and customer data. All scale items of the employee survey were captured with 7-point scales, ranging from 1 = "strongly disagree" to 7 = "strongly agree." Operationalization of group potency with six items was based on the scale developed by Guzzo et al. (1993). They conducted 10 in-depth interviews with employees to ascertain proper face validity of the scale. In this study, the group potency scale was aggregated to the group level.

The seven items that tapped into the measurement of management support were largely derived from scales developed by Hyatt and Ruddy (1997) and Campion, Medsker, and Higgs (1993). The measurement of interteam was predicated on scales developed by Campion, Medsker, and Higgs (1993). Next, team tenure quantified each employee's tenure on the team (in years). In addition, the operationalization of functional diversity was based on the Blau (1977) heterogeneity index. Social support scale was drawn from a scale developed and validated by Campion, Medsker, and Higgs (1993).

This article used customer survey ratings to measure customer-perceived service quality. The operationalization of service quality employed the SERVQUAL instrument developed by Parasuraman, Zeithaml, and Berry (1988). Items on service quality were measured on a 5-point scale ranging from 1 = "very dissatisfied" to 5 = "very satisfied." The customer-perceived service quality was aggregated to the group level to enable analysis on the group level. Service profitability was measured by a ratio of the work group's annual revenues and costs from the banks financial records.

### Development

Most items of this article came from previous studies and the article did not provide detailed information on the process to develop the scales.

### Sample

The data were collected from individual employees and their customers in self-managing teams (SMTs) within a large bank in the Netherlands. SMTs referred to "groups of interdependent employees who have the collective authority and responsibility of managing and performing relatively whole tasks" (p. 1610). A sample of 100 SMTs was randomly selected from the 848 boundary-spanning SMTs in the bank. Because of various reasons including respondent attrition, nonresponse, and lack of service profitability/customer data, a net usable sample of the study was 60 SMTs, with an average team size of two. For each team, both employee members and customers were surveyed. For the employee survey, 842 questionnaires were used in the analysis; and for the customer survey, 1,537 questionnaires were analyzed.

### Reliability and Validity

To empirically justify data aggregation of the employee variables, the authors examined within-group agreement, and interdependence $r_{wg(j)}$, ICC(1), and ICC(2) were calculated and compared. The authors performed a confirmatory factor analysis (CFA), using the measurement model of structural equation modeling (SEM) to assess the psychometric properties of the items. They tested construct reliabilities of the scales by means of composite reliability. All measures had coefficients of .66 and higher, which indicated reliability. In addition, they examined within-method convergent validity by investigating the significant and magnitude of the item loadings. All items loaded significantly on their respective construct (minimum *t*-value = 9.98).

Furthermore, discriminant validity was evaluated. All $\chi^2$ difference tests (d.f. = 1) were statistically significant ($p < .05$), indicating that all pairs of constructs were correlated less than one.

### Scores

The fit indices of the specified factor model, construct reliabilities of the scales, and CFA loadings with *t*-values for each item are indicated in Table 1 of the article. Table 2 depicts the results of multilevel analyses of antecedent group potency relationship.

### Other Evidence

Not available.

### References

Blau, P. M. 1977. *Inequality and heterogeneity: A primitive theory of social structure.* New York: Free Press.

Campion, M. A., G. J. Medsker, and C. A. Higgs. 1993. Relations between work group characteristics and effectiveness: Implications for designing effect work groups. *Personal Psychology* 46 (4): 823–50.

Guzzo, R. A., P. R. Yost, R. J. Campbell, G. P. Shea. 1993. Potency in groups: Articulating a construct. *British Journal of Social Psychology* 32 (1): 87–106.

Hyatt, D. E., and T. M. Ruddy. 1997. An examination of the relationship between work group characteristics and performance: Once more into the breech. *Personal Psychology* 50 (3): 533–85.

Parasuraman, A., V. A. Zeithaml, and L. L. Berry. 1988. SERVQUAL: A multiple-item scale for measuring consumer perceptions of service quality. *Journal of Retailing* 64 (1): 12–40.

---

## Dean and Snell (1991)

### Article Summarized

Dean, James W., Jr., and Scott A. Snell. 1991. Integrated manufacturing and job design: Moderating effects of organizational inertia. *Academy of Management Journal* 34 (4): 776–804.

**Scales (Actual Questions Used)**

*Advanced Manufacturing Technology*

1. Manufacturing resource planning
2. Computer-aided design
3. Numerical control (NC)
4. Computer numerical control (CNC)
5. Direct numerical control (DNC)
6. Flexible manufacturing systems
7. Robotics
8. Automated materials handling
9. Computer-aided test/inspection
10. Computer-aided process planning
11. Product design/development and production planning
12. Production planning and component manufacturing
13. Component manufacturing and assembly
14. Assembly and production scheduling
15. Production scheduling and maintenance
16. Maintenance and materials handling
17. Materials handling and quality control
18. Quality control and materials management

*Total Quality Management*

19. How much time does the plant management staff devote to quality improvement?
20. How much time is spent with the suppliers to improve their quality?
21. How well are you able to measure the "cost of quality" in your plant?
22. How would you describe your current approach to providing quality products?
23. What percentage of the plant's manufacturing processes is under statistical control?
24. What percentage of the plant's employees has quality as a major responsibility?
25. What percentage of the plant's employees is routinely given feedback about quality?
26. How would you describe the level of use within your plant of the following quality improvement methodologies?
    - Quality function deployment
    - Taguchi methods
    - Continuous process improvement

*JIT Inventory Control*

How much has each of the following changed in the past 5 years?

27. Number of your suppliers
28. Size of deliveries
29. Length of product runs
30. Number of total parts
31. Amount of buffer stock

*Job Characteristics*

Complexity

32. How much technical knowledge do the jobs in the unit require?
33. To what extent do jobs involve solving problems?
34. How complicated are the jobs in this unit?

Variety

35. How much variety in tasks, clients, or things do members of your work unit generally encounter in a working day?
36. How routine is the work of members in your unit? (reverse scored).
37. How much opportunity do members have in this unit to do a number of different things?
38. How similar are the tasks performed by the members in a typical day?
39. People in this unit do the same job in the same way most of the time.
40. In doing their jobs from day to day, unit members generally have to adopt different methods or procedures (reverse scored).
41. There are different types or kinds of work to do every day in this job (reverse scored).

Interdependence

42. How often do members start work that is finished by others?
43. How often do members finish work that is started by others?
44. To what extent is dealing with other people part of jobs in this unit?
45. How often do individuals in this group work by themselves?
46. How much does success in this unit depend on cooperation among people?
47. How much do people in this unit depend on people in other units?

*Performance*

Compared with your industry's average, how would you rate your plant's current performance on each of the following:

48. Product quality
49. Employee morale
50. On-time delivery
51. Inventory management
52. Employee productivity
53. Equipment utilization
54. Production lead time
55. Scrap minimization

## Construct Description

The authors examined the moderating effect of organizational "inertia" on the job characteristics with the introduction of integrated manufacturing (IM). IM was seen as the combination of advance manufacturing technology (AMT), just-in-time (JIT) inventory control, and total quality management (TQM). Task complexity, task variety, and task interdependence were chosen as the salient job characteristics. Based on Hannan and Freeman (1984), the authors defined organizational inertia as the "limitations on the ability of organizations to adapt" (p. 784). Performance, size, and dependency (sources of inertia) were used as constructs that influence the relationship between IM and job design.

## Measurement Description

Fifty-two items grouped into five categories (i.e., AMT, TQM, JIT inventory control, job characteristics, performance) were used to evaluate managers' and nonmanagers' attitudes toward integrated management, organizational inertia, and the job characteristics. AMT was assessed with an 18-item scale that captured the extent to which a firm had implemented and integrated computer technologies for manufacturing. TQM was measured using an eight-item scale assessing the extent to which the firm strove for continuous quality improvements in manufacturing. JIT employed a five-item scale that represented the extent to which a firm had attempted to cut costs through reduced inventories and lead times. Job characteristics were measured based on the work by Perrow (1967), Van De Ven and Delbecq (1974), and Van De Ven, Delbecq, and Koenig (1976). Task complexity was measured using a three-item scale reflecting the extent to which a job was mentally demanding and involved problem solving and technical knowledge. Task variety was formed by a four-item scale that gauges the extent to which a job involved many different tasks, clients, methods, and procedures. Task independence had six items that connoted the extent to which a job required interactions and collaboration with others. Size was measured as an objective measure and captured by the number of full-time employees at the plant. Performance was based on questions pertaining to productivity, lead time, and product quality. Dependence was measured by ascertaining the plant's status using the *Harris Pennsylvania Industrial Directory*.

### Development

This article employed a survey methodology to collect data to test the hypotheses that were developed. The data for IM were obtained from the plant and functional managers. Because of substantial interrater reliabilities, these responses were averaged to form organizational-level variables. The job design data from the functional mangers and nonmanagers were averaged to form unit-level variables. Because of high correlation between complexity and variety, these measurement scales were averaged to form the overall composite score for task uncertainty.

### Sample

A potential pool of 512 manufacturing firms in Pennsylvania was drawn from several segments of the metal-working industry: primary metals, U.S. Department of Commerce, Standard Industrial Classification (SIC) code 33; fabricated metal products, SIC 34; industrial and metal-working machinery, SIC 35; transportation equipment, SIC 36; and precision instruments, SIC 37. These industries were chosen because they have acknowledged adoption of advanced manufacturing processes. Plants in these industries were identified using the *Harris Pennsylvania Industrial Directory*, choosing plants, rather than entire firms, as the unit of analysis. A final total of 123 plant managers (24%) participated in the study. Their plants were representative of the original population in terms of both size and SIC code. One hundred and one operations managers (82%), 109 quality managers (89%), and 97 production control managers (79%) participated in the study.

### Reliability and Validity

Direct evidence of validity for the items was not reported for this exploratory study.

### Scores

Means, standard deviations, coefficient alphas, interrater reliabilities, and correlations are reported in Table 2 in the article.

### Other Evidence

Not available.

### References


Hannan, M. T., and J. Freeman. 1984. Structural inertia and organizational change. *American Sociological Review* 49 (2): 149–64.

Perrow, C. 1967. A framework for the comparative analysis of organizations. *American Sociological Review* 32 (2): 194–208.

Van De Ven, A. H., and A. L. Delbecq. 1974. A task contingent model of work unit structure. *Administrative Science Quarterly* 19 (2): 183–97.

Van De Ven, A. H., A. L. Delbecq, and R. Koenig Jr. 1976. Determinants of coordination modes within organizations. *American Sociological Review* 41 (2): 322–38.

# Dean and Snell (1996)

**Article Summarized**

Dean, James W., Jr., and Scott A. Snell. 1996. The strategic use of integrated manufacturing: An empirical examination. *Strategic Management Journal* 17 (6): 459–80.

**Scales (Actual Questions Used)**

*Advanced Manufacturing Technology*

To what extent are each of the following technologies used in your plant? (1 = not at all; 3 = moderately; 5 = extensively)

1. Manufacturing resource planning
2. Computer-aided design
3. Numerical control
4. Computer numerical control
5. Direct numerical control
6. Flexible manufacturing systems
7. Robotics
8. Automated material handling
9. Computer-aided test/inspection
10. Computer-aided process planning

To what extent are transactions between the following production processes integrated using computers? (1 = not computer integrated at all; 3 = moderately computer integrated; 5 = completely computer integrated)

11. Product design/development and production planning
12. Production planning and component manufacturing
13. Component manufacturing and assembly
14. Assembly and production scheduling
15. Production scheduling and maintenance
16. Maintenance and materials handling
17. Materials handling and quality control
18. Quality control and materials management

*Total Quality Management*

19. How much time does the plant management staff devote to quality improvement? (1 = very little; 4 = moderate amount; 7 = great deal)
20. How much time is spent working with suppliers to improve their quality? (1 = very little; 4 = moderate amount; 7 = great deal)
21. How well are you able to measure the cost of quality in your plant? (1 = not at all; 4 = to some extent; 7 = precisely)
22. How would you describe your current approach to provide quality products? (1 = inspecting it in; 4 = some of each; 7 = building it in)
23. What percentage of the plant's manufacturing processes are under statistical control?
24. What percentage of the plant's employees have quality as a major responsibility?
25. What percentage of the plant's employees are routinely given feedback about quality?
26. How would you describe the level of use within your plant of the following quality improvement methodologies? (1 = little or none; 4 = moderate use; 7 = consistent use)

- Quality function deployment
- Taguchi methods
- Continuous process improvements

*Just-in-Time*

How much has each of the following changed in the past 5 years? (1 = huge decrease; 4 = same; 7 = huge increase—reverse scored)

27. The number of your suppliers
28. The size of their deliveries
29. The length of product runs
30. The number of total parts
31. The amount of buffer stock

*Manufacturing Strategy*

32. Product quality
33. High product reliability
34. Exceptional product performance
35. Conformance to specifications
36. Dependability
37. Zero defects
38. Product serviceability
39. Durability
40. On-time delivery
41. Meeting release dates for new products
42. Flexibility
43. Scale up/down production quickly
44. Short lead time from order to delivery
45. High efficiency/productivity
46. Economies of scale
47. Adapting to changes in product mix
48. Handling difficult/nonstandard orders
49. Products made to order
50. Small lots
51. Low unit costs
52. Low labor costs
53. Low material costs
54. Solving customer problems immediately
55. Meeting customer expectations
56. Providing customers "peace of mind"
57. Taking lead in new product introduction
58. Low life cycle costs
59. Economies of scope
60. Juggling orders to ensure rapid delivery
61. Unique features
62. High operating margins

**Construct Description**

The concept of integrated manufacturing (IM) consists of these elements in this study: advanced manufacturing technology (AMT), total quality management (TQM), and just-in-time (JIT) inventory control.

Specifically, AMT was considered to be "the manufacturing subset of information technology and comprised such specific technologies as flexible manufacturing systems (FMS), as well as the integration aspects of manufacturing into computer-integrated manufacturing systems (CIM)" (p. 459). JIT is defined as "a set of practices for reducing lead time and inventory and is associated with reductions in number of parts and suppliers, and increased frequency of parts delivery" (p. 459). TQM was framed as "a philosophy of management consisting of principles, such as continuous improvement and teamwork with suppliers to improve quality" (p. 459).

The authors viewed manufacturing strategy in terms of the competitive priorities in manufacturing, including cost, quality, delivery, and flexibility. Consistent with Porter's (1980) definition, the construct of competition focused on intensity of rivalry among existing competitors (p. 465). Competition was conceptualized in terms of munificence, which measured the growth or decline in sales over time in an industry, and complexity, which reflected the industry concentration.

### Measurement Description

Three components of IM, that is, AMT, TQM, and JIT, were measured by multiple-item scales and using multiple respondents. Each item was operationalized on a 5-point or 7-point Likert scale. A single score was generated for each variable for each manufacturing site by averaging values across items related to the constituent construct variables and then across respondents.

Thirty-one items were chosen to operationalize the manufacturing strategy, including cost, quality, delivery, and flexibility. No detail was provided regarding how these items were measured. The competition construct was formed using statistic analysis techniques. The first element munificence was computed by using regression analysis to calculate the slope of the trend line for industry sales for the period 1982–86. The second variable—complexity—was assessed by using a variation of Herfindahl index called the MINL formula (Schmalensee 1977) for sales concentration. Finally, performance was derived from an eight-item scale that assessed the firm's current performance relative to its industry in terms of productivity, lead time, product quality, and so on.

### Development

Except that the IM measures were pilot tested on a group of manufacturing managers, few details were provided by the study regarding the development of scales.

### Sample

Data collection was conducted in two stages. In the first stage, the questionnaires measuring the IM and performance were mailed to the general managers of the plants in a pool of 512 manufacturing firms that were drawn randomly from the metalworking industry by using the *Harris Pennsylvania Industrial Directory*. A total of 160 general managers (31%) responded. Of the 160 participating general managers, 123 provided the names of managers in the functions of operations, quality, and production control. Different from the general managers, functional managers were only asked about the facet of IM that was most relevant to them and their unit's performance. Of the completed responses returned, 82% (102) held positions as operations managers, 89% (109) were quality managers, and 79% (97) were production control managers.

One and a half years later, the second stage of data collection was started. The questionnaires measuring manufacturing strategy and performance were sent to all the participating managers in the first stage. Ninety-two firms responded and thus retained in this study.

### Reliability and Validity

Multiple items and multiple respondents were used to ascertain the psychometric properties of the measurement scales. Table 1 in the article reported the Cronbach's coefficient alpha and interrater reliability scores. The fact that all coefficient alphas exceeded .70 and all interrater reliabilities exceeded .80 provided strong evidence of both internal consistency and interrater reliability. Factor analysis was employed to examine the unidimensionality of the scales. The results demonstrated the construct validity (pp. 465–67). In addition, the IM measures were also subjected to a pilot test on a group of manufacturing managers to ensure construct validity.

Empirical support for the theoretical propositions, whether the use of IM techniques influences performance, and whether these effects are decreased or increased by both the competitive environment and manufacturing strategy, demonstrated the evidence of predictive validity.

### Scores

Means, standard deviations, and correlations of all the variables are presented in Table 1 in the article. The factor loadings and structure of the manufacturing strategy are reported in Appendix 2.

### Other Evidence

Not available.

### References

Dean, J. W., Jr., and D. E. Bowen. 1994. Management theory and total quality: Improving research and practice through theory development. *Academy of Management Review* 19 (3): 392–418.

Majchrzak, A. 1988. *The human side of factory automation: Managerial and human resource strategies for making automation succeed.* San Francisco, CA: Jossey-Bass.

Porter, M. E. 1980. *Competitive strategy: Techniques for analyzing industries and competitors.* New York: Free Press.

Schmalensee, R. 1977. Using the H-Index of concentration with published data. *The Review of Economics and Statistics* 59 (2): 186–93.

Schonberger, R. J. 1986. *World class manufacturing: The lessons of simplicity applied.* New York: Free Press.

## Deane, McDougall, and Gargeya

### Article Summarized

Deane, Richard H., Patricia P. McDougall, and Vidyaranya B. Gargeya. 1991. Manufacturing and marketing interdependence in the new venture firm: An empirical study. *Journal of Operations Management* 10 (3): 329–43.

### Scales (Actual Questions Used)

*Manufacturing and Marketing Decision Variables: Seven-Point Scale*

Manufacturing Decision Variables

1. Emphasis on specialty versus commodity products
2. Emphasis on new product development (NPD)
3. Emphasis on cost reduction
4. Size of customer orders
5. Level of product quality
6. Long- versus short-term supplier contracts

Marketing Decision Variables

7. Size of geographic market served
8. Level of advertising and promotion expense

9. Profitability versus market share growth emphasis
10. Frequency of customer purchases
11. Number of customers
12. Number of distribution channels

*Industry Hostility and Entry Barrier Perception Barriers (Binary Variable)*

13. Growth in industry demand
14. Presence of restrictive government policies
15. Presence of industry price wars
16. Extent of domestic competition
17. Extent of industrial competition
18. Access to distribution channels
19. Retaliation to new entrants
20. Industry dominance by large firms
21. Efficient manufacturing plant size
22. Presence of economies of scale
23. Significance of proprietary knowledge
24. Customer loyalty

*Variables Used to Reflect Strategic Breadth*

25. Range of products offered (1 = narrow, 7 = broad)
26. Breadth of geographic market served (1 = limited, 7 = broad)
27. Market segments served (1 = one, 7 = numerous)
28. Number of different customers served (1 = small #, 7 = large #)
29. Number of distribution channels served (1 = single, 7 = many)
30. Degree of backward integration (1 = none, 7 = extensive)
31. Degree of forward integration (1 = none, 7 = extensive)
32. Scale of market entry (1 = small, 7 = large)

### Construct Description

Not available.

### Measurement Description

The items were measured by a blend of 7-point Likert scales as well as by binary variables.

### Development

The authors reported that the "research is a part of an on-going, comprehensive study of new venture firm strategy and performance. . . . The targeted new ventures operated in nine SIC codes in the computer and communications manufacturing industries" (p. 334).

### Sample

Not available.

### Reliability and Validity

The authors suggested that their instruments were reliable. "Reliability was examined using a sample survey of second respondents. At the request of the researcher, a different senior executive in fifty randomly selected new ventures in the sample completed an abbreviated survey form. Pearson correlation coefficients of the strategy variables for each of the fifty pairs of respondents were used to measure of reliability" (p. 334).

### Scores

The scores are presented in Tables 3 and 4 in the article.

### Other Evidence

Not available.

### Reference

None.

---

## Detert, Schroeder, and Cudeck

### Article Summarized

Detert, James R., Roger G. Schroeder, and Robert Cudeck. 2003. The measurement of quality management culture in schools: Development and validation of the SQMCS. *Journal of Operations Management* 21 (3): 307–28.

### Scales (Actual Questions Used)

*Shared Vision*

1. In setting classroom goals, I consider the overall vision and goals of our school.
2. I understand our school mission as it applies to my work.
3. The school's overall vision and goals guide my day-to-day work with students.

*Customer Focus*

4. Standards for student performance are determined by people outside the school.
5. People outside the school drive decisions about student discipline.
6. Educational professionals are the primary decision makers on curriculum for our school (reverse coded).
7. Curriculum is determined with significant input from people outside the school.

*Long-Term Focus*

8. Our long-term objectives change with the composition of the school board.
9. Our school board has similar goals from year to year.
10. Every time we get a new administrator, the long-term objectives seem to change (reverse coded).
11. When we introduce a major school improvement program, we give it at least 3 years to show results.

*Continuous Improvement*

12. I use student feedback to improve my courses each time I teach.
13. I tend to maintain things as they are, unless someone demonstrates a better way (reverse coded).
14. I do not change things unless they are not working (reverse coded).
15. I not only teach my classes, but constantly improve them.

*Teacher Involvement*

16. Part of my job includes working on projects aimed at schoolwide improvement.
17. I feel some personal responsibility when our school improvement goals are not met.
18. I am responsible for improving things within the school, even when they do not directly involve my own classroom.

*Collaboration*

19. There is ongoing collaborative work across subject areas in this school.
20. I frequently have conversations about my teaching practices with teachers from other subject areas/departments.
21. Work time is structured to provide me with opportunities to work with other teachers.

*Data-Based Decision Making*

22. I use data from surveys to assess teaching and learning.
23. If I propose a change, I bring data to support my proposal.
24. I use a breakdown of students' test results to evaluate my teaching.
25. I test my assumptions about the causes of student behavior and performance with data.

*Systems Focus*

26. When a student is performing poorly, I try to identify where the system is failing him or her.
27. When something goes wrong, I typically look for the cause in our processes rather than in specific staff members.
28. When there is a problem in my classroom, I identify where the systems need to be improved to keep the problem from happening again.

*Quality at Same Cost*

29. Improving the quality of education for students requires more money (reverse coded).
30. My approach to educating students can be improved without increasing the budget.
31. I have made changes to improve student outcomes without additional resources.

## Construct Description

Construct definitions were given below as the same as presented in Table 1 in the article:

"Construct 1 [Shared vision]: A shared vision and shared goals among faculty, staff, and administrators are critical for school success.

Construct 2 [Customer focus]: Educational needs should be determined primarily by parents, community groups, students, and other stake holders.

Construct 3 [Long-term focus]: Improving education requires a long-term commitment.

Construct 4 [Continuous improvement]: A school should strive to make continuous changes to improve education.

Construct 5 [Teacher involvement]: Teachers should be active in improving the overall school operation.

Construct 6 [Collaboration]: Collaboration is necessary for an effective school.

Construct 7 [Data-based decision making]: Decision making should rely on factual information.

Construct 8 [System focus]: Quality problems are caused by poor systems and processes, not by teachers.

Construct 9 [Quality at same cost]: Quality can be improved with the existing resources." (p. 310)

## Measurement Description

The measures were literature-based. Schein's (1992) *Organizational Culture and Leadership* and Hofstede et al. (1990) were the primary sources. After review of the literature and elimination of unnecessary dimensions, the authors identified eight unique dimensions for organizational culture. They used some key concepts related to quality management in TQM literature: customer focus (National Institute of Technology [NIST] 1998; Flynn, Sakakibara, and Schroeder 1994; Dean and Bowen 1994), continuous improvement (NIST 1998; Anderson, Rungtusanatham, and Schroeder 1994), and fact-based management (NIST 1998; Flynn, Sakakibara, and Schroeder 1994).

The respondents were asked to indicate their level of agreement on the constructs, first indicating the current situation in their school by "ARE," and second, how they think things should be by "SHOULD BE." In the article, the ARE column represents the current behavioral norms in school where as SHOULD BE column represents the intended behavioral forms to get at underlying values or beliefs.

## Development

According to the authors, the main purpose of their study was to explicitly define the cultural philosophy of quality management and "to measure the specific content of this philosophy applied in education" (p. 309). A measurement scale was developed that could be applied to the education sector. Nine constructs were used for the first survey version. "For each construct, at least one question was included to tap the opposite side" (p. 312) of the construct definition to be reverse scored. The face validity of the questions was ensured by the members of the expert panel and several practicing teachers. Fifteen questions out of 40 "were deemed to have desirable properties at the end" (p. 313) of the analysis of version 1. Then, version 2 was run to construct and select new questions. The research team agreed on 86 new questions. After exploratory factor analysis (EFA), 25 questions were finalized at the end of version 2. With a similar process, the number of questions was finalized as 39 at the end of version 3, which was the last version.

## Sample

The data for the final version were collected from 36 school districts in five states. The sample included 17 elementary schools, 10 middle schools/junior high schools, and 9 high schools. The number of students in the schools ranged from less than 500, which were several rural schools, to more than 2,500, which was suburban schools. Only licensed teachers were asked to fill in the survey. Most of the schools set aside part of a staff meeting to complete the survey. A total of 1,743 surveys were received and 1,740 of them were stated to be usable. The number of surveys per site ranged from 21 to 148.

## Reliability and Validity

Content validity was evaluated with thorough literature syntheses and interaction with teachers, administrators, and members of the expert panel. Convergent and discriminant validity were checked with multitrait-multimethod using confirmatory factor analysis (MTMM CFA). MTMM CFA resulted in consistent finding with their a priori assumption. In addition, "the pattern of factor loadings and RMSEA of .07 suggested that the model was a reasonably good approximation of the underlying data" (p. 321). Inter-item reliabilities were computed using Cronbach's alpha for both the ARE and SHOULD BE domains. In the ARE domain, alpha values ranged from .43 (CI) to .71 (shared vision). In the SHOULD BE domain, alpha values ranged from .41 (long-term focus) to .62 (CI).

## Scores

Parameter estimates and portioning of variance from CFA model with multiple traits and multiple methods can be found in Table 11 in the article.

## Other Evidence

Not available.

## References

Anderson, J. C., M. Rungtusanatham, and R. G. Schroeder. 1994. A theory of quality management underlying the Deming management method. *Academy of Management Review* 19 (3): 472–509.

Dean, J. W., Jr., and D. E. Bowen. 1994. Management theory and total quality: Improving research and practice through theory development. *Academy of Management Review* 19 (3): 392–418.

Flynn, B. B., R. G. Schroeder, and S. Sakakibara. 1994. A framework for quality management research and an associated measurement instrument. *Journal of Operations Management* 11 (4): 339–66.
Hofstede, G., B. Neuijen, D. D. Ohayv, and G. Sanders. 1990. Measuring organizational cultures: A qualitative and quantitative study across twenty cases. *Administrative Science Quarterly* 35: 286–316.
National Institute of Technology. 1998. *Malcolm Baldrige national quality award 1998 education criteria for performance excellence.* Washington, DC: Department of Commerce.
Schein, E. H. 1992. *Organizational culture and leadership.* San Francisco, CA: Jossey-Bass.

# Devaraj, Hollingworth, and Schroeder

**Article Summarized**

Devaraj, Sarv, David G. Hollingworth, and Roger G. Schroeder. 2004. Generic manufacturing strategies and plant performance. *Journal of Operations Management* 22 (3): 313–33.

**Scales (Actual Questions Used)**

*Generic Manufacturing Strategy*

Process Structure Complexity

1. The production process(es) in this plant is(are) best characterized (percentage in each category):
   Percentage one of a kind
   Percentage small batch
   Percentage large batch
   Percentage repetitive/semicontinuous
   Percentage continuous
2. We have laid out the shop floor so that processes and machines are in close proximity to each other (5-point Likert scale).
3. We use a kanban pull system for production control (5-point Likert scale).
4. The master production schedule is level loaded in our plant from day to day (5-point Likert scale).

Product Line Complexity

5. Extent of product customization (percentage in each category):
   Percentage highly customized
   Percentage somewhat customized
   Percentage standard with custom options
   Percentage somewhat standardized
   Percentage highly standardized

Organizational Scope (Degree of Vertical Integration)

6. The degree to which our firm is vertically integrated (i.e., owns elements of the total chain from transforming a raw material to putting it in the hands of the consumers) can be described as (a) not at all, (b) low, (c) medium, and (d) high.

*Plant Performance*

Subjective Measures of Performance

Indicate your opinion about how your plant compares with its competitors in your industry on a global basis in each of the areas below:

7. Unit cost of manufacturing
8. Inventory turnover
9. Cycle time (from receipt of raw materials to shipment)
10. Flexibility to change product mix
11. Flexibility to change volume
12. Quality of product conformance
13. Product capability and performance
14. Speed of new product introduction
15. Delivery performance (on-time delivery)
16. Fast delivery

Objective Measures of Plant Performance

17. Capacity utilization: What was the average percentage of plant capacity utilization during the past year?
18. Mix flexibility: What is the time horizon for the fixed production schedule?
19. Conformance quality: What is the percentage of products that undergo scrap or rework?
20. New product on introduction speed (innovation): What percentage of plant sales are from products that were introduced in the past 5 years?
21. Delivery dependability: What percentage of the orders are shipped on time?

#### Construct Description

To gauge process structure complexity, the authors used Woodward's typology (Woodward 1958, 1965). The study generated an index providing values from "one-of-a-kind" to "continuous process" operations, with continuous process being the most complex. The production process in each plant was characterized using percentages as one of a kind, small batch, large batch, repetitive/semicontinuous, and continuous.

The study operationalized the dimension "organizational scope" with measures recommended by Kotha and Orne (1989): the degree of vertical integration and geographic market focus. This dimension was predicated on the fact that "the organizational scope of a business unit is likely to increase as the level of vertical integration increases" (p. 322). Thus, vertical integration was defined as the number of process stages coordinated within a single business unit. Also, the organizational scope of a business unit tended to increase as the geographic coverage of its marketing efforts expanded, which was called geographic market focus in the article.

#### Measures

The subjective items used in this study were measured by 5-point Likert scales.

#### Development

The data were extracted from world class manufacturing (WCM) database. For further information on the development of the survey, please refer to Flynn, Sakakibara, and Schroeder (1995) and Flynn et al. (1994).

#### Sample

The WCM database (e.g., Flynn, Sakakibara, and Schroeder 1995; Flynn et al. 1994) was used as a source for this study. The study included multiple countries to accommodate possible differences in "practices, performance, and strategies" of different countries. Four industrialized countries, the United States,

Japan, Germany, and Italy, were used in the study. This approach was chosen in line with the one used by Noble (1995). "The data includes 143 manufacturing plants from three common industries: electronics, machinery, and suppliers of automobile/truck manufacturing, representing important sectors of industrialized production" (p. 320). The authors stated that they used the same number of plants in each industry to balance the samples across industries.

### Reliability and Validity

The authors suggested that content validity was obtained by a proper conceptualization of the constructs. They also compared the operationalization of their measures with previous studies when possible. In addition, a panel of five manufacturing executives reviewed the items for external content validity, indicating that the measures used were "reasonably valid assessments" of the constructs.

Subjective performance measures were also assessed for reliability using the "alternate forms approach" when possible. The plant's performance as assessed by the plant manager was compared with those assessed from other individuals, using objective performance data and company records or other reliable sources.

### Scores

The scores are presented in Tables 2–5 in the article.

### Other Evidence

Not available.

### References

Flynn, B. B., R. G. Schroeder, and S. Sakakibara. 1994. A framework for quality management research and an associated measurement instrument. *Journal of Operations Management* 11 (4): 339–66.

Flynn, B. B., S. Sakakibara, and R. G. Schroeder. 1995. Relationship between JIT and TQM: Practices and performance. *Academy of Management Journal* 38 (5): 1325–60.

Flynn, B. B., S. Sakakibara, R. G. Schroeder, K. A. Bates, and E. J. Flynn. 1990. Empirical research methods in operations management. *Journal of Operations Management* 9 (2): 250–84.

Kotha, S., and D. Orne. 1989. Generic manufacturing strategies: A conceptual synthesis. *Strategic Management Journal* 10 (3): 211–31.

Noble, M. A. 1995. Manufacturing strategy: Testing the cumulative model in a multiple country context. *Decision Sciences* 26 (5): 693–721.

Woodward, J. 1958. *Management and technology. Problems of progress in industry.* Series No. 3. London, UK: Her Majesty's Stationery Office.

———. 1965. *Industrial organization.* Oxford, UK: Oxford University Press.

## Diáz, Machuca, and Alvarez-Gil

### Article Summarized

Diáz, Macarena Sacristán, José A. D. Machuca, and María José Álvarez-Gil. 2003. A view of developing patterns of investment in AMT through empirical taxonomies: New evidence. *Journal of Operations Management* 21 (5): 577–606.

**Scales (Actual Questions Used)**

How great an importance do you think the following factors have had in determining your investments in AMT?

*Information Elements*

1. Information from suppliers
2. Information from workers
3. Other companies
4. Trade fairs
5. Journals and magazines
6. Government departments and agencies

*Catalyst Elements*

7. Arrival of new employee/executive
8. Plans for expansion
9. Rising profits
10. Injection of outside capital
11. Existence of skilled labor

To what degree do you think the following factors have had an adverse effect on the adoption and implementation process of your investments in AMT?

*Difficulties*

12. Lack of skilled labor
13. Loss of flexibility
14. Equipment breaking down
15. Reorganization of departments
16. Reticence among employees
17. Reticence among executives
18. Difficulties with evaluation
19. Difficulties with performance measurement
20. Difficulties with financing

*Design (AMTD)*

21. Computer-aided design
22. Computer-aided engineering
23. Computer-aided process planning
24. Group technology

*Manufacturing (AMTF)*

25. Computer-aided manufacturing
26. Numerical Control
27. Computer Numerical Control
28. Robotics (PF)
29. Automated guided vehicles (AGV)
30. Automated storage/retrieval systems (AS/RS)
31. Flexible manufacturing systems
32. Computer-aided inspections (CAI)

*Planning (AMTP)*

33. Manufacturing resource planning
34. Just-in-time
35. Computerized preventive maintenance (CPM)
36. Activity-based costing (ABC)
37. Shop floor control (SFC)

*Competitive Priorities*

Cost

38. Reduce inventory
39. Reduce production costs
40. Increase labor productivity

Quality

41. Consistent quality with low defect rate
42. Supply of reliable products
43. Establish a culture of quality

Delivery

44. Meet promised delivery dates

Flexibility

45. Fast introduction of new products
46. Adjust capacity quickly
47. Fast changes in volume
48. Offer a wide range of products
49. Fast changes in product mix

Integration

50. Between product design and process planning
51. Between product design and manufacturing
52. Between product design and production planning
53. Between process planning and manufacturing
54. Between production planning and manufacturing
55. Between various items of manufacturing equipment

*Performance*

Growth

56. Market share growth
57. Sales growth

Profit

58. Return on investment
59. Return on sales

**Construct Description**

There were three broad categories of constructs, each of which was used to detect differences among the three clusters that emerge from the study: The first category was competitive priorities with measures of cost, flexibility, and quality. Delivery priority was a single-item construct. These competitive priority constructs captured the relative importance that a company placed on each of the capabilities. The second category was integration, which is concerned with the extent that partial transactions between activities are computerized. The third area was performance, which contained two constructs—growth and profit.

### Measurement Description

The measurements of multi-item measurement scales were adapted from other studies. The objective of this study was to perform cluster analysis of advanced manufacturing technology (AMT) investment in a different setting than that of the two previous studies (Johnson 2000; Boyer, Ward, and Leong 1996).

### Development

The stated purpose of this study was to replicate earlier cluster analyses in a different environment and to evaluate differences among the clusters in this study and prior studies. Scale development was not a priority; and existing scales were mostly used. However, the article did add one item to the quality priority scale—establish a culture of quality—and also generated interesting single-item scales for information and catalyst elements that were attributed to investments in AMT.

### Sample

The study population was composed of manufacturing plants in the Andalusian aeronautical sector. There were 3 plants and 17 small- to medium-sized ancillary companies. The authors studied the entire population and administered the survey via interviews. The typical respondent held senior positions as managing directors and owners of the smaller companies and heads or assistant heads of engineering for the larger companies.

### Reliability and Validity

The authors considered the scales to be reliable and valid because the ones they used were scales previously validated by other studies and because all obtained high reliability scores for this study.

### Scores

Scale and reliability coefficients are reported in various tables in the article—Table 6 (AMT investments), Table 7 (operations competitive priorities), Table 8 (integration), and Table 9 (performance). Analysis of variance (ANOVA) and least significant difference (LSD) test results are given in Tables 10 and 13–19. Correlation between activity and groups is given in Table 11.

### Other Evidence

Not available.

### References

Boyer, K. K., P. T. Ward, and G. K. Leong. 1996. Approaches to the factory of the future: An empirical taxonomy. *Journal of Operations Management* 14 (4): 297–313.

Johnson, P. 2000. An empirical taxonomy of advanced manufacturing technology. *International Journal of Operations and Production Management* 20 (12): 1446–74.

# Dong, Carter, and Dresner

**Article Summarized**

Dong, Yan, Craig R. Carter, and Martin E. Dresner. 2001. JIT purchasing and performance: An exploratory analysis of buyer and supplier perspectives. *Journal of Operations Management* 19 (4): 471–83.

**Scales (Actual Questions Used)**

*Core JIT*

1. Order size reduction
2. Negotiation process simplification
3. Open-order status paperwork reduction
4. Expediting, receiving count, and inspection cost reduction
5. Order lead time reduction

*Facilitating JIT*

6. Quality assurance program
7. Formal supplier evaluation and selection program
8. Sole sourcing

*Supply Chain Integration*

9. EDI connections
10. Information sharing (e.g., demand forecasts and costs) with this supplier
11. Sharing joint cost savings with this supplier
12. Working with this supplier to improve the management of its own suppliers

*Supplier JIT Manufacturing*

13. Reduced manufacturing lot sizes
14. Reduced manufacturing lead times
15. Enhancement of quality assurance (TQM) programs

*Buyer Logistics Costs*

16. Your inventory costs
17. Your inbound transportation costs
18. Your purchase prices

**Construct Description**

There were no formal definitions of the constructs provided in the article. Only citations were given for the sources of the constructs and the items used in the study.

**Measurement Description**

Except the cost items, 7-point Likert scales with anchors 1 = "to no extent" and 7 = "to a greater extent" were used. Cost items employed 7-point Likert scales with anchors 1 = "very much decreased" and 7 = "very much increased."

### Development

Before the actual data collection, the "preliminary questionnaire was pretested with logistics managers working for major manufacturing companies, and with logistics professors. Comments were collected and modifications to the questionnaire were made before the final survey was mailed" (p. 475).

### Sample

The survey targeted buyers from companies that operate in manufacturing extensive industries with U.S. Census Bureau, Standard Industrial Classification (SIC) codes 35, 36, and 37. Suppliers were only chosen from industries with SIC 36. A total of 159 surveys were returned from the buyer sample with a response rate of 7%; and 197 surveys were obtained from the suppliers, yielding a response rate of 7.4%.

### Reliability and Validity

The authors used confirmatory factor analyses (CFA) to evaluate the validity and reliability of the scales. The factor loadings of the CFA were significant ($p < .01$) and the overall fit of CFA models were above .90 for all three widely used fit measures (i.e., goodness of fit index (GFI) comparative fit index (CFI), and non-normed fit index (NNFI) indicating a good fit. Indicating good reliability, composite reliability values were above .60 threshold, except for the facilitating JIT scale. Last, the authors used $\chi^2$ difference tests to assess the discriminant validity of the constructs. All the $\chi^2$ differences were significant ($p < .001$), indicating that the constructs are different from each other.

### Scores

The scores are presented in Figures 2 and 3 as well as Appendixes A and B in the article.

### Other Evidence

Not available.

### Reference

None.

---

## Douglas and Fredendall

### Article Summarized

Douglas, Thomas J., and Lawrence D. Fredendall. 2004. Evaluating the Deming management model of total quality in services. *Decision Sciences* 35 (3): 393–422.

### Scales (Actual Questions Used)

*Top Management Team Involvement*

1. The top health care organization executive assumes responsibility for quality performance.
2. The major department heads participate in the quality improvement process.
3. The organization's top management (top administrator and major department heads) has objectives for quality performance.
4. The goal-setting process for quality within the health care organization is comprehensive.
5. Importance is attached to quality by the organization's top management in relation to cost objectives.
6. Quality issues are reviewed in the organization's top management meetings.

*Quality Philosophy*

7. There is a strong commitment to quality at all levels of this organization.
8. People in this organization are aware of its overall mission.
9. Members of this organization show concern for the need for quality.
10. Continuous quality improvement is an important goal of this organization.
11. Managers here try to plan ahead for changes that might affect our performance.

*Total Quality Training*

12. Quality-related training is given to hourly employees throughout the organization.
13. Quality-related training is given to managers and supervisors throughout the organization.
14. Training is given in the "total quality concept" (i.e., philosophy of company-wide responsibility for quality) throughout the organization.
15. Training is given in the basic statistical techniques (such as histograms and control charts) in the organization as a whole.
16. The organization's top management is committed to employee training for quality.
17. Resources are provided for employee training in quality.

*Customer-Driven Information*

18. Associates know who their customers are.
19. Associates attempt to measure their internal customers' needs (customers inside this organization).
20. Associates attempt to measure their external customers' needs (customers outside this organization).
21. The organization uses customer requirements as the basis for quality.
22. Our organization is more customer focused than our competitors.

*Continuous Improvement*

23. Associates in the organization try to improve the quality of their service.
24. Associates in the organization believe that quality improvement is their responsibility.
25. Associates in the organization analyze their work products to look for ways of doing a better job.

*Management by Fact*

26. Quality data (defects, complaints, outcomes, time, satisfaction, etc.) are available.
27. Quality data are timely.
28. Quality data are used as tools to manage quality.
29. Quality data are available to hourly workers.
30. Quality data are available to managers and supervisors.
31. Quality data are used to evaluate supervisor and managerial performance.

*Total Quality Methods*

32. Associates use the basic statistical techniques (such as histograms and control charts) to study their work processes.
33. Associates analyze the time taken to get the job done.
34. Associates keep records and charts measuring the quality of work displayed in their work area.
35. Statistical techniques are used to reduce variation in processes in the organization.
36. TQM procedures (such as brainstorming, cause-and-effect diagrams, Pareto charts) are used to analyze information for process improvement.

*Supplier Involvement*

37. Suppliers are selected based on quality rather than price.
38. The organization's supplier rating system is thorough.
39. The organization relies on reasonably few, but dependable, suppliers.

40. The organization provides education to its suppliers.
41. Longer-term relationships are offered to suppliers.
42. Clear specifications are provided to suppliers.

*Perceived Financial Performance*

43. Growth in earnings
44. Growth in revenue
45. Changes in market share
46. Return on assets
47. Long-run level of profitability

*Perceived Customer Satisfaction*

48. Patient satisfaction
49. Average length of stay
50. Clinical outcomes

*Structural Exploration*

51. Highly structured channels of communication and highly restricted access to important financial and operating information
52. Open channels of communication with important financial and operating information flowing quite freely throughout the organization
53. A strong emphasis on holding fast to true and tried management principles despite any changes in business conditions
54. A strong emphasis on adapting freely to changing circumstances without too much concern for past practices

## Construct Description

The following definitions were provided in Table 1 in the article:

"Visionary leadership: The ability of management to establish, practice, and lead a long-term vision for the organization, driven by changing customer requirements, as opposed to an internal management control role.

Internal and external cooperation: The propensity of the organization to engage in noncompetitive activities internally among employees and externally with respect to suppliers.

Learning: The organizational capability to recognize and nurture the development of its skills, abilities, and knowledge base.

Process management: The set of methodological and behavioral practices emphasizing the management of process or means of actions, rather than results.

Continuous improvement: The propensity of the organization to pursue incremental and innovative improvements of its processes, products, and services.

Employee fulfillment: The degree to which employees of an organization feel that the organization continually satisfies their need.

Customer satisfaction: The degree to which an organization's customers continually perceive that their needs are being met by the organization's products and services." (p. 395)

## Measurement Description

The items used in study were measured by 5-point Likert scales.

### Development

The authors used previously published scales in the quality management literature.

### Sample

Hospitals in the General Medical Hospitals (U.S. Census Bureau, Standard Industrial Classification [SIC] code 8062) industry were the target population. The authors randomly selected 19 metropolitan areas across the United States and mailed questionnaires to the CEO and the Director of Quality at each hospital. Of the 512 hospitals in the sampling, 193 responded with at least one completed survey, resulting in an overall response rate of 38%.

In an effort to assess the potential for response bias, comparisons were made across a number of available variables for both the responding and the nonresponding hospitals for the 19 Standard Metropolitan Statistical Areas (SMSAs) using data from the 1995 American Hospital Association Survey. The mean results of the nonrespondents did not differ significantly from the responding firms on assets, number of employees, profitability, or services offered.

### Reliability and Validity

The reliability and validity of these scales were tested in the original studies. The authors mentioned that "additional factor and reliability analyses were conducted in this study" (p. 401), but they did not explicitly report the results.

### Scores

Factor loadings and standard errors were not reported. Measurement model was inclusive of the structural equation modeling and was not separately reported.

### Other Evidence

Survey data were combined with secondary information available for the responding hospitals.

### Reference

None.

---

## Dröge, Claycomb, and Germain

### Article Summarized

Dröge, Cornelia, Cindy Claycomb, and Richard Germain. 2003. Does knowledge mediate the effect of context on performance? Some initial evidence. *Decision Sciences* 34 (3): 541–68.

### Scales (Actual Questions Used)

*Production Technology Routineness*

1. Custom technology (production of a single unit or a few units to customer specification)
2. Small batch/job shop technology (batches of less than 1 week)
3. Large batch technology (e.g., of components for subsequent assembly as in fabricating shops, of finished products such as bottles, cans, drugs, chemicals)

4. Mass production technology (as in assembly lines)
5. Continuous process technology (as in production of liquids, gases, or solid shapes, e.g., oil refining)

*Technological Turbulence*

6. Logistics processes change slowly . . . rapidly.
7. Core production processes change slowly . . . rapidly.
8. Products become obsolete slowly . . . quickly.
9. New products are introduced infrequently . . . frequently.

*Demand Unpredictability*

10. Sales are predictable . . . unpredictable.
11. Market trends are easy to monitor . . . difficult to monitor.
12. Sales forecasts are likely to be accurate . . . inaccurate.

*Knowledge Creation*

13. Product R&D expenditures (as a percentage of sales)
14. Process R&D expenditures (as a percentage of sales)

*New Knowledge Creation*

15. Product R&D expenditures (as a percentage of sales)
16. Process R&D expenditures (as a percentage of sales)

*Applied Knowledge*

17. Internal knowledge application: mean of eight items
18. Customer knowledge application (*see* above)
19. Supplier knowledge application (*see* above)

*Financial Performance*

20. Average ROI over the past 3 years
21. Average profit over the past 3 years
22. Profit growth over the past 3 years

*Measurement of Applied Knowledge*

Internal Knowledge Application

23. Mechanisms such as SPC, Pareto charts, and so on, to improve the quality of processes/products
24. Total-preventive maintenance methods
25. Demand-pull support systems
26. Methods for reducing machine setup times
27. Direct labor's understanding of machinery/processes through cross-training
28. Direct labor's understanding of defects or errors in products and processes
29. Cellular plant layout
30. Kanban support systems

Customer Knowledge Application

31. Information from customers on their expected product quality levels
32. Joint design of products with customers
33. Information from customers on how they use your goods or component parts
34. Outbound warehouse staging systems proximate to customers to provide them with JIT-type delivery
35. Information from customers on their future production plans

36. Information from customers that lowers your production costs
37. Information from customers that improves outbound delivery and inventory management
38. Information from customers that improves your product quality

Supplier Knowledge Application

39. Information from alternative suppliers on their product quality levels
40. Joint design of products with suppliers
41. Information from suppliers that lowers your production costs
42. Information from suppliers that improves inbound delivery and product quality
43. Information from suppliers that improves product quality
44. Supplier's application of your firm's production plans because of information you provide
45. Supplier's application of how you use their goods in your production processes because of information you provide
46. Supplier's application of warehouse staging systems proximate to you that provide you with JIT service

**Construct Description**

In this study, size was determined by "the scale of a firm's operations" (p. 546). Production technology routineness was defined as "the means for creating outputs from inputs" (p. 547). Technological turbulence was "the rate of product and process change" (p. 547). Demand unpredictability was "a dimension of environmental uncertainty and refers to the predictability of demand (e.g., the accuracy of sales forecasts)" (p. 548). New knowledge creation represented the focus on "product *and* process knowledge . . . created . . . by manufacturers" (p. 550). Applied knowledge focused on "product *and* process knowledge . . . applied by manufacturers" (p. 550).

Internal knowledge application was related to firm's internal total quality management (TQM) and just-in-time (JIT) processes. Customer knowledge application suggested that "customer demands drive the specific objectives of product design, timelines, production scheduling, and product quality" (p. 553). Supplier knowledge application focused on "significant opportunities for integration of suppliers into firm processes" (p. 553).

The financial performance construct represented the business financial performance as traditionally "measured by return on investment, profit and profit growth" (p. 554).

**Measurement Description**

Size was computed as the natural logarithm of the number of employees. Production technology routineness was evaluated using Khandwalla's (1974) weighted mass output orientation scale, which "measures reliance on five types of production technology: custom production; small batch (or job shop) production; large batch production; mass assembly production; and continuous process production. This scale was created by weighing each of the five scores by 1 (custom) to 5 (continuous) and taking the sum" (p. 554). Technological turbulence and demand unpredictability were measured by seven semantic scales. Financial performance was assessed by a 7-point Likert scale with endpoints of 1 = "well below industry average" and 7 = "well above industry average." Respondents were asked to rate performance over the past 3 years to offset particularly good or bad years attributable to unusual circumstances (Miller 1991). Each variable in applied knowledge was calculated as the mean of eight items.

**Development**

The main purpose of the article was to explore the relations among the constructs. Thus, the details of scale development were not provided. Sources of items were based in the knowledge, marketing, TQM, and JIT literatures (e.g., Benson, Saraph, and Schroeder 1991; Davy et al. 1992; Flynn, Schroeder, and Sakakibara 1994; Nonaka et al. 1994; Sakakibara, Flynn, and Schroeder 1993).

### Reliability and Validity

Confirmatory factor analysis (CFA) was conducted to verify the measurement instrument. Composite scale reliabilities and variance extracted were determined. Two types of construct validity were evaluated. First, convergent validity was demonstrated because all item loadings were significant ($p < .01$). Second, discriminant validity was demonstrated using $\chi^2$ difference tests.

### Scores

In the article, the CFA results are given in Table 3, while model results are reported in Table 4.

### Other Evidence

Not available.

### References


Benson, P. G., J. V. Saraph, and R. G. Schroeder. 1991. The effects of organizational context on quality management: An empirical investigation. *Management Science* 37 (9): 1107–124.

Davy, J. A., R. E. White, N. J. Merritt, and K. Gritzmacher. 1992. A derivation of the underlying constructs of just-in-time management systems. *Academy of Management Journal* 35 (3): 653–70.

DeCarolis, D. M., and D. L. Deeds. 1999. The impact of stocks and flows of organizational knowledge on firm performance: An empirical investigation of the biotechnology industry. *Strategic Management Journal* 20 (10): 953–68.

Flynn, B. B., S. Sakakibara, and R. G. Schroeder. 1995. Relationship between JIT and TQM: Practices and performance. *Academy of Management Journal* 38 (5): 1325–60.

Hurley, R. F., and G. T. M. Hult. 1998. Innovation, market orientation, and organizational learning: An integration and empirical examination. *Journal of Marketing* 62 (3): 42–54.

Khandwalla, P. N. 1974. Mass output orientation of operations technology and organizational structure. *Administrative Science Quarterly* 19 (1): 74–97.

Miller, C. C., W. H. Glick, Y.-D. Wang, and G. Huber. 1991. Understanding technology-structure relationships: Theory development and meta-analytic theory testing. *Academy of Management Journal* 34 (2): 370–99.

Nonaka, I., P. Byosiere, C. C. Borucki, and N. Konno. 1994. Organizational knowledge creation theory: A first comprehensive test. *International Business Review* 3 (4): 337–51.

Sakakibara, S., B. B. Flynn, and R. B. Schroeder. 1993. A framework and measurement instrument for just-in-time manufacturing. *Production and Operations Management* 2 (3): 177–94.


## Dröge, Jayaram, and Vickery

### Article Summarized

Dröge, Cornelia, Jayanth Jayaram, and Shawnee K. Vickery. 2004. The effects of internal versus external integration practices on time-based performance and overall firm performance. *Journal of Operations Management* 22 (6): 557–73.

### Scales (Actual Questions Used)

*Strategic Design Integration (External Integration)*

1. Supplier development: implementing policies, procedures, and practices for assessing and improving supplier capability and performance in multiple areas such as quality, design support, and delivery
2. Supplier partnership: bringing all the participants in the product life cycle into the process early on so even suppliers and customers can provide input to each others' processes
3. Closer customer relationships: determining customers' (both inside and outside the firm) requirements, then meeting those requirements no matter what it takes

*Design-Process Integration (Internal Integration)*

4. Concurrent engineering: overlapping activities in product and process development to ensure a match between design requirements and process capabilities, reducing time-to-market
5. Design for manufacturability: an approach (using concepts such as design for assembly, design for serviceability, and design for test) for designing products that can be more effectively manufactured
6. Standardization: the use of standard procedures, materials, parts, and/or processes for designing and manufacturing a product
7. CAD/CAE: the use of computers in interactive engineering drawing and storage of design to obtain graphical views of a part and its relationship with other parts
8. CAM: the use of a computer to program, direct, and control an independent machine in the fabrication of manufactured items

*Time-to-Market*

9. Product development time: the ability to minimize the time it takes to develop new products
10. Product introduction time: the ability to minimize the time to make product improvements/variations to existing products, or to introduce completely new products

*Time-to-Product*

11. Procurement lead time: the ability to minimize the time from order placement to the delivery of the procured item, which includes supplier lead time, transportation, and receiving and inspection
12. Manufacturing lead time: the ability to minimize the time from when the order was released to the shop floor to the time of its completion
13. Delivery speed: the ability to minimize the time between receipt of customer order and final delivery to as close to zero as possible

*Responsiveness*

14. Presale customer service: the ability to service the customer during the purchase decision process (i.e., before the customer buys the product)
15. Product support: the ability to service the customer in providing product support after the sale of the product to ensure continuing customer satisfaction
16. Responsiveness to customers: the ability to minimize the time it takes to cater to customer needs by processing and solving customer complaints by rapid confirmation of orders and by minimizing customer information lead time

**Construct Description**

Strategic design integration, which reaches across firm boundaries to involve suppliers and customers, was formed as a composite index consisting of (1) supplier partnerships, (2) supplier development, and (3) closer customer relationships. Taken together, the authors claimed that these practices effectively integrate a firm's suppliers and customers "into a synergistic network that facilitates product design and development activities (hence the nomenclature, strategic designs integration)" (p. 558).

Design-process integration that consists of more tactically oriented, integration practices that match design requirements and process capabilities was computed as an index consisting of the following: "(1) concurrent engineering, (2) design for manufacturability, (3) standardization, and (4) CAD/CAM" (p. 558).

### Measurement Description

The "extent of use" scale had seven points with endpoints labeled 1 = "extremely low" and 7 = "extremely high use of item." Respondents were told to circle "not used" (coded as zero) if a particular initiative was not used at their strategic business units (SBUs). Time-to-market capability was defined by product development time and new product introduction time. Three types of time-to-product capability—procurement lead time, manufacturing lead time, and delivery speed—were measured. Finally, the three items measuring responsiveness were (1) presale customer service, (2) product support, and (3) responsiveness to customers. These items were also measured by 7-point Likert scales.

### Development

According to the authors, the measures were developed using knowledgeable experts. "A panel of Automotive Industry Action Group (AIAG) experts ensured the content validity of the items and assisted in the pretest" (p. 564).

### Sample

The unit of analysis for this study was composed of SBU and individual firms for first-tier suppliers to the large automobile manufacturers in North America. The top 150 first-tier suppliers (ranked by yearly sales) were used for the purpose. The AIAG, a professional association with more than 1,000 members (Actionline 1995) (p. 564) and their professional experts provided the sampling frame list of companies.

### Reliability and Validity

Experts from the AIAG reassured the content validity of the items. Also, the authors requested the respondents to provide objective measures of firm performance. A majority of the firms (28 of 57) responded to this request. The authors confirmed a high "concordance" between the objective and subjective performance measures (market share: $r = .49$, $p < .01$; growth in market share: $r = .34$, $p < .05$; ROA: $r = .61$, $p < .01$; ROI: $r = .34$, $p < .05$; ROS: $r = .61$, $p < .01$). More respondents answered to subjective measures, however. The authors also conducted a confirmatory factor analysis (CFA) to verify the overall measurement model fit (reported in the article in Table 2). The overall fit was adequate (i.e., $\chi^2 = 192.48$; d.f. = 149; $p = .009$; Bentler-Bonnet non-normed fit index (NNFI) = .98; comparative fit index (CFI) = .97; and standardized root mean-squared residual [SRMSQ] = .046). Factor loadings were considered statistically significant, noting suitable convergent validity.

Lagrange multiplier tests were also conducted to check for "omitted paths." The check revealed no significant "cross loadings," which is an indicator of discriminant validity. The authors seemed particularly concerned with discriminant validity between internal and external integration. They also conducted an exploratory factor analysis (EFA), which revealed two major factors with eigenvalues above 1. Thus, the unidimensionality of the measures was in line with the CFA results. The authors checked for internal consistency using Cronbach's coefficient alpha with results above .60, which is the standard threshold for exploratory research according to the authors. The authors did note that alpha values for internal versus external integration constructs are in the low .60s. Also some of the CFA standardized factor loadings are in the low range.

### Scores

Factor analysis results for each construct and the Cronbach's coefficient alpha scores, including factor loadings and *t*-values are listed in Table 2 of the article.

**Other Evidence**

Not available.

**References**

Aiken, L. S., and S. G. West. 1991. *Multiple regression: Testing and interpreting interactions.* Newbury Park, CA: Sage.

Narasimhan, R., and J. Jayaram. 1998. An empirical investigation of the antecedents and consequences of manufacturing goal achievement in North American, European, and Pan Pacific firms. *Journal of Operations Management* 16 (2/3): 159–76.

Sanchez, A. M., and M. P. Perez. 2003. Cooperation and the ability to minimize the time and cost of new product development within the Spanish automotive supplier industry. *Journal of Product Innovation Management* 20 (1): 57–69.

Vickery, S. K., C. Dröge, and R. E. Markland. 1997. Dimensions of manufacturing strength in the furniture industry. *Journal of Operations Management* 15 (4): 317–30.

# Dröge, Vickery, and Markland

**Article Summarized**

Dröge, Cornelia, Shawnee Vickery, and Robert E. Markland. 1994. Sources and outcomes of competitive advantage: An exploratory study in the furniture industry. *Decision Sciences* 25 (5/6): 669–89.

**Scales (Actual Questions Used)**

*Competitive Items*

[For each item:

a. Rate importance on 7-point scale with endpoints "least important" (1) and "extremely important" (7).
b. Rate firm performance on 7-point scale with endpoints "poor" (1) and "excellent" (7). These ratings were subsequently recoded to a -3 to +3 scale.
c. Rate percentage responsibilities of marketing, PD&D, and manufacturing. Percentages did not need to sum up to 100.]

1. Product flexibility
2. Volume flexibility
3. Process flexibility
4. Low production cost
5. New product introduction
6. Delivery speed
7. Delivery dependability
8. Production lead time
9. Production reliability
10. Production durability
11. Quality (conform to specifications)
12. Design quality/innovation
13. Product development cycle time
14. Product technological innovation

15. Product improvement
16. New product development
17. Original product development
18. Brand image
19. Competitive pricing
20. Low price
21. Advertising/promotion
22. Target market identification/selection
23. Responsive to target market
24. Presale customer service
25. Postsale customer service
26. Broad product line
27. Widespread distribution coverage
28. Low cost distribution
29. Selective distribution
30. Personal sales proficiency
31. Company reputation

*Performance*

[Evaluate performance relative to major competitors for each of the six measures on a 7-point scale with endpoints "worst in industry" (1) and "best in industry" (7)]

32. Return on investment
33. ROI growth
34. Market share
35. Market share growth
36. Return on sales
37. ROS growth

## Construct Description

Functional competence was broadly defined as "the total performance of that area across a broad spectrum of competitive items or priorities" (p. 670). Three functional competency constructs—marketing competency, product design and development (innovation) competency, and manufacturing competency—were developed in this study. Each refered to "the weighted performance on a comprehensive set of competitive elements" (pp. 670–71).

## Measurement Description

Marketing competency, product design and development (innovation) competency, and manufacturing competency were computed as the total weighted sum of performance across the 31 competitive priorities, which were listed on the survey, with importance and functional area responsibility as weighting factors. The importance of each competitive priority was rated using a 7-point scale with endpoints of 1 = "least important" and 7 = "extremely important." The performance was measured based on a 7-point scale with 1 = "poor," which was recoded as -3, and 7 = "excellent," which was recoded as 3.

Six performance items were used to evaluate overall performance relative to firms' major competitors (*see* Scales). Each item was measured on a 7-point scale with endpoints 1 = "worst in industry" and 7 = "best in industry."

## Development

The scales were developed from the strategy, innovation, marketing, and manufacturing literature. The entire questionnaire was validated in advance through several personal interviews conducted on site.

### Sample

The sample focused on strategic business units (SBUs) and firms in the office and residential furniture industry with sales exceeding $10 million. The authors considered this industry as highly competitive although no explanation as to the reason for this categorization was offered. The CEO was the target respondent. The response rate was approximately 20%. Efforts were made to separate out parent firms from constituent SBUs. If a CEO of a parent firm was interviewed, then all related SBU interviews were deleted. Sixty-five firms with mean sales of $121.7 million constituted the final sample. These firms had a mean number of employees at around 1,364, with a standard deviation of 2,713. A majority of the firms were from the Southeast region and West Coast regions (32 firms each), followed by the Midwest region (18 firms) and the Northeast (seven firms).

### Reliability and Validity

The authors used an alternate calculation method to test the validity of the competency scores. The factor (percentage) × (importance) × (performance) was originally used to calculate the competency factors of MKTCOMP, MFGCOMP, and PDDCOMP. A secondary competency score was developed by calculating the (importance) × (performance) factor for select areas, namely the ones with major responsibility. High correlations between the two sets of scores calculated in two alternative approaches for each area ranged from .75 to .87; and therefore, provided some support for the convergent validity of the constructs. Lower correlations between the set of scores across different functional areas varied from .31 to .46. These results indicated "a reasonable degree" of discriminant validity. The correlations between subjective and objective measures of performance ranged from .38 to .65. Therefore, the subjective ratings were judged to show satisfactory validity.

### Scores

Means for the percentage responsibilities are given in Table 1 in the article. Overall, manufacturing showed responsibility for flexibility (volume and process), cost (low production), delivery (speed and dependability), product durability, and conformance quality. Marketing had more responsibility for brand image, advertising and promotion, customer service (pre- and postsales), distribution coverage (widespread and selective), personal sales proficiency, and company reputation. Other items did not have as clear a "mean percent responsibility" distinction, as might have been predicted. By comparison, product development responsibilities seemed to be more "diffuse" than core production or marketing activities. Means and rank order data for the importance and performance ratings are listed in Table 2. Top items showed a considerable degree of consensus among the samples. Means, standard deviations, and correlations for the three competency constructs and the six performance measures are reported in Table 3. Overall performance measures were higher than the scale midpoint of 4. All performance measures were correlated to one another.

### Other Evidence

Not available.

### References

Campbell, D. T., and D. W. Fiske. 1959. Convergent and discriminant validation by the multitrait-multimethod matrix. *Psychological Bulletin* 56 (2): 81–105.

Cleveland, G., R. G. Schroeder, and J. C. Anderson. 1989. A theory of production competence. *Decision Sciences* 20 (4): 655–68.

# Escrig-Tena and Bou-Llusar

### Article Summarized

Escrig-Tena, Ana Belén, and Juan Carlos Bou-Llusar. 2005. A model for evaluating organizational competencies: An application in the context of a quality management initiative. *Decision Sciences* 36 (2): 221–57.

### Scales (Actual Questions Used)

*Leadership*

1. The way management acts makes it easier for employees to accept proposed changes voluntarily.
2. Management is skilled at reaching agreements on objectives and/or important projects.
3. Management behaves in such a way as to allow the integration and mobilization of members of a team.
4. Management continually acquires and updates valuable knowledge for the organization.

*Enacting Organizational Environment*

5. All the members of the firm have a clear idea about what the firm's position in the market should be.
6. All the members of the firm have a clear idea about what is expected of them, making their contribution to the company as beneficial as possible.
7. All the members of the organization know and share the firm's mission and goals.
8. We know the type of products and services the client requires.
9. We know the type of resources, competencies, abilities, and technologies the company requires.
10. We identify new customer and market opportunities because an IS about the environment has been set up.

*Employee Know-how*

11. Employees are able to identify and offer solutions to the problems that may arise in their workplace.
12. Employees at all levels are kept up-to-date on the progress made in their respective fields (new abilities, knowledge, usage of new technologies, and so forth).
13. Employees learn skills and knowledge in the workplace itself as a result of measures made available to them for that purpose.

*External Cooperation Skills*

14. Thanks to the cooperation we maintain with our suppliers, we have raw materials, resources, and services that are better than those of our competitors.
15. Our close relationship with suppliers and clients enables us to find out about new products or services, needs, resources, new technologies, or machinery before our competitors.
16. When we want to make some kind of improvement, we can collaborate with other firms in such a way that they help us to improve.
17. In general, our capacity for outside cooperation is very high.

*Creation of a Collective Mind*

18. Communication between employees is kept smooth, which goes beyond the formal structure of the organization.
19. Employees have been working together for a long time, which ensures they are well coordinated.

20. Internal communication is totally open and transparent.
21. Employees voluntarily transmit useful information to each other.

*Employee Commitment to the Organization*

22. If necessary, employees devote more time to the firm than those stipulated in their normal working hours.
23. Employees play an important part in deciding what work is to be carried out.
24. Employee participation in setting goals and how they are to be achieved is high.
25. We consider workers' level of loyalty to the organization to be high.

*Capacity to Stimulate the Organizational Learning Process*

26. Work processes have been designed in such a way that they are capable of developing standards of conduct at all levels of the firm.
27. Employees are capable of taking the initiative and assimilating better ways of doing their job.
28. There is an important spirit of dialogue and acceptance of diverse opinions in all areas of the firm.
29. Any one person's knowledge is transmitted and made readily available to the rest of the employees.

*Speed and Flexibility in Designing New Products or Services*

30. We are capable of keeping a step ahead of competitors when developing a new product or incorporating a new service.
31. We are capable of making fast changes in design and/or quickly introducing new products or services.
32. The way the firm operates is characterized by being able to provide the customer with a service more quickly.

*Reputation*

33. We have the ability to attract, develop, and maintain valuable personnel.
34. We are able to apply a higher price than our competitors.
35. The reputation of the products or services offered by my firm is better than that of my competitors.
36. We give guarantees for all our products.
37. My firm has built up a better brand image than that of its competitors.

## Construct Description

Competencies were defined as the abilities and specific skills that the firm possessed in the deployment of its resources, as well as its cognitive characteristics. Cognitive characteristics were geared toward the accomplishment of activities that permit the attainment of certain objectives.

## Measurement Description

This article adopted a subjective self-classification approach to measure four unobservable competences associated with quality management. Forty-six indicator variables were first established. After consulting the experts, 37 indicators were retained. A 7-point Likert scale was used for subjective measurement.

## Development

To verify the suitability of the indicators used in the study, the authors consulted a group of experts specialized in the competence-based perspective. This group consisted of 13 experts from a total of 20 academics consulted at various Spanish universities. These experts answered a questionnaire asking them how relevant they thought each item was to the nine competencies. After incorporating the suggestions of the experts, the authors ended up with 37 items that were used in the study.

### Sample

The sample data were provided by the Spanish national ARDAN database, a database that provides information of more than 100,000 firms in Spain. Stratified sampling method was employed to avoid biased sampling. The complexity of the transaction of the sectors chosen varied and the sectors selected were industrial ceramics, paints and glazes, and machinery.

The fieldwork was carried out during October and November, 2000, by face-to-face interviews with CEO or quality managers and by the use of a structured questionnaire. Final sample included 231 companies with 46% from the industrial sector and 54% from the service sector. Forty-five percent of the sampled firms were small firms, 46% were medium firms, and 9% were large firms.

### Reliability and Validity

The constructs were derived from an extensive bibliographic review. Thus, according to the authors, the content validity of the scale was ensured. A confirmatory factor analysis (CFA) analysis was conducted using EQS 5.7. After iteration, seven items were dropped from the scales depending on the individual reliability and the Lagrange multiplier test. As a result, four competences made up of nine factors, which in turn were made up of 30 indicators were included in the model. The goodness-of-fit statistics was reported in Table 4 in the article. To assess discriminant validity, pairwise tests were conducted for all competencies. The test results indicated, statistically, differences among the constructs; and thus, the discriminant validity was affirmed. Chi-square values were shown in Table 6. The proposed causal relationships were shown in Figure 7.

### Scores

Factor loadings, the measurement errors, and the random disturbances for each item are reported in Table 3 in the article. Reliability of the competency measurement scales are provided in Table 5.

### Other Evidence

Not available.

### Reference

None.

---

## Ettlie (1995)

### Article Summarized

Ettlie, John E. 1995. Product-process development integration in manufacturing. *Management Science* 41 (7): 1224–37.

### Scales (Actual Questions Used)

*Design-Manufacturing Integration Scale1*

Coordination and Control Integration

1. Design for assembly (DFA), design for manufacturability (DFM) training
2. Manufacturing sign-off
3. New structures (e.g., teams)

Personnel Integration

4. Job rotation design/manufacturing
5. Design/manufacturing job mobility

**Comparison of 1987 and 1991 Design Practices**

1. We have people who are trained in DFA or DFM. (If yes, Who was trained for what?)
2. A manufacturing representative is required to sign-off on design reviews for new products. (If yes, When are design reviews signed off?)
   a. Concept design
   b. Preliminary design
   c. Prototype
   d. Production release
3. We have developed and implemented new structures to coordinate design and manufacturing. (If yes, what are these structures?)
4. Job rotation between design and manufacturing engineering is practiced in this firm.
5. Personnel from design engineering are sometimes moved to manufacturing engineering or vice versa.

**Construct Description**

Based on the works of Ettlie and Reza (1992), the author defined product-process development integration as "a set of focused, disciplined, rigorous practices designed to concrete efforts on evolving concepts to market introduction." The author linked this definition to the works of Oral, Kettani, and Lang (1991) which considered how discipline could be introduced into the product development process, in a manner similar to the R&D project selection process. As a result, the product development process can be *more* or *less* structured. The author indicated how "policies, structures and practices that focus development on key design issues" (p. 1226) could be included as part of the project selection process.

**Measurement Description**

The product-process development integration was measured using two scales by estimating "the degree of coordination and cooperation between design engineering and the manufacturing function" (p. 1228). Originally these scales were developed as a single multi-item measure composed of five indicators by Ettlie and Stoll (1990). Because of unsatisfactory results in scale development, the scale was divided into two separate scales consisting of two and three items, respectively. Cronbach's coefficient alpha for the three-item scale showed a .54 value, with the interitem correlation equaling .28. Cronbach's alpha for the two-item scale was found to be .67, and the interitem correlation was recorded at .50.

**Development**

While some of the items and scales were based on previous works of Ettlie and Reza (1992) and Ettlie and Stoll (1990), there was no information available for the development of the new items used in the study.

**Sample**

A cross-sectional sample from the mailing list of the Office of Manufacturing Management Research (OMMR) at University of Michigan and a list of select members from National Center for Manufacturing Sciences (NCMS) were used for the development of the sample. Data were compiled using divisions of "well-known" firms with mean sales of $16.7 billion and 77,663 in number of employees. From a total of 122 survey questions, a total of 43 firms or divisions responded (35% usable response rate). Considering multiple company responses, a 47% response rate was achieved. Respondents were middle managers representing a variety of industries (31 product types in 4 U.S. Department of Commerce's Standard Industrial Classification [SIC] codes), including auto, aerospace, machine tools, and appliance manufacturers.

### Validity and Reliability

Validation of the results were made using open-ended questionnaires. The respondents were iteratively asked about the purpose of the new approach to design and the determinants of success in their new approach. Last, they were asked about the barriers to achieving "good" designs quickly. As noted earlier, measurement scale reliability was determined using Cronbach's coefficient alpha and corrected item-total correlation.

### Scores

The scores are presented in Tables 1 and 2 in the article. Both design manufacturing integration scales were noted as influential in the equation, and all three predictors of benchmarking were statistically significant $p < .05$) with 32% of variance explained. Seventy-two percent of the complete data cases were correctly grouped by the discriminant function used.

### Other Evidence

Not available.

### Note

1. Response format: Yes = 3, No = 1, In Process = 2.

### References

Ettlie, J. E., and E. M. Reza. 1992. Organizational integration and process innovation. *Academy of Management Journal* 35 (4): 795–827.

Ettlie, J. E., and H. W. Stoll. 1990. *Managing the design-manufacturing process*. New York: McGraw-Hill.

Oral, M., O. Kettani, and P. Lang. 1991. A methodology for collective evaluation and selection of industrial R&D projects. *Management Science* 37 (7): 871–85.

---

## Ettlie (1997)

### Article Summarized

Ettlie, John E. 1997. Integrated design and new product success. *Journal of Operations Management* 15 (1): 33–55.

### Scales

*Background, Policies, and Practices*

Company Background (to Verify Some Published Data)

1. Principal products (SIC codes in the United States).
2. Current total number of year-round, full-time employers in the firm (to verify published data).
3. Percent shipments (business) out of home country.
4. Please estimate to the nearest 5% the total manufacturing cost represented by purchased and outside costs (material, purchased parts, and subcontracts).

Product Development

5. Does your firm or business unit currently have a program to upgrade the product development process? Yes/No (skip to question 3).
6. What areas does this program cover: (Rank 1 = most important, etc., for all that apply) (a) quality (b) time to market (c) suppliers (d) plant modernization (e) other.
7. What is the current life cycle of your main product(s)? Projected?
8. How long did it take (concept to market) to introduce your last new product? (Years) Goal?
9. What percentage of your annual revenues comes from products introduced during the past 5 years?

*The Product Development Process*

10. The product development process has often been depicted as a sequence of stages such as that given below.

Product Concept → Product Plan → Product Design → Process Design

Consider only *your last major new product* launch that has a track record (no jury out products) when answering the following questions.

11. Name of the last major new product?
12. Date launched?

With regards to just the product *concept development* phase of this product.

13. What percentage of total project duration is devoted to concept development?
14. What proportion of total project cost is determined by the concept development phase?
15. What percentage of total project duration is devoted to product concept, product plan, and product design?
16. What percentage of total project duration is devoted to process design, prototype production, and testing?
17. Is simultaneous or concurrent engineering used for concept development?
18. Is simultaneous or concurrent engineering used for generating ideas before concepts are developed?

*Product Development Strategy*

19. We are supporting at least one major alliance or joint venture arrangement specifically to develop or apply new technology to new products.
20. The first principle in developing new products here is "know how to educate your customer."
21. We are actively engaged in a campaign to recruit the best qualified technical personnel available in engineering or production.
22. We always like to be the first in the industry to introduce a new product.
23. We advertise our new processing technology to our customers.
24. We have a long tradition and reputation in our industry of attempting to be the first to try out new methods and equipment.
25. We are strongly committed to technological forecasting. (If yes) please name the method used.
26. Which of the following statements best describes your new product? (Circle only one).

    Our firm was first in the world to introduce the product................................1
    Our firm was first in the United States to introduce the product........................2
    Our firm was first in the industry to introduce the product..............................3
    Our firm was second or third in our industry to introduce the new product........4

27. At the time of introduction, did this new product incorporate technology that was a *significant* break from past knowledge, technology, or practice in the industry? (Circle only one).

    The most significant breakthrough in the industry for many years.....................1
    A very significant break with the past, but not the most significant...................2
    It represents an improvement on past technology—not a breakthrough.............3
    The new product is a modest improvement on current practice.........................4
    The product is similar to competitors' offerings with some different features.......5
    The product is the same or almost the same as our competitors.......................6
    Don't know.......................................................................................7

28. On the following scale, how could you describe the new product?

    Evolutionary 1 2 3 4 5 6 7 Revolutionary

*Technologies of Integration*

Enterprise Product Definition Tools

29. Initial graphics exchange specification (IGES)
30. Product definition exchange specification (PDES)
31. Quality management tools using the ISO 9000 standards
    - ISO 9001
    - ISO 9002
    - ISO 9003
    - ISO 9004

*Communication Standards*

32. Electronic data interchange
33. Paperless product development
34. Distributed computing environment (DCE)

*Computing Standards*

35. Platform independent software
36. Interoperability
37. Common user interfaces

*Organizational Integration Tools*

38. Design for assembly
39. Design for manufacturability
40. Design for reusability (DFR)
41. Design for serviceability (DFS)
42. Design for disposability (DFD)
43. Proprietary CAD-CAM-CIM (computer integrated manufacturing) software
44. Quality function deployment

*Design Manufacturing Integration*

45. We have people who are trained in DFA or DFM.
46. A manufacturing representative is required to sign-off on design reviews for new products on this system.
47. CAD for product and purchasing are compatible.
48. We have a team for product development that includes OUTSIDE members (nonengineers, e.g., marketing). (If yes, Who [by function] is on this team?)

49. We have implemented new policies or practices to integrate design and manufacturing. (If yes, What are these policies or practices?)
50. We have developed and implemented new structures to coordinate design and manufacturing. (If yes, What are these structures?)
51. Job rotation between design and manufacturing engineering is practiced in this firm.
52. Personnel from design engineering are sometimes moved to manufacturing engineering or vice versa.
53. Do design engineers and purchasing agents/engineers have the same CAD/CAM database access?
54. Do cost accountants rotate through other positions (e.g., industrial engineering)?

*Origin of the Project and Realized Outcomes and Contributions of This New Product*

55. Who first *suggested* that this project (product) be undertaken? Check more than one box if necessary.

| | |
|---|---|
| Inside the firm | Outside the firm |
| R&D Staff | Customer |
| R&D first level supervision | Government representative |
| R&D middle management | Vendor/supplier |
| VP of R&D | University consultant |
| General management | Private consultant |
| Marketing/distribution/sales | Technical/professional colleague, but not paid |
| Production/engineering/technical | Services consultant |
| Other | Other |

56. How *well defined* was the *user need* that this project was intended to fill at the time the project was *initiated*?
57. How *well defined* was the *user need* that this project was intended to fill *late* in the life of the project?
58. How *well defined* was the *business purpose* of this project at the time the project was *initiated*?
59. How *well defined* was the *business purpose* of this project *late* in the life of the project?
60. At the time the project was *initiated*, who was the *intended* user? Check more than one box if necessary.

| | |
|---|---|
| Inside the firm | Outside the firm |
| R&D organization | An external customer: another firm |
| An organizational unit in the firm with responsibility for this line of business | Consumer |
| Marketing/distribution/sales | Government |
| Production | Vendor/supplier |
| Engineering | |
| Finance | |
| Technical services | Some other organizational unit not listed above |
| Other | Other |

61. Was the new product a technical success? (We define technical success as achievement of technical performance required in the project specification.)
62. Was technical success achieved at or very near budgeted cost?
63. Was technical success achieved during the required time period?
64. Overall, was the new product a commercial success (met commercial success expectations)?

65. Was the market share attained by the new product above, about the same as, or below expectations? (Circle one)

    Market share above expectations.......................1
    Market share about same as expectations.........2
    Market share below expectations......................3
    Too soon to tell..............................................4
    Don't know.....................................................5

66. Which one of the following statements best describes the ROI for the new product to date? (Circle only one).

    Below total costs.............................................1
    About equal to operating costs..........................2
    About equal to total costs..................................3
    Moderately above total costs.............................4
    A good multiple of investment............................5
    Too soon to tell..............................................6
    Don't know.....................................................7

67. Were "in-process" measures of project performance used for this new product?
68. Number of design change requests before fully released to production? (Fill in number)
69. Number of actual design change orders actually made after released to production? (Fill in number)
70. Dependence on supplier(s) reduced.
71. Quality improvements (e.g., Cpk. Sigma or scrap and rework?).
72. Other (please indicate)
73. Do you *benchmark* (make visits to other firms and gauge their practices because of their known good reputation) in design approaches?
74. Which organizations do you think are good benchmarks in design approach?

*Marketing*

75. Marketing is a worthwhile investment.
76. I understand the contribution marketing makes to the product development process.
77. Our engineering personnel rotate through marketing training.

## Construct Description

Integrated design was defined as "the coordinated development effort in timing and substance of the various disciplines and organizational functions that span the life-cycle of new products and services. This life-cycle starts with research and development or the invention and capture of new ideas, and ends with the recycling or disposal of product remnants" (pp. 33–34).

## Measurement Description

The author measured the construct of technology adaptation innovativeness by following the approach suggested by Mohr (1969). This approach was "confirmed by Damanpour (1991) and others as the preferred method. This approach used multiple firms with multiple technologies with several 'states' of adoption" (p. 39). Market need understanding "was measured with a summed, four item scale constructed as modified from Baker and Green (1985) which was originally included in the project origins of the questionnaire" (p. 41).

## Development

The scales used in this study were built on earlier work of Zurn (1991), Ettlie and Reza (1992), Susman (1992), and Ettlie (1995). They captured "some aspect of actual behaviors and practices used to integrate the design (often research, development and engineering) with manufacturing functions" (p. 40).

### Sample

"Durable goods firms were used because they have experienced significant global competition in the last decade . . . A total of 126 usable questionnaires were returned before the cut off date of 1 February 1993, for a usable response rate of 29%" (p. 38).

### Validity and Reliability

The construct of new product commercial success was validated as follows: "First, the measure was directly validated for construct validity by correlating archival measures for sales growth (1988–1992, since most of these products were introduced in 1990–1991) and the summed (and averaged) scale measure of commercial success" (p. 41). Reliability was measured by Cronbach's coefficient alpha and corrected item-total correlation.

### Scores

The scores are presented in Table 1 and Figure 1 in the article.

### Other Evidence

Not available.

### References

Baker, N. R., and S. C. Green. 1985. Project characteristics product survey. Report, University of Cincinnati, Cincinnati, OH.

Damanpour, F. 1991. Organizational innovation: A meta analysis of effects of determinants and moderators. *Academy of Management Journal* 34 (3): 555–90.

Ettlie, J. E. 1995. Product-process development integration in manufacturing. *Management Science* 41 (7): 1224–37.

Ettlie, J. E., and E. M. Reza. 1992. Organizational integration and process innovation. *Academy of Management Journal* 35 (4): 795–827.

Susman, G. I., ed. 1992. *Integrating design and manufacturing for competitive advantage*. New York: Oxford University Press.

Zurn, J. T. 1991. Problem discovery function: A useful tool for assessing new product introduction. *IEEE Transactions on Engineering Management* 38 (2): 110–19.

## Fedor, Ghosh, Caldwell, Maurer, and Singhal

### Article Summarized

Fedor, Donald B., Soumen Ghosh, Steven D. Caldwell, Todd J. Maurer, and Vinod R. Singhal. 2003. The effects of knowledge management on team members' ratings of project success and impact. *Decision Sciences* 34 (3): 513–39.

### Scales (Actual Questions Used)

*Team Leadership*

1. Our team leader was effective in getting us to work as a team.
2. Our team leader facilitated the ongoing exchange of information, opinions, and ideas.
3. Our team was managed in a way that maximized the creation of new knowledge.

4. Errors and mistakes were openly discussed within the team.
5. We felt free to critique each other's work.
6. During the project, we were not afraid to experiment with new ideas, even if it took extra time to do so.
7. When we disagreed, we usually worked out our differences in an honest, healthy way.
8. During problem-solving sessions, our team made a concerted effort to get all team members' opinions and ideas before moving forward to a decision.
9. Our team developed a clear, shared vision of what we were trying to accomplish.

*Organizational Support*

10. The team had a designated facilitator who was trained and skilled in team coordination.
11. The team was well trained in how to use systematic problem-solving tools.
12. Our team was given the proper training to function well.
13. Our team had access to the necessary resources (e.g., facilitators, outside resources, databases) to facilitate our learning and effectiveness.
14. We relied on common frameworks, processes, and systems within our team.
15. Decision and support systems were sufficiently standardized to make the team's task easier.

*Project Success*

16. Our group accomplished what it set out to do.
17. I am happy with what we accomplished.
18. Members of our group were generally satisfied with the outcome of the project.
19. Our group performed well.
20. We were able to exceed our initial expectations.

*Expected Impact*

21. What we learned from our project has had a beneficial impact on subsequent projects.
22. What we learned in doing our project has become a valuable resource for the rest of he organization.
23. Our team has been successful in disseminating the "lessons learned" from our project.
24. The results from our project will have far-reaching effects throughout the organization.

**Construct Description**

Constructs were operationally defined in the article as follows: Team leadership was defined as "the quality of direct leadership provided the team in terms of facilitation of open exchange of ideas and critiques" (p. 523). Organizational support included six items and it represented "such as training, structured approaches (e.g., decision support systems), and required resources provided to the team" (p. 523). Project success was defined as "the individual team members' assessment of the degree to which the project's goals were met and whether team members were satisfied with the outcome of the project" (p. 522). Expected impact indicated "the degree to which the individual team members believed that the project would have a positive impact both in terms of time (continual benefit) and organizational breadth (benefit to overall organization)" (p. 522). External generation represented "the processes of obtaining relevant knowledge by means of accessing knowledge from external repositories, the intranet, and the Internet" (p. 524). Internal generation represented "the development of knowledge from internal sources, specifically experimentation and research and development (R&D), creating new prototypes, and tapping into the knowledge of internal experts" (p. 524). Implicit dissemination represented "the process of disseminating relevant knowledge more as a natural course of daily activities, specifically groupware, job rotation, and knowledge databases/warehouses" (p. 525). Finally, explicit dissemination was reported as representing "the process of disseminating relevant knowledge through more formal means, specifically sharing rallies for success stories, lessons-learned presentations, shows and demonstrations, and success and failure stories" (p. 525).

### Measurement Description

A survey of team members were used to assess project success and expected impact as well as "independent variables capturing the team members' perceptions of Leadership and Support" (p. 521). All the items were measured on a 5-point Likert scale ranging from 1 = "strongly disagree" to 5 = "strongly agree." A team leader survey was "used to assess independent variables capturing the team leader's perspective on processes to generate or acquire relevant knowledge and to disseminate knowledge within the course of the project" (p. 523). All the items in the measurement instrument were on a 5-point Likert scale for *extent of use* ranging from 1 = "not at all" to 5 = "to a great extent."

### Development

The project was made up of two stages. In stage 1, semistructured interviews were performed to be able to specify the variables to represent each category. In stage 2, empirical data were gathered and analyses were done.

### Sample

Ten Fortune 100 companies participated in the study. The firms were from the following industries: "automotive, networking equipment, chemicals, textiles, pharmaceuticals, glass, optical fiber, engineering, and information technology services consulting" (p. 520). In the final sample, responses of 48 teams were used. Both team leader and team members' ratings were available for these teams. One hundred and fifty team members were included in the study. Response rate was 62.5% among the team members.

### Validity and Reliability

Cronbach's coefficient alpha values for team members' survey ranged from .87 for the expected impact construct to .94 for the team leadership construct. The team leader survey had alpha values ranging from .68 for the internal generation construct to .79 for the explicit dissemination construct.

### Scores

Factor analysis results are presented in Tables 1a–d in the article. Coefficients from hierarchical linear modeling (HLM) results are reported in Table 3.

### Other Evidence

Not available.

### Reference

None.

---

## Flynn and Flynn

### Article Summarized

Flynn, Barbara B., and E. James Flynn. 2004. An exploratory study of the nature of cumulative capabilities. *Journal of Operations Management* 22 (5): 439–57.

## Scales (Actual Questions Used)

*Strategic Initiative Scales*

Competitive Strategy

1. Product selling price
2. Percent of sales spent on R&D
3. Percent of sales spent on marketing expenses
4. Product quality
5. Brand image

Communication of Strategy

6. In our plant, goals, objectives and strategies are communicated to me.
7. Strategies and goals are communicated primarily to managers.
8. I know how we are planning to be competitive at this plant.
9. I understand the long-run competitive strategy of this plant.

*Top Management Leadership for Quality*

10. All major department heads within our plant accept their responsibility for quality.
11. Plant management provides personal leadership for quality products and quality improvement.
12. The top priority in evaluating plant management is quality performance.
13. All major department heads within our plant work toward encouraging quality production.
14. Our top management strongly encourages employee involvement in the production process.
15. Plant management creates and communicates a vision focused on quality improvement.
16. Plant management is personally involved in quality improvement projects.

*Rewards for Quality*

17. Workers are rewarded for quality improvement.
18. Supervisors are rewarded for quality improvement.
19. If we improve quality, management will reward us.
20. We pay a group incentive for quality improvement ideas.
21. Nonfinancial incentives, such as jackets, coffee cups, and so on, are used to reward quality improvement.

*JIT Delivery by Suppliers*

22. Our suppliers deliver to us on a JIT basis.
23. We receive daily shipments from most suppliers.
24. Our suppliers are certified, or qualified, for quality.
25. We have long-term agreements with our suppliers.
26. Our suppliers deliver to us on short notice.
27. We can depend on on-time delivery from our suppliers.
28. Our suppliers are linked with us by a pull system.

*Supplier Quality Involvement*

29. We strive to establish long-term relationships with suppliers.
30. Our suppliers are actively involved in our NPD process.
31. Quality is our number one criterion in selecting suppliers.
32. We use mostly suppliers that we have certified.
33. We maintain close communications with suppliers about quality.
34. Considerations and design changes.

*Cleanliness and Organization*

35. Our plant emphasizes putting all tools and fixtures in their place.
36. We take pride in keeping our plant neat and clean.
37. Our plant is kept clean at all times.
38. Employees often have trouble finding the tools they need (reverse scaled).
39. Our plant is disorganized and dirty (reverse scaled).

*Setup Time Reduction*

40. We are aggressively working to lower setup times in our plant.
41. We have converted most of the setup time to external time while the machine is running.
42. We have low setup times of equipment in our plant.
43. Our crews practice setups to reduce the time required.
44. Our workers are trained to reduce setup time.

*Interfunctional Design Efforts*

45. Direct labor employees are involved to a great extent (on teams or consulted) before introducing new products or making product changes.
46. Manufacturing engineers are involved to a great extent before the introduction of new products.
47. There is little involvement of manufacturing and quality people in the early design of products, before they reach the plant.
48. We work in teams, with members from a variety of areas (marketing, manufacturing, etc.) to introduce new products.

*Product Design Simplicity*

49. The emphasis in part design is on minimizing the part count.
50. Our engineers make an effort to simplify our product designs.
51. The parts we produce are designed for ease in manufacturability and assembly.

*Activity-Based Costing*

52. Our cost accounting system guides us to eliminate non-value-added activities.
53. We use ABC.
54. We have good traceability of costs to their cost drivers.

*Process Information*

55. Process data gathered from manufacturing inspections are stored for subsequent analysis.
56. Results if in-house product performance testing is easily available.
57. Data on product defects are used as a resource for improvement.

## Construct Description

Not available.

## Measurement Description

The subjective items were measured by 5-point Likert scales.

## Development

The data used in the study were taken from the world class manufacturing (WCM) database, Round II, for further information on the development on this survey please refer to Flynn et al. (1997).

### Sample

The WCM database, Round II was used for this study. The second round of WCM used an extended realm of data collection using a global sample, including plants in Europe (Germany, Italy, England) and far east (Japan) along with the United States. The data included manufacturing plants from three common industries: electronics, machinery, and suppliers of automobile/truck manufacturing, representing "important sectors of industrialized production." The plant was chosen as the level of analysis and samples were arbitrarily chosen from "master lists of traditional and world-class plants" (p. 443). These samples were assembled using published sources with assistance from industry experts. A total of 165 plants participated in this study (60% response rate). The authors pointed out that an equal amount of participation across industries within each country was noted. The authors used a series of questionnaires to request information on various related topics on manufacturing. Many of the topics asked were not used in the study.

### Reliability and Validity

For the strategic initiatives, the Cronbach's coefficient alpha value was higher than .60 as shown in parentheses in Table 1 in the article for all measures. All measures loaded onto a single factor, with eigenvalues higher than 1. The authors noted that there was a possibility for common method bias in the study since the capabilities were measured by the plant manager. To rectify this issue, the authors used a triangulation of data approach. The results of their findings—summarized in Table 2—showed how they provided each of the independent measures to respondents other than the plant manager. Respondents included process engineers, accountants, and quality managers. The authors also justified their findings by noting that "the independent measures were all objective data" (p. 444) as opposed to perceptual data for the capability measures. Appendix A provided factor loadings for the scales.

### Scores

The scores are presented in Tables 1–10 in the article.

### Other Evidence

Not available.

### Reference

Flynn, B. B., R. G. Schroeder, S. Sakakibara, and K. A. Bates. 1997. World-class manufacturing project: Overview and selected results. *International Journal of Operations and Production Management* 17 (7): 671–85.

## Flynn, Sakakibara, and Schroeder

### Article Summarized

Flynn, Barbara B., Sadao Sakakibara, and Roger G. Schroeder. 1995. Relationship between JIT and TQM: Practices and performance. *Academy of Management Journal* 38 (5): 1325–60.

**Scales (Actual Questions Used)**

*Unique TQM Practices*

Customer Focus

1. We frequently are in close contact with our customers.
2. Our customers seldom visit our plant (reverse coded).
3. Our customers give us feedback on quality and delivery performance.

Product Design

4. There is little involvement of manufacturing and quality people in the early design of products, before they reach the plant (reverse coded).
5. We design for producibility.
6. We make an effort, in the design process, to list only the specifications that are clearly needed.
7. The emphasis in part design is on minimizing the part count.
8. We are not concerned about the number of parts in an end item (reverse coded).
9. New product designs are thoroughly reviewed before the product is produced and sold.
10. Manufacturing engineers are involved to a great extent before the introduction of new products.

Statistical Process Control

11. A large number of the equipment or processes on the shop floor are currently under SPC.
12. We make extensive use of statistical techniques to reduce variance in processes.
13. Charts showing defect rates are posted on the shop floor.

*Unique JIT Management Practices*

Kanban

14. Vendors fill our kanban containers, rather than filling purchase orders.
15. Our suppliers deliver to us in kanban containers without the use of separate packaging.
16. We use a kanban pull system for production control.
17. We use kanban squares, containers of signals for production control.

Lot Size Reduction Practices

18. We have large lot sizes in our plant (reverse coded).
19. We tend to have large lot sizes in our master schedule (reverse coded).
20. We are aggressively working to lower lot sizes in our plant.

Setup Time Reduction Practices

21. Our crews practice setups to reduce the time required.
22. We are aggressively working to lower setup times in our plant.
23. We have low setup times of equipment in our plant.

JIT Scheduling

24. We usually meet the production schedule each day.
25. There is no time in the schedule for machine breakdowns or production stoppages (reverse coded).
26. Our schedule is designed to allow time for catching up because of production stoppages for quality problems.

*Common Infrastructure Practices*

Information Feedback

27. I am never told whether I am doing a good job (reverse coded).
28. Information on quality performance is readily available to employees.
29. Information on productivity is readily available to employees.
30. My manager never comments about the quality of my work (reverse coded).

Management Support

31. All major department heads within our plant accept their responsibility for quality.
32. Plant management provides personal leadership for quality products and quality improvement.
33. Management outside the plant is primarily concerned with short-range financial performance (reverse coded).

Plant Environment

34. Our equipment is in a high state of readiness for production at all times.
35. Our plant emphasizes putting all tools and fixtures in their places.
36. We take pride in keeping our plant neat and clean.
37. Our plant is kept clean at all times.
38. Our plant is disorganized and dirty (reverse coded).

Workforce Management

39. Managers in this plant believe in using a lot of face-to-face contact.
40. Direct labor technical competence is high in this plant.
41. Supervisors encourage the persons who work for them to work as a team.
42. We pay a group incentive for quality improvement ideas.
43. Supervisors encourage people who work for them to exchange opinions and ideas.
44. Direct labor undergoes training to perform multiple tasks in the production process.
45. Our plant is organized into permanent production teams.
46. Supervisors frequently hold group meetings where the people who work for them can really discuss things together.
47. Plant employees are rewarded for learning new skills.

Supplier Relationship

48. We strive to establish long-term relationships with suppliers.
49. Our suppliers are actively involved in the NPD process.
50. Quality is our number one criterion in selecting suppliers.
51. We rely on a small number of high-quality suppliers.
52. Our suppliers are certified, or qualified, for quality.

*Performance Variables*

Quality Performance

53. Our plant has superior quality of product and service, compared with its competition in our industry, on a global basis.
54. Our customers have been well satisfied with the quality of our products over the past 3 years.
55. In general, our plant's level of quality performance over the past 3 years has been low, relative to industry norms (reverse coded).
56. Our plant has superior customer relations, compared with its competition in our industry, on a global basis

JIT Performance

57. JIT performance was measured as cycle time defined as the total time from the receipt of raw materials by the plant until the customer receives the product in days, averaged across products.

## Construct Description

Total quality management (TQM) was defined as the effort of a manufacturer to improve the quality of its goods and services and achieve continuous improvement of processes, customer-driven quality, production without defects, focus on improvement of processes rather than criticism of people, and data-based decision making. The practices for achieving these goals were classified into three dimensions: statistic process control (SPC), product design, and customer focus. The principle behind just-in-time (JIT) practices was seen to be that of eliminating waste by simplifying manufacturing processes that include reduction of excess inventories and large lot sizes. These practices were classified into four categories: kanban, lot size reduction practices, JIT scheduling, and setup time reduction practices. Infrastructure practices were defined as those practices that supported both JIT and TQM and were classified into five dimensions: information feedback, plant environment, management support, supplier relationship, and workforce management.

## Measurement Description

A total of 56 items grouped under 13 categories were measured on 5-point Likert scales ranging from 1 = "strongly agree" to 5 = "strongly disagree."

## Development

This study employed a survey-based methodology. An initial set of 50 perceptual scales and 200 items were developed and collected into nine different questionnaires—each targeted at a different response group. The final instrument was set up after a pretest at 12 plants located in the United States. A smaller set of scales was developed from a preliminary set of scales based on factor analysis of items and the opinion of a panel of experts. Finally those items, which did not satisfy the minimum Cronbach's coefficient alpha value of .60, were eliminated.

## Sample

A total of 75 manufacturing plants from the electronics, transportation components, and machinery industries formed the sample for this study. Of these, 42 plants finally participated in the study, yielding a response rate at 60%. The unit of analysis in this study was the plant with responses aggregated to form one response per item per plant.

## Reliability and Validity

Reliability, in terms of internal consistency, was measured by Cronbach's coefficient alpha. Setting the minimum value of alpha at .60 ensured internal consistency. Table 4 in the article listed the alpha values for the scales. Within-scale factor analysis was performed to ensure construct validity. In support of construct validity, the eigenvalue for each of the scales was found to exceed 1.0, and the item factor loadings exceeded .40 on their intended constructs.

## Scores

Mean, standard deviation, and variance of each variable are listed in Table 6 in the article. The correlations are listed in Table 7.

### Other Evidence

Triangulation of data and the opinions of a panel of experts were used to provide additional evidence of construct validity.

### References

None.

---

## Flynn and Saladin

### Article Summarized

Flynn, Barbara B., and Brooke Saladin. 2001. Further evidence on the validity of the theoretical models underlying the Baldrige criteria. *Journal of Operations Management* 19 (6): 617–52.

### Scales (Actual Questions Used)

*Senior Corporate Leadership*

1. Plant management creates and communicates a vision focused on quality improvement.
2. Plant management provides personal leadership for quality products and quality improvement.

*Policy*

3. The top priority in evaluating plant management is quality performance.
4. Our top management strongly encourages employee involvement in the production process.

*Management Systems and Quality Improvement Process*

5. All major department heads within our plant work toward encouraging JIT production.
6. All major department heads within our plant accept their responsibility for quality.

*Use of Analytical Techniques*

7. Process data gathered from manufacturing inspections are stored for subsequent analysis.
8. We use statistical methods to recognize the source of problems.

*Use of Product Quality Data*

9. We use charts to determine whether our manufacturing processes are in control.
10. We monitor our processes using statistical control.

*Customer Data and Analysis*

11. Quality is the number one criterion used by our customers in selecting us as a supplier.
12. Our processes are certified, or qualified, by our customers.

*Supplier Quality Data and Analysis*

13. We require evidence of SPC from suppliers of critical parts.
14. We can easily use data from tests of quality, conducted by our suppliers or an independent laboratory.
15. Our suppliers have to send us information certifying the results of specified tests and inspections on materials.

*Employee Relations Data and Analysis*

16. I receive information about quality performance that helps me with my job.
17. I receive information about waste reduction that helps me with my job.

*Operations and Strategic Goals*

18. We have a regular system of monitoring plant performance against formal criteria.
19. Our plant is well focused.
20. Manufacturing provides competitive strength for our business.

*Planning Function*

21. Our plant has a formal strategic planning process that results in a written mission, long-range goals, and strategies for implementation.
22. Plant management is not included in the formal strategic process. It is conducted at higher levels in the corporation.
23. We have a well-developed manufacturing strategy in our plant.

*Management and Operations*

24. Management takes all product and process improvement suggestions seriously.
25. Management tells us why our suggestions are implemented or not used.
26. We select employees who are able to work well in small groups.
27. Problem-solving teams have helped improve manufacturing processes at this plant.

*Employee Quality Involvement*

28. We are encouraged to make suggestions for improving performance at this plant.
29. Many useful suggestions are implemented at this plant.
30. Our plant forms teams to solve problems.
31. In the past 3 years, many problems have been solved through small group sessions.
32. Employee teams are encouraged to try to solve their problems as much as possible.

*Quality Training and Education*

33. Direct labor undergoes training to perform multiple tasks in the production process.
34. Plant employees receive training and development in workplace skills on a regular basis.

*Evaluation and Recognition Systems*

35. Quality of team participation is a significant part of performance evaluation at this plant.
36. Workers are rewarded for quality improvement.
37. Our incentive system encourages us to vigorously pursue plant objectives.

*Customer Product and Service Input*

38. There is a strong customer focus in our design process.
39. Customer requirements are thoroughly analyzed in the NPD process.

*Planning for New Products and Services*

40. We pursue long-range programs to acquire manufacturing capabilities in advance of our needs.
41. We are constantly thinking of the next generation of technology.

*Design of New Products and Services*

42. Our engineers make an effort to simplify our product designs.
43. New product designs are thoroughly reviewed before the product is produced and sold.

*Measurement and Standards*

44. Quality is the number one criterion used by our customers for selecting us as a supplier.

*Documentation*

45. Written operating procedures are easily accessible to workers on the shop floor.
46. Our written manufacturing procedures are clear and easy to use.
47. Actual operating procedures are very different from our written shop-floor procedures.

*Assurance and Validation*

48. A large percentage of the equipment or processes on the shop floor are currently under statistical quality control.
49. We make extensive use of statistical techniques to reduce variance in processes.

*How My Plant Compares with Its Competition in Its Industry, on a Global Basis*

50. Quality of product performance
51. Product capability and performance
52. Customer support and service
53. Comparison with our competition, on a global basis

*Customer Views of Quality*

54. Our customers are pleased with the products and services we provide for them.
55. Our customers seem happy with our responsiveness to their problems.
56. We have a large number of repeat customers.

*Competitive Comparisons*

57. There is a very small chance that our customers will turn to our competitors.
58. In general, our plant's level of quality performance over the past 3 years has been low, relative to industry norms.

*Customer Service*

59. We strive to be highly responsive to our customers' needs
60. Customer standards are always met by our plant.

*Scope of Quality Data and Information*

61. Charts showing defect rates are posted on the shop floor.
62. Charts showing schedule compliance are posted on the shop floor.
63. Charts plotting the frequency of the machine breakdowns are posted on the shop floor.
64. Information on quality performance is readily available to employees.
65. Information on productivity is readily available to employees.

*Human Resources Management*

66. Management takes all product and process improvement suggestions seriously.
67. We select employees who are able to work well in small groups.
68. Employees at this plant have skills that are above average in industry.

*Employee Involvement*

69. We are encouraged to make suggestions for improving performance at this plant.
70. Many useful suggestions are implemented at this plant.

71. During problem-solving sessions, we make an effort to get all team members' opinions and ideas before making a decision.
72. Our plant forms teams to solve problems.
73. Problem-solving teams have helped improve manufacturing processes at this plant.
74. Employee teams are encouraged to try to solve their problems as much as possible.
75. Quality of team participation is a significant part of performance evaluation at this plant.

*Employee Well-being and Morale*

76. I find that my values and the organization's values are very similar.
77. I am proud to tell others that I am part of this organization.

*Employee Recognition*

78. Workers here are paid for the number of different tasks that they are able to perform.

*Design of Quality Products and Services*

79. We design for producibility.
80. Manufacturing engineers are involved to a great extent before the introduction of new products.
81. We work in teams with members from a variety of areas (marketing, manufacturing, etc.) to introduce new products.
82. Our engineers make an effort to simplify our product designs.

*Product and Service Processes*

83. Our equipment is in a high state of readiness for production at all times.
84. We emphasize good maintenance as a strategy for achieving quality and schedule compliance.
85. Our planning system promotes revision of the long-term production schedule to reach a frozen and feasible short-term schedule.

*Commitment to Customers*

86. Our customers can rely on us for quality products and processes.

*Customer Relations Management*

87. We are frequently in close contact with our customers.

*Customer Satisfaction Determination*

88. Our customers give us feedback on quality and delivery performance.

*Future Requirements of Customers*

89. Our customers are actively involved in the product design process.
90. Customer requirements are thoroughly analyzed in the new product design process.

*Company Specific Results*

91. Innovative manufacturing
92. JIT manufacturing
93. Degree of vertical integration
94. Fast delivery

*Financial and Market Results*

95. Comparison with our competition
96. Unit cost of manufacturing

*Customer Satisfaction Enhancement*

97. We strive to be highly responsive to our customers' needs.
98. Our customers involve us in their quality improvement efforts.
99. Our customers can rely on us for quality products and processes.

*Customer and Market Knowledge*

100. Our customers give us feedback on quality and delivery performance.
101. Our customers are actively involved in the product design process.
102. We regularly survey our customers' requirements.
103. Customer requirements are thoroughly analyzed in new product design process.

### Construct Description

Not available.

### Measurement Description

Most of the items used in this study were 5-point Likert scales, taken from WCM database, Phase II. The details of this study were presented by Flynn, Schroeder, and Sakakibara (1996).

### Development

For details, please refer to Flynn, Schroeder, and Sakakibara (1996).

### Sample

For details on the sample, please refer to Flynn, Schroeder, and Sakakibara (1996).

### Reliability and Validity

The reliabilities of the scores were assessed by Cronbach's coefficient alpha. Item-to-total correlations were used to assess discriminant validity of the scales.

### Scores

The scores are presented in Tables 4–12 as well as Figures 7–9 in the article.

### Other Evidence

Not available.

### Reference

Flynn, B. B., R. G. Schroeder, and S. Sakakibara. 1996. The relationship between quality management practices and performance: Synthesis of findings from the World Class Manufacturing (WCM) project. In *Advances in the management of organizational quality*, eds. D. G. Fedor and S. Ghosh, 141–85. Greenwich, CT: JAI Press.

## Flynn, Schroeder, and Sakakibara (1994)

### Article Summarized

Flynn, Barbara B., Roger G. Schroeder, and Sadao Sakakibara. 1994. A framework for quality management research and an associated measurement instrument. *Journal of Operations Management* 11 (4): 339–66.

**Scales (Actual Questions Used)**

*Dimension I: Top Management Support*

Quality Leadership

1. All major department heads within our plant accept their responsibility for quality.
2. Plant management provides personal leadership for quality products and quality improvement.
3. The top priority is evaluating plant management in quality performance.
4. All major department heads within our plant work toward encouraging JIT production.
5. Our top management strongly encourages employee involvement in the production process.

Quality Improvement Rewards

6. Workers are rewarded for quality improvement.
7. Supervisors are rewarded for quality improvement
8. If I improve quality, management will reward me.
9. We provide a group incentive for quality improvement ideas.
10. Our plant has an annual bonus system based on plant productivity
11. Nonfinancial incentives, such as jackets, coffee cups, and so on, are used to reward quality improvement.

*Dimension II: Quality Information*

Process Control

12. Processes in our plant are designed to be "foolproof."
13. A large percentage of the equipment or processes on the shop floor are currently under statistical quality control.
14. We make extensive use of statistical techniques to reduce variance in processes.

Feedback

15. Charts showing defect rates are posted on the shop floor.
16. Charts showing schedule compliance are posted on the shop floor.
17. Charts plotting the frequency of machine breakdowns are posted on the shop floor.
18. I am never told whether I am doing a good job (reverse coded).
19. Information on quality performance is readily available to employees.
20. Information on productivity is readily available to employees.
21. My manager never comments about the quality of my work (reverse coded).

*Dimension III: Process Management*

Cleanliness and Organization

22. Our plant emphasizes putting all tools and fixtures in their place.
23. We take pride in keeping our plant neat and clean.
24. Our plant is kept clean at all times.
25. I often have trouble finding the tools I need (reverse coded).
26. Our plant is disorganized and dirty (reverse coded).

*Dimension IV: Product Design*

New Product Quality

27. New product designs are thoroughly reviewed before the product is produced and sold.
28. Customer requirements are thoroughly analyzed in the new product design process.
29. Reducing the cost of new products is a more important priority than new product quality (reverse coded).
30. Scheduled concerns are more important than quality in the NPD process (reverse coded).

Interfunctional Design Process

31. Direct labor employees are involved to a great extent (on teams or consulted) before introducing new products or making product changes.
32. Manufacturing engineers are involved to a great extent before the introduction of new products.
33. There is little involvement of manufacturing and quality people in the early design of products, before they reach the plant (reverse coded).
34. We work in teams, with members from a variety of areas (marketing, manufacturing, etc.) to introduce new products.
35. Routine product modifications are made by design engineering or the R&D lab, rather than manufacturing engineering (reverse coded).

*Dimension V: Workforce Management*

Selection for Teamwork Potential

36. We use ability to work in a team as a criterion in employee selection.
37. We use problem-solving ability as a criterion in selecting employees.
38. We use work values and ethics as a criterion in employee selection.

Teamwork

39. Our plant is organized into permanent production teams.
40. During problem-solving sessions, we make an effort to get all team members' opinions and ideas before making a decision.
41. Our plant forms teams to solve problems.
42. In the past 3 years, many problems have been solved through small group sessions.

*Dimension VI: Supplier Involvement*

Supplier Relationship

43. We strive to establish long-term relationships with suppliers.
44. Our suppliers are actively involved in our NPD process.
45. Quality is our number one criterion in selecting suppliers.
46. We rely on a small number of high-quality suppliers.

*Dimension VII: Customer Involvement*

Customer Interaction

47. We are frequently in close contact with our customers.
48. Our customers seldom visit our plant (reverse coded).
49. Our customers give us feedback on quality and delivery performance.

## Construct Description

The overarching construct of quality management was defined by the authors as "an integrated approach to achieving and sustaining high quality output, focusing on the maintenance and continuous improvement of processes and defect prevention at all levels and in all functions of the organization, to meet or exceed customer expectations" (p. 342). According to the authors, quality management was proposed to have seven dimensions: top management support, quality information, process management, product design, workforce management, supplier involvement, and customer involvement.

## Measurement Description

Eleven scales with 49 items were retained in the final instrument to measure the quality management practices. Responses to the items ranged from 1 = "strongly agree" to 5 = "strongly disagree." Approximately one-fourth of the original items were reverse coded. Items within each of the 11 scales averaged per plant.

## Development

Fourteen scales were developed from the existing quality literature to measure seven core dimensions of quality management. The instrument was pretested at 12 plants located throughout the United States, through interviews, plant tours, and administration of the pilot questionnaires. The questionnaire was refined after the pilot study. Item analysis was conducted to further improve the scales. Three scales, Maintenance, Product Design Simplicity, and Labor Skills, were dropped because of the low reliability. The final version of scales was made after the principal component factor analysis. Items that were "nuisance factors" or "clearly represented more than a single domain" were dropped.

## Sample

A total of 75 plants with more than 100 employees were selected, with 25 each from three industries: electronics, transportation components, and machinery. These plants were stratified into plants that had world class reputations, Japanese-owned plants in the United States, and general plants. General plants were randomly selected from *Dun's Industrial Guide: The Metalworking Directory* (1986). Japanese-owned plants were randomly selected from the Japanese External Trade Organization (JETRO). Schonberger's (1986) honor roll and communication with industry leaders served as the source for the master list of world class plants, where the 25 world class plants were randomly chosen from.

A total of seven questionnaires, targeted at various respondents within a plant, were sent to the plant manager, who served as the plant research coordinator. The plant manager selected workers and supervisors at random from the entire plant, distributed the relevant questionnaires to them and collected the completed questionnaires from them. In addition, the plant manager distributed the managerial questionnaires to the appropriate respondents.

A total of 45 plants returned the completed questionnaire set. Three sets were removed because they were deemed inappropriate for the study. The overall response rate was 56%. Detailed information of the plants is provided in Tables 2 and 3.

## Reliability and Validity

To ensure the reliability of each scale, Cronbach's coefficient alpha was used to test the internal consistency among the items included in each scale. A threshold level of .60 was applied for acceptable reliability. The internal consistency was further assessed by computing the Cronbach's coefficient alpha on subsamples by plant ownership and by industry. After deleting Maintenance, Product Design Simplicity, and Labor Skills, the other scales all have Cronbach's coefficient alpha larger than .66.

The content validity of the scales was demonstrated through the extensive literature review and the structured interviews conducted during the pretest plant visits. Principal components factor analysis was used to assess construct validity. The final version of each of the scales was loaded on a single construct with eigenvalues greater than 1.0. Factor loadings were all significant ($p < .05$), which indicated construct validity. In addition, construct validity was also demonstrated by the strong univariate correlations between selected scales and independent measures of the same or similar constructs.

Canonical correlation was used to assess the interrelationship between the scales and two quality performance measures. The analysis showed that most of the individual scales were strongly related to the set of performance measures, and taken as a set, they had a correlation of .80 with the quality performance measures. These results indicated criterion-related validity.

### Scores

The results of factor analysis are presented in Table 6 in the article. The results of canonical correlations are presented in Table 10.

### Other Evidence

Not available.

### Reference

Schonberger, R. J. 1986. *World class manufacturing: The lessons of simplicity applied.* New York: Free Press.

## Flynn, Schroeder, and Sakakibara (1995)

### Article Summarized

Flynn, Barbara B., Roger G. Schroeder, and Sadao Sakakibara. 1995. The impact of quality management practices on performance and competitive advantage. *Decision Sciences* 26 (5): 659–91.

### Scales (Actual Questions Used)

*Top Management Support*

1. All major department heads within our plant accept their responsibility for quality.
2. Plant management provides personal leadership for quality products and quality improvement.
3. Our top management strongly encourages employee involvement in the production process.
4. We have a regular system of monitoring plant performance against formal criteria.
5. We have a well-developed manufacturing strategy in our plant.
6. Our plant is well focused.
7. We have products and/or processes that sometimes place conflicting demands on plant personnel (reverse coded).
8. Management outside the plant is primarily concerned with short-range financial performance (reverse coded).
9. Short-term losses affect our decision making but are less important than pursuing long-term goals.

*Customer Relationship*

10. We are frequently in close contact with our customers.
11. Our customers seldom visit our plant (reverse coded).
12. Our customers give us feedback on quality and delivery performance.

*Supplier Relationship*

13. We strive to establish long-term relationships with suppliers.
14. Our suppliers are actively involved in our NPD process.
15. Quality is our number one criterion in selecting suppliers.
16. We rely on a small number of high-quality suppliers.
17. Our suppliers are certified, or qualified, for quality.

*Workforce Management*

18. Our plant is organized into permanent production teams.
19. Our plant forms teams to solve problems.
20. In the past 3 years, many problems have been solved through small group sessions.
21. Workers are rewarded for quality improvement.
22. Supervisors are rewarded for quality improvement.
23. If I improve quality, management will reward me.
24. We pay a group incentive for quality improvement ideas.
25. Our plant has an annual bonus system based on plant productivity (reverse coded).
26. Nonfinancial incentives, such as jackets, coffee cups, and so on, are used to reward quality improvement.
27. Direct labor undergoes training to perform multiple tasks in the production process.
28. Plant employees are rewarded for learning new skills.
29. Our plant has a low skill level compared with our industry (reverse coded).
30. Direct labor technical competence is high in this plant.
31. Supervisors encourage the persons who work for them to work as a team.
32. Supervisors encourage the people who work for them to exchange opinions and ideas.
33. Supervisors frequently hold group meetings where the people who work for them can really discuss things together.

*Work Attitudes*

34. I talk up this organization to my friends as a great organization to work for.
35. I find that my values and the organization's values are very similar.
36. I am proud to tell others that I am part of this organization.
37. This organization really inspires the best in me in the way of job performance.
38. I am extremely glad that I chose this organization to work for over others I was considering at the time I joined.
39. This plant doesn't have a very definite idea about how things should be done (reverse coded).
40. This plant produces a very special kind of employee.
41. This plant has a clear view about how to achieve goals.
42. Sayings are often told within the plant, which embody organizational wisdoms.
43. Generally speaking, everyone in the plant works well together.
44. Departments in the plant communicate frequently with each other.
45. Departments within the plant seem to be in constant conflict.
46. Management works together well on all important decisions.

*Product Design Process*

47. We make an effort, in the design process, to list only the specifications that are really needed.
48. The emphasis in part design is on minimizing the part count.
49. We are not concerned about the number of parts in an end item (reverse coded).
50. Our new product introduction control process is very formalized with frequent reporting and monitoring.
51. Direct labor employees are involved to a great extent (on teams or consulted) before introducing new products or making product changes.
52. Manufacturing engineers are involved to a great extent before the introduction of new products.
53. There is little involvement of manufacturing and quality people in the early design of products before they reach the plant (reverse coded).
54. We work in teams, with members from a variety of areas (marketing, manufacturing, etc.) to introduce new products.

55. We design for producibility.
56. New product designs are thoroughly reviewed before the product is produced and sold.
57. Customer requirements are thoroughly analyzed in the new product design process.

*Process Flow Management*

58. Processes in our plant are designed to be "foolproof."
59. We dedicate a portion of every day solely to maintenance.
60. We have a separate shift or part of a shift reserved each day for maintenance activities.
61. Our plant emphasizes putting all tools and fixtures in their place.
62. We take pride in keeping our plant neat and clean.
63. Our plant is kept clean at all times.
64. I often have trouble finding the tools I need (reverse coded).
65. Our plant is disorganized and dirty (reverse coded).
66. Our schedule is designed to allow time for catching up because of production stoppages for quality problems.
67. We usually meet the production schedule every day.
68. Production is stopped immediately for quality problems.
69. We have laid out the shop floor so that process and machines are in close proximity to each other.
70. Direct labor is authorized to stop production for quality problems.
71. We hardly ever see managers on the shop floor (reverse coded).

*Statistical Control/Feedback*

72. Charts showing defect rates are posted on the shop floor.
73. Charts showing schedule compliance are posted on the shop floor.
74. Charts plotting the frequency of machine breakdowns are posted on the shop floor.
75. I am never told whether I am doing a good job.
76. Information on quality performance is readily available to employees.
77. Information on productivity is readily available to employees.
78. My manager never comments about the quality of my work.

*Perceived Quality Market Outcomes*

79. The quality of our plant's product and service is superior to the competition on a global basis.
80. Our plant's customer relations are superior to the competition on a global basis.
81. Our customers have been well satisfied with the quality of our products over the past 3 years.
82. In general, our plant's level of quality performance over the past 3 years has been low relative to industry norms (reverse coded).

*Competitive Advantage*

Opinion about how your plant compares with its competition in your industry on a global basis.

83. Unit cost of manufacturing
84. Fast delivery
85. Flexibility to change volume
86. Inventory turnover
87. Cycle time (from receipt of raw materials to shipment)

**Construct Description**

Quality management practices were grouped into two categories: core quality management practices, which lead to improved quality performance directly; and quality management infrastructure practices, which created "an environment supportive of the use of core quality management practices"

(p. 659). The fundamental quality management practices addressed were process flow management, product design process, and statistical control and feedback. The infrastructure components were customer relationship, supplier relationship, work attitudes, workforce management, and top management support.

The quality performance included two constructs: perceived quality market outcomes and percent of items that pass final inspection without requiring rework. Perceived quality market outcomes focused "on management's perception of the product quality and customer service" (p. 665) compared with its competitors, whereas the latter percentage metric was considered to be "an internal measure of the plant's ability to control its processes so that quality is designed and built into its products" (p. 665). The construct of competitive advantage described how a plant created "value for its customers by outperforming its" (p. 668) competitors on "the dimensions of low cost, fast delivery, volume flexibility, inventory turnover and cycle time" (p. 668).

### Measurement Description

There were 11 variables in the framework. Except for the single item, objective measure—percentage of items that passed final inspection without requiring rework—the other 10 variables were measured "as the mean value on a perceptual scale, where a value of one indicated the best performance and a value of five indicated the worst performance" (p. 668).

### Development

The quality management scales were built on the literature after discussion with managers. These scales were assembled into seven questionnaires, each of which targeted at different respondents in a plant who were expected to be most knowledgeable about the content. Altogether, 11 managers and 10 workers in each plant received questionnaires. Responses from different respondents were averaged into a single plant response per scale. The final instrument was set up after pretests at 12 plants located in the United States.

### Sample

As part of a larger data collection effort, data were collected by questionnaires from a stratified random sample of 75 manufacturing plants with greater than 100 employees in the machinery, electronics, and transportation components industries. In the random sample, there were three different types of plants: Japanese-owned and operating in the United States, world-class reputation and U.S.-owned, and traditional, U.S.-owned. In addition, all plants represented different parent corporations. Of the 75 plants, 60% (45 plants) responded. After removing 3 plants that were not appropriate to the sample design, 42 plants were retained for analyses.

### Reliability and Validity

Reliability, in terms of internal consistency, was measured by Cronbach's coefficient alpha. The final Cronbach's coefficient alpha values for all scales exceeded .60, which indicated internal consistency. Table 5 reported the alpha value for each scale.

Construct validity was examined using within-scale factor analysis. Eigenvalues for each of the 11 factors exceeded 1.00. The fact that factor loadings for each item were larger than .40 provided supportive evidence of construct validity.

Some evidence of predicative validity was provided by the mixed results from the tests of the proposed model based on path analysis. The revised model along with all estimates of path coefficients is presented in Figure 2.

### Scores

Mean, standard deviation, and variance of each variable and its zero-level correlation and covariance with all other variables are listed in Table 3.

### Other Evidence

Not available.

### Reference

None.

---

# Flynn, Schroeder, and Flynn

### Article Summarized

Flynn, Barbara B., Roger G. Schroeder, and E. James Flynn. 1999. World class manufacturing: An investigation of Hayes and Wheelwright's foundation. *Journal of Operations Management* 17 (3): 249–69.

### Scales (Actual Questions Used)

*WCM Practices*

Dimension 1: Workforce Skills and Capabilities

Employee Development

1. Direct labor undergoes training to perform multiple tasks in the production process.
2. Plant employees are rewarded for learning new skills.
3. Our plant has a low skill level compared with our industry (reverse coded).
4. Direct labor technical competence is high in this plant.
5. We use knowledge and skill level as criteria in selecting employees.
6. We use ability to work in a team as a criterion in employee selection.
7. We use problem-solving ability as a criterion in selecting employees.
8. We use work values and ethics as criteria in employee selection.

Dimension 2: Management Technical Competence

Management Technical Competence

Percentage of the staff having engineering or technical degrees.

Dimension 3: Competing Through Quality

Design for Customer Needs

9. We frequently are in close contact with our customer.
10. Our customers seldom visit our plant (reverse coded).
11. A very important objective is to obtain satisfied customers.
12. Our customers give us feedback on quality and delivery performance.
13. Customer requirements are thoroughly analyzed in the new product design process.
14. There is a strong customer focus in our design process.
15. Direct labor employees are involved to a great extent (on teams or consulted) before introducing new products or making product changes.
16. Manufacturing engineers are involved to a great extent before the introduction of new products.
17. There is little involvement of manufacturing and quality people in the early design of products before they reach the plant (reverse coded).
18. We work in teams, with members from a variety of areas (marketing, manufacturing, etc.), to introduce new products.

Dimension 4: Workforce Participation

Worker Participation

19. Quality of team participation is significant part of performance evaluation at this plant.
20. Strategies and goals are communicated primarily to managers (reverse coded).
21. I know how we are planning to be competitive at this plant.
22. Supervisors encourage the persons who work for them to work as a team.
23. Supervisors encourage people who work for them to exchange opinions and ideas.
24. Supervisors frequently hold group meetings where the people who work for them can really discuss things together.
25. Managers here are more likely to send a memo than to tell us something face-to-face (reverse coded).
26. During problem-solving sessions, we make an effort to get all team members' opinions and ideas before making a decision.
27. Our plant forms teams to solve problems.
28. In the past 3 years, many problems have been solved through small group sessions.

Dimension 5: Rebuilding Manufacturing Engineering

Proprietary Equipment

The sum of the percentage of the plants' equipment: vendor equipment, which we modified for our use; proprietary equipment designed by the company; and proprietary equipment designed and built by the company.

Dimension 6: Incremental Improvement Approaches

Continuous improvement

29. All employees believe that it is their responsibility to improve quality in the plant.
30. Continuous improvement of quality is stressed in all work processes throughout our plant.
31. I am constantly working to improve quality.
32. Quality improvement is not a high priority for me (reverse coded).
33. Workers are rewarded for quality improvement.
34. Supervisors are rewarded for quality improvement.
35. If I improve quality, management will reward me.
36. Managers are rewarded for making continuous improvements.

*Core Quality Practices*

Process Control

37. Processes in our plant are designed to be "foolproof."
38. We have standardized process instructions that are given to personnel.
39. A large percentage of the equipment or processes on the shop floor are currently under statistical quality control.
40. We make extensive use of statistical techniques to reduce variance in processes.

Feedback of Information

41. Charts showing defect rates are posted on the shop floor.
42. Charts showing schedule compliance are posted on the shop floor.
43. Charts plotting the frequency of machine breakdowns are posted on the shop floor.
44. Information in quality performance is readily available to employees.
45. Information on productivity is readily available to employees.

*Core JIT Practices*

Pull System

46. We have laid out the shop floor so that processes and machines are in close proximity to each other.
47. Direct labor is authorized to stop production for quality problems.
48. We use a pull system to control our production.
49. We use a kanban pull system for production control.
50. We use kanban squares, containers, or signals for production control.

JIT Supplier Relations

51. Our vendors supply us on a JIT basis.
52. We receive daily shipments from most suppliers.
53. Our suppliers are certified, or qualified, for quality.
54. We have long-term arrangements with our suppliers.

**Construct Description**

Ten independent constructs were identified from the literature. Six of them (worker development, management technical competence, competing through quality, workforce participation, rebuilding manufacturing engineering, and incremental improvement approach) corresponded to Hayes and Wheelwright's six world class manufacturing (WCM) practices, and the other four constructs, which represent quality management process improvement and core just-in-time (JIT) practices, were developed based on the literature of new manufacturing practices, especially the work of WCM by Schonberger (1986) and by Giffi, Roth, and Seal (1990).

The description of these 10 constructs is listed as follows. Worker development focused "on training, skill level, and criteria for employee selection, measuring Hayes and Wheelwright's 'workforce skills and capabilities'" (p. 260). Management technical competence was defined as "the technical literacy as a prerequisite for management careers" (p. 266). Competing through quality measured true customer orientation and coordination among functional areas in designing products and focused on the design process and how the customer is integrated into it. Workforce participation represented the real worker participation, including the use of teams and the culture change that accompanied it. Rebuilding manufacturing engineering was defined as "the ability to design and manufacture equipment for their own factories, as well as perform major repairs and modifications and the ability to compete on the basis of unique process technology" (p. 267). Incremental improvement approach was operationalized as continuous improvement. It measured the ability to survive and thrive in a competitive environment where success was based on a series of small steps rather than on a few dramatic breakthroughs. Process control dealt "with techniques to control process variability, including the use of SPC, fool proofing, inspection and the use of standardized process instruction" (p. 260). Feedback of information was described as "the extent of process feedback received by employee, including defect rates, schedule compliance, machine breakdown frequency, and quality performance" (p. 260). The pull system described "the extent to which production is driven by customer demand. JIT supplier relations describe the extent of coordination with suppliers to ensure JIT deliveries" (p. 260).

Based on Hayes and Wheelwright (1984), eight dependent variables were defined. They were cost, quality-performance, quality-features, dependability-specifications, dependability-on-time delivery, dependability-service, product flexibility, and volume flexibility. Complete definitions of the dependent variables can be found in Table 3 in the article.

**Measurement Description**

Ten independent variables were grouped into three sets. The first set corresponded to Hayes and Wheelwright's (1984) six WCM practices. The second set measured quality management process improvement. The third set consisted of the last two independent variables that were associated with core JIT practices. Among them, management technique competence and proprietary equipment were measured objectively, while all the others were measured perceptually. Seven dependent variables were chosen to represent Hayes and Wheelwright's description of the dimensions of competitive priorities. They were a mix of objective and perceptual measures.

### Development

Little detail was provided regarding the development of the final instrument. The final scales of both independent and dependent variables were constructed by selecting the perceptual and objective measures that corresponded most closely to Hayes and Wheelwright's description of world class practices from the existing WCM project data set. When necessary, a new scale was constructed by combining several items from the original WCM project scales. However, the quality management process focus and core JIT scales were not modified from the original scales in the WCM project data set.

### Sample

Data were collected from a stratified sample of three types of manufacturing plants: world-class reputation, traditional, and Japanese-owned plants. These plants were randomly selected from machinery, electronics, and transportation components industries. A master list of world-class manufacturers was used as the base of choosing world-class reputation plants. The traditional plants were randomly selected from Dunn's Guide. The Japanese-owned plants that operate in the United States were randomly selected from a Japanese-language source published by JETRO.

A packet of 21 questionnaires was sent to multiple respondents in each participating plant, the corresponding managers, and a random sample of 10 direct labors. A subset of the information gathered through the questionnaires was used for this study. The overall response rate was 60% and no respondent bias existed.

### Reliability and Validity

The authors state that since all the Cronbach's coefficient alpha values were larger than .70, the scales were proved to be reliable. Evidence of divergent validity mainly came from two sources. First, alpha values for each variable were higher than the average interscale correlation. Second, the correlations between items and the scales they were associated with were higher than the correlations between items and the remaining scales. However, the convergent validity was not tested because clearly Hayes and Wheelwright's WCM practices were not unidimensional.

Predictive validity was demonstrated by the empirical support for the hypothesis testing, that is, "the use of world class manufacturing practices, alone and in combination with new manufacturing practices, led to the achievement of simultaneous competitive advantages" (p. 255).

### Scores

The mean and standard deviation of each variable is reported in Table 4 in the article. The results of the regression analysis are presented in Table 8. In addition, Table 6 contains the intercorrelation matrix.

### Other Evidence

Not available.

### References

Giffi, C., A. V. Roth, and G. M. Seal. 1990. *Competing in world class manufacturing: America's 21st century challenge*. Homewood, IL: Business One Irwin.

Hayes, R. H., and S. C. Wheelwright. 1984. *Restoring our competitive edge: Competing through manufacturing*. New York: Wiley.

Schonberger, R. J. 1986. *World class manufacturing: The lessons of simplicity applied*. New York: Free Press.

# Forker

### Article Summarized

Forker, Laura B. 1997. Factors affecting supplier quality performance. *Journal of Operations Management* 15 (4): 243–69.

### Scales (Actual Questions Used)

*Role of Top Management and Quality Policy*

1. Assumption of responsibility for quality performance by the most senior executive responsible for profit and loss (P&L)
2. Acceptance of responsibility for quality by major department heads
3. Importance of quality results in top management performance appraisals
4. Support by top management of long-term quality improvement process
5. Participation by department heads in the quality improvement process
6. Degree to which objectives are set by top management for quality performance
7. Specific quality goals set within the firm
8. Extent of functional involvement (# of functions included) in the firm's quality goal-setting process
9. Clear understanding by top management of quality goals and policy set within the firm
10. Importance attached to quality by top management in relation to costs and schedules
11. Review of quality issues in top management meetings
12. Belief by top management that quality improvement is a way to increase profits
13. Existence of a complete quality plan in the firm

*Product/Service Design*

14. Thorough new product/service design reviews before the product/service is produced and marketed
15. Coordination among affected departments in the product/service development process
16. Emphasis on quality of new products/services instead of cost or schedule objectives
17. Unambiguous product specifications and procedures
18. Consideration of implementation/producibility in the product/service design process
19. Emphasis on quality by sales, customer service, and public relations (PR) personnel

*Supplier Quality Management*

20. Extent to which you select suppliers based on quality rather than price or schedule
21. Thoroughness of your supplier rating system
22. Reliance by you on a few dependable suppliers
23. Amount of education you provide your suppliers
24. Extent of technical assistance you provide your suppliers
25. Involvement of suppliers in your product development process
26. Extension of long-term contracts to your suppliers
27. Clarity of specifications provided to your suppliers

*Role of the Quality Department*

28. Visibility of the quality department in the firm
29. Degree of access the quality department has to top management
30. Degree of decision-making influence of the quality department
31. Coordination between the quality department and other departments
32. Effectiveness of the quality department at influencing quality improvement

*Process Management/Operating Procedures*

33. Use of preventive equipment maintenance
34. Automation of inspection, review, checking of work
35. Evenness of production schedules/work distribution
36. Automation of processes
37. "Foolproofing" of process design to minimize chances of employee errors
38. Unambiguous work or process instructions given to employees

*Quality Data and Reporting*

39. Data available on quality costs in your firm
40. Data available on quality shortfalls (error rates, defect rates, scrap, number of defects)
41. Timeliness of the quality data
42. Use of quality data as tools to manage quality
43. Relevance of the quality data made available to hourly employees
44. Relevance of the quality data made available to managers and supervisors
45. Use of quality data to evaluate supervisor and managerial performance
46. Display of quality data, control charts, and so on at employee work stations

*Employee Relations*

47. Implementation of quality-related employee involvement programs
48. Effectiveness of implemented quality-related employee involvement programs
49. Responsibility assigned to employees for error-free output
50. Feedback provided to employees on their quality performance
51. Participation in quality decisions by nonsupervisory employees
52. Continual enhancement of quality awareness among employees
53. Recognition of employees for superior quality performance
54. Extent of supervisors' effectiveness in solving quality problems

*Training*

55. Specific work-skills training (technical and vocational) given to hourly employees in the firm
56. Quality-related training given to hourly employees throughout the firm
57. Quality-related training given to managers and supervisors throughout the firm
58. Firm-wide training in the total quality concept (philosophy of company-wide responsibility for quality)
59. Firmwide training in basic statistical techniques (e.g., histograms and control charts)
60. Firmwide training in advanced statistical techniques (e.g., design of experiments and regression analysis)
61. Commitment of top management to employee training
62. Available resources for employee training

**Construct Description**

Eight practice-based scales based on the 62 items listed above constituted a measurement instrument for total quality management (TQM). TQM was defined as "an integrated system of principles and procedures that utilizes quantitative (technical) and human resource (behavioral) methods to improve the quality of material and service inputs, intra- and interorganizational processes, and an organization's focus on meeting customer needs" (p. 244). The collection of eight practices that operationalized TQM in this research included: (1) role of top management and quality policy, (2) product/service design, (3) supplier quality management (SQM), (4) role of the quality department, (5) process management/operating procedures, (6) quality data and reporting, (7) employee relations, and (8) training.

The construct of quality performance in this study was narrowed and defined in terms of the "conformance" dimension—in other words, "the extent to which a product's design and operating characteristic meet predetermined standards" (p. 244).

## Measurement Description

The multi-item measurement scales that were intended to capture the implementation of the quality practice listed above were adapted from the original Saraph, Benson, and Schroeder's (1989) research instrument. Several modifications were made in the present study, however. First, while Saraph, Benson, and Schroeder (1989) used a scale that evaluated level of use (from very low to very high) of current and ideal practice of each item, the survey instrument used in the present study employed a scale measuring "Current extent of use" (from no extent to great extent) based on the consideration that a desired scale for the perceptual measures of quality management practice should reflect the "degree" of quality (i.e., conformance to specification). Second, 5-point scales were chosen over 7-point scales because of the findings of Lissitz and Green (1975) who showed through a Monte Carlo simulation that the improvement in reliability (as evidenced by coefficient alpha) levels off after 5 scale points were exceeded. The scales were assigned as 1 = "no extent" and 5 = "to great extent."

To determine the relative efficiency that indicated the structural differences among the suppliers, data envelopment analysis (DEA) was used. DEA scores indicated the relative efficiency of each supplier. They were calculated as the maximum ratio of weighted atomic parts per million (APPM; output) to weighted TQM practices (inputs), subject to the conditions that similar ratios for every supplier be less than or equal to 1 and that weights chosen for the various inputs and output be greater than or equal to 0.

Two variables, supplier dependence (SUPD) and customer dependence (CUSD), were operationalized to measure the construct of bilateral dependence between the buyer and supplier firms. SUPD was measured as the percentage of business the common customer firm accounted for in each supplier's operations for the primary product or product line supplied to this customer. Similarly, CUSD was measured as the percentage of the common customer's purchases each supplier firm accounted for, for the primary product or product line procured.

## Development

The research instrument developed by Saraph, Benson, and Schroeder (1989) for measuring the critical factors of quality management was chosen to measure quality practices because of its empirical verification in a different production (and geographic) setting. There were 62 quality management practices in total that were included in this study's survey instrument. A total of 16 items from the original research instrument were deleted either to improve the instrument's reliability or to keep the questions updated.

In addition, the instrument was also pretested with four firms before the final instruments were mailed to the whole sample.

## Sample

The aerospace firms contacted for this study were all suppliers to a common customer fabricator of aerospace subassemblies. The common customer firm was a division of a Fortune 500 conglomerate corporation. The division supplied various subassemblies and services to aviation customers, both military and civilian, in the government, commercial, and overseas markets.

Among the 348 aerospace component suppliers that were mailed survey instruments to, 264 usable responses were received for a response rate of 76%. Respondent firms ranged in size from 3 employees to 3,700 employees, with average firm size around 253 workers. Respondents were located in geographic areas across North America and represented a variety of product lines.

## Reliability and Validity

Each construct was factor analyzed and checked for reliability. Component loadings for the constructs stayed within a bandwidth of from .58 to .88. Average item-to-total correlations for the constructs ranged from .80 to .66. Cronbach's coefficient alpha ranged from .94 to .81 for the eight TQM constructs. No TQM construct was significantly correlated with an objective measure of quality performance, but the purpose of the study was to demonstrate the nonlinear relationship between TQM practices and quality performance. This criterion-related validity was established through the statistical significance of five interaction terms and five TQM practices when interaction terms were included in the model (adjusted $R^2$ for the model = .876).

### Scores

The scores of the study are presented in Tables 3–11 in the article.

### Other Evidence

This same survey instrument also had been deployed by Forker, Mendez, and Hershauer (1997) in the electronic components industry, using a similar methodology (surveying the supply base of a common customer firm). Two hundred and ninety-two responses were received for a usable response rate of 69%. Similar results were obtained from the electronic components suppliers' survey with respect to reliability and criterion-related validity: component loadings remained in the .86 to .64 range; average item-to-total correlations were as high as .82 for the employee relations construct and as low as .70 for the SQM construct; and coefficient alphas ranged from .94 to .81 for role of top management and quality policy constructs to .81 for the process management/operating procedures construct. No TQM practice was directly correlated with quality performance but several interaction variables emerged significant when regressed with the TQM variables on the objective quality performance variable.

### References

Forker, L. B., D. Mendez, and J. C. Hershauer. 1997. Total quality management in the supply chain: What is its impact on performance? *International Journal of Production Research* 35 (6): 1681–701.

Lissitz, R. W., and S. B. Green. 1975. Effect of the number of scale points on reliability: A Monte Carlo approach. *Journal of Applied Psychology* 60 (1): 10–13.

Saraph, J., P. G. Benson, and R. Schroeder. 1989. An instrument for measuring the critical factors of quality management. *Decision Sciences* 20 (4): 810–29.

---

## Forker, Mendez, and Hershauer

### Article Summarized

Forker, Laura B., David Mendez, and James C. Hershauer. 1997. Total quality management in the supply chain: What is its impact on performance? *International Journal of Production Research* 35 (6): 1681–701.

### Scales (Actual Questions Used)

*Role of Top Management and Quality Policy*

1. Assumption of responsibility for quality performance by the most senior executive responsible for profit and loss (P&L)
2. Acceptance of responsibility for quality by major department heads
3. Importance of quality results in top management performance appraisals
4. Support by top management of long-term quality improvement process
5. Participation by department heads in the quality improvement process
6. Degree to which objectives are set by top management for quality performance
7. Specific quality goals set within the firm

8. Extent of functional involvement (# of functions included) in the firm's quality goal-setting process
9. Clear understanding by top management of quality goals and policy set within the firm
10. Importance attached to quality by top management in relation to costs and schedules
11. Review of quality issues in top management meetings
12. Belief by top management that quality improvement is a way to increase profits
13. Existence of a complete quality plan in the firm

*Product/Service Design*

14. Thorough new product/service design reviews before the product/service is produced and marketed
15. Coordination among affected departments in the product/service development process
16. Emphasis on quality of new products/services instead of cost or schedule objectives
17. Unambiguous product specifications and procedures
18. Consideration of implementation/producibility in the product/service design process
19. Emphasis on quality by sales, customer service, and PR personnel

*Supplier Quality Management*

20. Extent to which you select suppliers based on quality rather than price or schedule
21. Thoroughness of your supplier rating system
22. Reliance by you on a few dependable suppliers
23. Amount of education you provide your suppliers
24. Extent of technical assistance you provide your suppliers
25. Involvement of suppliers in your product development process
26. Extension of long-term contracts to your suppliers
27. Clarity of specifications provided to your suppliers

*Role of the Quality Department*

28. Visibility of the quality department in the firm
29. Degree of access the quality department has to top management
30. Degree of decision-making influence of the quality department
31. Coordination between the quality department and other departments
32. Effectiveness of the quality department at influencing quality improvement

*Process Management/Operating Procedures*

33. Use of preventive equipment maintenance
34. Automation of inspection, review, checking of work
35. Evenness of production schedules/work distribution
36. Automation of processes
37. "Fool-proofing" of process design to minimize chances of employee errors
38. Unambiguous work or process instructions given to employees

*Quality Data and Reporting*

39. Data available on quality costs in your firm
40. Data available on quality shortfalls (error rates, defect rates, scrap, number of defects)
41. Timeliness of the quality data
42. Use of quality data as tools to manage quality
43. Relevance of the quality data made available to hourly employees
44. Relevance of the quality data made available to managers and supervisors
45. Use of quality data to evaluate supervisor and managerial performance
46. Display of quality data, control charts, and so on at employee work stations

*Employee Relations*

47. Implementation of quality-related employee involvement programs
48. Effectiveness of implemented quality-related employee involvement programs
49. Responsibility assigned to employees for error-free output
50. Feedback provided to employees on their quality performance
51. Participation in quality decisions by nonsupervisory employees
52. Continual enhancement of quality awareness among employees
53. Recognition of employees for superior quality performance
54. Extent of supervisors' effectiveness in solving quality problems

*Training*

55. Specific work-skills training (technical and vocational) given to hourly employees in the firm
56. Quality-related training given to hourly employees throughout the firm
57. Quality-related training given to managers and supervisors throughout the firm
58. Firmwide training in the total quality concept (philosophy of company-wide responsibility for quality)
59. Firmwide training in basic statistical techniques (e.g., histograms and control charts)
60. Firmwide training in advanced statistical techniques (e.g., design of experiments and regression analysis)
61. Commitment of top management to employee training
62. Available resources for employee training

## Construct Description

Eight scales, comprised of the 62 items that were listed above, tap into a measurement instrument for total quality management (TQM). TQM was defined as "an integrated system of principles and procedures whose goal is to improve the quality of an organization's goods and services" (p. 1681). TQM was operationalized in this research as the collection of eight practices: (1) role of top management and quality policy, (2) product/service design, (3) supplier quality management (SQM), (4) role of the quality department, process management/operating procedures, quality data and reporting, employee relations, and training.

## Measurement Description

Multi-item measurement scales for the implementation of the quality practices listed above were adapted from the original Saraph, Benson, and Schroeder's (1989) research instrument. Several modifications were made in the present study. First, while Saraph, Benson, and Schroeder (1989) used a scale that evaluated level of use (from 1 = "very low" to 7 = "very high") of current and ideal practice of each item, the survey instrument used in the present study employed a scale measuring "current extent of use" (from 1 = "no extent" to 5 = "great extent") based on the consideration that a desired scale for the perceptual measures of quality management practice should reflect the "degree" of quality (i.e., conformance to specification). Second, 5-point scales were chosen over 7-point scales because the findings of Lissitz and Green (1975) showed through a Monte Carlo simulation that the improvement in reliability, as evidenced by Cronbach's coefficient alpha, levels off when 5-scale points were exceeded. The items assigned to each construct by the original three researchers (Saraph, Benson, and Schroeder 1989) were averaged together to come up with an overall score for each scale.

## Development

The research instrument developed by Saraph, Benson, and Schroeder (1989) for measuring the critical factors of quality management was chosen to measure quality practices because of its empirical verification in a different production (and geographic) setting. A total of 62 quality management practices were included on this study's survey instrument. A total of 16 items from the original research instrument were deleted for the following reasons: (1) either to improve the instrument's reliability or (2) to keep the questions updated. In addition, the instrument was also pretested with four firms before the final instruments were mailed to the entire sample.

### Sample

The sample consists of all suppliers to a common customer fabricator of electronic systems and equipment that were used in civilian government, commercial, and military applications. After pretesting the survey instrument with four firms, survey instruments were mailed to 421 suppliers of electronic components; 292 responses were received for a usable response rate of 69%. Respondent firms ranged in size from 3 employees to 25,000 employees, with average firm size around 551 workers. Respondents were located in geographic areas across North America and represented a variety of product lines.

### Reliability and Validity

Each construct was factor analyzed and checked for reliability. Component loadings for the constructs stayed within a narrow bandwidth of .86 to .64. Average item-to-total correlations for the constructs ranged from .82 to .70. Coefficient alpha ranged from .94 to .81 for the eight TQM constructs. No TQM construct was significantly correlated with an objective measure of quality performance but the purpose of the study was to demonstrate the *nonlinear* relationship between TQM practices and quality performance. This criterion-related validity was established through the statistical significance of five interaction terms and one TQM practice when interaction terms were included in the model (adjusted $R^2$ for the model = .507).

### Scores

Data on the suppliers' quality performance were provided by the common customer firm. These were the actual data that the customer firm uses to evaluate its suppliers' quality performance for contractual compliance and contractual renewal purposes. The electronics firm's most comprehensive measure of quality performance was defective parts per million (DPPM). The DPPM number included failures (defectives) of both critical and noncritical parts found in source inspection, receiving inspection, failures on the production/assembly line, and field failures to the degree possible. Only around 30% of field failures can be traced back to a specific part.

Because DPPM included failures from all inspection sources and was the most comprehensive supplier quality measure computed, it was chosen as the quality measure to use in this research. To facilitate interpretation of the statistical results and to avoid scaling problems, the DPPM numbers were inverted and normalized to the interval 0 to 1. Extent of use of the eight TQM practices ranged from "no extent" (1) to "great extent" (5) with means ranging from 4.12 to 3.27 for the role of the quality department and SQM constructs, respectively. Standard deviations were as high as .79 for training and as low as .61 for the role of the quality department.

### Other Evidence

This same survey instrument also has been deployed by Forker (1997) in the aerospace components industry. This article used a similar methodology, which surveyed the supply base of common customer firms. Two hundred and sixty-four responses were received for a usable response rate of 76%. Similar results were obtained from the aerospace components suppliers' survey with respect to reliability and criterion-related validity: (1) component loadings remained in the .88 to .58 range; average item-to-total correlations were as high as .80 for the role of the quality department and product/service design constructs and as low as .56 for SQM; (2) coefficient alphas ranged from .94 for the role of top management and quality policy constructs to .81 for process management/operating procedures. No TQM practice was directly correlated with quality performance but several interaction variables and stand-alone TQM practices emerged significant when regressed together on the objective quality performance variable.

**References**

Forker, L. B. 1997. Factors affecting supplier quality performance. *Journal of Operations Management* 15 (4):243–69.
Lissitz, R. W., and S. B. Green. 1975. Effect of the number of scale points on reliability: A Monte Carlo approach. *Journal of Applied Psychology* 60 (1): 10–13.
Saraph, J. V., P. G. Benson, and R. G. Schroeder. 1989. An instrument for measuring the critical factors of quality management. *Decision Sciences* 20 (4): 810–29.

# Froehle and Roth

**Article Summarized**

Froehle, Craig M., and Aleda V. Roth. 2004. New measurement scales for evaluating perceptions of the technology-mediated customer service experience. *Journal of Operations Management* 22 (1): 1–21.

**Scales (Actual Questions Used)**

*Information Richness Belief (IRB)*

1. How close to actual face-to-face interaction was your commutation with Iotanet customer service?
2. How much did your commutation with Iotanet customer service feel like a face-to-face, in-person conversation?
3. How much did your communication with the service provider feel like face-to-face, in-person conversation?

*Learning Belief (LB)*

4. After your communication with Iotanet customer service, how much more knowledgeable were you about your issue?
5. I believe my communication with the Iotanet customer service enabled me to look at the situation from a new perspective.
6. I believe my communication with the Iotanet customer service was educational.
7. I believe my communication with the Iotanet customer service provided me with new knowledge.

*Usefulness Belief (UB)*

8. I believe communicating with Iotanet customer service was a useful experience.
9. How much additional value did the experience of communicating with Iotanet customer service add for you?
10. The experience of communicating with Iotanet customer service was how useful to you?
11. I believe that the experience of communicating with Iotanet customer service added value to the service.

*Duration Appropriateness Belief (DAB)*

12. I believe the time I spent actively communicating (talking to someone, reading or writing e-mail, chatting) with Iotanet customer service should have been . . .
13. I believe the overall length of time I spent actively communicating (talking to someone, reading or writing e-mails, chatting) with Iotanet customer service was . . .

*Intimacy Appropriateness Belief (IAB)*

14. How impersonal did you consider communication with Iotanet customer service to be?
15. How intimate do you believe your communication with the Iotanet customer service was?
16. How friendly and personal was your communication with Iotanet customer service?

*Attitude toward the Medium (AM)*

17. I was pleased by using [this medium].
18. How satisfying was using [this medium]?
19. I enjoyed using [this medium].

*Attitude toward the Episode (AE)*

20. I was pleased by the experience of communicating with Iotanet customer service.
21. How satisfying was the experience of communicating with Iotanet customer service?
22. How disappointing was the experience of communicating with Iotanet customer service?

*Attitude toward the Service Provider (AP)*

23. I am pleased with Iotanet.
24. How satisfied are you with Iotanet?
25. I enjoy using Iotanet.

*Intention toward the Medium (IM)*

26. I would use [this medium] again to contact Iotanet customer service.
27. I intend to use [this medium] the next time I need to contact Iotanet customer service.
28. How likely are you to use Iotanet again?
29. I intend to use Iotanet again in the future.

**Construct Description**

Five constructs were reported to be associated about a customer's beliefs pertaining to attributes of communications technologies during a service encounter, which the authors referred to as tapping into the "customer belief domain" (CBD): (1) Information richness connoted "the customer's cognitive assessment of the complexity and vividness of the communication between the provider and the customer parallel to the original description of Media Richness offered by Daft and Lengel (1984, 1986)" (p. 5). (2) Learning belief was characterized "as the belief that he/she increased his/her own knowledge, capacity for understanding, or perspective-taking during the contact episode (Boland and Tenkasi, 1995)" (p. 5). (3) Usefulness belief extended "previous definitions of customer contact by also considering the degree to which the contact episode fulfills the customer's perceived needs and desires" (p. 5). (4) The duration appropriateness belief represented "the customer's belief about the duration of the contact episode" (p. 5). (5) Intimacy appropriateness belief related "to the level of *mutual confiding and trust* established during the customer episode, and is among the key customer variables discovered by Kellogg and Chase (1995)" (p. 6).

The article also captured three measures of customer's attitudes during a service encounter, or "customer belief domain" (CBD): (1) Attitude toward the medium reflected "the immediate favorableness (or customer-perceived satisfaction) or unfavorableness (dissatisfaction) created by using the communication medium (e.g., telephone, e-mail, or instant messaging) employed during the contact episode" (p. 6). (2) Attitude toward the contact episode was defined as "the immediate favorableness customer-perceived satisfaction) or unfavorableness (dissatisfaction) with the service content of the entire contact episode" (p. 6). (3) Attitude toward the service provider was defined as "the level of general satisfaction or dissatisfaction the customer has with the service provider or the company from whom the customer is currently seeking service, at the end of the contact episode" (p. 6).

Finally two customer loyalty measures were recorded for the customer service encounters, as indicated by the "customer intention domain" (CID): (1) Intention to use medium again assessed "the customer's internally estimated likelihood that he will carry out future contact with the service provider via the same communication medium as was used for his most recent contact episode" (p. 6). (2) Intention to use service provider again assessed "the customer's internally estimated likelihood that he will make use of the firms' services again at some future time (or continue the relationship if ongoing)" (p. 7).

Except for the duration appropriateness belief (DAB) items and first two items of intimacy appropriateness belief (IAB) that used 13-point Likert scales, all other items were measured on 7-point Likert scales.

**Development**

The main purpose of the research was to define "new constructs associated with the technology-mediated customer service experience after the development of new multi-item measurement scales for measuring these constructs" (p. 15). A rigorous approach to new scale development employed two distinct phases with independent samples: (1) exploratory pretesting and pilot studies to guide the iterative development and refinement of construct definitions and items and (2) confirmatory testing on independent samples. In the first phase, items were generated for each construct, which were then refined in using the following three steps: First, pretesting and item refinement was employed on a convenience sample of 39 MBA students to "enhance the readability and clarity of the questions as well as to enhance the items' and emerging scales' content validity. Second, pilot testing on second convenience sample of 35 students was used to test the Web-based survey instrument and make further modifications on the items as needed. Third, because students are not representative of the intended population, a second pilot study involved 305 Internet users. In the second phase, two separate confirmatory factor analyses (CFA) were conducted using data gathered from random sample customers of a large Internet service provider. The initial wave of 999 respondents constituted the calibration sample; and second wave of 999 respondents served as the hold-out sample, whereby the measurement model was confirmed. Methodological steps followed are given in Figure 3 (p. 8) in the article.

**Sample**

The first pretest survey was administered on 39 MBA students as a pencil-and-paper survey. Two pilot tests of the survey instrument were conducted on the Web. A convenient sample of MBA and graduate students responded to the first pilot test of multi-item measurement; 35 responses were received. The second pilot test was conducted on 3,117 randomly selected users of an Internet-based company. The response rate was 9.8%, or 305 responses were received. The Internet service provider company was referred to as Iotanet in the article. Iotanet was one of the world's largest Internet service providers with more than 10 million subscribers. Out of 12,050 surveys sent out, 2,001 responses, yielding a response rate of 16.6%. "In order to address the possibility of non response bias" (p. 10), overall descriptive statistics about Iota's database was requested. The sample was consistent with the data (*see* Table 3, p. 11 in the article).

**Reliability and Validity**

In the first phase of the research, tentative reliability and validity were first established in the exploratory, second pilot study with 305 respondents. Content validity was determined based on thorough literature reviews and feedback from respondents. In the second, applying independent samples to further establish reliability and validity, confirmatory factor analysis (CFA) was performed using the measurement model of structural equation modeling on both calibration and hold-out samples. First, on the calibration sample, the $\chi^2$ goodness-of-fit test was used to assess "the magnitude of discrepancy between the sample and fitted covariance matrices" (p. 12). goodness-of-fit index (GFI) and root mean square error approximation (RMSEA) were calculated. Incremental fit indices comparative fit index (CFI), nonnormed fit index (NNFI) Bollen's normed Rho1, Bollen's Delta2) were computed. These CFA results depicted convergent validity and reliability in the calibration sample after some modifications were made in the scales. Second, for revised scale using the hold-out sample, validity and reliability values were determined for each item and construct. Completing the analyses, each of the CFA test statistics listed above indicated good fit. Pairwise discriminant validity tests were also repeated in the second round of confirmation testing. Strong evidence of item and construct reliability and validity was found. (For reliability and validity values, refer to Appendix B, p. 18 in the article.)

### Scores

Results of CFA for the initial measurement model are presented in Table 4 in the article. Global fit statistics for CFA of the revised model using calibration sample (999) and hold-out sample (999) are presented in Table 6.

### Other Evidence

Not available.

### References

Boland, R. J., Jr., and R. V. Tenkasi. 1995. Perspective making and perspective taking in communities of knowing. *Organization Science* 6 (4): 350–72.

Daft, R. L., and R. H Lengel. 1984. Information richness: A new approach to managerial information processing and organizational design. In *Research in organizational behavior*, eds. B. M. Staw and L. Cummings, 191–223. Greenwhich, CT: JAI Press.

———. 1986. Organizational information requirements, media richness, and structural design. *Management Science* 35 (8): 982–1003.

Kellogg, D. L., and R. B. Chase. 1995. Constructing an empirically derived measure for customer contact. *Management Science* 41 (11): 1734–49.

## Frohlich and Westbrook (2001)

### Article Summarized

Frohlich, Markham T., and Roy Westbrook. 2001. Arcs of integration: An international study of supply chain strategies. *Journal of Operations Management* 19 (2): 185–200.

### Scales (Actual Questions Used)

*Integration Measures*

1. Access to planning systems
2. Sharing production plans
3. Joint EDI access/networks
4. Knowledge of inventory mix/levels
5. Packaging customization
6. Delivery frequencies
7. Common use of logistical equipment/containers
8. Common used of third-party logistical services

### Construct Description

Not available.

### Measurement Description

All items were measured on 5-point Likert scales.

### Development

The authors used the data from the 1998 round of the International Manufacturing Strategy Survey (IMSS) to test what they describe as the arc of integration hypothesis. "The IMSS was founded in 1992 to gather data about the practice and performance related to manufacturing strategy in a global setting (*see* Voss and Blackmon (1998) and Ettlie (1998) for more details on IMSS study)" (p. 187).

### Sample

The IMSS focuses on the International Standard Industrial Classification (ISIC) Division 38 that manufactures fabricated metal products, machinery, and equipment. The original database had 703 observations from 23 countries. Given that some of the observations had relatively little reported performance data, the authors used a subset of 322 companies to conduct their investigation. They provide the breakdown of the observations by region in Table 1 in the article.

### Reliability and Validity

The authors ensured content validity by considering the inputs of researchers from various business schools that contribute to IMSS study as well as pretesting the items. Also, confirmatory factor analysis (CFA) was used to ensure the reliability and the validity of the scales. According to the authors, the construct validity was supported by the empirical results indicating that all items loaded on their theoretical constructs. The authors assessed divergent or discriminant validity by analyzing bivariate correlations among each of the scales, and also with other potentially confounding demographic variables included in the study such as country responding, company size, market focus, product focus, and geographical focus.

### Scores

The scores are presented in Tables 2–7 in the article.

### Other Evidence

Not available.

### References

Ettlie, J. E. 1998. R&D and global manufacturing performance. *Management Science* 44 (1): 1–11.

Voss, C. A., and K. Blackmon. 1998. Differences in manufacturing strategy decisions between Japanese and Western manufacturing plants: The role of strategic time orientation. *Journal of Operations Management* 16 (2/3): 147–58.

---

## Frohlich and Westbrook (2002)

### Article Summarized

Frohlich, Markham T., and Roy Westbrook. 2002. Demand chain management in manufacturing and services: Web-based integration, drivers and performance. *Journal of Operations Management* 20 (6): 729–45.

### Scales (Actual Questions Used)

*Supply Integration*

1. To what extent have you implemented Web-based processes for integrated inventory planning with suppliers?
2. To what extent have you implemented Web-based processes for integrated supply chain management with suppliers?

3. To what extent have you implemented Web-based processes for integrated demand/forecasting with suppliers?
4. To what extent have you implemented Web-based processes for integrated order scheduling and tracking with suppliers?

*Demand Integration*

5. To what extent have you implemented Web-based processes for targeted marketing/customer profiling with customers?
6. To what extent have you implemented Web-based processes for online order taking/receipt with customers?
7. To what extent have you implemented Web-based processes for integrated demand/forecasting with customers?
8. To what extent have you implemented Web-based processes for customer relationship management with customers?

*Drivers of Change*

9. Improving speed of response
10. Improving service/support
11. Improving reliability and delivery
12. Anticipated cost reduction
13. Access to European single market
14. Access to global markets
15. Lack of local partners
16. Greater market valuation
17. Peer pressure "to get onboard"
18. Pressure from suppliers
19. Pressure from customers
20. Threat from traditional competitors

*Performance*

21. Faster delivery time
22. Reduced transaction costs
23. Greater profitability
24. Enhanced inventory turnover

## Construct Description

Not available.

## Measurement Description

All the items were measured on 5-point Likert scales.

## Development

The survey was developed in three stages. In the first stage, the authors identified relevant measures of Web-based demand and supply integration, drivers, and performance from the literature. In the second stage, the authors held a series of meetings with managers to ensure content and face validity of the instrument. Last, they pretested the survey with 30 manufacturing and service firms to gauge the content validity and overall readability of the survey.

### Sample

The data were collected from a stratified random sample of manufacturing and service companies from across the United Kingdom. The typical respondents were vice presidents (VPs) of operations or general managers who would know about their companies' up and downstream integration, demand chain drivers, and performance. A total of 890 usable surveys were returned with a response rate of 20%. The authors present the industry breakdown of the sample in Table 2.

### Reliability and Validity

The authors ensured the unidimensionality of the items by using principal component analyses (PCAs). The items had acceptable levels of reliability based on Cronbach's coefficient alpha values. The authors assessed construct validity by testing whether the items in a scale all loaded on a common factor when within-scale factor analysis was run. Bivariate correlations, average interscale correlations, and average correlations among scale and nonscale items were used to test the discriminant validity of the items.

### Scores

The scores are presented in Tables 3–9 in the article.

### Other Evidence

Not available.

### Reference

None.

---

## Fry, Steele, and Saladin

### Article Summarized

Fry, Timothy D., Daniel C. Steele, and Brooke A. Saladin. 1995. The role of management accounting in the development of a manufacturing strategy. *International Journal of Operations and Production Management* 15 (12): 21–31.

### Scales (Actual Questions Used)

*Indicate your plant's production orientation.*

1. Make to stock
2. Make to stock/assemble to order
3. Make to order
4. Assemble to order only

*I would characterize my plant as:*

5. High volume production with low product variety
6. Average volume production with average productivity
7. Low volume production with high product variety

Please estimate the percentage of total manufacturing cost for each of the categories below:

8. Fixed and variables overhead
9. Direct labor
10. Direct materials
11. Total

Please rank by 1, 2, 3, or 4, the importance of each criterion in acquiring orders from customers:

12. Product quality
13. Product price/cost
14. On-time delivery
15. Flexibility/lead time

Please indicate the importance of each success factor below to ensure long-term competitiveness:

16. Product quality
17. Inventory reductions
18. Product cost reductions
19. Lead-time reductions
20. Direct labor cost reductions

Rank by 1, 2, 3, and so on the emphasis given to the following reports to run your plant:

21. Labor variances or efficiencies
22. Other budget variances
23. Scrap or yield reports
24. Cash flow statement
25. Machine utilization reports
26. Plant P & L
27. Shipment reports
28. Inventory reports

## Construct Description

Manufacturing strategy was defined as "the link between the marketplace and the manufacturing process and is reflected in the decision of order-winners" (p. 22).

## Measurement Description

The decision of order winners was captured by two questions (*see* Scales). One question used the ordinal scale from 1 to 4 to measure the order of importance of each of the four criteria. The other question used a 5-point Likert scale ranging from 1 = "not important" to 5 = "critical importance" to measure the importance of success factors. Questions 7 to 9 were used "to identify the types of information used by operations managers" (p. 23) and "the role of the management accountant in each class of companies" (p. 23). Question 7 was measured with a 5-point Likert scale ranging from 1 = "none" to 5 = "high." Question 8 was ordinal data ranked by the level of emphasis. Question 9(b) was measured with a 5-point Likert scale ranging from 1 = "strongly disagree" to 5 = "strongly agree."

## Development

The authors reported that an "initial survey instrument was developed with the help of several local manufacturing companies" (p. 23) and was pretested in ten manufacturing companies. "Based on their responses and suggestions, the survey completed by the 85 companies was developed" (p. 23).

### Sample

The overall sample consisted of 85 U.S. manufacturing companies. "The chief operations officer (COO) from each company was asked to complete the survey based on one particular plant since different plants in the same company could manufacture different products on different processes" (p. 23).

### Reliability and Validity

Not available.

### Scores

The scores are given in Figure 2 in the article.

### Other Evidence

Not available.

### Reference

None.

---

## Fullerton, McWatters, and Fawson

### Article Summarized

Fullerton, Rosemary R., Cheryl S. McWatters, and Chris Fawson. 2003. An examination of the relationships between JIT and financial performance. *Journal of Operations Management* 21 (4): 383–404.

### Scales (Actual Questions Used)

*Survey Items Measuring JIT Implementation Factors and Control Variables*

JIT Manufacturing

Indicate the extent to which your firm has implemented the following techniques:

1. Focused factory
2. Group technology
3. Action plan to reduce setup times
4. Total productive maintenance
5. Multifunction employees
6. Uniform work load

JIT Quality

Indicate the extent to which your firm has implemented the following techniques:

7. Product quality improvement
8. Process quality improvement

JIT Unique

Indicate the extent to which your firm has implemented the following techniques:

9. Kanban system
10. JIT purchasing

*Innovation Strategy*

What most closely matches your firm's strategy related to innovation in

11. product technology,
12. process design, and
13. product design?

*Organizational Structure*

What is the organizational structure of your firm's

14. Overall company?
15. Individual operations?
16. Individual departments?

**Construct Description**

The constructs were as follows: just-in-time (JIT) manufacturing, JIT quality, JIT unique, innovation strategy, and organizational structure. The first construct indicates "the interrelatedness of the streamlining components of an advanced manufacturing system" (p. 390). JIT quality was a quality dimension that explains the extent of implementation of "procedures for improving product and process quality" (p. 390). This construct was grounded on Banker, Potter, and Schroeder (1993), Imai (1998), Sim and Killogh (1998), Swanson and Lankford (1998), and Young, Shields, and Wolf (1988). The third construct identified the extent to which companies have implemented JIT purchasing and kanban. The innovation strategy construct indicated if the company was on the follower side or the leader side in terms of product technology, process, and product design. The last construct, organizational strategy, specified the extent to which company was centralized or decentralized.

**Measurement Description**

A 6-point Likert scale was used for all items, except for innovations strategy and organizational structure. Instead, to measure those two constructs, 5-point Likert scales were used. The items were borrowed from Conner (2001), Davy et al. (1992), Fullerton and McWatters (2001, 2002), Jusko (1999), Koufteros, Vonderembse, and Doll (1998), Mehra and Inman (1992), Monden (1998), Moshavi (1990), Sahin (2000), Sakakibara, Flynn, and Schroeder (1993), Spencer and Guide (1995), White and Ruch (1990), White (1993), White and Prybutok (2001), Womack and Jones (1996), and Yasin, Small, and Wafa (1997).

Other salient constructs were defined as follows: Focused factory was operationalized "a production strategy that is based on corporate strategy. It centers on simplifying the organizational structure, reducing the numbers of products or processes, and minimizing the complexities of physical constraints" (p. 389). Group technology was characterized as "collecting and organizing common concepts, principles, problems, and tasks. It avoids unnecessary duplication through standardization. It includes sequencing similar parts through the same machine and creating manufacturing cells for processing" (p. 389). Reduced setup times was based on "reduction of the time and costs involved in changing tooling and other aspects required in moving from producing one product to another. This reduces lot sizes and the need for buffer inventories" (p. 389). Total productive maintenance was viewed as "rigorous, regularly scheduled preventive maintenance and machine replacement programs. Operators are actively responsible for the maintenance of their machines" (p. 389). The construct of multifunction employees was given as the "extended training of employees on several different machines and in various tasks" (p. 389). Uniform workload highlighted the "reduction of the fluctuations of the daily workload through line balancing, level schedules, stable cycle rates, and market-paced final assembly rates" (p. 389). Kanban was defined as "a card or information system that is used to 'pull' the necessary parts into each operation as they are needed" (p. 389).

### Development

The study employed a five page survey instrument, which gathered "specific information about the manufacturing operations, product costing methods, information and incentive systems, JIT practices employed. . . . To evaluate the survey instrument for readability, completeness, and clarity, a limited pretest was conducted by soliciting feedback from several business professors and managers of five manufacturing firms who were familiar with JIT practices" (pp. 386–87).

### Sample

The empirical investigation was carried out in a two-stage process. Data from 253 U.S. manufacturing firms were collected to determine the static relationship between firm profitability and the degree of JIT implementation. Then, the sample was stratified to focus on the subsets "of firms that have sufficient pre-JIT and post-JIT history" (p. 384). The longitudinal perspectives were based on the traditional annual performance measures.

The firms were selected from Compaq Disclosure Database. Eligibility for the survey was decided based on a primary two-digit U.S. Department of Commerce's Standard Industrial Classification (SIC) codes within the manufacturing ranging from 20 to 39, sales between $2 million and $2 billion, significant operations in the United States, and inclusion in the COMPUSTAT database. After refinement, 447 firms were included in the final sample. Two hundred and fifty-four firms returned completed surveys for a response rate of 56.8%. No response bias was found related to firm size or industry. One survey was defined to be not usable. Ninety-five out of the remaining usable surveys identified themselves as JIT firms.

### Reliability and Validity

Construct validity was supported by the factor solutions for the defined constructs. Multiple-item loadings for each factor also ensured the convergent validity. Cronbach's coefficient alpha values ranged from .52 for JIT unique to .90 for JIT quality. Discriminant validity was checked by factor analyses. None of the items have loadings in excess of .30 on more than one factor.

### Scores

Regression results with control variables can be found in Table 6 in the article. Pooled cross-section time series results are reported in Tables 7–9.

### Other Evidence

Not available.

### References

Banker, R., G. Potter, and R. G. Schroeder. 1993. Reporting manufacturing performance to workers: An empirical study. *Journal of Management Accounting Research* 5: 33–53.

Conner, G. 2001. *Lean manufacturing for the small shop*. Dearborn, MI: Society of Manufacturing Engineers.

Davy, J., R. White, N. Merritt, and K. Gritzmacher. 1992. A derivation of the underlying constructs of just-in-time management systems. *Academy of Management Journal* 35 (3): 653–70.

Fullerton, R. R., and C. S. McWatters. 2001. The production performance benefits from JIT implementation. *Journal of Operations Management* 19 (1): 81–96.

———. 2002. The role of performance measures and incentive systems in relation to the degree of JIT implementation. *Accounting, Organizations and Society* 27 (8): 711–35.

Imai, M. 1998. Will America's corporate theme song be "just in time"? *Journal for Quality and Participation* 21(3/4): 26–28.

Jusko, J. 1999. A look at lean. *Industry Week* 248 (22): 88–92.

Koufteros, X. A., M. A. Vonderembse, and W. J. Doll. 1998. Developing measures of time-based manufacturing. *Journal of Operations Management* 16 (1): 21–41.

Mehra, S., and R. A. Inman. 1992. Determining the critical elements of just-in-time implementation. *Decision Sciences* 23 (1): 160–74.

Monden, Y. 1998. *Toyota production system: An integrated approach to just-in-time*. Norcross, GA: Engineering and Management Press.

Moshavi, S. 1990. Well made in America: Lessons from Harley-Davidson on being the best. New York: McGraw-Hill.

Sahin, F. 2000. Manufacturing competitiveness: Different systems to achieve the same results. *Production and Inventory Management Journal* 41 (1): 56–65.

Sakakibara, S., B. B. Flynn, and R. G. Schroeder. 1993. A framework and measurement instrument for just-in-time manufacturing. *Production and Operations Management* 2 (3): 177–94.

Sim, K. L., and L. N. Killough. 1998. The performance effects of complementarities between manufacturing practices and management accounting systems. *Journal of Management Accounting Research* 10: 325–46.

Spencer, M. S., and V. D. Guide. 1995. An exploration of the components of JIT. *International Journal of Operations and Production Management* 5 (5): 72–83.

Swanson, C., and W. M. Lankford. 1998. Just-in-time manufacturing. *Business Process Management Journal* 4 (4): 333–41.

White, R. E. 1993. An empirical assessment of JIT in US manufacturers. *Production and Inventory Management* 34 (2): 38–42.

White, R. E., and V. Prybutok. 2001. The relationship between JIT practices and type of production system. *Omega* 29:113–24.

White, R. E., and W. A. Ruch. 1990. The composition and scope of JIT. *Operations Management Review* 7 (3/4): 9–18.

Womack, J. P., and D. T. Jones. 1996. *Lean thinking: Banish waste and create wealth in your corporation*. New York: Simon & Schuster.

Yasin, M. M., M. Small, and M. Wafa. 1997. An empirical investigation of JIT effectiveness: An organizational perspective. *Omega* 25 (4): 461–71.

Young, S. M., M. D. Shields, and G. Wolf. 1988. Manufacturing controls and performance: An experiment. *Accounting, Organizations and Society* 13 (6): 607–18.

## Germain and Dröge

### Article Summarized

Germain, Richard, and Cornelia Dröge. 1997. An empirical study of the impact of just-in-time task scope versus just-in-time workflow integration on organizational design. *Decision Sciences* 28 (3): 615–35.

### Scales (Actual Questions Used)

*JIT Task Scope (TS)*

1. Pareto charts, fishbone diagrams, and other analytic techniques are used to identify sources of defects in products.
2. Factory labor is encouraged to spot defects in materials or production/assembly processes.
3. Total preventive maintenance is used.

4. Reduced machine setup times are an important goal.
5. Cross-training of direct labor is relied on.
6. Our staff visits suppliers' plants on an informal basis.
7. We involve suppliers in new product/materials design.
8. We certify our suppliers concerning product quality.

*JIT Workflow Integration (WI)*

9. Small amounts of in-process inventory are used.
10. Small lots are manufactured.
11. Orders are placed to suppliers and delivered on a daily basis.
12. Suppliers' warehouses/factories are located nearby.
13. Small lot size orders are placed with suppliers.
14. Inspection of incoming materials has been reduced.

*Specialization (SP)*

15. Plant facilities design
16. Warehouse facilities design
17. Material handling
18. Sales forecasting
19. Plant facility location
20. Warehouse facility location
21. Production scheduling
22. Transportation scheduling
23. Manufacturing quality control
24. Distribution equipment procurement
25. Market research

*Decentralization (DE)*

26. The number of workers required
27. Allocation of work among available workers
28. Internal labor disputes
29. Overtime at the plant level
30. Plant machinery or equipment to be used
31. Delivery dates to customers and priority orders
32. Production scheduling
33. Selecting suppliers
34. Production volume
35. Goods to be manufactured
36. The number of factories to operate
37. The location of factories

*Internal Control (IC)*

38. Functional cost (e.g., manufacturing)
39. Customer service (e.g., fill rate, cycle time)
40. Cost controls by fixing standard costs and analyzing variation
41. Productivity analysis
42. Customer satisfaction and follow-up
43. Profitability

*Benchmark Control (BC)*

44. Functional cost (e.g., manufacturing)
45. Customer service (e.g., fill rate, cycle time)

46. Productivity levels
47. Operations (e.g., manufacturing)
48. Profitability

*Integration: Committees (IC)*

49. Distribution strategy
50. Marketing strategy
51. Production strategy
52. Purchasing strategy
53. Capital budgeting (the selection of long-term investments)
54. Long-term strategies (of growth or diversification) and decisions related to the firm's operating philosophy

*Integration: Mechanisms (IM)*

55. Interdepartmental committees that are set up to allow departments to engage in joint decision making.
56. Task forces that are temporary bodies set up to facilitate interdepartmental collaboration on a specific project.
57. Liaison personnel whose specific job it is to coordinate the efforts of several departments for the purposes of a project.

## Construct Description

The authors defined "JIT task scope as the amount and variety of JIT knowledge" (p. 617). As stated by the authors, this definition is based on Hage's (1980) definition of task scope. Hage (1980) defined task scope as "the amount and variety of knowledge employed by the organization in its production of goods and services" (p. 383). The authors conceptualized workflow integration as "routineness of production continuity, and indicates the degree of serial interdependence between successive stages of production (Thompson, 1967)" (p. 617). According to the authors, workflow integration was based on Hickson, Pugh, and Pheysey's (1969) definition of the "degree of automated, continuous, fixed-sequence operations" (p. 384).

## Measurement Description

The measures were drawn from the literature. Based on Mintzberg (1979), the authors defined specialization "as the creation of units concentrating on specific occupational tasks" (p. 620). From Child (1972), the authors defined decentralization as the "delegation or decrease in the vertical locus of decision-making authority" (p. 620). Last, based on Mintzberg (1979), the authors defined integration as "horizontal as opposed to hierarchical communication" (p. 621). The authors used 7-point Likert scales to measure the items.

## Development

All measures were borrowed from existing literature whenever possible. No further details on scale development are provided in the article.

## Sample

The authors obtained the initial sampling frame from the membership list provided by The Council of Logistics Management. Their list originally contained 3,069 members. They reduced this number to 1,002 "by eliminating non-US residents and retaining at most one individual from any given firm" (p. 622). They obtained 199 usable responses. The sample frame consisted of U.S. Department of Commerce's Standard Industrial Classification (SIC) codes such as "food and kindred products (SIC 20), 15.1%; chemicals and allied products (SIC 28), 14.1%; miscellaneous manufacturing industries (SIC 39), 12.6%; electronic and other electric equipment and components, except computer equipment (SIC 36), 8.5%; paper and allied products (SIC 26), 6.5%; rubber and miscellaneous plastic products (SIC 30), 5.5%; fabricated metal products except machinery and computer equipment (SIC 34), 5.5%; and measuring, analyzing, and controlling instruments, photographic medical and optical goods, watches and clocks (SIC 38), 5.5%. The rest were spread across the remaining 2-digit SICs" (p. 623).

### Reliability and Validity

Measures of reliability were given. "Cronbach's reliabilities are listed for all summed 7-point scales, while Kuder-Richardson 20 reliability is provided for the one scale that is the sum of dichotomous items. All reliabilities exceeded .60 and most were around .80" (p. 623).

### Scores

The scores are presented in Tables 1 and 2 in the article.

### Other Evidence

Not available.

### References

Child, J. 1972. Organization structure and strategies of control: A replication of the Aston study. *Administrative Science Quarterly* 17 (2): 163–77.
Hage, J. 1980. *Theories of organizations: Form, process, and transformation*. New York: Wiley.
Hickson, D. J., D. S. Pugh, and D. C. Pheysey. 1969. Operations technology and organization structure: An empirical reappraisal. *Administrative Science Quarterly* 14 (3): 378–97.
Mintzberg, H. 1979. *The structuring of organizations*. Englewood Cliffs, NJ: Prentice Hall.
Thompson, J. D. 1967. *Organizations in action*. New York: McGraw-Hill.

## Germain, Dröge, and Christensen

### Article Summarized

Germain, Richard, Cornelia Dröge, and William Christensen. 2001. The mediating role of operations knowledge in the relationship of context with performance. *Journal of Operations Management* 19 (4): 453–69.

### Scales (Actual Questions Used)

*Demand Unpredictability*

1. Sales are predictable . . . unpredictable.
2. Market trends are easy to monitor . . . difficult to monitor.
3. Sales forecasts are likely to be accurate . . . inaccurate.

*Mass Output Orientation*

4. Custom technology: production of a single unit or a few units at a time to customer specification
5. Small batch (job shop) technology (batches of less than 1 week)
6. Large batch technology (e.g., of components for subsequent assembly as in fabricating shops; of finished products such as bottles, cans, drugs, chemicals)

7. Mass-production technology, as in assembly lines
8. Continuous process technology, as in production of liquids, gases, or solid shapes (e.g., oil refining)

*Formal Performance Control*

9. A comprehensive management control and information system
10. Use of cost centers for cost control
11. Use of profit centers for cost control
12. Quality of operations using sampling and other methods
13. Formal appraisal for personnel

*Benchmark Performance Control*

14. Product quality
15. Production techniques
16. Functional costs (e.g., distribution)
17. Overall profitability

*Technocratic Specialization*

18. Sales forecasting
19. Location planning
20. Assesses and devises ways of producing output (work-study methods, operations study, etc.)
21. Devises new outputs, equipment, and processes
22. Obtains and controls materials and equipment (buying and stock control)
23. Controls workflow (planning and scheduling)
24. Carries outputs/resources from one place to another
25. Takes cake of quality control (inspection)
26. Advertising
27. Acquires and allocates human resources
28. Develops and trains personnel
29. Maintains and erects buildings and equipment
30. Develops and carries out administrative procedures (statistics, information systems)
31. Acquires information on the market
32. Disposes/distributes/services output
33. Takes care of welfare, security, or social services
34. Records and control financial resources
35. Deals with legal and insurance

*Integration*

36. Interdepartmental committees, which are set up to allow departments to engage in joint decision-making on an ongoing basis.
37. Cross-functional teams, which are temporary bodies set up to facilitate interdepartmental collaboration on a specific project.
38. Liaison personnel whose specific job it is to coordinate the efforts of several departments for the purposes of a specific project.

*Operations/Product Variance*

39. Production lead time (fixed production schedule)
40. Production lot size
41. Product quality
42. Individual factory machine speeds
43. Daily production output rate

*Inventory Variance*

44. Raw materials/components inventory level
45. Finished goods inventory level
46. In-process inventory level

*Financial Performance*

47. Average return on investment (ROI) over the past 3 years
48. Average profit over the past 3 years
49. Profit growth over the past 3 years

## Construct Description

The meta-scale of design knowledge intensity consisted of three constructs: technocratic specialization, formal performance control, and cross-functional integration. The authors defined design knowledge intensity as the "ability of the firm to collect, process, and integrate knowledge at various levels" (pp. 454–55). Based on this definition, technocratic specialization referred to employment of indirect labor that was responsible of handling technical, operations management related tasks. Formal performance control corresponded to various performance inputs as well as performance itself. Last, cross-functional integration connoted the integration of broad-based functional knowledge. Throughput variance was characterized as the "level of variability in the flow and quality of goods into, through, and out of the firm" (p. 455).

## Measurement Description

Demand unpredictability was measured with 7-point Likert scales, whereas mass output orientation was quantified by scales that range from "not applicable to principle products" to "used almost exclusively." Each item was given a respective weight from 1 to 5 and the sum of the items was used in the actual analyses. Formal performance control was captured by 7-point scales with endpoints of "rarely used" and "frequently used" in response to the extent to which the control devices were used to gather information about the performance of the firm.

Benchmark performance control was gauged by 7-point Likert scales ranging from "rarely used" to "frequently used" in response to the extent that the firm benchmarks its performance relative to industry leaders or industry standards. Technocratic specialization was quantified as binary variables with response to "are the following activities being dealt with exclusively by at least one full-time person." Integration was appraised by 7-point Likert scales in response to the extent that efforts were made to ensure the compatibility of decisions in one area (e.g., purchasing) was consistent with those in other areas (e.g., production).

## Development

Not available.

## Sample

The data were collected using a list of executives provided by National Association of Purchasing Managers. The sample frame consisted of companies ranging from U.S. Department of Commerce's Standard Industrial Classification (SIC) codes 20 (food and kindred products) to 39 (miscellaneous manufacturing industries). A total of 225 surveys were returned from 480 surveys faxed, leading to a response rate of 47%.

## Reliability and Validity

The authors used item-to-total correlation and Cronbach's coefficient alphas to measure item and measurement scale reliabilities. The minimum level of Cronbach's coefficient alpha, .72, was deemed satisfactory. For the binary scale, the authors used the Kuder Richardson 20 reliability estimate, which had a value of .78, and was also deemed acceptable. The authors assessed the validity of the scales by using confirmatory factor analysis (CFA).

### Scores

The scores are presented in Tables 2–5 in the article.

### Other Evidence

Not available.

### Reference

None.

---

## Gilgeous

### Article Summarized

Gilgeous, Vic. 1995. Strategic concerns and capability impeders. *International Journal of Operations and Production Management* 15 (10): 4–29.

### Scales (Actual Questions Used)

*Culture*

1. Inadequate time is spent on planning for the future.
2. Priorities are unclear.
3. Much time is spent on unnecessary work.
4. There is no written statement spelling out objectives in measurable terms.
5. Short-term expediency is seen as more important than building for the future.
6. Organizational values are inconsistent.
7. People "on the front line" feel that top management "keeps them in the dark."
8. Leaders/managers pay insufficient attention to the needs of individuals.
9. Top management fails to demonstrate belief/commitment in plans.

*Infrastructure*

10. Lines of responsibility/accountability are unclear.
11. There is insufficient flexibility to make rapid changes.
12. Managers are unable to cope with all the demands on their time.
13. Rules and procedures are often inappropriate/ineffective.
14. Manufacturing methods are not examined periodically for improvement.
15. There is too much unnecessary red tape.
16. Lessons learned in one department do not get transferred to others.
17. Insufficient effort is devoted to improving the way in which people from different functional areas work together

*Ability*

18. Skills are "picked up" rather than learned systematically.
19. People are not encouraged to update/increase their skills.

20. A significant "skills deficit" exists within the organization.
21. Managers are promoted without being given further training.
22. There is a lack of personal communication skills.
23. The organization fails to recruit and retain high-caliber personnel.
24. Existing incentive and reward systems are inadequate/inappropriate for employee involvement and development.
25. Independent consultants/outside expertise is often called on to undertake key roles in development and implementation of projects.

*Resources*

26. Investment in training is not evaluated.
27. Training is given a low priority.
28. Senior managers are insufficiently involved in establishing training policies.
29. Some projects/teams/departments are understaffed.
30. Lack of resources is a major source of plan/project failure.
31. Managers are often unaware of the capabilities of their subordinates.
32. Labor turnover is high.
33. Records of employee experience acquired on the job are not maintained.
34. Managers often have to rely on the skills of planning experts.
35. Planning timescales often have to be adjusted to accommodate shortages in resources availability.

*Information*

36. Physical barriers (e.g., different buildings, sites) inhibit communication.
37. The basic assumptions/premises of planning activities are unclear.
38. Functional areas (i.e., manufacturing, design, purchasing, sales, etc.) do not employ a database that is common to all.
39. Access to information systems/sources is overly restrictive.
40. Few managers/employees are versed in how to use available information systems.
41. Feedback from the implementation of plans is infrequent/unregulated.
42. Information within databases is frequently found to be out of date.
43. Production planning/scheduling is not an integral part of a management information system.
44. Information needed to make decisions is not readily available.
45. Those involved in implementing plans are not involved in their development.

## Construct Description

The constructs were described as follows. Ability was defined as "the availability of necessary skills, knowledge and competences of personnel within the organization (and the use of consultants) and their application to the planning process. This category embodies personal attributes and interactions such as training, skills, creativity, etc." (pp. 15–16). Resources were classified as "the provision of the necessary manpower, equipment, facilities support, funding, and time for planning. Similarly, this category refers to information on the availability, condition and capability of such resources" (p. 16). Information was "concerned with the availability and transfer of data when and where required, i.e. not only the content of data, but also its communication and regulation" (p. 16). The authors characterized culture as "the prevailing beliefs, attitudes, norms and values within an organization, which affect an employee's behavior and emphasis in certain circumstances. Such components of culture may relate to how work should be organized, authority exercised, how people are rewarded, and how they are controlled" (p. 16). Infrastructure was delineated as the "structure of the organization, i.e. the framework of formal relationships in the organization and among members of the organization, and includes defining tasks, responsibilities, work roles, relationships and channels of communication. Similarly, it relates to the planning and organizing of meetings, task teams and other management activities within the organization" (p. 16).

### Measurement Description

The items were measured by 6-point Likert scales.

### Development

The development was described as follows: "A questionnaire was sent to 8396 engineering based companies to enquire how they thought each of the five capability areas affected their planning" (p. 18).

### Sample

The sample consisted of 31 companies, with an 8% response rate.

### Reliability and Validity

Not available.

### Scores

The scores are presented in Tables 1–9 in the article.

### Other Evidence

Not available.

### Reference

None.

---

## Goffin, Lemke, and Szwejczewski

### Article Summarized

Goffin, Keith, Fred Lemke, and Marek Szwejczewski. 2006. An exploratory study of "close" supplier-manufacturer relationships. *Journal of Operations Management* 24 (2): 189–209.

### Scales (Actual Questions Used)

*Complaint Handling*

1. Good handling of complaints—the supplier accepts faults in a product, reacts quickly, and eliminates the fault once and for all.
2. Poor handling of complaints—the manufacturer has to convince the supplier that the product is faulty. He reacts slowly and supposedly eliminated faults reappear in the future.

*Dependency*

3. Independent—the manufacturer has got the opportunity to switch to alternative suppliers in the short term. The market is a buyer market based on open competition.
4. Dependent—switching to another supplier is time-consuming as the supplier has got a monopoly (sellers' market).

*Feedback*

5. Fast feedback—the conversational supplier replies to all enquiries of the manufacturer promptly.
6. No feedback—there is a "silent atmosphere" between the supplier and manufacturer and the supplier does not reply to the manufacturer's enquiries. The manufacturer has to "run after" the supplier, as he does not reply to the manufacturer's enquiries.

*New Product Development/Innovation*

7. New product development—the supplier becomes involved in developing and enhancing products due to his high quality technical input.
8. No new product development—in NPD processes, the manufacturer does not consider the supplier to take part. In general, the supplier is unable to submit any technical input, and he does not have the farsightedness for new products.

*Organizational Size*

9. Small family enterprise—the supplying organization consists of a small number of employees and is family owned.
10. Big enterprise—the organization has often more than 500 employees and has many subsidiaries (worldwide), e.g., a full public company.

*Relationship Maintenance*

11. Active—the relationship is very interactive and the supplier as well as the manufacturer nurture their relationship by contacting the partner and visiting the partner's company on a regular basis.
12. None—neither the supplier nor the manufacturer nurtures the relationship. The supplier initially aimed at an easy "customer catch," and he does not develop the relationship to anything more than that.

*Special Product Capability*

13. Special—the supplier delivers specially designed parts that fulfill the requirements of the manufacturer (e.g., parts are based on the manufacturer's drawings or that need be specially designed to suit the manufacturer tools and machines).
14. Special—the vendor supplies raw material, norm and DIN[1] parts, or OEM components.

*Personal Relationship*

15. Personal—there exists an intensive and familiar contact between the supplier and manufacturer at a "human level." Both parties have an interest to establish the personal relationship further and to keep it that way.
16. Business—the relationship between the supplier and manufacturer is formal, impersonal, and superficial and purely aims at processing orders.

*Volume of Turnover as Bought from the Supplier*

17. High—the supplier delivers a high volume of turnover to the manufacturer over the year, and he is one of the main suppliers. The manufacturer describes the supplier as his "A-supplier."
18. Low—either the supplier delivers parts sporadically or he supplies merely low volumes over the year ("C-supplier").

**Construct Description**

This was a case study and the items used above also indicated the construct description.

**Measurement Description**

Not available.

### Development

A technique called repertory grid (Hussey and Hussey, 1997) was used in the conduct case research. The authors explained this technique with an example. Interviewers asked an interviewee to name "nine suppliers with which they work, three in 'close' relationships. Each of these suppliers' names was written on a separate postcard-sized card, which had been randomly numbered in advance. The interviewee was then presented with a random set of three cards (termed a 'triad' in repertory grid terminology) and asked: 'why is working with two of these suppliers similar and different from working with the third?' From the many combinations possible, triads should be selected to include strongly contrasting elements (Bender, 1974) and explanation of this process can be found in Goffin (2002)" (p. 196). The authors termed the interviewee's response as a construct. After each construct was identified, "each of nine suppliers was rated against it on a 5-point scale [with 1 'very good,' 3 'neutral' and 5 'very poor,' as recommended by Tindall (1994) and Gammack and Stephens (1994)]" (p. 196).

### Sample

Germany was chosen as a suitable national context in which to investigate supplier relationships since many German writers have acknowledged the importance of supplier management there (Homburg 1995) and that close supplier relationships were a critical success factor (e.g., Snijder 1996). The repertory grid interviews formed part of a larger program of research into supplier management at German manufacturing companies and was linked to the International Best Factory Awards program, which has been the basis for a wide range of investigations of manufacturing performance. A previous study of supplier management took a database of 110 of mainly midsized, German manufacturers as its starting point and then conducted telephone interviews with a stratified random subsample of 34 companies in three sectors (Lemke et al 2000). In the current study, the authors contacted 28 of these companies and 18 agreed to participate in the research (corresponding to a response of 64%). The 18 companies represented German medium-sized companies that had an average of 377 employees and an average turnover of 57 million Euros and were deemed suitable as an exploratory sample. In engineering, the automotive industry was well represented, as this was a major sector in Germany.

### Reliability and Validity

Not available.

### Scores

Not available.

### Other Evidence

Not available.

### Note

1. DIN is a German Industrial Standard, similar to American Standards Association (ASA) in the United States.

### References

Bender, M. P. 1974. Provided versus elicited constructs: An explanation of Warr and Coffman's anomalous finding. *British Journal of Social and Clinical Psychology* 13: 329–30.

Gammack, J. G., and R. A. Stephens. 1994. Repertory grid technique in constructive interaction. In *Qualitative Methods in Organizational Research: A Practical Guide*, eds. C. Casell and G. Symon, 72–90, London: Sage.

Goffin, K. 2002. Repertory grid technique. In *Essential skills for management research*, ed. D. Partington, 199–225. London, Sage.

Homburg, C. 1995. Closeness to the customer in industrial markets: Towards a theory-based understanding of measurement, organizational antecedents, and performance outcomes. *Zeitschrift fur Betriebswirtschaft* 65 (3): 309–31.

Hussey, J., and R. Hussey. 1997. *Business research*. London, Macmillan Press.

Lemke, F., K. Goffin, M. Szwejczewski, R. Pfeiffer, and B. Lohmuller. 2000. Supplier base management: Experiences from the UK and Germany. *International Journal of Logistics Management* 11 (2): 45–48.

Snijder, J. 1996. Global sourcing: Weltweite Einkaufsmarktaufklarung und Lieferantenauswahl. In *Logistikmanagement: Strategische Wettbwerbsvorteile durch Logistik*, eds. G. Schuh, H. Weber, and P. Kajuter, 241–52. Stuttgart, Germany: Schaffer Poeschel Verlog.

Tindall, C. 1994. Personal construct approaches. In *Qualitative methods in psychology*, eds. P. Banister, E. Burman, I. Parker, M. Taylor, and C. Tindall, 72–91. Buckingham, UK: Open University Press.

# Goldstein

### Article Summarized

Goldstein, Susan Meyer. 2003. Employee development: An examination of service strategy in a high contact service environment. *Production and Operations Management* 12 (2): 186–203.

### Scales (Actual Questions Used)

*Employee Development*

Work Systems

1. Employees are given a broad range of tasks.
2. Employees are given decision-making responsibility.
3. We tie compensation and recognition to our strategic goals.
4. Employees are rewarded for learning new skills.
5. We motivate employees by improving job design (such as cross training, job rotation, etc.).

*Staff Training and Development*

6. We use training to build the capabilities of our staff.
7. Frontline employees are trained on how to handle service failures ("recoveries" from patient property theft, long waiting times, etc.).
8. Employees are trained with problem-solving skills.
9. We evaluate the benefits of staff training by measuring changes in skills or behavior.

*Staff Well-being*

10. Our work environment supports the well-being and development of all employees.
11. We use a variety of methods to measure employee satisfaction.
12. We work to improve employee health and safety (such as ergonomic training for jobs requiring lifting).
13. Employees receive career development services.
14. Employee turnover is evaluated in each department.

*Employee Outcomes*

15. Worker turnover (low turnover = better; high turnover = worse)
16. Efficiency (costs and timeliness) of services
17. Employee productivity
18. Overall satisfaction of employees (nonphysician)
19. Labor/management relationships are cooperative

*Customer Satisfaction*

20. Overall satisfaction of patients
21. Number of patients who return for future visits
22. Overall patient satisfaction
23. Number or severity of patient complaints

*Organization and Market Factors*

24. Using profit as financial performance measure
25. Location (urban/rural) [one dummy variable]
26. Number of beds
27. Teaching status (major teaching, resident training only, or nonteaching)
28. Proportion of market-managed care

*Using Revenue Growth as Financial Performance Measure*

29. Location (urban/rural) [one dummy variable]
30. Number of beds
31. Teaching status (major teaching, resident training only, or nonteaching) [two dummy variables]
32. Proportion of market-managed care

## Construct Description

Schlesinger and Heskett's (1991) article indicated that employee development was a multidimensional construct, and it motivated the construct development here. Employee development was explained as "a bundle of management issues and practices" (p. 193). The dimensions of this construct were also stated to be very similar to HR development and management category of Malcolm Baldrige National Quality Award Criteria. Work systems were "defined as the work and job designs that organizations establish for their employees" (p. 193). Work systems had been studied in Anderson and Wootton (1991), Counte et al. (1992), and NIST (1999).

Staff training and development connoted how these efforts were "focused on accomplishing key organizational plans and addressing organizational needs" (p. 193). This construct had been studied by Schweikhart and Strasser (1993) and NIST (1999). Staff well-being portrayed how the organization maintained "an environment and climate that support the well being and motivation of employees" (p. 193). This construct had been studied by Williams, Sobti, and Aw (1994) and NIST (1999).

Measures of employee outcomes were related to "key desirable results of employee development practices" and "employee satisfaction, employee turnover, labor/management relationships and workforce productivity and efficiency" (p. 193). Customer satisfaction focused on items related to satisfaction and satisfaction against the competitors.

## Measurement Description

Employee development was measured on a 7-point Likert scale: 1 = "not at all," 4 = "sometimes," and 7 = "always." Employee outcomes were similarly captured but the meanings of the points differed and were presented as: 1 = "significantly worse," 4 = "about the same," and 7 = "significantly better." For customer satisfaction, the following scale was used: 1 = "low/poor," 4 = "average," and 7 = "high/excellent." The remaining constructs were measured with open-ended questions.

**Development**

The main purpose of the study was to test the relationships among employee development constructs, which also led to internal service quality, employee outcomes, and customer satisfaction. Constructs were developed based on the existing literature.

**Sample**

Data were collected from 814 hospitals. People in the positions of director of quality, VP of quality, or quality manager filled in the surveys. Two hundred and ninety-nine surveys returned. In total, 220 surveys remained because some were dropped from the analyses because of missing data. Size of the hospitals ranged from less than 100 beds to more than 500 beds. Type of hospitals according to ownership fell into one of the following categories: for-profit, nonprofit, and government.

**Reliability and Validity**

Goldstein and Schweikhart (2001) discussed "validation and reliability of the measurement items for the three dimensions of employee development" (p. 193). Composite reliability values ranged from .74 for the employee outcomes construct to .89 for staff training and development; and variance extracted ranged from .48 to .76 for the employee outcomes and staff training and development constructs, respectively.

**Scores**

Measures and comparisons of fit are presented in Tables 1 and 2 in the article. Path coefficients are reported in Table 3.

**Other Evidence**

Not available.

**References**

Anderson, K., and B. Wootton. 1991. Changes in hospital staffing patterns. *Monthly Labor Review* 114 (3): 3–9.

Counte, M. A., G. L. Glandon, D. M. Oleske, and J. P. Hill. 1992. Total quality management in health care organizations: An analysis of employee impacts. *Hospital and Health Service Administration* 37 (4): 503–18.

Goldstein, S. M., and S. B. Schweikhart. 2001. Empirical support for the Baldrige award framework in U.S. hospitals. *Health Care Management Review* 27 (1): 62–75.

NIST (National Institute of Standards and Technology). 1999. *Health care criteria for performance excellence, Malcolm Baldrige National Quality Award: 1999 award criteria*. Gaithersburg, MD: NIST.

Schlesinger, L. A., and J. L. Heskett. 1991. Customer satisfaction is rooted in employee satisfaction. *Harvard Business Review* 69 (6): 148–49.

Schweikhart, S. B., and S. Strasser. 1993. Service recovery in health service organizations. *Hospital and Health Services Administration* 38 (1): 3–23.

Williams, N., A. Sobti, and T. C. Aw. 1994. Comparison of perceived occupational health needs among managers, employee representatives and occupational physicians. *Occupational Medicine* 44 (4): 205–208.

# Goldstein and Naor

**Article Summarized**

Goldstein, Susan Meyer, and Michael Naor. 2005. Linking publicness to operations management practices: A study of quality management practices in hospitals. *Journal of Operations Management* 23 (2): 209–28.

**Scales (Actual Question Used)**

*Publicness Dimensions*

1. Ownership: categorized as for-profit, nonprofit, or government.
2. Goal setting: categorized as major teaching, minor (resident only) teaching, nonteaching.
3. Funding: proportion of revenue provided by Medicare and Medicaid (both government funded) are summed, resulting in total proportion of revenue from government sources.
4. Control.

*Public Responsibility*

5. We integrate public responsibility into performance improvement efforts.
6. Our employees follow a formal code of ethics.
7. We lead efforts to improve community services, including education and environmental programs.
8. We provide free services for those who cannot pay.

*Compliance*

9. Results of regulatory reviews
10. Maintaining licensure of hospital employees
11. Compliance with standard care patterns

*Quality Management Practices*

12. Our information systems are *standardized* across departments (patient care, accounting, etc.).
13. Our information systems are *integrated* across departments.
14. Our information systems support frontline employees.
15. Both hardware and software are reliable.
16. Information systems are used to link caregivers' actions with patient outcomes.

*Selection and Use of Comparative Data*

17. We have adequate sources of benchmarking information.
18. We use benchmarking information to identify areas that need improvement.
19. We have information on "best-of-class" performance by our competitors for various hospital services.

*Analysis and Review of Organizational Performance*

20. Organizational planning is based on objective data which we have collected and analyzed.
21. We use objective data to identify our competitive strengths.
22. Our data analysis shows improvement in cycle times (reduced length of stay, reduced waiting times, etc.).
23. Training costs can be linked to positive changes in performance (quality of patient care, productivity, etc.).

24. We compare performance measurements with our competitors (such as comparing cost per diagnostic related group [DRG]).
25. We use our data to identify trends that help us set priorities in how our resources are used.

*Work Systems*

26. We motivate employees by improved job design (such as cross-training, job rotation, etc.).
27. Employees are given a broad range of tasks.
28. Employees are given decision-making responsibility.
29. We tie compensation and recognition to our strategic goals.
30. Employees are rewarded for learning new skills.

*Staff Education, Training, and Development*

31. We use training to build the capabilities of our staff.
32. Frontline employees are trained on how to handle service failures ("recoveries" from patient property theft, long waiting times, etc.).
33. Employees are trained with problem-solving skills.
34. We evaluate the benefits of staff training by measuring changes in skills or behavior.

*Staff Well-being and Satisfaction*

35. Our work environment supports the well-being and development of all employees.
36. We use a variety of methods to measure employee satisfaction.
37. We work to improve employee health and safety (such as ergonomic training for jobs requiring lifting).
38. Employees receive career development services.
39. Employee turnover is evaluated in each department.

*Design and Delivery of Patient Health Care Services*

40. New and revised health care services are reviewed and tested before they are introduced to patients.
41. Patient preferences are analyzed when designing new and revised patient services.
42. Performance standards for new and revised services are addressed during the design phase.
43. Design requirements are considered by all appropriate departments to ensure integration.
44. Our service design process is continuously improved.
45. We evaluate services on the basis of efficiency, including cost and timeliness.
46. We evaluate services on the basis of effectiveness, including appropriateness and risk.
47. Procedures and possible outcomes are explained to patients so they know what to expect.
48. Measurements/observations of patient services will indicate when corrective actions are needed.

*Management of Support Processes*

49. We measure the performance of our administrative services.
50. Analytical techniques such as process mapping and error proofing are used for addressing problems.
51. Feedback on administrative services is obtained from internal customers (other departments).
52. Feedback on administrative services is obtained from external customers (patients and other stakeholders).
53. All requirements (internal and external) are addressed in the design of support services.
54. We measure the performance of our support services.
55. We obtain feedback on support services from patients.
56. Quality is our most important criterion for selecting suppliers.
57. Suppliers are involved in designing new and revised services.

## Construct Description

Organizational publicness was classified by four dimensions that characterize organizations as public or private: ownership, goal setting, funding, and control (Bozeman 1987; Bozeman and Bretschneider 1994; Bozeman and Crow 1990). The study included quality management practices such as information and analysis, staff focus, and process management.

## Measurement Description

The construct of ownership was gauged by categorical data (i.e., for-profit, nonprofit, government) obtained from publicly published data. The goal-setting construct was evaluated by teaching role of each hospital (i.e., major, minor—resident training only, nonteaching). Public responsibility and quality management constructs were measured by 7-point Likert scales.

## Development

The data gathered for this study were part of a study on quality management practices by Meyer and Collier (2001).

## Sample

General acute care hospitals in the United Stated were the targeted population for this study. Unit of analysis was the facility. Using survey mailers, 814 quality managers and quality executives were the targeted informants, of which 228 completed and returned the surveys. The authors noted that nonresponse bias was not significant based on the hospital size and hospital ownership. Sixteen surveys included missing survey data and were thus eliminated from the data set, while 17 others did not have data available and were also dropped, resulting in 195 usable hospital responses.

## Reliability and Validity

The authors developed and pilot tested a measurement scale for each subcategory (Goldstein and Schweikhart 2002; Meyer and Collier 2001). They also assessed the validity and reliability of each scale. A multistep process was used to obtain each hospital's score on the quality management practice constructs. The score for this construct was derived from the scores from information analysis, staff focus, and process management. To derive the quality management practice construct score, the authors first used principal components analysis (PCA). They then weighed the subcategory scores using Baldrige Criteria points (the authors describe this as "subcategory scores multiplied by their Baldrige point value" shown in Appendix A). They then added the weighted subcategory scores deriving a three-weighted summed score, for information and analysis, staff focus, and process management, for every hospital.

Common method bias was a concern for the measures of publicness control and quality practices since these were derived from the same survey. The authors used a Harman's one-factor test to assess common method bias (Podsakoff and Organ 1986). Seven factors with eigenvalues greater than 1.0 resulted from the factor analysis, including all items for publicness control and quality practices. The authors noted that their empirical results suggested that variance in the measurement items was as a result of factors other than common method bias.

## Scores

The scores are presented in Tables 2, 3, and 5 in the article.

## Other Evidence

Not available.

### References

Bozeman, B. 1987. *All organizations are public: Bridging public and private organizational theories.* San Francisco, CA: Jossey-Bass.

Bozeman, B., and S. Bretschneider. 1994. The "Publicness Puzzle" in organizations theory: A test of alternative explanations of differences between public and private organizations. *Journal of Public Administration Research and Theory* 4 (2): 197–223.

Bozeman, B., and M. Crow. 1990. The environments of U.S. R&D laboratories: Political and market influences. *Policy Sciences* 23: 25–56.

Goldstein, S. M., and S. B. Schweikhart. 2002. Empirical support for the Baldrige Award framework in U.S. hospitals. *Health Care Management Review* 27 (1): 62–75.

Meyer, S. M., and D. A. Collier. 2001. An empirical test of the causal relationships in the Baldrige health care pilot criteria. *Journal of Operations Management* 19 (4): 403–25.

Podsakoff, P. M., and D. W. Organ. 1986. Self-reports in organizational research: Problems and prospects. *Journal of Management* 12 (4): 531–44.

## Goldstein, Ward, Leong, and Butler

### Article Summarized

Goldstein, Susan Meyer, Peter T. Ward, G. Keong Leong, and Timothy W. Butler. 2002. The effect of location, strategy, and operations technology on hospital performance. *Journal of Operations Management* 20 (1): 63–75.

### Scales (Actual Questions Used)

*Marketing Strategy Factor*

1. Reputation within industry
2. Innovation in health care services
3. Hospital name recognition
4. Extensive advertising
5. Forecasting market growth
6. Beating the competition to market with new services

*Operations Strategy Factor*

7. High level of customer service
8. Service quality control
9. Experienced/trained personnel
10. Capability to provide specialty health care
11. Dependable service provider

### Construct Description

Not available.

### Measurement Description

The items were measured on 7-point Likert scales.

### Development

Not available.

### Sample

The sample consisted of 160 general acute care hospitals in Michigan. The survey was sent to CEOs and VPs of operations. Sixty-seven hospitals returned at least one survey with a response rate of 41.9% while 30 hospitals returned two completed surveys.

### Reliability and Validity

The authors used Cronbach's coefficient alpha to measure reliability of the items. The minimum level of Cronbach's alpha was .73 and was deemed satisfactory.

### Scores

The scores are presented in Tables 1–4 in the article.

### Other Evidence

Not available.

### Reference

None.

---

## Griffith, Harvey, and Lusch

### Article Summarized

Griffith, David A., Michael G. Harvey, and Robert F. Lusch. 2006. Social exchange in supply chain relationships: The resulting benefits of procedural and distributive justice. *Journal of Operations Management* 24 (2):85–98.

### Scales (Actual Questions Used)

*Procedural Justice (PJ)*

1. Have fair policies regarding those they deal with
2. Generally treat us fairly
3. Are equitable in their treatment of those they deal with

*Distributive Justice (DJ)*

4. Our firm's contribution to this relationship
5. The supplier's contributions to this relationship
6. The outcomes or rewards we receive from this relationship
7. The outcomes or rewards the supplier receives from this relationship

*Long-Term Orientation (LTO)*

8. We expect our relationship with our major supplier to continue for a long time.
9. Renewal of the relationship with our major supplier is virtually automatic.

10. Our relationship with our major supplier is enduring.
11. Our relationship with our major supplier is a long-term alliance.

*Relational Behavior (RB)*

12. We are flexible when dealing with our major supplier.
13. We expect to make adjustments in dealing with our major supplier to cope with changing circumstances.
14. We provide any information that might help our major supplier.
15. We provide information to our major supplier frequently and informally and not only according to a prespecified agreement.
16. We will provide proprietary information to our major supplier if it can help.
17. We keep our major supplier informed about events or changes that may affect them.
18. When our major supplier incurs problems, we try to help.
19. We share in the problems that arise in the course of dealing with our major supplier.
20. We are committed to improvements that may benefit relationships with our major supplier as a whole and not only ourselves.

*Conflict (CONFL)*

21. Credit terms
22. Inventory levels
23. Product quality
24. Promotional programs
25. Pricing issues
26. Warranty policies
27. Backorders
28. Packaging
29. Delivery delay
30. Sales representatives

*Satisfaction (SATIS)*

31. Credit terms
32. Inventory levels
33. Product quality
34. Promotional programs
35. Pricing issues
36. Warranty policies
37. Backorders
38. Packaging
39. Delivery delay
40. Sales representatives

*Performance (PERF)*

41. Sales growth
42. Profit growth
43. Overall profitability
44. Liquidity
45. Cash flow

### Construct Description

The constructs were operationalized as follows: Procedural justice (PJ) was given as "the process, and the perceived fairness of that process, associated with the distribution and/or allocation of goods/services in limited supply relative to demand (Lind and Tyler, 1988; Konovsky, 2000)" (p. 87). The authors stated that PJ focused "on perceived fairness of decision-making procedures itself and on the attitudes of those directly involved in or affected by those decisions (Korsgaard et al., 1995) and as such can be viewed as a social policy of supply chain management" (p. 87). Closely tied to PJ, distributive justice (DJ) was defined as "the perceived fairness with the decision outcome (Sheppard et al., 1992; Konovsky, 2000) and as such can be viewed as an economic policy of supply chain management" (p. 87).

Long-term orientation was reported as "when an exchange partner believes that the on-going relationship with another is so important as to warrant maximum effort in maintaining the relationship (Ganesan, 1994; Morgan and Hunt, 1994; Li-Ping Tang and Sarsfield-Baldwin, 1996)" (p. 88). Relational behaviors was referred to as the "desired behaviors on the part of one or more partners in the exchange (Hewett and Bearden, 2001), such as flexibility, sharing of information and solidarity (Heide and John, 1992; Lusch and Brown, 1996). When a firm perceives its supply chain partner as offering fair administration (i.e., PJ), it behaves in a manner to continue the relationship to receive its benefits (cf. success and value proposition)" (p. 88).

The authors described conflict as "the tension between exchange partners that arises from incompatibility of actual or desired responses (Deutsch, 1969; Ross et al., 1997)" (p. 89). They stated that conflict referred "to the manifest conflict, or the behavioral response to perceived and/or affective conflict, of the distributor" (p. 89). Satisfaction was identified "as an affective state resulting from the appraisal of all aspects of a firm's exchange relationship. The study examined the distributor's performance according to the rational goal model that views organizations as striving for efficiency and productivity (Kumar et al., 1992). Thus, business performance was operationalized as the distributor's performance relative to other firms in its industry in terms of its sales growth, profit growth, overall profitability, liquidity, and cash flow (cf. Lusch and Brown, 1996)" (p. 89).

### Measurement Description

The items were measured by 7-point Likert scales.

### Development

The development of survey consisted of three stages. First the authors reviewed the relevant academic and practitioner literature. Then, two wholesale distributors and two industry consultants reviewed the preliminary instrument. After modifications were made, a random sample of 100 firms was employed for pretesting. The authors indicated that the pretest results indicated that no further modifications were needed to the questionnaire and they proceeded with final data collection.

### Sample

A supplier-distributor supply chain context was used to test the hypotheses. A systematic random sample of 3,225 merchant wholesale and agent distributors were drawn from a mailing list of all U.S. distributors in 16 four-digit U.S. Department of Commerce's Standard Industrial Classification (SIC) codes. The authors specifically chose SIC codes reflecting eight lines of nondurable goods and eight SIC codes reflecting eight lines of durable goods. They selected the lines of trade selected primarily consisting of small distributors; for example, the census of wholesalers indicated that 82% of merchant wholesalers have fewer than 20 employees. Based on Lusch and Brown (1996), the authors stated that by sampling small firms, they minimized the single informant concerns because of the nature of the respondent and their position within the firm. To increase the response rate, one U.S. dollar bill was included with the survey as an incentive and the targeted respondents were also offered a copy of the survey findings. An overall response rate of 28.8% was obtained. The resulting sample was composed of 290 merchant wholesale distributors who reported on their relationship with their primary supplier.

### Reliability and Validity

The authors used confirmatory factor analysis (CFA) to test whether the psychometric properties of the measures used in the posited model fit the data. Results of the CFA indicated acceptable model fit ($\chi^2$ = 773.265, d.f. = 307, p = .00; goodness-of-fit index (GFI) = .838, comparative fit index (CFI) = .903) with all factor loadings being statistically significant. Thus evidence of convergent validity was obtained. The authors referred to the Bagozzi and Yi (1988) guidelines for composite reliability and note that their results, ranging from .86 to .93, meet the threshold values. Cross-construct correlations were used to assess discriminant validity. The 95% confidence intervals were computed for each correlation coefficient and the interitem correlations were found to be less than one at the .05 significance level. These results provided further support for discriminant validity.

### Scores

The scores are presented in Tables 1–3 and in Figure 2 in the article.

### Other Evidence

Not available.

### References

Bagozzi, R. P., and Y. Yi. 1988. On the evaluation of structural models. *Journal of the Academy of Marketing Science* 16 (1): 74–94.

Deutsch, M. 1969. Conflicts: Productive and destructive. *Journal of Social Issues* 25 (1): 7–41.

Ganesan, S. 1994. Determinants of long-term orientation in buyer-seller relationships. *Journal of Marketing* 58 (2): 1–19.

Heide, J. B., and G. John. 1992. Do norms matter in marketing relationships? *Journal of Marketing* 56 (2): 32–44.

Hewett, K., and W. O. Bearden. 2001. Dependence, trust and relational behavior on the part of foreign subsidiary marketing operations: Implications for managing global marketing operations. *Journal of Marketing* 65 (4): 51–66.

Konovsky, M. A. 2000. Understanding procedural justice and its impact on business organizations. *Journal of Management* 26 (3): 489–511.

Korsgaard, M. A., D. M. Schweiger, and H. J. Sapienza. 1995. Building commitment, attachment, and trust in strategic decision-making teams: The role of procedural justice. *Academy of Management Journal* 38 (1): 60–84.

Kumar, N., L. Stern, and R. Achrol. 1992. Assessing reseller performance from the perspective of the supplier. *Journal of Marketing Research* 29 (2): 238–53.

Lind, E. A., and T. Tyler. 1988. *The social psychology of procedural justice*. New York: Plenum Press.

Li-Ping Tang, T., and L. J. Sarsfield-Baldwin. 1996. Distributive and procedural justice as related to satisfaction and commitment. *SAM Advanced Management Journal* 61 (3): 25–31.

Lusch, R. F., and J. R. Brown. 1996. Interdependency, contracting, and relational behavior in marketing channels. *Journal of Marketing* 60 (4): 19–38.

Morgan, R. M., and S. D. Hunt. 1994. The commitment-trust theory of relationship marketing. *Journal of Marketing* 58 (3): 20–38.

Ross, W. T., Jr., E. Anderson, and B. Weitz. 1997. Performance in principal-agent dyads: The causes and consequences of perceived asymmetry of commitment to the relationship. *Management Science* 43 (5): 680–704.

Sheppard, B. H., R. J. Lewicki, and J. W. Minton. 1992. *Organizational justice: The search for fairness in the workplace*. New York: Lexington Books.

# Grover and Malhotra

### Article Summarized

Grover, Varun, and Manoj K. Malhotra. 2003. Transaction cost framework in operations and supply chain management research: Theory and measurement. *Journal of Operations Management* 21 (4): 457–73.

### Scales (Actual Questions Used)

*In Developing an Association with Supplier S (with Respect to Component C)*

1. It was understood in advance what this relationship would involve.
2. Significant effort was required to gather the information necessary to outline the working relationship with supplier S.
3. It was straightforward and easy to work out the main issues and necessary details of the relationship with supplier S.
4. There were many unspecified terms which had to be worked out as the relationship with supplier S developed.
5. It required significant effort to determine individual roles to be performed by our firm and supplier S.

*In Monitoring the Performance of Supplier S*

6. It is easy to tell if we were receiving fair treatment from supplier S.
7. It takes significant effort to detect whether or not supplier S conforms to specifications and quality standards.
8. We are in a good position to evaluate how fairly our supplier S deals with us.
9. Accurately evaluating supplier S requires a lot of effort.
10. There is not much concern about supplier S taking advantage of this relationship.
11. It is costly, in time and effort, to clearly monitor the performance of supplier S.

*In Addressing Problems That Might Arise in the Relationship with Supplier S*

12. The approach to solving problems in our relationship with supplier S is clear-cut.
13. There are standard solutions or approaches to problems that might occur with supplier S.
14. Problem solving is often challenging due to the nature of component C.
15. Although solutions to problems can be achieved, they would often need to be highly customized.

*Concerning the Likelihood of Supplier S Taking Advantage of Its Relationship with Our Firm*

16. There are no incentives for supplier S to pursue their interests at the expense of our interests.
17. It is easy for supplier S to alter the facts to get what they wanted.
18. There is a strong temptation for supplier S to withhold or distort information for their benefit.
19. It is difficult for supplier S to promise to do things and get away without actually doing them later.
20. There exists, from supplier S's perspective, a significant motivation to take advantage of unspecified or unenforceable contract terms.

### Construct Description

The constructs studied were derived from the transaction cost theory by Williamson (1975). Transaction costs corresponded to the combination of coordination and transaction risk. Coordination cost was specified as the cost of exchanging risk and the cost of incorporating that information into the decision process. While transaction risk characterized the risk that the other party might shirk their agreed on responsibilities, the asset specificity construct was related "to the transferability of the assets that support a given transaction" (p. 49). Uncertainty referred to the "unanticipated changes in circumstances surrounding a transaction. This uncertainty could preclude both the formulation of a contract ex ante and/or the ability to verify compliance ex post. The former (environmental uncertainty) can be reflected in constructs such as unpredictability of the environment, technology, and demand volume and variety. The latter (behavioral uncertainty) includes performance evaluation and information asymmetry problems" (p. 460). In this study, market and hierarchy constructs were reported as representing "governance mechanisms in their purest mode. Each firm has different mechanisms for coordinating the flow of materials and services through steps in the value chain (Malone et al., 1987). Hierarchies, firms, or vertically integrated entities control and direct this flow at a higher level in the management hierarchy" (p. 460).

### Measurement Description

The measures for the study were drawn from the scales developed by Pilling et al. (1994), but the authors reversed some of the scales to reduce method bias. Transaction cost was a second-order construct and was reflected by the first-order constructs of effort, monitor, problem, and advantage. Effort was characterized as the effort required for building and maintaining the relationship, and monitor was defined as the effort required to monitor the performance of the supplier. Problem was operationalized as how the problems were resolved as they arise with the supplier, and last advantage was operationalized as whether the supplier engaged in opportunistic behavior.

### Development

The article borrowed from transaction cost literature to operationalize the "transaction cost" construct. The theoretical foundations for the research were drawn from the transaction cost theory (Williamson 1975, 1985).

### Sample

The unit of interest for this survey was buyer-supplier dyads. The data on the original equipment manufacturers (OEM) relationships were gathered from organizational buyers within a dyadic relationship. The respondents were drawn from a list of 1,000 purchasing managers who were obtained from a professional information service. A total of 730 companies satisfied the criteria of having an established supplier with whom there was an ongoing relationship, who provided an important input/component for the production process. The final response received was 203 with a response rate of 27% (of 730 firms).

### Reliability and Validity

The value of the benchmark alpha used was .60 (Nunnally 1978; Churchill 1979). Discriminant validity was assessed by the correlations among the constructs, which are presented in Table 5 in the article. The $\chi^2$ test for differences in these cases suggested that the correlations were different from one, indicating that the constructs were distinct.

### Scores

The confirmatory factor analysis (CFA) loadings are depicted in Table 4 in the article, and in Table 5 the correlations between the first-order constructs are presented.

### Other Evidence

Not available.

**References**

Churchill, G. A., Jr. 1979. A paradigm for developing better measures of marketing constructs. *Journal of Marketing Research* 16: 64–73.

Malone, T. W., J. Yates, and R. Benjamin. 1987. Electronic markets and electronic hierarchies: Effects of information technology on market structure and corporate strategies. *Communications of the ACM* 30 (6): 484–97.

Nunnally, J. C. 1978. *Psychometric theory*. New York: McGraw-Hill.

Pilling, B. K., L. A., Crosby, and D. W. Jackson. 1994. Relational bonds in industrial exchange: An experimental test of the transaction cost economic framework. *Journal of Business Research* 30 (3): 237–51.

Williamson, O. E. 1975. *Markets and hierarchies: Analysis and antitrust implications*. New York: Free Press.

———. 1985. *The economic institutions of capitalism: Firms, markets, relational contracting*. London: Free Press.

# Harrison-Walker

**Article Summarized**

Harrison-Walker, L. Jean. 2001. The measurement of word-of-mouth communication and an investigation of service quality and customer commitment as potential antecedents. *Journal of Service Research* 4 (1): 60–75.

**Scales (Actual Questions Used)**

*Affective Commitment*

1. For me, this is one of the best service organizations of its kind.
2. I am proud that I use the services of this organization.
3. I usually agree with this organization's policies and procedures on important matters.
4. This is a good service organization to use.
5. I care about the fate of this service organization.
6. This organization inspires the best in me in the way of being a good customer.
7. I like the way this service organization operates.
8. This service organization understands my needs.
9. If I were in charge of this service organization, I wouldn't run it any differently.
10. I like this service organization.
11. I have a special relationship with this service organization.
12. I want to help this service organization achieve its goals.
13. Doing business with this service organization is enjoyable.
14. I do business with this service organization because I like it.

*High Sacrifice Commitment*

15. The longer I stay with this service organization, the harder it is to leave.
16. It would be difficult for me to adapt to a new service organization.
17. Many changes would have to occur in my present circumstances to cause me to stop doing business with this service organization.
18. If I decided to stop doing business with this service organization, it would be difficult to explain to my friends and my family.
19. I would give up a lot if I stopped doing business with this service organization.
20. If I left this service organization for another service organization, it would be hard to come back.
21. It would be hard on my significant other(s) if I decided to stop using this service organization.
22. It would be impractical to change to a new service organization.
23. I continue to do business with this service organization because it would be difficult to make a change.
24. There are certain costs associated with switching to another service organization.

*Word of Mouth*

Frequency

25. Since I have been with this service organization, I have mentioned the name of this service organization very rarely.
26. I mention this service organization to others quite frequently.
27. I rarely have occasion to mention the name of this service organization to others.

Number of Contacts

28. I've told more people about this service organization than I've told about most other service organizations.
29. I seldom miss an opportunity to tell others about this service organization.
30. I've told very few people about this service organization.

Detail

31. When I tell others about this service organization, I tend to talk about the organization in great detail.
32. I seldom do more than mention the name of this service organization to others.
33. Once I get talking about this service organization, it's hard for me to stop.

Praise

34. I have only good things to say about this service organization.
35. Although I use this service organization, I tell others that I do not recommend it.

## Construct Description

The constructs were defined as follows. Word of mouth (WOM) connoted the "informal, person-to-person communication between a perceived noncommercial communicator and a receiver regarding a brand, a product, an organization, or a service" (p. 63). Affective commitment captured "the strength of an individual's identification with, and involvement in, a particular organization" (p. 65). Organizational commitment was referred to as "the tendency to engage in consistent lines of activity because of the perceived costs of doing otherwise" (p. 65). The service quality construct was conceptualized as "an attitude that is defined by an individual's importance-weighted evaluation of the performance of the specific dimensions of a service" (p. 66).

## Measurement Description

The service quality scale was drawn primarily on Parasuraman and Zeithaml (1988). A 22-item scale was adopted to tap into five dimensions of service quality. The actual question items used, however, were not provided in the article. Other constructs were also measured using multi-item scales, where each response was gauged on a 7-point Likert scale.

## Development

Measurement scales for three constructs—affective commitment, high sacrifice commitment, and service quality—were adapted from existing scales. The sources of each construct were reported in Appendix A in the article. The new measurement scale for WOM was developed following the recommendations from Churchill (1979). Based on the literature review, the authors initially generated 13 items to capture different aspects of WOM. The scale was empirically validated using a split-sample approach, where survey data were randomly divided into two half samples. The first subsample of data was used for scale development, and the second subsample was used to reaffirm the reliability of the refined scale. As a result, 6 out of the initial 13 items were dropped after the purification process. The remaining 7 items captured two dimensions of WOM: WOM activity and WOM praise.

## Sample

The survey sample consisted "of 471 individual consumers residing in two midsize college towns located in two southern states that were recruited by student assistants. Respondents were asked to complete the survey based on the specific service provider for which they were ongoing customers" (p. 63). Industrial sectors that respondents could report on were the veterinarian or hairdressing professions.

### Validity and Reliability

The reliability for the WOM activity and WOM praise scales using the first sample of pooled data were found to have acceptable levels of Cronbach coefficient alpha that equaled .80 and .78, respectively (Nunnally 1978). To assess the discriminant validity of the subsets of measures, the procedure recommended by Anderson and Gerbing (1988) was used. That is, for each pair of constructs in the conceptual model, two different models were conceptualized: The first model allows phi to vary, whereas the second model constrains the phi correlation to unity. The difference between the $\chi^2$ values for the models is itself asymptotically distributed as $\chi^2$ distribution, with degrees of freedom equal to the difference in degrees of freedom for the two models (Anderson and Gerbing 1988). An $\chi^2$ difference test was conducted for each pair of constructs. In each case, the $\chi^2$ value for the unconstrained model was found to be significantly lower ($p < .001$) than the constrained model, which indicated discriminant validity (*see* Table 3 in the article). Of particular importance, discriminant validity was demonstrated between WOM Activity and WOM Praise, two constructs initially thought to be two aspects of a single, more generalized WOM construct.

### Scores

The scores are presented in Tables 1–3 of the article.

### Other Evidence

Not available.

### References

Anderson, J. C., and D. W. Gerbing. 1988. Structural equation modeling in practice: A review and recommended two-step approach. *Psychological Bulletin* 103 (3): 411–23.

Churchill, G. A., Jr. 1979. A paradigm for developing better measures of marketing constructs. *Journal of Marketing Research* 16 (1): 64–73.

Nunnally, J. C. 1978. *Psychometric theory.* New York: McGraw-Hill.

Parasuraman, A., and V. A. Zeithaml. 1988. SERVQUAL: A multiple-item scale for measuring consumer perceptions of service quality. *Journal of Retailing* 64 (1): 12–40.

## Hausman, Montgomery, and Roth

### Article Summarized

Hausman, Warren H., David B. Montgomery, and Aleda V. Roth. 2002. Why should marketing and manufacturing work together? Some exploratory empirical results. *Journal of Operations Management* 20 (3): 241–57.

### Scales (Actual Questions Used)

*Marketing Importance*

1. Importance of marketing to the strategy of this business unit

*Manufacturing Importance*

2. Importance of manufacturing to the strategy of this business unit

*M/M Interface Harmony*

3. How well marketing and manufacturing work together

*Profit*

4. Profit performance

*Competitive Position*

5. Competitive position

*Manufacturing Morale*

6. Morale of the manufacturing personnel

*Marketing Morale*

7. Morale of the marketing personnel

**Construct Description**

Not available.

**Measurement Description**

Single-item scales were used to measure each construct. Each question was gauged on a 7-point, bipolar scale with response categories ranging from 1 = "much lower (worse or low)" to 4 = "average" to 7 = "much higher (better or high)."

**Development**

The constructs were literature based.

**Sample**

The sampling frame employed for this study included participants in four executive education programs at Stanford University over a 2-year period. The data were collected from two independent convenience samples at two different points of time. In the first year, 215 executives responded out of 273 requests, which yielded a response rate of 79%. In the second year, 175 out of 337 executives returned surveys, resulting at a 52% response rate. Overall, the two pooled sample has an effective response rate of 64%. Respondents in the sample came from major functional areas and had a variety of job titles ranging from middle to top managers.

**Reliability and Validity**

Item reliability and validity were not determined; however, the overall model was found to be valid.

**Scores**

The scores are reported in Tables 4–7 of the article.

**Other Evidence**

Not available.

**Reference**

None.

# Hays and Hill

### Article Summarized

Hays, Julie M., and Arthur V. Hill. 2001. A preliminary investigation of the relationships between employee motivation/vision, service learning, and perceived service quality. *Journal of Operations Management* 19 (3): 335–49.

### Scales (Actual Questions Used)

*Employee Motivation and Vision (EMV)*

Motivation

1. Our employees always make customer satisfaction their top goal.
2. Our employees go out of their way to listen when customers complain.
3. Our employees try very hard to fix customer problems when they know about them.
4. Our employees feel a strong sense of accountability and ownership for service quality.
5. Customer satisfaction is an extremely important part of my job.

Vision

6. Our service quality priorities are clear to our employees.
7. Our employees have a clear understanding of the role that service quality plays in helping our company compete in our market.
8. We have very well-defined standards for service quality.

*Learning through Service Failure (LTSF)*

Discovery

9. When a service problem occurs, we are almost always aware of the problem.
10. Our employees are very aware of customer complaints and why they occur.
11. Customers with a service problem almost always complain to us.

Data

12. We have accurate information on how many complaints we receive.
13. We have accurate information on why our customers complain.
14. Information on customer satisfaction trends is communicated to all our employees.

Improvement

15. Collecting customer feedback helps us to regularly improve our service quality.
16. We have improved our service quality over the past year based on customer complaint information.

### Construct Description

The construct of employee motivation and vision (EMV) was defined as "the degree to which a firm's employees have a desire to provide high quality service and have a clear vision of the role that service quality plays in the company's overall strategy" (p. 340). The EMV construct was conceptually broken down to two dimensions—motivation and vision. Motivation referred to "the degree to which a firm's employees have a desire to provide high quality service" (p. 340). Vision was developed to capture "the degree to which management has communicated priorities clearly and the firm's employees (managers through front-line workers) have an awareness of the key role that service quality plays in the company's strategy" (p. 340).

The construct of learning through service failure (LTSF) was conceptualized as "the efficiency with which a firm is able to learn from its customers by discovering dissatisfied customers, collecting information from these customers, and improving their systems based on the information collected in order to improve the quality of its offerings" (p. 340). The LTSF consisted of three dimensions—discovery, data, and improvement. First, the discovery dimension was defined as "the degree to which a firm is able to detect service failures" (p. 340). Second, the data dimension reflected "the degree to which a firm collects and communicates information on service failures" (p. 340). Finally, improvement indicated "the degree to which a firm uses the failure to improve quality" (p. 340).

### Measurement Description

Each item was measured on a 7-point Likert scale.

### Development

Before the large-scale survey, a small-scale pilot survey was administered to a sample of local business managers and frontline personnel over a wide variety of service companies. The results of this survey revealed that all respondents had difficulty with reverse-scaled items. As a result, all items were positively worded. The authors also conducted exploratory factor analysis (EFA) to validate these scales. Several items were dropped because of poor psychometric performance.

### Sample

The survey was sent to a sample of 25 North American hotels, which were part of a multinational hotel corporation. The sample consisted of different sizes and types of hotels. Both the frontline personnel and the management were surveyed. More than 250 surveys were returned.

### Reliability and Validity

The perceived service quality (i.e., dependent variable) "is obtained partly by using the firm's customer response data. This measure should be both more reliable and more valid than other commonly employed measures such as employee's ratings of the quality of their service offering" (p. 340). The authors used EFA to assess the convergent and discriminant validity of the scales. The authors stated that the factor loadings of the items on their theoretical constructs indicated validity. They determined reliability by using Cronbach's coefficient alpha, with values greater or equal to .70.

### Scores

The scores are presented in Tables 2–4 and Figure 4 of the article.

### Other Evidence

Not available.

### Reference

None.

---

## Heineke

### Article Summarized

Heineke, Janelle. 1995. Strategic operations management decisions and professional performance in U.S. HMOs. *Journal of Operations Management* 13 (4): 255–72.

## Scales (Actual Questions Used)

*Model Type*

1. Please check the health maintenance organization (HMO model type that most closely describes your organization.
   - Staff
   - Group
   - Network
   - IPA

*Non-Clinical Factors*

2. Do 90% or more of your members deliver their babies in the same hospital?
   - If no, go to question 11.
   - If yes, what is that hospital's annual number of deliveries?
3. What is the teaching level?
4. What is the ownership type?
5. Does that hospital have a NICU?

*Cesarean Policies*

For each of the three groupings of items that follow, please check the item that describes an existing POLICY (POL) or a RECOMMENDATION (REC) for practice, and also check the item that describes the USUAL PRACTICE (UP) at your HMO.

6. In the absence of medical contraindications, women who have had previous cesarean sections have the following options:
   - Are required to try labor
   - Are strongly encouraged to try labor
   - Are given the option to try labor or to have a repeat cesarean section
   - Are encouraged to have repeat cesarean sections
   - Are required to have repeat cesarean sections
7. Elective repeat cesarean sections:
   - Will only be performed after the onset of labor.
   - May be scheduled prior to onset of labor.
8. A committee reviews all candidates for repeat cesarean section prior to scheduling to determine appropriateness of trial of labor.
9. A second physician opinion is obtained for repeat cesarean section.

*Length of Stay (LOS) Standard*

10. Does your HMO have a standard for length of stay for obstetrics?

*Algorithm Use*

11. Are clinical algorithms* in use in obstetrics at your HMO?
    (* Specific, step-by-step procedures or protocols.)

*Office Practice Review*

12. Does your HMO have a formal procedure for reviewing office obstetric care?

*Hospital Practice Review*

13. Does your HMO have a formal procedure for reviewing hospital obstetric care?

*Cesarean Feedback*

14. Is information regarding cesarean section rates provided to practicing physicians?
    - If yes, how often?

*Adverse Outcome Management*

15. When an adverse obstetrical outcome occurs, what, if any, steps are taken by the HMO?
    - Review of medical record by clinician committee.
    - Presentation of event by attending physician to grand rounds (or equivalent).
    - Confidential letter to attending physician by HOM manager (physician or non-physician).
    - Follow-up is left to hospital's quality assurance system.
    - Other (please describe) ______________________

*Utilization Feedback*

16. Is feedback on resource utilization in obstetrics provided to your physicians?

*MD Payment*

17. How are individual OB/GYN physicians paid?
    - Straight salary
    - Salary with incentive based on clinical performance
    - Salary with incentive based on utilization (cost containment)
    - Modified fee-for-serve (e.g., contractually reduced FFS payment with holdback)
    - Fee for service
    - Other (specify)____________________

*Workforce Configuration*

18. Other than obstetricians, please check which of the following clinician types function within your HMO. Are they employed, contracted directly, or practicing with physicians with whom the HMO contracts?
    - Perinatologist
    - Family practice or general practice physicians
    - Nurse practitioners
    - Midwives
    - Physician assistants

*Access Standards*

19. Has your HMO adapted access standards for obstetrical care?

**Construct Description**

Workforce management decisions covered "those regarding the composition of the workforce and how the workforce will be scheduled and paid" (p. 259). The workforce management variables used in this study included provider type and mode of physician payment. The management of quality within the organization covered the "policies and procedures regarding establishing measures of quality, collecting data on those measures, and using the data to influence the way work is done" (p. 259). "Quality management variables in this research included whether HMOs conducted reviews of office practice and hospital practice. Feedback of cesarean information and resource utilization were also assessed, as was the way HMOs managed adverse outcomes of care" (p. 259).

"In professional service organizations, planning and control systems comprise workforce practice guidelines, and protocols and mechanisms for controlling demand" (p. 259). The variables associated with planning and control systems in this study included policies regarding repeat cesarean section, access standards, and clinical algorithms. "The process measure is the length of hospital stay, and the outcome measure is cesarean section rate" (p. 260) and these constituted the performance measures.

### Measurement Description

All survey items were objective measures.

### Development

All Health Maintenance Organizations (HMOs) in the United States received a survey. "The survey elicited respondent identifier information, HMO descriptions and specific performance responses" (p. 260).

### Sample

The target population comprised all HMOs in the United States. Within each HMO, a single respondent—the manager responsible for obstetrics—was the target respondent. "One-hundred fifty-two usable questionnaires were returned an overall response rate of 28.2%. All of the respondents held managerial positions. Ninety-six percent of respondents ($n$ = 144) also had clinical training" (p. 260).

### Reliability and Validity

"Content validity, which depends on the extent to which an empirical measurement reflects a specific domain of content, was established through the literature review and mapping of each survey item to the conceptual framework, and through a pilot study which involved interviews and administration of the survey to OB/GYN managers in three staff and three IPA HMOs (Carmines and Zeller, 1979; Flynn et al., 1990)" (p. 260).

### Scores

The scores are presented in Tables 2 and 3 and Appendix B of the article.

### Other Evidence

Not available.

### References

Carmines, E. G., and R. A. Zeller. 1979. *Reliability and validity assessment.* Sage University Paper Series on Quantitative Applications in the Social Sciences, Series 07/017. Beverly Hills, CA: Sage.

Flynn, B. B., S. Sakakibara, R. G. Schroeder, K. A. Bates, and E. J. Flynn. 1990. Empirical research methods in operations management. *Journal of Operations Management* 9 (2): 250–85.

## Hennig-Thurau, Langer, and Hansen

### Article Summarized

Hennig-Thurau, Thorsten, Markus F. Langer, and Ursula Hansen. 2001. Modeling and managing student loyalty: An approach based on the concept of relationship quality. *Journal of Service Research* 3 (4): 331–44.

**Scales (Actual Questions Used)**

*Quality*

1. Academic staff
2. Infrastructure
3. Teaching on offer
4. Student care
5. Examinations/tests
6. Administrative services
7. Outcome

*Student Loyalty*

8. I'd recommend my course to someone else.
9. I'd recommend my university to someone else.
10. I'm very interested in keeping in touch with "my faculty."
11. If I was faced with the same choice again, I'd still choose the same course.
12. If I was faced with the same choice again, I'd still choose the same university.
13. I'd become a member of any alumni organization at my old university or faculty.

*Trust*

14. Integrity is a word I'd use when describing the university staff.
15. I was sure that the university staff were always acting in my best interest.
16. I trusted the university staff completely.
17. University staff always kept their promises to me.

*Emotional Commitment*

18. I felt very attached to my university.
19. I felt very attached to my faculty.
20. I was proud to be able to study at my university.
21. I was proud to be able to take the course I did.

*Cognitive Commitment*

22. I chose this university for practical reasons (fixed parameter).

*Goal Commitment*

23. When I set targets for myself, I always reach them (fixed parameter).

*Social Integration*

24. I regularly took part in university-related leisure activities, such as sports or fairs.
25. I always had intensive contact with my fellow students.
26. I regularly did things with fellow students outside the university.

*Academic Integration*

27. I regularly took part in extra-academic courses or events.
28. I was a regular member of student academic groups set up on their own initiative.
29. I regularly got involved with university committee work.

*Commitment to Nonuniversity Activities*

30. I made sure I still had plenty of time for my hobbies while I was a student (fixed parameter).

*Family Commitment*

31. I still had very close contact with my family and relatives (e.g., parents) while I was a student.

*Job Commitment*

32. While I was at the university, some of my time was taken up with paid work.

**Construct Description**

Student loyalty was conceptualized as the loyalty of a student during and after his or her time at the university. This construct contained both an attitudinal component and a behavioral component. The behavioral component was associated with a student's willingness to use the institution's offerings on a regular basis, while the attitudinal component reflected the student's positive cognitive-emotive attitude toward the institution.

**Measurement Description**

With the exception of job commitment, all other constructs were captured through multiple indicator variables.

**Development**

Most scales, except student loyalty, were adapted from the existing scales. The scales used to measure quality were from Hansen, Hennig-Thurau, and Wochnowski (1997). Trust and emotional commitment were modified versions of items used by Morgan and Hunt (1994). Cognitive commitment was derived from Geyskens et al. (1996). Goal commitment, social and academic integration, job commitment, family commitment, and nonuniversity activity commitment were drawn from Tinto (1993).

The scale for student loyalty was newly designed to cover different facets of loyalty—namely, questions regarding the students' repurchasing intention, items measuring referral, and alumni-related behavioral intentions.

**Sample**

A questionnaire was mailed to 5,994 students from six northern German universities, of which 1,162 questionnaires were returned. The sample contained both graduates and dropouts. There were no significant differences between the answers of early respondents and late respondents. The students were from different courses.

**Reliability and Validity**

"To ensure a high degree of reliability and result validity, the final operationalization of the variables was based on the three-step procedure recommended by leading researchers (e.g., Churchill, 1979; Fornell and Larcker, 1981). In the first step, an exploratory principal component analysis [PCA] was performed for each construct in order to assess its dimensionality. In the second step, where a construct was found to be two dimensional instead of one dimensional, the discrimination of the two dimensions was tested using the chi-square procedure and the Fornell-Larcker discrimination coefficient (Fornell and Larcker, 1981). The exploratory analysis suggested this: the service quality construct should have a two-factor structure but the high interfactor correlation demonstrated using the Fornell-Larcker coefficient meant that the proposed one-factor approach could be considered adequate. In the third step, we performed confirmatory factor analysis on each construct and deleted single indicators where necessary in order to increase the homogeneity of the respective construct" (p. 337).

**Scores**

The means, standard deviations, Cronbach's coefficient alphas for each construct as well as the correlations are reported in Table 1 of the article. Tables 2–5 depict the results of factor analysis.

### Other Evidence

Not available.

### References

Churchill, G. A., Jr. 1979. A paradigm for developing better measures of marketing constructs. *Journal of Marketing Research* 16 (1): 64–73.

Fornell, C., and D. F. Larcker. 1981. Evaluating structural equation models with unobservable variables and measurement error. *Journal of Marketing Research* 18 (1): 39–50.

Geyskens, I., J.–B. E. M. Steenkamp, L. K. Scheer, and N. Kumar. 1996. The effects of trust and interdependence on relationship commitment: A trans-Atlantic study. *International Journal of Research in Marketing* 13 (4): 303–17.

Hansen, U., T. Hennig-Thurau, and H. Wochnowski. 1997. Teach-Q: Ein valides und handhabbares instrument zur bewertung von vorlesungsleistungen. *Die Betriebswirtschaft* 57 (3): 376–96.

Morgan, R. M., and S. D. Hunt. 1994. The commitment-trust theory of relationship marketing. *Journal of Marketing* 58 (3): 20–38.

Tinto, V. 1993. *Leaving college: Rethinking the causes and cures of student attrition.* Chicago, IL: University of Chicago Press.

## Huete and Roth

### Article Summarized

Huete, Luis M., and Aleda V. Roth. 1988. The industrialisation and span of retail banks' delivery systems. *International Journal of Operations and Production Management* 8 (3): 46–66.

### Scales (Actual Questions Used)

*Banking Transactions*

The questionnaire provided a banking unit transaction versus means of customer interface matrix.

The matrix depicted the means by which the customers can interface with the bank to execute particular transactions. Respondents were asked to address the following three questions for each row in the matrix:

- Place an "X" by each means of interface your retail banking unit currently offers to its customers to execute transactions named in the row.
- Place one "7" (1987) in each row to indicate the currently most emphasized (in terms of managerial attention and resources deployed) means of interface to execute the transactions for your primary market.
- Place one "0" (1990) in each row to indicate the planned most emphasized (in terms of managerial attention and resources deployed) means of interface to execute the transactions for your target market.

*Customer Enquiries*

The questionnaire provided a banking unit product versus means of handling customer inquiries matrix. The matrix depicted the means by which the retail banking unit provides information in response to customer enquiries. Respondents were asked to address the following three questions for each row.

- Place an "X" by each means of interface your retail banking unit currently offers to its customers to execute transactions named in the row.

- Place one "7" (1987) in each row to indicate the currently most emphasized (in terms of managerial attention and resources deployed) means of interface to execute the transactions for your primary market.
- Place one "0" (1990) in each row to indicate the planned most emphasized (in terms of managerial attention and resources deployed) means of interface to execute the transactions for your target market.

**Banking Services Scales**

*Banking Transactions*

Depository Transactions

1. Withdrawals from current accounts
2. Withdrawals from savings accounts
3. Deposits to current accounts
4. Deposits to savings accounts
5. Cash advances

Applications for Loans

6. Applications for installment loans
7. Applications for home equity loans
8. Applications for home mortgages

Bill Payments

9. Payments to the bank
10. Payments to third parties (utilities)
11. Payments to third parties (other bills)

Asset Transactions

12. Applications for deposit accounts
13. Applications for discount brokerage
14. Applications for club accounts
15. Financial planning
16. Securities
17. Trust management

*Banking Enquiries*

Credit Enquiries

18. Enquiries on credit cards
19. Enquiries on installment plans
20. Enquiries on home equity loans
21. Enquiries on home mortgage
22. Enquiries on educational loans
23. Enquiries on personal credit lines

Asset Enquiries

24. Enquiries on securities brokerage
25. Enquiries on IRAs [the internet retirement alliance] and Keogh accounts
26. Enquiries on trust management

Protection Enquiries

27. Enquiries on travelers' checks
28. Enquiries on credit life insurance

Account Enquiries

29. Enquiries on deposit accounts
30. Enquiries on money market funds

**Construct Description**

The constructs in this study were developed to test a service operations management analog to the well-known Hayes and Wheelwright (1979) product-process matrix. The industrialization construct meant taking a manufacturing approach to service by substituting "technology and systems for people" (p. 49). The span construct was defined to capture the effect "on the management of a service system by having several delivery channels coexisting within the same system" (p. 49).

**Measurement Description**

The constructs associated with banking services were all operationalized using multi-item measures. Each item was assessed on an 8-point scale referring to the service delivery option (ranging from "personal visit to customer" to "home banking").

**Development**

The authors created the instruments for all the variables studied in this project based on an extensive literature search and interviews with banking executives. Factor analysis was conducted to empirically verify the scales. During the scale refinement process, several items were dropped because of low inter-item correlations.

**Sample**

The target population was a stratified, cross-sectional group of U.S. retail banks. Secondary data were obtained from the 1987 Retail Banking Delivery System Survey administered jointly by Boston University School of Management and the Bank Administration Institute. The details of the study were discussed at length by Roth and van der Velde (1988). "For the purposes of this article a reduced sample of 90 banks was used in parts of the analysis due to problems of missing data. The reduced sample was found not be statistically significant from the full sample in respect of any of the dimensions listed in Table 1" (p. 51) in the article.

**Validity and Reliability**

The authors followed suggestions by Nunnally (1978) for exploratory analysis and development of new scales. To check for internal consistency, they used Cronbach's coefficient alpha and "item-to-scale" correlations. The results indicated Cronbach's values ranging from .74 to .97. All "item-to-total" correlations showed positive and significant p-levels (<.01).

**Scores**

The scores are presented in Tables 1–9 of the article.

**Other Evidence**

Not available.

**References**

Hayes, R. H., and S. C. Wheelwright. 1979. Link manufacturing process and product life cycles. *Harvard Business Review* 57 (1): 133–40.
Nunnally, J. C. 1978. *Psychometric theory.* New York: McGraw-Hill.
Roth, A. V., and M. van der Velde. 1988. *The strategic role of operations in retail banking delivery systems.* Boston University Working Paper Series. Boston, MA: Boston University.

# Hill and Scudder

**Article Summarized**

Hill, Craig A., and Gary D. Scudder. 2002. The use of electronic data interchange for supply chain coordination in the food industry. *Journal of Operations Management* 20 (4): 375–87.

**Scales (Actual Questions Used)**

*Use of EDI with Your Customers/Suppliers*

1. Invoices
2. Purchases
3. Pricing
4. Item maintenance
5. Promotion information
6. Advanced shipping notices
7. Warehouse orders
8. Notices of order receipt
9. Schedule information
10. Current production activities
11. Current sales activities

*Degree of Supply Chain Coordination Regarding Customers*

12. Our company strives to be the preferred supplier to our customers.
13. Our company plays an active role in developing innovative business practices between our customers and ourselves.
14. We developed different procedures and systems to accommodate each customer's preferences for purchase orders, billing, and delivery.
15. We consider our customers to be our partners.
16. Our company is taking an active role in the implementation of efficient consumer response incentives with our customers.

*Degree of Supply Chain Coordination Regarding Suppliers*

17. Our company strives to reduce the number of suppliers that are used for a specific item.
18. Our company plays an active role in developing innovative business practices between our suppliers and ourselves.
19. We developed different procedures and systems to accommodate different suppliers' preferences for purchase orders, billing, and delivery.
20. We consider our suppliers to be our partners.
21. Our company is taking an active role in the implementation of efficient consumer response incentives with our suppliers.

### Construct Description

Not available.

### Measurement Description

The items for use of electronic data interchange (EDI) with customers and suppliers were measured by 5-point quasi-objective Likert scales that ranged from "0–5%" to "76–100%." The items for degree of supply chain coordination were measured with 5-point Likert scales that ranged from 1 = "strongly disagree" to 5 = "strongly agree."

### Development

The questionnaire was built on the insights gained by the interviews held by the authors with food industry professionals. Later, the questionnaire was modified according to the inputs from professionals and academicians.

### Sample

The data were collected through the database obtained from the American Production and Inventory Control Society (APICS). The respondents were mainly food manufacturers, raw material suppliers to food manufacturers, and food service providers. The authors obtained 185 usable questionnaires leading to an effective response rate of 41.5%.

### Reliability and Validity

Not available.

### Scores

The scores are presented in Tables 1–3 of the article.

### Other Evidence

Not available.

### Reference

None.

---

## Ho

### Article Summarized

Ho, Chin-Fu. 1996. A contingency theoretical model of manufacturing strategy. *International Journal of Operations and Production Management* 16 (5): 74–98.

### Scales (Actual Questions Used)

*Environmental Uncertainty*

Customer Component

1. Number of actual users of your product
2. Pattern of customers' purchasing behavior
3. Customers' capability of price negotiation

Supplier Component

4. Number of suppliers of material, equipment, and product parts
5. Lead times of purchased items
6. Quality of vendor shipments
7. Cost of purchased items
8. Vendor influence in price negotiation
9. Sources of labor supply
10. Quality of labor forces
11. Wage structure of labor forces

Competitor Component

12. Competitors for your customers
13. Potential competitors for your customers

Social-Political Component

14. Government regulatory control over your industry
15. Public attitude toward the industry and its particular products

Technological Component

16. The emergence and life cycle of relevant new technology
17. Improving and developing new products by implementing new technological advances in the industry

*Risk Taking*

18. Your operations can be characterized as high risk.
19. You seem to adopt a rather conservative view when making major decisions (reverse scored).
20. New projects are approved on a "stage-by-stage" basis rather than with "blanket" approval (reverse scored).
21. A tendency to support projects where the expected returns are certain (reverse scored).
22. Operations have generally followed the "tried and true" paths (reverse scored).

*Manufacturing Flexibility*

23. Average volume fluctuations that occur over a given time period (largest in the industry to smallest in the industry)
24. Product varieties offered in a time period (widest range in the industry to narrowest range in the industry)
25. Number of design changes made to a component per time period (most frequent in the industry to least frequent in the industry)
26. Possible to continue production and remain unaffected by machine stoppage (most capable in the industry to none)
27. Extent of variations in key dimensional and metallurgical properties handled by the equipment (most capable in the industry to none)
28. The ability to rearrange the order in which different kinds of parts are fed into the manufacturing process (most capable in the industry to none)
29. Worker transfer in a given time period (most frequent in the industry to least frequent in the industry)

*Manufacturing Strategy Process*

Role of Manufacturing Function

30. The extent to which manufacturing-related decisions are made by manufacturing managers.
31. The degree of involvement that manufacturing managers have in designing company's strategy or policy.
32. The degree of cooperation that the manufacturing department has shown in meeting the target or objective set by the top management.

Manufacturing Planning Activities

33. The extent to which manufacturing planning is formalized.
34. The degree of understanding that manufacturing managers have displayed in controlling costs, delivery, and quality.

Environmental Interaction

35. The degree of manufacturing managers' exposure to external environmental information.
36. The degree of utilization of environmental information in improving company's products.

Worker Participation

37. Impact of workers' suggestions on manufacturing policy
38. Frequency of workers' suggestions

Performance

39. Average annual rate of growth in return on total asset
40. Average annual rate of return on total asset
41. Average annual rate of growth in sales
42. Average annual rate of sales
43. Average annual rate of growth in ROS
44. Average annual rate of ROS

## Construct Description

In this study, the definition of environment was identified as the physical and social factors outside an organization's boundaries, which are directly relevant to the organization in achieving its goals. Typically, it included customers, trade associations, public pressure groups, and current technology. Uncertainty arose from the dynamic nature of the environment, in which factors external to the organization changed over time. The environmental uncertainty used in this study represented "the environmental factors predictability to be recognized by management" (p. 79).

Risk and manufacturing strategy were key managerial factors in this research. Risk was treated as an ex ante construct associated with "the expected value of resources commitments" (p. 79). The construct of risk taking in this study reflected managerial attitudes toward risk. Manufacturing strategy included both content and process variables. Manufacturing strategy content was conceptually defined as manufacturing flexibility in this article, while manufacturing strategy process was developed to capture "the role of the manufacturing function in strategic decision making, manufacturing planning activities, environmental interaction, and internal employee participation" (p. 76).

Two financial indicators—growth and profitability—were employed as the criteria for performance. Growth reflected the performance trend of the business and profitability provided an efficient view of current performance.

## Measurement Description

Environmental uncertainty was measured perceptually. All items were scored on a 5-point scale ranging between "always predictable" to "never predictable." The items were divided into five components. Risk-taking items were based on Venkatraman (1989). The items were scored on a 5-point Likert scale ranging from "strongly agree" to "strongly disagree." Manufacturing flexibility was based on Gerwin (1987). All items were scored on 5-point scales. Manufacturing strategy process items were scored on a 5-point scale ranging from "highest" to "lowest."

Both growth and profitability were operationalized using multiple-item measures. All items were scored on a 9-point scale ranging between "best performance," to "average performance," to "worst performance," compared with industry average during the past 5 years.

## Development

Wherever possible, the scales were adapted from the existing ones in the literature. A pilot study was conducted to ensure the appropriateness of the questionnaire form. The data were collected from participating firms predominantly via face-to-face interviews with chief executives or equivalents (general managers or vice presidents) and executives/managers in charge of the manufacturing function.

## Sample

Data were collected from three industries in Taiwan that together served as the reference population—namely, electronic parts, personal computer and machine tools. "Firms in each industry group were identified by four-digit [U. S. Department of Commerce, Standard Industrial Classification code] SIC categories to provide the necessary control for industry type" (p. 84). Within each industry, the authors selected 25 firms for the study. "Most of the responding firms in the electronic parts industry are located in the southern part of Taiwan, the personal computer industry is in the North, and the machine tools industry is more evenly distributed throughout the country. The registered capital of each participating firm is at least 1 million dollars (NT)" (New Taiwan $) (p. 84). Data were gathered "through interviews with chief executives or equivalents and executives/managers in charge of the manufacturing function" (p. 83).

## Reliability and Validity

Confirmatory factor analysis (CFA) was used to assess the reliability and validity. The composite measure reliability, which "examines the ratio of trait variance to the sum of trait and error variances" (p. 85), was calculated to examine reliability. The value for the eight measures in this study ranged from an acceptable .71 to .90, which provided the evidence of reliability.

The author assessed predictive validity by applying path analysis to the data. The statistical investigation provided the standardized regression coefficients (path coefficients), their p-values, and the coefficients of determination for the electronic parts, personal computer, and machine tools industry, respectively. The Simon-Blalock technique was applied to test for the existence of linkages not included in the recursive model by computing the zero-order correlations between pairs of variables hypothesized to be unrelated. The results showed that zero-order correlations between pairs of variables hypothesized to be unrelated were near zero.

## Scores

The standardized regression coefficients, p-values, and the coefficients of determination are displayed in Tables 1–3 of the article.

## Other Evidence

Not available.

## References

Gerwin, D. 1987. An agenda for research on the flexibility of manufacturing processes. *International Journal of Operations and Production Management* 7 (1): 38–49.

Venkatraman, N. 1989. Strategic orientation of business enterprises: The construct, dimensionality, and measurement. *Management Science* 35 (8): 942–62.

# Hoegl, Parboteeah, and Munson

### Article Summarized

Hoegl, Martin, K. Praveen Parboteeah, and Charles L. Munson. 2003. Team-level antecedents of individuals' knowledge networks. *Decision Sciences* 34 (4): 741–70.

### Scales (Actual Questions Used)

*Team's Perception of Strength of the Organizational Knowledge-Sharing Climate*

1. Project-relevant information was made accessible by the organization.
2. Colleagues from outside the team were willing to share their knowledge, information, and experiences.
3. It was easy to draw on existing knowledge inside the organization.

*Team's Level of Networking Preference*

4. The team members were generally motivated to collaborate with experts from different disciplines and functions.
5. The team members were interested in working with people from other organizations.

*Team's Perceived Importance of Networking for Project Success*

To successfully complete the project it was important to

6. acquire team-external knowledge,
7. coordinate team-external work contributions, and
8. seek feedback outside the team.

*Team's Strength of Networking Resources*

From the start of the project,

9. the team had relationships with team-external colleagues that helped the progress of the project,
10. the team had useful contacts outside our organization, and
11. the team had enough contacts that could help out if problems arose.

*Team's Perception of the Adequacy of Its Technical Competency*

12. The team had the necessary programming skills.
13. The team had the necessary knowledge regarding the application field of the software.
14. The team possessed the necessary knowledge regarding the software and hardware environment.
15. Through its composition, the team had, at all times, all the necessary know-how for this project.

*Team's Perception of the Adequacy of Its Material Resources*

16. The team was given an adequate budget for this project.
17. Overall, the team was supplied with the necessary material resources.

*Individuals' Extent of Network Building through This Team Project*

18. I have gotten to know people from other functional areas and divisions.
19. I have acquired interesting contacts outside our organization through this project.
20. This cross-functional project has increased the number of my personal contacts within our greater organization (including other companies within our group of companies).
21. The project has allowed me to acquire more contacts than a line position would have.

**Construct Description**

Team's perception of the strength of the organizational knowledge-sharing climate was represented by a "set of shared understandings about providing employees access to relevant information as well as building and using knowledge networks within organizations. This can include training and technical consultation." (p. 745). Team's networking resources were defined as "the aggregate of all the team member's knowledge networks" (p. 748). Team's level of network preference was conceptualized as the level of general (i.e., not project-specific) motivation of team members to develop networks and work with colleagues from different disciplines and organizations. Team's perceived importance of networking for project success was defined as the degree of importance that team members attach to the use of external contacts to complete a specific project successfully.

**Measurement Description**

Not available.

**Development**

All items were generated by the authors based on a literature review and a pretest was conducted on 23 members of a product development team in a machine tool manufacturing unit. The authors developed German language measurement scales based on descriptions and measures of related constructs in literature. The final data were collected from 430 team leaders and members. The factor loadings of the items on their theoretical constructs is given in Table 2 in the article, and Table 3 shows the loadings on a confirmatory factor analysis (CFA). The reliability ratings for each of the scale are reported in the article.

**Sample**

The sample of the study consisted of 145 software development teams from four German software development laboratories. Two companies out of the four had the same U.S. parent company, and the other two were headquartered in Germany. Each lab had 100 to 500 software developers. Table 1 of the article provided an extensive description of the sample. Interviews were conducted with the participants, resulting in 430 interviews. Multiple respondents from each team participated to obtain the team-level data. The teams averaged 6.3 members per team; the average age was 36.6 years; and the sample contained 26% female respondents.

**Reliability and Validity**

Cronbach's coefficient alpha was calculated for each of the constructs, and an alpha of .7 (Nunnally 1978) was used as a benchmark. The authors also verified the interrater reliability, and the scores are given in Table 4 of the article. Construct validity and reliability were further supported through both exploratory and confirmatory factor analyses—EFA and CFA. The composite reliabilities, reported in Table 3 in the article, ranged between .77 and .91.

**Scores**

Table 4 of the article reports details of the descriptive statistics and interitem correlations. Table 3 depicts the CFA results.

**Other Evidence**

Not available.

**Reference**

Nunnally, J. C. 1978. *Psychometric theory.* New York: McGraw-Hill.

# Hong, Vonderembse, Doll, and Nahm

### Article Summarized

Hong, Paul, Mark A. Vonderembse, William J. Doll, and Abraham Y. Nahm. 2005. Role change of design engineers in product development. *Journal of Operations Management* 24 (1): 63–79.

### Scales (Actual Questions Used)

*Role Change of Design Engineers (RCDE)*

1. Qualifications required for design engineers have been upgraded.
2. Training required for design engineers has been more extensive.
3. Power of design engineers in product development team has increased.
4. Influence of design engineers in product development team has increased.
5. Technical skills required for design engineers have been more rigorous.
6. Behavioral skills (e.g., team work, intercommunication) required for design engineers have been more important.
7. Design engineers' jobs have become more complex.
8. Design engineers' jobs have been enlarged.
9. Design engineers' jobs have been enriched.
10. Overall, design engineers feel more satisfied with their work.

*Clarity of Project Targets (CLARITY)*

11. A clear set of project targets guided development efforts.
12. Project targets were clearly understood by all team members.
13. Project targets were clearly communicated to all team members.
14. Project targets were clear.
15. Project targets clearly defined customer requirements.

*Shared Knowledge about Customers (SKCUST)*

This product development team shared knowledge about

16. how customer needs were changing,
17. customer requirements,
18. how well we were doing on customer satisfaction ratings,
19. how customers make purchase decisions,
20. which features were most valued by target customers,
21. which customer groups we were targeting,
22. current customer needs,
23. what our customers want, and
24. our target customers.

*Product Development Productivity (DEVPROD)*

This product development team

25. allocated personnel realistically,
26. was productive,
27. used financial resources sensibly,
28. used all product development resources rationally, and
29. used product engineering hours efficiently.

### Construct Description

The construct descriptions obtained from the article are as follows: Role change of design engineers was defined as "the degree of change in technical and interpersonal skills needed for cross-functional product development" (p. 65). Clarity of project targets referred to "the extent to which project goals are communicated and understood" (p. 65). Shared knowledge about customers was conceptualized as "the level of understanding of customer needs that is common to product development team members" (p. 65). Product development productivity demonstrated "the team's efficiency in creating new products (e.g., allocating resources rationally and effectively)" (p. 66).

### Measurement Description

For each indicator variable, a 5-point scale was used to quantify the respondent's agreement or lack thereof with a set of statements that were linked to its theoretical construct.

### Development

Survey items were grouped by their theoretical construct and presented to 10 product development engineers during structured interviews. These interviews resulted in dropping some items. Then, the refined survey instrument was pretested on 12 knowledgeable informants, and a pilot test was performed.

### Sample

In the administration of a large-scale survey, a total of 2,262 questionnaires were mailed. Of these, 205 usable surveys were returned. These potential informants were derived from a member listing of the *Society of Automotive Engineers,* which served as the sampling frame. To check for response bias, the U.S. Department of Commerce, Standard Industrial Classification codes (SIC) and firm size were examined using $\chi^2$ analyses of the responding firms in comparison with those in the sampling frame.

### Reliability and Validity

The responses ($n$ = 205) were divided into two groups for analyses: a measurement model and a structural model. A confirmatory factor analysis model (CFA) was implemented using the measurement model in LISREL. Several indicators of model fit (non-normed fit index [NNFI], comparative fit index [CFI], root-mean square error approximation [RMSEA], $\chi^2$/d.f.) were examined to determine the model adequacy. Small residual loadings and significant *t*-values associated with completely standardized coefficients provided evidence for high convergent validity. Discriminant validity was assessed using the standard measurement model methodology of comparing fixed versus freed correlations between pairs of latent variables within the model. The resulting $\chi^2$ analysis indicated that the two models were dissimilar at a significance level of p = .001, which supported discriminant validity. Second, average variance extracted versus the squared correlation between constructs was compared and further demonstrated discriminant validity. Model fit was assessed with NNFI, CFI, and RMSEA, and the resulting findings indicated that the model had sufficient fit.

### Scores

The scores are presented in Tables 1–4.

### Other Evidence

Not available.

### Reference

None.

# Hult, Hurley, Giunipero, and Nichols

## Article Summarized

Hult, G. Tomas M., Robert F. Hurley, Larry C. Giunipero, and Ernest L. Nichols, Jr. 2000. Organizational learning in global purchasing: A model and test of internal users and corporate buyers. *Decision Sciences* 31 (2): 293–325.

## Scales (Actual Questions Used)

*Centralization (C)*

1. There can be little purchasing action until purchasing management approves a decision.
2. If we wanted to make our own decisions, we would quickly be discouraged.
3. Even small matters have to be referred to purchasing management for a final answer.
4. We have to ask purchasing management before we do almost anything.
5. Any decision we make has to be approved by purchasing management.

*Formalization (F)*

6. We feel that we are our own boss in most purchasing matters.
7. We can make our own purchasing decisions without checking with anybody else.
8. How things are done in the purchasing process is left to us.
9. We are allowed to do almost as we please in the purchasing process.
10. We make our own rules in the purchasing process.

*Transformational Leadership (TL)*

11. We go beyond our own self-interest for the good of the purchasing process.
12. We talk enthusiastically about what needs to be accomplished in the purchasing process.
13. We spend time teaching and coaching participants about the purchasing process.
14. We seek different perspectives when solving purchasing problems.
15. We clarify the central purpose underlying our purchasing actions to participants.

*Participativeness (P)*

16. It is easy to talk with the purchasing participants, regardless of their rank or position.
17. There is ample opportunity for informal hall talk in the purchasing process.
18. We feel comfortable calling our purchasing management when need arises.
19. Our purchasing management is quite accessible.
20. Purchasing participants can easily schedule meetings with purchasing management.

*Reflectiveness (R)*

21. We are susceptible to influencing each other's purchasing ideas.
22. We are committed to sharing our views about the purchasing process.
23. We are continuously willing to challenge each other's thinking about the purchasing process.
24. We continually judge the quality of our purchasing decisions taken over time.

*Team Orientation (TO)*

25. A team spirit pervades our ranks in the purchasing process.
26. Cross-functional teamwork is the common way of working in the purchasing process.
27. There is a commonality of purpose in the purchasing process.

28. There is total agreement on our organizational vision in the purchasing process.
29. We are committed to sharing our vision with each other in the purchasing process.

*Systems Orientation (SO)*

30. All activities that take place in the purchasing process are clearly defined.
31. We understand how our work fits into the value chain of the purchasing process.
32. We have a good sense of the interconnectedness of all parts of the purchasing process.
33. We understand where all activities fit in the purchasing process.

*Learning Orientation (LO)*

34. The sense around here is that employee learning is an investment, not an expense.
35. The basic values of this purchasing process include learning as a key to improvement.
36. Once we quit learning in the purchasing process, we endanger our future.
37. We agree that our ability to learn is the key to improvement in the purchasing process.

*Memory Orientation (MO)*

38. Organizational conversation keeps alive the lessons learned from purchasing history.
39. We always audit unsuccessful purchasing endeavors and communicate the lessons learned.
40. We have specific mechanisms for sharing lessons learned in the purchasing process.
41. Formal routines exist to uncover faulty assumptions about the purchasing process.

*Information Acquisition (IA)*

42. We meet regularly to find out what products or services we need in the future.
43. We do a lot of in-house research on products and services we may need.
44. We are fast to detect changes in our product and service preferences.
45. We are fast to detect fundamental shifts in the purchasing environment.

*Information Dissemination (ID)*

46. We frequently have interdepartmental meetings to discuss trends in purchasing.
47. We spend time discussing future purchasing needs.
48. We immediately know when something important happens in the purchasing process.
49. We alert participants when something important happens in the purchasing process.

*Subjective Cycle Time (SCT)*

50. The length of the purchasing process is getting shorter every time.
51. We are satisfied with the speediness of the purchasing process.
52. Based on our knowledge of the purchasing process, we think it is short and efficient.
53. The length of the purchasing process could not be much shorter than it is today.

*Objective Cycle Time (OCT)*

54. What is the average length of our purchasing process from initiation to completion?

**Construct Description**

To conceptualize purchasing-specific organizational learning, the authors proposed a four-dimensional construct. The four dimensions of organizational learning included the following. Team orientation was defined as "the degree to which the corporate buyer and the internal user in the focal purchasing unit stress collaboration and cooperation in performing purchasing activities and in making purchasing decisions" (p. 295). Systems orientation captured "the degree to which the corporate buyer and the internal user in the focal purchasing unit stress the broad picture of the activities in the purchasing process and the justification that certain activities exist" (p. 297). Learning orientation was related to "the degree to which the corporate buyer and the internal user in the focal purchasing unit stress the value of learning for the long-term benefit of the purchasing process and the specific purchasing unit" (p. 297). Memory orientation reflected "the degree to which the corporate buyer and the internal user in the focal purchasing unit stress communication and distribution of purchasing knowledge" (p. 297).

Transformational leadership was also portrayed as a multidimensional construct. The five underlying dimensions were (1) attributed charisma, (2) inspirational leadership, (3) individualized consideration, (4) intellectual stimulation, and (5) idealized influence (*see* p. 298 for definitions).

### Measurement Description

Five-point Likert scales were employed for centralization, formalization, information acquisition, and information dissemination. Seven-point Likert scales were used for other constructs, including transformational leadership, participativeness, reflectiveness, team orientation, systems orientation, learning orientation, memory orientation, and subjective cycle time. Objective cycle time was a numerical score based on number of weeks in the user sample and number of days in the buyer sample.

### Development

All measurement scales were taken directly from existing literature. The sources of each scale were reported in the article's appendix. The instrument was then evaluated and refined by two pretests. Based on the inputs from the National Association of Purchasing Management (NAPM) managers, the authors reduced the scales to shorten the questionnaire.

### Sample

The authors conducted two studies to test their hypotheses. Study 1 collected data from internal purchasing field managers of one major multinational corporation's strategic business units worldwide. Of the 416 questionnaires sent, 355 strategic business units responded. The response rate was 85.3%. In study 2, the authors sent the survey to the purchasing directors of 200 multinational corporations in the NAPM membership directory. A total of 1,873 questionnaires were mailed. One hundred and sixty two responses were received from the initial mailings. An additional 38 responses were received in a second wave after follow-up calls were made. The overall response rate was 10.7%. Nonresponse bias was tested using two groups based on early and late return status. The results indicated no statistically significant differences between the two groups on the variables of interest.

### Validity and Reliability

Three separate confirmatory factor analyses (CFAs) using the measurement model in LISREL were conducted to evaluate the quality of the scales—one model for the antecedents (i.e., localness, transformational leadership, and openness), one for the organizational learning scales, and one for scales reflecting outcomes (i.e., purchasing information and cycle time). Evaluation criteria used for assessing the measurement model, included (1) overall model fit indices, and (2) modification index, residual covariation, and error variances for specific items. All criteria provided support for the model. All item loadings on the theoretical constructs were significant at the $p < .01$. As a result, construct convergent validity was established. Discriminant validity was established by comparing the shared variances between construct pairs and the average variances extracted for the individual constructs. In addition, the composite scores derived from the CFA model estimates demonstrated good construct reliabilities.

### Scores

The scores are given in Tables 1–4, and Figures 1 and 2 of the article.

### Other Evidence

The organizational-learning-related scales, including team orientation, systems orientation, learning orientation, and memory orientation, were also studied in Hult, Ketchen, and Nichols (2003).

### References

Hult, G. T. M., D. G. Ketchen Jr., and E. L. Nichols Jr. 2003. Organizational learning as a strategic resource in supply management. *Journal of Operations Management* 21 (5): 541–56.

## Hult, Ketchen, and Nichols

### Article Summarized

Hult, G. Tomas M., David G. Ketchen Jr., and Ernest L. Nichols, Jr. 2003. Organizational learning as a strategic resource in supply management. *Journal of Operations Management* 21 (5): 541–56.

### Scales (Actual Questions Used)

*Team Orientation*

1. A team spirit pervades our ranks in the purchasing process.
2. Cross-functional teamwork is the common way of working in the purchasing process.
3. There is a commonality of purpose in the purchasing process.
4. There is total agreement on our organizational vision in the purchasing process.
5. We are committed to sharing our vision with each other in the purchasing process.

*Systems Orientation*

6. All activities that take place in the purchasing process are clearly defined.
7. We understand how our work fits into the value chain of the purchasing process.
8. We have a good sense of the interconnectedness of all parts of the purchasing process.
9. We understand where all activities fit in the purchasing process.

*Learning Orientation*

10. The sense around here is that employee learning is an investment, not an expense.
11. The basic values of this purchasing system include learning as a key to improvement.
12. Once we quit learning in the purchasing process, we endanger our future.
13. We agree that our ability to learn is the key to improvement in the purchasing process.

*Memory Orientation*

14. Organizational conversation keeps alive the lessons learned from purchasing history.
15. We always audit unsuccessful purchasing endeavors and communicate the lessons learned.
16. We have specific mechanisms for sharing lessons learned in the purchasing process.
17. Formal routines exist to uncover faulty assumptions about the purchasing process.

*Learning Consequence*

18. We are fast to detect fundamental shifts in the purchasing environment.
19. We immediately know when something important happens in the purchasing process.

20. We develop a shared understanding of the available purchasing information.
21. We have a great deal of knowledge about the purchasing process.

*Supply Management Consequence*

22. We are committed to each other in the purchasing process.
23. Our assigned buyer tries to find out what kind of products would be most helpful to us.

*Management Consequence*

24. We actively seek innovative purchasing ideas.
25. We have a strong proclivity for high-risk projects.

*Performance Consequence*

26. Based on our knowledge of the ordering process, we think it is short and efficient.
27. Overall performance of our organization/unit last year was very good.

**Construct Description**

The resource-based view (RBV) of the firm provided the theoretical underpinnings for the research. Indicator variables of the learning constructs were built on prior related research by the author (Hult 1998; Hult et al. 2000). Accordingly, learning was loosely conceptualized as a function of four different types of orientations stressed by supply management members. Listed below are the definitions of these four orientation constructs.

Team orientation was defined as "the degree to which the members of the focal supply management unit stress collaboration and cooperation in performing supply management activities and in making supply management decisions" (p. 544). Systems orientation connoted "the degree to which the members of the focal supply management unit stress the interconnectedness and mutual dependence of the activities in the supply management process" (p. 544). Learning orientation captured "the degree to which the members of the focal supply management unit stress the value of learning for the long-term benefit of the supply management system" (p. 544). Memory orientation reflected "the degree to which the members of the focal supply management unit stress the distribution and preservation of supply management knowledge" (p. 544).

**Measurement Description**

All items except for those reflecting learning consequence were measured using 7-point Likert scales. The items for learning consequence were evaluated on 5-point Likert scales.

**Development**

The constructs were, for the most part, used directly or adapted from other studies.

**Sample**

The sample came entirely from one Fortune 500 company. The sample was split into three groups: (1) users, who included customers of the firm's strategic business units (141 respondents out of 346, 4.8%); (2) buyers, who were corporate buyering agents of the company (115 out of 338, 34.0%); and (3) suppliers, who provided the firm with inputs (58 out of 235, 24.7%). Each respondent was asked to focus their group's orientation for responding to the survey.

**Reliability and Validity**

According to the authors, content validity was achieved by "a pretest involving eight marketing academics and seven supply management executives was conducted to assess the face validity of the scale items. Next, a pilot study of 36 marketing and supply management executives was conducted to assess the general quality of the research design" (p. 546). To further evaluate the psychometric properties of the scales, the authors conducted confirmatory factor analysis (CFA). Various criteria, including overall fit indices and item-specific statistics suggested good model fit. Measurement scale reliabilities were checked based on the values of composite reliabilities, which were all above .80. Discriminant validity was assessed on nested models. Support for discriminant validity was obtained by showing the statistical significance of the $\chi^2$ difference test. This test considered the differences in model fit between a constrained model, where the correlations between each pair of factors were set to 1.0, and an unconstrained model, where the correlations were estimated freely.

### Scores

The correlations are presented in Table 2 of the article. Descriptive statistics are reported in Table 3. The results of the CFA are depicted in Table 4. The results of regression analyses are given in Tables 5 and 6.

### Other Evidence

Not available.

### References

Hult, G. T. M. 1998. Managing the international strategic sourcing process as a market-driven organizational learning system. *Decision Sciences* 29 (1): 193–216.

Hult, G. T. M., R. F. Hurley, L. C. Giunipero, and E. L. Nichols Jr. 2000. Organizational learning in global purchasing: A model and test of internal users and corporate buyers. *Decision Sciences* 31 (2): 293–325.

## Ittner and Larcker

### Article Summarized

Ittner, Christopher D., and David F. Larcker. 1997. The performance effects of process management techniques. *Management Science* 43 (4): 522–34.

### Scales (Actual Questions Used)

*Indicators for Statistical Quality Control (SQC)*

1. What percentage of employees regularly use statistical process control (SPC) charting when it is applicable?
2. How often do you use SPC as a process improvement practice?
3. How often do you use process capability studies?

*Indicators for Process*

4. How often do you use process value analysis as a process improvement practice?
5. How often do you use process simplification?
6. How often do you use process cycle time analysis?

*Indicators for Project*

7. Does management have to approve the formation of teams?
8. Does management have to approve team projects?

*Indicators for Training*

9. What is the average number of hours per year spent in required and optional training programs by senior management?
10. What is the average number of hours per year spent in required and optional training programs by middle management?
11. What is the average number of hours per year spent in required and optional training programs by first-line supervisors?
12. What is the average number of hours per year spent in required and optional training programs by nonmanagement?

*Indicators for Team*

13. What percentage of the workforce is involved in departmental improvement teams/quality circles?
14. What percentage of the workforce is involved in cross-functional improvement teams?

*Indicators for Empower*

15. To what degree are employees in the marketing/selling mode empowered to make decisions within their realm of activity without prior supervisor approval?
16. To what degree are employees in the service delivery mode empowered to make decisions within their realm of activity without prior supervisor approval?
17. To what degree are employees in after-sales service empowered to make decisions within their realm of activity without prior supervisor approval?
18. To what degree are employees in the resolution of after-sales problems empowered to make decisions within their realm of activity without prior supervisor approval?

*Indicators of Reward*

19. How important is team performance in the assessment criteria used for compensation of senior management?
20. How important is team performance in the assessment criteria used for compensation of middle management?
21. How important is team performance in the assessment criteria used for compensation of nonmanagement?
22. How important is organizational quality performance in the assessment criteria used for compensation of senior management?
23. How important is organizational quality performance in the assessment criteria used for compensation of middle management?
24. How important is organizational quality performance in the assessment criteria used for compensation of nonmanagement?

*Indicators for Tools*

25. What percentage of employees use the following tools whenever they are applicable?

Affinity diagrams, cause and effect diagrams, histograms, flowcharting, interrelationship diagrams, matrix diagrams, Pareto analysis, standard PERT/critical path method (CPM), process decision charts, scatter diagrams, SPC charting, and tree diagrams.

*Indicators for Bench*

26. How often is benchmarking of marketing systems used to monitor the position of your organization?
27. How often is benchmarking of marketing systems used to monitor the position of your sales systems?
28. How often is benchmarking of marketing systems used to monitor the position of your distribution systems?

29. How often is benchmarking of marketing systems used to monitor the position of your delivery systems?
30. How often is benchmarking of marketing systems used to monitor the position of your process methods, products, and services?

*Indicators for Cdesign*

31. How often are customer expectations translated into design specifications for a new product/service by a cross-functional team including the customer?
32. How often are meetings with customers employed to identify product or service features that go beyond meeting customer requirements and add performance and excitement?
33. How often are customer representatives on the review team used to verify that the design of your product/service meets your customer requirements?
34. How often are customer pilot runs used to verify that design of your product/service meets your customer requirements?
35. How often are design reviews by customers used to verify that the design of your product/service meets your customer requirements?
36. How important are the customer visits to the development of new products/services?
37. How important are feedback offered by current customers?

*Indicators for Ltrel*

38. Are customers involved (either formally or informally) in the development of the strategic plan?
39. Are suppliers involved (either formally or informally) in the development of the strategic plan?

*Indicators for Sdesign*

40. How important are suppliers selected to build a strong, long-term, strategic partnership?

*Indicators for Select*

41. How frequently are suppliers selected to build a strong, long-term, strategic partnership?
42. How important is quality in selecting suppliers?
43. How important is on-time delivery?
44. How important is uninterrupted supply?

*Indicators for Commit*

45. In your personal opinion, is this organization concerned about quality?

What is your personal agreement with

46. no organization can get away ignoring the wishes of consumers these days?
47. the best way to solve problems is for a group of people to work together, including both management and nonmanagement employees?
48. a sense of community or togetherness among people working for this organization is important?
49. an organization should always analyze these weak points?

## Construct Description

Process focus referred to the use of statistical quality control (SQC) and other broad process improvement initiatives. Three dimensions were identified to tap into the domain of process focus—SQC, process, and project. The operational definitions of these constructs were provided later.

Other constructs considered were: human resource management, which covered innovative workforce practices that emphasized training, team-based activities, employee empowerment, and team performance-based rewarding systems. Second was information utilization that was based on the workers having process and problem-solving information to facilitate problem identification and correction, and also encouraged "closer communication and coordination between work groups, allowing more rapid cross-functional problem-solving and smoother production flows" (p. 523). Third, customer/supplier relations reflected an organization's effort in extending their process improvement efforts beyond their own boundaries to incorporate their customers and suppliers. Fourth, organizational commitment was associated with the level of management support and organizational culture that was committed to teamwork and continuous improvement.

## Measurement Description

With the exception of organizational commitment, most concepts discussed above were operationalized as multidimensional constructs. The operational definitions for each construct were as follows. First are constructs related to process focus—SQC, process, and project. SQC referred to "an organization's use of statistical quality control methods statistical process control (SPC) and process capability studies to reduce operational variability" (p. 525). Process was operationalized as "an organization's use of process-focused improvement techniques such as process value analysis, process simplification, and process cycle time analysis" (p. 525). Project measured "the level of management responsibility for approving the selection of process improvement projects and the formation of project teams" (p. 525).

Second are those constructs related to human resource management that were operationalized by training, team, empower, and reward. Training assessed "the amount of training for top management, middle management, first-line supervisors, and non-management personnel" (p. 525). Team reflected "the percentage of employees involved in departmental and cross-functional improvement programs" (p. 525). Empower referred to "the extent to which employees are empowered to make customer-related decisions during the sales and after-sales processes without supervisor approval" (p. 525). Reward was operationally defined as "the importance of quality and team-related performance in determining compensation" (p. 525).

Third, information utilization consisted of two constructs—tools and bench. Tools gauged "the use of data gathering and analysis tools such as Pareto charts, statistical process control charts, and cause and effect diagrams" (p. 525). Bench captured "the frequency with which organizations benchmark products, services, and processes" (p. 525).

Fourth, customer and supplier relations constructs were cdesign ltrel, sdesign, and select. Cdesign indicated "the frequency with which customers are involved in design reviews and the identification and development of new products and processes" (p. 525). Ltrel focused on "the involvement of customers and suppliers in the development of the strategic plan, an indicator of the extent to which organizations have established long-term strategic relations with other members of the value chain" (p. 525). Sdesign was associated with "the extent of supplier involvement in the product development process" (p. 525). Select reflected "the importance of non-price factors (e.g. quality, reliability, technical capabilities, and the development of long-term strategic relationships) in supplier selection" (p. 525).

Finally, commit indicated "the degree to which the organization exhibits a commitment to continuous improvement and teamwork" (p. 525).

Each construct was measured using multi-item indicators on Likert-type scales. The response categories for each scale varied. The detailed information on the response categories are presented in Appendix A in the article.

## Development

A total of 61 questions were first developed by the authors based on the conceptual definitions of the constructs. The initial scales were subject to principal components analysis (PCA). Two out of the 16 factors generated in the initial PCA were dropped because these two factors explained less than 2% of the shared variance among items and their eigenvalues were marginally above 1.

## Sample

The empirical data "were taken from a 1991 consulting company survey of organizational practices covering the automobile and computer industries in Canada, Germany, Japan, and the United States. All automobile assemblers and a random sample of their suppliers were invited to participate. In the computer industry, the consulting company contacted a random sample of Canadian firms classified by Dun & Bradstreet as electronics and telecommunications manufacturers, all West German computer and peripheral manufacturers or suppliers to the industry, all Japanese mainframe assemblers and a random selection of their suppliers, and American computer firms on the Gartner Group "Top 100" list (excluding those identified as software, services, data communication, or CAD/CAM suppliers) (p. 524). A total of 249 organizations participated, which corresponded to a response rate of 85%".

### Reliability and Validity

Principal components analysis (PCA) was used to evaluate measurement scales. "Construct validity is supported by the fact that only one of the questions (the use of SPC) loaded greater than .50 on more than one factor (.61 on SQC and .51 on TOOLS)" (p. 525). "Cronbach coefficient alphas range from .57 to .93 (mean = .82), above minimum acceptable level suggested by Nunnally (1967)" (p. 525).

### Scores

The scores are presented in Tables 2 and 3 and Appendix B of the article.

### Other Evidence

Not available.

### Reference

Nunnally, J. C. 1967. *Psychometric theory.* New York: McGraw-Hill.

---

## Jambulingam, Kathuria, and Doucette

### Article Summarized

Jambulingam, Thanigavelan, Ravi Kathuria, and William R. Doucette. 2005. Entrepreneurial orientation as a basis for classification within a service industry: The case of retail pharmacy industry. *Journal of Operations Management* 23 (1): 23–42.

### Scales (Actual Questions Used)

*Entrepreneurial Orientation Scales*

Risk Taking

1. RISK1: Taking gambles is part of our strategy for success.
2. RISK2: We take above-average risks in our business.
3. RISK3: Taking chances is an element of our business strategy.
4. RISK4: Our strategy can be characterized by a strong tendency to take risks.

Innovativeness

5. INNOV1: Our pharmacy is known as an innovator among pharmacies in our area.
6. INNOV2: We promote new, innovative services in our pharmacy.
7. INNOV3: Our pharmacy provides leadership in developing new services.
8. INNOV4: Our pharmacy constantly experiments with new services.

Motivation

9. MOTIV1: We consider ourselves as having high motivation toward work.
10. MOTIV2: Our employees are a group of hard-working individuals.
11. MOTIV3: At our pharmacy, we are very ambitious about our work.
12. MOTIV4: At our pharmacy, we like challenges.

Proactiveness

13. PROACT1: Our pharmacy usually takes action in anticipation of future market conditions.
14. PROACT2: We try to shape our business environment to enhance our presence in the market.
15. PROACT3: Because market conditions are changing, we continually seek out new opportunities.
16. PROACT4: We consistently try to position ourselves to meet emerging demands.

Competitive Aggressiveness

17. COMPAG1: We directly challenge our competitors.
18. COMPAG2: We are responsive to maneuvers of our rivals.
19. COMPAG3: Our actions toward competitors can be termed aggressive.
20. COMPAG4: We always respond to actions of our competitors.

Autonomy

21. AUTON1: New service ideas suggested by employees are acted on by decision makers.
22. AUTON2: Management approves of independent activity by employees to develop new services.
23. AUTON3: Identifying new business opportunities is the concern of all employees.
24. AUTON4: All employees are encouraged to develop ideas for new service.

*Environmental Factors*

Competitive Intensity

25. COMPIN1: There is substantial competition among pharmacies in our area.
26. COMPIN2: Our local market is noted for competition between pharmacies.
27. COMPIN3: Competition among pharmacies in our market is intense.
28. COMPIN4: There are promotional wars among pharmacies in our local market.

Munificence

29. MUNIF1: There are ample opportunities for growth in our pharmacy's business environment.
30. MUNIF2: Our business environment will support continued growth of our pharmacy.
31. MUNIF3: Prospects for pharmacy growth in our current business environment are good.
32. MUNIF4: Our business environment is rich with opportunities for pharmacy growth.

Environmental Stability

33. DYNAM1: Growth of pharmacies in our local market
34. DYNAM2: Contract terms with third-party payers
35. DYNAM3: Services provided to pharmacy customers in our local market
36. DYNAM4: The proportion of cash-paying customers during the next year
37. DYNAM5: The local health care environment next year

*Organizational Factors*

Organicity

For each pair of statements, please circle the number that best represents the management at your pharmacy. In general, the management philosophy at my pharmacy factors.

38. ORGSTR1: Tight formal control based on rules and procedures (1) coordination through informal relationships based on cooperation (7)
39. ORGSTR2: A strong emphasis on getting personnel to follow formal procedures (1) a strong emphasis on getting things done even if this means disregarding formal procedures (7)
40. ORGSTR3: A strong emphasis on getting personnel to adhere to formal job descriptions (1) a strong tendency to let requirements of the job and the individual's personality define proper on-the-job behavior (7)

Adaptability

41. ADAPT1: We are able to change to meet the needs of our business environment.
42. ADAPT2: We keep pace with changes required by our business environment.
43. ADAPT3: We adapt to demands of our business environment.

Tolerance for Ambiguity

44. TOLAMB1: Management is comfortable handling a vague situation.
45. TOLAMB2: Our decision makers think that it's OK to have ambiguity present.
46. TOLAMB3: The managers here can live with an ambiguous situation.
47. TOLAMB4: Our managers are tolerant of ambiguity about our situation.

*Performance Measures*

Effectiveness

48. We consistently meet our organizational performance goals.
49. Our pharmacy always achieves its stated goals.
50. More often than not, we attain our annual objectives.

Customer Orientation

51. The welfare of our customers is a primary concern for us.
52. The customers' interests always come first, ahead of our owners'.
53. We regularly ask our customers about the value of our services.
54. Our service development is based on good customer information.
55. Our success comes from meeting our customers' needs.

**Construct Description**

The construct definitions in the article were given as follows. Entrepreneurial orientation was "defined as the processes, practices, and decision-making activities that lead to the development and delivery of new and innovative services that can differentiate an organization from others in its market (Lumpkin and Dess, 1996). . . . The dimensions of entrepreneurial orientation include a firm's ability and willingness to: (1) innovate (innovativeness), (2) take action in anticipation of changes (proactiveness), (3) encourage independent activity by employees (autonomy), (4) respond to maneuvers of rivals (competitive aggressiveness), (5) take chances (risk taking), and (6) motivate employees to work hard and face challenges (motivation). Firms might possess different levels of these intangible resources in a market place" (p. 25).

Risk taking referred to a firm's "proclivity to engage in risky projects and reflects" (p. 26) managers' "preferences for bold acts to achieve organizational objectives (Gasse, 1982)" (p. 26). Innovativeness captured "an organization's tendency to engage in and support new ideas, novelty, experimentation, and creative processes that may result in new services (Lumpkin and Dess, 1996). It reflects an important way in which organizations address new opportunities" (p. 26). Motivation connoted "an organization's ability to enhance employees' attitude and morality toward work. Favorable attitudes toward and moral belief in hard work will contribute to employees' motivation toward a high level of job performance" (p. 26).

Proactiveness characterized a "firm's processes aimed at anticipating and acting on future needs (Venkatraman, 1989). Autonomy refers to the extent to which all employees of an organization have freedom to bring forth an idea or vision and carrying it through to completion" (p. 26).

Competitive aggressiveness corresponded to "an organization's propensity to directly and intensely challenge its competitors to achieve entry or improve market position (Lumpkin and Dess, 1996). In contrast to proactiveness, competitive aggressiveness captures the reactive tendencies of a firm" (p. 26). Autonomy signified "the extent to which all employees of an organization have freedom to bring forth an idea or vision and carrying it through to completion" (p. 26). The competitive intensity of a firm's environment reflected "the level of competition among firms in a market (Covin and Slevin, 1989)" (p. 27). Munificence described "the extent to which an environment can support sustained growth (Dess and Beard, 1984; Starbuck, 1976). A firm exists in a munificent environment when it is able to identify adequate opportunities for growth" (p. 27). Environmental stability indicated "high predictability of future influences in the marketplace (Miller and Friesen, 1978). For example, a pharmacy in a dynamic or less stable environment may have difficulty predicting the actions of competitors, the influence of managed care on demand for its services, or the preferences of consumers" (p. 26).

Organicity was "defined as an organization's use of informal control and cooperation to govern their employees" (p. 27). Adaptability was characterized "as the willingness to change as the business environment changes (Lumpkin and Dess, 1996). Firms that tend to be more proactive, competitive aggressive, and risk taking are expected to be more adaptable. Proactiveness and competitive aggressiveness require awareness of the firm's environment and an ability to react to it. These intangible resources will support adaptability" (p. 27). Tolerance for ambiguity was described "as the willingness and ability to handle a vague situation (Lumpkin and Dess, 1996). Firms that intend to develop new services (e.g. innovativeness) are more likely to face, and be more willing to handle, a vague situation than those who prefer status quo" (p. 27).

Effectiveness signified "the organization's ability to consistently meet organizational goals and performance objectives" (p. 28). Customer orientation captured "the organization's ability to meet customer needs through the services provided, and to keep customers' interests ahead of the owners'" (p. 28).

### Measurement Description

The authors used four-item scales to evaluate six entrepreneurial orientation constructs—(1) environmental munificence, (2) competitive intensity, and (3) tolerance for ambiguity. In addition, three-item scales were used to measure organicity, adaptability, customer orientation, and effectiveness. All these items were assessed using 7-point Likert scales, anchored by 1 = "strongly disagree" and 7 = "strongly agree."

Five items that were associated with the predictability of the pharmacy's business environment were used to quantify environmental stability. Each item was evaluated on a 5-point scale, with 1 = "very low" and 5 = "very high." Last, a single-item, 3-point scale was used to capture the growth relative to the largest competitor of the respondent, where 1 = "less," 2 = "similar," and 3 = "more."

### Development

All measurement scales were newly developed and tested by the authors.

### Sample

The survey was mailed to a random sample of 630 pharmacies. The authors were careful to include at least one pharmacy from each of the nine U.S. census divisions within each of the nine states surveyed. Excluding 15 undeliverable surveys, 251 responses were returned, giving a response rate of 40.8%. The responses included different types of pharmacies. The authors reported absence of nonresponse bias since the $\chi^2$ test did not reveal significant differences between the proportion of pharmacy types in the responding sample and the population statistics obtained from the National Council for Prescription Drug Programs files.

### Validity and Reliability

As estimated by Cronbach's coefficient alpha, the reliability coefficients of the independent variables range between .63 and .90; and reliability coefficients for the performance scales, effectiveness, and customer orientation were .86 and .65, respectively. A principal component factor (PCA) analysis with oblimin rotation was used to assess unidimensionality. The PCA analyses resulted in multiple factors, with the largest factor loadings distributed across the factors representing separate measurement scales.

### Scores

The scores for each scale were obtained by taking the average of the individual scores of the corresponding measures. The factor loadings for each construct, along with eigenvalues and variance explained, are reported in Tables 1–3 in the article.

### Other Evidence

Not available.

### References

Covin, J. G., and D. P. Slevin. 1989. Strategic management of small firms in hostile and benign environments. *Strategic Management Journal* 10 (1): 75–87.

Dess, G. G., and D. W. Beard. 1984. Dimensions of organizational task environments. *Administrative Science Quarterly* 29 (1): 52–73.

Gasse, Y. 1982. Elaborations on the psychology of the entrepreneur. In *Encyclopedia of Entrepreneurship,* ed. C. A. Kent, D. L. Sexton, and K. H. Vesper, 57–71. Englewood Cliffs, NJ: Prentice Hall.

Lumpkin, G. T., and G. G. Dess. 1996. Clarifying the entrepreneurial orientation construct and linking it to performance. *Academy of Management Review* 21 (1): 135–72.

Miller, D., and P. H. Friesen. 1978. Archetypes of strategy formulation. *Management Science* 24 (9): 921–33.

Starbuck, W. H. 1976. Organizations and their environments. In *Handbook of industrial and organizational psychology,* ed. M. D. Dunnette, 1069–123. Chicago, IL: Rand McNally.

Venkatraman, N. 1989. Strategic orientation of business enterprises: The construct, dimensionality, and measurement. *Management Science* 35 (8): 942–62.

---

## Janz and Prasarnphanich

### Article Summarized

Janz, Brian D., and Pattarawan Prasarnphanich. 2003. Understanding the antecedents of effective knowledge management: The importance of a knowledge-centered culture. *Decision Sciences* 34 (2): 351–84.

### Scales (Actual Questions Used)

*Organizational Climate*

Risk

1. Decision making in this organization is too cautious for maximum effectiveness.
2. Our management is willing to take a chance on a good idea.
3. Our business has been built by taking calculated risks at the right time.

4. The philosophy of our management is that in the long run we get ahead fastest by playing it slow, safe, and sure.
5. We have to take some pretty big risks occasionally to keep ahead of the competition in the business we're in.

Reward

6. There is not enough reward and recognition given in this organization for doing good work.
7. There is a great deal of criticism in this organization.
8. In this organization, people are rewarded in proportion to the excellence of their job performance.
9. We have a promotion system here that helps the best person to rise to the top.
10. In this organization, the rewards and encouragements you get usually outweigh the threats and the criticism.
11. If you make a mistake in this organization, you will be punished.

Warmth

12. A friendly atmosphere prevails among the people in this organization.
13. It's very hard to get to know people in this organization.
14. This organization is characterized by a relaxed, easygoing working climate.
15. There is a lot of warmth in the relationships between management and workers in this organization.
16. People in this organization tend to be cool and aloof toward each other.

Support

17. The philosophy of our management emphasizes the human factor, how people feel, etc.
18. Management makes an effort to talk with you about your career aspirations within the organization.
19. When I am on a difficult assignment I can usually count on getting assistance from my boss and coworkers.
20. People in this organization don't really trust each other enough.
21. You don't get much sympathy from higher-ups in this organization if you make a mistake.

*Autonomy*

People-Related Autonomy

22. Fire members of the team
23. Determine compensation plans for the team
24. Conduct peer evaluations
25. Recruit/hire team members
26. Handle discipline problems on the team

Planning-Related Autonomy

27. Develop budgets
28. Plan the team's work
29. Set team goals or objectives
30. Determine the team's training needs
31. Schedule the team's work

Process-Related Autonomy

32. Develop system and end-user documentation.
33. Specify which development tools will be used by the team.
34. Determine appropriate system quality and assurance (i.e., testing) procedures.
35. Determine information and application requirements.
36. Specify which development methods will be used by the team.

*Cooperative Learning*

Positive Interdependence

37. When we work together on our team, we try to make sure everyone on the team learns from each other.
38. When we work together as a team, our job is not finished until everyone on the team has finished his/her job.
39. When we work together on the team, we all receive the same performance evaluation.
40. When we work together on the team, our performance evaluations depend, in part, on how much all members learn.
41. When we work together on the team, I have to make sure the other members of the team learn if I want to do well on the project.
42. When we work together on our team, we cannot complete a project unless everyone contributes.
43. When we work together on our team, the work is divided so that everyone has a part and everyone has to share.
44. When we work together on the team, we have to share work material to complete the project.
45. When we work together on the team, everyone's ideas are needed if we are going to be successful.
46. When we work together on the team, I have to find out what everyone else knows if I am going to be able to complete my part of the project.

Promotive Interaction

47. On this team, I like to share my ideas and work material with other members of the team.
48. On this team, I can learn important things from other team members.
49. On this team, I like to help my teammates.
50. On this team, I like to share my ideas and work materials with my teammates when I think it will help them.
51. On this team, it is a good idea for teammates to help each other learn.
52. On this team, I like to cooperate with my teammates.
53. Members of my team learn a lot of important things from each other.

Group Process

54. We take the time as a team to examine areas in which we need more skill or experience.
55. We rarely stop to consider how we can work better as a team.
56. We have recently discussed what we did right or wrong on a particular project or job.

General Job Satisfaction

57. Generally speaking, I am very satisfied with this job.
58. I frequently think of quitting this job.
59. I am generally satisfied with the kind of work I do in this job.
60. Most people doing this job are very satisfied with the job.
61. People doing this job often think of quitting.

Growth Satisfaction

62. The amount of personal growth and development I get from doing my job
63. The feeling of worthwhile accomplishment I get from doing my job
64. The amount of independent thought and action I can exercise in my job
65. The amount of challenge in my job

Efficiency

66. The efficiency of team operations
67. The team's adherence to budgets
68. The amount of work the team produces

Effectiveness

69. Effectiveness of the team's interactions with people outside the team
70. The quality of work the team produces
71. The team's ability to meet the goals of the project

Timeliness

72. The team's adherence to schedules
73. The team could have done its work faster with the same level of quality
74. The team met the goals as quickly as possible

### Construct Description

As given in the article, the constructs were defined as follows: Cooperative learning was said to exist "when team members work together to maximize their own" (p. 358) and other team members' performance and learning. Autonomy denoted the extent to which "an individual or group of individuals have the freedom, independence, and direction to determine what actions are required and how best to execute them" (p. 359). Organizational climate referred to "the organization's value system in terms of risk taking, reward system and providing a warm and supportive environment" (p. 360).

Work performance was not explicitly defined and was, in turn, captured by three measures: efficiency, effectiveness, and timeliness. General job satisfaction was defined as "a measure of how satisfied the worker is with the work he/she does. Growth satisfaction was a measure of the opportunity for personal learning and growth offered by the work itself" (p. 362).

### Measure Description

Organizational climate had 21 indicator variables that were parsed into four key dimensions: (1) risk (five items), (2) reward (six items), (3) warmth (five items), and (4) support (five Items). The construct of risk measured the orientation of the organization toward undertaking potentially innovative initiatives with uncertain outcomes, whereas reward measured how well the organization recognized employee performance with rewards. The construct of warmth was a measure of the friendliness of the atmosphere in the organization and support was a measure of the organization's interest in the employee. The items were measured by 7-point Likert scales.

In this study, autonomy was divided into people-related autonomy, planning-related autonomy, and work-process-related autonomy. The autonomy items were captured on 5-point Likert scales. The scales for the first two dimensions—the people-related and planning-related autonomy were adapted from Beyerlein, Beyerlein, and Richardson (1993). Level of cooperative learning was measured by 20 survey items, which tapped into three dimensions: (1) Ten items measuring positive interdependence; (2) seven items indicating promotive interaction that were adopted from Johnson et al. (1988); and (3) three items capturing group process that were adopted from Campbell and Hallams (1994). Items were quantified using 7-point Likert scales.

The work satisfaction construct had nine measurements that were derived from Hackman and Oldham (1980). Work performance employed a nine-item scale used by Henderson and Lee (1992). For these items, 7-point Likert scales were also used.

### Development

Most scales used in the study were adapted from existing literature, with the exception of process-related autonomy scale. The initial item pool for this new scale—process-related autonomy—was derived from theories and inputs from a panel of experts with an extensive experience of systems development practices. The items were refined during the scale validation process.

### Sample

The data for the study were collected from 270 team members in 28 teams belonging to 13 organizations in the United States. The authors received usable responses from 231 team members (85.6%),

27 teams (96.4%), and 114 stakeholders (81.4%). The majority of the stakeholders were the internal customers of the team and the rest were management, external customers, and others. More than 75% of the respondents had college degrees.

### Validity and Reliability

The scale assessment process involved two steps. First, assessment was performed on the dimensional scale level and the individual items were used as the indicators in the models. Second, detailed evaluations were conducted on the construct level and the composite scores of dimensional scales were served as indicators in the model. In both cases, confirmatory factor analysis (CFA) was used. On the dimensional scale level, Cronbach's coefficient alpha value for each dimensional scale was calculated, which demonstrated scale reliability. The results of CFA for each dimensional scale (i.e., the first-order factor) indicated that each model had achieved reasonable fit. On the construct level, all five constructs were assessed for convergent and discriminant validity. The authors used the individual item reliability, composite reliability of each constructs, and average variance extracted as the measures for convergent validity. Discriminant validity was evaluated using two approaches. First, the standard $\chi^2$ test on the nested models was computed—one of which constrained the correlation between two constructs to one, and the other freed up this constraint. Second, comparisons of the squared correlations between two constructs with the respective average variance extracted were made. Overall, the analyses indicated evidence of convergent validity and discriminant validity.

### Scores

The factor loadings, *t*-values, results of convergent and discriminant validity tests are provided in Tables 2–4 of the article.

### Other Evidence

Not available.

### References

Beyerlein, M., S. T. Beyerlein, and S. Richardson. 1993. *1993 survey of technical professionals in teams: Summary report.* Center for the Study of Work Teams University of North Texas.

Campbell, D., and G. Hallam. 1994. *Manual for the Campbell-Hallam team development survey.* Minneapolis, MN: National Computer Systems.

Hackman, J. R., and G. R. Oldham. 1980. *Work redesign.* Reading, MA: Addison-Wesley.

Henderson, J. C., and S. Lee. 1992. Managing I/S design teams: A control theories perspective. *Management Science* 38 (6): 757–77.

Johnson, D. W., R. T. Johnson, L. A. Buckman, and P. S. Richards. 1985. The effect of prolonged implementation of cooperative learning on social support within the classroom. *Journal of Psychology* 119 (5): 405–11.

## Jap and Anderson

### Article Summarized

Jap, Sandy D., and Erin Anderson. 2003. Safeguarding interorganizational performance and continuity under ex post opportunism. *Management Science* 49 (12): 1684–701.

## Scales (Actual Questions Used)

*Time 1: Measures of Ex-Post Opportunism and Safeguards*

Bilateral Idiosyncratic Investments

1. If this relationship were to end, they would be wasting a lot of knowledge that's tailored to their relationship.
2. If either company were to switch to competitive buyer or vendor, they would lose a lot of the investments made in the present relationship.
3. They have invested a great deal in building up their joint business.

Goal Congruence

4. The firms share the same goals in the relationship.
5. They have compatible goals.
6. They support each other's objectives.
7. They have different goals (reverse coded).

Interpersonal Trust

8. Our promises to each other are reliable.
9. We are very honest in dealing with each other.
10. We trust each other.
11. We would go out of our way to help each other.
12. We consider each other's interests when problems arise.

Ex-Post Opportunism

When a problem occurs, how often will the buyer (supplier) do the following?

13. They make hollow promises.
14. They are aloof toward us.
15. They "window dress" their efforts to improve.
16. They expect us to pay for more than our fair share of the costs to correct the problem.
17. They are unwilling to accept responsibility.
18. They make false accusations.
19. They provide false information.
20. They fail to provide proper notification.

*Time 2: Measures of Performance*

Evaluation of the Counterpart's Performance

21. Our association with this buyer/supplier has been a successful one.
22. The buyer/supplier leaves a lot to be desired from an overall performance standpoint (reverse coded).
23. If we had to give the buyer/supplier a performance appraisal, it would be outstanding.
24. Overall, the results of our relationship with the buyer/supplier have fallen short of expectations (reverse coded).

Achievement of Competitive Advantages

25. They have both gained advantages over their competitors.
26. The relationship has not resulted in strategic advantages for them (reverse coded).
27. The relationship has not resulted in strategically important outcomes (reverse coded).

Joint Profit Performance

28. They have achieved a high level of joint profits between them.
29. They have generated a lot of profits together.
30. They have increased joint profits shared between them.

Expectations of Relational Continuity

31. Our relationship with this firm will last far into the future.
32. We expect to continue working with this firm on a long-term basis.

## Construct Description

Constructs were described in the article as follows. Ex-post opportunism represented "self-interest seeking with guile" (p. 1686). Exchange outcomes consisted of two parts—short- and long-term strategic outcomes—that were based on four constructs. Evaluation of the counterpart's performance was a holistic, economically significant short-term outcome. Achievement of competitive advantages referred to the "strategic benefits gained over competing firm, such as superior access to resources, or the development of unique process technologies" (p. 1686). For long-term outcomes, joint profit performance represented "indexes financial outcomes that result from interdependence of effort and investments that reside within the dyad" (p. 1687). Expectations of relationship continuity reflected "focal firm's perspective of long-term viability of the relationship" (p. 1687).

Three constructs were used to tap into the domain of relationship safeguards. The first construct—bilateral idiosyncratic investments referred to the investments in the exchange, either tangible or intangible, by the partners. The second construct—goal congruence captured "the extent to which firms perceive the possibility of achieving compatible, if not identical, objectives" (p. 1688). The last construct—interpersonal trust was associated with "the willingness of a party to be vulnerable to the actions of another party based on the expectation that the other will perform a particular action important to the trustor, irrespective of the ability to monitor or control that other party" (p. 1688).

## Measurement Description

Indicators for each scale were captured on 7-point Likert scales. Some of the items reflected the focal firm's perspective on what the two organizations were doing together while the others reflected the view of the focal firm. The entire set of constructs were measured at two points in time.

## Development

Wherever possible, the authors made use of the existing scales from past interorganizational relations research. Sources of the adapted scales were presented in the appendix of the article. The only exceptions were two newly developed scales for this study—ex-post opportunism and expectations of relational continuity.

## Sample

A longitudinal survey method was applied for data collection. The time lag between time 1 and time 2 was 1 year. A total of 200 buyers from the procurement division of four Fortune 50 companies were requested for reporting two different supply relationships, creating an initial sampling frame of 400 dyadic relationships. A total of 275 buyer surveys were returned at time 1 for a 69% response rate. A total of 275 corresponding suppliers also received the survey after the first batch arrived. For a response rate of 80%, 220 of the supplier surveys returned completed. At time 2, the prior 275 buyers were surveyed. At 61% response rate, 167 of them returned the survey. A total of 220 corresponding suppliers were surveyed and 154 of them responded (70% response). "These dyads had worked with each other over an average of 3.7 years. Annual transactions between the buyer and supplier involved over $63 billion in materials and services" (p. 1689).

## Validity and Reliability

For validity, the authors used confirmatory factor analyses (CFA). They stated that "all the factor loadings and measurement errors are in acceptable ranges and significant at $p \leq .05$, providing evidence of convergent validity. Discriminant validity among the constructs is stringently examined using the procedure recommended by Fornell and Larcker (1981). Every pair of latent factors passes this test" (p. 1691). The authors used Cronbach's coefficient alpha to check for scale reliability. The results indicated all scales were reliable.

### Scores

The standardized parameter estimates of the test of hypothesis are given in Tables 2A and B of the article.

### Other Evidence

Not available.

### Reference

None.

## Johnson, Klassen, Leenders, and Fearon

### Article Summarized

Johnson, P. Fraser, Robert D. Klassen, Michiel R. Leenders, and Harold E. Fearon. 2002. Determinants of purchasing team usage in the supply chain. *Journal of Operations Management* 20 (1): 77–89.

### Scales (Actual Questions Used)

*Team Usage*

1. Cross-functional teams
2. Commodity teams (purchasing personnel only)
3. Purchasing councils (purchasing managers only)
4. Teams involving supplier(s)
5. Teams involving customer(s)
6. Supplier councils (primarily key suppliers)
7. Teams involving both supplier(s) and customer(s)

*Purchasing's Strategic Role*

8. Outsourcing
9. IS planning
10. Capital project/investment planning
11. Corporate strategic planning
12. New product development
13. Financial/cash flow planning
14. Risk management/hedging
15. Technology planning
16. Environmental planning
17. Government relations
18. International counter trade/offer planning
19. Mergers, acquisitions, and alliances
20. Marketing planning

### Construct Description

Not available.

### Measurement Description

The items for team usage and purchasing's strategic role were measured with 5-point Likert scales that were anchored by 1 = "not available" and 5 = "extensive."

### Development

The questionnaire was pretested by eight purchasing executives, and minor changes were made on the questionnaire.

### Sample

The sampling frame was a list of firms in the United States and Canada, generated from "a *Fortune* listing of large service and manufacturing firms, the National Association of Purchasing Management (NAPM) and the Purchasing Management Association of Canada (PMAC)" (p. 81). The target respondent was the chief purchasing officer in each firm. A total of 602 surveys were mailed and 236 responses were returned, which yielded a response rate of 39%. The authors performed an independence test regarding the firm size between the respondent group and the targeted sample. No evidence was found that indicated nonresponse bias.

### Reliability and Validity

The authors used Cronbach's coefficient alpha to assess construct reliability. In addition, exploratory factor analysis by means of principal components analysis (PCA) with varimax rotation was implemented. This procedure revealed the underlying factor structure for both team usage and purchasing's strategic role. The PCAs indicated multidimensional nature of scales for both cases.

### Scores

The scores are presented in Tables 1–7 of the article.

### Other Evidence

Not available.

### Reference

None.

---

## Johnston, McCutcheon, Stuart, and Kerwood

### Article Summarized

Johnston, David A., David M. McCutcheon, F. Ian Stuart, and Hazel Kerwood. 2004. Effects of supplier trust on performance of cooperative supplier relationships. *Journal of Operations Management* 22 (1): 23–38.

## Scales (Actual Questions Used)

*Supplier's Perception of Buyer's Benevolence (Supplier's Response)*

1. We feel that it is important not to use any proprietary information to the other party's disadvantage.
2. A characteristic of this relationship is that neither party is expected to make demands that might be damaging to the other.
3. The parties expect that the more powerful party to restrain the use of their power in attempting to get its way.

*Supplier's Perception of Buyer's Dependability (Supplier's Response)*

4. We have strong personal confidence in one another.
5. We have strong business confidence in one another.
6. We can always rely on one another when it counts.
7. I believe that this purchaser will work hard in the future to maintain a close relationship with my company.

*Joint Responsibility*

8. In most aspects of this relationship, the parties are jointly responsible for making sure that tasks are completed.
9. Problems that arise in the course of this relationship are treated as joint rather than individual responsibilities.
10. The responsibility for making sure that the relationship works for both the other party and us is shared jointly.

*Shared Planning*

11. It is expected that we keep each other informed about events or changes that may affect the other party.
12. We plan together the terms by which our future business relationship will be determined.
13. We make joint decisions about the ways to improve (1) cost efficiency, (2) order entry procedures, (3) delivery schedules, (4) product/service design, and (5) quality monitoring/improvement.

*Flexibility in Arrangements*

14. A characteristic of this relationship is flexibility in response to requests for changes.
15. When some unexpected situation arises, the parties would rather work out a new deal than to hold each other to the original terms.
16. It is expected that the parties will be open to modifying their agreements when unexpected events occur.

*Buyers Perception of Relationship's Performance*

To what extent has each of the following possible performance objectives of this buyer-supplier relationship been met?

17. Long-term profitability
18. Net profits over past year
19. Growth
20. Innovation of products/services
21. Lower long-term costs
22. Lower short-term costs
23. Increased quality
24. Increased product/service base

*Buyer's Satisfaction (Buyer Responses)*

25. In general, how satisfied has your firm been with the overall performance of this buyer-supplier relationship?
26. In general, how satisfied has your purchasing organization been with the overall performance of this buyer-supplier relationship?

## Construct Description

Construct descriptions were provided in the article as follows: Supplier's perception of buyer's benevolence reflected the supplier's perception of buyer's 'goodwill' that grows from "acts or behaviors that demonstrate trustworthiness" (p. 27). Supplier's perception of buyer's dependability captured the supplier's perception of buyers to "fulfill obligations and behave predictably" (p. 27). These two constructs—supplier's perception of buyer's benevolence and dependability, altogether, were developed to model the multidimensional construct—trust in buyer-supplier relationship.

Joint responsibility was defined as both dyad members' perceptions of shared responsibility for problem solving and/or design work, "the integration of decision making between supply chain partners" (p. 25). Shared planning was based on both dyad members' perceptions of "planning that involves both the buyer and the seller . . . the provision of information to the other party about planned changes (capacity changes, future project changes) or, in the shorter term, production data" (p. 25). Flexibility in arrangements focused on both dyad members' perceptions of "willingness to vary from fixed contractual terms as conditions change" (p. 25).

Buyer's assessment of relationship's performance was defined to capture buyer's perception of what they call performance; "different buyers would have a wide range of possible performance objectives for particular suppliers" (p. 26). Buyer satisfaction was conceptualized as the "buying firm's satisfaction with the supplier relationship" (p. 26).

## Measurement Description

With the exception of overall performance, the multi-item measurement scales for the other six constructs were characterized by reflective indicators. Seven-point Likert-type scales were used to quantify each item. For the "cooperative relationship" scales—joint responsibility, shared planning, and flexibility in arrangements, each item score was calculated by summing the buyer and supplier's responses. For other scales, dependent upon the underlying construct, the item score was either the supplier's response or the buyer's response. The overall performance, on the other hand, was developed using a 7-point Likert-type formative scale. The performance index was created by calculating "the average response from those dimensions to which the buyer respondent provided answers" (p. 28).

## Development

All scales were modified from existing scales in the literature (*see* p. 28 in the article for detailed information on the sources of preexisting scales). The survey instrument was then reviewed by three faculty members who were familiar with psychometric measurement to examine the logic of the questionnaire design. Finally, the questionnaire was pretested using five MBA students who had experience in sales and purchasing. The authors revised the instrument regarding the order and phrasing of the survey items accordingly based on the feedback on the clarity and meaning.

## Sample

The survey was mailed to members of the Purchasing Management Association of Canada, to managers who "judged to be at a high enough organizational level to be involved with strategic supply decisions" (p. 30). The buyers then gave the researchers the contact information for their "most cooperative supplier." A total of 1,094 surveys were sent to purchasers and 270 usable surveys were returned (24.7%). Of those 270 sent to suppliers, 164 were received (62.4%). Of the total responses, 89 were from manufacturing firms, 16 from service firms, and 58 from the public sector. Other descriptive organization information are provided in Table 2 in the article.

### Validity and Reliability

Convergent validity was evaluated by assessing both Cronbach coefficient alpha as a measure of internal consistency of the scale and the factor loading of each item on its theoretical construct. All coefficient alpha values exceeded. 70, and all but one item passed the threshold of .7 for its factor loading. However, as the authors stated, "this loading was not so low as to render this construct's measure unacceptable" (p. 32). Discriminant validity was evaluated by examining the correlations among the constructs. The authors reported: "In all cases, the variance shared by constructs was much less than the average variance extracted for any one of the constructs' measurement items (shown in Table 3). Thus, we can conclude that each measure was tapping into distinct and different concepts" (p. 33). The authors discussed the relatively high correlations within three cooperative behavior dimensions, and provided possible explanation. They also noted that the two trust measures were quite distinct, which offered support for the multidimensional nature of trust as conceptualized in the article.

### Scores

Descriptive statistics of all the items are given in Table 1 of the article. Path coefficients and $R^2$ values are presented in Figure 2. Convergent validity checks (including reliability) are given in Table 3. A correlation matrix of the latent constructs is displayed in Table 4.

### Other Evidence

Not available.

### Reference

None.

---

## Joshi, Kathuria, and Porth

### Article Summarized

Joshi, Maheshkumar P., Ravi Kathuria, and Stephen J. Porth. 2003. Alignment of strategic priorities and performance: An integration of operations and strategic management perspectives. *Journal of Operations Management* 21 (3): 353–69.

### Scales (Actual Questions Used)

*Manufacturing Manager's Survey*

Quality-of-Conformance

1. Ensuring conformance of final product to design specifications
2. Ensuring consistency in manufacturing
3. Ensuring accuracy in manufacturing

Flexibility

4. Handling changes in the product mix quickly
5. Handling variations in customer delivery schedule

6. Introducing new designs or new products into production quickly
7. Customizing product to customer specifications
8. Adjusting capacity rapidly within a short period

Quality-of-Design

9. Manufacturing durable and reliable products
10. Meeting and exceeding customer needs and preferences
11. Making design changes in the product as desired by customer

Cost

12. Controlling production costs
13. Improving labor productivity
14. Running equipment at peak efficiency

Delivery

15. Meeting delivery dates
16. Making fast deliveries
17. Reducing manufacturing lead time

*General Manager's Survey*

Quality-of-Conformance

18. Consistent quality
19. Conformance to product specifications
20. Accuracy in manufacturing

Cost

21. Low price
22. A standard, no-frills product

Flexibility

23. Frequent design changes or new product introductions
24. Product variety
25. Rapid volume changes
26. Speed in product changeover

Quality-of-Design

27. High product performance
28. Customized product
29. Large number of product features or options
30. High durability (long life) of product

Delivery

31. Short delivery time
32. Dependable delivery promises
33. Delivery on due date (ship on time)
34. Fast delivery

Manufacturing Unit's Performance

35. Accuracy of work
36. Quality of work

37. Productivity of the group
38. Customer satisfaction
39. Operating efficiency
40. Quantity of work
41. Timeliness in meeting
42. Delivery schedules

### Construct Description

The constructs studied in the article included cost, flexibility, quality-of-conformance, quality-of-design, delivery, and manufacturing's unit performance. The first five constructs were defined as manufacturing priorities. They were conceptualized slightly differently for the manufacturing managers (MMs) versus the general managers' (GMs) perspectives. For MMs, these manufacturing priorities were defined as competencies, while, for GMs, they were defined more from the competitiveness perspective.

### Measurement Description

Multiple items were used to measure the manufacturing priorities in both MMs and GMs' surveys. Each item was rated on a 5-point Likert scale with anchors of 1 = "not at all important" and 5 = "extremely important." Perceptual measures of performance were used. Each of the eight items was gauged on a 7-point scale anchored by 1 = "unsatisfactory" and 7 = "excellent."

### Development

The instrument was constructed based on the existing literature. For instance, the scale items on manufacturing survey were developed based on earlier studies (Morrison and Roth 1993; Nemetz 1990; Roth and Miller 1990). Items of performance of a manufacturing unit are borrowed from the performance rating scale of Touliatos et al. (1987). The instrument was modified during the scale validation process, as several items were dropped because of low construct reliability.

### Sample

The surveys were sent to the manufacturers based in the mid-Atlantic region. Data were collected from matched pairs of managers, that is, from the general manager and the manufacturing manager of the same company. More than 13,000 letters were mailed to solicit participation. Of them, 100 came back undelivered. Of the 1,200 remaining companies, approximately 300 companies responded and 158 of the responding companies agreed to participate. This yielded a response rate of 53%. A total of 316 surveys (two for each of the 158 participating companies) were distributed at manufacturing and general manager level.

The sample consisted of 17 industries. A comparison of two-digit U.S. Department of Commerce, Standard Industrial codes (SIC) revealed that the article industry was overrepresented, and petroleum refining, food, and transportation equipment sectors were somewhat underrepresented. The average plant in the sample had 2,785 employees and annual sales of $43 million.

### Validity and Reliability

Cronbach's coefficient alpha values were used to check the reliability of the scales. Manufacturing managers survey results showed that except for quality-of-design ($\alpha$ = .46), alpha values exceeded .60. Thus, quality-of-design was dropped from the study. The results of general managers' survey indicated that alpha values for flexibility, quality-of-conformance, quality-of-design, and delivery scales were above .60. The cost scale was based on Porter (1980). "Given the theoretical soundness of the scale" (p. 360), the authors did not calculate alpha value for this scale. Alpha value of the performance measurement scale was .80.

**Scores**

Descriptive statistics are reported in Table 3. Regression results are presented in Tables 4 and 5 in the article.

**Other Evidence**

Not available.

**References**

Morrison, A., and K. Roth. 1993. Relating Porter's configuration/coordination framework to competitive strategy and structural mechanisms: Analysis and implications. *Journal of Management* 19 (4): 797–818.

Nemetz, P. L. 1990. Bridging the strategic outcome measurement gap in manufacturing organizations. In *Manufacturing strategy: The research agenda for the next decade,* eds. J. E. Ettlie, M. C. Burstein, and A. Fiegenbaum, 63–74. Boston, MA: Kluwer Academic.

Porter, M. E. 1980. *Competitive strategy: Techniques for analyzing industries and competitors.* New York: Free Press.

Roth, A. V., and J. G. Miller. 1990. Manufacturing strategy, manufacturing strength, managerial success, and economic outcomes. In *Manufacturing strategy: The research agenda for the next decade,* eds. J. E. Ettlie, M. C. Burstein, and A. Fiegenbaum, 97–108. Boston, MA: Kluwer Academic.

Touliatos, J., A. G. Bedeian, K. W. Mossholder, and A. I. Barkman. 1984. Job-related perceptions of male and female government, industrial, and public accountants. *Social Behavior and Personality* 12 (1): 61–68.

# Karlsson and Ahlstrom

### Article Summarized

Karlsson, Christer, and Pär Ahlström. 1995. Change processes towards lean production: The role of the remuneration system. *International Journal of Operations and Production Management* 15 (11): 80–99.

### Scales (Actual Questions Used)

This is a case study and the authors assessed the constructs with the broad measures.

### Fixed Part of Remuneration

A competence ladder, with four different levels, comparable to the rungs of the ladders. A new employee starts at the bottom. The employee then moves up the ladder as he or she learns to perform new jobs. To attain the highest level, the employee must be able to perform five different team tasks (*see* below for *Team Skills*). As the employee moves up the ladder, each additional ring is linked to a wage increase.

*Team Skills (Tasks)*

1. Ability to be a team leader?
2. Has been team leader?
3. External flexibility?
4. Ability to do maintenance?
5. Ability to do setups?

*Achievements of the Team*

6. Productivity, measured as standard time as compared to actual time (adjusted for new employees). A bonus is awarded only if actual time is equal to or less than standard time, which corresponds to a productivity of 1.0 or more. To avoid suboptimization, productivity must reach at least 0.95 for the bonus for quality and time accuracy to be paid out.
7. Quality, measured as the number of defects from a sampling of goods to be delivered. Bonus is paid only if zero defects are reached.
8. Time accuracy, measured as the number of orders delivered on time. Bonus only if all orders are delivered on time.

*The Output of Changes*

9. Quality, based on the periodical review of the completed products, essentially corresponding to quality from the customer's point of view. Products are graded based on the frequency and type of defects. Zero indicates that the products were fault-free.
10. Time accuracy, measured as the percentage of orders delivered on time.
11. Manufacturing lead time, measured as the average number of work days needed to manufacture a complete product from raw material.
12. Delivery lead time, measured as the number of weeks from order to delivery.

### Construct Description

This was a case study and formal measures were not presented.

### Measurement Description

The study did not use any formal measures. For the definitions of the measures, please refer to the scales section.

### Development

The study was developed based on three different data collection methods: direct observation, interviews, and content analysis of documents. The authors obtained in-depth information through interviews. They gathered facts through documentation and direct observations that provided them with access to group processes and revealed the discrepancies between what was said and what was actually done.

### Sample

The study was conducted in a single manufacturing site that produced mechanical and electronic office equipment, mostly for export in Sweden.

### Reliability and Validity

Not available.

### Scores

Not available.

### Other Evidence

Not available.

### Reference

None.

---

## Karuppan and Ganster

### Article Summarized

Karuppan, Corinne M., and Daniel C. Ganster. 2004. The labor-machine dyad and its influence on mix flexibility. *Journal of Operations Management* 22 (6): 533–56.

### Scales (Actual Questions Used)

*Competitive Priorities: Flexibility (Range)*

1. Process a large variety of boards
2. Process boards of a very limited range of sizes and thicknesses (reversed coded)

*Competitive Priorities: Speed*

3. Meet the production schedule
4. Reduce the time it takes to complete your work
5. Increase the time it takes to process units (reversed coded)

*Competitive Priorities: Quality*

6. Improve conformance to design specifications
7. Provide quality products consistently

*Competitive Priorities: Cost*

8. Reduce inventory levels
9. Increase the amount of resources (time, money, material) used in completing your work (reversed coded)

*Competitive Priorities: Flexibility (Time)*

10. Adjust quickly to the changes in order volume (i.e., quantity)
11. Adjust quickly to changes in order mix (i.e., variety)

*Labor Flexibility: Range-Number (RN)*

12. Number of different tasks currently performed by the operator at his or her work center
13. Number of different machines operated by the individual at his or her work center
14. Number of on the job training certificates obtained by the individual for his or her current job

*Labor Flexibility: Range-Heterogeneity (RH)*

15. Number of different jobs held by the individual at the plant over the last year
16. Number of departments in which the individual has worked over the past year
17. Number of different areas in which the individual has received on-the-job training certificates

*Labor Flexibility: Uniformity (UN)*

18. Standard deviation of defects associated with the individual over the past year (reversed coded)
19. Consistency of employee's performance in terms of quality across all tasks/jobs

*Machine Flexibility: Range-Number*

20. This machine can use many different tools.
21. This machine can use many different programs.
22. A number of programs can be typically loaded on this machine.
23. A number of tools can be typically used simultaneously on this machine.

*Machine Flexibility: Range-Heterogeneity*

24. This machine can perform operations that vary greatly from one another.
25. A number of types of operations can be performed by this machine.

*Machine Flexibility: Mobility (MOB)*

26. Machine setups between operations are quick.
27. The tools on this machine can be changed or replaced quickly.
28. Average setup time between operations.
29. Average time to switch tools when loaded on magazine.

*Mix Flexibility: Range-Number*

30. Average number of board models processed monthly without incurring a major setup
31. Average number of board models processed simultaneously
32. Ratio of the number of boards processed in this department to the total number processed at the plant

*Mix Flexibility: Range-Heterogeneity*

33. Average number of different board sizes processed monthly in this department
34. Range of board thickness processed in this department in a typical month

*Mix Flexibility: Mobility*

35. Average changeover time between lots
36. Ratio of average lot size to monthly output

*Mix Flexibility: Uniformity*

37. Range of scrap rate
38. Average monthly output

### Construct Description

The authors first defined the domain of flexibility. Range-number (RN) flexibility was given as the number of options that could be achieved for a given flexibility dimension (Slack 1983; Upton 1994). Range-heterogeneity (RH) flexibility was characterized as the variety of options, i.e., differences between operations, tasks, products, etc. (Upton 1994). Mobility signified the ease with which a firm moves from one state to another (Upton 1994). Next, uniformity was defined as the similarity of performance outcomes in terms of quality, cost, time, etc. (Gupta and Buzacott 1989; Upton 1994). Last, the authors connoted mix flexibility as the "capability of a manufacturing system to respond quickly and economically to different product mix changes in the market (Chen et al., 1992)" (p. 535).

### Measurement Description

Constructs representing competitive priorities were measured by asking supervisors to rate the emphasis they placed on cost, speed, quality, and flexibility in their department on a scale of 1 = "very little" to 5 = "very much." These items were adopted from Boyer (1998) and Kathuria (2000). Labor flexibility was captured by asking operators and supervisors to estimate RN and RH measures of flexibility and the time it took to adjust to new job assignments (MOB). Machine flexibility was quantified by 26 subjective and 6 objective items. After the reliability analysis, 15 items were retained for the analyses. Mix flexibility was measured by using binary items indicating 1 = "high flexibility" and 0 = "low flexibility."

### Development

Not available.

### Sample

"This study was conducted in a single PCB (printed circuit boards) assembly plant" (p. 540).

### Reliability and Validity

The authors used Cronbach's coefficient alpha to assess construct reliability. They used factor analyses to assess the dimensionality of the scales.

### Scores

The scores are presented in Tables 1–3 and 5–8 in the article.

### Other Evidence

Not available.

### References


Boyer, K. K. 1998. Longitudinal linkages between intended and realized operations strategies. *International Journal of Operations and Production Management* 18 (4): 356–73.

Chen, I. J., R. J. Calantone, and C. H. Chung. 1992. The marketing-manufacturing interface and manufacturing flexibility. *Omega* 20 (4): 431–43.

Gupta, D., and J. A. Buzacott. 1989. A framework for understanding flexibility of manufacturing systems. *Journal of Manufacturing Systems* 8 (2): 89–97.

Kathuria, R. 2000. Competitive priorities and managerial performance: A taxonomy of small manufacturers. *Journal of Operations Management* 18 (6): 627–41.

Slack, N. 1983. Flexibility as a manufacturing objective. *International Journal of Operations and Production Management* 3 (3): 4–13.

Upton, D. M. 1994. The management of manufacturing flexibility. *California Management Review* 36 (2): 72–89.

# Kaynak

## Article Summarized

Kaynak, Hale. 2003. The relationship between total quality management practices and their effects on firm performance. *Journal of Operations Management* 21 (4): 405–35.

## Scales (Actual Questions Used)

*Total Quality Management*

Management Leadership

1. Extent to which the top business unit/organization executive (responsible for organization profit and loss) assumes responsibility for quality performance
2. Acceptance of responsibility for quality by major department heads within the organization
3. Degree to which organization top management (top organization executive and major department heads) is evaluated for quality performance
4. Extent to which the organization top management supports long-term quality improvement process
5. Degree of participation by major department heads in the quality improvement process
6. Extent to which the organizational top management has objectives for quality performance
7. Specificity of quality goals within the organization
8. Comprehensiveness of the goal-setting process for quality within the organization
9. Extent to which quality goals and policy are understood within the organization
10. Importance attached to quality by the organizational top management in relation to cost and schedule objectives
11. Amount of review of quality issues in organizational top management meetings
12. Degree to which the organizational top management considers quality improvement as a way to increase profits
13. Degree of comprehensiveness of the quality plan within the organization

Training

14. Specific work-skills training (technical and vocational) given to hourly employees throughout the organization
15. Quality-related training given to hourly employees throughout the organization
16. Quality-related training given to managers and supervisors throughout the organization
17. Training in the "total quality concept" (i.e., philosophy of companywide responsibility for quality) throughout the organization
18. Training in the basic statistical techniques (such as histogram and control charts) in the organization as a whole
19. Training in advanced statistical techniques (such as design of experiments and regression analysis) in the organization as a whole
20. Commitment of the organizational top management to employee training
21. Availability of resources for employee training in the organization

Employee Relations

22. Extent to which quality circles or employee involvement-type programs are implemented in the organization
23. Effectiveness of quality circles or employee involvement-type programs in the organization
24. Extent to which employees are held responsible for error-free output
25. Amount of feedback provided to employees on their quality performance

26. Degree of participation in quality decisions by hourly/nonsupervisory employees
27. Extent to which building quality awareness among employees is ongoing
28. Extent to which employees are recognized for superior quality performance
29. Effectiveness of supervisors in solving problems/issues

Quality Data and Reporting

30. Availability of cost of quality data in the organization
31. Availability of quality data (error rates, defect rates, scrap, defects, etc.)
32. Timeliness of the quality data
33. Extent to which quality data (cost of quality, defects, errors, scrap, etc.) are used as tools to manage quality
34. Extent to which quality data are available to hourly employees
35. Extent to which quality data are available to managers and supervisors
36. Extent to which quality data are used to evaluate supervisor and managerial performance
37. Extent to which quality data, control charts, etc. are displayed at employee work stations

Supplier Quality Management

38. Extent to which long-term relationships are offered to suppliers
39. Reduction in the number of suppliers since implementing JIT purchasing and/or total quality management
40. Extent to which suppliers are evaluated according to *quality, delivery performance,* and *price,* in that order
41. Extent to which suppliers are selected based on quality rather than price or delivery schedule
42. Reliance on a reasonably few dependable suppliers
43. Thoroughness of your organization's supplier rating system
44. Amount of education provided for suppliers by your organization
45. Technical assistance provided to the suppliers by your organization
46. Involvement of the supplier in your product/service development process
47. The extent to which the inspection of incoming parts has been reduced since you implemented JIT purchasing and/or total quality management
48. Extent to which supplier conforms to the exact quality attributes required on your incoming parts

Product/Service Design

49. Thoroughness of new product/service design reviews before the product/service is produced and marketed
50. Coordination among affected departments in the product/service development process
51. Quality of new products/services emphasized in relation to cost or schedule objectives
52. Clarity of product/service specifications and procedures
53. Extent to which implementation/producibility is considered in the product/service design process
54. Quality emphasis by sales, customer service, marketing, and public relations personnel

Process Management

55. Use of acceptance sampling to accept/reject lots or batches of work
56. Amount of preventive equipment maintenance
57. Extent to which inspection, review, or checking of work is automated
58. Amount of incoming inspection, review, or checking
59. Amount of in-process inspection, review, or checking
60. Amount of final inspection, review, or checking
61. Stability of production schedule/work distribution
62. Degree of automation of the process
63. Extent to which process design is "fool-proof" and minimizes the chances of employee errors
64. Clarity of work or process instructions given to employees

*Relative Perceived Performance*

Inventory Management Performance

65. Purchase material turnover
66. Total inventory turnover

Quality Performance

67. Product/service quality
68. Productivity
69. Cost of scrap and rework as a percentage of sales
70. Delivery lead time of purchased materials
71. Delivery lead time of finished products/services to customer

Financial and Market Performance

72. Return on investment
73. Sales growth
74. Profit growth
75. Market share
76. Market share growth

### Construct Description

The research investigated the relationships between the following constructs: management leadership, training, employee relations, quality data and reporting, supplier quality management, process management, product/service design, quality performance, financial and market performance, and inventory management performance. Management leadership was defined as a factor in total quality management (TQM) implementation that improved performance by influencing other TQM practices. Training was presented as the efforts shown by the organization to "help employees discover innovative ways to improve the organization" (p. 415). Employee relations connoted "a variety of organizational development (OD) techniques to facilitate changes such as employee participation in decisions" (p. 415). Quality data and reporting were viewed as providing information by "using costs of poor quality such as rework, scrap and warranty costs, and control charts to identify quality problems" (p. 416).

Supplier quality management was characterized as obtaining quality materials and/or services by establishing long-term, cooperative relationships with as few suppliers as possible. Product/service design was defined as "designing manufacturable products and designing quality into the products" (p. 417). Process management entailed "taking a preventive approach to quality improvement such as designing processes that are foolproof and that provide stable production schedules and work distribution (Flynn et al., 1995; Saraph et al., 1989) to reduce process variation (Flynn et al., 1995) by building quality into the product during the production stage (Handfield et al., 1999)" (p. 417).

Definitions of inventory management performance, quality performance, and financial and market performance were not clearly articulated in the article. However, each of these three constructs were referred to as a firm performance measure.

### Measurement Description

The items used to measure the TQM constructs were mostly based on Saraph, Benson, and Schroeder (1989). Instead of using Likert-type scales, the authors used "a continuous scale 100-mm long" (p. 419) that ranged from 0 = "none" to 100 = "very high."

### Development

The instrument is developed by using the existing literature. One contribution of the study is a refined version of a questionnaire constructed by Saraph, Benson, and Schroeder (1989). Pilot tests were conducted at a joint dinner of the American Production and Inventory Control Society (APICS) and the Institute for Supply Management (ISM). Pilot test results were based on 11 respondents.

### Sample

The target population of the survey was chosen as the industries most likely to implement TQM and just-in-time production (JIT). Based on the results of the pilot study, the survey was e-mailed to 1,884 subjects. Three hundred and eighty-three of them returned the survey. One of the responses was unusable. Survey achieved a 20.3% response rate. The majority of the respondents were presidents, vice presidents, directors, managers, and coordinators. The organizations that comprised the sample represent various manufacturing industries with the U.S. Department of Commerce, Standard Industrial Classification (SIC) codes 20 to 39, and service industries, which accounted for 15% of the sample. Manufacturing firms were from the following sectors: rubber and miscellaneous products, fabricated material, machinery and computer, electrical and electronic, measuring instruments, and analyzing and controlling instruments. The number of employees in the sample ranged from 100 to more than 55. The annual sales of the companies ranged from $12.5 million or less to $50 million.

### Reliability and Validity

Cronbach's coefficient alpha was used to check the reliability of each scale. Several items in the TQM factors that did not contribute to reliability were dropped. The authors evaluated the unidimensionality of the scales using exploratory factor analysis (EFA) using principal components extraction with a varimax rotation. Then, by using confirmatory factor analysis (CFA), the authors checked the convergent validity by using the t values of each item's coefficient. Each item's coefficient was greater than twice its *t* value. The authors stated that "an instrument has discriminant validity if the correlations between the measures of different factors using the same method of measurement are lower than the reliability coefficients (Crocker and Algina, 1986). . . . Nevertheless, the correlation coefficients were lower than the reliability coefficients, suggesting that measures have discriminant validity" (p. 424).

### Scores

The scores are reported in Tables 3 and 4 in the article.

### Other Evidence

Not available.

### References

Bagozzi, R. P., Y. Yi, and L. W. Phillips. 1991. Assessing construct validity in organizational research. *Administrative Science Quarterly* 36 (3): 421–58.

Churchill, G. A., Jr. 1979. A paradigm for developing better measures of marketing constructs. *Journal of Marketing Research* 16: 64–73.

Crocker, L., and J. Algina. 1986. *Introduction to classical and modern test theory.* Forth Worth, TX: Harcourt, Brace & Jovanovich.

Flynn, B. B., R. G. Schroeder, and S. Sakakibara. 1995. The impact of quality management practices on performance and competitive advantage. *Decision Sciences* 26 (5): 659–91.

Handfield, R., J. Jayaram, and S. Ghosh. 1999. An empirical examination of quality tool deployment patterns and their impact on performance. *International Journal of Production Research* 37 (6): 1403–26.

Hoskisson, R., M. Hitt, R. Johnson, and D. Moesel. 1993. Construct validity of an objective (entropy) categorical measure of diversification strategy. *Strategic Management Journal* 14 (3): 215–35.

Saraph, J. V., G. P. Benson, and R. G. Schroeder. 1989. An instrument for measuring the critical factors of quality management. *Decision Sciences* 20 (4): 810–29.

# Kearns and Lederer

**Article Summarized**

Kearns, Grover S., and Albert L. Lederer. 2003. A resource-based view of strategic IT alignment: How knowledge sharing creates competitive advantage. *Decision Sciences* 34 (1): 1–29.

**Scales (Actual Questions Used)**

*Information Intensity of the Value Chain*

1. Information is used to a great extent in our production or service operations.
2. Information used in our production or service operations is frequently updated.
3. Information used in our production or service operations is usually accurate.
4. Many steps in our production or service operations require the frequent use of information.

*The Chief Information Officer (CIO) Participates in Business Planning: The IT Executive*

5. regularly attends business planning meetings,
6. contributes to the formulation of business goals,
7. has regular informal contacts with top management, and
8. has easy access to the CEO.
9. has frequent contacts with the CEO.

*The CEO Participates in IT Planning: The CEO*

10. plays an important role in the corporate IS steering committee,
11. becomes knowledgeable about competitors' use of IS,
12. has frequent informal contacts with IS management,
13. becomes knowledgeable about IS opportunities within the firm,
14. regards spending on IS as strategic investments rather than expenses to be controlled.

*IT Planning (ITP)-Reflects-Business Plan*

15. The IS plan reflects the business plan mission.
16. The IS plan reflects the business plan goals.
17. The IS plan supports the business strategies.
18. The IS plan recognizes external business environment forces.
19. The IS plan reflects the business plan resource constraints.

*Business Plan-Reflects-ITP*

20. The business plan refers to the IS Plan.
21. The business plan refers to specific IS applications.
22. The business plan refers to specific information technologies.
23. The business plan uses the strategic capability of IS.
24. The business plan contains reasonable expectations of IS.

*IT Is Used to Create a Competitive Advantage*

With respect to our company's core products or services and major customers and suppliers, IS has been used to

25. provide advantages such as lower costs or product differentiation,
26. make it more costly for our customers to change suppliers,
27. create barriers to keep competitors from entering our markets,

28. establish electronic links with suppliers or customers, and
29. influence the buyer's decision to switch to our products.

### Construct Description

The constructs in this study were based on the resource-based theory of the firm, where a number of different adaptations of this theory were found to be of use in the management information systems (MIS) literature. The construct of information intensity of the value chain was expressed as "the significance of the information component in the value chain activities" (p. 5), and it was "demonstrated by the level of accuracy, frequency of updates and the magnitude and extent of information employed in operations" (p. 5).

Explicit definitions of the other constructs were not specified. In general, the constructs reflected the paradigm of aligning the business plan with the IT plan of the firm and the resulting competitive advantage that accrued to the organization.

### Measurement Description

The authors used 7-point Likert scales ranging from 1 = "strongly agree" to 7 = "strongly disagree" to measure the items.

### Development

A two-stage process to refine the questionnaire was followed. The authors first contacted "four MIS professors at a doctoral-granting university [to] initially [critique] the instrument. Second, the instrument was piloted on four CIOs and four other executives from four different industries. Comments and suggestions were incorporated into the final instrument" (p. 11).

### Sample

A list of 12,000 firms representing all the industries, except for the nonprofit and government organizations, served as the sampling frame. The mailing list for the study was brought from Lighthouse Lists, Fort Lauderdale, Florida. From the list that was obtained from Lighthouse Lists, a random sample of 1,200 firms was drawn. The firms that were isolated for the purpose of administering the survey had a minimum revenue of $75 million. The responses that were finally received and used after accounting for the nondelivery and discarding by the office of the CEO secretary in many firms was 161. Based on the initial sample frame, the unadjusted response rate was 13.4%. Also, some of the surveys posted were returned back to the authors because of address changes, or they reached their intended respondents without their knowledge. As a result, the authors achieved an adjusted response rate of 20.5%.

### Reliability and Validity

The authors used Cronbach's coefficient alpha and also presented a composite reliability index to assess reliability. The benchmark for the reliability coefficients was .70. Discriminant validity was ensured through multiple methods, which were the variance extraction test (more than 50% of the variance explained by the constructs); the $\chi^2$ test, which measured whether the correlation between the constructs was statistically different from 1; and a confidence interval test that checked for the rejection of the hypotheses that the population correlation between the individual factors was 1.0.

### Scores

The results of the model fit of the structural equation model are given in Table 9 in the article. The correlation coefficients for the constructs are presented in Table 5.

### Other Evidence

Not available.

### Reference

None.

---

## Ketoviki and Schroeder

### Article Summarized

Ketokivi, Mikko A., and Roger G. Schroeder. 2004. Strategic, structural contingency and institutional explanations in the adoption of innovative manufacturing practices. *Journal of Operations Management* 22 (1): 63–89.

### Scales (Actual Questions Used)

*Cross-Functional Corporation*

1. Direct labor employees are involved to a great extent (on teams or consulted) before introducing new products or making product changes.
2. Manufacturing engineers are involved to a great extent before the introduction of new products.
3. There is little involvement of manufacturing and quality people in the early design of products before they reach the plant.
4. We work in teams with members from a variety of areas (marketing, manufacturing, etc.) to introduce new products.

*Supply Chain Relationship*

Supplier Relationships

5. We strive to establish long-term relationships with suppliers.
6. Our suppliers are actively involved in our NPD process.
7. Quality is our number one criterion in selecting suppliers.
8. We use monthly suppliers that we have certified.
9. We maintain close communication with suppliers about quality considerations and design changes.

Customer Relationships (CRs)

10. We are frequently in close contact with our customers.
11. Our customers give feedback on quality and delivery performance.
12. Our customers are actively involved in the product design process.
13. We strive to be highly responsible to our customers' needs.
14. We regularly survey our customers' requirements.

*Design for Manufacturability*

15. We make an effort, in the design process, to list only the specifications that are really needed.
16. The emphasis in part design is on minimizing the part count.
17. Our engineers make an effort to simplify our product designs.
18. The parts we produce are designed for ease in manufacturability and assembly.

*Just-in-Time*

Frequent Delivery by Suppliers

19. Our suppliers deliver to us on a JIT basis.
20. We receive daily shipments from most suppliers.

21. Our suppliers are certified, or qualified, for quality.
22. We have long-term arrangements with our suppliers.
23. We can depend on on-time delivery from our suppliers.

Setup Reduction

24. We are aggressively working to lower setup times in our plant.
25. We have converted most of the setup time to external time while the machine is running.
26. We have low setup times of equipment in our plant.
27. Our crews practice setups to reduce the time required.
28. Our workers are trained to reduce setup time.
29. Management emphasizes importance of setup time reduction.

Pull System Support

30. We have laid out the shop floor so that processes and machines are in close proximity to each other.
31. Direct labor is authorized to stop production for quality problems.
32. We use kanban pull system for production control.
33. We have low work-in-process inventory on the shop floor.
34. When we have a problem on the production floor, we can identify its location easily.

Cross-Training

35. Employees at this plant learn how to perform a variety of tasks/jobs.
36. The longer an employee has been at this plant, the more tasks and jobs they learn to perform.
37. Employees are cross-trained at this plant so that they can fill in for others if necessary.
38. At this plant, employees only learn how to do one job/task.

Quality Management Philosophy

39. All major department heads within our plant accept their responsibility for quality.
40. Plant management provides personal leadership for quality products and quality improvement.
41. The top priority in evaluating plant management is quality performance.
42. Our top management strongly encourages employee involvement in the production process.
43. Plant management creates and communicates a vision focused on quality improvements.
44. Plant management is personally involved in quality improvement projects.

**Construct Description**

The constructs developed in this article were defined as follows. Cross-functional corporation indicated "the degree to which different departments and individuals within the plant coordinate their activities and efforts" (p. 71). JIT manufacturing was expressed as "the degree to which the manufacturing plant seeks to eliminate waste and minimize inventories through measures such as setup time, frequent supply and delivery, and plant layout" (p. 71). Cross-training was given as "the degree to which shop-floor employees receive training to perform multiple operational tasks" (p. 71).

Long-term supply chain relationship was defined as "the degree to which the plant emphasizes the development of recurring arrangements, supplier involvement, and close communications with its suppliers, instead of focusing on competitive bidding and arm's length relationships" (p. 71). Design for manufacturability pertained to "the degree to which the plant's products are designed such that manufacturing them is easy through practices such as simplified design and reduced part counts" (p. 71). Quality management philosophy was described as "the degree to which management has adopted the quality management philosophy" (p. 73).

Just-in-time (JIT) was derived and operationalized as a second-order factor and reflected by three first-order factors: (1) frequent delivery by suppliers, (2) setup reduction, and (3) pull system support. The supply chain relationships construct was estimated from two first-order constructs: (1) long-term supplier relationships and (2) long-term customer relationships.

### Measurement Description

Five-point Likert scales were used to measure the items. A high value on the scales indicated high intensity of implementation. A high value meant that there was a high degree of internalization for quality management philosophy.

### Development

Not available.

### Sample

Data collected as a part of the second round of the world class manufacturing (WCM) Project (Flynn, Schroeder, and Sakakibara 1994; Schroeder and Flynn 2001) were used in the study. Surveys were obtained from 164 manufacturing companies, with at least 100 employees in Germany, Italy, Japan, the United Kingdom, and the United States from 1994 to 1997. The sample was drawn from three industries: automotive suppliers, machinery, and electronics. To avoid interdependence of observations, only one plant per business unit or corporation was included. Sixty-five percent of the plants sampled participated in the study.

### Reliability and Validity

Confirmatory factor analysis (CFA) was used to check discriminant validity. Discriminant validity was tested by checking the impact of freeing the constrained between the latent variable correlations, which were set to 1—one correlation at a time. Factor loadings, composite reliabilities, and discriminant validity data are given in Appendix A1 (p. 79) in the article. Based on the CFA, composite reliability values ranged from .58 (pull system support) to .86 (quality management philosophy).

### Scores

Convergent and discriminant validity and reliability results are reported in Appendix A1 (p. 79) of the article.

### Other Evidence

Not available.

### References

Flynn, B. B., R. G. Schroeder, and S. Sakakibara. 1994. A framework for quality management research and an associated measurement instrument. *Journal of Operations Management* 11 (4): 339–66.

Schroeder, R. G., and B. B. Flynn, eds. 2001. *High performance manufacturing: Global perspectives.* New York: Wiley.

---

## Kim and Arnold (1993)

### Article Summarized

Kim, Jay S., and Peter Arnold. 1993. Manufacturing competence and business performance: A framework and empirical analysis. *International Journal of Operations and Production Management* 13 (10): 4–25.

### Scales (Actual Questions Used)

*Competitive Capabilities*

Dimension 1: Price

1. Price

Dimension 2: Flexibility

2. Design change
3. New Products
4. Volume change
5. Mix change
6. Broad line

Dimension 3: Quality

7. Conformance
8. Performance
9. Reliable products

Dimension 4: Delivery

10. Fast delivery
11. On-time delivery

Dimension 5: Service

12. After sales service
13. Support
14. Distribution
15. Customize

*Strength in Competitive Capabilities*

Dimension 1: Price

16. Price

Dimension 2: Flexibility

17. Design change
18. New products
19. Volume change
20. Mix change
21. Broad line

Dimension 3: Quality

22. Conformance
23. Performance
24. Reliable products

Dimension 4: Delivery

25. Fast delivery
26. On-time delivery

Dimension 5: Service

27. After-sales service
28. Support
29. Distribution
30. Customize

*Performance*

31. Pretax return of assets (pretax profit/total assets)
32. Net pretax ratio (pretax profit/total sales)
33. Annual growth rate in unit sales
34. Market share of primary product

### Construct Description

The authors used the traditional notion of competitive priorities as the main vehicle to operationalize the concept. Behind this view of competitive priorities was that "in order to develop a manufacturing policy and infrastructure that are consistent with the goals and objectives of business strategy, a firm must make prudent trade-off decisions regarding the desirable level of several key manufacturing capabilities, such as cost, quality, dependability, and flexibility" (pp. 9–10). The authors presented manufacturing competence as "the degree of consistency between importance given to a capability and the firm's strength with regard to that particular strategy" (p. 10). In turn, they defined manufacturing strategy as a construct that captured "the degree of fit between competitive priorities and manufacturing strength" (p. 10).

### Measurement Description

The importance of competitive priorities was quantified using a 7-point Likert scale where 1 = "not important" and 7 = "very important." Strength in competitive capabilities was a perceptual measure of the business's relative capabilities versus its primary competitors in the same industry based on a 7-point Likert scale where 1 = "substantially weaker" and 7 = "substantially stronger." These raw scores were then converted into normalized scores calculated by "finding the differences between a score of each capability and the average of all dimensions" (pp. 16–17). This relative measure was said to eliminate "the inter-firm bias from further analysis" (p. 17).

A manufacturing competence index was constructed to measure the degree of match between priorities and strength. The general formula for the quantitative manufacturing competence index was as follows:

$$C = f_j \in J \; (I_j, S_j)$$

where

$C$ = general competence index,

$I_j$ = normalized importance of competitive capability $j$,

$S_j$ = normalized strength in competitive capability $j$,

$J$ = set of all competitive capabilities

Two models were developed to compute the manufacturing competence index. In Model I, $C = \Sigma_j I_j S_j$, while in Model II, $C = \Sigma_j I_j S_j$, based on whether the relative importance capability is negative or not. Four other metrics were used to evaluate the market and finance performance (*see* Scales).

### Development

The authors used the data "from the 1990 U.S. Manufacturing Futures Survey conducted by Boston University Manufacturing Roundtable. The project was initiated in 1981 with the purpose of developing a comprehensive data set that can be used to study the strategic aspects of manufacturing management" (p. 8).

### Sample

There were 182 respondents to the 1990 survey. They included firms from various industries, such as consumer package goods, electronics, basic machinery, and industry products. Typically, large successful manufacturing companies responded to the survey. The unit of analysis was the "manufacturing business unit (MBU) and divisional vice presidents were the typical individuals to fill out the questionnaire" (p. 9).

### Reliability and Validity

Not available.

### Scores

The results of scores are presented in Figures 2–8 in the article.

**Other evidence**

Not available.

**Reference**

None.

---

# Kim and Arnold (1996)

**Article Summarized**

Kim, Jay S., and Peter Arnold. 1996. Operationalizing manufacturing strategy: An exploratory study of constructs and linkage. *International Journal of Operations and Production Management* 16 (12): 45–73.

**Scales (Actual Questions Used)**

*Manufacturing Strategy Process*

Dimension 1: Competitive Capabilities

Price

1. Ability to profit in price competitive markets

Flexibility: Ability to

2. make rapid changes in design,
3. introduce new products quickly,
4. make rapid volume changes,
5. make rapid product mix changes, and
6. offer broad product line.

Quality: Ability to

7. offer consistently low defect rates,
8. provide high-performance products, and
9. provide reliable/durable products.

Delivery: Ability to

10. provide fast deliveries and
11. make dependable delivery promises.

Service: Ability to

12. provide effective after-sales service,
13. provide product support effectively,
14. make product easily available, and
15. customize products and services to customer needs.

Dimension 2: Manufacturing Objectives

16. Improve conformance quality
17. Reduce unit costs
18. Improve safety record
19. Reduce manufacturing lead time

20. Increase capacity
21. Reduce procurement lead time
22. Reduce NPD cycle
23. Reduce material costs
24. Improve direct labor productivity
25. Increase throughput
26. Reduce number of vendors
27. Improve vendor quality
28. Reduce inventories
29. Increase delivery reliability
30. Increase delivery speed
31. Improve ability to make rapid product mix changes
32. Improve to make rapid volume changes
33. Reduce break-even points
34. Raise employee morale
35. Maximize cash flow
36. Increase environmental safety/protection
37. Reduce capacity
38. Increase product/materials standardization
39. Improve labor relations
40. Improve white-collar productivity
41. Increase range of products produced by existing facilities
42. Meet financial shipping goals
43. Improve presales service and technical support
44. Improve after-sales service
45. Change culture of manufacturing organization
46. Improve interfunctional communication
47. Improve communication with external partners
48. Reduce setup/changeover times

Dimension 3: Improvement Action Plan

49. Giving workers a broad range of tasks or more responsibility
50. Activity-based costing
51. Manufacturing reorganization
52. Worker training
53. Management training
54. Supervisor training
55. Computer-aided manufacturing
56. Computer-aided design
57. Value analysis/product redesign
58. Interfunctional work teams
59. Quality function deployment
60. New processes for new products
61. New processes for old products
62. IS in manufacturing
63. IS across functions
64. Reconditioning physical plants
65. Just-in-time
66. Robots
67. Flexible manufacturing systems
68. Design for manufacture

69. Statistical quality control
70. Closing and/or relocating plants
71. Quality circles
72. Production-inventory control systems
73. Hiring in new skills from outside
74. Linking manufacturing strategy to business strategy

## Construct Description

The research was conceptualized "around three constructs: competitive priorities, manufacturing objectives and action plans" (p. 47). Each construct differed "from the others in the level of abstraction, with the competitive priorities being the most abstract and the action programs being the most specific" (p. 49). The authors defined competitive priorities as "what the manufacturing function should achieve with regard to cost, quality, flexibility and delivery, in order to support the business strategy effectively" (p. 49). The authors stated that after the competitive priorities were set, the manufacturing function could establish measurable performance targets. According to the authors, some "researchers argued that the manufacturing function's decisions on various investment alternatives should be guided by the firm's strategic objectives rather than traditional cost accounting measures alone. Therefore, the relative emphasis on various performance measures defined in this model as manufacturing objectives" (p. 50).

## Measurement Description

Fifteen competitive variables from the five dimensions of price, flexibility, quality, delivery, and service were used to indicate competitive priorities. Thirty-four different manufacturing objectives—ranging from financial measures, to time-related dimensions, and to quality-improvement-related items—were used in the study. The relative importance given to each of the 33 objectives was determined by a 7-point Likert scale where 1 = "very unimportant" and 7 = "very important."

Twenty-six manufacturing action plans were listed. The relative emphasis on each action plan given by managers for the next 2 years was measured using a 7-point Likert scale with 1 = "little emphasis" and 7 = "great emphasis."

## Development

The data were obtained "from the 1990 Manufacturing Futures Survey conducted by Boston University's Manufacturing Roundtable. The project was initiated in 1981 to develop a comprehensive data set that can be used to study strategic aspects of manufacturing management. For the past 10 years, the content of the survey has been continually refined through review of the previous year's survey results, discussion with the manufacturing executives participating in Boston University's Manufacturing Roundtable meetings, and pilot testing performed with ten member companies, in order to improve the reliability and validity of the survey instrument" (p. 52).

## Sample

The survey sampling frame consisted of 1,306 companies, which included participants in various executive education programs, respondents from prior survey years, and 422 randomly selected firms from the 1986 Dun's business rankings. The manufacturing business unit (MBU) was selected as the unit of analysis because of the "diversity of organizational structures where functional strategies are developed" (p. 54). "After two rounds of follow-up mailings, 182 usable responses were returned, representing a 13.9 percent response rate" (p. 53). "Among the 182 respondents, 66 chose the entire company as an MBU, while 86 chose the division and 20 the plant" (p. 54). Moreover, respondents to this survey covered a wide variety of industrial sectors, such as consumer products and electronics. On average, the sample was prone to be "biased towards larger and rather successful manufacturing companies with an average market share of 38.7% and annual unit sales growth rate of 7.6%" (p. 54).

### Reliability and Validity

Principal components analysis (PCA) with varimax rotation was used in an exploratory way for scale development. A series of PCA analyses were run, and after each, "factors with eigenvalues larger than 1.0 were carried for further analysis. Also the procedure used by Sethi and King was applied and after each run all the items that showed loadings of less than 0.35 on all factors, and items whose loadings were greater than 0.35 on two or more factors were dropped. This procedure was repeated until no such item was present" (p. 58). Composite reliability was determined by Cronbach's coefficient alpha, which indicated the internal consistency of the items that loaded significantly on a factor. "Since this study was exploratory in its purpose, a threshold level of 0.50 was applied to eliminate internally inconsistent factors, as used by Sethi and King on the basis of Nunnally's recommendation" (p. 59).

### Scores

The results of factor analysis are presented in Tables 5–8 in the article.

### Other Evidence

Not available.

### References

Miller, J. G., and A. V. Roth. 1988. Manufacturing strategies: Executive summary of the 1988 North American manufacturing futures survey. Boston University Manufacturing Roundtable Report Series.

Nunnally, J. 1967. *Psychometric theory.* New York: McGraw-Hill.

Sethi, V., and W. R. King. 1991. Construct measurement in information systems research: An illustration in strategic systems *Decision Sciences* 22 (3): 455–72.

## Koste, Malhotra, and Sharma

### Article Summarized

Koste, Lori L., Manoj K. Malhotra, and Subhash Sharma. 2004. Measuring dimensions of manufacturing flexibility. *Journal of Operations Management* 22 (2): 171–96.

### Scales (Actual Questions Used)

*Machine Flexibility: Range-Number*

1. A typical machine can perform a large percentage of the total number of operations performed in the plant.
2. A large number of operations can be performed by more than one machine.
3. A typical machine can use many different tools.
4. The number of different operations that a typical machine can perform is high.

*Machine Flexibility: Range-Heterogeneity*

5. Machines can perform operations that are not very similar to one another.
6. Machines can perform various types of operations.

7. Existing machines cannot be used to perform new operations.
8. Machines can perform a variety of operations.
9. Machines can perform operations that differ greatly from one another.

*Machine Flexibility: Mobility*

10. Machine changeovers between operations are easy.
11. Machine setups between operations are quick.
12. A lot of available capacity is used in changing between machine operations.
13. Machine tools can be changed quickly.

*Machine Flexibility: Uniformity*

14. All machines achieve similar performance across all operations.
15. Machines are equally effective, in terms of productivity, for all operations.
16. Machines are equally efficient for all processing operations.
17. Machines are equally effective, in terms of quality, for all operations.
18. Machines are equally reliable for all operations.
19. The processing cost (in dollars) of an operation is not affected by machine choice.

*Labor Flexibility: Range-Number*

20. Workers can perform a large number of tasks.
21. Workers are responsible for more than one task.
22. A large number of job classifications exist in the workforce.
23. Workers are cross-trained to perform many different tasks.
24. Workers posses many different skills.

*Labor Flexibility: Range-Heterogeneity*

25. The tasks that workers perform are very similar to one another.
26. Workers perform a diverse set of tasks.
27. Workers can perform various types of tasks.
28. Workers can perform tasks that differ greatly form one another.

*Labor Flexibility: Mobility*

29. A short time delay occurs when workers are moved between different tasks.
30. It is easy to move workers between different tasks.
31. A small cost is incurred (in dollar) when workers are moved between different tasks.
32. A small cost is incurred (in terms of lost productivity) when workers are moved between different tasks.
33. Workers can move easily between different tasks.

*Labor Flexibility: Uniformity*

34. Workers are equally effective, in terms of quality, for all tasks.
35. Workers are equally efficient at all tasks.
36. Workers achieve similar performance levels for all tasks.
37. Worker choice does not affect the processing cost (in dollars) of a task.
38. Workers are equally reliable for all tasks.
39. Workers are equally effective, in terms of productivity, for all tasks.

*Material Handling Flexibility: Range-Number*

40. Material can be routed along many paths.
41. There are many different material-handling paths between processing centers.
42. Many processing centers are linked by the material handling system.

43. There are a large number of material-handling paths.
44. There are a limited number of material-handling paths between processing centers.

*Material Handling Flexibility: Range-Heterogeneity*

45. The material handling system can transport materials of different shapes.
46. The material-handling paths used by the system are very different from one another.
47. The material handling system uses a large proportion of general purpose pallets.
48. The material handling system uses a large proportion of general purpose fixtures.
49. The material handling system can transport materials of different sizes.
50. The material handling system can transport a wide variety of materials.

*Material Handling Flexibility: Mobility*

51. Changing a material-handling path is easy.
52. Changing a material-handling path is inexpensive.
53. Changing a material-handling path is quick.
54. Material-handling paths can be easily added.
55. Material-handling paths can be easily removed.

*Material Handling Flexibility: Uniformity*

56. The choice of material-handling path does not affect the material transfer time.
57. The choice of material-handling path does not affect the efficiency of material transfer.
58. The quality of materials is not affected by the material-handling path used.
59. The choice of material-handling path does not affect the material transfer cost (in dollars).
60. All material-handling paths exhibit similar performance.

*Mix Flexibility: Range-Number*

61. A large number of products are produced in the plant.
62. The average number of products produced in the plant is large.
63. A large number of product lines are produced in the plant.
64. A limited number of products are produced in the plant.
65. Existing product lines are very broad.

*Mix Flexibility: Range-Heterogeneity*

66. The variety of products produced in the plant is extensive.
67. The processing requirements for the products produced in the plant vary greatly from one product to another.
68. The products produced in the plant are very different from one another.
69. Products are only slightly different from one another.
70. A diverse set of products is produced in the plant.
71. The material requirements for the products produced in the plant vary greatly from one product to another.

*Mix Flexibility: Mobility*

72. The cost (in dollars) of including a product in the product mix is small.
73. The product mix produced by the plant can be changed easily.
74. The time required to change to a different product mix is short.
75. The manufacturing system can quickly changeover to a different product mix.
76. The cost of changing to a different product mix is small.

*Mix Flexibility: Uniformity*

77. Productivity levels are not affected by changes in product mix.
78. The efficiency of the production process is not affected by changes in product mix.

79. Product quality is not affected by changes in product mix.
80. The performance of the system is not affected by changes in product mix.

*New Product Flexibility: Range-Number*

81. The number of new products introduced into production each year is high.
82. A limited number of new products are introduced each year.
83. A large number of new prototypes are produced in the system each year.
84. A large proportion of our products have been introduced within the past year.
85. A large number of new products are introduced each year.

*New Product Flexibility: Range-Heterogeneity*

86. New products are very similar to existing products.
87. New products are incremental improvements of existing products.
88. New product variety is extensive.
89. New products are often extensions of existing product lines.
90. New products are often improvements of existing products.
91. New products are very innovative.
92. New products are very different form existing products.
93. New products are refinements of existing products.

*New Product Flexibility: Mobility*

94. The managerial effort required to introduce a new product into full-scale production is low.
95. The cost (in dollars) required to design and develop new products is extremely high.
96. The start-up cost (in dollars) required to design and develop new products is extremely high.
97. The number of months from the earliest stage of design to production of a saleable product is low.
98. The time required to develop and introduce new products is extremely low.

*New Product Flexibility: Uniformity*

99. Manufacturing system performance is not affected when a new product is introduced into the production system.
100. The quality of existing products is not affected when a new product is introduced into the production system.
101. The average cost/unit of products is not affected when a new product is introduced into the production system.
102. Productivity levels are not affected when a new product is introduced into the production system.

*Modification Flexibility: Range-Number*

103. A large number of products are modified to the customer's specifications.
104. There are a limited number of modified products produced each year.
105. The features of existing products are often modified.
106. Engineering change orders are often used to modify products.
107. There are a large number of modified products produced each year.
108. Existing product lines are frequently modified.

*Modification Flexibility: Range-Heterogeneity*

109. The product modifications made are fairly similar to one another.
110. The variety of product modifications made is extensive.
111. Modified products are very similar to existing products.
112. Modified products are very different from each other.
113. Modified products are very different from existing products.

*Modification Flexibility: Mobility*

114. Modified products can be made quickly.
115. The average cost of introducing modified products into full-scale production is low.
116. Product modifications are performed quickly.
117. The time to produce modified products is small.
118. Product modifications are easy to make.

*Modification Flexibility: Uniformity*

119. Productivity levels are not affected when a modified product is introduced into the manufacturing system.
120. Manufacturing system performance is not affected by the production of modified products.
121. The average cost/unit of products is not affected when a modified product is introduced into the production system.
122. The quality of existing products is not affected when a modified product is introduced into the manufacturing system.

## Construct Description

There were four major constructs of flexibility presented in this article: (1) range number (R-N), (2) range heterogeneity (R-H), (3) mobility (M), and (4) uniformity (U). The R-N element of flexibility was defined as "a strict numerical count of the number of possible options that a system or resource can achieve" (p. 172). The R-H element addressed "the degree of difference between different options" (p. 172). The M element represented "the ease with which the organization moves from one state to another" (p. 172), whereas the U element of flexibility captured "any alteration or deterioration of the system associated with invoking a flexible response" (p. 172).

## Measurement Description

The items were measured by 7-point Likert scales that ranged from 1 = "strongly disagree" to 7 = "strongly agree."

## Development

The survey was pretested by sending it to a small sample of manufacturing members listed in the 1998 National Edition of the *Harris Manufacturers Directory*. Fifteen respondents returned the pretest survey items and also "provided written qualitative feedback on the clarity of both the instructions and the survey items. The respondents provided notes on any words or items that were ambiguous or imprecise" (p. 177).

## Sample

The 1998 National Edition of the *Harris Manufacturers Directory* served as the sampling frame. The authors initially sent 1,000 surveys to potential respondents. Of the 1,000 initial surveys returned, 20 had incorrect addresses. Checking the list of nonrespondent firms revealed that 218 of the original sample did not have correct contact information, and they were removed from the eligible sample. As a result, 158 surveys were obtained, which yielded an effective response rate of 20.9%. The authors presented the profile of the respondent firms in Table 2 in the article.

## Reliability and Validity

The authors suggested that "analysis of the inter-item correlations among the scale items supported the content validity of the scales" (p. 178). They stated that the content validity was supported as long as these correlations were lower than .80. There was only one construct that had an average interitem correlation greater than .80 (mobility element of material-handling flexibility). The authors evaluated the convergent validity of the items by examining the statistical significance of the loadings, squared standardized loadings, and average variance extracted. The authors stated that after the modification of the measurement models, all the items showed the necessary statistics for convergent validity. Interrater agreement was determined by collecting a second questionnaire from 28 of the participating organizations. The interrater agreement values were deemed acceptable by the authors.

The authors assessed discriminant validity by $\chi^2$ test as proposed by Bagozzi's (1980) test, where they assessed whether the correlations between the latent constructs were statistically different from 1, and by the technique suggested by Fornell and Larcker (1981). Both techniques indicated that the constructs had discriminant validity. Last, they assessed predictive validity by correlating the flexibility measures to an external single-item variable called "overall flexibility." The correlation between the composite score of flexibility that encompassed all the items used in the study and this single item had a value of .35, which was statistically significant ($p <. 01$).

### Scores

The scores are presented in Tables 3–5, Appendixes A1–A6, and Appendix B in the article.

### Other Evidence

Not available.

### References

Bagozzi, R. P. 1980. *Casual models in marketing.* New York: Wiley.

Fornell, C., and D. F. Larcker. 1981. Evaluating structural equation models with unobservable variables and measurement error. *Journal of Marketing Research* 18: 39–50.

---

## Koufteros

### Article Summarized

Koufteros, Xenophon A. 1999. Testing a model of pull production: A paradigm for manufacturing research using structural equation modeling. *Journal of Operations Management* 17 (4): 467–88.

### Scales (Actual Questions Used)

*Preventive Maintenance*

1. We emphasize good preventive maintenance.
2. We do preventive maintenance.
3. We do preventive maintenance during nonproductive time.
4. We maintain our equipment regularly.

*Setup Improvement Practices*

5. Standard setups are developed for new processes.
6. Employees work on setup improvement.
7. Employees redesign or reconfigure equipment to shorten setup time.
8. Our employees are trained to reduce setup time.

*Pull Production*

9. We do not produce unless there is demand in the next station.
10. Production is pulled by the shipment of finished goods.

11. Production at stations is pulled by the current demand on the next station.
12. We use a pull production system.

*Delivery Dependability*

13. Our capability of providing dependable deliveries
14. Our capability of providing on-time deliveries
15. Our capability of delivering the kind of products needed on time
16. Our capability of delivering the correct quantity of products needed on time

### Construction Description

Some general information about the constructs was discussed in the article. However, no formal definitions were provided except for the constructs indicated by the 16 items previously listed in the scales section.

### Measurement Description

Based on the analyses, the 16 items were grouped into four constructs: (1) setup improvement practices, (2) preventive maintenance practices, (3) pull production, and (4) delivery dependability. Each of the four constructs was operationalized by four indicator variables. The first 12 items used 5-point Likert scales to quantify the extent to which setup improvement practices, preventive maintenance practices, and pull production were used by a firm. Similarly, the delivery dependability construct was measured on a 7-point Likert scale, where a firm was compared with the average in the industry.

### Development

The initial scales were developed based on the established literature and interviews with 10 practitioners. After that, the scales were evaluated first in a formal pretest study using 14 practitioners and academicians; and second, in a pilot test with 34 firms. The resultant measurement scales were further modified after the assessment of reliability and validity.

### Sample

The data were collected from 244 firms. Among them, about 92% came from fabricated metal products, industrial and commercial machinery, electronic and electrical equipment and components, and transportation equipment manufacturing industries. Over 43% of the respondents were top executives, and the rest held the title of director or manager.

### Reliability and Validity

Unidimensionality was assessed by examining the model fit using confirmatory factor analysis (CFA) along with four diagnostics (i.e., standardized residuals, Q-plots, modification indices, and expected change in $\Lambda_x$). All fit indices were well within the acceptable limits; for example, the $\chi^2$ per degree of freedom was 1.11, and the comparative fit index (CFI) and non-normal fit index (NNFI) indices were both .99. These results indicated a good fit, which consequently provided strong evidence of unidimensionality. In addition, observations from other four diagnostics could not identify abnormal indicators that might be complex or contained unusual amounts of random variation. Taken together, unidimensionality was confirmed.

The convergent validity was estimated using *t*-values, which were the ratios of factor loadings to their respective standard errors in the first-order level of measurement models. These *t*-values all exceeded the critical values at the .01 significant level, which suggested strong posited relationships among indicators and constructs. Besides, on the first-order level of measurement models, $R^2$ was calculated as the estimate of the item reliability. Three items were dropped from the scales because their item reliabilities were less than .50, while the reliabilities of all the other items ranged from .51 to .90.

Evidence of discriminant validity was provided by three different methods. In the first method, all the differences between the fixed and free solutions in $\chi^2$ were reported to be statistically significant. In the second method, the comparison of the average variance extracted (AVE) with the squared correlation between constructs showed that the AVE was substantially higher. Finally, the discriminant validity was further confirmed since the confidence intervals calculated in the third method did not include 1.

The estimates of composite reliability were .91, .85, .89, and .96 based on the LISREL output. Additional evidence of construct reliability was provided by the estimates of AVE, all of which exceeded the critical value of .50. The test of the structural model showed that the model fitted the data adequately ($\chi^2$ per degree of freedom was 1.32, and the CFI and NNFI indices were both .98). Nomological validity was reported based on the fact that the hypotheses stated in the study were supported.

### Scores

Factor loadings, *t*-values, fit indices, and $R^2$ for full model, trimmed model after iteration, and trimmed model using the validation sample are reported in Tables 5–7 in the article.

### Other evidence

Not available.

### Reference

None.

---

## Koufteros, Vonderembse, and Doll (1998)

### Article Summarized

Koufteros, Xenophon A., Mark A. Vonderembse, and William J. Doll. 1998. Developing measures of time-based manufacturing. *Journal of Operations Management* 16 (1): 21–41.

### Scales (Actual Questions Used)

*Shop-Floor Employee Involvement in Problem Solving*

1. Shop-floor employees are involved in problem-solving efforts.
2. Shop-floor employees are involved in suggestion programs.
3. Shop-floor employees are involved in designing processes and tools that focus on improvement.
4. Shop-floor employees are involved in improvement efforts.
5. Shop-floor employees are involved in problem-solving teams.

*Reengineering Setup*

6. Employees work on setup improvement.
7. Employees redesign or reconfigure equipment to shorten setup time.
8. Employees redesign jigs or fixtures to shorten setup time.
9. We use special tools to shorten setup.
10. Our employees are trained to reduce setup time.

*Cellular Manufacturing*

11. Products that share similar design or processing requirements are grouped into families of products.
12. Products are classified into groups with similar processing requirements.
13. Products are classified into groups with similar routing requirements.

14. Equipment is grouped to produce families of products.
15. Families of products determine our factory layout.

*Quality Improvement Efforts*

16. We use fishbone-type diagrams to identify causes of quality problems.
17. We use design of experiments (i.e., Taguchi methods).
18. Our employees use quality control charts (e.g., SPC charts).
19. We conduct process capability studies.

*Preventive Maintenance*

20. We emphasize good preventive maintenance.
21. Records of routine maintenance are kept.
22. We do preventive maintenance.
23. We do preventive maintenance during nonproductive time.
24. We maintain our equipment regularly.

*Dependable Suppliers*

25. We receive parts from suppliers on time.
26. We receive the correct number of parts from suppliers.
27. We receive the correct type of parts from suppliers.
28. We receive parts from suppliers that meet our specifications.
29. Our suppliers accommodate our needs.
30. We receive high-quality parts from suppliers.

*Pull Production*

31. Production is "pulled" by the shipment of finished goods.
32. Production at stations is "pulled" by the current demand of the next stations.
33. We use a "pull" production system.

### Construct Description

The authors described time-based manufacturing as a construct whose "primary purpose is to reduce end-to-end time in manufacturing" (p. 22) and as "an externally focused production system that emphasizes quick response to changing customer needs" (p. 22).

Seven, key, time-based manufacturing practices were identified in the study: shop-floor employee involvement in problem solving, reengineering setup, cellular manufacturing, quality improvement efforts, preventive maintenance, dependable suppliers, and pull production. Among these seven key components, shop-floor employee involvement was specified as an antecedent to other time-based manufacturing practices. Enhanced shop-floor employee problem-solving skills facilitated the reengineering of setups, the implementation of cellular manufacturing, the establishment of quality improvement efforts, the initiation of effective preventative maintenance programs, and the creation of dependable suppliers. The authors stated that with these practices in place, time-based manufacturers sought to achieve pull production to cut response time to customers and enhance competitive capabilities.

In the study, shop-floor employee involvement in problem solving was defined as the participation of first-level employees in problem-defining and problem-solving activities. Reengineering setup time referred to the "efforts taken to reduce set up time" (p. 23). Cellular manufacturing referred to production in a product-oriented layout. Quality improvement efforts connoted the methods that were "developed and used to reduce defects and enhance quality" (p. 23). Preventive maintenance was described as the maintenance of the equipment on a routinely proactive basis. Dependable suppliers referred to those suppliers that facilitated customer needs for service quality. Pull production signified the type of production that was "driven by demand from the next work station and ultimately from the customer" (p. 23).

### Measurement Description

Thirty-three items were grouped into seven categories that were used to measure the extent of usage of manufacturing practices for the firm's dominant product line. A 5-point Likert scale was used where 1 = "not at all," 2 = "a little," 3 = "moderately," 4 = "much," and 5 = "a great deal."

### Development

The initial 52 items that reflected the seven time-based manufacturing practices were generated based on the literature review and structured interviews with practitioners. To provide additional support for content validity, the items were refined in a pretest by 14 experts, including 9 faculty members from business and engineering colleges and 5 practitioners. Based on their evaluation, items were added, changed, or deleted to form a revised instrument that contained 66 items. The instrument was then subjected to a pilot study that targeted a sample of manufacturing and engineering executives from discrete part-manufacturing firms. Thirty-four responses were analyzed to purify the scales, assess unidimensionality and reliability.

The large-scale data analysis was based on responses from 244 firms. The items in each construct were subjected to further purification through corrected item-total correlation analysis. At this stage, 12 items were eliminated from further consideration, which produced the final instrument with 33 items grouped into seven categories.

### Sample

Two thousand and five hundred organizations that were engaged in discrete part manufacturing and with more than 100 employees were selected from the Society of Manufacturing Engineers (SME). A survey and cover letter were mailed to the senior manufacturing executive at these firms. Out of 253 responses received, 244 were usable, resulting in a response rate of 9.9%. "The usable responses were from fabricated metal products (35%), industrial and commercial machinery (30%), electrical equipment and components (12%), transportation equipment (15%), and miscellaneous (8%). The respondent's position is: president (12%), vice-president (31%), director (11%), manager (19%), and miscellaneous (27%). Seventy percent of the responses are from firms with less than 500 employees, and firms with more than 1,000 employees account for 15% of the sample" (p. 27).

### Reliability and Validity

Content validity was supported by the careful exploratory development of the scales described above. In addition, construct validity was assessed by an exploratory factor analysis (EFA) as the means of extraction and method of rotation, respectively. Only the items referring to six of the practices were included because shop-floor employee involvement was viewed as a theoretical antecedent (Monden 1983) to the other constructs and was factor analyzed separately. A simple structure factor solution was obtained, as all the items had loadings less than .60 on their intended factors and there were no cross-loadings greater than .30 on the other factors.

In addition to factor analysis, convergent validity was evaluated by testing the lowest within-group correlation to determine if it is significant at $p < .01$. All were found significant. As reported by the authors, discriminant validity was assessed at the item level using a single-method, multitrait approach (Campbell and Fiske 1959), and zero violations were detected. Structural equation modeling (SEM) methodology (Bagozzi and Philips 1982) was also used to test discriminant validity between pairs of constructs. In addition, discriminant validity was tested by comparing the average variance extracted (AVE) with the squared correlation between constructs. These tests have provided evidence for discriminant validity. The reliability of each of the scales was examined using Cronbach's coefficient alpha and the AVE. To assess predictive validity, the seven time-based, manufacturing scales were each correlated with a composite measure of competitive capabilities.

### Scores

Scores are presented in Tables 1–5 in the article.

### Other Evidence

A number of authors have used all or parts of the items that were included in the Koufteros, Vonderembse, and Doll (1998) battery of scales. Rondeau (1997) developed a framework to evaluate the relationship between manufacturing and information system practices and their effects on competitive capabilities and firm performance. He used most of the items across the seven time-based manufacturing constructs and provides evidence for validity through corrected item-total correlation, within block factor analysis, and EFA across the six constructs as tested in Koufteros, Vonderembse, and Doll (1998). Tu (1999) used the time-based manufacturing constructs within the context of mass customization and absorptive capacity.

### References

Bagozzi, R. P., and L. W. Philips. 1982. Representing and testing organizational theories: A holistic construal. *Administrative Science Quarterly* 27 (3): 459–89.

Campbell, D. T., and D. W. Fiske. 1959. Convergent and discriminant validation by the multitrait-multimethod matrix. *Psychological Bulletin* 56 (1): 81–105.

Monden, Y. 1983. *Toyota production system: A practical approach to production management.* Norcross, GA: Industrial Engineers and Management Press.

Rondeau, P. J. 1997. A framework to evaluate the relationship between manufacturing and information system practices: The effect on competitive capabilities and firm performance. PhD diss, University of Toledo, Toledo, OH.

Tu, Q. 1999. Achieving mass customization through technology application and absorptive capacity: A customer driven framework. PhD diss, University of Toledo, Toledo, OH.

## Koufteros, Vonderembse, and Doll (2001)

### Article Summarized

Koufteros, Xenophon A., Mark A. Vonderembse, and William J. Doll. 2001. Concurrent engineering and its consequences. *Journal of Operations Management* 19 (1): 97–115.

### Scales (Actual Questions Used)

*Change*

1. What best describes the percentage of products in your industry whose performance has improved over the past 2 years because of technological change?
2. In this industry, what best describes the degree of improvement in product performance within the past 2 years?
3. In this industry, how quickly do new products capture market share from existing products?
4. In this industry, what best describes the frequency of product change within the past 2 years by you or your competition?
5. What best describes the percentage of products in your industry whose quality has improved over the past 2 years because of technological change?
6. What best describes the percentage of products in your industry whose manufacturing practices have been substantially improved over the past 2 years because of technological change?
7. In this industry, how extensive is the typical product change?

*Concurrent Work-Flow*

8. Product and process designs are developed concurrently by a group of employees from various disciplines.
9. Our organization uses formal techniques, such as quality functional deployment, to translate customer preferences into product and process parameters.
10. Much of process design is done concurrently with product design.
11. Product development activities are concurrent.

*Early Involvement*

12. Purchasing managers are involved from the early stages of product development.
13. Process engineers are involved from the early stages of product development.
14. Top management is involved from the early stages of product development.
15. Manufacturing is involved from the early stages of product development.
16. Various disciplines are involved in product development from the early stages.

*Product Development Teams*

17. Product development group members share information.
18. Product development group members represent a variety of disciplines.
19. Product development group members trust each other.
20. Product development employees work as a team.
21. Product development group members seek integrative solutions.

*Quality*

22. Our capability of offering products that function according to customer needs over a reasonable lifetime
23. Our capability of offering a high value product to the customers
24. Our capability of offering safe-to-use products that meet customer needs
25. Our capability of offering reliable products that meet customer needs
26. Our capability of offering durable products that meet customer needs
27. Our capability of offering quality products that meet customer expectations
28. Our capability of offering high-performance products that meet customer needs

*Product Innovation*

29. Our capability of developing customized products
30. Our capability of developing unique features
31. Our capability of developing new products and features
32. Our capability of developing a number of "new" features
33. Our capability of developing a number of "new" products

*Premium Pricing*

34. Our capability of commanding premium prices
35. Our capability of selling at prices above average
36. Our capability of selling at high prices that only a few firms can achieve

**Construct Description**

In the article product innovation was characterized as the "capability of the organization to introduce new products and new features" (p. 101). Quality was described based on prior research as "the capability of the firm to produce products that would satisfy customer needs for quality and performance (Hall et al., 1991; Doll and Vonderembse, 1991)" (p. 101). The authors did not provide formal definitions of change, concurrent work flow, early involvement, product development teams, quality, and premium pricing.

### Measurement Description

The construct of change was captured by a 5-point Likert scale that ranged from 1 = "less than 10% of products" to 5 = "over 90% of products." The authors measured the items tapping into concurrent workflow, early involvement, and product development teams by 5-point Likert scales that ranged from 1 = "not at all" to 5 = "a great deal." The constructs of quality, product innovation, and premium pricing were quantified by 5-point Likert scales that ranged from 1 = "much below" to 7 = "much above."

### Development

The survey was pretested with responses from 34 firms and revised accordingly.

### Sample

The survey was sent to executives in 2,500 discrete-part-manufacturing firms with more than 100 employees each. The companies were selected from the member database of the Society of Manufacturing Engineers (SME). The companies were drawn from four two-digit U.S. Department of Commerce, Standard Industrial Classification (SIC) code industries (SIC 34, fabricated metal products; SIC 35, industrial and commercial machinery; SIC 36, electronics, electrical equipment and components; and SIC 37, transportation equipment). Two hundred and forty-four usable surveys were received, leading to an effective response rate of 10%. The details of the respondent profiles are depicted in Table 1 in the article.

### Reliability and Validity

The authors assessed the reliability and validity of the items in an iterative, exploratory way. First, they ensured content validity by literature review and interviews with practitioners and experts on the area. Then, they conducted a pilot study on the items and assessed item-total correlations and the results of the exploratory factor analyses (EFA). Last, they split the final sample into two: exploratory and validation. They modified the scales in the exploratory sample based on the results of the item-total correlations, EFA, and Cronbach's coefficient alpha values. Then they confirmed these results through confirmatory factor analysis (CFA) using the validation sample.

### Scores

The scores are presented in Tables 2–7 in the article.

### Other Evidence

Not available.

### References

Doll, W. J., and M. A. Vonderembse. 1991. The evolution of manufacturing systems: Towards the post industrial enterprise. *OMEGA* 19 (5): 401–11.

Hall, R. W., H. T. Johnson, and P. B. B. Turney. 1991. *Measuring up: Charting pathways to manufacturing excellence.* Homewood, IL: Business One, Irwin.

# Koufteros, Vonderembse, and Doll (2002)

**Article Summarized**

Koufteros, Xenophon A., Mark A. Vonderembse, and William J. Doll. 2002. Integrated product development practices and competitive capabilities: The effects of uncertainty, equivocality, and platform strategy. *Journal of Operations Management* 20 (4): 331–55.

**Scales (Actual Questions Used)**

*Heavy Weight Product Development Managers*

1. Product development managers are given "real" authority over personnel.
2. Product development managers have enough influence to make things happen.
3. Product development managers have a final say in budget decisions.
4. Product development managers have a final say in product design decisions.

*Concurrent Engineering*

5. Product and process designs are developed concurrently by a group of employees.
6. Much of process design is done concurrently with product design.
7. Product development activities are concurrent.
8. Product development group members share information.
9. Product development group members represent a variety of disciplines.
10. Product development group members trust each other.
11. Product development employees work as a team.
12. Product development group members seek integrative solutions.
13. Purchasing managers are involved from the early stages of product development.
14. Process engineers are involved from the early stages of product development.
15. Manufacturing is involved from the early stages of product development.
16. Various disciplines are involved in product development from the early stages.

*Computer Use*

17. We use computers to improve designs.
18. We use computerized systems for product development.
19. Computers help us in making engineering changes.
20. We use computers to develop product prototypes.
21. We use computers to coordinate product development activities.

*Product Innovation*

22. Our capability of developing unique features
23. Our capability of developing new products and features
24. Our capability of developing a number of "new" features

*Quality*

25. Our capability of offering products that function according to customer needs over a reasonable lifetime
26. Our capability of offering a high-value product to the customers
27. Our capability of offering safe-to-use products that meet customer needs
28. Our capability of offering reliable products that meet customer needs

29. Our capability of offering durable products that meet customer needs
30. Our capability of offering quality products that meet customer expectations
31. Our capability of offering high-performance products that meet customer needs

*Premium Pricing*

32. Our capability of commanding premium prices
33. Our capability of selling at prices above average
34. Our capability of selling at high prices that only a few firms can achieve

*Profitability*

35. What is your profitability relative to the average in the industry?

*Uncertainty*

36. What best describes the percentage of products in your industry whose performance has improved over the past 2 years because of technological change?
37. In this industry, what best describes the degree of improvement in product performance within the past 2 years?
38. In this industry, how quickly do new products capture market share from existing products?
39. In this industry, what best describes the frequency of product change within the past 2 years by you or your competition?
40. What best describes the percentage of products in your industry whose quality has improved over the past 2 years because of technological change?
41. What best describes the percentage of products in your industry whose manufacturing practices have been substantially improved over the past 2 years because of technological change?
42. In this industry, how extensive is the typical product change?

*Equivocality*

43. What is the degree of process complexity in your dominant product line?
44. In your dominant product line, what best describes the complexity of your most complex process?
45. What is the degree of product complexity in your dominant product line?

*Product Strategy*

46. Our core products are designed as platforms for multiple generations of products to come.
47. Our product designs enable us to accommodate several generations of products.
48. Our product designs are drawn to accommodate future generations of products.

## Construct Description

The construct definitions offered in this article were as follows: Concurrent engineering was described as the "early involvement of a cross-functional team in a process to plan product, process and manufacturing activities, simultaneously" (p. 334). Product innovation was characterized as "the capability of organizations to introduce new products and features" (p. 336). Building on prior literature, quality was defined as "the capability of the firm to design and produce products that would fulfill customer expectations (Hall et al. 1997; Doll and Vonderembse, 1991)" (p. 336). The authors indicated that premium pricing was the capability of the firm to command superior prices.

## Measurement Description

The authors operationalized items tapping into heavyweight product development managers, concurrent engineering, computer usage, and product strategy by 5-point Likert scales that ranged from 1 = "not at all" to 5 = "a great deal." The constructs of quality, product innovation, and premium pricing were measured by items using 7-point Likert scales that ranged from 1 = "much below" to 7 = "much above." The construct of profitability was quantified by a single 7-point Likert scale with an anchor, from 1 = "considerably low" to 7 = "considerably above."

## Development

The authors developed the measurement items and scales from theory, literature review, and structured interviews with 10 practitioners. Next, the resulting scales were evaluated by 14 practitioners and academicians in a formal pretest. Last, the scales were pilot tested with 34 companies.

## Sample

The survey was sent to executives in 2,500 discrete-part-manufacturing firms with more than 100 employees each. The companies were selected from the member database of the Society of Manufacturing Engineers (SME). The companies were basically from four two-digit U.S. Department of Commerce, Standard Industrial Classification (SIC) code industries (SIC 34, fabricated metal products; SIC 35, industrial and commercial machinery; SIC 36, electronics, electrical equipment, and components; and SIC 37, transportation equipment). The authors received 244 usable surveys, leading to an effective response rate of 10%.

## Reliability and Validity

Following Gerbing and Anderson (1988) and Anderson and Gerbing (1982, 1988), the authors assessed the reliability and validity of the items by confirmatory factor analysis (CFA). They assessed convergent validity by examining the significance of the individual item loadings and model fit. They assessed unidimensionality of the scales through the examination of cross-loadings of the items. The discriminant validity was assessed by comparing the average variance extracted (AVE) with the squared correlation between constructs (Fornell and Larcker 1981).

## Scores

The scores are presented in Tables 1–5 in the article.

## Other Evidence

Not available.

## References

Anderson, J. C., and D. W. Gerbing. 1982. Some methods for respecifying measurement models to obtain unidimensional construct measurement. *Journal of Marketing Research* 19 (4): 453–60.

———. 1988. Structural equation modeling in practice: A review and recommended two-step approach. *Psychological Bulletin* 103 (3): 411–23.

Doll, W. J., and M. A. Vonderembse. 1991. The evolution of manufacturing systems: Towards the post industrial enterprise. *OMEGA* 19 (5): 401–411.

Fornell, C., and D. F. Larcker. 1981. Evaluating structural equations models with unobservable variables and measurement error. *Journal of Marketing Research* 18 (1): 39–50.

Gerbing, D. W., and J. C. Anderson. 1988. An updated paradigm for scale development incorporating unidimensionality and its assessment. *Journal of Marketing Research* 25 (2): 186–92.

Hall, R. W., H. T., Johnson, and P. B. B. Turney. 1991. *Measuring up: Charting pathways to manufacturing excellence.* Homewood, IL: Business One, Irwin.

# Koufteros, Vonderembse, and Jayaram

## Article Summarized

Koufteros, Xenophon A., Mark A. Vonderembse, and Jayanth Jayaram. 2005. Internal and external integration for product development: The contingency effects of uncertainty, equivocality, and platform strategy. *Decision Science* 36 (1): 97–133.

## Scales (Actual Questions Used)

*Concurrent Engineering (Internal Integration)*

1. Much of process design is done concurrently with product design.
2. Product development activities are concurrent.
3. Product development group members share information.
4. Product development group members trust each other.
5. Product development employees work as a team.
6. Product development group members seek integrative solutions.
7. Purchasing managers are involved from the early stages of product development.
8. Process engineers are involved from the early stages of product development.
9. Manufacturing is involved from the early stages of product development.
10. Various disciplines are involved in product development from the early stages.

*Customer Integration*

11. In developing the product concept, we listen to our customer needs.
12. We visit our customers to discuss product development issues.
13. We study how our customers use our products.
14. Our product development people meet with customers.

*Supplier Product Integration*

15. Our suppliers do the product engineering of component parts for us.
16. Our suppliers develop component parts for us.
17. Our suppliers develop whole subassemblies for us.

*Supplier Process Integration*

18. Our suppliers are involved in the early stages of product development.
19. We ask our suppliers for their input on the design of component parts.
20. We make use of supplier expertise in the development of our products.

*Product Innovation*

21. Our capability of developing unique features
22. Our capability of developing new product and features
23. Our capability of developing a number of new features
24. Our capability of developing a number of new products

*Quality*

25. Our capability of offering products that function according to customer needs over a reasonable lifetime
26. Our capability of offering a high-value product to the customers
27. Our capability of offering safe-to-use products that meet customer needs

28. Our capability of offering reliable products that meet customer needs
29. Our capability of offering durable products that meet customer needs
30. Our capability of offering quality products that meet customer expectations
31. Our capability of offering high-performance products that meet customer needs

*Profitability*

32. What is your profitability relative to the average in the industry?

### Construct Description

The constructs were defined in the article as follows: Concurrent engineering was characterized "to include cross-functional teams, concurrent workflows, and early involvement" (p. 100). Supplier integration connoted "the supplier's engineers work alongside the customer's engineers to jointly design the product so the supplier's process can be effectively integrated with the design" (p. 102). Product innovation referred "to the capability of organizations to introduce new products and features" (p. 106). Quality was defined as the "capability of the firm to design and produce products that would fulfill customer expectations" (p. 106).

### Measurement Description

Thirty-two items emerged from the pilot study, including ten for concurrent engineering and four for customer integration. Two constructs—supplier product integration and supplier process integration—constituted supplier integration, with three items for each of these constructs. Measures of these items was based on 5-point Likert scales, where 1 = "not at all" and 5 = "a great deal."

Four items comprised product innovation; seven represented quality; and one item was used for profitability. These 12 items were quantified on 7-point Likert Sscales, where 1 = "much below" and 7 = "much above." These 12 items were measured to compare with the average in the industry.

### Development

Several items were generated for each construct after literature review and structured interviews with 10 practitioners. Professors and practitioners reviewed the items. Fourteen practitioners from product development, engineer managers, and faculty from three universities participated in the pretest.

### Sample

To collect the data, a large-scale mail survey was conducted and co-administrated with the Society of Manufacturing Engineers (SME). The pool of respondents included "executives of 2500 discrete-part manufacturing firms with more than 100 employees each" (p. 109) and was targeted at four U.S. Department of Commerce, Standard Industrial Classification (SIC) codes, SIC 34 to 37. The authors indicated that the choice of SIC codes was based on their gained popularity as key segments in reported manufacturing research. The unit of analysis was the firm.

Out of 253 responses, 244 were useable, resulting in a response rate of 10%. Response/nonresponse bias was assessed by a $\chi^2$ test, and no statistically significant difference on any of the testing variables was found. Most of the respondents were small-sized firms (fewer than 500 employees). High- and middle-level executives were targeted because they were reported to have knowledge of both product development practice and competitive environment.

### Reliability and Validity

Confirmatory factor analysis (CFA) was performed using maximum likelihood estimation. The overall fit was assessed by comparative fit index (CFI), non-normed fit index (NNFI), parsimony goodness-of-fit index (PGFI), and parsimony normed fit index (PNFI). These indices were .94, .93, .70, and .79, respectively. The root mean residual (RMR) and root mean square error approximation (RMSEA) were .48 and .58, respectively, and all items had statistically significant relationships with their factors. Discriminant validity was assessed by comparing the squared correlation of two constructs against their individual AVE and correlations among the constructs. The authors reported that the composite reliability and the AVE estimates for each construct exceeded customary acceptable levels and can be found in Table 2 in the article.

### Scores

The factor loadings were above .63, and most of the items were above .80. Factor loadings and t-value of the 32 items are shown in Table 1 in the article.

### Other Evidence

Not available.

### Reference

None.

---

## Krause

### Article Summarized

Krause, Daniel R. 1999. The antecedents of buying firms' efforts to improve suppliers. *Journal of Operations Management* 17 (2): 205–24.

### Scales (Actual Questions Used)

*Buying Firm's Top Management Support*

1. Top management is supportive of our efforts to improve the purchasing department.
2. In this company, purchasing is considered a vital part of our corporate strategy.
3. Purchasing's views are considered important in most top managers' eyes.

*Importance of Purchased Inputs to the Buying Firm*

4. Purchased inputs represent a large expenditure for this company.
5. Purchased inputs have become a key area in which improvements are possible.
6. Purchased inputs have caught the attention of top management.

*Interfirm Communication Effort*

7. In this relationship, any information that might help the supplier will be provided to them.
8. Exchange of information in this relationship takes place frequently and informally and not only according to a prespecified agreement.
9. It is expected that we keep each other informed about events or changes that may affect the other party.

*Buying Firm's Perspective toward Suppliers*

10. We view our suppliers as an extension of our company.
11. Our suppliers' problems are our problems.
12. Continuous improvement of our supplier's product/service is an objective of our purchasing department.

*Supplier Commitment*

13. This supplier has a strong sense of loyalty to us.
14. This supplier is willing to make a long-term investment in helping us.
15. This supplier sees our relationship as a long-term alliance.
16. This supplier is willing to dedicate whatever people and resources it takes to make us a satisfied customer.

*Buying Firm's Expectation of Relationship Continuity*

17. We expect our relationship with this supplier to last a long time.
18. The relationship we have with this supplier is essentially "evergreen."
19. It is assumed that renewal of agreements in this relationship will occur.
20. The parties make plans not only for terms of current purchases, but also for the continuance of the relationship.

*Transaction-Specific Supplier Development Activities*

21. Assessment of supplier's performance through formal evaluation, using established guidelines and procedures
22. Use of a supplier certification program to certify supplier's quality, thus making incoming inspection unnecessary
23. Site visits by your firm to supplier's premises to help supplier improve its performance
24. Inviting supplier's personnel to your site to increase their awareness of how their product is used
25. Recognition of supplier's achievements/performance in the form of awards
26. Training/education of the supplier's personnel

*Buying Firm Market Competition*

27. The business climate for our firm's end products is very competitive.
28. Winning in the marketplace is a very tough battle.
29. What used to be good enough to succeed in the marketplace is no longer sufficient for success.

*Rate of Technological Change in Buying Firm's Industry*

30. Our industry is characterized by rapidly changing technology.
31. If we don't keep up with changes in technology, it will be difficult for us to remain competitive.
32. The rate of process obsolescence is slow (reversed).

## Construct Description

This study examined the factors that preceded buying firms' "time and resource investments in supplier development" (p. 205). These investments were defined as "any effort by a buying firm with a supplier to improve" (p. 205) the supplier's performance and/or capabilities and to meet the buying firm's short- and/or long-term supply needs. Specific constructs addressed in the study included buying the firm's top management support, importance of purchased inputs to the buying firm, interfirm communication effort, buying firm's perspective toward suppliers, supplier commitment, buying firm's expectation of relationship continuity, transaction-specific supplier development activities, buying firm market competition, and rate of technological change in the buying firm's industry. No formal definitions of these constructs were provided in the study.

## Measurement Description

All items except the ones pertaining to transaction-specific supplier development activities were evaluated using 5-point Likert scales that ranged between 1 = "strongly agree" and 5 = "strongly disagree." The supplier development items were captured on 5-point Likert scales where 1 = "always," 2 = "often,"

3 = "sometimes," 4 = "seldom," and 5 = "never." Reverse-scored items were designated as such in the list of measures above.

## Development

Of the nine constructs employed in the study, supplier development, the buying firm's perspective toward suppliers, and rate of technological changes were newly developed for the study; and the remainder were adapted from the existing literature. The survey instrument was first pretested with six purchasing executives and three academics. Then, confirmatory factor analysis (CFA) was used to further purify the scales. Scale items with high residuals and/or insignificant factor loading were deleted.

## Sample

The data were collected by mail survey. The authors targeted 1,504 Title 1 members of the National Association of Purchasing Management (NAPM) for the sample. "Title 1 NAPM members are high ranking purchasing executives with titles such as Director of Purchasing, Vice-President of Purchasing, Vice-President of Materials Management and Purchasing Manager. The sample was drawn across industries. From the 1,504 subjects in the target sample, 546 responses were received. Nineteen surveys were set aside from the analysis because of incomplete information; thus the effective response rate was 35.0 percent" (p. 211).

## Reliability and Validity

The measurement model was estimated by maximum likelihood using the SAS program's "CALIS" procedure. Most fit indices indicated an acceptable fit of the measurement model to the data. For example, the AGFI was .90, which was over the threshold of .80. Confirmatory factor analysis (CFA) was used to evaluate convergent and discriminant validity. Table 3 (p. 214) reported the results from the testing of the measurement model. The results showed that the coefficients for each individual item were statistically significant and, in turn, provided empirical evidence of convergent validity. Table 4 (p. 215) reported correlations between factors as output from CFA. Most of the correlations were low, ranging from −.08 to +.47. Chi-square difference tests were applied to two correlations that were above .60, including the correlation between the interfirm communication and the buying firm's perspective toward suppliers and the correlation between the interfirm communication and supplier commitment. The test results indicated that discriminant validity was achieved. In addition, the confidence intervals around the correlation estimates for all pairs of factors were also constructed. None of the confidence intervals included 1.0, which also proved discriminant validity acceptable. Cronbach's coefficient alpha values were calculated to test the scale reliability. Alpha values ranged from .73 to .87. Therefore, reasonable scale reliability was achieved.

## Scores

The results of measurement model and structural model are reported in Tables 3–5 of the article.

## Other Evidence

Not available.

## Reference

None.

# Krause, Handfield, and Scannell

**Article Summarized**

Krause, Daniel R., Robert B. Handfield, and Thomas V. Scannell. 1998. An empirical investigation of supplier development: Reactive and strategic processes. *Journal of Operations Management* 17 (1): 39–58.

**Scales (Actual Questions Used)**

*Identification and Prioritization of Supplier Development Opportunities*

1. Describe the process you use to select commodities requiring supplier development.
2. Describe the process you use to select suppliers requiring supplier development.
3. Discuss the five most important events or requirements that would be classified as drivers for supplier development.
4. Describe the methods you use to determine how much time, effort and resources should be dedicated to supplier development.

*Supplier Development Strategies, Practices, and Methods*

5. Please provide a detailed description of all the strategies, practices, tools, methods you use for supplier development.
6. Describe organizational strategies or structural changes used to carry out your supplier development strategy.
7. Describe any system (automated or manual) you use to carry out supplier development strategies.
8. Describe how cooperation between functional groups is achieved to implement your supplier development strategy.
9. Describe critical success factors underlying your supplier development program.
10. Identify three most important or key measurable results typically achieved from your supplier development strategy.
11. List other key soft results from your supplier development strategy.
12. What continuous improvement efforts could you have done to improve the implementation process and results derived relative to your supplier development strategy?
13. What are your future plans for supplier development?

*Tools/Practices to Identify Suppliers for Development Efforts*

14. Formal process to identify suppliers requiring development
15. Identification of high-performing critical suppliers for cost reduction and other improvement opportunities
16. Regular joint meetings with commodity managers and plant managers to identify key suppliers for cost/quality improvement projects

*Cross-Functional Involvement in Supplier Development*

17. Operations production/process engineering
18. Senior management
19. Purchasing executive management
20. Design/engineering/R&D

*Strategies for Identifying Critical Performance Areas for Improvement*

21. A supplier-focused total cost management program to assist in identifying and eliminating non-value-added costs
22. Development of targeted quality and other improvement benchmarks within the supply base

23. Criteria established about when to enter into supplier development
24. Formal process to identify supplier cost reduction targets
25. Coordination of supplier quality engineers worldwide (across facilities)

*Agreement on Performance Improvement Metrics*

26. Development of objective supplier quality metrics (percent reject, PPM, etc.)
27. A formal supplier assessment system to measure cost, quality, service, delivery performance, technology, and environment
28. A formal supplier assessment system to determine capabilities

*Implementation Strategies for Supplier Development Efforts*

29. Colocation of engineers to supplier facilities for supplier development
30. Direct investment in supplier training
31. Formation of total cost reduction teams (suppliers and engineers)
32. Joint cost/quality improvement work sessions held regularly
33. Direct investment in supplier facilities

*Supplier Resources Dedicated to Supplier Development Activities*

34. Supplier has hired additional engineering and other personnel to support our development needs.
35. Supplier has dedicated personnel to us specifically to improve performance.
36. Supplier has invested in employee training to support our development proposals.
37. Supplier has provided discrete and/or additional investment in generalized (as opposed to specific) production capacity in the expectation of supporting our requirements.
38. Supplier has invested dedicated equipment specifically to improve capability/performance for our business unit.

*Continuous Improvement Activities*

39. Internal program to respond to suppliers' needs for development
40. Ongoing communication with supplier community via supplier councils
41. Regularly work with suppliers to improve performance of second-tier suppliers
42. Joint cost/quality improvement work sessions held regularly
43. Supplier is part of supplier council that provides feedback on our performance

## Construct Description

In this research, supplier development was defined as "any systematic organizational effort to create and maintain a network of competent suppliers (Hahn et al. 1990)" (p. 41). No other formal construct definitions were offered.

## Measurement Description

Not available.

## Development

The authors conducted interviews with selected companies to identify factors that would aid in the development of the survey instrument. Then, "the questionnaire was developed and reviewed by five operations and purchasing management academicians, pretested with five industry executives, and revised as necessary. The survey instrument included extensive use of open ended questions, as well Likert scale and categorical scales" (p. 42).

## Sample

As indicated by the authors, "This study was part of a larger research effort, the Global Procurement and Supply Chain Electronic Benchmarking Network (GEBN) initiative at Michigan State University. . . . A total of 84 companies responded to this survey (a response rate of 40%)" (p. 42).

### Reliability and Validity

To ensure the validity of their conceptual framework, the authors took a triangulated approach. "The qualitative data were used to build the process model and operationalize the two distinct approaches to supplier development: strategic and reactive. The quantitative data were used to statistically validate and differentiate between the strategic and reactive approaches to supplier development" (p. 43).

### Scores

The scores are presented in Tables 2–10 in the article.

### Other Evidence

Not available.

### References

Hahn, C. K., C. A. Watts, and K. Y. Kim. 1990. The supplier development program: A conceptual model. *International Journal of Purchasing Materials Management* 26 (2): 2–7.

---

## Krause, Pagell, and Curkovic

### Article Summarized

Krause, Daniel R., Mark Pagell, and Sime Curkovic. 2001. Toward a measure of competitive priorities for purchasing. *Journal of Operations Management* 19 (4): 497–512.

### Scales (Actual Questions Used)

*Quality*

1. The ability of a supplier to provide you with reliable inputs
2. The ability of a supplier to provide your plant with durable products
3. The ability of suppliers to conform to your specifications

*Delivery*

4. The ability, willingness, and cost for a supplier to expedite a rush order
5. The amount of time it takes a supplier to develop a new part
6. The ability of supplier to provide JIT delivery
7. How quickly a supplier can deliver an order
8. The ability of a supplier to consistently deliver its products on promised due dates
9. Supplier location

*Flexibility*

10. The ability, willingness, and cost for a supplier to change order volumes
11. The ability, willingness, and cost for a supplier to change the mix of ordered items
12. The ability of the supplier to design new products or make design changes in existing products

*Cost*

13. The total cost associated with the item, including price, transportation, inspection and testing, cost of supplier nonconformance, customer returns, and other associated costs
14. The ability and willingness of the supplier to share cost data
15. The unit price of an item

*Innovation*

16. The ability of the supplier to design new products or make changes in existing products
17. The level of technological capabilities the supplier possesses and is willing to use for your products
18. The willingness of the supplier to share key technological information

## Construct Description

Not available.

## Measurement Description

The authors developed the quality factor "in terms of suppliers' ability to provide inputs that are reliable, durable, and that conform to the buying firm's specifications" (p. 503). All items were measured on 7-point Likert scales that ranged from 1 = "extremely unimportant" to 7 = "extremely important."

## Development

The authors prested the survey "with purchasing executives, who were asked to review the questionnaire for readability, ambiguity, and completeness (Dillman, 1978). The questionnaire was also critiqued by several academics who were asked to review survey items for ambiguity and clarity, and evaluate whether individual items appeared to be appropriate measures of their perspective constructs (DeVellis, 1991)" (p. 504).

## Sample

The survey was sent to 1,283 Title 1 members of the National Association of Purchasing (NAPM). The final sample consisted of 137 directors of purchasing or materials managers, 50 vice presidents, 22 purchasing managers, and 41 other titles. The effective response rate was 19.6%. The authors have provided the details of the respondents in Tables 2 and 3 in the source article.

## Reliability and Validity

The measurement properties of the constructs evaluated included (1) unidimensionality, (2) convergent validity, (3) discriminant validity, (4) nomological validity, and (4) reliability (Peter 1981; Venkatraman 1989). Scale reliability was assessed by Cronbach's coefficient alpha. All the validity measures, except nomological validity, were assessed by confirmatory factor analysis (CFA). Nomological validity reported to be ensured by literature review and the feedback from the practitioners.

## Scores

The scores are presented in Tables 4–6 in the article.

## Other Evidence

Not available.

## References


DeVellis, R. F. 1991. *Scale development: Theory and applications.* Newbury Park, CA: Sage.

Dillman, D. A. 1978. *Mail and telephone surveys: The total design method.* New York: Wiley.

Peter, P. J. 1981. Construct validity: A review of basic issues and marketing practices. *Journal of Marketing Research* 18 (2): 33–45.

Venkatraman, N. 1939. Strategic orientation of business enterprises: The construct, dimensionality, and measurement. *Management Science* 35 (8): 942–62.

# Krause, Scannell, and Calantone

## Article Summarized

Krause, Daniel R., Thomas V. Scannell, and Roger J. Calantone. 2000. A structural analysis of the effectiveness of buying firms' strategies to improve supplier performance. *Decision Sciences* 31 (1): 33–55.

## Scales (Actual Questions Used)

*Dimension 1: Direct Involvement*

1. Site visits by your firm to supplier's premises to help supplier improve its performance
2. Training/education of the supplier's personnel

*Dimension 2: Supplier Incentives*

3. Promise of current benefits such as higher volume order of the present item
4. Promise of the future business such as consideration for future business

*Dimension 3: Competitive Pressure*

5. Use of two or three suppliers for this purchased item to create competition among suppliers.
6. Although quality is our first priority, when competition is fierce, we might switch suppliers to cut costs.

*Dimension 4: Supplier Assessment*

7. Assessment of supplier's performance through formal evaluation, using established guidelines and procedures
8. Providing supplier with feedback about results of its evaluation

*Dimension 5: Performance Improvement*

9. This supplier development effort has contributed to increasing our product/service sales.
10. Our products can be produced faster because of our efforts to improve this supplier's performance.
11. Because of this supplier development effort, we expect this supplier to help us improve our product design.
12. The supplier development effort has helped improve our product/service quality.

## Construct Description

Constructs were formally defined in this research. Direct involvement was explained as the efforts of the buying firm to internalize supplier development by directly involving itself in the improvement effort. Supplier incentive was referred to as "increased volumes of present business and priority consideration for future business to the supplier as incentives for improvement" (p. 41). Competitive pressure captured the degree of multiple suppliers used to create competition. Supplier assessment was used to find whether a formal evaluation program and feedback are provided to the suppliers. Performance improvement indicated "the supplier development on the buying firm's product" (p. 42).

## Measurement Description

The items were measured by 5-point Likert scales.

## Development

According to the authors, the survey was developed using a "modified approach to Dillman's Total Design Method was used. The first mailing included a cover letter describing the research and the questionnaire; in the second mailing, a postcard was sent to remind nonrespondents of the importance of the research and request their response; the third and final mailing, which was sent to all remaining nonrespondents, included another copy of the survey and a new cover letter" (p. 40).

### Sample

After three mailings to a random sample of 1,504 purchasing executives who were the members of the National Association of Purchasing Managers (NAPM), 527 usable responses were returned, yielding a response rate of 35%. The industrial sectors as categorized by U.S. Department of Commerce, Standard Industrial Classification (SIC) codes are given in Table 1.

### Reliability and Validity

The magnitude and sign of the factor loading of the indicator variables onto their intended latent variables served as an indicator of convergent validity. "Each loading was in the anticipated direction and magnitude, and each was significantly different from 0 at $p \leq .05$" (p. 43). "Discriminant validity was assessed by examining the cross-factor loadings of each manifest variable onto all other latent variables on which high loadings were not expected. This was accomplished by examining the matrix of factor loadings as well as by using Lagrange Multiplier Tests. Factor loadings of the individual items on their respective factors were greater magnitude than with other latent factors in the measurement model. The Langrage Multiplier Tests revealed no parameters that could be released to significantly improve model fit" (pp. 43, 45).

### Scores

The scores are given in Figures 3–5 and in Table 3 in the article.

### Other Evidence

Not available.

### Reference

None.

## LaForge, Wood, and Sleeth

### Article Summarized

LaForge, R. Lawrence, D. Robley Wood Jr., and Ronall G. Sleeth. 1984. An application of the survey-feedback method in a service operation. *Journal of Operations Management* 5 (1): 103–18.

### Scales (Actual Questions Used)

*Communication in the Organization*

1. To what extent is work time lost because of a failure of communications between the construction department and the customer service department?
2. To what extent does your foreman listen to your ideas on improving aspects of your work?
3. To what extent does your foreman inform you about changes in company policies?

*Organizational Rewards*

4. To what extent do you think company pay scales accurately match the amount of pay with the amount of responsibility in a job classification?
5. To what extent does a well-done job get recognized?
6. To what extent does a hard worker get rewarded in terms of promotions and pay raises?

*Job Scheduling*

7. To what extent are the team scheduling worksheets accurate?
8. To what extent do you feel proper vehicles, tools, and equipment are assigned to each job?
9. To what extent are daily jobs scheduled well?

*Supervision*

10. To what extent do you feel your supervisor knows what you are doing each day?
11. To what extent does your foreman have control over your work group?
12. To what extent does your foreman help your work group solve problems on the job?

*Job Satisfaction*

13. To what extent do you enjoy performing the actual day-to-day activities that make your job?
14. All in all, how satisfied are you with your job?
15. To what extent do people, policies, or working conditions discourage you from working hard?

*Note: The three survey questions listed under each construct are only a sample of the survey questions from that construct. The complete list was not provided in the article.*

**Construct Description**

This study was intended to "determine if the survey-feedback method could be employed to improve the work performance of the crews" (p. 105). The research was predicated on managerial concerns related to worker nonproductive time, which was defined by the company as "idle time and personal time that could be avoided, unscheduled or unauthorized breaks, extended lunch periods, lost time due to poor planning, and lost time due to inclement weather" (p. 105). The constructs were formed around the perceptions and attitudes concerning a number of aspects of a construction operation that the management felt might be related to the high nonproductive index. Five constructs were considered: (1) communication in the organization, (2) organization rewards, (3) job scheduling, (4) supervision, and (5) job satisfaction.

No formal definitions of these five constructs were provided in the study. In general, however, items pertaining to communication within the organization captured the communication between different workers and different jobs in the organization. Organization rewards considered the extent of reasonable rewards in the organization. Job-scheduling items were predicated on how well the job schedules were made and followed in the organization. Supervision connoted the extent and properness of supervision in the organization. Job satisfaction explained how satisfied the workers were with the job, working conditions, people around, and so on.

**Measurement Description**

A total of 56 items were used to tap into the theoretical meaning of the five latent variables: communication in the organization (13 items), organization rewards (5 items), job scheduling (9 items), supervision (18 items), and job satisfaction (11 items). Each item was measured using a 5-point Likert scale that ranged from 1 = "to a very little extent," to 5 = "to a very great extent." The score for each construct was the sum of responses from all the items under the corresponding latent variable.

### Development

Most survey questions on the instrument were selected from Taylor and Bowers (1972). Some items were specifically developed for this study by the authors, in consultation with management, to address specific problems unique to the operation under study.

### Sample

The research was conducted in a major electrical utility in the Southeast. Two districts in the construction division of the company that were separated geographically by a mountain range were selected as the test district and the control district. Employees in each district were classified as lower-level employees (groundmen, linemen, and lead linemen) or upper-level employees (foremen, construction supervisors, and district manager). The survey instrument was administered separately to employees in both the test district and the control district, with district and job level being the only demographic data collected. After three feedback meetings, 2 years later, the survey instrument was administered for a second time. No other detailed description about the population or sample was provided in the article.

### Reliability and Validity

Cronbach's coefficient alpha values were calculated to test the scale reliability for each construct. Cronbach's coefficient alpha values ranged from .73 to .89 (Table 1, p. 107) in the article. Therefore, reasonable multi-item measurement scale reliability was achieved.

### Scores

Table 4 (p. 110) shows the mean attitude scores for both the test and the control districts. A three-way ANOVA (ANalysis Of VAriance) was conducted separately for each attitude variable to test the null hypotheses of no difference in attitudes over time, between districts, or between job levels. Table 5 (p. 110) summarizes the main findings of the ANOVA models. Tables 6 and 7 (p. 112) indicate the mean job satisfaction scores and the mean nonproductive indexes, respectively.

### Other Evidence

Not available.

### Reference

Taylor, J. C., and D. G. Bowers. 1972. Survey of organizations: A machine-scored standardized questionnaire instrument. Ann Arbor, MI: University of Michigan.

---

## Lawrence and Hottenstein

### Article Summarized

Lawrence, John J., and Michael P. Hottenstein. 1995. The relationship between JIT manufacturing and performance in Mexican plants affiliated with U.S. companies. *Journal of Operations Management* 13 (1): 3–18.

### Scales (Actual Questions Used)

*Manufacturing Strategy*

Factor 1: Manufacturing Strategy

1. Manufacturing kept in step with business strategy
2. Make effort to anticipate new manufacturing practices

3. Have manufacturing strategy that is actively pursued
4. Pursue programs to acquire capabilities in advance of needs
5. Entire workforce understands long run strategy

Factor 2: Interaction with Other Functions

6. Manufacturing involved in marketing and engineering decisions
7. Investments are screened for consistency with strategy

Factor 3: Communication of Strategy

8. Objectives and strategies communicated to production workers
9. Strategies and goals communicated primarily to managers (reverse coded)

*Employee Participation*

Factor 1: Employee Involvement

10. Workers are rewarded for learning new skills.
11. Workers are selected for problem-solving ability.
12. Workers are selected for ability to work in a team.
13. Teams are formed to solve production problems.
14. Many problems are solved from workers' suggestions.
15. Workers are responsible for inspecting own work.
16. Workers collect and analyze process control data.
17. Entire workforce understands long run strategy.

Factor 2: Employee Responsibility

18. Only managers have authority to stop production (reverse coded).
19. Plant employs many quality control inspectors (reverse coded).
20. Workers rarely involved in day to day decisions (reverse coded).
21. Strategies are communicated primarily to managers (reverse coded).

*Factor 3: Flexible Workforce*

22. Workers are frequently moved between workstations.
23. Workers can perform many production operations.

Factor 4: Maintenance and Strategy

24. Workers are expected to perform some maintenance.
25. Strategies are communicated to production workers.

*Supplier Participation*

Factor 1: Supplier Involvement

26. Calling means the supplier made a mistake (reverse coded).
27. Suppliers should communicate frequently about improvements.
28. Suppliers understand products and processes.
29. Suppliers frequently visit plant.
30. Suppliers should strive for long-term relationships.

Factor 2: JIT Deliveries

31. Deliveries arrive on time.
32. Deliveries are made directly to the production.
33. Deliveries are made frequently.
34. Keep large inventory of purchased materials. (reverse coded)
35. Keep minimal safety stock of purchased materials.

Factor 3: Supplier Selection

36. It is preferable to have multiple suppliers (reverse coded).
37. Cost is number one criteria in selection (reverse coded).
38. It is good to rely on a small number of high-quality suppliers.

Factor 4: Inspection

39. Do not perform incoming inspection.

*Waste Elimination*

Factor 1: Process Modification

40. Processes designed to be mistake proof
41. Processes under statistical quality control
42. Workstations arranged into manufacturing cells
43. Equipment setup time converted to external time

Factor 2: Inventory Reduction

44. Aggressively working to reduce inventories
45. Aggressively working to reduce lot sizes
46. Aggressively working to reduce setup times

Factor 3

47. Working to make parts right the first time
48. Subsequent processes are in close proximity

Factor 4

49. Expect that a percentage of production will require rework (reverse coded)
50. Equipment takes a long time to setup (reverse coded)
51. Tend to have large lot sizes (reverse coded)

*Technology*

52. Please comment on the extent that the plant uses advanced production technologies. Technology = 1, if very extensive use; Technology = 5, if very little use.

*Integration*

53. Please comment on the level of vertical integration of plant. Integration = 1, if very high; Integration = 5, if very low.

## Construct Description

The research definition of just-in-time (JIT) was based on Golhar and Stamm's (1991) four basic tenets of a JIT management philosophy: (1) the elimination of waste, (2) employee involvement, (3) supplier participation, and (4) total quality control. The four tenets and the activities associated with each were reconfigured into a model of JIT that focused on three groups responsible for the use of JIT in the plant—employees, managers, and suppliers.

## Measurement Description

Seven multi-item measurement scales captured the dimensions of JIT. The response to each item associated with each construct was captured on a 5-point Likert scale where 1 = "strongly agree," 2 = "agree," 3 = "neither agree nor disagree," 4 = "disagree," and 5 = "strongly disagree." A single overall JIT scale was calculated by averaging the seven retained scales. This overall JIT scale demonstrated the extent to which plants have implemented the complete JIT philosophy.

Plant performance was computed as an aggregate measure of four dimensions of performance: (1) quality, (2) lead time, (3) productivity, and (4) customer service. Two indicator items were included to measure quality: (1) the percentage of product shipped that did not require rework and (2) the percentage of product found to be defective at final inspection. These two items, which required respondents to select a quantitative answer from seven response choices, were combined to form a single measure of quality. Single items were included in the study to measure lead time, productivity, and customer service. The lead time indicator variable was based on the selection of one quantitative answer from seven response choices. A 5-point Likert scale ranging from "best in industry" to "below industry average" was used to quantify items for both productivity and customer service. The overall performance measure was then calculated as the simple combination of these four performance dimensions. Z-scores were used instead of the raw data.

### Development

Scales developed by Sakakibara, Flynn, and Schroeder (1993) to study JIT in the United States served as a starting point for the development of the JIT scales in the research. The initial version of the questionnaire was pretested on operations management and business logistics researchers, and after incorporating the suggestions and recommendations of these individuals, an intermediate version of the questionnaire was pretested on five manufacturing managers and five general managers from 10 different plants in Mexico. The final version of the questionnaire contained 49 items to permit assessment of the extent to which responding plants were using JIT.

### Sample

The questionnaire was delivered to manufacturing or general managers of all 504 plants with U.S. Department of Commerce, Standard Industrial Classification (SIC) codes in the 3,000 range in the American Chamber of Commerce of Mexico's 1991 Directory of American Companies Operating in Mexico. The mail survey was sent both in English and in Spanish. Of the 504 questionnaires sent out, 137 returned usable questionnaires (29% response rate). After deleting plants with fewer than 30 production employees, 124 plants remained.

Most of the responding plants (65.3%) belonged either to the commercial machinery industry or the electronic and electrical equipment industry. All of them were affiliated with a U.S. company; almost half were subsidiaries. The majority of the plants (73.4%) were not Maquiladoras. The sample is biased toward small plants, with 70% having fewer than 500 production employees and 40% having fewer than 150 production employees. Most plants in the sample performed a relatively large range of manufacturing tasks. The majority of the respondents were at the general manager level (69.4%) or were in charge of manufacturing (21.8%). Most of them were Mexican citizens (65.3%) and had been at the plant for more than 5 years (70.1%).

### Reliability and Validity

The authors refined the items by using principal components analysis (PCA) with varimax rotation. After the refinement of the items, Cronbach's coefficient alpha for the retained five-item manufacturing strategy scale was .71; for the retained two scales of employee participation, the alpha values were .85 and .60; for the retained two scales of supplier participation, the alpha values were .73 and .70; and for the retained two scales of waste elimination, they were .70 and .61.

### Scores

The factor loadings for each item are presented in Tables 2–5 in the article.

### Other Evidence

Not available.

**References**

Golhar, D. Y., and C. L. Stamm. 1991. The just-in-time philosophy: A literature review. *International Journal of Production Research* 29 (4): 657–76.

Sakakibara, S., B. B., Flynn, and R. G. Schroeder. 1993. A framework and measurement instrument for just-in-time manufacturing. *Production and Operations Management* 2 (3): 177–94.

# Leonard-Barton and Deschamps

**Article Summarized**

Leonard-Barton, Dorothy, and Isabelle Deschamps. 1988. Managerial influence in the implementation of new technology. *Management Science* 34 (10): 1252–65.

**Scales (Actual Questions Used)**

*Management Influence*

1. Management message
2. Perceived management support

*Personal Characteristics and Skills of Targeted Users*

3. Personal innovativeness toward this type of innovation
4. Job-determined importance (need)
5. Subjective importance of the task
6. Configuration skills (task related)
7. Skill in software use (technology related)
8. Job performance

*Physical Accessibility*

9. Physical accessibility

*Social Influence*

10. Interpersonal communication
11. Modeled behavior (acquaintance with users)

*Measure of Use*

12. Measure of use

**Construct Description**

The article focused on the role of the end user's individual characteristics. In particular, it addressed the mediating role of these characteristics on the relationship of the perceived managerial behavior about the innovation and the end user's own individual adoption decision after controlling for environmental factors. The end user's individual characteristics represented the individual target user's skills relative to peers and in relation to his or her job and, therefore, were context dependent. They included skills, attitudes, need (job-determined importance), and job performance.

**Measurement Description**

Management message was measured by multiplying two scales: the first capturing the power of message source (0 = "no message," 1 = "message from senior rep," 2 = "message from district manager,"

3 = "message from sales unit manager"), and the second capturing the degree of requirement (0 = "not suggested/required," 1 = "suggested only," 2 = "required"). The items and scales are described in Appendix A (p. 1263) in the article. Perceived management support was quantified by combining scores on three items each measuring agreement/disagreement (on a 1–5 scale) with statements about perceived support for layout use from the district manager, sales unit manager, and sales management in the general range.

Personal innovativeness toward this type of innovation was determined by combined scores on three measures of agreement/disagreement with statements about the respondents' tendency to 1 = "be among the first to try new sales tools," 2 = "use only sales tools that have a 'proven track record,'" and 3 = "leave it to others to work out the 'bugs' in the new sales tools before using them."

Job-determined importance was measured by the percentage of sales quotations made in the last quarter by the respondents that necessitated major changes in configuration. This percentage was taken as an indicator of a greater need to use layout. Responses ranged from 0% to 100%, with a median of about 60%, since sales representatives who sold similar systems repeatedly did not need to reconfigure for each new sale.

Subjective importance of the task was computed by the addition of two rankings: the importance of the task of configuring systems and the satisfaction derived from it, ranked relative to the importance of and satisfaction with five other tasks: (1) face-to-face selling, (2) sales planning, (3) answering technical questions, (4) administrative work, and (5) other internal corporation work. In the pilot study, sales representatives identified these six tasks as absorbing all their time outside of meeting and travel.

Configuration skills was measured by the combination of two responses. First, self-rating on a 7-point Likert scale as 1 = "adequate, but beginner" to 7 = "expert, as good as anyone can be." Skill in software use was measured by combination of (1) whether or not (yes/no) each of the six descriptive statements about software-related behaviors (with specific examples appended) applied, such as use of internal corporate software, experience with other systems, playing with software as hobby, past proficiency in at least one programming language, current programming activity, and past or current career experience as a professional programmer and (2) self-reported ability on a scale that ranged from 1 = "limited use of software" to 7 = "real computer jock."

Job performance was based on a single item—the percentage of sales goal achieved last year. Physical accessibility was measured by a combination of responses to three items, each measured on a scale from 1 to 5: (1) the layout's accessibility—the extent to which the respondent has the necessary hardware, (2) its availability—the extent to which the software is running on a machine the respondent can use, and (3) the response time of the system—poor to excellent. These three items loaded together on one factor when 18 characteristics of the layout were evaluated by respondents.

Interpersonal communication was measured by the type of information about the layout heard through the grapevine, from 1 = "very negative" to 5 = "very positive."

Modeled behavior was measured by number of layout users known by the respondents, including people outside their own office (responses ranged from 0 to 100, condensed for analysis into quintiles).

Use was measured by a 6-point scale: 1 = "never tried"; 2 = "tried only once"; 3 = "used it in the past, but discontinued"; 4 = "currently using it for less than 10% of the sales quotations issued"; 5 = "currently used for 10% to 50% of the quotations"; and 6 = "currently used for more than 50% of the quotations."

## Development

Measures used in this study were developed based on unstructured in-depth interviews, a pilot study, and two previous annual surveys about the same innovation. The scales measuring personal characteristics were confirmed through factor analysis.

## Sample

A telephone survey was conducted with a representative sample of 93 salespeople working in a multinational computer manufacturing corporation. The managerial influence was predominantly that of the sales unit manager. The innovation investigated was a software package called Layout, which guided the selection of parts and system design. Layout offered expert advice as well as prods for the salesperson's memory about available components.

### Reliability and Validity

The measurement properties of the scales were assessed using exploratory factor analyses and interitem reliability tests. Cronbach's coefficient alpha was used to evaluate the reliability of the scales. For the following scales, the alpha values were .56, .66, .58, .77, and .70, respectively: perceived management support, personal innovativeness, subjective importance of the task, configuration skills, skill in software use, and physical accessibility.

### Scores

The findings from hierarchical regressions are presented in Tables 2–4 in the article.

### Other Evidence

Not available.

### Reference

None.

---

## Levin and Cross

### Article Summarized

Levin, Daniel Z., and Rob Cross. 2004. The strength of weak ties you can trust: The mediating role of trust in effective knowledge transfer. *Management Science* 50 (11): 1477–90.

### Scales (Actual Questions Used)

*Perceived Receipt of Useful Knowledge*

The information/advice I received from this person made (or is likely to make) the following contribution to

1. client satisfaction with this project,
2. this project team's overall performance,
3. this project's value to my organization,
4. this project's quality,
5. this project's coming in on budget or closer to coming in on budget,
6. reducing costs on this project,
7. my being able to spend less time on this project, and
8. shortening the time this project took.

*Tie Strength*

Prior to seeking information/advice from this person on this project

9. How close was your working relationship with each person? (reverse coded)
10. How often did you communicate with each person? (reverse coded)
11. To what extent did you typically interact with each person?

*Benevolence-Based Trust*

Prior to seeking information/advice from this person on this project,

12. I assumed that he or she would always look out for my interests,
13. I assumed that he or she would go out of his or her way to make sure I was not damaged or harmed, and
14. I felt like he or she cared what happened to me.

*Competence-Based Trust*

Prior to seeking information/advice from this person on this project,

15. I believed that this person approached his or her job with professionalism and dedication, and
16. given his or her track record, I saw no reason to doubt this person's competence and preparation.

*Tacit Knowledge*

17. Was all this information/advice sufficiently explained to you in writing (in written reports, manuals, e-mails, faxes, etc.)?
18. How well documented was the information/advice that you received from this person? Consider all the information or advice.
19. What type of information/advice came from this person?

*Organizational Proximity*

20. Please indicate each person's location at the time of this project (reverse coded).

*Physical Proximity*

21. Please indicate each person's physical proximity to you at the time of this project (reverse coded).

*Hierarchical Level*

22. Please indicate each person's hierarchical level relative to your own at the time of this project.

*Receiver's Expertise*

Prior to seeking information/advice from this person on this project,

23. I had a full understanding of the subject matter regarding which I turned to this person,
24. I did not have adequate expertise to feel comfortable with the subject matter regarding which I turned to this person (reverse coded), and
25. I was confident in my ability to perform successfully all the activities myself in the subject matter regarding which I turned to this person.

*Friendship*

Prior to seeking information/advice from this person on this project,

26. I would have felt awkward talking to this person about a nonwork-related problem (reverse coded) and
27. I knew this person well outside work-related areas.

*Availability*

Prior to seeking information/advice from this person on this project, I assumed that:

28. it would generally be hard for me to get in touch with this person (reverse coded),
29. in general, I could find this person if I wanted to talk to him or her, and
30. he or she would usually be around if I were to need him or her.

**Construct Description**

Tie strength was defined as "closeness of a working relationship and communication frequency" (p. 1482). Tacit knowledge was denoted as knowledge that is difficult to articulate. Benevolence-based trust and competence-based trust were two trust-based constructs. In this article, these two constructs represented knowledge seekers' trust in a knowledge source's benevolence and competence.

**Measurement Description**

Eight items adapted from Hansen (1999), Hansen and Hass (2001), Keller (1994), and Szulanski (1996) were employed to measure perceived receipt of useful knowledge. Four of the eight items were related to both project efficiency in terms of time and budget, while the other four were related to project effectiveness. Each item was quantified on a 7-point scale with 1 = "contributed very negatively" and 7 = "contributed very positively." Three items were used to gauge tie strength. The first two were adapted from Hansen (1999), and the third item was added to indicate interaction frequency. The first two items were also quantified on 7-point Likert scales with the following anchors: for the first item, 1 = "very close," 4 = "somewhat close," 7 = "distant"; for the second item, 1 = "daily," 2 = "twice a week," 3 = "once a week," 4 = "twice a month," 5 = "once a month," 6 = "once every second month," 7 = "once every 3 months or less (or never)." The last item was measured on 5-point Likert scales that ranged from 1 = "to no extent" to 5 = "to a very great extent." Because of the differences in the range of the Likert scales across these three items, the authors normalized the items.

Three items were adapted from Johnson et al. (1996) to measure benevolence-based trust. Competence-based trust scale was taken from the two top-loading items from McAllister's (1995) cognition-based trust. Both items tapping into these constructs were captured by 7-point Likert scales. Three items from Hansen's (1999) were taken to assess tacit knowledge. Each item was measured with a 7-point scale (*see* Appendix p. 1488 in the article).

## Development

Most of the scale items were adapted from existing scales in the literature. A pretest was conducted to collect feedback. One item—interaction frequency—was added to measure tie strength to increase reliability and validity.

## Sample

Samples were collected through employees within three divisions: one in an American pharmaceutical company, one in a British bank, and one in a Canadian oil and gas company, with a total of 127 respondents—42 from the pharmaceutical company, 41 from the bank, and 44 from the oil and gas company. "Each respondent reported on four relationships, thereby generating an initial total sample of 508 observations. Respondents, 61% of whom were men, did not significantly differ by gender or office location from the group of people sent surveys. Most respondents (70%) were in their 30s or 40s, with a median age in the early 40s. The average respondent had worked in his or her division for 5.2 years. Nearly half (47%) of the respondents had a graduate or professional degree, and more than two-thirds (68%) had graduated from college" (p. 1481).

## Reliability and Validity

All multi-item constructs were assessed for discriminant validity based on factor analysis, using scree plots of eigenvalues and principal axis factoring with direct oblimin rotation. Factor analysis results showed that all items loaded on the expected factors and all expected factor loadings were above .40. The authors reported that all constructs show good discriminant and convergent validity. Cronbach's coefficient alphas were calculated to evaluate construct reliability. All Cronbach's alphas were above .70, which provided evidence of reliability.

## Scores

Scores for each multi-item variable were calculated as unweighted averages of relevant items.

## Other Evidence

Not available.

## References

Hansen, M. T. 1999. The search-transfer problem: The role of weak ties in sharing knowledge across organization subunits. *Administrative Science Quarterly* 44 (1): 82–111.

Hansen, M. T., and M. R. Haas. 2001. Different knowledge, different benefits: Toward a productivity perspective on knowledge sharing in organizations. Paper presented at the annual meeting of the Academy of Management, Washington, DC, August.

Johnson, J. L., J. B. Cullen, T. Sakano, and H. Takenouchi. 1996. Setting the stage for trust and strategic integration in Japanese-U.S. cooperative alliances. *Journal of International Business Studies* 27 (5): 981–1004.

Keller, R. T. 1994. Technology-information processing fit and the performance of R&D project groups: A test of contingency theory. *Academy of Management Journal* 37 (1): 167–79.

McAllister, D. J. 1995. Affect- and cognition-based trust as foundations for interpersonal cooperation in organizations. *Academy of Management Journal* 38 (1): 24–59.

Szulanski, G. 1996. Exploring internal stickiness: Impediments to the transfer of best practice within the firm. *Strategic Management Journal* 17 (Winter): 27–43.

---

# Lewis

### Article Summarized

Lewis, Kyle. 2004. Knowledge and performance in knowledge-worker teams: A longitudinal study of transactive memory systems. *Management Science* 50 (11): 1519–33.

### Scales (Actual Questions Used)

*Complexity*

1. Has a more complicated problem to solve
2. Is fairly simple and straightforward (reversed) interdependence
3. Requires that group members rely on one another's work products to succeed
4. Demands that the ideas of all group members be shared to succeed uncertainty
5. Was well-defined by the client from the beginning (reversed)
6. [Project's] client is apt to request significant modifications in scope during the course of the engagement

*Transactive Memory Systems*

7. Each team member has specialized knowledge of some aspect of the project.
8. I have knowledge about an aspect of the project that no other team member has.
9. Different team members are responsible for expertise in different areas.
10. The specialized knowledge of several different team members was needed to complete the project deliverables.
11. I know which team members have expertise in specific areas.
12. I was comfortable accepting procedural suggestions from other team members.
13. I trusted that other members' knowledge about the project was credible.
14. I was confident relying on the information that other team members brought to the discussion.
15. When other members gave information, I wanted to double-check it for myself. (reverse coded)
16. I did not have much faith in the other members' expertise. (reverse coded)
17. Our team worked together in a well-coordinated fashion.
18. Our team had very few misunderstandings about what to do.
19. Our team needed to backtrack and start over a lot. (reverse coded)
20. We accomplished the task smoothly and efficiently.
21. There was much confusion about how we would accomplish the task. (reverse coded).

Performance

22. The team's deliverables were of excellent quality.
23. The team managed time effectively.
24. The team met important deadlines on time.
25. The team did a good job of meeting (the client's) needs.

Viability

26. This team would perform well together in the future.
27. If I had the choice of working on this team again, I would do it.
28. If we were assigned to another project, I am confident that this team would work well together.

## Construct Description

The concept of transactive memory systems (TMSs) was conceptualized by Wegner (1987) to explain how people in close relationships organize and remember information important for joint tasks. Familiarity was defined as "the extent to which members knew one another before the consulting project began" (p. 1525).

## Measurement Description

Twenty-eight items were grouped into four factors: (1) TMSs, (2) task demands, (3) performance, and (4) viability. Among these four factors, items to measure TMS, performance, and viability were derived from previous studies. Most items were operationalized using 5-point Likert scales with 1 = "strongly disagree" and 5 = "strongly agree." The familiarity construct used a 4-point scale, with the anchors of 1 = "do not know," 2 = "acquaintance," 3 = "know well," 4 = "know very well," and communication process was measured by the relative frequency and type of communication with face-to-face (FTF) and non-FTF types of communications.

Three dimensions were associated with the task demand: (1) complexity, (2) interdependence, and (3) uncertainty. The task demand was assessed by the degree to which the focal project was more (or less) demanding than an average project on each dimension.

## Development

Three surveys were conducted for this research. The first survey, a paper-and-pencil questionnaire asking about members' demographics and familiarity, was administered before the projects began. The other two surveys were Web-based asking about the team processes and were conducted to focus on the planning and implementation phases, respectively. E-mails were sent to the participants within 1 week of the end of the planning phase and implementation phase as a reminder. Participants who completed the survey were entered in to win $25-lottery (second survey), $50-lottery (third survey), or $100-lottery (final lottery) to encourage responses.

## Sample

The data were collected from "second-year MBA students of a large, mid-Atlantic university and their corporate clients" (p. 1524). The data were "gathered during the fall semester of two consecutive academic years" (p. 1524). The first year data contained 164 students: 36 teams of 4 to 6 members. The second year data contained 182 students: 35 teams of 4 to 6 members. Thus, total data included 346 students, or 71 teams, across the two time periods. Of the 346 students, 268 completed the entire study, yielding a response rate of 77.5%. Of the 71 teams, 33 had 100% response rate, while the remaining 38 teams had some nonresponses. Teams that had fewer than three member responses were dropped. Consequently, there were 64 teams that were made up of 261 members.

The average age of the respondents was 27 years, with 5 years of full-time working experience on the average. Twenty-nine percent of the respondents were female. Of the 64 teams, 39 had a majority of male members, 10 had an equal number of males and females, while females were the majority for the other 15 teams.

### Reliability and Validity

The difficulty of the project—the task demand—was judged by the program director, who was familiar with the tasks of each consulting project assigned to the team members. The average of the respondents' answers to the six indicator items formed a composite scale, with the higher score indicating a more difficult project. Cronbach's coefficient alpha for the scale was .72.

### Scores

The scores in the planning phase and the implementation phase are shown in Table 1 of the article. Detailed regression results are shown in Table 2.

### Other Evidence

Not available.

### Reference

Wegner, D. M. 1987. Transactive memory: A contemporary analysis of the group mind. In *Theories of group behavior,* eds. B. Mullen and G. R. Goethals, 185–208. New York: Springer-Verlag.

---

## Li, Benton, and Leong

### Article Summarized

Li, Ling X., W. C. Benton, and G. Keong Leong. 2002. The impact of strategic operations management decisions on community hospital performance. *Journal of Operations Management* 20 (4): 389–408.

### Scales (Actual Questions Used)

*Outpatient Service*

1. Ambulatory service capacity (e.g., examination rooms) expansion
2. Outpatient surgery capacity (e.g., operation rooms) expansion
3. Home health care service (e.g., folding beds) expansion
4. Opening clinic(s) at different location(s)

*Health Service Network*

5. Forging a partnership with physicians to improve facility utilization rate (census and outpatient utilization)
6. Forging a partnership with local hospitals (within 1-hr drive, 55 mph) to improve facility utilization rate
7. Forging a partnership with hospitals within 1- to 4-hr driving time to improve facility utilization rate

*Invest in Office Technology*

8. Computers in doctor's offices
9. Paging system
10. Teleradiography
11. E-mail system
12. Fax machines in every department

*Invest in Clinical Technology*

13. Laboratory equipment and IS
14. Radiology equipment and IS
15. Pharmacy equipment and IS
16. Dietary IS

*Invest in Patient Medical IS*

17. Computerized patient clinical records
18. An integrated IS for tracking patient information
19. Computers in doctor's offices

*Demand Prediction*

20. Preadmission review is required by the payer.
21. Expected LOS is considered on admission.
22. Patient diagnose group are considered on admission.

*Managing Demand*

23. Patients are shifted to other units when the most appropriate unit is not available.
24. Emergency patients are delayed when capacity is not available.
25. Early discharge is solicited when there are more patients than beds.

*Staff Reduction*

26. Reducing the number of registered nurses (RNs)
27. Reducing the number of licensed practical nurses (LPNs)
28. Reducing the number of nurse aides
29. Reducing the number of professional staff (other than nursing staff)
30. Reducing the number of nonprofessional staff

*Staff Composition*

31. Increase the number of LPNs
32. Increasing the number of nurse aides
33. Changing nursing staff mix (RN/licensed registered nurse (LRN)/nurse aids) to meet cost containment goals
34. Reducing the number of professional staff (other than nursing staff)

*Staff Increase*

35. Increasing the number of RNs
36. Increasing the number of professional staff (other than nursing staff)
37. Increasing the number of nonprofessional staff

*Staff Shortage Management*

38. Use voluntary overtime
39. Extend hours of part-time staff
40. Call in staff on assigned day off
41. Use hospital "pool" nurses

*Staff Overage Management: Nonpay-Related Measures*

42. Use voluntary vacation time
43. Use mandated vacation time
44. Send excess nursing staff to other units
45. Assign excess nursing staff to other duties within unit

*Staff Overage Management: Pay-Related Measures*

46. Use voluntary unpaid time off
47. Use mandated unpaid time off
48. Send unneeded nursing staff home without pay

*Staff Training*

49. Creating opportunities for staff members to learn and use skills that go beyond current job assignment
50. Providing cross-training program for creating flexible staffs
51. Providing training for staffs to learn new technology

*Staff Competence*

52. Providing training to supervisors to improve leadership capabilities
53. Providing training to improve staff members' clinical competence
54. Staff members have the knowledge and skills required to perform their jobs
55. Staff members effectively use all equipment in their activities

*Job Enrichment*

56. Assigning a broader range of tasks to staff members
57. Giving staff members more quality control responsibility
58. Implementing employee empowerment programs
59. Increasing the level of job enlargement
60. Implementing job sharing

*Cost Performance*

61. Holding down inpatient costs
62. Attaining high labor productivity
63. Maintaining high capacity utilization

*Quality Performance*

64. Clinical quality
65. Customer (patient) satisfaction
66. Responding to patient requests
67. Responding to patient complaints

*Financial Performance*

68. Market share growth
69. Return on assets
70. Operating profit

**Construct Description**

Not available.

**Measurement Description**

The authors used 7-point Likert scales to measure the items. The items tapping into constructs for outpatient service, health service network, invest in office technology, staff reduction, staff composition, staff increase had anchors from 1 = "no emphasis" to 7 = "extreme emphasis." The indicator variables for demand prediction, managing demand, staff shortage management, and staff overage management were fixed from 1 = "seldom" to 7 = "always." The items that represent invest in clinical technology and invest in patient medical IS were anchored by 1 = "no investment" to 7 = "extreme investment." Measures of staff training, staff competence, job enrichment ranged from 1 = "not important" to 7 = "very important."

Last, items for the performance constructs used Likert scales that varied from 1 = "significantly lower" to 7 = "significantly higher."

### Development

The survey was pilot tested at three hospitals. The authors revised the instrument based on the suggestions of the practicing health care managers.

### Sample

The questionnaire was mailed to 492 community hospitals. One hundred and sixty-five hospital administrators and/or chief operating managers replied.

### Reliability and Validity

The authors assessed the reliability of the constructs by using Cronbach's coefficient alpha. They reported ensuring content validity by extensive interviews with practicing health service administrators. Last, they evaluated the measurement properties of the items by using confirmatory factor analysis (CFA).

### Scores

The scores are presented in Table 1 and Figure 2 in the article.

### Other Evidence

Not available.

### Reference

None.

---

## Li, Rao, Ragu-Nathan, and Ragu-Nathan

### Article Summarized

Li, Suhong, S. Subba Rao, T. S. Ragu-Nathan, and Bhanu Ragu-Nathan. 2005. Development and validation of a measurement instrument for studying supply chain management practices. *Journal of Operations Management* 23 (6): 618–41.

### Scales (Actual Questions Used)

*Strategic Supplier Partnership (SSP)*

1. We rely on a few dependable suppliers.
2. We rely on a few high-quality suppliers.
3. We consider quality as our number one criterion in selecting suppliers.
4. We strive to establish long-term relationship with our suppliers.
5. We regularly solve problems jointly with our suppliers.
6. We have helped our suppliers to improve their product quality.
7. We have continuous improvement programs that include our key suppliers.
8. We include our key suppliers in our planning and goal-setting activities.
9. We actively involve our key suppliers in NPD processes.
10. We certify our suppliers for quality.

*Customer Relationship*

11. We frequently evaluate the formal and informal complaints of our customers.
12. We frequently interact with customers to set reliability, responsiveness, and other standards for us.
13. We have frequent follow-up with our customers for quality/service feedback.
14. We frequently measure and evaluate customer satisfaction.
15. We frequently determine future customer expectations.
16. We facilitate customers' ability to seek assistance from us.
17. We share a sense of fair play with our customers.
18. We periodically evaluate the importance of our relationship with our customers.

*Information Sharing*

19. We share our business units' proprietary information with trading partners.
20. We inform trading partners in advance of changing needs.
21. Our trading partners share proprietary information with us.
22. Our trading partners keep us fully informed about issues that affect our business.
23. Our trading partners share business knowledge of core business processes with us.
24. We and our trading partners exchange information that helps establishment of business planning.
25. We and our trading partners keep each other informed about events or changes that may affect the other partners.

*Information Quality (IQ)*

26. Information exchange between our trading partners and us is timely.
27. Information exchange between our trading partners and us is accurate.
28. Information exchange between our trading partners and us is complete.
29. Information exchange between our trading partners and us is adequate.
30. Information exchange between our trading partners and us is reliable.

*Internal Lean Practices (ILP)*

31. Our firm reduces setup time.
32. Our firm has continuous quality improvement program.
33. Our firm uses a "Pull" production system.
34. Our firm pushes suppliers for shorter lead times.
35. Our firm streamlines ordering, receiving, and other paperwork from suppliers.

*Postponement (POS)*

36. Our products are designed for modular assembly.
37. Our production process modules can be rearranged so that customization can be carried out later at distribution centers.
38. We delay final product assembly activities until customer orders have actually been received.
39. We delay final product assembly activities until the last possible position (or nearest to customers) in the supply chain.
40. Our goods are stored at appropriate distribution points close to the customers in the supply chain.

*Delivery Dependability*

41. We deliver the kind of products needed.
42. We deliver customer orders on time.
43. We provide dependable delivery.

*Time to Market: An Organization Is Capable of Introducing New Products Faster Than Major Competitors*

44. We deliver product to market quickly.
45. We are first in the market in introducing new products.

46. We have time-to-market lower than industry average.
47. We have fast product development.

**Construct Description**

The constructs were defined in the article as follows. Strategic supplier partnership was designated as the long-term relationship between the organization and its suppliers. It was designed to leverage the strategic and operational capabilities of individual participating organizations to help them achieve significant ongoing benefits (Balsmeier and Voisin 1996; Monczka et al. 1998; Noble 1997; Stuart 1997). A strategic partnership emphasized direct, long-term association and encouraged mutual planning and problem-solving efforts (Gunasekaran, Patel, and Tirtiroglu 2001).

Customer relationship comprised the entire array of practices that are employed for the purpose of managing customer complaints, building long-term relationships with customers, and improving customer satisfaction (Aggarwal 1997; Claycomb, Dröge, and Germain 1999; Tan, Kannan, and Handfield 1998). Noble (1997) and Tan, Kannan, and Handfield (1998) considered customer relationship management as an important component of supply chain management (SCM) practices.

Information sharing referred to the extent to which critical and proprietary information was communicated to one's supply chain partner (Monczka et al. 1998). Shared information could vary from strategic to tactical in nature and from information about logistics activities to general market and customer information (Mentzer, Min, and Zacharia 2000).

Information quality included aspects such as the accuracy, timeliness, adequacy, and credibility of the information exchanged (Monczka et al. 1998). While information sharing was important, the significance of its impact on SCM depended on what information is shared, when and how it is shared, and with whom (Chizzo 1998; Holmberg 2000). Jarrell (1998) notes that sharing information within the entire supply chain could create flexibility, but this required accurate and timely information.

Internal lean practices were associated with eliminating waste (e.g., cost, time, etc.) in a manufacturing system and were characterized by reduced setup times, small lot sizes, and pull-production (Womack and Jones 1996; McIvor 2001; Taylor 1999). The term *lean* was used to refer to a system that uses less input to produce at a mass production speed, while offering more variety to the end customers. Elimination of waste was a fundamental idea within the lean system. In *Lean Thinking,* written by Womack and Jones (1996), five principles were identified as fundamental to the elimination of waste.

Postponement was described as the practice of moving forward one or more operations or activities (making, sourcing, and delivering) to a much later point in the supply chain (Beamon 1998; Naylor, Naim, and Berry 1999). In general, there were three types of postponement: form, time, and place postponement. "Form postponement entails delaying activities that determine the form and function of products in the chain until customer orders have been received. Time postponement means delaying the forward movement of goods until customer orders have been received. Place postponement refers to the positioning of inventories upstream in centralized manufacturing or distribution operations, to postpone the forward or downward movement of goods" (Van Hoek, Voss, and Commandeur 1999, 623).

Delivery dependability was characterized as the ability of an organization to provide products on time and of the type and in the volume required by the customers (Hall 1993; Koufteros, Vonderembse, and Doll 1997; Rondeau, Vonderembse, and Ragu-Nathan 2000).

**Measurement Description**

A total of 44 items were developed to tap the six concepts that according to the authors underlie SCM. Five-point Likert scales were used for all items.

**Development**

The items used to measure the constructs were developed from a thorough review of the literature in each substantive domain area as specified above. Six academics reviewed these items, and the items were further reviewed via structured interviews with three practitioners, who were asked to comment on the appropriateness of the item. Redundant and ambiguous items were eliminated. A pilot study was undertaken, and a Q-sort procedure was used to assess construct validity and reliability. A total of 44 items were validated in this way.

## Sample

"Mailing lists were obtained from the Society of Manufacturing Engineers and attendees of the Council of Logistics Management conference in New Orleans" (p. 626). Responses were solicited from companies of more than 100 employees from six U.S. Department of Commerce, Standard Industrial Classification (SIC) codes (25, 30, 34, 35, 36, 37), and surveys were mailed to 3,137 target respondents. Of these, 196 were returned and usable.

## Reliability and Validity

Reliability was assessed for each construct using the Werts-Linn-Jöreskog coefficient and Cronbach's coefficient alpha. All indicated acceptable construct reliability. Discriminant validity was examined using the $\chi^2$ comparison between pairs of constrained and unconstrained models. The constructs were found to be independent.

Predictive validity was examined using the standard *t*-test to examine the relationship between the latent and the dependent variables, and these results were shown to be significant. Further examination of unidimensionality, convergent validity, and reliability were also assessed and found to be significant.

## Scores

The scores are presented in Tables 4–8 in the article.

## References


Aggarwal, S. 1997. Flexibility management: The ultimate strategy. *Industrial Management* 39 (1): 26–31.

Balsmeier, P. W., and W. Voisin. 1996. Supply chain management: A time-based strategy. *Industrial Management* 38 (5): 24–27.

Beamon, B. M. 1998. Supply chain design and analysis: Models and methods. *International Journal of Production Economics* 55 (3): 281–94.

Chizzo, S. A. 1998. Supply chain strategies: Solutions for the customer-driven enterprise. *Supply Chain Management Directions Supplement* (Software Magazine) January: 4–9.

Claycomb, C., C. Dröge, and R. Germain. 1999. The effect of just-in-time with customers on organizational design and performance. *International Journal of Logistics Management* 10 (1): 37–58.

Gunasekaran, A., C. Patel, and E. Tirtiroglu. 2001. Performance measures and metrics in a supply chain environment. *International Journal of Operations and Production Management* 21 (1/2): 71–87.

Hall, R. W. 1993. A framework for linking intangible resources and capabilities to sustainable competitive advantage. *Strategic Management Journal* 14 (8): 607–18.

Holmberg, S. 2000. A systems perspective on supply chain measurements. *International Journal of Physical Distribution and Logistics Management* 30 (10): 847–68.

Jarell, J. L. 1998. Supply chain economics. *World Trade* 11(11): 58–61.

Koufteros, X. A., M. A. Vonderembse, and W. J. Doll. 1997. Competitive capabilities: Measurement and relationships. *Proceedings Decision Science Institute* 3: 1067–68.

McIvor, R. 2001. Lean supply: The design and cost reduction dimensions. *European Journal of Purchasing and Supply Chain Management* 7 (4): 227–42.

Mentzer, J. T., S. Min, and Z. G. Zacharia. 2000. The nature of inter-firm partnering in supply chain management. *Journal of Retailing* 76 (4): 549–68.

Monczka, R. M., K. J. Petersen, R. B. Handfield, and G. L. Ragatz. 1998. Success factors in strategic supplier alliances: The buying company perspective. *Decision Sciences* 29 (3): 5553–77.

Naylor, J. B., M. M. Naim, and D. Berry. 1999. Legality: Integrating the lean and agile manufacturing paradigms in the total supply chain. *International Journal of Production Economics* 62 (1/2): 107–18.

Noble, D. 1997. Purchasing and supplier management as a future competitive edge. *Logistics Focus* 5 (5): 23–27.

Rondeau, P. J., M. A. Vonderembse, and T. S. Ragu-Nathan. 2000. Exploring work system practices for time-based manufacturers: Their impact on competitive advantage. *Journal of Operations Management* 18 (5): 509–29.
Stuart, F. I. 1997. Supply-chain strategy: Organizational influence through supplier alliances. *British Academy of Management* 8 (3): 223–36.
Tan, K. C., V. R. Kannan, and R. B. Handfield. 1998. Supply chain management: Supplier performance and firm performance. *International Journal of Purchasing and Materials Management* 34 (3): 2–9.
Taylor, D. H. 1999. Supply chain improvement: The lean approach. *Logistics Focus* 7 (1): 14–20.
Van Hoek, R. I., R. I. Voss, H. R. Commandeur. 1999. Restructuring European supply chain by implementing postponement strategies. *Long Range Planning* 32 (5): 505–18.
Womack, J., and D. Jones. 1996. *Lean thinking.* New York: Simon & Schuster.

## Malhotra, Heine, and Grover

### Article Summarized

Malhotra, Manoj K., Michelle L. Heine, and Varun Grover. 2001. An evaluation of the relationship between management practices and computer aided design technology. *Journal of Operations Management* 19 (3): 307–33.

### Scales (Actual Questions Used)

*Perceptual Measures of Functionality*

1. This CAD (computer-aided design) technology allows the design of a wide variety of parts and products.
2. This CAD system has a lot of extra features and is not just a basic system.
3. This CAD technology has just about any feature we could want.
4. This CAD technology has a lot of features compared with available CAD technologies.

*Sophistication*

5. In terms of its hardware
6. In terms of its electronics and use of IT
7. In terms of all its features
8. In terms of its placement on a state of the art timeline

*Formalization*

9. Comprehensive rules exist for all routine procedures and operations with regard to CAD usage.
10. Whenever a situation arises in the CAD area, we have procedures to follow in dealing with it.
11. When rules and procedures exist in the CAD area, they are in written form.
12. There are significant penalties for CAD designer for violating procedures.
13. The CAD designer's job has up-to-date job description.
14. The job description for the CAD designer's job contains all the duties performed by individual CAD designers.
15. The actual job duties are shaped more by the CAD designer than by a specific job description.

*Decentralization*

16. CAD designers are involved in decisions related to the investment of new equipment and technology.
17. CAD designers work autonomously with little or no management guidance.
18. CAD designers have a high degree of participation in the adoption or change in the organization policies affecting their area.

19. CAD designers have a high degree of participation in hiring and staffing decisions.
20. CAD designers determine their own workflow, scheduling, or order tasks.
21. CAD designers are rarely involved in day-to-day decisions on product design issues.

*Extent of the Use of Teams*

22. CAD designers are organized into formal product design teams that are organized for new product design or introduction.
23. CAD designers are involved in temporary teams that form to solve problems or accomplish specific goals.
24. CAD designers frequently work in teams with members from a variety of areas (marketing, manufacturing, etc.) to introduce new products.
25. CAD designers are involved in teams that form to solve problems.

*Extent of Training*

26. How extensive is the training process for CAD designers?
27. How much priority is placed on training CAD designers?
28. How much money is spent on training CAD designers?
29. How formal or structured is the training process?
30. What percentage of designers have received training last year?
31. On average, how many hours of formal training does a typical CAD designer receive per year?
32. How many different kinds of training programs are available for CAD designers to attend?
33. Do you feel training is viewed as cost or an investment?

*Equity of Incentives*

34. How would you rate pay levels in this work unit compared with other firms?
35. How do you rate the pay levels in this work unit relative to past years?
36. The wages in our product design area are not very competitive with the industry.
37. To what extent are CAD designers paid their worth compared with others in this work unit?
38. How much emphasis is placed on paying CAD designers what they would be paid on similar jobs in other companies?
39. To what extent do differences in pay across CAD designers represent differences in their contribution?
40. How wide is the range in pay across CAD designers?
41. How closely is pay tied to individual performance?

*Flexibility*

42. Ability to customize product per design specifications
43. Ability to produce more variety in designs
44. Ability to make design changes easily
45. Design speed
46. Time to introduce new products into production

*Quality*

47. Quality of design presentations
48. Features shown on design
49. Design conformance to engineering specifications
50. Product quality as perceived by the customer
51. Drawing quality

*Performance Measures: Overall CAD Process*

52. How would you rate the overall performance of this CAD technology based on corporate performance criteria?
53. How would you rate the overall performance of this CAD technology based on increasing the number of nonprofessional staff?

*Scale Measures*

54. Please state the approximate replacement value of the hardware and software only for this system.
55. How many work stations are there in this CAD system?
56. The size of this CAD system is large in comparison to other CAD technologics available in the industry.

## Construct Description

In this article, scale was defined in two ways: (1) relative scale indicated the "size of the technology investment relative to similar systems used by competitors" (p. 311) and (2) absolute scale referred to the "number of workstations, pieces of equipment or employees, and replacement dollar value of the system" (p. 311). Functionality meant the "number of features the technology possesses, plus its ability to handle different products, parts, materials, dimensions, and functions" (p. 311). Sophistication referred to the "extent to which the technology is 'state of the art'" (p. 311).

Formalization was identified as the "formal reporting relationships and procedures within the firm and/or process" (p. 311). Decentralization was portrayed as the "levels where decisions are to be made, including how much the occupants of positions participate in decisions about the allocation of resources and determination of organizational policies" (p. 311).

Extent of team use was characterized as the "use of formally organized groups of employees to handle specific job-related issues, share things they have learned about their technology, make improvements in the process and technology use, or form for a limited time to handle specific problem or accomplish specific goals" (p. 311). Extent of training described the training activities that are "formally organized, paid by the employer, and related to the work in the company" (p. 311). Equity of incentives referred to the "fairness of the means by which employees are enticed to perform their work" (p. 311).

Quality was identified as "high product quality and higher conformance to specifications" (p. 311). Flexibility connoted "customization, design variety, ease of changes to designs, and design change speed" (p. 311). Last, process performance referred to the "overall performance compared to corporate performance criteria or use of similar technology by the competitors" (p. 311).

## Measurement Description

Most of the items tapping into the intended constructs were quantified on 7-point Likert scales that ranged from 1 = "strongly disagree" to 7 = "strongly agree." Those constructs that were measured differently are reported in Appendix A in the article.

## Development

Not available.

## Sample

The potential respondents were chosen from membership listing for various automotive and equipment manufacturing organizations such as Equipment Manufacturers Institute, American Gear Manufacturers Association, Society of Automotive Engineers, the Outdoor Power Equipment Industry as well as the *Harris Directory*. The final sample consisted of 143 responses out of 581 surveys administered, leading to a response rate of 24.6%.

## Reliability and Validity

The authors assessed the reliability of the constructs by using Cronbach's coefficient alpha. The authors reported that they ensured the convergent and discriminant validity of the measurement scales by exploratory factor analysis (EFA).

## Scores

The scores are presented in Tables 2–13.

### Other Evidence

Not available.

### Reference

None.

---

## Malhotra, Steele, and Grover

### Article Summarized

Malhotra, Manoj K., Daniel C. Steele, and Varun Grover. 1994. Important strategic and tactical manufacturing issues in the 1990s. *Decision Sciences* 25 (2): 189–214.

### Scales (Actual Questions Used)

*Strategic Issues*

1. Capacity planning: Planning the timing, size, and location of long-term capacity.
2. Process technology: Adopting new process technology and integrating it with product design, materials, handling, and manufacturing planning and control systems.
3. Process planning: Selecting the type of production process and its organization and flow.
4. Product planning: Planning the introduction, modification, and discontinuation of products with respect to timing, product characteristics, and fit with process capabilities.
5. Quality management: Creating quality objectives, programs, and organizational values that have the appropriate priority, scope, and focus.
6. Location: Selecting the firm's manufacturing, distribution, and service facility sites.
7. Layout: Physical arrangement of people, equipment, and space for production.
8. Manufacturing planning and control: Defining the approach to material/capacity planning and control, the role of inventory and capacity utilization, and the level of centralization.
9. Organizational development: Defining and implementing organizational structure, control, and reward systems, role of staff, worker authority, and participation levels.
10. Workforce: Acquiring, developing, and maintaining desired workforce.
11. Manufacturing strategy: Statement and development of manufacturing strategy that integrates all the other issues consistent with the business strategy.
12. Interfunctional: Interaction between all other issues and nonmanufacturing functions such as accounting, engineering, marketing, and finance.

*Tactical Issues*

13. Purchasing: Sourcing of raw materials, and vendor development and selection, based on negotiations of price, quality, and flexibility.
14. Production planning: Evaluating alternative approaches to determine aggregate production rates, and workforce and inventory levels of product families.
15. Distribution management: Planning, implementing, and controlling the efficient cost-effective flow and storage of finished goods and related information.
16. Materials management: Integrating planning and control of materials flow, including purchasing, manufacturing, and physical distribution into a single department.
17. Master production scheduling: Constructing disaggregated product schedules, which are used for deriving component schedules and other dependent requirements.

18. Inventory control: Determining timing, quantity, and positioning of inventory.
19. Manufacturing planning and control systems: Designing policies, procedures, decision rules, and/or software to determine material/capacity requirements and to control execution.
20. Scheduling: Timing and sequencing of production lots.
21. Quality control: Using techniques that ensure that product specifications are met.
22. Workforce supervision: Implementing supervisory styles, work standards training programs, incentive schemes, and similar activities that enhance worker performance.
23. Maintenance: Determining the intensity and type of maintenance management.

### Construct Description

The article identified and ranked major strategic and tactical manufacturing issues (*see* Tables 1, 2, and 5 for more details) that American manufacturing managers and academics should focus in the 1990s to be competitive on a global basis. "An issue must be related to the content and subject of manufacturing related topics that are commonly researched and taught within the academic production and operations management community. It is an aspect or a decision area of manufacturing which is important to the success of the organization, is relevant across diverse industry groups, and has some degree of controversy associated with it" (pp. 190–91).

### Measurement Description

The Delphi methodology was used in the study. In each round, the panelists ranked the relative importance of each strategic and tactical manufacturing issue. The rankings were then averaged over all the respondents, and their comments were summarized by issue (Tables 3 and 4). After each round, the issues were modified based on the responses. A revised list along with the ranking summaries was sent to the next round panelist to evaluate. The process stopped after the third round, where a significant degree of consensus between the panelists was reached and the relative ranking of each issue didn't change considerably.

### Development

Existing frameworks, such as the ones proposed by Hayes and Wheelwright (1984), Hill (1989), and Krajewski and Ritzman (1992), were used to establish the initial list of manufacturing issues. A rationale for the importance of each issue was developed too (Tables 1 and 2). A pilot testing of the Delphi questionnaire was conducted through personal interviews with two vice presidents of manufacturing and four production and operations management professors. Changes were made to the initial instruments.

### Sample

A total of 675 letters explaining the Delphi study and requesting participation were mailed to vice presidents of manufacturing for American companies with sales in the vicinity of $50 million or higher per year. These vice presidents were selected from the Standard and Poor Corporation Description. Out of 112 executives who initially agreed to participate in the study, 86 vice presidents actually answered to the first round, 76 to the second round, and 73 to the third round. This group of executives was a diverse one, representing companies of different sizes from several different industries across the United States. The demographic profile of the Delphi panel is summarized in Figure 1 in the article.

### Reliability and Validity

Validity of the results was assessed by collecting an alternative measurement for the final round study, where the panelists provided not only relative rank of the issues, but also an importance score for each issue on 7-point Likert scales. There was full congruence between the rankings and the Likert scale scores, which implied that the panelists were conducting correct trade-offs between different issues by assigning them similar average ranks on two different measures. Factor analysis with orthogonal varimax rotation on the seven-point importance ranking scores was also conducted for both strategic and tactical issues separately to understand the underlying relationship between them.

### Scores

The Kendall coefficients of concordance are given in Table 5 of the article. Factor analysis results are presented in Tables 6–8.

### Other Evidence

Not available.

### References

Hayes, R. H., and S. C. Wheelwright. 1984. *Restoring our competitive edge: Competing through manufacturing.* New York: Wiley.
Hill, T. 1989. *Manufacturing strategy.* Homewood, IL: Richard D. Irwin.
Krajewski, L. J., and L. P. Ritzman. 1992. *Operations management: Strategy and analysis.* 3rd ed. Reading, MA: Addison-Wesley.

## Marley, Collier, and Goldstein

### Article Summarized

Marley, Kathryn A., David A. Collier, and Susan Meyer Goldstein. 2004. The role of clinical and process quality in achieving patient satisfaction in hospitals. *Decision Sciences* 35 (3): 349–69.

### Scales (Actual Questions Used)

*Participatory Leadership*

1. Our senior executives are involved in quality activities.
2. Our senior executives focus on improving patient care.
3. Our senior executives are accessible to patients.

*Clinical Quality*

4. Patient unplanned readmissions
5. Clinical outcomes measured internally (relative to competitors)
6. Clinical outcomes measured externally (relative to competitors)

*Process Quality*

7. Patient preferences are analyzed when designing new and revised patient services.
8. Our service design is continuously improved.
9. Easing customer access to information that they need (degree of emphasis).

*Patient Satisfaction*

10. Overall patient satisfaction (relative to competitors)
11. Overall satisfaction of patients
12. Number of patients who return for future visits

### Construct Description

The constructs as described by the authors are given next. Participatory leadership was defined as "the level of motivation exhibited by administrators and executives of the hospital in setting strategic quality goals, improving the overall well-being of the patients and employees, and directing employees in all improvement initiatives" (p. 352).

Clinical quality was defined as "the ability of hospitals to achieve high standards of patient health through medical diagnosis, procedures and treatment, and ultimately creating physical or physiological effects on patients" (p. 353). Process quality was represented as "the result of the service (non-technical) delivery process engaged during and outside of the medical procedures. Process quality results from patients' perception of 'how' the service was created and delivered" (p. 353).

### Measurement Description

Each item was quantified using a 7-point Likert-type scale. For participatory leadership, respondents were asked to indicate how often the said situations occurred in their hospital. For clinical quality, relative positions to competitors were asked.

### Development

The authors first conducted a pilot study using data from 51 hospitals. Next, they administered the main survey to 814 hospitals. "Each survey question was developed based on a thorough review and understanding of the Malcolm Baldrige National Quality Award Criteria and the content and wording of the items are directly traceable to the Baldrige Health Care Criteria" (p. 358).

### Sample

The sampling frame consisted of hospitals with 60 or more patient beds. The target respondents were members of "hospital management such as the Director of Quality, Vice President of Quality, or Quality Manager. Two hundred twenty eight surveys were received, with a response rate of 28 percent. After discarding responses with missing data, data from 202 hospitals were used in this study to build the four constructs and test the structural model" (p. 358). Tests for non-response bias were made "to determine if those who completed the questionnaire were significantly different from the study sample (n = 814). The $\chi^2$ test statistics for hospital size and ownership were non-significant" (p. 358).

### Reliability and Validity

Cronbach's coefficient alpha values for the four multi-item scales—participatory leadership, clinical quality, process quality, and patient satisfaction—were .83, .80, .81, and 76, respectively. Discriminant validity was examined by computing the difference between the Cronbach's coefficient alpha and average interscore correlation for each factor. All the differences exceeded the acceptable level, .37. Scale unidimensionality was evaluated by using Carmines and Zeller's (1979) criterion. Accordingly, the first component from principal components analyses (PCA) for each scale should explain a large proportion of the variance in the items—at least 40%. The factor loadings in Table 1 exceeded Carmines and Zeller's heuristic. Each scale loaded on one component and had a single eigenvalue that was greater than 1. Structural equation modeling (SEM) methods were deemed to suggest predictive validity.

### Scores

The survey questions and factor loadings for the four constructs are shown in Table 1 in the article.

### Other Evidence

Not available.

### Reference

Carmines, E. G., and R. A. Zeller. 1979. *Reliability and validity assessment.* Beverly Hills, CA: Sage.

# McCollough, Berry, and Yadav

## Article Summarized

McCollough, Michael A., Leonard L. Berry, and Manjit S. Yadav. 2000. An empirical investigation of customer satisfaction after service failure and recovery. *Journal of Service Research* 3 (2): 121–37.

## Scales (Actual Questions Used)

*Failure Expectations*

1. In general, I am not surprised if I encounter some kind of problem when I fly.
2. I would consider myself lucky if I did not experience some kind of problem with my flight today.
3. I consider the odds of running into a problem when I fly as being pretty high.

*Service Performance*

4. The airline's on-time performance was very poor. (reverse coded)
5. The airline's reliability was very high.

*Recovery Expectations*

6. My expectations were high that I would receive compensation if I encountered a long delay.
7. For the situation described, I had very high expectations concerning actions the airline would take to deal with a lengthy delay.
8. After reading the posted sign, I expected the airline to do whatever it took to guarantee my satisfaction.
9. I didn't expect this airline to do much for me if I encountered a long delay. (reverse coded)

*Recovery Performance*

10. I would rate the performance of the airline in dealing with the cancellation as exceptional.
11. For the situation described, I would rate the efforts of the airline to deal with my problem as superior.

*Initial Disconfirmation*

12. The airline's reliability was about what I expected.
13. This airline's on-time performance was much better than I expected.

*Recovery Disconfirmation*

14. I expected the airline would do more in response to the canceled flight. (reverse coded)
15. The compensation for my problem was much better than I expected the airline would provide.
16. After reading the airline's posted policy, I expected the airline would do more for me. (reverse coded)

*Final Satisfaction/Postrecovery Satisfaction*

17. Overall, how satisfied or dissatisfied did this experience leave you feeling?
18. How well did this service experience meet your need?
19. Overall, I am very satisfied with this experience.

## Construct Description

The two disconfirmation constructs given in the article were described. Initial disconfirmation was defined as "the discrepancy between expectations that the service may fail (failure expectations) and initial service performance perceptions (service performance)" (p. 122). Recovery disconfirmation was expressed as "the discrepancy between the expectations by the consumer regarding what the service provider will do when a failure occurs (recovery expectations) and the perceptions regarding steps by the service provider in response to the failure (recovery performance)" (p. 122).

### Measurement Description

The authors measured all the items with 7-point Likert scales. To limit skewness, the authors indicated two exceptions. Two of the satisfaction scale questions were quantified using a 9-point scale.

### Development

The research setting was airline travel. To test the hypothesis, two separate studies were developed, because of excessive length of the research tools. "Three pretests were conducted. The first two employed student participants and assisted in determining the realism of the scenarios and in the development and refinement of the measures. The final pretest with N = 240 was intended to mirror the final data collection plan as closely as possible. It was conducted at a small airport" (pp. 125–26).

### Sample

The studies were conducted at a medium-sized regional airport in the southwestern United States. A total of 1,005 airline passengers were approached, of whom 727 agreed to cooperate. Six hundred and fifteen passengers returned the survey. Passengers from 50 departures were included in the sample.

### Reliability and Validity

The authors used the standardized loadings, item reliabilities, and composite reliabilities scales to measure the latent variables in the disconfirmation model of recovery that were presented in Table 1. The total samples size available for the structural model was N = 117. "Standardized loadings (all significant at $p < 0.001$) and the item reliabilities suggest that the constructs' items cohere reasonably well. Bagozzi and Yi (1988) suggest as a guideline that composite reliability should be equal to or greater than about 0.60. All scales with the exception of service performance (0.55) and initial disconfirmation (0.56) meet this criterion" (p. 128).

Anderson's (1987) criterion, "that the correlation between two latent constructs plus or minus two standard error does not include one" (p. 128), was used. The results indicated that with the exception of measurement scale pairs between recovery disconfirmation and recovery performance [$0.93 \pm 2(.05) = 1.03, .83$], the criterion was met. Even here, however, Anderson's "rule is violated only marginally. The discriminant validity of the scales was also assessed using confirmatory factor analysis (Anderson and Gerbing, 1988), focusing specifically on the conceptually similar constructs that could potentially overlap: initial disconfirmation, recovery disconfirmation, and satisfaction. The results of this analysis suggest that the three-factor solution is better than a one-factor solution (three-construct solution: $\chi^2$ [20] = 65.76; $\chi^2$ [3] difference = 39.59, $p < .001$). Thus, the measures of these conceptually similar constructs are empirically distinct" (p. 128).

### Scores

The scores are presented in Tables 1–4 in the article.

### Other Evidence

Not available.

### References

Anderson, J. C. 1987. An approach for confirmatory measurement and structural equation modeling of organizational properties. *Management Science* 33 (4): 525–41.

Anderson, J. C., and D. W. Gerbing. 1988. Structural equation modeling in practice: A review and recommended two-step approach. *Psychological Bulletin* 103 (3): 411–23.

Bagozzi, R. P., and Y. Yi. 1988. On the evaluation of structural equation models. *Journal of the Academy of Marketing Science,* 16 (1): 74–94.

# McDermott and Stock

### Article Summarized

McDermott, Christopher M., and Gregory N. Stock. 1999. Organizational culture and advanced manufacturing technology implementation. *Journal of Operations Management* 17 (5): 521–33.

### Scales (Actual Questions Used)

*AMT Implementation Outcomes*

Operational Benefits
1. Output levels
2. Efficiency
3. Reliability
4. Repeatability
5. Quality
6. Flexibility

*Organizational and Managerial Benefits*
7. The extent to which technology has improved work flows
8. Communication
9. Integration of business activities
10. Management control
11. Realization of goals

*Competitive Performance*
12. Sales growth
13. Market share
14. Return on investment
15. Cost

*Satisfaction*
16. Satisfaction with technical aspects of the system
17. Satisfaction with the implementation process
18. Satisfaction with how the technology will affect jobs within the organization
19. Satisfaction with time required

### Construct Description

This article investigates how organizational culture was "related to outcomes associated with advanced manufacturing technology (AMT) implementation" (p. 521). In the article, the authors followed the definition of AMT given by Pennings (1987, p. 198), as "an automated production system of people, machines, and tools for the planning and control of the production process, including the procurement of raw materials, parts, and components, and the shipment and service of finished products" (p. 521).

Organizational culture was described as "a pattern of basic assumptions—invented, discovered, or developed by a given group as it learns to cope with its problems of external adaptation and internal integration—that has worked well enough to be considered valid and, therefore, to be taught to new members as the correct way to perceive, think, and feel in relation to those problems (Schein, 1985)" (p. 524).

The competing values framework (Denison and Spreitzer 1991) was used as the conceptual framework of organizational culture in the article, which was labeled by a two-dimensional space. The first dimension was the flexibility-control axis, and the second was the internal-external axis, which focused on activities occurring within or outside the organization.

## Measurement Description

A total of nine variables were studied. Organizational culture was drawn from a previously validated scale published in Quinn and Spreitzer (1991). The scale consisted of four variable groupings corresponding to the four ideal culture types as per the competing values model. A set of items associated with each ideal type was used to measure each culture variable. "Technology implementation benefits were measured along four dimensions: operational benefits, organizational benefits, competitive performance, and satisfaction" (p. 527). Items under each of these dimensions are listed in the article. Five-point Likert scales were used to quantify each item.

## Development

Questionnaires were sent to respondents, which required them to consider a specific AMT implementation project in answering the items. The authors used principal component loading analysis "to reduce the raw questionnaire data to a set of meaningful variables corresponding to the construct scale developed. Component scores calculated from the principal components analysis were then used as the variables in the next step of the analysis, multiple regression, to test the relationships predicted in the hypotheses" (p. 528).

## Sample

The sampling frame was developed in conjunction with the American Production and Inventory Control Society (APICS) and comprised a wide array of industries. Target respondents were plant managers and vice presidents of manufacturing. Four hundred and seventy mail surveys were administered, and of these 97 were returned, yielding a 20.6% response rate. "In total, 11 industries were represented among the respondents: textiles, furniture, article and printing, chemicals and plastics, primary metals, fabricated metals, machinery, electrical and electronic products, transportation equipment, lumber and wood, and other" (p. 526).

## Reliability and Validity

Reliability was gauged by Cronbach's coefficient alpha. The alpha values for each scale "ranged from 0.64 to 0.87, indicating an acceptable level of reliability" (p. 529). Table 3 in the article depicts the alpha values for all the variables. Regression analysis was employed to test the hypotheses.

## Scores

Mean, standard deviation, and variance of each variable are shown in Table 3 in the article. The correlations between the variables are listed in Table 4. Factor loadings are given in Table 2.

## Evidence

Not available.

## References

Denison, D. R., and G. M. Spreitzer. 1991. Organizational culture and organizational development: A competing values approach. *Research in Organizational Change and Development* 5: 1–21.

Pennings, J. M. 1987. Technological innovations in manufacturing. In *New technology as an organizational innovation: The development and diffusion of microelectronics,* eds. J. M. Pennings and A. Buitendam, 197–216. Cambridge, MA: Ballinger.

Quinn, R. E., and G. M. Spreitzer. 1991. The psychometrics of the competing values culture instrument and an analysis of the impact of organizational culture on quality of life. *Research in Organizational Change and Development* 5: 115–42.

Schein, E. H. 1985. *Organizational culture and leadership.* San Francisco, CA: Jossey-Bass.

# McKone, Schroeder, and Cua

### Article Summarized

McKone, Kathleen E., Roger G. Schroeder, and Kristy O. Cua. 1999. Total productive maintenance: A contextual view. *Journal of Operations Management* 17 (2): 123–44.

### Scales (Actual Questions Used)

*Total Productive Maintenance (TPM) Implementation Level*

Autonomous Maintenance

*Housekeeping*

1. Our plant emphasizes putting all tools and fixtures in their place.
2. We take pride in keeping our plant neat and clean.
3. Our plant is kept clean at all times.
4. I often have trouble finding the tools I need (reverse coded).
5. Our plant is disorganized and dirty (reverse coded).

*Cross-Training*

6. Employees receive training to perform multiple tasks.
7. Employees at this plant learn how to perform a variety of tasks/jobs.
8. The longer an employee has been at this plant, the more tasks or jobs he or she learns to perform.
9. Employees are cross-trained at this plant so that they can fill in for others if necessary.
10. At this plant, employees only learn how to do one job/task (reverse coded).

*Teams*

11. During problem-solving sessions, we make an effort to get all team members' opinions and ideas before making a decision.
12. Our plant forms teams to solve problems.
13. In the past 3 years, many problems have been solved through small group sessions.
14. Problem-solving teams have helped improve manufacturing processes at this plant.
15. Employee teams are encouraged to try to solve their problems as much as possible.

*Operator Involvement*

16. What percentage of the maintenance on the machines involved in the production of this product is performed by the workers rather than by a separate maintenance crew?

Planned Maintenance

*Disciplined Planning*

17. We devote a portion of every day solely to maintenance.
18. We emphasize good maintenance as a strategy for achieving quality and schedule compliance.
19. We have a separate shift, or part of a shift, reserved each day for maintenance activities.
20. Our maintenance department focuses on assisting machine operators perform their own preventive maintenance.

*Information Tracking*

21. Charts plotting the frequency of machine breakdowns are posted on the shop floor.
22. Information on productivity is readily available to employees.

23. A large percentage of the equipment or processes on the shop floor are currently under statistical quality control.
24. We use charts to determine whether our manufacturing processes are in control.
25. We monitor our processes using SPC.

*Schedule Compliance*

26. What percentage of the time is the maintenance schedule (for equipment used to produce this product) followed?

Just-in-Time (JIT) Implementation Level

*JIT Delivery by Suppliers*

27. Our suppliers deliver to us on a JIT basis.
28. We receive daily shipments from most suppliers.
29. Our suppliers are certified, or qualified, for quality.
30. We have long-term arrangements with our suppliers.
31. Our suppliers deliver to us on short notice.
32. We can depend on on-time delivery from our suppliers.
33. Our suppliers are linked with us by a pull system.

*JIT Link with Customers*

34. Our customers receive JIT deliveries from us.
35. Most of our customers receive frequent shipments from us.
36. We are expected to supply on short notice to our customers.
37. We always deliver on time to our customers.
38. We can adapt our production schedule to sudden production stoppages by our customers.
39. Our customers have a pull type link with us.

*Pull System Support*

40. We use a back-flushing system, where components are subtracted from inventory every time a product is made.
41. We have laid out the shop floor so that process and machines are in close proximity to each other.
42. Direct labor is authorized to stop production for quality problems.
43. We use a pull system for production control.
44. The control of production is in the hands of the workers.
45. Generally, workers on the production floor have the authority to decide how to handle production problems.
46. We have low work-in-process inventory on the shop floor.
47. When we have a problem on the production floor, we can identify its location easily.

*Repetitive Nature of Master Schedule*

48. Our master schedule repeats the same mix of products from hour to hour and day to day.
49. The master schedule is level-loaded in our plant from day to day.
50. We make every model every day.
51. A fixed sequence of items is repeated throughout our master schedule.
52. We are able to use a mixed model schedule because our lot sizes are small.
53. Within our schedule, the mix of items is designed to be similar to the forecasted demand mix.

*Setup Reduction*

54. We are aggressively working to lower setup times in our plant.
55. We have converted most of the setup time to external time while the machine is running.
56. We have low setup times of equipment in our plant.

57. Our crews practice setups to reduce the time required.
58. Our workers are trained to reduce setup time.
59. Management emphasizes importance of setup time reduction.
60. TQM implementation level

*Customer Involvement*

61. We are frequently in close contact with our customers.
62. Our customers seldom visit our plant (reverse coded).
63. Our customers give us feedback on quality and delivery performance.
64. Our customers are actively involved in the product design process.
65. We strive to be highly responsive to our customers' needs.
66. We regularly survey our customers' requirements.

*Rewards for Quality*

67. Workers are rewarded for quality improvement.
68. Supervisors are rewarded for quality improvement.
69. If I improve quality, management will reward me.
70. We pay a group incentive for quality improvement ideas.
71. Our plant has an annual bonus system based on plant productivity.
72. Nonfinancial incentives, such as jackets, coffee cups, etc., are used to reward quality improvement.

*Supplier Quality Management*

73. We strive to establish long-term relationships with suppliers.
74. Our suppliers are actively involved in our NPD process.
75. Quality is our number one criterion in selecting suppliers.
76. We rely on a small number of high-quality suppliers.
77. We use mostly suppliers whom we have certified.
78. We maintain close communication with suppliers about quality considerations and design changes.

*Top Management Leadership for Quality*

79. All major department heads within our plant accept their responsibility for quality.
80. Plant management provides personal leadership for quality products and quality improvement.
81. The top priority in evaluating plant management is quality performance.
82. All major department heads within our plant work toward encouraging JIT production.
83. Our top management strongly encourages employee involvement in the production process.
84. Plant management creates and communicates a vision focused on quality improvements.
85. Plant management is personally involved in quality improvement projects.

*Employee Involvement (EI) Implementation Level*

Centralization of Authority

86. I can do almost anything I want without consulting my boss (reverse coded).
87. Even small matters have to be referred to someone higher up for a final answer.
88. This plant is a good place for a person who likes to make his own decisions (reverse coded).
89. Any decision I make has to have my boss's approval.
90. There can be little action taken here until a supervisor approves a decision.

## Construct Description

In this article addressing total productive maintenance (TPM), the construct was broadly focused "on equipment maintenance through a comprehensive productive-maintenance delivery system covering the entire life of the equipment and involving all employees from production and maintenance personnel to top management" (p. 123). Accordingly, the implementation of TPM was "considered in terms of the short-term maintenance efforts that could normally be found at the plant level of an organization" (p. 125).

Based on the work of Nakajima (1988), Tajiri and Gotoh (1992), and Suzuki (1992), the authors considered seven elements of TPM: "four elements of autonomous maintenance—housekeeping on the production line, cross-training of operators to perform maintenance tasks, teams of production and maintenance personnel, and operator involvement in the maintenance delivery system; and three elements of planned maintenance—disciplined planning of maintenance tasks, information tracking of equipment and process condition and plans, and schedule compliance to the maintenance plan" (p. 126).

Various just-in-time (JIT) practices discussed in Sakakibara, Flynn, and Schroeder (1993) and Sakakibara et al. (1997) were deliberated in the measurement of the implementation level of JIT. These were JIT delivery by suppliers, JIT delivery to customers, pull system support, repetitive nature of the master production schedule, and setup reduction efforts within the plant. The implementation level of total quality management (TQM) was viewed in terms of the level of customer involvement, rewards for quality, supplier quality management, and top management leadership for quality. Previous studies had found that these aspects of TQM adequately represent a broad-based view of the construct (Flynn, Schroeder, and Sakakibara 1994, 1996). The level of employee involvement construct focused on the level of responsibility given to each employee and is considered in terms of the extent of (de)centralization of authority.

### Measurement Description

The constructs were measured using perceptual questions that formed multi-item scales—except for operator involvement and schedule compliance, which were measured by objective one-item questions. The responses to the perceptual questions were in scale score formats, with 1 = "strongly disagree" and 5 = "strongly agree." The answers to the two objective questions were expressed as percentages. All scale scores were obtained by taking the average of the items for a scale and then aggregating over all respondents from the same manufacturing plant. The measurements for the implementation level of JIT and TQM were in the form of a superscale obtained by taking the average of the scores of their respective subscales. Other items that were used to measure environmental and organizational contextual factors that may affect the level of TPM implementation are given in the article.

### Development

The items of the JIT, TQM, and employee involvement (EI) were based on existing scales. The items for the different TPM elements were selected from the World Class Manufacturing (WCM) Database (Flynn, Schroeder, and Sakakibara 1994, 1996) and fit well with the literature review.

### Sample

The data were collected as part of the WCM study. Two-thirds of the plants randomly selected within strata (country and industry) joined the study. These 97 plants included in this study belonged to three countries—Japan, Italy, and the United States—and three industries—electronics, machinery, and automobile. The article provides a summary of the respondents in Table 1, describing the profile of the plants with respect to the different organizational contextual variables used in the study. There were multiple respondents from each plant (i.e., 11 managers and 12 production workers in each plant).

### Reliability and Validity

Content validity was evaluated by the fit of the items for each construct fit with the existing TPM literature. Cronbach's coefficient alpha scores for each of the scales ranged from .76 to .90. When the scales were evaluated by the country where a plant is located, the alpha scores ranged from .72 to .96. Using factor analysis, the authors verified that each TPM scale contained only one dimension (e.g., an eigenvalue greater than 1.0 for only one factor) and the loadings of each item on the scales were all greater than .59. In addition, the results from the hypothesis testing also provided some evidence of validity.

### Scores

The scores of the different scales are not reported in the article but a table of correlations is included in the article.

### Other Evidence

The scales for TPM, JIT, and TQM were also used in McKone, Schroeder, and Cua (2001). Plants located in Germany were also included in this study.

### Reference

Flynn, B. B., R. G. Schroeder, and S. Sakakibara. 1994. A framework for quality management research and an associated measurement instrument. *Journal of Operations Management* 11 (4): 339–66.

———. 1996. The relationship between quality management practices and performance: Synthesis of finding from the world class manufacturing project. In *Advances in the Management of Organizational Quality,* Vol. 1, eds. D. Fedor and S. Ghosh, 141–86. Greenwich, CT: JAI Press.

McKone, K. E., R. G. Schroeder, and K. O. Cua. 2001. The impact of total productive maintenance practices on manufacturing performance. *Journal of Operations Management* 19 (1): 39–58.

Nakajima, S. 1988. *Introduction to TPM.* Cambridge, MA: Productivity Press.

Sakakibara, S., B. B. Flynn, and R. G. Schroeder. 1993. A framework and measurement instrument for just-in-time manufacturing, *Production and Operations Management* 2 (3): 177–94.

Sakakibara, S., B. B. Flynn, R. G. Schroeder, and W. T. Morris. 1997. The impact of just-in-time manufacturing and its infrastructure on manufacturing performance. *Management Science* 43 (9): 1246–57.

Suzuki, T. 1992. *New Directions for TPM. Cambridge, MA:* Productivity Press.

Tajiri, M., and F. Gotoh. 1992. *TPM implementation: A Japanese approach.* New York: McGraw-Hill.

## Mehra and Inman

### Article Summarized

Mehra, Satish, and R. Anthony Inman. 1992. Determining the critical elements of just-in-time implementation. *Decision Sciences* 23 (1): 160–74.

### Scales (Actual Questions Used)

*Critical Elements of JIT Implementation*

Management Commitment

1. During the implementation process, did your company have or use a formal means whereby top management listens to operator suggestions?
2. During the implementation process, did top management investigate operator suggestions and implement those of merit?
3. During the implementation process, did your company have or use production employees with the authority to halt the production process (stop the line)?
4. During the implementation process, did your company have or use QC circles in progress?

JIT Production Strategy

5. By what percentage has "in-house" setup time been reduced?
6. Made "in-house" products have had their lot sizes reduced by an average of approximately what percentage?
7. During the implementation process, did your company make any alteration of plant layout?

8. During the implementation process, did your company make an effort to identify the "sameness" of parts, equipment, or processes?
9. What percentage of your goods are manufactured in a cellular type production equipment layout?
10. What percentage of your production employees were "cross-trained" as part of JIT implementation?
11. During the implementation process, did your company have or use machine operators who performed preventive maintenance on their own machines?
12. During the implementation process, did your company have or use time scheduled each day for checking and maintenance for *all* machines.

JIT Vendor Strategy

13. By what approximate percentage have purchased products had their lot sizes reduced?
14. What percentage of your purchased items are "sole sourced"?
15. Overall, vendor lead time has been reduced by what percentage?
16. What percentage of your suppliers use SPC?
17. What percentage of your suppliers have made a delivery commitment?
18. What percentage of you suppliers have a quality assurance plan (set procedures written down)?
19. What percentage of your suppliers were part of a formal education program on your part?

JIT Education Strategy

20. During the implementation process, did your company have or use a pilot project?
21. During the implementation process, did your company have or use a formal "JIT team"?
22. During the implementation process, did top management participate in the education process?
23. During the implementation process, did your company have or use outside consultants to introduce JIT implementation?
24. During the implementation process, did your company have or use a project leader or someone who championed the cause of JIT within your company?
25. During the implementation process, did your company make a formal presentation of the objectives of your company's JIT program to the employees?

*Level of Success Criteria*

Inventory Elements

26. What percentage decrease in total inventory resulted?
27. What percentage increase in inventory turns resulted?
28. Approximately, what percentage workspace reduction resulted?
29. What percentage decrease in scrap and rework resulted?

Utilization Elements

30. By what extent did equipment utilization increase (percentage)?
31. To what extent did labor utilization increase (percentage)?
32. What percentage decrease in downtime resulted from JIT implementation?

## Construct Description

The authors presented a battery of items to identify the elements of a successful just-in-time (JIT) implementation. Four factors were proposed to be crucial components: (1) management commitment, (2) JIT production strategy, (3) JIT vendor strategy, and (4) JIT education strategy. Each of the four factors was composed of relevant implementation elements. For instance, JIT production strategy was the group of implementation elements that were directly related to the production area or the transformation process. To judge the level of JIT implementation of success, seven criteria had been selected: downtime reduction, inventory reduction, workspace reduction, increased quality, labor utilization, equipment utilization, and increased inventory turns. These seven criteria were further grouped into two factors: inventory elements and utilization elements.

### Measurement Description

Nineteen items were chosen to measure the JIT implementation. The measures were typically based on answers to a single question. The exceptions were three multi-item scales: (1) group technology, (2) preventive maintenance, and (3) quality certification of suppliers. For these three constructs, the indicator variables were summed and divided by the number of questions to reach a value for the overall item. In addition, seven items were used to assess the level of success criteria, with four indicating inventory elements and three indicating utilization elements.

### Development

The item generation was grounded in an extensive literature review and with structured interviews with five managers directly responsible for implementing JIT within their respective firms. The item makeup of each construct was hypothesized and tested through factor analysis. Some items did not load as hypothesized on the intended factor; hence, refinements were made according to the results. Factor scales were constructed for each of the revised factors representing the elements of JIT implementation. Regression was used to weigh each variable proportional to the strength of its relationship to the common factor.

### Sample

Questionnaires were mailed to 550 manufacturing firms known, through the JIT literature, to be using JIT or believed to be a JIT user because of their affiliation with other JIT users. This sample consisted of many different types of manufacturing firms throughout the United States, who had large ranges in size and differing classes of products manufactured. Of the 550 questionnaires mailed, 42 were returned as undeliverable, and a total of 114 usable questionnaires were obtained for the analyses. The response rate was 22.44%.

### Reliability and Validity

Face validity of the questionnaire was indicated by querying five mangers directly responsible for implementing JIT within their respective firms. Each manager reviewed the proposed questionnaire to clarify any confusing terms or concepts, identify any irrelevant questions, and determine if they could disclose all the information requested. Reliability coefficients for the implementation factors and the criteria for judging level of success factor scores were calculated. The coefficient values ranged from .71 to .87.

### Scores

Scores are reported in Tables 5–7 in the article.

### Other Evidence

The level of success scales was also used to compare JIT success with financial success in Inman and Mehra (1993). Acceptable Spearman-Brown reliability coefficients—a special case of Cronbach's coefficient alpha—were reported for each implementation and level of success factor.

### Reference

Inman, R. A., and S. Mehra. 1993. Financial justification of JIT implementation. *International Journal of Operations and Production Management* 13 (4): 32–39.

# Melnyk, Sroufe, and Calantone

### Article Summarized

Melnyk, Steven A., Robert P. Sroufe, and Roger Calantone. 2003. Assessing the impact of environmental management systems on corporate and environmental performance. *Journal of Operations Management* 21 (3): 329–51.

### Scales (Actual Questions Used)

1. Total annual sales of your "company": ($000) __________
2. Is your company ☐ publicly traded ☐ privately owned?
3. What is the status of the following developments in your company? ISO 14000
4. If your company does have a formal environmental management system in place, how long has that system been in place? ______________ years

Environmental activities within your firm have

5. Significantly reduced overall costs
6. Significantly reduced lead times
7. Significantly improved product quality
8. Significantly improved its position in the market place
9. Helped enhance the reputation of your company
10. Helped your company design/develop better products
11. Significantly reduced waste within the production process
12. Significantly reduced waste within the equipment selection process
13. Had benefits that have definitely outweighed any cost incurred
14. Improved its chances of successfully selling its products in international markets

To what extent are the following options considered within your company?

15. *Production design:* redesigning the product to eliminate any potential environmental problems (manufacturing or recycling)
16. *Process design:* redesigning the process to eliminate any potential environmental problems
17. *Disassembly:* redesigning the product or process so as to simplify disassembly and disposal at the end of the product's useful life
18. *Substitution:* replacing a material that can cause environmental problems with another material that is not problematic
19. *Reduce:* reducing the level of material and/or components (which are contributing to environmental problems) within products
20. *Recycling:* making more use of recycled components or making a product that is more easily/readily recycled
21. *Rebuilding:* rebuilding a product where some of the parts or components are recovered while others are replaced
22. *Remanufacturing:* like rebuilding except that none of the parts are reduced to raw materials
23. *Consume internally:* consuming waste internally (e.g., wood pallets used in shipping or product storage used to generate electrical power in a cogeneration facility)
24. *Prolonging use:* reducing environmental problems by increasing the overall life of the product (e.g., engines that now last longer before having to be replaced or rebuilt)
25. *Returnable packaging:* using packaging and pallets that can be returned after they are finished being used

26. *Spreading risks:* shifting responsibilities for environmental problems to a third party or expert better able to deal with issues
27. *Creating a market for waste products:* treating waste as an input to another product that can be made and sold at profit
28. *Waste segregation:* an intermediate action in which waste steams are separated from each other into their individual components before being recycled, reused, or consumed internally
29. *Relocation:* changing the location of a process or plant to take advantage of more favorable environmental regulations and conditions
30. *Alliances:* working with either suppliers or customers to address environmental problems and/or issues

### Construct Description

The study did not have multi-item constructs. It used single item metrics, which were defined in the scales section above.

### Measurement Description

The survey instrument was extensive, with five major sections as next described by the authors:

> "The first section gathered information about the respondent, their position, professional affiliations (if any), and extent of involvement in various corporate initiatives. The second section focused on the business unit (the basic unit of analysis). This included products manufactured, extent of uncertainty facing the business unit and its personnel, and the status of various initiatives. Section three dealt with the impact of the ISO/QS 9000 certification process on the business unit and its competitive position in the market place. In Section four, the respondent was asked to evaluate a series of questions pertaining to ISO 14001. These questions assessed the respondent's level of knowledge of the ISO 14001 certification process, as well as the factors affecting its implementation and use. The fifth and final section gathered information about the business unit's environmental management system, the effectiveness and efficiency of this system, and the types of options used to improve environmental performance." (p. 335)

### Development

The main purpose of the study was to evaluate (1) the influence of having a formal environmental management system (EMS) on both operations and environmental options, (2) the benefits of having a formal and certified EMS, and (3) the relative effects of having a formal and certified EMS compared with a formal but uncertified EMS.

"While the development of EMS research is new, an exploratory approach to the selection of variables was not used. Instead, identification of the variables was based on the literature (Cascio, 1996; Tibor and Feldman, 1996), discussion with practitioners, the experiences of the researchers, and a confirmatory factor analysis [CFA] with coefficient alphas > 0.7. For the independent variables, four were selected and/or developed, where each corresponded to one of the four constructs discussed previously" (p. 337).

A four-stage process was used to analyze the data gathered. First, the normality of the data is checked using the Shapiro-Wilk test (D'Agostino, Balanger, and D'Agostino 1990). Second, consistency of data with the assumptions of ordinary least squares (OLS) procedure for regression analysis was determined. Third, ANOVA was used to analyze the effects of variables. Finally, regression models were tested based on the results of ANOVA using the guidelines in Berk (1990).

### Sample

Mailing lists were taken from the National Association of Purchasing Managers (NAPM), the American Production and Inventory Control Society (APICS), and one anonymous group. Using Dillman's (1978) method, surveys were sent. The response rate was 10.35%, and the number of usable responses was

1,510. Data were collected from the following industries: industrial and commercial machinery and computer equipment, transportation equipment, electronic and other electrical equipment and components except computer equipment, fabricated metal products, except machinery and transportation equipment and measuring, analyzing, and controlling instruments such as optical goods or watches. "To ensure whether the surveys went only to manufacturing firms or not, the respondents were asked to list main products produced in their plants. 89.2% (1347) of the responses came from the targeted U.S. department of Commerce Standard Industrial Classification (SIC) codes, 7.3% (110) came from industries out of the targeted SIC codes and the remaining did not identify their industries" (p. 336).

### Validity and Reliability

Content validity was gauged primarily on the experience of the researchers, the literature, and practitioners. According to the authors, a number of safeguards were employed to ensure the psychometric properties of the variables. They stated:

> "First, the specific form we use sets conditions (i.e., strong situation specificity) very high so the ambiguity (which is the usual source of difficulty and confusion) is very low. Specificity of conditions leads to less confusion and higher accuracy of responses in complex assessment questions (Warshaw, 1980; Davis et al., 1989). Second, considerable time was spent in case studies, pilot tests (at two major corporations), and pretesting the survey during personal interviews with executives and experts to ensure that there was little or no ambiguity in the questions and their interpretation. These safeguards help support to the validity of our survey instrument and items." (p. 335)

There were no multi-item scales. No reliability results were reported.

### Scores

Full-factorial ANOVA results of performance variables are presented in Table 3 in the article. Regression results for performance variables are presented in Table 4. Table 5 summarizes the variables with significant findings.

### Other Evidence

Not available.

### References


Berk, R. A. 1990. A primer on robust regression. In *Modern methods of data analysis,* eds. J. Fox and J. S. Long, 292–324. Newbury Park, CA: Sage.

Cascio, J. 1996. *The ISO 14001 handbook.* Fairfax, VA: CEEM Information Systems.

D'Agostino, R. B., A. Balanger, and R. B. D'Agostino Jr. 1990. A suggestion for using powerful and informative tests of normality. *American Statistician* 44 (4): 316–21.

Davis, F., R. Bagozzi, and P. Warshaw. 1989. User acceptance of computer technology. *Management Science* 35 (8): 982–1003.

Dillman, D. A. 1978. *Mail and telephone surveys: The total design method.* New York: Wiley.

Tibor, T., and I. Feldman. 1996. *ISO 14001: A guide to the new environmental management standards.* Burr Ridge, IL: Irwin.

Warshaw, P. 1980. Predicting purchase and other behaviors from general and contextual specific intentions. *Journal of Marketing Research* 17 (3): 26–33.

# Menda and Dilts

### Article Summarized

Menda, Rafael, and David Dilts. 1997. The manufacturing strategy formulation process: Linking multifunctional viewpoints. *Journal of Operations Management* 15 (4): 223–41.

### Scales (Actual Questions Used)

*Candidate Order-Winning Criteria*

Participants were asked to assign a percentage value (0 to 100) to each criterion based on its importance relative to other criteria.

1. Price
2. Quality conformance
3. Delivery speed
4. Delivery reliability
5. Product range
6. Volume flexibility
7. Product mix flexibility
8. Changeover flexibility
9. Routing flexibility
10. Design flexibility
11. Employee relations
12. Inventory turnover
13. Innovativeness
14. Product performance
15. After-sales service
16. Advertising
17. Broad distribution
18. New product lead time to market
19. Customer service
20. Return on investment
21. Design capability
22. Existing/preferred supplier; corporate reputation
23. Technical support
24. Unique/value-added features and services
25. Package leadership

### Construct Description

Eight order-winning criteria were used in the survey and are based on the definitions provided in the article (pp. 231–32). According to the authors, price was given "as competing on the basis of low selling price." Delivery speed was described "as delivering faster than competitors." Delivery reliability connoted "meeting delivery due dates consistently." Unique/value-added features and services indicated the "product's differentiation attributes, providing trade and consumer support services." Lead time to market was explained "as getting to market with new products and line extensions faster than competitors." Preferred-supplier status and corporate reputation was expressed as "exploitation of the existing positive relations with trade customers." Product range was described "as offering a wide range of product variations within each brand." Package leadership was presented "as reliance on innovative packaging as a selling feature."

### Measurement Description

None.

### Development

The first list of potential order-winning criteria was developed by conducting literature research (Hayes and Wheelwright 1984, Hill 1994, Skinner 1985, among others). "The list was then evaluated for applicability to Rumack's [i.e. the firms] situation; a subset of relevant criteria was extracted . . . Following discussions, the group arrived at a consensus on the final list of eight characteristics to be used in the survey" (p. 231).

### Sample

This study was based on a single case at an operating unit of a large multinational corporation based in North American, which marketed over-the-counter pharmaceuticals. "In total, twenty-eight individual interviews and group meetings were conducted, involving sixteen senior managers from seven functional areas in the firm. Information gathered during the focused interviews was recorded in survey forms; comments during the open-ended interviews and group discussions, and their results were recorded in point form" (p. 228).

### Validity and Reliability

Not available.

### Scores

Scores are presented in Table 4 and Figure 5 in the article.

### Other Evidence

Not available.

### References

Hayes, R. H., and S. C. Wheelwright. 1984. *Restoring our competitive edge.* New York: Wiley.
Hill, T. J. 1994. *Manufacturing strategy: Text and cases.* 2nd ed. Homewood, IL: Irwin.
Skinner, W. 1985. *Manufacturing: The formidable competitive weapon.* New York: Wiley.

---

## Menor, Roth, and Mason

### Article Summarized

Menor, Larry J., Aleda V. Roth, and Charlotte H. Mason. 2001. Agility in retail banking: A numerical taxonomy of strategic service groups. *Manufacturing & Service Operations Management* 3 (4): 273–92.

### Scales (Actual Questions Used)

*Relative Performance Dimensions of Competitive Capabilities*

Service Quality

1. Courteous services
2. Consistency (reliability)
3. Customer perceived quality

4. Accurate information (credibility)
5. Empathy
6. Timely information (customer responsiveness)
7. Conformance

Delivery

8. Delivery speed (wait times)
9. Convenient services (access)
10. On-time delivery
11. Handling customer complaints

Flexibility

12. System responsiveness
13. New product introduction speed
14. Rapid staffing changes
15. Customization

*Nonfinancial Business Performance*

Business Sustainability

16. Gross chargeoffs/loans ratio
17. Reserve/loans ratio

Quality of Customer Interface

18. Responsiveness to customer inquiries
19. Accuracy of account statements
20. Overall customer requirements
21. Meet customer service levels
22. Timeliness of mailing account statements
23. Account turnover rate performance
24. Customer complaint volume
25. Processing errors/exception performance
26. Overall system response time

Factor Performance

27. Back office labor productivity
28. Front office labor productivity
29. Overall reliability of delivery systems
30. Cost effective backroom technology innovations
31. Online systems availability
32. Adherence to budgets/plans
33. Transaction processing costs

*Resource Competencies*

Employee Knowledge

34. Employee understanding of goals/strategy
35. Superior customer information support services
36. Enhanced employee skills and knowledge (competence)

Market Acuity

37. Implementing and managing sales concept
38. Cross-selling products

39. Understanding markets/competition
40. Enlarging range of relationships
41. Offering a broad line of financial products
42. Understanding customer requirements

*Heskett, Sasser, and Hart (1990) Attributes*

Relative Characteristics of Primary Retail Banking Offerings

| | | |
|---|---|---|
| 43. Standardized | 1 2 3 4 5 6 7 | Personalized/customized |
| 44. Self-service channels | 1 2 3 4 5 6 7 | Full-service (broad mix of delivery channels) |
| 45. Slow response | 1 2 3 4 5 6 7 | Rapid response |
| 46. Premium price | 1 2 3 4 5 6 7 | Low price |

Relative Characteristics of Retail Delivery System, Policies, and Processes

47. Relatively high emphasis on cost control/productivity 1 2 3 4 5 6 7 Relatively high emphasis on service quality.

*Long-Term/Short-Term Strategic Orientation*

48. What is the *current balance* between short-term and long-term thinking (5 to 10 years) for your retail banking unit?
49. To what degree are strategic resource commitments maintained despite short-term performance shortfalls?

**Construct Description**

The purpose of this article was to operationalize the construct of operational agility in services and to test specific hypotheses about the factors related to it. Building on theory and practice, the authors described operations agility as "the ability to excel simultaneously on operations capabilities of quality, delivery, flexibility, and cost in a coordinated fashion" (p. 273). Besides operational agility, the constructs found in this research fall into six categories developed by Roth (1993): (1) relative dimensions of competitive capabilities in services, including service quality, delivery, flexibility and cost; (2) nonfinancial business performance measures covering business sustainability, quality of customer interface, and factor productivity; (3) financial measures on return on assets (ROA) and change in ROA; (4) resource competencies capturing first-order variables for employee knowledge, technological leadership, and market acuity; (5) Heskett et al.'s (1990) attributes, including characteristics of the bank's product offerings and the retail delivery system, policies and processes; and (6) strategic orientation.

**Measurement Description**

The measures of operational agility are rooted in the theory-based literature and observations in practice. For example, the theoretical grounding for operational agility is found in Roth's competitive progression theory (1996), which counters the traditional operations logic of trading off one capability for another. The article also employed the resource-based view (RBV) in that "generic resource competencies of technology, people, and market acuity" (p. 288) will differ for agile operations versus those those trade-off capabilities. The authors note, "Operationally agile banks apparently take a more holistic approach, with more highly integrated, cross-functional strategies. While higher investments in technology and capacity were typically associated with operational agility, perhaps even more striking was the agile group's attention to understanding their customers and competitors and to cultivating a skilled and knowledgeable workforce" (p. 288). They also indicate that agility can in part be explained by the laws of requisite variety. Moreover, the authors indicated that the 2000 Malcolm Balridge National Quality Award Criteria for Performance Excellence (NIST) referenced agility as an important performance criterion for practice. Most of the perceptual multi-item measures were captured on Likert-type scales.

## Development

The authors used the "data from the Survey of Retail Banking Strategy and Performance (SRBSP), administrated biennially by the Bank Administration Institute (BAI) from 1987 to 1992. This mail survey was specifically designed to gather data on operations strategy and performance with refinements over time to improve construct validity and reliability of measures (Roth, 1993; Roth and Jackson, 1995; Roth and van der Velde, 1991, 1992)" (p. 278).

## Sample

The sampling frame comprised U.S. banks developed for the *Survey of Retail Banks and Performance* in conjunction with the Bank Administration Institute. "Data from executive teams representing 140 retail-banking units (RBU) in 1992 were used for our analyses. The RBU represents the highest point in the firm where strategic retail delivery system decisions are made. Almost three-quarters of the RBUs in our study were individual banks; the remainder were primarily 'holding companies' or divisions" (p. 278). The sample was biased to larger banks that were market leaders. Because of missing data, two banks were eliminated for the purposes of this analysis, leaving 38 RBUs. Care was taken to seek the most knowledgeable individuals who understood the bank's strategies and were able to gauge performance. Appendix A in the article provides descriptive statistics on the study participants and the sample database.

## Reliability and Validity

The psychometric properties of the multi-item measurement scales used in this study were developed and refined in prior related research over an extended time period, from 1987 to 1992. The survey instrument and measures were shown to be reliable and valid; however, to evaluate predictive validity, archival performance data was collected from a secondary source—Sheshunoff Information Services' *Bank Quarterly Ratings and Analysis*. For this study, longitudinal data were taken at the time of the survey and 2 years later. Discriminant validity for the strategic groups that were obtained from cluster analyses was provided in the article, and multiple criteria for assessment were applied, including a jackknife cross-validation procedure.

## Scores

Scores are presented in Tables 1–6 in the article. Appendix B contains detailed listings of the individual items, the measurement scales used, and the multi-item indices of the theoretically important constructs. It also contains evidence for measurement scale reliabilities and correlations among the constructs.

## Other Evidence

Not available.

## References

Heskett, J. L., W. E. Sasser, and C. W. Hart. 1990. *Service breakthroughs.* New York: Free Press.

Roth, A. V. 1993. Performance dimensions in services: An empirical investigation of strategic performance. In *Services quality:* Vol. 2, *Advances in services marketing and management,* eds. T. A. Swartz, D. E. Bowen, and S. W. Brown, 1–47. Greenwich, CT: JAI Press.

———. 1996. Neo-operations strategy: linking capabilities-based competition to technology. In *The handbook of technology management,* eds. G. H. Gaynor, 38.1–38.44. New York: McGraw-Hill.

Roth, A. V., and W. J. Jackson. 1995. Strategic determinants of service quality and performance: Evidence from the banking industry. *Management Science* 41 (11): 1720–33.

Roth, A. V., and M. van der Velde. 1991. Operations as marketing: A competitive service strategy. *Journal of Operations Management* 10 (3): 303–28.

———. 1992. *World class banking: Benchmarking the strategies of the retail leaders.* Chicago, IL: Bank Administration Institute.

# Monczka, Petersen, Handfield, and Ragatz

## Article Summarized

Monczka, Robert M., Kenneth J. Petersen, Robert B. Handfield, and Gary L. Ragatz. 1998. Success factors in strategic supplier alliances: The buying company perspective. *Decision Sciences* 29 (3): 553–77.

## Scales (Actual Questions Used)

*Indicators of Success*

Past Success

1. In this strategic supplier alliance/partnership relationship, the parties work together to solve problems.
2. This strategic supplier is flexible in response to requests we make.
3. This strategic supplier makes an effort to help us during emergencies.
4. When an agreement is made, we can always rely on the strategic supplier to fulfill the requirements.
5. Please indicate the overall degrees of results satisfaction with your most/least successful strategic supplier alliance/partnership.

Success Difference

6. Please indicate your degree of satisfaction with this strategic supplier alliance/partnership.
7. What is your business unit's overall degree of satisfaction with strategic supplier alliances/partnerships?

*Attributes of the Alliance*

Trust

8. We trust that our strategic supplier alliance/partnership will be beneficial to our business unit.
9. We do not get an equitable deal from our strategic supplier in this alliance (reversed scored).
10. This strategic supplier alliance/partnership is marked by a high degree of harmony.

Coordination

11. Please rate the business unit's most and least successful strategic supplier alliance/partnership in terms of coordination with your strategic supplier.

Commitment

12. Time commitment of your business unit's key personnel
13. Supplier training
14. Capital investment in the supplier
15. Direct dollar investment in the supplier

Interdependence

16. It would be very easy to terminate these most or least successful strategic supplier alliance/partnerships and establish another strategic supplier.
17. The time to establish another strategic supplier alliance/partnership for this commodity/purchase family would be extremely long.
18. The cost to establish another strategic supplier alliance/partnership for this commodity/purchase family would be extremely high.

*Communication Behavior*

Information Quality

19. Timely
20. Accurate

21. Adequate
22. Complete
23. Credible

Information Participation

24. We actively seek advice, counsel, and information from our strategic supplier alliance/partnership.
25. The strategic supplier participates in our planning and goal-setting activities.
26. We participate in our strategic supplier's planning and goal-setting activities that are relevant to this strategic supplier alliance/partnership.
27. We actively encourage improvement suggestions from this strategic supplier.
28. We take timely action on this strategic supplier's suggestion(s) for this alliance/partnership.

Information Sharing

29. We share our business unit's proprietary information with this strategic supplier for this strategic supplier alliance/partnership.
30. Our strategic supplier shares proprietary information with us.
31. We inform this strategic supplier in advance of changing needs.
32. In this relationship, it is expected that any information that might help the other party will be provided.
33. The parties are expected to keep each other informed about events or changes that may affect the other party.
34. It is expected that the parties will only provide information according to prespecified agreements (reverse coded).
35. This strategic supplier keeps us fully informed about issues that affect our business.

*Conflict Resolution Techniques*

36. Smooth over the problem
37. Persuasive attempts by either party
38. Joint problem solving
39. Harsh words
40. Outside arbitration

*Commodity/Supplier Selection Process*

41. How comprehensive is your business unit's process to select commodities/purchase items as candidates for strategic supplier alliances/partnerships compared with what you may consider best practice?
42. How comprehensive is your business unit's strategic supplier assessment and selection process compared with what you consider best practice?

**Construct Description**

The authors stated that they built the definition of strategic supplier alliance "on a comparison of both theoretical and managerial descriptions" (p. 553). From the theoretical standpoint, this concept followed the framework of alliance proposed by Yoshina and Rangan (1995). The final working definition was further developed based on the responses from managers in 77 firms. According to their opinion, strategic supplier alliances were defined as "long-term, cooperative relationships designed to leverage the strategic and operational capabilities of individual participating companies to achieve significant ongoing benefits to each party. These alliances continue as long as significant value accrues to both parties. Among the primary benefits of such relationships are enhanced supply chain synchronization, total cost reduction, improved quality and cycle time, and a strengthened overall competitive position, which exceeds the contributions possible from other traditional relationships" (pp. 555–56).

The authors examined four major dimensions of the strategic supplier alliance in the study: "attributes of the alliance, communication behavior, conflict resolution techniques, and commodity/supplier selection process" (p. 557). Attributes of the alliance were described by three constructs: (1) commitment,

(2) trust and coordination, and (3) interdependence. Commitment referred to "the willingness of buyers and suppliers to exert effort on behalf of the relationship" (p. 557). Interdependence measured "the extent to which one actor controls all of the conditions necessary for achievement of an action or a desired outcome" (p. 558).

The construct of communication behavior was based on literature such as Mohr and Nevin (1990). Three communication behaviors were considered: information sharing, information quality, and information participation. Information sharing referred "to the extent to which critical and proprietary information is communicated to one's supply chain partner." Information quality included "such aspects as the accuracy, timeliness, adequacy, and credibility of information exchanged." Information participation referred "to the extent to which partners engage jointly in planning and goal setting" (p. 559).

The construct of conflict resolution was based on literature such as Patterson and Handfield (1996). It measured conflict resolution orientations and constructive conflict resolution techniques applied to resolve potential conflicts. The construct of commodity/supplier selection processes was based on literature such as Monczka and Trent (1995). It measured how formal the commodity selection process and the supplier selection processes were.

### Measurement Description

Measurement scales for all the constructs except one are shown in the scales section above. Besides the two perceptual measures listed above, objective measures of alliance performance was also "used to assess the extent to which each alliance was successful" (p. 561). In particular, the respondents were required to estimate the percentage improvements their company had achieved on several performance dimensions (purchased material price, purchased material quality, access to new technologies, NPD time, and order cycle time) "through each of the strategic alliances they were reporting on" (p. 561).

### Development

All the measures except the supplier and commodity selection processes were adapted from measures validated by Mohr and Spekman (1994). All these measures were taken from the perspective of the customer (buying company) in the alliance.

### Sample

"The data in this study were collected as part of a questionnaire focusing on strategic supplier alliances. Questionnaires were sent to 205 [Global Procurement and Supply Chain Electronic Benchmarking Network] GEBN member companies" (p. 560). Eighty-four of them responded with a response rate of 41% and 77 responses were usable. The companies "were located in the United States, Canada, Mexico, Western Europe, and Australia." The individual respondents "were procurement professionals who provided data on their companies' experience as a customer in strategic supplier alliance relationships with its suppliers." The authors asked each respondent to provide two independent observations, one about his or her company's most successful strategic alliance and the other about the least successful strategic alliance. The final sample size was 154 alliances.

### Reliability and Validity

Before the survey, all measures were thoroughly examined by a group of industry executives and subject-area experts to ensure face validity. "Principle components factor analysis [PCA] was applied to test the extent of convergence validity for the trust and coordination, interdependence, commitment, information quality and participation, and information sharing constructs" (p. 561). The resulting principle components factor loadings for these multi-item measures ranged from .52 to .91, with most of them over .70. Cronbach's coefficient alpha was used to evaluate the reliability of the scales. All the Cronbach's coefficient alpha values were higher than .70 and were regarded as sufficient for reliability.

Criterion validity was assessed by calculating the bivariate correlations between the two perceptual measures of success and the five objective measures of alliance performance (price, quality, cycle time, technology, and NPD time). All the correlations but one were statistically significant at the .10 level in the expected direction, thereby providing support for the criterion validity of the measures.

### Scores

The means, standard deviation, and correlation coefficients for each construct are presented in Table 3 in the article. Regression analysis was employed in this study. The regression coefficients for testing various hypotheses are reported in Table 7.

### Other Evidence

Not available.

### References

Mohr, J., and J. Nevin. 1990. Communication strategies in marketing channels: A theoretical perspective. *Journal of Marketing* 54 (4): 36–51.

Mohr, J., and E. Spekman. 1994. Characteristics of partnership success: Partnership attributes, communication behavior, and conflict resolution techniques. *Strategic Management Journal* 15 (2): 135–52.

Monczka, R., and R. Trent. 1995. *Purchasing and sourcing strategy: Trends and implications*. Tempe, AZ: NAPM/CAPS.

Patterson, J., and R. Handfield. 1996. Managing buyer-supplier conflict: A conceptual model. Working paper, Michigan State University, East Lansing, MI.

Yoshina, M., and S. Rangan. 1995. *Strategic alliance: An entrepreneurial approach to globalization*. Boston, MA: Harvard Business School Press.

## Morgan, Zou, Vorhies, and Katsikeas

### Article Summarized

Morgan, Neil A., Shaoming Zou, Douglas W. Vorhies, and Constantine S. Katsikeas. 2003. Experiential and informational knowledge, architectural marketing capabilities, and the adaptive performance of export ventures: A cross-national study. *Decision Sciences* 34 (2): 287–321.

### Scale (Actual Questions Used)

*Individual Experiential Knowledge*

1. Knowledge of export marketing personnel
2. Experience of our export marketing personnel
3. The skills of our export marketing people

*Venture Experiential Knowledge*

4. Company experience with operating in this export market
5. International orientation of our company's culture
6. Company's international experience

*Venture Market Information Knowledge*

7. Customer knowledge in this export market
8. Knowledge of competitors in this market

9. Information related to doing business in this market
10. Knowledge of distributors in this export market

*Marketing Planning Capabilities*

11. Export marketing planning skills
12. Setting clear export marketing goals
13. Formulating creative export marketing strategies
14. Thoroughness of export marketing planning process

*Marketing Implementation Capabilities*

15. Effectively translating planned export marketing strategies into action
16. Allocating appropriate resources to execute export marketing strategies
17. Monitoring the performance of export marketing strategies
18. Organizing to deliver planned export marketing strategies effectively

*Competitive Intensity*

19. Competition in this export market is cutthroat.
20. There are many "promotion" wars in this export market.
21. Price competition is a hallmark of this export market.
22. One hears of a new competitive move in this market almost every day.

*Adaptive Performance*

23. Responding to competitors' product changes in this export market.
24. Time to market for new export venture products.
25. Number of successful new export venture products; revenue from new export venture.
26. Products (less than 3 years old).

## Construct Description

This research was based on the research in knowledge management (Brown and Duguid 1991; Nonaka 1994) and literature on export ventures (Ambler, Styles, and Xiucum 1999; Cavusgil and Zou 1994). Experiential knowledge was characterized as "knowledge concerning accumulated skills that require required tasks to be effectively and efficiently accomplished" (p. 291). Informational knowledge was given as "knowledge concerning data that have been organized to give meaning, experience related to performing exporting activities and the venture's foreign market context" (p. 291). Marketing planning capability was expressed as "the processes used to orchestrate the integration of the venture's specialized marketing capabilities (such as product development, advertising, channel management, etc.), and the combinations of resources (e.g., brand equity, channel relationships, etc.) they are designed to leverage, in ways that optimize venture goal achievement" (p. 295).

Market implementation capability was defined as "the routines by which export ventures transform intended export marketing strategy into realized actions and resource deployments" (p. 295).

## Measurement Description

The authors used 7-point scales to measure the items.

## Development

This study developed a framework for export venture knowledge management by examining the relationship between different types of individual and organizational level knowledge relevant to the market environment, the firm's organizational capabilities, and its adaptive performance.

### Sample

The sample for this data came from two countries: the United Kingdom and China. The data for the United Kingdom sample were obtained by random selection of publicly available sources such as Dun and Bradstreet directories, and responses were obtained from 567 firms. The Chinese sample consisted of firms from the Jiangsu province, which is one of the major exporting provinces of China. Two hundred and twenty-three firms agreed to participate. The final responses consisted of 243 companies in the United Kingdom (43% response) and 198 from China (88% response). Some surveys were dropped because of inadequate self-reported knowledge of the respondent of the export market, which reduced the final sample to 287 in the United Kingdom and 173 in China.

### Validity and Reliability

The authors reported the composite reliability of each scale for both Chinese and UK samples (Fornell and Larcker 1981). Discriminant validity was examined by looking at average variance extracted (AVE) for each of the constructs. These results are reported in Table 2 of the article.

### Scores

The statistics from the confirmatory factor analyses (CFA) output are presented in Table 1, and the descriptive statistics are presented in Table 2. The structural model is shown in Figures 3 and 4.

### Other Evidence

Not available.

### References

Ambler, T., C. Styles, and W. Xiucum. 1999. The effect of channel relationships and guanxi on the performance of interprovince export ventures in the People's Republic of China. *International Journal of Research in Marketing* 16 (1): 75–87.

Brown, J. S., and P. Duguid. 1991. Organizational learning and communities-of-practice: Toward a unified view of working, learning, and innovation. *Organization Science* 2 (1): 40–57.

Cavusgil, S. T., and S. Zou. 1994. Marketing strategy-performance relationship: An investigation of the empirical link in export market ventures. *Journal of Marketing* 58 (1): 1–21.

Fornell, C., and C. Larcker. 1981. Structural equation models with unobservable variables and measurement error: Algebra and statistics. *Journal of Marketing Research* 18 (3): 382–88.

Nonaka, I. 1994. A dynamic theory of organizational knowledge creation. *Organization Science* 5 (1): 14–37.

## Morita and Flynn

### Article Summarized

Morita, Michiya, and E. James Flynn. 1997. The linkage among management systems, practices and behaviour in successful manufacturing strategy. *International Journal of Operations and Productions Management* 17 (10): 967–93.

### Scales (Actual Questions Used)

*Working on the Floor*

1. Documentation of shop-floor procedures
2. Supervisory interaction facilitation

3. Employee suggestion
4. Shop-floor contact
5. Small group problem solving

*Management Practices*

6. Functional integration
7. Coordination with corporation
8. Dynamic performance measures
9. Coordination of decision making
10. Performance feedback
11. Pride in work (single scale)
12. Commitment (single scale)

*Human Resource Development*

13. Manufacturing/HR fit
14. Multifunctional employee
15. Recruiting and selection
16. Task-related training for employee
17. Compensation for breadth of skills

*Operational System for Quality*

18. Continuous improvement
19. Customer satisfaction
20. Feedback
21. (Statistical) process control
22. Rewards for quality
23. Cleanliness and organization

*Organizational System for Quality*

24. Supplier quality involvement
25. Customer involvement
26. Top management leadership for quality
27. Internal quality information
28. External information: supplier quality control

*Production Control System*

29. Manufacturing plans
30. Rewards and manufacturing coordination
31. Accounting
32. Benefits of IS
33. Stability/predictability of short-term production
34. Daily schedule adherence
35. Repetitive nature of master schedule
36. Maintenance

*Production System: JIT Orientation*

37. Equipment layout
38. JIT delivery by suppliers
39. Kanban

40. Setup time reduction
41. Small lot size
42. JIT link with customers

*Technological Adaptation*

43. Interfunctional efforts
44. Product design simplicity
45. Effective process implementation
46. Anticipation of new technologies
47. Proprietary equipment

*Strategic Adaptation*

48. Manufacturing strategy strength
49. Manufacturing-business strategy linkage
50. Product competitive performance comparison
51. Formal strategic planning
52. Communication of manufacturing strategy

**Construct Description**

In this study, the authors followed "the definition of manufacturing strategy synthesized by Voss (1995) and Voss and Winch (1996)" (p. 968) and the initial definitions of world-class manufacturing by Hill (1993) and Schonberg (1986). A total of 11 characteristics comprising the management practices and systems as well as managerial characteristics and behavior of the firms were identified during the study as the drivers of factory management and operations.

The constructs and their definitions are as follows. Strategic adaptation was defined as the "planning and implementation of manufacturing strategy" (p. 972). It involved linkages "with business strategy and organizational commitment to strategy" (p. 972). Technological adaptation was characterized as the "adaptive behavior to technological progress and opportunities" (p. 972). Management practices were defined as the "front line and middle managers' activities" (p. 972). It involved organizational goal congruence and cooperative behavior to achieve goals.

Production system connoted the "physical production system and operations" (p. 972). Production control system was described as the "production control of physical production activities" (p. 972). Organizational system for quality was defined as the "organizational support and environment for quality control activities" (p. 972).

Operational system for quality was presented as the "quality control activities on the floor" (p. 972).

Human resource development was defined as the "culture and system for human resource development" (p. 972). Commitment was treated as the "status of employee's minds toward organization" (p. 972). Pride in work signified the "employees' valuation of works" (p. 972). Working on the floor was defined as the "workers' behaviors on the working floor" (p. 972).

**Measurement Description**

Multiple respondents answered a total of 250 items grouped under 53 "multi-item scales measuring management practices, systems and behavior and competitive performance. Likert-type scales with 5 representing "strongest agreement" and 1 representing the "least agreement" were used for all scales except the performance scale, which quantified the manager's perception of the factory's performance relative to its industry" (p. 971), where 1 = "substantially worse" and 5 = "substantially better."

**Development**

Not available.

### Sample

Data were collected from 12 factories from the machinery industry, 12 from the electronics industry, 8 from the automobile industry, which collectively formed the world-class subgroup, and from 14 randomly selected factories. The factories chosen were Japanese for their higher levels of best practice management. An 80% response rate from the world-class subgroup and a 20% response rate from the randomly selected group were observed.

### Reliability and Validity

For reliability, the authors reported Cronbach's coefficient alpha with a minimum value of .50. Factor analysis was also used for the validity and reliability tests for the multi-item scales.

### Scores

The average values for the subgroups for the extent of their use of the 11 characteristics are listed in Table 3 in the article.

### Other Evidence

Not available.

### References

Hill, T. J. 1993. *Manufacturing strategy: The strategic management of the manufacturing function.* 2nd ed. London: Macmillan.

Schonberg, R. 1986. *World class manufacturing: The lessons of simplicity applied.* New York: Free Press.

Voss, C. A. 1995. Alternative paradigms for manufacturing strategy. *International Journal of Operations and Production Management* 15 (4): 5–16.

Voss, C. A., and G. Winch. 1996. Including engineering in operations strategy. *Production and Operations Management* 5 (1): 78–90.

# Nahm, Vonderembse, and Koufteros (2003)

## Article Summarized

Nahm, Abraham Y., Mark A. Vonderembse, and Xenophon A. Koufteros. 2003. The impact of organizational structure on time-based manufacturing and plant performance. *Journal of Operations Management* 21 (3): 281–306.

## Scales (Actual Questions Used)

*Locus of Decision Making*

1. Our work teams cannot take significant actions without supervisors' or middle managers' approval. (reverse coded)
2. Our workers have the authority to correct problems when they occur.
3. Our workers handle job-related problems themselves.
4. Our work teams have control over their job.
5. Our supervisors or middle managers are supportive of the decisions made by our work teams.
6. Our workers are encouraged to make suggestions to change current rules and procedures.
7. We encourage workers to be creative in dealing with problems at work.
8. Our workers are involved in writing policies and procedures.
9. Our workers are involved in developing standard methods.

*Nature of Formalization*

10. We have written rules and procedures that show how workers can make suggestions for changes.
11. We have written rules and procedures that describe how workers can make changes on their job.
12. We have written rules and procedures that show how workers can experiment with their job.
13. We have written rules and procedures that guide quality improvement efforts.
14. We have written rules and procedures that guide creative problem solving.

*Number of Layers in Hierarchy*

15. There are many management layers between plant operators and the CEO (more than six).
16. There are few layers in our organizational hierarchy.
17. We are a lean organization.
18. There are only few management layers between plant operators and the CEO.

*Level of Horizontal Integration*

19. Our tasks are done through cross-functional teams.
20. Our workers are assigned to work in cross-functional teams.
21. Our workers are trained to work in cross-functional teams.
22. Our workers are required to work in cross-functional teams.
23. Our managers are assigned to lead various cross-functional teams.
24. Our most important tasks are carried out by cross-functional teams.

*Level of Communication*

25. Lots of communications are carried out among managers.
26. Communications are easily carried out among workers.
27. Strategic decisions are quickly passed on to relevant work groups.
28. Communication between different levels in hierarchy is easy.
29. Workers can easily meet and communicate with upper management.

*Time-Based Manufacturing Practices*

30. Reengineering setups
31. Cellular manufacturing
32. Quality improvement efforts
33. Preventive maintenance
34. Dependable suppliers
35. Pull production

*Plant Performance*

36. Sales growth
37. Return on investment
38. Market share gain
39. Overall competitive position

## Construct Description

The following definitions of the organizational structure constructs were taken from Table 1 (p. 285) of the document. Nature of formalization was defined as "the degree to which workers are provided with rules and procedures that deprive versus encourage creative, autonomous work and learning" (p. 285). Number of layers in the hierarchy captured "the degree to which an organization has many versus few levels of management" (p. 285). Level of organizational integration signified "the degree to which departments and workers are functionally specialized versus integrated in their works, skills, and training" (p. 285). Locus of decision making indicated the "degree to which decisions are made high versus low in the organizational hierarchy" (p. 285). Level of communication was indicated as "the degree to which vertical and horizontal communications are slow, difficult, and limited versus fast, easy, and abundant" (p. 285). Last, time-based manufacturing practices were described as processes to compress time in order to achieve higher productivity, increased market share, and improved customer service.

## Measurement Description

Most of the items were measured on 5-point Likert scales. Time-based manufacturing was treated as a metaconstruct that consisted of six subscales. (1) Reengineering setups referred to the "extent to which efforts are taken to reduce setup time" (p. 288). (2) Cellular manufacturing was defined as "the extent to which units are produced in a product oriented layout" (p. 288). (3) The construct of quality improvement efforts corresponded to the "extent to which methods are developed and used to reduce defects and enhance quality" (p. 288). (4) Preventive maintenance indicated the "extent to which equipment is routinely maintained on a proactive basis" (p. 288). (5) Dependable suppliers referred to "the extent to which suppliers facilitate customer needs for service quality" (p. 288). (6) Pull production was explained as "the extent to which production is driven by demand from the next station and ultimately from customer" (p. 288). For more details on these measures, please refer to Koufteros, Vonderembse, and Doll (1998).

## Development

The authors developed the scales based on literature review, structured interviews, and Q-sorting. With a few exceptions, most of the items came from existing scales. The survey instrument was also first pretested by six academic experts and two industry experts and then evaluated in a pilot study with 40 responses collected from manufacturing executives/managers in different industries.

## Sample

The questionnaires were sent to 3,000 manufacturing companies in four industries: U.S. Department of Commerce, Standard Industrial Classification (SIC) codes 34 to 37, with the number of employees greater than 100. The mailing list was provided by the Society of Manufacturing Engineers (SME). A total of 224 questionnaires were returned. Most respondents in the sample had job tiles of president/CEO, vice president, director, and managers. Chi-square tests of homogeneity were performed to examine nonresponse bias in SIC code and firm size. The authors noted that when the target population (i.e., the 3,000 companies on the mailing list) was compared with the total responses (i.e., the 224 responding companies), "there was a bias involving SIC codes 34 and 35. Firms in SIC 34 responded at a higher rate than expected (110 responses received and 60 expected), and SIC 35 was significantly underrepresented (34 responses received and 56 expected)" (p. 292). The authors also reported that there was no bias in firm size.

**Reliability and Validity**

Reliability of the latent variables was evaluated by (1) calculating Cronbach's coefficient alpha using the data obtained from the pilot study and (2) computing composite reliability based on the confirmatory factor analysis (CFA) results from the large-scale data. According to the authors, composite reliabilities ranged from .84 for the locus of decision-making construct to .92 for the level of horizontal integration, which offered support for reliability.

The authors addressed the validity of the constructs by following a two-step approach. First, they randomly sampled 104 observations from the whole sample and conducted CFAs. Various fit indices including the nonnormed fit index (NNFI) and the comparative fit index (CFI) showed that the model fit was moderated. Based on the CFA results, they modified the measures and dropped seven problematic items. The authors asserted that the deletion of these items had minimal effect on content validity because the domains of the constructs were adequately covered by other items retained in the model. The resulting trimmed model fitted the data well, and the completely standardized coefficients were all large in magnitude and statistically significant ($p < .01$). Hence, convergent validity was supported. Discriminant validity was examined in three ways: (1) by counting the number of "violations"—that is, the "correlation of item to outer-scale items being higher than the minimum inner-scale item-to-item correlation" (p. 294); (2) by comparing the constrained model (where the correlation between two latent variables was fixed at 1) and the nonconstrained model (where the correlation was free) for each construct pair; and (3) by comparing the average variance extracted with the squared correlation between constructs. All three methods provided support for discriminant validity. In the second stage, the authors validated their results with the validation sample that consisted of 120 observations.

**Scores**

The scores are presented in Tables 2—6 in the article.

**Other Evidence**

The scales for time-based manufacturing practices were also used in Nahm, Vonderembse, and Koufteros (2004).

**Reference**

Koufteros, X. A., M. A. Vonderembse, and W. J. Doll. 1998. Developing measures of time-based manufacturing. *Journal of Operations Management* 16 (1): 21–41.

Nahm, A.Y., M. A.Vonderembse, and X. A. Koufteros. 2004. The impact of organizational culture on time-based manufacturing and performance. *Decision Sciences* 35 (4): 579–607.

# Nahm, Vonderembse, and Koufteros (2004)

### Article Summarized

Nahm, Abraham Y., Mark A. Vonderembse, and Xenophon A. Koufteros. 2004. The impact of organizational culture on time-based manufacturing and performance. *Decision Sciences* 35 (4): 579–607.

### Scales (Actual Questions Used)

*Customer Orientations*

1. We believe that managers should focus on finding customer wants and needs.
2. We believe that managers should focus on finding ways to satisfy our customers.
3. We believe that managers should focus on providing value to customers.
4. We believe that we should strive to get closer to our customers.

*Beliefs on Investing in Facilities and Equipment*

5. Through investments in facilities and equipment, we want to encourage our workers to work in innovative ways.
6. Through investments in facilities and equipment, we want to increase intellectual work among our workers.
7. Through investments in facilities and equipment, we want to increase creativity among our workers.
8. Through investments in facilities and equipment, we want to support product improvement efforts among our workers.

*Beliefs on Working with Others*

9. We believe that functional departments should work together as a team.
10. We believe that employees from one department should work with employees from other departments.
11. We believe employees should work together as a team.
12. We believe that workers should understand the nature of work in other departments.

*Beliefs on Making Decisions That Are Global*

13. We believe that departments should discuss important decisions with other departments.
14. We believe that departmental managers should make decisions that benefit the whole company.
15. We believe that when making decisions, the overall effects of a decision should be considered.
16. We believe that decisions should be based on overall company objectives.
17. We believe that we should be willing to make suboptimal decisions in local scale for maximum performance in global scale.
18. We believe that decision making should include input from many areas.

*Beliefs on Management Control*

19. We believe that managers should take tight control on their subordinates (reverse coded).
20. We believe that command and control are the best way to manage (reverse coded).
21. We believe that workers should simply follow the directions given by their managers (reverse coded).

*Beliefs on Integrating with Suppliers*

22. We believe that our suppliers can be part of our success in our business.
23. We believe that our suppliers are strategic partners in building up our competitive capabilities.

24. We believe that the best suppliers are the ones who enable us to provide value to customers.
25. We believe that suppliers should be involved in decision making about product design.

*Time-Based Manufacturing Practices*

26. Reengineering setups
27. Cellular manufacturing
28. Quality improvement efforts
29. Preventive maintenance
30. Pull production

*Performance*

31. Sales growth
32. Return on investment
33. Market share gain
34. Overall competitive position

## Construct Description

The authors provided descriptions of constructs as follows. Customer orientation was defined "as the degree to which a company focuses on getting closer to its customers to identify their desires to provide higher levels of quality of service and products" (p. 583). Beliefs on investing in facilities and equipment connoted the "degree to which the objective for investing in facilities and equipment is to leverage intellectual work and promote innovation and creativity" (p. 584). Beliefs on working with others indicated the "degree to which workers are expected to work together on integrative tasks" (p. 585). Beliefs on making decisions that are global signified the "degree to which decisions are expected to be made from an integrated perspective" (p. 585) Beliefs on management control characterized the "degree to which management tasks are expected to be carried out by collaboration and consensus" (p. 586). Beliefs on integrating with suppliers described the "degree to which the primary goal of supplier-relationship management is to achieve long-term strategic partnership for competitive advantage" (p. 586).

## Measurement Description

A large-scale survey was conducted to gather the data. Items were detailed in the appendix of the article. Items for customer orientation, beliefs (i.e., the espoused values), and time-based manufacturing practices were measured on a 5-point scale where 1 = "not at all" and 5 = "to a great extent." Time-based measurement items were based on Koufteros, Vonderembse, and Doll's (1998) study. Performance items were also measured on a 5-point scale where 1 = "unacceptable" and 5 = "superior." Respondents were asked to compare their own performance with that of all the competitors in their primary market segment.

## Development

A total of 37 items were generated for each construct after literature review and evaluated through structured interviews with managers from five manufacturing firms. The pretest was conducted using six academic and two industry experts. Pilot study was conducted using 40 responses from firms that belong to the same industries. Exploratory factor analysis (EFA) was conducted based on the data collected from the pilot study. After assessment, seven items were dropped. The resultant measurement model can be found in Table 1 in the article. Reliability was assessed by Cronbach's coefficient alpha. Detailed information about the pilot study and instrument evaluation were available on request to authors.

## Sample

A large-scale questionnaire was mailed to 3,000 manufacturing executives/managers, mainly from four industries with U.S. Department of Commerce, Standard Industrial Classification (SIC) codes

34 to 37. The mailing list was provided by the Society of Manufacturing Engineers (SME). Of the 224 responses included in the sample, 49% came from SIC code 34, 15% from SIC code 35, 17% from SIC code 36, 16% from SIC code 37; 2% were for other industries, and the remainder were not specified. Response/nonresponse bias was checked by the $\chi^2$ test with no evidence of bias in firm size. However, the authors noted the existence of nonresponse bias in SIC codes when they compared the target population with the responding companies.

### Reliability and Validity

CFA was performed using maximum likelihood estimation. The overall fit of the measurement model was assessed by comparative fit index (CFI) and nonnormed fit index (NNFI) with .94 and .93, respectively. The root mean residual (RMR) and root mean square error of approximation (RMSEA) were .05 and .053, respectively. Detailed information was shown in Table 1 of the article. Convergent validity was assessed by examining the significance of item loadings estimated in the CFA. According to Table 1, all the completely standardized coefficients had significant *t*-values at $p < .01$, which provided support for convergent validity. The discriminant validity was assessed by comparing the squared correlation of two constructs against their individual average variance extracted (AVE). The results showed that the highest squared correlation was lower than the respective AVEs, and therefore discriminant validity was demonstrated.

The construct reliability was examined by computing the composite reliabilities and the AVEs. The composite reliability estimates were all above .75, and the AVE estimates for each construct were greater than .5. Refer to Table 2 (p. 591) of the article for details. Thus, these scales were shown to be reliable.

### Scores

The factor loadings of the resultant measurement model are shown in Table 1 of the article. All the loadings were greater than .54, with most of the loadings greater than .7.

### Other Evidence

Not available.

### Reference

Koufteros, X. A., M. A. Vonderembse, and W. J. Doll. 1998. Developing measures of time-based manufacturing. *Journal of Operations Management* 16 (1): 21–41.

## Narasimhan, Jayaram, and Carter

### Article Summarized

Narasimhan, Ram, Jayanth Jayaram, and Joseph R. Carter. 2001. An empirical examination of the underlying dimensions of purchasing competence. *Production and Operations Management* 10 (1): 1–15.

### Scales (Actual Questions Used)

*Empowerment*

1. Involvement: job-related decisions
2. Involvement: operational decisions
3. Autonomy in jobs
4. Job security

*Employee Competence*

5. Training for purchasing in quality and customer satisfaction
6. Training for suppliers in quality and customer satisfaction
7. Performance evaluation related to quality improvement

*Interaction Frequency: Tactical*

8. Interaction of purchasing with production
9. Interaction of purchasing with quality control

*Interaction Effectiveness: New Product Development*

10. Interaction of purchasing with engineering
11. Interaction of purchasing with R&D

*Buyer-Seller Relationship Management*

12. Risk sharing for capital investment with suppliers
13. Technical assistance and information sharing with suppliers
14. Joint production planning with suppliers
15. Sharing of cost savings with suppliers

### Construct Description

Purchasing competence was conceptualized as a multidimensional concept. It consisted of performance along a range of key enabling areas in which the purchasing function has a primary responsibility.

### Measurement Description

Purchasing competence was measured by five dimensions: "empowerment, employee competence, interaction frequency—tactical, interaction effectiveness—NPD, and buyer-seller relationship management" (p. 4). The operational definitions of each dimension are provided in the article on p. 4.

The human resources constructs (including employee and employee competence) and the buyer-seller relationship management construct were measured on a 5-point Likert scale with the endpoints labeled 1 = "strongly disagree" and 5 = "strongly agree." The interaction frequency—tactical and interaction effectiveness—NPD were both measured on a 5-point Likert-type scale. The response categories for the former were 1 = "very infrequent" to 5 = "very frequent." The response categories for the latter were 1 = "adversarial" to 5 = "very cooperative."

### Development

The research instrument was validated in two phases. In the first phase, an ad hoc committee of senior purchasing executives was formed. This committee developed (1) a list of firms that could be used for in-depth field case studies and (2) a list of issues that should be examined during site visits. In the second phase, informants in 10 companies identified in Phase 1 were interviewed. Inputs on the survey instrument were collected from purchasing personnel and other key executives in each company. The authors then incorporated these inputs in their final design of the questionnaire.

### Sample

Approximately "3000 questionnaires were mailed to a stratified random sample of potential respondents selected from the National Association of Purchasing Management (NAPM) membership database. Since the NAPM database is arbitrarily segmented into three subsets based on professional position within purchasing, surveys were sent out in equal numbers to each of these three segments" (p. 6). Of the "3000 questionnaires, 302 were returned, constituting a response rate of 10%. Complete data were available for 172 firms. Among the respondents, there was no evidence of overrepresentation of any of the three categories of members. Mean sales for the sample was $1,175.44 million with a standard deviation of $4,338.52 million. The mean number of employees was 8,401 with a standard deviation of 47,372" (p. 6).

### Reliability and Validity

The reliability of the measures was assessed by using Cronbach's coefficient alpha. The "Cronbach's alpha values for the scales comprising each of the five factors were ranging from 0.667 to 0.784" (p. 8). The authors claimed that content validity was ensured by expert judgment obtained through their interaction with purchasing executives during the scale development stage and through extensive literature search. Convergent validity was investigated by subjecting the 15 practices constituting the purchasing competence construct to a second-order factor model. Based on multiple fit criteria, the authors noted that the overall fit of the model estimated in LISREL 7.0 using the maximum likelihood method of estimation was acceptable. Moreover, all first- and second-order factor loadings were found to be statistically significant and positive. Therefore, the authors claimed that a high degree of convergent validity was found.

According to the authors, the discriminant validity was checked by examining the modification indices (MI) reported as part of the second-order factor model estimation results. "The rule of thumb for evidence of a lack of discriminant validity is modification indices that are higher than 10" (p. 10). The factor analysis showed that most of the MI values were less than 1, with the largest MI being 6.182. The authors argued that this result demonstrated a high level of discriminant validity, as indicated by the lack of cross-loadings. Predictive validity was demonstrated by examining the correlations among factors constituting purchasing performance and performance measure. As predicted, the empowerment dimension "was found to be significantly correlated with TQM and with customer satisfaction" (p. 11).

### Scores

The scores are reported in Tables 1–6 in the article.

### Other Evidence

Not available.

### Reference

None.

## Nassimbeni

### Article Summarized

Nassimbeni, Guido. 2003. Local manufacturing systems and global economy: Are they compatible? The case of the Italian eyewear district. *Journal of Operations Management* 21 (2): 151–71.

### Scales (Actual Questions Used)

*Technology*

1. Production technologies
2. Design technologies
3. Information technologies
4. Communication technologies

*Management*

JIT Practices

5. Our main suppliers deliver to us on a just-in-time basis.
6. The layout of our factory facilitates fast throughput.
7. We are actively working to lower setup times in our plant.
8. Our lot size is equal to present requirements.

Concurrent Engineering Practices

9. We are actively involved in the design activities of our customers.
10. We use design for manufacturing/design for assembly techniques.
11. Component reduction is very important for us and we focus on it.
12. We make every effort to us standard components
13. Product modularization is very important for us and we focus on it.

TQC Practices

14. Our firm has established and formalized procedures and norms for total quality achievement.
15. We use a defect analysis technique (such as Pareto diagram, ABC diagrams, etc."
16. We have defined measures to control the flow coming from main suppliers.
17. We have defined measures to control the flow directed to main customers.
18. We invest in preventive maintenance
19. We use statistical process control to monitor the process.

Innovation

20. New materials
21. New product functions
22. New production technology
23. New working methods

**Construct Description**

Two important constructs in this article were technology and management. Technology was defined as "the importance and up-to-datedness of the technology adopted in the main areas (manufacturing, quality control, management, design, communication, handling, storage)" (p. 168).The construct of management comprised three constructs: (1) just-in-time (JIT) practices, (2) concurrent engineering practices, and (3) total quality control (TQC) practices. JIT practices had four items, including layout, suppliers, lot size, and setup times. Concurrent engineering practices considered how well products are designed for manufacture and whether clients are involved in design. TQC practices covered the usage of common TQM practices (e.g., preventive maintenance [PM], statistical process control [SPC], etc.). Innovation signified the amount of "new" things occurring at the company (e.g., materials, product functions, technology, and working methods).

**Measurement Description**

Technology was measured in two ways. First, perceptive 5-point Likert scales were used to evaluate the adoption of technologies in the main areas. Second, the authors collected objective data on the nature of adoption (*see* Appendix A in the article for details.) The management constructs (including JIT, concurrent engineering practices, and TQC) were first measured using 5-point Likert scales, and then a dichotomous variable was used to assess whether the firm had been certified by an institutional agency.

Innovation was measured by assessing the level of investments by the firm in the past 5 years and the level of intended investment by the firm in the next 5 years. Each question was rated on 5-point Likert scales. "In addition, dichotomous variables were used to capture the firm's resort to outside services (technological and management consultancy) and the kind of material used (nickel-silver, stainless, brass, titanium, nickel-free, copper-beryllium, and carbonium alloys)" (p. 170).

### Development

A large portion of the survey was adapted from Sakakibara, Flynn, and Schroeder (1993), whereas the remaining parts of the scales were based on Lefebvre and Lefebvre (1993).

### Sample

The sample contained five main contractors and 49 subcontractors in the Italian eyewear district. Eight main contractors—the eighth largest producers in the district—were approached, and five agreed to participate. These five represented 60% of the overall district sales. The sample focused on "small" suppliers—those with less than 22 employees. Compared with the nonresponders, this group was a little smaller (a mean of 8.92 employees vs. a mean of 11.8 employees).

### Validity and Reliability

Not available.

### Scores

Table 4 presents a comparison of "preferred" versus "marginal" suppliers on several variables.

### Other Evidence

Not available.

### References

Lefebvre, E., and L. A. Lefebvre. 1992. Firm innovativeness and CEO characteristics in small manufacturing firms. *Journal of Engineering and Technology Management* 9 (3/4): 243–77.

Sakakibara, S., B. B. Flynn, and R. G. Schroeder. 1993. A framework and measurement instrument for just-in-time manufacturing. *Production and Operations Management* 2 (3): 177–94.

## Naveh and Marcus

### Article Summarized

Naveh, Eitan, and Alfred Marcus. 2005. Achieving competitive advantage through implementing a replicable management standard: Installing and using ISO 9000. *Journal of Operations Management* 24 (1): 1–26.

### Scales (Actual Questions Used)

*Catalyst for Change*

1. To what extent was design and development of your ISO 9000 system a springboard to introduce new practices?
2. To what extent has ISO 9000 led to the discovery of improvement opportunities?
3. To what extent was your investment of time and resources in ISO 9000 a starting point for other more advanced practices?

4. To what extent was your investment of time and resources in ISO 9000 a catalyst for rethinking the way you do business?
5. To what extent was your investment of time and resources in ISO 9000 understood as an opportunity to innovate?

*Daily Practice*

6. To what extent are the documents created for the purpose of ISO 9000 registration used in daily practice?
7. To what extent are preparations for external audits made at the last minute?
8. To what extent is the system regularly ignored?
9. To what extent is the system an unnecessary burden?
10. To what extent has it become part of your regular routine?

*Internally Integrated*

11. To what extent was design and development of your ISO 9000 system coordinated and led by employees who were trained and developed inside the organization?
12. To what extent was design and development of your ISO 9000 system integrated with practices already in place?
13. To what extent was design and development of your ISO 9000 system customized to the needs of your company?

*Externally Coordinated*

14. To what extent was design and development of your ISO 9000 system coordinated with suppliers?
15. To what extent was design and development of your ISO 9000 system coordinated with customers?
16. To what extent was design and development of your ISO 9000 system based on learning from other companies that already were registered?

### Construct Description

The authors define internal integration as "designing and developing new systems to conform to the standard based on the analysis of a company's existing internal processes" (p. 4).

### Measurement Description

A total of 16 items were used to measure four independent variables: (1) internally integrated, (2) externally coordinated, (3) daily practice, and (4) catalyst for change. The corresponding items were averaged to create the composite measure for each construct.

### Development

The measurement scales were all adapted from existing studies. The sources of the items are reported on p. 10 of the article. The questionnaire was developed in an iterative process with 19 leading practitioners in the quality field, followed by a pilot study with several dozens of respondents. As a result, the questionnaire was refined to incorporate the inputs collected from the pilot study.

### Sample

The questionnaires were sent to 4,233 ISO 9000 certified organizations in North America. The list of these 4,233 organizations was obtained from *Quality System Update,* a newsletter published by McGraw-Hill, which "routinely collects lists of all facilities in the U.S. that have demonstrated through external auditing that they have implemented ISO 9000" (p. 7). At the time of the survey of the article, the 4,233 organizations were the entire population of ISO-certified organizations in North America that appeared on the list. A total of 1,150 managers from 924 organizations completed the survey, which yielded a response rate of 27%. The responding organizations were located in six industries: (1) agriculture, forestry, and mining; (2) services, trades, and construction; (3) food, tobacco, textiles, and wood products; (4) petrochemicals and plastics; (5) manufacturing, metals, and machinery; and (6) electronics and instruments. Seventy-five percent of the respondents were from manufacturing, while 25% were from services. Nonrespondent bias was assessed using several different methods. None of these analyses detected any signs of nonrespondent bias.

### Reliability and Validity

The authors assessed the validity of the constructs by confirmatory factor analyses (CFA). Overall, the authors reported that the model had a good fit and the item loadings were all significant. The authors also computed Cronbach's coefficient alpha values to gauge reliability. All multi-item measurement scales had an alpha value above .90, which provided evidence for composite reliability.

### Scores

The scores are presented in Tables 2–7 in the article.

### Other Evidence

Not available.

### Reference

None.

## New and Szwejczewski

### Article Summarized

New, C. C., and M. Szwejczewski. 1995. Performance measurement and the focused factory: Empirical evidence. *International Journal of Operations and Production Management* 15 (4): 63–79.

### Scales (Actual Questions Used)

*Dimension 1: Descriptor (What)*

1. Size of plant
2. Number of products
3. Number of different raw materials
4. Number of components per product
5. Processing time per order
6. Basic manufacturing cost structure
7. Number of employees

*Dimension 2: Management (Why)*

8. Management style
9. Push or pull approach to production
10. Performance measurement systems

*Dimension 3: Intermediate (How)*

11. Proportion

    Make-to-order (MTO)
    Assemble-to-order (ATO)
    Make-to-stock (MTS)

12. Procurement lead times
13. Manufacturing lead times
14. Customer lead times
15. Setup times
16. Inventory levels

*Dimension 4: Performance (Result)*

17. Quality
18. Cost
19. Flexibility
20. Dependability

**Construct Description**

Descriptor variables portrayed the manufacturing plant in terms of "what" is being done. They defined the general task of the manufacturing operation and tended to be long term in nature. For example, consider the width of the product range that the plant will manufacture, the number of components per product (complexity), and the basic cost structure of products. Management variables related to the approach taken by management to the operations of the manufacturing plant and drove "why" things are done in certain ways. Intermediate variables were those "which management team can influence directly through policy, layout, etc. with a greater degree and on a shorter time scale" (pp. 69–70).

**Measurement Description**

Not available.

**Development**

Not available.

**Sample**

This study was conducted based on the 1993 UK Best Factory Awards database, in which 262 plants submitted entries covering a full spectrum of industries. The data were collected at the plant level, and multiple respondents were sought to complete the survey questionnaires.

**Reliability and Validity**

Not available.

**Scores**

The scores are listed in Tables 1—6 in the article.

**Other Evidence**

Not available.

**Reference**

None.

# Noble

## Article Summarized

Noble, Margaret A. 1997. Manufacturing competitive priorities and productivity: An empirical study. *International Journal of Operations and Production Management* 17 (1): 85–99.

## Scales (Actual Questions Used)

*Manufacturing Capabilities*

Dimension 1: Quality

1. Chief areas of recent productivity accomplishment:
   - Improved quality; less rework, inspection,
   - Higher materials yields; less waste
   - Machine "up-time,"
2. Degree to which quality control staff is the source of productivity ideas,
3. Perceived strength of quality control/assurance function within the plant, and
4. Percentage of output reworked.

Dimension 2: Dependability

5. Perceived strength of the following functions within the plant:
   - Maintenance
   - Materials handling/logistics
   - Production planning/scheduling
   - Production control
6. Expediting of orders through plant (%)
7. Chief area of recent productivity accomplishment:
   - Materials-handling improvements

Dimension 3: Delivery

8. Important product lines compete in market place via
   - Quick delivery (short lead times)
   - Reliable deliveries

Dimension 4: Cost

9. Perceived strength of inventory control function in the plant
10. Important product lines compete in marketplace via low-cost product
11. Chief areas of recent productivity accomplishment:
    - Material substitution
    - Machine or line speed improvements
    - Lower work-in-process inventories
    - Materials shortage reduction
    - Reduction of overhead
12. Linking of process segments so that materials/products flow more smoothly.

Dimension 5: Flexibility

13. Frequency of product mix changes
14. Fluctuation in monthly output volume (%)

15. Change in throughput time over past five years
16. Important product lines compete in marketplace via:
    - Product customization
    - Production rate flexibility

Dimension 6: Innovation

17. Important product lines compete in marketplace via:
    - Rapid new product introduction
    - Frequency of new product introduction

*Productivity Measures*

Dimension 1: Productivity

18. Labor productivity gain from one year to the next in terms of percentage

Dimension 2: Relative productivity

19. Based on productivity/performance, plant's rank in same industry
20. Based on productivity/performance, plant's rank in parent corporation
21. Productivity advance in plant in recent years

## Construct Description

In this study, manufacturing capabilities were defined as competitive priorities, which consisted of six dimensions: quality, dependability, delivery, cost, flexibility, and innovation.

## Measurement Description

Measurement items related to the manufacturing capabilities were selected from the database if they were found to be consistent with the conceptual meaning of the constructs being operationalized. When necessary, these items were recoded so that "the higher the score, the 'better' or more 'focused' the capability" (p. 89). Composite variables by means of summated scales were used to capture the value of the latent factor. Performance was measured in two ways. "The first, labor productivity gain, as a percentage, from one year to the next—often referred to in this article as 'productivity' for the sake of simplicity—served as the primary measure of performance. Frequently a surrogate for a more general productivity measure, labor productivity is more widely used and understood in industry and hence was more readily available than other, more inclusive measures, such as total factor productivity" (p. 89).

## Development

This study utilized a proprietary database designed and developed by Schmenner (1988) for a productivity study. The survey instrument was eight pages long and contained 227 questions. A translation was made when the survey was prepared for data collection in Korea.

## Sample

Data were collected from "265 North American, 129 predominantly European and 167 mostly Korean plants, for a total of 561 factories worldwide" (p. 88). In the United States, the primary targets were U.S. plants from larger companies. The response rate was 3%. However, the author claimed that, "as statistically determined, the responses were found to be representative of the population, with no geographical or industry biases. Additionally, a comparison of the earliest with the latest returns indicated no statistically significant differences in the productivity measures, implying that the responding firms were not likely to be either better or worse performing than were those which did not respond. Nor did another 53 variables suggest bias in the sample" (p. 88).

In Europe, the surveys were sent to "past participants of IMEDE [currently, Institute for Management Development] (now IMD), the international business school in Lausanne, Switzerland. The true response rate for the European sample is not known because some of the IMD respondents were from the same companies" (p. 88). In Korea, the surveys were mailed through the auspices of the Korean Traders' Scholarship Association. According to the author, a comparison between early returns and late returns yielded no signs of nonresponse bias.

### Reliability and Validity

Not available.

### Scores

The results are given in Tables 4—6 in the article.

### Other Evidence

Not available.

### References

Schmenner, R. W. 1988. Behind labor productivity gains in the factory. *Journal of Manufacturing and Operations Management* 1 (4): 323–38.

Skinner, W. 1974. The focused factory. *Harvard Business Review* 52 (3): 113–21.

---

## Olson, Belohlav, and Boyer

### Article Summarized

Olson, John R., James A. Belohlav, and Kenneth K. Boyer. 2005. Operational, economic and mission elements in not-for-profit organizations: The case of the Chicago Symphony Orchestra. *Journal of Operations Management* 23 (2): 125–42.

### Scales (Actual Questions Used)

*Ordering Tool Usage*

1. Event descriptions
2. Seat selection tool
3. Concert search tool
4. Season calendar
5. E-mail order confirmation
6. E-mail concert reminder

*Educational Tool Usage*

7. Program notes
8. Music samples
9. Concert information tool
10. Chicago Symphony Orchestra (CSO) e-mailing list
11. Orchestra tour
12. Musician biographies
13. CSO Rosenthal archives

*Value*

System Effectiveness

14. The time to place an order
15. The delivery time from when an order is placed to receipt of all items
16. The thoroughness of order documentation
17. The ease of interpretation for documentation
18. The reliability of delivery

*Web Site Interaction*

Perspective

19. I like using Internet ordering.
20. Internet ordering is fun to use.
21. Internet ordering provides an attractive ordering method.
22. One of my favorite leisure activities is exploring the Internet.

Overall Impression

23. Ordering tickets online is more attractive than other ordering methods.
24. I will use the CSO site in the future.

Ease of Interaction

25. It is easy for me to remember how to perform tasks using Internet ordering.
26. It is easy to get Internet ordering to do what I want it to do.
27. My interaction with Internet ordering is clear and understandable.
28. Overall, I believe that Internet ordering is easy to use.

Patron Strategy

29. Cost
30. Convenience
31. Delivery speed
32. Faster access to ticket information

Transactional Accuracy

33. Ordering speed
34. Order accuracy
35. Customer service of system
36. Security of system

**Construct Description**

Web site interaction referred to the patron's interaction with the Web site. The authors note a well-developed research literature relating to technology acceptance within organizations. Patron strategy consisted of "preexisting patron characteristics that reflect individual preferences or perceived value required in the purchase of a product or service" (p. 133).

**Measurement Description**

The context for the study was the Chicago Symphony Orchestra (CSO). Ordering tools and educational tools are the two independent variables in this research model. The two scales included questions that "measure the degree to which consumers use various items on the CSO website" (p. 140). The authors rated these items on a 1 = "never" to 4 = "frequently" to 7 = "always" Likert scale. "The overall usage of economic elements of the CSO website was evaluated by creating a variable measuring the average score of all ordering tool features" (p. 132). The authors then conducted a median split on the composite variables to create the "high and low" usage categories. An identical process was used to create the "educational tool" variable.

Three groups of dependent variables including multiple scales were generated for this study. The authors noted that the larger group of dependent variables as value, Web site interaction, and patron's strategy. The dependent variable that captured value consisted of a single scale on system effectiveness. This scale measured the degree of improvement when the tasks/events were conducted using the Internet for ordering tickets through the CSO in comparison with traditional methods (order by phone, in person, by fax, or by mail). These items were rated on a 1 ("large decrease") to 7 ("larger increase") Likert scale. Patron utility is measured by the system effectiveness dependent variable. The concept of utility in individual decision making has been developed in several disciplines. The authors evaluated customers through online interactions, using the level of improvement patrons receive through online interactions relative to traditional methods. The authors evaluated the dependent variable using a single multi-item measurement scale—system effectiveness. This scale employed five items related to order fulfillment and included the measurement of time to place an order, delivery time, order documentation and accuracy, and reliability of delivery (Torkzadeh and Dhillon 2002; Zeithaml, Parasuraman, and Malhotra 2000; Palvia and Palvia 1999).

The Web site interaction dependent variable consists of scales that were primarily derived from the technology acceptance model (TAM) (Davis, Bagozzi, and Warshaw 1989). Research has clearly shown that these scales are extremely important to the overall interaction of individuals and Internet-based technology (Devaraj, Fan, and Kohli 2002). The patron perceptions were measured using a four-item scale on perspective, a two-item scale on overall impression, and a four-item scale on ease of interaction.

The authors measured patron strategy perceptions in three areas: cost (one item), convenience (three items), and transactional accuracy (four items). The first scale measured the patron's perceptions of cost. The second scale, convenience, captured various aspects comprising convenience, including delivery speed and access to additional ticket information. Early research on e-commerce suggested that the primary motive for switching to e-commerce-based systems was transaction costs and easy access to product availability (Lynch and Ariely 2000).

### Development

The authors used existing scales whenever possible. A few new scales were developed specifically for CSO.

### Sample

The targeted population of the study was the patrons of the CSO "who had placed at least one order over the Internet during the past concert season" (p. 131). The initial database included approximately 5,100 patrons. A total of 518 individuals were selected to be part of the study. Of the 518 surveys mailed out, 242 useable surveys were returned. This yielded an effective response rate of 46.7%.

### Reliability and Validity

No discussion of validity and reliability verification was included in the article.

### Scores

Mean, standard deviation, and correlation are reported in Table 1 of the article.

### Other Evidence

Not available.

**References**

Davis, F. D., R. P. Bagozzi, and P. R. Warshaw. 1989. User acceptance of computer technology: A comparison of two theoretical models. *Management Science* 35 (8): 982–1003.

Devaraj, S., M. Fan, and R. Kohli. 2002. Antecedents of B2C channel satisfaction and preference: Validating e-commerce metrics. *Information Systems Research* 13 (3): 316–33.

Lynch, J. G., Jr., and D. Ariely. 2000. Wine online: Search costs affect competition on price, quality, and distribution. *Marketing Science* 19 (1): 83–103.

Palvia, P. C., and S. C. Palvia. 1999. An examination of the IT satisfaction of small-business users. *Information and Management* 35 (3): 127–37.

Torkzadeh, G., and G. Dhillon. 2002. Measuring factors that influence the success of Internet commerce. *Information Systems Research* 13 (2): 187–204.

Zeithaml, V. A., A. Parasuraman, and A. Malhotra. 2000. *A conceptual framework for understanding e-service quality: Implications for future research and managerial practice.* Working paper No. 00–115. Cambridge, MA: Marketing Science Institute.

## Olson and Boyer

**Article Summarized**

Olson, John R., and Kenneth K. Boyer. 2003. Factors influencing the utilization of Internet purchasing in small organizations. *Journal of Operations Management* 21 (2): 225–45.

**Scales (Actual Questions Used)**

*Internet Purchasing Acceptance Factors*

Perceived Usefulness

1. Using Internet purchasing enables me to accomplish tasks such as order placement, order estimating, and order tracking more quickly.
2. Using Internet purchasing improves my job performance.
3. Using Internet purchasing gives me greater control over my work.
4. Using Internet purchasing improves the quality of the work I do.
5. Using Internet purchasing improves my productivity.
6. Using Internet purchasing enhances my effectiveness on the job.
7. Using Internet purchasing makes it easier to do my job.
8. Overall, I find Internet purchasing technology useful in my job.

Perceived Ease

9. It is easy for me to remember how to perform tasks using Internet purchasing.
10. It is easy to get Internet purchasing to do what I want it to do.
11. My interaction with Internet purchasing is clear and understandable.
12. Overall, I believe that Internet purchasing is easy to use.

Attitude

13. I like using Internet purchasing.
14. Internet purchasing is fun to use.

15. I dislike using Internet purchasing (reverse coded).
16. Internet purchasing provides an attractive working environment.

Comfort

17. I am knowledgeable about personal computer usage.
18. I am comfortable and experienced with the Internet.
19. I am proficient at fixing glitches when working on the computer.
20. I am good at resolving problems with computers.

*Contextual Factors: Strategy*

Goals

21. Cost
22. Convenience
23. Delivery speed

Administrative

24. Ability to track inventory
25. Reduces paperwork
26. Faster access to information
27. Flexibility in order size

Delivery

28. Order-site accuracy
29. Delivery of system
30. Security of system

*Outcome Factors*

Organizational Performance

<u>Internet Improvement</u>

31. The time to place an order
32. The delivery time from when an order is placed to receipt of all items
33. The thoroughness of order documentation
34. The ease of interpretation for documentation
35. The reliability of delivery

<u>Cost Reduction</u>

36. Cost of activities associated with purchasing (reverse coded)
37. Cost of training new personnel associated with ordering systems (reverse coded)

<u>Purchasing Efficiency</u>

38. Site accuracy of your billing
39. Availability of supplies and materials

Site Performance

<u>Site Ease</u>

40. I can get on the site when I want to.
41. The site loads quickly.
42. The site is easy to navigate.

43. The site has a logical sequence of pages.
44. Office Depot Web site is easy to search.

<u>Site Accuracy</u>

45. Contents on the Web page are current with respect to *price*.
46. Contents on the Web page are current with respect to *new items*.
47. Contents on the Web page are current with respect to *in-stock items*.
48. Contents on the Web page are current with respect to *promotions*.
49. Office Depot has my products in stock when I place an order.

<u>Transaction</u>

50. I experience difficulties *placing an order* when using the online ordering system (reverse coded).
51. I experience *Web page navigation* (i.e., page would not upload or server time was expired) problems when using the online ordering system (reverse coded).
52. I experience *billing* problems when using the online ordering system (reverse coded).

Items That Did Not Load on Any Scale

53. Office Depot sends order confirmation in a timely fashion.
54. The company delivers the items when they promised delivery.
55. Office Depot provides good technical support.

### Construct Description

The authors' working definitions of constructs are as follows: Perceived ease connoted "the extent to which the target technology's use of implementation is free from undue effort on the part of the end user" (p. 233). Perceived usefulness was defined as "potential user's subjective views of the new technology as offering benefits relative to alternatives" (p. 233). Attitude was characterized as the general feelings toward the technology, and comfort is defined as the overall level of familiarity with computers. Goals were described as the "importance of cost, delivery speed, and convenience" (p. 233). Administrative indicated the "importance of various standard purchasing administrative functions" (p. 233). Internet improvement captured "the degree that the internet improves purchasing transactions" (p. 233). Cost performance indicated the "degree to which the internet improves general purchasing costs and personnel training costs" (p. 233). Last, site ease was defined as the "ease of navigation and loading of site" (p. 233).

### Measurement Description

The 13 constructs studied in the article were all measured using multi-item scales. Each item was quantified by a 7-point Likert scale ranging from 1 = "strongly disagree," to 7 = "strongly agree."

### Development

Four constructs of the acceptance factors—namely, usefulness, ease, attitude, and comfort—were based on the Technology Acceptance Model (Davis, Bagozzi, and Warshaw 1989). The constructs of strategic contextual factors (i.e., goals, administrative, and delivery) scales were developed for this survey. The scales for the constructs of Internet improvement, cost reduction, purchasing efficiency, which represent organizational performance scales, were developed for this survey. Site performance was developed for this study by starting with a list of 17 items that referred to specific aspects of a particular Internet site. The exploratory factor analysis (EFA) resulted in three eigenvalues greater than 1. This finding, together with the retained items with loadings greater than .40, indicated three factors, which the authors labeled (1) site ease, (2) site accuracy, and (3) transaction.

### Sample

The sampling frame contained individual customers of Office Depot who had placed their orders on the Web site within the last calendar year of the study. The data were collected using both a printed survey and an electronic survey. A total of 1,045 customers were sampled. Among them, a total of 416 usable surveys were received, with a response rate of 39.8%. Office Depot gave a $15 rebate to all respondents. The responses that came from companies with greater than 1,000 individuals were removed from the database. As a result, the final sample contained 395 observations, with respondents emanating from a variety of industries including engineering/architecture/consulting, business services, manufacturing/ printing, and others. The breakdown of respondents in terms of industry membership is provided in Table 2 of the article.

Chi-square tests were conducted "on the proportion of positive responses for three variables: the percent of respondents that received computer-based versus printed surveys, the proportion of respondents within each of the seven categories shown in Table 1 and industry membership (17 categories, self-typed by customers when ordering)" (p. 232). None of the $\chi^2$ tests revealed any signs of nonresponse bias.

### Validity and Reliability

Validity was not explicitly discussed in the article except for the site performance scale as previously discussed. To evaluate unidimensionality, EFA was performed on the 17 items related to the site performance, and a three-factor solution was found. As part of this analysis, the three items that did not load on a specific factor were dropped along with items that had loadings less than .40. Interitem reliability was assessed using Cronbach's coefficient alphas, which ranged from a low of .63 for the composite variable—goals—to a high of .90 for Internet improvement. According to the authors, these alpha values demonstrated a sufficiently high degree of interitem reliability.

### Scores

Tables 1–3 of the article present information about the sample. Table 4 gives descriptive and reliability data for the scales. Table 5 shows the Internet purchasing clusters. The authors presented contextual factors (Table 6), outcome factors (Table 7), and purchasing and percent Internet orders (Table 8) by Internet purchasing groups.

### Other Evidence

Not available.

### Reference

Davis, F. D., R. P. Bagozzi, and P. R. Warshaw. 1989. User acceptance of computer technology: A comparison of two theoretical models. *Management Science* 35 (8): 982–1003.

## Pagell

### Article Summarized

Pagell, Mark. 2004. Understanding the factors that enable and inhibit the integration of operations, purchasing and logistics. *Journal of Operations Management* 22 (5): 459–87.

**Scale (Actual Questions Used)**

*Strategy*

1. How does the plant/company compete—in other words why does a customer buy your product as opposed to the competition?
2. Who do you compete with (locations/numbers/etc.)?
3. Uncertainty—number of competitors?
4. Speed of growth/retrenchment?
5. Speed of technological change?
6. Ease of predicting demand?
7. Ability to predict/direct changes in the competitive space?
8. Delineating order winners versus order qualifiers, based on the competitive priorities of quality, delivery, cost, flexibility innovation, and service.
9. Which of these order winners and qualifiers are most important to your functional area? In other words, if you had to prioritize them for your function what order would you put them in? If this differs from the overall company's prioritization, please explain.
10. We are going to ask managers of the other functional areas the same question. How will they answer it? Can you explain any deviations they have from the overall company's/plant's prioritization?

*Integration*

11. How much cross-functional integration does your company have? Focusing on key internal supply chain activities, such as manufacturing, purchasing, and logistics,
12. Why do you say you have levels of integration? In other words, what does integration mean to you, and how have you determined how much you have?
13. Can you give me a few examples?
14. Is this integration mostly aimed at solving problems or preventing problems?
15. What mechanisms does your company use to create/discourage integration?
16. How integrated is your company/plant with the rest of the supply chain (external members)? Do you mainly work to solve problems (reactive) or to prevent problems and leverage opportunities (proactive)?
17. Why do you feel you have levels of external integration?
18. Can you give me a few examples?
19. Is this external integration mostly aimed at solving problems or preventing problems?
20. What mechanisms does your company use to create/discourage external integration?
21. When you make decisions in your function how much do you consider the impact of these decisions on other functions?
22. When they make decisions in other functions how often do they consider the impact of these decisions on your function?
23. Do you use cross-functional teams? If so, how often and where (managerial or operational)?
24. Do managerial employees rotate from function to function?

*Measurement*

25. How is your function's performance evaluated?
26. What are the key things your function tracks (i.e., defects, efficiency, etc.)? What do you do with this information?
27. How are you (as an individual) assessed and rewarded?

    In other words, what percentages of your rewards depend on
    Individual performance

Functional performance (including teams within the function)
The performance of the entire plant (including cross-functional teams)
The company's performance (for multi-plant systems).

28. If rewards are at least somewhat cross-functional—ask them to explain.

*Performance*

29. How well does your company/plant perform in the market it serves? Please explain why you say you have levels of performance.
30. How does your function perform in terms of meeting the goals of your organization? Please explain why you say you have levels of performance.
31. How does your function perform compared to others in the industry? Please explain why you say you have levels of performance.
32. How do the other functions perform in terms of meeting organizational goals (we can offer confidentiality if desired)? Please explain why you say they have levels of performance.

## Construct Description

The author used Kahn and Mentzer's (1998) definition of integration as "a process of interdepartmental interaction and interdepartmental collaboration that brings departments together into a cohesive organization" (p. 56). This definition was similar to the definition by O'Leary-Kelly and Flore (2002), where "integration refers to the extent to which separate parties work together in a cooperative manner to arrive at mutually acceptable outcomes" (p. 226). As a result, their definition of integration encompassed constructs pertaining to the degree of (1) cooperation, (2) coordination, (3) interaction, and (4) collaboration.

## Measurement Description

A structured interview protocol was used to collect information from each plant. Each individual plant's level of integration was assessed by multiple researchers by triangulating from all respondents. Appendix B (p. 484) provides examples of coding integration.

## Development

The initial protocol was developed based on the existing strategy literature. The author constantly updated and improved the protocol after each case replication.

## Sample

Eleven different plants, from 11 distinct companies within 200 miles of the primary researcher's employment location were used for the purpose of this study. An effort was made to ensure that the plants selected used a variety of different production processes. The range of size for the plants varied from approximately 30 employees to more than 1,000 employees. According to the author, company-wide employment ranged from approximately 30 to 150,000 employees. Various industries represented, including printing, food production, and machined metal parts, were noted in this study. The details of the sample are provided in Table 2 of the article. The authors also indicated that the study sample "was limited to plants where different managers were in charge of at least two of the three key internal supply chain functions of purchasing, operations and logistics" (p. 464).

## Reliability and Validity

To observe the organization in operation, multiple researchers were used. This approach also helped to minimize potential sources of bias. The author interviewed multiple managers from different functional areas to gain a compound perspective of the same construct. Additional data were gathered to help eliminate any inconsistencies. A secondary researcher, who was a graduate student in management, was used to check the validity of the data. To remedy possible "a priori beliefs" on the drivers of integration, the author used a series of approaches: (1) The primary researcher organized and rewrote their notes prior to coding attempts, and the secondary researcher(s)—a variety of secondary researchers were apparently used for the study—reviewed the notes. This helped minimize the bias. (2) Using follow-up contacts with the respondent organizations, inconsistencies between primary and secondary researchers were resolved.

### Scores

Measures and comparisons of fit are shown in Tables 1 and 2 of the article. Path coefficients are reported in Table 3.

### Other Evidence

Not available.

### References

Kahn, K. B., and J. T. Mentzer. 1998. Marketing's integration with other departments. *Journal of Business Research* 42 (1): 53–62.

O'Leary-Kelly, S. W., and B. E. Flores. 2002. The integration of manufacturing and marketing/sales decisions: Impact on organizational performance. *Journal of Operations Management* 20 (3): 221–40.

## Pagell and Krause

### Article Summarized

Pagell, Mark, and Daniel R. Krause. 2004. Re-exploring the relationship between flexibility and the external environment. *Journal of Operations Management* 21 (6): 629–49.

### Scales (Actual Questions Used)

*Environmental Uncertainty*

1. Actual users of your products
2. Competitors for your supply of raw materials
3. Competitors for your customers
4. Government regulation controlling your industry
5. The public's political views and attitudes toward your industry

*Flexibility Items*

6. Delivery flexibility: the ability to effectively respond to changes in planned delivery dates.
7. Volume flexibility: the ability to effectively increase or decrease aggregate production in response to customers.
8. Mix flexibility: the ability of a manufacturing system to effectively produce a wide variety of different products.
9. Changeover flexibility: the ability of a manufacturing system to effectively handle additions and subtractions to the product mix over time.
10. Modification flexibility: the ability of a manufacturing system to effectively implement minor changes in current products that result from corrective actions or changing customer requirements.

*Alternative Measure of Flexibility to Reflect Approximation of Swamidass and Newell (1987)*

11. Product innovation
12. Process innovation
13. Mix flexibility—the ability of a manufacturing system to effectively produce a wide variety of products
14. Changeover flexibility—the ability of a manufacturing system to effectively handle additions and subtractions to the product mix over time
15. New product development time—the ability to minimize the time to make product improvements, variations to existing products, or to introduce completely new products

*Performance*

16. Unit price of manufacturing
17. Total cost
18. Product quality
19. Delivery speed
20. Delivery dependability
21. Flexibility and new product introduction

*Alternative Measure of Performance*

22. Average annual rate of growth in return on total assets over the past 3 years
23. Average annual sales growth over the past 3 years
24. Average annual market share growth over the past 3 years

## Construct Descriptions

The constructs studied in this article were uncertainty, flexibility, and firm performance. This research was positioned as a replication of two previous studies: (1) Swamidass and Newell (1987) and (2) Pagell and Krause (1999). No explicit construct definitions were provided.

## Measurement Descriptions

The measures for external environment were derived from Duncan (1972). The items used in the measure are given in the Scales section. One of the items, which had to do with predictability of the unions, was dropped from the study (p. 633). All items were rated on 7-point Likert scales ranging from 1 = "always predictable" to 7 = "never predictable."

The research used objective measures of environmental uncertainty to complement Duncan (1972), and the following measures were evaluated. Munificence captured changes in sales for a particular industry over time. This was measured by regressing 5-year sales data against time. Shipments were used as proxy for sales data. Instability, or demand uncertainty, signified the volatility or unpredictability of a firm's environment. This indicator was derived from the regression that was performed for measuring munificence, and antilog of the standard error for the regression slope coefficient indicated a measure for instability. Complexity provided a measure of concentration. "The more concentrated a market, the less competition a plant faces" (p. 634). Complexity was measured using the MINL formulation (an approximation of the H index for industry concentration) proposed by Schmalensee (1977).

Flexibility was measured using two different scales. First, a five-item scale was used, which defined the construct as one of the competitive priorities commonly found in the manufacturing strategy literature. The second scale was created to mirror the operationalization of Swamidass and Newell (1985). In both cases, the 7-point Likert scales with the endpoints labeled as 1 = "extremely unimportant" and 7 = "extremely important" were used to measure each item.

Performance was also operationalized in two ways. First, performance was gauged as the plant's relative performance on unit price of manufacturing, total cost, product quality, delivery speed, delivery dependability, flexibility, and new production compared with its major industry competitors. The alternative measure focused on the relative financial performance on growth, sales, and market share, which mirrored the operationalization of Swamidass and Newell (1985). Both scales were evaluated using a 7-point Likert scale where 1 represented "far worse than competitors" and 7 represented "far better than competitors."

## Development

This study was a replication study of the Swamidass and Newell (1987) and Pagell and Krause (1999) articles. All the scales used in the article were based on existing scales. Minor changes were made to the survey instrument based on the inputs from executives and academics who were asked to participate in the pretest.

## Sample

The target sample was assembled based on the membership list provided by the Institute of Supply Management (ISM). The sampling frame contained 1,283 high-ranking purchasing executives in manufacturing-based industries with the U.S. Department of Commerce, Standard Industrial Classification (SIC) codes 20 to 39. This study collected plant-level data from these purchasing executives and their high-level manufacturing counterparts in each of the 1,283 plants. Of the 1,283 purchasing executives (i.e., the primary respondent) sampled, 252 returned usable responses. The response rate for purchasing executives was 19.6%. From the 252 plants where the purchasing executives responded, a total of 168 manufacturing executives responded as well. The response rate for manufacturing executives was 66.7%. The respondent profile consisted of directors (44%), vice presidents (25%), operations or production managers (20%), and others (11%), and the key industries that were sampled are electrical and electronic equipment, miscellaneous manufacturing, food, transportation equipment, and chemicals. The respondents were from medium to large companies (with more than 500 employees).

Nonresponse bias was investigated using two approaches. In the first approach, *t*-tests were performed on the responses collected from the early- and late-returned groups. The scores from 20 randomly selected survey items were compared, and no significant differences were found. In the second approach, a comparison was made between the plants with responses only from the purchasing area and the plants with responses from both functional areas. The comparisons did not yield any significant differences either.

## Reliability and Validity

For the flexibility and performance measures, reliability was determined by Cronbach's coefficient alpha values, which ranged from .85 to .92. In addition, the authors computed the interrater reliabilities for the external environment and performance constructs, based on the responses from the manufacturing managers and the purchasing managers. High interrater reliabilities on both the environment and performance were reported in the article. There was no reliability computed for the metric of uncertainty used in this study, which was an index.

## Scores

The correlation matrix for all the measures are given in Table 3 (p. 638) of the article.

## Other Evidence

Not available.

### References

Duncan, R. B. 1972. Characteristics of organizational environments and perceived environmental uncertainty. *Administrative Science Quarterly* 17 (3): 313–27.

Pagell, M., and D. R. Krause. 1999. A multiple-method study of environmental uncertainty and manufacturing flexibility. *Journal of Operations Management* 17 (3): 307–25.

Schmalensee, R. 1977. Using the H–index of concentration with published data. *Review of Economics and Statistics* 59 (2): 186–93.

Swamidass, P. M., and W. T. Newell. 1987. Manufacturing strategy, environmental uncertainty and performance: A path analytic model. *Management Science* 33 (4): 509–24.

## Pannirselvam, Siferd, and Ruch

### Article Summarized

Pannirselvam, Gertrude P., Sue P. Siferd, and William A. Ruch. 1998. Validation of the Arizona Governor's Quality Award criteria: A test of the Baldrige criteria. *Journal of Operations Management* 16 (5): 529–50.

### Scales (Actual Questions Used)

*Leadership*

1. Senior executive leadership
2. Management for quality
3. Public responsibility

*Information and Analysis*

4. Scope and management of quality and performance data and information
5. Competitive comparisons and benchmarks
6. Analysis and use of company-level data

*Strategic Quality Planning*

7. Strategic quality and company performance-planning process
8. Quality and performance plans

*Human Resources Development and Management*

9. Human resource management
10. Employee involvement
11. Employee education and training
12. Employee performance and recognition
13. Employee well-being and morale

*Management of Process Quality*

14. Design and introduction of quality products and services
15. Process management—product and service production and delivery process
16. Process management—business and support services
17. Supplier quality
18. Quality assessment

*Quality and Operational Results*

19. Product and service quality results
20. Company operational results
21. Business processes and support services results
22. Supplier quality results

*Customer Focus and Satisfaction*

23. Customer expectations—current and future
24. Customer relationship management
25. Commitment to customers
26. Customer satisfaction determination
27. Customer satisfaction results
28. Customer satisfaction comparison

### Construct Description

The authors stated that the Arizona Governor's Quality Awards (AGQA) criteria closely followed the Malcolm Baldrige National Quality Award (MBNQA). As a result, in this study, the constructs and the measures are based on MBNQA. The Baldrige criteria assessed organizational quality through seven categories—leadership, information and analysis, strategic quality planning, human resources (HR) development and management, management of process quality, quality and operational results, and customer focus and satisfaction. The Baldrige criteria have four basic elements: (1) driver, (2) systems, (3) measures of progress, and (4) goals. Accordingly, the driver is viewed as senior leadership, which in turn creates values and goals and guides the pursuit of quality and is captured by the first category, leadership. The system consisted of processes for meeting the company's quality goals and performance requirements and is measured by four categories in the assessment. The measures of progress were product and service quality, internal quality and productivity, and supplier quality, which formed the sixth category. The goal of the quality process, as specified in the seventh category, was improved value to the customer.

### Measurement Description

Based on the Baldrige criteria, 28 items were grouped into seven factors—leadership, information and analysis, strategic quality planning, HR development and management, management of process quality, quality and operational results, and customer focus and satisfaction. A scale of 0 to 100 measured at 10-point intervals was used to rate each item.

### Development

The instrument was based on the AGQA criteria. AGQA criteria closely follows the MBNQA criteria; the only difference is that AGQA includes government and not-for-profit-organizations, whereas MBNQA only includes private sector manufacturing and service firms.

### Sample

The sample consisted of the 69 applicants to the 1993 AGQA. Of these, 19 were manufacturing businesses, 36 were service businesses, 4 were health care organizations, 4 were educational institutions, and 6 were government agencies. Small businesses (less than 100 employees), medium-size businesses (between 100 and 500 employees), and large businesses (greater than 500 employees) accounted for 38%, 38%, and 24% of the sample, respectively. The number of employees ranged from seven to more than 6,000. Some of the applicants were divisions of national or multinational corporations.

"The individual scores that the applicants received in the first stage of the evaluation process were used in this research to test the validity of the AGQA criteria. There were fifty-one examiners. Three or four examiners evaluated each of the sixty-nine applicants in 1993. The evaluation was done on a scale of 0 to 100 (in 10-point increments) for each of the twenty-eight examination items. The 272 individual examiner responses were used to test the validity of the criteria" (p. 535).

### Reliability and Validity

Confirmatory factor analysis (CFA) was used to assess construct reliability and validity. Reliabilities of the seven factors were established through Cronbach's coefficient alpha and Fornell and Larcker's (1981) $\rho_{vc}$. Cronbach's coefficient alpha values for the seven factors were .85, .87, .77, .90, .88, .85, and .88, respectively. The corresponding $\rho_{vc}$ values were .65, .68, .62, .64, .60, .59, and .55, respectively.

Based on CFA, all the goodness-of-fit measures were above .90, with the exception of goodness-of-fit index (GFI), which was .84. The authors noted that since a large number of parameters were estimated and the sample size was not very big, confidence intervals for the factor loadings were estimated by using a bootstrap algorithm. Nevertheless, all the factor loadings were found to be significant. These results supported convergent validity. Discriminant validity was examined by comparing a correlation-constrained model with its counterpart nonconstrained model for each construct pair. Discriminant validity was confirmed by the high (i.e., $p = .001$) significance level for the $\chi^2$ difference test for each pair of the latent factors. In addition, predicative validity of the latent variables that measured the quality management practices was also reported in the study. Predictive validity was established through canonical correlation analysis of the criteria with the factors that measured results. Finally, the authors asserted that content validity was warranted by the extensive review of the literature.

### Scores

The factor loadings for the 28 items are provided in Table 5 in the article.

### Other Evidence

The following researchers have used Baldrige criteria to address issues of applicability of the criteria and to study the relationships between the categories. Moser (1992) studies the applicability of the criteria to health care. Wilson (1997) surveyed businesses in the United States to study the relationship between the Baldrige categories.

### References

Fornell, C., and D. F. Larcker. 1981. Evaluating structural equation models with unobservable variables and measurement error. *Journal of Marketing Research* 18 (1): 39–50.

Moser, J. M. 1992. The applicability of the Malcolm Baldrige National Quality Award criteria to the evaluation of quality in hospitals as perceived by the chief executive nurse. Unpublished PhD diss., Ohio State University, Columbus, OH.

Wilson, D. D. 1997. An empirical study to test the causal linkages implied in the MBNQA. Unpublished PhD diss., Ohio State University, Columbus, OH.

## Parasuraman

### Article Summarized

Parasuraman, A. 2000. Technology Readiness Index (TRI): A multiple-item scale to measure readiness to embrace new technologies. *Journal of Service Research* 2 (4): 307–20.

**Scales (Actual Questions Used)**

*Optimism*

1. Technology gives people more control over their daily lives.
2. Products and services that use the newest technologies are much more convenient to use.
3. You like the idea of doing business via computers because you are not limited to regular business hours.
4. You prefer to use the most advanced technology available.
5. You like computer programs that allow you to tailor things to fit your own needs.
6. Technology makes you more efficient in your occupation.
7. You find new technologies to be mentally stimulating.
8. Technology gives you more freedom of mobility.
9. Learning about technology can be as rewarding as the technology itself.
10. You feel confident that machines will follow through with what you instructed them to do.
11. Computers are easier to deal with than people performing the same service.
12. You find you are doing more things now with advanced technology than a couple of years ago.
13. You like the idea of doing business by computer because there is no person to pressure you.
14. People can solve problems more effectively than computers (reverse scored).
15. Society should not depend heavily on technology to solve its problems (reverse scored).
16. People often become too dependent on technology to do things for them (reverse scored).
17. The benefits of new technologies are often grossly overstated (reverse scored).
18. People tell you that you are too optimistic about technology (reverse scored).
19. You find that technology designed to make life easier usually has disappointing results (reverse scored).
20. You want to see the benefits of technology demonstrated before you buy it (reverse scored).

*Innovativeness*

21. Other people come to you for advice on new technologies.
22. It seems your friends are learning more about the newest technologies than you are (reverse scored).
23. In general, you are among the first in your circle of friends to acquire new technology when it appears.
24. You can usually figure out new high-tech products and services without help from others.
25. You keep up with the latest technological developments in your areas of interest.
26. You enjoy the challenge of figuring out high-tech gadgets.
27. You find you have fewer problems than other people in making technology work for you.
28. You have avoided trying new high-tech things because of the time it takes to learn them (reverse scored).
29. You are always open to learning about new and different technologies.
30. There is no sense trying out new high-tech products when what you have already is working fine (reverse scored).

*Discomfort*

31. Technical support lines are not helpful because they don't explain things in terms you understand.
32. Sometimes, you think that technology systems are not designed for use by ordinary people.
33. There is no such thing as a manual for a high-tech product or service that's written in plain language.
34. When you get technical support from a provider of a high-tech product or service, you sometimes feel as if you are being taken advantage of by someone who knows more than you do.
35. If you buy a high-tech product or service, you prefer to have the basic model over one with a lot of extra features.

36. It is embarrassing when you have trouble with a high-tech gadget when people are watching.
37. There should be caution in replacing important people/tasks with technology because new technology can breakdown or get disconnected.
38. Many new technologies have health or safety risks that are not discovered until after people have used them.
39. New technology makes it too easy for governments and companies to spy on people.
40. Technology always seems to fail at the worst possible time.
41. New technology is often too complicated to be useful.
42. You get overwhelmed with how much you need to know to use the latest technology.
43. With new technology, you too often risk paying a lot of money for something that is not worth much.
44. It is helpful to have a new high-tech product or service explained to you by a knowledgeable person.
45. You find it limiting to use high-tech products that are designed to be overly simple (reverse scored).
46. It is not really critical to have a detailed manual for a high-tech product or service (reverse scored).
47. You like to try out all the special features available in a new high-tech product to see what they can do (reverse scored).
48. People miss out on the benefits of technology when they delay a purchase for something better to come out (reverse scored).
49. You feel you are usually in control of new technologies (reverse scored).
50. When you have a problem with technology, you prefer to solve the problem on your own rather than call for help (reverse scored).
51. The hassles of getting new technology to work for you usually make it not worthwhile.

*Insecurity*

52. You do not consider it safe giving out a credit card number over a computer.
53. You do not consider it safe to do any kind of financial business online.
54. You worry that information you send over the Internet will be seen by other people.
55. You do not feel confident doing business with a place that can only be reached online.
56. Any business transaction you do electronically should be confirmed later with something in writing.
57. Whenever something gets automated, you need to check carefully that the machine or computer is not making mistakes.
58. The human touch is very important when doing business with a company.
59. When you call a business, you prefer to talk to a person rather than a machine.
60. If you provide information to a machine or over the Internet, you can never be sure it really gets to the right place.
61. Revolutionary new technology is usually a lot safer than what critics lead people to believe (reverse scored).
62. A machine or computer is going to be a lot more reliable in doing a task than a person (reverse scored).
63. It can be risky to switch to a revolutionary new technology too quickly.
64. If you purchased something from a machine using a credit card, you would usually NOT require a receipt (reverse scored).
65. If you buy products that are too high-tech, you may get stuck with replacement parts or service.
66. Technological innovations always seem to hurt a lot of people by making their skills obsolete.

### Construct Description

In this article, the technology-readiness referred "to people's propensity to embrace and use new technologies for accomplishing goals in home life and at work. The construct can be viewed as an overall state of mind resulting from a gestalt of mental enablers and inhibitors that collectively determine a person's predisposition to use new technologies" (p. 308). A "combination of positive and negative feelings about technology underlies the domain of technology readiness" (p. 309).

Dimensions in the technological readiness domain were described as follows. Optimism was defined as "a positive view of technology and a belief that it offers people increased control, flexibility, and efficiency in their lives" (p. 311). Innovativeness was reported as a "tendency to be a technology pioneer and thought leader" (p. 311). Discomfort connoted "a perceived lack of control over technology and a feeling of being overwhelmed by it" (p. 311). Insecurity was described as "distrust of technology and skepticism about its ability to work properly" (p. 311).

### Measurement Description

Each technology-readiness item was evaluated on a 5-point Likert scale ranging from 1 = "strongly disagree" to 5 = "strongly agree."

### Development

The instrument was developed as follows. "An initial pool of 44 technology-readiness items was generated from focus group interviews with customers of companies in a variety of sectors and from a literature search. In an empirical evaluation, 1,200 respondents answered each technology-readiness item on a 5-point scale indicating level of agreement or disagreement" (p. 310). The results were used to analyze the pool of items. Exploratory factor analysis (EFAs) and evaluations of scale reliabilities led to a pool of 30 items and five factors with eigenvalues greater than 1.0. Subsequently, one factor containing two items was deleted because of poor predictive power. The resulting four dimensions in the so-called National Technology Readiness Survey (NTRS) were optimism (10 items, $\alpha = .78$), innovativeness (five items, $\alpha = .82$), discomfort (eight items, $\alpha = .79$), and insecurity (five items, $\alpha = .72$). Two additional studies of more limited extent supported the four-factor structure.

A review of the interview transcripts was used to generate additional items to reduce the Internet and online specificity of the pool of items. The list given above (in the section Scales [Actual Questions Used]) contains the totality of these items.

### Sample

The data were collected through 1,000 interviews. The respondents were individual adults (18 years or older) selected through random-digit dialing from all over the United States. According to the authors, these individuals were a good representation of a national cross-section of adults.

### Reliability and Validity

The authors evaluated construct reliabilities by means of Cronbach's coefficient alpha. The construct validity was assessed mainly through both EFA and confirmatory factor analysis (CFA) approaches. According to the authors, "The high reliabilities [optimism (10 items, alpha = .81), innovativeness (7 items, alpha = .80), discomfort (10 items, alpha = .75), and insecurity (9 items, alpha = .74)] and consistent factor structure of the TRI's four dimensions provide support for the scale's trait validity" (p. 314). However, the author argued that although high reliability and consistent dimensionality were important, they were not sufficient for establishing construct validity. Construct validity was further evaluated on other conceptual and empirical criteria. First, content validity was assessed as the primary conceptual yardstick. The author stated that the iterative scale development and refinement process based on extensive qualitative research, including an extensive literature review, ensured content validity. Second, investigations of the relationships between technological readiness index (TRI) scores and the constructs of "having technology-based products and services," "use of technology-based services," and "perceived future desirability of various technology-based services" further empirically supported "the TRI's construct validity by demonstrating the scale's ability to discriminate well across different levels of ownership (or subscriptions to) those products/services for which one might a priori expect consumers' technology readiness levels to be especially relevant" (p. 316).

### Scores

The summary statistics and pairwise correlations for the TRI and its scales are given in Table 7 of the article. The factor loadings are reported in Tables 2 and 3.

### Other Evidence

Not available.

### Reference

None.

---

## Park, Hartley, and Wilson

### Article Summarized

Park, Seungwook, Janet L. Hartley, and Darryl Wilson. 2001. Quality management practices and their relationship to buyer's supplier ratings: A study in the Korean automotive industry. *Journal of Operations Management* 19 (6): 695–712.

### Scales (Actual Questions Used)

*Information Management*

1. Collect feedback data
2. Clear guideline for data selection
3. User-friendly information system
4. Information system focusing on key business
5. Collect data across business units
6. Using benchmarking information for improvement
7. Evaluating process for selecting benchmarking information
8. Training employees on data collection and analysis

*Strategic Planning*

9. Strategic plans are aligned with performance.
10. Communicating the business strategy to employees.
11. Employees understand the business unit's strategic plans.
12. Strategic plans are translated into key business drivers.
13. Work unit performance measures are linked to strategies.
14. Strategic plans always include reduction in waste targets.
15. Short-term and long-term strategic plans are well aligned.
16. Long-term strategies include projection on product quality.
17. Strategic plans are fully deployed.

*Employee Satisfaction*

18. Human resource plans are aligned with business strategies.
19. Employee development objectives are derived from strategy.

20. Employee grievance resolution program is effective.
21. Work environment is conductive to employee well-being.
22. Improvement activities include employee well-being factors.
23. A variety of methods are used to measure employee satisfaction.
24. Work environment is conductive to the development of all the employees.

*Empowerment*

25. Giving Workers a broader range of works.
26. Giving Workers more planning and responsibility.
27. Giving Workers more inspection/quality responsibility.

*Employee Education*

28. Management training in quality principles
29. Employee training in quality principles
30. Employee training in problem-solving skills
31. Involving employees and line managers in training development
32. Involving employees and line managers for decision of training needs

*Process Management*

33. Extensive use of statistical techniques in processes
34. Reducing cycle time is a priority for all processes
35. Process performance charts are found on shop floor
36. Processes in our plant are continuously improved

*Supplier Management*

37. We strive to establish long-term relationship with suppliers.
38. Suppliers are actively involved in new product development process.
39. Quality is our number one criterion in selecting suppliers.
40. We rely on a small number of high-quality suppliers.

## Construct Description

The quality practice constructs were derived from the production system category in the 1995 Malcolm Baldrige National Quality Award criteria (MBNQAC), National Institute of Standards and Technology.

## Measurement Description

A total of 50 survey questions were initially used to measure quality management practices by suppliers. All these items were measured using a 7-point Likert-type scale. Ten items were dropped in the final analysis to improve construct validity. The overall performance of suppliers was rated by the purchasing department of the assembler, using data collected by purchasing, manufacturing, quality, finance, accounting, and after-sales service, on a 1 to 4 scale: (1) excellent world-class suppliers, (2) domestic suppliers providing consistently good performance, (3) suppliers that need minor internal improvements, and (4) suppliers that are inconsistent and unreliable. This overall performance rating was evaluated based on the actual performance points and the quality systems points received by the supplier. The actual performance points were scored based on five factors with a total of 120 points: (1) conformance quality (42%), (2) the supplier's financial performance (25%), (3) cost reduction (17%), (4) delivery (12%), and (5) accuracy of electronic data exchange (4%). The quality systems were designed to assess whether suppliers follow specific operations to documented stated requirements. On top of the actual performance points, a supplier can potentially receive a total of 180 points from the quality system points accrued. The overall performance of a supplier was the combination of the points gathered from actual performance points and the points accrued from quality systems.

### Development

The survey instrument was developed based on the 1995 MBNQAC. Existing scales that aligned with the MBNQAC were adopted whenever possible. An English version of the survey was first presented to the Executive Committee of the Columbus, Ohio, Section of the American Society for Quality Control (ASQC) and a former MBNQAC examiner, and then was refined to increase content validity and clarity based on these experts' comments. Finally, a bilingual native of Korea proofed the instrument and made several revisions. After these revisions, the survey was translated to Korean.

The Korean version of survey was reviewed by several Korean scholars who are familiar with quality management, followed by a pilot study. In the pilot study, the questionnaire was mailed to Korean suppliers to the automotive and shipbuilding industries. Of 50 surveys, 31 were returned. The pilot study suggested that the instrument was a valid representation of the MBNQAC.

### Sample

The data on quality management practices were collected from first-tier automotive suppliers in the Korean automotive industry. The entire set of qualified first-tier production material suppliers to a major Korean automotive assembler was chosen as the survey population, which included 490 firms. Surveys were answered by quality managers or plant managers when quality managers did not exist. After removing 16 returned, uncompleted surveys because of an incorrect address, a total of 121 usable surveys were retained, with a response rate of 25.7%. The responding suppliers represented 11 different industries. The average number of employees was 297. The authors claimed, "The findings are more representative of the larger first-tier suppliers" (p. 701).

### Reliability and Validity

Content validity was ensured because the survey questions were derived from the MBNQAC and existing scales in the quality management literature and had been subjected to rigorous pilot testing.

A principal components factor analysis (PCA) with varimax rotation was conducted for the initial set of 50 measurement items. Ten out of 50 items were dropped because their factor loadings were lower than .50. The remaining items clearly and significantly loaded on seven individual factors, which provided evidence of construct validity. Cronbach's coefficient alpha value was used to evaluate construct reliability. All seven quality management constructs had an alpha value above .70, which demonstrated internal consistency.

### Scores

Factor scores were calculated using a PCA on each construct. Table 2 in the article reports the factor analysis results for all measurement items. Table 3 provides the factor analysis results by construct and the associated Cronbach's coefficient alpha values.

### Other Evidence

Not available.

### Reference

None.

# Petersen, Handfield, and Ragatz

## Article Summarized

Petersen, Kenneth J., Robert B. Handfield, and Gary L. Ragatz. 2005. Supplier integration into new product development: Coordinating product, process and supply chain design. *Journal of Operations Management* 23 (3/4): 371–88.

## Scale (Actual Questions Used)

*Supplier Integration Measures*

Technical Assessment

1. The supplier was involved in establishing technical performance measures.
2. The supplier was involved in establishing technical performance targets.
3. Technical performance targets were clearly defined and agreed on by both parties.

Business Assessment

4. The supplier was involved in establishing business performance measures.
5. The supplier was involved in establishing business performance targets.
6. Business performance targets were clearly defined and agreed on by both parties.

Detailed Supplier Assessment

7. There was consensus within my business unit at the start of this project that the right supplier was selected.
8. The capabilities of the supplier in this effort complemented my business unit's capabilities.
9. The business culture of the supplier chosen for this effort matched well with my business unit's culture.
10. We had an effective process for selecting the supplier to be integrated in this effort.

*Project Team Effectiveness*

11. My business unit's project team functioned more smoothly as a result of supplier involvement in the design process.
12. The supplier's involvement in this project led to better decisions by the project team.
13. The supplier's involvement in this project led to faster problem resolution during the design process.
14. The supplier's involvement in this project led to greater consensus on decisions made by the project team.
15. The supplier's involvement in this project resulted in more realistic project objectives being set.

*Firm Financial Performance*

16. The supplier's involvement in this project enabled more sales to be made.
17. The supplier's involvement in this project increased our profits beyond what could have been expected without integration.
18. The supplier's involvement in this project increased our return on investment beyond what could have been expected without integration.

*Design Performance*

19. The project resulted in a design that was easier for the supplier to execute than if the supplier had not been integrated.
20. This project resulted in a design that was less costly for the supplier to execute than if the supplier had not been integrated.

21. The supplier's involvement in this project resulted in a better design of the procured item.
22. The supplier's involvement in this project resulted in a better design/technology for the finished product/service.

**Construct Description**

In this article, supplier integration into new product development (NPD) indicated that suppliers can provide information and are direct participants of the decision-making processes for purchased items used in the new product, process, or service. The authors defined suppliers as those external business entities that were linked to customers' business and/or technical processes. Furthermore, participation or involvement by a supplier can occur at any point in time within the new product/process/service development process.

The authors considered three antecedents for successful supplier integration into new product development (NPD): (1) a "detailed assessment of the suppliers being considered for involvement," which should lead to choosing suppliers that had the requisite competencies and were aligned with the buying company's requirements; (2) "supplier input and involvement in the assessment of the technical elements associated with the project such as quality, reliability, functionality, etc." (p. 374); and (3) "supplier input and involvement in the assessment of the cost, schedule and other business factors critical to the ultimate success of the NPD project" (p. 374). The authors also indicated that early agreements on schedules and pricing alongside costs and commitment levels are significant considerations in the success of a supplier's involvement.

**Measurements Description**

Multiple items were used to operationalize the constructs studied in the article. Respondents were asked to rate the degree of agreement of each statement in the survey instrument relative to the procured item for which the supplier was integrated.

**Development**

To generate and pretest the survey instrument, the authors used a team of industry experts and a team of academics from marketing, organizational behavior, operations, and purchasing areas.

**Sample**

More than 3,000 companies in 18 countries around the world were contacted with a two-page "commitment letter" to solicit participation. No information was provided in the article regarding how these 3,000 companies were chosen. The target respondents were purchasing/sourcing managers and executives. Of these, 225 indicated an interest in the study. Ultimately, 134 surveys were received, which yielded a response rate of 60%. Respondents represented a "wide range" of industry groups including aerospace, automotive, chemical, computer and electronics, medical services, and others. Approximately 12.5% of the responses were from outside the manufacturing arena. A majority of the responses were from North America (68%). Nonresponse bias was evaluated using two approaches: a "wave analysis" on early and late responses and a comparison of annual sales and total employees of the U.S. respondents in the sample to a benchmark of the 500 largest companies in the United States. Neither analysis spotted the presence of nonresponse bias.

**Reliability and Validity**

The authors calculated Cronbach's coefficient alpha values to assess construct reliabilities. They reported that all the multi-item measures had an alpha value of .75 or above, which was "an indication of sufficient reliability" (Cook and Campbell 1979). The authors also used a group of purchasing and sourcing managers and executives to thoroughly review all measures and, hence, ensured the face validity of the measures.

### Scores

Measurement statistics are provided in Table 2 of the article.

### Other Evidence

Not available.

### Reference

Cook, T. D., and D. T. Campbell. 1979. *Quasi-experimentation: Design and analysis issues for field settings.* Chicago, IL: Rand McNally.

---

## Pflughoeft, Ramamurthy, Soofi, Yasai-Ardekani, and Zahedi

### Article Summarized

Pflughoeft, Kurt A., K. Ramamurthy, Ehsan S. Soofi, Masoud Yasai-Ardekani, Fatemeh (Mariam) Zahedi. 2003. Multiple conceptualizations of small business Web use and benefit. *Decision Sciences* 34 (3): 467–512.

### Scales (Actual Questions Used)

*Market Pressure*

1. Competitors' use
2. Customers' expectation
3. Suppliers' expectation

*Scope of Operations*

4. The company's markets are regional or national.
5. The company's markets are international.
6. The company's suppliers are regional or national.
7. The company's suppliers are international.

*IT Sophistication*

8. General office activities (e.g., word processing, appointment setting)
9. Data management (e.g., Access, Paradox, other database systems)
10. Accounting (e.g., receivable, payable, general ledger, budgeting)
11. Personnel management (e.g., payroll, benefits, career planning)
12. Sales and marketing

*Web-Related Costs*

13. Initial setup costs
14. Annual operating costs
15. Training costs

*Information Search*

16. Customers
17. Suppliers
18. Competitors

*Extent of Electronic Commerce Infusion*

19. Receiving orders
20. Receiving payments
21. Servicing customers

*Strategic Benefits*

22. Geographic expansion of firm's markets
23. Sales revenue
24. Number of potential customers (prospects)
25. Number of actual customers

*Operational Efficiency*

26. Productivity
27. Speed of conducting business activities
28. Ability of employees to work away from office
29. Ability to meet customer needs

*Face-to-Face Contacts*

30. Direct contact (face-to-face or by phone) with customers
31. Direct contact (face-to-face or by phone) with suppliers
32. Direct contact (face-to-face or by phone) among employees

**Construct Descriptions**

This article investigated relationships among an organization's contextual characteristics, its IT infrastructure, Web use, and Web benefits. There were two constructs identified to tap into the domain of an organization's context—market pressure and scope of operations. Market pressure was defined as the "pressure to use the Web from key external stakeholders" (p. 501). Scope of operations captured the geographical scope of the firm's market and suppliers.

IT infrastructure consisted of IT sophistication and Web-related cost. IT sophistication was "represented by the extent of software use in various business functions" (p. 503). Web-related costs reflected "the commitment of the firm to providing the necessary resources for Web-based services" and were composed "of the initial investment for setting up the system as well as the ongoing operating and training costs" (p. 504).

Similarly, two constructs—information search and e-commerce infusion—accounted for Web use. Information search connoted the use of the Web to "search for and capture information about their customers and suppliers as well as for surveillance of their competitors" (p. 504). The second construct—electronic commerce infusion—was defined as the "use of the firm's Web site for conducting key business activities" (p. 508).

Finally, the Web benefits were characterized as the use of IT for competitive advantage and consisted of three constructs: (1) strategic benefit, (2) operational efficiency, and (3) direct contacts. Strategic benefits referred to "the effect of Web use on geographic expansion of the firm's markets, sales revenue, number of potential customers, and number of actual customers" (p. 508). Operational efficiency reflected the "speed of conducting business activities, the ability of the firm's employees to work away from the office (i.e., telecommute and telework), and the firm's ability to meet customers' needs" (p. 508). Direct contact indicated the "effects of Web use on contact with customers, contact with suppliers, and contact among the firm's employees on a face-to-face basis or by telephone" (p. 508).

### Measurement Descriptions

Market pressure was gauged using three, 6-point Likert-type scales with the endpoints labeled as 0 for "none" and 5 for "very great." For speed of operations, four binary indicators were created. Two indicators were used to identify the firm's market type—one to show if the firm served regional or national markets and the other to indicate if the firm operates in the North American Free Trade Agreement (NAFTA) countries of Canada and Mexico or in other international markets. Two other binary variables captured whether the firm has either regional and national suppliers or suppliers from Canada, Mexico, or other countries. IT sophistication was gauged by five Likert-type scales ranging from 0 = "no use" and 1 = "very little use" through 5 = "very great use." Three Likert-type scales were used to measure Web-related costs, information search, e-commerce infusion, and direct contacts. The response categories ranged from 0 = "none" to 5 = "very great." Four 5-point Likert-type scales were used to quantify operational efficiency and strategic benefits.

### Development

Measures for organizational context, IT infrastructure, Web use, and the metaconstruct of Web benefits, which consisted of constructs of strategic benefits, operational efficiency, and direct contacts, were all developed based on the existing literature. They were specifically designed for small businesses.

### Sample

Surveys were sent to small business. Target respondents were titled as CEOs/owners of the firms. Two independent samples were drawn from the American Business Information (ABI) database. A total of 52,000 small businesses with the number of employees ranging between 10 and 500 and falling within the ABI's "Web Sites USA" database were identified for the sampling frame. The first sampling frame was partitioned into size-industry-region strata. From each stratum, a random sample of 6,000 firms were selected and were mailed surveys. Of these, 297 responses were received. A low response rate was anticipated because of the length of the survey and the high-level executives, who were the targeted respondents. The authors claimed that representativeness of this first sample was ensured by the stratified sampling design.

For the second sampling frame, all the remaining small businesses with between 10 and 500 employees that were not identified as having a Web site in the ABI database were selected. This frame was far larger than the first one and included more than 2 million small businesses in the ABI database. For this frame, no information regarding Web usage was available; and therefore, it was possible that there might have been companies that had Web usage included in the mailing. The same stratified sampling design as used for the first sample was also employed for the second. From a set of 16,000 mailed surveys, 536 responses were received, and among these, 461 adopters and 75 nonadopters were found. Because of the nature of the research questions in this article, only the data from the adopters are considered from the second sample.

### Reliability and Validity

Convergent validity and discriminant validity were assessed by first checking on the correlations among the indicators and then examining the results from both exploratory factor analysis (EFA) and confirmatory factor analysis (CFA). The factor loadings of the indicators of each intended latent construct were moderate to high, which indicated convergent validity. The good model fit based on the CFA analysis provided further evidence to support convergent validity. Discriminant validity was checked by the fact that "in each set, the correlations within the indicators of a construct *were* considerably higher than those between the indicators of different constructs" (p. 484). In addition, the authors stated that the clear factor patterns found in the factor analysis supported discriminant validity as well. Construct reliability was assessed by means of Cronbach's coefficient alpha and construct variance. According to Table 4 of the article, all the alpha values were above .70, and the variance extracted for each factor was above .60.

### Scores

Descriptive statistics, correlations, and EFA results are reported in Appendix A of the article. Estimates of structural equation parameters are given in Appendix B.

### Other Evidence

Not available.

### Reference

None.

---

## Pinto, Pinto, and Prescott

### Article Summarized

Pinto, Mary Beth, Jeffrey K. Pinto, and John E. Prescott. 1993. Antecedents and consequences of project team cross-functional cooperation. *Management Science* 39 (10): 1281–97.

### Scale (Actual Questions Used)[1]

*Superordinate Goals*

1. All project team members are committed to the same project goals.

*Organizational Rules and Procedures*

2. For most problems that arise on this project, there are rules and procedures for dealing with them.

*Project Team Rules and Procedures*

3. We established our own rules and procedures to facilitate the progress of the project.

*Physical Proximity*

4. How many project team members were conveniently located near you in the hospital?

*Accessibility*

5. How many members of the project team are inaccessible to you for reasons other than their physical location in the hospital?

*Cross-Functional Cooperation*

6. Open communication of relevant information occurs among project team members.

*Implementation Success: Perceived Task Outcomes*

7. To date, the project is on schedule.

---

[1]This list contains a partial list of the actual survey items.

*Implementation Success: Perceived Psychosocial Outcomes*

8. I enjoy working with the members of this project team.

## Construct Description

This article investigated "the influence of four antecedent constructs (superordinate goals, accessibility, physical proximity, and formalized rules and procedures) on the attainment of both cross-functional cooperation and perceived project outcomes" (p. 1281). Superordinate goals referred to "goals that are urgent and compelling for all groups involved but whose attainment requires the resources and efforts of more than one group" (Sherif 1962, p. 19). Rules and procedures were defined to capture "the degree to which activities or tasks on the project team were mandated or controlled" (p. 1284). Physical proximity focused on the physical distance and it establishes a context for interactions. Accessibility was defined as "an individual's perception of his/her liberty or ability to approach or communicate with another organizational member" (p. 1286). It determines the type and frequency of interactions that occur. Cross-functional cooperation was conceptualized as "the degree, extent and nature of interpersonal relationships among project team members from multiple functional areas" (p. 1286).

The construct of implementation success was assessed by two distinct outcomes: task and psychosocial outcomes. Task outcomes referred to "factors involved in the actual implementation of the project and its subsequent usage by the clients for whom it was intended" (p. 1287). Psychosocial outcomes indicated "whether or not the implementation process was considered to be worthwhile, satisfying and productive" (p. 1287).

## Measurement Descriptions

A four-item scale was used to quantify the construct of superordinate goals. Each item was assessed based on a 7-point Likert scale ranging from "strongly disagree" to "strongly agree."

Two scales, organizational rules and procedures, were operationally defined to capture (1) the formalized rules and procedures created by the organization and (2) the project-specific rules and procedures developed by the project team. Items tapping into these two constructs were assessed on 5-point Likert scales ranging from "strongly disagree" to "strongly agree." Two 7-point Likert scales with anchors from "none" to "all" were employed to gauge single-item indicators of physical proximity and accessibility, respectively. Moreover, 7-point Likert scales were developed to capture the degree of cross-functional cooperation achieved. A five-item Likert scale, adapted from Slevin and Pinto (1986), was used to measure perceived task outcomes. Similarly, perceived psychosocial outcomes were measured using five-item Likert scales developed from the literature.

## Development

The initial pool of scale items was constructed from the existing literature. The clarity of the scale items used in the constructs was then determined by three formal pretests. After the pretests were concluded, minor revisions were made to the questionnaire.

## Sample

Hospitals were the population of interest for this study. A total of 131 hospitals from Pennsylvania, Ohio, and New York were chosen from the *American Hospital Association Guide* (American Hospital Association 1986). The sampling frame was developed based on four criteria: (1) the Joint Commission on Accreditation, (2) general hospital care, (3), nongovernment and not-for-profit, and (4) bed size within 200 to 550. To gain the hospitals' cooperation, telephone contacts were initiated, and 73 of them agreed to participate. One of these was eliminated because of the inappropriateness of the project.

Project team members from each hospital were chosen as the target respondents. These team members came from a variety of functional areas, both clinical and nonclinical. Team members also varied with respect to their previous project experience and project duration. Questionnaires were administered to 299 project team members from the 72 project teams. The majority of projects focused on the development of a new program or service in the hospital. A total of 273 responses were received with the individual response rate of 91.3%. There were 62 usable teams out of the original 73 teams that agreed to participate, with a project team response rate of 85%.

### Reliability and Validity

Cronbach's coefficient alpha values were calculated to test the scale reliability for constructs with multi-attribute indexes. The authors reported that all alpha values ranged from .72 to .92. No validity tests were reported in the article.

### Scores

Path analysis was applied to study the relationships among different constructs in this study. The direct, indirect, and total effects of antecedent variables on cross-functional cooperation and outcomes are shown in Table 2 (p. 1292) in the article. Final perceived task and psychosocial outcomes path model are given in Figure 2 (p. 1293).

### Other Evidence

Not available.

### References

American Hospital Association. 1986. *American Hospital Association guide to the health care field.* Chicago, IL: American Hospital Association.

Sherif, M. 1962. Intergroup relations and leadership: Introductory statement. In *Intergroup relations and leadership: Approaches and research in industrial, ethnic, cultural, and political areas,* ed. M. Sherif, 3–21. New York: Wiley.

Slevin, D. P., and J. K. Pinto. 1986. The project implementation profile: New tool for project managers. *Project Management Journal* 17 (4): 57–70.

## Powell

### Article Summarized

Powell, Thomas C. 1995. Total quality management as competitive advantage: A review and empirical study. *Strategic Management Journal* 16 (1): 15–37.

### Scale (Actual Questions Used)

*Industry*

Participants were asked to circle the best response to each statement on 1 to 5 scale (5 = "agree strongly," 1 = "disagree strongly").

Entry Barriers

1. Our industry is very difficult for new firms to enter successfully.
2. In our business, existing firms have insurmountable advantages over new entrants.
3. Large firms have definite cost advantages in our industry.
4. Our industry is dominated by a few large competitors.

Rivalry

5. In our industry, customers are loyal—they rarely switch to new firms or competitors.
6. Competition in our industry is mainly on price, not product or service differentiation.
7. Compared with other industries, rivalry in our industry is extremely intense.
8. Firms in our industry advertise heavily compared with other industries.
9. Demand in our industry has been growing rapidly in the past 3 years.
10. Innovation and R&D are more prevalent in our industry than in most industries.
11. Over the past 3 years, our industry has been more profitable than most.
12. We have a serious excess capacity problem in our industry.
13. Our industry is still in early growth and infancy.
14. Our industry would be characterized as a high-technology industry.

*TQM General*

Respondents were asked the following two general TQM questions:

15. Has your organization ever made a significant commitment to Total Quality Management or a similar Total Quality Program?
    A. Yes
    B. No
16. Please tell us how advanced the implementation of the program is compared with quality programs of other organizations you are familiar with.
    A. Far more advanced in implementation than most other organizations I am familiar with.
    B. Somewhat more advanced in implementation than most other organizations I am familiar with.
    C. About equally advanced in implementation than most other organizations I am familiar with.
    D. Somewhat less advanced in implementation than most other organizations I am familiar with.
    E. Far less advanced in implementation than most other organizations I am familiar with.
    F. No significant involvement with a quality program.

*TQM Factors*

Respondents were asked to indicate their implementation of the quality features given below on a 0 to 5 scale (5 = highly advanced in implementation, 1 = have not begun implementation but intend to, and 0 = do not intend to implement).

Executive Commitment

17. A top executive decision to commit fully to a quality program
18. Top executives actively championing our quality program
19. Executives actively communicating a quality commitment to employees

Adopting the Philosophy

20. Quality principles included in our mission statement
21. An overall theme based on our quality program
22. Entering a Baldrige Award competition

Closer to Customers

23. Increasing the organization's direct personal contacts with customers
24. Actively seeking customer inputs to determine their requirements
25. Using customer requirements as the basis for quality
26. Involving customers in product or service design

Closer to Suppliers

27. Working more closely with suppliers
28. Requiring suppliers to meet stricter quality specifications
29. Requiring suppliers to adopt a quality program

Benchmarking

30. An active competitive benchmarking program
31. Researching best practices of other organizations
32. Visiting other organizations to investigate best practices firsthand

Training

33. Management training in quality principles
34. Employee training in quality principles
35. Employee training in problem-solving skills
36. Employee training in teamwork

Open Organization

37. A more open, trusting organizational culture
38. Less bureaucracy
39. Frequent use of cross-departmental means
40. Use of empowered work teams

Employee Empowerment

41. Increased employee involvement in design and planning
42. A more active employee suggestion system
43. Increased employee autonomy in decision making
44. Increased employee interaction with customers and suppliers

Zero-Defects Mentality

45. An announced goal of zero defects
46. A program for continuous reduction in defects
47. A plan to reduce rework drastically

Flexible Manufacturing

48. Design for assembly (DFA) or design for manufacturability (DMA)
49. A flexible manufacturing system
50. A JIT inventory system
51. Cellular manufacturing
52. Process capability studies
53. Statistical process control
54. Taguchi methods, or design of experiments (DOE)

Process Improvement

55. A program to reduce order-processing cycle time
56. A program to reduce new product or service development cycle times
57. A program to reduce overall product or service delivery cycle times
58. A program to reduce paperwork
59. A program to find wasted time and costs in all internal processes

Measurement

60. Measurement of quality performance in all areas
61. Charts and graphs to measure and monitor quality
62. Statistical methods to measure and monitor quality
63. Employee training in statistical methods for measuring quality

*Total Performance*

Using the "agree–disagree" scale shown earlier, respondents were asked to rate their firms' overall performance over the past 3 years:

64. Over the past 3 years, our financial performance has been outstanding.
65. Over the past 3 years, our financial performance has exceeded our competitors.'
66. Over the past 3 years, our revenue (sales) growth has been outstanding.
67. Over the past 3 years, we have been more profitable than our competitors.
68. Over the past 3 years, our revenue growth rate has exceeded our competitors.'

*Total Quality Management (TQM) Program Performance*

Using the "agree-disagree" scale shown earlier, respondents were asked to indicate how their TQM programs had affected performance by answering each question.

69. Our quality program has dramatically increased our organization's productivity.
70. Our quality program has dramatically improved our competitive position.
71. Our quality program has dramatically increased our profitability.
72. Our quality program has dramatically increased our revenues.
73. Our quality program has dramatically improved our overall performance.
74. Our quality program has been a positive development for our organization.
75. Our quality program has had a negative impact on our profitability.
76. We would have been better off without a quality program.

### Construct Description

TQM was defined by Ross (1993) as " an integrated management philosophy and set of practices that emphasizes, among other things, continuous improvement, meeting customer's requirements, reducing rework, long-range thinking, increased employee involvement and teamwork, process redesign, competitive benchmarking, team-based problem solving, constant measurement of results, and closer relationships with suppliers."

### Measurement Descriptions

The final scale contained 76 items under five broad categories. The TQM measurement scale contained 47 items covering 12 variables. Industry effects were captured using a scale of 14 industry items classified into two variables, entry barriers and rivalry, as an index of industry differences. Overall financial performance, including profitability and sales growth, was measured using a scale of five items. The specific response categories used in the scales were listed in the above Scale section.

### Development

After an extensive review of the literature and some TQM training, researchers first developed measurement scales for the TQM dimensions. Then, these scales were pretested, which included review and feedback from TQM consultants, trainers, and executives.

### Sample

This study was done in three phases. The first phase included the scale development as described above. The second phase included a mail survey, the sample for which included all firms with 50 or more employees within selected zip codes in the northeastern United States. Of the 143 surveys mailed out, 36 complete responses were returned. The useable response rate was 25.2%. The third phase included on-site personal interviews, the sample for which included 30 firms chosen from selected zip codes in the northeastern United States but not in zip codes included in the mail survey. The usable response rate for this phase was 78.3%. The target respondent for this survey was either the CEO or a senior executive responsible for the quality program implementation.

### Validity and Reliability

Cronbach's coefficient alpha values were computed to test the reliabilities of the TQM scales. The coefficients for the 12 variables ranged from .78 to .90. The correlations can be found in Table 3 of the article. According to the author, to test the convergent validity of the total performance measure, objective financial measures for 15 publicly held survey participants were obtained. The author reported that the commonly used objective financial measure—return on sales—was significantly correlated with the subjectively derived total performance measures.

### Scores

The mean values are given in Table 3 of the article.

### Other Evidence

Not available.

### Reference

Ross, J. E. 1993. *Total quality management: Text, cases, and readings.* Delray Beach, FL: St. Lucie Press.

---

## Prahinski and Benton

### Article Summarized

Prahinski, Carol, and W. C. Benton. 2004. Supplier evaluations: Communication strategies to improve supplier performance. *Journal of Operations Management* 22 (1): 39–62.

### Scales (Actual Questions Used)

*Indirect Influence Strategy*

1. Assessment of your firm's performance through formal evaluation using guidelines and procedures
2. Use of a supplier certification program to certify your firm's process control
3. Public recognition of your firm's achievements/performance
4. Site visits by <<Mfg>> to your premises to help your firm improve its performance
5. Inviting your personnel to <<Mfg>>'s site to increase your awareness of how the product is used
6. Training and education of your personnel

*Formality*

7. In coordinating our activities with <<Mfg>>, formal communication channels are followed (i.e., channels that are regularized, structured modes vs. casual, informal, word-of-mouth modes).
8. <<Mfg>> has a formal system to track the performance of their suppliers.
9. <<Mfg>> has a formal program for evaluating and recognizing suppliers.
10. The source of our information about <<Mfg>>'s evaluation program is predominantly word-of-mouth (reverse coded).
11. <<Mfg>>'s evaluation process is conducted through standard procedures.

*Feedback*

12. To clarify their expectations of our firm's performance
13. Regarding their evaluation of our firm's performance
14. Regarding ideas for performance improvement
15. To establish goal activities for performance improvement

*Buying Firm's Commitment*

16. <<Mfg>> is loyal to our firm.
17. <<Mfg>> is continually on the lookout to reduce dependence on our firm (reverse coded).
18. <<Mfg>> expects to buy our products for a long time.
19. <<Mfg>> sees this relationship as a long-term partnership.
20. How strong is <<Mfg>>'s commitment to your firm?
21. How significant are <<Mfg>>'s investments in your firm as compared with investments provided by other customers?

*Cooperation*

22. <<Mfg>> is concerned about our firm's success.
23. <<Mfg>> will not take advantage of a strong bargaining position.
24. <<Mfg>> and our firm must work together to achieve our mutual goals.
25. Our relationship with <<Mfg>> is better described as a cooperative effort rather than an adversarial effort.
26. When our firm has a problem, <<Mfg>> helps us solve it.
27. How flexible is <<Mfg>> in response to requests your firm makes?
28. When we are solving problems jointly, how flexible is <<Mfg>> in resolving them?

*Operational Linkages*

29. Our business activities are closely linked with <<Mfg>>.
30. We feel like we never know what we are supposed to be doing for <<Mfg>> (reverse coded).
31. Our activities with <<Mfg>> are well coordinated.
32. We have a routine and well-established system that facilitates the links of our operations with <<Mfg>>'s operations.

*Supplier's Commitment*

33. Our firm is loyal to <<Mfg>>.
34. Our firm is continually on the lookout to reduce dependence on <<Mfg>> as a customer (reverse coded).
35. Our firm expects <<Mfg>> to buy our products for a long time.
36. Our firm sees this relationship as a long-term partnership.
37. How strong is your firm's commitment with <<Mfg>>?

38. How significant are your firm's investments in equipment dedicated to <<Mfg>> as compared with investments dedicated to other customers?
39. Compared with your competitors, how well does your firm perform on the following aspects?

*Supplier's Performance*

40. Product quality (reverse coded)
41. Delivery performance (reverse coded)
42. Price (reverse coded)
43. Responsiveness to requests for changes (reverse coded)
44. Service support (reverse coded)
45. Overall performance (reverse coded)

### Construct Description

In the article, buyer-supplier relationship was defined as "the supplier's perception of the buying firm's behavioral and operational relationship attributes" (p. 42). It was conceptualized as a high-order construct containing three subdimensions: (1) the buying firm's commitment, (2) cooperation, and (3) operational linkage. According to the authors, buying firm's commitment was described as the "suppliers' perception of the degree to which the buying firm feels pledged or obligated to continue business with a specific supplier" (p. 42); the cooperation dimension was included to capture "the supplier's perceptions of the degree to which the two trading partners work together to solve problems, establish strategic directions and achieve their mutual goals" (p. 42); and the last dimension—operational linkage—represented "the supplier's perceptions of the degree to which the buying and selling firms coordinate their systems, procedures, and routines to facilitate operations" (p. 42).

Another multidimensional construct studied in the article was the collaborative communication construct. This construct covered three communication strategies: (1) indirect influence strategy, (2) formality, and (3) feedback. Indirect influence strategy was described as integration of business partners toward a common language and shared objectives by education, training, and site visits. Formality focused on the structure and routine embedded in the communication process and reflected "the degree to which the inter-organizational communication of the supplier evaluation is established through structured rules and fixed procedures" (p. 41). Finally, feedback emphasized two-way communication between the buyer and the supplier.

This article also included two one-dimensional constructs: (1) supplier's commitment and (2) supplier's performance. The former was defined as "the degree to which the supplier feels obligated to continue business with the particular buying firm" (p. 42), while the latter was "an operational measure of key success factors—namely, product quality, delivery performance, price, responsiveness to change requests, service support, and overall performance" (p. 43).

### Measurement Description

There were a total of eight first-order constructs. Each was measured by multi-item scales; and 7-point Likert scales were used to gauge each item. During the scale validation process, some of the items were dropped because of "weak loadings, cross loadings, multiple loadings, communalities, error residuals and theoretical determination" (p. 480).

### Development

Wherever possible, the authors relied on existing scales (such as Anderson and Weitz 1992; Cannon and Perreault 1999; Carr and Pearson 1999; Krause 1995; Maloni and Benton 2000; Mohr and Sohi 1995; Mohr and Spekman 1994), with a minor wording change to reflect the supplier's perspective. The survey items for the feedback, formality, cooperation, commitment, and operational linkages constructs were newly developed. These new items were subjected to extensive scale refinement and validation, including a pretest by three first-tier automotive supplier executives and five experienced researchers. As a result of scale validation, a few items dropped from the initial instrument along with some changes in wording and format modification.

### Sample

The sample contained the critical suppliers for the four largest North American automotive manufacturers—Honda, Daimler-Chrysler, Ford, and General Motors. In the first two cases, the manufacturers provided the contact information for their most critical suppliers. For the other two manufacturers, the list of critical suppliers was developed based on recent publicized awards recognition. The surveys were mailed to the chief executive officers of the supplier companies. Of the 660 surveys sent out, 139 usable surveys were received, constituting a response rate of 24.3%. Nonresponse bias was analyzed by comparing the responses from the early and late returns. The nonsignificant *t*-tests on 12 randomly selected survey items indicated absence of nonresponse bias.

### Reliability and Validity

According to the authors, content validity of the survey instrument was established through an extensive literature review, followed by in-depth interviews with business executives and researchers. The authors continued with a validation process that included an assessment of unidimensionality, construct reliability, convergent validity, and discriminant validity. During the validation process, a target rotation factor analysis was performed. The results showed that the lowest significant factor loading purported to measure the underlying construct was above .30 and all the *t*-values were above 2.0. These significant factor loadings provided evidence to support unidimensionality and convergent validity. Discriminant validity was assessed by calculating the 95% confidence interval of the correlations between each factor pair. In addition, the authors provided validation of the second-order factors. They noted that the loadings of the first-order constructs onto the high-order factors were all significant, which indicated the existence of second-order factors. Cronbach's coefficient alpha values, as a yardstick of construct reliability, were all above .70. The alpha-if-item-deleted was also checked to provide additional support to construct reliabilities.

### Scores

Tables 1 and 2 in the article provide information about the sample. Table 3 reports the descriptive statistics on the survey items. Table 4 lists the final factor loadings. Table 5 presents measures of model fit and statistical power. Table 6 reports correlations and standard errors of latent variables. Table 7 shows second-order factor loadings. Figures 2–5 and Table 8 give the results of structural analyses.

### Other Evidence

Not available.

### References

Anderson, E., and B. Weitz. 1992. The use of pledges to build and sustain commitment in distribution channels. *Journal of Marketing Research* 29 (1): 18–34.

Cannon, J. P., and W. D. Perreault Jr. 1999. Buyer-seller relationships in business markets. *Journal of Marketing Research* 36 (4): 439–60.

Carr, A. S., and J. N. Pearson. 1999. Strategically managed buyer-supplier relationships and performance outcomes. *Journal of Operations Management* 17 (5): 497–519.

Krause, D. R. 1995. Interorganizational cooperation in supplier development: Influencing factors. Unpublished PhD diss., Arizona State University, Tempe, AZ.

Maloni, M., and W. C. Benton. 2000. Power influences in the supply chain. *Journal of Business Logistics* 21 (1): 49–73.

Mohr, J. J., and R. S. Sohi. 1995. Communication flows in distribution channels: Impact on assessments of communication quality and satisfaction. *Journal of Retailing* 71 (4): 393–416.

Mohr, J., and R. Spekman. 1994. Characteristics of partnership success: Partnership attributes, communication behavior, and conflict resolution techniques. *Strategic Management Journal* 15 (2): 135–52.

## Prasad, Tata, and Madan

### Article Summarized

Prasad, Sameer, Jasmine Tata, and Manu Madan. 2005. Build to order supply chains in developed and developing countries. *Journal of Operations Management* 23 (5): 551–68.

### Scales (Actual Questions Used)

*Uncertainty*

1. Demand for items
   - Deterministic
   - Known probability with known parameters
   - Normal distribution with known parameters
   - Poisson distribution with known parameters
   - Special known distribution such as intermittent or erratic demand
   - Known distribution, but parameters are not assumed to be known
   - Other
2. Demand mean and variance
   - Stationary
   - Nonstationary

*Information Complexity*

3. Number of items analyzed by model
   - Single item analyzed
   - Budget of space constraint for a group of items
   - Coordinated control to save replenishment costs
   - Substitute items permissible
   - Complimentary demand
   - Dependency due to product structure
   - Other
4. Time period for the analysis
   - Single period
   - Finite multiple time period with rolling time horizon
   - Finite multiple time period with no rolling time horizon
   - Infinite time period
5. Nature of the supply process
   - Lead time is known
   - Random lead time with known mean and variance
   - Random portion of material is received
   - Finite replenishment rate
   - Other

*Operational Independence*

6. Out-of-stock policy
   - Back order
   - Last sales
   - Both

7. Number of stocking points
   - Single stocking point
   - Single echelon at several locations
   - Other

8. Repair
   - No repair
   - Repair system

*Replenishment Volumes*

9. Procurement structure
   - No discount
   - Discounts
10. Order size
    - No limit
    - Limits
    - Other
11. Order quantity
    - Obtained/calculated
    - Predetermined
12. Other systems
    - s, Q
    - s, S
    - R, S
    - s, S, R

*Supplier Integration*

13. Suppliers
    - Tight coupling with suppliers
    - Loose coupling with suppliers

**Construct Description**

Following Pope and Prasad's (1998) classification system, build-to-order (BTO) supply chains and make-to-stock (MTS) supply chains were defined along five dimensions—uncertainty, information complexity, operational independence, replenishment volumes, and supplier integration. Compared with BTO supply chains, MTS supply chains were characterized by lower levels of postponement, uncertainty, information complexity, replenishment volumes, and supplier integration and a higher level of operational independence.

**Measurement Descriptions**

The authors asked for a self-description from the respondents on each variable during the structured interviews.

### Development

The instrument was adopted from Pope and Prasad (1998).

### Sample

Structured interviews were conducted with materials managers within 30 companies, comprising 86 product lines. A total of 57% of the companies were located in the United States, 30% in Latin America, 10% in Europe, and the rest in Asia. The companies also spanned a variety of industries, including electronics, office material, food suppliers, maintenance suppliers, and so on. However, the article does not provide information regarding the sampling frame of the study.

### Reliability and Validity

The dimensions assessed were validated by the original authors (Pope and Prasad 1998) and had theoretical support in the literature. The structured interview technique adopted in the study used standardized definitions and hence avoided confusion. Furthermore, reliability was assessed by multiple interviews. Open-ended questions were also used as part of the instrument and the answers coded. These answers, as well as multiple respondents, allowed for internal validity of the conclusions.

### Scores

Descriptive statistics and $\chi^2$ differences are included in Table 2.

### Other Evidence

Not available.

### Reference

Pope, J. A., and S. Prasad. 1998. The measurement of international inventory systems. *Logistics Information Management* 11 (6): 375–85.

## Primo and Amundson

### Article Summarized

Primo, Marcos A. M., and Susan D. Amundson. 2002. An exploratory study of the effects of supplier relationships on new product development outcomes. *Journal of Operations Management* 20 (1): 33–52.

### Scales (Actual Questions Used)

*Supplier Involvement*

1. How active are suppliers in the NPD process?
2. Do key suppliers provide input in NPD projects?
3. How close are communications with suppliers about quality considerations and design changes?
4. Does the company provide a fair return to suppliers?
5. Does the company strive to establish long-term relationships with suppliers?
6. Does the company help suppliers to improve their quality?

*Supplier Quality Control*

7. Data about the quality of parts and components under consideration for purchasing is at our disposal.
8. We can easily use data from tests of quality conducted by our suppliers.
9. We have a system for supplier certification.
10. We require evidence of statistical control from suppliers of critical parts.
11. Our suppliers have to send us information certifying the results of specific tests and inspections on materials.

*Supplier Obstructionism*

12. The progress of this project was hampered by uncooperative suppliers.
13. We could have completed this project sooner, if we had not had to wait for critical suppliers.
14. Our suppliers considered other customers to be a higher priority than we are.
15. Our suppliers consider us to be their highest priority (reverse coded)

*Project Speed*

16. This project was completed in significantly less time than similar projects undertaken by this organization.
17. The time to complete this project was about normal for this organization (reverse coded).
18. This project took longer than the usual amount of time for a project like this, in this organization (reverse coded).
19. My organization holds this project up as an example of fast product development.
20. This was one of the fastest projects ever undertaken by this organization.

*Project Quality*

21. Primary product performance characteristics
22. Secondary options for features—characteristics that supplement the basic functioning of the product
23. Reliability of the product—probability of failure in a specified time
24. Conformance to established standards
25. Durability—the amount of use before the product deteriorates or needs to be replaced
26. Serviceability—ease of repair
27. Aesthetics—how the product looks, feels, sounds, tastes, or smells
28. Overall product quality perceived by customers

*Projected R&D Budget/Time-to-Market Objective/Projected Unit Cost of the Product*

29. To what extent was the projected R&D budget/time-to-market objective/projected unit cost of the product met, relative to your original expectations?

*Technical Difficulty*

30. If the level of technical difficulty of the NPD project is within the bounds of the firm's current technical capabilities or requires the development of new technology capabilities, and if so, the amount of innovation required.

**Construct Description**

Supplier involvement was defined in terms of both the extent of supplier participation and the quality of the relationship a firm develops with its suppliers. Supplier quality control was defined as "the extent to which suppliers provide quality control information to their customers (Flynn et al., 1994)" (p. 37). It reflected the availability and easy use of quality data provided by suppliers. Supplier obstructionism was developed to capture "damage to NPD projects due to dependence on uncooperative suppliers" (p. 35). This construct included the information of delays caused by suppliers in NPD project activities and also the information of the lack of priority and cooperation by suppliers involved with the NPD project. NPD project outcomes included three individual constructs: project development time, project costs, and product quality. Product quality was conceptualized as an index consisting of eight quality dimensions proposed by Garvin (1987). The definition of technical difficulty followed the description provided by Tatikonda (1995). It captured "the difficulty of developing the scientific solution to the problem" (p. 42).

## Measurement Description

Multi-item scales were used for supplier involvement, supplier obstructionism, supply quality control, and project speed. Specifically, seven items were used to measure supplier involvement. Some items were related to the extent of supplier involvement and others were related to the nature of supplier involvement. Four items were used to measure supplier obstructionism, while supplier quality control was measured using a five-item scale.

Two different measures were used for project development time. First, project speed was evaluated using a five-item scale that reflected the progress of a specific project compared with other projects developed in the company. Second, a single item was used to measure the extent to which the time-to-market objective was met relative to the company's original expectations. A 7-point scale was developed to measure this item: 1 = "significantly worse than expected," 2 = "worse than expected," 3 = "a little worse than expected," 4 = "on target," 5 = "a little better than expected," 6 = "better than expected," and 7 = "significantly better than expected."

Project costs were also measured in two different ways—projected R&D budget and projected unit cost of the product. The first one indicated the extent to which the projected R&D budget objective was met, and the other indicated the extent to which the projected product unit cost was met. Both items were evaluated using a 7-point scale: 1 = "significantly worse than expected," 2 = "worse than expected," 3 = "a little worse than expected," 4 = "on target," 5 = "a little better than expected," 6 = "better than expected," and 7 = "significantly better than expected."

Product quality was measured using eight items. Each item indicated one quality dimension. Respondents compared each of the quality dimensions with the correspondent quality dimensions in their competitor's product or substitute products and reported on a 7-point scale. The anchors for the 7-point scale were as follows: 1 = "significantly worse than competitors," 2 = "worse than competitors," 3 = "a little worse than competitors," 4 = "on target," 5 = "a little better than competitors," 6 = "better than competitors," and 7 = "significantly better than competitors."

Technical difficulty was quantified based on a single item using a 7-point scale with the following anchors: 1 = "within the bounds of our current technology capability (a step, with little or no innovation)," 4 = "requires some stretch, but related to our current capabilities (a stretch, with some innovation)," and 7 = "requires developing new technology capabilities (a leap, requiring radical innovation)."

## Development

Whenever available, existing scales were used for the relevant constructs (e.g., technical difficulty and product quality outcomes). New scales were developed based on case studies, which used interviews and focus groups.

## Sample

Data were collected from 38 NPD projects in five companies in the electronic industries. Multiple respondents were target for each project. These respondents included the team leader, up to five team members, and the team sponsor, as well as various levels of management and product development support, quality managers and procurement managers. The total number of individual respondents for each question varied from 2 to 7. No further information regarding the sampling approach, for instance, the sampling frame, was provided in the article.

**Reliability and Validity**

Before data from multiple respondents within a project were aggregated, interrater reliability was evaluated using several interrater reliability measures, including the F statistic, the intraclass correlation ($\eta$), and $\eta^2$. Overall, the analyses indicated a satisfactory level of interrater reliability of most items. The Cronbach's coefficient alpha values were computed to evaluate internal consistency for four multi-item scales—project speed, supplier involvement, supplier quality control, and supplier obstructionism. The values were .78, .79, .65, and .68, respectively, which provided empirical evidence of construct reliability. These four multi-item scales were also subject to construct validity tests. First, the unidimensionality test indicated one large major component in each scale according to the results from exploratory factor analysis (EFA). Although, in three cases, a second dimension was suggested according to the criterion of eigenvalue larger than 1, the authors believed that the values for the second dimension were much smaller and that the second components were not representative of all items. Hence, all scales were treated as unidimensional.

EFA with the principal components analysis (PCA) method was used to test discriminate validity of supplier involvement and supplier obstructionism. The unrotated factor solution showed that all items of the supplier involvement scale clearly loaded on factor 1 while all items from the supplier obstructionism scale loaded on factor 2, with the exception of only one cross-loading item originally designed for the supplier obstructionism scale. Therefore, the authors claimed that discriminant validity was achieved.

**Scores**

The factor analysis results for unidimensionality and discriminant validity are reported in Tables 5 and 6, respectively. The interrater reliability measures are provided in Table 3.

**Other Evidence**

Not available.

**References**

Flynn, B. B., R. G. Schroeder, and S. Sakakibara. 1994. A framework for quality management research and an associated measurement instrument. *Journal of Operations Management* 11 (4): 339–66.

Garvin, D. A. 1987. Competing on the eight dimensions of quality. *Harvard Business Review* 65 (6): 101–109.

Tatikonda, M. V. 1995. *Technology planning and implementation in product development projects: An empirical study of innovation type, organization, and performance.* Unpublished doctoral dissertation, Graduate School of Management, Boston University, Boston, MA.

---

# Rabinovich, Dresner, and Evers

**Article Summarized**

Rabinovich, Elliot, Martin E. Dresner, and Philip T. Evers. 2003. Assessing the effects of operational processes and information systems on inventory performance. *Journal of Operations Management* 21 (1): 63–80.

**Scales (Actual Questions Used)**

1. What percentage of the product line's inventory is managed through a computer-based, enterprise-wide inventory management system linking supply, manufacturing, distribution, and order reception operations (circle one)?

| | | | | | |
|---|---|---|---|---|---|
| 0–10% | 11–20% | 21–30% | 31–40% | 41–50% | 51–60% |
| 61–70% | 71–80% | 81–90% | 91–100% | No response | |

2. What percentage of the product line's inventory categories listed below is managed through JIT and MRP techniques (complete all)?

   Raw material inventory bound for manufacturing
   Work-in-process inventory
   Finished goods inventory bound from manufacturing

3. Which one of the following descriptions most typifies the manufacturing of your business unit's product line (circle one)?

   Standard product with no options
   Standard product with standard options but not at the request of individual buyers
   Standard product modified to customer specification using standardized components
   Standard product modified to customer specification using customized components
   Customized product manufactured and designed to customer specification

4. Processes and equipment can be organized in various ways. Please use the following options in answering question 5:

   *Flow process:* Products are produced in a continuous flow; work centers are laid out in the sequence in which the products are produced.
   *Assembly line:* Products are produced in large batches; work centers are laid out in the sequence in which the products are produced.
   *Batch shop:* Products are produced in moderately large batches; similar equipments performing the same functions are grouped together or manufacturing cells are used.
   *Job shop:* Products are produced in small batches; similar equipments performing the same functions are grouped together or manufacturing cells are used.

   Which one of the following categories comes closest to characterizing your product line's dominant manufacturing process (circle one)?

   Flow process
   Assembly line
   Batch shop
   Job shop

5. Of the total number of units manufactured, what percentage is built to inventory (circle one)?

| | | | | | |
|---|---|---|---|---|---|
| 0–10% | 11–20% | 21–30% | 31–40% | 41–50% | 51–60% |
| 61–70% | 71–80% | 81–90% | 91–100% | No response | |

6. What is the average elapsed time in days between receiving a customer request and delivering the product line that accounts for the largest percentage of your business unit's revenues (circle one)?

| | | | | | |
|---|---|---|---|---|---|
| <1 | 1–2 | 2.1–4 | 4.1–7 | 7.1–14 | 14–21 |
| 21.1–30 | 30.1–60 | 60.1–90 | >90 | No response | |

7. What is the current annual inventory-turnover ratio of the product line that accounts for the largest percentage of your business unit's revenues (circle one)?

| | | | | | |
|---|---|---|---|---|---|
| <0.5 | 0.5–1 | 1.1–2 | 2.1–4 | 4.1–8 | 8.1–12 |
| 12.1–16 | 16.1–20 | 20.1—30 | >30 | No response | |

8. What is the level of annual sales of the product line that accounts for the largest percentage of your business unit's revenues (circle one)?

   US$ 100 million or less
   More than US$ 100 million, up to US$ 200 million

More than US$ 200 million, up to US$ 300 million
More than US$ 300 million, up to US$ 400 million
More than US$ 400 million, up to US$ 500 million
More than US$ 500 million, up to US$ 600 million
More than US$ 600 million, up to US$ 700 million
More than US$ 700 million, up to US$ 800 million
More than US$ 800 million, up to US$ 900 million
More than US$ 900 million, up to US$ 1000 million
More than US$ 1000 million

9. What is the current market share of the product line that accounts for the largest percentage of your business unit's revenues (circle one)?

| | | | | | |
|---|---|---|---|---|---|
| 0–10% | 11–20% | 21–30% | 31–40% | 41–50% | 51–60% |
| 61–70% | 71–80% | 81–90% | 91–100% | No response | |

### Construct Description

JIT adoption was defined as "the extent to which JIT techniques are implemented throughout the enterprise" (p. 69). Similarly, MRP adoption was given in the article as "the extent to which MRP techniques are implemented throughout the enterprise" (p. 69). Adoption of enterprise-wide IS was characterized as "the extent to which the firm's inventory is managed using a computer-based, enterprise-wide information system" (p. 67). Product customization captured the extent to which the product offered to customers is manufactured to their specifications. The construct of manufacturing flexibility and modularization reflected "the manufacturing methods through which product characteristics are altered in order to satisfy customer demands" (p. 69). Inventory speculation represented "the efficiency with which firms use their inventories" (p. 69). Inventory effectiveness connoted "the quality of the process output" (p. 69).

### Measurement Description

Constructs were operationally defined based on the data related to the product line that represented the largest share of the responding company's revenues. The specific response categories for each variable were reported in the Scales section.

### Development

Survey items all had theoretical support in the literature. The authors adopted existing scales that had already been validated as much as possible. For example, the manufacturing flexibility and modularization scales were based on the works of Hayes and Wheelwright (1979) and were empirically validated by Safizadeh et al. (1996).

### Sample

The authors sampled 1,527 high-level managers working for manufacturing firms in the United States. The source of the sample was a list of 10,906 logistics practitioners affiliated with one major (unnamed) professional association. A total of 272 returned responses yielded a response rate of 18.3%. Among them, 256 questionnaires were usable and were analyzed. Approximately 86.8% of the respondents "were managers, directors, vice presidents, and chief operating officers in such fields as logistics, manufacturing, distribution and transportation" (pp. 69–70). The range of industries covered in the sample data included 19 different two-digit U.S. Department of Commerce's Standard Industrial Classification (SIC) code sectors.

### Validity and Reliability

Confirmatory factor analysis (CFA) was used to assess the psychometric properties of the constructs studied in the article. According to the CFA results, the unidimensionality was validated by multiple fit indices and the absence of large negative or possible residuals. Construct reliability was computed based on standardized loadings and their corresponding standard errors. The author noted that the composite reliability estimates were .69 for JIT adoption and .68 for MRP adoption, and the variance extracted measures were .63 and .52, respectively. These findings provided some support for construct reliability.

Furthermore, the CFA results indicated that all standardized factor loadings were significant and substantial (i.e., >.65), which suggested convergent validity. The discriminant validity was "assessed by constraining the estimated correlation parameter between MRP adoption and JIT adoption to 1 and then performing a $\chi^2$ difference test on the values obtained for the constrained and unconstrained models" (p. 78). The resulting statistically significant $\chi^2$ difference reported in the article provided evidence for discriminant validity. Finally, the predictive validity was verified by looking at the covariance coefficients between the latent constructs and the corresponding criterion constructs that they were theoretically intended to predict. The presence of statistically significant correlations provided evidence of predictive validity.

### Scores

Table 1 in the article shows the descriptive statistics. Table 2 provides a summary of statistically significant standardized effects. Figure 2 gives the CFA model results. The standardized structural model results are displayed in Figure 3.

### Other Evidence

Not available.

### References

Hayes, R. H., and S. C. Wheelwright. 1979. Link manufacturing process and product life cycles. *Harvard Business Review* 57 (1): 133–40.

Safizadeh, M. H., L. P. Ritzman, D. Sharma, and C. Wood. 1996. An empirical analysis of the product-process matrix. *Management Science* 42 (11): 1576–91.

## Raffi and Swamidass

### Article Summarized

Raffi, Farshad, and Paul M. Swamidass. 1987. Towards a theory of manufacturing overhead cost behavior: A conceptual and empirical analysis. *Journal of Operations Management* 7 (1/2): 121–37.

### Scales (Actual Questions Used)

*Competitive Priorities*

1. Ability to provide high-performance products
2. Ability to make dependable delivery promises
3. What is the approximate number of engineering (product design) changes in a month for the business unit?

*Degree of Product Customization*

4. Overall, how extensively are products customized in the business unit?

*Process Rationalization*

5. The production process in this business unit is one of a kind, small batch, large batch, repetitive/semicontinuous, continuous

*Growth Rate on Sales*

6. What was the approximate average annual growth rate of sales (in units) in the last three years for the business unit?

*Trend in Capacity Utilization*

7. What has been the trend in utilization of manufacturing capacity in the last five years?

*Order-Filling Method*

8. Place an (X) in the box or boxes that describe the production in the business unit:

| | |
|---|---|
| Make-to-stock | ☐ |
| Make-to-order | ☐ |
| Assemble-to-order | ☐ |

**Construct Description**

Manufacturing overhead cost was defined as an aggregation of several individual overhead cost items. These cost items accounted for four types of costs—"indirect materials, indirect labor, facilities cost, and service departments related cost" (p. 123). Strategy variables were "those with long-term implications, or with potential to change the competitive position of the firm" (p. 127). They fell into three categories of generic strategies: (1) low cost, (2) differentiation, and (3) focus. The six strategy variables investigated in the study were reliance on delivery dependability, rates of sales growth, capacity utilization, level of product standardization, reliance on high-performance products, and degree of process rationalization.

**Measurement Description**

The manufacturing overhead costs were quantified as percentages of total manufacturing costs for a typical final product. Order-filling method was captured using a categorical variable. Respondents could choose more than one alternative from the three categories—MTS, MTO, and ATO—as the order-filling methods. Most items for strategy variables were measured on Likert-type scales. Please see the Appendix (p. 136) of the original article for details.

**Development**

Not available.

**Sample**

The data for the study were obtained from the 1983 North American Manufacturing Futures (Miller 1983) survey undertaken by the Manufacturing Roundtable, School of Management, Boston University. In the 1983 North American Manufacturing Futures survey, the questionnaires were sent to all firms in the Fortune 500 listing of industrial firms, as well as a number of executives who had participated in an earlier survey conducted in 1982. A total of 213 completed questionnaires were returned, out of which 209 were usable. The participants were high-level manufacturing executives, typically holding a vice-president position. The average 1982 sales of the responding business units were $751 million. Table 2 described the distributions of industries in the survey.

### Reliability and Validity

Not available.

### Scores

Not available.

### Other Evidence

Not available.

### Reference

Miller, Jeffrey G. 1983. *The 1983 manufacturing futures project.* Research report series. Manufacturing Roundtable, School of Management, Boston University, Boston, MA.

---

## Rho and Yu

### Article Summarized

Rho, Boo-Ho, and Yung-Mok Yu. 1998. A comparative study on the structural relationships of manufacturing practices, lead time and productivity in Japan and Korea. *Journal of Operations Management* 16 (2/3): 257–70.

### Scales (Actual Questions Used)

*Design and Engineering Change*

1. Product line change
2. Number of product lines
3. Number of engineering change orders per month
4. Change in engineering change orders
5. Change in documentation of new product release
6. Change in design engineering and manufacturing interface

*Production Planning*

7. Product mix change
8. Plant order expedition
9. Change in plant order expedition
10. Vendor expedition
11. Change in vendor expedition
12. Production schedule frozen period

*Materials Management*

13. Total inventory level in weekly demand
14. Change in work-in-progress (WIP inventory
15. Change in materials handling
16. Change in materials tracking
17. Parts shortages
18. Change in parts shortages

*Process and Process Technologies*

19. Process technology similarity
20. Process hardware advances
21. Change in process flow
22. Change in plant layout
23. Percent of new equipment
24. Proprietary of the production process and/or equipments

*Quality*

25. Change in scrap rate
26. Change in quality complaints
27. Percent of output reworked

*Lead Time*

28. Production throughput time
29. Change in throughput time

*Productivity*

30. Labor productivity gain
31. General productivity gain
32. Industry productivity growth

**Construct Description**

The causal manufacturing practices consisted of five manufacturing practice constructs: (1) design and engineering changes, (2) production planning, (3) materials management, (4) process and process technologies, and (5) quality. Each construct was defined as follows. Design and engineering changes connoted "the extensiveness of product design and engineering changes and how well these changes are adopted by manufacturing process" (p. 261). Production planning was defined as "the production planning capability of well reflecting product mix and customer order changes" (p. 261).

Materials management referred to "the ability of providing and maintaining right amount of materials for assuring continuous process flow" (p. 261). Process and process technology represented the "rationalizing process layout and aggressive adoption of new technologies" (p. 261). The quality construct studied in the article focused on conformance quality.

Two performance-oriented constructs—lead time and productivity—were employed to capture the manufacturing performance. Lead time was viewed as a measure of time wasted in the production flow. Productivity was defined in terms of labor productivity, general productivity, and industry productivity growth.

**Measurement Description**

A total of 32 indicator variables were grouped into five manufacturing practice constructs and two performance constructs. These indicator variables were either static measures, which captured the characteristic "of the addressed variables at a certain time" (p. 261), or dynamic measures, which took "into account the cumulative or time-lagged effect" (p. 261) of manufacturing practices. All the dynamic indicator variables were measured on a Likert-type scale—for example, change in engineering change orders: One scale item pertaining to the design and engineering change construct was gauged using a three-place response format, where a value of 1 indicated "less now" and a value of 3 indicated "more now." As for the static indicator variables, some of them, such as number of product lines, were measured objectively, and the others, such as proprietary of the production process and/or equipments, were measured perceptually using Likert-type scales. A detailed description of the measurement is given in Table 1.

## Development

The questionnaire was largely adopted from the factory productivity survey instrument initially developed by Schmenner (1986). Five main categories were included in this questionnaire: product management, process management, workforce management, productivity performances, and some descriptive productivity relevant statistics and programs. Among the 220 items in the original instrument, 32 relevant items were selected for this study. After evaluating the measurement model of the Japanese sample, the authors further dropped 12 out of the 32 items to improve the overall model fit.

## Sample

The data were collected by two mail surveys, one in Korea and the other in Japan. A total of 1,200 questionnaires were sent to the large manufacturing companies listed in Korea Productivity Center's mailing database, and 136 responses were usable. In Japan, 120 usable responses were collected from 500 large manufacturers listed on the Tokyo Stock Exchange. The authors noted a significant difference of industrial backgrounds between the Korean and Japanese samples. (Detailed information regarding the company size and industry type of the sampled companies is given in Table 2 of the article.) However, the authors argued, "This biasedness of the Japanese sample in industry distribution will not give a serious restriction to our study since it is not focusing on the practices of specifically designated manufacturing industries but on the practices of overall manufacturing industries" (p. 263). They also asserted that Japanese and Korean samples shared a consistent factor pattern based on their confirmatory factor analysis (CFA) results on the final measurement model.

## Reliability and Validity

CFA was used to examine the construct validity. The final measurement model calibrated with Japanese data revealed acceptable model fit and significant factor loadings and, therefore, provided support for construct validity. In addition, multisample tests were performed to compare the factor pattern between the Japanese and Korean samples. Based on the results of the unconstrained model, which allowed different factor-loading estimates between the two samples and used pseudo-indicators to replace the insignificant indicators identified in the Korean sample, the authors reported an acceptable fit between two countries in the multisample test. In addition, the $\chi^2$ statistics and t-values listed in Tables 4 and 5 of the article provided some evidence of predicative validity. Particularly, the accepted fit demonstrated by $\chi^2$ statistics in both the Japanese and the Korean samples indicated that the proposed causal relationship fitted the data well.

## Scores

The structural model fitness test results are displayed in Tables 4 and 5 in the article.

## Other Evidence

Not available.

## Reference

Schmenner, R. W. 1986. *Comparative factory productivity.* Research report to the Research and Evaluation Division, Economic Development Administration, U.S. Department of Commerce.

# Robinson and Satterfield

### Article Summarized

Robinson, E. Powell Jr., and Ronald K. Satterfield. 1998. Designing distribution systems to support vendor strategies in supply chain management. *Decision Sciences* 29 (3): 685–706.

### Scales (Actual Questions Used)

*Minimum Delivery Lead Time Available*

1. Same-day delivery
2. One-day minimum
3. Two-day minimum

*Dependability of Delivery Lead Time*

4. A total of 85% or more of deliveries on time
5. A total of 60% to 85% of deliveries on time
6. A total of 60% or less of deliveries on time

*Distance to Supplier Distribution Terminal*

7. Under 50 miles
8. Between 50 to 150 miles
9. Over 150 miles

*Product Price Compared with Competition*

10. Slightly lower
11. Same
12. Slightly higher

*Breadth of Product Line*

13. Narrow range of specialty items
14. Moderately broad line
15. Full-line supplier

*Note: The scales listed above were only one part of the questionnaire. It collected data about each respondent's top three chemical vendors. It was also the most important part of the questionnaire. The complete questionnaire was not provided in the article.*

### Construct Description

Robinson and Satterfield (1988) described a multidisciplinary framework that considers the interactions among a firm's distribution strategy, market share, and distribution costs in the design of "profit-maximizing" distribution networks. To illustrate the potential effectiveness of this framework, they tested it on a specific design problem facing a leading distributor of chemical products. Six criteria were identified in this article as the most important vendor selection criteria: (1) product quality, (2) price, (3) lead time, (4) average delivery lead time, (5) breadth of product line, and (6) supplier proximity. Among them, supplier proximity "represents a composite of service elements including: local inventories, local technical expertise, local sales personnel, ability to pick up emergency items at the distribution terminal, short delivery lead time, and others" (p. 695).

### Measurement Description

Not available.

### Development

The questionnaire was developed based on the literature (Heskett 1971; Gilmour 1977; LaLonde and Zinszer 1976) and the interviews with practitioners. The earlier version of the questionnaire was pretested on a sample of 30 chemical purchasers. Minor revisions to the questionnaire were made based on the feedback.

### Sample

A total of 1,964 recipients were randomly selected from a list of Class A and B chemical purchasers (top 80% in terms of sales dollars) in the test market zones. Of the 1,964 questionnaires mailed out, 356 usable surveys were returned with a response rate of 18.13%. No analysis of nonbias was reported in this article.

### Reliability and Validity

Not available.

### Scores

Correlation coefficients for the data aggregation schemes are reported in Table 1 (p. 697) in the article.

### Other Evidence

Not available.

### References

Gilmour, P. 1977. Customer service: Differentiating by marketing segment. *International Journal of Physical Distribution* 7 (3):141–49.

Heskett, J. L. 1971. Controlling customer logistics service. *International Journal of Physical Distribution* 1 (3): 141–45.

La Londe, B. J., and P. H. Zinszer. 1976. *Customer service: Meaning and measurement.* Chicago, IL: National Council of Physical Distribution Management.

Robinson, E. P., and R. K. Satterfield. 1988. Distribution system design with customer service dependent demand. In J. R. Grabner (Ed.) *Proceedings of the Eighteenth Annual Transportation and Logistics Educators Conference.* Chicago, IL: Council of Logistics Management.

---

## Rosenzweig, Roth, and Dean

### Article Summarized

Rosenzweig, Eve D., Aleda V. Roth, and James W. Dean Jr. 2003. The influence of an integration strategy on competitive capabilities and business performance: An exploratory study of consumer products manufacturers. *Journal of Operations Management* 21 (4): 437–56.

### Scales (Actual Questions Used)

*Industrial Sector Measure*

1. Which industry best describes your manufacturing focus?

   Automotive
   Chemicals

Pharmaceuticals
Consumer goods/products
High-tech
Aerospace and defense
General manufacturing

*Integration Intensity Measures*

2. How integrated is your business unit's supply chain?

   Integrated closely within your own organization (e.g., cross-functional management)
   Integrated closely with raw material suppliers
   Integrated closely with distributors/retailers
   Integrated closely with customers

*Competitive Capability Measures*

Listed below are critical success factors for competing in an industry. Please indicate how strong you feel your business unit is for each capability relative to your primary competition in the same markets.

Product Quality

3. Conformance quality
4. Product durability
5. Product reliability
6. Performance quality
7. Overall product quality as perceived by the customer

Delivery Reliability

8. Reliability of delivery times (on time)
9. Promptly handle customer complaints

Process Flexibility

10. Ability to rapidly change product mix
11. Ability to rapidly change production volumes
12. Manufacture broad product mix within same facilities
13. Rapidly handle custom orders or engineer-to-order

Cost Leadership

14. Offer lower priced products than competitors.
15. Manufacture products at lower internal costs than competition.

*Business Performance Measures*

About how has your business unit performed against internal performance measures over the past 3 years?

16. Pretax return on assets (ROA)
17. Percentage of revenues from new products
18. Overall customer satisfaction ratings
19. How would you rate your business unit's sales growth in your target markets relative to your primary competitors over last 3 years?

*Criterion-Related Validity Measures*

20. To what extent does cooperation exist between the various internal functions or business units of your organization when it comes to pursuing overall strategic objectives?

*Marketing and Customer Service*

21. Listed below are critical success factors for competing in an industry. Please indicate how strong you feel your business unit is for each capability relative to your primary competitors in the same markets.

*Quality of Customer Relationships*

22. What was your business unit's profit level (before taxes) for the most recent fiscal year?
23. About what percent of your total business unit sales revenues can concurrently be attributed to new products?
24. About how was your business unit performed against internal performance measures over the past 3 years?

## Construct Description

This research investigates the influence of supply chain integration on performance and the mediating influence of manufacturing-based competitive capabilities. It expands the work of Frohlich and Westbrook (2001). Integration intensity was defined as the linkages among various supply chain elements. It captured both the internal linkages among "the departments, functions or business units within the firm that 'source,' 'make,' and 'deliver' products" (p. 439) and the external linkages "with entities outside the enterprise, including the network of direct suppliers and their suppliers and direct customers and their customers" (p. 440). Competitive capabilities on product quality, delivery reliability, process flexibility, and cost leadership were defined in terms of the indicator variables and broadly captured manufacturers' relative competitive strength versus primary competitors in their target markets.

## Measurement Description

The integration intensity construct was operationally defined by the relative degree of the internal and external manufacturing business unit's (MBU) supply chain integration. Particularly, "to assess the MBU's achievement of Steven's (1989) internal integration stage, respondents were asked how closely integrated their internal organization is. To gauge Steven's (1989) external integration stage, respondents were asked to indicate how closely integrated their MBU is with their (1) raw material suppliers; (2) distributions and retailers; and (3) end customers" (p. 444). Each item was then evaluated using a 5-point Likert-type scale ranging from 1 = "none" to 5 = "high."

Competitive capability scales were developed to capture the organization's capability relative to its primary competitors in the same market. The resulting scales included multiple items, where each item was rated on 5-point self-anchoring scales. Business performances included two financial measures—return on assets (ROA) and the percentage of revenues from new products, one customer satisfaction measure capturing the customer perspective and one sales growth measure. The first three performance metrics reflected the MBU's performance relative to its internal goals over the past 3 years and were rated on a 5-point scale with 1 = "poor performance" and 5 = "exceptional performance." The last variable, sales growth, was also captured on a 5-point scale and indicated "the direction of the MBU sales growth in target markets relative to primary competitors over the past 3 years" (p. 446).

## Development

The authors drew on a multidisciplinary literature base and prior related research for developing the constructs of integration intensity, competitive capabilities, and performance. The survey instrument used in this research was part of the 1997 Vision in Manufacturing (VIM) questionnaire. VIM is an industry-academic research project conducted biennially by Deloitte Consulting and Professor Aleda Roth, now at Clemson University, since 1989 (*see* Roth et al., 1997 for details of the study). The authors largely relied on existing scales to select relevant items from the VIM database except for the integration intensity scale.

The competitive capabilities scales were further developed from those described in Roth (1996), which were developed in a prior administration of the VIM survey with another sample. The integration intensity scale was a newly developed scale. It was grounded in the literature and verified through pretests and follow-up interviews with senior executives.

## Sample

The sample of consumer products manufacturers was constructed based on the 1997 VIM survey. The unit of analysis was MBU, "defined by the level in the organization at which the manufacturing strategy is formulated for the primary product (Ferdows and DeMeyer, 1990; Miller and Roth, 1994)" (p. 442). The target population for VIM consisted of manufacturers in the top quartile of sales revenues in 35 countries. A stratified, probability-sampling approach was used to select manufacturers from the sample frame derived from the databases of public companies. The overall survey response rate was 10%, and the total sample size was 867. Among them, 27.5% of the entire sample (n = 238) were consumer products manufacturers, which was the focus of the study.

## Reliability and Validity

The authors argued that the scale had content validity since the items were grounded in the literature and supported by inputs from senior executives during the pretest and interviews. Principal components factor analysis (PCA) with varimax rotation was conducted to evaluate the multi-item integration intensity scale. The PCA results indicated scale unidimensionality. Cronbach's coefficient alpha value for integration intensity was .71, which demonstrated construct reliability (Nunnally, 1978). Besides, criterion-related validity was established by the significant and positive correlations between the integration intensity scale and two other measures related from theory—"the extent cooperation exists between the various internal functions or business units of the organization when it comes to pursuing overall strategic objectives [$p \leq 0.001$], and quality of customer relationships relative to primary competitors in the same markets [$p \leq 0.001$]" (p. 444).

For the competitive capability scales, the authors computed Cronbach's coefficient alpha values to assess construct reliabilities. According to the article, the, "resulting measures of reliability are reasonable for each competitive capability scale: product quality (Cronbach's coefficient $\alpha = .83$), delivery reliability (Pearson correlation coefficient = .52; [$p \leq .001$]), process flexibility (Cronbach's coefficient $\alpha = .75$) and cost leadership (Pearson correlation coefficient = .46; [$p = .001$]" (p. 444).

For the business performance measures, criterion-related validity was evaluated. Each perceptual performance measure was correlated with one objective measure. The findings of significant correlations provided evidence of criterion-related validity.

## Scores

The scores are reported in Tables 2–4 of the article.

## Other Evidence

The competitive capability scales were also studied in Roth (1996 and 1998) using similar data from prior administrations of the VIM with other samples.

## References

Ferdows, K., and A. De Meyer. 1990. Lasting improvements in manufacturing performance: In search of a new theory. *Journal of Operations Management* 9 (2): 168–84.

Frohlich, M. T., and R. Westbrook. 2001. Arcs of integration: An international study of supply chain strategies. *Journal of Operations Management* 19 (2): 185–200.

Miller, J. G., and A. V. Roth. 1994. A taxonomy of manufacturing strategies. *Management Science* 40 (3): 285–304.

Nunnally, J. C. 1978. *Psychometric theory.* New York: McGraw-Hill.

Roth, A. V. 1996. Neo-operations strategy: Linking capabilities-based competition to technology. In *Handbook of technology management,* ed. G. H. Gaynor, 38.1–38.44. New York: McGraw-Hill.

———. 1998. The second generation of quality: Global supply chain integration in Japan and the United States. In *The quality yearbook: 1998 edition,* eds. J. W. Cortada and J. A. Woods, 49–57. New York: McGraw-Hill.

Roth, A. V., A. E. Gray, J. Singhal, and K. Singhal. 1997. International technology and operations management: Resource toolkit for research and teaching. *Production and Operations Management* 6 (2): 167–87.

Steven, G. C. 1989. Integrating the supply chain. *International Journal of Physical Distribution and Materials Management* 19 (8): 3–8.

## Rosenzweig and Roth

### Article Summarized

Rosenzweig, Eve D., and Aleda V. Roth. 2004. Towards a theory of competitive progression: Evidence from high-tech manufacturing. *Production and Operations Management* 13 (4): 354–68.

### Scales (Actual Questions Used)

*Competitive Capability Measures*

1. Conformance quality
2. Reliability of delivery times (on time)
3. Ability to rapidly change production volumes
4. Manufacture products at lower internal costs than competition

*Operational Know-how Measures*

5. Overall workforce flexibility
6. Organization's learning capabilities/knowledge base

*Non-Value-Added Measure*

7. About how has your business unit performed against internal performance measures over the past 3 years?
    - Total manufacturing indirect costs

*Profitability Measure*

8. What was your business unit's profit level (before taxes) for the most recent fiscal year?

### Construct Description

The constructs used in this article to develop Roth's (1996) competitive progression theory (CPT) path model included conformance quality, delivery reliability, volume flexibility, low cost, non–value added, operational know-how, and profitability. Taking from Roth (1996, p. 38.15), "Conformance quality . . . 'affords effective and efficient approaches to process variance reduction [i.e., produces consistent output]'" (p. 357). Delivery reliability is characterized by on-time or predictable delivery cycles and dates. Low-cost capability is indicated by a manufacturer's ability to produce with lower internal costs than the primary competitors. These definitions for low cost, delivery reliability, and conformance quality were taken directly from previous literature in these areas (Roth, 1996; Dostaler 2001; Ferdows and De Meyer 1990).

In Roth's CPT, flexibility is specifically "cast in terms of volume flexibility, which is consistent with traditional manufacturing strategy" (p. 356). Likewise, the definition for volume flexibility was based on previous work that used this specific type of flexibility (Gerwin 1993; Gupta and Somers 1996; Jack and Raturi 2003; Koste and Malhotra 1999). The definition for non-value-added measure was derived from earlier research on statistical variation in work processes (Anderson, Rungtusunatham, and Schroeder 1994; Blocher, Garrett, and Schmenner 1999; Giffi, Roth, and Seal 1990; Kerkhoff, Eagar, and Utterback 1998; Roth 1996; Schmenner and Swink 1998; Wacker 1996). No formal definitions were given for the other constructs in the article, however operational know-how was loosely defined in the article as "the absorptive capacity to value, assimilate, and apply new knowledge" (p. 356).

### Measurement Description

Eight items were grouped into four dimensions (competitive capabilities, operational know-how, non–value added, and profitability). The first two dimensions (competitive capabilities and operational know-how) included six items (conformance quality, delivery reliability, volume flexibility, low cost, workforce flexibility, and learning capabilities/knowledge base) that were operationalized using a 5-point Likert-type scale (i.e., ranging from 1 = "lower" to 3 = "average" to 5 = "market leader"). The third dimension (non–value added) had one item (total manufacturing indirect cost) that was also operationalized using a 5-point Likert-type scale, except with different response categories (i.e., where 1 = "poor performance," 3 = "okay/met goals," and 5 = "exceptional performance"). The last dimension (profitability) included one item (profit level) that was measured with a forced 7-point Likert-type scale.

### Development

All survey items came directly from the vision in manufacturing (VIM) database. No further information was provided in the article.

### Sample

The data in this study were taken from a larger ongoing study, the VIM, which included more than 900 items of perceptual and objective manufacturing strategy and performance data collected from global manufacturing firms. The sampling frame for these data was the manufacturing business unit (MBU) and it encompassed the top 25% of sales in 35 countries. The overall response rate was 10% for a total sample size of 867 respondents (senior executives in the firm's MBU). The sub-sample for this study was the manufacturers in the "global high-tech" industrial sector (n = 119 or 13.7% of the 867 respondents). Of the 119 high-tech firms, 38 firms had incomplete responses of variables of interests. Hence, the final sample size of this study was 81.

### Reliability and Validity

The authors assumed that because the CPT constructs listed above were based on the operations strategy literature, they were content valid. Nonetheless, to ensure criterion-related validity, they checked for and found positive and significant ($p \leq .01$) correlation of the conformance quality measure with Garvin's (1987) quality dimensions. Likewise, they did the same for the volume flexibility and delivery reliability measures and found positive and significant correlation ($p \leq .001$) of these two constructs with the ability to achieve short lead times and fast deliveries. Volume flexibility, in particular, was also found to correlate positively and significantly ($p \leq .01$) to several dimensions of Gerwin's (1993) flexibility framework. The measure used for low cost was also positively and significantly ($p \leq .001$) correlated with the capability of providing low-priced products to customers. In addition, the measures used for operational know-how ($p \leq .01$), non–value added ($p \leq .05$), and profitability ($p \leq .05$) were all positively and significantly correlated to their corresponding outcomes. Furthermore, the overall CPT model was evaluated using LISREL 8.6 software and the resulting $\chi^2$ statistic showed an indication of excellent overall model fit.

### Scores

Means, standard deviation, and correlations are reported in Table 2 of the article.

### Other Evidence

Formal specification of the competitive progression theory (CPT) was first specified by Roth (1996) to explain the Ferdows and De Meyer (1990) observation of a sand-cone effect of combinative capabilities in manufacturing.

### References

Anderson, J. C., M. Rungtusanatham, and R. G. Schroeder. 1994. A theory of quality management underlying the Deming management method. *Academy of Management Review* 19 (3): 472–509.

Blocher, J. D., R. W. Garrett, and R. W. Schmenner. 1999. Throughput time reduction: Taking one's medicine. *Production and Operations Management* 8 (4): 357–73.

Dostaler, I. 2001. Beyond practices: A qualitative inquiry into high performance electronics assembly. *Production and Operations Management* 10 (4): 478–93.

Ferdows, K., and A. De Meyer. 1990. Lasting improvements in manufacturing performance: In search of a new theory. *Journal of Operations Management* 9 (2): 168–84.

Garvin, D. 1987. Competing on the eight dimensions of quality. *Harvard Business Review* 65 (6): 101–109.

Gerwin, D. 1993. Manufacturing flexibility: A strategic perspective. *Management Science* 39 (4): 395–410.

Giffi, C., A. V. Roth, and G. M. Seal. 1990. *Competing in world-class manufacturing: America's 21st century challenge*. Homewood, IL: Richard D. Irwin.

Gupta, Y. P., and T. M. Somers. 1996. Business strategy, manufacturing flexibility, and organizational performance relationships: A path analysis approach. *Production and Operations Management* 5 (3): 204–233.

Jack, E. D., and A. S. Raturi. 2003. Measuring and comparing volume flexibility in the capital goods industry. *Production and Operations Management* 12 (4): 480–501.

Kerkhoff, J., T. W. Eagar, and J. Utterback. 1998. A systematic strategy for optimizing manufacturing operations. *Production and Operations Management* 7 (1): 67–85.

Koste, L. L., and M. K. Malhotra. 1999. A theoretical framework for analyzing the dimensions of manufacturing flexibility. *Journal of Operations Management* 18 (1): 75–93.

Roth, A. V. 1996. Neo-operations strategy: linking capabilities-based competition to technology. In *Handbook of technology management,* ed. G. H. Gaynor, 38.1–38.44. New York: McGraw-Hill.

Schmenner, R. W., and M. L. Swink. 1998. On theory in operations management. *Journal of Operations Management* 17 (1): 97–113.

Wacker, J. G. 1996. A theoretical model of manufacturing lead times and their relationship to a manufacturing goal hierarchy. *Decision Sciences* 27 (3): 483–517.

## Roth (1993)

### Article Summarized

Roth, Aleda V. 1993. Performance dimensions in services: An empirical investigation of strategic performance. In *Advances in services marketing and management,* Vol. 2, eds. S. Swartz, D. E. Bowen, and S. W. Brown, 1–47. Greenwich, CT: JAI Press.

### Scales (Actual Questions Used)

*Business Unit Performance*

Market Performance

1. Overall retail banking unit (RBU) performance
2. Overall profitability

3. Profitability of the "brick & mortar"
4. Overall productivity of retail delivery system
5. Relative market share for primary products

Stakeholder Value

6. Price/earnings ratio
7. Return on assets
8. Return on equity
9. Net income/employees

Business Sustainability

10. Gross charge-offs/loan ratio
11. Reserve/loans ratio

*Competitive Capabilities Service Quality*

12. Courteous services
13. Consistency (Reliability)
14. Customer perceived quality
15. Accurate info (Credibility)
16. Empathy
17. Timely info (Responsiveness)
18. Conformance

*Technological Leadership*

19. Streamlined self-services
20. Technological leadership
21. Consumer-oriented technology
22. Innovative products/services
23. Enhanced features
24. Increased distribution channels
25. Technologically superior workforce

*Market Acuity*

26. Implement and manage sales concept
27. Cross-sell products
28. Understand markets/competition
29. Enlarge range of relationships
30. Broad line of financial products
31. Understand customer requirements

*Flexibility*

32. System responsiveness
33. New product introduction speed
34. Rapid staffing changes
35. Customizations

*Knowledge*

36. Employee understanding of goals/strategy
37. Superior customer info support services
38. Enhanced employee skills and knowledge (competency)

*Delivery*

39. Delivery speed (wait times)
40. Convenient services (access)
41. On-time delivery
42. Handle customer complaints

*Niche Profile*

43. Specialty image
44. Focused/niche markets

*Low Cost*

45. Low cost
46. Unique low-tech processes

*Process Performance*

Quality of Customer Interface

47. Responsive to customer inquiries
48. Accuracy of account statements
49. Overall customer requirements
50. Meet customer service levels
51. Overall customer satisfaction
52. Timeliness of mailing account statements
53. Account turnover rate performance
54. Customer complaint volume
55. Processing errors/exception performance
56. Overall system response time

Factor Productivity

57. Back office labor productivity
58. Front office labor productivity
59. Overall reliability of delivery systems
60. Cost-effective back-room tech innovations
61. Online systems availability
62. Adherence to budget/plans
63. Transaction processing costs

Innovation

64. Number of product innovations
65. Speed of new product introduction
66. Percentage of new products introduced
67. Number of service innovations

Headcount

68. Overhead performance
69. Employee headcount
70. Total labor cost
71. Ratio of management/supervisors

Quality of work life

72. Employee morale
73. Teller retention
74. Percentage of employee suggestions implemented
75. Internal communications
76. Customer service representative retention

Streamlining

77. Standardizing of procedures
78. Forms and document simplification

**Construct Description**

This article was the first to develop operational constructs in service operations management that paralleled those in the traditional manufacturing strategy literature in the early 1990s. First, competitive capabilities were constructed to exemplify "the service business' relative competitive strength" (p. 18) in operations and marketing and therefore to reflect the service business's competitive positioning. This concept was defined as a multidimensional construct, which included first-order operations and marketing capabilities, captured by eight generic, theory-based competitive capabilities: (1) service quality, (2) technological leadership, (3) market acuity, (4) flexibility, (5) knowledge, (6) delivery, (7) niche profile, and (8) low cost.

Among the eight capability dimensions, *technological leadership* indicated "the ability to use technological muscle in capturing and servicing customers" (p. 22). It was defined by "the technological content of three major components of the service enterprises: (a) *the delivery channels* (streamlined self-services and distribution), (b) the *service offerings* (e.g., enhanced product features, innovations and high consumer-oriented contents) and (c) a technologically superior workforce" (p. 22). *Market acuity* described "the combined competitive strength of marketing and sales" (p. 22). This dimension captured the "ability to see the competitive environment clearly, and thus to anticipate and respond to customers' evolving needs and wants" (p. 22). *Flexibility* was associated with the "ability to respond quickly to customer or market demands and to incorporate new ideas and technologies quickly into products (Stalk et al. 1992, p. 63)." The dimension of *knowledge* was a general competency construct which focused on "possession of the required skills and knowledge to perform the service—as illustrated by the knowledge and skill of the contact personnel (and) the knowledge and skill of operational support personnel" (p. 24). The author also noted that this construct "transcends task proficiency to include an understanding of the rationale for the purpose of work" (p. 24). Finally, *niche profile* referred to the "firm's ability to develop a specialty image and to develop highly focused/niche markets" (p. 25).

Second, overall process performance captured "the actual attributes of service delivery system process outputs and the managerial prowess to achieve operation targets" (p. 27). It was viewed as "a function of general management's ability to control cross-functional processes and insure that they are 'capable' of delivering desired product attributes" (p. 27). Similarly, this construct was characterized by six underlying dimensions: (1) quality of customer interface, (2) factor productivity, (3) innovation, (4) headcount, (5) quality of work life, and (6) streamlining.

Third, the article developed constructs related to business performance in services. Business unit viability implied a firm's ability to "not only survive but also retain its competitive posture or value over the long run" (p. 15). To sufficiently characterize the domain of this concept, the author proposed three first-order constructs: (1) market performance, (2) stakeholder value, and (3) business sustainability. The market performance construct was developed to combine "overall sales effectiveness and the ability of the service firm's delivery system to provide a 'product' bundle that meets customer needs, wants and expectations at a profit" (p. 17). Stakeholder value was constructed to capture "service enterprise's ability to leverage and to access capital in financial markets" (p. 17). Finally, business sustainability was defined to indicate "long-term solvency as represented by the business unit's ability to meet its debt obligations" (p. 17).

### Measurement

The competitive capability construct was measured using multiple items. The final set of retained items for this construct assessed eight related dimensions as discussed earlier. Each item was gauged on 7-point self-anchored scales, where 1 = "substantially weaker," 4 = "about the same," and 7 = "substantially stronger." The operational definition of process performance involved a set of items "which reflect average front- and back-room performance relative to goals over the past three years" (p. 27). The items retained in the final analysis covered all six dimensions constituting the process performance construct. A total of 11 items were used to operationalize the construct of business unit viability. Of these 11 items, 5 were used to measure the market performance dimension, 4 for stakeholder value, and 2 for the dimension of business sustainability. Each item was rated on 7-point self-anchoring scales, where 1 = "very poor performance," 4 = "met goals," and 7 = "outstanding performance."

### Development

The initial survey instrument was developed based on extensive literature review and interviews with banking executives and academic experts in the strategy area. "Over the three administrations of the survey from 1987 to 1991" (p. 14), the instrument was consistently reviewed, modified, and updated. After the data were collected, the survey items were subjected to a series of factor analyses. As a result, several items were dropped to improve construct reliability and validity.

### Sample

Empirical data used in this article were obtained through the 1991 survey of retail banking strategy and performance. This survey was a part of the Retail Banking Futures Project (RBFP), which administrated a large-scale mail survey every 2 years by the Bank Administration Institute in conjunction with Professor Aleda V. Roth, currently at Clemson University. The sampling frame used in the project was constructed based on the Federal Deposit Insurance Corporation (FDIC) Call Report tapes of all commercial banks in the United States (as of January 1990). The unit of analysis was retail banking units (RBUs), which represented "the highest level in the bank where strategic retail delivery system decisions are made" (p. 11). In the 1991 survey, the overall response rate was 11.3%, with a total sample size of 140. Of the 140 RBUs, more than 75% were banks, and the remaining 25% included holding companies and divisions. Approximately 71% of the respondents were senior/executives vice presidents. An investigation of nonrespondents suggested the existence of potential nonresponse bias. The author reported that "the sample is systematically biased towards competitive and market leaders or world-class banks" (p. 11).

### Validity and Reliability

To validate construct validity, the author performed an exploratory investigation at two different stages. First, at the initial scale development stage, qualitative evidence from the literature was sought to tentatively support content validity. Second, after the survey data were collected, the author followed Ghiselli's guidance (1964) and used Pearson product moment correlations as the convergent validity coefficient. According to the authors, the findings of significant validity coefficients between index scores and "held out" variables pertaining to the same constructs provided additional evidence for construct convergent validity. In addition, since the scales were developed based on a thorough analysis of the relevant literature and feedback from both bank executives and expert academic colleagues, the authors also claimed that reasonable evidence of content validity was established.

To further ensure construct reliability, the author relied on three different pieces of information: the factor loadings, the item-to-total correlations, and Cronbach's coefficient alpha. Several items were dropped when their factor loadings were below .50 and/or their item-to-total correlations were low. For the remaining items, Cronbach's coefficient alpha was calculated. According to the article, all three dimensions of business unit viability, all six dimensions of process performance, and six of the eight dimensions of competitive capability exhibited adequate reliability, evidenced by high Cronbach's coefficient alpha values (>.70). For the remaining two dimensions of competitive capability, one had a Cronbach's coefficient alpha value of .65, and the other was considered to be unreliable with a Cronbach's coefficient alpha value of .45.

### Scores

The scores are presented in Tables 2–6 of the article. Indexes were computed to summarize a respondent's responses to related items as a single score for the underlying latent constructs.

### Other Evidence

These constructs have been developed and applied in several related books, including Roth and van der Velde (1987, 1990, and 1992), and articles (Roth and van der Velde 1991; Roth and Jackson 1995; and Menor, Mason, and Roth 2001).

### References

Ghiselli, E. E. 1964. *Theory of psychological measurement.* New York: McGraw-Hill.

Menor, L. J., A. V. Roth, and C. H. Mason. 2001. Agility in retail banking: A numerical taxonomy of strategic service groups. *Manufacturing and Service Operations Management* 3 (4); 273–92.

Roth, A. V., and W. E. Jackson III. 1995. Strategic determinants of service quality and performance: Evidence from the banking industry. *Management Science* 41 (11): 1720–33.

Roth, A. V., and M. van der Velde. 1987. *The future of retail banking delivery systems: Executive summary of findings.* Chicago, IL: Bank Administration Institute.

———. 1990. *Retail banking strategies: Opportunities for the 1990's.* Chicago, IL: Bank Administration Institute.

———. 1991. Operations as marketing: A competitive service strategy. *Journal of Operations Management* 10 (3): 303–28.

———. 1992. *World class banking: Benchmarking the market leaders.* Chicago, IL: Bank Administration Institute.

Stalk, G., P. Evans, and L. E. Shulman. 1992. Competing on capabilities: The new rules of corporate strategy. *Harvard Business Review* 70 (2): 57–69.

## Roth (1996)

### Article Summarized

Roth, Aleda V. 1996. Neo-operations strategy: Linking capabilities-based competition to technology. In *Handbook of technology management,* ed. G. H. Gaynor, 38.1–38.44. New York: McGraw-Hill.

**Scales (Actual Questions Used)**

*Quality Index*

1. Reliability (Reduced probability of product breakdowns)
2. Perceived quality (Customer perceived quality order delivery date)
3. Conformance (Degree to which product meets standards)
4. Durability (Functionality of design)

*Delivery Index*

5. Delivery reliability (Ship on time)
6. Order Confirmation (Rapidly confirm customer order)
7. Complaint handling (Promptness in handling customer complaints)

*Flexibility Index*

8. Mix flexibility (Rapidly change product mix)
9. Variety (Manufacture broad product mix in same facilities)
10. Volume flexibility (Rapidly change production volumes)
11. Customization (Rapidly handle "customer" orders)
12. Changeover times (Reduce product changeover time)

*Price Leader Index*

13. Low price (Offer lower-priced products than competitors)
14. Low Mfg costs (Manufacturing similar products and lower cost)
15. Meet competition (Meet competitor's prices)

*Process Technological Leadership Index*

16. State-of-the-Art (Develop state-of-the-art manufacturing processes)
17. Skilled workers (Workforce with superior technological skills)
18. Unique Mfg process (Develop unique manufacturing process capabilities)
19. Organization knowledge (Superior technological know-how in organization)

*Process Enables Index*

20. Robotics (Robotics)
21. CAD (Computer-aided design)
22. CAT (Computer-aided testing)
23. BC-SF (Bar coding for shop floor)
24. AS/AR (Automated storage and retrieva)
25. AMH (Automated materials handling)
26. Vision (Vision systems)
27. Kaeyoke (Fail-safing production processes)

*Information Technology Index*

28. RDMS (Relational database management systems)
29. EDI (Electronic data interchange)
30. LAN (Local area networks)
31. PC (Personal computers)
32. E-mail (Electronic mail)

33. Org Info Integration (Integrated information systems across functions)
34. Mfg Integration (Integration of manufacturing and engineering systems)
35. AI (Artificial intelligence and expert systems)

*Design-Manufacturing Interfaces Index*

36. CAD (Computer-aided design)
37. CAPP (Computer-aided process planning)
38. CAE (Computer-aided engineering)
39. S_ENG (Simultaneous or concurrent engineering)
40. DFM (Design for manufacturing)
41. VA/VE (Value analysis and value engineering)

*Production Planning and Control (PPC) Index*

42. JIT (Just-in-Time)
43. MRP-II (Manufacturing resource planning)
44. Kanban (Kanban)
45. TPM (Total productive maintenance)
46. TMS (Tool management systems)

*Flexible Automation*

47. CNC (Computer numerical control)
48. DNC (Direct numerical control)

### Construct Description

The constructs were formed around traditional measures of competitive capabilities and technology in manufacturing and were used to describe what Roth calls competitive progression theory. Quality was given an index that consisted of "five attributes generally associated with superior product quality: product reliability, customer perceived quality, the degree to which the product conforms to standards, durability, and the general functionality of design. These five items represent the 'tangible' attributes indicated by Garvin's (1987) dimensions of quality" (p. 38.21). Delivery comprised three attributes that characterize delivery reliability. "The first is manufacturing's ability to ship on schedule. This requires a high degree of internal coordination. The remaining two attributes indicate information flows with customers, either by having the process capability to rapidly confirm orders or to be able to promptly resolve complaints" (pp. 38.21, 38.24). Flexibility was described as the ability "to respond quickly to the macro forces surrounding markets and customers, manufacturers must have responsive business processes. This degree of responsiveness requires a significant degree of coordination and process integration cross-functionally and cross-organizationally with customers and suppliers. Five items that connote process flexibility are the ability to rapidly change product mix, to produce a wide variety within the same facilities, to rapidly change production volumes, rapidly handle custom orders, and reduce product changeover times. Economies of scope, speed and economies of integration are implied by the aforementioned attributes" (p. 38.24). Finally, price leadership was represented "by three items: the ability to offer lower priced products than competitors, the ability to manufacture similar products at a lower cost, and the ability to meet competitor's prices. Price leaders are able to garner higher margins and can be more price responsive than the competition. Therefore, they will have more resources for investment and can simultaneously satisfy customers and stakeholders" (p. 38.24).

Technological leadership was the fifth capability to be added, which was described "as a sociotechnical measure of three critical measures: "hardware," "orgware," and "thoughware." The four-item index consists of superior manufacturing processes in terms of the state-of-the-art applications and their unique capabilities. The third attribute reflects the firm's overall technical know-how in the organization. This reflects, in part, the firm's ability to leverage its organizational knowledge. The fourth item is a workforce with superior technological skills. Taken together, they are manifestations of the firm's potential absorptive capacity" (p. 38.24).

In addition to competitive capabilities, a number of technology constructs were operationalized in the article. Advanced manufacturing technologies were described as follows. "Although literally hundreds of different types of advanced technologies are available to manufacturers, this research is restricted to advanced hardware, software, and methods technologies which can be broadly applied to manufacturing operations, including those for product and process design, automating production, enhancing production planning and contro , and information technologies" (p. 38.24). The process enablers' index comprised "eight items which provide advanced support functions for production. One set of support activities is used to monitor the production activities by gathering information about the process. These include computer aided inspection, computer aided testing, vision systems, and fail-safing processes . . . A second category of enablers supports materials handling and storage" (p. 38.25). "The information system index represents eight basic information technologies (ITs) for communications, integration and coordination, intelligence, and control. Information technologies are used to automate administrative information processing tasks internally, such as electronic mail (e-mail), and externally integrating information cross-functions and electronic data interchange with suppliers and customers" (p. 38.25).

For evaluating design interfaces, six items formed "an index of product and process design tools that are used to enhance the productivity of engineers and facilitate the effective coupling of engineering and manufacturing activities" (p. 38.25). The production planning and control index covered "four disciplines and control mechanisms that enable the organization to plan, schedule, and execute production and materials requirements effectively" (p. 38.25). The four disciplines and control mechanism covered were just-in-time (JIT), kanban system, MRP-II, and total productive maintenance (TPM). Finally, the flexible automation construct was represented by a two-item index that was given as "production equipment that enables the production of a variety of products with little time for changeovers" (p. 38.25).

### Measurement Description

Two distinct sets of survey items were used to tap the domains of generic competitive capabilities and advanced operations technologies. The generic competitive capabilities included five dimensions: quality, delivery, flexibility, price leader, and process technological leadership. Each dimension was operationalized through multiple items designed to capture the current business unit's competitive strength relative to their primary competitors in the same market. A 5-point Likert-type scale anchored with 1 = "relatively weak competitive strength," 3 = "strength," and 5 = "market leader" was adopted to gauge the measurement items.

Similarly, multip e items were used to measure the advanced operations technologies. The operational definition of advanced operations technologies covered five underlying dimensions: process enablers, information technology, design-manufacturing interface, production planning and control, and flexible automations. Respondents were asked to rate their manufacturing business unit's relative experience with the technologies listed as the measurement items under each dimension. The scale adopted to gauge each item was a 5-point self-anchoring scale ranging from 1 = "no experience" to 5 = "state-of-the-art experience."

### Development

The survey instrument was continuously refined from 1989 to 1993 during the progression of Vision in Manufacturing (VIM) from what was called at the time of this study the Global Manufacturing and Technology Strategy Vision Project (GMTSV) (*see* Giffi, Roth, and Seal 1990; and Roth et al. 1997). Inputs from executives and new findings in the extant literature were incorporated into the survey instrument development.

### Sample

The empirical data were collected through the Global Manufacturing Technology and Strategy Vision Project, a collaborative survey research effort between Deloitte Touche Tohmatsu International and Professor Aleda V. Roth, currently at Clemson University. The sampling frame was "the Fortune 1000 manufacturers supplemented by additional lists from directories of manufacturing firms reporting at least $50 million in annual revues" (p. 38.18). In the 1992 to 1993 study, the sample data were obtained from about 1,300 manufacturing business units (MBUs) around the world. "For the purposes of analyses presented in this report, 254 MBUs from Europe, 291 from Japan, and 676 from North America were included. The breakdown of industries and revenues of responding MBUs are given in Fig. 38.3" (p. 38.19). The author noted the fact that the MBUs sampled in this project had potential bias toward manufacturing leaders.

### Reliability and Validity

To establish content validity, extensive literature review and field research on world-class manufacturing were conducted. Expert opinion from executives was also collected to provide additional support for content validity. Regarding construct validity, exploratory factor analysis (EFA) was adopted as the main approach to determine whether each index corresponded to the underlying construct. The author reported that "each index possesses the property of unidimensionality" (p. 38.21). Cronbach's coefficient alpha and item-to-total correlations were examined to evaluate construct reliability. Tables 38.3 and 38.4 of the article report the reliability scores for the constructs.

### Scores

The scores are presented in Tables 38.2–38.10 in the article. The index was constructed by averaging the items related to the underlying constructs.

### Other Evidence

This study evolved out of a larger study of world-class manufacturing (Giffi, Roth, and Seal, 1990).

### Reference

Garvin, D. 1987. Competing on the eight dimensions of quality. *Harvard Business Review* 65 (6): 101–109.

Giffi, C., A. V. Roth, and G. Seal. 1990. *Competing in world-class manufacturing: America's 21st century challenge*. Homewood, IL: Richard D. Irwin.

Roth, A. V., A. E. Gray, J. Singhal, and K. Singhal. 1997. International technology and operations management: Resource toolkit for research and teaching. *Production and Operations Management* 6 (2): 167–87.

---

## Roth and Jackson

### Article Summarized

Roth, Aleda V., and William E. Jackson III. 1995. Strategic determinants of service quality and performance: Evidence from the banking industry. *Management Science* 41 (11): 1720–33.

**Scales (Actual Questions Used)**

*Market Performance*

1. Overall RBU performance
2. Overall RBU profitability
3. Relative market share for primary products
4. Overall productivity of the retail delivery system
5. Overall productivity of the retail delivery system

*Service Quality*

6. Courteous service
7. Consistency (reliability)
8. Customer perceived quality
9. Conformance (degree to which service meets standards)
10. Empathy in the treatment of customers
11. Accurate information (credibility)
12. Timely information (responsiveness)

*Knowledge*

13. Employees understanding of the organization's goals/strategies
14. Enhanced employee abilities and knowledge to perform required work (competency)
15. Superior customer information and support capabilities

*Technological Leadership*

16. Overall technological leadership
17. Streamlined self-services
18. Increased distribution networks (delivery channel advancements)
19. Enhanced product features
20. Innovative products and services
21. High consumer-oriented technology (service offerings)
22. Technologically superior workforce

*Market Acuity*

23. Understanding markets/competition
24. Understanding customer requirements
25. Enlarging the range of relationships or relationship marketing
26. Implementing and managing the sales concept
27. Cross-selling products
28. Offering a broad line of financial products

*Quality of Customer Interface*

29. Responsiveness to customer inquiries
30. Accuracy of account statements
31. Overall customer requirements met
32. Meeting customer service levels
33. Overall customer satisfaction
34. Timeliness of mailing account statements
35. Account turnover rates
36. Customer complaint volume

37. Processing errors/exception performance
38. Overall system response times

*Factor Productivity*

39. Front-office labor productivity
40. Back-office labor productivity
41. Overall reliability of delivery systems
42. Online systems availability
43. Cost-effectiveness of back-room technological innovations
44. Adherence to budgets and plans
45. Transaction processing costs

## Construct Description

Based on existing literature (Chase and Hayes 1992; Roth and van der Velde 1992, etc.), technological leadership capabilities, people capabilities, business process capabilities, and factor productivity were conceptualized as four generic operational capabilities developed by world-class service performers. Of these four, business process capabilities harbored "the institutional knowledge that governs behavior in the form of rules, procedures, shared values, and communication flows across boundaries" (p. 1724); people capabilities represented "the stock of individual knowledge acquired by employees (Schneider 1990)" (p. 1724); technological leadership represented "enhancing state-of-the-art technology" (p. 1731); and factor productivity indicated the firm's internal capabilities to use resources efficiently.

In addition, market acuity was also identified as an important capability for a service firm. This construct was defined as "the ability to see the competitive environment clearly, and thus to anticipate and respond to customers' evolving needs and wants" (Stalk, Evans, and Shulman 1992).

Service quality was defined by "how well the delivery system is structured to meet specific expectations of customers relative to its strategic positioning" (p. 1731). This definition was congruent with the prevailing theory of service quality capabilities.

## Measurement Description

Multiple items were used to measure each construct. All items were assessed on 7-point Likert scales with different response categories. The response categories for market performance, quality of customer interface, and factor productivity were 1 = "very poor performance," 4 = "met goals," and 7 = "outstanding performance." For service quality, knowledge, market acuity, and technological leadership, the Likert scale ranged from 1 = "substantially weaker" to 4 = "same" to 7 = "substantially stronger."

## Development

All scales were adopted from prior research (Roth 1993) and were proven reliable and valid. Descriptive statistics and Cronbach's coefficient alpha values for each multi-item index are given in the article's appendix.

## Sample

This study was conducted in the banking industry. The data were gathered from the 1991 Survey of Retail Banking Strategy and Performance, which was part of the Retail Banking Futures Project (RBFP) (Roth 1993; Roth and van der Velde 1988, 1989, 1990, 1992). There were 140 respondents, 135 of whom had complete data on each of the indexes required for testing the hypotheses. No response rate was reported in the article.

### Reliability and Validity

Cronbach's coeff cient alpha values were calculated to assess the scale reliability for each construct. According to the article, all alpha values ranged from .71 to .90, which provided the evidence of interitem reliability. Unidimensional indexes were constructed based on exploratory factor analysis (EFA) (using loadings of ≥ 50 as a minimum value for inclusion of an item in an index) and reliability analysis (item to total correlations and Cronbach's coefficient values). The market performance index was validated using absolute measures of net pretax profitability ($r = 0.42$, $p < .001$) and return on assets (ROA) ($r = .24$, $p < .05$) derived from secondary sources.

### Scores

Sample mean and standard deviation for each scale are reported in Appendix A (p. 1731).

### Other Evidence

This research builds on a larger study of banking strategies, and other studies have followed (*see* Menor, Roth, and Mason 2001; Roth 1993; Roth and van der Velde 1987, 1989, 1990, 1991).

### References

Chase, R. B., and R H. Hayes. 1991. Beefing up operations in service firms. *Sloan Management Review* 33 (1): 15–26.

Menor, L. J., A. V. Roth, and C. H. Mason. 2001. Agility in retail banking: A numerical taxonomy of strategic service groups. *Manufacturing and Service Operations Management* 3 (4): 273–92.

Roth, A. V. 1993. Performance dimensions in services: An empirical investigation of strategic performance. In *Advances in services marketing and management,* Vol. 2, eds. S. Swartz, D. E. Bowen, and S. W. Brown, 1–47. Greenwich, CT: JAI Press.

Roth, A. V., and M. van der Velde. 1987. *The future of retail banking delivery systems: Executive summary of findings.* Chicago, IL: Bank Administration Institute.

———. 1989. Investing in retail delivery system technology. *Journal of Retail Banking* 11 (2): 23–34.

———. 1990. *Retail banking strategies: Opportunities for the 1990's.* Chicago, IL: Bank Administration Institute.

———. 1991. Operations as marketing: A competitive service strategy. *Journal of Operations Management* 10 (3): 303–28.

———. 1992. *World class banking: Benchmarking the market leaders.* Chicago, IL: Bank Administration Institute.

Schneider, B. 1990. Alternative strategies for creating service-oriented organizations. In *Service management effectiveness: Balancing strategy, organization and human resources, operations, and marketing,* ed. D. E. Bowen, R. B. Chase, and T. G. Cummings, 126–51. San Francisco, CA: Jossey-Bass.

Stalk, G., P. Evans, and L. E. Shulman. 1992. Competing on capabilities: The new rules of corporate strategy. *Harvard Business Review* 70 (2): 57–69.

## Roth and van der Velde

### Article Summarized

Roth, Aleda V., and Marjolijn van der Velde. 1991. Operations as marketing: A competitive service strategy. *Journal of Operations Management* 10 (3): 303–28.

**Scales (Actual Questions Used)**

*Critical Success Factors*

1. Courteous service
2. Consistent service
3. Enlarge customer relationships
4. Accurate information
5. Timely information
6. Efficient back-office processing
7. Price services adequately
8. High-value services
9. Convenient service (easy access)
10. Highly personalized services

*Process Technology*

11. Increase ATM investments
12. Increase point of sale (POS) investments
13. Increase home banking investments

*Facilities and Retail Outlets*

14. Increase full-service branches
15. Increase limited-service branches
16. Increase ATM minibranches
17. Relocate branches
18. Downsize branches
19. Shared facilities
20. Increase specialized facilities
21. Improve facilities maintenance

*Capacity*

22. Increase direct customer contact capacity
23. Decrease direct customer contact capacity
24. Improve space utilization
25. Central support services centers

*Vertical Integration*

26. Tailored distribution channels
27. Increase internal technical staff
28. Increase internal R&D

*Information Systems*

29. New software/old products
30. Improve budgeting & reporting

*Human Resources*

31. Overall investment in human assets
32. Increase new employee training
33. Retrain for new skills

34. Supervisor training
35. Improve recruiting efforts
36. Increase teller/sup sales reps
37. Job enlargement for teller/sup

*Performance Management*

38. Improve fringe benefits
39. Improve physical work conditions
40. Increase financial incentives
41. Upgrade wages/salaries
42. Work measurement

*Quality Management Program*

43. Quality control procedures
44. Standardize procedures
45. Quality circles

*Integration Choices*

46. Improve internal communications
47. Reduce Mgt levels
48. Change labor/Mgt culture
49. Overall systems integration
50. Central operations/communications

*Marketing Choices*

51. Product line expansion
52. Supplementary services
53. Product bundling/packaging
54. Customize products/target management

## Construct Description

Critical success factors were identified as a combination of competitive priorities and competitive capabilities in services. Retail banks provided the context. Critical success factors were referred to as "a limited number of areas in which satisfactory achievement will ensure successful competitive performance for the organization" (p. 324). Competitive priorities were defined as "capabilities which are needed to build and maintain future market share; they are planned, but not necessarily yet obtained" (p. 306). In this sense, a bank's competitive capabilities connoted its market orientation, which exemplifies its "collective source of positional advantage relative to the group average" (p. 315). On the other hand, competitive capabilities reflected "the firm's relative areas of current competitive strength vis-à-vis its primary competitors" (p. 306), and the bank's current capabilities represented its competitive orientation. Banks that are more adept at converting their resources into capabilities than their competitors were posited to pose significant barriers to entry, and the relative size of the gaps indicated their competitor orientation.

These two dimensions—market orientation and competitor orientation—formed the dimensions of what the authors labeled the Customer/Account Base (CAB) matrix, where the top 10 critical success factors were "arrayed by the sample banks' average scores on dimensions of competitive priorities and competitive capability gaps" (p. 313). The four quadrants in the CAB matrix—(1) revolving doors, (2) minimum daily requirements, (3) gateways, and (4) golden handcuffs—were said to coincide with Hayes and Wheelwright's (1984) four stages of capability development as they pertain to services. Critical success factors that were classified as minimum daily requirements were composed of two types of service quality (p. 311): (1) external service quality, which was defined as "the bank's ability to provide courteous and consistent services" and (2) internal service quality, which tapped into "the provision of timely and accurate information." Those that were golden handcuffs were based on relationship banking, which was described in terms of "enlarging relationships with customers," and those that were called gateways were basic ways to differentiate themselves in attracting new customers to the bank, including personalized services, adequate pricing, convenience, and back-office efficiency.

The study also investigated service operations strategy choices that were associated with critical success factors in each CAB quadrant: information systems, human resources investments, human resources performance management, quality management programs, marketing practices, and integration practices. From a list of 49 practice-based initiatives, 43 represented behavioral measures of operations strategy and the remainder tapped into strategic marketing choices. The RBU's profile of responses "over the set of action programs are proxy variables for a bank's 'intended' operations and marketing strategy" (p. 310).

### Measurement Description

Each item pertaining to competitive priorities was measured on 7-point, self-anchoring scales that ranged from 1 = "not important" to 7 = "critically important" in successfully competing in the bank's target market over the next 5 years. The size of a competitive capability gap, which indicated the difference between a bank's current capability and that required in the next 5 years, was quantified on 7-point, self-anchoring scales where 1 = "no gap" and 7 = "large gap."

For the practice-based questions that captured elements of operations and marketing strategy, the items reflected the relative degree of managerial emphasis, in terms of firm plans to adopt or emphasize over the next 3 years; and were captured on 7-point, self-anchoring scales ranging from 1 = "none/little" to 7 = "significant emphasis."

### Development

The measures and data were obtained from the Retail Banking Futures Project (RBFP) database, which was joint research between the Bank Administration Institute and Professor Aleda V. Roth, currently at Clemson University (Roth and van der Velde 1987, 1990, 1992). The development of the banking operations strategy measures in the RBFP was patterned after the International Manufacturing Futures Project; and it was the first to apply a manufacturing strategy framework to service management (*see* Figure 1, p. 306, in the article). Items were also developed from a multidisciplinary, academic, and practitioner literature base and were modified after interviews with bankers to be consistent with service management and especially to be appropriate to the context of retail banking marketing and operations strategy. Questions were pretested and refined further with focused groups of bankers in conjunction with the Bank Administration Institute's research staff. The survey instrument was then pilot tested on a small sample of retail banks.

### Sample

The data were collected through the RBFP, originated in 1986 by the authors in conjunction with the Bank Administration Institute (Roth and van der Velde 1987, 1990, 1992). "In this longitudinal research project, the Survey of Retail Banking Delivery Systems' Strategies and Performance is administered to banking executives biennially through a mail questionnaire" (p. 309). "The population of approximately 16,000 retail banks was stratified into five groups by bank asset size: less than \$100 million, \$100–\$499 million, \$500–\$999 million, \$1 billion–\$3 billion and over \$3 billion. Mail surveys were sent to a stratified probability sample of 1,244 banks, resulting in 117 usable surveys" (p. 309). Table 1 of the article provided the details of the respondent retail banks. Follow-up studies were performed to ensure that no serious nonrespondent bias existed on questions of interest; however, the responses were biased toward larger, market leader banks.

### Validity and Reliability

Content validity was established through a thorough review of the literature and interviews with experienced practitioners. The authors reported that "tests of internal reliability were computed and follow-ups with samples of banking executives were made to ensure construct validity" (p. 311). The authors referred the readers to Roth and van der Velde (1987) for details of the psychometric properties of their measures. Canonical correlation was used to ensure that the two dimensions forming the CAB matrix were independent.

### Scores

The scores are presented in Tables 2 and 3 of the article.

### Other Evidence

Not available.

### References

Roth, A. V., and M. van der Velde. 1987. *The future of retail banking delivery systems: Executive summary of findings.* Chicago, IL: Bank Administration Institute.

———. 1990. *Retail banking strategies: Opportunities for the 1990's.* Chicago, IL. Bank Administration Institute.

———. 1992. *World class banking: Benchmarking the market leaders.* Chicago, IL: Bank Administration Institute.

---

## Rungtusanatham, Forze, Koka, Salvador, and Nie

### Article Summarized

Rungtusanatham, M., C. Forza, B. R. Koka, F. Salvador, and W. Nie. 2005. TQM across multiple countries: Convergence hypothesis versus national specificity arguments. *Journal of Operations Management* 23 (1): 43–63.

### Scales (Actual Questions Used)

*Seven Deming-Based TQM Constructs*

Visionary Leadership

1. All major department heads within our plant accept their responsibility for quality.
2. Plant management provides personal leadership for quality products and quality improvement.
3. Our top management strongly encourages employee involvement in the production process.

Internal and External Cooperation

4. During problem-solving sessions, we make an effort to get all team members' opinions and ideas before making a decision.
5. In the past 3 years, many problems have been solved through small group sessions.
6. We maintain close communication with suppliers about quality consideration and design changes.
7. We regularly survey our customers' requirements.

Learning

8. Employees receive training to perform multiple tasks.
9. Employees are cross-trained at the plant so that they can fill in for others if necessary.
10. Plant employees receive training and development in workplace skills on a regular basis.

Process Management

11. A large percentage of the equipment or processes on the shop floor are currently under statistical quality control.
12. We make extensive use of statistical techniques to reduce variance in processes.
13. We use charts to determine whether our manufacturing processes are in control.

Continuous Improvement

14. All employees believe that it is their responsibility to improve quality in the plant.
15. Continuous improvement of quality is stressed in all work processes throughout our plant.
16. We search for continuing learning and improvement after installation of the equipment.

Employee Fulfillment

17. I am proud to tell others that I am part of this organization.
18. I am extremely glad that I chose this organization to work for over others I was considering at the time I joined.

Customer Satisfaction

19. Our customers have been well satisfied with the quality of our products over the past 3 years.
20. Our customers are pleased with the products and services we provide for them.
21. Our customers seem happy with our responsiveness to their problems.

**Construct Description**

The Deming Management Method encompassed Deming's prescriptive set of "14 points" and identified "seven deadly diseases" that impeded organizational performance and numerous "obstacles" that prevented the attainment of organizational quality (Deming 1986). Accordingly, Anderson, Rungtusanatham, and Schroeder (1994) developed seven constructs and proposed their interrelationships that, in their opinion, reflected a definition and a theory of TQM. This article investigated the same set of Deming-based TQM constructs and followed the same definitions. The specific definitions are provided below.

Visionary leadership was defined as "the ability of management to establish, practice and lead a long term vision for the organization, driven by changing customer requirements as opposed to an internal management control role" (p. 47). Internal and external cooperation referred to "the propensity of the organization to engage in non-competitive activities internally among employees and externally with respect to suppliers" (p. 47). Learning captured the "organizational capability to recognize and nurture the development of its skills, abilities and knowledge base" (p. 47). Process management constituted "the set of methodological and behavioral practices emphasizing the management of process or means of actions rather than results" (p. 47). Continuous improvement was identified as "the propensity of the organization to pursue incremental and innovative improvements of its processes, products and services" (p. 47). Employee fulfillment reflected "the degree to which employees of an organization feel that the organization continually satisfies their needs" (p. 47). Customer satisfaction captured "the degree to which an organization's customers continually perceive that their needs are being met by the organization's products and services" (p. 47).

**Measurement Description**

To operationalize the seven constructs, multiple items were used. Each of them was measured on a 5-point Likert scale ranging from "strongly disagree" to "strongly agree."

### Development

The measurement items were assembled based on the survey instruments used in the second round of the World Class Manufacturing (WCM) study. The survey questionnaires were initially pilot tested in Round One (Flynn et al. 1997) and were further modified and refined in Round Two. Most perceptual measurement scales included in the questionnaires had been found to be reliable and valid in the existing literature. For the current study, the authors selected a list of relevant items from the refined instruments based on the nominal definitions of those seven constructs of interest.

### Sample

The Round-Two data source from the WCM database was used for this study. In the second round of the WCM project, the data were collected from three industries (electronics, machinery, and transportation related) and five countries (Germany, Italy, Japan, the United Kingdom, and the United States) with a target population of medium- to large-sized plants (i.e., plants with more than 100 employees). Within each country, the researchers deliberately included plants with either a "World-Class" or a non–"World-Class" reputation. For the current article, the sample size was 110 plants. Their distribution is provided in Table 1 of the article. During the data collection process, the authors distributed survey questionnaires (15 in total) to different plant informants (26 in total), ranging from managerial and engineering positions to supervisors and process operators in each plant. A plant-level score was constructed by averaging the scores gained from each of the "relevant" informants from the plant.

### Reliability and Validity

Cronbach's coefficient alpha for each measurement scale and for each country was calculated to assess internal consistency reliability. For all countries (except the United Kingdom), the measurement scales for the seven constructs were found to be reliable with Cronbach's coefficient alpha larger than .60. For the U.K. data, the authors noted that the alpha values for the continuous improvement and employee fulfillment measurement scales were .58 and .54, respectively, which did not appear to be adequately reliable.

To establish construct validity, the dimensionality of each measurement scale was examined using the exploratory factor analysis (EFA) approach (Cronbach and Meehl 1955; Kim and Mueller 1978). The authors argued that within the context of factor analysis, a measurement scale was unidimensional when the second eigenvalue was less than 1.00 and when factor loadings for measurement items were larger than .30 (Hair et al. 1979). Based on these two criteria, the factor analyses demonstrated strong support for scale unidimensionality.

### Scores

A single average plant-level score was derived by averaging the plant-level scores for each corresponding measurement scale.

### Other Evidence

Not available.

### References


Anderson, J. C., M. Rungtusanatham, and R. G. Schroeder. 1994. A theory of quality management underlying the Deming management method. *Academy of Management Review* 19 (3): 472–509.

Cronbach, L. J., and P. E. Meehl. 1955. Construct validity in psychological tests. *Psychological Bulletin* 52 (4): 281–302.

Deming, W. E. 1986. *Out of the crisis.* Cambridge: MIT Center for Advanced Engineering Study.

Flynn, B. B., R. G. Schroeder, E. J. Flynn, S. Sakakibara, and K. A. Bates. 1997. World-class manufacturing project: Overview and selected results. *International Journal of Operations and Production Management* 17 (7/8): 671–85.

Hair, J. F., Jr., R. E. Anderson, R. L. Tatham, and B. J. Grablowsky. 1979. *Multivariate data analysis with readings.* Tulsa, OK: Petroleum Publishing.

Kim, J.-O. and C. W. Mueller. 1978. *Introduction to factor analysis: what it is and how to do it.* Beverly Hills, CA: Sage.

# Sabherwal and Becerra-Fernandez

**Article Summarized**

Sabherwal, Rajiv, and Irma Becerra-Fernandez. 2003. An empirical study of the effect of knowledge management processes at individual, group, and organizational levels. *Decision Sciences* 34 (2): 225–60.

**Scales (Actual Questions Used)**

Measurement of perceived knowledge management (KM) effectiveness

*Perceived Individual-Level KM Effectiveness*

1. You are satisfied with the availability of knowledge for your tasks.
2. The available knowledge improves your effectiveness in performing your tasks.
3. You are satisfied with the management of knowledge you need.

*Perceived Group-Level KM Effectiveness*

4. You are satisfied with knowledge sharing among individuals at your directorate.
5. The available knowledge improves the effectiveness of your directorate.
6. You are satisfied with the management of knowledge at your directorate.

*Perceived Organizational-Level KM Effectiveness*

7. You are satisfied with the knowledge available for various tasks across NASA's John F. Kennedy Space Center (KSC).
8. You are satisfied with knowledge sharing among various directorates at KSC.
9. You are satisfied with the management of knowledge at KSC.

*Measurement of KM Processes*

Externalization

10. A problem-solving system based on a technology such as case-based reasoning
11. Groupware and other team collaboration tools
12. Pointers to expertise (skills "yellow pages")
13. Modeling based on analogies and metaphors
14. Capture and transfer of experts' knowledge

Combination

15. Web-based access to data
16. Web pages (Intranet and Internet)
17. Databases
18. Repositories of information, best practices, and lessons learned

Socialization

19. Cooperative projects across directorates
20. The use of apprentices and mentors to transfer knowledge
21. Brainstorming retreats or camps
22. Employee rotation across areas

Internalization

23. On-the-job training
24. Learning by doing
25. Learning by observation

## Construct Description

Construct of internalization was based on Nonaka (1994). Nonaka (1994) viewed internalization as a process that helped convert explicit knowledge into tacit knowledge. Externalization, on the other hand, involved the expression of tacit knowledge and its translation into comprehensible forms that others could understand (Nonaka 1994; Nonaka and Takeuchi 1995). Combination processes involved the conversion of explicit knowledge into more complex sets of explicit knowledge (Nonaka 1994). Individuals' perception of knowledge depended on the perceptual filters they used to interpret events and actions (Daft and Weick 1984; Fiol 1994; Starbuck and Milliken 1988). The authors stated that knowledge was transmitted from individual to group via social interaction as well as through the use of beliefs shared across groups to create organizational routines (Probst, Büchel, and Raub 1998). Nonaka (1994) described organizational knowledge creation as a spiral process that, starting at the individual level, expands to the group and organizational levels.

## Measurement Description

Except for the items related to perception of knowledge management (KM), all the items were borrowed from the existing literature as shown in the scale. Except for the fourth item measuring externalization, all the items were borrowed from Nonaka and Konno (1998). The fourth item was borrowed from Nonaka (1994). All the items except the last item measuring combination were borrowed from Nonaka and Takeuchi (1995). The last item was taken from Nonaka and Konno (1998). The first and third items measuring socialization were adapted from Nonaka and Takeuchi (1995). The second and last items were adapted from Nonaka and Konno (1998) and Nonaka (1994), respectively. All the items measuring internalization were adapted from Nonaka and Konno (1998). The authors used 5-point Likert scales.

## Development

The main purpose of this study was to define the relations among constructs of KM processes and perceived KM effectiveness. Thirty-seven KM tools were used to prepare a list of tools. Then, the number of KM tools was limited to 25 for survey purposes. There existed a question about the usage of quality tools in the questionnaire (on a 5-point scale).

Eleven questions were developed on perceived effectiveness of KM. Feedback was obtained from three employees of the John F. Kennedy Space Center (KSC) CIO's office (they were not used for the actual survey). The questionnaire was finalized after some minor modifications. The questionnaires used for the eight groups differed in these knowledge areas and in the name of the group on the cover page.

## Sample

The sample came from the KSC of the National Aeronautics and Space Administration. Two hundred questionnaires were distributed to potential respondents. Out of 200 surveys distributed, 159 questionnaires were returned in total. As a result of listwise deletion, 156 surveys were deemed to be usable.

Survey was administered to different groups of people in the KSC: Administration Office, Space Station Hardware Integration Office, Biomedical Office, Shuttle Processing Directorate, Payload Processing Directorate, and Engineering Development Directorate. The overall difference between groups was not significant. In addition, since the sample contained people from different hierarchical levels, groups, and experiences, the authors stated that "the sample of respondents seems to be quite diverse" (p. 235).

### Reliability and Validity

Cronbach's coefficient alpha was used to measure the reliability of the scale for each construct. Nine items in the KM processes scale were dropped as a result of confirmatory factor analysis (CFA). Convergent validity was measured according to Anderson and Gerbing (1988) by using the t statistics for the path coefficients. Discriminant validity was assessed by "the confidence interval for each pairwise correlation estimate" (p. 238), the percentage of variance extracted, and a $\chi^2$ test, by which the impact of constraining correlation between each pair of construct to 1 was measured.

### Scores

Validity, intercorrelation, and descriptive statistics are reported in Table 3. Results for the structural model proposed are given in Table 4 in the article.

### Other Evidence

Not available.

### References

Anderson, J. C., and D. W. Gerbing. 1988. Structural equation modeling in practice: A review and recommended two-step approach. *Psychological Bulletin* 103 (3): 411–23.

Daft, R. L., and K. E. Weick. 1984. Toward a model of organizations as interpretation systems. *Academy of Management Review* 9 (2): 284–95.

Fiol, C. M. 1994. Consensus, diversity, and learning in organizations. *Organization Science* 5 (3): 403–20.

Nonaka, I. 1994. A dynamic theory of organizational knowledge creation. *Organization Science* 5 (1): 14–37.

Nonaka, I., and N. Konno. 1998. The concept of "ba": Building a foundation for knowledge creation. *California Management Review* 40 (3): 40–54.

Nonaka, I., and H. Takeuchi. 1995. *The knowledge creating company: How Japanese companies create the dynamics of innovation.* New York: Oxford University Press.

Probst, G., B. Büchel, and S. Raub. 1998. Knowledge as a strategic resource. In *Knowing in firms: Understanding, managing, and measuring knowledge,* eds. G. von Krogh, J. Roos, and D. Kleine, 240–52. Thousand Oaks, CA: Sage.

Starbuck, W. H., and F. J. Milliken. 1988. Executives perceptual filters: What they notice and how they make sense. In *The executive effect: Concepts and methods of studying top managers,* ed. D. Hambrick, 35–65. Greenwich, CT: JAI Press.

## Safizadeh, Field, and Ritzman

### Article Summarized

Safizadeh, M. Hossein, Joy M. Field, and Larry P. Ritzman. 2003. An empirical analysis of financial services processes with a front-office or back-office orientation. *Journal of Operations Management* 21 (5): 557–76.

### Scales (Actual Questions Used)

These scales were given in the Appendix of the original article (pp. 572–75).

*Orientation*

1. In terms of the *length* of the service process, to what extent does the service process entail interacting directly with your customer (vs. the back office)?
2. In terms of the *value added* of the service process, to what extent does the service process entail interacting directly with your customer (vs. the back office)?

*Mode of Interaction*

3. In dealing with the *primary customers* of your process, how frequently do you use the following types of "delivery channels" (mark one box for each item)?
   - Face-to-face
   - Telephone
   - Mail
   - E-mail
   - World Wide Web
   - Fax

*Customization*

4. "Every service process has some level of customization driven by the needs to its customers and the service offered by the competitors. For example, a law office often tailors its service to the specific needs of a specific client for a specific visit. On the other hand public transportation offers a service that is minimally customized. Please rate the level of customization that your *primary customers* currently expect from your process" (p. 572).

   Seven options to check were as follows: standard service with no options, standard service with a few standard options, standard service with some standard options, standard service with many standard options, standard service with some customized options, customized service with some standard service modules, and highly customized service.

*Range of Products, Customer's Choice, and Customer Involvement*

5. How would you characterize your process in terms of customer choice?
   - The customer can select from a range of products.
   - The customer has considerable choice in determining how each step in the service process is carried out.
   - Active involvement in the service encounter gives the customer increased control over the service encounter.

*Labor Intensity*

6. Service processes have different levels of *labor intensity*. The greater the proportion of a service's cost that is attributed to human resources (wages and salaries), the greater the labor intensity. Please rate the level of labor intensity of your process.

   Seven options to check were as follows: minimal labor intensity, very low amount, low amount, average amount, high amount, very high amount, and exceptionally high labor intensity.

*Capital Expenditure*

7. Service processes have different levels of *capital intensity*. Capital intensity depends on the level of investment in the facility and equipment (including computer technology) used by a process. The greater the proportion of cost attributed to the investment in equipment and facilities, the greater the capital intensity. Capital intensity deals with investment expenditures that are depreciated or leased

(rather than expensed). It includes office equipment, special equipment (such as check processing equipment or ATMs at banks), floor space (which can be hundreds of dollars per square foot at prime locations), and computer equipment. How would you rate the capital intensity of your process?

Seven options to check were as follows: minimal capital intensity (<$10,000 per employee), very low amount, low amount, average amount, high amount, very high amount, and exceptionally high capital intensity (>$100,000 per employee).

To determine the capital intensity of your process, estimate the annual cost of investments in facility and equipment per average employee at this process. For shared resources, roughly estimate how much depreciation of the assets is allocated to this process.

*Routineness*

8. To what extent does your process match the following statement?
   There are hardly any exceptional cases in the production of this service; the process is routine.

*Cross-Training*

9. For some processes, employees are able to perform a wide variety of tasks and have considerable latitude as to how to do their jobs. In other processes, employees are more specialized. How would you characterize the employees involved in your process?
10. How many employees are cross-trained to perform alternate jobs?

*Utilization*

11. The following question is intended to measure the capacity utilization at your process. Please express capacity numbers as a percentage of full capacity for this process.
    What has been the actual utilization of your *facility* capacity during the last year? ____%

*Use of Appointment System*

12. To what extent do you use an appointment system to assign specific times to customers at your process?

    Seven options to check were as follows: never, very infrequently, infrequently, average frequency, frequently, very frequently, and always.

*Competitive Priorities and Capabilities*

Please answer the following questions about your process performance for each performance measure.

Quality of Customer Interface

13. Responsiveness to customer inquiries
14. Meet overall customer requirements
15. Meet overall customer service levels
16. Overall customer satisfaction
17. Customer complaints volume
18. Processing errors/exceptional performance
19. Overall system response times

Service Quality

20. Provide courteous service
21. Provide consistent level of service (reliability)
22. Perceived quality (customer's perception)
23. Provide accurate information (credibility)
24. Provide personal attention in treatment of customers

25. Provide timely information (responsiveness)
26. Conformance (degree to which service meets standards)

Process Flexibility

27. Make system changes in response to fluctuation in demand/volume
28. Rapidly introduce new product/service
29. Make rapid staffing changes to match supply with demand/volume

Product Flexibility

30. Customize products/service

Delivery

31. Speed of service/wait times
32. Provide convenient (simple/easy access) services
33. Perform promised services on time
34. Promptness in handling customer complaints/problems

Low Cost

35. Provide low-cost service
36. High labor productivity
37. Cost-effectiveness of process technology
38. Low overhead cost
39. Adherence to budget/plans

Performance

40. How would you rate the overall performance of your process?
    - Based on corporate performance criteria
    - Based on the performance of similar processes in other companies in the industry.

### Construct Description

There were 10 multi-item scales in this survey. They were both about the importance and performance of the following five performance measures: quality of customer interface, service quality, process flexibility, delivery, and low cost. Quality was specifically discussed, "Although there are multiple dimensions of quality in the manufacturing literature, they seem to be correlated in the service sector and make up one construct (Roth, 1993). This construct incorporates the multiple dimensions related to both internal and external quality. These ten constructs are essentially defined by their scales" (pp. 562–63).

The constructs "front-office orientation" and "back-office orientation" were not concisely defined in the article. The differences between the two were discussed in detail beginning on p. 560. A basic difference was the amount of customer contact. Modes of interaction were how the service interacts with the customer. Customization and customer choice gave information about how many options were available to customers and their level of involvement in the service. Design characteristics were each individually defined, essentially by the question in the scale. Competitive priorities were made up of the multi-item constructs above. Performance was how well the operation was doing.

### Measurement Description

The measures covered design and improvement issues, customer contact and participation, operations policies, and performance. Questions 11 to 39 were adapted from Roth and van der Velde (1991) and Roth (1993), with the following adjustment: in the "quality of customer interface" construct, two questions were eliminated that dealt with the accuracy of account statements and account turnover rate. Question 40 was a perceptual question used for performance. The authors note based on their unit of analysis shows that there was no way to get objective data, even from within the company.

**Development**

This research used processes, which is a lower-level unit of analysis than most empirical studies of service organizations. The 27 sets of questions used to develop the scales for competitive priorities were taken from Roth and van der Velde (1991) and also used by Roth (1993). The others (all single-item scales) were developed by the authors.

**Sample**

The authors received 108 completed surveys from a convenience sample of 350 professionals in the financial services industry North American Industry Classification System (NAICS 52), primarily in the northeastern United States.

**Reliability and Validity**

Validity was not explicitly discussed. The authors expressed confidence in the scales because most of them had been used before, and the reliability scores (including interrater reliability) were generally high. Two types of reliability measures were given: interrater reliability for every question and Cronbach's coefficient alpha for every multi-item scale.

**Scores**

Means of modes of interface (Table 3), customer's options (Table 4), design characteristics (Table 5), and competitive priorities (Table 6) versus process type (front office/back office) are presented in the article.

**Other Evidence**

Not available.

**References**

Roth, A. V. 1993. Performance dimensions in services: An empirical investigation of strategic performance. In *Advances in service marketing and management,* Vol. 2, eds. S. Swartz, D. E. Bowen, and S. W. Brown, 1–47. Greenwich, CT: JAI Press.

Roth, A. V., and M. van der Velde. 1991. Operations as marketing: A competitive service strategy. *Journal of Operations Management* 10 (3): 303–28.

---

# Safizadeh and Ritzman

**Article Summarized**

Safizadeh, M. Hossein, and Larry P. Ritzman. 1997. Linking performance drivers in production planning and inventory control to process choice. *Journal of Operations Management* 15 (4): 389–403.

**Scales (Actual Questions Used)**

*Process Choice*

1. Which of the following categories come closest to characterizing your dominant processes?

*Aggregate Plan*

2. What percentage of the production is planned based on actual customer orders for future delivery?
3. What percentage of the production is planned based on demand forecast?
4. To what extent does the actual demand differ from the forecasted demand in terms of quantity for your primary product line?
5. To what extent does the actual demand differ from the forecasted demand in terms of timing for your primary product line?
6. How frequently is capacity varied in your dominant processes?

*Order Backlog*

7. What is the amount of order backlogs expressed in weeks of production?

*Planning Horizon*

8. How far ahead (planning horizon) do you plan the master production schedule (planning production for your end products)?

*Material Management: Batch Size Rationale*

9. What is the amount of consideration given to the minimization of down time for setup in determining batch size or production lot size in the dominant processes at your plant?
10. What is the amount of consideration given to the maximization of equipment utilization in determining batch size or production lot size in the dominant processes at your plant?
11. What is the actual capacity utilization that is currently being experienced?

*Material Management: Inventory Level*

12. Indicate days on hand for raw material or purchased inventory.
13. Indicate days on hand for work-in-process inventory.
14. Indicate days on hand for finished goods inventory.

*Performance*

15. How would you rate the overall performance of manufacturing in your plant based on corporate performance criteria?
16. How would you rate the overall performance of manufacturing in your plant based on the performance of manufacturing plants owned by other companies in the industry?
17. Relative to your significant competitors, please indicate your position on dependability of on-time delivery.

**Construct Description**

This research investigated how process choice relates to production planning and inventory control decisions. Process choice consisted of two alternatives: job/batch shops and production line/continuous flow plants. This definition was built up on the work of Hayes and Wheelwright (1979) and Pesch and Schroeder (1996). The constructs of aggregate plan, planning horizon, and order backlog were partly based on Ashton and Cook (1989). They indicated whether a plant was pursuing a chase strategy or a level strategy in production plan. The construct of batch size rationale was partly based on Abell and Hammond (1979) and Taylor (1980). It measured the emphasis that a firm places on maximizing equipment utilization and minimizing the downtime related to setup.

**Measurement Description**

Some of the variables, such as weeks of order backlog or days of inventory on hand (Questions 7, 8, 12, 13, and 14) were collected using objective data. Other variables were collected using perceptual measures. The process choice question asked respondents to choose one of the production types listed as follows: job shop, batch shop, production line, and continuous shop.

### Development

The pilot test was applied to eliminate potential problems in interpreting the questions. In the final version of the questionnaire, changes were made to the wording of a few questions after the pilot test.

### Sample

The participants were chosen from the *Harris Industrial and Manufacturing Directory,* located primarily in the Midwest and Northeast. Two hundred firms were contacted by telephone, and 175 agreed to participate. Among the 175 firms, 110 actually returned the completed surveys, which led to a response rate of 55%. Another 200 firms were contacted by mail without telephone contact, and 34 returned the completed surveys with a response rate of 17%. The survey was sent to the person with overall responsibility for manufacturing (i.e., vice president of manufacturing). The respondents provided information in relation to the primary product line at an individual plant. Size and industry were compared between respondents who were contacted by telephone and those who were not, and no difference was found on either factor. Subsequent examination of the characteristics did not reveal any nonrespondent bias. The 144 plants in the final sample had 22% job shops, 32% batch shops, 25% production lines, and 21% continuous flow shops. These plants represented 15 different industries (*see* Table 2 for details, p. 394), and the average plant had 450 employees and an asset value of U.S.$103 million.

### Reliability and Validity

To assess the reliability of the perceptual measures, a shorter version of the survey was mailed to the respondents in the primary database. But this time, the questionnaire was required to be completed by a different respondent. The paired responses were compared using the reliability coefficient. The average interrater agreement was .77, which showed a reasonably high level of agreement between different respondents in the same plant. In addition, the mean difference between respondents was examined, and no statistically significant difference was found for either objective or perceptual measures.

### Scores

Means for decision areas, classified by process choice, are reported in Table 3 in the article (p. 396). Correlations between operations performance and type of decision are reported in Table 4 (p. 398).

### Other Evidence

Not available.

### References

Abell, D. F., and J. S. Hammond. 1979. *Strategic market planning: Problems and analytical approaches.* Englewood Cliffs, NJ: Prentice Hall.

Ashton, J. E., and F. X. Cook Jr. 1989. Time to reform job shop manufacturing. *Harvard Business Review* 67 (2): 106–11.

Hayes, R. H., and S. C. Wheelwright. 1979. Link manufacturing process and product life cycles. *Harvard Business Review* 57 (1): 133–40.

Pesch, M. J., and R. G. Schroeder. 1996. Measuring factory focus: An empirical study. *Production and Operations Management* 5 (3): 234–54.

Taylor, S. G. 1980. Are process industries different? The 23rd annual conference proceedings, American Production and Inventory Control Society, Los Angeles, CA.

# Safizadeh, Ritzman, Sharma, and Wood

**Article Summarized**

Safizadeh, M. Hossein, Larry P. Ritzman, Deven Sharma, and Craig Wood. 1996. An empirical analysis of the product-process matrix. *Management Science* 42 (11): 1576–91.

**Scales (Actual Questions Used)**

*Quality*

Relative to your significant competitors, please indicate your position on the following dimensions of performance (check one box for each item).

1. Product performance
2. Number of features on the product
3. Product quality consistency
4. Product quality as perceived by the customer

*Time*

Relative to your significant competitors, please indicate your position on the following dimensions of performance (check one box for each item).

5. Delivery time
6. Dependability on delivery

*Cost*

Relative to your significant competitors, please indicate your position on the following dimensions of performance (check one box for each item).

7. Product cost
8. Product price

*Product Flexibility*

Listed below are several alternatives for competing in an industry. Please indicate the importance that you attach to each alternative in selling the products in your primary product line (check one box for each item).

9. Customizing product to customer specification

   Which one of the following descriptions most typify the production in your plant?

   - Degree of product standardization
   - Standard product with no options
   - Standard product with standard option
   - Standard product modified to customer specification
   - Standard product with options modified to customer specification
   - Customized product manufactured to customer specification

*Development Speed*

Listed below are some items that describe some management priorities in manufacturing. Please indicate the importance given to each item in your plant.

10. Ability to introduce new products into production quickly
11. Ability to make design changes in the product after production has started

**Process Choice**

The process and equipment can be categorized in various ways. Please use the following definitions in answering the following question.

*Job shop:* Products are produced in small batches; similar equipment performing the same functions are grouped together.

*Batch shop:* Products are produced in moderately large batches; similar equipment performing the same function are grouped together.

*Production:* Products are produced in batches; work centers are laid out in the line sequence in which the products are produced.

*Continuous:* Products are produced in large batches or in a continuous flow; shop work centers are laid out in the sequence in which the products are manufactured.

12. Which one of the following categories does come closest to characterizing your dominant process?
    [1 = job shop, 2 = batch shop, 3 = production line, 4 = continuous shop]

## Construct Description

These measured variables for competitive priorities and process choice originated in Sharma (1987). Part of the initial purpose was to test the concepts of Hayes and Wheelwright (1979a, 1979b) on interdependence of marketing and manufacturing decisions and, specifically, how process choice related with competitive priorities. The measures also drew from scales being used in Manufacturing Futures studies at Boston University (*see* Miller and Roth 1994; Roth, Gray, Singhal, and Singal 1997 for a description of the Boston University study). The measures covered process choice and five competitive priorities for a major product and main process at a single plant. Product flexibility focused more on make-to-order customization instead of assemble-to-order customization (i.e., mass customization or MC).

## Measurement Description

The 12 items grouped into five categories of competitive priorities (quality, time, cost, product flexibility, and development speed) were related to process choice (the 13th item) to assess the frequency and desirability of several decision patterns in operations management.

## Development

Not available.

## Sample

The population of firms came from the *Harris Industrial and Manufacturing Directory*, from which 400 companies were selected for inclusion in this research.

> Half of these companies were subsequently contacted by telephone to request their participation in the study. A total of 175 firms agreed to participate, though only 110 firms returned their questionnaires. Questionnaires were also mailed to the remaining 200 firms, of which 34 responded. Subsequent analysis did not show nonrespondent bias. . . . Respondents consisted of 22 percent job shops, 32 percent batch shops, 25 percent production lines, and 21 percent continuous shops. The average plant has an asset value of $103 million, annual sales of $84 million, and 450 employees. The sample consistent of 15 different industries at the two-digit SIC code level. (pp. 1582–83)

## Reliability and Validity

Direct evidence of validity was not reported. Prior studies had documented evidence on the construct validity of the scales. The article did offer evidence of discriminant and association validity. Moreover, the study measured reliability (operationalized as internal consistency) with Cronbach's coefficient alpha, and the results were satisfactory.

### Scores

Factor loadings and average factor scores for the competitive priorities were reported. The average factor scores for plants on the main diagonal and those off the main diagonal of the product-process matrix were compared.

### Other Evidence

The relationships reported in this study and other studies (Safizadeh and Ritzman 1997; Ritzman and Safizadeh 1999) using different parts of the collected data concurred with the deductive arguments. Viewed together, the scales had produced results consistent with the theoretical expectation.

### References

Hayes, R. H., and S. C. Wheelwright. 1979a. Link manufacturing process and product life cycles. *Harvard Business Review* 57 (1): 133–40.

———. 1979b. The dynamics of process-product life cycles. *Harvard Business Review* 57 (2):127–36.

Miller, J. G., and A. V. Roth. 1994. A taxonomy of manufacturing strategies, *Management Science,* 40(3): 285–304.

Ritzman, L. P., and M. H. Safizadeh. 1999. Linking process choice with plant-level decisions about capital and human resources. *Production and Operations Management* 8 (4): 374–92.

Roth, A. V., A. E. Gray, J. Singhal, and K. Singhal. 1997. International technology and operations management: Resource toolkit for research and teaching, *Production and Operations Management* 6 (2): 167–87.

Safizadeh, M. H., and L. P. Ritzman. 1997. Linking performance drivers in production planning and inventory control to process choice. *Journal of Operations Management* 15 (4): 389–403.

Sharma, D. 1987. *Manufacturing strategy: An empirical analysis.* Unpublished doctoral dissertation, Ohio State University, Columbus, OH.

## Sakakibara, Flynn, and Schroeder

### Article Summarized

Sakakibara, Sadao, Barbara B. Flynn, and Roger G. Schroeder. 1993. A framework and measurement instrument for just-in-time manufacturing. *Production and Operations Management* 2 (3): 177–94.

### Scales (Actual Questions Used)

*Setup Time Reduction*

1. We are aggressively working to lower setup times in our plant.
2. We have converted most of the setup time to external time while the machine is running.
3. We have low setup times of equipment in our plant.
4. Our crews practice setups to reduce the time required.

*Small Lot Sizes*

5. We have large lot sizes in out plant (reversed scale).
6. We are aggressively working to lower lot sizes in our plant.
7. We tend to have large lot sizes in our master schedule (reversed scale).

*JIT Deliveries from Suppliers*

8. Our vendors supply us on a JIT basis.
9. We receive daily shipments from most suppliers.
10. Our suppliers are certified, or qualified, for quality.
11. We have long-term arrangements with our suppliers.

*Supplier Quality Level*

12. We strive to establish long-term relationships with suppliers.
13. Our suppliers are actively involved in our new product development process.
14. Quality is our number one criterion in selecting suppliers.
15. We rely on a small number of high-quality suppliers.

*Multifunction Workers*

16. I usually do not perform my own machine setups (reversed scale).
17. I inspect my own output.
18. I am capable of performing several different tasks.
19. When my machine is stopped, I am idle (reversed scale).

*Small Group Problem Solving*

20. During problem-solving sessions, we make an effort to get all team members' opinions and ideas before making a decision.
21. Our plant forms teams to solve problems.
22. In the past 3 years, many problems have been solved through small group sessions.

*Training*

23. Direct labor undergoes training to perform multiple tasks in the production process.
24. Plant employees are rewarded for learning new skills.
25. Our plant has a low skill level compared with our industry (reversed scale).
26. Direct labor technical competence is high in this plant.

*Daily Schedule Adherence*

27. Our schedule is designed to allow time for catching up because of production stoppages for quality problems.
28. We usually meet the production schedule each day.
29. There is no time in the schedule for machine breakdown or production stoppages (reversed scale).

*Repetitive Master Schedule*

30. Our master schedule repeats the same mix of products from hour to hour and day to day.
31. The master schedule is level loaded in our plant from day to day.
32. We make every model every day.

*Preventive Maintenance*

33. Our equipment is in a high state of readiness for production at all time.
34. We devote a portion of every day solely to preventive maintenance.
35. We emphasize good maintenance as a strategy for achieving quality and schedule compliance.
36. We have a separate shift, or part of a shift, reserved each day for maintenance activities.
37. We have a relatively high rate of downtime for repair compared with our industry (reversed scale).

*Equipment Layout*

38. We have laid out the shop floor so that our machines and processes are laid out in close proximity to each other.
39. We have organized our plant floor by means of manufacturing cells.
40. We have eliminated many long conveyors to move materials.

*Product Design Simplicity*

41. We make an effort, in the design process, to list only the specifications that are really needed.
42. The emphasis in part design is on minimizing the part count.
43. We are not concerned about the number of parts in an end item (reversed scale).

*Kanban*

44. Vendors fill our kanban containers rather than filling purchase orders.
45. Our suppliers deliver to us in kanban containers without the use of separate packaging.
46. We use a kanban pull system for production control.
47. We use kanban squares, containers, or signals for production control.

*Pull System Support*

48. We use a back-flushing system where components are subtracted from inventory every time a product is made.
49. We emphasize effective equipment layout to increase our process efficiency.
50. Direct labor is authorized to stop production for quality problems.
51. We use a pull system to control our production.
52. The control of production is in the hands of the workers.

*MRP Adaptation to JIT*

53. We use a run schedule (pull system) rather than work orders.
54. We use MRP for major event planning only, such as a product change or a shift in run size.
55. We use work orders extensively to maintain shop-floor information (reversed scale).

*Accounting Adaptation to JIT*

56. We use a job order accounting system where costs are assigned by the cost prebatch (reversed scale).
57. We use time standards to measure direct labor (reversed scale).
58. We monitor cost variances frequently (reversed scale).

## Construct Description

The authors described just-in-time (JIT) as a comprehensive approach to continuous manufacturing improvement based on the notion of eliminating all waste in the manufacturing process. From the sources of literature and the discussion with experts at the plant, 16 core JIT components and 5 supporting fields were identified. However, this JIT manufacturing scale focused on measuring only the core JIT components that were useful in assessing JIT's impact in manufacturing environments. The 16 dimensions of core JIT components were further grouped into six categories: production floor management, scheduling, process and product design, workforce management, supplier management, and the information system.

The components of JIT were defined as follows. Setup time reduction was defined as "the extent to which the plant is taking an active role in reducing set-up times" (p. 184). Small lot sizes indicated "the level of activities the plant is taking to lower lot sizes" (p. 184). JIT deliveries from suppliers connoted "the extent to which suppliers have been integrated into production, making frequent deliveries and achieving quality certification" (p. 184). Supplier quality level indicated "the steps to maintain long-term relationship with suppliers involving suppliers in the planning and quality improvement process" (p. 184). The construct of multifunction workers was identified as "to what extent workers are performing multiple tasks such as setups, maintenance, inspection, and tasks that demand initiative" (p. 184). Small group problem solving indicated "the use of small groups of workers, staff, and management for solving production problems, and encouraging workers to bring production-related problems to ream problem-solving sessions" (p. 184). Training referred to the "plant management's commitment to train workers for multiple tasks and to maintain high worker skill levels relative to industry" (p. 184).

Daily schedule adherence implied "the time allotted for meeting each day's schedule, including catching up after stoppages for quality considerations or machine breakdowns" (p. 184). Representative master schedule described "the extent of use of a repetitive level daily production schedule in the plant" (p. 184). Preventive maintenance was defined as "the steps plant management has taken to introduce preventative maintenance practices to workers daily routines, reserved a part of the shift for preventative maintenance, and incorporated preventative maintenance into manufacturing strategy" (p. 184). Equipment layout was explained as "the use of manufacturing cells, machine and process layout, and the use of equipment designed for flexible floor layout" (p. 184).

Product design simplicity referred to "the simplicity of design specifications, minimizing part counts, and customer orientation in new product design" (p. 184). Kanban was defined as "the integration of plant and suppliers into production, in terms of using kanban cards and containers" (p. 184). Pull system support indicated "the features the plant has introduced supporting pull systems, such as stopping for quality problems, efficient floor layout, and worker-directed production" (p. 184). MRP adaptation to JIT represented "the extent the plant has integrated JIT concepts with MRP" (p. 184). Last, accounting adaptation to JIT was given as "how well the plant's accounting practices support a JIT orientation" (p. 184).

## Measurement Description

Fifty-eight items were grouped into 16 dimensions. Each item was operationalized using a 5-point Likert scale that ranged from 1 = "strongly agree" to 5 = "strongly disagree." The response to each scale was the sum of the responses to all the items under the scale. In addition, some items were reverse scaled (*see* Scales).

## Development

The initial measurement instrument with 65 items was developed based on the extensive review of the literature and the discussion with experts at the plant level. Preliminary tests on the measurement instrument were conducted at 12 plants. Special attention was placed on the possibility of cultural bias. Based on the reliability analysis using Cronbach's coefficient alpha value, the authors dropped seven items from the original instrument.

## Sample

Forty-one plants were randomly selected from lists of U.S.- and Japanese-owned plants in three industries: transportation, electronics, and machinery. On average, 12 to 16 plants were from each industry. Among them were 13 Japanese-owned and 28 American-owned plants that were all located in the United States. Multiple respondents were used in the data collection. The types of respondents consisted of supervisors, process engineers, production and inventory managers, quality managers, human resource managers, workers, plant accountants, plant superintendents, and plant managers. The total number of respondents was 822 (*see* Table 4 for detailed information). The overall participation rate was larger than 60%.

## Reliability and Validity

Reliability was assessed using Cronbach's coefficient alpha method. "The level of reliability of the scales ranged from .43 to .88. Of the 16 scales, 12 had an alpha value > .60 (p. 186)." Results of the reliability test analysis are reported in Table 5 in the article. Content validity was demonstrated by the review of the literature and extensive discussion with practitioners in the manufacturing plants. Factor analysis was used to assess the construct validity. The results showed that all 12 scales left after the reliability assessment loaded on single factors. Factor loadings for each item in these scales were greater than .40, with many loadings ranging from .70 to .90. Results of construct validity analysis are reported in Table 6.

Criterion-related validity in this study was assessed by using canonical correlation analysis technique to calculate the correlation coefficients between the JIT scales and the objective JIT performance criteria. In particular, three typical performance criteria, lead time to fill orders, cycle time, and inventory turns per year, were chosen. The relatively high overall correlation between the JIT scale and the performance criteria indicated good criterion validity. Particularly, the correlation coefficient for the first canonical function was .84 ($p < .08$), while the correlation coefficients for the second and third functions were lower and insignificant at the .10 level. In addition, the bivariate correlation between each scale and the canonical performance variate also provided some evidence of criterion validity. Six of the JIT scales were shown to be significantly correlated with the canonical performance variate. Results of criterion-related validity of analysis are reported in Table 7.

High intercorrelation among the JIT scales supported the assumption that JIT practices were strongly related to each other. Factor analysis further grouped the 12 JIT scales into three independent factors: management of people and schedules, simplified physical flow, and supplier management.

### Scores

Correlations between JIT practices and composite performance variate are reported in Table 5 in the article. The scale intercorrelation matrix is presented in Table 8.

### Other Evidence

Not available.

### Reference

None.

---

## Sakakibara, Flynn, Schroeder, and Morris

### Article Summarized

Sakakibara, Sadao, Barbara B. Flynn, Roger G. Schroeder, and William T. Morris. 1997. The impact of just-in-time manufacturing and its infrastructure on manufacturing performance. *Management Science* 43 (9): 1246–57.

### Scales (Actual Questions Used)

*JIT Practices*

1. Setup time reduction
2. Schedule flexibility
3. Maintenance
4. Equipment layout
5. Kanban
6. JIT supplier relationship

*Product Design*

7. New product quality
8. Design characteristics
9. Interfunctional design efforts

*Workforce Management*

10. Supervisor leadership
11. Incentives for group performance
12. Labor flexibility
13. Small group problem solving
14. Recruiting and selection
15. Supervisors as team leaders

*Organizational Characteristics*

16. Coordination of decision making
17. Decentralization of authority
18. Plantwide philosophy

*Quality Management*

19. Process control
20. Feedback
21. Rewards for quality
22. Top management quality leadership
23. Supplier quality involvement

*Manufacturing Strategy*

24. Communication of strategy
25. Long-range orientation
26. Manufacturing strategy strength
27. Stage 3 manufacturing
28. Stage 4 manufacturing

**Construct Description**

A conceptual framework to study just-in-time (JIT), in terms of practices, manufacturing performance, and competitive advantage was used to test the hypotheses suggested. Infrastructure practices included quality management, workforce management, manufacturing strategy, organizational characteristics, and product design. Six key JIT practices, such as setup time reduction, scheduling flexibility, maintenance, equipment layout, kanban, and JIT supplier relationships, were studied.

**Measurement Description**

In this study, 24 measurement scales were newly developed; and five were derived from those existing in the literature. Five-point Likert scales quantified responses that ranged from 1 = "strongly agree" to 5 = "strongly disagree." The responses tapping into each construct were averaged to arrive at the overall scale score. Manufacturing performance was captured using four quantitative variables—inventory turnover, cycle time, lead time, and on-time delivery rate. Each of these was obtained from the plant accountant. Competitive advantage was measured by five perceptual variables that assessed the "plant management's opinion of the plant's performance relative to global competition, in terms of unit cost of manufacturing, quality of product and service, fast delivery, and flexibility to change volume, relative competition" (p. 1250).

### Development

"A set of questionnaires was developed to correspond to the groups of JIT practices and infrastructure practices. The measures were targeted at the respondents who were expected to be the most knowledgeable in providing the desired information. The items from the various scales were intermixed, so that scale membership was not readily apparent in the questionnaires. Each scale appeared on at least two different questionnaires to ensure better reliability" (p. 1250).

### Sample

The plants were randomly selected from lists of U.S.-owned and Japanese transplants in transportation components, electronics, and machinery industries. The participation rate was at 60% with a total of 822 responses from the 41 plants. For details on the data, please see Sakakibara, Flynn, and Schroeder (1993).

### Reliability and Validity

Reliability, in terms of internal consistency, was measured by Cronbach's coefficient alpha. The final Cronbach's coefficient alpha values for all scales exceeded .60, which indicated internal consistency. Table 1 in the article reports the alpha scales for each scale. Factor analysis by principal components analysis (PCA) was found to yield "eigenvalues greater than 1, and the item loadings were all found to be greater than the minimum of .40 indicating good construct validity" (p. 1251).

### Scores

The scores are presented in Tables 1–7 in the article.

### Other Evidence

Not available.

### Reference

Sakakibara, S., B. B. Flynn, and R. G. Schroeder. 1993. A framework and measurement instrument for just-in-time manufacturing. *Production and Operations Management* 2 (3): 177–94.

## Samson and Terziovski

### Article Summarized

Samson, Danny, and Mile Terziovski. 1999. The relationship between total quality management practices and operational performance. *Journal of Operations Management* 17 (4): 393–409.

### Scales (Actual Questions Used)

*Leadership*

1. Senior managers actively encourage change and implement a culture of trust, involvement, and commitment in moving toward "best practice."
2. There is a high degree of unity of purpose throughout our site, and we have eliminated barriers between individuals and/or departments.

3. "Champion(s) of change" are effectively used to drive best practice at this site.
4. At this site, we proactively pursue continuous improvement rather than reacting to crisis "fire-fighting."
5. Ideas from production operators are actively used in assisting management.
6. Environmental ("green") protection issues are proactively managed at this site.

*People Management*

7. The concept of the "internal customer" (i.e., the next person or process down the line and including all employees) is well understood at this site.
8. We have an organization-wide training and development process, including career path planning, for all our employees.
9. Our site has effective "top-down" and "bottom-up" communication processes.
10. Employee satisfaction is formally and regularly measured.
11. Our Occupational Health and Safety practices are excellent.
12. Employee flexibility, multi-skilling, and training are actively used to support improved performance.
13. All employees believe that quality is their responsibility.

*Customer Focus*

14. We know our external customers' current and future requirements (both in terms of volume and product characteristics).
15. These customer requirements are effectively disseminated and understood throughout the workforce.
16. In designing new products and services, we use the requirements of domestic customers.
17. We have an effective process for resolving external customers' complaints.
18. Customer complaints are used as a method to initiate improvements in our current processes.
19. We systematically and regularly measure external customer satisfaction.

*Planning*

20. We have a mission statement that has been communicated throughout the company and is supported by our employees.
21. We have a comprehensive and structured planning process that regularly sets and reviews short- and long-term goals.
22. Our plans focus on achievement of best practice.
23. When we develop our plans, polices, and objectives, we always incorporate customer requirements, supplier capabilities, and needs of other stakeholders, including the community.
24. We have a written statement of strategy covering all manufacturing operations, which is clearly articulated and agreed to by our senior managers.
25. Our site's manufacturing operations are effectively aligned with the central business mission.

*Process Management*

26. Our suppliers work closely with us in product development.
27. We work closely with our suppliers to improve each other's processes.
28. Our suppliers have an effective system for measuring the quality of the materials they send to us.
29. We have well-established methods to measure the quality of our products and services.
30. We have site wide, standardized and documented operating procedures.

*Information and Analysis*

Benchmarking

31. Relative cost position
32. Operating processes
33. Technology
34. Quality procedure

Customer Service

Estimate the total number of business days your site invest per year in reviewing the following information relating to other firms in your industry:

35. Other firms' product quality and procedures
36. Other firms' HR practices and policies
37. Other firms' processes in bringing new products to market

*Organizational Performance*

38. Customer satisfaction
39. Employee morale
40. Productivity
41. Defects as a percentage of production volume
42. Warranty claims cost as a percentage of total sales
43. Cost of quality (error, scrap, rework, and inspection) as percentage of total sales
44. Delivery in full on time to our customer

## Construct Description

Total quality management (TQM) consisted of seven elements that were based on the main criteria of quality awards frameworks, particularly the Malcolm Baldrige National Quality Award (MBNQA) criteria (1994). These are given as follows. (1) Leadership examined senior executives' leadership and "personal involvement in setting strategic directions and building and maintaining a leadership system that will facilitate high organizational performance, individual development, and organizational learning" (p. 396). (2) People management was "how well the human resource practices tie into and are aligned with the organization's strategic directions" (p. 396). (3) Customer focus addressed "how and how well the organization determines current and emerging customer requirements and expectations, provides effective customer relationship management, and determines customer satisfaction (Evans and Lindsay, 1995)" (p. 396). The authors also included "the extent to which customer related information is disseminated through the organization and the extent of customer complaint resolution" (p. 396) into this construct. (4) Strategic planning focused on the "organization's strategic and business planning and deployment of plans, along with the organization's attention to customer and operational performance requirements" (p. 396). (5) Customer quality and operational performance excellence were treated as key strategic business issues that were part of the overall strategic planning. (6) Information and analysis was described as the "scope, management, and use of data and information to maintain a customer focus, to drive quality excellence, and to improve performance (MBNQA 1994)" (p. 397). (7) Process management was "concerned with how the organization designs and introduces products and services, integrates production and delivery requirements and manages the performance of suppliers" (p. 397).

The performance construct focused "on quality performance, operational and business performance indicators: customer satisfaction, employee morale, productivity, quality of output and delivery performance" (p. 397).

## Measurement Description

Fifty-three TQM-related variables were allocated to seven constructs. Four of the variables were measured based on continuous scales. All the remaining variables were operationalized using interval scales; predominantly 5-point Likert-type scales. Appendix A in the article presents the summary of the scales for each of the 53 variables.

## Development

The initial questionnaire was developed by a committee of academics, site managers, and the chairman of the Australian Quality Awards Foundation using various sources of quality awards criteria. Revision was made after six pilot tests in Australia. Little evidence of bias such as "respondent fatigue" and "awareness" of change in the tone and/or measurement scale of the questionnaire were found.

Fifty-three TQM-related variables were chosen from the initial 246 questions. After screening outliers and treating the incomplete response, the measurement items retained were subject to reliability and validity testing. Several items were dropped based on factor analyses.

**Sample**

Approximately 4,000 manufacturing sites across all manufacturing industries were randomly selected from manufacturing sites "that employ 20 to 3000 employees and were registered with the Australian Bureau of Statistics, or Statistics New Zealand in 1993" (p. 399), using 12 industry codes and 3 size categories. Among the 4,000 manufacturing sites, the Australian sample had at least 15 respondents from each site and 3,000 sites in total, while New Zealand sample had 1,000 sites. "Responses from 1289 sites, 962 in Austria and 327 in New Zealand, were received" (p. 399). The response rates were 32% and 38%, respectively. No significant response bias was detected. However, considering the quality (i.e., correctness and completeness) of the responses, only 1,024 usable responses were left for further analysis.

**Reliability and Validity**

Reliability was assessed by Cronbach's coefficient alpha. The value of Cronbach's coefficient alpha for each construct based on the final measurement items exceeded .60, which satisfied the general reliability requirement for survey study. Table 1 reports the initial measurement items, the items dropped from the scale, and the corresponding reliability coefficients. In light of the initial selection of measurement items based on the extensive review of international literature and the evaluation criteria of major international quality awards, content validity was considered valid.

The construct validity was evaluated by using principal components factor analysis (PCA). Tables 1 and 2 report the factor loadings for each item. The initial loadings ranged from .35 to .93. After deleting the items whose loadings were less than .45, all the factors loaded acceptably well. Evidence of criterion validity was provided by the strong relationship between TQM practice and organizational performance. The multiple R coefficient was computed for the first six constructs and the last performance measurement was .46, which indicated that when taken together, the six TQM components explained a significant proportion of variance in performance. Thus, the six TQM element constructs were reported to have a reasonably high degree of criterion-related validity.

**Scores**

The factor loadings for the six independent variable TQM elements and the dependent variable performance are reported in Tables 1 and 2, respectively, in the article. Correlation matrix of independent variable construct factor scores is shown in Table 3. The results from the multiple regression analysis are reported in Table 4.

**Other Evidence**

Not available.

**References**

Evans, J. R., and W. M. Lindsay. 1995. *The management and control of quality.* New York: West.

Malcolm Baldrige National Quality Award Criteria [MBNQA]. 1994. United States Department of Commerce, National Institute of Standards and Technology, Washington, DC.

# Sarin and McDermott

**Article Summarized**

Sarin, Shikhar, and Christopher McDermott. 2003. The effect of team leader characteristics on learning, knowledge application, and performance of cross-functional new product development teams. *Decision Sciences* 34 (4): 707–39.

**Scales (Actual Questions Used)**

*Participative Behavior*

1. Team members can exert influence regarding how the team should function.
2. Team members can influence decisions of the team leader regarding things concerning the team.
3. Our team leader frequently asks the team members for their opinion when a problem comes up that involves the project.
4. Our team leader frequently makes decisions concerning the team, without consulting the team members. (reverse coded)

*Consideration*

5. Our team leader is friendly and approachable.
6. Our team leader gives advance notice of changes.
7. Our team leader makes my job pleasant.
8. Our team leader does little things to make it pleasant to be a member of this team.
9. Our team leader treats all members of the team as his or her equal.

*Process Structure*

10. Our team leader encourages the use of uniform procedures.
11. Our team leader decides what shall be done and how it will be done.
12. Our team leader schedules the work to be done.
13. Our team leader maintains definite standards of performance.
14. Our team leader asks the team members to follow standard rules and regulations.

*Goal Structure*

15. Our team leader lets the team know what is expected of them.
16. Our team leader makes his or her attitudes clear to the team members.
17. Our team leader makes sure that his or her part in the team is understood by the team members.

*Team Leader Position*

18. Our team leader is well respected in the organization for his or her management skills.
19. Our team leader is well respected in the organization for his or her technical skills.
20. Our team leader is widely "networked" in the organization.
21. Our team leader occupies a high position in the organization.
22. Our team leader enjoys authority in the organization.
23. Our team leader has significant decision-making responsibility in our organization.

*Team Learning*

24. Being a part of this team has been a great learning experience for the team members.
25. Member's experience with the team is likely to help them perform better in cross-functional teams in the future.

26. Member's experience with the project is likely to help them perform better on product development projects in the future.
27. Team members are likely to repeat the mistakes made here on other projects. (reverse coded)
28. Because of their experience on this project, team members will be better prepared to handle similar situations.
29. Members are likely to apply the lessons learned on this project to other areas in the organization.

*Speed to Market*

30. This product was developed much faster than other comparable products developed by our organization.
31. This product was developed much faster than similar products developed by our nearest competitors.
32. This product could have been developed in a shorter time. (reverse coded)
33. The product concept formation (i.e., opportunity identification and product design) took longer than expected. (reverse coded)
34. The product commercialization (i.e., product/market testing, production, distribution, promotion, sales) took longer than expected. (reverse coded)

*Degree of Innovation*

35. Several product-related innovations were introduced during the development of this product.
36. High quality technical innovations were introduced during the development of this product.
37. Compared with similar products developed by our competitors, our product will offer unique features/attributes/benefits to the customers.
38. Our product introduces many completely new features to this class of products.
39. Compared with similar products developed by our organization, our product will offer unique features.
40. Check one of the following statements that best (or most closely) describes the product developed by your team:
    - The product is new to both our firm as well as the customers.
    - The product is new to the customer but not very new to our firm.
    - The product is new to our firm but not very new to the customers.
    - The product is neither new to our firm nor new to the customers.
    - Our product is an imitation of an existing product.

*Project Complexity*

41. The product developed by our team was technically complex to develop.
42. Our team had to use nonroutine technology to develop the product.
43. The development process associated with the product was relatively simple (reverse coded).
44. Development of this product required pioneering innovation.
45. The product developed by our team is/was complex.

*Project Risk*

46. Our organization has a lot riding on this project.
47. Poor market performance by this product will have serious consequences for our business.
48. Our organization has made a significant investment in the development of this product.
49. The outcome of this project has high strategic value for our organization.

*Functional Diversity*

50. Please indicate how many members of your product team belong to the following functional areas:
    - Marketing ____
    - Manufacturing ____
    - Engineering ____

### Construct Description

The constructs for the study were derived from a varying range of literature that included articles on organizational learning, new product development (NPD) teams, and leadership in product teams. The appropriate references can be found in the Measurement Description section below, which summarizes the literature from where the scales were drawn. The following construct definitions were reported in the article.

Facilitative behavior was defined as "the degree to which the team leader is considered friendly. Facilitative behavior is measured by the underlying dimensions of participation and consideration" (p. 734). There were no scales that separately measured facilitative behavior. Participative behavior was indicated by "the degree to which the team leader is perceived to be democratic in his/her interactions with the team members" (p. 734). Consideration was characterized as "the degree to which the team leader is perceived to demonstrate concern for the well being of team members" (p. 734).

Initiation of goal and process structure was given as "the degree to which the team leader assigns tasks and prescribes behaviors to the team members in order to achieve the desired results" (p. 734). This construct was measured by two other constructs, process structure and goal structure. Process structure was defined as "the degree to which the team leader organizes and defines the activities of team members" (p. 734). Goal structure was explained as "the degree to which the team leader lets team members know what is expected of them and makes his/her desires known to the group" (p. 734).

Team leader position was identified as "the team leader's position is an indication of the formal and informal status enjoyed by the team leader" (p. 734). Team learning was defined as "the degree to which processing of team experience changes the nature and range of potential team actions" (p. 734). Team size was presented as "the number of members who form the core/primary part of your product development team" (p. 738). Functional diversity was "the degree of functional heterogeneity in the team" (p. 738).

Speed to market was "a time measure of the pace at which the product was developed by the team" (p. 734). Degree of innovation connoted "the degree of 'newness' of the product under development" (p. 734). Project complexity was defined as "the degree to which the development process was complicated and difficult" (p. 737). Project risk was "the magnitude of failure associated with the project" (p. 738).

### Measurement Description

New scales were developed for measuring team learning and team leader position. Some of the items in these scales were derived from Fleishman (1957), House and Dressler (1974), and Stogdill (1963). For team learning, the items were derived from Arygris and Schön (1978), Barabba and Zaltman (1991), Huber (1991), Fiol and Lyles (1985), and Moenaert and Caeldries (1996). Participative behavior, consideration, process structure, goal structure, degree of innovation and speed to market scales were based on Teas (1981, 1983), Sarin and Mahajan (2001), Olson, Walker, and Rueckert (1995). Project complexity, project risk, and functional diversity scales were based on Sarin and Mahajan (2001), and Ancona and Cladwell (1992a, 1992b).

### Development

The goal of the study was to examine the impact of the leadership characteristics in NPD teams on learning, application of knowledge, and subsequent performance of the teams. The development of the measures mainly borrowed from the NPD literature and leadership literature.

### Sample

This study chose NPD projects in the high-tech industries that had the following three characteristics: (1) only intraorganizational NPD projects were chosen, (2) all the NPD projects were product introductions bound for the external market, and (3) projects were in advanced stages of development and those introduced within the previous 12 months of development. The first phase qualitative data gathering was conducted in nine organizations with 26 leaders, team members, and NPD managers. In the second phase, 246 individuals from 64 different NPD teams were surveyed. The samples reported in the study were from the following functional spread: R&D and lab (27%), engineering (24%), software (7%), manufacturing

(7%), marketing (11%), management and administration (9%), and 14% nonresponses. The final usable number contained 229 completed surveys from 52 teams.

### Reliability and Validity

To ensure the reliability of each factor, Cronbach's coefficient alpha was used to test the internal consistency among the items included in each factor. A threshold level of .70 (Nunnally 1978) was applied for acceptable reliability for newly developed scales. The discriminant validity and the convergent validity were established using confirmatory factor analysis (CFA).

### Scores

The results of the correlation are given in Table 2 of the article. The results of the hierarchical regression are given in Table 3 of the article.

### Other Evidence

Not available.

### References

Ancona, D. G., and D. F. Caldwell. 1992a. Demography and design: Predictors of new product team performance. *Organization Science* 3 (3): 321–41.

———. 1992b. Bridging the boundary: External activity and performance in organizational teams. *Administrative Science Quarterly* 37 (4): 634–65.

Argyris, C., and D. A. Schön. 1978. *Organizational learning: A theory of action perspective.* Reading, MA: Addison-Wesley.

Barabba, V. P., and G. Zaltman. 1991. *Hearing the voice of the market: Competitive advantage through creative use of market information.* Boston, MA: Harvard Business School Press.

Fiol, C. M., and M. A. Lyles. 1985. Organizational learning. *Academy of Management Review* 10 (4): 803–13.

Fleishman, E. A. 1957. A leader behavior description for industry. In *Leader behavior: Its description and measurement,* eds. R. M. Stogdill and A. E. Coons, 103–19. Columbus: Bureau of Business Research, Ohio State University.

House, R. J., and G. Dressler. 1974. The path-goal theory of leadership: Some post hoc and a priori tests. In *Contingency approaches to leadership: A symposium held at Southern Illinois University, Carbondale, May 17-18, 1973,* eds. J. G. Hunt and L. L. Larson, 29–55. Carbondale: Southern Illinois University Press.

Huber, G. P. 1991. Organizational learning: The contributing processes and the literatures. *Organization Science* 2 (1): 88–115.

Moenaert, R. K., and F. Caeldries. 1996. Architectural redesign, interpersonal communication, and learning in R&D. *Journal of Product Innovation Management* 13 (4): 296–310.

Nunnally, J. C. 1978. *Psychometric Theory.* New York: McGraw-Hill.

Olson, E. M., O. C. Walker Jr., and R. W. Ruekert. 1995. Organizing for effective new product development: The moderating role of product innovativeness. *Journal of Marketing* 59 (1): 48–62.

Sarin, S., and V. Mahajan. 2001. The effect of reward structures on the performance of cross-functional product development teams. *Journal of Marketing* 65 (2): 35–53.

Stogdill, R. M. 1963. *Manual for leadership behavior description questionnaire-Form XII: An experimental revision.* Columbus: Bureau of Business Research, Ohio State University.

Teas, R. K. 1981. An empirical test of models of salespersons' job expectancy and instrumentality perceptions. *Journal of Marketing Research* 18 (2): 209–26.

———. 1983. Supervisory behavior, role stress, and the job satisfaction of industrial salespeople. *Journal of Marketing Research* 20 (1): 84–91.

# Sawhney and Piper

### Article Summarized

Sawhney, Rajeev, and Chris Piper. 2002. Value creation through enriched marketing–operations interfaces: An empirical study in the printed circuit board industry. *Journal of Operations Management* 20 (3): 259–72.

### Scales (Actual Questions Used)

*Marketing-Operations Interface (MOI) Quality Construct*

1. Operations consults marketing before making process changes.
2. Marketing consults operations before accepting early delivery requests.
3. Marketing consults operations before accepting special feature requests.
4. Order entry system provides information on existing orders, their completion time, and available capacity.

*Product Complexity*

5. Typical hole size
6. Typical line width
7. Typical number of layers

*MOI Speed*

8. Time taken by marketing to pass order information to production (days)

*Customer Value*

Quality

9. Defect rate (rework plus rejects)

Cost

10. Product cost relative to competition

Lateness

11. Orders delivered after agreed date

Product Lead Time

12. Lead time promised to the customers (days)

Plant Size

13. Number of employees representing plant size

### Construct Description

Two dimensions were used in defining the construct of marketing-operations interface (MOI) effectiveness: (1) MOI quality and (2) MOI speed. MOI quality "was defined by the extent to which product mix decisions were made in the light of both market and process needs" (p. 265). MOI speed was defined as "the time taken by marketing to pass order information to production" (p. 265).

Customer value was defined based on four dimensions: (1) quality, (2) cost, (3) lateness, and (4) product lead time. Product complexity was determined along three attributes: (1) typical hole size, (2) typical line width, and (3) typical number of layers.

## Measurement Description

A few constructs were derived from multiple items. MOI quality was measured using four items, two assessing operations' contribution to interface effectiveness and the other two assessing marketing's contributions. Each item was evaluated on a 7-point Likert scale ranging from 1 = "not at all" to 7 = "a great extent." Product complexity was operationalized as an index of three items. Each item was measured by open-ended questions, where respondents provided numerical estimates. These responses were subsequently sorted on a 7-point scale, where the intervals represented increasing complexity. The scale for the first item—hole size ranged from >30 to <10 mil; the scale for the second item—line width—ranged from >14 to <3 mil; and the scale for the last item—number of layers—ranged from 2 to >12 layers. The simple average of three numerical item scores was computed and used as the measure for overall product complexity.

All the other constructs, including MOI speed, plant size, and the four dimensions of customer value, were measured by a single item. Respondents provided direct numeric estimates for MOI speed, plant size, and product lead time. The other three dimensions of customer value—quality, cost, and lateness—were reported, on the other hand, on 7-point interval scales. Specifically, the scales for quality and lateness ranged from "0%" to ">30%," and the scale for cost ranged from "far worse than competitors" to "far better than competitors."

## Development

The development of instruments relied heavily on the field study where extensive interviews of people at different levels, factory visits, and analysis of company documents were conducted. Inputs from both industry experts and academic researchers were also requested to refine the survey. Finally, the revised questionnaire was pretested with managers at beta sites.

## Sample

A stratified sampling approach was used to chose plants from the population of 300-plus of the North American printed circuit board (PCB) industry. The authors classified plants into three strata according to plant size information (i.e., number of employees). A total of 167 plants within the sample frame were selected, with approximately equal numbers of plants from each plant-size stratum. Overall, 74 usable responses were received. These 74 responding firms accounted for nearly 70% of total industry sales. The response rate from each plant-size stratum ranged from 39% to 47%, with the overall response rate of 45%. A comparison of the profiles of responding plants and nonresponding plants suggested that no significant nonresponse bias existed.

The target respondent in each plant was the senior manager responsible for operations. Typically, these respondents were the vice president (VP) of operations, the VP of manufacturing, or the director of operations. Phone calls were made to these respondents to complete missing response and cross-check the information provided in the questionnaire, when necessary.

## Reliability and Validity

Multiple sources of information, including responses from different people, company documents, company archival data collected from the respondents' public Web sites, and from third-party information providers, were used, whenever possible, to provide a pseudo test-rest reliability check. The Cronbach's coefficient alpha values were also computed for the two multi-item scales—MOI quality and product complexity. Both constructs have an alpha value over .63.

The content validity was supported by extensive on-site interviews, factory visits, and reviews by experts from both industries and academe. The two multi-item constructs—MOI quality and product complexity—were also subjected to exploratory factor analysis (EFA) to evaluate convergent and discriminant validity. For the single-item construct, a correlation analysis was performed to test for discriminant validity. "Most of the correlations between the variables were under .30 and the greatest was <.45, thus, providing a good indication of discriminant validity" (p. 266).

### Scores

The factor loadings, mean, standard deviation of each item are reported in Table 2 (p. 267) in the article.

### Other Evidence

Not available.

### Reference

None.

---

## Schmenner and Cook

### Article Summarized

Schmenner, Roger W., and Randall L. Cook. 1985. Explaining productivity differences in North Carolina factories. *Journal of Operations Management* 5 (3): 273–89.

### Scales (Actual Questions Used)

*Labor Productivity*

1. Units per man-hour
2. Actual versus standard for direct labor
3. Value added per worker or per worker dollar
4. Cost per worker or per worker dollar
5. Other

*General Productivity*

6. Actual versus standard for direct and indirect labor
7. Effectiveness (labor efficiency times utilization)
8. Gross margin measures
9. Value added per all labor
10. Ratio of indirect to direct labor
11. Plotting of learning/experience curves for products
12. Other
13. Plant's rank within the industry
14. Plant's rank within the parent company
15. Plant's rate of change of productivity advance

*Product and Product Changes*

16. Major products lines manufactured
17. Number of product lines manufactured
18. Whether these product lines are also manufactured at other company plants
19. Whether this plant's products "inputs" to other company plants
20. Whether this plant receives as input the output of other company plants
21. Percentage of this plant's supply needs satisfied from other company plants
22. Whether product designs are dictated by industry standards, competitor initiation, or company initiative
23. Approximate number of parts (stock-keeping units) at plant

*Product-Related Changes since 1975*

24. Breadth of product line
25. Extent of product mix change
26. Change in complexity of product
27. Frequency of change to product design
28. Degree of engineering change orders
29. Extent of materials substitution
30. Change in product versatility
31. Change in product reliability
32. Change in product life
33. Change in product cost in real terms
34. Change in new product introduction in the plant
35. Degree of new product introduction in the plant

*Production Process and Process Changes*

36. Percentage to which direct labor at plant is devoted to the following process types: job shop, batch flow, line flow, continuous flow
37. Whether plant is controlled as a profit center or a cost center

Whether the Following Functions Are Performed at the Plant

38. New product design or redesign
39. Process engineering
40. Methods engineering
41. All production planning and scheduling
42. Purchasing of all major raw materials
43. Direct receipt of customer orders
44. Warehousing and distribution of finished goods
45. Which of the following functions are viewed as the two strongest and which as the two weakest: operations supervision, maintenance, materials handling/logistics, labor relations, personnel, quality control/assurance, purchasing, production planning/scheduling, inventory control, production control, industrial engineering, maintenance engineering, product design engineering
46. Degree of automation of the following types: computerized automatic machines, noncomputerized mechanization, automated materials handling
47. Percentage of equipment in various age categories
48. What kinds of process hardware advances the plant has pursued: computer controlled machines, process control computers, programmable controllers, robots, computer controlled test equip– CAD/CAM, automatic storage/retrieval system, programmable operator-less materials handling carts/trucks, others solicited
49. Degree of involvement by plant in process hardware advances
50. How proprietary is production process or equipment
51. Production cycle time (receipt of first materials through shipment) in weeks
52. Nature of any change in production cycle time since 1975
53. Frequency of occurrence of the following: expediting of orders through the plant, expediting of materials from vendors, products mix changes, parts shortages, engineering change orders
54. Direction of process-related change, if any, since 1975, in the following: nature of process flow, plant layout, materials handling, materials scrap rate, degree of rework, quality complaints, engineering changes, release of new products, parts shortages, vendor expediting, expediting in plant, work-in-process inventory, materials tracking, machine monitoring, design engineering/manufacturing interface
55. Whether plant operates a computer-based MRP system

56. Special features of any MRP system: simulation of work center loads, sharing demand patterns and lead time with vendors, computer-generated work center priorities, computer-based tracking of inventories
57. Period of time the production schedule is frozen
58. Number of weeks of inventory presently held
59. Percentage of inventory held as raw material, work-in-process, finished goods

*The Workforce*

60. Average employment and maximum employment since 1975
61. Number of shifts run
62. Year company first occupied the plant
63. Percentage of workforce characterized as skilled, semiskilled, and low skilled
64. Typical value for annual labor turnover
65. Nature of wage system
66. Whether plant is unionized and, if so, characterization of union attitude
67. Year of last union organizing campaign of last election
68. Number of labor grades
69. Number of management layers between production worker and plant managers
70. Importance of time standards for direct labor force
71. Nature of any recent change in worker responsibilities
72. Degree of cross-training

*Productivity Programs and Miscellaneous Variables*

73. Character of rate of growth of productivity in the industry.
74. Character of competition in the industry.
75. Which of the following areas designated as chief areas of recent productivity accomplishment and which designated as targets for future productivity gains: automation of tasks previously un-automated, improved automation of tasks previously automated, production cycle time reduction, improved quality, smoother linking of process segments, speed improvements, morale, methods, worker participation, layout, parts shortage reduction, product redesign, materials substitution, vendor performance, yields, lower work-in-process, machine "up-time" overhead reduction, worker training, materials handling improvements
76. Key sources of productivity ideas from among the following: operators/assemblers, first line supervisors, manufacturing/industrial engineers, middle level management, top level management at plant, trade journals/conventions, companies in industry, maintenance/repair workers, quality control staff, materials handlers, design engineers, materials vendors, equipment vendors, customers, companies in other industries, others possible
77. Nature of any worker suggestion plan
78. Average number of suggestions per worker per year
79. Nature and frequency of plant management meetings with workers
80. Whether there is a separate salaried personnel suggestion plan
81. Whether target levels of cost reduction plant savings are built into the budget
82. Whether quality circles have been initiated and their level of success

*Labor Productivity: Percent Average Annual Increase*

Industry Productivity Growth

83. The industry's rate of productivity growth

Simpler Flow of Materials through the Process

84. Production cycle time changes
85. Frequency of order expediting through plant

86. Frequency of product mix changes
87. Production planning and scheduling done at plant
88. Parts shortage reduction is the key future productivity target
89. Percentage of raw materials that are products of other company-owned plants
90. Cycle time reduction is the key future productivity target

People Valued

91. Degree of cross-training of workers

Attention to Quality

92. Materials costs are tracked
93. Importance of quality control staff productivity ideas

Hardware Advances

Miscellaneous

94. Importance of mid-management productivity ideas

*General Productivity: Percent Average Annual Increase*

Industry Productivity Growth

95. The industry's rate of productivity growth

Simpler Flow of Materials through the Process

96. Percentage of inventory held in raw materials
97. Change in level of plant expediting
98. Production planning and scheduling done at plant
99. Process engineering performed at the plant
100. New or rearranged layout is the key future productivity target
101. Vendor performance improvements have been accomplished

People Valued

102. Operator/assembler methods improvement has been accomplished

Attention to Quality

103. Importance of quality control staff productivity ideas
104. Materials costs are tracked

Hardware Advances

Miscellaneous

105. Design engineering and manufacturing interface
106. Plant's productivity performance rank relative to the industry

Industry Productivity Growth

107. The industry's rate of productivity growth

Simpler Flow of Materials through the Process

108. Percentage of direct labor working in job-shop process
109. Production planning and scheduling function in the plant
110. Process engineering performed at plant

111. Reduced work-in-process inventory is the key future productivity target
112. Product designs are dictated by
    - Industry standards
    - Imitation of certain competitors
    - Company

People Valued

113. Operations supervision function relative to other functions
114. Typical annual labor turnover rate

Attention to Quality

115. Improved quality/less rework is the key future productivity target

Hardware Advances

116. Degree of automation for noncomputerized machines, relative to the industry
117. Involvement in hardware advances
118. The year this plant was first occupied
119. Degree of automation for computerized machines relative to the industry
120. Degree of computer monitoring of equipment since 1975

*Productivity Achievements Relative to the Industry's Rate of Productivity Growth*

Industry Productivity Growth

Simpler Flow of Materials through the Process

121. Product mix changes
122. Production planning and scheduling function
123. Warehousing of finished goods at plant
124. Purchasing function

People Valued

125. Supervision of operations function
126. Labor relations function

Attention to Quality

127. Changes in product design affecting reliability
128. Improved quality/less rework is the key future productivity target

Miscellaneous

129. Percentage of inputs that are products of other company-owned plants
130. Percentage of direct labor involved in continuous flow process
131. Product designs are dictated by industry standards, imitation of certain competitors, company
132. Targeted cost reduction plan savings are included in budgets
133. Plant's rank relative to other plants in the parent corporation based on productivity performance

Simpler Flow of Materials through the Process

134. Percentage of direct labor working in a line-flow process
135. New or rearranged layout the key future productivity target
136. Linking of process segments for smoother flow the key future productivity target

People Valued

137. Operator/assembler methods improvement has been accomplished.
138. Increased workforce morale and effort has been accomplished.

Attention to Quality

139. Product changes affecting reliability
140. The maintenance engineering function in the plant

Hardware Advances

141. Involvement in hardware advances
142. Importance of equipment vendor productivity ideas

Dependent Variables

143. Change in Rate of Change in Productivity

Industry Productivity Growth

144. Industry's rate of productivity growth

Simpler Flow of Materials through the Process

145. Production planning and scheduling function
146. Purchasing all raw materials done at plant
147. Number of weeks of inventory
148. Nature of products changes

People Valued

149. Degree of worker responsibility
150. Maintenance worker productivity ideas

Attention to Quality

151. Maintenance engineering function

Hardware Advances

152. Percentage of equipment <5 years old

## Construct Description

This study focused on productivity and measured it as a ratio, with the numerator being an output measure (e.g., units, dollars) and the denominator being an input measure (e.g., labor hours, dollars). The authors asked plant managers to rate their plants according to the following five measures (p. 274):

1. Approximate average annual rate of improvement (or decline) of labor productivity in recent years
2. Approximate average annual rate of improvement (or decline) of a general measure of productivity in recent years
3. From the standpoint of productivity/performance, the plant's rank among other plants within the same industry
4. From the standpoint of productivity/performance, the plant's rank among other plants within the parent corporation
5. The recent rate of change of productivity advance at the plant.

### Measurement Description

This study employed a variety of measures ranging from Likert-type scales to objective measures. Even though the authors did not provide a formal measurement description, Tables 1 and 2 in the article offer some details about the operationalization of the scales.

### Development

The study was developed in two parts. First, there was a series of 20 interviews with plant (or manufacturing) managers in North Carolina. Second, based on these interviews, an eight-page survey was developed.

### Sample

An eight-page survey was delivered to 860 factories in North Carolina that had more than 250 employees each. Ninety-five surveys were completed and returned. No further details on the data were provided in the article.

### Reliability and Validity

Not available.

### Scores

The scores are presented in Tables 3–8 in the article.

### Other Evidence

Not available.

### Reference

None.

---

## Schroeder, Anderson, and Cleveland

### Article Summarized

Schroeder, Roger G., John C. Anderson, and Gary Cleveland. 1986. The content of manufacturing strategy: An empirical study. *Journal of Operations Management* 6 (3/4): 405–15.

### Scales (Actual Questions Used)

*Business Strategy Elements*

Product

1. The highest quality and most reliable products
2. Better product features than most competitors
3. A complete line of products
4. The first to market (new product innovator)
5. Products that are simple and easy to use

Price

6. To sell at the highest price in the market
7. To sell at a medium price
8. To sell at the lowest price

Service

9. To provide the best delivery and service performance in the industry

Operations

10. The most people-oriented company
11. Effective use of the learning curve
12. Focused operations
13. The latest process technology
14. Low inventories
15. Best location of facilities
16. High vertical integration

*Manufacturing Strategy Elements*

Manufacturing Mission

17. Quality and reliability
18. Customer service (delivery, warranty, field service)
19. Economic performance (efficiency, productivity, unit cost)
20. Flexibility (volume, product)
21. Resource and equipment utilization (capacity, output)
22. Technology (product, process)
23. Organizational development
24. Employee and community relations
25. Inventory control

Manufacturing Objectives

26. Quality
27. Delivery performance
28. Unit cost
29. Flexibility to change volume
30. Flexibility to change product
31. Employee relations
32. Inventory turnover
33. Equipment utilization

Manufacturing Policies (Areas with Written Policies Established)

34. Quality of the product
35. Management of the workforce
36. Treatment of suppliers and vendors
37. Professional and managerial development
38. Inventory and distribution levels
39. Development of new process technology
40. Outside hiring versus inside development
41. Focus of facilities

42. Facilities location
43. Vertical integration

*Assessment of Strategy*

44. The current business strategy helps us compete in the marketplaces.
45. The business has performed up to our expectations.
46. The elements of business strategy are consistent among marketing, finance, manufacturing, and personnel.
47. Manufacturing has lent competitive strength to the business.
48. We have a well-developed manufacturing strategy.
49. Manufacturing strategy follows from marketing strategy.
50. Manufacturing has performed up to our expectations.
51. Marketing strategy lends competitive strength to the business.

### Construct Description

This study empirically investigated the content of manufacturing strategy. Manufacturing strategy content, as defined by the authors, included "the type of strategies used, the way they are defined, the linkage with business strategies, and ultimately whether they help the business gain a competitive advantage" (p. 406). It consisted of mission, objectives, policies, and distinctive competences. Manufacturing mission specified what operations must accomplish for the business to succeed, so it states the purpose of the manufacturing function. Manufacturing objectives were specific statements of expected results—a refinement of the mission. Manufacturing policy was defined by resources or functions that must be performed by manufacturing. It supported manufacturing mission and objectives. Manufacturing distinctive competence was what sets manufacturing apart from the competition and, thus, could be viewed in terms of uniqueness.

### Measurement Description

To measure the relationship between manufacturing strategy and business strategy, eight items were constructed. Each item was assessed on 5-point Likert scales ranging from 1 = "strongly agree" to 5 = "strongly disagree." The questionnaire for the manufacturing strategy content contained both open-ended and close-ended questions. For most close-ended questions, respondents were asked to rank the order of priority and/or importance for items listed in the questionnaire.

### Development

The questionnaire was constructed based on the literature and the opinion of the managers.

### Sample

The questionnaires were administered to 39 manufacturing managers enrolled in two sections of a 1-week executive program on manufacturing strategy that was sponsored by the University of Minnesota. These individuals were "generally plant managers, manufacturing vice-presidents, or manufacturing managers who were knowledgeable about business strategies and manufacturing strategies" (p. 406). These companies represented a variety of sizes and industries. About 25% of the sample were divisions of large multinational companies, and the remaining were smaller companies. About 50% of the companies were in the electronics industry, while the rest were from diverse industries such as metal working, equipment suppliers, etc.

### Reliability and Validity

Not available.

### Scores

The assessment of relationships between business strategy and manufacturing strategy is reported in Table 1 in the article.

**Other Evidence**

Not available.

**Reference**

None.

---

# Schroeder, Anderson, Tupy, and White

**Article Summarized**

Schroeder, Roger G., John C. Anderson, Sharon E. Tupy, and Edna M. White. 1981. A study of MRP benefits and costs. *Journal of Operations Management* 2 (1): 1–9.

**Scales (Actual Questions Used)**

*MRP Benefit Questions*

1. Inventory turnover
2. Delivery lead time (days)
3. Percentage of time meeting delivery promises (%)
4. Percentage of orders requiring "splits" because of unavailable material (%)
5. Number of expeditors (# people)
6. Average unit production cost

To What Degree Have the Following Benefits Been Achieved from Your MRP System?

7. Improved competitive position
8. Improved customer satisfaction
9. Better production scheduling
10. Improved plant efficiency
11. Reduced safety stocks
12. Better cost estimating
13. Better control of inventory
14. Improved coordination with marketing and finance
15. Improved morale in production

*Costs of MRP Systems*

16. Current cost $ ____________
17. Total eventual cost $ ______

*Company Characteristics*

Company Size

18. Sales
19. Number of employees
20. Inventory level

Type of Products and Process

21. Industry
22. Make-to-order or make-to-stock

23. Assembly or fabrication
24. Job shop, continuous process, or assembly line

Complexity of the Product Structure

25. Number of parts and components
26. Number of levels in the bill of material

Pre-MRP Conditions

27. Year MRP development was started
28. Type of system in use prior to MRP

*Type of MRP System*

Degree of Computerization

29. The number of MRP system elements that were computerized
30. The percentage of system integration
31. Whether the company was a class A, B, C, or D company

Data Accuracy

32. The accuracy of a number of MRP system elements
33. The problems encountered with data accuracy

*Type of Implementation Approach*

Degree of Management Support

34. Who initiated the MRP effort
35. Problems encountered with various types of management support

*The Implementation Methods Used*

36. Source of expertise used
37. Source of software development
38. Degree of formality of the MRP project

*Starting Levels*

Starting Levels of Performance

39. Inventory turnovers
40. Delivery lead time
41. Percentage of delivery promises met
42. Percentage of split orders
43. Number of expeditors

### Construct Description

Not available.

### Measurement Description

The benefits of material requirements planning (MRP) were measured by (1) improvement in tangible measures of manufacturing performance and (2) subjective ratings of benefits. Five tangible performance measures were given as (1) percentage of delivery promise met, (2) inventory turnover, (3) delivery lead time, (4) percentage of split orders, and (5) number of expeditors. For each measure, respondents described (1) the current level of performance (LOP), (2) the performance levels prior to MRP installation under comparable economic conditions, and (3) the expected future performance levels when the MRP was fully installed. Current benefits and potential future benefits were defined as the difference between these performance measures. The subjective benefits were assessed by measures such as better production control, improved competitive position and improved morale in manufacturing. The subjective benefits were rated on a nominal scale ranging from little/none to very much. In addition, cost was measured as the estimation of the current and total eventual cost of the MRP system installation. Company characteristics were captured by the company size, type of products and process, complexity of the product structure, and pre-MRP conditions. Type of MRP system was described by the degree of computerization and data accuracy. Type of implementation approach was given by the degree of management support and the implementation method used. Starting levels were determined by the starting levels of performance. Summation variables were constructed as the scores for each factor.

### Development

Not available.

### Sample

A comprehensive six-page survey instrument was used to collect data on company description, MRP system status, MRP benefits and costs, implementation problems, and implementation approach used. Questionnaires were sent to the production and inventory control or materials managers in 1,700 companies. These respondents were selected from the APICS (founded as the American Production and Inventory Control Society, currently as the Association for Operations Management) membership lists in the Midwest. This selection process made the sample not a representative one of manufacturing companies, but rather a large sample of companies with APICS representation in the Midwest. Only one survey was sent to each company location to avoid multiple responses from the same site. The response rate was 40% (i.e., 679 companies). Only 422 companies (62% of the respondents) reported that they have an MRP system.

### Reliability and Validity

In this exploratory study, to assess which items correspond to latent variables, a factor analysis was conducted on 20 variables that described company characteristics and computerization of the MRP systems. At the end of the factor analysis, the following six factors emerged: (1) computerization, (2) front-end computerization, (3) size, (4) product complexity, (5) process complexity, and (6) inventory.

Then, the 422 companies with MRP systems were randomly divided into two samples: Three fourths were in the first part of the sample and one fourth in a holdout sample. Model validity was defined in terms of the $R^2$ and overall F-test achieved from the first sample, the *t*-scores of the coefficients of individual variables in the model, and the predictive accuracy of the models in the holdout sample. The benefits of MRP are reported in Table 1 in the article. The findings from the regression analyses are reported in Tables 5 and 6.

### Scores

The scores are presented in Tables 5 and 6 in the article.

### Other Evidence

Not available.

### Reference

None.

# Schroeder, Bates, and Junttila

## Article Summarized

Schroeder, Roger G. Kimberly A. Bates, and Mikko A. Junttila. 2002. A resource-based view of manufacturing strategy and the relationship to manufacturing performance. *Strategic Management Journal* 23 (2): 105–17.

## Scales (Actual Questions Used)

*Process and Equipment*

1. We have equipment that is protected by the firm's patents.
2. Proprietary equipment helps us gain a competitive advantage.
3. How does the process technology at your plant compare to industry competition on a global basis?
4. What term below describes your production equipment relative to your industry? (Reverse coded)

*Internal Learning*

5. Employees are cross-trained at this plant so that they can fill in for others if necessary.
6. Employees receive training to perform multiple tasks.
7. Management takes all product and process improvement suggestions seriously.
8. Many useful suggestions are implemented at this plant.

*External Learning*

9. We strive to establish long-term relationships with suppliers.
10. We maintain close communication with suppliers about quality considerations and design changes.
11. Our customers give us feedback on quality and delivery performance.
12. Our customers are actively involved in the product design process.

*Manufacturing Performance*

13. Manufacturing cost as a percentage of sales
14. Scrap rate (conformance quality)
15. Percentage of deliveries customers receive on time
16. Number of days from receipt of raw materials to customer receipt (cycle time)
17. Length of fixed production schedule (flexibility)

## Construct Description

The constructs used in the study are described as follows. Internal learning included "the training of multifunctional employees and incorporating employee suggestions into process and product development" (p. 107). External learning was defined as "interorganizational learning through problem solving with customers and suppliers" (p. 108). Proprietary manufacturing process and equipment included "equipment protected by patents as well as unpatented processes and equipment held in secret" (p. 108). Manufacturing performance included "cost as a percentage of sales, conformance quality, percentage of on-time deliveries, days from receipt of raw materials to customer receipt, and the length of the fixed production schedule" (p. 108).

## Measurement Description

The items used 5-point Likert scales indicating degree of agreement or disagreement unless otherwise stated. This study also used multiple respondents for various parts of the questionnaire to overcome mono-respondent bias.

### Development

Please refer to Flynn, Schroeder, and Sakakibara (1994).

### Sample

The data were collected through written questionnaires from a total of 164 manufacturing plants in Germany, Italy, Japan, the United Kingdom, and the United States. Sixty-five percent of the plants contacted attended the study. Both objective data on performance and perceptual data on the constructs of interest were collected from 23 respondents in each plant using the survey instrument developed by Flynn, Schroeder, and Sakakibara (1994).

### Reliability and Validity

To evaluate convergent validity, the authors used confirmatory factor analysis (CFA). The factor loadings range from .48 to .83 with an average of .67. These measures provide evidence of adequate convergent validity of the constructs; all loadings were statistically significant and positive. Discriminant validity was assessed by constraining interconstruct correlations in the measurement model to unity one at a time and by measuring the change in $\chi^2$ statistics. The changes in $\chi^2$ statistics were highly significant; thus, discriminant validity was reached. The reliability was assessed by using composite reliabilities. The composite reliabilities for the internal learning, external learning, and process and equipment were .82, .74, and .70; thus, construct reliabilities appear to be adequate.

### Scores

The scores are provided in Tables 2 and 3 in the article.

### Other Evidence

Not available.

### Reference

Flynn B. B., R. G. Schroeder, and S. Sakakibara. 1994. A framework for quality management research and an associated measurement instrument. *Journal of Operations Management* 11 (4): 339–66.

---

## Shah and Ward

### Article Summarized

Shah, Rachna, and Peter T. Ward. 2003. Lean manufacturing: Context, practice bundles, and performance. *Journal of Operations Management* 21 (2): 129–49.

### Scales (Actual Questions Used)

*Contextual Variables*

1. How many employees are there at this location?
2. How many years has it been since plant start-up?
3. Approximately what percentage of plant production workers is represented by a union(s)?
(None, 1% to 25%, 26% to 50%, 51% to 75%, 76% to 99%, 100%)

*Operational Performance (Six-Item Scale)*

How has the *following* changed over the past 5 years?

4. Finished product first-pass quality yield (reverse coded) (improved more than 40%, improved 21% to 40%, improved 1% to 20%, stayed the same, declined 1% to 20%, declined more than 20%)
5. Scrap and rework costs (increased more than 20%, increased 1% to 20%, stayed the same, decreased 1% to 20%, decreased 21% to 40%, decreased more than 40%)
6. Productivity, defined as dollar volume of shipments per employee (reverse coded) (increased more than 80%, increased 41% to 80%, increased 21% to 40%, increased 11% to 20%, increased 1% to 20%, stayed the same, decreased 1% to 10%, decreased more than 10%)
7. Per unit manufacturing costs, excluding purchased material (increased more than 20%, increased 11% to 20%, increased 1% to 10%, stayed the same, decreased 1% to 20%, decreased more than 20%)
8. Manufacturing cycle time (no reduction, decreased 1% to 10%, decreased 11% to 20%, decreased 21% to 50%, decreased 51% to 75%, decreased more than 75%)
9. Customer lead time (increased more than 20%, increased 1% to 20%, stayed the same, decreased 1% to 20%, decreased 21% to 40%, decreased more than 40%)

*Lean Bundles*

10. Just-in-time
11. Total quality management
12. Total productive maintenance
13. Human resources management

## Construct Description

The three contextual factors—age, size, union—were single-item constructs and were defined by the way they were given in the questionnaire. Operational performance was intended to assess the overall operational performance of a manufacturing plant.

## Measurement Description

The subjective items of lean manufacturing practices were measured with 3-point Likert-type scales with anchors ranging from 1 = "no implementation" to 3 = "extensive implementation." The measurement properties of the other scales are provided in the Scales section.

## Development

The lean bundles were developed empirically in this model. Also, the six-item operational performance scales were newly developed for this study. Using principal components analysis (PCA), the authors argued that each derived factor was unidimensional enough to be used in this context.

## Sample

There were 1,757 completed surveys of 28,000 sent out by Penton Media Inc. in 1999. These surveys were filled out by plant managers, plant leaders, and manufacturing managers. The unit of analysis was the manufacturing plant. The sample was representative of the population profile of the 1997 U.S. Census of Manufacturers. The details of the sample characteristics are provided in Table 2 (p. 135) of the article.

## Reliability and Validity

The authors presented an argument that whether operational performance was unidimensional in the conceptual sense was different from the issue of whether it was unidimensional in the empirical sense. "Two competing and equally valid conceptual views on performance are the tradeoff view and the production competence view popularized by Skinner (1969) and Vickery (1991), respectively. We argue that firms are capable of developing multiple internal competences. Further, global competition requires that firms develop and possess these multiple competences in order to succeed. Our measure focuses on three underlying aspects that are highly related: lead time, cost, and conformance quality. The very basis of JIT is that manufacturing processes that are faster and more precise with regard to first-time-through quality are also inherently less costly. Thus, we contend that these six measures are conceptually and empirically related and represent a single dimension of operational performance" (pp. 138–39).

The unidimensionality of the four lean bundles were assessed by PCA.

### Scores

Correlations are presented in Table 3 in the article. PCA results are presented in Table 4. Operations performance—factor loading, means, standard deviation, and Spearman's correlations—are given in Table 5. Pearson's $\chi^2$ values to test the association between contextual variables and implementation of lean practices are given in Table 6. Table 7 presents results of a hierarchical regression analysis. Table 8 presents an ANOVA of industry effects.

### Other Evidence

Not available.

### References

Skinner, W. 1969. Manufacturing-missing link in corporate strategy. *Harvard Business Review* 47 (3): 136–45.
Vickery, S. K. 1991. A theory of production competence revisited. *Decision Sciences* 22 (3): 635–43.

## Small and Yasin

### Article Summarized

Small, Michael H., and Mahmoud M. Yasin. 1997. Advanced manufacturing technology: Implementation policy and performance. *Journal of Operations Management* 15 (4): 349–70.

### Scales (Actual Questions Used)

*Effort Expended on Planning and Installation Activities*

On Strategic Planning for AMT Adoption

1. Effort expended on linking business and manufacturing strategies
2. Effort expended on coordinating marketing and manufacturing strategies
3. Effort expended on developing a long-term automation strategy
4. Effort expended on monitoring AMTs

On Worker Preparation

5. Effort expended on emphasizing teamwork/group activities
6. Effort expended on communicating the likely impact of AMT to all plant workers
7. Effort expended on having multi-skilled production workers
8. Effort expended on preinstallation training for all project participants

On Team-Based Project Management

9. Effort expended on establishing multidisciplinary planning teams
10. Effort expended on establishing multidisciplinary installation teams
11. Effort expended on choosing knowledgeable project leader(s)

On Technology Consistency

12. Effort expended on matching capabilities of AMT to the benefits expected by the firm
13. Effort expended on ensuring compatibility of AMT with existing systems

*Performance*

Time-Based Performance Factor

14. Time for major design change in existing product
15. Time-to-market for a new product
16. Production changeover time

Organizational Effectiveness Factor

17. Plant revenues from manufacturing operations
18. Operator output rates
19. Product quality

Operational Efficiency Factor

20. Delivery lead times
21. Inventory turnover rates
22. Ability to change production lot sizes

## Construct Description

This study investigated "the relationships between adoption of various advanced manufacturing technologies (AMT), the way that firms plan for and implement them, and their eventual performance" (p. 349). Four planning and installation factors/strategies—strategic planning factor, technology consistency factor, worker preparation for AMT adoption factor, and team-based project management factor—were proposed based on previous literature (e.g., Anderson, Cleveland, and Schroeder 1989; Primrose 1991). No detailed definitions except the measure items were offered for these four constructs.

## Measurement Description

All items in the scales of planning and installation activities were measured on 7-point Likert scales that anchored from 1 = "no effort at all" to 7 = "an extremely high level of effort." Factor scores were constructed for each of the four derived AMT implementation process scales using regression. A composite implementation score used to represent overall implementation effort was also derived by summing the four planning and installation factor scores. Performance was measured using firms' self-assessment of changes in manufacturing performance on 12 performance variables since the adoption of AMT. These variables were also measured on 7-point Likert scales anchored at 1 = "declined significantly" and 7 = "increased significantly." The data were recorded using a new 7-point Likert scale, anchored at one end by –3, representing "substantial decline" in performance and at the other end by 3, representing "substantial improvement" in performance, with 0 representing "no change" in performance. A composite performance score was also derived by summing the three individual performance factor scores.

**Development**

Several academic experts, AMT consultants, operations managers at various firms that had installed AMT, and a few board members of the American Production and Inventory Control Society (APICS) were asked to critique the content, structure, and relevance of the survey instrument. Some minor changes were made to the survey instrument based on these reviewers' comments.

**Sample**

The surveyed population consisted of firms whose major products were classified in several subgroups of U.S. Department of Commerce, Standard Industrial Classification code (SIC) Major Groups 35 to 37 (the discrete parts, durable goods manufacturing classifications). Firms in these classifications were major adopters of AMT. The population list was developed using several national corporate directories of U.S. manufacturing firms. Nine-hundred and fifteen firms with the highest sales-per-employee ratios from among the directories were identified as the target population. Questionnaire packets were mailed to top-level corporate managers with responsibility for technology, manufacturing, or engineering at a randomly selected sample of 584 of the 915 firms. A total of 125 responses were obtained in which 9 were unusable, with a survey response rate of 22% and a usable response rate of 20.4%.

ANOVA and goodness-of-fit $\chi^2$ tests were applied to analyze the potential nonresponse bias. Analysis did not reveal any significant differences between respondents and nonrespondents with respect to annual sales distributions or employee levels at the .05 level.

**Reliability and Validity**

Convergent and discriminant validity of the four proposed planning and installation scales were tested using confirmatory factor analysis (CFA) with LISREL. As evidence of convergent validity, the comparative fit index (CFI) for this model was .93, which was above the .90 rule-of-thumb heuristic. Convergent validity was further supported by the fact that all 13 of the observable variables were significantly related to their criterion, and the mean squared multiple correlation (SMC) for the 13 variables was .61 with 11 of the 13 SMCs exceeding the .50 level and none of them falling below the .45 level.

The Anderson and Gerbing (1988) approach was applied to assess the discriminant validity of the four proposed planning and installation scales. Accordingly, the correlations between the latent constructs were tested to see whether they are statistically different from 1. The single-degree-of-freedom contrasts of the four- and one-factor models was significant at the .05 level. This result supported the discriminant validity of the measurement scales.

The reliability of each scale was assessed using Cronbach's coefficient alpha values. All but one of the alpha values was more than .70. The operational efficiency scale has an alpha value of .66; however, the authors indicated that alphas as low as .60 may be acceptable in exploratory situations (Flynn, Schroeder, and Sakakibara 1994). Therefore, all scales were deemed to be reliable.

**Scores**

Tables 2 and 3 in the article report the orthogonal factor analysis of the planning and installation variables and performance variables, respectively.

**Other Evidence**

Not available.

**References**

Anderson, J. C., G. Cleveland, and R. G. Schroeder. 1989. Operations strategy: A literature review. *Journal of Operations Management* 8 (2): 133–58.

Anderson, J. C., and D. W. Gerbing. 1988. Structural equation modeling in practice: A review and recommended two-step approach. *Psychological Bulletin* 103 (3): 411–23.
Flynn, B. B., R. G. Schroeder, and S. Sakakibara. 1994. A framework for quality management research and an associated measurement instrument. *Journal of Operations Management* 11 (4): 339–66.
Primrose, P. L. 1991. *Investment in manufacturing technology.* New York: Chapman and Hall.

# Snell and Dean

**Article Summarized**

Snell, Scott A., and James W. Dean Jr. 1992. Integrated manufacturing and human resource management: A human capital perspective. *Academy of Management Journal* 35 (3): 467–504.

**Scales (Actual Questions Used)**

*Advanced Manufacturing Technology*

*To What Extent Are Each of the Following Technologies Used in Your Plant?*

1. Manufacturing resource planning
2. Computer-aided design
3. Numerical control
4. Computer numerical control
5. Direct numerical control
6. Flexible manufacturing systems
7. Robotics
8. Automated materials handling
9. Computer-aided test/inspection
10. Computer-aided process planning

*To What Extent Are Transactions between the Following Production Processes Accomplished Using Computers?*

11. Product Design/Development and Production Planning
12. Production planning and component manufacturing
13. Component manufacturing and assembly
14. Assembly and production scheduling
15. Production scheduling and maintenance
16. Maintenance and materials handling
17. Materials handling and quality control
18. Quality control and materials management

Total Quality Management

19. How much time does the plant management staff devote to quality improvement?
20. How much time is spent with the suppliers to improve their quality?
21. How well are you able to measure the "cost of quality" in your plant?
22. How would you describe your current approach to providing quality products?
23. What percentage of the plant's manufacturing processes is under statistical control?
24. What percentage of the plant's employees has quality as a major responsibility?
25. What percentage of the plant's employees is routinely given feedback about quality?

*How Would You Describe the Level of Use within Your Plant of the Following Quality Improvement Methodologies?*

26. Quality function deployment
27. Taguchi methods
28. Continuous process improvement

JIT Inventory Control

29. Number of your suppliers
30. Size of deliveries
31. Length of product runs
32. Number of total parts
33. Amount of buffer stock

Selective Staffing

34. How extensive is the employee selection process for a job in this unit (e.g., use of tests, interviews, etc.)?
35. How important is it to select the best person for a given job?
36. In general, how long does it take to select someone for a position in this unit once the job becomes open?
37. How many people are involved in the selection decision?
38. How much money is generally spent in selecting people for a job?
39. How many applicants are screened for each person hired for a job?
40. How much importance is placed on the staffing process in this unit?

Comprehensive Training

41. How extensive is the training process for members of your work unit?
42. How much priority is placed on training employees in your unit?
43. How formal or structured is the training process?
44. What percentage of people has received training in the past year?
45. On average, how many hours of formal training does a typical member of your work unit receive per year?
46. How many different kinds of training are available for members of your work unit to attend?
47. How much money is spent on training individuals in your work unit?
48. Do you feel training is viewed as a cost or an investment?

Development Performance Appraisal

49. How much effort is given to measuring employees?
50. How would you describe the performance standards in your unit?
51. How much do employees participate in goal setting and appraisal?
52. How often is performance discussed with the employees?
53. Do discussions focus on present performance or future performance?
54. When performance is discussed, how much emphasis is placed on finding avenues of personal development for an employee?
55. How closely are raises, promotions, etc., tied to performance appraisal?
56. How would you describe the approach used to discuss performance?
57. How many people provide input to the performance evaluation of each employee?

Equitable Reward Systems

58. How would you rate pay levels in this unit relative to the other firms?
59. How would you rate the pay levels in this unit area relative to past years?

60. Are the wages in this work unit competitive for this industry?
61. How much emphasis is placed on paying people in this work unit compared with what they would be paid on similar jobs in other companies?
62. How closely is pay tied to individual performance?
63. How wide is the range in pay across members in this work unit?
64. To what extent do differences in pay across members of this work unit represent differences in their contribution?
65. To what extent are people paid what they are worth compared with others in the work unit?

### Construct Description

This study examined the relationship between integrated manufacturing and human resources management (HRM) from a human capital perspective. The concept of human capital that was used in the study was that people possessed skills, experience, and knowledge that had economic value to firms. HRM practices were seen as investments in human capital. Integrated manufacturing was defined as a combination of advanced manufacturing technologies (AMT), just-in-time (JIT) inventory control, and total quality management (TQM) practices. It eliminated the barriers between stages, functions, and the goals of production to create a streamlined value-added system.

### Measurement Description

In total, 57 items grouped into seven categories were used in the study. Multiple-item scales were developed to measure manager's perceptions of AMT, TQM, JIT inventory control, the size, and performance of the firm and the nonmanager's perception of the job characteristics—complexity, variety, and interdependence.

AMT was measured with an 18-item scale assessing the extent to which a firm had implemented and integrated computer technologies for manufacturing. TQM was captured on a 10-item scale assessing the extent to which the firm strove for continuous quality improvements in manufacturing. JIT was measured with a 10-item scale assessing the extent to which a firm had attempted to cut costs through reduced inventories and lead times and by controlling features such as the number of suppliers, size of deliveries, and the total number of parts. Selective staffing was quantified by a seven-item scale assessing the extensiveness of a firm's selection process as shown for instance by the time and money spent and the number of people involved. An eight-item scale was used to gauge comprehensive training that indicated the extensiveness of training and development opportunities, such as the frequency and variety of training, the money spent, and the percentage of employees trained.

Developmental appraisal was a nine-item scale measuring whether performance appraisal was used for developing employee, as exemplified by diagnosing training needs, frequent feedback, problem solving, and discussing future issues. Equitable rewards was an eight-item scale that tapped into the degree to which pay was competitive for the industry (external equity) and based on individual performance (individual equity). Organizational size was obtained from a natural logarithmic transformation of the number of full-time employees obtained from Standard & Poor's *Directory of Corporate Unionization* was a single-item scale measure asking whether a union represented a firm's workforce. Responses were coded 0 for "no" and 1 for "yes." Growth was assessed by regressing the natural logarithm of sales against time, and the antilogarithm of this regression slope was used as an index of the munificence while the antilogarithm of the standard error term from the same regression slope was used to assess dynamism. The MINL formula (Schamalansee 1977) of sales concentration was used as a surrogate for the Herfindahl-Hirschman-index of complexity.

### Development

The measures for integrated manufacturing survey were pilot tested on an independent group of manufacturing managers using multiple items and multiple respondents to ensure both internal consistency and interrater reliability.

### Sample

A potential pool of 512 manufacturing firms in Pennsylvania was drawn from several segments of the metal-working industry using the *Harris Pennsylvania Industrial Directory:* primary metals, U.S. Department of Commerce, Standard Industrial Classification code (SIC) 33; fabricated metal products, SIC 34; industrial and metal working machinery, SIC 35; transportation equipment, SIC 36; and precision instruments, SIC 37. These industries were chosen because they had an acknowledged adoption of advanced manufacturing processes. The unit of analysis was plants rather than entire firms. In each plant, focus was of four functions: (1) operations, (2) quality, (3) production control, and (4) human resource. A final total of 160 plant managers, 102 operations managers, 109 quality managers, 97 production managers, 90 human resource managers, and at least 90 employees participated in the study.

### Reliability and Validity

Principal components analysis (PCA) with varimax rotation was used to assess the convergence validity within each latent variable as well as the divergence between latent variables. Tables 1 and 2 in the article provide the factor values. The authors also assessed the interrater reliability measures, which are presented in Table 3.

### Scores

Means, standard deviations, alphas, interrater reliabilities, and zero-order correlations for all variables are reported in Table 3 in the article.

### Other Evidence

Not available.

### Reference

Schmalensee, R. 1977. Using the H index of concentration with published data. *Review of Economics and Statistics* 59 (2): 186–93.

---

## Somers, Nelson, and Karimi

### Article Summarized

Somers, Toni M., Klara Nelson, and Jahangir Karimi. 2003. Confirmatory factor analysis of the end-user computing satisfaction instrument: Replication within an ERP domain. *Decision Sciences* 34 (3): 595–621.

### Scales (Actual Questions Used)

*Content*

1. Does the system provide precise information you need?
2. Does the system provide reports that seem to be just about exactly what you need?
3. Does the system provide sufficient information?

*Accuracy*

4. Is the system accurate?
5. Are you satisfied with the accuracy of the system?

*Format*

6. Do you think the output is presented in a useful format?
7. Is the information clear?

*Ease of Use*

8. Is the system user friendly?
9. Is the system easy to use?

*Timeliness*

10. Do you get the information you need in time?
11. Does the system provide up-to-date information?

## Construct Description

Content, accuracy, format, ease of use, timeliness, and end-user satisfaction were the key constructs used in this study. None of the constructs was newly developed. Each was adapted from Doll and Torkzadeh (1988). Content, accuracy, timeliness, and format were related to product usefulness, while ease of use considered "the user friendliness of the application" (p. 598).

## Measurement Description

The measurement instrument of Doll and Torkzadeh (1988) was tested for reliability and validity. Thus, no measurement instrument was developed in this article. Items were measured on a 5-point scale: 1 = "almost never," 2 = "some of the time," 3 = "about half the time," 4 = "most of the time," and 5 = "always."

## Development

The main purpose of the article was "to test structure and dimensionality, and reliability and validity of the end-user computing satisfaction (EUCS) instrument" (p. 595) and to test four different models posited by Doll, Xia, and Torkzadeh (1994) based on the empirical data.

## Sample

Data were collected by a nationwide mail survey of users of ERP systems. The sample was drawn from the *Directory of Top Computer Executives* (2000). Only companies with ERP systems were included. Introductory letters along with three questionnaires were sent to the CIOs or other top-level executives of 1,162 firms in the United States who identified the major end users and applications. Four hundred and seven usable surveys came back. Most of the respondents "implemented commercial off-the shelf systems from vendors such as Baan, J. D. Edwards, Oracle, PeopleSoft, and SAP, and many organizations reported implementing ERP systems from more than one vendor" (p. 600).

## Reliability and Validity

Based on the confirmatory factor analysis, significance of factor loadings, construct reliabilities, and average variance were employed to evaluate convergent validity based on Fornell and Larcker (1981). Values .80 and .50 were used as cutoff values for reliability and average variance extracted, respectively.

## Scores

The correlation matrix is given in the appendix. A comparison of Model 4 indices is given in Table 6. A comparison of Model 4 standardized parameter estimates is reported on p. 611.

### Other Evidence

Not available.

### References

*Directory of top computer executives.* 2000. Phoenix, AZ: Applied Computer Research.
Doll, W. J., and G. Torkzadeh. 1988. The measurement of end-user computing satisfaction. *MIS Quarterly* 12 (2): 259–74.
Doll, W. J., W. Xia, and G. Torkzadeh. 1994. A confirmatory factor analysis of the end-user computing satisfaction instrument. *MIS Quarterly,* 18 (4): 453–61.
Fornell, C., and D. F. Larcker. 1981. Evaluating structural equation models with unobservable variables and measurement error. *Journal of Marketing Research* 18 (1): 39–50.

## Soteriou and Chase

### Article Summarized

Soteriou, Andreas C., and Richard B. Chase. 1998. Linking the customer contact model to service quality. *Journal of Operations Management* 16 (4): 495–508.

### Scales (Actual Questions Used)

*Intimacy*

1. The customer shares all relevant to the incident information with the service provider.
2. The service provider shares all relevant to the incident information with the customer.
3. The service episode was (not) intimate.

*Service Complexity*

4. All the steps involved in the service production are well understood.
5. There are hardly any exceptional cases in the production of this service.
6. Little judgment is necessary in the production of this service; there are standard ways of solving the problems that might arise.
7. There is nothing very intricate or complicated about the work this service requires.
8. This is a one-person job; there is little need to check or work with others.
9. To perform this service properly, workers must collaborate extensively with others.
10. This service is about the same from case to case and from time to time.

### Construct Description

The construct of customer contact referred to the interface between the customer and the service provider. The authors employed Kellogg and Chase's customer contact model, which identified three dimensions of customer contact: (1) communication time, (2) intimacy, and (3) information richness. Among these three customer contact dimensions, communication time and intimacy were the two independent variables, and information richness was one of the control variables in the study. Specifically, intimacy was defined as the mutual confiding and trust, and communication time was given as the total time spent in communication between customer and server.

The construct of service quality used in the study follows the definition of Parasuraman, Zeithaml, and Berry (1988). There were five dimensions associated with the service quality construct: reliability, tangibles, responsiveness, assurance, and empathy. Detailed descriptions of each dimension can be found in Table 1 (p. 497) in the article.

Service complexity and divergence were the other two control variables in the study. Complexity was defined by Shostack (1987) as the number and intricacy of steps required to perform the service, and divergence was the exectutional latitude of the service.

### Measurement Description

Three items were used to capture intimacy and seven items to capture service complexity. Each item was operationalized using 7-point Likert scales. Service quality data were collected using the modified SERVQUAL instrument (Parasuraman, Zeithaml, and Berry 1988) with 21 items. Service divergence was quantified by the frequency distributions of all services offered at the reception area over the period of 2 months.

### Development

An exploratory study was used in the development and validation of the constructs. Initial intimacy items were based on the definition provided by Kellogg and Chase (1995). Kellogg and Chase (1995) also used the construct of task analyzability (Perrow 1967; Van de Ven and Delbecq 1974), which was in turn used by Soteriou and Chase (1995) to identify an initial set of items for service complexity. The service quality instrument was based on the SERVQUAL instrument (Parasuraman, Zeithaml, and Berry 1988), which had been validated in prior research. To assess the face validity of the instrument, the general managers of the hotel and the head receptionist were contacted. The item that addressed the dimension of safety was deleted since it did not reflect the episode level of analysis and the hospitality environment.

### Sample

Intimacy data were collected via personal interviews with randomly selected customers using a combination of cluster and systematic sampling at the reception desk of a five-star hotel. A total of 117 interviews were conducted in a period of 6 weeks with a reported response rate of 28%. Service complexity items were used as the basis for interviews with the service providers during their break or at the end of their shifts.

### Reliability and Validity

Given the exploratory nature of this study, no in-depth validity checks were reported. However, the Cronbach's coefficient alpha for the five service quality dimensions and the intimacy construct are reported in Table 2 in the article (p. 501). All the alpha values were above .80. In addition, confirmatory factor analysis (CFA) was used to examine the distinctiveness of the latent variables for empathy and intimacy. The results, listed in Table 4 (p. 501), provide evidence of discriminant validity.

### Scores

The scores are reported in Tables 2–8 in the article.

### Other Evidence

Despite the similarity between customer contact intimacy and service quality empathy (Parasuraman, Zeithaml, and Berry 1988), CFA further supported an assumption of two separate constructs.

### References

Kellogg, D., and R. B. Chase. 1995. Constructing and empirically derived measure for customer contact. *Management Science* 41 (11): 1734–49.

Parasuraman, A., A. V. Zeithaml, and L. L. Berry. 1988. SERVQUAL: A multiple-item scale for measuring perceptions of service quality. *Journal of Retailing* 64 (1): 12–40.
Shostack, G. L. 1987. Service positioning through structural change. *Journal of Marketing* 51 (1): 34–43.
Van de Ven, A. H., and A. L. Delbecq. 1974. A task-contingent model of work-unit structure. *Administrative Science Quarterly* 19 (2): 183–97.

# Stahl and Zimmerer

### Article Summarized

Stahl, Michael J., and Thomas W. Zimmerer. 1983. Using decision modeling to examine management consensus: A study of a maintenance management control system. *Journal of Operations Management* 3 (2): 93–98.

### Scales (Actual Questions Used)

*Criteria for the Maintenance Management System*

1. Cost efficiency
2. Productivity improvement
3. Materials management
4. Unification of work control
5. Planning and scheduling
6. Information and retrieval

*Maintenance Management System Decision*

7. Indicate your recommendation regarding approval or disapproval of this system for maintenance management control.

### Construct Description

The maintenance management control system (MMCS) was designed to incorporate the full cycle of maintenance functions into a total comprehensive management system. It was programmed to manage and control materials and human resources. It offered an overall maintenance review system through an online system with visual display modes.

A single definition was given for each MMCS criterion. For instance, cost efficiency captured the trade-off of downtime cost and maintenance cost. Productivity improvement was defined as maximum utilization of maintenance resources. Materials management was ordering, cataloguing, and locating material inventories. Unification of work control connoted the entire maintenance work control cycle from planning through scheduling, performance, measurement, reporting, and revision unified in one system. Planning and scheduling described the ability of a system to plan and schedule all but emergency maintenance. Information and retrieval was equal to the ability of a system to organize and disseminate maintenance data.

### Measurement Description

Each criterion variable was measured as either "adequate" or "excellent" and was coded as –1 or +1, respectively. Adequate was described as "barely meets minimally acceptable value or requirements" (p. 94). Excellent was defined as "considerably better than minimally acceptable value or requirements" (p. 94). The rating of adequate was used as the lowest possible rating because managers implied that any factor below adequate in a system would cause rejection of the system. The recommendations regarding approval or disapproval of each MMCS system were captured on scales ranging from –5 = "strongly recommended disapproval" to +5 = "strongly recommended approval."

### Development

The instrument was developed based on the interviews at a large construction company with division vice president (VP), two regional VPs, group regional managers, project managers, and maintenance engineers. Through interviews, criteria for effective MMCS and the definitions for these criteria were set up. The actual instrument was based on a hypothetical MMCS by varying the quality of each of the six criteria. Each criterion in the hypothetical MMCS was rated as either adequate or excellent. The only differences between the systems were the extent to which the six criteria differed for each hypothetical system.

### Sample

The instrument was administered to 120 managers. Seventy-two managers responded to the request. Of the 72 responses, 60 were found usable. No further details of the sample were provided in the article.

### Reliability and Validity

Not available.

### Scores

The scores are presented in Tables 3–4 in the article.

### Other Evidence

Not available.

### Reference

None.

---

## Stank, Goldsby, and Vickery

### Article Summarized

Stank, Theodore P., Thomas J. Goldsby, and Shawnee K. Vickery. 1999. Effect of service supplier performance on satisfaction and loyalty of store managers in the fast food industry. *Journal of Operations Management* 17 (4): 429–47.

### Scales (Actual Questions Used)

*Service Performance Measures*

Operational Performance

1. Delivers when they say they will
2. Delivers when the restaurant requests
3. Orders shipped complete
4. Products delivered in good condition
5. Ease of returning products
6. Provides the best price

Relational Performance

7. Driver courtesy
8. Distribution center personnel courtesy
9. Distribution center personnel responsiveness
10. Develops relationships using same driver for every delivery
11. Develops relationships using distribution center account service representative

*Customer Satisfaction*

12. I am delighted with my firm's overall relationship with our primary distributor.
13. I wish more of my firm's distributors were like this one.
14. It is a pleasure dealing with this distributor.
15. There is some problem or another with this distributor (reverse scored).

*Customer Loyalty*

16. The relationship that my firm has with this distributor is something we are very committed to.
17. The relationship that my firm has with this distributor is something we intend to maintain indefinitely.
18. The relationship that my firm has with this distributor deserves our maximum effort to maintain.
19. Maintaining a long-term relationship with this distributor is very important to my firm.
20. I would recommend that my successor continue using this distributor.
21. Other things being equal (price, product, quality, etc.), I intend to continue buying from this distributor because of their distribution service.

## Construct Description

The activities contributing to consistent quality, productivity, and efficiency were considered as the operational elements, which included "physical features of the service, e.g., characteristics of delivery that define and capture form, time, and place utilities of the service" (p. 430). Those activities that enhanced the service firm's closeness to the customer and thus helped in understanding their "needs and expectations and develop[ing] processes to fulfill them" (p. 430) were incorporated to evaluate the relational performance of the firm.

Customer satisfaction was seen as the customer's overall judgment concerning the extent to which their expectations were met by the product or service. Customer loyalty was defined as "a long-term commitment to repurchase involving both a favorable cognitive attitude toward the selling firm and repeated patronage" (p. 433).

## Measurement Description

A total of 21 items grouped into four categories—operational performance, relational performance, customer satisfaction, and customer loyalty—were used. Items under each category were operationalized using 7-point Likert scales.

## Development

"A comprehensive listing of service elements capturing the dimensions of operational and relational performance were generated from the service priorities identified by Roth and van der Velde (1991) as well as the SERVQUAL scale (Parasuraman et al., 1985)" (p. 436). "Customer satisfaction measures were drawn from scales used and validated in existing literature (Leuthesser and Kohli, 1995). . . . Loyalty measures were also literature based, utilizing the work of Cronin and Morris (1989) and Morgan and Hunt (1994)" (p. 436). "Based on the measures derived from the literature, telephone interviews of managers representing nine customer firms and five service providers from the fast food industry were then used to develop a complete customer survey instrument" (p. 435).

### Sample

This study focused on the industrial distributors in the fast-food service industry. A total of 560 samples were randomly chosen from among the total population of restaurants representing the six largest fast-food restaurant chains in the United States as listed in the *American Business Directory* (1996). A usable database of 287 responses was obtained from the survey administered, giving an overall response of 51.3%. The target respondent was the restaurant manager, who was asked to evaluate their primary food distributor, regardless of whether they could choose them or not. The wording of the survey questions related to loyalty and repurchase intentions reflected the manager's recommendations regarding the continued use of the distributor and the importance of the distributor to the restaurant's business.

### Reliability and Validity

Cronbach's coefficient alpha values were used for reliability. The zero-order correlations between the indicator variables and latent constructs as a preliminary assessment of construct validity are tabulated in Table 2. Further validity assessment of the measurement model was inferred using confirmatory factor analysis (CFA).

### Scores

The scores are presented in Tables 2–4 and Figure 3 in the article.

### Other Evidence

Not available.

### References

*American business directory.* 1996. Omaha, NE: American Business Information.

Cronin, J. J., and M. H. Morris. 1989. Satisfying customer expectations: The effect on conflict and repurchase intentions in industrial marketing channels. *Journal of Academy of Marketing Science* 17 (1): 41–49.

Leuthesser, L., and A. K. Kohli. 1995. Relational behavior in business markets. *Journal of Business Research* 34 (3): 221–33.

Morgan, R. M., and S. D. Hunt. 1994. The commitment-trust theory of relationship marketing. *Journal of Marketing* 58 (3): 20–38.

Parasuraman, A., V. A. Zeithaml, L. L. Berry. 1985. A conceptual model of service quality and its implications for future research. *Journal of Marketing* 49 (4): 41–50.

Roth, A. V., and M. van der Velde. 1991. Operations as marketing: A competitive service strategy. *Journal of Operations Management* 10 (3): 303–28.

---

## Stanley and Wisner

### Article Summarized

Stanley, L. L., and J. D. Wisner. 2001. Service quality along the supply chain: Implications for purchasing. *Journal of Operations Management* 19 (3): 287–306.

### Scales (Actual Questions Used)

*Cooperative Purchasing/Supplier Relationship*

1. Periodic audits of supplier facilities
2. Hold meetings with suppliers on regular basis to solve problems
3. Require certification of suppliers on key materials

4. Providing training on quality requirements to suppliers
5. Formal, periodic written evaluation of suppliers
6. Involve key suppliers in design stage of new products
7. Operate in a JIT purchasing environment
8. Contact with one or two suppliers on key materials

*Purchasing's Service Quality Performance*

9. Overall service level
10. Reliable delivery of information (reports, updates)
11. Ability to meet internal customer expectations
12. Responsive to customers' needs
13. Communication level
14. On-time delivery of products/services
15. On-time delivery of information (reports, updates)
16. Quality of delivered products/services
17. Flexible to internal customer's changing needs
18. Explanation of product/service delivery problems

*Internal Suppliers' Service Quality Performance*

19. Overall service quality
20. Ability to meet purchasing's expectations
21. Responsive to purchasing's needs
22. On-time delivery of products/services
23. Quality of delivered products/services
24. On-time delivery of information (reports, updates)
25. Reliable delivery of information (reports, updates)
26. Flexible to purchasing's changing needs
27. Explanation of products/service delivery problems
28. Communication level

*Service Quality to External Customers*

29. Ability to meet customers expectations
30. Resolution of product/service delivery problems
31. Fast delivery of products/services
32. Reliable delivery
33. Resolution of product quality problems
34. Quality of delivered products/services
35. Flexibility to meet customer's changing needs

## Construct Description

Four constructs of interest were proposed in the article. Service quality to external customers reflected the respondent firms' performance in the delivery of service and product quality to external customers. Purchasing's service quality performance and internal suppliers' service quality performance were two internal service quality constructs. These internal service quality constructs were conceptualized as performance rather than perceptions and expectations. Cooperative purchasing/supplier relationship represents the respondent firms' efforts in cultivating a cooperative relationship between purchasing and suppliers.

## Measurement Description

Cooperative purchasing/supplier relationship was measured using eight items, which represented a set of supplier programs and activities that would suggest a cooperative relationship. Possible responses for each question item ranged from 1 = "not at all" to 7 = "always," indicating the different utilization levels of each supplier program at the data collection time. Purchasing's service quality performance was operationalized as 10 question items. The same set of questions was also used in parallel to gauge the internal supplier's service quality performance. In both cases, each item was measured using a 7-point Likert scale with 1 = "poor" and 7 = "excellent." The option of "N/A" was also provided. Service quality to external customers was quantified with seven items. Similarly, the performance items were measured using 7-point Likert scales ranging from 1 = "poor" to 7 = "excellent," along with the option of "N/A."

### Development

The survey instrument was initially developed based on extensive literature review and inputs from three academic experts in the purchasing field. It was modified based on the feedback from participants at the 1994 Decision Sciences Meeting after the instrument was presented. After that, pretests with five purchasing executives who were familiar with the internal service quality concept were conducted to further refine the instrument.

### Sample

A total of 500 senior-level purchasing executives was randomly selected from Title I membership list of the National Association of Purchasing Management (NAPM), a not-for-profit organization with a membership spanning service, manufacturing, and not-for-profit organizations. The responding firms varied regarding their annual revenue in 1994, represented a wide variety of industries, including manufacturing, services, construction, and not-for-profit agencies. Of the 500 surveys mailed, 118 usable responses were received, which generated a response rate of 23.6%. Nonresponse bias was investigated by comparing early and late responses on a number of survey items. No significant differences were found.

### Reliability and Validity

Content validity of the constructs was ensured by careful assessment of existing theory and empirical literature. In addition, the feedback from both executives and academia in the purchasing area helped purify the questionnaire. Convergent validity was analyzed by performing exploratory factor analysis (EFA) using a principal components analysis (PCA) method on each construct separately. Discriminant validity was examined for three service quality related constructs—purchasing's service quality performance, internal suppliers' service quality performance, and service quality to external customers. All questionnaire items for these three constructs were entered into one factor model once. The results from the PCA on this model suggested a three-factor model, which accounted for 73.4% of variance. Discriminant validity was further evaluated by performing $\chi^2$ tests for each factor pairs. The $\chi^2$ test results showed that the correlation between each factor was significantly different from 1, supporting discriminant validity. Construct reliability was analyzed through the calculation of Cronbach's coefficient alpha values. All alpha values were above .86, indicating internal consistency for each construct.

### Scores

The factor analysis results and the Cronbach's coefficient alpha are reported in Tables 2 and 3 in the article.

### Other Evidence

Not available.

### Reference

None.

# Stratman and Roth

### Article Summarized

Stratman, Jeff K., and Aleda V. Roth. 2002. Enterprise resource planning (ERP) competence constructs: Two-stage multi-item scale development and validation. *Decision Sciences* 33 (4): 601–28.

### Scales (Actual Questions Used)

*Strategic IT Planning*

1. We constantly review our IT capabilities against strategic goals
2. IT goals are designed as required to meet evolving conditions.
3. Strategic IT planning is a continuous process.
4. Written guidelines exist to structure strategic IT planning in our organization.
5. Top management is not involved in strategic IT planning (reverse coded).
6. Strategic IT planning includes inputs from all functional areas.

*Executive Commitment*

7. Functional managers willingly assign resources to the ERP project as they are needed.
8. The need for long-term ERP support resources is recognized by management.
9. Executive management is enthusiastic about the possibilities of ERP.
10. Executives have invested the time needed to understand how ERP will benefit the enterprise.
11. Executives mandate that ERP requirements have priority over unique functional concerns.
12. Top management has clearly defined the ERP entity's business goals.
13. All levels of management support the overall goals of the ERP entity.

*Project Management*

14. The tasks to be performed during the ERP project are clearly defined.
15. The responsibilities of project team members are clearly defined.
16. There is a formal management process to track external contractor activities.
17. Problems found during reviews of external project members are not tracked to closure (reverse coded).
18. Measurements are used to determine the status of project tasks.
19. Project tasks are reviewed on a periodic basis.
20. The ERP project leader is able to track project tasks to completion.
21. The ERP project leader is experienced in project management.

*IT Skills*

22. The internal IT staff have the ability to conduct routine ERP system maintenance.
23. There is a high degree of technical expertise in the IT organization.
24. The database administrator is an expert in the ERP database management system.
25. Internal IT team members understand custom ERP software programs.
26. The IT staff are able to efficiently implement ERP system upgrades.
27. The IT staff have the technical ability to conduct a formal validation of all system changes.
28. IT staff are able to analyze the technical impact of proposed system changes.
29. The IT staff actively build relationships with business managers.
30. IT staff offer ideas on how IT can be used to achieve business goals.
31. IT staff communicate with functional use groups in the ERP entity.
32. The IT organization provides a service to the business.

*Business Process Skills*

33. There is a high level of business process knowledge within the ERP entity.
34. Employees understand how their actions impact the operations of other functional areas.
35. Employees understand how their daily business activities support the goals of the ERP entity.
36. Managers are not clear on how ERP focused business processes support the goals of the ERP entity.
37. The operational processes of the ERP entity are formally documented.
38. Our ERP entity's business process documentation reflects actual operational activities.
39. Functional managers are able to document cross-functional business process flows.
40. Business process design is driven by customer requirements.
41. Managers are skilled at analyzing business processes for customer benefits.

*ERP Training*

42. Specific user training needs were identified early in the implementation.
43. A formal training program has been developed to meet the requirements of ERP system users.
44. Training materials have been customized for each specific job.
45. We seldom update training materials to reflect system changes.
46. Training materials target the entire business task, not just the ERP screens and reports.
47. Employees are tracked to ensure that they have received the appropriate ERP system training.
48. All users have been trained in basic ERP system skills.
49. ERP system training review sessions are scheduled.
50. The training needs of each user group have not been identified.
51. Training is conducted by consultants.

*Learning*

52. Benchmarking is used to identify cutting-edge ERP techniques.
53. We keep track of ERP developments related to our industry.
54. Cross-functional groups meet regularly to discuss new uses for the ERP system.
55. Internal groups meet regularly to share new methods of using the ERP system.
56. ERP improvement suggestions are regularly collected from multiple employee levels.
57. Business experiments are conducted to evaluate potential improvements in the way we use ERP.
58. ERP experimentation is encouraged even if the proposed improvement is unsuccessful.
59. External ERP experts are invited to suggest better ways to use the ERP system.

*Change Readiness*

60. Employees understand how they fit into new ERP entity.
61. Employees have input into how their jobs will change with new ERP business processes.
62. Management actively works to alleviate employee concerns about ERP.
63. An ERP support group is available to answer concerns about ERP job changes.
64. The roles of all employees under the ERP system have been clearly communicated.
65. The change readiness of employees affected by the ERP system is regularly assessed.
66. Employees are not prepared for a series of ERP-related changes as the system evolves (reverse coded).
67. ERP-focused changes to the employee reward system have been communicated.

*Improved Business Performance*

68. Company business processes have been rationalized through the use of the ERP system.
69. Business flexibility has been diminished through the use of the ERP system.
70. The ERP system allows for better control of business operating expenses.
71. New market opportunities have been identified through the use of ERP.
72. The ERP system has improved customer satisfaction.

73. The ERP entity facilitates have been rationalized because of information provided by the ERP system.
74. The ERP system allows users to generate supply-chain schedules addressing customer needs.
75. The efficiency of the ERP entity's supplier network has been improved.
76. The efficiency of the procurement function has been improved.
77. The efficiency of the distribution function has been improved.
78. Business benefits have been realized from the reengineered ERP processes.
79. Internal integration across functions has been achieved.
80. Internal integration across the lines of business has been achieved.
81. There is overall organizational agility.
82. External integration with suppliers has been achieved.
83. External integration with customers has been achieved.
84. Customer responsiveness has improved.

## Construct Description

This article provided for nine new multi-item measurement scales. Eight of these tapped into first-order constructs that reflected enterprise resource planning (ERP) competence, which is a second-order latent variable. ERP competence was defined as "a portfolio of managerial, technical and organizational skills and expertise posited as antecedents to improved business performance occurring after an ERP system is operational and functionally stable" (p. 601). In addition, the article developed a construct that captured "improved business performance."

The authors characterized four managerial and technical domains in terms of four interrelated elements: (1) strategic IT planning, (2) executive commitment, (3) project management, and (4) IT skills. Strategic IT planning was characterized as "an organization's competence in matching IT capabilities with the changing, cross-functional business requirements of the enterprise" (p. 610). Executive commitment referred "to top management's willingness to champion ERP within the resources required for successful ERP infusion" (p. 610). Project management involved "the use of skills and knowledge in coordinating the scheduling and monitoring of defined activities to ensure that the stated objectives of implementation projects are achieved" (p. 611). A competency in IT skills referred "to the ability to configure and maintain information systems in support of the business" (p. 611).

There were four organizational elements associated with ERP competence as well: business process skills, ERP training, learning, and change readiness. Business process skills represented "an understanding of how the business operates, and the ability to predict the impact of a particular decision or action on the rest of the enterprise" (p. 611). ERP training indicated "the processes involved in teaching each of the various user groups to use the ERP system efficiently in their day-to-day activities" (p. 612). The learning competency referred "to activities designed to identify cutting-edge ERP techniques from both internal and external sources" (p. 612). Change readiness signified "the managerial strategies used to overcome workforce resistance to the operational changes resulting from the implementation of the ERP system" (p. 612).

## Measurement Description

The items were measured by 7-point Likert scales anchored on "agree" to "disagree."

## Development

The authors developed the new multi-item measurement scales following a rigorous two-stage normative process. In the first stage, the authors developed the constructs and items based on extensive cross-disciplinary literature reviews and site visits to companies that implemented ERP, where multiple interviews were conducted with system "users, including IT technicians, engineers, production planners, supervisors and managers. Visits were supplemented by structured and unstructured interviews with executives knowledgeable about ERP systems and adoption practices. This iterative process resulted in the identification of eight theoretically important competency constructs" (p. 602). Then, these items and scales were tested for clarity and content validity by a series of manual item-sorting exercises, iteratively with independent samples of knowledgeable practitioners, who served as expert judges. Based on each iteration of the sorting exercises, items and construct were refined in their questionnaire, and this continued until sufficient levels of item and scale reliabilities were determined statistically. "In the second stage, survey data was collected from a sample of 79 North American manufacturing firms with operational ERP systems" (p. 603), which enabled the confirmation of the items and measurement scales.

### Sample

The target population was the set of North American manufacturers that had an implemented ERP system, which was up-and-running and operationally stable. The sampling frame of 623 firms was generated from three sources. "(1) The top five ERP vendors (SAP, PeopleSoft, ORACLE, J. D. Edwards, and Baan) [were selected] . . . (2) North American manufacturing firms were also extracted from PC Week's 1999 Top 100 Innovative Manufacturers and from Industry Week's 1999 Top 1000 Manufacturers . . . (3) Since this research was supported by the American Production and Inventory Control Society (APICS) Educational and Research Foundation, as well as by the Canadian Association of Supply Chain and Logistics Management, contact information for supply chain and manufacturing managers were extracted from these organization's mailing list" (p. 616).

The survey was administered using an adaptation of Dillman's (1978) procedures. "A total of 85 surveys were returned, 79 of which were usable for scale development, for a response rate of 13%" (p. 616). The distribution of responses is summarized in the article (pp. 617–618), and checks for sample nonresponse bias indicated that none differed from the other reported ERP studies.

### Reliability and Validity

The first-stage results indicated tentative reliability and validity. "The literature review and input from expert industry judges together establish the content validity of construct scales" (p. 618). For reliability analyses please refer to Table 4 (p. 619). In the second stage, confirmatory factor analyses (CFA) were implemented using the measurement model of structural equation modeling and following the guidelines of Anderson and Gerbing (1991). Interitem reliabilities of the measurement scales were found to be adequate, and with refinement, the composite reliability exceeded .85. "Since each factor loading was in the anticipated direction and magnitude, and was statistically significant at $p < 0.05$, each scale can be considered to exhibit adequate convergent validity" (p. 619).

"Discriminant validity was assessed using a series of chi-square difference tests between CFA models for all construct pairs. CFA is run on a pair of scale construct measurement models in which the latent construct variables are allowed to freely correlate (the unconstrained model). The chi-square value for this model is noted. A second confirmatory analysis is run with the latent variable correlation constrained to one. The chi-square value of the unconstrained model is subtracted from that of the constrained model to give the chi-square difference. A statistically significant chi-square value indicates two distinct constructs" (p. 620). Please refer to Table 5 for more details.

Criterion validity was established by correlations of COMPUSTAT metrics (i.e., secondary data) with the perceptual measures obtained in the survey, and predictive validity was indicated by correlations of the latent variables with the improved business performance latent variable (*see* Table 6 in the article).

### Scores

Scores are given in Tables 1–6 in the article.

### Other Evidence

Not available.

**References**

Anderson, J. C., and D. W. Gerbing. 1991. Predicting the performance of measures in a confirmatory factor analysis with a pretest assessment of their substantive validities. *Journal of Applied Psychology* 76 (5): 732–41.

Dillman, D. A. 1978. *Mail and telephone surveys: The total design method.* New York: Wiley.

---

# Swafford, Ghosh, and Murthy

**Article Summarized**

Swafford, Patricia M., Soumen Ghosh, and Nagesh Murthy. 2006. The antecedents of supply chain agility of a firm: Scale development and model testing. *Journal of Operations Management* 24 (2): 170–88.

**Scales (Actual Question Used)**

*Procurement/Sourcing Flexibility*

Procurement/Sourcing Range

1. Range of supplier delivery frequencies (weekly, daily, etc.)
2. Extent to which supplier lead time can be expedited/changed
3. Extent to which supplier short-term capacity can be influenced
4. Number of suppliers selected per component on a global basis
5. Extent of flexibility (options) within supplier contracts
6. Number of components purchased per supplier
7. Range of possible order sizes from suppliers

Procurement/Sourcing Adaptability

8. Influence supplier's short-term capacity
9. Change volume allocation among existing suppliers on a global basis
10. Locate and procure services and products when required
11. Change quantity of supplier's order
12. Change delivery times of order placed with suppliers
13. Influence suppliers' ability to implement engineering change orders
14. Consolidate global demand for purchase orders of components.
15. Change suppliers on a global scale when required

*Manufacturing Flexibility*

Manufacturing Range

16. Range of products manufactured by your business unit
17. Number of products that each manufacturing facility, on average, can produce
18. Number of product changeovers per facility, on average, made each month
19. Range of production capacity across which manufacturing can adjust
20. Number of different tasks the typical worker can perform
21. Range of production volume over which manufacturing can operate cost-effectively
22. Number of different manufacturing routings for each product

Manufacturing Adaptability

23. Change production volume capacity when necessary
24. Accommodate changes in production mix as required
25. Implement engineering change orders in production
26. Reduce manufacturing throughput times to satisfy customer delivery
27. Adjust manufacturing process capabilities
28. Rotate workers among different manufacturing tasks
29. Reallocate production product mix among global facilities

*Distribution/Logistic Flexibility*

Distribution/Logistics Range

30. Number of carriers used for each type of delivery mode, on average
31. Number of items handled by each distribution facility, on average
32. Number of worldwide storage/distribution facilities
33. Number of items per order handled by each distribution facility, on average
34. Number of customers supported by each distribution facility, on average
35. Number of customer delivery frequencies used
36. Range of volume over which distribution can operate cost-effectively

Distribution/Logistics Adaptability

37. Alter delivery schedules to meet changing customer requirements
38. Fill customer orders from alternate global facilities
39. Adjust worldwide storage capacity
40. Adjust global delivery capacity
41. Redistribute finished products among global storage facilities
42. Change delivery modes when necessary
43. Adjust to different distribution delivery requirements to meet customer delivery

Supply Chain Agility

44. Reduce manufacturing leadtimes
45. Reduce product development cycle time
46. Increase frequency of new product introductions
47. Increase level of customization
48. Adjust worldwide delivery capacity/capability
49. Improve level of customer service
50. Improve delivery reliability
51. Improve responsiveness to changing market needs
52. Reduce setup/changeover time
53. Increase production capacity
54. Decrease ramp-up time for new products
55. Reduce delivery time

**Construct Description**

Constructs in this article were described as follows. Procurement/sourcing flexibility was defined "as the availability of a range of options and the ability of the purchasing process to effectively exploit them so as to respond to changing requirements related to the supply of purchased components" (p. 174). Manufacturing flexibility was explained "as the availability of a range of options and the ability of the manufacturing process to effectively exploit them so as to produce quality products in response to changing product characteristics, material supply and demand, or to employ technological process enhancements" (p. 174). Distribution/logistics flexibility referred to "the availability of a range of options and the ability to effectively exploit them so as to adapt the process of controlling the flow and storage of materials, finished goods, services, and related information from origin to destination in response to changing marketplace conditions" (p. 176).

### Measurement Description

The items were measured by 5-point Likert scales.

### Development

The authors developed the scales based on a thorough literature review and Q-sort analyses.

### Sample

The initial sample frame consisted of a mailing list of manufacturing firms from Dunn and Bradstreet and membership lists from the Council of Logistics Management and Supply Chain Council (2004) organizations. Surveys were mailed to high-ranking executives (i.e., general managers) in manufacturing firms with at least 100 employees. Of the 664 surveys administered, 57 had incorrect contact information and were returned by the postal service. A total of 121 responses were received, of which 6 had missing data, thus yielding a sample size of 115 with a response rate of 19%.

The profile information of respondents indicated that multiple industries were represented. Participating organizations had an average sales volume in the range of U.S. $101 to $250 million per year and an average number of employees in the range of 501 to 1,000. More than 60% of the firms provided some level of product customization and achieved low to moderate volumes of sales. Respondents consisted mostly of VPs of supply chain, manufacturing, operations, or logistics with the predominant respondent being a VP of manufacturing. For more details on the sample, please refer to Table 2 (p. 178) of the article.

### Reliability and Validity

To achieve higher statistical power in testing, the authors followed Jöreskog and Sörbom's (1993) recommendation and analyzed each measurement model individually. Item measures with insignificant factor loadings were removed from the scale if content validity was not sacrificed. All factor loadings for the constructs were significant except for MR4, which was retained to maintain content validity. As for discriminant validity, statistically significant $\chi^2$ tests of the difference between the models indicated that the latent variables representing each construct were different from each other (Byrne 1998) and, in turn, supported the existence of discriminant validity. All the $\chi^2$ tests were significant at $p < .001$.

All latent constructs in confirmatory factor analysis (CFA) had reliabilities that exceed the level of .60, except for manufacturing range, which was close with a value of .59. Thus, they were judged to possess acceptable reliability.

### Scores

The scores are presented in Table 3 and Figures 2 and 3.

### Other Evidence

Not available.

### References

Byrne, B. M. 1998. *Structural equation modeling with Lisrel, Prelis, and Simplis, basic concepts, applications and programming.* Mahwah, NJ: Lawrence Erlbaum.

Jöreskog, K. G., and D. Sörbom. 1993. *LISREL 8: User's reference guide.* Chicago, IL: Scientific Software International.

# Swamidass and Kotha

## Article Summarized

Swamidass, Paul M., and Suresh Kotha. 1998. Explaining manufacturing technology use, firm size and performance using a multidimensional view of technology. *Journal of Operations Management* 17 (1): 23–37.

## Scales (Actual Questions Used)

*Advanced Manufacturing Technologies*

1. Local area network for factory use
2. Computers used for control on factory floor
3. Local area network for technical data
4. Computers for production scheduling
5. Electronic data interchange
6. MRPI and MRPII systems
7. Intercompany networks
8. Automated drafting technologies
9. Computer-aided design
10. Computer-aided engineering
11. Computer-aided quality control performed on final products
12. Computer-aided inspection performed on incoming or in-process material
13. Robots others than pick and place
14. Pick and place robots
15. Manufacturing automation protocol
16. Numerical control/computer numerical control
17. Programmable controllers
18. Computer-aided design/computer-aided manufacturing
19. FMC/flexible manufacturing systems

*Performance*

20. After-tax return on total assets
21. After-tax return on total sales
22. Net profit position relative to competition's
23. Market share gains relative to competition's
24. Sales growth position relative to competition
25. Overall firm performance success rating

## Construct Description

Four dimensions of advanced manufacturing technology (AMT) were first established in the conceptual model with 19 items: (1) product design technologies (PDT), (2) process technologies (PT), (3) logistics/planning technologies (LPT), and (4) information exchange technologies (IET). PDT included "technologies that focus primarily on product definition, design, and related information processing functions. PT encompasses technologies that focus on the process related aspects in manufacturing, especially those that are used on the shop floor. LPT covers technologies that control and monitor the material flow from the acquisition of raw materials to the delivery of finished products, and the related counter flows of logistical information. IET facilitates the storage and exchange of information among process, product, and logistics technologies" (p. 25). Except for the actual items, no further description of these four dimensions was given in the study.

## Measurement Description

Nineteen items were chosen to measure the use of AMT. Each item was operationalized using a 5-point Likert-type scale ranging from 1 = "not used" to 5 = "used extensively." Based on the factor analysis technique, these 19 items were classified into four factors. Each factor score was computed as the sum of the weighted raw scores across all the 19 items in the instrument. Six items were used to measure performance. Each of these six items was rated based on 5-point Likert-type scales. Different from the technology scale, larger values in the performance scale represented inferior performance—that is, 1 = "top 20%" to 5 = "lowest 20%." Two factors, profitability and growth factor were found according to the factor analysis. Firm size was measured as the logarithm of employment.

## Development

The initial measurement instrument of assessing "technology use" was adapted from published work by U.S. Department of Commerce (1988). After the discussion by academic researchers on the preliminary drafts, the questionnaire was subject to a pilot test with five firms. Clarity, comprehensives, and relevance of the research instrument were improved.

## Sample

The data were collected by mail survey from a target sample of 851 firms listed in the 1990 Compustat Compact Disclosure Database in six discrete products/parts manufacturing industries (U.S. Department of Commerce, Standard Industrial Classification code [SIC] 34–39). Approximately 10% of the 851 firms, randomly selected, were sent two questionnaires, each to be filled out by a different senior manager in the firm. Thirty-one "firms declined to attend the study citing the company policy and 22 questionnaires were undeliverable" (p. 27), resulting in 798 potential respondents. The authors randomly selected approximately 10% of the firms to send two surveys; as a result, 86 firms received two surveys to be completed by two different managers. Of those 86 companies, a total of 17 firms returned both questionnaires. In sum, there were 177 completed responses, including the firms that received two surveys, from 798 potential respondents, which produced a response rate of 22.2%. Of these 177 returns, 160 surveys were completed by only one respondent, who was typically a senior manager, and in the case of multiple respondents, 40% were CEOs or presidents, and approximately 70% held titles such as vice president or higher. A detailed description of the data is presented in Table 2 of the article.

## Reliability and Validity

To assess criterion validity, correlation analysis was conducted between standardized values of return on assets and return on sales for the industry, which were obtained from the Compustat II database, and the self-reported, perceptual data from the survey for 32 randomly selected firms from the total 160 firms. The correlations were .72 and .82, respectively, which provided evidence of validity. Besides, the instrument development process provided additional information on construct and content validity. Reliability was examined by using interrater agreement analysis on a sample of 17 firms that returned both of the surveys. Out of the 317 possible combinations for AMT use, 74% of the responses from two different respondents in the same firm were within one interval or less. A total of 91% of the possible 102 matches in the performance responses were identical or within one interval on the 5-point scale.

## Scores

Results of factor analysis on the AMT and the performance measures are presented in Tables 4 and 6, respectively, in the article. Table 7 reports the results of the regression analysis on performance and AMT use.

## Other Evidence

Not available.

### Reference

U.S. Department of Commerce. 1988. *Manufacturing technology 1988.* A Bureau of Census Report. Washington, DC: U.S. Government Printing Office.

## Swamidass and Newell

### Article Summarized

Swamidass, Paul M., and William T. Newell. 1987. Manufacturing strategy, environmental uncertainty and performance: A path analytic model. *Management Science* 33 (4): 509–24.

### Scales (Actual Questions Used)

*Manufacturing Flexibility*

[All items were scored on 10-point scales. Extremities of scales are shown in parentheses.]

1. New products introduction
   [Most frequent in the industry to least frequent in the industry]
2. Introducing new production processes
   [Most frequent in the industry to least frequent in the industry]
3. Product varieties
   [Widest range in the industry to narrowest range in the industry]
4. Product features
   [Widest range in the industry to narrowest range in the industry]
5. R&D effort
   [Most aggressive in the industry to none]

*Perceived Environmental Uncertainty*

[All items were scored on five-point scales between the extremities "always predictable and never predictable"]

6. Actual users of your products
7. Competition for your supply of raw materials and parts
8. Competitors for your customers
9. Government regulations controlling your industry
10. The public's political views and attitudes toward your industry
11. Your relationship with trade unions

*Role of Manufacturing Managers in Strategic Decision Making (RMMSDM)*

[All items were scored on five-point scales between the extremities "strongly agree" and "strongly disagree"]

12. I feel that the manufacturing functional managers (MFMs) have a good understanding of how the divisional strategy is formed.
13. I feel the MFMs are an integral part of the strategy formulation process and that their inputs are part of the divisional (or corporate) strategy.
14. I feel that the MFMs know exactly what the most important parameters or criteria for manufacturing jobs are (i.e., low cost, delivery, quality, etc.).
15. MFMs are responsible for initiating and modifying long-range changes in manufacturing strategy.

*Performance Measure*

[All items were scored on 10-point scales between the extremities "above average performance" and "below average performance" compared with industry average during 1977 to 1981.]

16. Average annual rate of growth in return on total assets during 1977 to 1981
17. Average annual rate of growth in sales during 1977 to 1981
18. Average annual rate of growth in return on sales during 1977 to 1981

**Construct Description**

Construct definitions were presented in the article as follows. Manufacturing strategy was viewed as the effective use of manufacturing strengths as a competitive weapon for the achievement of business and corporate goals. For the successful practice of manufacturing strategy, its content (manufacturing flexibility) as well as its process were important. Manufacturing flexibility was attained and maintained by several coordinated policies and actions. Flexibility offered the capability to cope with environmental uncertainty. The role of manufacturing managers in strategic decision making (RMMSDM) was explained as being a function of "numerous variables such as size, structure, intra-organizational power and influence, environmental factors, the strategic planning system, top-management coalition, resource and information constraints, formalization of strategic planning, etc." (p. 515).

"Environmental uncertainty was cast in two ways—one that is based on resource scarcity and the other based on information complexity" (p. 514). Environmental uncertainty was termed perceived environmental uncertainty to recognize the fact that the study employed perceptual measures.

**Measurement Description**

A pair of survey questionnaires was used for this analysis: one for chief executives and the other for responsible executives in charge of the manufacturing function. The four variables in the model were all included in the form of multi-item instruments (*see* the Scales section). For every firm participating in the study, a single measure of flexibility was computed by averaging the ratings by the two executives.

**Development**

A modified version of the instrument used by Duncan (1972) was used for the environmental uncertainty construct. The measure of RMMSDM was adapted from the questionnaire "The Manufacturing Management Survey" from Skinner and Associates, Cambridge, Massachusetts. Following Churchill's (1979) recommendations for developing reliable measures, items with low interitem correlations were dropped from the instrument. For each variable, item scores were summed and averaged to compute the measure.

**Sample**

The data were gathered from a field study and stemmed from 35 participating manufacturing firms (out of 77 contacted firms). Of those 35 firms, 27 participated the study through face-to-face interviews, and 8 responded to a mailed questionnaire. To control for process type and industry type, the sample was limited to the machinery and machine tools industry with predominantly small batch production. The average participating firm had an employment of 210 in 1982. No further details about the data were presented in the article.

**Reliability and Validity**

Cronbach's coefficient alphas that measured the reliability of the scales ranged from .69 to .88.

**Scores**

The scores are presented in Table 1 and Figure 4 in the article.

**Other Evidence**

Not available.

### References

Churchill, G. A. 1979. A paradigm for developing better measures of marketing constructs. *Journal of Marketing Research* 16 (1): 64–73.

Duncan, R. B. 1972. Characteristics of organizational environments and perceived environmental uncertainty. *Administrative Science Quarterly* 17 (3): 313–27.

# Swink, Narasimhan, and Kim

### Article Summarized

Swink, Morgan, Ram Narasimhan, and Soo Wook Kim. 2005. Manufacturing practices and strategy integration: Effects on cost efficiency, flexibility, and market-based performance. *Decision Sciences* 36 (3): 427–57.

### Scales (Actual Questions Used)

*Workforce Development*

1. Performance reviews are handled by empowered teams.
2. Employees are cross-trained to perform a variety of activities.
3. Our employees have strong problem-solving abilities.
4. Employees are rewarded for learning new skills.
5. Production scheduling is handled by empowered teams.
6. Certification and training are handled by empowered teams.
7. Labor scheduling/job assignments are handled by empowered teams.

*Process Quality Management*

8. Design of experiments is used.
9. Continuous improvement of quality is expected in all work processes.
10. SPC is used.
11. Processes on the shop floor are under statistical quality control.
12. We use statistical techniques to reduce variance in processes.
13. We measure process capability.

*JIT Flow*

14. We use a pull system in production.
15. We produce in small lot sizes in this plant.
16. We use JIT flow production methods.
17. Manufacturing operations are organized around product families with similar customer needs.
18. We have a "focused factory" (e.g., product or process focused) production system.
19. Our production flow uses manufacturing cells.

*Supplier Relationship Management*

20. We provide technological assistance to suppliers.
21. We share our cost information with our major suppliers.
22. We require cost information sharing by our suppliers.
23. We establish long-term contracts with suppliers.
24. We pursue joint investments with suppliers.

*Product-Process Development*

25. We use design-for-manufacturing and assembly (DFMA) methods.
26. Manufacturing sign-off is required for new products.
27. We develop dedicated technologies for specific product families/customer segments.
28. We practice job rotation between design and manufacturing engineering.
29. We have created new ways to coordinate design and manufacturing issues.
30. Our product designers make use of manufacturability guidelines/checklists.
31. Product designers and manufacturing staff have equal status in NPD projects.
32. CAM is used.

*Manufacturing Capabilities*

Cost Efficiency

33. Unit cost
34. Total manufacturing overhead cost
35. Productivity

Process Flexibility

36. Ability to customize products
37. Ability to adjust production volumes
38. Ability to respond to changes in delivery requirements
39. Ability to produce a range of products

New Product Flexibility

40. Lead time to introduce new products
41. Number of new products introduced each year

Strategy Integration

42. Manufacturing strategy is well aligned with corporate strategy.
43. We have clearly defined strategic manufacturing goals and objectives.
44. Our firm's strategy leverages existing capabilities.
45. Manufacturing strategies and goals are clearly communicated to all employees.
46. Manufacturing strategy is frequently reviewed and revised.

Market-Based Performance

47. Profitability
48. Market share of major product/product line
49. Unit growth rate in sales

**Construct Description**

In this article, manufacturing practices consisted of five major constructs: (1) workforce development, (2) process quality management, (3) just-in-time (JIT) flow, (4) supplier relationship management, and (5) product-process development. "Workforce development practices are aimed at improving workers' technical and problem-solving skills through empowerment, incentives for learning, cross-training, idea sharing, and teams (Giffi, Roth, & Seal 1990; Schonberger 1996)" (p. 432). "Process quality management practices make use of associated tools to promote the continuous improvement of process capabilities. Important related practices include a focus on quality performance, measurement, and communications (i.e., feedback) of quality related data for improvement and control purposes, and statistical quality control techniques (Giffi et al. 1990; Kinni 1997)" (p. 432).

"Just-in-time flow practices have the primary goal of eliminating wastes in terms of material movement, work-in-process inventories, and delays (Sugimori, Kusunoki, Cho, & Uchikawa 1977)" (p. 432). "Important practices include lot-size reduction, setup time reduction, facility layouts (e.g., cells) to promote smooth flow, and pull or kanban-based production systems (references in Table 1; Giffi et al. 1990; Schonberger 1996; Kinni 1997)" (p. 432). "Supplier relationship management practices promote closer involvement with fewer, select suppliers by establishing long-term relationships, information sharing systems, certification and training, and joint investments (Kinni 1997)" (p. 432). "Product-process development practices facilitate collaboration between product and process designers as they seek to make the most effective use of manufacturing technologies. These practices include developing and integrating advanced manufacturing technologies as well as ensuring that the constraints and capabilities of these technologies are considered during product design" (p. 432).

Manufacturing capability in this article consisted of two primary dimensions: (1) cost efficiency and (2) flexibility. "Cost efficiency is defined as the demonstrated ability to execute plant operations using relatively few total input resources, and flexibility is the demonstrated ability to adapt or change plant-level operations with relatively little time or cost penalties. Both definitions involve *relative* comparisons of capability, that is, relative to industry competitors" (p. 432).

This conceptualization of strategy integration is consistent with the arguments of Skinner (1969) and others (Wheelwright 1984; Miles and Snow 1978; Miller and Friesen 1978; Burgelman 1983) "that a manufacturing plant's investments and practices should be consistent with the demands placed upon it by the limits of its own internal capabilities and by the objectives of higher order business and functional strategies . . . Strategy integration is consideration and synthesis of internal constraints, strengths, and weaknesses, along with external market demands, opportunities, and threats" (p. 434). The definition of market-based performance construct was not explicitly given in the article, but it can be derived from a reference (Rosenzweig, Roth, and Dean 2003) that the author made as referring to combination of customer satisfaction and sales growth.

### Measurement Description

The manufacturing practices were assessed by using or adapting "measures from previous research where possible. Measures were also developed from construct descriptions in case-oriented studies when needed (Hayes & Wheelwright 1984; Giffi et al. 1990; Schonberger 1996)" (p. 437). Additionally, adapted and included were "measures from the *IndustryWeek* survey, and from the published plant case reports (Kinni 1997)" (p. 437).

The measures of manufacturing capabilities were based on seminal manufacturing research works (Hayes and Wheelwright 1984; Wheelwright 1984; Giffi et al. 1990), and on manufacturing capability studies (Ferdows and DeMeyer 1990; Miller and Roth 1994; Safizadeh et al. 1996; White 1996; Kathuria 2000; Boyer and Lewis 2002; Rosenzweig, Roth, and Dean 2003). Measurement items of the strategy integration were drawn from previous manufacturing strategy studies (Flynn, Schroeder, and Sakakibara 1994; Sakakibara et al. 1997; Dow, Samson, and Ford 1999; Cua, McKone, and Schroeder 2001). Market-based performance measures were similar to those used in Vickery, Droge, and Markland (1993) and Boyer (1999).

### Development

The authors used two additional qualitative sources of information in the study to aid their interpretations of the study findings: *Industry Week*'s case descriptions of the practices and performance improvements at each winning plant and personal conversations with plant managers by telephone and in person at a national conference sponsored by *Industry Week* (p. 437).

### Sample

The "study sample included the past winners and finalists for each of the years from 1990 to 1999 in the *Industry Week's* 'America's Best' competition as the target population" (p. 436). "130 plants either agreed to participate or to receive the questionnaire and consider participation" (p. 437), 57 plants were chosen as the final sample size with a 39% response rate. The sample spans a variety of industries, plant size, and process types. For more information on the sample, please refer to Table 2 of the article.

**Reliability and Validity**

In this study, content validity was ensured by building the scales based on a comprehensive analysis of well-established empirical and conceptual research literatures. "Additionally, the scales were purified and validated first by conducting three iterations of an item-sorting procedure, and second by confirmatory factor analyses (CFA) of the survey data. Inter-judge agreement scores (Perreault & Leigh 1989) and item placement ratios (Moore & Benbasat 1991) were assessed to determine construct reliability and validity associated with the item-sorting procedures. Agreement scores far exceeded the acceptable level of .65, thus suggesting a high degree of reliability for the scales. The item placement ratios also far exceeded the commonly accepted percentage of 70% correctly placed items, indicating a high degree of construct validity as well as a high potential to be reliable" (p. 439).

After applying the sorting procedures, data from field research were input into confirmatory factor analysis (CFA) to further validate the multi-item measurement scales. "A measurement model was specified for each construct and evaluated goodness-of-fit indices for evidence of a lack of unidimensionality" (p. 439). The authors stated that most of the results from reliability and validity analysis showed acceptable criterion values (Fornell and Larker 1981; Hu and Bentler 1999): reliability ≥ .70, average variance extracted (AVE) ≥ .50, comparative fit index (CFI) ≥ .95, and $\chi^2$ over degrees of freedom ≤ 3. However, "because the limited sample size prevented a test of a complete CFA model, convergent and discriminant validities were further assessed by constructing all" (p. 439) 45 combinations of pairwise construct models (Hatcher 1994; Ahire, Golhar, and Waller 1996). The results indicated acceptable evidence of convergent validity, and discriminant validity was verified using the approach prescribed by Fornell and Larker (1981).

The predictive validity of each of the manufacturing practice scales was indicated by a significant correlation of each practice to at least one of the manufacturing capabilities (Table 4). In addition, each of the three manufacturing capability scales was significantly correlated to market-based performance, thus collectively suggesting their predictive validity. Likewise, scores for the strategy integration scale were correlated with manufacturing capabilities and with market-based performance scores. The criterion validity of the market-based performance scale was evaluated by computing its correlation with a ration-scale measure of market share. The correlation was .46 (p = .004), indicating strong criterion-related validity for the scale.

**Scores**

The results of construct scale validity analysis are shown in Table 3 in the article. Correlation results are provided in Table 4. Standard loading (t-value) for each scale item is given in the appendix. The results of hierarchical moderated regression models are depicted in Table 5, and in Table 6, the results of regression of market-based performance on strategy integration and manufacturing capabilities are shown.

**Other Evidence**

Not available.

**References**

Ahire, S. L., D. Y. Golhar, and M. A. Waller. 1996. Development and validation of TQM implementation constructs. *Decision Sciences* 27 (1): 23–56.

Boyer, K. K. 1999. Evolutionary patterns of flexible automation and performance: A longitudinal study. *Management Science* 45 (6): 824–42.

Boyer, K. K., and M. W. Lewis. 2002. Competitive priorities: Investigating the need for trade-offs in operations strategy. *Production and Operations Management* 11 (1): 9–20.

Burgelman, R. A. 1983. A model of the interaction of strategic behavior, corporate context, and the concept of strategy. *Academy of Management Review* 8 (1): 61–70.

Cua, K. O., K. E. McKone, and R. G. Schroeder. 2001. Relationships between implementations of TQM, JIT, and TPM and manufacturing performance. *Journal of Operations Management* 19 (6): 675–94.

Dow, D., D. Samson, and S. Ford. 1999. Exploding the myth: Do all quality management practices contribute to superior quality performance? *Production and Operations Management* 8 (1): 1–27.

Ferdows, K., and A. DeMeyer. 1990. Lasting improvements in manufacturing performance: In search of a new theory. *Journal of Operations Management* 9 (2): 168–84.

Flynn, B. B., R. G. Schroeder, and S. Sakakibara. 1994. A framework for quality management research and an associated measurement instrument. *Journal of Operations Management* 11 (4): 339–66.

Fornell, C., and D. F. Larcker. 1981. Evaluating structural equation models with unobservable variables and measurement error. *Journal of Marketing Research* 18 (1): 39–50.

Giffi, C., A. Roth, and G. M. Seal. 1990. *Competing in world class manufacturing: America's 21st century challenge.* Homewood, IL: Business One Irwin.

Hatcher, L. 1994. *A step-by-step approach to using the SAS system for factor analysis and structural equation modeling.* Cary, NC: SAS Institute.

Hayes, R. H., and S. C. Wheelwright. 1984. *Restoring our competitive edge: Competing through manufacturing.* New York: Wiley.

Hu, L., and P. M. Bentler. 1999. Cutoff criteria for fit indexes in covariance structure analysis: Conventional criteria versus new alternatives. *Structural Equation Modeling* 6 (1): 1–55.

Kathuria, R. 2000. Competitive priorities and managerial performance: A taxonomy of small manufacturers. *Journal of Operations Management* 18 (6): 627–41.

Kinni, T. B. 1997. *America's best:* IndustryWeek's *guide to world-class manufacturing plants.* New York: Wiley.

Miles, R. E., and C. C. Snow. 1978. *Organization strategy, structure, and process.* Burr Ridge, IL: McGraw-Hill.

Miller, D., and P. H. Friesen. 1978. Archetypes of strategy formulation. *Management Science* 24 (9): 921–33.

Miller, J. G., and A. V. Roth. 1994. A taxonomy of manufacturing strategies. *Management Science* 40 (3): 285–304.

Moore, G. C., and I. Benbasat. 1991. Development of an instrument to measure the perceptions of adopting an information technology innovation. *Information Systems Research* 2 (3): 192–222.

Perreault, W. D., Jr., and L. E. Leigh. 1989. Reliability of nominal data based on qualitative judgments. *Journal of Marketing Research* 26 (2): 135–48.

Rosenzweig, E. D., A. V. Roth, and J. W. Dean Jr. 2003. The influence of an integration strategy on competitive capabilities and business performance: An exploratory study of consumer products manufacturers. *Journal of Operations Management* 21 (4): 437–56.

Safizadeh, M. H., L. P. Ritzman, D. Sharma, and C. Wood. 1996. An empirical analysis of the product-process matrix. *Management Science* 41 (11): 1576–91.

Sakakibara, S., B. B. Flynn, R. G. Schroeder, and W. T. Morris. 1997. The impact of just-in-time manufacturing and its infrastructure on manufacturing performance. *Management Science* 43 (9): 1246–57.

Schonberger, R. J. 1996. *World class manufacturing: The next decade.* New York: Free Press.

Skinner, W. 1969. Manufacturing: Missing link in corporate strategy. *Harvard Business Review* 47 (3): 136–45.

Sugimori, Y., F. Kusunoki, F. Cho, and S. Uchikawa. 1977. Toyota production system and kanban system: Materialization of just-in-time and respect for human system. *International Journal of Production Research* 15 (6): 553–64.

Vickery, S. K., C. Dröge, and R. E. Markland. 1993. Production competence and business strategy: Do they affect business performance. *Decision Sciences* 24 (2): 435–55.

Wheelwright, S. C. 1984. Manufacturing strategy: Defining the missing link. *Strategic Management Journal* 5 (1): 77–91.

White, G. P. 1996. A meta-analysis model of manufacturing capabilities. *Journal of Operations Management* 14 (4): 315–31.

# Tan

**Article Summarized**

Tan, Keah Choon. 2001. A structural equation model of new product design and development. *Decision Sciences* 32 (2): 195–226.

**Scales (Actual Questions Used)**

*Supplier Assessment Strategy*

1. Quality level
2. Service level
3. Correct quality
4. On-time delivery
5. Price/cost of product
6. Use of EDI
7. Willingness to share sensitive information
8. Presence of certification or other documentation
9. The flexibility to respond to unexpected demand changes
10. Communication skills/systems (phone, fax, e-mail, Internet)
11. Quick response time in case of emergency, problem, or special request
12. Willingness to change their products and services to meet your changing needs
13. Willingness to participate in you firm's new product development and value analysis

*JIT Strategy*

How important are the following JIT principles in your operations?

14. Reducing lot size
15. Reducing setup time
16. Reducing supplier base
17. Preventive maintenance
18. Buying from JIT suppliers
19. Increasing delivery frequencies
20. Reducing inventory, which in turn frees up capital investment
21. Reducing inventory to expose manufacturing and scheduling problems

*Quality Strategy*

How important are the following quality practices in your firm?

22. Inspection
23. Using benchmark data
24. Simplifying the product
25. Statistical process control
26. Using standard component parts
27. Designing quality into the product
28. Modular design of component parts
29. Process improvement (modification of process)
30. Employee training in quality management and control
31. Empowerment of shop operators to correct quality problems
32. Top management communication of quality goals to the organization

33. Emphasis on quality instead of price in the supplier selection process
34. Considering manufacturability and assembly in the product design stage

*New Product Design and Development Strategy*

35. Modular design of parts
36. Early supplier involvement
37. The use of concurrent engineering
38. Simplification of component parts
39. Standardization of component parts
40. The use of value analysis/value engineering
41. Quick product development and introduction time
42. The use of QFD (house of quality)

### Construct Description

The authors defined the term *practice* "as an approach used by managers and workers to achieve a specific objective, whereas 'strategy' is a construct used to represent a collective set of practices. For example, a firm's JIT strategy comprises of various JIT practices, including reducing set up times, lot sizes and supplier base, increasing preventive maintenance activities, buying from JIT suppliers, and requiring more frequent deliveries" (p. 196).

### Measurement Description

Items were grouped into four factors—supplier assessment, JIT strategy, quality strategy, new product design, and development strategy. Items were operationalized using 5-point Likert scales.

### Development

The authors pretested the survey with 30 managers for content validity and clarity of the items. They reworded some of the items based on the pretest of the survey.

### Sample

The authors mailed the survey instrument to 3,000 senior managers who were members of the American Production and Inventory Control Society (APICS). The authors received 310 surveys back, leading to a 10.33% response rate. "Table 2 shows the respondents profile. Approximately 13% of the respondents were raw material and component manufacturers, whereas slightly more than 38% were final product manufacturers. Wholesalers and retailers made up 18.3% of the respondents, and 30.1% of the respondents identified themselves as Services/Others" (p. 209). There is no information provided in the article about which industries were represented in the final sample.

### Reliability and Validity

The measurement properties of the items were tested by using confirmatory factor analysis (CFA).

### Scores

The scores are reported in Table 3 in the appendix.

### Other Evidence

Not available.

### Reference

None.

# Tatikonda and Montoya-Weiss

**Article Summarized**

Tatikonda, Mohan V., and Mitzi M. Montoya-Weiss. 2001. Integrating operations and marketing perspectives of product innovation: The influence of organizational process factors and capabilities on development performance. *Management Science* 47 (1): 151–72.

**Scales (Actual Questions Used)**

*Organizational Process Factors*

Process Concurrency

1. What percentage of the design engineering effort was complete when manufacturing engineering started active involvement in this project?

Process Formality

2. To what degree were project management rules and procedures formalized via documents such as contract books, sign-off forms, and so on?
3. To what degree were formal project management rules and procedures actually followed for this project?
4. To what degree were formal progress reviews held (sometimes also called design, gate, phase, or stage reviews)?

Process Adaptability

With respect to upper management, how free was project management to

5. determine interim schedule targets,
6. determine the project management approach, and
7. choose the format of progress reviews.

Technical Uncertainty

8. Product technology novelty
9. How new, on average, were the product modules?[1]
10. How new was the product configuration?
11. Overall, how new were the product technologies to be employed in this project?

Process Technology Novelty

12. How new, on average, were the individual manufacturing stages?[2]
13. How new was the process layout?
14. Overall, how new were the manufacturing technologies to be employed with this project?

*Operational Outcomes*

Product Quality

15. Original product performance objective met?

---

[1] A product is made up of major subsections called modules. Modules may be subassemblies, subsystems, major components, etc. The way the modules are linked together is the product configuration also called product architecture or systems design.

[2] The manufacturing process is made up of major individual manufacturing stages. A manufacturing stage can be fabrication, machining, assembly or packaging process. The order of the stages, and linkages among stages, constitutes the process layout.

Unit Cost

16. Original product unit-cost objective met?

Time-to-Market

17. Original product time-to-market objective met?

*Market and Environmental Uncertainty*

Market Newness

18. How was the target market to your company?

*Environmentally-Caused Disruption*

19. To what degree did events external to project impact the project?

*Market Outcomes*

Customer Satisfaction

20. To what degree were customers satisfied with the product that resulted from this development effort?

Relative Sales

21. As of today, this product's actual sales results are relative to sales expectations.

**Construct Description**

The key constructs in this article were described as follows. Process concurrency represented "the degree to which different organizational functions simultaneously conduct project work" (p. 155). Process formality indicated "the degree to which rules, policies, and procedures govern the product development work activities" (p. 155). Process adaptability was defined as "the degree of discretion available to development project managers regarding work activities and decisions during the project constitutes process adaptability" (p. 155). Technological uncertainty connoted "the degree of familiarity with the given technology or degree of change in the technologies relative to products previously developed or manufactured by the company. They consider two aspects of technology novelty that apply in the assembled products context: product and process technology novelty" (p. 157).

According to the authors, the operational perspective of "product quality typically refers to the technical performance and reliability of the product relative to specifications. However, from a marketing perspective, product quality simply means that each element of the product design and positioning is aimed at satisfying customers" (p. 158). Time-to-market was the approximate date for which first customer shipment was planned. Market newness was presented as the degree to which the firm was familiar and had experience with the target market for the new product. Environmentally caused disruption was characterized as the degree to which events external to the development effort influence it.

**Measurement Description**

Most measures were developed from the existing literature. The process concurrency scale was based on the cross-functional integration concepts of Wheelwright and Clark (1992). This scale was reverse coded. The process formality scale was an adaptation of Oldham and Hackman's (1981) formality measure. The process adaptability scale was Van de Ven and Ferry's (1980) measure of work group discretion. The technology novelty scales were developed from the field experience of the authors and built on the notions of architecture and modularity presented by Henderson and Clark (1990) and Ulrich (1995). Product technology novelty was measured by the degree to which product modules, the product architecture, and the product technologies overall were new to the firm at the start of project execution. Process technology novelty was measured by the degree to which manufacturing stages, the process layout, and manufacturing technologies overall were new.

Three individual operational performance outcome measures were the employed to assess "the degree of achievement of the product *quality, unit cost* and *time-to-market* objectives of the project" (p. 161). The two individual market performance outcome measures were the perceived degree of customer satisfaction with the product that resulted from the development effort and relative product *sales* compared with sales expectations. The market newness measure was adopted from Olson, Walker, and Ruekert (1995), who described newness as a function of the firm's experience and familiarity. The environmentally caused disruption measure was an adoption of Tyre's (1988) measure of disruptiveness.

### Development

Solicitation mailings were sent to selected members of the Product Development Management Association (PDMA) and the Manufacturing Executives Forum (MEF). The PDMA membership and executive education program participants had served as samples for previous studies of product development (Zirger and Maidique 1990; Zirger and Hartley 1996).

### Sample

The resulting sample had the greatest representation from the medical/scientific instruments and imaging product categories. The other industries comprising the sample included computers, chip sets, video and audio systems, communication transmission equipment, process controls, and manufacturing. The sample consisted of 120 projects from 57 companies. Most projects (81%) were completed within a 36-month period. The respondents were project managers who were responsible for a particular new product development project.

### Reliability and Validity

For the multi-item constructs, a confirmatory factor analysis (CFA) was performed to assess the convergent and discriminant validity of the measurement items. Examination of the patterns of item-item correlations and item-total correlation indicated that there were no deviations from the internal consistency and external consistency criteria (Anderson and Gerbing 1988). The internal reliability of the multi-item scales were assessed by Cronbach's coefficient alpha.

### Scores

The scores are presented in Tables 1–3 in the article.

### Other Evidence

Not available.

### References

Anderson, J. C., and D. W. Gerbing. 1988 Structural equation modeling in practice. A review and recommended two-step approach. *Psychological Bulletin* 103 (3): 411–23.

Henderson, R. M., and K. B. Clark. 1990. Architectural innovation: The reconfiguration of existing product technologies and the failure of established firms. *Administrative Science Quarterly* 35 (1): 9–30.

Oldham, G. R., and J. R. Hackman. 1981. Relationships between organizational structure and employee reactions: Comparing alternative frameworks. *Administrative Science Quarterly* 26 (1): 66–83.

Olson, E. M., O. C. Walker Jr., and R. W. Ruekert. 1995. Organizing for effective new product development: The moderating role of product innovativeness. *Journal of Marketing* 59 (1): 48–62.

Tyre, M. J. 1988. Managing the introduction of new process technology. Unpublished doctoral dissertation, Harvard University, Cambridge, MA.

Ulrich, K. T. 1995. The role of product architecture in manufacturing firm. *Research Policy* 24 (3): 419–40.

Van de Ven, A. H, and D. L. Ferry. 1980. *Measuring and assessing organizations.* New York: Wiley.

Wheelwright, S. C., and K. B. Clark. 1992. *Revolutionizing product development: Quantum leaps in speed, efficiency, and quality.* New York: Free Press.

Zirger, B. J., and J. L. Hartley. 1996. The effect of acceleration techniques on product development time. *IEEE Transactions on Engineering Management* 42 (2): 143–52.

Zirger, B. J., and M. A. Maidique. 1990. A model of new product development: An empirical test. *Management Science* 36 (7): 867–83.

# Teigland and McLure Wasko

## Article Summarized

Teigland, Robin, and Molly McLure Wasko. 2004. Integrating knowledge through information trading: Examining the relationship between boundary spanning communication and individual performance. *Decision Sciences* 34 (2): 261–86.

## Scales (Actual Questions Used)

*Knowledge Sources*

Sources in your everyday work

1. Coworkers in my location
2. Cap Gemini colleagues in another location
3. Cap Gemini electronic communities
4. NCN MS electronic communities
5. Other contacts outside Cap Gemini
6. Internet: discussion forums/electronic communities

Information Trading

How many times during the past year have the following happened?

7. You were contacted by someone in Cap Gemini for some specific technical information.
8. You gave out some specific technical information to someone at Cap Gemini.
9. You sent formal, written communications in the form of reports or data to someone inside Cap Gemini.
10. You sent informal, written communications in the form of reports or data to someone inside Cap Gemini.
11. You were contacted by someone outside Cap Gemini for some specific technical information.

Information Trading

How many times during the past year have the following happened?

12. You gave out some specific technical information to a person working outside Cap Gemini.
13. You sent formal, written communications in the form of reports or data to someone outside Cap Gemini.
14. You sent informal, written communications in the form of reports or data to someone outside Cap Gemini.

*Performance*

15. My work tasks demand creative and totally new ideas and solutions.
16. The others at Cap Gemini think that I am creative.

17. My colleagues at Cap Gemini consider me to be a guru.
18. I have a high level of expertise in the technology with which I work.
19. You are able to meet objectives set by your immediate superior relative to your colleagues at Cap Gemini.
20. You are able to meet my deadlines relative to your colleagues at Cap Gemini.

## Construct Description

Key constructs were operationally defined in the article. Collocated workers were the workers who "share the same physical space, and are more likely to frequently interact with each other and develop a common language of discourse" (p. 266). The construct of noncollocated coworkers connoted the employees who worked within the same organization but were located across intraorganizational boundaries. Intraorganizational electronic discussion networks were presented as "internet-based electronic networks, individuals are able to share information and know-how through mechanisms that support posting and responding to questions, sharing stories of personal experience, and discussing and debating issues relevant to the professional community" (p. 269). Contacts at other firms referred to external contact with people who do not belong to the same organization. External information trading was defined as the "act of reciprocation while accessing knowledge from contacts in occupational community" (p. 269). Internal information trading signified "accessing advice and knowledge from non-collocated coworkers with the expectation of reciprocity in return" (p. 267). General performance was presented as the ability to meet one's job demand, and creativity was defined as the ability to develop creative solutions to business problems.

## Measurement Description

The authors used self-reported scores for the measures for the constructs specified. The scales were mentioned in the Scales section of this summary. Information trading was measured separately with three items measuring external information trading. The scales measured all the sources of information under a single heading using five items mentioned in the scales.

## Development

The questionnaire was validated by a pilot test on a group of 15 programmers. The pilot test made them drop some of the items since the initial questionnaire was long. No mention was made of the items that were dropped.

## Sample

All the respondents were from a single company (Cap Gemini) and members of a single electronic network (i.e., the NSN MS Community). A total of 350 participants yielded 83 usable responses with a response rate of 24%. The average age of the respondents was 35.6 years, and they were employed with the company for 4.0 years and had 7.7 years experience in the competence area.

## Reliability and Validity

The authors reported the internal composite reliabilities. They assessed discriminant validity by comparing the square root of average variance extracted for each latent variable with the correlations between the latent constructs. Convergent validity was assessed by looking at the factor loadings that are provided in the partial least squares (PLS) analysis. Evidence of convergent and discriminant validity can be found in data provided in Tables 1 and 2 of the article, respectively.

### Scores

The results of the article are presented in Tables 2 and 3 of the article. The results of the partial least squares are given in Table 3. Table 2 also presents the interitem correlation numbers.

### Other Evidence

Not available.

### Reference

None.

---

## Terziovski, Samson, and Dow

### Article Summarized

Terziovski, Milé, Danny Samson, and Douglas Dow. 1997. The business value of quality management systems certification: Evidence from Australia and New Zealand. *Journal of Operations Management* 15 (1): 1–18.

### Scales (Actual Questions Used)

*Operating Performance*

1. Reliability (warranty claims cost as a percentage of total sales)
2. Timeliness (delivery in full on time to customers)
3. Cost of quality (error, scrap, rework, and inspection) as a percentage of total sales
4. Defects as a percentage of production volume
5. Productivity

*Customer Satisfaction*

6. Customer complaints (fewer complaints, higher customer retention)
7. Employee morale

*Business Performance*

8. Cash flow (per capital investment)

*Innovation*

9. In 1992 to 1993, what was the percentage of total sales from "new" products (i.e., those produced for <5 years)?

*Employee Growth*

10. What was the total number of full-time employees at this site for the years 1900 to 1991, 1991 to 1992, and 1992 to 1993?

*Market Share Growth*

11. For your principal product, in its major market, please indicate its level of market share for the years 1900 to 1991 and 1992 to 1993 (percentage market share).

*Sales Growth*

12. Please indicate the total sales from your site for the years 1990 to 1991 and 1992 to 1993 ($AUS or $NZ).

*Export Growth*

13. Please indicate the export sales from your site for the years 1990 to 1991 and 1992 to 1993 ($AUS or $NZ).

*Status in Terms of ISO 9000 Certification*

14. Where does your site fit in relation to quality certification in the ISO 9000 series?

*Total Quality Management*

15. Mission statement is communicated and supported.
16. Shop-floor ideas are used by management.
17. Customer requirements are understood.
18. Quality is each employee's responsibility.
19. Customer satisfaction is measured.
20. There is effective "top-down" and "bottom-up" communication.
21. Continuous improvement is proactively pursued.
22. There is understanding of internal customer concept.
23. Management encourages trust and involvement.
24. There is organization-wide training and development.

**Construct Description**

The definition of total quality management (TQM) followed the framework developed by the U.S. General Accounting Office (GAO). According to the GAO, TQM had six common features that contribute to improved performance. They were as follows: (1) corporate attention is focused on meeting customers' quality requirements; (2) top management leads the way in disseminating TQM values throughout the organization; (3) employees are asked and empowered to continuously improve all key business processes; (4) management nurtures a flexible and responsive corporate culture; (5) management systems support fact-based decision making; and (6) partnerships with suppliers are used to improve product or service quality.

**Measurement Description**

Each firm's status in terms of ISO 9000 certification was measured using an ordinal scale. "Firms reporting a value of 1 or 2 on this ISO 9000 certification variable were labeled 'certified companies.' Firms reporting a value of 4 or 5 were labeled 'non-certified companies.' Firms reporting a value of 3 were discarded to reduce any uncertainty regarding their status" (p. 6). Organization performance was captured with 13 variables from the Australian Manufacturing Council (AMC) survey. "These variables ranged from objective business performance measures such as percentage growth in sales to subjective estimates given by the site managers concerning employee morale" (p. 6). Company size was computed by taking the natural logarithm of the number of full-time employees and was used as a covariate in data analysis.

Based on GAO's framework of TQM, 10 items were developed to measure firm's extent of adoption of the TQM philosophies. Each item in the TQM model was measured using a five-point Likert-type scale. Firms were developed into two categories dependent on their score on the TQM construct. Firms that had scores greater than the sample mean were classified as having "strong TQM environment," while those that had scores equal to or below the sample mean were defined as having "weak TQM environment."

All four growth measures were calculated in the percentage annual increase from 1990 to 1991 and 1992 to 1993 as follows. To calculate market share growth, the level of market share was sought for 1990 to 1991 and from 1992 to 1993. "The average percentage growth is calculated by determining the percentage growth in market share from 1990-1991 and the percentage growth in market share from

1992-1993, and then averaging these figures" (p. 15). To determine sales growth, the average sales growth was calculated by determining the growth from 1990 to 1991 and from 1992 to 1993 and then averaging these results. A method similar to that employed for sales growth was used for export growth and employee growth.

### Development

The goal of the AMC study was to investigate the extent of "best practice" adoption by the Australian and New Zealand manufacturing firms and its impact on organizational performance. The AMC built a framework and questionnaire based on the academic literature and international quality awards such as the Malcolm Baldrige National Quality Award, the Australian Quality Award, and the European Quality Award (Garvin 1991).

Ergas and Wright (1994) conducted a number of statistical quality tests on the AMC questionnaire. First, "the data were tested for evidence of 'respondent fatigue' (i.e. inconsistent responses to similar questions in different parts of the questionnaire). Second, a number of 'awareness tests' were applied (i.e. where certain questions had a different tone or measurement scale to surrounding questions, correlation coefficients were calculated to test the hypothesis that respondents failed to pay attention to the change" (p. 7). It was found that none of these biases existed. The questions pertaining to TQM were selected from the AMC survey instrument and review of literature.

### Sample

Data were collected by the AMC (1994). The AMC delivered questionnaires to 3,000 randomly selected Australian manufacturing sites and 1,000 randomly selected New Zealand manufacturing sites. A total of 962 Australian sites (32% response rate) and 379 New Zealand sites (38% response rate) answered the questionnaire, which was filled out by the most senior manufacturing executive at the site. In both the countries, stratification of the sample was conducted based on 12 industry codes (ASIC and NZSIC) and three company-size categories. These categories were "small" (20 to 49 employees), "medium" (50 to 99 employees), and "large" (100 or more employees). Statistical analysis was conducted to assess potential nonrespondent bias. No significant respondent bias in the sample was found.

### Reliability and Validity

The internal consistency of the TQM model was checked using reliability analysis. Cronbach's coefficient alpha for this single construct comprising 10 items was .82, which indicated the reliability of this construct. "The ten items of the TQM model . . . loaded on a single TQM factor. Each item had a factor loading greater than .40. This supports construct validity of the model. Content validity is supported by comparing the ten items of our model with models from the literature, for example the TQM features identified by the GAO" (p. 17). No further details on the measurement properties of the items were presented in the study.

### Scores

The scores are reported in Tables 1–5 in the article.

### Other Evidence

Not available.

### References

Australian Manufacturing Council [AMC]. 1994. Leading the way: A study of best manufacturing practices in Australia and New Zealand, Melbourne, Australia, 59–63.

Ergas, H., and M. Wright. 1994. Internationalisation, firm conduct, and productivity. In *International integration of the Australian economy,* eds. Lowe and Dwyer, pp. 55–105. Sydney, Australia: Reserve Bank of Australia.

Garvin, D. A. 1991. How the Baldrige Award really works. *Harvard Business Review* 69 (6): 80–93.

# Tracey, Vonderembse, and Lim

### Article Summarized

Tracey, Michael, Mark A. Vonderembse, and Jeen-Su Lim. 1999. Manufacturing technology and strategy formulation: Keys to enhancing competitiveness and improving performance. *Journal of Operations Management* 17 (4): 411–28.

### Scales (Actual Questions Used)

*Advanced Manufacturing Technology*

1. We apply computer-enhanced technology to improve the flexibility of manufacturing.
2. We have incorporated real-time process control into our production systems.
3. We use production technology that is among the most flexible in our industry.

*Manufacturing Manager's Participation (MMP) in Strategy Formulation*

4. The input of manufacturing plant managers is an integral part of the strategy formation process.
5. Manufacturing plant managers have a good understanding as to how company/divisional strategy is formed.
6. Manufacturing plant managers are involved in decisions related to strategies for company growth.

*Price Offered (PR)*

7. We offer competitive prices.
8. We are able to compete based on our prices.
9. We are able to offer prices as low or lower than our competitors.

*Quality of Products (QP)*

10. We are able to compete based on quality.
11. We offer products that are highly reliable.
12. We offer products that are very durable.
13. We offer high-quality products to our customers.

*Product Line Breadth (PLB)*

14. We respond well to changing customer preferences regarding products.
15. We respond well to changing customer preferences regarding accompanying services.
16. We alter our product offerings to meet client needs.
17. We respond well to customer demand for "new" features.

*Delivery Capability (DC)*

18. We supply accurate projected shipping dates.
19. Orders submitted to us are delivered on time as defined by the customer.
20. We supply accurate projected delivery dates.
21. We provide on-time delivery of customer orders.
22. Our customers are pleased with the frequency of our delivery.
23. Our customers are satisfied with our level of completeness for *routine* shipments.
24. Our frequency of customer backorders is low.
25. We work with each customer to develop a delivery schedule that is acceptable.

*Level of Performance*

26. Customers perceiving they receive their money's worth when they purchase our products
27. Customer retention rate
28. Generating new business through customer referrals
29. Sales growth position
30. Market share gain
31. Overall competitive position

**Construct Description**

Constructs were derived from the literature. Advanced manufacturing technology (AMT) was defined as "the application of computer-enhanced, applied science to a firm's production system" (p. 413). Investment in AMT enabled the firm to respond to rapid market change by designing and producing high-quality, custom designed products (Goldhar and Jelinek 1983; Doll and Vonderembse 1990; Roth 1996; Wheelwright and Clark 1992). Manufacturing manager's participation (MMP) in strategy formulation was explained as "the extent to which manufacturing plant managers are involved in organizational level strategy development" (p. 414).

Competitive capabilities were "the attributes of an organization that attract customers; they are potential points of differentiation between an organization and its competitors" (p. 414). In this study, four competitive capabilities were defined as follows: "Price offered (PR) is one of the key determinants of customer satisfaction (Innis & LaLonde, 1994; Bergman 1995). Quality of products (QP) is defined as fitness for use and includes product performance, reliability, and durability. It has become a key competitive issue in the global marketplace (Garvin 1988; Flynn et al., 1995). Product line breadth (PLB) is defined as the ability to offer customers the various products and features that satisfy their individual requirements (Meredith et al., 1994). Delivery capability (DC) encompasses satisfactory order fill rates, cycle times, shipment information, and frequency of delivery (Bockerstette & Shell, 1993; Holcomb 1994; Vonderembse et al., 1995)" (p. 414).

Level of performance (LOP) was defined as the combination of customer satisfaction—that is, perception of value, retention, and referrals—and market performance, which pertains to sales gains and overall position (Venkatraman and Ramanujan 1986; Narver and Slater 1995).

**Measurement Description**

Thirty-one items were grouped into seven categories to assess upper managers' perceptions of their firms' levels of AMT, MMP, competitive capabilities (i.e., PR, QP, PLB, DC), and LOP. Each item was quantified using a 5-point Likert scale. For the AMT, MMP, PR, QP, PLB, and DC metrics, the "strongly disagree" to "strongly agree" format was used with the "not relevant"/"do not know" response also available for each item. For the LOP scale, the "unacceptable" to "superior" format was used with the "not relevant"/"do not know" response also available for each item.

**Development**

An extensive literature review facilitated the item generation. The initial list of items and definitions for each construct was presented to two consultants, six executives from six manufacturing firms, and eight academics as a pretest. A pilot-study mailing of the instrument resulted in 50 usable responses that were used to purify the instrument. The responses from a large-scale survey were then employed to refine the instrument further. Throughout scale development, exploratory factor analysis (EFA) was conducted and the objectives were reliability, parsimony, and convergent, discriminant, and predictive validity.

**Sample**

The large-scale mailing resulted in 474 acceptable responses from upper-level managers of manufacturing firms from across the United States. The effective response rate was 14.5%. The 474 organizations were mainly from four U.S. Department of Commerce, Standard Industrial Classification (SIC) codes: 25, furniture and fixtures; 34, fabricated metal products; 35, industrial and commercial machinery; and 36, electronic and other electrical equipment. The respondents had from 50 to 1,000 employees at their location (about 75% had fewer than 500). The types of manufacturing operations reported were uniformly distributed across the spectrum from continuous flow to job shop.

### Reliability and Validity

Internal/convergent validity was assessed by subjecting the items related to a specific dimension of a latent variable to EFA. Items that did not load at .60 were either dropped or designated for modification. External discriminant validity was then assessed by subjecting the items remaining for an entire construct "to exploratory factor analysis to uncover significant cross-loadings"(p. 417). "The KMO measure of sampling adequacy (Kaiser 1970) was first calculated for each construct and in each case factor analysis was found to be appropriate. Where significant cross-loadings were discovered, items were either dropped or modified. Predictive validity was assessed by correlating composite measures of the constructs" (p. 417).

Cronbach's coefficient alpha values for the individual scales were computed to test the reliability. These values ranged from .75 to .93, which demonstrated good reliability. Moreover, to demonstrate the generalizability of the scales, Cronbach's coefficient alpha was calculated for several industries with sufficient responses. The results showed, for all scales, no significant differences in reliability across these industries.

### Scores

Means and standard deviations were not provided in the article. The corrected-item total correlations, factor loadings (dimension and construct levels), and Cronbach's coefficient alpha for the scales are presented in Tables 1–4 in the article.

### Other Evidence

Not available.

### References


Bockerstette, J. A., and R. L. Shell. 1993. *Time based manufacturing.* New York: McGraw-Hill.

Bregman, R. L. 1995. Integrating marketing, operations, and purchasing to create value. *Omega* 23 (2): 159–72.

Doll, W. J., and M. A. Vonderembse. 1991. The evolution of manufacturing systems: Towards the post-industrial enterprise. *Omega* 19 (5): 401–11.

Flynn, B. B., R. G. Schroeder, S. Sakakibara. 1995. The impact of quality management practices on performance and competitive advantage. *Decision Sciences* 26 (5): 659–91.

Garvin, D. A. 1988. *Managing quality.* New York: Free Press.

Goldhar, J. D., and M. Jelinek. 1983. Plan for economies of scope. *Harvard Business Review* 61 (6): 141–48.

Holcomb, M. C. 1994. Customer service measurement: A methodology for increasing customer value through utilization of the Taguchi strategy. *Journal of Business Logistics* 15 (1): 29–52.

Innis, D. E., and B. J. La Londe. 1994. Customer service: The key to customer satisfaction, customer loyalty, and market share. *Journal of Business Logistics* 15 (1): 1–27.

Kaiser, H. F. 1970. A second-generation little jiffy. *Psychometrika* 35 (4): 401–15.

Meredith, J. R., D. M. McCutcheon, J. Hartley. 1994. Enhancing competitiveness through the new market equation. *International Journal of Operations and Production Management* 14 (11): 7–22.

Roth, A. V. 1996. Achieving strategic agility through economics of knowledge. *Strategy and Leadership* 24 (2): 30–37.

Slater, S. F., and J. C. Narver. 1995. Market orientation and the learning organization. *Journal of Marketing* 59 (3): 63–74.

Venkatraman, N., and V. Ramanujan. 1986. Measurements of business performance in strategy research: A comparison of approaches. *Academy of Management Review* 11 (10): 801–14.

Vonderembse, M. A. M. Tracey, C. L. Tan, and E. J. Bardi. 1995. Current purchasing practices and JIT: Some of the effects on inbound logistics. *International Journal of Physical Distribution & Logistics Management* 25 (3): 33–48.
Wheelwright, S. C., and K. B. Clark. 1992. *Revolutionizing product development: Quantum leaps in speed, efficiency, and quality.* New York: Free Press.

# Tsikriktsis, Lanzolla, and Frohlich

## Article Summarized

Tsikriktsis, Nikos, Gianvito Lanzolla, and Mark Frohlich. 2004. Adoption of e-processes by service firms: An empirical study of antecedents. *Production and Operations Management* 13 (3): 216–29.

## Scales (Actual Questions Used)

*Barriers of Web-Based Integration*

Internal Barriers

1. Our culture of resistance to change
2. Our lack of management skills
3. Our lack of technical skills
4. Our technology costs
5. Our benefits not demonstrated
6. Our IT systems integration

Customer Barriers

7. Customers' culture of resistance to change
8. Customers' lack of technical skills
9. Customers' technology costs
10. Customers' reluctance because of benefits not demonstrated
11. Customers' reluctance because of IT systems integration

*Drivers of Web-Based Integration*

Expected Performance Benefits

12. Improving speed of response
13. Improving reliability and delivery
14. Improving service quality
15. Anticipated cost reduction
16. Improving after sales support

New Markets

17. Access to European single market
18. Access to global markets
19. Lack of local partners

External Pressure

20. Threat from traditional competitors
21. Pressure from customers

22. Pressure from suppliers
23. Peer pressure "to get onboard"

*e-Processes*

e-CRM

24. Targeted marketing/customer profiling
25. Electronic catalog/product info
26. After-sales support

e-Transactions

27. Order taking/receipt
28. Billing
29. Electronic payments
30. Order tracking
31. Integrated demand/forecasting

### Construct Description

The constructs used in this article included expected performance benefits, access to new markets, external pressure, internal barriers, customer barriers, adoption of e-CRM, and adoption of e-transactions. The definitions for each of these constructs came from previous literature (O'Leary-Kelly and Vokura 1998). The study also referred to several prior case examples from managerial journals for anecdotal evidence of item and scale efficacy. For instance, the authors cited Coltman et al. (2001), Winer (2001), and Willcocks and Plant (2001) regarding customer and internal barriers to e-business. In addition, they cited case examples from Holweg and Pil (2001), Barua et al. (2001), and Venkatraman (2000) to develop their construct definition for expected performance benefits. Although no formal definitions were given for the constructs in the article, they were self-evident from the items in the scales that were developed for all of them.

### Measurement Description

Thirty-one items were grouped into seven factors: internal barriers, customer barriers, expected performance benefits, new markets, external pressure, adoption of e-CRM, and adoption of e-transactions. These were further grouped under three broad factor headings: (1) barriers of Web-based integration, (2) drivers of Web-based integration, and (3) e-processes. The first broad category of factors—barriers—included internal and customer barriers. All were quantified using 5-point Likert scales ranging from 1 = "highly insignificant" to 5 = "highly significant." The second broad category of factors—drivers—included expected performance benefits, access to new markets, and external pressure. These drivers were also operationalized using 5-point Likert scales, except that this time they ranged from 1 = "not at all" to 5 = "fully." The last broad category of factors—adoption of e-processes—included e-CRM and e-transactions, and these were captured with 5-point Likert scales ranging from 1 = "not at all" to 5 = "fully."

### Development

The scales in this study were developed through a three-stage process. The first stage was the construction of the survey instrument from the initial measures and antecedents that were found in the existing literature. After this was established, stage 2 was to test the preliminary survey instrument for content and face validity. This was accomplished through a series of meetings with managers involved in e-business, who provided early feedback on the readability and validity of the scales. The third stage was to actually pretest the revised survey instrument with a group of 30 firms in order to determine content validity.

## Sample

The data in this study came from a stratified random sample of service companies from all 13 regions of the United Kingdom, including firms in the manufacturing, retailing, agriculture, finance, transportation, and consulting sectors. The sampling frame was 1,600 of these firms; the overall response rate was 21% for a total final sample size of 338 respondents, who were managers/executives with knowledge about their companies' e-services and performance. The authors checked the final sample data to ensure that nonresponse bias and common method bias, using Harmon's one-factor test, were not significantly present in the study.

## Reliability and Validity

The authors indicated that exploratory factor analysis was used to check for construct validity (Kim and Mueller 1978). All scales demonstrated unidimensionality and acceptable reliability (Nunnally 1968). In addition, construct validity was checked using common factor loading. Furthermore, discriminant validity was tested for by using the bivariate correlations between each measure and any other possibly confounding variables. Also, Cronbach's coefficient alphas were calculated and compared with the average interscale correlations. Because the alphas were found to be greater, this provided more evidence of discriminant validity.

## Scores

The factor loadings, percentage of variances explained, and Cronbach's coefficient alphas for each of the factors are shown in the appendix at the end of the article.

## Other Evidence

Not available.

## References

Barua, A., P. Konana, A. B. Whinston, and F. Yin. 2001. Driving e-business excellence. *Sloan Management Review* 43 (1): 36–44.

Coltman, T., T. M. Devinney, A. Latukefu, and D. F. Midgley. 2001. E-business: Revolution, evolution, or hype? *California Management Review* 44 (1): 57–88.

Holweg, M., and F. K. Pil. 2001. Successful build-to-order strategies start with the customer. *Sloan Management Review* 43 (1): 74–83.

Kim, J., and C. W. Mueller. 1978. *Factor analysis: Statistical methods and practical issues.* Beverly Hills, CA: Sage.

Nunnally, J. C. 1968. *Psychometric theory.* New York: McGraw-Hill.

O'Leary-Kelly, S. W., and R. J. Vokurka. 1998. The empirical assessment of construct validity. *Journal of Operations Management* 16 (4): 387–405.

Venkatraman, N. 2000. Five steps to a dot.com strategy: How to find your footing on the Web. *Sloan Management Review* 41 (3): 15–28.

Willcocks, L. P., and R. Plant. 2001. Pathways to e-business leadership: Getting from bricks to clicks. *Sloan Management Review* 42 (3): 50–59.

Winer, R. S. 2001. A framework for customer relationship management. *California Management Review* 43 (4): 89–107

# Tu, Vonderembse, and Ragu-Nathan

**Article Summarized**

Tu, Qiang, Mark A. Vonderembse, and T. S. Ragu-Nathan. 2001. The impact of time-based manufacturing practices on mass customization and value to customer. *Journal of Operations Management* 19 (2): 201–17.

**Scales (Actual Questions Used)**

*Time-Based Manufacturing Practices (TBMP)*

Shop-Floor Employee Involvement in Problem Solving

1. Shop-floor employees are involved in improvement efforts.
2. Shop-floor employees are involved in problem-solving teams.
3. Shop-floor employees are involved in suggestion programs.

Reengineering Setup

4. We use special tools to shorten setup time.
5. Our employees are trained to reduce setup time.
6. Employees work on setup improvement.
7. We redesign or reconfigure equipment to shorten setup time.

Cellular Manufacturing

8. Products are classified into groups with similar routing requirements.
9. Products are classified into groups with similar processing requirements.
10. Equipment is grouped to produce families of products.
11. Families of products determine our factory layout.

Preventive Maintenance

12. We maintain our equipment regularly.
13. We emphasize good preventive maintenance.
14. Records of routine maintenance are kept.

Quality Assurance

15. We use fishbone-type diagrams to identify causes of quality problems.
16. Our employees use quality control charts.
17. We conduct process capability studies.

Dependable Suppliers

18. We receive parts from suppliers on time.
19. We receive the correct number of parts from suppliers.
20. We receive high-quality parts from suppliers.
21. We receive the correct type of parts from suppliers.

Pull Production

22. Production at stations is "pulled" by the current demand of the next stations.
23. Production is "pulled" by the shipment of finished goods.

24. We use a "pull" production system.
25. Production is "pulled" by an open kanban/bin position.

*Mass Customization (MC)*

26. Our capacity of customizing products on a large scale is high.
27. Our capability of adding product variety without increasing cost is high.
28. Our capability of customizing products while maintaining a large volume is high.
29. Our capability of setting up for a different product at low cost is high.
30. Our capability of responding to customization requirements quickly is high.
31. Our capability of adding product variety without sacrificing overall production volume is high.

*Value to Customer (VC)*

32. Our customers are satisfied with the quality of our products.
33. Our customers are satisfied with the features that our products provide.
34. Our customers are loyal to our products.
35. Our customers refer new customers to purchase our products.
36. Our customers feel that we offer products with high value.

## Construct Description

The constructs were presented in the article as follows. Mass customization (MC) was defined as "the ability of a firm to quickly produce customized products on a large scale at a cost comparable to non-customized products" (p. 203). Time-based manufacturing practice (TBMP) connoted "an externally focused production system that emphasizes quick response to changing customer needs" (p. 204). This definition was consistent with the definition provided by Koufteros, Vonderembse, and Doll (1998). Value to customer (VC) was "an external measure that assesses the customers' degree of satisfaction with the organization's products" (p. 204). It captured customers' perceptions of the values of products that were important to them.

## Measurement Description

TBMP was operationalized as a second-order factor with seven dimensions: (1) shop-floor employee involvement in problem solving, (2) reengineering setups, (3) cellular manufacturing, (4) preventive maintenance, (5) quality improvement efforts, (6) dependable suppliers, and (7) pull production. Each dimension was measured using multiple items that were adapted from Koufteros, Vonderembse, and Doll (1998). Each item was measured using a 5-point Likert scale with 1 = "strongly disagree" and 5 = "strongly agree." VC was conceptualized as a single-dimension construct. The measurement items for VC were adapted from Tracey (1996). Similarly, each item was measured using a 5-point Likert scale with 1 = "strongly disagree" and 5 = "strongly agree." A final list of six items was used to measure MC as a single-dimension construct, which was newly developed for this study. The scale for the MC items followed a 5-point Likert-type scale response format with 1 = "much below average" and 5 = "much above average." In addition to the Likert-scale anchors, a choice of "not applicable" or "do not know" was also offered for each item representing TBMP, VC, and MC

## Development

The authors followed four major phases to develop the instrument for the MC items: (1) item generation, (2) pre–pilot study, (3) pilot study, and (4) large-scale data collection and analysis. The initial list of MC items was generated based on a comprehensive literature review and structured interviews with manufacturing executives, followed by a pre–pilot study. During the pre–pilot study, six faculty members evaluated the MC items and suggested changes if necessary according to the copies of the initial item list and the definition of MC provided to them. Third, a pilot study was conducted to evaluate the reliability and validity of the MC scale. The questionnaire was sent to 1,000 senior manufacturing managers in medium to large companies. Forty usable responses were received. Scales were modified based on the information of corrected item-total correlation (CITC) and Cronbach's coefficient alpha values. In general, CITC above .50, factor loadings above .60, and Cronbach's coefficient alpha above .70 were considered acceptable. Last, the list of nine items identified in the pilot study was subjected to final assessment in Phase 4—large-scale analysis. Three items were dropped to improve the psychometric properties of the scale based on the results obtained from the LISREL measurement model.

## Sample

The sample for the large-scale empirical analysis was obtained from the Society of Manufacturing Engineers (SME), which has 65,000 members (manufacturing managers and engineers) from all over the world in almost every industry. A total of 2,831 manufacturing managers were randomly selected from SME's U.S. membership database. The authors first mailed the respondents a copy of the final version of questionnaire along with a cover letter describing the purpose and significance of the study. Two follow-up letters were also sent to each target respondent—the first, 2 weeks later and the second, 4 weeks later. A total of 303 usable responses were received, representing an overall response rate of 10.7%.

Nonresponse bias was tested by comparing early respondents and late respondents. Two groups were compared on the basis of firm size, industry type, and sales volume. The authors reported, "No significant differences were found between two groups using the $\chi^2$ statistic and $p < 0.05$" (p. 207). The respondents consisted of the vice president of manufacturing, manufacturing manager, plant manager, manufacturing director, production manager, or plant operations manager. The final sample included the following U.S. Department of Commerce, Standard Industrial Classification codes (SIC): 25, furniture and fixtures; 30, rubber and miscellaneous plastics products; 34, fabricated metal products; 35, industrial machinery and equipment; 36, electronic and other electronic equipment; 37, transportation equipment; and 38, instruments and related products.

## Reliability and Validity

Exploratory factor analysis (EFA) with varimax rotation and mean substitution was performed to check the unidimensionality of MC and VC. In both cases, EFA produced one single factor with all factor loadings above .60. A single-factor LISREL measurement model was also constructed for both MC and VC constructs. In the former case, the final MC measurement model specifying a single-factor model with six items demonstrated a very good model fit (i.e., fit indices were above .90 and all factor loadings were above .60). In the latter case, the single-factor LISREL measurement for VC also revealed very good measurement properties.

Given the fact that TBMP was conceptualized as a second-order factor with seven dimensions, two separate analyses were conducted. First, discriminant validity assessment was performed using 21 pairwise tests on the dimension level. Each pair of dimensions under the TBMP construct was evaluated using two LISREL models—one constrained model with correlation of 1 between two dimensions and the other unconstrained model with free correlation instead. All $\chi^2$ differences were significant at $p < .01$ level, indicating strong support for the discriminant validity. Second, a second-order factor model with seven dimensions was evaluated using LISREL. The fit statistics provided evidence of acceptable fit for the overall model. The $\lambda$ coefficients were all significant at $p < .01$ level. The target coefficient index was 94.9%, indicating strong evidence of a higher-order TBMP.

All three constructs (MC, VC, and TBMP) were subjected to reliability assessment. The Cronbach's coefficient alphas for the final MC instrument and VC were .84 and .80, respectively. The alpha values for the seven dimensions of TBMP vary from .77 to .88.

## Scores

The factor loadings for the final MC model are reported in Figure 3. The mean and standard deviation of each measurement item for TBMP and VC are reported in Appendix A in the article. Assessment of discriminant validity of TBMP measures are provided in Table 3 of the article. Figure 4 shows the overall results from the LISREL structural equation model.

### Other Evidence

Not available.

### References

Koufteros, X. A., M. A. Vonderembse, and W. J. Doll. 1998. Developing measures of time-based manufacturing. *Journal of Operations Management* 16 (1): 21–41.

Tracey, M. A. 1996. Logistics/purchasing effectiveness, manufacturing flexibility and firm performance: Instrument development and causal model analysis. Unpublished doctoral dissertation, University of Toledo, OH.

## Tu, Vonderembse, Ragu-Nathan, and Ragu-Nathan

### Article Summarized

Tu, Qiang, Mark A. Vonderembse, T. S. Ragu-Nathan, and Bhanu Ragu-Nathan. 2004. Measuring modularity-based manufacturing practices and their impact on mass customization capability: A customer-driven perspective. *Decision Sciences* 35 (2): 147–68.

### Scales (Actual Questions Used)

*Modularity-Based Manufacturing Practices*

Dynamic Teaming (DT)

1. Production teams that can be reorganized are used in our plant.
2. Production teams can be reorganized in response to production/process changes.
3. Production teams can be reassigned to different production tasks.
4. Production teams are not permanently linked to a certain production task.
5. Production team members can be reassigned to different teams.
6. Production team members are capable of working on different teams.
7. Production teams have no difficulty accessing necessary resources.

Product Modularity (PM)

8. Our products use modularized design.
9. Our products share common modules.
10. Our product features are designed around a standard base unit.
11. Our products can be customized by adding feature modules as requested.
12. Product modules can be reassembled into different forms.
13. Product feature modules can be added to a standard base unit.
14. Product modules can be rearranged by end users to suit their needs.

Process Modularity (PRM)

15. Our product process is designed as adjustable modules.
16. Our production process can be adjusted by adding new process modules.

17. Production process modules can be adjusted for changing production needs.
18. Our product process can be broken down into standard subprocesses that produce standard base units and customization subprocesses that further customize the base units.
19. Production process modules can be rearranged so that customization subprocesses occur last.
20. Production process modules can be rearranged so that customization subprocesses can be carried out later at distribution centers.

*Customer Closeness (CC)*

21. We monitor changes in customer needs through close contacts.
22. We try to understand customers' exact needs through close contacts.
23. We help customers clarify their needs through close contacts.
24. We involve customers in the customization processes through close contacts.
25. We have a well-designed system to ensure close contact with customers.

*Mass Customization*

26. Our capacity of customizing products on a large scale is high.
27. Our capability of adding product variety without increasing cost is high.
28. Our capability of customizing products while maintaining a large volume is high.
29. Our capability of setting up for a different product at low cost is high.
30. Our capability of responding to customization requirements quickly is high.
31. Our capability of adding product variety without sacrificing overall production volume is high.

**Construct Description**

The following constructs were employed in this study. Modularity-based manufacturing practices (MBMP) were defined as a "set of actions that enable firms to achieve modularity in product design, product process design and organizational design" (p. 148). In general, modularity connotes the degrees to which a system's components can be separated and recombined (Schilling 2000).

The authors indicated three elements of MBMP. First, product modularity was characterized as "the practice of using standardized product modules so they can be easily reassembled/rearranged into different functional forms or shared across different product line" (p. 150). Second, process modularity was given as "the practice of standardizing manufacturing process modules so that they can be resequenced easily or new modules can be added quickly in response to changing product requirements" (p. 151). Third, dynamic teaming was defined as "the practice of using modular structures to reorganize manufacturing teams quickly and link them to necessary resources in response to product design or manufacturing changes" (p. 152).

Customer closeness (CC) was "the practice of keeping close contact with customers, to communicate with customers effectively and to understand customers' individual needs" (p. 150). Mass customization (MC) capability was defined as the "ability to produce varieties of customized products quickly, on a large scale and at a cost comparable to mass-production through technical managerial innovations" (p. 152).

**Measurement Description**

MBMP was operationalized as a second-order construct with three subdimensions, while CC and MC were operationalized as single-dimension constructs. MBMP's three subdimensions—product modularity, process modularity, and dynamic teaming—each comprised multiple items. PM had seven items; PRM, six items; and DT, seven items. Following large-scale reliability analysis, the authors dropped some items to improve the psychometric properties. Both CC and MC were single-dimension variables, and the number of items for these variables were 5 and 6, respectively.

### Development

The authors followed four major phases to develop the instrument for MBMP and CC: (1) item generation, (2) pre–pilot study, (3) pilot study, and (4) large-scale data collection and analysis. Regarding MC, the authors adapted items from Tu, Vonderembse, and Ragu-Nathan (2001). "A comprehensive literature review was completed to define the constructs and to identify an initial list of items. To improve contend validity, a pre-pilot study was completed that involved four manufacturing managers and six academic experts. During the structural interviews, the definitions of MBMP, CC and the items that were developed to measure them were presented. A pilot study was completed that targeted senior manufacturing managers. Forty usable responses were received. Corrected item-total correlation (CITC) was used to purify scales (Kerlinger, 1978). An item was eliminated if its correlation with the corrected item total was below 0.50. Cronbach's alpha was used to evaluate the scale reliability (over 0.7)" (p. 154).

### Sample

The sample was derived from the Society of Manufacturing Engineers (SME). "The SME has 65,000 members (manufacturing managers and engineers) from all over the world in almost every industry. Final version of the questionnaire was administered through a large-scale mailing to 2,831 manufacturing managers who were randomly selected from SME's U.S. membership database. There were 303 usable responses from both mailings. Nonresponse bias was tested by comparing early respondents and late respondents. Two groups were compared on the basis of firm size, industry type, and sales volume. No statistically significant differences were found using the chi-square statistic at $p < 0.05$" (p. 155). Further information on the sample characteristics is provided in Appendix A of the article.

### Reliability and Validity

Unidimensionality, discriminant validity, and reliability were tested for MBMP and CC. But regarding MC, the results from Tu, Vonderembse, and Ragu-Nathan (2001) were presented as the evidence of reliability and validity. MBMP was the second-order construct with three dimensions. Therefore, to check its validity, the authors conducted three analyses. Reliability analysis was conducted by examining the CITC scores. Exploratory factor analysis (EFA) was used to ensure the unidimensionality of each of the three dimensions in MBMP. All MBMP items were submitted together to a latent-variable-level analysis. To check the unidimensionality of CC items, EFA was performed. Alpha score was .91 for the five items of CC constructs.

### Scores

MBMP's large-scale reliability and construct level factor analysis results appear in Tables 2 and 3 in the article. Unidimensionality values of CC appear in Table 4. Figure 2 shows the overall results from the LISREL structural equation model.

### Other Evidence

Not available.

### References


Kerlinger, F. N. 1978. *Foundations of behavioral research.* New York: McGraw-Hill.

Schilling, M. A. 2000. Toward a general modular systems theory and its application to interfirm product modularity. *Academy of Management Review* 25 (2): 312–34.

Tu, Q., M. A. Vonderembse, and T. S. Ragu-Nathan. 2001. The impact of time-based manufacturing practices on mass customization and value to customer. *Journal of Operations Management* 19 (2): 201–17.

# Tucker

## Article Summarized

Tucker, Anita L. 2004. The impact of operational failures on hospital nurses and their patients. *Journal of Operations Management* 22 (2): 151–69.

## Scales (Actual Questions Used)

*Interruption*

1. Inconsequential interruption, such as when between tasks
2. Tasks that posed low risk to patient safety if interrupted but involved cognitive setup time
3. Tasks that could result in medical errors if RN was distracted (i.e., preparing medications)
4. Direct patient care tasks done in the presence of patient (i.e., patient bathing, assessment, or passing medications)

*Delay*

5. Tasks not related to immediate patient care (i.e., personal time and assigning patients to rooms or nurses to patients).
6. Indirect patient care with no time requirements (i.e., documentation).
7. Patient care tasks that were moderately time-sensitive because of patient comfort or health but were scheduled at the discretion of RN (i.e., meals, bathing, or changing linens)
8. Patient care tasks scheduled for specific times (i.e., medication administration, preparing patients for surgery, laboratory tests, vital sign assessments, treatments)

*Risk*

9. No foreseeable risk to patient such as looking for ordering forms, housekeeping
10. Failure caused discomfort to patient (i.e., delayed food tray)
11. Potential for risk given other conditions being present (i.e., confusing orders, missing medication)
12. Failure by itself could potentially cause patient harm (i.e., last minute medication cancellations or missed orders)

*Losses*

13. Wasted material or medication
14. Patient or RN aware of failure potentially causing a loss of confidence in quality of care provided in hospital
15. Patient procedure delayed by a few hrs or a procedure performed unnecessarily
16. Failure postponed patient's procedure until following day

## Construct Description

The term *construct* was not used in the article until the appendix. The author stated that "PCA [principal components analysis] is a statistical technique that can be used to determine if a subset of the variables are correlated and collectively account for a large enough percentage of the total variance to be considered as a distinguishable dimension, or construct. These distinguishable constructs are called components" (p. 167). Three "constructs" were thus derived using PCA: (1) complexity, (2) patient care efficiency, and (3) interaction. The constructs were named based on the associated factor loadings.

### Measurement Description

The measures fell into two broad categories—description of the failures and failure impacts. The measures were recorded by the author through her direct close observation. "At the outset, we defined a "failure" as a problem in the supply of information, material, equipment, or services that interrupted the nurse's work" (p. 155). This definition was revised as "whether there were failures in work system design that resulted in the worker being less effective than he or she otherwise might have been . . . Two general categories of operational failures emerged: problems and errors" (p. 155). A problem was defined as "a disruption in ability to execute a prescribed task," and a system error was given as "the execution of a task that is subsequently determined to be unnecessary or wrong" (p. 155).

### Development

This article used qualitative data involving floor observations of nurses by the author. The development of the measures "emerged" from observation and interviews.

### Sample

The author spent "239 hours shadowing 26 different nurses at nine hospitals and recording detailed information about their work activities. . . . The nurses observed typically were experienced employees who had worked for at least 3 years on their care unit. . . . The observation process entailed close shadowing of a nurse" (p. 154). A total of 194 errors were observed during the study period.

### Reliability and Validity

The coding scheme was changed because of low internal validity of the original working definition. Other than this, validity was not specifically discussed. Since there were no multi-item scales, there were no traditional reliability measures. However, the reliability of the coding scheme was assessed. The author notes, "To test reliability of the coding scheme, we performed two sets of analyses. First, the author and another person unaffiliated with the research project independently coded 41 excerpts as either a failure or not a failure. Second, we coded the sources of 20 different failures. Agreements between our ratings were evaluated using the kappa statistic, which is appropriate to use for interrater reliability when there are a fixed number of choices. Kappa accounts for the expected probability that codes will match because of random chance. A kappa value of 0 means that the amount of agreement is the same as would be expected by guessing randomly, a negative value is worse than chance, and a positive value is better than chance. The kappa value for whether an excerpt was or was not a failure was .81 (standard error .15), which is considered almost perfect agreement (Landis and Koch, 1977). We had complete agreement for failure type, yielding a kappa of 1.0. The high level of interrater reliability increased our confidence in the validity of the coding scheme and the reliability of having one person code the remaining transcripts" (p. 156).

### Scores

Descriptive statistics for operational failure impact measures are given in Table 4 in the article. Cost and impact of operational failures are reported in Table 5. Factor loadings for measure of operational failure impact are specified in Table A.1 in the article.

### Other Evidence

Not available.

### Reference

Landis, J. R., and G. G. Koch. 1977. The measurement of observer agreement for categorical data. *Biometrics* 33 (1): 159–74.

# Venkatesh, Speier, and Morris

## Article Summarized

Venkatesh, Viswanath, Cheri Speier, and Michael G. Morris. 2002. User acceptance enablers in individual decision making about technology: Toward an integrated model. *Decision Sciences* 33 (2): 297–316.

## Scales (Actual Questions Used)

*Intrinsic Motivation (IM)*

1. I find the system to be enjoyable.
2. The actual process of using the system is pleasant.
3. I have fun using the system.

*Perceived Ease of Use (EOU)*

4. My interaction with the system is clear and understandable.
5. Interacting with the system does not require a lot of my mental effort.
6. I find the system to be easy to use.
7. I find it easy to get the system to do what I want it to do.

*Perceived Usefulness (U)*

8. Using the system improves my performance in my job.
9. Using the system in my job increases my productivity.
10. Using the system enhances my effectiveness on the job.
11. I find the system to be useful in my job.

*Behavioral Intention (BI)*

12. Assuming I had access to the system, I intend to use it.
13. Given that I had access to the system, I predict that I would use it.

## Construct Description

The constructs studied in the article were all identified by previous research in the technology acceptance literature. No explicit definitions were provided in the current article.

## Measurement Description

All constructs were operationalized using multi-item perceptual scales. Each item was measured using a 7-point Likert scale.

## Development

Previously developed and validated scales were adopted to measure the different constructs. Among the four scales, three—perceived usefulness (U), perceived ease of use (EOU), and behavioral intention (BI)—were constructed and tested in Davis, Bagozzi, and Warshaw (1989) and validated in other studies (Davis, Bagozzi, and Warshaw 1992; Venkatesh 1999; Venkatesh and Speier 1999). "The scale for intrinsic motivation (IM) was developed and tested in Davis et al. (1992)" (p. 306).

### Sample

The empirical data from the Venkatesh (1999) and Venkatesh and Speier (1999) were reanalyzed in the article. In addition, "the current work extends the cross-sectional analysis presented in the initial study by collecting field data for an additional six months. Specifically, in order to provide a longitudinal perspective, user reactions are measured after three months, and usage is measured for the six-month period after the first wave of data collection (post-training)" (p. 305).

### Validity and Reliability

Structural equation modeling was used to estimate the measurement model. The authors reported that "all constructs satisfied the criteria of reliability (Cronbach's alpha greater than .90) and convergent and discriminant validity" (p. 306).

### Scores

The scores are presented in Tables 2 and 3 in the article.

### Other Evidence

Not available.

### References

Davis, F. D., R. P. Bagozzi, and P. R. Warshaw. 1989. User acceptance of computer technology: A comparison of two theoretical models. *Management Science* 35 (8): 982–1002.

———. 1992. Extrinsic and intrinsic motivation to use computers in the workplace. *Journal of Applied Social Psychology* 22 (14): 1111–32.

Venkatesh, V. 1999. Creation of favorable user perceptions: Exploring the role of intrinsic motivation. *MIS Quarterly* 23 (2): 239–60.

Venkatesh, V., and C. Speier. 1999. Computer technology training in the workplace: A longitudinal investigation of the effect mood. *Organizational Behavior and Human Decision Process* 79 (1): 1–28.

## Veuglers and Cassiman

### Article Summarized

Veuglers, Reinhilde and Bruno Cassiman. 1999. Make and buy in innovation strategies: Evidence from Belgian manufacturing firms. *Research Policy* 28 (1): 63–80.

### Scales (Actual Questions Used)

*Importance of Internal Information Sources of the Firm for Innovation*

1. Information within the company
2. Information within the group
3. Importance of close competitors as information sources of the firm for innovation

*Importance of Scientific Information Sources*

4. Information from universities
5. Information from public research institutes
6. Information from technical institutes

*Importance of Cost-Efficiency Goal of the Firm*

7. Increasing flexibility
8. Lowering wage cost
9. Lowering material usage
10. Lowering energy usage
11. Lowering design cost
12. Lowering setup time
13. Lessen environmental effects
14. Improve work environment and job security

*Importance of Quality Improvement Goal of the Firm*

15. Increase product quality
16. Replace older products

*Importance of Protection Mechanisms for Product and Process Innovations of the Firm*

17. Legal: patents, registration (brands, copy rights, etc.)
18. Secrecy
19. Complexity of product or process design
20. Lead time on competitors

*Importance of Cost and Risk Obstacle for Innovation by the Firm*

21. Risk too high
22. No suitable financing available
23. High costs of innovation
24. Payback period too long
25. Innovation cost hard to control
26. Uncertainty about introduction times

*Importance of Lack of Information for Innovation as an Obstacle to Innovation by the Firm*

27. Lack of qualified personnel
28. Lack of personnel to innovate
29. Lack of information on technology
30. Lack of market information

*Importance of No Need for Innovation as an Obstacle to Innovation by the Firm*

31. No need for innovation because of earlier innovations
32. Little interest for innovations by the customers

*Importance of Lack of Opportunities for Innovation as an Obstacle to Innovation by the Firm*

33. Lack of external technical services
34. Few opportunities for cooperation
35. Lack of technological opportunities
36. Importance of resistance within the firm as an obstacle to innovation by the firm
37. Importance of ease of imitation of innovations as an obstacle to innovation by the firm

## Construct Description

Not available.

### Measurement Description

A 13-page questionnaire, in which "respondents were asked to rate the importance to their innovation strategy of different information sources for the innovation process, goals for innovation, protection of innovations and obstacles to innovation. Firms had to rate their answer on a 5-point Likert scale [from unimportant (1) to crucial (5)]" (p. 70). The details of the measurement description can be found in Eurostat Community Innovation Survey (1993).

### Development

Not available.

### Sample

The data used in the study were obtained as part of the Community Innovation Survey (CIS) conducted by Eurostat in the different member countries in 1993. The subsample used in the analysis focused innovation data on the Belgian manufacturing industry. The 13-page questionnaires were mailed out to a representative sample of 1,335 Belgian manufacturing firms. The response rate was greater than 50% with an overall sample size of 748, and no systematic nonrespondent bias could be detected.

### Reliability and Validity

Not available.

### Scores

The scores are presented in Tables 2–5 in the article.

### Other Evidence

Not available.

### Reference

None.

---

## Vickery

### Article Summarized

Vickery, Shawnee K. 1991. A theory of production competence revisited. *Decision Sciences* 22 (3): 635–43.

### Scales (Actual Questions Used)

*Production Competence*

- Adaptive manufacturing
- Cost efficiency of labor
- Delivery performance
- Logistics
- Production economies of scale
- Process technology

- Quality performance
- Throughput and lead time
- Vertical integration

### Construct Description

Production competence is meta-construct that is composed of nine items and "is closely tied to the development and implementation of manufacturing strategy and can best be understood within this context" (p. 641). According to the authors, production competence provided "a 'snapshot' of the performance or effectiveness of manufacturing with respect to its current set of competitive priorities" (p. 641).

### Measurement Description

The operational definition of production competence covered nine areas presented in the scale section above. For each area, the importance of the area was first ranked on a 9-point scale ranging from 1 = "lowest importance," to 9 = "highest importance," and subsequently the performance of the company in the area was evaluated as +1 = "strong," 0 = "neutral," or –1 = "weak." Finally, a single score numerical value of production competence was calculated as the sum of the products of rank and evaluation of the nine areas.

### Development

The measure of production competence was offered as a correction of the numerical measure of production competence proposed by Cleveland, Schroeder, and Anderson (1989). The ranking scheme was revised so that higher priority areas were now assigned higher numbers (ranks) to demonstrate the greater importance of the area. Modification was also made in measuring business performance. To avoid overlap in the measures of production competence and business performance, and to reduce redundancy, the authors excluded the manufacturing-related items from Cleveland, Schroeder, and Anderson's (1989) aggregate index of business performance. Instead, the current study formed the overall business performance index by only summing three ratings—pretax return on assets, market share, and growth rate.

### Sample

The measures were applied to the example firms presented in Cleveland, Schroeder, and Anderson (1989). Detailed information regarding sampling approaches was not reported in this article.

### Validity and Reliability

Not available.

### Scores

Production competence scores are given in Table 2 (p. 638) in the article. Business performance scores are provided on p. 637 in the article.

### Other Evidence

Not available.

### Reference

Cleveland, G., R. G. Schroeder, and J. C. Anderson. 1989. A theory of production competence. *Decision Sciences* 20 (4): 655–68.

# Vickery, Dröge, and Germain

### Article Summarized

Vickery, Shawnee K. Cornelia Dröge, and Richard Germain. 1999. The relationship between product customization and organizational structure. *Journal of Operations Management* 17 (4): 377–91.

### Scales (Actual Questions Used)

*Formal Benchmarking Control*

1. Functional costs (e.g., transportation, manufacturing, selling)
2. Customer service (e.g., fill rate, cycle time, on-time delivery)
3. Productivity levels
4. Operations (e.g., warehousing, manufacturing, transportation)

*Formal Internal Control*

5. Functional costs (e.g., selling, transportation, manufacturing)
6. Customer service (e.g., fill rate, cycle time, on-time delivery)
7. Cost controls by fixing standard costs and analyzing variation
8. Productivity analysis
9. Customer satisfaction and follow-up

*Formal Supplier Control*

10. Distribution services (e.g., on-time delivery, fill rate)
11. Product quality (e.g., number of defects)
12. Competitive price
13. Personnel/management quality
14. Manufacturing compatibility/capacity
15. Engineering capability

*Operations Decentralization*

16. The number of workers required
17. Allocation of work among available workers
18. Internal labor disputes
19. Overtime at the plant level
20. Plant equipment or machinery to be used

*Layers*

21. Business unit
22. Manufacturing function
23. Distribution
24. Marketing

*Spans*

25. CEO
26. Senior marketing executive
27. Senior manufacturing executive
28. Senior distribution executive

*Environmental Uncertainty*

29. Marketing practices
30. Competitor actions
31. Demand and customer tastes
32. Production processes

## Construct Description

This study examined the "relationship between the extent of use of a product customization strategy and organizational structure" (p. 377). There were seven constructs in this study: (1) product customization, (2) formal control, (3) operations decentralization, (4) layers, (5) spans, (6) size, and (7) environmental uncertainty.

Formal control, operations decentralization, layers, and spans were dependent variables that represented organizational structure. Formal control was taken as synonymous with after-the-fact measurement of performance, which encompassed the measurement of competitive, internal, and supplier performance. Operations decentralization referred to the vertical locus of production decision-making authority in the firm. Layers were the levels in a chain of command. Spans of the control were equal to the number of subordinates reporting directly to a supervisor.

Size and environmental uncertainty were two control variables. The former indicated the scale of the firm, while the latter connoted "uncertainty as opposed to stability with respect to an organization's markets, demand, customer tastes, technology, government regulations" (p. 379).

The independent variable product customization captured a company's make-to-order (MTO) capability. It focused on measuring the degree to which production was undertaken after customers' orders were received.

## Measurement Description

Product customization was assessed in terms of a company's MTO capability. It was quantified on a continuum ranging from 0% to 100%. Besides, three other variables were captured: (1) number of finished goods field warehouses (mean = 12.9), (2) percentage of sales made on a just-in-time (JIT) basis (mean = 19.9%), and (3) percentage of inbound shipments made on a JIT basis (mean = 25.6%). These variables were measured on open-ended scales.

Items representing formal control, which consisted of formal benchmarking control, formal internal control, and formal supplier control were operationalized on Likert-type scales. For example, formal benchmarking control was measured as the sum of four 7-point scales with endpoints, ranking from "used rarely or for small part of operations" to "used frequently or throughout the firm" for the extent to which performance was compared with industry standards or competitors. Similarly, operations decentralization was quantified as the sum of five Likert-type scales with endpoints ranging from "decision made above chief executive" to "individual below first-level supervisors." However, the other two organizational design variables, layers and spans, were measured as the sum of open-ended scales. Environmental uncertainty was measured as the sum of four 7-point scales with endpoints describing environmental opposites. The other control variable size was calculated by taking the natural logarithm of annual sales.

## Development

Few details were provided regarding the development of the items and scales. Most of the scales used in the study were adapted from the existing literature. For instance, the formal internal control was based on the control scale by Khandwalla (1974), and environmental uncertainty was measured using the summed scale of Miller and Dröge (1986).

## Sample

The data were collected by mail surveys from a sample of 1,000 randomly selected companies from the Council of Logistics Management manufacturers' membership list. The target respondents were logistics managers. Of the 1,000 questionnaires administered, 261 surveys were returned and 44 of them were non-deliverable. Hence, the response rate was 22.7%. In addition, eight responses were discarded due to missing values and 26 were deleted "because they were completed by retailers, wholesalers or distributor subsidiaries of manufacturing concerns" (p. 382). This yielded a final sample of 183 useful responses. According to the 183 effective responses obtained, the sample covered various companies across different industries and company sizes. Detailed information can be found on p. 382 of the article.

### Reliability and Validity

Item-to-item correlations and Cronbach's coefficient alpha were calculated to assess scale reliability. Since all alpha values were larger than .70, the scales were deemed to be reliable. Construct validity was assessed by using confirmatory factor analysis (CFA). The fit indices of the measurement model revealed an acceptable level of model fit. According to the authors, these CFA results obtained indicated support for construct validity.

### Scores

The correlation matrix and summary statistics of the variables, the path estimates and *t*-values obtained by fitting the structural model, and the subgroup analysis results obtained using multiple regressions are presented in Tables 1–3 of the article.

### Other Evidence

Not available.

### References

Khandwalla, P. 1974. Mass output orientation of operations technology and organizational structure. *Administrative Science Quarterly* 19: 74–97.

Miller, D., and C. Dröge. 1986. Psychological and traditional determinants of structure. *Administrative Science Quarterly* 31: 539–60.

## Vickery, Dröge, Stank, Goldsby, and Markland

### Article Summarized

Vickery, Shawnee K., Cornelia Dröge, Theodore P. Stank, Thomas J. Goldsby, and Robert E. Markland. 2004. The performance implications of media richness in a business-to-business service environment: Direct versus indirect effects. *Management Science* 50 (8): 1106–19.

### Scales (Actual Questions Used)

*Media Richness*

1. The third-party logistics (3PL) provider uses visual (in person) modes of communication.
2. The 3PL uses audio (telephone) modes of communication.
3. The 3PL uses electronic (e-mail, EDI) modes of communication.

*Relational Performance*

4. The 3PL knows customers' needs well.
5. The 3PL cooperates with us to help do the job well.

6. The 3PL provides valuable feedback.
7. The 3PL makes recommendations for continuous improvement on an ongoing basis.

*Customer Satisfaction*

8. Please rate your overall satisfaction with the quality of the 3PL's logistical service.
9. I am delighted with my firm's overall relationship with this service provider.
10. I wish more of my firm's service providers were like this one.
11. There is always some problem or another with this provider (reverse-scaled item).

*Customer Loyalty*

12. The relationship that my firm has with this service provider is something we are very committed to.
13. The relationship that my firm has with this service provider is something we intend to maintain indefinitely.
14. Maintaining a long-term relationship with this provider is very important to my firm.

**Construct Description**

The constructs used in this article included media richness, relational performance, customer satisfaction, and customer loyalty. The definition of media richness followed the conceptualization developed by Daft and Lengel (1984) through their five-stage continuum framework. Specifically, for the purpose of this study, the authors looked at the feedback, channel, source, and language characteristics of the medium to define its richness. Likewise, the definition for relational performance in a business-to-business (B2B) context was adapted from previous work by Stank, Goldsby, and Vickery (1999) and Leuthesser (1997) and was given as "the extent of activities/behaviors directed toward initiating, developing, and/or maintaining successful industrial relational exchanges" (p. 1110). Customer satisfaction was described by the authors as "cumulative overall satisfaction" as adapted from the previous literature by Leuthesser and Kohli (1995). Finally, the authors defined customer loyalty as "a long-term commitment to repurchase involving both a favorable attitude toward the seller and repeated patronage" (p. 1111). Previous work by Cronin and Morris (1989) and Morgan and Hunt (1994) highlighted the need for this long-term focus.

**Measurement Description**

A total of 14 items were grouped into four factors: (1) media richness, (2) relational performance, (3) customer satisfaction, and (4) customer loyalty. The first factor—media richness—included three items that were operationalized using a Likert-type 7-point response format ranging from 1 = "strongly disagree" to 7 = "strongly agree." The second factor—relational performance—had four items that were operationalized in the same way. The third factor—customer satisfaction—also had four items. With the exceptions of question 4 (a reverse-scaled item) and question 1, which had a different response categories (i.e., ranging from 1 = "very poor" to 7 = "excellent"), the remaining items were gauged on the same 7-point Likert scales as factors 1 and 2. The last factor—customer loyalty—included three items that were again operationalized like the first two factors. Respondents were given the option to answer "N/A" ("not applicable") to any question that they felt did not apply to them.

**Development**

The scales in this study were developed from the existing literature and input from a panel of experts, who included two logistics researchers, two executives from third-party logistics (3PLs) organizations, and one executive from a consulting firm. This panel pretested the survey instrument to determine its validity.

**Sample**

This study focused on all 3PLs organizations that offered a comprehensive set of logistics services in the United States. Therefore, the sampling frame for this study was the 68 U.S. 3PL firms, minus two firms that were acquired by others for a total of 66 firms. The overall response rate was 53% for a total sample size of 35 respondents, who were the top executives of the firms. The top executive was then asked to identify their customers. If they could not, the *Armstrong & Associates Directory* (Armstrong & Associates 1999) was used to locate executives. A total of 129 customers, with 99 identified by the executives and 30 from the directory, were listed as the sampling frame and e-mailed the questionnaire. The overall response rate was 89%. Thus, the final sample data for this study came from 113 customer respondents, who were identified as the persons who worked closest with the 3PL.

### Reliability and Validity

The authors used confirmatory factor analysis (CFA) to determine the validity of the measurement scales used in the study (Anderson and Gerbing 1988). The CFA results, including $\chi^2$, comparative fit index (CFI), and goodness-of-fit index (GFI) statistics, among others (Bentler 1990; Bollen 1989), showed an acceptable model fit. The CFA also revealed that all measurement items loaded significantly on their designated latent factors as evidenced by the standardized factor loading estimates. Hence, convergent validity was supported. Discriminant validity was assessed using nested models. The authors reported that "all alternative models having a correlation between latent variables fixed to one fit worse than the original model" (p. 1115), which demonstrated discriminant validity. In addition, Cronbach's coefficient alphas were computed. All the measurement scales were found to be reliable with alpha values above .80.

### Scores

The Cronbach's coefficient alphas for each of the factors and the fit statistics for the initial model are shown in Tables 4–6 of the article.

### Other Evidence

Not available.

### References

Anderson, J. C., and D. W. Gerbing. 1988. Structural equation modeling in practice: A review and recommended two-step approach. *Psychological Bulletin* 103 (3): 411–23.

Armstrong & Associates. 1999. *Armstrong's guide to third party logistics services providers.* Vol. 7. Stoughton, WI: Armstrong & Associates.

Bentler, P. M. 1990. Fit indexes, Lagrange multipliers, constraint changes, and incomplete data in structural models. *Multivariate Behavioral Research* 25 (2): 163–72.

Bollen, K. A. 1989. *Structural equations with latent variables.* New York: Wiley.

Cronin, J. J., Jr., and M. H. Morris. 1989. Satisfying customer expectations: The effect on conflict and repurchase intentions in industrial marketing channels. *Journal of the Academy of Marketing Science* 17 (1): 41–9.

Daft, R.L., and R. H. Lengel, 1984. Information richness: A new approach to managerial behavior and organizational design. In *Research in organizational behavior,* Vol. 6, eds. L. L. Cummings and B. M. Staw, 191–233. Homewood, IL: JAI Press.

Leuthesser, L. 1997. Supplier relational behavior: An empirical assessment. *Industrial Marketing Management* 26 (3): 245–54.

Leuthesser, L., and A. K. Kohli. 1995. Relational behavior in business markets: Implications for relationship management. *Journal of Business Research* 34 (3): 221–33.

Morgan, R. M., and S. D. Hunt. 1994. The commitment-trust theory of relationship marketing. *Journal of Marketing* 58 (3): 20–38.

Stank, T. P., T. J. Goldsby, and S. K. Vickery. 1999. Effect of service supplier performance on satisfaction and loyalty of store managers in the fast food industry. *Journal of Operations Management* 17 (4): 429–47.

# Vickery, Dröge, Yeomans, and Markland

### Article Summarized

Vickery, Shawnee K., Cornelia L. M. Dröge, James M. Yeomans, Robert E. Markland. 1995. Time-based competition in the furniture industry. *Production and Inventory Management Journal* 36 (4): 14–21.

### Scales (Actual Questions Used)

*Strategic Importance*

1. Product development cycle time
2. New product introduction
3. Production lead time
4. Delivery speed

*Responsibility*

5. Product development cycle time
6. New product introduction
7. Production lead time
8. Delivery speed

*Performance*

9. Product development cycle time
10. New product introduction
11. Production lead time
12. Delivery speed

*Business Performance*

Financial Measures

13. After-tax return on assets
14. Before-tax return on assets
15. Return on investment (ROI)
16. Growth in ROI
17. Sales growth
18. Return on sales (ROS)
19. Growth in ROS

Marketing Measures

20. Market share
21. Market share growth

### Construct Description

Time-based competition was defined as "a competitive strategy that seeks to compress the time required to propose, develop, manufacture, market, and deliver products" (p. 14). Four constructs were developed to cover the domain of this construct. The definitions of each are provided below.

Product development cycle time reflected "the ability to minimize the time it takes to develop new products" (p. 15). New product introduction was developed to capture "the ability to rapidly introduce large numbers of product improvements/variations or completely new products" (p. 15). Production lead time was conceptualized as "the ability to reduce the time it takes to manufacture products" (p. 15).

Delivery speed was related to "the ability to reduce the time between order taking and customer delivery to as close to zero as possible" (p. 15).

### Measurement Description

All perceptual multi-item scales were quantified on 7-point Likert-type scales. Additional objective data were also used to measure performance.

### Development

Much of the initial survey development was based on the literature and several months of interviews and refinement. "The face validity . . . was established through pretesting. Several personal interviews were conducted, some on site" (p. 15). Based on the feedback from the interviews, modifications were made, including the addition of financial performance.

### Sample

The target population of the study was strategic business units (SBUs) or autonomous divisions and individual firms in the furniture industry. "All firms, SBUs, and/or autonomous divisions listed under relevant Standard Industrial Codes whose sales revenues exceeded approximately $10million" (p. 15) were contacted for participation. A total of 65 SBUs, autonomous divisions, and individual firms in the furniture industry agreed to participate. The response rate was approximately 20%, "based on the total number of firms (inclusive of parent companies or SBUs according to applicability) in the original population" (p. 15). The empirical data were mainly collected through telephone interviews with CEOs or directors from these participating companies. Among the 65 companies in the final sample, mean sales were about 122 million dollars and mean number of employees was about 1,364.

### Reliability and Validity

The face validity of the questionnaire was established by interviews conducted with managers. Based on these interviews, some wordings of the items were changed. The further discussion on reliability or validity is provided in the article.

### Scores

The summary statistics are given in Table 2 of the article.

### Other Evidence

Not available.

### Reference

None.

## Vickery, Jayaram, Dröge, and Calantone

### Article Summarized

Vickery, Shawnee K., Jayanth Jayaram, Cornelia Dröge, and Roger Calantone. 2003. The effects of an integrative supply chain strategy on customer service and financial performance: An analysis of direct versus indirect relationships. *Journal of Operations Management* 21 (5): 523–39.

### Scales (Actual Questions Used)

*Integrative Information Technologies*

1. Integrated EDI
2. Integrated IS
3. Computerized production systems

*Supply Chain Integration*

4. Supplier partnering
5. Closer customer relationships
6. Cross-functional teams

*Customer Service*

7. Presale customer service
8. Product support
9. Responsiveness to customers
10. Delivery speed
11. Delivery dependability

*Financial Performance*

12. Pretax ROA
13. Return on investment
14. Return on sales

### Construct Description

Four constructs were investigated in this study. Two of them—customer service and financial performance—were performance constructs. The customer service construct captured service and delivery-related issues, and reflected general performance dimensions and those germane to a manufacturing context, while the financial performance construct was defined solely from the financial perspective.

The remaining two constructs—integrative information technologies and supply chain integration were developed to tap the domain of integrated supply chain strategy from two aspects: technologies and practices, both inter- and intrafirm. Specifically, integrative information technologies increased "the flow of relevant information amongst process participants" (p. 525), both within the firm (e.g., computerized production systems for manufacturing integrated IS) and external (e.g., EDI). Supply chain integration encompassed both intrafirm as well as interfirm integration, since the internal functions were as much a part of the supply chain as the external.

### Measurement Description

A total of 14 items were used to operationalize the four constructs. The operational definitions of these measurement items are provided in Appendix A of the article (p. 536). The six items comprising the constructs of integrated information technologies and supply chain integration constructs were measured on 7-point Likert scales with endpoints of 1 = "extremely low use of initiative" and 7 = "extremely high use of initiative." The option of "not used" was offered as well. Similarly, the four-item scale for customer service and three-item scale for financial performance were also gauged on 7-point scales but with different response categories. The former had responses categories ranging from 1 = "poor" to 7 = "excellent," while the latter had endpoints of 1 = "worse in industry" and 7 = "best in industry."

### Development

Most measurement items were adapted from the existing scales. For instance, the measurement scales for the customer service construct followed Stank, Daugherty, and Ellinger (1999). The measurement items included in the integrative information technologies were grounded in the existing literature.

### Sample

The sampling frame of this study was constructed "with the assistance of a panel of experts from the Automotive Industry Action Group (AIAG), a professional association with over 1000 members" (p. 530). Based on these experts' opinion, the top 150 in terms of annual sales and that were independently owned, first-tier suppliers of GM, Ford, and Chrysler were selected for sampling. "These suppliers account for over 90% of the purchasing sales volume by North American automobile manufacturers" (p. 530). Questionnaires were mailed to the CEOs, or directors, of these 150 companies. The final sample consisted of 57 firms that yielded a response rate of 38%. Follow-up investigation on nonrespondents and late respondents indicated that no statistically significant nonresponse bias was detected.

### Reliability and Validity

The authors used a panel of experts to assist "in the development and pre-testing of the questionnaire. The only substantive changes made were to ensure that the definitions of items were meaningful and comprehensive for the sample. This ensured content validity" (p. 530). A confirmatory factor analysis (CFA) was performed on the measurement model. The overall model fit was good, and "all specified factor loadings were highly significant, which indicates good convergent validity among the measures of each construct. The Lagrange Multiplier (LM) test for omitted paths revealed no significant cross-loadings among the items, indicating discriminant validity. Good convergent and discriminant validities are indicators of construct validity" (p. 533).

### Scores

Correlations and summary statistics are given in Table 2 of the article. The results of CFA are displayed in Table 3. Path model results are presented in Table 4.

### Other Evidence

Not available.

### Reference

Stank, T. P., P. J. Daugherty, and A. E. Ellinger. 1999. Marketing/logistics integration and firm performance. *International Journal of Logistics Management* 10 (1): 11–24.

## Voss and Blackmon

### Article Summarized

Voss, Chris, and Kate Blackmon. 1998. Differences in manufacturing strategy decisions between Japanese and Western manufacturing plants: The role of strategic time orientation. *Journal of Operations Management* 16 (2/3): 147–58.

### Scales (Actual Questions Used)

*Measures of Short-Term Orientation*

1. To what degree is manufacturing driven by the need to meet short-term financial, budget, and output requirements?

*Measures of Long-Term Orientation*

2. To what degree is there a process for translating corporate and marketing goals into a manufacturing strategy?
3. How much can manufacturing influence the development of corporate strategies and goals?

*Adoption of Strategic Manufacturing Practices*

4. Total productive maintenance
5. Quality policy deployment
6. Kaizen/continuous improvement
7. Total quality management
8. Quality function deployment
9. Zero defects
10. Single-minute die exchange
11. Statistical process control
12. Simultaneous engineering

**Construct Description**

The research examined constructs pertaining to strategic orientation and the adoption of best manufacturing practices. Strategic time orientation was defined as "the extent to which an organization focuses on either the long-term or the short-term" (p. 150). It was described "in terms of planning time horizons, the number of time periods over which an individual or organization plans its activities" (p. 150). Best manufacturing practices were characterized by the practice items listed in the Scales section above.

**Measurement Description**

Strategic time orientation was examined in two ways. First, the authors "sought indicators of strategic time orientation in the degree to which corporate and manufacturing strategic practices were linked" (p. 152). They "also questioned managers about the degree to which they were subjected to short-term pressures" (p. 152). Second, they "examined the adoption of manufacturing practices and performance that could be taken as indicators of longer-term orientation" (p. 152).

Three questions were used to assess the links between corporate and manufacturing strategy. The response to each question was measured on a 5-point Likert-type scale, with 1 = "being low" and 5 = "being high." A number of programs were selected as the key action programs. "Respondents were asked to identify the degree of use and perceived payoff from" (p. 154) these programs based on a 5-point Likert-type scale, from 1 = "being low" to 5 = "being high."

**Development**

Not available.

**Sample**

Data used in the study were taken from the International Manufacturing Strategy Survey, which was designed to gather data about practices and performance associated with manufacturing strategy in an international context. The mail survey was administered by research coordinators in 20 countries on a country-by-country basis. The survey instruments were delivered to companies in the International Standard Industrial Classification (ISIC) Division 38, manufacturer of fabricated metal products, machinery, and equipment. This study focused on the machinery industry. Overall 600 responses from managers in these 20 countries were received, of which 26 were from Japan. Please see Table 2 of the article for detailed information.

### Reliability and Validity

Not available.

### Scores

The scores on the links between corporate and manufacturing strategy are reported in Table 3 of the article. The differences in adoption and perceived payoff for selected strategic manufacturing practices are reported in Table 4.

### Other Evidence

Not available.

### Reference

None.

---

## Voss, Tsikriktsis, Funk, Yarrow, and Owen

### Article Summarized

Voss, Chris, Nikos Tsikriktsis, Benjamin Funk, David Yarrow, and Jane Owen. 2005. Managerial choice and performance in service management: A comparison of private sector organizations with further education colleges. *Journal of Operations Management* 23 (2): 179–95.

### Scales (Actual Questions Used)

*Human Resource Management Practices*

1. Recognition and reward
   (5-point scale): 1 = no feedback or recognition of service performance at the employee level, 5 = recognition is everyone's responsibility and is based on exceeding internal and external expectations.
2. Education and training for quality
   (5-point scale): 1 = limited training for quality, 5 = comprehensive quality training plan, training in quality values, tools, and techniques.
3. Employee involvement
   (5-point scale): 1 = blocked by attitudes of both management and employees, limited teamwork, 5 = employees are highly involved and able to make real contributions to business improvement, extensive teamwork.

*Quality Procedures*

4. Quality procedures and framework
   (5-point scale): 1 = no procedures for quality management in place, 5 = comprehensive framework followed for quality management.
5. Management involvement in quality leadership
   (5-point scale): 1 = managers are generally disinterested in quality issues, 5 = senior executives exert personal leadership of organization's overall quality program.

6. Collection and use of data on quality
   (5-point scale): 1 = fragmentary data collection of quality measures, 5 = actively collects data from a variety of sources on customer feedback, quality improvement, and competitors, as a basis of improvement and strategic planning.

*Service Quality*

7. Reliability
   (5-point scale): 1 = customers frequently feel let down, 5 = seen as an organization that you can always rely on to deliver the promised service.
8. Quality performance, relative to industry
   (5-point scale): 1 = poor overall quality record, compared with industry, 5 = achieved a reputation for excellence in quality services and products that is notable in the industry and significantly better than the competition.
9. Staff responsiveness
   (5-point scale): 1 = staff seen as slow to respond to customer needs, 5 = staff go out of their way to respond to customer needs even when not part of the core service.

*Employee Satisfaction*

10. Employee satisfaction
    (5-point scale): 1 = moderate or serious internal morale problems, 5 = optimism and confidence, highest levels of employee satisfaction.
11. Employee loyalty, relative to industry
    (5-point scale): 1 = high turnover, worse than industry average, 5 = staff turnover at low-end of industry, very high levels of loyalty and commitment.
12. Employee attitude
    (5-point scale): 1 = little respect for the services they deliver, 5 = understand and are fully committed to customer service.

*Customer Satisfaction*

13. Customer retention
    (5-point scale): 1 = high rate of customer turnover, 5 = customers are exceptionally loyal.
14. Customer base
    (5-point scale): 1 = the overall customer base is declining faster than competitors, 5 = the customer base is expanding, with many defecting from competitors.
15. Perceived value
    (quality/price): 1 = customer perception of value is lower than competitors, 5 = the organization is perceived in the market as offering high value.

## Construct Description

There were five constructs studied in the article. Of these five, three were performance constructs. The first construct—employee satisfaction—focused on the organizations' "overall human resource management performance" (p. 183). The other two—service quality and customer satisfaction—indicated the level of organizations' service quality and market performance, respectively. The remaining two constructs were developed to describe related practices adopted by the organization. Specifically, the human resource management construct defined the nature of the human resource management systems, while the quality procedure construct described "the quality procedures and frameworks that organizations have in place to help maintain and drive service quality" (p. 185).

### Measurement Description

Multi-item scales were employed to measure each construct and were derived from the International Service Study (ISS; Roth, Chase, and Voss 1997). The items for employee satisfaction included measures of employee loyalty, attitude, and satisfaction. The operational definition of service quality was based on the measures of staff responsiveness, courtesy, reliability, and relative performance. Measures of customer satisfaction, retention, and base were used to build the scale for customer satisfaction. To gauge all these measure items, 5-point scales were used. The specific response categories for each scale were presented early.

### Development

The ISS questionnaire was designed to investigate service management related issues in both public and private sector organizations (Roth, Chase, and Voss 1997). The initial survey instrument was pilot tested with public sector organizations and modified accordingly.

### Sample

The U.K. subset of the ISS (Roth, Chase, and Voss 1997) was used for this study. The data set consisted of 291 organizations with 229 representing the private and 62 representing the public sector (mainly education colleges). The authors noted that the study sample was biased toward leading service organizations, but they continued to argue that "such sampling is suitable for exploratory research investigating unique or complex phenomena" (p. 184).

### Reliability and Validity

To ensure reliability and validity, the ISS survey was "field tested, reviewed by subject experts, and where appropriate, revised before final use" (p. 184) (*see* Roth, Chase, and Voss 1997). For this study, Cronbach's coefficient alpha reliability values were all above acceptable values (.60), which proved scales to be internally consistent. Each scale was also validated with "factor analysis using maximum likelihood extraction" (p. 184). All the tests indicated that internal validity was achieved. In addition, the authors verified external validity by comparing the model against three established models: the Malcolm Baldrige National Quality Award (NIST 1996), the European Quality Award (European Foundation for Quality Management 1986), and from the United Kingdom, the Citizens' Charter 1996. Support was found for external validity.

### Scores

Correlations, descriptive statistics, and construct reliabilities are provided in Tables 1 and 2 of the article.

### Other Evidence

This research was based on the International Service Study, which was developed by Professor Chris Voss (London Business School) in the United Kingdom and Professors Aleda V. Roth (Clemson University) and Richard Chase (University of Southern California) in the United States (Roth, Chase, and Voss 1997; Roth, Gray, Singhal, and Singhal 1997). Several related articles provide other evidence and use of the ISS data in other sectors and countries (Chase, Roth, and Voss 1999; Froehle et al. 2000; Roth, Chase, and Voss 1997; Meyer et al. 1999; Voss et al. 1997, 2004).

### References

Chase R. B., A. V. Roth, and C. Voss, 1999. How do financial services stack up? Findings from a benchmarking study of the U.S. financial service sector. In *Creating value in financial services: Strategies, operations, and technologies,* eds. E. Melnick, P. Nayyar, M. Pinedo, and S. Seshardri, 427–47. Boston, MA: Kluwer Publishers.

European Foundation for Quality Management. 1986. *The European model for business excellence.* Brussels, Belgium: European Foundation for Quality Management.

Froehle, C. M., A. V. Roth, R. B. Chase, and C. A. Voss. 2000. Antecedents of new service development effectiveness: An exploratory examination of strategic operations choices. *Journal of Service Research* 3 (1): 3–17.

Meyer, A., R. Chase, A. V. Roth, C. Voss, K. U. Sperl, L. Menor, and K. Blackmon. 1999. Service competitiveness: An international benchmarking comparison of service practice and performance in Germany, UK, and USA. *International Journal of Service Industry Management* 10 (4): 369–79.

National Institute of Standards and Technology (NIST). 1996. *Malcolm Baldrige National Quality Award.* Gaithersburg, MD: National Institute of Standards and Technology.

Roth, A. V., Chase, R., and Voss, C. 1997. *Service in the US: Progress towards global service leadership.* Birmingham, UK: Severn Trent.

Roth, A. V., A. E. Gray, J. Singhal, and K. Singhal. 1997. International technology and operations management: Resource toolkit for research and teaching, *Production and Operations Management* 6 (2): 167–87.

Voss, C. A., K. Blackmon, R. Chase, E. L. Rose, and A. V. Roth. 1997. Service competitiveness: An Anglo-US study. *Business Strategy Review* 8 (1): 7–22.

Voss, C. A., A. V. Roth, E. D. Rosenzweig, K. Blackmon, and R. Chase. 2004. A tale of two countries' conservatism, service quality, feedback on customer satisfaction. *Journal of Service Research* 6 (3): 212–30.

---

# Wallace, Keil, and Rai

**Article Summarized**

Wallace, Linda, Mark Keil, and Arun Rai. 2004. How software project risk affects project performance: An investigation of the dimensions of risk and an exploratory model. *Decision Sciences* 35 (2): 289–321.

**Scales (Actual Questions Used)**

*Organizational Environment Risk*

1. Change in organizational management during the project
2. Corporate politics with negative effect on project
3. Unstable organizational environment
4. Organization undergoing restructuring during the project

*User Risk*

5. Users resistant to change
6. Conflict between users
7. Users with negative attitudes toward the project
8. Users not committed to the project
9. Lack of cooperation from users

*Requirements Risk*

10. Continually changing system requirements
11. System requirements not adequately identified
12. Unclear system requirements
13. Incorrect system requirements

*Project Complexity Risk*

14. Project involved the use of new technology
15. High level of technical complexity

16. Immature technology
17. Project involves use of technology that has not been used in prior projects

*Planning and Control Risk*

18. Lack of an effective project management methodology
19. Project progress not monitored closely enough
20. Inadequate estimation of required resources
21. Poor project planning
22. Project milestones not clearly defined
23. Inexperienced project manager
24. Ineffective communication

*Team Risk*

25. Inadequately trained development team members
26. Inexperienced team members
27. Team members lack specialized skills required by the project

*Product Performance Measure*

28. The application developed is reliable.
29. The application is easy to maintain.
30. The users perceive that the system meets intended functional requirements.
31. The system meets user expectations with respect to response time.
32. The overall quality of the developed application is high.

*Process Performance Measures*

33. The system was completed within budget.
34. The system was completed within schedule.

## Construct Description

Six dimensions of software project risk were identified. The first dimension—organizational environment risk—was related to "the risk or uncertainty surrounding the organizational environment in which a software project takes place" (p. 293). Second, user risk meant "the lack of user involvement during system development" (p. 293). The third dimension—requirements risk—was conceptualized as the uncertainty surrounding system requirements. The fourth dimension—project complexity risk—focused on "the risk related to inherent complexity of a software project, in terms of the difficulty of the project being undertaken" (p. 293). Next, planning and control risk captured the risk associated with unrealistic schedules and budgets added during the planning and control of the software development process. The last dimension—team risk—referred to "the issues associated with the project team members that can increase the uncertainty of project outcomes" (p. 293).

These six risk dimensions were employed to conceptualize three higher-level latent risk constructs: project management risk, technical subsystem risk, and social subsystem risk. The project management risk referred to variations in the distribution of possible outcomes from project management, which included planning and control risk and team risk. Social subsystem risk captured "the notion that a software is embedded within a social context that may be unstable or highly politicized, causing reductions in commitment and resources needed to successfully complete the project" (p. 295). Organizational environment risk and user risk were the two dimensions that constituted this second-order risk construct. Finally, technical subsystem risk reflected "the notion that a software project involves the creation of a technical artifact or some complexity that is described by a set of requirements" (p. 295). The requirements risk and project complexity risk were the two dimensions that tapped into the domain of technical subsystem risk construct.

In addition, project performance was the outcome construct investigated in the article. It was defined in terms of product and process performance. Product performance referred to the successfulness of the systems that were developed and process performance referred to the successfulness of the development process itself (i.e., extent to which the project was delivered on schedule and within budget).

### Measurement Description

In this article, risk was defined as three second-order constructs, each having two first-order constructs. Multiple items were developed to operationalize the associated dimension of risk.

### Development

This article conducted five phases to develop and to validate the instrument based on previous work by Churchill (1979) and Smith, Milberg, and Burke (1996). Figure 2 of the article depicted an overview of this methodology by phase: (1) specified the domain and dimensionality of the construct, (2) generated the item pool and sort items into dimensions of software project risk, (3) administered the instrument to practicing project managers and assess the reliability of the scales and modify items, (4) administered the instrument to a large sample of project managers, and (5) provided statistical refinement of measures (isolated scale analysis, scale pair analysis, and full-measurement model analysis).

After identifying the six dimensions from the literature, the authors conducted interviews with practicing software project managers to determine if they were consistent with how practitioners viewed the software project risk construct. Changes were made to generate the final measurement instrument. The scales were further refined through repeated model fittings based on an examination of the standardized loadings, modification indices, overall fit indices, interpretability, and content validity implications (Frohlich, 2002)" (p. 298). Regarding the two performance variables—product performance and process performance, measures were adapted from Rai and Al-Hindi (2000) and Nidumolu (1996).

### Sample

A Web-based survey was conducted to collect the data from software project managers. The participants selected were members of the Information Systems Special Interest Group (ISSIG) of Project Management Institute (PMI). An electronic newsletter was sent to individuals who shared their e-mail addresses with PMI-ISSIG and asked project managers to fill out the Web survey. At the time of the survey administration, there were about 7,200 members, and approximately 3,800 of them shared their e-mail addresses. A few weeks later, a paper newsletter was mailed out to all 7,200 members. A total of 507 survey responses were collected with a response rate of about 13.34%. The authors believed that most of the participants came from the 3,800 members who received an electronic request for participation. The sample "covered a wide variety of projects and varied from very small to very large projects" (p. 296). Of the 507 responding software project managers, 371 were males, 127 female, and the other 9 did not report the information on gender. More information on the respondents can be found in Appendix 1 (p. 320) of the article.

### Reliability and Validity

Structural equation modeling (SEM) using AMOS 4.01 was adopted to assess the psychometric properties of the scale. "Each scale model was examined in isolation, in pairs, and in a full-measurement model containing all indicators" (p. 296). Maximum likelihood estimation was selected as the estimation method. Analysis of the isolated models based on the refined scales indicated an acceptable level of model fit. The composite reliabilities for each of the six software project risk dimensions were .78 or above, which exceeded the threshold levels.

To evaluate the discriminant validity of the six, risk, multi-item measurement scales, models of each pair of latent variables were estimated (15 possible combinations of construct pairs). Confidence interval tests were performed as a way to further establish discriminant validity. In addition, according to the authors, the variance-extracted test was used to establish both discriminant and convergent validity.

### Scores

Table 3 shows the variance-extracted test for six dimensions of risk. Figure 3 displays details of measurement model of software project risk. The final SEM results appear in Figure 5 of the article.

### Other Evidence

Not available.

### References

Churchill, G. A. 1979. A paradigm for developing better measures of marketing constructs. *Journal of Marketing Research* 16 (1): 64–73.

Frohlich, M. T. 2002. E-integration in the supply chain: Barriers and performance. *Decision Sciences* 33 (4): 537–56.

Nidumolu, S. R. 1996. A comparison of the structural contingency and risk-based perspectives on coordination in software development projects. *Journal of Management Information Systems* 13 (2): 77–113.

Smith, H. J., S. J. Milberg, and S. J. Burke. 1996. Information privacy: Measuring individuals' concerns about organizational practices. *MIS Quarterly* 20 (2): 167–96.

Rai, A., and H. Al-Hindi. 2000. The effects of development process modeling and task uncertainty on development quality performance. *Information and Management* 37 (6): 335–46.

## Ward, Duray, Leong, and Sum

### Article Summarized

Ward, Peter T., Rebecca Duray, G. Keong Leong, and Chee-Chuong Sum. 1995. Business environment, operations strategy, and performance: An empirical study of Singapore manufacturers. *Journal of Operations Management* 13 (2): 99–115.

### Scales (Actual Questions Used)

*Environment*

Business Costs

1. Rising labor cost
2. Rising material cost
3. Rising transport cost
4. Rising telecommunication cost
5. Rising utilities cost
6. Rising rental cost
7. Rising health care cost
8. Strong Singapore dollar

Labor Availability

9. Shortage of managerial and administrative staff
10. Shortage of technicians
11. Shortage of clerical and related workers
12. Shortage of skilled workers

13. Shortage of production workers
14. Inability to operate third shift

Competitive Hostility

15. Keen competition in local markets
16. Keen competition in foreign markets
17. Low profit margins
18. Declining demand in local market
19. Declining demand in foreign market
20. Producing to the required quality standards
21. Unreliable vendor quality

Dynamism

22. Rate at which products and services become outdated
23. Rate of innovation of new products and services
24. Rate of innovation of new operation processes
25. Rate of change in taste and preferences of customers in your industry

*Competitive Priorities*

Cost

26. Reduce unit costs
27. Reduce material costs
28. Reduce overhead costs
29. Reduce inventory level

Quality

30. Reduce defective rates
31. Improve product performance and reliability
32. Improve vendor's quality
33. Implement quality control circles
34. Obtaining ISO 9000 certification

Flexibility

35. Reduce manufacturing lead time
36. Reduce procurement lead time
37. Reduce new product develop cycle
38. Reducing setup/changeover time

Delivery

39. Increase delivery reliability
40. Increase delivery speed
41. Improve presales service and technical support
42. Improve after-sales service

*Business Performance in 1992*

How did the company perform in 1992 as compared with the same period in 1991 for the following?

43. Profit before tax

### Construct Description

Four constructs were developed to characterize two important environmental dimensions identified in the literature (Dess and Beard 1984). Three of them—business costs, labor availability, and competitive hostility—were used to define environmental munificence, which was "the extent to which an environment supports growth of organizations within it" (p. 104). The dynamism construct captured "unpredictable change in environmental conditions faced by firms" (p. 104). The concept of competitive priorities was used to describe a manufacturer's choice of emphasis among key capabilities. Consistent with the literature, this study used low cost, quality, delivery performance, and flexibility to characterize the manufacturing competitive priorities.

### Measurement Description

Environment was measured in four dimensions: business costs (eight items), labor availability (six items), competitive hostility (seven items), and dynamism (four items). Competitive priorities were described as costs (four items), quality (five items), flexibility (four items), and delivery (four items). The measurement items related to environment and competitive priorities were rated on a 5-point Likert scale. Similarly, performance was measured perceptually as well. It was defined in terms of the manager's perception about the change in business performance between 1991 and 1992 (i.e., "increased," "remained the same," "decreased").

### Development

The measures were based on the existing literature.

### Sample

The data stemmed from "The Survey on Business Operations in Singapore" that was sponsored by the Singapore Manufacturers' Association (SMA). The questionnaires were sent to 1,000 companies "representing the manufacturing businesses in the populating of SMA member companies in 1993" (p. 106). Top executives (usually managing directors or general managers) were addressed, and responses were received from 319 firms (response rate 32%). Analysis of nonrespondents showed no proportional difference with respect to industry, and the asset value and employment data (given in Table 4) fitted the profile of Singaporean manufacturing as a whole. In addition, "Any firms that reported no change in profits are dropped from the analysis . . . High performers account for 124 respondents, and the low-performers category includes 112 responses" (p. 105).

### Reliability and Validity

Interitem analyses were performed to check the scales for internal consistency and reliability. Cronbach's coefficient alpha for each scale exceeded "by a comfortable margin the .50 to .60 criterion generally considered adequate for exploratory work" (p. 107). The author also claimed that theoretical validity was established through the extensive literature review of operations strategy and environment.

To further check the unidimensionality of each scale, factor analysis was conducted. The scales met all the criteria suggested by Carmines and Zeller (1979) for establishing the unidimensionality of scales using principal components. In addition, criterion-related validity was investigated. The authors argued that the findings of the article provided evidence to support criterion validity. "The cross-validation index for the covariance structure model developed in this research is .55, indicating a high probability that the model results are consistent with population parameters" (p. 108).

### Scores

Factor scores were used to form the scores for each scale. The correlation matrix is reported in Table 5 of the article.

**Other Evidence**

Not available.

**References**

Carmines, E. G., and R. A. Zeller. 1979. *Reliability and validity assessment*. Beverly Hills, CA: Sage.
Dess, G. G., and D. W. Beard. 1984. Dimensions of organizational task environments. *Administrative Science Quarterly* 29 (1): 52–73.

---

# Ward, Leong, and Boyer

**Article Summarized**

Ward, Peter T., G. Keong Leong, and Kenneth K. Boyer. 1994. Manufacturing proactiveness and performance. *Decision Sciences* 25 (3): 337–58.

**Scales (Actual Questions Used)**

*Manufacturing Involvement*

1. To what extent is the head of manufacturing involved in specifying the strategy of the business unit?
2. To what extent is the head of manufacturing responsible for strategic changes in manufacturing?

To what extent are the following decisions based on participative, cross-functional discussions?

3. Product or service decisions concerning production, marketing, and R&D strategies
4. Capital budget decisions: the selection and financing of long-term investments
5. Decisions related to changes in the business unit's operating philosophy and strategies for growth

*Capability Building Programs*

Structural Programs

6. Computer-aided manufacturing
7. Computer-aided design
8. Robotics
9. Updating process equipment
10. Real-time process controls
11. Flexible manufacturing systems
12. Computerized numerical control machines
13. Distributed numerical control machines
14. Automated material handling systems
15. Vision systems

Infrastructural Programs

16. Giving workers a broader range of tasks
17. Giving workers more planning responsibility
18. Giving workers more inspection/quality responsibility
19. Changing labor/management relationships
20. Improving direct labor motivation
21. Increasing the level of job automation

22. Improving supervisor training
23. Improving direct labor training

*Performance*

24. Market share
25. Sales growth

### Construct Description

Two major dimensions of manufacturing proactiveness were identified in the article. The first dimension, manufacturing involvement, was developed to capture the relative "degree of involvement of the top manufacturing executive in formulating business strategy compared to executives from other functions" (p. 342). The second dimension, capability-building programs, indicated "the existence of long-term commitment to investments in manufacturing capability building program" (p. 342). It was aimed at building capabilities in anticipation of the company's need.

### Measurement Description

The survey items were all measured on 7-point Likert scales. The manufacturing involvement scales included items associated with the manufacturing executive's involvement in the strategic process, and the items related to the extent to which strategic decisions result from cross-functional processes. Capability-building programs were operationalized using two multi-item scales. The first of these captured the structural, technology-oriented programs over the next 2 years. The second was based on a "measure of commitment of infrastructural programs" (p. 342). It focused on capturing the improvement of skills and their involvement in the plant, which the authors noted as "infrastructural programs" (p. 342).

### Development

The authors used existing scales wherever possible to develop the initial items. For instance, the manufacturing involvement scales were mainly adapted from Swamidass and Newell (1987) and Miller (1987). The scales for capability-building programs were adopted from Miller and Vollmann (1984). After that, the initial survey instrument was first pretested and then further purified using large-scale data. Minor changes were made to the scales for structural and infrastructural programs.

### Sample

A sample of manufacturing firms in Ohio with primary products in hand tools, fabricated metal products, plating and polishing, current-carrying wiring devices, and industrial controls were targeted for the study. The source was *Harris Industrial Directory* of Ohio, and the plant size was restricted to 150 or more employees at each location. The chosen firms exhibited higher productivity than other firms in the region.

Phone conversations and contact letters were first used to solicit participation from general managers in the sample. After the general manager agreed to participate, the questionnaires were mailed to their plant manager, marketing manager, and manufacturing manager, whose names were provided by the general manager. Excluding the incomplete data surveys received, the final sample included 60 business units across five industries (a response rate of 37%). The authors noted that there was no "significant pattern of responses" by industry type (i.e., no industry effect). They also tested for nonresponse bias with no pattern of difference identified.

### Validity and Reliability

Cronbach's coefficient alpha values were the key measures of reliability and internal consistency found in this research. The scale for manufacturing involvement was found to be reliable. However, slight modifications were made to the scales for structural and infrastructural programs to improve scale reliability.

After the changes, the final alpha values for manufacturing involvement, structural programs, and infrastructural program were .83, .81, and .85, respectively, showing a high level of internal consistency.

In addition, unidimensionality of the scales was tested through principal components analysis (PCA), with a large proportion of the variance explained by the first factor.

### Scores

Factor scores were used in the analysis. The scores are given in Tables 1–3 of the article.

### Other Evidence

Not available.

### References

Miller, D. 1987. Strategy making and structure: Analysis and implications for performance. *Academy of Management Journal* 30 (1): 7–32.

Miller, J. D., and T. E. Vollmann. 1984. *1984 North American manufacturers' survey: Summary of survey responses.* Boston University Manufacturing Roundtable Report Series, Boston, MA.

Swamidass, P. M., and W. T. Newell. 1987. Manufacturing strategy, environmental uncertainty and performance: A path analytic model. *Management Science* 33 (4): 509–24.

## Ward, McCreery, Ritzman, and Sharma

### Article Summarized

Ward, Peter T., John K. McCreery, Larry P. Ritzman, and Deven Sharma. 1998. Competitive priorities in operations management. *Decision Sciences* 29 (4): 1035–46.

### Scales (Actual Questions Used)

*Cost Importance*

1. Importance of production cost in management priorities in manufacturing
2. Importance of labor productivity in management priorities in manufacturing
3. Importance of capacity utilization in management priorities in manufacturing
4. Importance of reducing inventory in management priorities in manufacturing
5. Importance of cost as criterion in evaluating line managers' performance
6. Importance of productivity as criterion in evaluating line managers' performance

*Quality Importance*

7. Importance of high product performance in selling the products in the primary product line
8. Importance of high product durability in selling the products in the primary product line
9. Importance of high product reliability in selling the products in the primary product line
10. Importance of ease (cost and time) to service product in selling the products in the primary product line
11. Importance of promptness in solving customer complaints in selling the products in the primary product line
12. Importance of conformance to design specifications in management priorities in manufacturing

*Delivery Time Importance*

13. Importance of short delivery time in selling the products in the primary product line
14. Importance of delivery on due date in selling the products in the primary product line
15. Importance of reduce production lead time in management priorities in manufacturing
16. Importance of on-time delivery as a criterion in evaluating line managers' performance
17. Importance of production cycle time as a criterion in evaluating line managers' performance

*Flexibility Importance*

18. Importance of large number of product features or options in selling the products in the primary product line
19. Importance of quick new-product introduction in management priorities in manufacturing
20. Importance of rapid capacity adjustment in management priorities in manufacturing
21. Importance of ability to make design changes in production in management priorities in manufacturing

### Construct Description

Following the large existing literature (e.g., Fine and Hax 1985; Wheelwright 1984), the authors developed four commonly accepted manufacturing competitive priorities. In particular, cost importance captured the importance firms placed on each of the following cost categories: production cost, productivity, capacity utilization, and inventory reduction. The definition of quality followed the first six of Garvin's (1987) quality dimensions: (1) performance, (2) features, (3) reliability, (4) conformance, (5) durability, and (6) serviceability. Delivery time consisted of the idea of on-time delivery, which was related to the ability to deliver according to a promised schedule and delivery speed. Flexibility was based on the first four of Gerwin's (1993) dimensions of flexibility: (1) product mix, (2) volume, (3) changeover, and (4) modification.

### Measurement Description

All the items were measured on a 5-point Likert scale where 1 = "not important," 2 = "somewhat important," 3 = "quite important," 4 = "very important," and 5 = "extremely important."

### Development

In terms of the measurement items, the quality importance items were based on Garvin (1987), and the flexibility importance items were partly based on Gerwin (1993). The authors developed the measurement items for cost importance and delivery time importance specifically for this study.

### Sample

A total of 400 companies were selected from the *Harris Industrial and Manufacturing Directory*. Of them, 200 were contacted by phone; "175 firms agreed to participate and 110 firms actually responded with a response rate of 55%" (p. 1037). Questionnaires were also sent to the remaining 200 firms directly without telephone contact. Of them, 34 responded with a response rate of 17%. No differences in terms of size or industry were found between the two groups of respondents. No evident nonrespondent bias was revealed through subsequent examination. The final sample of 144 firms were located in the Midwest and Northeast and were "weighted more heavily toward durable goods manufacturing than is the U.S. population of plants" (p. 1037).

Plants that were not discrete-part manufacturers were eliminated from the respondents, and this resulted in a usable sample of 114 observations. These plants belonged to the following industries: furniture, fabricated metals, industrial equipment (including computers), electronic equipment, transformation equipment, instruments, and miscellaneous manufacturing. Questionnaires were sent to individuals with titles of "president, vice president of manufacturing, vice president of operations, director of manufacturing, director of operations, plant manager, manufacturing manager, controller, and strategic planning manager" (p. 1038).

**Reliability and Validity**

Factor analysis with principal components analysis (PCA) extraction was used to evaluate each scale. According to the authors, "The factor loadings were substantial (>.45) for each variable on its expected factor and high loadings for a variable on multiple factors are minimal" (p. 1038). These results suggested that "all four of the competitive priority constructs are considered by the managers surveyed as unidimensional in nature" (p. 1038). Cronbach's coefficient alpha value was "used to measure the internal consistency of the items included in each of the four constructs" (p. 1038). The alpha values ranged from .70 to .80, which indicated an "acceptable level of internal consistency for the constructs as measured" (p. 1038).

"A second executive in a sample of the responding companies was asked to answer a shorted version of the original questionnaire. There were 27 usable responses to the second questionnaire" (p. 1039). The 27 matched pairs were used to examine inter-rater agreements with the method developed by James, Demaree, and Wolf (1984). The reliability coefficients for the four constructs were .94 for cost, .84 for quality, .85 for delivery time, and .89 for flexibility. These values indicated a high level of inter-rater agreement. Predictive validity was established by using data collected from an instrument to explain or predict current or future performance. The results were as predicted by the literature, so the measures of competitive priorities fit in the context of manufacturing strategy theory.

**Scores**

The results of factor analysis are reported in Table 1 of the article.

**Other Evidence**

Not available.

**References**

Fine, C. H., and A. C. Hax. 1985. Manufacturing strategy: A methodology and an illustration. *Interfaces* 15 (6): 28–46.

Garvin, D. A. 1987. Competing on the eight dimensions of quality. *Harvard Business Review* 65 (6): 101–09.

Gerwin, D. 1993. Manufacturing flexibility: A strategic perspective. *Management Science* 39: 395–410.

James, L. R., R. G. Demaree, and G. Wolf. 1984. Eliminating within-group inter-rater reliability with and without response bias. *Journal of Applied Psychology* 69 (1): 85–98.

Wheelwright, S. C. 1984. Manufacturing strategy: Defining the missing link. *Strategic Management Journal* 5 (1): 77–91.

# Wathen

**Article Summarized**

Wathen, Samuel. 1995. Manufacturing strategy in business units: An analysis of production process focus and performance. *International Journal of Operations and Production Management* 15 (8): 4–13.

**Scales (Actual Questions Used)**

1. What percentage (nearest 10%) of the business's sales were derived from products manufactured in small batches (production runs normally under 200)?
2. What percentage (nearest 10%) of the business's sales were derived from products manufactured in large batches or on an assembly line?
3. What percentage (nearest 10%) of the business's sales were derived from products manufactured using a continuous process?

### Construct Description

The production process focus construct could be characterized based on the degree to which business units use small-batch, large-batch/assembly, or continuous processes. Production process focus was operationally defined as the degree to which a business unit uses different production processes as part of the manufacturing operation.

### Measurement Description

The purpose of these scales was to provide a qualitative, three-point description of production process focus. Each point on the scale indicated the relative degree of focus—that is, (1) "unfocused" (each item accounted for a significant proportion of sales, or Items 1 and 3 accounted for a significant proportion of sales), (2) "quasi-focused" (Items 1 and 2, or 2 and 3 accounted for a significant proportion of sales), and (3) "focused" (nearly 100% of sales were indicated by one of the items). Note that the three-item responses were required to sum up to 100%.

### Development

The three items discussed had not been previously used as a measure of production process focus. However, similar items that assessed the characteristics of a company's process (e.g., material flow, degree of departmentalization, and type of equipment) and/or characteristics of a company's products (e.g., standardized vs. customized and high vs. low volume) had been previously used (e.g., Safizadeh et al. 1996; Bozarth and Edwards 1997) as measures of focus. The items selected in this study were taken from the Profit Impact of Marketing Strategy (PIMS) database.

### Sample

The sample data were drawn from the PIMS database. The database contained self-reports from business units or strategic business units (SBUs). PIMS defined this unit of analysis as an operating unit that sells a distinct set of products to an identifiable group of customers in competition with a well-defined set of operating units (Schoeffler 1977). Two criteria determined the selection of a business unit for this study. First, each business unit had a U.S. Department of Commerce, Standard Industrial Classification (SIC) code and belonged to a two-digit SIC manufacturing industry. The SIC codes ranged inclusively from 20 to 39. Second, at least 90% of the business unit's sales were from manufactured products. Based on these criteria, 1,004 of the 2,044 manufacturing SBUs were selected for the analysis of production process focus.

### Reliability and Validity

Not available.

### Scores

Table 1 in the article provides the results of the cluster analysis, which revealed three classes of "production process focus": (1) focused-production processes, (2) quasi-focused production processes, and (3) unfocused production processes. Focused production processes generated nearly all their sales from products produced with one process type. Quasi-focused production processes generated sales primarily from two production processes that have similarities in terms of batch size (small vs. large) and assembly/continuous flow production. Unfocused production processes generate sales with all three production process types or with two divergent process types, that is, small batch and continuous processes. The other scores are presented in Tables 2 and 3 of the article.

### Other Evidence

Not available.

**References**

Bozarth, C., and S. Edwards. 1997. The impact of market requirement focus and manufacturing characteristics focus on plant performance. *Journal of Operations Management* 15 (3): 161–80.
Safizadeh, M. H., L. P. Ritzman, D. Sharma, and C. Wood. 1996. An empirical analysis of the product-process matrix. *Management Science* 42 (11): 1576–91.
Schoeffler, S. 1977. Cross-sectional study of strategy, structure, and performance. In *Strategy and structure = performance,* ed. H. B. Thorelli, 108–21. Bloomington: Indiana University Press.

# White

**Article Summarized**

White, Gregory P. 1996. A meta-analysis model of manufacturing capabilities. *Journal of Operations Management* 14 (4): 315–31.

**Scales (Actual Questions Used)**

*Component of Production Competence for Which Manufacturing Responsibility Exceeds 30%*

1. Product flexibility
2. Volume flexibility
3. Process flexibility
4. Low product cost
5. Delivery speed
6. Delivery dependability
7. Production lead time
8. Product reliability
9. Product durability
10. Quality
11. Competitive pricing
12. Low price

Dimensions of Quality

13. Performance
14. Features
15. Reliability
16. Conformance
17. Durability
18. Serviceability
19. Aesthetics
20. Perceived quality

Dimensions of Flexibility

21. Machine flexibility
22. Material handling flexibility
23. Operational flexibility
24. Process flexibility

25. Product flexibility
26. Routing flexibility
27. Volume flexibility
28. Expansion flexibility
29. Program flexibility
30. Production flexibility
31. Market flexibility

### Construct Description

This study integrated the findings from several published articles to collectively illustrate the relationships among competitive capabilities, manufacturing strategy, and business performance. The definitions of constructs analyzed in the article followed the well-accepted definitions in the existing literature. For instance, both quality and flexibility were conceptualized as multidimensional constructs. In particular, the quality construct was defined by eight underlying dimensions proposed by Garvin (1984), and the flexibility construct had 11 dimensions identified by Sethi and Sethi (1990).

### Measurement Description

Data were drawn from the reported data.

### Development

Not available.

### Sample

The analyses in this study were based on previously published articles such as Ferdows and De Meyer (1990), Wood (1991), Sluti (1992), Noble (1995), Whybark and Vastag (1993), Sethi and Sethi (1990), and Vickery, Dröge, and Markland (1993).

### Reliability and Validity

Not available.

### Scores

The scores are provided in Tables 1–9 of the article.

### Other Evidence

Not available.

### References

Ferdows, K., and A. De Meyer. 1990. Lasting improvements in manufacturing performance: In search of a new theory. *Journal of Operations Management* 9 (2): 168–84.

Garvin, D. A. 1984. What does "product quality" really mean? *Sloan Management Review* 26 (1): 25–43.

Noble, M. A. 1995. Manufacturing strategy: Testing the cumulative model in a multiple country context. *Decision Sciences* 26 (5): 693–720.

Sethi, A. K., and S. P. Sethi. 1990. Flexibility in manufacturing: A survey. *International Journal of Flexibility Manufacturing Systems* 2 (4): 289–328.

Sluti, D. G. 1992. Linking process quality with performance: An empirical study of New Zealand manufacturing plants. Unpublished PhD diss., University of Auckland, Auckland, New Zealand.

Vickery, S. K., and C. Dröge. 1993. Production competence and business strategy: Do they affect business performance? *Decision Sciences* 24 (2): 435–55.
Whybark, D. C., and G. Vastag, eds. 1993. *Global manufacturing practices: A worldwide survey of practices in production planning and control.* Amsterdam, The Netherlands: Elsevier.
Wood, C. H. 1991. Operations strategy: Decision patterns and measurement. Unpublished PhD diss., The Ohio State University, Columbus, OH.

## Williams, D'Souza, Rosenfeldt, and Kassaee

### Article Summarized

Williams, Frank P., Derrick E. D'Souza, Martin E. Rosenfeldt, and Massoud Kassaee. 1995. Manufacturing strategy, business strategy, and firm performance in a mature industry. *Journal of Operations Management* 13 (1): 19–33.

### Scales (Actual Questions Used)

*Level of Differentiation*

1. Industry-wide cost leadership strategy
2. Industry-wide differentiation strategy
3. Segment cost leadership strategy
4. Segment differentiation strategy

*Technology Orientation*

Production Planning and Control System

5. Complexity of production planning techniques; scale

Quality Assurance Programs

6. Level of quality assurance process sophistication

Capacity Planning

7. Frequency of capacity changes; scale

Innovative Process

8. Level of emphasis on innovative manufacturing processes

Special Purpose Machines

9. Level of emphasis on special purpose machines

*Market Orientation*

General Purpose Machines

10. Level of emphasis on general purpose equipment

Capacity Slack

11. Level of capacity slack

Product Quality

12. Level of emphasis on superior product quality

Variety of Products

13. Variety of final product

Product Customization

14. Level of product customization

Facility Focus

15. Level of facility focus

Performance

16. Return on sales

### Construct Description

This study examined the relationship between manufacturing strategy, business strategy, and firm performance. Business strategy was regarded as the "strategic posture" of the business unit and was defined by the level of differentiation. Manufacturing strategy was characterized by technology orientation and market orientation. Technology orientation was defined as "a focus on process and product technology that strongly influences the types of products created and the processes and material used" (p. 22). Market orientation referred to "the focus on market opportunities and customer needs" (p. 22).

### Measurement Description

Business strategy captured by the level of differentiation was quantified on a 7-point Likert-type scale. Business performance was measured by return on sales (ROS) using a 5-point scale. Manufacturing strategy was operationalized by 10 variables; each variable was indicated by a single item on a 7-point Likert-type scale.

### Development

The manufacturing strategy scale was developed from the existing manufacturing strategy studies, which was predicated on Hayes and Wheelwright (1984). The measurement items for business strategy were developed based on Porter's (1980) conceptual model of business level strategy.

### Sample

The data were collected from the questionnaires sent to 334 plants in a sector within the textile industry—that is, U.S. Department of Commerce, Standard Industrial Classification code (SIC) 2211, broad-woven cotton fabric mills. The survey population was identified based on Davidson's *Textile Blue Book* (1990) and the *Textile Red Book* (1991). A total of 88 usable responses were received, providing a response rate of 26.3%. Three observations were dropped because of missing data. The final sample data used consisted of 85 business units across the states. Nonresponse bias was assessed by comparing the distribution of responding firms with the distribution of the population on the variable of facility location. According to the authors, no nonresponse bias was detected.

### Reliability and Validity

Not available.

### Scores

The correlation matrix of study variables is presented in Table 3. The parameter estimates and significance tests of four different multiple regression analyses are presented in Table 4 of the article.

**Other Evidence**

Not available.

**References**

Davidson's *Textile Blue Book*. 1990. Davidson's Publishing Company. Ridgewood, New Jersey.
Davidson's *Textile Red Book*. 1991. America's Textile's International, Atlanta, GA.
Hayes, R. H., and S. C. Wheelwright. 1984. *Restoring our competitive edge*. New York: Wiley.
Porter, M. 1980. *Competitive strategy: Techniques for analyzing industries and competition*. New York: Free Press.

# Wisner, Stringfellow, Youngdahl, and Parker

**Article Summarized**

Wisner, Priscilla S., Anne Stringfellow, William E. Youngdahl, and Lenore Parker. 2005. The service volunteer—loyalty chain: An exploratory study of charitable not-for-profit service organizations. *Journal of Operations Management* 23 (2): 143–61.

**Scales (Actual Questions Used)**

*Schedule Flexibility*

1. The organization's demands are so great that they take away time from my other activities (e.g., family, work, outside interests) (reverse coded).
2. In my volunteer activities, I have so much to do that it takes away time from my personal interests (reverse coded).
3. My volunteer activities take up time that I'd rather spend with family/friends (reverse coded).
4. The hours that I volunteer fit my schedule just fine.
5. Short-term assignments are available in this organization.

*Orientation and Training*

6. Volunteers receive training prior to beginning work in this organization.
7. Training is part of this organization's volunteer management program.
8. The organization has an orientation program for all new volunteers.
9. The organization provides an orientation packet to volunteers.
10. Volunteers are regularly trained during their time with this organization.
11. The organization provides minimal training to new volunteers (reverse scored).

*Empowerment*

12. Volunteers are actively involved in planning and development of activities.
13. The organization provides leadership opportunities for volunteers.
14. The organization modifies its processes in response to volunteer feedback.
15. Volunteers do not have contact with our organization's clients (reverse scored).
16. Volunteers have direct contact with the people the organization serves.

*Social Interaction*

17. Volunteers have the opportunity to interact with each other.
18. Volunteers interact with our paid employees on a regular basis.
19. People in this organization are friendly.
20. The organization makes sure that I get along well with my fellow volunteers.
21. The organization facilitates social interactions between volunteers.
22. Staff members of this organization are very pleasant to deal with.

*Reflection*

23. The organization provides information to volunteers about the mission of the organization.
24. The organization provides information to volunteers about policy issues related to the mission of the organization.
25. The organization provides opportunities for volunteers to reflect on their experiences.
26. The organization frequently reminds volunteers about the impact that they have on the people whom we serve.
27. The organization makes sure that all new volunteers understand the positive impact they have on the people it serves.
28. Volunteers receive feedback on the impact of their work.
29. Volunteers understand how much they matter in fulfilling the organization's mission.

*Rewards*

30. The organization arranges parties or luncheons to thank volunteers.
31. Volunteers receive thank you letters or certificates of appreciation from our organization.
32. The organization has a volunteer reward program.
33. Staff members constantly express their appreciation for our volunteer efforts.
34. The organization recognizes outstanding volunteers.

*Satisfaction*

35. Overall, I am satisfied with my volunteer experience.
36. I am satisfied with the people who manage the organization.
37. I am satisfied with the organization's policies.
38. I am satisfied with the support provided by the organization.
39. I am satisfied with the opportunities for advancement in the organization.

*Intent to Remain*

40. I intend to continue volunteering for this organization.
41. I would like to remain a volunteer here.
42. I do not intend to remain a long-term volunteer for this organization.
43. I plan to quit volunteering here soon.

*Intent to Donate*

44. I have donated to this organization in the past.
45. I donate to this organization on a regular basis.
46. I intend to donate to this organization in the future.
47. I would be prepared to support this organization financially.
48. I would like to contribute money as well as time to this organization.

*Intent to Recommend Organization to Others*

49. I would encourage friends and/or family to volunteer for this organization.
50. I would not recommend doing volunteer work for this organization (reverse scored).

51. I would discourage those close to me from volunteering here (reverse scored).
52. I would recommend that others consider volunteering for this organization.

*Altruism*

53. I want to help others.
54. I am concerned about those less fortunate than myself.
55. I feel compassion toward people in need.
56. I feel it is important to help others.
57. I want to do something for a cause that is important to me.
58. I want to give back to the community.
59. I want to do something worthwhile.
60. By volunteering, I help to create a better society.
61. I am genuinely concerned about the particular group I am serving.

*Career Advancement*

62. I want to make new contacts that might help my business or career.
63. Volunteer experience will look good on my resume.

## Construct Description

The authors provided detailed reasoning on why the constructs used in the study are important from a theoretical and practical perspective, but they did not provide any formal definitions of the constructs.

## Measurement Description

Each construct was operationally described by perceptual measures evaluated on 5-point Likert-type scales. In particular, schedule flexibility was characterized by a three-item scale measuring volunteers' perception that the organization makes reasonable demands on their time. The four-item scale for orientation and training measured the extent to which volunteers participate in orientation and training programs. The measure for contact with clients was a single item that assessed the amount of direct interaction between the volunteers and the nonprofit organization's clients.

The empowerment scale included three items. It captured the extent to which volunteers are given autonomy within the organization. The 6-item scale measuring social interaction indicated the extent to which volunteers interacted with paid staff and with one another. The 7-item scale for reflection demonstrated the extent to which the organization facilitates volunteer reflection on the results of their volunteer activities. The 6-item scale for rewards captured the extent to which the organization expressed its gratitude for their volunteer efforts.

The outcome measures analyzed in the article included (1) a 5-item satisfaction scale assessing the extent to which volunteers were satisfied with their volunteer experience; (2) a 4-item scale for intent to remain, which measured the extent to which volunteers planned to continue volunteering for the organization in the future; (3) a 5-item intent to donate scale, measuring volunteers' intention to give money to the organization for which they volunteered; and (4) a 4-item intent to recommend scale focusing on the extent to which volunteers were prepared to recommend that their friends and acquaintances volunteer for the organization.

In addition, two scales were constructed to measure volunteer motivation. The first scale—a 4-item altruism scale—assessed "the extent to which a desire to help others motivated volunteers" (p. 152). The other was a 2-item scale for career advancement, which was developed to measure "the extent to which a desire to gain contacts or experience for career purpose motivated volunteers" (p. 152).

## Development

The measurement items were developed based on extensive literature review. Then, scales were purified after being subjected to several validation analyses. As a result, several items were dropped from the final measurement instrument.

### Sample

A commercial Web-based survey was used for data collection. Volunteers from 246 organizations in a "large southwestern city" in the United States were asked for participation using an e-mail correspondence. The volunteers were provided a link to a survey site. Responses from 288 volunteers (43 organizations) were considered usable. Demographic data are listed in Table 1 of the article. Information on the source of the participating organization was not available in the article.

### Validity and Reliability

To ensure construct validity, the authors used previous literature to develop and verify the items for each construct. Furthermore, they used exploratory factor analysis (EFA) to examine item intercorrelations and to purify the scales. Additionally, a confirmatory factor analysis (CFA) was used to check for unidimensionality. Results from these factor analyses provided consistent support for construct validity.

The authors also conducted reliability tests on each scale. The resulting Cronbach's coefficient alpha values ranged from .76 to .91, which were all above the acceptable minimum per Nunnally and Bernstein (1994). Hence, the scales were said to be reliable.

### Scores

Table 2 of the article summarizes the means, standard deviations, and correlation matrix for the measures. Table 3 reports the results of the regression analyses.

### Other Evidence

Not available.

### Reference

Nunnally, J. C., and I. H. Bernstein. 1994. *Psychometric theory.* 3rd ed. New York: McGraw-Hill.

## Youngdahl and Kellogg

### Article Summarized

Youngdahl, William E., and Deborah L. Kellogg. 1997. The relationship between service customers' quality assurance behaviors, satisfaction, and effort: A cost of quality perspective. *Journal of Operations Management* 15 (1): 19–32.

### Scales (Actual Questions Used)

*Service Type*

1. What specific service was this?

*Critical Incident (Actual Customer Behavior)*

2. What was the primary thing that you either did or tried to do to affect the quality?

*Motivation for Quality Assurance Behaviors*

3. Why did you feel it was necessary to take this action (or not take action) to affect the quality of the service?

*Degree of Effort Incurred*

4. Please indicate your level of effort in terms of time.
5. Please indicate your level of effort in terms of thought or intellectual effort.
6. Please indicate your level of emotional effort.

### Construct Description

This article investigated customers' roles in service quality assurance by identifying four customer costs of service quality. These four customer costs were (1) preparation, (2) relationship building, (3) information exchange, and (4) intervention. Each of these is described next.

Preparation was defined as "preparing for the service by such actions as seeking referrals, researching competitors, and arriving early" (p. 23). Relationship building referred to "building a relationship with the service provider through such actions as smiling, offering words of kindness, getting to know providers, trying to build loyalty, and asking for servers by names" (p. 23). Information exchange was associated with "providing and seeking information to clarify service expectations and seeks status" (p. 23). Intervention connoted the provision of "negative performance feedback and involving oneself in problem diagnosis and resolution" (p. 23).

### Measurement Description

The first three questions presented early were answered using respondents' own words. Questions 4 to 6 were based on a Likert scale that ranged from "none" to "very much."

### Development

Before the survey, pilot testing of the questionnaire was conducted. Personal interviews were also applied to verify respondents' understanding of the survey instrument. As a result, minor changes were made to the instrument.

### Sample

The respondent group consisted of diverse groups of part-time, student, subject volunteers, ranging in age from 20 to 62 years, from the authors' respective universities (Arizona State University and University of Colorado, Denver). Most students in the sample were fully employed, and their positions ranged from fast-food employees to medical doctors. Each respondent contributed two responses to be judged for inclusion as critical incidents, one for satisfactory and the other for dissatisfactory. The data were screened against four criteria for being critical incidents. Finally, 521 out of the 547 responses were usable, with 250 from satisfactory encounters and 271 from dissatisfactory encounters.

### Reliability and Validity

Three independent judges, the two authors and a third person who was not directly associated with the research project, performed the classification of customer cost of service quality behaviors using the critical incident technique (CIT). Interrater reliability was assessed with the procedure outlined by Roman and Latham (1974). In this study, reliability was determined as the intersection of each judge's categorization divided by the union of the categorization. The reliability percentages for the four categories were 93.4%, 99.5%, 90.0%, and 88.3%, respectively, which were higher than the 80% threshold value; and therefore, indicated reliability.

The content validity of the categories was assessed through two procedures. The first procedure was proposed by Anderson and Nilsson (1964), which determined that the classification of the last 100 incidents resulted in the addition of no more than two additional categories. The second procedure applied a simple ratio analysis proposed by Roman and Latham (1974). This approach suggests that content validity is deemed satisfactory if 90% of the categories appear when 75% of the data have been categorized. Both tests supported the validity of the categories.

### Scores

The four customer costs of service quality or quality assurance behaviors yielded from the CIT classification are reported in Table 2 of the article (p. 23). The model that integrated these quality assurance behaviors into service design and delivery are shown in Figure 4 of the article (p. 29).

### Other Evidence

Not available.

### References

Anderson, B. E., and S. G. Nilsson. 1964. Studies in the reliability and validity of the Critical Incident Technique. *Journal of Applied Psychology* 48 (6): 398–403.

Roman, W. W., and G. P. Latham. 1974. The reliability and validity of the Critical Incident Technique: A closer look. *Studies in Personal Psychology* 6 (1): 53–64.

Youngdahl, W. E., and D. L. Kellogg. 1994. Customer costs of service quality: A critical incident study. In *Service marketing and management effectiveness,* Vol. 3, ed. T. A. Swartz, D. E. Bowen, and S. W. Brown, 149–73. Greenwich, CT: JAI Press.

---

## Youngdahl, Kellogg, Nie, and Bowen

### Article Summarized

Youngdahl, William E., Deborah L. Kellogg, Winter Nie, and David E. Bowen. 2003. Revisiting customer participation in service encounters: Does culture matter? *Journal of Operations Management* 21 (1): 109–20.

### Scales (Actual Questions Used)

*Cultural Dimension Scales*

Power Distance

1. People in higher positions should make most decisions without consulting people in lower positions.
2. People in higher positions should not ask the opinions of people in lower positions too frequently.
3. People in higher positions should avoid social interaction with people in lower positions.
4. People in lower positions should not disagree with decisions by people in higher positions.

Collectivism

5. Individuals should sacrifice self-interest for the group (either at the school or at the workplace).
6. Individuals should stick with the group even through difficulties.
7. Group welfare is more important than individual rewards.
8. Group success is more important than individual success.
9. Individuals should only pursue their goals after considering the welfare of the group.
10. Group loyalty should be encouraged even if individual goals suffer.

Uncertainty Avoidance

11. It is important to have instructions spelled out in detail so that I always know what I am expected to do.
12. It is important to closely follow instructions and procedures.
13. Rules and regulations are important because they inform me what is expected of me.

14. Standardized work procedures are helpful.
15. Instructions for operations are important.

Masculinity

16. It is more important for men to have a professional career than it is for women.
17. Men usually solve problems with logical analysis; women usually solve problems with intuition.
18. Solving difficult problems usually requires an active forcible approach, which is typical of men.
19. There are some jobs in which a man can always do better than a woman.

Time Orientation

20. Careful management of money (thrift)
21. Long-term planning
22. Giving up today's fun for success in the future
23. Working hard for success in the future

### Construct Description

Based on Hofstede's work, five constructs were identified to tap into the domain of culture. Among the five constructs, four of them—power distance, uncertainty avoidance, individualism, and masculinity—were built on Hofstede (1980), and the fifth construct—time orientation—was proposed by Hofstede and Bond (1988). The definitions of these constructs are listed below.

Power distance described "the degree to which a person accepts power inequality in dealings with others" (p. 111). Individuality referred to "the value placed on individual effort and achievement" (p. 112). Uncertainty avoidance defined "how an individual feels in uncertain or unknown situations" (p. 112). Masculinity indicated "what is valued and how one relates to others" (p. 112). Time orientation captured "the tension between long-term and short-term perspectives" (p. 112).

The definitions of another two constructs in the article—effort and satisfaction—were not explicitly specified.

### Measurement Description

The culture dimensions were measured using 5-point scale items. Similarly, "effort was measured with a series of five items each with five-point scales. Overall satisfaction was also measured with a series of five-point scale items" (p. 113).

### Development

The measurement items used for culture dimension were developed and prevalidated by Donthu and Yoo (1998). The measures for effort and satisfaction were new and developed by the research team.

### Sample

The data used were collected from "two U.S. universities with [the Center for International Business Education and Research] CIBER designations, one of which has a majority of students coming from countries outside the U.S." (p. 113). The sample consisted of 245 graduate students from 40 different countries. Each respondent selected one satisfactory incident and one unsatisfactory incident to report. A total of 454 usable cases were obtained after excluding the missing and incomplete data. Response rate was not reported in the article. The authors did note that "the sample also presented some potential biases and limitations associated with the use of student volunteers and asking respondents to recall service experiences that happened in a different cultural context" (p. 113).

### Validity and Reliability

Validity, according to the authors, "was assured through iterative pre-screening and editing of the instrument and by using survey items that had been used and validated in prior studies" (p. 114). In addition, the results from factor analysis using orthogonal principal components analysis (PCA) provided empirical support for an acceptable level of construct validity. The reliability for each of the constructs was evaluated using Cronbach's coefficient alpha values. The analysis showed that all alpha values ranged between .61 and .96.

### Scores

The results are reported in Tables 1–4 of the article.

### Other Evidence

Not available.

### References

Donthu, N., and B. Yoo. 1998. Cultural influences on service quality expectations. *Journal of Service Research* 1 (2): 178–85.
Hofstede, G. 1980. *Culture's consequences: International differences in work-related values.* Beverly Hills, CA: Sage.
Hofstede, G., and M. H. Bond, 1988. Confucius and economic growth: New trends in culture's consequences. *Organizational Dynamics* 16 (4): 4–21.

---

## Zahay and Griffin

### Article Summarized

Zahay, Debra, and Abbie Griffin. 2004. Customer learning processes, strategy selection, and performance in business-to-business service firms. *Decision Sciences* 35 (2): 169–203.

### Scales (Actual Questions Used)

Although Table 1 of the article presents sources of major items and brief descriptions, this article did not present a list of items used in the survey. The following are simplified items appearing in the article.

*Customer IS*

1. Information quality

   Accuracy
   Consistency
   Timeliness
   Overall quality

2. Person specificity, sales

   Have contact name
   Have contact type
   Have response to contact names of others in purchase

3. Person specificity, marketing

   Marketing offers made
   Offers responded to

Method of contact
Response time for offers

4. Time-specific purchase history

   First purchase date
   Contact renewal date
   Purchase history
   Last purchase date

5. Database capabilities

   Base contact information available
   No purchase last year
   Extend information
   Contact in 3 months

6. Dissemination

   Circulate customer documents
   Spread important information on major customers
   Disseminate customer purchase patterns
   Exchange customer information across units

7. Shareability—R&D and operations

   R&D access customer information
   Operations access customer information
   R&D modify customer information
   Operations modify customer information

8. Knowledge share of wallet

   Know share of wallet unit
   Know share of wallet company

*Customization*

9. Use information to create products for individual customers

*Personalization*

10. Respond to customer by taking into account customer's individual response to prior communication

*Positioning (Strategic Excellence)*

11. Low cost versus differentiation, generic positioning strategies as defined by Porter (1985)

*Customer-Based Performance*

12. Retention, lifetime customer value, share of wallet, ROI

*Business Growth*

13. Increases in sales and net income, self-reports

**Construct Description**

Six major constructs—customer information system (CIS), customization, personalization, positioning, customer-based performance, and business growth—were investigated in the article. Most constructs were defined based on the widely accepted definitions in the literature. For instance, the strategic positioning construct followed Porter's (1985) framework and was conceptualized as position in the market depicted by a firm's choices of two generic strategies: low costs and differentiation.

Personalization was given as the ability to individualize customer communications. This construct included "both responding individually to customer-initiated communications and providing only the information desired about the firm and its products" (p. 174). Business growth was related to overall strategic performance. It was defined by commonly used metrics such as profit and sales growth. These performance measures tapped outcomes from all the tactical decisions made across all the functions of the firm.

CIS was a new construct. The authors defined it as a high-order latent construct with eight underlying dimensions: (1) quality, (2) time specific, (3) person-specific marketing, (4) person-specific sales, (5) database capabilities, information within unit, (6) knowledge share of wallet, (7) shareability—R&D, and (8) operations.

### Measurement Description

This article indicated the sources of items used in the survey but did not include detailed information on how each construct was actually measured. Some descriptions on positioning and CIS constructs were as follows. CIS was operationalized on a 30-item scale: four items each for seven out of the eight dimensions and two items for the last underlying dimension. The overall score for CIS was the sum for all eight dimensions. Positioning—strategic excellence—was "a summed mean of the differentiation and low-cost variables, indicating a progression toward the 'both' strategy" (p. 180).

### Development

With the exception of CIS, for the most part, existing scales in the previous literature were used to measure the underlying constructs. Regarding the new scale for CIS, a total of 30 managers were interviewed to understand CIS management. Based on this interview, concepts were operationalized and developed into specific items.

The initial survey was pretested with three marketing managers in the target industries for item clarification. A modified instrument was then paper-and-pencil pretested by 47 managers. A marketing research company contacted firms from the sample to prescreen for the person in the division with the most relevant knowledge. Interview requests were mailed to that person. Within 1 week, the research firm scheduled telephone appointments. A copy of the survey was mailed or faxed to respondents so that they could see the "scales and questions" during the interview. The final measurement instrument was developed through correlation analysis and factor analysis based on large-scale data. The authors reported that a few items were dropped from the early instrument.

### Sample

Respondents were selected from stratified random samples of business-to-business (B2B) property and casualty insurers (U.S. Department of Commerce, Standard Industrial Classification [SIC] code 6331, NAICS code 524126) and software companies (SIC code 7372, NAICS code 51121) from Dun & Bradstreet and *Ward's Business Directory* of U.S. private and public companies. Managers responsible for B2B product and market decisions in the software and insurance industries were used in all phase-of-scale and survey development. Response rate to the survey was 48% on a company base (209 of 433) and 31% on a per contact basis (209 of 684 mailed contacts). The authors noted that the response rates were consistent across industries.

### Reliability and Validity

Cronbach's coefficient alpha (a) was computed to test scale reliability of each multi-item measurement scale. All composite scales met the criteria of a >.60 for exploratory research, and most items were well above .70. Exceptions for this rule (a >.70) were customization and positioning. However, because of previous validation in other studies, the authors decided to maintain these constructs and items.

Several exploratory factor analyses (EFA) employed with the principal components analyses (PCA) procedure and varimax rotation were performed on indicator items. The cutoffs used in these analyses were .50 for individual item factor loadings and 1.0 for eigenvalues. The EFA results then served as guidance for the following confirmatory factor analyses (CFA). The CFA results indicated that "the CIS construct itself had good overall fit statistics," but this was not true for all CIS subconstructs (p. 198). The authors stated that "CIS subconstructs were retained in the measurement based on their contribution to the overall model fit" (p. 198). In addition, a post hoc PCA provided evidence to support the discriminant validity of CIS-subconstruct-related variables. For the non-CIS constructs, CFA exhibited good fit.

**Scores**

Table A.2.2 in the article shows the CFA results for CIS subconstructs. The CFA results of non-CIS constructs appear in Table A.2.3. The initial model and the alternative one are displayed in Figures 5 and 6. Correlations and descriptive statistics are reported in Table 4. Comparison of means by strategic category (positioning constructs) is shown in Table 5.

**Other Evidence**

Not available.

**Reference**

Porter, M. 1985. *Competitive advantage.* New York: Free Press.

## Zellmer-Bruhn

**Article Summarized**

Zellmer-Bruhn, Mary E. 2003. Interruptive events and team knowledge acquisition. *Management Science* 49 (4): 514–28.

**Scales (Actual Questions Used)**

*Knowledge Transfer Effort*

1. Searching outside the team for practices.
2. Implementing new processes adopted from outside sources.
3. Finding out how other teams within your organization complete similar tasks.
4. (Others available from author, not printed.)
5. Team score is average of individual scale scores by team.

*Knowledge Acquisition*

6. Did the team adopt work practices from outside the team?

*Interruptions*

7. Did the team lose any members?
8. Did the team hold a formal planning session?
9. Did the team have changes in machines, tools, or other technologies?
10. Did the organization experience a restructuring?

*External Contact*

11. This team depends on other teams to get our work done.
12. Members of this team have frequent contact with members of other similar teams.

13. This team often must interact with other teams to complete our tasks.
14. Members of this team regularly attend meetings with members of other teams.
15. Team size, length of time the team has existed, and organization are also controls.

### Construct Description

The constructs were developed from the literature on interruptions and knowledge. No conceptual definitions of these constructs were provided in the article.

### Measurement Description

The measures used for the constructs above were perceptual. Each construct was operationalized by multi-item scales. The following were the operational definitions. The composite scale for interruption consisted of a list of 13 items, each representing one disruptive event that triggered changes in group routines. Interruption then was defined as the frequency of these 13 disruptions (events) faced by the team. Knowledge acquisition was captured on one item that assessed whether or not the team adopted a work practice from outside the team in a given month. The variable "was coded 1 if a team member reported adopting new practices in the specified month, and 0 if a team member did not report practice adoption" (p. 520).

Knowledge transfer effort reflected how much effort the team spends examining current work methods outside the team and seeking to implement them. To measure it, an 8-item, composite scale was developed, and each item was rated on a 5-point scale with endpoints of 1 = "not effort" and 5 = "a very high amount of effort." External contact was determined by how much the team interacts with other similar teams. The scale for external contact included four items, and each of them was evaluated on a 7-point Likert-type scale.

### Development

This research focused on team-level knowledge acquisition information and interruptions. The scales were created by the author using the literature and interviews as a guide.

### Sample

The survey was administered to a total of 158 teams in three organizations, 12 teams in the first organization, 11 teams in the second organization, and 135 teams in the third organization. A total of 90 teams had at least two responses (57% of teams, 26% overall response rate) and were therefore used in the survey. Among these 90 teams, the within-team responses ranged from 2 to 12, with an average of 5. This corresponded to the within-team response rate of 14% to 100%. Team size in the sample varied from 3 to 21 members, with a mean of 10. However, the authors did not specify the characteristics of the three organizations and the selection criteria of the 158 teams.

### Reliability and Validity

Prior to administering the survey, the authors interviewed 98 individuals from 46 teams outside the targeted sample. According to the authors, validity was ensured during the interview process. Excerpts obtained from the interviews were used to determine what language the team members used. For multi-item scales, Cronbach's coefficient alpha values were computed, and all the reliability scores ranged between .76 and .96, which exhibited evidence of scale reliabilities.

### Scores

All the individual-level data were aggregated before analysis to get team-level data. Descriptive statistics and correlations are given in Table 1 of the article. Regression results are given in Table 2.

**Other Evidence**

Not available.

**Reference**

None.

---

# Zhang, Vonderembse, and Lim

**Article Summarized**

Zhang, Qingyu, Mark A. Vonderembse, and Jeen-Su Lim. 2003. Manufacturing flexibility: Defining and analyzing relationships among competence, capability, and customer satisfaction. *Journal of Operations Management* 21 (2): 173–91.

**Scales (Actual Questions Used)**

*Machine Flexibility*

1. Machine setup can be done quickly.
2. A typical machine can perform many types of operations.
3. A typical machine can effectively use many different tools.*
4. Machines often become obsolete when new operations are required.
5. Machine tools can be changed quickly.
6. Machine setups are easy.

*Labor Flexibility*

7. Workers can perform many types of operations effectively.
8. A typical worker can use many different tools effectively.
9. Cross-trained workers can perform a broad range of manufacturing tasks effectively in the organization.
10. Workers can operate various types of machines.
11. Workers can be transferred easily between organizational units.

*Material Handling Flexibility*

12. A typical material handling system can handle different part types.
13. A typical material handling system can link different processing centers.
14. Material handling system can move different part types through manufacturing facilities.
15. Material handling changeovers between parts are quick.
16. Material handling tools can be changed or replaced quickly.*

*Routing Flexibility*

17. A typical part operation can be routed to different machines.
18. A typical part can use many different routes.
19. The system has alternative routes in case machines break down.
20. The operating sequence through which the parts flow can be changed.

21. Machine visitation sequence can be changed or replaced quickly.
22. Route changeovers are easy.

*Volume Flexibility*

23. We can operate efficiently at different levels of output.
24. We can operate profitably at different production volumes.
25. We can economically run various batch sizes.
26. We can quickly change the quantities for our products produced.
27. We can vary aggregate output from one period to the next.
28. We can easily change the production volume of a manufacturing process.

*Mix Flexibility*

29. We can produce a wide variety of products in our plants.
30. We can produce different product types without major changeover.
31. We can build different products in the same plants at the same time.
32. We can produce, simultaneously or periodically, multiple products in a steady-state operating mode.
33. We can vary product combinations from one period to the next.
34. We can change over quickly from one product to another.

*Customer Satisfaction*

35. Customers keep doing business with us.
36. Customers are satisfied with ratio of price and functions of our products.
37. Customers perceive they receive their money's worth when they purchase our products.
38. Our customers are satisfied with the quality of our products.
39. Our firm has a good reputation for our products.
40. Our customers are loyal to our products.

*Note:* *Item was dropped during large-scale measurement analysis.

## Construct Description

Constructs were operationally defined as follows. Manufacturing flexibility was given as "the ability of the organization to manage production resource and uncertainty to meet various customer requests" (p. 177). To conceptualize this construct, the authors proposed six different types of manufacturing flexibilities. Their definitions are given below.

Machine flexibility was characterized as "the ability of a piece of equipment to perform different operations economically and effectively" (p. 177). Labor flexibility referred to "the ability of the workforce to perform a broad range of manufacturing tasks economically and effectively" (p. 177). Material handling flexibility described "the ability to transport different work pieces between various processing centers over multiple paths economically and effectively" (p. 177). Routing flexibility was defined as "the ability to process a given set of part types using multiple routes economically and effectively" (p. 177). Volume flexibility connoted "the ability of the organization to operate at various batch sizes and/or at different production output levels economically and effectively" (p. 177). Mix flexibility was associated with "the ability of the organization to produce different combinations of products economically and effectively given certain capacity" (p. 177).

In addition, customer satisfaction was analyzed in the article as the performance construct. It was constructed to capture "the degree to which customers perceive that they received products and services that are worth more than the price they paid" (p. 177).

## Measurement Description

All the constructs were measured using multi-item composite variables, with items quantified on 5-point Likert scales. Within each composite variable, six or fewer items were included. The response categories ranged from 1 = "strongly disagree" to 5 = "strongly agree."

**Development**

All the multi-item composite scales, except customer satisfaction, were newly developed for the study. The initial list of scale items were generated based on extensive literature review and structured interviews with manufacturing executives, followed by a pretest with 10 faculty members in the operations management, information systems, and marketing areas. After incorporating the changes, the revised instrument was subjected to a pilot study using 33 responses collected from manufacturing management executives to further purify the scales. "During the pilot study, items with low CITC [corrected item-to-total correlation], factor loadings, or reliability were deleted or reworded. In some cases, items were added to cover the domain of the construct" (p. 180).

For the customer satisfaction construct, the scale used in the article was adapted from Tracey (1996), with two revised items. "Customer retention rate" was changed to "customers keep doing business with us," and "generating new business through customer referrals" was changed to "our firm has a good reputation for our products."

**Sample**

A large-scale survey was conducted using a mailing list of the Society of Manufacturing Engineers (SME). Of the 3,000 surveys sent, 273 were usable. The response rate was 9.2%. The targeted respondents were CEOs, vice presidents, managers, and directors. Five U.S. Department of Commerce, Standard Industrial Classification (SIC) codes were covered in the survey: 34, fabricated metal products; 35, industrial and commercial machinery; 36, electronic and electrical equipment and components; 37, transportation equipment; and 38, instruments and measurements equipment. The $\chi^2$ test did not detect the existence of nonresponse bias. Furthermore, the construct means computed based on the sample responses across the five SIC codes were found to be consistent.

**Reliability and Validity**

Exploratory factor analysis (EFA) was conducted to check for the underlying factor structure. For the 32 items retained in the final measurement instrument, the analysis showed that all the items loaded on their respective factors and the lowest factor loading was .59 with the majority of them above .70. The cumulative variance explained by the six factors was 69.4%.

The correlation matrix was examined for evidence of convergent and discriminant validity. "The smallest within-factor items correlations are: machine flexibility = 0.34, labor flexibility = 0.54, material handling flexibility = 0.66, routing flexibility = 0.60, volume flexibility = 0.22, and mix flexibility = 0.51. These correlations are significantly different from zero ($p < 0.01$)" (p. 182). According to the authors, these results indicated that there was an acceptable level of convergent validity within the factors. Discriminant validity was tested "by comparing the lowest correlation for a particular item and any other item within the factor (within factor correlation) to correlations of that item and all items outside of the factor (between factor correlations). If the former correlation is less than the latter, then a violation occurs. An examination of the correlation matrix in Table [4 of the article] reveals a total of 11 violations. In no case does the count for the violations for an item exceed half the potential comparisons. [According to the authors, these results support] the claim that there is good discriminant validity between the factors (Campbell and Fiske, 1959; Koufteros et al., 1998)" (p. 184).

In addition, Cronbach's coefficient alpha was calculated to check for construct reliability. The resulting alpha values were all high, ranging between .79 and .92. To sum up, the authors claimed that "the instruments exceed generally accepted validity and reliability standards for basic research" (p. 188).

**Scores**

Factor loadings for manufacturing flexibility are given in Table 3 of the article. Correlations for manufacturing flexibility are given in Table 4. Completely standardized loadings and errors in the LISREL model are given in Table 6.

### Other Evidence

Not available.

### References

Campbell, D. T., and D. W. Fiske. 1959. Convergent and discriminant validation by the multitrait-multimethod matrix. *Psychological Bulletin* 56 (1): 81–105.

Koufteros, X. A., M. A. Vonderembse, and W. J. Doll. 1998. Developing measures of time-based manufacturing. *Journal of Operations Management* 16 (1): 21–41.

Tracey, M. A. 1996. Logistics/purchasing effectiveness, manufacturing flexibility and firm performance: Instrument development and causal model analysis. Unpublished diss., University of Toledo, Toledo, OH.

## Zhu and Sarkis

### Article Summarized

Zhu, Qinghua, and Joseph Sarkis. 2004. Relationships between operational practices and performance among early adopters of green supply chain management practices in Chinese manufacturing enterprises. *Journal of Operations Management* 22 (3): 265–89.

### Scales (Actual Questions Used)

*Green Supply Chain Management (GSCM) Practices*

External GSCM Practices

1. Providing design specification to suppliers that include environmental requirements for purchased items
2. Cooperation with suppliers for environmental objectives
3. Environmental audit for suppliers' internal management
4. Suppliers' ISO 14000 certification
5. Second-tier supplier's environment-friendly practice evaluation
6. Cooperation with customer for eco-design
7. Cooperation with customers for cleaner production
8. Cooperation with customers for green packaging

Investment Recovery

9. Investment recovery (sale) of excess inventories/materials
10. Sale of scrap and used materials
11. Sale of excess capital equipment

Eco-Design

12. Design of products for reduced consumption of material/energy
13. Design of products for reuse, recycle, recovery of material, and component parts
14. Design of products to avoid or reduce use of hazardous products and/or their manufacturing process

Internal Environmental Management

15. Commitment of GSCM from senior managers
16. Support for GSCM from mid-level managers
17. Cross-functional cooperation for environmental improvements

18. Total quality environmental management
19. Environmental compliance and auditing programs
20. ISO 14001 certification
21. EMS exists

Quality Management

22. ISO 9000 serial certification
23. TQM type programs

Just-in-Time

24. JIT systems implemented

*GSCM Performance Influences*

Environmental Performance

25. Reduction of air emission
26. Reduction of waste water
27. Reduction of solid wastes
28. Decrease of consumption for hazardous/harmful/toxic materials
29. Decrease of frequency for environmental accidents
30. Improve an enterprise's environmental situation

Negative Economic Performance

31. Increase of investment
32. Increase of operational cost
33. Increase of training cost
34. Increase of costs for purchasing environmentally friendly materials

Positive Economic Performance

35. Decrease of cost for material purchasing
36. Decrease of cost for energy consumption
37. Decrease of fee for waste treatment
38. Decrease of fee for waste discharge
39. Decrease of find for environmental accidents

## Construct Description

Green supply chain management (GSCM) practices were defined in terms of four factors based on the literature—internal environment management, external GSCM practices, inventory recovery, and eco-design (i.e., design for the environment). Quality management (QM) was defined as two main activities—total quality management (TQM) and ISO 9000 standards certification. Regarding just-in-time (JIT), the authors focused on "the implementation of a logistics-based JIT system, considering the overall management of materials flow of a JIT system" (p. 272). Organizational performance included both environmental performance and economic performance.

## Measurement Description

GSCM practices were quantified using 21 items, where each was answered on a 5-point Likert-type scale (1 = "not considering it," 2 = "planning to consider it," 3 = "considering it currently," 4 = "carrying out to some degree," and 5 = "carrying it out fully"). GSCM performance, including both environmental and operational financial performance, was measured using 15 items. Each item was answered using a 5-point scale (1 = "not at all," 2 = "a little bit," 3 = "to some degree," 4 = "relatively significant," and 5 = "significant").

## Development

The questionnaire was developed based on the existing literature and inputs from expert opinion to ensure that construct domains have been adequately covered. Items for the performance measures were also pretested using managers from the Bureau of Environmental Protection in Tianjin Economic and Development Zone and Dalian Economic and Technological Development Zone and several environmental managers of companies from these two zones. The survey questionnaire was initially developed in English and then translated into Chinese by one research team member. Copies of the draft questionnaire were sent to experts from academia, governmental agencies, and companies in China to confirm that questions can be understood by respondents. During the data collection process, the research team remained available to most of the respondents to address any questions related to the instrument.

## Sample

The survey was conducted using a convenience sampling approach. A total of 281 questionnaires were administered to mid-level Chinese managers participating in training workshops on environmental management, the representatives from several Chinese enterprises during site visits, and some executive MBA students from Shandong province (for details, see the appendix in the article, p. 286). The respondents sampled come from mainly Chinese manufacturing and processing industries, including automobile, power generation, electrical and electronic, chemical, steel, petroleum, pharmaceutical, and others. The target company fell into three major enterprise types in China: foreign direct investment enterprise and joint ventures, enterprises exporting products or becoming suppliers of foreign enterprises, and traditional heavy polluters. Company sizes ranged from 500 to over 8,000 employees. Out of these 281 questionnaires, 186 usable responses were received.

## Reliability and Validity

Exploratory factor analysis (EFA) with a varimax rotation technique was conducted to evaluate construct validity. The factor analysis results supported the four-factor model of GSCM practices, the three-factor model of performance, and the two-factor models of moderators—QM and JIT. Cronbach's coefficient alpha was used to measure the reliability of the scale for each construct. The alpha values for the four GSCM factors were .94, .92, .85, and .86, respectively. The alpha values for the three performance measures were .93, .90, and .87. The high values of Cronbach's coefficient alpha proved that the scales were reliable.

## Scores

The factor analysis results for GSCM practices and organizational performance are reported in Tables 3 and 4 of the article respectively. The mean and standard deviations for GSCM practices are provided in Table 5 of the article.

## Other Evidence

Not available.

## Reference

None.

# Appendix 1

# Classification of Scales

## Context and Environment Scales

| *Categories* | *Scale Name from the Paper* | *Paper* |
|---|---|---|
| Competition | Business costs | Amoako-Gyampah and Boye (2001) |
| | Business costs | Ward, Duray, Leong, and Sum (1995) |
| | Buying firm market competition | Krause (1999) |
| | Competitive hostility | Ward, Duray, Leong, and Sum (1995) |
| | Competitive hostility | Amoako-Gyampah and Boye (2001) |
| | Competitive intensity | Jambulingam, Kathuria, and Doucette (2005) |
| | Competitive intensity | Morgan, Zou, Vorhies, and Katsikeas (2003) |
| | Entry barriers | Powell (1995) |
| | Industry hostility and entry barrier perception barriers | Deane, McDougall, and Gargeya (1991) |
| | Labor availability | Ward, Duray, Leong, and Sum (1995) |
| | Labor availability | Amoako-Gyampah and Boye (2001) |
| | Marketplace environment | Benson, Saraph, and Schroeder (1991) |
| | Munificence | Jambulingam, Kathuria, and Doucette (2005) |
| | Rivalry | Powell (1995) |
| Uncertainty | Agility assessment | Cao and Dowlatshahi (2005) |
| | Change | Koufteros, Vonderembse, and Doll (2001) |
| | Demand uncertainty | Chen and Paulraj (2004) |
| | Demand unpredictability | Dröge, Claycomb, and Germain (2003) |
| | Demand unpredictability | Germain, Dröge, and Christensen (2001) |
| | Dynamism | Ward, Duray, Leong, and Sum (1995) |
| | Dynamism | Amoako-Gyampah and Boye (2001) |
| | Environment: dynamism | Ward, Duray, Leong, and Sum (1995) |
| | Environmental stability | Jambulingam, Kathuria, and Doucette (2005) |
| | Environmental uncertainty | Pagell and Krause (2004) |

*(Continued)*

(Continued)

| | | |
|---|---|---|
| | Environmental uncertainty | Vickery, Dröge, and Germain (1999) |
| | Environmental uncertainty: competitor component | Ho (1996) |
| | Environmental uncertainty: customer component | Ho (1996) |
| | Environmental uncertainty: social-political component | Ho (1996) |
| | Environmental uncertainty: supplier component | Ho (1996) |
| | Environmental uncertainty: technological component | Ho (1996) |
| | Environmentally caused disruption | Tatikonda and Montoya-Weiss (2001) |
| | Equivocality | Koufteros, Vonderembse, and Doll (2002) |
| | Market newness | Tatikonda and Montoya-Weiss (2001) |
| | Perceived environmental uncertainty | Swamidass and Newell (1987) |
| | Process technology novelty | Tatikonda and Montoya-Weiss (2001) |
| | Product technology novelty | Tatikonda and Montoya-Weiss (2001) |
| | Production technology routineness | Dröge, Claycomb, and Germain (2003) |
| | Rate of technological change in buying firm's industry | Krause (1999) |
| | Supply uncertainty | Chen and Paulraj (2004) |
| | Supply uncertainty | Carter and Carter (1998) |
| | Technological turbulence | Dröge, Claycomb, and Germain (2003) |
| | Technology uncertainty | Chen and Paulraj (2004) |
| | Uncertainty | Prasad, Tata, and Madan (2005) |
| | Uncertainty | Calantone, Dröge, and Vickery (2002) |
| | Uncertainty | Koufteros, Vonderembse, and Doll (2002) |
| | Unpredictability | Anand and Ward (2004) |
| | Volatility | Anand and Ward (2004) |
| Industry type | Competitive sector | Carter and Carter (1998) |
| | Industrial sector | Rosenzweig, Roth, and Dean (2003) |
| | Industry | Lawrence and Hottenstein (1995) |
| | Industry productivity growth | Schmenner and Cook (1985) |
| | Input sector | Carter and Carter (1998) |
| | Output sector | Carter and Carter (1998) |
| | Regulatory sector | Carter and Carter (1998) |
| Plant/process/ product type | Capacity utilization | Cua, McKone, and Schroeder (2001) |
| | Characteristics of plant | Lawrence and Hottenstein (1995) |
| | Degrees of product customization | Raffi and Swamidass (1987) |
| | Descriptor (what) | New and Szwejczewski (1995) |
| | Information complexity | Prasad, Tata, and Madan (2005) |
| | Intermediate (how) | New and Szwejczewski (1995) |
| | Manufacturing flexibility and modularization | Rabinovich, Dresner, and Evers (2003) |
| | Mass output orientation | Germain, Dröge, and Christensen (2001) |
| | Number of employees | Cua, McKone, and Schroeder (2001) |
| | Order filling method | Raffi and Swamidass (1987) |

| | | |
|---|---|---|
| | Plant age | Shah and Ward (2003) |
| | Plant environment | Flynn, Sakakibara, and Schroeder (1995) |
| | Plant size | Shah and Ward (2003) |
| | Plant size | Sawhney and Piper (2002) |
| | Plant type | Fry, Steele, and Saladin (1995) |
| | Process choice | Safizadeh, Ritzman, Sharma, and Wood (1996) |
| | Process choice | Safizadeh and Ritzman (1997) |
| | Process rationalization | Raffi and Swamidass (1987) |
| | Process structure complexity | Devaraj, Hollingworth, and Schroeder (2004) |
| | Process-orientation | Cua, McKone, and Schroeder (2001) |
| | Product and product changes | Schmenner and Cook (1985) |
| | Product/process environment | Benson, Saraph, and Schroeder (1991) |
| | Production orientation | Fry, Steele, and Saladin (1995) |
| | Production process and process changes | Schmenner and Cook (1985) |
| | Production process focus | Wathen (1995) |
| | Service type | Youngdahl and Kellogg (1997) |
| | Type of products and process | Schroeder, Anderson, Tupy, and White (1981) |
| | Union | Shah and Ward (2003) |
| Task type | Product complexity | Sawhney and Piper (2002) |
| | Task demands: complexity | Lewis (2004) |
| | Technical difficulty | Primo and Amundson (2002) |

## Operations Strategy Scales

| *Categories* | *Scale Name from the Paper* | *Paper* |
|---|---|---|
| Competitive priorities | Competitive capabilities: delivery | Kim and Arnold (1992) |
| | Competitive capabilities: flexibility | Kim and Arnold (1992) |
| | Competitive capabilities: price | Kim and Arnold (1992) |
| | Competitive capabilities: quality | Kim and Arnold (1992) |
| | Competitive capabilities: service | Kim and Arnold (1992) |
| | Competitive priorities | Roth and van der Velde (1991) |
| | Competitive priorities | Chen and Paulraj (2004) |
| | Competitive priorities | Raffi and Swamidass (1987) |
| | Competitive priorities | Dröge, Vickery, and Markland (1994) |
| | Competitive priorities | Safizadeh, Ritzman, Sharma, and Wood (1996) |
| | Competitive priorities: cost | Boyer and McDermott (1999) |
| | Competitive priorities: cost | Karuppan and Ganster (2004) |
| | Competitive priorities: cost | Ward, Duray, Leong, and Sum (1995) |
| | Competitive priorities: delivery | Ward, Duray, Leong, and Sum (1995) |
| | Competitive priorities: delivery | Boyer and McDermott (1999) |
| | Competitive priorities: flexibility | Ward, Duray, Leong, and Sum (1995) |
| | Competitive priorities: flexibility | Boyer and McDermott (1999) |
| | Competitive priorities: flexibility (range) | Karuppan and Ganster (2004) |
| | Competitive priorities: flexibility (time) | Karuppan and Ganster (2004) |

*(Continued)*

(Continued)

| | |
|---|---|
| Competitive priorities: quality | Ward, Duray, Leong, and Sum (1995) |
| Competitive priorities: quality | Boyer and McDermott (1999) |
| Competitive priorities: quality | Karuppan and Ganster (2004) |
| Competitive priorities: speed | Karupan and Ganster (2004) |
| Competitive strategy | Flynn and Flynn (2004) |
| Cost | Diáz, Machuca, and Alvarez-Gil (2003) |
| Cost | Krause, Pagell, and Curkovic (2001) |
| Cost | Joshi, Kathuria, and Porth (2003) |
| Cost importance | Ward, McCreery, Ritzman, and Sharma (1998) |
| Delivery | Joshi, Kathuria, and Porth (2003) |
| Delivery | Safizadeh, Field, and Ritzman (2003) |
| Delivery | Diáz, Machuca, and Alvarez-Gil (2003) |
| Delivery | Krause, Pagell, and Curkovic (2001) |
| Delivery performance | Amoako-Gyampah and Boye (2001) |
| Delivery time importance | Ward, McCreery, Ritzman, and Sharma (1998) |
| Flexibility | Joshi, Kathuria, and Porth (2003) |
| Flexibility | Pagell and Krause (2004) |
| Flexibility | Diáz, Machuca, and Alvarez-Gil (2003) |
| Flexibility | Krause, Pagell, and Curkovic (2001) |
| Flexibility | Amoako-Gyampah and Boye (2001) |
| Flexibility importance | Ward, McCreery, Ritzman, and Sharma (1998) |
| Innovation | Nassimbeni (2003) |
| Innovation | Krause, Pagell, and Curkovic (2001) |
| Labor flexibility: mobility | Koste, Malhotra, and Sharma (2004) |
| Labor flexibility: range-heterogeneity | Karuppan and Ganster (2004) |
| Labor flexibility: range-number | Karuppan and Ganster (2004) |
| Labor flexibility: range-heterogeneity | Koste, Malhotra, and Sharma (2004) |
| Labor flexibility: range-number | Koste, Malhotra, and Sharma (2004) |
| Labor flexibility: uniformity | Koste, Malhotra, and Sharma (2004) |
| Labor flexibility: uniformity | Karuppan and Ganster (2004) |
| Low cost | Safizadeh, Field, and Ritzman (2003) |
| Low cost priority | Amoako-Gyampah and Boye (2001) |
| Machine flexibility: mobility | Koste, Malhotra, and Sharma (2004) |
| Machine flexibility: mobility | Karuppan and Ganster (2004) |
| Machine flexibility: range-heterogeneity | Koste, Malhotra, and Sharma (2004) |
| Machine flexibility: range-number | Koste, Malhotra, and Sharma (2004) |
| Machine flexibility: range-heterogeneity | Karuppan and Ganster (2004) |
| Machine flexibility: range-number | Karuppan and Ganster (2004) |
| Machine flexibility: uniformity | Koste, Malhotra, and Sharma (2004) |
| Manufacturing decision variables | Deane, McDougall, and Gargeya (1991) |
| Manufacturing mission | Schroeder, Anderson, and Cleveland (1986) |
| Manufacturing objectives | Kim and Arnold (1996) |
| Manufacturing objectives | Schroeder, Anderson, and Cleveland (1986) |
| Manufacturing strategy | Dean and Snell (1996) |
| Material handling flexibility: mobility | Koste, Malhotra, and Sharma (2004) |

| | | |
|---|---|---|
| | Material handling flexibility: range-heterogeneity | Koste, Malhotra, and Sharma (2004) |
| | Material handling flexibility: range-number | Koste, Malhotra, and Sharma (2004) |
| | Material handling flexibility: uniformity | Koste, Malhotra, and Sharma (2004) |
| | Mix flexibility: mobility | Karuppan and Ganster (2004) |
| | Mix flexibility: mobility | Koste, Malhotra, and Sharma (2004) |
| | Mix flexibility: range-heterogeneity | Karuppan and Ganster (2004) |
| | Mix flexibility: range-heterogeneity | Koste, Malhotra, and Sharma (2004) |
| | Mix flexibility: range-number | Karuppan and Ganster (2004) |
| | Mix flexibility: range-number | Koste, Malhotra, and Sharma (2004) |
| | Mix flexibility: uniformity | Karuppan and Ganster (2004) |
| | Mix flexibility: uniformity | Koste, Malhotra, and Sharma (2004) |
| | Mobility | Anand and Ward (2004) |
| | Modification flexibility: mobility | Koste, Malhotra, and Sharma (2004) |
| | Modification flexibility: range-heterogeneity | Koste, Malhotra, and Sharma (2004) |
| | Modification flexibility: range-number | Koste, Malhotra, and Sharma (2004) |
| | Modification flexibility: uniformity | Koste, Malhotra, and Sharma (2004) |
| | New product flexibility: mobility | Koste, Malhotra, and Sharma (2004) |
| | New product flexibility: range-heterogeneity | Koste, Malhotra, and Sharma (2004) |
| | New product flexibility: range-number | Koste, Malhotra, and Sharma (2004) |
| | New product flexibility: uniformity | Koste, Malhotra, and Sharma (2004) |
| | New product introduction rate | Calantone, Dröge, and Vickery (2002) |
| | Order winners | Menda and Dilts (1997) |
| | Order winners | Fry, Steele, and Saladin (1995) |
| | Process flexibility | Safizadeh, Field, and Ritzman (2003) |
| | Quality | Diáz, Machuca, and Alvarez-Gil (2003) |
| | Quality | Amoako-Gyampah and Boye (2001) |
| | Quality | Krause, Pagell, and Curkovic (2001) |
| | Quality importance | Ward, McCreery, Ritzman, and Sharma (1998) |
| | Quality of customer interface | Safizadeh, Field, and Ritzman (2003) |
| | Quality-of-conformance | Joshi, Kathuria, and Porth (2003) |
| | Quality-of-design | Joshi, Kathuria, and Porth (2003) |
| | Range | Anand and Ward (2004) |
| | Service quality | Safizadeh, Field, and Ritzman (2003) |
| | Strategic importance | Vickery, Dröge, Yeomans, and Markland (1995) |
| | Success factors | Fry, Steele, and Saladin (1995) |
| Strategy contents (structural/ infrastructural choices) | Adoption of strategic manufacturing practices | Voss and Blackmon (1998) |
| | Alternative ways to change capacity: decreases | Chikan and Demeter (1995) |

*(Continued)*

(Continued)

| | | |
|---|---|---|
| | Alternative ways to change capacity: increases | Chikan and Demeter (1995) |
| | Capability building programs | Ward, Leong, and Boyer (1994) |
| | Capacity | Roth and van der Velde (1991) |
| | Causes of late delivery | Chikan and Demeter (1995) |
| | Causes of priority changes | Chikan and Demeter (1995) |
| | Degree of computerization | Chikan and Demeter (1995) |
| | Degree of similarity across focused work cells or PWPs | Bozarth and Edwards (1997) |
| | Delivery speed | da Silveira (2005) |
| | Facilities and retail outlets | Roth and van der Velde (1991) |
| | Health service network | Li, Benton, and Leong (2002) |
| | Human resources | Roth and van der Velde (1991) |
| | Identifying traditional and enlightened plants | Brown (1998) |
| | Improvement action plan (manufacturing strategy) | Kim and Arnold (1996) |
| | Information systems | Roth and van der Velde (1991) |
| | Infrastructural investments: QLEAD | Boyer and McDermott (1999) |
| | Infrastructural investments: TEAM | Boyer and McDermott (1999) |
| | Infrastructural investments: WEMP | Boyer and McDermott (1999) |
| | Integration choices | Roth and van der Velde (1991) |
| | Invest in clinical technology | Li, Benton, and Leong (2002) |
| | Invest in office technology | Li, Benton, and Leong (2002) |
| | Invest in patient medical information systems demand prediction | Li, Benton, and Leong (2002) |
| | Level of capital investment | da Silveira (2005) |
| | Managing demand | Li, Benton, and Leong (2002) |
| | Manufacturing characteristics focus | Bozarth and Edwards (1997) |
| | Manufacturing flexibility | Ho (1996) |
| | Manufacturing flexibility | Swamidass and Newell (1987) |
| | Manufacturing importance | Hausman, Montgomery, and Roth (2002) |
| | Manufacturing policies (areas with written policies established) | Schroeder, Anderson, and Cleveland (1986) |
| | Manufacturing strategy: technology orientation | Williams, D'Souza, Rosenfeldt, and Kassaee (1995) |
| | Manufacturing strategy: market orientation | Williams, D'Souza, Rosenfeldt, and Kassaee (1995) |
| | Marketing choices | Roth and van der Velde (1991) |
| | Marketing importance | Hausman, Montgomery, and Roth (2002) |
| | Operations strategy | Ahmed, Montagno, and Firenze (1996) |
| | Operations strategy factor | Goldstein, Ward, Leong, and Butler (2002) |
| | Outpatient service | Li, Benton, and Leong (2002) |
| | Performance management | Roth and van der Velde (1991) |
| | Price | da Silveira (2005) |
| | Process choice | Safizadeh, Ritzman, Sharma, and Wood (1996) |
| | Process choice | da Silveira (2005) |
| | Process technology | Roth and van der Velde (1991) |
| | Product plan | Safizadeh, Ritzman, Sharma, and Wood (1996) |

| | | |
|---|---|---|
| | Production competence | Cleveland, Schroeder, and Anderson (1989) |
| | Production process | Cleveland, Schroeder, and Anderson (1989) |
| | Production process focus | Wathen (1995) |
| | Quality management program | Roth and van der Velde (1991) |
| | Reasons for subcontracting | Chikan and Demeter (1995) |
| | Relative characteristics of primary retail banking offerings | Menor, Roth, and Mason (2001) |
| | Relative characteristics of retail delivery system, policies, and processes | Menor, Roth, and Mason (2001) |
| | Staff composition | Li, Benton, and Leong (2002) |
| | Staff increase | Li, Benton, and Leong (2002) |
| | Staff overage management: | Li, Benton, and Leong (2002) |
| | non-pay-related measures | Li, Benton, and Leong (2002) |
| | Staff overage management: | |
| | pay-related measures | Li, Benton, and Leong (2002) |
| | Staff reduction | |
| | Staff shortage management | Li, Benton, and Leong (2002) |
| | Strategic breadth of the new venture | Deane, McDougall, and Gargeya (1991) |
| | firms | Malhotra, Steele, and Grover (1994) |
| | Strategic(manufacturing) issues | |
| | Strategic(manufacturing) issues | Malhotra, Steele, and Grover (1994) |
| | Structural investments : design | Boyer and McDermott (1999) |
| | Structural investments: admin | Boyer and McDermott (1999) |
| | Structural investments: manufacturing | Boyer and McDermott (1999) |
| | Tactical (manufacturing) issues | Malhotra, Steele, and Grover (1994) |
| | Tactical (manufacturing) issues | Malhotra, Steele, and Grover (1994) |
| | Trend in capacity utilization | Raffi and Swamidass (1987) |
| | Type of product | da Silveira (2005) |
| | Unique design capability | da Silveira (2005) |
| | Vertical integration | Roth and van der Velde (1991) |
| | Work-in-progress | da Silveira (2005) |
| Strategy process | Ability | Gilgeous (1995) |
| | Communication of strategy | Sakakibara, Flynn, Schroeder, and Morris (1997) |
| | Communication of strategy | Ahmad and Schroeder (2001) |
| | Communication of strategy | Flynn and Flynn (2004) |
| | Communication of strategy | Lawrence and Hottenstein (1995) |
| | Communication of strategy | Ahmad and Schroeder (2003) |
| | Critical success factors | Roth and van der Velde (1991) |
| | Culture | Gilgeous (1995) |
| | Customer focus | Chen and Paulraj (2004) |
| | Identifying traditional and enlightened plants | Brown (1998) |
| | Information | Gilgeous (1995) |
| | Infrastructure | Gilgeous (1995) |
| | Interaction with other functions | Lawrence and Hottenstein (1995) |
| | Long-term/short-term strategic orientation | Menor, Roth, and Mason (2001) |

*(Continued)*

(Continued)

| | | |
|---|---|---|
| | Long-range orientation | Sakakibara, Flynn, Schroeder, and Morris (1997) |
| | Management practices | Morita and Flynn (1997) |
| | Manufacturing involvement | Ward, Leong, and Boyer (1994) |
| | Manufacturing manager's participation in strategy formulation | Tracey, Vonderembse, and Lim (1999) |
| | Manufacturing strategy | Lawrence and Hottenstein (1995) |
| | Manufacturing strategy process: environmental interaction | Ho (1996) |
| | Manufacturing strategy process: manufacturing planning activities | Ho (1996) |
| | Manufacturing strategy process: role of manufacturing function: | Ho (1996) |
| | Manufacturing strategy process: worker participation | Ho (1996) |
| | Manufacturing strategy scales: communication of strategy | Bates, Amundson, Schroeder, and Morris (1995) |
| | Manufacturing strategy scales: formal strategic planning | Bates, Amundson, Schroeder, and Morris (1995) |
| | Manufacturing strategy scales: long-range orientation | Bates, Amundson, Schroeder, and Morris (1995) |
| | Manufacturing strategy scales: manufacturing strategy strength | Bates, Amundson, Schroeder, and Morris (1995) |
| | Manufacturing strategy scales: strategic role-stage 1 | Bates, Amundson, Schroeder, and Morris (1995) |
| | Manufacturing strategy scales: strategic role-stage 2 | Bates, Amundson, Schroeder, and Morris (1995) |
| | Manufacturing strategy scales: strategic role-stage 3 | Bates, Amundson, Schroeder, and Morris (1995) |
| | Manufacturing strategy scales: strategic role-stage 4 | Bates, Amundson, Schroeder, and Morris (1995) |
| | Manufacturing strategy strength | Sakakibara, Flynn, Schroeder, and Morris (1997) |
| | Measures of long-term orientation | Voss and Blackmon (1998) |
| | Measures of short-term orientation | Voss and Blackmon (1998) |
| | Resources | Gilgeous (1995) |
| | Responsibility | Vickery, Dröge, Yeomans, and Markland (1995) |
| | Risk taking | Ho (1996) |
| | Role of manufacturing managers in strategic decision making | Swamidass and Newell (1987) |
| | Stage 3 manufacturing | Sakakibara, Flynn, Schroeder, and Morris (1997) |
| | Stage 4 manufacturing | Sakakibara, Flynn, Schroeder, and Morris (1997) |
| | Strategic adaptation | Morita and Flynn (1997) |
| | Technological adaptation | Morita and Flynn (1997) |
| | Top management support | Chen and Paulraj (2004) |
| Lean manufacturing strategy | Discipline | Collins, Cordon, and Julien (1998) |
| | Flexibility | Collins, Cordon, and Julien (1998) |
| | Internal lean practices | Li, Rao, Ragu-Nathan, and Ragu-Nathan (2005) |

| | | |
|---|---|---|
| | Lean manufacturing | Karlsson and Ahlstrom (1995) |
| | Leaning manufacturing practices | Shah and Ward (2003) |
| | Simplicity | Collins, Cordon, and Julien (1998) |
| Time-based strategy | Time-based manufacturing practices | Nahm, Vonderembse, and Koufteros (2004) |
| | Time-based manufacturing practices | Nahm, Vonderembse, and Koufteros (2003) |
| Mass customization | Customer closeness | Tu, Vonderembse, Ragu-Nathan, and Ragu-Nathan (2004) |
| | Customization | Zahay and Griffin (2004) |
| | Dynamic teaming | Tu, Vonderembse, Ragu-Nathan, and Ragu-Nathan (2004) |
| | Mass customization | Tu, Vonderembse, Ragu-Nathan, and Ragu-Nathan (2004) |
| | Mass customization | Tu, Vonderembse, and Ragu-Nathan (2001) |
| | Personalization | Zahay and Griffin (2004) |
| | Postponement | Li, Rao, Ragu-Nathan, and Ragu-Nathan (2005) |
| | Process modularity | Tu, Vonderembse, Ragu-Nathan, and Ragu-Nathan (2004) |
| | Product customization | Rabinovich, Dresner, and Evers (2003) |
| | Product customization | Vickery, Dröge, and Germain (1999) |
| | Product modularity | Tu, Vonderembse, Ragu-Nathan, and Ragu-Nathan (2004) |
| Service strategy | Academic integration | Hennig-Thurau, Langer, and Hansen (2001) |
| | Access standards | Heineke (1995) |
| | Adverse outcome management | Heineke (1995) |
| | Algorithm use | Heineke (1995) |
| | Banking enquiries | Heute and Roth (1988) |
| | Banking transactions | Heute and Roth (1988) |
| | Capital expenditure | Safizadeh, Field, and Ritzman (2003) |
| | Cesarean feedback | Heineke (1995) |
| | Cesarean policies | Heineke (1995) |
| | Cognitive commitment | Hennig-Thurau, Langer, and Hansen (2001) |
| | Commitment to nonuniversity activities | Hennig-Thurau, Langer, and Hansen (2001) |
| | Cross-training | Safizadeh, Field, and Ritzman (2003) |
| | Customer enquiries | Heute and Roth (1988) |
| | Customization | Safizadeh, Field, and Ritzman (2003) |
| | Emotional commitment | Hennig-Thurau, Langer, and Hansen (2001) |
| | Family commitment | Hennig-Thurau, Langer, and Hansen (2001) |
| | Goal commitment | Hennig-Thurau, Langer, and Hansen (2001) |
| | Hospital practice review | Heineke (1995) |
| | Intimacy | Soteriou and Chase (1998) |
| | Job commitment | Hennig-Thurau, Langer, and Hansen (2001) |
| | Labor intensity | Safizadeh, Field, and Ritzman (2003) |
| | Length of stay standard | Heineke (1995) |
| | Medical doctor payment | Heineke (1995) |
| | Mode of interaction | Safizadeh, Field, and Ritzman (2003) |
| | Model type | Heineke (1995) |
| | Nonclinical factors | Heineke (1995) |

*(Continued)*

(Continued)

| | | |
|---|---|---|
| | Office practice review | Heineke (1995) |
| | Orientation of process | Safizadeh, Field, and Ritzman (2003) |
| | Range of products, customer's choice, and customer involvement | Safizadeh, Field, and Ritzman (2003) |
| | Routineness | Safizadeh, Field, and Ritzman (2003) |
| | Social integration | Hennig-Thurau, Langer, and Hansen (2001) |
| | Trust | Hennig-Thurau, Langer, and Hansen (2001) |
| | Use of appointment system | Safizadeh, Field, and Ritzman (2003) |
| | Utilization | Safizadeh, Field, and Ritzman (2003) |
| | Utilization feedback | Heineke (1995) |
| | Workforce configuration | Heineke (1995) |

## Business Strategy Scales

| *Categories* | *Scale Name from the Paper* | *Paper* |
|---|---|---|
| Business strategy | Business strategy | Cleveland, Schroeder, and Anderson (1989) |
| | Business strategy elements: operations | Schroeder, Anderson, and Cleveland (1986) |
| | Business strategy elements: price | Schroeder, Anderson, and Cleveland (1986) |
| | Business strategy elements: product | Schroeder, Anderson, and Cleveland (1986) |
| | Business strategy elements: service | Schroeder, Anderson, and Cleveland (1986) |
| | Differentiation | Zahay and Griffin (2004) |
| | Level of differentiation | Williams, D'Souza, Rosenfeldt, and Kassaee (1995) |
| | Low cost | Zahay and Griffin (2004) |
| | Niche profile | Roth (1993) |
| | Strategic excellence | Zahay and Griffin (2004) |
| | Strategy | Pagell (2004) |
| Marketing and other functional strategy | Importance of scientific information sources | Veuglers and Cassiman (1999) |
| | Importance of close competitors as information sources of the firm for innovation | Veuglers and Cassiman (1999) |
| | Importance of cost and risk obstacle for innovation by the firm | Veuglers and Cassiman (1999) |
| | Importance of cost-efficiency goal of the firm | Veuglers and Cassiman (1999) |
| | Importance of ease of imitation of innovations as an obstacle to innovation by the firm | Veuglers and Cassiman (1999) |
| | Importance of internal information sources of the firm for innovation | Veuglers and Cassiman (1999) |
| | Importance of lack of information for innovation as an obstacle to innovation by the firm | Veuglers and Cassiman (1999) |
| | Importance of lack of opportunities of innovation as an obstacle to innovation by the firm | Veuglers and Cassiman (1999) |

| | | |
|---|---|---|
| | Importance of no need for innovation as an obstacle to innovation by the firm | Veuglers and Cassiman (1999) |
| | Importance of protection mechanisms for product and process innovations of the firm | Veuglers and Cassiman (1999) |
| | Importance of quality improvement goal of the firm | Veuglers and Cassiman (1999) |
| | Importance of resistance against change within the firm as an obstacle to innovation by the firm | Veuglers and Cassiman (1999) |
| | Market requirements focus | Bozarth and Edwards (1997) |
| | Marketing decision variables | Deane, McDougall, and Gargeya (1991) |
| | Marketing implementation capabilities | Morgan, Zou, Vorhies, and Katsikeas (2003) |
| | Marketing planning capabilities | Morgan, Zou, Vorhies, and Katsikeas (2003) |
| | Marketing strategy factor | Goldstein, Ward, Leong, and Butler (2002) |
| Integration between strategies | Marketing-manufacturing (M/M) interface harmony | Hausman, Montgomery, and Roth (2002) |
| | Manufacturing evaluation of marketing communication | Calantone, Dröge, and Vickery (2002) |
| | Marketing knowledge of manufacturing | Calantone, Dröge, and Vickery (2002) |
| | Marketing-manufacturing integration | Calantone, Dröge, and Vickery (2002) |
| | Marketing-manufacturing relationship quality | Calantone, Dröge, and Vickery (2002) |
| | Marketing-operations interface (MOI) quality | Sawhney and Piper (2002) |
| | MOI speed | Sawhney and Piper (2002) |
| | Strategy integration | Swink, Narasimhan, and Kim (2005) |

## CORE QUALITY PRACTICES

| *Categories* | *Scale Name from the Paper* | *Paper* |
|---|---|---|
| Quality leadership/ management support | Committed leadership | Curkovic, Vickery, and Dröge (2000) |
| | Committed leadership | Cua, McKone, and Schroeder (2001) |
| | Corporate quality culture | Black and Porter (1996) |
| | Corporate support for quality | Benson, Saraph, and Schroeder (1991) |
| | Executive commitment | Powell (1995) |
| | Leadership | Escrig-Tena and Bou-Llusar (2005) |
| | Leadership | Samson and Terziovski (1999) |
| | Leadership | Pannirselvam, Siferd, and Ruch (1998) |
| | Leadership: director of nursing | Chesteen, Helgheim, Randall, and Wardell (2005) |

*(Continued)*

(Continued)

| | | |
|---|---|---|
| | Leadership: immediate supervisor | Chesteen, Helgheim, Randall, and Wardell (2005) |
| | Leadership: patient focus | Chesteen, Helgheim, Randall, and Wardell (2005) |
| | Management support | Flynn, Sakakibara, and Schroeder (1995) |
| | Management systems and quality improvement process | Flynn and Saladin (2001) |
| | Managerial knowledge | Benson, Saraph, and Schroeder (1991) |
| | Organizational system for quality | Morita and Flynn (1997) |
| | Participatory leadership | Marley, Collier, and Goldstein (2004) |
| | Policy | Flynn and Saladin (2001) |
| | Quality improvement: Behavioral | Adam (1994) |
| | Role of top management and quality policy | Forker, Mendez, and Hershauer (1997) |
| | Role of top management and quality policy | Forker (1997) |
| | Senior corporate leadership | Flynn and Saladin (2001) |
| | Senior executive involvement | Adam, Corbett, Flores, Harrison, Lee, Rho, Ribera, Samson, and Westbrook (1997) |
| | Shared vision | Detert and Schroeder (2003) |
| | Strategic quality management | Black and Porter (1996) |
| | Top management commitment | Ahire, Golhar, and Waller (1996) |
| | Top management leadership for quality | Flynn and Flynn (2004) |
| | Top management leadership for quality | McKone, Schroeder, and Cua (1999) |
| | Top management support | Flynn, Schroeder, and Sakakibara (1995) |
| | Top management support: quality improve rewards | Flynn, Schroeder, and Sakakibara (1994) |
| | Top management support: quality leadership | Flynn, Schroeder, and Sakakibara (1994) |
| | Top management team involvement | Douglas and Fredendall (2004) |
| | Top management quality leadership | Sakakibara, Flynn, Schroeder, and Morris (1997) |
| | Total quality management: management leadership | Kaynak (2003) |
| | Vision | Hays and Hill (2001) |
| | Visionary leadership | Rungtusanatham, Forza, Koka, Salvador, and Nie (2005) |
| | Visionary leadership | Anderson, Rungtusanatham, Schroeder, and Devaraj (1995) |
| Strategic quality planning | Adopting the philosophy | Powell (1995) |
| | Attention to quality | Schmenner and Cook (1985) |
| | Infrastructure: QLEAD | Boyer, Leong, Ward, and Krajewski (1997) |
| | Long-term focus | Detert and Schroeder (2003) |
| | Operational quality planning | Black and Porter (1996) |
| | Operations and strategic goals | Flynn and Saladin (2001) |
| | Planning function | Flynn and Saladin (2001) |
| | Role of the quality department | Forker, Mendez, and Hershauer (1997) |
| | Role of the quality department | Forker (1997) |
| | Strategic planning | Samson and Terziovski (1999) |

| | | |
|---|---|---|
| | Strategic planning | Cua, McKone, and Schroeder (2001) |
| | Strategic planning | Park, Hartley, and Wilson (2001) |
| | Strategic quality planning | Choi and Eboch (1998) |
| | Strategic quality planning | Pannirselvam, Siferd, and Ruch (1998) |
| Information and analysis | Benchmark control | Germain and Dröge (1997) |
| | Benchmarking | Curkovic, Vickery, and Dröge (2000) |
| | Benchmarking | Ahire, Golhar, and Waller (1996) |
| | Benchmarking | Powell (1995) |
| | Communications of improvement information | Black and Porter (1996) |
| | Customer data and analysis | Flynn and Saladin (2001) |
| | Customer driven information | Douglas and Fredendall (2004) |
| | Data | Hays and Hill (2001) |
| | Data-based decision making | Detert and Schroeder (2003) |
| | Documentation | Flynn and Saladin (2001) |
| | Employee relations data and analysis | Flynn and Saladin (2001) |
| | Feedback | Sakakibara, Flynn, Schroeder, and Morris (1997) |
| | Feedback | Ahmad and Schroeder (2001) |
| | Feedback of information | Flynn, Schroeder, and Flynn (1999) |
| | Information and analysis | Goldstein and Naor (2005) |
| | Information and analysis | Pannirselvam, Siferd, and Ruch (1998) |
| | Information and analysis | Samson and Terziovski (1999) |
| | Information and analysis | Choi and Eboch (1998) |
| | Information and feedback | Cua, McKone, and Schroeder (2001) |
| | Information and retrieval | Stahl and Zimmerer (1983) |
| | Information feedback | Flynn, Sakakibara, and Schroeder (1995) |
| | Information management | Park, Hartley, and Wilson (2001) |
| | Information utilization | Ittner and Larcker (1997) |
| | Internal quality information usage | Ahire, Golhar, and Waller (1996) |
| | Knowledge dissemination: feedback | Chesteen, Helgheim, Randall, and Wardell (2005) |
| | Knowledge dissemination: task expectation | Chesteen, Helgheim, Randall, and Wardell (2005) |
| | Management by fact | Douglas and Fredendall (2004) |
| | Measurement | Curkovic, Vickery, and Dröge (2000) |
| | Measurement | Powell (1995) |
| | Measurement and standards | Flynn and Saladin (2001) |
| | Process information | Flynn and Flynn (2004) |
| | Quality data and reporting | Forker, Mendez, and Hershauer (1997) |
| | Quality data and reporting | Forker (1997) |
| | Quality improvement measurement systems | Black and Porter (1996) |
| | Quality information: feedback | Flynn, Schroeder, and Sakakibara (1994) |
| | Quality information: process control | Flynn, Schroeder, and Sakakibara (1994) |
| | Rewards for quality | Flynn and Flynn (2004) |
| | Rewards for quality | Sakakibara, Flynn, Schroeder, and Morris (1997) |
| | Scope of quality data and information | Flynn and Saladin (2001) |
| | Supplier quality data and analysis | Flynn and Saladin (2001) |

*(Continued)*

(Continued)

| | | |
|---|---|---|
| | Total quality management (TQM): quality data and reporting | Kaynak (2003) |
| | TQM implementation: rewards for quality | McKone, Schroeder, and Cua (1999) |
| | Use of analytical techniques | Flynn and Saladin (2001) |
| | Use of product quality data | Flynn and Saladin (2001) |
| Process management | Assurance and validation | Flynn and Saladin (2001) |
| | Autonomous and planned maintenance | Cua, McKone, and Schroeder (2001) |
| | Continuous improvement (CI) communication | Choi and Liker (1995) |
| | CI effectiveness | Choi and Liker (1995) |
| | Continuous improvement | Curkovic, Vickery, and Dröge (2000) |
| | Continuous improvement | Rungtusanatham, Forza, Koka, Salvador, and Nie (2005) |
| | Continuous improvement | Douglas and Fredendall (2004) |
| | Continuous improvement | Detert and Schroeder (2003) |
| | Continuous improvement | Flynn, Schroeder, and Flynn (1999) |
| | Continuous improvement | Anderson, Rungtusanatham, Schroeder, and Devaraj (1995) |
| | Flexible manufacturing | Powell (1995) |
| | Improvement | Hays and Hill (2001) |
| | Maintenance | Sakakibara, Flynn, Schroeder, and Morris (1997) |
| | Maintenance and strategy | Lawrence and Hottenstein (1995) |
| | Management of process quality | Choi and Eboch (1998) |
| | Management of process quality | Pannirselvam, Siferd, and Ruch (1998) |
| | Management technical competence | Flynn, Schroeder, and Flynn (1999) |
| | Operational system for quality | Morita and Flynn (1997) |
| | Preventive maintenance | Koufteros, Vonderembse, and Doll (1998) |
| | Preventive maintenance | Koufteros (1999) |
| | Preventive maintenance | Sakakibara, Flynn, and Schroeder (1993) |
| | Preventive maintenance | Tu, Vonderembse, and Ragu-Nathan (2001) |
| | Process control | Ahmad and Schroeder (2001) |
| | Process control | Flynn, Schroeder, and Flynn (1999) |
| | Process control | Sakakibara, Flynn, Schroeder, and Morris (1997) |
| | Process flow management | Flynn, Schroeder, and Sakakibara (1995) |
| | Process focus | Ittner and Larcker (1997) |
| | Process improvement | Powell (1995) |
| | Process management | Rungtusanatham, Forza, Koka, Salvador, and Nie (2005) |
| | Process management | Goldstein and Naor (2005) |
| | Process management | Samson and Terziovski (1999) |
| | Process management | Anderson, Rungtusanatham, Schroeder, and Devaraj (1995) |
| | Process management | Cua, McKone, and Schroeder (2001) |
| | Process management | Park, Hartley, and Wilson (2001) |
| | Process management/operating procedures | Forker, Mendez, and Hershauer (1997) |

| | | |
|---|---|---|
| | Process management/operating procedures | Forker (1997) |
| | Process management: cleanliness and organization | Flynn, Schroeder, and Sakakibara (1994) |
| | Process management: procedures | Chesteen, Helgheim, Randall, and Wardell (2005) |
| | Process management: responsiveness | Chesteen, Helgheim, Randall, and Wardell (2005) |
| | Process quality management | Swink, Narasimhan, and Kim (2005) |
| | Product and service processes | Flynn and Saladin (2001) |
| | Productivity improvement | Adam (1994) |
| | Productivity programs and miscellaneous variables | Schmenner and Cook (1985) |
| | Proprietary equipment | Flynn, Schroeder, and Flynn (1999) |
| | Proprietary equipment development | Cua, McKone, and Schroeder (2001) |
| | Quality assurance | Tu, Vonderembse, and Ragu-Nathan (2001) |
| | Quality at same cost | Detert and Schroeder (2003) |
| | Quality improvement | Adam (1994) |
| | Quality improvement efforts | Koufteros, Vonderembse, and Doll (1998) |
| | Quality procedures | Voss, Tsikriktsis, Funk, Yarrow, and Owen (2005) |
| | Statistical Process Control (SPC) usage | Ahire, Golhar, and Waller (1996) |
| | Statistical control/feedback | Flynn, Schroeder, and Sakakibara (1995) |
| | Statistical process control | Curkovic, Vickery, and Dröge (2000) |
| | Statistical process control | Flynn, Sakakibara, and Schroeder (1995) |
| | Technology emphasis | Cua, McKone, and Schroeder (2001) |
| | Total quality control practices | Nassimbeni (2003) |
| | Total quality management: process management | Kaynak (2003) |
| | Total preventive maintenance (TPM): autonomous maintenance-teams | McKone, Schroeder, and Cua (1999) |
| | TPM: autonomous maintenance-cross-training | McKone, Schroeder, and Cua (1999) |
| | TPM: autonomous maintenance-housekeeping | McKone, Schroeder, and Cua (1999) |
| | TPM: autonomous maintenance-operator involvement | McKone, Schroeder, and Cua (1999) |
| | TPM: planned maintenance-disciplined planning | McKone, Schroeder, and Cua (1999) |
| | TPM: planned maintenance-information tracking | McKone, Schroeder, and Cua (1999) |
| | TPM: planned maintenance-schedule compliance | McKone, Schroeder, and Cua (1999) |
| | Traditional industrial engineering | Adam (1994) |
| | Value orientation | Choi and Liker (1995) |
| Supplier/customer quality management | Closer customer relationships | Curkovic, Vickery, and Dröge (2000) |
| | Closer to customers | Powell (1995) |
| | Closer to suppliers | Powell (1995) |

*(Continued)*

(Continued)

| | | |
|---|---|---|
| | Customer involvement | Cua, McKone, and Schroeder (2001) |
| | Customer involvement: customer interaction | Flynn, Schroeder, and Sakakibara (1994) |
| | Customer relations management | Flynn and Saladin (2001) |
| | Customer satisfaction determination | Flynn and Saladin (2001) |
| | Future requirements of customers | Flynn and Saladin (2001) |
| | Internal and external cooperation | Anderson, Rungtusanatham, Schroeder, and Devaraj (1995) |
| | Supplier development | Curkovic, Vickery, and Dröge (2000) |
| | Supplier involvement | Douglas and Fredendall (2004) |
| | Supplier involvement | Primo and Amundson (2002) |
| | Supplier involvement: supplier relationship | Flynn, Schroeder, and Sakakibara (1994) |
| | Supplier management | Park, Hartley, and Wilson (2001) |
| | Supplier performance | Ahire, Golhar, and Waller (1996) |
| | Supplier quality control | Primo and Amundson (2002) |
| | Supplier quality involvement | Sakakibara, Flynn, Schroeder, and Morris (1997) |
| | Supplier quality involvement | Ahmad and Schroeder (2001) |
| | Supplier quality level | Sakakibara, Flynn, and Schroeder (1993) |
| | Supplier quality management | Forker, Mendez, and Hershauer (1997) |
| | Supplier quality management | Forker (1997) |
| | Supplier quality management | Cua, McKone, and Schroeder (2001) |
| | Supplier quality management | Ahire, Golhar, and Waller (1996) |
| | Total quality management (TQM): supplier quality management | Kaynak (2003) |
| | TQM implementation: customer involvement | McKone, Schroeder, and Cua (1999) |
| | TQM implementation: supplier quality management | McKone, Schroeder, and Cua (1999) |
| Quality dimensions | Behavioral outcomes | Brady and Cronin (2001) |
| | Clinical quality | Marley, Collier, and Goldstein (2004) |
| | Company reputation | Curkovic, Vickery, and Dröge (2000) |
| | Conformance to specifications | Curkovic, Vickery, and Dröge (2000) |
| | Customer satisfaction | Brady and Cronin (2001) |
| | Design quality management | Curkovic, Vickery, and Dröge (2000) |
| | Information systems (IS) service quality: assurance | Carr (2002) |
| | IS service quality: empathy | Carr (2002) |
| | IS service quality: reliability | Carr (2002) |
| | IS service quality: responsiveness | Carr (2002) |
| | Overall service quality | Brady and Cronin (2001) |
| | Performance service quality | Brady and Cronin (2001) |
| | Physical goods quality | Brady and Cronin (2001) |
| | Presale customer service | Curkovic, Vickery, and Dröge (2000) |
| | Process quality | Marley, Collier, and Goldstein (2004) |
| | Product durability | Curkovic, Vickery, and Dröge (2000) |
| | Product quality | Ahire, Golhar, and Waller (1996) |
| | Product reliability | Curkovic, Vickery, and Dröge (2000) |
| | Product support | Curkovic, Vickery, and Dröge (2000) |

| | | |
|---|---|---|
| | Responsiveness to customers | Curkovic, Vickery, and Dröge (2000) |
| | Service quality | Harrison-Walker (2001) |
| | Servicescape quality | Brady and Cronin (2001) |
| | Value | Brady and Cronin (2001) |
| Customer focus | Customer focus | Detert and Schroeder (2003) |
| | Customer focus | Samson and Terziovski (1999) |
| | Customer focus | Ahmad and Schroeder (2001) |
| | Customer focus | Adam (1994) |
| | Customer focus | Flynn, Sakakibara, and Schroeder (1995) |
| | Customer focus | Ahire, Golhar, and Waller (1996) |
| | Customer focus and satisfaction | Pannirselvam, Siferd, and Ruch (1998) |
| | Customer orientation | Brady and Cronin (2001) |
| | Customer orientation | Jambulingam, Kathuria, and Doucette (2005) |
| | Customer product and service input | Flynn and Saladin (2001) |
| | Customer satisfaction orientation | Black and Porter (1996) |
| | Customers | Adam, Corbett, Flores, Harrison, Lee, Rho, Ribera, Samson, and Westbrook (1997) |
| | Employee motivation and vision | Hays and Hill (2001) |
| Quality management philosophies/ systems | Catalyst for change | Naveh and Marcus (2005) |
| | Daily practice | Naveh and Marcus (2005) |
| | Environmental options | Melnyk, Sroufe, and Calantone (2003) |
| | Externally coordinated | Naveh and Marcus (2005) |
| | Internally integrated | Naveh and Marcus (2005) |
| | Just-in-time (JIT) quality | Fullerton, McWatters, and Fawson (2003) |
| | Quality management | Zhu and Sarkis (2004) |
| | Quality management philosophy | Ketokivi and Schroeder (2004) |
| | Quality philosophy | Douglas and Fredendall (2004) |
| | Quality strategy | Tan (2001) |
| | State of the EMS (environmental management system) | Melnyk, Sroufe, and Calantone (2003) |
| | Status in terms of ISO 9000 certification | Terziovski, Samson, and Dow (1997) |
| | Systems focus | Detert and Schroeder (2003) |
| | Total quality management | Snell and Dean (1992) |
| | Total quality management | Dean and Snell (1996) |
| | Total quality management | Dean and Snell (1991) |
| | Total quality methods | Douglas and Fredendall (2004) |
| | Total quality management | Terziovski, Samson, and Dow (1997) |
| | Zero-defects mentality | Powell (1995) |
| Service recovery/failure | Adaptive recovery behavior | de Jong and de Ruyter (2004) |
| | Critical incident (actual customer behavior) | Youngdahl and Kellogg (1997) |
| | Customer complaint management | de Jong and de Ruyter (2004) |
| | Degree of effort incurred | Youngdahl and Kellogg (1997) |

*(Continued)*

(Continued)

| | | |
|---|---|---|
| | Delay | Tucker (2004) |
| | Discovery | Hays and Hill (2001) |
| | Failure expectations | McCollough, Berry, and Yadav (2000) |
| | Initial disconfirmation | McCollough, Berry, and Yadav (2000) |
| | Interruption | Tucker (2004) |
| | Losses | Tucker (2004) |
| | Motivation for quality assurance behaviors | Youngdahl and Kellogg (1997) |
| | Proactive recovery behavior | de Jong and de Ruyter (2004) |
| | Recovery disconfirmation | McCollough, Berry, and Yadav (2000) |
| | Recovery expectations | McCollough, Berry, and Yadav (2000) |
| | Risk | Tucker (2004) |

## Planning and Control Scales

| *Categories* | *Scale Name from the Paper* | *Paper* |
|---|---|---|
| Schedule and plan | Aggregate plan | Safizadeh and Ritzman (1997) |
| | Daily schedule adherence | Ahmad and Schroeder (2001) |
| | Daily schedule adherence | Sakakibara, Flynn, and Schroeder (1993) |
| | Just-in-time (JIT) implementation: repetitive nature of master schedule | McKone, Schroeder, and Cua (1999) |
| | JIT scheduling | Flynn, Sakakibara, and Schroeder (1995) |
| | Job scheduling | LaForge, Wood, and Sleeth (1984) |
| | Order backlog | Safizadeh and Ritzman (1997) |
| | Planning and scheduling | Stahl and Zimmerer (1983) |
| | Planning horizon | Safizadeh and Ritzman (1997) |
| | Production planning | Rho and Yu (1998) |
| | Repetitive master schedule | Sakakibara, Flynn, and Schroeder (1993) |
| | Schedule adherence | Cua, McKone, and Schroeder (2001) |
| | Schedule flexibility | Sakakibara, Flynn, Schroeder, and Morris (1997) |
| Process modification and material flow | Dependable suppliers | Tu, Vonderembse, and Ragu-Nathan (2001) |
| | Frequent delivery by suppliers | Ketokivi and Schroeder (2004) |
| | Just-in-time (JIT) deliveries from suppliers | Sakakibara, Flynn, and Schroeder (1993) |
| | JIT delivery by suppliers | Flynn and Flynn (2004) |
| | JIT delivery by suppliers | Ahmad and Schroeder (2001) |
| | JIT implementation: JIT delivery by suppliers | McKone, Schroeder, and Cua (1999) |
| | JIT implementation: JIT link with customers | McKone, Schroeder, and Cua (1999) |
| | JIT link with customers | Ahmad and Schroeder (2001) |
| | JIT supplier relations | Flynn, Schroeder, and Flynn (1999) |
| | JIT supplier relationship | Sakakibara, Flynn, Schroeder, and Morris (1997) |
| | JIT vendor strategy | Mehra and Inman (1992) |
| | JIT workflow integration | Germain and Dröge (1997) |

| | | |
|---|---|---|
| | JIT flow | Swink, Narasimhan, and Kim (2005) |
| | Material management | Stahl and Zimmerer (1983) |
| | Product design simplicity | Sakakibara, Flynn, and Schroeder (1993) |
| | Simpler flow of materials through the process | Schmenner and Cook (1985) |
| | Waste elimination: process modification | Lawrence and Hottenstein (1995) |
| Setup and lot size | Just-in-time (JIT) implementation: setup reduction | McKone, Schroeder, and Cua (1999) |
| | Lot size reduction practices | Flynn, Sakakibara, and Schroeder (1995) |
| | Material management-batch size rationale | Safizadeh and Ritzman (1997) |
| | Reengineering setup | Koufteros, Vonderembse, and Doll (1998) |
| | Reengineering setup | Tu, Vonderembse, and Ragu-Nathan (2001) |
| | Setup improvement | Koufteros (1999) |
| | Setup time reduction | Ketokivi and Schroeder (2004) |
| | Setup time reduction | Flynn and Flynn (2004) |
| | Setup time reduction | Ahmad and Schroeder (2001) |
| | Setup time reduction | Sakakibara, Flynn, Schroeder, and Morris (1997) |
| | Setup time reduction | Sakakibara, Flynn, and Schroeder (1993) |
| | Setup time reduction | Cua, McKone, and Schroeder (2001) |
| | Setup time reduction practices | Flynn, Sakakibara, and Schroeder (1995) |
| | Small-lot sizes | Sakakibara, Flynn, and Schroeder (1993) |
| Production control | Core JIT | Dong, Carter, and Dresner (2001) |
| | Facilitating JIT | Dong, Carter, and Dresner (2001) |
| | Intermediate (how) | New and Szwejczewski (1995) |
| | JIT implementation: pull system support | McKone, Schroeder, and Cua (1999) |
| | JIT manufacturing | Fullerton, McWatters, and Fawson (2003) |
| | JIT production strategy | Mehra and Inman (1992) |
| | Kanban | Ahmad and Schroeder (2001) |
| | Kanban | Flynn, Sakakibara, and Schroeder (1995) |
| | Kanban | Sakakibara, Flynn, Schroeder, and Morris (1997) |
| | Kanban | Sakakibara, Flynn, and Schroeder (1993) |
| | Management (why) | New and Szwejczewski (1995) |
| | Material requirements planning (MRP) adaptation to JIT | Sakakibara, Flynn, and Schroeder (1993) |
| | MRP adoption | Rabinovich, Dresner, and Evers (2003) |
| | Production control system | Morita and Flynn (1997) |
| | Production system: JIT orientation | Morita and Flynn (1997) |
| | Pull production | Koufteros, Vonderembse, and Doll (1998) |
| | Pull production | Koufteros (1999) |
| | Pull production | Tu, Vonderembse, and Ragu-Nathan (2001) |
| | Pull system | Flynn, Schroeder, and Flynn (1999) |
| | Pull system production | Cua, McKone, and Schroeder (2001) |
| | Pull system support | Ketokivi and Schroeder (2004) |
| | Pull system support | Sakakibara, Flynn, and Schroeder (1993) |
| | Supplier JIT manufacturing | Dong, Carter, and Dresner (2001) |
| | Unification of work control | Stahl and Zimmerer (1983) |
| | Working on the floor | Morita and Flynn (1997) |

*(Continued)*

(Continued)

| | | |
|---|---|---|
| Layout | Cellular manufacturing | Koufteros, Vonderembse, and Doll (1998) |
| | Cellular manufacturing | Tu, Vonderembse, and Ragu-Nathan (2001) |
| | Cleanliness and organization | Flynn and Flynn (2004) |
| | Equipment layout | Ahmad and Schroeder (2001) |
| | Equipment layout | Sakakibara, Flynn, Schroeder, and Morris (1997) |
| | Equipment layout | Sakakibara, Flynn, and Schroeder (1993) |
| | Equipment layout | Cua, McKone, and Schroeder (2001) |
| | Plant environment | Flynn, Sakakibara, and Schroeder (1995) |
| Inventory control | | |
| | Effective inventory planning and control | Adam (1994) |
| | Inventory reduction | Adam, Corbett, Flores, Harrison, Lee, Rho, Ribera, Samson, and Westbrook (1997) |
| | JIT inventory control | Snell and Dean (1992) |
| | JIT inventory control | Dean and Snell (1991) |
| | Material management-inventory level | Safizadeh and Ritzman (1997) |
| | Materials management | Rho and Yu (1998) |
| | Waste elimination: inventory reduction | Lawrence and Hottenstein (1995) |
| Overall JIT and other related constructs | Accounting adaptation to JIT | Sakakibara, Flynn, and Schroeder (1993) |
| | JIT adoption | Rabinovich, Dresner, and Evers (2003) |
| | JIT unique | Fullerton, McWatters, and Fawson (2003) |
| | Just-in-time | Dean and Snell (1996) |
| | Just-in-time | Zhu and Sarkis (2004) |
| | JIT strategy | Tan (2001) |
| | JIT practices | Nassimbeni (2003) |
| | Management commitment | Mehra and Inman (1992) |

## Human Resources/Organizational Issues Scales

| *Categories* | *Scale Name from the Paper* | *Paper* |
|---|---|---|
| Organizational culture/structure | Accessibility | Pinto, Pinto, and Prescott (1993) |
| | Adaptability | Jambulingam, Kathuria, and Doucette (2005) |
| | Autonomy | Jambulingam, Kathuria, and Doucette (2005) |
| | Autonomy: people-related autonomy | Janz and Prasarnphanich (2003) |
| | Autonomy: planning-related autonomy | Janz and Prasarnphanich (2003) |
| | Autonomy: process-related autonomy | Janz and Prasarnphanich (2003) |
| | Beliefs on integrating with suppliers | Nahm, Vonderembse, and Koufteros (2004) |
| | Beliefs on investing in facilities and equipment | Nahm, Vonderembse, and Koufteros (2004) |
| | Beliefs on making decisions that are global | Nahm, Vonderembse, and Koufteros (2004) |

| | |
|---|---|
| Beliefs on management control | Nahm, Vonderembse, and Koufteros (2004) |
| Beliefs on working with others | Nahm, Vonderembse, and Koufteros (2004) |
| Centralization | Hult, Hurley, Giunipero, and Nichols (2000) |
| Change readiness | Stratman and Roth (2002) |
| Cohesiveness | Brockman and Morgan (2003) |
| Collectivism | Youngdahl, Kellogg, Nie, and Bowen (2003) |
| Commitment | Morita and Flynn (1997) |
| Competitive aggressiveness | Jambulingam, Kathuria, and Doucette (2005) |
| Coordination of decision making | Sakakibara, Flynn, Schroeder, and Morris (1997) |
| Creation of a collective mind | Escrig-Tena and Bou-Llusar (2005) |
| Cultural congruence scales: loyalty | Bates, Amundson, Schroeder, and Morris (1995) |
| Cultural congruence scales: philosophy | Bates, Amundson, Schroeder, and Morris (1995) |
| Customer orientations | Nahm, Vonderembse, and Koufteros (2004) |
| Decentralization | Germain and Dröge (1997) |
| Decentralization of authority | Sakakibara, Flynn, Schroeder, and Morris (1997) |
| Developmental culture | McDermott and Stock (1999) |
| Enacting organizational environment | Escrig-Tena and Bou-Llusar (2005) |
| Entrepreneurship | Brockman and Morgan (2003) |
| Formalization | Hult, Hurley, Giunipero, and Nichols (2000) |
| Group culture | McDermott and Stock (1999) |
| Hierarchical culture | McDermott and Stock (1999) |
| Hierarchical level | Levin and Cross (2004) |
| Individualism-collectivism scales: coordination of decision making | Bates, Amundson, Schroeder, and Morris (1995) |
| Individualism-collectivism scales: rewards for group performance | Bates, Amundson, Schroeder, and Morris (1995) |
| Individualism-collectivism scales: small group problem solving | Bates, Amundson, Schroeder, and Morris (1995) |
| Individualism-collectivism scales: supervisors as team leaders | Bates, Amundson, Schroeder, and Morris (1995) |
| Innovativeness | Jambulingam, Kathuria, and Doucette (2005) |
| Interteam support | de Jong and de Ruyter (2004) |
| Interteam support | de Jong, de Ruyter, and Wetzels (2005) |
| Intrateam support | de Jong and de Ruyter (2004) |
| Layers | Vickery, Dröge, and Germain (1999) |
| Level of communication | Nahm, Vonderemse, and Koufteros (2003) |
| Level of horizontal integration | Nahm, Vonderemse, and Koufteros (2003) |
| Locus of decision making | Nahm, Vonderemse, and Koufteros (2003) |
| Management support | de Jong and de Ruyter, and Wetzels (2005) |
| Masculinity | Youngdahl, Kellogg, Nie, and Bowen (2003) |
| Motivation | Jambulingam, Kathuria, and Doucette (2005) |
| Nature of formalization | Nahm, Vonderemse, and Koufteros (2003) |
| Number of layers in hierarchy | Nahm, Vonderemse, and Koufteros (2003) |
| Open organization | Powell (1995) |
| Operations decentralization | Vickery, Dröge, and Germain (1999) |
| Organicity | Jambulingam, Kathuria, and Doucette (2005) |
| Organization structure | Brockman and Morgan (2003) |
| Organizational climate: reward | Janz and Prasarnphanich (2003) |

*(Continued)*

(Continued)

| | | |
|---|---|---|
| | Organizational climate: risk | Janz and Prasarnphanich (2003) |
| | Organizational climate: support | Janz and Prasarnphanich (2003) |
| | Organizational climate: warmth | Janz and Prasarnphanich (2003) |
| | Organizational commitment | Ahmad and Schroeder (2003) |
| | Organizational commitment | Ahmad and Schroeder (2001) |
| | Organizational commitment | Escrig-Tena and Bou-Llusar (2005) |
| | Organizational commitment | Ittner and Larcker (1997) |
| | Organizational proximity | Levin and Cross (2004) |
| | Organizational support | Fedor, Ghosh, Caldwell, Maurer, and Singhal (2003) |
| | Physical proximity | Pinto, Pinto, and Prescott (1993) |
| | Physical proximity | Levin and Cross (2004) |
| | Plant-wide philosophy | Sakakibara, Flynn, Schroeder, and Morris (1997) |
| | Power distance | Youngdahl, Kellogg, Nie, and Bowen (2003) |
| | Power distance scales: centralization of authority | Bates, Amundson, Schroeder, and Morris (1995) |
| | Power distance scales: hierarchical index | Bates, Amundson, Schroeder, and Morris (1995) |
| | Power distance scales: shop-floor contact | Bates, Amundson, Schroeder, and Morris (1995) |
| | Proactiveness | Jambulingam, Kathuria, and Doucette (2005) |
| | Rational culture | McDermott and Stock (1999) |
| | Risk taking | Jambulingam, Kathuria, and Doucette (2005) |
| | Social support | de Jong, de Ruyter, and Wetzels (2005) |
| | Spans | Vickery, Dröge, and Germain (1999) |
| | Systems orientation | Hult, Hurley, Giunipero, and Nichols (2000) |
| | Time orientation | Youngdahl, Kellogg, Nie, and Bowen (2003) |
| | Tolerance for ambiguity | Jambulingam, Kathuria, and Doucette (2005) |
| | Uncertainty avoidance | Youngdahl, Kellogg, Nie, and Bowen (2003) |
| Organizational process | Benchmark control | Germain and Dröge (1997) |
| | Formal benchmark control | Vickery, Dröge, and Germain (1999) |
| | Formal internal control | Vickery, Dröge, and Germain (1999) |
| | Formal supplier control | Vickery, Dröge, and Germain (1999) |
| | Goal structure | Sarin and Mcdermott (2003) |
| | Integration: committees | Germain and Dröge (1997) |
| | Integration: mechanisms | Germain and Dröge (1997) |
| | Internal control | Germain and Dröge (1997) |
| | Management and operations | Flynn and Saladin (2001) |
| | Organizational rules and procedures | Pinto, Pinto, and Prescott (1993) |
| | Process adaptability | Tatikonda and Montoya-Weiss (2001) |
| | Process concurrency | Tatikonda and Montoya-Weiss (2001) |
| | Process formality | Tatikonda and Montoya-Weiss (2001) |
| | Process structure | Sarin and Mcdermott (2003) |
| | Superordinate goals | Pinto, Pinto, and Prescott (1993) |
| | Supervision | LaForge, Wood, and Sleeth (1984) |
| Hiring/ selection | Behavior and attitude | Ahmad and Schroeder (2003) |

| | | |
|---|---|---|
| | Behavior and attitude | Ahmad and Schroeder (2001) |
| | Employee selection and development | Adam, Corbett, Flores, Harrison, Lee, Rho, Ribera, Samson, and Westbrook (1997) |
| | Manufacturing and human resources fit | Ahmad and Schroeder (2003) |
| | Manufacturing and human resources fit | Ahmad and Schroeder (2001) |
| | Recruiting and selection | Sakakibara, Flynn, Schroeder, and Morris (1997) |
| | Selective staffing | Snell and Dean (1992) |
| | Workforce management: selection for teamwork potential | Flynn, Schroeder, and Sakakibara (1994) |
| Employee development/ training | Comprehensive training | Snell and Dean (1992) |
| | Cross-training | Ketokivi and Schroeder (2004) |
| | Cross-functional training | Cua, McKone, and Schroeder (2001) |
| | Employee development | Goldstein (2003) |
| | Employee development | Flynn, Schroeder, and Flynn (1999) |
| | Employee education | Park, Hartley, and Wilson (2001) |
| | Employee training | Ahire, Golhar, and Waller (1996) |
| | ERP training | Stratman and Roth (2002) |
| | Human resource development | Morita and Flynn (1997) |
| | Job enrichment | Li, Benton, and Leong (2002) |
| | Orientation and training | Wisner, Stringfellow, Youngdahl, and Parker (2005) |
| | Quality training and education | Flynn and Saladin (2001) |
| | Quality training | Curkovic, Vickery, and Dröge (2000) |
| | Staff competence | Li, Benton, and Leong (2002) |
| | Staff focus: training | Chesteen, Helgheim, Randall, and Wardell (2005) |
| | Staff training | Li, Benton, and Leong (2002) |
| | Staff training and development | Goldstein (2003) |
| | Total quality management: training | Kaynak (2003) |
| | Total quality training | Douglas and Fredendall (2004) |
| | Training | Forker (1997) |
| | Training | Forker, Mendez, and Hershauer (1997) |
| | Training | Powell (1995) |
| | Training | Sakakibara, Flynn, and Schroeder (1993) |
| | Training in multiple functions | Ahmad and Schroeder (2003) |
| | Training in multiple functions | Ahmad and Schroeder (2001) |
| | Training on job skills | Ahmad and Schroeder (2001) |
| | Training on the job skills | Ahmad and Schroeder (2003) |
| | Workforce development | Swink, Narasimhan, and Kim (2005) |
| Teamwork | Collaboration | Detert and Schroeder (2003) |
| | Consideration | Sarin and McDermott (2003) |
| | Cross-functional quality teams | Curkovic, Vickery, and Dröge (2000) |
| | Incentives for group performance | Sakakibara, Flynn, Schroeder, and Morris (1997) |
| | Interaction facilitation | Ahmad and Schroeder (2003) |
| | Interaction facilitation | Ahmad and Schroeder (2001) |
| | Participative behavior | Sarin and McDermott (2003) |

*(Continued)*

(Continued)

| | | |
|---|---|---|
| | Project team rules and procedures | Pinto, Pinto, and Prescott (1993) |
| | Small group problem solving | Sakakibara, Flynn, Schroeder, and Morris (1997) |
| | Small group problem solving | Sakakibara, Flynn, and Schroeder (1993) |
| | Social interaction | Wisner, Stringfellow, Youngdahl, and Parker (2005) |
| | Staff focus: teamwork | Chesteen, Helgheim, Randall, and Wardell (2005) |
| | Supervisors as team leaders | Sakakibara, Flynn, Schroeder, and Morris (1997) |
| | Supervisory leadership | Sakakibara, Flynn, Schroeder, and Morris (1997) |
| | Team activities | Ahmad and Schroeder (2003) |
| | Team activities | Ahmad and Schroeder (2001) |
| | Team leader position | Sarin and Mcdermott (2003) |
| | Team leadership | Fedor, Ghosh, Caldwell, Maurer, and Singhal (2003) |
| | Team orientation | Hult, Hurley, Giunipero, and Nichols (2000) |
| | Team skills | Karlsson and Ahlstrom (1995) |
| | Teamwork structures for improvement | Black and Porter (1996) |
| | Workforce management: teamwork | Flynn, Schroeder, and Sakakibara (1994) |
| | Working on the floor | Morita and Flynn (1997) |
| Measurement/ rewards | Compensation | Adam, Corbett, Flores, Harrison, Lee, Rho, Ribera, Samson, and Westbrook (1997) |
| | Development performance appraisal | Snell and Dean (1992) |
| | Employee recognition | Flynn and Saladin (2001) |
| | Equitable reward systems | Snell and Dean (1992) |
| | Evaluation and recognition systems | Flynn and Saladin (2001) |
| | Feedback on performance | Ahmad and Schroeder (2001) |
| | Feedback on performance | Ahmad and Schroeder (2003) |
| | Incentives to meet objectives | Ahmad and Schroeder (2003) |
| | Incentives to meet objectives | Ahmad and Schroeder (2001) |
| | Measurement | Pagell (2004) |
| | Organizational rewards | LaForge, Wood, and Sleeth (1984) |
| | Reflection | Wisner, Stringfellow, Youngdahl, and Parker (2005) |
| | Rewards | Wisner, Stringfellow, Youngdahl, and Parker (2005) |
| Employee satisfaction/ attitude | Affective commitment | Harrison-Walker (2001) |
| | Employee fulfillment | Rungtusanatham, Forza, Koka, Salvador, and Nie (2005) |
| | Employee morale | Terziovski, Samson, and Dow (1997) |
| | Employee outcomes | Goldstein (2003) |
| | Employee satisfaction | Adam, Corbett, Flores, Harrison, Lee, Rho, Ribera, Samson, and Westbrook (1997) |
| | Employee satisfaction | Voss, Tsikriktsis, Funk, Yarrow, and Owen (2005) |
| | Employee satisfaction | Park, Hartley, and Wilson (2001) |
| | Employee well-being and morale | Flynn and Saladin (2001) |
| | High sacrifice commitment | Harrison-Walker (2001) |
| | Intent to donate | Wisner, Stringfellow, Youngdahl, and Parker (2005) |

| | | |
|---|---|---|
| | Intent to recommend organization to others | Wisner, Stringfellow, Youngdahl, and Parker (2005) |
| | Intent to remain | Wisner, Stringfellow, Youngdahl, and Parker (2005) |
| | Job satisfaction | LaForge, Wood, and Sleeth (1984) |
| | Pride in work | Morita and Flynn (1997) |
| | Quality of work life | Roth (1993) |
| | Satisfaction | Wisner, Stringfellow, Youngdahl, and Parker (2005) |
| | Staff well-being | Goldstein (2003) |
| | Work attitudes | Flynn, Schroeder, and Sakakibara (1995) |
| | Work satisfaction: effectiveness | Janz and Prasarnphanich (2003) |
| | Work satisfaction: efficiency | Janz and Prasarnphanich (2003) |
| | Work satisfaction: general job satisfaction | Janz and Prasarnphanich (2003) |
| | Work satisfaction: growth satisfaction | Janz and Prasarnphanich (2003) |
| | Work satisfaction: timeliness | Janz and Prasarnphanich (2003) |
| Work design/ employee empowerment | Complexity (job) | Dean and Snell (1991) |
| | Employee empowerment | Powell (1995) |
| | Employee empowerment | Ahire, Golhar, and Waller (1996) |
| | Employee empowerment | Curkovic, Vickery, and Dröge (2000) |
| | Employee fulfillment | Anderson, Rungtusanatham, Schroeder, and Devaraj (1995) |
| | Employee involvement | Lawrence and Hottenstein (1995) |
| | Employee involvement | Adam, Corbett, Flores, Harrison, Lee, Rho, Ribera, Samson, and Westbrook (1997) |
| | Employee involvement | Cua, McKone, and Schroeder (2001) |
| | Employee involvement | Flynn and Saladin (2001) |
| | Employee involvement | Ahire, Golhar, and Waller (1996) |
| | Employee involvement implementation: centralization of authority | McKone, Schroeder, and Cua (1999) |
| | Employee quality involvement | Flynn and Saladin (2001) |
| | Employee relations | Forker, Mendez, and Hershauer (1997) |
| | Employee relations | Forker (1997) |
| | Employee responsibility | Lawrence and Hottenstein (1995) |
| | Empowerment | de Jong and de Ruyter (2004) |
| | Empowerment | Wisner, Stringfellow, Youngdahl, and Parker (2005) |
| | Empowerment | Narasimhan, Jayaram, and Carter (2001) |
| | Empowerment | Park, Hartley, and Wilson (2001) |
| | Flexible workforce | Lawrence and Hottenstein, M.P. (1995) |
| | Interdependence (job) | Dean and Snell (1991) |
| | Labor flexibility | Sakakibara, Flynn, Schroeder, and Morris (1997) |
| | Multifunction workers | Sakakibara, Flynn, and Schroeder (1993) |
| | Schedule flexibility | Wisner, Stringfellow, Youngdahl, and Parker (2005) |
| | Shop-floor employee involvement in problem solving | Tu, Vonderembse, and Ragu-Nathan (2001) |
| | Shop-floor employee involvement in problem solving | Koufteros, Vonderembse, and Doll (1998) |

*(Continued)*

(Continued)

| | | |
|---|---|---|
| | Specialization | Germain and Dröge (1997) |
| | Staff focus | Goldstein and Naor (2005) |
| | Staff focus: cross-functional | Chesteen, Helgheim, Randall, and Wardell (2005) |
| | Teacher involvement | Detert and Schroeder (2003) |
| | Total quality management: employee relations | Kaynak (2003) |
| | Variety (job) | Dean and Snell (1991) |
| | Work systems | Goldstein (2003) |
| | Worker participation | Flynn, Schroeder, and Flynn (1999) |
| Other human resource management | Human resource management practices | Voss, Tsikriktsis, Funk, Yarrow, and Owen (2005) |
| | Human resources development and management | Choi and Eboch (1998) |
| | Human resources development and management | Pannirselvam, Siferd, and Ruch (1998) |
| | Human resources management | Flynn and Saladin (2001) |
| | Human resources management | Das and Narasimhan (2001) |
| | Human resources management practices | Ittner and Larcker (1997) |
| | People and customer management | Black and Porter (1996) |
| | People management | Samson and Terziovski (1999) |
| | The workforce | Schmenner and Cook (1985) |
| | Workforce management | Flynn, Sakakibara, and Schroeder (1995) |
| | Workforce management | Flynn, Schroeder, and Sakakibara (1995) |

## Organizational Learning Scales

| *Categories* | *Scale Name from the Paper* | *Paper* |
|---|---|---|
| Learning/ knowledge transfer | Access | Borgatti and Cross (2003) |
| | Availability | Levin and Cross (2004) |
| | Benevolence-based trust | Levin and Cross (2004) |
| | Combination | Sabherwal and Becerra-Fernandez (2003) |
| | Competence-based trust | Levin and Cross (2004) |
| | Cooperative learning: group process | Janz and Prasarnphanich (2003) |
| | Cooperative learning: positive interdependence | Janz and Prasarnphanich (2003) |
| | Cooperative learning: promotion interaction | Janz and Prasarnphanich (2003) |
| | Cost | Borgatti and Cross (2003) |
| | Explicit knowledge dissemination | Fedor, Ghosh, Caldwell, Maurer, and Singhal (2003) |
| | External contact | Zellmer-Bruhn (2003) |
| | External knowledge generation | Fedor, Ghosh, Caldwell, Maurer, and Singhal (2003) |

| | |
|---|---|
| External learning | Schroeder, Bates, and Juntilla (2002) |
| Externalization | Sabherwal and Becerra-Fernandez (2003) |
| Friendship | Levin and Cross (2004) |
| Implicit knowledge dissemination | Fedor, Ghosh, Caldwell, Maurer, and Singhal (2003) |
| Individuals' extent of network building | Hoegl, Parboteeah, and Munson (2003) |
| Information | Borgatti and Cross (2003) |
| Information acquisition efficiency | Brockman and Morgan (2003) |
| Information trading | Teigland and McLure Wasko (2004) |
| Innovative information | Brockman and Morgan (2003) |
| Internal knowledge generation | Fedor, Ghosh, Caldwell, Maurer, and Singhal (2003) |
| Internal Learning | Schroeder, Bates, and Junttila (2002) |
| Internalization | Sabherwal and Becerra-Fernandez (2003) |
| Interruptions | Zellmer-Bruhn (2003) |
| Knowing | Borgatti and Cross (2003) |
| Knowledge sources | Teigland and McLure Wasko (2004) |
| Knowledge transfer effort | Zellmer-Bruhn (2003) |
| Learning | Rungtusanatham, Forza, Koka, Salvador, and Nie (2005) |
| Learning | Anderson, Rungtusanatham, Schroeder, and Devaraj (1995) |
| Learning | Stratman and Roth (2002) |
| Learning consequence | Hult, Ketchen, and Nichols (2003) |
| Learning orientation | Hult, Hurley, Giunipero, and Nichols (2000) |
| Memory orientation | Hult, Hurley, Giunipero, and Nichols (2000) |
| Organizational learning | Escrig-Tena, and Bou-Llusar (2005) |
| Perceived group-level KM effectiveness | Sabherwal and Becerra-Fernandez (2003) |
| Perceived individual-level KM effectiveness | Sabherwal and Becerra-Fernandez (2003) |
| Perceived organizational-level KM effectiveness | Sabherwal and Becerra-Fernandez (2003) |
| Perceived receipt of useful knowledge | Levin and Cross (2004) |
| Receiver's expertise | Levin and Cross (2004) |
| Shared interpretation | Brockman and Morgan (2003) |
| Socialization | Sabherwal and Becerra-Fernandez (2003) |
| Team learning | Sarin and McDermott (2003) |
| Team's level of networking preference | Hoegl, Parboteeah, and Munson (2003) |
| Team's perceived importance of networking for project success | Hoegl, Parboteeah, and Munson (2003) |
| Team's perception of strength of the organizational knowledge-sharing climate | Hoegl, Parboteeah, and Munson (2003) |
| Team's perception of the adequacy of its material resources | Hoegl, Parboteeah, and Munson (2003) |

*(Continued)*

(Continued)

| | | |
|---|---|---|
| | Team's perception of the adequacy of its technical competency | Hoegl, Parboteeah, and Munson (2003) |
| | Team's strength of networking resources | Hoegl, Parboteeah, and Munson (2003) |
| | Tie strength | Levin and Cross (2004) |
| | Value | Borgatti and Cross (2003) |
| Knowledge | Benchmark performance control | Germain, Dröge, and Christensen (2001) |
| | Business process skills | Stratman and Roth (2002) |
| | Customer knowledge application | Dröge, Claycomb, and Germain (2003) |
| | Employee knowledge | Menor, Roth, and Mason (2001) |
| | Formal performance control | Germain, Dröge, and Christensen (2001) |
| | Individual experiential knowledge | Morgan, Zou, Vorhies, and Katsikeas (2003) |
| | Internal knowledge application | Dröge, Claycomb, and Germain (2003) |
| | Just-in-time (JIT) task scope | Germain and Dröge (1997) |
| | Know-how | Escrig-Tena and Bou-Llusar (2005) |
| | Knowledge | Adam, Corbett, Flores, Harrison, Lee, Rho, Ribera, Samson, and Westbrook (1997) |
| | Knowledge | Roth and Jackson (1995) |
| | Knowledge | Roth (1993) |
| | Operational know-how | Rosenzweig and Roth (2004) |
| | Supplier knowledge application | Dröge, Claycomb, and Germain (2003) |
| | Tacit knowledge | Levin and Cross (2004) |
| | Technocratic specialization | Germain, Dröge, and Christensen (2001) |
| | Transactive memory systems | Lewis (2004) |
| | Venture experiential knowledge | Morgan, Zou, Vorhies, and Katsikeas (2003) |
| | Venture market information knowledge | Morgan, Zou, Vorhies, and Katsikeas (2003) |

## PERFORMANCE/CAPABILITIES SCALES

| *Categories* | *Scale Name from the Paper* | *Paper* |
|---|---|---|
| Operational performance/ capabilities | Advanced manufacturing technology (AMT) implementation outcome: competitive performance | McDermott and Stock (1999) |
| | AMT implementation outcomes: operational benefits | McDermott and Stock (1999) |
| | Breadth of product line | Robinson and Satterfield (1998) |
| | Buyer logistics costs | Dong, Carter, and Dresner (2001) |
| | Company specific results | Flynn and Saladin (2001) |
| | Competitive advantage | Flynn, Schroeder, and Sakakibara (1995) |
| | Competitive capability | Rosenzweig and Roth (2004) |
| | Conformance quality | White (1996) |
| | Cost | Flynn, Schroeder, and Flynn (1999) |
| | Cost | Menor, Roth, and Mason (2001) |
| | Cost | Sawhney and Piper (2002) |
| | Cost efficiency | Swink, Narasimhan, and Kim (2005) |
| | Cost efficiency | Stahl and Zimmerer (1983) |

| | |
|---|---|
| Cost leadership | Rosenzweig, Roth, and Dean (2003) |
| Cost performance | Li, Benton, and Leong (2002) |
| Costs of material requirements planning (MRP) systems | Schroeder, Anderson, Tupy, and White (1981) |
| Customization responsiveness performance | Das and Narasimhan (2001) |
| Degree of innovation | Sarin and McDermott (2003) |
| Delivery | Safizadeh, Field, and Ritzman (2003) |
| Delivery | Roth (1993) |
| Delivery | Menor, Roth, and Mason (2001) |
| Delivery | Roth (1996) |
| Delivery capabilities | Tracey, Vonderembse, and Lim (1999) |
| Delivery dependability | Li, Rao, Ragu-Nathan, and Ragu-Nathan (2005) |
| Delivery dependability | Koufteros (1999) |
| Delivery dependability | White (1996) |
| Delivery lead time | Karlsson and Ahlstrom (1995) |
| Delivery performance | Das and Narasimhan (2001) |
| Delivery reliability | Rosenzweig, Roth, and Dean (2003) |
| Delivery speed | White (1996) |
| Dependability of delivery lead time | Robinson and Satterfield (1998) |
| Dependability on-time delivery | Flynn, Schroeder, and Flynn (1999) |
| Dependability service | Flynn, Schroeder, and Flynn (1999) |
| Dependability specifications | Flynn, Schroeder, and Flynn (1999) |
| Design and engineering change | Rho and Yu (1998) |
| Distance to supplier distribution terminal | Robinson and Satterfield (1998) |
| Expected impact | Fedor, Ghosh, Caldwell, Maurer, and Singhal (2003) |
| Factor performance | Menor, Roth, and Mason (2001) |
| Factor productivity | Roth and Jackson (1995) |
| Factor productivity | Roth (1993) |
| Flexibility | Roth (1996) |
| Flexibility | Menor, Roth, and Mason (2001) |
| Flexibility | Malhotra, Heine, and Grover (2001) |
| Flexibility | Roth (1993) |
| General productivity | Schmenner and Cook (1985) |
| Headcount | Roth (1993) |
| Innovation | Roth (1993) |
| Interaction effectiveness—new product development (NPD) | Narasimhan, Jayaram, and Carter (2001) |
| Interaction frequency—tactical | Narasimhan, Jayaram, and Carter (2001) |
| Inventory management performance | Kaynak (2003) |
| Inventory variance | Germain, Dröge, and Christensen (2001) |
| Just-in-time (JIT) performance | Flynn, Sakakibara, and Schroeder (1995) |
| Labor flexibility | Zhang and Vonderembse (2003) |
| Labor productivity | Schmenner and Cook (1985) |
| Lateness | Sawhney and Piper (2002) |
| Lead time | Rho and Yu (1998) |
| Level of success criteria: inventory elements | Mehra and Inman (1992) |

*(Continued)*

(Continued)

| | | |
|---|---|---|
| | Level of success criteria: utilization elements | Mehra and Inman (1992) |
| | Low cost | Safizadeh, Field, and Ritzman (2003) |
| | Low Cost | Roth (1993) |
| | Machine flexibility | Zhang and Vonderembse (2003) |
| | Manufacturing capabilities: cost | Noble (1997) |
| | Manufacturing capabilities: delivery | Noble (1997) |
| | Manufacturing capabilities: dependability | Noble (1997) |
| | Manufacturing capabilities: flexibility | Noble (1997) |
| | Manufacturing capabilities: quality | Noble (1997) |
| | Manufacturing capabilities: innovation | Noble (1997) |
| | Manufacturing competency | Dröge and Vickery (1994) |
| | Manufacturing cost reduction | Das and Narasimhan (2001) |
| | Manufacturing flexibility | Swamidass and Newell (1987) |
| | Manufacturing lead time | Karlsson and Ahlstrom (1995) |
| | Manufacturing morale | Hausman, Montgomery, and Roth (2002) |
| | Manufacturing performance | Bozarth and Edwards (1997) |
| | Manufacturing performance | Cleveland, Schroeder, and Anderson (1989) |
| | Manufacturing performance | Schroeder, Bates, and Juntilla (2002) |
| | Manufacturing performance | Cua, McKone, and Schroeder (2001) |
| | Market acuity | Roth (1993) |
| | Material handling flexibility | Zhang and Vonderembse (2003) |
| | Minimum delivery lead time available | Robinson and Satterfield (1998) |
| | Mix flexibility | Zhang and Vonderembse (2003) |
| | MRP benefit | Schroeder, Anderson, Tupy, and White (1981) |
| | New product developments | Brown (1998) |
| | New product flexibility | Swink, Narasimhan, and Kim (2005) |
| | New product innovativeness | Brockman and Morgan (2003) |
| | New product introduction | Das and Narasimhan (2001) |
| | New product performance | Brockman and Morgan (2003) |
| | Non-value added | Rosenzweig and Roth (2004) |
| | Objective cycle time | Hult, Hurley, Giunipero, and Nichols (2000) |
| | Operating performance | Terziovski, Samson, and Dow (1997) |
| | Operational outcomes | Tatikonda and Montoya-Weiss (2001) |
| | Operational performance | Shah and Ward (2003) |
| | Operational performance | Ahmad and Schroeder (2003) |
| | Operations/product variance | Germain, Dröge, and Christensen (2001) |
| | Past quality performance | Benson, Saraph, and Schroeder (1991) |
| | Patient satisfaction | Marley, Collier, and Goldstein (2004) |
| | Perceived quality market outcomes | Flynn, Schroeder, and Sakakibara (1995) |
| | Performance | Joshi, Kathuria, and Porth (2003) |
| | Performance | Safizadeh, Ritzman, Sharma, and Wood (1996) |
| | Performance | Frohlich and Westbrook (2002) |
| | Performance (result) | New and Szwejczewski (1995) |
| | Performance: flexibility | Boyer, Leong, Ward, and Krajewski (1997) |

| | |
|---|---|
| Performance measures—overall CAD process | Malhotra, Heine, and Grover (2001) |
| Performance quality | Adam, Corbett, Flores, Harrison, Lee, Rho, Ribera, Samson, and Westbrook (1997) |
| Performance: operational efficiency factor | Small and Yasin (1997) |
| Performance: time-based performance factor | Small and Yasin (1997) |
| Plant performance | Devaraj, Hollingworth, and Schroeder (2004) |
| Plant performance | Nahm, Vonderemse, and Koufteros (2003) |
| Plant performance: cost | Choi and Eboch (1998) |
| Plant performance: delivery | Choi and Eboch (1998) |
| Plant performance: quality | Choi and Eboch (1998) |
| Plant's rank within the industry | Schmenner and Cook (1985) |
| Plant's rank within the parent company | Schmenner and Cook (1985) |
| Plant's rate of change of productivity advance | Schmenner and Cook (1985) |
| Price leader | Roth (1996) |
| Price offered | Tracey, Vonderembse, and Lim (1999) |
| Process flexibility | Safizadeh, Field, and Ritzman (2003) |
| Process flexibility | Swink, Narasimhan, and Kim (2005) |
| Process flexibility | Rosenzweig, Roth, and Dean (2003) |
| Process performance | Wallace, Keil, and Rai (2004) |
| Process technological leadership | Roth (1996) |
| Product design and development competency | Dröge and Vickery (1994) |
| Product development productivity | Hong, Vonderembse, Doll, and Nahm (2005) |
| Product flexibility | Safizadeh, Field, and Ritzman (2003) |
| Product flexibility | White (1996) |
| Product flexibility | Flynn, Schroeder, and Flynn (1999) |
| Product innovation | Koufteros, Vonderembse, and Jayaram (2005) |
| Product innovation | Koufteros, Vonderembse, and Doll (2001) |
| Product innovation | Koufteros, Vonderembse, and Doll (2002) |
| Product lead-time | Sawhney and Piper (2002) |
| Product line breadth | Tracey, Vonderembse, and Lim (1999) |
| Product performance | Wallace, Keil, and Rai (2004) |
| Product price compared to competition | Robinson and Satterfield (1998) |
| Product quality | Rosenzweig, Roth, and Dean (2003) |
| Product quality | Tatikonda and Montoya-Weiss (2001) |
| Product quality | Robinson and Satterfield (1998) |
| Production competence | Vickery (1991) |
| Productivity | Rho and Yu (1998) |
| Productivity improvement | Stahl and Zimmerer (1983) |
| Productivity measures: productivity | Noble (1997) |
| Productivity measures: relative productivity | Noble (1997) |
| Project quality | Primo and Amundson (2002) |

*(Continued)*

(Continued)

| | | |
|---|---|---|
| | Project speed | Primo and Amundson (2002) |
| | Project success | Fedor, Ghosh, Caldwell, Maurer, and Singhal (2003) |
| | Projected research and development (R&D) budget/time-to-market objective/projected unit cost of the product | Primo and Amundson (2002) |
| | Purchasing competency | Narasimhan, Jayaram, and Carter (2001) |
| | Quality | Koufteros, Vonderembse, and Jayaram (2005) |
| | Quality | Roth (1996) |
| | Quality | Rho and Yu (1998) |
| | Quality | Hennig-Thurau, Langer, and Hansen (2001) |
| | Quality | Karlsson and Ahlstrom (1995) |
| | Quality | Koufteros, Vonderembse, and Doll (2001) |
| | Quality | Koufteros, Vonderembse, and Doll (2002) |
| | Quality | Sawhney and Piper (2002) |
| | Quality | Malhotra, Heine, and Grover (2001) |
| | Quality | Carter and Carter (1998) |
| | Quality and operational results | Pannirselvam, Siferd, and Ruch (1998) |
| | Quality of customer interface | Safizadeh, Field, and Ritzman (2003) |
| | Quality of customer interface | Roth and Jackson (1995) |
| | Quality of customer interface | Menor, Roth, and Mason (2001) |
| | Quality of customer interface | Roth (1993) |
| | Quality of products | Tracey, Vonderembse, and Lim (1999) |
| | Quality performance | Kaynak (2003) |
| | Quality performance | Flynn, Sakakibara, and Schroeder (1995) |
| | Quality performance | Das and Narasimhan (2001) |
| | Quality performance | Li, Benton, and Leong (2002) |
| | Quality features | Flynn, Schroeder, and Flynn (1999) |
| | Quality performance | Flynn, Schroeder, and Flynn (1999) |
| | Responsiveness | Dröge, Jayaram, and Vickery (2004) |
| | Results from quality assurance of products and services/quality and operational results | Flynn and Saladin (2001) |
| | Routing flexibility | Zhang and Vonderembse (2003) |
| | Satisfaction | McDermott and Stock (1999) |
| | Service quality | Safizadeh, Field, and Ritzman (2003) |
| | Service quality | Voss, Tsikriktsis, Funk, Yarrow, and Owen (2005) |
| | Service quality | Roth (1993) |
| | Service quality | Menor, Roth, and Mason (2001) |
| | Service quality | Roth and Jackson (1995) |
| | Service quality to external customers | Stanley and Wisner (2001) |
| | Speed and flexibility in the design of new products and services | Escrig-Tena and Bou-Llusar (2005) |
| | Speed to market | Sarin and McDermott (2003) |
| | Streamlining | Roth (1993) |
| | Strength in competitive capabilities: delivery | Kim and Arnold (1992) |

| | | |
|---|---|---|
| | Strength in competitive capabilities: flexibility | Kim and Arnold (1992) |
| | Strength in competitive capabilities: price | Kim and Arnold (1992) |
| | Strength in competitive capabilities: quality | Kim and Arnold (1992) |
| | Strength in competitive capabilities: service | Kim and Arnold (1992) |
| | Strength/weakness in manufacturing performance areas | Cleveland, Schroeder, and Anderson (1989) |
| | Subjective cycle time | Hult, Hurley, Giunipero, and Nichols (2000) |
| | Supplier's performance | Prahinski and Benton (2004) |
| | Technological leadership | Roth and Jackson (1995) |
| | Technological leadership | Menor, Roth, and Mason (2001) |
| | Technological leadership | Roth (1993) |
| | Time accuracy | Karlsson and Ahlstrom (1995) |
| | Time-to-market | Li, Rao, Ragu-Nathan, and Ragu-Nathan (2005) |
| | Time-to-market | Dröge, Jayaram, and Vickery (2004) |
| | Time-to-market | Tatikonda and Montoya-Weiss (2001) |
| | Time-to-product | Dröge, Jayaram, and Vickery (2004) |
| | Total performance | Powell (1995) |
| | TQM program performance | Powell (1995) |
| | Unit cost | Tatikonda and Montoya-Weiss (2001) |
| | Volume flexibility | Zhang and Vonderembse (2003) |
| | Volume flexibility | Flynn, Schroeder, and Flynn (1999) |
| Customer satisfaction | Billing | Athanassopoulos and Iliakopoulos (2003) |
| | Branch network | Athanassopoulos and Iliakopoulos (2003) |
| | Commitment to customers | Flynn and Saladin (2001) |
| | Competitive comparisons | Flynn and Saladin (2001) |
| | Corporate image | Athanassopoulos and Iliakopoulos (2003) |
| | Customer and market knowledge | Flynn and Saladin (2001) |
| | Customer loyalty | Vickery, Dröge, Stank, Goldsby, and Markland (2004) |
| | Customer loyalty | Stank, Goldsby, and Vickery (1999) |
| | Customer responsiveness | Chen, Paulraj, and Lado (2004) |
| | Customer results | Escrig-Tena and Bou-Llusar (2005) |
| | Customer satisfaction | Rungtusanatham, Forza, Koka, Salvador, and Nie (2005) |
| | Customer satisfaction | Terziovski, Samson, and Dow (1997) |
| | Customer satisfaction | Vickery, Dröge, Stank, Goldsby, and Markland (2004) |
| | Customer satisfaction | Voss, Tsikriktsis, Funk, Yarrow, and Owen (2005) |
| | Customer satisfaction | Zhang and Vonderembse (2003) |
| | Customer satisfaction | Goldstein (2003) |
| | Customer satisfaction | Anderson, Rungtusanatham, Schroeder, and Devaraj (1995) |
| | Customer satisfaction | Tatikonda and Montoya-Weiss (2001) |
| | Customer satisfaction | Terziovski, Samson, and Dow (1997) |

*(Continued)*

(Continued)

| | | |
|---|---|---|
| | Customer satisfaction | Stank, Goldsby, and Vickery (1999) |
| | Customer satisfaction enhancement | Flynn and Saladin (2001) |
| | Customer satisfaction: cost | Choi and Eboch (1998) |
| | Customer satisfaction: delivery | Choi and Eboch (1998) |
| | Customer satisfaction: quality | Choi and Eboch (1998) |
| | Customer service | Vickery, Jayaram, Dröge, and Calantone (2003) |
| | Customer service | Flynn and Saladin (2001) |
| | Customer views of quality | Flynn and Saladin (2001) |
| | Customer-based performance | Zahay and Griffin (2004) |
| | Customer-perceived service quality | de Jong, de Ruyter, and Wetzels (2005) |
| | Directory inquiries | Athanassopoulos and Iliakopoulos (2003) |
| | Fault repair | Athanassopoulos and Iliakopoulos (2003) |
| | Final satisfaction/postrecovery satisfaction | McCollough, Berry, and Yadav (2000) |
| | Loyalty intentions | de Jong and de Ruyter (2004) |
| | Perceived customer satisfaction | Douglas and Fredendall (2004) |
| | Perceived performance | Athanassopoulos and Iliakopoulos (2003) |
| | Recovery performance | McCollough, Berry, and Yadav (2000) |
| | Satisfaction from the product | Athanassopoulos and Iliakopoulos (2003) |
| | Service performance | McCollough, Berry, and Yadav (2000) |
| | Service performance measures: operational performance | Stank, Goldsby, and Vickery (1999) |
| | Service performance measures: relational performance | Stank, Goldsby, and Vickery (1999) |
| | Service provisioning | Athanassopoulos and Iliakopoulos (2003) |
| | Service recovery satisfaction | de Jong and de Ruyter (2004) |
| | Share of customer | de Jong and de Ruyter (2004) |
| | Student loyalty | Hennig-Thurau, Langer, and Hansen (2001) |
| | Value to customer | Tu, Vonderembse, and Ragu-Nathan (2001) |
| | Word of mouth: activity | Harrison-Walker (2001) |
| | Word of mouth: praise | Harrison-Walker (2001) |
| Supply chain capabilities | Adaptive performance | Morgan, Zou, Vorhies, and Katsikeas (2003) |
| | Distribution/logistics adaptability | Swafford, Ghosh, and Murthy (2006) |
| | Distribution/logistics range | Swafford, Ghosh, and Murthy (2006) |
| | Manufacturing adaptability | Swafford, Ghosh, and Murthy (2006) |
| | Manufacturing range | Swafford, Ghosh, and Murthy (2006) |
| | Performance consequence | Hult, Ketchen, and Nichols (2003) |
| | Performance improvements | Krause, Handfield, and Scannell (1998) |
| | Procurement/sourcing adaptability | Swafford, Ghosh, and Murthy (2006) |
| | Procurement/sourcing range | Swafford, Ghosh, and Murthy (2006) |
| | Supply chain agility | Swafford, Ghosh, and Murthy (2006) |
| Financial/ business/ marketing/ organizational performance | After-tax return on assets (ROA) | Curkovic, Vickery, and Dröge (2000) |

| | |
|---|---|
| AMT implementation outcomes: organizational and managerial benefits | McDermott and Stock (1999) |
| Business growth | Zahay and Griffin (2004) |
| Business performance | Vickery, Dröge, Yeomans, and Markland (1995) |
| Business performance | Terziovski, Samson, and Dow (1997) |
| Business performance | da Silveira (2005) |
| Business performance | Rosenzweig, Roth, and Dean (2003) |
| Business performance | Ward, Duray, Leong, and Sum (1995) |
| Business performance | Rosenzweig, Roth, and Dean (2003) |
| Business sustainability | Roth (1993) |
| Business sustainability | Menor, Roth, and Mason (2001) |
| Company reputation | Cao and Dowlatshahi (2005) |
| Competitive position | Hausman, Montgomery, and Roth (2002) |
| Economic results | Escrig-Tena and Bou-Llusar (2005) |
| Effectiveness | Jambulingam, Kathuria, and Doucette (2005) |
| Environmental performance | Zhu and Sarkis (2004) |
| Financial and market performance | Kaynak (2003) |
| Financial and market results | Flynn and Saladin (2001) |
| Financial performance | Vickery, Jayaram, Dröge, and Calantone (2003) |
| Financial performance | Cao and Dowlatshahi (2005) |
| Financial performance | Dröge, Claycomb, and Germain (2003) |
| Financial performance | Dröge, Jayaram, and Vickery (2004) |
| Financial performance | Adam, Corbett, Flores, Harrison, Lee, Rho, Ribera, Samson, and Westbrook (1997) |
| Financial performance | Cleveland, Schroeder, and Anderson (1989) |
| Financial performance | Chen, Paulraj, and Lado (2004) |
| Financial performance | Germain, Dröge, and Christensen (2001) |
| Financial performance | Li, Benton, and Leong (2002) |
| Firm financial performance | Petersen, Handfield, and Ragatz (2005) |
| Firm's financial performance over the past five years | Carr and Pearson (1999) |
| Growth | Diáz, Machuca, and Alvarez-Gil (2003) |
| Growth in market share | Curkovic, Vickery, and Dröge (2000) |
| Growth in return on investment | Curkovic, Vickery, and Dröge (2000) |
| Growth rate on sales | Raffi and Swamidass (1987) |
| Improved business performance | Stratman and Roth (2002) |
| Level of performance | Tracey, Vonderembse, and Lim (1999) |
| Market acuity | Roth and Jackson (1995) |
| Market acuity | Menor, Roth, and Mason (2001) |
| Market growth | Cao and Dowlatshahi (2005) |
| Market outcomes | Tatikonda and Montoya-Weiss (2001) |
| Market performance | Christensen, Germain, and Birou (2005) |
| Market performance | Roth (1993) |
| Market performance | Roth and Jackson (1995) |
| Market share | Dröge, Jayaram, and Vickery (2004) |
| Market share | Curkovic, Vickery, and Dröge (2000) |
| Market-based performance | Swink, Narasimhan, and Kim (2005) |
| Marketing competency | Dröge and Vickery (1994) |

*(Continued)*

(Continued)

| | | |
|---|---|---|
| | Marketing morale | Hausman, Montgomery, and Roth (2002) |
| | Marketing performance | Cleveland, Schroeder, and Anderson (1989) |
| | Negative economic performance | Zhu and Sarkis (2004) |
| | Organizational performance | Samson and Terziovski (1999) |
| | Overall performance | Safizadeh, Field, and Ritzman (2003) |
| | Perceived financial performance | Douglas and Fredendall (2004) |
| | Performance | Nahm, Vonderembse, and Koufteros (2004) |
| | Performance | Pagell and Krause (2004) |
| | Performance | Pagell, M. (2004) |
| | Performance | Griffith, Harvey, and Lusch (2006) |
| | Performance | Williams, D'Souza, Rosenfeldt, and Kassaee (1995) |
| | Performance | Vickery, Dröge, Yeomans, and Markland (1995) |
| | Performance | Ho (1996) |
| | Performance | Dröge and Vickery (1994) |
| | Performance | Swamidass and Kotha (1998) |
| | Performance | Boyer, Ward, and Leong (1996) |
| | Performance | Williams, D'Souza, Rosenfeldt, and Kassaee (1995) |
| | Performance | Safizadeh and Ritzman (1997) |
| | Performance | Dean and Snell (1991) |
| | Performance : profit | Boyer, Leong, Ward, and Krajewski (1997) |
| | Performance measure | Swamidass and Newell (1987) |
| | Performance measure | Ahmed, Montagno, and Firenze (1996) |
| | Performance: growth | Boyer, Leong, Ward, and Krajewski (1997) |
| | Performance: organizational effectiveness factor | Small and Yasin (1997) |
| | Positive economic performance | Zhu and Sarkis (2004) |
| | Premium pricing | Koufteros, Vonderembse, and Doll (2001) |
| | Premium pricing | Koufteros, Vonderembse, and Doll (2002) |
| | Pretax return on assets (ROA) | Curkovic, Vickery, and Dröge (2000) |
| | Product innovation | Cao and Dowlatshahi (2005) |
| | Profit | Diáz, Machuca, and Alvarez-Gil (2003) |
| | Profitability | Koufteros, Vonderembse, and Jayaram (2005) |
| | Profitability | Koufteros, Vonderembse, and Doll (2002) |
| | Profitability | Rosenzweig and Roth (2004) |
| | Profits | Hausman, Montgomery, and Roth (2002) |
| | Relative sales | Tatikonda and Montoya-Weiss (2001) |
| | Reputation | Escrig-Tena and Bou-Llusar (2005) |
| | Return on investment | Curkovic, Vickery, and Dröge (2000) |
| | Stakeholder value | Roth (1993) |
| | The impact of environmental management system (EMS) on performance | Melnyk, Sroufe, and Calantone (2003) |
| Individual/team performance | Design performance | Petersen, Handfield, and Ragatz (2005) |
| | Employee competence | Narasimhan, Jayaram, and Carter (2001) |
| | Group potency | de Jong, de Ruyter, and Wetzels (2005) |
| | Implementation success-perceived psychosocial outcomes | Pinto, Pinto, and Prescott (1993) |
| | Implementation success-perceived task outcomes | Pinto, Pinto, and Prescott (1993) |

| | | |
|---|---|---|
| | People valued | Schmenner and Cook (1985) |
| | Performance | Teigland and McLure Wasko (2004) |
| | Performance | Lewis (2004) |
| | Project team effectiveness | Petersen, Handfield, and Ragatz (2005) |
| Supply chain relationship performance | Achievement of competitive advantages | Jap and Anderson (2003) |
| | Buyer financial performance | Chen and Paulraj (2004) |
| | Buyer operational performance | Chen and Paulraj (2004) |
| | Buyer's perception of relationship's performance | Johnston, McCutcheon, Stuart, and Kerwood (2004) |
| | Buyer's satisfaction | Johnston, McCutcheon, Stuart, and Kerwood (2004) |
| | Evaluation of the counterpart's performance | Jap and Anderson (2003) |
| | Expectations of relational continuity | Jap and Anderson (2003) |
| | Internal suppliers' service quality performance | Stanley and Wisner (2001) |
| | Joint profit performance | Jap and Anderson (2003) |
| | Performance-manufacturer | Benton and Maloni (2004) |
| | Performance-supplier | Benton and Maloni (2004) |
| | Performance-supply chain | Benton and Maloni (2004) |
| | Product freshness | Boyer and Hult (2006) |
| | Product quality | Boyer and Hult (2006) |
| | Purchasing's service quality performance | Stanley and Wisner (2001) |
| | Relational performance | Vickery, Dröge, Stank, Goldsby, and Markland (2004) |
| | Satisfaction | Benton and Maloni (2004) |
| | Satisfaction | Griffith, Harvey, and Lusch (2006) |
| | Service quality | Boyer and Hult (2006) |
| | Supplier operational performance | Chen and Paulraj (2004) |

## Information Systems/e-Business Scales

| *Categories* | *Scale Name from the Paper* | *Paper* |
|---|---|---|
| IT strategy/ management | BP-reflects-ITP | Kearns and Lederer (2003) |
| | CAPIS (competitive advantage provided by information systems): primary activity efficiency | Byrd and Turner (2001) |
| | CAPIS (competitive advantage provided by information systems): resource management functionality | Byrd and Turner (2001) |
| | CAPIS (competitive advantage provided by information systems): support activity efficiency | Byrd and Turner (2001) |

*(Continued)*

(Continued)

| | | |
|---|---|---|
| | CAPIS (competitive advantage provided by information systems): threat | Byrd and Turner (2001) |
| | Contextual factors-strategy: administrative | Olson and Boyer (2003) |
| | Contextual factors-strategy: delivery | Olson and Boyer (2003) |
| | Contextual factors-strategy: goals | Olson and Boyer (2003) |
| | Executive commitment | Stratman and Roth (2002) |
| | Flexible information systems (IS) infrastructure: data transparency | Byrd and Turner (2001) |
| | Flexible IS infrastructure: IS compatibility | Byrd and Turner (2001) |
| | Flexible IS infrastructure: IS connectivity | Byrd and Turner (2001) |
| | Flexible IS infrastructure: applications functionality | Byrd and Turner (2001) |
| | Information intensity of the value chain | Kearns and Lederer (2003) |
| | Information technology (IT) is used to create a competitive advantage | Kearns and Lederer (2003) |
| | Flexible IS infrastructure: data transparency | Byrd and Turner (2001) |
| | Flexible IS infrastructure: IS compatibility | Byrd and Turner (2001) |
| | Flexible IS infrastructure: IS connectivity | Byrd and Turner (2001) |
| | Flexible IS infrastructure: applications functionality | Byrd and Turner (2001) |
| | IT skills | Stratman and Roth (2002) |
| | Information technology planning (ITP) reflects-business planning (BP) | Kearns and Lederer (2003) |
| | Project management | Stratman and Roth (2002) |
| | Scope of operations | Pflughoeft, Ramamurthy, Soofi, Yasai-Ardekani, and Zahedi (2003) |
| | Strategic IT planning | Stratman and Roth (2002) |
| | The CEO participates in IT planning | Kearns and Lederer (2003) |
| | The CIO participates in business planning | Kearns and Lederer (2003) |
| Usefulness/value/ satisfaction (perceived or belief) | Accuracy | Somers, Nelson, and Karimi (2003) |
| | Content | Somers, Nelson, and Karimi (2003) |
| | Convenience | Olson, Belohlav, and Boyer (2005) |
| | Cost | Olson, Belohlav, and Boyer (2005) |
| | Cost reduction | Olson and Boyer (2003) |
| | Duration appropriateness belief | Froehle and Roth (2004) |
| | Expected performance benefits | Tsikriktsis, Lanzolla, and Frohlich (2004) |

| | | |
|---|---|---|
| | Face-to-face contacts | Pflughoeft, Ramamurthy, Soofi, Yasai-Ardekani, and Zahedi (2003) |
| | Format | Somers, Nelson, and Karimi (2003) |
| | Information richness belief | Froehle and Roth (2004) |
| | Internet improvement | Olson and Boyer (2003) |
| | Internet purchasing acceptance factors: perceived usefulness | Olson and Boyer (2003) |
| | Intimacy appropriateness belief | Froehle and Roth (2004) |
| | Learning belief | Froehle and Roth (2004) |
| | Media richness | Vickery, Dröge, Stank, Goldsby, and Markland (2004) |
| | Operational efficiency | Pflughoeft, Ramamurthy, Soofi, Yasai-Ardekani, and Zahedi (2003) |
| | Perceived usefulness | Venkatesh, Speier, and Morris (2002) |
| | Purchasing efficiency | Olson and Boyer (2003) |
| | Site accuracy | Olson and Boyer (2003) |
| | Strategic benefits | Pflughoeft, Ramamurthy, Soofi, Yasai-Ardekani, and Zahedi (2003) |
| | System effectiveness | Olson, Belohlav, and Boyer (2005) |
| | Time savings | Boyer and Hult (2006) |
| | Timeliness | Somers, Nelson, and Karimi (2003) |
| | Transaction | Olson and Boyer (2003) |
| | Transactional accuracy | Olson, Belohlav, and Boyer (2005) |
| | Usefulness belief | Froehle and Roth (2004) |
| | Web site interaction: overall impression | Olson, Belohlav, and Boyer (2005) |
| | Web site interaction: perspective | Olson, Belohlav, and Boyer (2005) |
| Ease of use (perceived or belief) | Ease of use | Somers, Nelson, and Karimi (2003) |
| | Internet purchasing acceptance factors: comfort | Olson and Boyer (2003) |
| | Internet purchasing acceptance factors: perceived ease | Olson and Boyer (2003) |
| | Perceived ease of use | Venkatesh, Speier, and Morris (2002) |
| | Site ease | Olson and Boyer (2003) |
| | Web site interaction: ease of interaction | Olson, Belohlav, and Boyer (2005) |
| Use/adoption | Customer information system | Zahay and Griffin (2004) |
| | e-CRM (customer relationship management) | Tsikriktsis, Lanzolla, and Frohlich (2004) |
| | Educational tool usage | Olson, Belohlav, and Boyer (2005) |
| | Electronic commerce infusion | Pflughoeft, Ramamurthy, Soofi, Yasai-Ardekani, and Zahedi (2003) |
| | e-Transactions | Tsikriktsis, Lanzolla, and Frohlich (2004) |
| | Information search | Pflughoeft, Ramamurthy, Soofi, Yasai-Ardekani, and Zahedi (2003) |

*(Continued)*

(Continued)

| | | |
|---|---|---|
| | Information technology | Cao and Dowlatshahi (2005) |
| | Information technology | Chen and Paulraj (2004) |
| | Integrative information technologies | Vickery, Jayaram, Dröge, and Calantone (2003) |
| | Ordering tool usage | Olson, Belohlav, and Boyer (2005) |
| | Virtual enterprise | Cao and Dowlatshahi (2005) |
| Barriers/ motivations/ pressure | Customer barriers | Tsikriktsis, Lanzolla, and Frohlich (2004) |
| | External pressure | Tsikriktsis, Lanzolla, and Frohlich (2004) |
| | Internal barriers | Tsikriktsis, Lanzolla, and Frohlich (2004) |
| | Intrinsic motivation | Venkatesh, Speier, and Morris (2002) |
| | IT sophistication | Pflughoeft, Ramamurthy, Soofi, Yasai-Ardekani, and Zahedi (2003) |
| | Market pressure | Pflughoeft, Ramamurthy, Soofi, Yasai-Ardekani, and Zahedi (2003) |
| | New markets | Tsikriktsis, Lanzolla, and Frohlich (2004) |
| | Web-related costs | Pflughoeft, Ramamurthy, Soofi, Yasai-Ardekani, and Zahedi (2003) |
| Attitude | Attitude toward the episode | Froehle and Roth (2004) |
| | Attitude toward the medium | Froehle and Roth (2004) |
| | Attitude toward the service provider | Froehle and Roth (2004) |
| | Internet purchasing acceptance factors: attitude | Olson and Boyer (2003) |
| Intention | Behavioral intention | Venkatesh, Speier, and Morris (2002) |
| | Behavioral intentions | Boyer and Hult (2006) |
| | Intention toward the medium | Froehle and Roth (2004) |
| | Intention toward the provider | Froehle and Roth (2004) |

## Supply Chain Scales

| *Categories* | *Scale Name from the Paper* | *Paper* |
|---|---|---|
| Buyer-supplier relationship | Buyer-seller relationship management | Narasimhan, Jayaram, and Carter (2001) |
| | Buyer-supplier relationships | Carr and Pearson (1999) |
| | Buying firm's expectation of relationship continuity | Krause (1999) |
| | Buying firm's commitment | Prahinski and Benton (2004) |
| | Commitment | Monczka, Peterson, Handfield, and Ragatz (1998) |
| | Commitment | Benton and Maloni (2004) |
| | Complaint handling | Goffin, Lemke, and Szwejczewski (2006) |
| | Conflict resolution techniques | Monczka, Peterson, Handfield, and Ragatz (1998) |
| | Conflict | Benton and Maloni (2004) |
| | Conflict | Griffith, Harvey, and Lusch (2006) |
| | Conflict resolution | Benton and Maloni (2004) |
| | Cooperation | Prahinski and Benton (2004) |
| | Cooperation | Benton and Maloni (2004) |

| | |
|---|---|
| Cooperative purchasing/supplier relationship | Stanley and Wisner (2001) |
| Customer and supplier relations | Ittner and Larcker (1997) |
| Customer involvement: customer interaction | Flynn, Schroeder, and Sakakibara (1994) |
| Customer relationship | Flynn, Schroeder, and Sakakibara (1995) |
| Customer relationship | Li, Rao, Ragu-Nathan, and Ragu-Nathan (2005) |
| Customer relationships | Ketokivi and Schroeder (2004) |
| Dependency | Goffin, Lemke, and Szwejczewski (2006) |
| Distributive justice | Griffith, Harvey, and Lusch (2006) |
| Ex post opportunism | Jap and Anderson (2003) |
| Flexibility in arrangements | Johnston, McCutcheon, Stuart, and Kerwood (2004) |
| Goal congruence | Jap and Anderson (2003) |
| Importance of purchased inputs to the buying firm | Krause (1999) |
| Interdependence | Monczka, Peterson, Handfield, and Ragatz (1998) |
| Interpersonal trust | Jap and Anderson (2003) |
| Just-in-time (JIT) supplier relations | Flynn, Schroeder, and Flynn (1999) |
| Joint responsibility | Johnston, McCutcheon, Stuart, and Kerwood (2004) |
| Limited number of suppliers | Chen, Paulraj, and Lado (2004) |
| Long-term orientation | Griffith, Harvey, and Lusch (2006) |
| Long-term orientation | Chen, Paulraj, and Lado (2004) |
| Long-term relationship | Chen and Paulraj (2004) |
| Management consequence | Hult, Ketchen, and Nichols (2003) |
| Organizational size | Goffin, Lemke, and Szwejczewski (2006) |
| Personal relationship | Goffin, Lemke, and Szwejczewski (2006) |
| Procedural justice | Griffith, Harvey, and Lusch (2006) |
| Purchasing's strategic role | Johnson, Klassen, Leenders, and Fearon (2002) |
| Reasons for subcontracting | Chikan and Demeter (1995) |
| Relational behavior | Griffith, Harvey, and Lusch (2006) |
| Relationship | Choi and Hartley (1996) |
| Relationship maintenance | Goffin, Lemke, and Szwejczewski (2006) |
| Shared planning | Johnston, McCutcheon, Stuart, and Kerwood (2004) |
| Strategic purchasing | Carr and Pearson (1999) |
| Strategic purchasing | Chen and Paulraj (2004) |
| Strategic purchasing | Chen, Paulraj, and Lado (2004) |
| Strategic supplier partnership | Li, Rao, Ragu-Nathan, and Ragu-Nathan (2005) |
| Supplier commitment | Krause (1999) |
| Supplier involvement: supplier relationship | Flynn, Schroeder, and Sakakibara (1994) |
| Supplier relationship | Flynn, Schroeder, and Sakakibara (1995) |
| Supplier relationship | Flynn, Schroeder, and Sakakibara (1995) |
| Supplier relationship management | Swink, Narasimhan, and Kim (2005) |
| Supplier relationships | Ketokivi and Schroeder (2004) |
| Supplier's commitment | Prahinski and Benton (2004) |

*(Continued)*

(Continued)

| | | |
|---|---|---|
| | Suppliers' perception of buyer's benevolence | Johnston, McCutcheon, Stuart, and Kerwood (2004) |
| | Supplier's perception of buyer's dependability | Johnston, McCutcheon, Stuart, and Kerwood (2004) |
| | Supply base reduction | Chen and Paulraj (2004) |
| | Supply management consequence | Hult, Ketchen, and Nichols (2003) |
| | Supply network structure | Chen and Paulraj (2004) |
| | Trust | Benton and Maloni (2004) |
| | Trust and coordination | Monczka, Peterson, Handfield, and Ragatz (1998) |
| | Vertical coordination | Carter and Carter (1998) |
| | Volume of turnover as bought from the supplier | Goffin, Lemke, and Szwejczewski (2006) |
| Power | Coercive | Benton and Maloni (2004) |
| | Competitive pressure | Krause, Scannell, and Calantone (2000) |
| | Compliance | Benton and Maloni (2004) |
| | Expert | Benton and Maloni (2004) |
| | Legal legitimate | Benton and Maloni (2004) |
| | Referent | Benton and Maloni (2004) |
| | Reward | Benton and Maloni (2004) |
| | Supplier incentives | Krause, Scannell, and Calantone (2000) |
| Integration/ collaboration/ coordination | Bilateral idiosyncratic investments | Jap and Anderson (2003) |
| | Buying firm's top management support | Krause (1999) |
| | Closer customer relationships | Curkovic, Vickery, and Dröge (2000) |
| | Closer to customers | Powell (1995) |
| | Closer to suppliers | Powell (1995) |
| | Continuous improvement activities | Krause, Handfield, and Scannell (1998) |
| | Cross-functional cooperation | Ketokivi and Schroeder (2004) |
| | Cross-functional cooperation | Pinto, Pinto, and Prescott (1993) |
| | Cross-functional involvement in supplier development | Krause, Handfield, and Scannell (1998) |
| | Cross-functional teams | Chen and Paulraj (2004) |
| | Customer and supplier relations | Ittner and Larcker (1997) |
| | Degree of supply chain coordination regarding customers | Hill and Scudder (2002) |
| | Degree of supply chain coordination regarding suppliers | Hill and Scudder (2002) |
| | Demand integration | Frohlich and Westbrook (2002) |
| | Design-process integration | Dröge, Jayaram, and Vickery (2004) |
| | Direct involvement | Krause, Scannell, and Calantone (2000) |
| | Drivers of change | Frohlich and Westbrook (2002) |
| | External cooperation skills | Escrig-Tena and Bou-Llusar (2005) |
| | External interface management | Black and Porter (1996) |
| | Implementation strategies for supplier development efforts | Krause, Handfield, and Scannell (1998) |

| | |
|---|---|
| Integration | Pagell, M. (2004) |
| Integration | Diáz, Machuca, and Alvarez-Gil (2003) |
| Integration | Lawrence and Hottenstein (1995) |
| Integration | Germain, Dröge, and Christensen (2001) |
| Integration intensity | Rosenzweig, Roth, and Dean (2003) |
| Integration measures | Frohlich and Westbrook (2001) |
| Internal and external cooperation | Rungtusanatham, Forza, Koka, Salvador, and Nie (2005) |
| Just-in-time (JIT) deliveries | Lawrence and Hottenstein (1995) |
| JIT delivery by suppliers | Cua, McKone, and Schroeder (2001) |
| JIT implementation: JIT delivery by suppliers | McKone, Schroeder, and Cua (1999) |
| JIT implementation: JIT link with customers | McKone, Schroeder, and Cua (1999) |
| JIT supplier relationship | Sakakibara, Flynn, Schroeder, and Morris (1997) |
| JIT vendor strategy | Mehra and Inman (1992) |
| Logistics integration | Chen and Paulraj (2004) |
| Management practices | Morita and Flynn (1997) |
| New product development/innovation | Goffin, Lemke, and Szwejczewski (2006) |
| Operational independence | Prasad, Tata, and Madan (2005) |
| Operational linkages | Prahinski and Benton (2004) |
| Organizational scope | Devaraj, Hollingworth, and Schroeder (2004) |
| Participativeness | Hult, Hurley, Giunipero, and Nichols (2000) |
| Reflectiveness | Hult, Hurley, Giunipero, and Nichols (2000) |
| Replenishment volumes | Prasad, Tata, and Madan (2005) |
| Special product capability | Goffin, Lemke, and Szwejczewski (2006) |
| Strategic design integration | Dröge, Jayaram, and Vickery (2004) |
| Supplier development | Curkovic, Vickery, and Dröge (2000) |
| Supplier development strategies, practices and methods | Krause, Handfield, and Scannell (1998)<br>Prasad, Tata, and Madan (2005) |
| Supplier integration | |
| Supplier involvement | Chen and Paulraj (2004) |
| Supplier involvement | Lawrence and Hottenstein (1995) |
| Supplier obstructionism | Primo and Amundson (2002) |
| Supplier partnerships | Black and Porter (1996) |
| Supplier quality involvement | Flynn and Flynn (2004) |
| Supplier quality involvement | Sakakibara, Flynn, Schroeder, and Morris (1997) |
| Supplier resources dedicated to supplier development activities. | Krause, Handfield, and Scannell (1998) |
| Supply chain integration | Vickery, Jayaram, Dröge, and Calantone (2003) |
| Supply chain integration | Dong, Carter, and Dresner (2001) |
| Supply integration | Frohlich and Westbrook (2002) |
| Total quality management (TQM) implementation: customer involvement | McKone, Schroeder, and Cua (1999) |
| Transaction-specific supplier development activities | Krause (1999) |
| Transformational leadership | Hult, Hurley, Giunipero, and Nichols (2000) |

*(Continued)*

(Continued)

| | | |
|---|---|---|
| Assessment/ communication | Agreement on performance improvement metrics | Krause, Handfield, and Scannell (1998) |
| | Applied customer supply chain knowledge | Christensen, Germain, and Birou (2005) |
| | Applied supplier supply chain knowledge | Christensen, Germain, and Birou (2005) |
| | Business assessment | Petersen, Handfield, and Ragatz (2005) |
| | Buying firm's perspective toward suppliers | Krause (1999) |
| | Commodity/supplier selection process | Monczka, Peterson, Handfield, and Ragatz (1998) |
| | Communication | Chen and Paulraj (2004) |
| | Communication | Chen, Paulraj, and Lado (2004) |
| | Consistency | Choi and Hartley (1996) |
| | Dependable suppliers | Koufteros, Vonderembse, and Doll (1998) |
| | Detailed supplier assessment | Petersen, Handfield, and Ragatz (2005) |
| | Feedback | Goffin, Lemke, and Szwejczewski (2006) |
| | Feedback | Prahinski and Benton (2004) |
| | Finances | Choi and Hartley (1996) |
| | Flexibility | Choi and Hartley (1996) |
| | Formal supplier control | Vickery, Dröge, and Germain (1999) |
| | Formality | Prahinski and Benton (2004) |
| | Identification and prioritization of supplier development opportunities | Krause, Handfield, and Scannell (1998) |
| | Indirect influence strategy | Prahinski and Benton (2004) |
| | Information acquisition | Hult, Hurley, Giunipero, and Nichols (2000) |
| | Information dissemination | Hult, Hurley, Giunipero, and Nichols (2000) |
| | Information participation | Monczka, Peterson, Handfield, and Ragatz (1998) |
| | Information quality | Monczka, Peterson, Handfield, and Ragatz (1998) |
| | Information quality | Li, Rao, Ragu-Nathan, and Ragu-Nathan (2005) |
| | Information sharing | Monczka, Peterson, Handfield, and Ragatz (1998) |
| | Information sharing | Li, Rao, Ragu-Nathan, and Ragu-Nathan (2005) |
| | Inspection | Lawrence and Hottenstein (1995) |
| | Interfirm communication effort | Krause (1999) |
| | Price | Choi and Hartley (1996) |
| | Relationship | Choi and Hartley (1996) |
| | Reliability | Choi and Hartley (1996) |
| | Service | Choi and Hartley (1996) |
| | Strategies for identifying critical performance areas for improvement | Krause, Handfield, and Scannell (1998) |
| | Supplier assessment | Krause, Scannell, and Calantone (2000) |
| | Supplier assessment (Sassess) strategy | Tan (2001) |
| | Supplier evaluation system | Carr and Pearson (1999) |
| | Supplier performance | Ahire, Golhar, and Waller (1996) |
| | Supplier quality management | Forker (1997) |
| | Supplier quality management | Forker, Mendez, and Hershauer (1997) |
| | Supplier quality management | Ahire, Golhar, and Waller (1996) |

| | | |
|---|---|---|
| | Supplier selection | Lawrence and Hottenstein (1995) |
| | Supply management capabilities | Bowen, Cousins, Lamming, and Faruk (2001) |
| | Team usage | Johnson, Klassen, Leenders, and Fearon (2002) |
| | Technical assessment | Petersen, Handfield, and Ragatz (2005) |
| | Technological capability | Choi and Hartley (1996) |
| | Tools/practices to identify suppliers for development efforts | Krause, Handfield, and Scannell (1998) |
| | Total quality management (TQM) implementation: supplier quality management | McKone, Schroeder, and Cua (1999) |
| | Use of electronic data interchange (EDI) with your customers/suppliers | Hill and Scudder (2002) |
| Transaction cost | Advantage | Grover and Malhotra (2003) |
| | Effort | Grover and Malhotra (2003) |
| | Monitor | Grover and Malhotra (2003) |
| | Problem | Grover and Malhotra (2003) |
| | Resource dependence | Carter and Carter (1998) |
| Environmental supply chain practice | Eco-design | Zhu and Sarkis (2004) |
| | Environmental purchasing | Carter and Carter (1998) |
| | External green-supply-chain-management (GSCM) practices | Zhu and Sarkis (2004) |
| | Greening the supply process | Bowen, Cousins, Lamming, and Faruk (2001) |
| | Internal environmental management | Zhu and Sarkis (2004) |
| | Inventory recovery | Zhu and Sarkis (2004) |
| | Product-based green supply | Bowen, Cousins, Lamming, and Faruk (2001) |
| | Strategic purchasing | Bowen, Cousins, Lamming, and Faruk (2001) |

## Product/Service Development Scales

| *Categories* | *Scale Name from the Paper* | *Paper* |
|---|---|---|
| Development practices/ techniques/ strategy | Clarity of project targets | Hong, Vonderembse, Doll, and Nahm (2005) |
| | Comparison of 1987 and 1991 design practices | Ettlie (1995) |
| | Computer use | Koufteros, Vonderembse, and Doll (2002) |
| | Concurrent engineering | Koufteros, Vonderembse, and Doll (2002) |
| | Concurrent engineering (internal integration) | Koufteros, Vonderembse, and Jayaram (2005) |
| | Concurrent engineering practices | Nassimbeni (2003) |
| | Concurrent work-flow | Koufteros, Vonderembse, and Doll (2001) |
| | Cross-functional product design | Cua, McKone, and Schroeder (2001) |
| | Customer integration | Koufteros, Vonderembse, and Jayaram (2005) |

(Continued)

(Continued)

| | | |
|---|---|---|
| | Design and conformance | Adam, Corbett, Flores, Harrison, Lee, Rho, Ribera, Samson, and Westbrook (1997) |
| | Design and engineering change | Rho and Yu (1998) |
| | Design characteristics | Sakakibara, Flynn, Schroeder, and Morris (1997) |
| | Design for customer needs | Flynn, Schroeder, and Flynn (1999) |
| | Design for manufacturability | Ketokivi and Schroeder (2004) |
| | Design manufacturing integration | Ettlie (1997) |
| | Design of new products and services | Flynn and Saladin (2001) |
| | Design of quality products and services | Flynn and Saladin (2001) |
| | Design quality management | Ahire, Golhar, and Waller (1996) |
| | Design-Manufacturing Integration Scale | Ettlie (1995) |
| | Early involvement | Koufteros, Vonderembse, and Doll (2001) |
| | Heavy weight product development managers | Koufteros, Vonderembse, and Doll (2002) |
| | Interfunctional design efforts | Sakakibara, Flynn, Schroeder, and Morris (1997) |
| | Interfunctional design efforts | Flynn and Flynn (2004) |
| | Marketing | Ettlie (1997) |
| | New product design and development (NPDD) strategy | Tan (2001) |
| | New product quality | Sakakibara, Flynn, Schroeder, and Morris (1997) |
| | Planning for new products and services | Flynn and Saladin (2001) |
| | Product design | Flynn, Sakakibara, and Schroeder (1995) |
| | Product design process | Flynn, Schroeder, and Sakakibara (1995) |
| | Product design simplicity | Flynn and Flynn (2004) |
| | Product design: interfunctional design process | Flynn, Schroeder, and Sakakibara (1994) |
| | Product design: new product quality | Flynn, Schroeder, and Sakakibara (1994) |
| | Product development | Ettlie (1997) |
| | Product development strategy | Ettlie (1997) |
| | Product development teams | Koufteros, Vonderembse, and Doll (2001) |
| | Product strategy | Koufteros, Vonderembse, and Doll (2002) |
| | Product/service design | Forker, Mendez, and Hershauer (1997) |
| | Product/service design | Forker (1997) |
| | Product-process development | Swink, Narasimhan, and Kim (2005) |
| | Quality products and services | Adam (1994) |
| | Role change of design engineers | Hong, Vonderembse, Doll, and Nahm (2005) |
| | Shared knowledge about customers | Hong, Vonderembse, Doll, and Nahm (2005) |
| | Supplier process integration | Koufteros, Vonderembse, and Jayaram (2005) |
| | The product development process | Ettlie (1997) |
| | Total quality management: product/service design | Kaynak (2003) |
| Project selection | Functional diversity | Sarin and McDermott (2003) |
| | Organizational environment risk | Wallace, Keil, and Rai (2004) |
| | Origin of the project and realized outcomes and contributions of this new product | Ettlie (1997) |

| | | |
|---|---|---|
| | Planning and control risk | Wallace, Keil, and Rai (2004) |
| | Project complexity | Sarin and McDermott (2003) |
| | Project complexity risk | Wallace, Keil, and Rai (2004) |
| | Project risk | Sarin and McDermott (2003) |
| | Requirements risk | Wallace, Keil, and Rai (2004) |
| | Team risk | Wallace, Keil, and Rai (2004) |
| | User risk | Wallace, Keil, and Rai (2004) |

## TECHNOLOGY SCALES

| *Categories* | *Scale Name from the Paper* | *Paper* |
|---|---|---|
| Types of AMTs and other technologies | Administrative | Boyer, Ward, and Leong (1996) |
| | Advanced manufacturing technologies | Small and Yasin (1997) |
| | Advanced manufacturing technologies | Boyer, Leong, Ward, and Krajewski (1997) |
| | Advanced manufacturing technology | Snell and Dean (1992) |
| | Advanced manufacturing technology | Dean and Snell (1996) |
| | Advanced manufacturing technology | Dean and Snell (1991) |
| | Advanced manufacturing technology | Tracey, Vonderembse, and Lim (1999) |
| | Design | Boyer, Ward, and Leong (1996) |
| | Design | Diáz, Machuca, and Alvaraez-Gil (2003) |
| | Design-manufacturing interfaces | Roth (1996) |
| | Flexible automation | Roth (1996) |
| | Hardware advances | Schmenner and Cook (1985) |
| | High volume automation technology | Swamidass and Kotha (1998) |
| | Information exchange and planning technology | Swamidass and Kotha (1998) |
| | Information technology | Roth (1996) |
| | Integration | Boyer, Ward, and Leong (1996) |
| | Low volume process automation technology | Swamidass and Kotha (1998) |
| | Manufacturing | Boyer, Ward, and Leong (1996) |
| | Manufacturing | Diáz, Machuca, and Alvarez-Gil (2003) |
| | Manufacturing design | Das and Narasimhan (2001) |
| | Manufacturing infrastructure | Das and Narasimhan (2001) |
| | Manufacturing technology | Das and Narasimhan (2001) |
| | Planning | Diáz, Machuca, and Alvarez-Gil (2003) |
| | Process and process technologies | Rho and Yu (1998) |
| | Product design technology | Swamidass and Kotha (1998) |
| | Production planning and control (PPC) | Roth (1996) |
| | Proprietary manufacturing process and equipment | Schroeder, Bates, and Juntilla (2002) |
| | Technologies of integration | Ettlie (1997) |
| | Technology | Nassimbeni (2003) |
| | Type of MRP system | Schroeder, Anderson, Tupy, and White (1981) |

*(Continued)*

(Continued)

| | | |
|---|---|---|
| Technology adoption drivers/ enablers—organizational characteristics | Infrastructure: SOFT | Boyer, Leong, Ward, and Krajewski (1997) |
| | Management message | Leonard-Barton and Deschamps (1988) |
| | Perceived management support | Leonard-Barton and Deschamps (1988) |
| | Process enablers | Roth (1996) |
| | Perceptual measures of functionality | Malhotra, Heine, and Grover (2001) |
| | Sophistication | Malhotra, Heine, and Grover (2001) |
| Technology adoption drivers/ enablers—individual characteristics and skills | Configuration skills (task-related) | Leonard-Barton and Deschamps (1988) |
| | Discomfort | Parasuraman (2000) |
| | Innovativeness | Parasuraman (2000) |
| | Insecurity | Parasuraman (2000) |
| | Job performance | Leonard-Barton and Deschamps (1988) |
| | Job-determined importance (need) | Leonard-Barton and Deschamps (1988) |
| | Optimism | Parasuraman (2000) |
| | Personal innovativeness toward this type of innovation | Leonard-Barton and Deschamps (1988) |
| | Skill in software use (technology-related) | Leonard-Barton and Deschamps (1988) |
| | Subjective importance of the task | Leonard-Barton and Deschamps (1988) |
| | Training | Leonard-Barton and Deschamps (1988) |
| Technology adoption drivers/ enablers—social influence | Interpersonal communication | Leonard-Barton and Deschamps (1988) |
| | Modeled behavior (acquaintance with users) | Leonard-Barton and Deschamps (1988) |
| | Catalyst elements | Diáz, Machuca, and Alvarez-Gil (2003) |
| Technology adoption drivers/ enablers—other factors | Difficulties | Diáz, Machuca, and Alvarez-Gil (2003) |
| | Information elements | Diáz, Machuca, and Alvarez-Gil (2003) |
| | Physical accessibility | Leonard-Barton and Deschamps (1988) |
| Technology implementation strategy | Decentralization | Malhotra, Heine, and Grover (2001) |

| | | |
|---|---|---|
| | Effort expended on planning and installation activities | Small and Yasin (1997) |
| | Effort expended on strategic planning for AMT adoption | Small and Yasin (1997) |
| | Effort expended on team-based project management | Small and Yasin (1997) |
| | Effort expended on technology consistency | Small and Yasin (1997) |
| | Effort expended on worker preparation | Small and Yasin (1997) |
| | Equity of incentives | Malhotra, Heine, and Grover (2001) |
| | Extent of the use of teams | Malhotra, Heine, and Grover (2001) |
| | Extent of training | Malhotra, Heine, and Grover (2001) |
| | Formalization | Malhotra, Heine, and Grover (2001) |
| | Measure of use | Leonard-Barton and Deschamps (1988) |
| | Scale measures | Malhotra, Heine, and Grover (2001) |
| | Starting levels | Schroeder, Anderson, Tupy, and White (1981) |
| | Type of implementation approach | Schroeder, Anderson, Tupy, and White (1981) |

## OTHER SCALES

| *Categories* | *Scale Name from the Paper* | *Paper* |
|---|---|---|
| Others | Activity-based costing | Flynn and Flynn (2004) |
| | Altruism | Wisner, Stringfellow, Youngdahl, and Parker (2005) |
| | Career advancement | Wisner, Stringfellow, Youngdahl, and Parker (2005) |
| | Compliance | Goldstein and Naor (2005) |
| | Management accounting system | Fry, Steele, and Saladin (1995) |
| | Public responsibility | Goldstein and Naor (2005) |

# Appendix 2

# List of Scale Names

## Sorted Alphabetically by Scale Name

| *Scale Name* | *Paper* |
|---|---|
| Ability | Gilgeous (1995) |
| Academic integration | Hennig-Thurau, Langer, and Hansen (2001) |
| Access | Borgatti and Cross (2003) |
| Access standards | Heineke (1995) |
| Accessibility | Pinto, Pinto, and Prescott (1993) |
| Accounting adaptation to just-in-time (JIT) | Sakakibara, Flynn, and Schroeder (1993) |
| Accuracy | Somers, Nelson, and Karimi (2003) |
| Achievement of competitive advantages | Jap and Anderson (2003) |
| Activity-based costing | Flynn and Flynn (2004) |
| Adaptability | Jambulingam, Kathuria, and Doucette (2005) |
| Adaptive performance | Morgan, Zou, Vorhies, and Katsikeas (2003) |
| Adaptive recovery behavior | de Jong and de Ruyter (2004) |
| Administrative | Boyer, Ward, and Leong (1996) |
| Adopting the philosophy | Powell (1995) |
| Adoption of strategic manufacturing practices | Voss and Blackmon (1998) |
| Advanced manufacturing technologies | Boyer, Leong, Ward, and Krajewski (1997) |
| Advanced manufacturing technologies | Small and Yasin (1997) |
| Advanced manufacturing technology | Dean and Snell (1991) |
| Advanced manufacturing technology | Dean and Snell (1996) |
| Advanced manufacturing technology | Snell and Dean (1992) |
| Advanced manufacturing technology | Tracey, Vonderembse, and Lim (1999) |
| Advanced manufacturing technology (AMT) implementation outcome: competitive performance | McDermott and Stock (1999) |
| Advantage | Grover and Malhotra (2003) |
| Adverse outcome management | Heineke (1995) |
| Affective commitment | Harrison-Walker (2001) |
| After-tax ROA | Curkovic, Vickery, and Dröge (2000) |

| | |
|---|---|
| Aggregate plan | Safizadeh and Ritzman (1997) |
| Agility assessment | Cao and Dowlatshahi (2005) |
| Agreement on performance improvement metrics | Krause, Handfield, and Scannell (1998) |
| Algorithm use | Heineke (1995) |
| Alternative ways to change capacity: decreases | Chikan and Demeter (1995) |
| Alternative ways to change capacity: increases | Chikan and Demeter (1995) |
| Altruism | Wisner, Stringfellow, Youngdahl, and Parker (2005) |
| AMT implementation outcomes: operational benefits | McDermott and Stock (1999) |
| AMT implementation outcomes: organizational and managerial benefits | McDermott and Stock (1999) |
| Applied customer supply chain knowledge | Christensen, Germain, and Birou (2005) |
| Applied supplier supply chain knowledge | Christensen, Germain, and Birou (2005) |
| Assurance | Soteriou and Chase (1998) |
| Assurance and validation | Flynn and Saladin (2001) |
| Attention to quality | Schmenner and Cook (1985) |
| Attitude toward the episode | Froehle and Roth (2004) |
| Attitude toward the medium | Froehle and Roth (2004) |
| Attitude toward the service provider | Froehle and Roth (2004) |
| Autonomous and planned maintenance | Cua, McKone, and Schroeder (2001) |
| Autonomy | Jambulingam, Kathuria, and Doucette (2005) |
| Autonomy: people-related autonomy | Janz and Prasarnphanich (2003) |
| Autonomy: planning-related autonomy | Janz and Prasarnphanich (2003) |
| Autonomy: process-related autonomy | Janz and Prasarnphanich (2003) |
| Availability | Levin and Cross (2004) |
| Banking enquiries | Heute and Roth (1988) |
| Banking transactions | Heute and Roth (1988) |
| Behavior and attitude | Ahmad and Schroeder (2003) |
| Behavioral intention | Venkatesh, Speier, and Morris (2002) |
| Behavioral intentions | Boyer and Hult (2006) |
| Behavioral outcomes | Brady and Cronin (2001) |
| Beliefs on integrating with suppliers | Nahm, Vonderembse, and Koufteros (2004) |
| Beliefs on investing in facilities and equipment | Nahm, Vonderembse, and Koufteros (2004) |
| Beliefs on making decisions that are global | Nahm, Vonderembse, and Koufteros (2004) |
| Beliefs on management control | Nahm, Vonderembse, and Koufteros (2004) |
| Beliefs on working with others | Nahm, Vonderembse, and Koufteros (2004) |
| Benchmark control | Germain and Dröge (1997) |
| Benchmark performance control | Germain, Dröge, and Christensen (2001) |
| Benchmarking | Ahire, Golhar, and Waller (1996) |
| Benchmarking | Curkovic, Vickery, and Dröge (2000) |
| Benchmarking | Powell (1995) |
| Benevolence-based trust | Levin and Cross (2004) |
| Bilaterial idiosyncratic investments | Jap and Anderson (2003) |
| Billing | Athanassopoulos and Iliakopoulos (2003) |
| BP-reflects-ITP | Kearns and Lederer (2003) |
| Branch network | Athanassopoulos and Iliakopoulos (2003) |
| Breadth of product line | Robinson and Satterfield (1998) |
| Business assessment | Petersen, Handfield, and Ragatz (2005) |
| Business cost | Amoako-Gyampah and Boye (2001) |
| Business costs | Ward, Duray, Leong, and Sum (1995) |

*(Continued)*

(Continued)

| | |
|---|---|
| Business growth | Zahay, D., Griffin, A. (2004) |
| Business performance | da Silveira (2005) |
| Business performance | Rosenzweig, Roth, and Dean (2003) |
| Business performance | Terziovski, Samson, and Dow (1997) |
| Business performance | Terziovski, Samson, and Dow (1997) |
| Business performance | Vickery, Dröge, Yeomans, and Markland (1995) |
| Business performance | Ward, Duray, Leong, and Sum (1995) |
| Business process skills | Stratman and Roth (2002) |
| Business strategy | Cleveland, Schroeder, and Anderson (1989) |
| Business strategy elements: operations | Schroeder, Anderson, and Cleveland (1986) |
| Business strategy elements: price | Schroeder, Anderson, and Cleveland (1986) |
| Business strategy elements: product | Schroeder, Anderson, and Cleveland (1986) |
| Business strategy elements: service | Schroeder, Anderson, and Cleveland (1986) |
| Business sustainability | Menor, Roth, and Mason (2001) |
| Business sustainability | Roth (1993) |
| Buyer financial performance | Chen and Paulraj (2004) |
| Buyer logistics costs | Dong, Carter, and Dresner (2001) |
| Buyer operational performance | Chen and Paulraj (2004) |
| Buyer's perception of relationship's performance | Johnston, McCutcheon, Stuart, and Kerwood (2004) |
| Buyer's satisfaction | Johnston, McCutcheon, Stuart, and Kerwood (2004) |
| Buyer-seller relationship management | Narasimhan, Jayaram, and Carter (2001) |
| Buyer-supplier relationships | Carr and Pearson (1999) |
| Buying firm market competition | Krause (1999) |
| Buying firm's commitment | Prahinski and Benton (2004) |
| Buying firm's expectation of relationship continuity | Krause (1999) |
| Buying firm's perspective toward suppliers | Krause (1999) |
| Buying firm's top management support | Krause (1999) |
| Capability building programs | |
| Ward, Leong, and Boyer (1994) | |
| Capacity | Roth and van der Velde (1991) |
| Capacity utilization | Cua, McKone, and Schroeder (2001) |
| CAPIS (competitive advantage provided by information systems): primary activity efficiency | Byrd and Turner (2001) |
| CAPIS (competitive advantage provided by information systems): resource management functionality | Byrd and Turner (2001) |
| CAPIS (competitive advantage provided by information systems): support activity efficiency | Byrd and Turner (2001) |
| CAPIS (competitive advantage provided by information systems): threat | Byrd and Turner (2001) |
| Capital expenditure | Safizadeh, Field, and Ritzman (2003) |
| Career advancement | Wisner, Stringfellow, Youngdahl, and Parker (2005) |
| Catalyst elements | Diáz, Machuca, and Alvarez-Gil (2003) |
| Catalyst for change | Naveh and Marcus (2005) |
| Causes of late delivery | Chikan and Demeter (1995) |
| Causes of priority changes | Chikan and Demeter (1995) |
| Cellular manufacturing | Koufteros, Vonderembse, and Doll (1998) |
| Cellular manufacturing | Tu, Vonderembse, and Ragu-Nathan (2001) |
| Centralization | Hult, Hurley, Giunipero, and Nichols (2000) |

| | |
|---|---|
| Cesarean feedback | Heineke (1995) |
| Cesarean policies | Heineke (1995) |
| Change | Koufteros, Vonderembse, and Doll (2001) |
| Change readiness | Stratman and Roth (2002) |
| Characteristics of plant | Lawrence and Hottenstein (1995) |
| CI effectiveness | Choi and Liker (1995) |
| Clarity of project targets | Hong, Vonderembse, Doll, and Nahm (2005) |
| Cleanliness and organization | Flynn and Flynn (2004) |
| Clinical quality | Marley, Collier, and Goldstein (2004) |
| Closer customer relationships | Curkovic, Vickery, and Dröge (2000) |
| Closer to customers | Powell (1995) |
| Closer to suppliers | Powell (1995) |
| Coercive | Benton and Maloni (2004) |
| Cognitive commitment | Hennig-Thurau, Langer, and Hansen (2001) |
| Cohesiveness | Brockman and Morgan (2003) |
| Collaboration | Detert, Schroeder, and Cudeck (2003) |
| Collectivism | Youngdahl, Kellogg, Nie, and Bowen (2003) |
| Combination | Sabherwal and Becerra-Fernandez (2003) |
| Commitment | Benton and Maloni (2004) |
| Commitment | Monczka, Peterson, Handfield, and Ragatz (1998) |
| Commitment | Morita and Flynn (1997) |
| Commitment to customers | Flynn and Saladin (2001) |
| Commitment to nonuniversity activities | Hennig-Thurau, Langer, and Hansen (2001) |
| Committed leadership | Cua, McKone, and Schroeder (2001) |
| Committed leadership | Curkovic, Vickery, and Dröge (2000) |
| Commodity/supplier selection process | Monczka, Peterson, Handfield, and Ragatz (1998) |
| Communication | Chen and Paulraj (2004) |
| Communication | Chen, Paulraj, and Lado (2004) |
| Communication in the organization | LaForge, Wood, and Sleeth (1984) |
| Communication of strategy | Ahmad and Schroeder (2003) |
| Communication of strategy | Flynn and Flynn (2004) |
| Communication of strategy | Lawrence and Hottenstein (1995) |
| Communication of strategy | Sakakibara, Flynn, Schroeder, and Morris (1997) |
| Communications of improvement information | Black and Porter (1996) |
| Company reputation | Cao and Dowlatshahi (2005) |
| Company reputation | Curkovic, Vickery, and Dröge (2000) |
| Company specific results | Flynn and Saladin (2001) |
| Comparison of 1987 and 1991 design practices | Ettlie (1995) |
| Compensation | Adam, Corbett, Flores, Harrison, Lee, Rho, Ribera, Samson, and Westbrook (1997) |
| Competence-based trust | Levin and Cross (2004) |
| Competitive advantage | Flynn, Schroeder, and Sakakibara (1995) |
| Competitive aggressiveness | Jambulingam, Kathuria, and Doucette (2005) |
| Competitive capabilities: delivery | Kim and Arnold (1992) |
| Competitive capabilities: flexibility | Kim and Arnold (1992) |
| Competitive capabilities: price | Kim and Arnold (1992) |
| Competitive capabilities: quality | Kim and Arnold (1992) |
| Competitive capabilities: service | Kim and Arnold (1992) |
| Competitive capability | Rosenzweig and Roth (2004) |
| Competitive comparisons | Flynn and Saladin (2001) |
| Competitive hostility | Amoako-Gyampah and Boye (2001) |

*(Continued)*

(Continued)

| | |
|---|---|
| Competitive hostility | Ward, Duray, Leong, and Sum (1995) |
| Competitive intensity | Jambulingam, Kathuria, and Doucette (2005) |
| Competitive intensity | Morgan, Zou, Vorhies, and Katsikeas (2003) |
| Competitive position | Hausman, Montgomery, and Roth (2002) |
| Competitive pressure | Krause, Scannell, and Calantone (2000) |
| Competitive priorities | Chen and Paulraj (2004) |
| Competitive priorities | Dröge, Vickery, and Markland (1994) |
| Competitive priorities | Raffi and Swamidass (1987) |
| Competitive priorities | Roth and van der Velde (1991) |
| Competitive priorities | Safizadeh, Ritzman, Sharma, and Wood (1996) |
| Competitive priorities: cost | Boyer and McDermott (1999) |
| Competitive priorities: cost | Karuppan and Ganster (2004) |
| Competitive priorities: delivery | Boyer and McDermott (1999) |
| Competitive priorities: flexibility | Boyer and McDermott (1999) |
| Competitive priorities: flexibility (range) | Karuppan and Ganster (2004) |
| Competitive priorities: flexibility (time) | Karuppan and Ganster (2004) |
| Competitive priorities: quality | Boyer and McDermott (1999) |
| Competitive priorities: quality | Karuppan and Ganster (2004) |
| Competitive priorities: speed | Karuppan and Ganster (2004) |
| Competitive sector | Carter and Carter (1998) |
| Competitive strategy | Flynn and Flynn (2004) |
| Complaint handling | Goffin, Lemke, and Szwejczewski (2006) |
| Complexity (job) | Dean and Snell (1991) |
| Compliance | Benton and Maloni (2004) |
| Compliance | Goldstein and Naor (2005) |
| Comprehensive training | Snell and Dean (1992) |
| Computer use | Koufteros, Vonderembse, and Doll (2002) |
| Concurrent engineering | Koufteros, Vonderembse, and Doll (2002) |
| Concurrent engineering (internal integration) | Koufteros, Vonderembse, and Jayaram (2005) |
| Concurrent engineering practices | Nassimbeni (2003) |
| Concurrent work flow | Koufteros, Vonderembse, and Doll (2001) |
| Configuration skills (task-related) | Leonard-Barton and Deschamps (1988) |
| Conflict | Benton and Maloni (2004) |
| Conflict | Griffith, Harvey, and Lusch (2006) |
| Conflict resolution | Benton and Maloni (2004) |
| Conflict resolution techniques | Monczka, Peterson, Handfield, and Ragatz (1998) |
| Conformance quality | White (1996) |
| Conformance to specifications | Curkovic, Vickery, and Dröge (2000) |
| Consideration | Sarin and Mcdermott (2003) |
| Consistency | Choi and Hartley (1996) |
| Content | Somers, Nelson, and Karimi (2003) |
| Contextual factors—strategy: administrative | Olson and Boyer (2003) |
| Contextual factors—strategy: delivery | Olson and Boyer (2003) |
| Contextual factors—strategy: goals | Olson and Boyer (2003) |
| Continuous improvement | Anderson, Rungtusanatham, Schroeder, and Devaraj (1995) |
| Continuous improvement | Curkovic, Vickery, and Dröge (2000) |
| Continuous improvement | Detert, Schroeder, and Cudeck (2003) |
| Continuous improvement | Douglas and Fredendall (2004) |
| Continuous improvement | Flynn, Schroeder, and Flynn (1999) |

| | |
|---|---|
| Continuous improvement | Rungtusanatham, Forza, Koka, Salvador, and Nie (2005) |
| Continuous improvement (CI) communication | Choi and Liker (1995) |
| Continuous improvement activities | Krause, Handfield, and Scannell (1998) |
| Convenience | Olson, Belohlav, and Boyer (2005) |
| Cooperation | Benton and Maloni (2004) |
| Cooperation | Prahinski and Benton (2004) |
| Cooperative learning: group process | Janz and Prasarnphanich (2003) |
| Cooperative learning: positive interdependence | Janz and Prasarnphanich (2003) |
| Cooperative learning: promotion interaction | Janz and Prasarnphanich (2003) |
| Cooperative purchasing/supplier relationship | Stanley and Wisner (2001) |
| Coordination | Monczka, Peterson, Handfield, and Ragatz (1998) |
| Coordination of decision making | Sakakibara, Flynn, Schroeder, and Morris (1997) |
| Core just-in-time (JIT) | Dong, Carter, and Dresner (2001) |
| Corporate environmental proactivity | Bowen, Cousins, Lamming, and Faruk (2001) |
| Corporate image | Athanassopoulos and Iliakopoulos (2003) |
| Corporate quality culture | Black and Porter (1996) |
| Corporate support for quality | Benson, Saraph, and Schroeder (1991) |
| Cost | Borgatti and Cross (2003) |
| Cost | Diáz, Machuca, and Alvarez-Gil (2003) |
| Cost | Flynn, Schroeder, and Flynn (1999) |
| Cost | Joshi, Kathuria, and Porth (2003) |
| Cost | Krause, Pagell, and Curkovic (2001) |
| Cost | Menor, Roth, and Mason (2001) |
| Cost | Olson, Belohlav, and Boyer (2005) |
| Cost | Sawhney and Piper (2002) |
| Cost | Ward, Duray, Leong, and Sum (1995) |
| Cost efficiency | Stahl and Zimmerer (1983) |
| Cost efficiency | Swink, Narasimhan, and Kim (2005) |
| Cost importance | Ward, McCreery, Ritzman, and Sharma (1998) |
| Cost leadership | Rosenzweig, Roth, and Dean (2003) |
| Cost performance | Li, Benton, and Leong (2002) |
| Cost reduction | Olson and Boyer (2003) |
| Costs of material requirements planning (MRP) systems | Schroeder, Anderson, Tupy, and White (1981) |
| Creation of a collective mind | Escrig-Tena and Bou-Llusar (2005) |
| Critical incident (actual customer behavior) | Youngdahl and Kellogg (1997) |
| Critical success factors | Roth and van der Velde (1991) |
| Cross-functional cooperation | Ketokivi and Schroeder (2004) |
| Cross-functional cooperation | Pinto, Pinto, and Prescott (1993) |
| Cross-functional involvement in supplier development | Krause, Handfield, and Scannell (1998) |
| Cross-functional product design | Cua, McKone, and Schroeder (2001) |
| Cross-functional quality teams | Curkovic, Vickery, and Dröge (2000) |
| Cross-functional teams | Chen and Paulraj (2004) |
| Cross-functional training | Cua, McKone, and Schroeder (2001) |
| Cross-training | Ketokivi and Schroeder (2004) |
| Cross-training | Safizadeh, Field, and Ritzman (2003) |
| Cultural congruence scales: loyalty | Bates, Amundson, Schroeder, and Morris (1995) |
| Cultural congruence scales: philosophy | Bates, Amundson, Schroeder, and Morris (1995) |
| Culture | Gilgeous (1995) |
| Customer and market knowledge | Flynn and Saladin (2001) |
| Customer and supplier relations | Ittner and Larcker (1997) |

*(Continued)*

(Continued)

| | |
|---|---|
| Customer barriers | Tsikriktsis, Lanzolla, and Frohlich (2004) |
| Customer closeness | Tu, Vonderembse, Ragu-Nathan, and Ragu-Nathan (2004) |
| Customer complaint management | de Jong and de Ruyter (2004) |
| Customer data and analysis | Flynn and Saladin (2001) |
| Customer driven information | Douglas and Fredendall (2004) |
| Customer enquiries | Heute and Roth (1988) |
| Customer focus | Adam (1994) |
| Customer focus | Ahire, Golhar, and Waller (1996) |
| Customer focus | Ahmad and Schroeder (2001) |
| Customer focus | Chen and Paulraj (2004) |
| Customer focus | Detert, Schroeder, and Cudeck (2003) |
| Customer focus | Flynn, Sakakibara, and Schroeder (1995) |
| Customer focus | Samson and Terziovski (1999) |
| Customer focus and satisfaction | Pannirselvam, Siferd, and Ruch (1998) |
| Customer information system | Zahay, D., Griffin, A. (2004) |
| Customer integration | Koufteros, Vonderembse, and Jayaram (2005) |
| Customer involvement | Cua, McKone, and Schroeder (2001) |
| Customer involvement: customer interaction | Flynn, Schroeder, and Sakakibara (1994) |
| Customer knowledge application | Dröge, Claycomb, and Germain (2003) |
| Customer loyalty | Stank, Goldsby, and Vickery (1999) |
| Customer loyalty | Vickery, Dröge, Stank, Goldsby, and Markland (2004) |
| Customer orientation | Brady and Cronin (2001) |
| Customer orientation | Jambulingam, Kathuria, and Doucette (2005) |
| Customer orientations | Nahm, Vonderembse, and Koufteros (2004) |
| Customer product and service input | Flynn and Saladin (2001) |
| Customer relations management | Flynn and Saladin (2001) |
| Customer relationship | Flynn, Schroeder, and Sakakibara (1995) |
| Customer relationship | Li, Rao, Ragu-Nathan, and Ragu-Nathan (2005) |
| Customer relationships | Ketokivi and Schroeder (2004) |
| Customer responsiveness | Chen, Paulraj, and Lado (2004) |
| Customer results | Escrig-Tena and Bou-Llusar (2005) |
| Customer satisfaction | Anderson, Rungtusanatham, Schroeder, and Devaraj (1995) |
| Customer satisfaction | Brady and Cronin (2001) |
| Customer satisfaction | Goldstein (2003) |
| Customer satisfaction | Rungtusanatham, Forza, Koka, Salvador, and Nie (2005) |
| Customer satisfaction | Stank, Goldsby, and Vickery (1999) |
| Customer satisfaction | Tatikonda and Montoya-Weiss (2001) |
| Customer satisfaction | Terziovski, Samson, and Dow (1997) |
| Customer satisfaction | Terziovski, Samson, and Dow (1997) |
| Customer satisfaction | Vickery, Dröge, Stank, Goldsby, and Markland (2004) |
| Customer satisfaction | Voss, Tsikriktsis, Funk, Yarrow, and Owen (2005) |
| Customer satisfaction | Zhang, Vonderembse, and Lim (2003) |
| Customer satisfaction determination | Flynn and Saladin (2001) |
| Customer satisfaction enhancement | Flynn and Saladin (2001) |
| Customer satisfaction orientation | Black and Porter (1996) |
| Customer satisfaction: cost | Choi and Eboch (1998) |
| Customer satisfaction: delivery | Choi and Eboch (1998) |
| Customer satisfaction: quality | Choi and Eboch (1998) |

| | |
|---|---|
| Customer service | Flynn and Saladin (2001) |
| Customer service | Vickery, Jayaram, Dröge, and Calantone (2003) |
| Customer views of quality | Flynn and Saladin (2001) |
| Customer-based performance | Zahay, D., Griffin, A. (2004) |
| Customer-perceived service quality | de Jong, de Ruyter, and Wetzels (2005) |
| Customers | Adam, Corbett, Flores, Harrison, Lee, Rho, Ribera, Samson, and Westbrook (1997) |
| Customization | Safizadeh, Field, and Ritzman (2003) |
| Customization | Zahay, D., Griffin, A. (2004) |
| Customization responsiveness performance | Das and Narasimhan (2001) |
| Daily practice | Naveh and Marcus (2005) |
| Daily schedule adherence | Ahmad and Schroeder (2001) |
| Daily schedule adherence | Sakakibara, Flynn, and Schroeder (1993) |
| Data | Hays and Hill (2001) |
| Data-based decision-making | Detert, Schroeder, and Cudeck (2003) |
| Dealer belief | Conlon, Devaraj, and Matta (2001) |
| Decentralization | Germain and Dröge (1997) |
| Decentralization | Malhotra, Heine, and Grover (2001) |
| Decentralization of authority | Sakakibara, Flynn, Schroeder, and Morris (1997) |
| Degree of computerization | Chikan and Demeter (1995) |
| Degree of effort incurred | Youngdahl and Kellogg (1997) |
| Degree of innovation | Sarin and Mcdermott (2003) |
| Degree of similarity across focused work cells or PWPs | Bozarth and Edwards (1997) |
| Degree of supply chain coordination regarding customers | Hill and Scudder (2002) |
| Degree of supply chain coordination regarding suppliers | Hill and Scudder (2002) |
| Degrees of product customization | Raffi and Swamidass (1987) |
| Delay | Tucker (2004) |
| Delivery | Diáz, Machuca, and Alvarez-Gil (2003) |
| Delivery | Joshi, Kathuria, and Porth (2003) |
| Delivery | Krause, Pagell, and Curkovic (2001) |
| Delivery | Menor, Roth, and Mason (2001) |
| Delivery | Roth (1993) |
| Delivery | Roth (1996) |
| Delivery | Safizadeh, Field, and Ritzman (2003) |
| Delivery | Ward, Duray, Leong, and Sum (1995) |
| Delivery capabilities | Tracey, Vonderembse, and Lim (1999) |
| Delivery dependability | Koufteros (1999) |
| Delivery dependability | Li, Rao, Ragu-Nathan, and Ragu-Nathan (2005) |
| Delivery dependability | White (1996) |
| Delivery lead time | Karlsson and Åhlström (1995) |
| Delivery performance | Amoako-Gyampah and Boye (2001) |
| Delivery performance | Das and Narasimhan (2001) |
| Delivery reliability | Rosenzweig, Roth, and Dean (2003) |
| Delivery speed | da Silveira (2005) |
| Delivery speed | White (1996) |
| Delivery time importance | Ward, McCreery, Ritzman, and Sharma (1998) |
| Demand integration | Frohlich and Westbrook (2002) |

*(Continued)*

(Continued)

| | |
|---|---|
| Demand uncertainty | Chen and Paulraj (2004) |
| Demand unpredictability | Dröge, Claycomb, and Germain (2003) |
| Demand unpredictability | Germain, Dröge, and Christensen (2001) |
| Dependability of delivery lead time | Robinson and Satterfield (1998) |
| Dependability on-time delivery | Flynn, Schroeder, and Flynn (1999) |
| Dependability service | Flynn, Schroeder, and Flynn (1999) |
| Dependability specifications | Flynn, Schroeder, and Flynn (1999) |
| Dependable suppliers | Koufteros, Vonderembse, and Doll (1998) |
| Dependable suppliers | Tu, Vonderembse, and Ragu-Nathan (2001) |
| Dependency | Goffin, Lemke, and Szwejczewski (2006) |
| Descriptor (what) | New and Szwejczewski (1995) |
| Design | Boyer, Ward, and Leong (1996) |
| Design | Diáz, Machuca, and Alvarez-Gil (2003) |
| Design and conformance | Adam, Corbett, Flores, Harrison, Lee, Rho, Ribera, Samson, and Westbrook (1997) |
| Design and engineering change | Rho and Yu (1998) |
| Design characteristics | Sakakibara, Flynn, Schroeder, and Morris (1997) |
| Design for customer needs | Flynn, Schroeder, and Flynn (1999) |
| Design for manufacturability | Ketokivi and Schroeder (2004) |
| Design manufacturing integration | Ettlie (1997) |
| Design of new products and services | Flynn and Saladin (2001) |
| Design of quality products and services | Flynn and Saladin (2001) |
| Design performance | Petersen, Handfield, and Ragatz (2005) |
| Design quality management | Ahire, Golhar, and Waller (1996) |
| Design quality management | Curkovic, Vickery, and Dröge (2000) |
| Design-Manufacturing Integration Scale | Ettlie (1995) |
| Design-manufacturing interfaces | Roth (1996) |
| Design-process integration | Dröge, Jayaram, and Vickery (2004) |
| Detailed supplier assessment | Petersen, Handfield, and Ragatz (2005) |
| Development performance appraisal | Snell and Dean (1992) |
| Developmental culture | McDermott and Stock (1999) |
| Differentiation | Zahay, D., Griffin, A. (2004) |
| Difficulties | Diáz, Machuca, and Alvarez-Gil (2003) |
| Direct involvement | Krause, Scannell, and Calantone (2000) |
| Directory inquiries | Athanassopoulos and Iliakopoulos (2003) |
| Discipline | Collins, Cordon, and Julien (1998) |
| Discomfort | Parasuraman (2000) |
| Discovery | Hays and Hill (2001) |
| Distance to supplier distribution terminal | Robinson and Satterfield (1998) |
| Distribution/logistics adaptability | Swafford, Ghosh, and Murthy (2006) |
| Distribution/logistics range | Swafford, Ghosh, and Murthy (2006) |
| Distributive justice | Griffith, Harvey, and Lusch (2006) |
| Documentation | Flynn and Saladin (2001) |
| Drivers of change | Frohlich and Westbrook (2002) |
| Duration appropriateness belief | Froehle and Roth (2004) |
| Dynamic teaming | Tu, Vonderembse, Ragu-Nathan, and Ragu-Nathan (2004) |
| Dynamism | Amoako-Gyampah and Boye (2001) |
| Dynamism | Ward, Duray, Leong, and Sum (1995) |

| | |
|---|---|
| Early involvement | Koufteros, Vonderembse, and Doll (2001) |
| Ease of use | Somers, Nelson, and Karimi (2003) |
| Eco-design | Zhu and Sarkis (2004) |
| Economic results | Escrig-Tena and Bou-Llusar (2005) |
| e-CRM | Tsikriktsis, Lanzolla, and Frohlich (2004) |
| Educational tool usage | Olson, Belohlav, and Boyer (2005) |
| Effective inventory planning and control | Adam (1994) |
| Effectiveness | Jambulingam, Kathuria, and Doucette (2005) |
| Effort | Grover and Malhotra (2003) |
| Effort expended on planning and installation activities | Small and Yasin (1997) |
| Effort expended on strategic planning for advanced manufacturing technology (AMT) adoption | Small and Yasin (1997) |
| Effort expended on team-based project management | Small and Yasin (1997) |
| Effort expended on technology consistency | Small and Yasin (1997) |
| Effort expended on worker preparation | Small and Yasin (1997) |
| Electronic commerce infusion | Pflughoeft, Ramamurthy, Soofi, Yasai-Ardekani, and Zahedi (2003) |
| Emotional commitment | Hennig-Thurau, Langer, and Hansen (2001) |
| Empathy | Soteriou and Chase (1998) |
| Employee competence | Narasimhan, Jayaram, and Carter (2001) |
| Employee development | Flynn, Schroeder, and Flynn (1999) |
| Employee development | Goldstein (2003) |
| Employee education | Park, Hartley, and Wilson (2001) |
| Employee empowerment | Ahire, Golhar, and Waller (1996) |
| Employee empowerment | Curkovic, Vickery, and Dröge (2000) |
| Employee empowerment | Powell (1995) |
| Employee fulfillment | Anderson, Rungtusanatham, Schroeder, and Devaraj (1995) |
| Employee fulfillment | Rungtusanatham, Forza, Koka, Salvador, and Nie (2005) |
| Employee involvement | Adam, Corbett, Flores, Harrison, Lee, Rho, Ribera, Samson, and Westbrook (1997) |
| Employee involvement | Ahire, Golhar, and Waller (1996) |
| Employee involvement | Cua, McKone, and Schroeder (2001) |
| Employee involvement | Flynn and Saladin (2001) |
| Employee involvement | Lawrence and Hottenstein (1995) |
| Employee involvement implementation: centralization of authority | McKone, Schroeder, and Cua (1999) |
| Employee knowledge | Menor, Roth, and Mason (2001) |
| Employee morale | Terziovski, Samson, and Dow (1997) |
| Employee morale | Terziovski, Samson, and Dow (1997) |
| Employee motivation and vision | Hays and Hill (2001) |
| Employee outcomes | Goldstein (2003) |
| Employee quality involvement | Flynn and Saladin (2001) |
| Employee recognition | Flynn and Saladin (2001) |
| Employee relations | Forker (1997) |
| Employee relations | Forker, Mendez, and Hershauer (1997) |
| Employee relations data and analysis | Flynn and Saladin (2001) |
| Employee responsibility | Lawrence and Hottenstein (1995) |
| Employee satisfaction | Adam, Corbett, Flores, Harrison, Lee, Rho, Ribera, Samson, and Westbrook (1997) |
| Employee satisfaction | Park, Hartley, and Wilson (2001) |

*(Continued)*

(Continued)

| | |
|---|---|
| Employee satisfaction | Voss, Tsikriktsis, Funk, Yarrow, and Owen (2005) |
| Employee selection and development | Adam, Corbett, Flores, Harrison, Lee, Rho, Ribera, Samson, and Westbrook (1997) |
| Employee training | Ahire, Golhar, and Waller (1996) |
| Employee well-being and morale | Flynn and Saladin (2001) |
| Empowerment | de Jong and de Ruyter (2004) |
| Empowerment | Narasimhan, Jayaram, and Carter (2001) |
| Empowerment | Park, Hartley, and Wilson (2001) |
| Empowerment | Wisner, Stringfellow, Youngdahl, and Parker (2005) |
| Enacting organizational environment | Escrig-Tena and Bou-Llusar (2005) |
| Enterprise resource planning (ERP) training | Stratman and Roth (2002) |
| Entrepreneurship | Brockman and Morgan (2003) |
| Entry barriers | Powell (1995) |
| Environmental options | Melnyk, Sroufe, and Calantone (2003) |
| Environmental performance | Zhu and Sarkis (2004) |
| Environmental purchasing | Carter and Carter (1998) |
| Environmental stability | Jambulingam, Kathuria, and Doucette (2005) |
| Environmental uncertainty | Pagell and Krause (2004) |
| Environmental uncertainty | Vickery, Dröge, and Germain (1999) |
| Environmental uncertainty: competitor component | Ho (1996) |
| Environmental uncertainty: customer component | Ho (1996) |
| Environmental uncertainty: social-political component | Ho (1996) |
| Environmental uncertainty: supplier component | Ho (1996) |
| Environmental uncertainty: technological component | Ho (1996) |
| Environmentally caused disruption | Tatikonda and Montoya-Weiss (2001) |
| Environmentally-caused disruption | Tatikonda and Montoya-Weiss (2001) |
| Equipment layout | Ahmad and Schroeder (2001) |
| Equipment layout | Cua, McKone, and Schroeder (2001) |
| Equipment layout | Sakakibara, Flynn, and Schroeder (1993) |
| Equipment layout | Sakakibara, Flynn, Schroeder, and Morris (1997) |
| Equitable reward systems | Snell and Dean (1992) |
| Equity of incentives | Malhotra, Heine, and Grover (2001) |
| Equivocality | Koufteros, Vonderembse, and Doll (2002) |
| e-Transactions | Tsikriktsis, Lanzolla, and Frohlich (2004) |
| Evaluation and recognition systems | Flynn and Saladin (2001) |
| Evaluation of the counterpart's performance | Jap and Anderson (2003) |
| Ex post opportunism | Jap and Anderson (2003) |
| Executive commitment | Powell (1995) |
| Executive commitment | Stratman and Roth (2002) |
| Expectations of relational continuity | Jap and Anderson (2003) |
| Expected impact | Fedor, Ghosh, Caldwell, Maurer, and Singhal (2003) |
| Expected performance benefits | Tsikriktsis, Lanzolla, and Frohlich (2004) |
| Expert | Benton and Maloni (2004) |
| Explicit knowledge dissemination | Fedor, Ghosh, Caldwell, Maurer, and Singhal (2003) |
| Extent of the use of teams | Malhotra, Heine, and Grover (2001) |
| Extent of training | Malhotra, Heine, and Grover (2001) |
| External contact | Zellmer-Bruhn (2003) |
| External cooperation skills | Escrig-Tena and Bou-Llusar (2005) |
| External green-supply-chain-management (GSCM )practices | Zhu and Sarkis (2004) |

| | |
|---|---|
| External interface management | Black and Porter (1996) |
| External knowledge generation | Fedor, Ghosh, Caldwell, Maurer, and Singhal (2003) |
| External learning | Schroeder, Bates, and Juntilla (2002) |
| External pressure | Tsikriktsis, Lanzolla, and Frohlich (2004) |
| Externalization | Sabherwal and Becerra-Fernandez (2003) |
| Externally coordinated | Naveh and Marcus (2005) |
| Face-to-face contacts | Pflughoeft, Ramamurthy, Soofi, Yasai-Ardekani, and Zahedi (2003) |
| Facilitating JIT | Dong, Carter, and Dresner (2001) |
| Facilities and retail outlets | Roth and van der Velde (1991) |
| Factor performance | Menor, Roth, and Mason (2001) |
| Factor productivity | Roth (1993) |
| Factor productivity | Roth and Jackson (1995) |
| Failure expectations | McCollough, Berry, and Yadav (2000) |
| Family commitment | Hennig-Thurau, Langer, and Hansen (2001) |
| Fault repair | Athanassopoulos and Iliakopoulos (2003) |
| Feedback | Ahmad and Schroeder (2001) |
| Feedback | Goffin, Lemke, and Szwejczewski (2006) |
| Feedback | Prahinski and Benton (2004) |
| Feedback | Sakakibara, Flynn, Schroeder, and Morris (1997) |
| Feedback of information | Flynn, Schroeder, and Flynn (1999) |
| Feedback on performance | Ahmad and Schroeder (2003) |
| Final satisfaction/postrecovery satisfaction | McCollough, Berry, and Yadav (2000) |
| Finances | Choi and Hartley (1996) |
| Financial and market performance | Kaynak (2003) |
| Financial and market results | Flynn and Saladin (2001) |
| Financial performance | Adam, Corbett, Flores, Harrison, Lee, Rho, Ribera, Samson, and Westbrook (1997) |
| Financial performance | Cao and Dowlatshahi (2005) |
| Financial performance | Chen, Paulraj, and Lado (2004) |
| Financial performance | Cleveland, Schroeder, and Anderson (1989) |
| Financial performance | Dröge, Claycomb, and Germain (2003) |
| Financial performance | Dröge, Jayaram, and Vickery (2004) |
| Financial performance | Germain, Dröge, and Christensen (2001) |
| Financial performance | Li, Benton, and Leong (2002) |
| Financial performance | Vickery, Jayaram, Dröge, and Calantone (2003) |
| Firm financial performance | Petersen, Handfield, and Ragatz (2005) |
| Firm's financial performance over the past five years | Carr and Pearson (1999) |
| Flexibility | Amoako-Gyampah and Boye (2001) |
| Flexibility | Choi and Hartley (1996) |
| Flexibility | Collins, Cordon, and Julien (1998) |
| Flexibility | Diáz, Machuca, and Alvarez-Gil (2003) |
| Flexibility | Joshi, Kathuria, and Porth (2003) |
| Flexibility | Krause, Pagell, and Curkovic (2001) |
| Flexibility | Malhotra, Heine, and Grover (2001) |
| Flexibility | Menor, Roth, and Mason (2001) |
| Flexibility | Pagell and Krause (2004) |
| Flexibility | Roth (1993) |
| Flexibility | Roth (1996) |
| Flexibility | Ward, Duray, Leong, and Sum (1995) |

*(Continued)*

(Continued)

| | |
|---|---|
| Flexibility importance | Ward, McCreery, Ritzman, and Sharma (1998) |
| Flexibility in arrangements | Johnston, McCutcheon, Stuart, and Kerwood (2004) |
| Flexible automation | Roth (1996) |
| Flexible information systems (IS) infrastructure: data transparency | Byrd and Turner (2001) |
| Flexible IS infrastructure: applications functionality | Byrd and Turner (2001) |
| Flexible IS infrastructure: IS compatibility | Byrd and Turner (2001) |
| Flexible IS infrastructure: IS connectivity | Byrd and Turner (2001) |
| Flexible manufacturing | Powell (1995) |
| Flexible workforce | Lawrence and Hottenstein (1995) |
| Formal benchmark control | Vickery, Dröge, and Germain (1999) |
| Formal internal control | Vickery, Dröge, and Germain (1999) |
| Formal performance control | Germain, Dröge, and Christensen (2001) |
| Formal supplier control | Vickery, Dröge, and Germain (1999) |
| Formality | Prahinski and Benton (2004) |
| Formalization | Hult, Hurley, Giunipero, and Nichols (2000) |
| Formalization | Malhotra, Heine, and Grover (2001) |
| Format | Somers, Nelson, and Karimi (2003) |
| Frequent delivery by suppliers | Ketokivi and Schroeder (2004) |
| Friendship | Levin and Cross (2004) |
| Functional diversity | Sarin and Mcdermott (2003) |
| Future requirements of customers | Flynn and Saladin (2001) |
| | |
| General productivity | Schmenner and Cook (1985) |
| Goal commitment | Hennig-Thurau, Langer, and Hansen (2001) |
| Goal congruence | Jap and Anderson (2003) |
| Goal structure | Sarin and Mcdermott (2003) |
| Greening the supply process | Bowen, Cousins, Lamming, and Faruk. (2001) |
| Group culture | McDermott and Stock (1999) |
| Group potency | de Jong, de Ruyter, and Wetzels (2005) |
| Growth | Diáz, Machuca, and Alvarez-Gil (2003) |
| Growth in market share | Curkovic, Vickery, and Dröge (2000) |
| Growth in ROI | Curkovic, Vickery, and Dröge (2000) |
| Growth rate on sales | Raffi and Swamidass (1987) |
| | |
| Hardware advances | Schmenner and Cook (1985) |
| Headcount | Roth (1993) |
| Health service network | Li, Benton, and Leong (2002) |
| Heavy weight product development managers | Koufteros, Vonderembse, and Doll (2002) |
| Hierarchical culture | McDermott and Stock (1999) |
| Hierarchical level | Levin and Cross (2004) |
| High sacrifice commitment | Harrison-Walker (2001) |
| High-volume automation technology | Swamidass and Kotha (1998) |
| Hospital practice review | Heineke (1995) |
| Human resource development | Morita and Flynn (1997) |
| Human resource management practices | Voss, Tsikriktsis, Funk, Yarrow, and Owen (2005) |
| Human resources | Roth and van der Velde (1991) |
| Human resources development and management | Choi and Eboch (1998) |
| Human resources development and management | Pannirselvam, Siferd, and Ruch (1998) |
| Human resources management | Das and Narasimhan (2001) |

| | |
|---|---|
| Human resources management | Flynn and Saladin (2001) |
| Human resources management practices | Ittner and Larcker (1997) |
| Identification and prioritization of supplier development opportunities | Krause, Handfield, and Scannell (1998) |
| Identifying traditional and enlightened plants | Brown (1998) |
| Implementation strategies for supplier development efforts | Krause, Handfield, and Scannell (1998) |
| Implementation success—perceived psychosocial outcomes | Pinto, Pinto, and Prescott (1993) |
| Implementation success—perceived task outcomes | Pinto, Pinto, and Prescott (1993) |
| Implicit knowledge dissemination | Fedor, Ghosh, Caldwell, Maurer, and Singhal (2003) |
| Importance of close competitors as information sources of the firm for innovation | Veuglers and Cassiman (1999) |
| Importance of cost and risk obstacle for innovation by the firm | Veuglers and Cassiman (1999) |
| Importance of cost-efficiency goal of the firm | Veuglers and Cassiman (1999) |
| Importance of ease of imitation of innovations as an obstacle to innovation by the firm | Veuglers and Cassiman (1999) |
| Importance of internal information sources of the firm for innovation | Veuglers and Cassiman (1999) |
| Importance of lack of information for innovation as an obstacle to innovation by the firm | Veuglers and Cassiman (1999) |
| Importance of lack of opportunities of innovation as an obstacle to innovation by the firm | Veuglers and Cassiman (1999) |
| Importance of no need for innovation as an obstacle to innovation by the firm | Veuglers and Cassiman (1999) |
| Importance of protection mechanisms for product and process innovations of the firm | Veuglers and Cassiman (1999) |
| Importance of purchased inputs to the buying firm | Krause (1999) |
| Importance of quality improvement goal of the firm | Veuglers and Cassiman (1999) |
| Importance of resistance against change within the firm as an obstacle to innovation by the firm | Veuglers and Cassiman (1999) |
| Importance of scientific information sources | Veuglers and Cassiman (1999) |
| Improved business performance | Stratman and Roth (2002) |
| Improvement | Hays and Hill (2001) |
| Improvement action plan (manufacturing strategy) | Kim and Arnold (1996) |
| Incentives for group performance | Sakakibara, Flynn, Schroeder, and Morris (1997) |
| Incentives to meet objectives | Ahmad and Schroeder (2003) |
| Indirect influence strategy | Prahinski and Benton (2004) |
| Individual experiential knowledge | Morgan, Zou, Vorhies, and Katsikeas (2003) |
| Individualism-collectivism scales: coordination of decision making | Bates, Amundson, Schroeder, and Morris (1995) |
| Individualism-collectivism scales: rewards for group performance | Bates, Amundson, Schroeder, and Morris (1995) |
| Individualism-collectivism scales: small group problem solving | Bates, Amundson, Schroeder, and Morris (1995) |
| Individualism-collectivism scales: supervisors as team leaders | Bates, Amundson, Schroeder, and Morris (1995) |
| Individuals' extent of network building | Hoegl, Parboteeah, and Munson (2003) |
| Industrial sector | Rosenzweig, Roth, and Dean (2003) |
| Industry | Lawrence and Hottenstein (1995) |

*(Continued)*

(Continued)

| | |
|---|---|
| Industry hostility and entry barrier perception barriers | Deane, McDougall, and Gargeya (1991) |
| Industry productivity growth | Schmenner and Cook (1985) |
| Information | Borgatti and Cross (2003) |
| Information | Gilgeous (1995) |
| Information acquisition | Hult, Hurley, Giunipero, and Nichols (2000) |
| Information acquisition efficiency | Brockman and Morgan (2003) |
| Information and analysis | Choi and Eboch (1998) |
| Information and analysis | Goldstein and Naor (2005) |
| Information and analysis | Pannirselvam, Siferd, and Ruch (1998) |
| Information and analysis | Samson and Terziovski (1999) |
| Information and feedback | Cua, McKone, and Schroeder (2001) |
| Information and retrieval | Stahl and Zimmerer (1983) |
| Information complexity | Prasad, Tata, and Madan (2005) |
| Information dissemination | Hult, Hurley, Giunipero, and Nichols (2000) |
| Information elements | Diáz, Machuca, and Alvarez-Gil (2003) |
| Information exchange and planning technology | Swamidass and Kotha (1998) |
| Information feedback | Flynn, Sakakibara, and Schroeder (1995) |
| Information intensity of the value chain | Kearns and Lederer (2003) |
| Information management | Park, Hartley, and Wilson (2001) |
| Information participation | Monczka, Peterson, Handfield, and Ragatz (1998) |
| Information quality | Li, Rao, Ragu-Nathan, and Ragu-Nathan (2005) |
| Information quality | Monczka, Peterson, Handfield, and Ragatz (1998) |
| Information richness belief | Froehle and Roth (2004) |
| Information search | Pflughoeft, Ramamurthy, Soofi, Yasai-Ardekani, and Zahedi (2003) |
| Information sharing | Li, Rao, Ragu-Nathan, and Ragu-Nathan (2005) |
| Information sharing | Monczka, Peterson, Handfield, and Ragatz (1998) |
| Information systems | Roth and van der Velde (1991) |
| Information systems (IS) service quality: assurance | Carr (2002) |
| Information technology | Cao and Dowlatshahi (2005) |
| Information technology | Chen and Paulraj (2004) |
| Information technology | Roth (1996) |
| Information technology (IT) personnel skills: business skills | Byrd and Turner (2001) |
| Information Technology sophistication | Pflughoeft, Ramamurthy, Soofi, Yasai-Ardekani, and Zahedi (2003) |
| Information trading | Teigland and McLure Wasko (2004) |
| Information utilization | Ittner and Larcker (1997) |
| Infrastructural investments: QLEAD | Boyer and McDermott (1999) |
| Infrastructural investments: TEAM | Boyer and McDermott (1999) |
| Infrastructural investments: WEMP | Boyer and McDermott (1999) |
| Infrastructure | Gilgeous (1995) |
| Infrastructure: QLEAD | Boyer, Leong, Ward, and Krajewski (1997) |
| Infrastructure: SOFT | Boyer, Leong, Ward, and Krajewski (1997) |
| Infrastructure: WEMP | Boyer, Leong, Ward, and Krajewski (1997) |
| Initial disconfirmation | McCollough, Berry, and Yadav (2000) |
| Innovation | Krause, Pagell, and Curkovic (2001) |
| Innovation | Nassimbeni (2003) |
| Innovation | Roth (1993) |
| Innovation strategy | Fullerton, McWatters, and Fawson (2003) |

| | |
|---|---|
| Innovative information | Brockman and Morgan (2003) |
| Innovativeness | Jambulingam, Kathuria, and Doucette (2005) |
| Innovativeness | Parasuraman (2000) |
| Input sector | Carter and Carter (1998) |
| Insecurity | Parasuraman (2000) |
| Inspection | Lawrence and Hottenstein (1995) |
| Integration | Boyer, Ward, and Leong (1996) |
| Integration | Diáz, Machuca, and Alvarez-Gil (2003) |
| Integration | Germain, Dröge, and Christensen (2001) |
| Integration | Lawrence and Hottenstein (1995) |
| Integration | Pagell (2004) |
| Integration choices | Roth and van der Velde (1991) |
| Integration intensity | Rosenzweig, Roth, and Dean (2003) |
| Integration measures | Frohlich and Westbrook (2001) |
| Integration: committees | Germain and Dröge (1997) |
| Integration: mechanisms | Germain and Dröge (1997) |
| Integrative information technologies | Vickery, Jayaram, Dröge, and Calantone (2003) |
| Intent to donate | Wisner, Stringfellow, Youngdahl, and Parker (2005) |
| Intent to recommend organization to others | Wisner, Stringfellow, Youngdahl, and Parker (2005) |
| Intent to remain | Wisner, Stringfellow, Youngdahl, and Parker (2005) |
| Intention toward the medium | Froehle and Roth (2004) |
| Intention toward the provider | Froehle and Roth (2004) |
| Interaction effectiveness—new product development (NPD) | Narasimhan, Jayaram, and Carter (2001) |
| Interaction facilitation | Ahmad and Schroeder (2003) |
| Interaction frequency—tactical | Narasimhan, Jayaram, and Carter (2001) |
| Interaction with other functions | Lawrence and Hottenstein (1995) |
| Interdependence | Monczka, Peterson, Handfield, and Ragatz (1998) |
| Interdependence (job) | Dean and Snell (1991) |
| Interfirm communication effort | Krause (1999) |
| Interfunctional design efforts | Flynn and Flynn (2004) |
| Interfunctional design efforts | Sakakibara, Flynn, Schroeder, and Morris (1997) |
| Intermediate (how) | New and Szwejczewski (1995) |
| Internal and external cooperation | Anderson, Rungtusanatham, Schroeder, and Devaraj (1995) |
| Internal and external cooperation | Rungtusanatham, Forza, Koka, Salvador, and Nie (2005) |
| Internal barriers | Tsikriktsis, Lanzolla, and Frohlich (2004) |
| Internal control | Germain and Dröge (1997) |
| Internal environmental management | Zhu and Sarkis (2004) |
| Internal knowledge application | Dröge, Claycomb, and Germain (2003) |
| Internal knowledge generation | Fedor, Ghosh, Caldwell, Maurer, and Singhal (2003) |
| Internal lean practices | Li, Rao, Ragu-Nathan, and Ragu-Nathan (2005) |
| Internal learning | Schroeder, Bates, and Juntilla (2002) |
| Internal quality information usage | Ahire, Golhar, and Waller (1996) |
| Internal suppliers' service quality performance | Stanley and Wisner (2001) |
| Internalization | Sabherwal and Becerra-Fernandez (2003) |
| Internally integrated | Naveh and Marcus (2005) |
| Internet improvement | Olson and Boyer (2003) |
| Internet purchasing acceptance factors: attitude | Olson and Boyer (2003) |
| Internet purchasing acceptance factors: comfort | Olson and Boyer (2003) |
| Internet purchasing acceptance factors: perceived ease | Olson and Boyer (2003) |

*(Continued)*

(Continued)

| | |
|---|---|
| Internet purchasing acceptance factors: perceived usefulness | Olson and Boyer (2003) |
| Interpersonal communication | Leonard-Barton and Deschamps (1988) |
| Interpersonal trust | Jap and Anderson (2003) |
| Interruption | Tu, Vonderembse, Ragu-Nathan, and Ragu-Nathan (2004) |
| Interruptions | Zellmer-Bruhn (2003) |
| Interteam support | de Jong and de Ruyter (2004) |
| Interteam support | de Jong, de Ruyter, and Wetzels (2005) |
| Intimacy | Soteriou and Chase (1998) |
| Intimacy appropriateness belief | Froehle and Roth (2004) |
| Intrateam support | de Jong and de Ruyter (2004) |
| Intrinsic motivation | Venkatesh, Speier, and Morris (2002) |
| Inventory management performance | Kaynak (2003) |
| Inventory recovery | Zhu and Sarkis (2004) |
| Inventory reduction | Adam, Corbett, Flores, Harrison, Lee, Rho, Ribera, |
| Samson, and Westbrook (1997) | |
| Inventory variance | Germain, Dröge, and Christensen (2001) |
| Invest in clinical technology | Li, Benton, and Leong (2002) |
| Invest in office technology | Li, Benton, and Leong (2002) |
| Invest in patient medical information systems demand prediction | Li, Benton, and Leong (2002) |
| IS service quality: empathy | Carr (2002) |
| IS service quality: reliability | Carr (2002) |
| IS service quality: responsiveness | Carr (2002) |
| IT is used to create a competitive advantage | Kearns and Lederer (2003) |
| IT personnel skills: interpersonal skills | Byrd and Turner (2001) |
| IT personnel skills: technical skills | Byrd and Turner (2001) |
| IT personnel skills: technology management | Byrd and Turner (2001) |
| IT skills | Stratman and Roth (2002) |
| ITP-reflects-BP | Kearns and Lederer (2003) |
| JIT deliveries from suppliers | Sakakibara, Flynn, and Schroeder (1993) |
| JIT implementation: JIT link with customers | McKone, Schroeder, and Cua (1999) |
| JIT implementation: pull system support | McKone, Schroeder, and Cua (1999) |
| JIT implementation: repetitive nature of master schedule | McKone, Schroeder, and Cua (1999) |
| JIT implementation: setup reduction | McKone, Schroeder, and Cua (1999) |
| JIT link with customers | Ahmad and Schroeder (2001) |
| JIT production strategy | Mehra and Inman (1992) |
| JIT quality | Fullerton, McWatters, and Fawson (2003) |
| JIT scheduling | Flynn, Sakakibara, and Schroeder (1995) |
| JIT strategy | Tan (2001) |
| JIT unique | Fullerton, McWatters, and Fawson (2003) |
| JIT vendor strategy | Mehra and Inman (1992) |
| JIT workflow integration | Germain and Dröge (1997) |
| Job commitment | Hennig-Thurau, Langer, and Hansen (2001) |
| Job enrichment | Li, Benton, and Leong (2002) |
| Job performance | Leonard-Barton and Deschamps (1988) |
| Job satisfaction | LaForge, Wood, and Sleeth (1984) |

| | |
|---|---|
| Job scheduling | LaForge, Wood, and Sleeth (1984) |
| Job-determined importance (need) | Leonard-Barton and Deschamps (1988) |
| Joint profit performance | Jap and Anderson (2003) |
| Joint responsibility | Johnston, McCutcheon, Stuart, and Kerwood (2004) |
| Just-in-time | Dean and Snell (1996) |
| Just-in-time | Zhu and Sarkis (2004) |
| Just-in-time (JIT) adoption | Rabinovich, Dresner, and Evers (2003) |
| Just-in-time (JIT) deliveries | Lawrence and Hottenstein (1995) |
| Just-in-time (JIT) delivery by suppliers | Ahmad and Schroeder (2001) |
| Just-in-time (JIT) delivery by suppliers | Cua, McKone, and Schroeder (2001) |
| Just-in-time (JIT) education strategy | Mehra and Inman (1992) |
| Just-in-time (JIT) flow | Swink, Narasimhan, and Kim (2005) |
| Just-in-time (JIT) implementation: JIT delivery by suppliers | McKone, Schroeder, and Cua (1999) |
| Just-in-time (JIT) inventory control | Dean and Snell (1991) |
| Just-in-time (JIT) inventory control | Snell and Dean (1992) |
| Just-in-time (JIT) manufacturing | Fullerton, McWatters, and Fawson (2003) |
| Just-in-time (JIT) performance | Flynn, Sakakibara, and Schroeder (1995) |
| Just-in-time (JIT) supplier relations | Flynn, Schroeder, and Flynn (1999) |
| Just-in-time (JIT) supplier relationship | Sakakibara, Flynn, Schroeder, and Morris (1997) |
| Just-in-time (JIT) task scope | Germain and Dröge (1997) |
| Just-in-time delivery by suppliers | Flynn and Flynn (2004) |
| Just-in-time practices | Nassimbeni (2003) |
| Kanban | Ahmad and Schroeder (2001) |
| Kanban | Flynn, Sakakibara, and Schroeder (1995) |
| Kanban | Sakakibara, Flynn, and Schroeder (1993) |
| Kanban | Sakakibara, Flynn, Schroeder, and Morris (1997) |
| Know-how | Escrig-Tena and Bou-Llusar (2005) |
| Knowing | Borgatti and Cross (2003) |
| Knowledge | Adam, Corbett, Flores, Harrison, Lee, Rho, Ribera, Samson, and Westbrook (1997) |
| Knowledge | Brockman and Morgan (2003) |
| Knowledge | Roth (1993) |
| Knowledge | Roth and Jackson (1995) |
| Knowledge dissemination: feedback | Chesteen, Helgheim, Randall, and Wardell (2005) |
| Knowledge dissemination: task expectation | Chesteen, Helgheim, Randall, and Wardell (2005) |
| Knowledge sources | Teigland and McLure Wasko (2004) |
| Knowledge transfer effort | Zellmer-Bruhn (2003) |
| Labor availability | Amoako-Gyampah and Boye (2001) |
| Labor availability | Ward, Duray, Leong, and Sum (1995) |
| Labor flexibility | Sakakibara, Flynn, Schroeder, and Morris (1997) |
| Labor flexibility | Zhang, Vonderembse, and Lim (2003) |
| Labor flexibility: mobility | Koste, Malhotra, and Sharma (2004) |
| Labor flexibility: range-heterogeneity | Karuppan and Ganster (2004) |
| Labor flexibility: range-heterogeneity | Koste, Malhotra, and Sharma (2004) |
| Labor flexibility: range-number | Karuppan and Ganster (2004) |
| Labor flexibility: range-number | Koste, Malhotra, and Sharma (2004) |
| Labor flexibility: uniformity | Karuppan and Ganster (2004) |
| Labor flexibility: uniformity | Koste, Malhotra, and Sharma (2004) |

*(Continued)*

(Continued)

| | |
|---|---|
| Labor intensity | Safizadeh, Field, and Ritzman (2003) |
| Labor productivity | Schmenner and Cook (1985) |
| Lateness | Sawhney and Piper (2002) |
| Layers | Vickery, Dröge, and Germain (1999) |
| Lead time | Rho and Yu (1998) |
| Leadership | Escrig-Tena and Bou-Llusar (2005) |
| Leadership | Pannirselvam, Siferd, and Ruch (1998) |
| Leadership | Samson and Terziovski (1999) |
| Leadership: director of nursing | Chesteen, Helgheim, Randall, and Wardell (2005) |
| Leadership: immediate supervisor | Chesteen, Helgheim, Randall, and Wardell (2005) |
| Leadership: patient focus | Chesteen, Helgheim, Randall, and Wardell (2005) |
| Lean manufacturing | Karlsson and Åhlström (1995) |
| Leaning manufacturing practices | Shah and Ward (2003) |
| Learning | Anderson, Rungtusanatham, Schroeder, and Devaraj (1995) |
| Learning | Rungtusanatham, Forza, Koka, Salvador, and Nie (2005) |
| Learning | Stratman and Roth (2002) |
| Learning belief | Froehle and Roth (2004) |
| Learning consequence | Hult, Ketchen, and Nichols (2003) |
| Learning orientation | Hult, Hurley, Giunipero, and Nichols (2000) |
| Learning orientation | Hult, Ketchen, and Nichols (2003) |
| Legal legitimate | Benton and Maloni (2004) |
| Length of stay standard | Heineke (1995) |
| Level of capital investment | da Silveira (2005) |
| Level of communication | Nahm, Vonderembse, and Koufteros (2003) |
| Level of differentiation | Williams, D'Souza, Rosenfeldt, and Kassaee (1995) |
| Level of horizontal integration | Nahm, Vonderembse, and Koufteros (2003) |
| Level of performance | Tracey, Vonderembse, and Lim (1999) |
| Level of success criteria: inventory elements | Mehra and Inman (1992) |
| Level of success criteria: utilization elements | Mehra and Inman (1992) |
| Limited number of suppliers | Chen, Paulraj, and Lado (2004) |
| Locus of decision making | Nahm, Vonderembse, and Koufteros (2003) |
| Logistics integration | Chen and Paulraj (2004) |
| Long-range orientation | Sakakibara, Flynn, Schroeder, and Morris (1997) |
| Long-term focus | Detert, Schroeder, and Cudeck (2003) |
| Long-term orientation | Chen, Paulraj, and Lado (2004) |
| Long-term orientation | Griffith, Harvey, and Lusch (2006) |
| Long-term relationship | Chen and Paulraj (2004) |
| Long-term/short-term strategic orientation | Menor, Roth, and Mason (2001) |
| Losses | Tucker (2004) |
| Lot size reduction practices | Flynn, Sakakibara, and Schroeder (1995) |
| Low cost | Roth (1993) |
| Low cost | Safizadeh, Field, and Ritzman (2003) |
| Low cost | Zahay, D., Griffin, A. (2004) |
| Low cost priority | Amoako-Gyampah and Boye (2001) |
| Low-volume process automation technology | Swamidass and Kotha (1998) |
| Loyalty intentions | de Jong and de Ruyter (2004) |
| Machine flexibility | Zhang, Vonderembse, and Lim (2003) |
| Machine flexibility: mobility | Karuppan and Ganster (2004) |

| | |
|---|---|
| Machine flexibility: mobility | Koste, Malhotra, and Sharma (2004) |
| Machine flexibility: range-heterogeneity | Karuppan and Ganster (2004) |
| Machine flexibility: range-heterogeneity | Koste, Malhotra, and Sharma (2004) |
| Machine flexibility: range-number | Karuppan and Ganster (2004) |
| Machine flexibility: range-number | Koste, Malhotra, and Sharma (2004) |
| Machine flexibility: uniformity | Koste, Malhotra, and Sharma (2004) |
| Maintenance | Sakakibara, Flynn, Schroeder, and Morris (1997) |
| Maintenance and strategy | Lawrence and Hottenstein (1995) |
| Management (why) | New and Szwejczewski (1995) |
| Management accounting system | Fry, Steele, and Saladin (1995) |
| Management and operations | Flynn and Saladin (2001) |
| Management by fact | Douglas and Fredendall (2004) |
| Management commitment | Mehra and Inman (1992) |
| Management consequence | Hult, Ketchen, and Nichols (2003) |
| Management message | Leonard-Barton and Deschamps (1988) |
| Management of process quality | Choi and Eboch (1998) |
| Management of process quality | Pannirselvam, Siferd, and Ruch (1998) |
| Management practices | Morita and Flynn (1997) |
| Management support | Flynn, Sakakibara, and Schroeder (1995) |
| Management support | de Jong, de Ruyter, and Wetzels (2005) |
| Management systems and quality improvement process | Flynn and Saladin (2001) |
| Management technical competence | Flynn, Schroeder, and Flynn (1999) |
| Managerial knowledge | Benson, Saraph, and Schroeder (1991) |
| Managing demand | Li, Benton, and Leong (2002) |
| Manufacturing | Boyer, Ward, and Leong (1996) |
| Manufacturing | Diáz, Machuca, and Alvarez-Gil (2003) |
| Manufacturing adaptability | Swafford, Ghosh, and Murthy (2006) |
| Manufacturing and human resources fit | Ahmad and Schroeder (2003) |
| Manufacturing capabilities: cost | Noble (1997) |
| Manufacturing capabilities: delivery | Noble (1997) |
| Manufacturing capabilities: dependability | Noble (1997) |
| Manufacturing capabilities: flexibility | Noble (1997) |
| Manufacturing capabilities: innovation | Noble (1997) |
| Manufacturing capabilities: quality | Noble (1997) |
| Manufacturing characteristics focus | Bozarth and Edwards (1997) |
| Manufacturing competency | Dröge, Vickery, and Markland (1994) |
| Manufacturing cost reduction | Das and Narasimhan (2001) |
| Manufacturing decision variables | Deane, McDougall, and Gargeya (1991) |
| Manufacturing design | Das and Narasimhan (2001) |
| Manufacturing evaluation of marketing communication | Calantone, Dröge, and Vickery (2002) |
| Manufacturing flexibility | Ho (1996) |
| Manufacturing flexibility | Swamidass and Newell (1987) |
| Manufacturing flexibility and modularization | Rabinovich, Dresner, and Evers (2003) |
| Manufacturing importance | Hausman, Montgomery, and Roth (2002) |
| Manufacturing infrastructure | Das and Narasimhan (2001) |
| Manufacturing involvement | Ward, Leong, and Boyer (1994) |
| Manufacturing lead time | Karlsson and Åhlström (1995) |
| Manufacturing manager's participation in strategy formulation | Tracey, Vonderembse, and Lim (1999) |
| Manufacturing mission | Schroeder, Anderson, and Cleveland (1986) |

*(Continued)*

(Continued)

| | |
|---|---|
| Manufacturing morale | Hausman, Montgomery, and Roth (2002) |
| Manufacturing objectives | Kim and Arnold (1996) |
| Manufacturing objectives | Schroeder, Anderson, and Cleveland (1986) |
| Manufacturing performance | Bozarth and Edwards (1997) |
| Manufacturing performance | Cleveland, Schroeder, and Anderson (1989) |
| Manufacturing performance | Cua, McKone, and Schroeder (2001) |
| Manufacturing performance | Schroeder, Bates, and Juntilla (2002) |
| Manufacturing policies (areas with written policies established) | Schroeder, Anderson, and Cleveland (1986) |
| Manufacturing range | Swafford, Ghosh, and Murthy (2006) |
| Manufacturing strategy | Dean and Snell (1996) |
| Manufacturing strategy | Lawrence and Hottenstein (1995) |
| Manufacturing strategy process: environmental interaction | Ho (1996) |
| Manufacturing strategy process: manufacturing planning activities | Ho (1996) |
| Manufacturing strategy process: role of manufacturing function | Ho (1996) |
| Manufacturing strategy process: worker participation | Ho (1996) |
| Manufacturing strategy scales: communication of strategy | Bates, Amundson, Schroeder, and Morris (1995) |
| Manufacturing strategy scales: formal strategic planning | Bates, Amundson, Schroeder, and Morris (1995) |
| Manufacturing strategy scales: long-range orientation | Bates, Amundson, Schroeder, and Morris (1995) |
| Manufacturing strategy scales: manufacturing strategy strength | Bates, Amundson, Schroeder, and Morris (1995) |
| Manufacturing strategy scales: strategic role-stage 1 | Bates, Amundson, Schroeder, and Morris (1995) |
| Manufacturing strategy scales: strategic role-stage 2 | Bates, Amundson, Schroeder, and Morris (1995) |
| Manufacturing strategy scales: strategic role-stage 3 | Bates, Amundson, Schroeder, and Morris (1995) |
| Manufacturing strategy scales: strategic role-stage 4 | Bates, Amundson, Schroeder, and Morris (1995) |
| Manufacturing strategy strength | Sakakibara, Flynn, Schroeder, and Morris (1997) |
| Manufacturing strategy: market orientation | Williams, D'Souza, Rosenfeldt, and Kassaee (1995) |
| Manufacturing strategy: technology orientation | Williams, D'Souza, Rosenfeldt, and Kassaee (1995) |
| Manufacturing technology | Das and Narasimhan (2001) |
| Manufacturing-Marketing interface harmony | Hausman, Montgomery, and Roth (2002) |
| Market acuity | Menor, Roth, and Mason (2001) |
| Market acuity | Roth (1993) |
| Market acuity | Roth and Jackson (1995) |
| Market growth | Cao and Dowlatshahi (2005) |
| Market newness | Tatikonda and Montoya-Weiss (2001) |
| Market newness | Tatikonda and Montoya-Weiss (2001) |
| Market outcomes | Tatikonda and Montoya-Weiss (2001) |
| Market performance | Christensen, Germain, and Birou (2005) |
| Market performance | Roth (1993) |
| Market performance | Roth and Jackson (1995) |
| Market pressure | Pflughoeft, Ramamurthy, Soofi, Yasai-Ardekani, and Zahedi (2003) |
| Market requirements focus | Bozarth and Edwards (1997) |
| Market share | Curkovic, Vickery, and Dröge (2000) |
| Market share | Dröge, Jayaram, and Vickery (2004) |

| | |
|---|---|
| Market-based performance | Swink, Narasimhan, and Kim (2005) |
| Marketing | Ettlie (1997) |
| Marketing choices | Roth and van der Velde (1991) |
| Marketing competency | Dröge, Vickery, and Markland (1994) |
| Marketing decision variables | Deane, McDougall, and Gargeya (1991) |
| Marketing implementation capabilities | Morgan, Zou, Vorhies, and Katsikeas (2003) |
| Marketing importance | Hausman, Montgomery, and Roth (2002) |
| Marketing knowledge of manufacturing | Calantone, Dröge, and Vickery (2002) |
| Marketing morale | Hausman, Montgomery, and Roth (2002) |
| Marketing performance | Cleveland, Schroeder, and Anderson (1989) |
| Marketing planning capabilities | Morgan, Zou, Vorhies, and Katsikeas (2003) |
| Marketing strategy factor | Goldstein, Ward, Leong, and Butler (2002) |
| Marketing-manufacturing integration | Calantone, Dröge, and Vickery (2002) |
| Marketing-manufacturing relationship quality | Calantone, Dröge, and Vickery (2002) |
| Marketing-operations interface (MOI) quality | Sawhney and Piper (2002) |
| Marketplace environment | Benson, Saraph, and Schroeder (1991) |
| Masculinity | Youngdahl, Kellogg, Nie, and Bowen (2003) |
| Mass customization | Tu, Vonderembse, and Ragu-Nathan (2001) |
| Mass customization | Tu, Vonderembse, Ragu-Nathan, and Ragu-Nathan (2004) |
| Mass output orientation | Germain, Dröge, and Christensen (2001) |
| Material handling flexibility: mobility | Koste, Malhotra, and Sharma (2004) |
| Material handling flexibility: range-heterogeneity | Koste, Malhotra, and Sharma (2004) |
| Material handling flexibility: range-number | Koste, Malhotra, and Sharma (2004) |
| Material handling flexibility: uniformity | Koste, Malhotra, and Sharma (2004) |
| Material management | Stahl and Zimmerer (1983) |
| Material management—batch size rationale | Safizadeh and Ritzman (1997) |
| Material management—inventory level | Safizadeh and Ritzman (1997) |
| Material requirements planning (MRP) adaptation to JIT | Sakakibara, Flynn, and Schroeder (1993) |
| Material requirements planning (MRP) adoption | Rabinovich, Dresner, and Evers (2003) |
| Material-handling flexibility | Zhang, Vonderembse, and Lim (2003) |
| Materials management | Rho and Yu (1998) |
| Measure of use | Leonard-Barton and Deschamps (1988) |
| Measurement | Curkovic, Vickery, and Dröge (2000) |
| Measurement | Pagell (2004) |
| Measurement | Powell (1995) |
| Measurement and standards | Flynn and Saladin (2001) |
| Measures of long-term orientation | Voss and Blackmon (1998) |
| Measures of short-term orientation | Voss and Blackmon (1998) |
| Media richness | Vickery, Dröge, Stank, Goldsby, and Markland (2004) |
| Medical doctor payment | Heineke (1995) |
| Memory orientation | Hult, Hurley, Giunipero, and Nichols (2000) |
| Memory orientation | Hult, Ketchen, and Nichols (2003) |
| Minimum delivery lead time available | Robinson and Satterfield (1998) |
| Mix flexibility | Zhang, Vonderembse, and Lim (2003) |
| Mix flexibility: mobility | Karuppan and Ganster (2004) |
| Mix flexibility: mobility | Koste, Malhotra, and Sharma (2004) |
| Mix flexibility: range-heterogeneity | Karuppan and Ganster (2004) |
| Mix flexibility: range-heterogeneity | Koste, Malhotra, and Sharma (2004) |
| Mix flexibility: range-number | Karuppan and Ganster (2004) |
| Mix flexibility: range-number | Koste, Malhotra, and Sharma (2004) |
| Mix flexibility: uniformity | Karuppan and Ganster (2004) |

*(Continued)*

(Continued)

| | |
|---|---|
| Mix flexibility: uniformity | Koste, Malhotra, and Sharma (2004) |
| Mobility | Anand and Ward (2004) |
| Mode of interaction | Safizadeh, Field, and Ritzman (2003) |
| Model type | Heineke (1995) |
| Modeled behavior (acquaintance with users) | Leonard-Barton and Deschamps (1988) |
| Modification flexibility: mobility | Koste, Malhotra, and Sharma (2004) |
| Modification flexibility: range-heterogeneity | Koste, Malhotra, and Sharma (2004) |
| Modification flexibility: range-number | Koste, Malhotra, and Sharma (2004) |
| Modification flexibility: uniformity | Koste, Malhotra, and Sharma (2004) |
| MOI speed | Sawhney and Piper (2002) |
| Monitor | Grover and Malhotra (2003) |
| Motivation | Jambulingam, Kathuria, and Doucette (2005) |
| Motivation for quality assurance behaviors | Youngdahl and Kellogg (1997) |
| MRP benefit | Schroeder, Anderson, Tupy, and White (1981) |
| Multifunction workers | Sakakibara, Flynn, and Schroeder (1993) |
| Munificence | Jambulingam, Kathuria, and Doucette (2005) |
| Nature of formalization | Nahm, Vonderembse, and Koufteros (2003) |
| Negative economic performance | Zhu and Sarkis (2004) |
| New markets | Tsikriktsis, Lanzolla, and Frohlich (2004) |
| New product design and development strategy | Tan (2001) |
| New product development/innovation | Goffin, Lemke, and Szwejczewski (2006) |
| New product developments | Brown (1998) |
| New product flexibility | Swink, Narasimhan, and Kim (2005) |
| New product flexibility: mobility | Koste, Malhotra, and Sharma (2004) |
| New product flexibility: range-heterogeneity | Koste, Malhotra, and Sharma (2004) |
| New product flexibility: range-number | Koste, Malhotra, and Sharma (2004) |
| New product flexibility: uniformity | Koste, Malhotra, and Sharma (2004) |
| New product innovativeness | Brockman and Morgan (2003) |
| New product introduction | Das and Narasimhan (2001) |
| New product introduction rate | Calantone, Dröge, and Vickery (2002) |
| New product performance | Brockman and Morgan (2003) |
| New product quality | Sakakibara, Flynn, Schroeder, and Morris (1997) |
| Niche profile | Roth (1993) |
| Nonclinical factors | Heineke (1995) |
| Non-value added | Rosenzweig and Roth (2004) |
| Number of employees | Cua, McKone, and Schroeder (2001) |
| Number of layers in hierarchy | Nahm, Vonderembse, and Koufteros (2003) |
| Objective cycle time | Hult, Hurley, Giunipero, and Nichols (2000) |
| Office practice review | Heineke (1995) |
| Open organization | Powell (1995) |
| Operating performance | Terziovski, Samson, and Dow (1997) |
| Operating performance | Terziovski, Samson, and Dow (1997) |
| Operational efficiency | Pflughoeft, Ramamurthy, Soofi, Yasai-Ardekani, and Zahedi (2003) |
| Operational independence | Prasad, Tata, and Madan (2005) |
| Operational know-how | Rosenzweig and Roth (2004) |
| Operational linkages | Prahinski and Benton (2004) |
| Operational outcomes | Tatikonda and Montoya-Weiss (2001) |

| | |
|---|---|
| Operational performance | Ahmad and Schroeder (2003) |
| Operational performance | Shah and Ward (2003) |
| Operational quality planning | Black and Porter (1996) |
| Operational system for quality | Morita and Flynn (1997) |
| Operations and strategic goals | Flynn and Saladin (2001) |
| Operations decentralization | Vickery, Dröge, and Germain (1999) |
| Operations strategy | Ahmed, Montagno, and Firenze (1996) |
| Operations strategy factor | Goldstein, Ward, Leong, and Butler (2002) |
| Operations/product variance | Germain, Dröge, and Christensen (2001) |
| Optimism | Parasuraman (2000) |
| Order backlog | Safizadeh and Ritzman (1997) |
| Order filling method | Raffi and Swamidass (1987) |
| Order winners | Fry, Steele, and Saladin (1995) |
| Order winners | Menda and Dilts (1997) |
| Ordering tool usage | Olson, Belohlav, and Boyer (2005) |
| Organicity | Jambulingam, Kathuria, and Doucette (2005) |
| Organization structure | Brockman and Morgan (2003) |
| Organizational climate: reward | Janz and Prasarnphanich (2003) |
| Organizational climate: risk | Janz and Prasarnphanich (2003) |
| Organizational climate: support | Janz and Prasarnphanich (2003) |
| Organizational climate: warmth | Janz and Prasarnphanich (2003) |
| Organizational commitment | Ahmad and Schroeder (2003) |
| Organizational commitment | Escrig-Tena and Bou-Llusar (2005) |
| Organizational commitment | Ittner and Larcker (1997) |
| Organizational environment risk | Wallace, Keil, and Rai (2004) |
| Organizational learning | Escrig-Tena and Bou-Llusar (2005) |
| Organizational performance | Samson and Terziovski (1999) |
| Organizational proximity | Levin and Cross (2004) |
| Organizational rewards | LaForge, Wood, and Sleeth (1984) |
| Organizational rules and procedures | Pinto, Pinto, and Prescott (1993) |
| Organizational scope | Devaraj, Hollingworth, and Schroeder (2004) |
| Organizational size | Goffin, Lemke, and Szwejczewski (2006) |
| Organizational structure | Fullerton, McWatters, and Fawson (2003) |
| Organizational support | Fedor, Ghosh, Caldwell, Maurer, and Singhal (2003) |
| Organizational system for quality | Morita and Flynn (1997) |
| Orientation and training | Wisner, Stringfellow, Youngdahl, and Parker (2005) |
| Orientation of process | Safizadeh, Field, and Ritzman (2003) |
| Origin of the project and realized outcomes and contributions of this new product | Ettlie (1997) |
| Outpatient service | Li, Benton, and Leong (2002) |
| Output sector | Carter and Carter (1998) |
| Overall performance | Safizadeh, Field, and Ritzman (2003) |
| Overall service quality | Brady and Cronin (2001) |
| | |
| Participative behavior | Sarin and Mcdermott (2003) |
| Participativeness | Hult, Hurley, Giunipero, and Nichols (2000) |
| Participatory leadership | Marley, Collier, and Goldstein (2004) |
| Past quality performance | Benson, Saraph, and Schroeder (1991) |
| Past success | Monczka, Peterson, Handfield, and Ragatz (1998) |
| Patient satisfaction | Marley, Collier, and Goldstein (2004) |
| People and customer management | Black and Porter (1996) |

*(Continued)*

(Continued)

| | |
|---|---|
| People management | Samson and Terziovski (1999) |
| People valued | Schmenner and Cook (1985) |
| Perceived customer satisfaction | Douglas and Fredendall (2004) |
| Perceived ease of use | Venkatesh, Speier, and Morris (2002) |
| Perceived environmental uncertainty | Swamidass and Newell (1987) |
| Perceived financial performance | Douglas and Fredendall (2004) |
| Perceived group-level KM effectiveness | Sabherwal and Becerra-Fernandez (2003) |
| Perceived individual-level knowledge management (KM) effectiveness | Sabherwal and Becerra-Fernandez (2003) |
| Perceived management support | Leonard-Barton and Deschamps (1988) |
| Perceived organizational-level KM effectiveness | Sabherwal and Becerra-Fernandez (2003) |
| Perceived performance | Athanassopoulos and Iliakopoulos (2003) |
| Perceived quality market outcomes | Flynn, Schroeder, and Sakakibara (1995) |
| Perceived receipt of useful knowledge | Levin and Cross (2004) |
| Perceived usefulness | Venkatesh, Speier, and Morris (2002) |
| Perceptual measures of functionality | Malhotra, Heine, and Grover (2001) |
| Performance | Anand and Ward (2004) |
| Performance | Boyer, Ward, and Leong (1996) |
| Performance | Dean and Snell (1991) |
| Performance | Dröge, Vickery, and Markland (1994) |
| Performance | Frohlich and Westbrook (2002) |
| Performance | Griffith, Harvey, and Lusch (2006) |
| Performance | Ho (1996) |
| Performance | Joshi, Kathuria, and Porth (2003) |
| Performance | Lewis (2004) |
| Performance | Nahm, Vonderembse, and Koufteros (2004) |
| Performance | Pagell (2004) |
| Performance | Pagell and Krause (2004) |
| Performance | Safizadeh and Ritzman (1997) |
| Performance | Safizadeh, Ritzman, Sharma, and Wood (1996) |
| Performance | Swamidass and Kotha (1998) |
| Performance | Teigland and McLure Wasko (2004) |
| Performance | Vickery, Dröge, Yeomans, and Markland (1995) |
| Performance | Ward, Leong, and Boyer (1994) |
| Performance | Williams, D'Souza, Rosenfeldt, and Kassaee (1995) |
| Performance (result) | New and Szwejczewski (1995) |
| Performance : flexibility | Boyer, Leong, Ward, and Krajewski (1997) |
| Performance : PROFIT | Boyer, Leong, Ward, and Krajewski (1997) |
| Performance consequence | Hult, Ketchen, and Nichols (2003) |
| Performance improvement | Krause, Scannell, and Calantone (2000) |
| Performance improvements | Krause, Handfield, and Scannell (1998) |
| Performance management | Roth and van der Velde (1991) |
| Performance measure | Ahmed, Montagno, and Firenze (1996) |
| Performance measure | Swamidass and Newell (1987) |
| Performance measures—overall CAD process | Malhotra, Heine, and Grover (2001) |
| Performance quality | Adam, Corbett, Flores, Harrison, Lee, Rho, Ribera, Samson, and Westbrook (1997) |
| Performance service quality | Brady and Cronin (2001) |
| Performance: GROWTH | Boyer, Leong, Ward, and Krajewski (1997) |
| Performance: operational efficiency factor | Small and Yasin (1997) |

| | |
|---|---|
| Performance: organizational effectiveness factor | Small and Yasin (1997) |
| Performance: time-based performance factor | Small and Yasin (1997) |
| Performance-manufacturer | Benton and Maloni (2004) |
| Performance-supplier | Benton and Maloni (2004) |
| Performance-supply chain | Benton and Maloni (2004) |
| Personal innovativeness toward this type of innovation | Leonard-Barton and Deschamps (1988) |
| Personal relationship | Goffin, Lemke, and Szwejczewski (2006) |
| Personalization | Zahay, D., Griffin, A. (2004) |
| Physical accessibility | Leonard-Barton and Deschamps (1988) |
| Physical goods quality | Brady and Cronin (2001) |
| Physical proximity | Levin and Cross (2004) |
| Physical proximity | Pinto, Pinto, and Prescott (1993) |
| Planning | Diáz, Machuca, and Alvarez-Gil (2003) |
| Planning and control risk | Wallace, Keil, and Rai (2004) |
| Planning and scheduling | Stahl and Zimmerer (1983) |
| Planning for new products and services | Flynn and Saladin (2001) |
| Planning function | Flynn and Saladin (2001) |
| Planning horizon | Safizadeh and Ritzman (1997) |
| Plant age | Shah and Ward (2003) |
| Plant environment | Flynn, Sakakibara, and Schroeder (1995) |
| Plant performance | Devaraj, Hollingworth, and Schroeder (2004) |
| Plant performance | Nahm, Vonderembse, and Koufteros (2003) |
| Plant performance: cost | Choi and Eboch (1998) |
| Plant performance: delivery | Choi and Eboch (1998) |
| Plant performance: quality | Choi and Eboch (1998) |
| Plant size | Sawhney and Piper (2002) |
| Plant size | Shah and Ward (2003) |
| Plant type | Fry, Steele, and Saladin (1995) |
| Plant's rank within the industry | Schmenner and Cook (1985) |
| Plant's rank within the parent company | Schmenner and Cook (1985) |
| Plant's rate of change of productivity advance | Schmenner and Cook (1985) |
| Plantwide philosophy | Sakakibara, Flynn, Schroeder, and Morris (1997) |
| Policy | Flynn and Saladin (2001) |
| Positive economic performance | Zhu and Sarkis (2004) |
| Postponement | Li, Rao, Ragu-Nathan, and Ragu-Nathan (2005) |
| Power distance | Youngdahl, Kellogg, Nie, and Bowen (2003) |
| Power distance scales: centralization of authority | Bates, Amundson, Schroeder, and Morris (1995) |
| Power distance scales: hierarchical Index | Bates, Amundson, Schroeder, and Morris (1995) |
| Power distance scales: shop-floor contact | Bates, Amundson, Schroeder, and Morris (1995) |
| Premium pricing | Koufteros, Vonderembse, and Doll (2001) |
| Premium pricing | Koufteros, Vonderembse, and Doll (2002) |
| Presale customer service | Curkovic, Vickery, and Dröge (2000) |
| Pretax return-on-assets (ROA) | Curkovic, Vickery, and Dröge (2000) |
| Preventive maintenance | Koufteros (1999) |
| Preventive maintenance | Koufteros, Vonderembse, and Doll (1998) |
| Preventive maintenance | Sakakibara, Flynn, and Schroeder (1993) |
| Preventive maintenance | Tu, Vonderembse, and Ragu-Nathan (2001) |
| Price | Choi and Hartley (1996) |
| Price | da Silveira (2005) |
| Price leader | Roth (1996) |
| Price offered | Tracey, Vonderembse, and Lim (1999) |

*(Continued)*

(Continued)

| | |
|---|---|
| Pride in work | Morita and Flynn (1997) |
| Proactive recovery behavior | de Jong and de Ruyter (2004) |
| Proactiveness | Jambulingam, Kathuria, and Doucette (2005) |
| Proactivity | Conlon, Devaraj, and Matta (2001) |
| Problem | Grover and Malhotra (2003) |
| Procedural justice | Griffith, Harvey, and Lusch (2006) |
| Process adaptability | Tatikonda and Montoya-Weiss (2001) |
| Process adaptability | Tatikonda and Montoya-Weiss (2001) |
| Process and process technologies | Rho and Yu (1998) |
| Process choice | da Silveira (2005) |
| Process choice | Safizadeh and Ritzman (1997) |
| Process choice | Safizadeh, Ritzman, Sharma, and Wood (1996) |
| Process concurrency | Tatikonda and Montoya-Weiss (2001) |
| Process concurrency | Tatikonda and Montoya-Weiss (2001) |
| Process control | Ahmad and Schroeder (2001) |
| Process control | Flynn, Schroeder, and Flynn (1999) |
| Process control | Sakakibara, Flynn, Schroeder, and Morris (1997) |
| Process enablers | Roth (1996) |
| Process flexibility | Rosenzweig, Roth, and Dean (2003) |
| Process flexibility | Safizadeh, Field, and Ritzman (2003) |
| Process flexibility | Swink, Narasimhan, and Kim (2005) |
| Process flow management | Flynn, Schroeder, and Sakakibara (1995) |
| Process focus | Ittner and Larcker (1997) |
| Process formality | Tatikonda and Montoya-Weiss (2001) |
| Process formality | Tatikonda and Montoya-Weiss (2001) |
| Process improvement | Powell (1995) |
| Process information | Flynn and Flynn (2004) |
| Process management | Anderson, Rungtusanatham, Schroeder, and Devaraj (1995) |
| Process management | Cua, McKone, and Schroeder (2001) |
| Process management | Goldstein and Naor (2005) |
| Process management | Park, Hartley, and Wilson (2001) |
| Process management | Rungtusanatham, Forza, Koka, Salvador, and Nie (2005) |
| Process management | Samson and Terziovski (1999) |
| Process management/operating procedures | Forker (1997) |
| Process management/operating procedures | Forker, Mendez, and Hershauer (1997) |
| Process management: cleanliness and organization | Flynn, Schroeder, and Sakakibara (1994) |
| Process management: procedures | Chesteen, Helgheim, Randall, and Wardell (2005) |
| Process management: responsiveness | Chesteen, Helgheim, Randall, and Wardell (2005) |
| Process modularity | Tu, Vonderembse, Ragu-Nathan, and Ragu-Nathan (2004) |
| Process performance | Wallace, Keil, and Rai (2004) |
| Process quality | Marley, Collier, and Goldstein (2004) |
| Process quality management | Swink, Narasimhan, and Kim (2005) |
| Process rationalization | Raffi and Swamidass (1987) |
| Process structure | Sarin and Mcdermott (2003) |
| Process structure complexity | Devaraj, Hollingworth, and Schroeder (2004) |
| Process technological leadership | Roth (1996) |
| Process technology | Roth and van der Velde (1991) |
| Process technology novelty | Tatikonda and Montoya-Weiss (2001) |
| Process technology novelty | Tatikonda and Montoya-Weiss (2001) |
| Process-orientation | Cua, McKone, and Schroeder (2001) |

| | |
|---|---|
| Procurement/sourcing adaptability | Swafford, Ghosh, and Murthy (2006) |
| Procurement/sourcing range | Swafford, Ghosh, and Murthy (2006) |
| Product and product changes | Schmenner and Cook (1985) |
| Product and service processes | Flynn and Saladin (2001) |
| Product complexity | Sawhney and Piper (2002) |
| Product customization | Rabinovich, Dresner, and Evers (2003) |
| Product customization | Vickery, Dröge, and Germain (1999) |
| Product design | Flynn, Sakakibara, and Schroeder (1995) |
| Product design and development competency | Dröge, Vickery, and Markland (1994) |
| Product design process | Flynn, Schroeder, and Sakakibara (1995) |
| Product design simplicity | Flynn and Flynn (2004) |
| Product design simplicity | Sakakibara, Flynn, and Schroeder (1993) |
| Product design technology | Swamidass and Kotha (1998) |
| Product design: interfunctional design process | Flynn, Schroeder, and Sakakibara (1994) |
| Product design: new product quality | Flynn, Schroeder, and Sakakibara (1994) |
| Product development | Ettlie (1997) |
| Product development productivity | Hong, Vonderembse, Doll, and Nahm (2005) |
| Product development strategy | Ettlie (1997) |
| Product development teams | Koufteros, Vonderembse, and Doll (2001) |
| Product durability | Curkovic, Vickery, and Dröge (2000) |
| Product flexibility | Flynn, Schroeder, and Flynn (1999) |
| Product flexibility | Safizadeh, Field, and Ritzman (2003) |
| Product flexibility | White (1996) |
| Product freshness | Boyer and Hult (2006) |
| Product innovation | Cao and Dowlatshahi (2005) |
| Product innovation | Koufteros, Vonderembse, and Doll (2001) |
| Product innovation | Koufteros, Vonderembse, and Doll (2002) |
| Product innovation | Koufteros, Vonderembse, and Jayaram (2005) |
| Product lead time | Sawhney and Piper (2002) |
| Product line breadth | Tracey, Vonderembse, and Lim (1999) |
| Product modularity | Tu, Vonderembse, Ragu-Nathan, and Ragu-Nathan (2004) |
| Product performance | Wallace, Keil, and Rai (2004) |
| Product plan | Safizadeh, Ritzman, Sharma, and Wood (1996) |
| Product price compared to competition | Robinson and Satterfield (1998) |
| Product quality | Ahire, Golhar, and Waller (1996) |
| Product quality | Boyer and Hult (2006) |
| Product quality | Robinson and Satterfield (1998) |
| Product quality | Rosenzweig, Roth, and Dean (2003) |
| Product quality | Tatikonda and Montoya-Weiss (2001) |
| Product reliability | Curkovic, Vickery, and Dröge (2000) |
| Product strategy | Koufteros, Vonderembse, and Doll (2002) |
| Product support | Curkovic, Vickery, and Dröge (2000) |
| Product technology novelty | Tatikonda and Montoya-Weiss (2001) |
| Product technology novelty | Tatikonda and Montoya-Weiss (2001) |
| Product/process environment | Benson, Saraph, and Schroeder (1991) |
| Product/service design | Forker (1997) |
| Product/service design | Forker, Mendez, and Hershauer (1997) |
| Product-based green supply | Bowen, Cousins, Lamming, and Faruk (2001) |
| Production competence | Cleveland, Schroeder, and Anderson (1989) |
| Production competence | Vickery (1991) |
| Production control system | Morita and Flynn (1997) |

*(Continued)*

(Continued)

| | |
|---|---|
| Production orientation | Fry, Steele, and Saladin (1995) |
| Production planning | Rho and Yu (1998) |
| Production planning and control | Roth (1996) |
| Production process | Cleveland, Schroeder, and Anderson (1989) |
| Production process and process changes | Schmenner and Cook (1985) |
| Production process focus | Wathen (1995) |
| Production system: just-in-time (JIT) orientation | Morita and Flynn (1997) |
| Production technology routineness | Dröge, Claycomb, and Germain (2003) |
| Productivity | Rho and Yu (1998) |
| Productivity improvement | Adam (1994) |
| Productivity improvement | Stahl and Zimmerer (1983) |
| Productivity measures: productivity | Noble (1997) |
| Productivity measures: relative productivity | Noble (1997) |
| Productivity programs an miscellaneous variables | Schmenner and Cook (1985) |
| Product-process development | Swink, Narasimhan, and Kim (2005) |
| Profit | Diáz, Machuca, and Alvarez-Gil (2003) |
| Profitability | Koufteros, Vonderembse, and Doll (2002) |
| Profitability | Koufteros, Vonderembse, and Jayaram (2005) |
| Profitability | Rosenzweig and Roth (2004) |
| Profits | Hausman, Montgomery, and Roth (2002) |
| Project complexity | Sarin and Mcdermott (2003) |
| Project complexity risk | Wallace, Keil, and Rai (2004) |
| Project management | Stratman and Roth (2002) |
| Project quality | Primo and Amundson (2002) |
| Project risk | Sarin and Mcdermott (2003) |
| Project speed | Primo and Amundson (2002) |
| Project success | Fedor, Ghosh, Caldwell, Maurer, and Singhal (2003) |
| Project team effectiveness | Petersen, Handfield, and Ragatz (2005) |
| Project team rules and procedures | Pinto, Pinto, and Prescott (1993) |
| Projected research and development (R&D) budget/time-to-market objective/projected unit cost of the product | Primo and Amundson (2002) |
| Proprietary equipment | Flynn, Schroeder, and Flynn (1999) |
| Proprietary equipment development | Cua, McKone, and Schroeder (2001) |
| Proprietary manufacturing process and equipment | Schroeder, Bates, and Juntilla (2002) |
| Public responsibility | Goldstein and Naor (2005) |
| Pull production | Koufteros (1999) |
| Pull production | Koufteros, Vonderembse, and Doll (1998) |
| Pull production | Tu, Vonderembse, and Ragu-Nathan (2001) |
| Pull system | Flynn, Schroeder, and Flynn (1999) |
| Pull system production | Cua, McKone, and Schroeder (2001) |
| Pull system support | Ketokivi and Schroeder (2004) |
| Pull system support | Sakakibara, Flynn, and Schroeder (1993) |
| Purchasing competency | Narasimhan, Jayaram, and Carter (2001) |
| Purchasing efficiency | Olson and Boyer (2003) |
| Purchasing's service quality performance | Stanley and Wisner (2001) |
| Purchasing's strategic role | Johnson, Klassen, Leenders, and Fearon (2002) |
| Quality | Amoako-Gyampah and Boye (2001) |
| Quality | Carter and Carter (1998) |

| | |
|---|---|
| Quality | Diáz, Machuca, and Alvarez-Gil (2003) |
| Quality | Hennig-Thurau, Langer, and Hansen (2001) |
| Quality | Karlsson and Åhlström (1995) |
| Quality | Koufteros, Vonderembse, and Doll (2001) |
| Quality | Koufteros, Vonderembse, and Doll (2002) |
| Quality | Koufteros, Vonderembse, and Jayaram (2005) |
| Quality | Krause, Pagell, and Curkovic (2001) |
| Quality | Malhotra, Heine, and Grover (2001) |
| Quality | Rho and Yu (1998) |
| Quality | Roth (1996) |
| Quality | Sawhney and Piper (2002) |
| Quality | Ward, Duray, Leong, and Sum (1995) |
| Quality and operational results | Pannirselvam, Siferd, and Ruch (1998) |
| Quality assurance | Tu, Vonderembse, and Ragu-Nathan (2001) |
| Quality at same cost | Detert, Schroeder, and Cudeck (2003) |
| Quality data and reporting | Forker (1997) |
| Quality data and reporting | Forker, Mendez, and Hershauer (1997) |
| Quality features | Flynn, Schroeder, and Flynn (1999) |
| Quality importance | Ward, McCreery, Ritzman, and Sharma (1998) |
| Quality improvement | Adam (1994) |
| Quality improvement efforts | Koufteros, Vonderembse, and Doll (1998) |
| Quality improvement measurement systems | Black and Porter (1996) |
| Quality improvement: behavioral | Adam (1994) |
| Quality information: feedback | Flynn, Schroeder, and Sakakibara (1994) |
| Quality information: process control | Flynn, Schroeder, and Sakakibara (1994) |
| Quality management | Zhu and Sarkis (2004) |
| Quality management philosophy | Ketokivi and Schroeder (2004) |
| Quality management program | Roth and van der Velde (1991) |
| Quality of customer interface | Menor, Roth, and Mason (2001) |
| Quality of customer interface | Roth (1993) |
| Quality of customer interface | Roth and Jackson (1995) |
| Quality of customer interface | Safizadeh, Field, and Ritzman (2003) |
| Quality of products | Tracey, Vonderembse, and Lim (1999) |
| Quality of work life | Roth (1993) |
| Quality performance | Das and Narasimhan (2001) |
| Quality performance | Flynn, Sakakibara, and Schroeder (1995) |
| Quality performance | Flynn, Schroeder, and Flynn (1999) |
| Quality performance | Kaynak (2003) |
| Quality performance | Li, Benton, and Leong (2002) |
| Quality philosophy | Douglas and Fredendall (2004) |
| Quality procedures | Voss, Tsikriktsis, Funk, Yarrow, and Owen (2005) |
| Quality products and services | Adam (1994) |
| Quality Strategy | Tan (2001) |
| Quality training | Curkovic, Vickery, and Dröge (2000) |
| Quality training and education | Flynn and Saladin (2001) |
| Quality-of-conformance | Joshi, Kathuria, and Porth (2003) |
| Quality-of-design | Joshi, Kathuria, and Porth (2003) |
| | |
| Range | Anand and Ward (2004) |
| Range of products, customer's choice, and customer involvement | Safizadeh, Field, and Ritzman (2003) |

*(Continued)*

(Continued)

| | |
|---|---|
| Rate of technological change in buying firm's industry | Krause (1999) |
| Rational culture | McDermott and Stock (1999) |
| Reasons for subcontracting | Chikan and Demeter (1995) |
| Receiver's expertise | Levin and Cross (2004) |
| Recovery disconfirmation | McCollough, Berry, and Yadav (2000) |
| Recovery expectations | McCollough, Berry, and Yadav (2000) |
| Recovery performance | McCollough, Berry, and Yadav (2000) |
| Recruiting and selection | Sakakibara, Flynn, Schroeder, and Morris (1997) |
| Reengineering setup | Koufteros, Vonderembse, and Doll (1998) |
| Reengineering setup | Tu, Vonderembse, and Ragu-Nathan (2001) |
| Referent | Benton and Maloni (2004) |
| Reflection | Wisner, Stringfellow, Youngdahl, and Parker (2005) |
| Reflectiveness | Hult, Hurley, Giunipero, and Nichols (2000) |
| Regulatory sector | Carter and Carter (1998) |
| Relational behavior | Griffith, Harvey, and Lusch (2006) |
| Relational performance | Vickery, Dröge, Stank, Goldsby, and Markland (2004) |
| Relationship | Choi and Hartley (1996) |
| Relationship maintenance | Goffin, Lemke, and Szwejczewski (2006) |
| Relative characteristics of primary retail banking offerings | Menor, Roth, and Mason (2001) |
| Relative characteristics of retail delivery system, policies, and processes | Menor, Roth, and Mason (2001) |
| Relative sales | Tatikonda and Montoya-Weiss (2001) |
| Reliability | Choi and Hartley (1996) |
| Reliability | Soteriou and Chase (1998) |
| Repetitive master schedule | Sakakibara, Flynn, and Schroeder (1993) |
| Replenishment volumes | Prasad, Tata, and Madan (2005) |
| Reputation | Escrig-Tena and Bou-Llusar (2005) |
| Requirements risk | Wallace, Keil, and Rai (2004) |
| Resource dependence | Carter and Carter (1998) |
| Resources | Gilgeous (1995) |
| Responsibility | Vickery, Dröge, Yeomans, and Markland (1995) |
| Responsiveness | Dröge, Jayaram, and Vickery (2004) |
| Responsiveness | Soteriou and Chase (1998) |
| Responsiveness to customers | Curkovic, Vickery, and Dröge (2000) |
| Results from quality assurance of products and services/quality and operational results | Flynn and Saladin (2001) |
| Return on investment (ROI) | Curkovic, Vickery, and Dröge (2000) |
| Reward | Benton and Maloni (2004) |
| Rewards | Wisner, Stringfellow, Youngdahl, and Parker (2005) |
| Rewards for quality | Flynn and Flynn (2004) |
| Rewards for quality | Sakakibara, Flynn, Schroeder, and Morris (1997) |
| Risk | Tucker (2004) |
| Risk taking | Ho (1996) |
| Risk taking | Jambulingam, Kathuria, and Doucette (2005) |
| Rivalry | Powell (1995) |
| Role change of design engineers | Hong, Vonderembse, Doll, and Nahm (2005) |
| Role of manufacturing managers in strategic decision making | Swamidass and Newell (1987) |

| | |
|---|---|
| Role of the quality department | Forker (1997) |
| Role of the quality department | Forker, Mendez, and Hershauer (1997) |
| Role of top management and quality policy | Forker (1997) |
| Role of top management and quality policy | Forker, Mendez, and Hershauer (1997) |
| Routineness | Safizadeh, Field, and Ritzman (2003) |
| Routing flexibility | Zhang, Vonderembse, and Lim (2003) |
| | Benton and Maloni (2004) |
| Satisfaction | Griffith, Harvey, and Lusch (2006) |
| Satisfaction | McDermott and Stock (1999) |
| Satisfaction | Wisner, Stringfellow, Youngdahl, and Parker (2005) |
| Satisfaction from the product | Athanassopoulos and Iliakopoulos (2003) |
| Scale measures | Malhotra, Heine, and Grover (2001) |
| Schedule adherence | Cua, McKone, and Schroeder (2001) |
| Schedule flexibility | Sakakibara, Flynn, Schroeder, and Morris (1997) |
| Schedule flexibility | Wisner, Stringfellow, Youngdahl, and Parker (2005) |
| Scope of operations | Pflughoeft, Ramamurthy, Soofi, Yasai-Ardekani, and Zahedi (2003) |
| Scope of quality data and information | Flynn and Saladin (2001) |
| Selective staffing | Snell and Dean (1992) |
| Senior corporate leadership | Flynn and Saladin (2001) |
| Senior executive involvement | Adam, Corbett, Flores, Harrison, Lee, Rho, Ribera, Samson, and Westbrook (1997) |
| Service | Choi and Hartley (1996) |
| Service performance | McCollough, Berry, and Yadav (2000) |
| Service performance measures: operational performance | Stank, Goldsby, and Vickery (1999) |
| Service performance measures: relational performance | Stank, Goldsby, and Vickery (1999) |
| Service provisioning | Athanassopoulos and Iliakopoulos (2003) |
| Service quality | Boyer and Hult (2006) |
| Service quality | Harrison-Walker (2001) |
| Service quality | Menor, Roth, and Mason (2001) |
| Service quality | Roth (1993) |
| Service quality | Roth and Jackson (1995) |
| Service quality | Safizadeh, Field, and Ritzman (2003) |
| Service quality | Voss, Tsikriktsis, Funk, Yarrow, and Owen (2005) |
| Service quality to external customers | Stanley and Wisner (2001) |
| Service recovery satisfaction | de Jong and de Ruyter (2004) |
| Service satisfaction | Conlon, Devaraj, and Matta (2001) |
| Service type | Youngdahl and Kellogg (1997) |
| Servicescape quality | Brady and Cronin (2001) |
| Setup improvement | Koufteros (1999) |
| Setup time reduction | Ahmad and Schroeder (2001) |
| Setup time reduction | Cua, McKone, and Schroeder (2001) |
| Setup time reduction | Flynn and Flynn (2004) |
| Setup time reduction | Ketokivi and Schroeder (2004) |
| Setup time reduction | Sakakibara, Flynn, and Schroeder (1993) |
| Setup time reduction | Sakakibara, Flynn, Schroeder, and Morris (1997) |
| Setup time reduction practices | Flynn, Sakakibara, and Schroeder (1995) |
| Share of customer | de Jong and de Ruyter (2004) |
| Shared interpretation | Brockman and Morgan (2003) |

*(Continued)*

(Continued)

| | |
|---|---|
| Shared knowledge about customers | Hong, Vonderembse, Doll, and Nahm (2005) |
| Shared planning | Johnston, McCutcheon, Stuart, and Kerwood (2004) |
| Shared vision | Detert, Schroeder, and Cudeck (2003) |
| Shop floor employee involvement in problem solving | Tu, Vonderembse, and Ragu-Nathan (2001) |
| Shop-floor employee involvement in problem solving | Koufteros, Vonderembse, and Doll (1998) |
| Simpler flow of materials through the process | Schmenner and Cook (1985) |
| Simplicity | Collins, Cordon, and Julien (1998) |
| Site accuracy | Olson and Boyer (2003) |
| Site ease | Olson and Boyer (2003) |
| Skill in software use (technology-related) | Leonard-Barton and Deschamps (1988) |
| Small group problem solving | Sakakibara, Flynn, and Schroeder (1993) |
| Small group problem solving | Sakakibara, Flynn, Schroeder, and Morris (1997) |
| Small lot sizes | Sakakibara, Flynn, and Schroeder (1993) |
| Social integration | Hennig-Thurau, Langer, and Hansen (2001) |
| Social interaction | Wisner, Stringfellow, Youngdahl, and Parker (2005) |
| Social support | de Jong, de Ruyter, and Wetzels (2005) |
| Socialization | Sabherwal and Becerra-Fernandez (2003) |
| Sophistication | Malhotra, Heine, and Grover (2001) |
| Spans | Vickery, Dröge, and Germain (1999) |
| Special product capability | Goffin, Lemke, and Szwejczewski (2006) |
| Specialization | Germain and Dröge (1997) |
| Speed and flexibility in the design of new products and services | Escrig-Tena and Bou-Llusar (2005) |
| Speed to market | Sarin and Mcdermott (2003) |
| Staff competence | Li, Benton, and Leong (2002) |
| Staff composition | Li, Benton, and Leong (2002) |
| Staff focus | Goldstein and Naor (2005) |
| Staff focus: cross-functional | Chesteen, Helgheim, Randall, and Wardell (2005) |
| Staff focus: teamwork | Chesteen, Helgheim, Randall, and Wardell (2005) |
| Staff focus: training | Chesteen, Helgheim, Randall, and Wardell (2005) |
| Staff increase | Li, Benton, and Leong (2002) |
| Staff overage management—non-pay-related measures | Li, Benton, and Leong (2002) |
| Staff overage management—pay-related measures | Li, Benton, and Leong (2002) |
| Staff reduction | Li, Benton, and Leong (2002) |
| Staff shortage management | Li, Benton, and Leong (2002) |
| Staff training | Li, Benton, and Leong (2002) |
| Staff training and development | Goldstein (2003) |
| Staff well-being | Goldstein (2003) |
| Stage 3 manufacturing | Sakakibara, Flynn, Schroeder, and Morris (1997) |
| Stage 4 manufacturing | Sakakibara, Flynn, Schroeder, and Morris (1997) |
| Stakeholder value | Roth (1993) |
| Starting levels | Schroeder, Anderson, Tupy, and White (1981) |
| State of the EMS (environmental management system) | Melnyk, Sroufe, and Calantone (2003) |
| Statistical control/feedback | Flynn, Schroeder, and Sakakibara (1995) |
| Statistical process control | Curkovic, Vickery, and Dröge (2000) |
| Statistical process control | Flynn, Sakakibara, and Schroeder (1995) |
| Statistical process control (SPC) usage | Ahire, Golhar, and Waller (1996) |
| Status in terms of ISO 9000 certification | Terziovski, Samson, and Dow (1997) |
| Strategic (manufacturing) issues | Malhotra, Steele, and Grover (1994) |

| | |
|---|---|
| Strategic adaptation | Morita and Flynn (1997) |
| Strategic benefits | Pflughoeft, Ramamurthy, Soofi, Yasai-Ardekani, and Zahedi (2003) |
| Strategic breadth of the new venture firms | Deane, McDougall, and Gargeya (1991) |
| Strategic design integration | Dröge, Jayaram, and Vickery (2004) |
| Strategic excellence | Zahay, D., Griffin, A. (2004) |
| Strategic importance | Vickery, Dröge, Yeomans, and Markland (1995) |
| Strategic information technology (IT) planning | Stratman and Roth (2002) |
| Strategic planning | Cua, McKone, and Schroeder (2001) |
| Strategic planning | Park, Hartley, and Wilson (2001) |
| Strategic planning | Samson and Terziovski (1999) |
| Strategic purchasing | Bowen, Cousins, Lamming, and Faruk (2001) |
| Strategic purchasing | Carr and Pearson (1999) |
| Strategic purchasing | Chen and Paulraj (2004) |
| Strategic purchasing | Chen, Paulraj, and Lado (2004) |
| Strategic quality management | Black and Porter (1996) |
| Strategic quality planning | Choi and Eboch (1998) |
| Strategic quality planning | Pannirselvam, Siferd, and Ruch (1998) |
| Strategic supplier partnership | Li, Rao, Ragu-Nathan, and Ragu-Nathan (2005) |
| Strategies for identifying critical performance areas for improvement | Krause, Handfield, and Scannell (1998) |
| Strategy | Pagell (2004) |
| Strategy integration | Swink, Narasimhan, and Kim (2005) |
| Streamlining | Roth (1993) |
| Strength in competitive capabilities: delivery | Kim and Arnold (1992) |
| Strength in competitive capabilities: flexibility | Kim and Arnold (1992) |
| Strength in competitive capabilities: price | Kim and Arnold (1992) |
| Strength in competitive capabilities: quality | Kim and Arnold (1992) |
| Strength in competitive capabilities: service | Kim and Arnold (1992) |
| Strength/weakness in manufacturing performance areas | Cleveland, Schroeder, and Anderson (1989) |
| Structural (advanced manufacturing technology) investments: ADMIN | Boyer and McDermott (1999) |
| Structural (advanced manufacturing technology) investments: DESIGN | Boyer and McDermott (1999) |
| Structural (advanced manufacturing technology) investments: MANUFACTURING | Boyer and McDermott (1999) |
| Student loyalty | Hennig-Thurau, Langer, and Hansen (2001) |
| Subjective cycle time | Hult, Hurley, Giunipero, and Nichols (2000) |
| Subjective importance of the task | Leonard-Barton and Deschamps (1988) |
| Success difference | Monczka, Peterson, Handfield, and Ragatz (1998) |
| Success factors | Fry, Steele, and Saladin (1995) |
| Superordinate goals | Pinto, Pinto, and Prescott (1993) |
| Supervision | LaForge, Wood, and Sleeth (1984) |
| Supervisors as team leaders | Sakakibara, Flynn, Schroeder, and Morris (1997) |
| Supervisory leadership | Sakakibara, Flynn, Schroeder, and Morris (1997) |
| Supplier assessment | Krause, Scannell, and Calantone (2000) |
| Supplier assessment (Sassess) strategy | Tan (2001) |
| Supplier commitment | Krause (1999) |
| Supplier development | Curkovic, Vickery, and Dröge (2000) |
| Supplier development strategies, practices, and methods | Krause, Handfield, and Scannell (1998) |

*(Continued)*

(Continued)

| | |
|---|---|
| Supplier evaluation system | Carr and Pearson (1999) |
| Supplier incentives | Krause, Scannell, and Calantone (2000) |
| Supplier integration | Prasad, Tata, and Madan (2005) |
| Supplier involvement | Chen and Paulraj (2004) |
| Supplier involvement | Douglas and Fredendall (2004) |
| Supplier involvement | Lawrence and Hottenstein (1995) |
| Supplier involvement | Primo and Amundson (2002) |
| Supplier involvement: supplier relationship | Flynn, Schroeder, and Sakakibara (1994) |
| Supplier JIT manufacturing | Dong, Carter, and Dresner (2001) |
| Supplier knowledge application | Dröge, Claycomb, and Germain (2003) |
| Supplier management | Park, Hartley, and Wilson (2001) |
| Supplier obstructionism | Primo and Amundson (2002) |
| Supplier operational performance | Chen and Paulraj (2004) |
| Supplier partnerships | Black and Porter (1996) |
| Supplier performance | Ahire, Golhar, and Waller (1996) |
| Supplier process integration | Koufteros, Vonderembse, and Jayaram (2005) |
| Supplier product integration | Koufteros, Vonderembse, and Jayaram (2005) |
| Supplier quality control | Primo and Amundson (2002) |
| Supplier quality data and analysis | Flynn and Saladin (2001) |
| Supplier quality involvement | Ahmad and Schroeder (2001) |
| Supplier quality involvement | Flynn and Flynn (2004) |
| Supplier quality involvement | Sakakibara, Flynn, Schroeder, and Morris (1997) |
| Supplier quality level | Sakakibara, Flynn, and Schroeder (1993) |
| Supplier quality management | Ahire, Golhar, and Waller (1996) |
| Supplier quality management | Cua, McKone, and Schroeder (2001) |
| Supplier quality management | Forker (1997) |
| Supplier quality management | Forker, Mendez, and Hershauer (1997) |
| Supplier relationship | Flynn, Sakakibara, and Schroeder (1995) |
| Supplier relationship | Flynn, Schroeder, and Sakakibara (1995) |
| Supplier relationship management | Swink, Narasimhan, and Kim (2005) |
| Supplier relationships | Ketokivi and Schroeder (2004) |
| Supplier resources dedicated to supplier development activities | Krause, Handfield, and Scannell (1998) |
| Supplier selection | Lawrence and Hottenstein (1995) |
| Supplier's commitment | Prahinski and Benton (2004) |
| Supplier's perception of buyer's dependability | Johnston, McCutcheon, Stuart, and Kerwood (2004) |
| Supplier's performance | Prahinski and Benton (2004) |
| Suppliers' perception of buyer's benevolence | Johnston, McCutcheon, Stuart, and Kerwood (2004) |
| Supply base reduction | Chen and Paulraj (2004) |
| Supply chain agility | Swafford, Ghosh, and Murthy (2006) |
| Supply chain integration | Dong, Carter, and Dresner (2001) |
| Supply chain integration | Vickery, Jayaram, Dröge, and Calantone (2003) |
| Supply integration | Frohlich and Westbrook (2002) |
| Supply management capabilities | Bowen, Cousins, Lamming, and Faruk (2001) |
| Supply management consequence | Hult, Ketchen, and Nichols (2003) |
| Supply network structure | Chen and Paulraj (2004) |
| Supply uncertainty | Carter and Carter (1998) |
| Supply uncertainty | Chen and Paulraj (2004) |
| System effectiveness | Olson, Belohlav, and Boyer (2005) |

| | |
|---|---|
| Systems focus | Detert, Schroeder, and Cudeck (2003) |
| Systems orientation | Hult, Hurley, Giunipero, and Nichols (2000) |
| Systems orientation | Hult, Ketchen, and Nichols (2003) |
| | |
| Tacit knowledge | Levin and Cross (2004) |
| Tactical (manufacturing) issues | Malhotra, Steele, and Grover (1994) |
| Tangibles | Soteriou and Chase (1998) |
| Task demands: complexity | Lewis (2004) |
| Teacher involvement | Detert, Schroeder, and Cudeck (2003) |
| Team activities | Ahmad and Schroeder (2003) |
| Team leader position | Sarin and Mcdermott (2003) |
| Team leadership | Fedor, Ghosh, Caldwell, Maurer, and Singhal (2003) |
| Team learning | Sarin and Mcdermott (2003) |
| Team orientation | Hult, Hurley, Giunipero, and Nichols (2000) |
| Team orientation | Hult, Ketchen, and Nichols (2003) |
| Team risk | Wallace, Keil, and Rai (2004) |
| Team skills | Karlsson and Åhlström (1995) |
| Team usage | Johnson, Klassen, Leenders, and Fearon (2002) |
| Team's level of networking preference | Hoegl, Parboteeah, and Munson (2003) |
| Team's perceived importance of networking for project success | Hoegl, Parboteeah, and Munson (2003) |
| Team's perception of strength of the organizational knowledge-sharing climate | Hoegl, Parboteeah, and Munson (2003) |
| Team's perception of the adequacy of its material resources | Hoegl, Parboteeah, and Munson (2003) |
| Team's perception of the adequacy of its technical competency | Hoegl, Parboteeah, and Munson (2003) |
| Team's strength of networking resources | Hoegl, Parboteeah, and Munson (2003) |
| Teamwork structures for improvement | Black and Porter (1996) |
| Technical assessment | Petersen, Handfield, and Ragatz (2005) |
| Technical difficulty | Primo and Amundson (2002) |
| Technocratic specialization | Germain, Dröge, and Christensen (2001) |
| Technological adaptation | Morita and Flynn (1997) |
| Technological capability | Choi and Hartley (1996) |
| Technological leadership | Menor, Roth, and Mason (2001) |
| Technological leadership | Roth (1993) |
| Technological leadership | Roth and Jackson (1995) |
| Technological turbulence | Dröge, Claycomb, and Germain (2003) |
| Technologies of integration | Ettlie (1997) |
| Technology | Lawrence and Hottenstein (1995) |
| Technology | Nassimbeni (2003) |
| Technology emphasis | Cua, McKone, and Schroeder (2001) |
| Technology uncertainty | Chen and Paulraj (2004) |
| The chief executive officer (CEO) participates in information technology (IT) planning (ITP) | Kearns and Lederer (2003) |
| The chief information officer (CIO) participates in business planning (BP) | Kearns and Lederer (2003) |
| The impact of EMS on performance | Melnyk, Sroufe, and Calantone (2003) |
| The product development process | Ettlie (1997) |
| The workforce | Schmenner and Cook (1985) |
| Tie strength | Levin and Cross (2004) |

*(Continued)*

(Continued)

| | |
|---|---|
| Time accuracy | Karlsson and Åhlström (1995) |
| Time orientation | Youngdahl, Kellogg, Nie, and Bowen (2003) |
| Time savings | Boyer and Hult (2006) |
| Time to market | Li, Rao, Ragu-Nathan, and Ragu-Nathan (2005) |
| Time-based manufacturing practices | Nahm, Vonderembse, and Koufteros (2003) |
| Time-based manufacturing practices | Nahm, Vonderembse, and Koufteros (2004) |
| Timeliness | Somers, Nelson, and Karimi (2003) |
| Time-to-market | Dröge, Jayaram, and Vickery (2004) |
| Time-to-market | Tatikonda and Montoya-Weiss (2001) |
| Time-to-product | Dröge, Jayaram, and Vickery (2004) |
| Tolerance for ambiguity | Jambulingam, Kathuria, and Doucette (2005) |
| Tools/practices to identify suppliers for development efforts | Krause, Handfield, and Scannell (1998) |
| Top management commitment | Ahire, Golhar, and Waller (1996) |
| Top management leadership for quality | Flynn and Flynn (2004) |
| Top management quality leadership | Sakakibara, Flynn, Schroeder, and Morris (1997) |
| Top management support | Chen and Paulraj (2004) |
| Top management support | Flynn, Schroeder, and Sakakibara (1995) |
| Top management support: quality improve rewards | Flynn, Schroeder, and Sakakibara (1994) |
| Top management support: quality leadership | Flynn, Schroeder, and Sakakibara (1994) |
| Top management team involvement | Douglas and Fredendall (2004) |
| Total performance | Powell (1995) |
| Total preventive maintenance (TPM): autonomous maintenance—housekeeping | McKone, Schroeder, and Cua (1999) |
| Total quality control practices | Nassimbeni (2003) |
| Total quality management | Dean and Snell (1991) |
| Total quality management | Dean and Snell (1996) |
| Total quality management | Snell and Dean (1992) |
| Total quality management | Terziovski, Samson, and Dow (1997) |
| Total Quality Management (TQM) implementation: customer involvement | McKone, Schroeder, and Cua (1999) |
| Total quality management (TQM) program performance | Powell (1995) |
| Total Quality Management (TQM): management leadership | Kaynak (2003) |
| Total quality methods | Douglas and Fredendall (2004) |
| Total quality training | Douglas and Fredendall (2004) |
| TPM: autonomous maintenance—cross-training | McKone, Schroeder, and Cua (1999) |
| TPM: autonomous maintenance—operator involvement | McKone, Schroeder, and Cua (1999) |
| TPM: autonomous maintenance-teams | McKone, Schroeder, and Cua (1999) |
| TPM: planned maintenance—disciplined planning | McKone, Schroeder, and Cua (1999) |
| TPM: planned maintenance—information tracking | McKone, Schroeder, and Cua (1999) |
| TPM: planned maintenance—schedule compliance | McKone, Schroeder, and Cua (1999) |
| TQM implementation: rewards for quality | McKone, Schroeder, and Cua (1999) |
| TQM implementation: supplier quality management | McKone, Schroeder, and Cua (1999) |
| TQM implementation: top management leadership for quality | McKone, Schroeder, and Cua (1999) |
| TQM: employee relations | Kaynak (2003) |
| TQM: process management | Kaynak (2003) |
| TQM: product/service design | Kaynak (2003) |

| | |
|---|---|
| TQM: quality data and reporting | Kaynak (2003) |
| TQM: supplier quality management | Kaynak (2003) |
| TQM: training | Kaynak (2003) |
| Traditional industrial engineering | Adam (1994) |
| Training | Forker (1997) |
| Training | Forker, Mendez, and Hershauer (1997) |
| Training | Leonard-Barton and Deschamps (1988) |
| Training | Powell (1995) |
| Training | Sakakibara, Flynn, and Schroeder (1993) |
| Training in multiple functions | Ahmad and Schroeder (2003) |
| Training on the job skills | Ahmad and Schroeder (2003) |
| Transaction | Olson and Boyer (2003) |
| Transactional accuracy | Olson, Belohlav, and Boyer (2005) |
| Transaction-specific supplier development activities | Krause (1999) |
| Transactive memory systems | Lewis (2004) |
| Transformational leadership | Hult, Hurley, Giunipero, and Nichols (2000) |
| Trend in capacity utilization | Raffi and Swamidass (1987) |
| Trust | Benton and Maloni (2004) |
| Trust | Hennig-Thurau, Langer, and Hansen (2001) |
| Trust and coordination | Monczka, Peterson, Handfield, and Ragatz (1998) |
| Type of implementation approach | Schroeder, Anderson, Tupy, and White (1981) |
| Type of MRP system | Schroeder, Anderson, Tupy, and White (1981) |
| Type of product | da Silveira (2005) |
| Type of products and process | Schroeder, Anderson, Tupy, and White (1981) |
| | |
| Uncertainty | Calantone, Dröge, and Vickery (2002) |
| Uncertainty | Koufteros, Vonderembse, and Doll (2002) |
| Uncertainty | Prasad, Tata, and Madan (2005) |
| Uncertainty avoidance | Youngdahl, Kellogg, Nie, and Bowen (2003) |
| Unification of work control | Stahl and Zimmerer (1983) |
| Union | Shah and Ward (2003) |
| Unique design capability | da Silveira (2005) |
| Unit cost | Tatikonda and Montoya-Weiss (2001) |
| Unpredictability | Anand and Ward (2004) |
| Use of analytical techniques | Flynn and Saladin (2001) |
| Use of appointment system | Safizadeh, Field, and Ritzman (2003) |
| Use of electronic-data-interchange (EDI) with your customers/suppliers | Hill and Scudder (2002) |
| Use of product quality data | Flynn and Saladin (2001) |
| Usefulness belief | Froehle and Roth (2004) |
| User risk | Wallace, Keil, and Rai (2004) |
| Utilization | Safizadeh, Field, and Ritzman (2003) |
| Utilization feedback | Heineke (1995) |
| | |
| Value | Borgatti and Cross (2003) |
| Value | Brady and Cronin (2001) |
| Value orientation | Choi and Liker (1995) |
| Value to customer | Tu, Vonderembse, and Ragu-Nathan (2001) |
| Variety (job) | Dean and Snell (1991) |
| Venture experiential knowledge | Morgan, Zou, Vorhies, and Katsikeas (2003) |
| Venture market information knowledge | Morgan, Zou, Vorhies, and Katsikeas (2003) |

*(Continued)*

(Continued)

| | |
|---|---|
| Vertical coordination | Carter and Carter (1998) |
| Vertical integration | Roth and van der Velde (1991) |
| Virtual enterprise | Cao and Dowlatshahi (2005) |
| Vision | Hays and Hill (2001) |
| Visionary leadership | Anderson, Rungtusanatham, Schroeder, and Devaraj (1995) |
| Visionary leadership | Rungtusanatham, Forza, Koka, Salvador, and Nie (2005) |
| Volatility | Anand and Ward (2004) |
| Volume flexibility | Flynn, Schroeder, and Flynn (1999) |
| Volume flexibility | Zhang, Vonderembse, and Lim (2003) |
| Volume of turnover as bought from the supplier | Goffin, Lemke, and Szwejczewski (2006) |
| Waste elimination: inventory reduction | Lawrence and Hottenstein (1995) |
| Waste elimination: process modification | Lawrence and Hottenstein (1995) |
| Web site interaction: ease of interaction | Olson, Belohlav, and Boyer (2005) |
| Web site interaction: overall impression | Olson, Belohlav, and Boyer (2005) |
| Web site interaction: perspective | Olson, Belohlav, and Boyer (2005) |
| Web-related costs | Pflughoeft, Ramamurthy, Soofi, Yasai-Ardekani, and Zahedi (2003) |
| Word of mouth: activity | Harrison-Walker (2001) |
| Word of mouth: praise | Harrison-Walker (2001) |
| Work attitudes | Flynn, Schroeder, and Sakakibara (1995) |
| Work satisfaction: effectiveness | Janz and Prasarnphanich (2003) |
| Work satisfaction: efficiency | Janz and Prasarnphanich (2003) |
| Work satisfaction: general job satisfaction | Janz and Prasarnphanich (2003) |
| Work satisfaction: growth satisfaction | Janz and Prasarnphanich (2003) |
| Work satisfaction: timeliness | Janz and Prasarnphanich (2003) |
| Work systems | Goldstein (2003) |
| Worker participation | Flynn, Schroeder, and Flynn (1999) |
| Workforce configuration | Heineke (1995) |
| Workforce development | Swink, Narasimhan, and Kim (2005) |
| Workforce management | Flynn, Sakakibara, and Schroeder (1995) |
| Workforce management | Flynn, Schroeder, and Sakakibara (1995) |
| Workforce management: selection for teamwork potential | Flynn, Schroeder, and Sakakibara (1994) |
| Workforce management: teamwork | Flynn, Schroeder, and Sakakibara (1994) |
| Working on the floor | Morita and Flynn (1997) |
| Work-in-progress | da Silveira (2005) |
| Zero-defects mentality | Powell (1995) |

# APPENDIX 3

# LIST OF PAPERS SUMMARIZED


Adam, E. E., Jr. 1994. Alternative quality improvement practices and organization performance. *Journal of Operations Management* 12 (1): 27–44.

Adam, E. E., Jr., L. M. Corbett, B. E. Flores, N. J. Harrison, T. S. Lee, B. Rho, J. Ribera, D. Samson, and R. Westbrook. 1997. An international study of quality improvement approach and firm performance. *International Journal of Operations & Production Management* 17 (9): 842–73.

Ahire, S. L., D. Y. Golhar, and M. A. Waller. 1996. Development and validation of TQM implementation constructs. *Decision Sciences* 27 (1): 23–56.

Ahmad, S., and R. G. Schroeder. 2001. The impact of electronic data interchange on delivery performance. *Production and Operations Management* 10 (1): 16–30.

———. 2003. The impact of human resource management practices on operational performance: Recognizing country and industry differences. *Journal of Operations Management* 21 (1): 19–43.

Ahmed, N. U., R. V. Montagno, and R. J. Firenze. 1996. Operations strategy and organizational performance: An empirical study. *International Journal of Operations & Production Management* 16 (5): 41–53.

Amoako-Gyampah, K., and S. S. Boye. 2001. Operations strategy in an emerging economy: The case of the Ghanaian manufacturing industry. *Journal of Operations Management* 19 (1): 59–79.

Anand, G., and P. T. Ward. 2004. Fit, flexibility and performance in manufacturing: Coping with dynamic environments. *Production and Operations Management* 13 (4): 369–85.

Anderson, J. C., M. Rungtusanatham, R. G. Schroeder, and S. Devaraj. 1995. A path analytic model of a theory of quality management underlying the Deming management method: Preliminary empirical findings. *Decision Sciences* 26 (5): 637–58.

Athanassopoulos, A. D., and A. Iliakopoulos. 2003. Modeling customer satisfaction in telecommunications: Assessing the effects of multiple transaction points on the perceived overall performance of the provider. *Production and Operations Management* 12 (2): 224–45.

Bates, K. A., S. D. Amundson, R. G. Schroeder, and W. T. Morris. 1995. The crucial interrelationship between manufacturing strategy and organizational structure. *Management Science* 41 (10): 1565–80.

Benson, P. G., J. V. Saraph, and R. G. Schroeder. 1991. The effects of organizational context on quality management: An empirical investigation. *Management Science* 37 (9): 1107–24.

Benton, W. C., and M. Maloni. 2004. The influence of power driven buyer/seller relationships on supply chain satisfaction. *Journal of Operations Management* 23 (1): 1–22.

Black, S. A., and L. J. Porter. 1996. Identification of the critical factors of TQM. *Decision Sciences* 27 (1): 1–21.

Borgatti, S. P., and R. Cross. 2003. A relational view of information seeking and learning in social networks. *Management Science* 49 (4): 432–45.

Bowen, F. E., P. D. Cousins, R. C. Lamming, and A. C. Faruk. 2001. The role of supply management capabilities in green supply. *Production and Operations Management* 10 (2): 174–89.

Boyer, K. K., and G. T. M. Hult. 2006. Customer behavioral intentions for online purchases: An examination of fulfillment method and customer experience level. *Journal of Operations Management* 24 (2): 124–47.

Boyer, K. K., G. K. Leong, P. T. Ward, and L. J. Krajewski. 1997. Unlocking the potential of advanced manufacturing technologies. *Journal of Operations Management* 15 (4): 331–47.

Boyer, K. K., and C. McDermott. 1999. Strategic consensus in operations strategy. *Journal of Operations Management* 17 (3): 289–305.

Boyer, K. K., P. T. Ward, and G. K. Leong. 1996. Approaches to the factory of the future: An empirical taxonomy. *Journal of Operations Management* 14 (4): 297–313.

Bozarth, C., and S. Edwards. 1997. The impact of market requirements focus and manufacturing characteristics focus on plant performance. *Journal of Operations Management* 15 (3): 161–80.

Brady, M. K., and J. J. Cronin. 2001. Customer orientation: Effects on customer service perceptions and outcome behaviors. *Journal of Service Research* 3 (3): 241–51.

Brockman, B. K., and R. M. Morgan. 2003. The role of existing knowledge in new product innovativeness and performance. *Decision Sciences* 34 (2): 385–419.

Brown, S. 1998. Manufacturing seniority, strategy and innovation. *Technovation* 18 (3): 149–62.

Byrd, T. A., and D. E. Turner. 2001. An exploratory analysis of the value of skills of IT personnel: Their relationship to IS infrastructure and competitive advantage. *Decision Sciences* 32 (1): 21–54.

Calantone, R., C. Dröge, and S. Vickery. 2002. Investigating the manufacturing-marketing interface in new product development: Does context affect the strength of relationships? *Journal of Operations Management* 20 (3): 273–87.

Cao, Q., and S. Dowlatshahi. 2005. The impact of alignment between virtual enterprise and information technology on business performance in an agile manufacturing environment. *Journal of Operations Management* 23 (5): 531–50.

Carr, A. S., and J. N. Pearson. 1999. Strategically managed buyer-supplier relationships and performance outcomes. *Journal of Operations Management* 17 (5): 497–519.

Carr, C. L. 2002. A psychometric evaluation of the expectations, perceptions, and difference-scores generated by the IS-adapted SERVQUAL instrument. *Decision Sciences* 33 (2): 281–96.

Carter, C. R., and J. R. Carter. 1998. Interorganizational determinants of environmental purchasing: Initial evidence from the consumer products industries. *Decision Sciences* 29 (3): 659–84.

Chen, I. J., and A. Paulraj. 2004. Towards a theory of supply chain management: The constructs and measurements. *Journal of Operations Management* 22 (2): 119–50.

Chen, I. J., A. Paulraj, and A. A. Lado. 2004. Strategic purchasing, supply management, and firm performance. *Journal of Operations Management* 22 (5): 505–23.

Chesteen, S., B. Helgheim, T. Randall, and D. G. Wardell. 2005. Comparing quality of care in non-profit and for-profit nursing homes: A process perspective. *Journal of Operations Management* 23 (2): 229–42.

Chikan, A., and K. Demeter. 1995. Manufacturing strategies in Hungarian industry: The effects of transition from planned to market economy. *International Journal of Operations & Production Management* 15 (11): 5–19.

Choi, T. Y., and K. Eboch. 1998. The TQM paradox: Relations among TQM practices, plant performance, and customer satisfaction. *Journal of Operations Management* 17 (1): 59–75.

Choi, T. Y., and J. L. Hartley. 1996. An exploration of supplier selection practices across the supply chain. *Journal of Operations Management* 14 (5): 333–43.

Choi, T. Y., and J. K. Liker. 1995. Bringing Japanese continuous improvement approaches to U.S. manufacturing: The roles of process orientation and communications. *Decision Sciences* 26 (5): 589–620.

Christensen, W. J., R. Germain, and L. Birou. 2005. Build-to-order and just-in-time as predictors of applied supply chain knowledge and market performance. *Journal of Operations Management* 23 (5): 470–81.

Cleveland, G., R. G. Schroeder, and J. C. Anderson. 1989. A theory of production competence. *Decision Sciences* 20 (4): 655–68.

Collins, R. S., C. Cordon, and D. Julien. 1998. An empirical test of the rigid flexibility model. *Journal of Operations Management* 16 (2/3): 133–46.

Conlon E., S. Devaraj, and K. F. Matta. 2001. The relationship between initial quality perceptions and maintenance behavior: The case of the automotive industry. *Management Science* 47 (9): 1191–202.

Cua, K. O., K. E. McKone, and R. G. Schroeder. 2001. Relationships between implementation of TQM, JIT, and TPM and manufacturing performance. *Journal of Operations Management* 19 (6): 675–94.

Curkovic, S., S. Vickery, and C. Dröge. 2000. Quality-related action programs: Their impact on quality performance and firm performance. *Decision Sciences* 31 (4): 885–905.

da Silveira, G. J. C. 2005. Market priorities, manufacturing configuration, and business performance: An empirical analysis of the order-winners framework. *Journal of Operations Management* 23 (6): 662–75.

Das, A., and R. Narasimhan. 2001. Process-technology fit and its implications for manufacturing performance. *Journal of Operations Management* 19 (5): 521–40.

de Jong, A., and K. de Ruyter. 2004. Adaptive versus proactive behavior in service recovery: The role of self-managing teams. *Decision Sciences* 35 (3): 457–91.

de Jong, A., K. de Ruyter, and M. Wetzels. 2005. Antecedents and consequences of group potency: A study of self-managing service teams. *Management Science* 51 (11): 1610–25.

Dean, J. W., Jr., and S. A. Snell. 1991. Integrated manufacturing and job design: Moderating effects of organizational inertia. *Academy of Management Journal* 34 (4): 776–804.

———. 1996. The strategic use of integrated manufacturing: An empirical examination. *Strategic Management Journal* 17 (6): 459–80.

Deane, R. H., P. P. McDougall, and V. B. Gargeya. 1991. Manufacturing and marketing interdependence in the new venture firm: An empirical study. *Journal of Operations Management* 10 (3): 329–43.

Detert, J. R., R. G. Schroeder, and R. Cudeck. 2003. The measurement of quality management culture in schools: Development and validation of the SQMCS. *Journal of Operations Management* 21 (3): 307–28.

Devaraj, S., D. G. Hollingworth, and R. G. Schroeder. 2004. Generic manufacturing strategies and plant performance. *Journal of Operations Management* 22 (3): 313–33.

Diáz, M. S., J. A. D. Machuca, and M. J. Alvarez-Gil. 2003. A view of developing patterns of investment in AMT through empirical taxonomies: New evidence. *Journal of Operations Management* 21 (5): 577–606.

Dong, Y., C. R. Carter, and M. E. Dresner. 2001. JIT purchasing and performance: An exploratory analysis of buyer and supplier perspectives. *Journal of Operations Management* 19 (4): 471–83.

Douglas, T. J., and L. D. Fredendall. 2004. Evaluating the Deming management model of total quality in services. *Decision Sciences* 35 (3): 393–422.

Dröge, C., C. Claycomb, and R. Germain. 2003. Does knowledge mediate the effect of context on performance? Some initial evidence. *Decision Sciences* 34 (3): 541–68.

Dröge, C., J. Jayaram, and S. K. Vickery. 2004. The effects of internal versus external integration practices on time-based performance and overall firm performance. *Journal of Operations Management* 22 (6): 557–73.

Dröge, C., S. Vickery, and R. E. Markland. 1994. Sources and outcomes of competitive advantage: An exploratory study in the furniture industry. *Decision Sciences* 25 (5/6): 669–89.

Escrig-Tena, A. B., and J. C. Bou-Llusar. 2005. A model for evaluating organizational competencies: An application in the context of a quality management initiative. *Decision Sciences* 36 (2): 221–57.

Ettlie, J. E. 1995. Product-process development integration in manufacturing. *Management Science* 41 (7): 1124–237.

———. 1997. Integrated design and new product process. *Journal of Operations Management* 15 (1): 33–55.

Fedor, D. B., S. Ghosh, S. D. Caldwell, T. J. Maurer, and V. R. Singhal. 2003. The effects of knowledge management on team members' ratings of project success and impact. *Decision Sciences* 34 (3): 513–39.

Flynn, B. B., and E. J. Flynn. 2004. An exploratory study of the nature of cumulative capabilities. *Journal of Operations Management* 22 (5): 439–57.

Flynn, B. B., S. Sakakibara, and R. G. Schroeder. 1995. Relationship between JIT and TQM: Practices and performance. *Academy of Management Journal* 38 (5): 1325–60.

Flynn, B. B., and B. Saladin. 2001. Further evidence on the validity of the theoretical models underlying the Baldrige criteria. *Journal of Operations Management* 19 (6): 617–52.

Flynn, B. B., R. G. Schroeder, and S. Sakakibara. 1994. A framework for quality management research and an associated measurement instrument. *Journal of Operations Management* 11 (4): 339–66.

———. 1995. The impact of quality management practices on performance and competitive advantage. *Decision Sciences* 26 (5): 659–91.

Flynn, B. B., R. G. Schroeder, and E. J. Flynn. 1999. World class manufacturing: An investigation of Hayes and Wheelwright's foundation. *Journal of Operations Management* 17 (3): 249–69.

Forker, L. B. 1997. Factors affecting supplier quality performance. *Journal of Operations Management* 15 (4): 243–69.

Forker, L. B., D. Mendez, and J. C. Hershauer. 1997. Total quality management in the supply chain: What is its impact on performance? *International Journal of Production Research* 35 (6): 1681–701.

Froehle, C. M., and A. V. Roth. 2004. New measurement scales for evaluating perceptions of the technology-mediated customer service experience. *Journal of Operations Management* 22 (1): 1–21.

Frohlich, M. T., and R. Westbrook. 2001. Arcs of integration: An international study of supply chain strategies. *Journal of Operations Management* 19 (2): 185–200.

———. 2002. Demand chain management in manufacturing and services: Web-based integration, drivers and performance. *Journal of Operations Management* 20 (6): 729–45.

Fry, T. D., D. C. Steele, and B. A. Saladin. 1995. The role of management accounting in the development of a manufacturing strategy. *International Journal of Operations and Production Management* 15 (12): 21–31.

Fullerton, R. R., C. S. McWatters, and C. Fawson. 2003. An examination of the relationships between JIT and financial performance. *Journal of Operations Management* 21 (4): 383–404.

Germain, R., and C. Dröge. 1997. An empirical study of the impact of just-in-time task scope versus just-in-time workflow integration on organizational design. *Decision Sciences* 28 (3): 615–35.

Germain, R., C. Dröge, and W. Christensen. 2001. The mediating role of operations knowledge in the relationship of context with performance. *Journal of Operations Management* 19 (4): 453–69.

Gilgeous, V. 1995. Strategic concerns and capability impeders. *International Journal of Operations and Production Management* 15 (10): 4–29.

Goffin, K., F. Lemke, and M. Szwejczewski. 2006. An exploratory study of 'close' supplier-manufacturer relationships. *Journal of Operations Management* 24 (2): 189–209.

Goldstein, S. M. 2003. Employee development: An examination of service strategy in a high contact service environment. *Production and Operations Management* 12 (2): 186–203.

Goldstein, S. M., and M. Naor. 2005. Linking publicness to operations management practices: A study of quality management practices in hospitals. *Journal of Operations Management* 23 (2): 209–28.

Goldstein, S. M., P. T. Ward, G. K. Leong, and T. W. Butler. 2002. The effect of location, strategy, and operations technology on hospital performance. *Journal of Operations Management* 20 (1): 63–75.

Griffith, D. A., M. G. Harvey, and R. F. Lusch. 2006. Social exchange in supply chain relationships: The resulting benefits of procedural and distributive justice. *Journal of Operations Management* 24 (2): 85–98.

Grover, V., and M. K. Malhotra. 2003. Transaction cost framework in operations and supply chain management research: Theory and measurement. *Journal of Operations Management* 21 (4): 457–73.

Harrison-Walker, L. J. 2001. The measurement of word-of-mouth communication and an investigation of service quality and customer commitment as potential antecedents. *Journal of Service Research* 4 (1): 60–75.

Hausman W. H., D. B. Montgomery, and A. V. Roth. 2002. Why should marketing and manufacturing work together? Some exploratory empirical results. *Journal of Operations Management* 20 (3): 241–57.

Hays, J. M., and A. V. Hill. 2001. A preliminary investigation of the relationships between employee motivation/vision, service learning, and perceived service quality. *Journal of Operations Management* 19 (3): 335–49.

Heineke, J. 1995. Strategic operations management decisions and professional performance in U.S. HMOs. *Journal of Operations Management* 13 (4): 255–72.

Hennig-Thurau, T., M. F. Langer, and U. Hansen. 2001. Modeling and managing student loyalty: An approach based on the concept of relationship quality. *Journal of Service Research* 3 (4): 331–44.

Heute, L. M., and A. V. Roth. 1988. The industrialisation and span of retail banks' delivery systems. *International Journal of Operations and Production Management* 8 (3): 46–66.

Hill, C. A., and G. D. Scudder. 2002. The use of electronic data interchange for supply chain coordination in the food industry. *Journal of Operations Management* 20 (4): 375–87.

Ho, C. 1996. A contingency theoretical model of manufacturing strategy. *International Journal of Operations and Production Management* 16 (5): 74–98.

Hoegl, M., K. P. Parboteeah, and C. L. Munson. 2003. Team-level antecedents of individuals' knowledge networks. *Decision Sciences* 34 (4): 741–70.

Hong, P., M. A. Vonderembse, W. J. Doll, and A. Y. Nahm. 2005. Role change of design engineers in product development. *Journal of Operations Management* 24 (1): 63–79.

Hult, G. T. M., R. F. Hurley, L. C. Giunipero, and E. L. Nichols Jr. 2000. Organizational learning in global purchasing: A model and test of internal users and corporate buyers. *Decision Sciences* 31 (2): 293–325.

Hult, G. T. M., D. J. Ketchen Jr., and E. L. Nichols Jr. 2003. Organizational learning as a strategic resource in supply management. *Journal of Operations Management* 21 (5): 541–56.

Ittner, C. D., and D. F. Larcker. 1997. The performance effects of process management techniques. *Management Science* 43 (4): 522–34.

Jambulingam, T., R. Kathuria, and W. R. Doucette. 2005. Entrepreneurial orientation as a basis for classification within a service industry: The case of the retail pharmacy industry. *Journal of Operations Management* 23 (1): 23–42.

Janz, B. D., and P. Prasarnphanich. 2003. Understanding the antecedents of effective knowledge management: The importance of a knowledge-centered culture. *Decision Sciences* 34 (2): 351–84.

Jap, S. D., and E. Anderson. 2003. Safeguarding interorganizational performance and continuity under ex post opportunism. *Management Science* 49 (12): 1684–701.

Johnson, P. F., R. D. Klassen, M. R. Leenders, and H. E. Fearon. 2002. Determinants of purchasing team usage in the supply chain. *Journal of Operations Management* 20 (1): 77–89.

Johnston, D. A., D. M. McCutcheon, F. I. Stuart, and H. Kerwood. 2004. Effects of supplier trust on performance of cooperative supplier relationships. *Journal of Operations Management* 22 (1): 23–38.

Joshi, M. P., R. Kathuria, and S. J. Porth. 2003. Alignment of strategic priorities and performance: An integration of operations and strategic management perspectives. *Journal of Operations Management* 21 (3): 353–69.

Karlsson, C., and P. Åhlström. 1995. Change processes towards lean production: The role of the remuneration system. *International Journal of Operations and Production Management* 15 (11): 80–99.

Karuppan, C. M., and D. C. Ganster. 2004. The labor–machine dyad and its influence on mix flexibility. *Journal of Operations Management* 22 (6): 533–56.

Kaynak, H. 2003. The relationship between total quality management practices and their effects on firm performance. *Journal of Operations Management* 21 (4): 405–35.

Kearns, G. S., and A. L. Lederer. 2003. A resource-based view of strategic IT alignment: How knowledge sharing creates competitive advantage. *Decision Sciences* 34 (1): 1–29.

Ketokivi, M. A., and R. G. Schroeder. 2004. Strategic, structural contingency and institutional explanations in the adoption of innovative manufacturing practices. *Journal of Operations Management* 22 (1): 63–89.

Kim, J. S., and P. Arnold. 1992. Manufacturing competence and business performance: A framework and empirical analysis. *International Journal of Operations and Production Management* 13 (10): 4–25.

———. 1996. Operationalizing manufacturing strategy: An exploratory study of constructs and linkage. *International Journal of Operations and Production Management* 16 (12): 46–73.

Koste, L. L., M. K. Malhotra, and S. Sharma. 2004. Measuring dimensions of manufacturing flexibility. *Journal of Operations Management* 22 (2): 171–96.

Koufteros, X. A. 1999. Testing a model of pull production: A paradigm for manufacturing research using structural equation modeling. *Journal of Operations Management* 17 (4): 467–88.

Koufteros, X. A., M. A. Vonderembse, and W. J. Doll. 1998. Developing measures of time-based manufacturing. *Journal of Operations Management* 16 (1): 21–41.

———. 2001. Concurrent engineering and its consequences. *Journal of Operations Management* 19 (1): 97–115.

———. 2002. Integrated product development practices and competitive capabilities: The effects of uncertainty, equivocality, and platform strategy. *Journal of Operations Management* 20 (4): 331–55.

Koufteros, X. A., M. A. Vonderembse, and J. Jayaram. 2005. Internal and external integration for product development: The contingency effects of uncertainty, equivocality, and platform strategy. *Decision Sciences* 36 (1): 97–133.

Krause, D. R. 1999. The antecedents of buying firms' efforts to improve suppliers. *Journal of Operations Management* 17 (2): 205–24.

Krause, D. R., R. B. Handfield, and T. V. Scannell. 1998. An empirical investigation of supplier development: Reactive and strategic process. *Journal of Operations Management* 17 (1): 39–58.

Krause, D. R., M. Pagell, and S. Curkovic. 2001. Toward a measure of competitive priorities for purchasing. *Journal of Operations Management* 19 (4): 497–512.

Krause D. R., T. V. Scannell, and R. J. Calantone. 2000. A structural analysis of the effectiveness of buying firms' strategies to improve supplier performance. *Decision Sciences* 31 (1): 33–55.

LaForge, R. L., D. R. Wood Jr., and R. G. Sleeth. 1984. An application of the survey-feedback method in a service operation. *Journal of Operations Management* 5 (1): 103–18.

Lawrence, J. J., and M. P. Hottenstein. 1995. The relationship between JIT manufacturing and performance in Mexican plants affiliated with U.S. companies. *Journal of Operations Management* 13 (1): 3–18.

Leonard-Barton, D., and I. Deschamps. 1988. Managerial influence in the implementation of new technology. *Management Science* 34 (10): 1252–65.

Levin, D. Z., and R. Cross. 2004. The strength of weak ties you can trust: The mediating role of trust in effective knowledge transfer. *Management Science* 50 (11): 1477–90.

Lewis, K. 2004. Knowledge and performance in knowledge-worker teams: A longitudinal study of transactive memory systems. *Management Science* 50 (11): 1519–33.

Li, L. X., W. C. Benton, and G. K. Leong. 2002. The impact of strategic operations management decisions on community hospital performance. *Journal of Operations Management* 20 (4): 389–408.

Li, S., S. S. Rao, T. S. Ragu-Nathan, and B. Ragu-Nathan. 2005. Development and validation of a measurement instrument for studying supply chain management practices. *Journal of Operations Management* 23 (6): 618–41.

Malhotra, M. K., M. L. Heine, and V. Grover. 2001. An evaluation of the relationship between management practices and computer aided design technology. *Journal of Operations Management* 19 (3): 307–33.

Malhotra, M. K., D. C. Steele, and V. Grover. 1994. Important strategic and tactical manufacturing issues in the 1990s. *Decision Sciences* 25 (2): 189–214.

Marley, K. A., D. A. Collier, and S. M. Goldstein. 2004. The role of clinical and process quality in achieving patient satisfaction in hospitals. *Decision Sciences* 35 (3): 349–69.

McCollough, M. A., L. L. Berry, and M. S. Yadav. 2000. An empirical investigation of customer satisfaction after service failure and recovery. *Journal of Service Research* 3 (2): 121–37.

McDermott, C. M., and G. N. Stock. 1999. Organizational culture and advanced manufacturing technology implementation. *Journal of Operations Management* 17 (5): 521–33.

McKone, K. E., R. G. Schroeder, and K. O. Cua. 1999. Total productive maintenance: A contextual view. *Journal of Operations Management* 17 (2): 123–44.

Mehra, S., and R. A. Inman. 1992. Determining the critical elements of just-in-time implementation. *Decision Sciences* 23 (1): 160–74.

Melnyk, S. A., R. P. Sroufe, and R. L. Calantone. 2003. Assessing the impact of environmental management systems on corporate and environmental performance. *Journal of Operations Management* 21 (3): 329–51.

Menda, R., and D. Dilts. 1997. The manufacturing strategy formulation process: Linking multifunctional viewpoints. *Journal of Operations Management* 15 (4): 223–41.

Menor, L. J., A. V. Roth, and C. H. Mason. 2001. Agility in retail banking: A numerical taxonomy of strategic service groups. *Manufacturing & Service Operations Management* 3 (4): 273–92.

Monczka, R. M., K. J. Petersen, R. B. Handfield, and G. L. Ragatz. 1998. Success factors in strategic supplier alliances: The buying company perspective. *Decision Sciences* 29 (3): 553–77.

Morgan, N. A., S. Zou, D. W. Vorhies, and C. S. Katsikeas. 2003. Experiential and informational knowledge, architectural marketing capabilities, and the adaptive performance of export ventures: A cross-national study. *Decision Sciences* 34 (2): 287–321.

Morita, M., and E. J. Flynn. 1997. The linkage among management systems, practices, and behavior in successful manufacturing strategy. *International Journal of Operations and Production Management* 17 (10): 967–93.

Nahm, A. Y., M. A. Vonderembse, and X. A. Koufteros. 2003. The impact of organizational structure on time-based manufacturing and plant performance. *Journal of Operations Management* 21 (3): 281–306.

———. 2004. The impact of organizational culture on time-based manufacturing and performance. *Decision Sciences* 35 (4): 579–607.

Narasimhan, R., J. Jayaram, and J. R. Carter. 2001. An empirical examination of the underlying dimensions of purchasing competence. *Production and Operations Management* 10 (1): 1–15.

Nassimbeni, G. 2003. Local manufacturing systems and global economy: Are they compatible? The case of the Italian eyewear district. *Journal of Operations Management* 21 (2): 151–71.

Naveh, E., and A. Marcus. 2005. Achieving competitive advantage through implementing a replicable management standard: Installing and using ISO 9000. *Journal of Operations Management* 24 (1): 1–26.

New, C. C., and M. Szwejczewski. 1995. Performance measurement and the focused factory: Empirical evidence. *International Journal of Operations and Production Management* 15 (4): 63–79.

Noble, M. A. 1997. Manufacturing competitive priorities and productivity: An empirical study. *International Journal of Operations and Production Management* 17 (1): 85–99.

Olson, J. R., J. A. Belohlav, and K. K. Boyer. 2005. Operational, economic and mission elements in not-for-profit organizations: The case of the Chicago Symphony Orchestra. *Journal of Operations Management* 23 (2): 125–42.

Olson, J. R., and K. K. Boyer. 2003. Factors influencing the utilization of Internet purchasing in small organizations. *Journal of Operations Management* 21 (2): 225–45.

Pagell, M. 2004. Understanding the factors that enable and inhibit the integration of operations, purchasing and logistics. *Journal of Operations Management* 22 (5): 459–87.

Pagell, M., and D. R. Krause. 2004. Re-exploring the relationship between flexibility and the external environment. *Journal of Operations Management* 21 (6): 629–49.

Pannirselvam, G. P., S. P. Siferd, and W. A. Ruch. 1998. Validation of the Arizona Governor's Quality Award criteria: A test of the Baldrige criteria. *Journal of Operations Management* 16 (5): 529–50.

Parasuraman, A. 2000. Technology readiness index (TRI): A multiple-item scale to measure readiness to embrace new technologies. *Journal of Service Research* 2 (4): 307–20.

Park, S., J. L. Hartley, and D. Wilson. 2001. Quality management practices and their relationship to buyer's supplier ratings: A study in the Korean automotive industry. *Journal of Operations Management* 19 (6): 695–712.

Petersen, K. J., R. B. Handfield, and G. L. Ragatz. 2005. Supplier integration into new product development: Coordinating product, process and supply chain design. *Journal of Operations Management* 23 (3/4): 371–88.

Pflughoeft, K. A., K. Ramamurthy, E. S. Soofi, M. Yasai-Ardekani, and F. Zahedi. 2003. Multiple conceptualizations of small business Web use and benefit. *Decision Sciences* 34 (3): 467–512.

Pinto, M. B., J. K. Pinto, and J. E. Prescott. 1993. Antecedents and consequences of project team cross-functional cooperation. *Management Science* 39 (10): 1281–97.

Powell, T. C. 1995. Total quality management as competitive advantage: A review and empirical study. *Strategic Management Journal* 16 (1): 15–27.

Prahinski, C., and W. C. Benton. 2004. Supplier evaluations: Communication strategies to improve supplier performance. *Journal of Operations Management* 22 (1): 39–62.

Prasad, S., J. Tata, and M. Madan. 2005. Build to order supply chains in developed and developing countries. *Journal of Operations Management* 23 (5): 551–68.

Primo, M. A. M., and S. D. Amundson. 2002. An exploratory study of the effects of supplier relationships on new product development outcomes. *Journal of Operations Management* 20 (1): 33–52.

Rabinovich, E., M. E. Dresner, and P. T. Evers. 2003. Assessing the effects of operational processes and information systems on inventory performance. *Journal of Operations Management* 21 (1): 63–80.

Raffi, F., and P. M. Swamidass. 1987. Towards a theory of manufacturing overhead cost behavior: A conceptual and empirical analysis. *Journal of Operations Management* 7 (1/2): 121–37.

Rho, B.-H., and Y.-M. Yu. 1998. A comparative study on the structural relationships of manufacturing practices, lead time and productivity in Japan and Korea. *Journal of Operations Management* 16 (2/3): 257–70.

Robinson, E. P., Jr., and R. K. Satterfield. 1998. Designing distribution systems to support vendor strategies in supply chain management. *Decision Sciences* 29 (3): 685–706.

Rosenzweig, E. D., and A. V. Roth. 2004. Towards a theory of competitive progression: Evidence from high-tech manufacturing. *Production and Operations Management* 13 (4): 354–68.

Rosenzweig, E. D., A. V. Roth, and J. W. Dean Jr. 2003. The influence of an integration strategy on competitive capabilities and business performance: An exploratory study of consumer products manufacturers. *Journal of Operations Management* 21 (4): 437–56.

Roth, A. V. 1993. Performance dimensions in services: An empirical investigation of strategic performance. In *Advances in services marketing and management,* Vol. 2, eds. S. Swartz, D. E. Bowen, and S. W. Brown, 1–47. Greenwich, CT: JAI Press.

——— 1996. Neo-operations strategy: Linking capabilities-based competition to technology. In *Handbook of technology management*, ed. G. H. Gaynor, 38.1–38.44. New York: McGraw-Hill.

Roth, A. V., and W. E. Jackson III. 1995. Strategic determinants of service quality and performance: Evidence from the banking industry. *Management Science* 41 (11): 1720–33.

Roth, A. V., and M. van der Velde. 1991. Operations as marketing: A competitive service strategy. *Journal of Operations Management* 10 (3): 303–28.

Rungtusanatham, M., C. Forza, B. R. Koka, F. Salvador, and W. Nie. 2005. TQM across multiple countries: Convergence hypothesis versus national specificity arguments. *Journal of Operations Management* 23 (1): 43–63.

Sabherwal, R., and I. Becerra-Fernandez. 2003. An empirical study of the effect of knowledge management processes at individual, group, and organizational levels. *Decision Sciences* 34 (2): 225–60.

Safizadeh, M. H., J. M. Field, and L. P. Ritzman. 2003. An empirical analysis of financial services processes with a front-office or back-office orientation. *Journal of Operations Management* 21 (5): 557–76.

Safizadeh, M. H., and L. P. Ritzman. 1997. Linking performance drivers in production planning and inventory control to process choice. *Journal of Operations Management* 15 (4): 389–403.

Safizadeh, M. H., L. P. Ritzman, D. Sharma, and C. Wood. 1996. An empirical analysis of the product-process matrix. *Management Science* 42 (11): 1576–91.

Sakakibara, S., B. B. Flynn, and R. G. Schroeder. 1993. A framework and measurement instrument for just-in-time manufacturing. *Production and Operations Management* 2 (3): 177–94.

Sakakibara, S., B. B. Flynn, R. G. Schroeder, and W. T. Morris. 1997. The impact of just-in-time manufacturing and its infrastructure on manufacturing performance. *Management Science* 43 (9): 1246–57.

Samson, D., and M. Terziovski. 1999. The relationship between total quality management practices and operational performance. *Journal of Operations Management* 17 (4): 393–409.

Sarin, S., and C. McDermott. 2003. The effect of team leader characteristics on learning, knowledge application, and performance of cross-functional new product development teams. *Decision Sciences* 34 (4): 707–39.

Sawhney, R., and C. Piper. 2002. Value creation through enriched marketing-operations interfaces: An empirical study in the printed circuit board industry. *Journal of Operations Management* 20 (3): 259–72.

Schmenner, R. W., and R. L. Cook. 1985. Explaining productivity differences in North Carolina factories. *Journal of Operations Management* 5 (3): 273–89.

Schroeder, R. G., J. C. Anderson, and G. Cleveland. 1986. The content of manufacturing strategy: An empirical study. *Journal of Operations Management* 6 (4): 405–15.

Schroeder, R. G., J. C. Anderson, S. E. Tupy, and E. M. White. 1981. A study of MRP benefits and costs. *Journal of Operations Management* 2 (1): 1–9.

Schroeder, R. G., K. A. Bates, and M. A. Junttila. 2002. A resource-based view of manufacturing strategy and the relationship to manufacturing performance. *Strategic Management Journal* 23 (2): 105–17.

Shah, R., and P. T. Ward. 2003. Lean manufacturing: Context, practice bundles, and performance. *Journal of Operations Management* 21 (2): 129–49.

Small, M. H., and M. M. Yasin. 1997. Advanced manufacturing technology: Implementations policy and performance. *Journal of Operations Management* 15 (4): 349–70.

Snell, S. A., and J. W. Dean Jr. 1992. Integrated manufacturing and human resource management: A human capital perspective. *Academy of Management Journal* 35 (3): 467–504.

Somers, T. M., K. Nelson, and J. Karimi. 2003. Confirmatory factor analysis of the end-user computing satisfaction instrument: Replication within an ERP domain. *Decision Sciences* 34 (3): 595–621.

Soteriou, A. C., and R. B. Chase. 1998. Linking the customer contact model to service quality. *Journal of Operations Management* 16 (4): 495–508.

Stahl, M. J., and T. W. Zimmerer. 1983. Using decision modeling to examine management consensus: A study of a maintenance management control system. *Journal of Operations Management* 3 (2): 93–98.

Stank, T. P., T. J. Goldsby, and S. K. Vickery. 1999. Effect of service supplier performance on satisfaction and loyalty of store managers in the fast food industry. *Journal of Operations Management* 17 (4): 429–47.

Stanley, L. L., and J. D. Wisner. 2001. Service quality along the supply chain: Implications for purchasing. *Journal of Operations Management* 19 (3): 287–306.

Stratman, J. K., and A. V. Roth. 2002. Enterprise resource planning (ERP) competence constructs: Two-stage multi-item scale development and validation. *Decision Sciences* 33 (4): 601–28.

Swafford, P. M., S. Ghosh, and N. Murthy. 2006. The antecedents of supply chain agility of a firm: Scale development and model testing. *Journal of Operations Management* 24 (2): 170–88.

Swamidass, P. M., and S. Kotha. 1998. Explaining manufacturing technology use, firm size, and performance using a multidimensional view of technology. *Journal of Operations Management* 17 (1): 23–37.

Swamidass, P. M., and W. T. Newell. 1987. Manufacturing strategy, environmental uncertainty and performance: A path analytic model. *Management Science* 33 (4): 509–24.

Swink, M., R. Narasimhan, and S. W. Kim. 2005. Manufacturing practices and strategy integration: Effects on cost efficiency, flexibility, and market-based performance. *Decision Sciences* 36 (3): 427–57.

Tan, K. C. 2001. A structural equation model of new product design and development. *Decision Sciences* 32 (2): 195–226.

Tatikonda, M. V., and M. McLutre Montoya-Weiss. 2001. Integrating operations and marketing perspectives of product innovation: The influence of organizational process factors and capabilities on development performance. *Management Science* 47 (1): 151–72.

Teigland, R., and M. McLure Wasko. 2004. Integrating knowledge through information trading: Examining the relationship between boundary spanning communication and individual performance. *Decision Sciences* 34 (2): 261–86.

Terziovski, M., D. Samson, and D. Dow. 1997. The business value of quality management systems certification: Evidence from Australia and New Zealand. *Journal of Operations Management* 15 (1): 1–18.

Tracey, M., M. A. Vonderembse, and J. Lim. 1999. Manufacturing technology and strategy formulation: Keys to enhancing competitiveness and improving performance. *Journal of Operations Management* 17 (4): 411–28.

Tsikriktsis, N., G. Lanzolla, and M. Frohlich. 2004. Adoption of e-processes by service firms: An empirical study of antecedents. *Production and Operations Management* 13 (3): 216–29.

Tu, Q., M. A. Vonderembse, and T. S. Ragu-Nathan. 2001. The impact of time-based manufacturing practices on mass customization and value to customer. *Journal of Operations Management* 19 (2): 201–17.

Tu, Q., M. A. Vonderembse, T. S. Ragu-Nathan, and B. Ragu-Nathan. 2004. Measuring modularity-based manufacturing practices and their impact on mass customization capability: A customer-driven perspective. *Decision Sciences* 35 (2): 147–68.

Tucker, A. L. 2004. The impact of operational failures on hospital nurses and their patients. *Journal of Operations Management* 22 (2): 151–69.

Venkatesh, V., C. Speier, and M. G. Morris. 2002. User acceptance enablers in individual decision making about technology: Toward an integrated model. *Decision Sciences* 33 (2): 297–316.

Veuglers, R., and B. Cassiman. 1999. Make and buy in innovation strategies: Evidence from Belgian manufacturing firms. *Research Policy* 28 (1): 63–80.

Vickery, S. K. 1991. A theory of production competence revisited *Decision Sciences* 22 (3): 635–43.

Vickery, S. K., C. Dröge, and R. Germain. 1999. The relationship between product customization and organizational structure. *Journal of Operations Management* 17 (4): 377–91.

Vickery, S. K., C. Dröge, T. P. Stank, T. J. Goldsby, and R. E. Markland. 2004. The performance implications of media richness in a business-to-business service environment: Direct versus indirect effects. *Management Science* 50 (8): 1106–19.

Vickery, S. K., C. L. M. Dröge, J. M. Yeomans, and R. E. Markland. 1995. Time-based competition in the furniture industry. *Production and Inventory Management Journal* 36 (4): 14–21.

Vickery, S. K., J. Jayaram, C. Dröge, and R. Calantone. 2003. The effects of an integrative supply chain strategy on customer service and financial performance: An analysis of direct versus indirect relationships. *Journal of Operations Management* 21 (5): 523–39.

Voss, C., and K. Blackmon. 1998. Differences in manufacturing strategy decisions between Japanese and Western manufacturing plants: The role of strategic time orientation. *Journal of Operations Management* 16 (2/3): 147–58.

Voss, C., N. Tsikriktsis, B. Funk, D. Yarrow, and J. Owen. 2005. Managerial choice and performance in service management: A comparison of private sector organizations with further education colleges. *Journal of Operations Management* 23 (2): 179–95.

Wallace, L., M. Keil, and A. Rai. 2004. How software project risk affects project performance: An investigation of the dimensions of risk and an exploratory model. *Decision Sciences* 35 (2): 289–321.

Ward, P. T., R. Duray, G. K. Leong, and C-C. Sum. 1995. Business environment, operations strategy, and performance: An empirical study of Singapore manufacturers. *Journal of Operations Management* 13 (2): 99–115.

Ward, P. T., G. K. Leong, and K. K. Boyer. 1994. Manufacturing proactiveness and performance. *Decision Sciences* 25 (3): 337–58.

Ward, P. T., J. K. McCreery, L. P. Ritzman, and D. Sharma. 1998. Competitive priorities in operations management. *Decision Sciences* 29 (4): 1035–46.

Wathen, S. 1995. Manufacturing strategy in business units: An analysis of production process focus and performance. *International Journal of Operations & Production Management* 15 (8): 4–13.

White, G. P. 1996. A meta-analysis model of manufacturing capabilities. *Journal of Operations Management* 14 (4): 315–31.

Williams, F. P., D. E. D'Souza, M. E. Rosenfeldt, and M. Kassaee. 1995. Manufacturing strategy, business strategy and firm performance in a mature industry. *Journal of Operations Management* 13 (1): 19–33.

Wisner, P. S., A. Stringfellow, W. E. Youngdahl, and L. Parker. 2005. The service volunteer-loyalty chain: An exploratory study of charitable not-for-profit service organizations. *Journal of Operations Management* 23 (2): 143–61.

Youngdahl, W. E., and D. L. Kellogg. 1997. The relationship between service customers' quality assurance behaviors, satisfaction, and effort: A cost of quality perspective. *Journal of Operations Management* 15 (1): 19–32.

Youngdahl, W. E., D. L. Kellogg, W. Nie, and D. E. Bowen. 2003. Revisiting customer participation in service encounters: Does culture matter? *Journal of Operations Management* 21 (1): 109–120.

Zahay, D., and A. Griffin. 2004. Customer learning processes, strategy selection, and performance in business-to-business service firms. *Decision Sciences* 35 (2): 169–203.

Zellmer-Bruhn, M. E. 2003. Interruptive events and team knowledge acquisition. *Management Science* 49 (4): 514–28.

Zhang, Q., M. A. Vonderembse, J.-S. Lim. 2003. Manufacturing flexibility: Defining and analyzing relationships among competence, capability, and customer satisfaction. *Journal of Operations Management* 21 (2): 173–91.

Zhu, Q., and J. Sarkis. 2004. Relationships between operational practices and performance among early adopters of green supply chain management practices in Chinese manufacturing enterprises. *Journal of Operations Management* 22 (3): 265–89.

# ABOUT THE AUTHORS

**Aleda V. Roth** is the Burlington Industries Distinguished Professor of supply chain management at Clemson University. She is an internationally recognized empirical scholar in service and manufacturing operations strategy. Her research is motivated by theoretical and practical explanations of how firms can best deploy their global supply chains, operations, and technology strategies for competitive advantage. She has more than 150 publications to her credit, and her work has been distinguished by 49 research awards and 27 grants. She holds senior editorial positions for *Management Science, Production and Operations Management (POM), Journal of Operations Management (JOM), Decision Sciences Journal (DSJ), Journal of Supply Chain Management,* and others. She served as president of the Production and Operations Management Society (POMS); received the Lifetime Scholarship Achievement Award from the Academy of Management; and is a Fellow of the Decision Sciences Institute, POMS, and the U.K. Advanced Institute of Management Research (AIM). She is a member of the Conference Board's Performance Excellence Council and has consulted with corporate staff at leading global companies. She worked in top management for a decade before earning her PhD at Ohio State University, where she also received her BS. She received her MSPH in biostatistics from the University of North Carolina at Chapel Hill.

**Roger G. Schroeder** holds the Frank A. Donaldson Chair in operations management at the Carlson School of Management, University of Minnesota. He has published over 100 papers in academic journals on topics of quality management, operations strategy, and high-performance manufacturing. He is a leader in empirical research in operations management. He is a Fellow of the Decision Sciences Institute and Production and Operations Management Society (POMS), and received the Lifetime Scholarship Achievement Award from the Academy of Management, Operations Management Division. In 2005, he received the Dean's prize for best researcher in the Carlson School of Management and was inducted into the University of Minnesota Academy of Distinguished Teachers. According to ISI, he is the most highly cited scholar in the world in the operations management field. He is the author of the highly regarded textbook *Operations Management: Contemporary Concepts and Cases*. He received his PhD from Northwestern University.

**Xiaowen Huang** is an assistant professor of supply chain and operations management at the Richard T. Farmer School of Business, Miami University, Ohio. She teaches in the areas of operations management, supply chain management, and operations strategy. Her research interest primarily revolves around the question of "how can companies achieve competitive advantage through effective technology management, especially in the supply chain context?" Her current research falls into two main research streams. The first stream includes empirical investigation of use of information and Internet technologies (especially online auction) in the manufacturing setting and in the retail e-Bay setting. Her second research stream involves theoretical understanding and testing effective product modularity and mass customization strategies. Her research appears in *Journal of Operations Management* and other academic journals. She received her PhD from the Operations and Management Science Department, University of Minnesota.

**M. Murat Kristal** is an assistant professor of operations management at Schulich School of Business at York University, Toronto, Canada. He teaches in the areas of operations management/strategy, supply chain management, and statistical models. His research interests focus on the areas of supply chain management, operations management, and operations strategy. His current empirical research spans from how supply chains adapt to their competitive environments to how manufacturers achieve mass customization capabilities. He received his PhD from the Operations Management Department in the Kenan-Flagler Business School at the University of North Carolina at Chapel Hill.